The History of the ANCIENT WORLD

Also by Susan Wise Bauer

The Well-Educated Mind:
A Guide to the Classical Education You Never Had
(W. W. Norton, 2003)

The Story of the World: History for the Classical Child
(Peace Hill Press)

Volume 1: Ancient Times (rev. ed., 2006)

Volume 2: The Middle Ages (2003)

Volume 3: Early Modern Times (2004)

Volume 4: The Modern Age (2005)

Though the Darkness Hide Thee
(Multnomah, 1998)

With Jessie Wise

The Well-Trained Mind:
A Guide to Classical Education at Home
(rev. ed., W. W. Norton, 2004)

The History of the ANCIENT WORLD

From the Earliest Accounts to the Fall of Rome

SUSAN WISE BAUER

W · W · Norton New York London

Printed in the United States of America
First Edition

Maps designed by Susan Wise Bauer and Sarah Park and created by Sarah Park

Manufacturing by R. R. Donnelley, Bloomsburg Division
Book design by Margaret M. Wagner
Page makeup: Carole Desnoes
Production manager: Julia Druskin

Library of Congress Cataloging-in-Publication Data

Bauer, S. Wise
The history of the ancient world: from the earliest accounts to the fall of Rome /
Susan Wise Bauer. — 1st ed.
p. cm.
Includes bibliographical references and index.
ISBN-13: 978-0-393-05974-8 (hbk.)
ISBN-10: 0-393-05974-X (hbk.)
1. History, Ancient. I. Title.
D57.B38 2007
930—dc22
2006030934

W. W. Norton & Company, Inc.
500 Fifth Avenue, New York, NY 10110
www.wwnorton.com

W. W. Norton & Company Ltd.
Castle House, 75/76 Wells Street, London W1T 3QT

1 2 3 4 5 6 7 8 9 0

For
Christopher

Contents

Part Four
EMPIRES

Part Five
IDENTITY

Maps

Illustrations

Acknowledgments

FOR SEVERAL YEARS NOW, I've had trouble finding a good answer to the question, "What are you working on these days?" When I say, "I'm working on a history of the world," people inevitably laugh.

I really am writing a history of the world. But I wouldn't have ventured into a project like this unless my editor at Norton, Starling Lawrence, had suggested it first. His advice, encouragement, and editorial judgment have helped shape this first volume; a generous share of the credit (and a heaping helping of any punishment headed my way for the crime of hubris) should go to him. Thanks also to Star and Jenny for their hospitality, which is almost Southern in its kindness.

My able agent, Richard Henshaw, helps me manage my professional affairs with skill and efficiency. I continue to be grateful for his help and friendship.

Any general history like this one relies on the painstaking work of specialists. I am particularly indebted to Samuel Noah Kramer, for all things Sumerian; Gwendolyn Leick, for Mesopotamia and Babylon; Peter Clayton, for the chronology of the pharaohs; Daniel Luckenbill, for the Assyrian kings; Romila Thapar, for perspectives on India; Grant Frame, for the Babylonian kings; Robin Waterfield, for the translations from the Greek; and Burton Watson, for the translations from the Chinese. I made heavy use of the Electronic Text Corpus of Sumerian Literature, a wonderful resource made available by the Oriental Institute of Oxford University.

The librarians and interlibrary loan staff at my home library, the Swem Library of the College of William & Mary, were both helpful and tolerant. Many thanks also to Diane Bergman at the Sackler Library, Oxford University, for her assistance.

I feel very fortunate that the talented Sarah Park was able to work with me to create my maps, and I'm looking forward to moving on into the medieval landscape with her.

At Peace Hill, I'm grateful to Peter Buffington, for able assistance with permissions, library runs, e-mail, and a myriad of details (and also for saying how well I was getting along every time I told him I had advanced another fifteen years or so); Sara Buffington, for all the miles-to-inches and kilometers-tomillimeters calculations, for help with catalog copy, and for her friendship; Charlie Park, for website work, publicity, technical advice, and enthusiasm; Elizabeth Weber, for cheerful help with everything from references to diapers; and Nancy Blount, who took on the job of my assistant right at the most dreadful point in the process, when I had 364 books checked out of the university library and hadn't answered my mail for eight months. She set about bringing order out of chaos with both good humor and efficiency.

Thanks to the other historians, professional and amateur, who have encouraged me in this project: John Wilson of *Books & Culture*; Maureen Fitzgerald of the College of William and Mary, for support that went far, far beyond the call of duty; and my father (and business partner), James L. Wise Jr., M.D., who also built me an office in our old chicken shed and turned it into a thing of beauty.

Robert Eric Frykenberg, Rollin Phipps, Michael Stewart, and Martha Dart read early drafts; thanks to them for their suggestions. Elizabeth Pierson's expert copyediting caught more inconsistencies than I thought I was capable of.

Thanks to Lauren Winner for the sympathetic encouragement, and to Greg and Stephanie Smith for not giving up on the chance to do lunch, once a year or so. Susan Cunningham continues to remind me what I'm supposed to be doing.

My brother Bob Wise provided photographic expertise and kept in touch. (Bob and Heather: now that the first volume is out, I promise to start answering the phone AND my e-mail.) Jessie Wise is both my respected professional colleague and an extraordinary mother/grandmother; she taught Emily to read while I was wading through Sumerian inscriptions, and kept bringing me food from the garden even though I never weed anything. My son Christopher, the first student to use this for a high-school history text, gave me valuable feedback; Ben, Daniel, and Emily reminded me that life is "just great!" even when there's proofreading to be done. My deepest gratitude goes to my husband, Peter, who makes it possible for me to write and still have a life. *Sumus exules, vivendi quam auditores.*

Preface

Sometime around 1770 BC, Zimri-Lim, king of the walled city of Mari on the banks of the Euphrates, got exasperated with his youngest daughter.

A decade earlier, Zimri-Lim had married his older daughter Shimatum to the king of another walled and sovereign city called Ilansura. It was a good match, celebrated with enormous feasts and heaps of presents (mostly from the bride's family to the groom). Zimri-Lim's grandchildren would eventually be in line for the throne of Ilansura, and in the meantime the king of Ilansura would become an ally, rather than another competitor among the crowd of independent cities fighting for territory along the limited fertile stretches of the Euphrates.

Unfortunately, grandchildren didn't arrive as soon as hoped. Three years later Zimri-Lim, still hoping to make the alliance with Ilansura permanent, sent the king another daughter: Shimatum's younger sister Kirum. Kirum, sharp-tongued and ambitious, was expected to take her lawful place as second wife and servant to her sister. Instead, she decided to lobby for a position as the king's first wife. She involved herself in politics, commandeered servants for her personal use, sneered at her sister, and generally queened it about the palace—until Shimatum gave birth to twins.

Immediately the childless Kirum plummeted in the palace hierarchy. "No one asks my opinion any more," she complained, in letter after letter to her father. "My husband has taken away my very last servants. My sister says that she will do whatever she wants to me!"

Given Kirum's behavior to her sister in the early years of her marriage, it is unlikely that "whatever she wants" involved anything good; and indeed, Kirum's letters soon begged her father for rescue. The plea "Bring me home or I shall surely die!" progressed to "If you do not bring me back home to Mari, I will throw myself from the highest roof in Ilansura!"

Zimri-Lim had hoped to make the king of Ilansura his friend. Unfortunately, leaving Kirum in the the man's household wasn't doing much to increase the goodwill between the two families. Seven years after the wedding, Zimri-Lim gave up, made a royal journey north, and in the words of his own court records, "liberated the palace of Ilansura" by bringing Kirum home.[1]

THOUSANDS OF YEARS AGO, groups of hunters and gatherers roamed across Asia and Europe, following mammoth herds that fed on the wild grasses. Slowly the ice began to retreat; the patterns of the grass growth changed; the herds wandered north and diminished. Some hunters followed. Others, deprived of the meat that was central to their diet, harvested those wild grasses and, in time, began to plant some of the grasses for themselves.

Probably.

EVEN THOUGH world histories routinely begin with prehistoric times, I suspect that prehistory is the wrong starting place for the historian. Other specialists are better equipped to dig into the murk of the very distant past. Archaeologists unearth the remnants of villages built from mammoth bones; anthropologists try to reconstruct the lost world of the villagers. Both are searching for a hypothesis that fits the evidence, a lens that will reveal groups of people moving from east to west, abandoning mammoth meat for barley, and digging pits for their extra grain.

But for the historian who hopes not just to explain *what* people do, but in some measure *why* and *how* they do it, prehistory—the time before people began to write and tell stories about their kings, their heroes, and themselves—remains opaque. Whatever the archaeologist concludes about that group called "Neolithic man," I know nothing about the days and nights of a Neolithic potter, constructing his ring-rimmed pots in a village in the south of France. The tracks of the hunters and gatherers (pots, stone flakes, bones of people and animals, paintings on cliffs and cave walls) reveal a pattern of life, but no story emerges. There are no kings and wives in prehistory. Stripped of personality, prehistoric peoples too often appear as blocks of shifting color on a map: moving north, moving west, generating a field of cultivated grain or corralling a herd of newly domesticated animals. The story of these nameless people must be told in the impersonal voice that mars too many histories: "Civilization arose in the Fertile Crescent, where wheat was planted for the first time on the banks of the Euphrates. The development of writing soon followed, and cities were established."

Any time the historian is forced to resort to hugely general statements about "human behavior," she has left her native land and is speaking a foreign language—usually with a total lack of fluency and grace. This kind of impersonal history (heavy on the passive verbs) is stupefyingly dull. Worse, it is inaccurate. The Fertile Crescent had no monopoly on farming; small groups all over Asia and Europe began planting grain as the weather warmed, and in any case the Fertile Crescent was mostly a howling waste.

Anthropologists can speculate about human behavior; archaeologists, about patterns of settlement; philosophers and theologians, about the motivations of "humanity" as an undifferentiated mass. But the historian's task is different: to look for particular human lives that give flesh and spirit to abstract assertions about human behavior.

It was not easy to be a petty king in the ancient Near East. Zimri-Lim spends half of his time fighting the kings of other cities, and the other half trying to negotiate his complicated personal life. His queen, competent and politically astute Shiptu, runs the city of Mari while her husband goes off to fight yet another war. She writes to him, in the height of a Mediterranean summer, "Be sure to take care of yourself when you are in the full rays of the sun! . . . Wear the robe and cloak that I have made for you! . . . My heart has been greatly alarmed; write me and tell me that you are safe!" And Zimri-Lim writes back: "The enemy has not threatened me with weapons. All is well. Let your heart no longer be afflicted."[2] In thousands of cuneiform tablets unearthed on the banks of the Euphrates, Zimri-Lim emerges both as a typical Mesopotamian king, and as an individual: a much-married man with little talent for fatherhood.

So rather than beginning with cave paintings, or anonymous groups of nomads wandering across the plains, I have chosen to begin this history at the point where particular human lives and audible human voices emerge from the indistinct crowds of prehistory. You will find some prehistory, borrowed from archaeology and anthropology, in the chapters that follow (and along with it, some inevitable use of the impersonal voice). But where this prehistory appears, it serves only to set the stage for the characters who wait in the wings.

I have made careful use of epic tales and myths to flesh out this prehistory. The first personalities that bob up from the surface of ancient history seem to be part man and part god; the earliest kings rule for thousands of years, and the first heroes ascend to the heavens on eagle's wings. Since the eighteenth century (at least), western historians have been suspicious of such tales. Trained in a university system where science was revered as practically infallible, historians too often tried to position themselves as scientists: searching for cold hard facts and dismissing any historical material which seemed to depart from the realities of Newton's universe. After all, any document which begins, as the Sumerian king list does, "Kingship descended from heaven" can't possibly be trustworthy as history. Much better to rely on the science of archaeology, and to reconstruct the earliest days of Sumer and Egypt and the Indus valley settlements around tangible physical evidence.

But for the historian who concerns herself with the why and how of human behavior, potsherds and the foundations of houses are of limited use. They give no window into the soul. Epic tales, on the other hand, display the fears and hopes of the people who tell them—and these are central to any explanation of their behavior. Myth, as the historian John Keay says, is the "smoke of history." You may have to fan at it a good deal before you get a glimpse of the flame beneath; but when you see smoke, it is wisest not to pretend that it isn't there.

In any case, we should remember that all histories of ancient times involve a great deal of speculation. Speculation anchored by physical evidence isn't, somehow, more reliable than speculation anchored by the stories that people choose to preserve and tell to their children. Every historian sorts through evidence, discards what seems irrelevant, and arranges the rest into a pattern. The evidence provided by ancient tales is no less important than the evidence left behind by merchants on a trade route. Both need to be collected, sifted, evaluated, and put to use. To concentrate on physical evidence to the exclusion of myth and story is to put all of our faith in the explanations for human behavior in that which can be touched, smelled, seen, and weighed: it shows a mechanical view of human nature, and a blind faith in the methods of science to explain the mysteries of human behavior.

Nevertheless, history constructed around very ancient stories involves just as much theorizing as history constructed around very ancient ruins. So I have tried to indicate the point at which written records begin to multiply, and conjecture becomes a little less conjectural ("Part Two"). Historians don't always bother to give the reader this kind of heads-up; many leap from "Mesolithic man grew steadily better at making weapons" to "Sargon spread his rule across Mesopotamia" without noting that those two statements are based on very different kinds of evidence, and bear very different degrees of ambiguity.

In this volume, we will not spend a great deal of time in Australia, or the Americas, or for that matter Africa, but for a slightly different reason. The oral histories of these cultures, old as they are, don't stretch back nearly as far as the oldest lists of kings from Mesopotamia, or the first memorial tablets to Egyptian kings. However, the whole idea of linear time that gives us such a neat outline for history—prehistory, ancient history, medieval history, and on towards the future—is not African or Native American; it is a very western creation (which in no way diminishes its usefulness). As archaeologist Chris Gosden points out in his primer on prehistory, native peoples such as the Aborigines of Australia had no native concept of "prehistory." So far as we can tell, they thought of past and present as one until Westerners arrived, bringing "history" with them—at which point their prehistory came to a sudden end. We will meet them then: an approach which may not be ideal, but at least avoids doing violence to their own sense of time.

One additional note: Dating anything that happened before Hammurabi (c. 1750 BC) is problematic. Even Hammurabi's accession has an error factor of fifty years or so on either side, and by the time we go back to 7000 BC the error factor is closer to five or six hundred years. Before 7000 BC, assigning dates takes place in a polite free-for-all. Writing about anything that happened from the beginning of time through about 4000 BC is further complicated by the fact that there are several different systems in place for labelling the eras of "prehistory," none of which is in total agreement with any other, and at least one of which is just plain wrongheaded.

I have chosen to use the traditional designations BC and AD for dates. I understand why many historians choose to use BCE and CE in an attempt to avoid seeing history entirely from a Judeo-Christian point of view, but using BCE while still reckoning from Christ's birth seems, to me, fairly pointless.

Part One

THE EDGE OF HISTORY

Chapter One

The Origin of Kingship

Just north of the Persian Gulf, in the very distant past, the Sumerians discover that cities need rulers

MANY THOUSANDS of years ago, the Sumerian king Alulim ruled over Eridu: a walled city, a safe space carved out of the unpredictable and harsh river valley that the Romans would later name Mesopotamia. Alulim's rise to power marked the beginning of civilization, and his reign lasted for almost thirty thousand years.

The Sumerians, who lived in a world where the supernatural and the material had not yet been assigned to different sides of the aisle, would not have choked over the last part of that sentence. On the other hand, they would have found Alulim's placement at "the beginning of civilization" extremely hard to swallow. In their own minds, the Sumerians had always been civilized. Alulim's kingship, recorded in the Sumerian king list (perhaps the oldest historical record in the world), "descended from heaven" and was already perfect when it arrived on earth.

But looking back, we see the coming of the first king in different perspective. It is a sea change in the condition of man, the beginning of a whole new relationship between people, their land, and their leaders.

We can't date Alulim's reign, since he is not mentioned in any other records, and since we don't know how old the Sumerian king list itself is. The list was set down on clay tablets sometime after 2100 BC, but it undoubtedly preserves a much older tradition. More than that: the chronology given by the Sumerian king list doesn't exactly match the past as we know it. "After kingship had descended from heaven," the king list tells us, "Alulim reigned 28,000 years as king; [his heir] Alalgar reigned 36,000 years."[1]

The length of these reigns may suggest that both of these kings are actually demigods, drawn from mythology rather than history; or perhaps, simply that Alulim and his heir ruled for a very long time. According to the Sumerians, eight kings ruled before the enormous catastrophe of Sumerian history occurred and "the Flood swept over" the land. Each reign lasted for a multiple of thirty-six hundred years, which suggests that the king list involves a kind of reckoning we don't understand.*

What we *can* do is place the first Sumerian king in the distant past. Whenever he reigned, Alulim lived in a land probably quite different from the Mesopotamia we know today, with its familiar two rivers—the Tigris and the Euphrates—running into the Persian Gulf. Geologists tell us that, just before the beginning of history (the date 11,000 BC, although far from precise, gives us a reference point), ice spread down from the polar caps far to the south, down almost to the Mediterranean Sea. With so much water contained in ice, the oceans and seas were lower; the northern end of the Gulf itself was probably a plain with streams running through it, and the ocean lapped up against a shore that lay roughly level with modern Qatar. Rain fell regularly, so that the land was watered.

As the climate began to warm and the ice caps began to melt—a process that geologists assign to the five thousand years between 11,000 and 6000 BC—the ocean crept up past Qatar, past the modern territory of Bahrain. Settlements retreated before the rising water. By 6000 BC, Britain—previously a peninsula jutting off from Europe—had become an island, and the shore of the Persian Gulf had crept up to the southern border of Kuwait. The plain that lay to its north was watered, not by two rivers, but by a whole complex of powerful streams, their paths still visible in satellite photos; the book of Genesis describes one river with "four heads" running through the plain.[2]

But although the land was watered by this braided riverway, it grew drier. As the ice retreated, the temperature rose. Just north of the Gulf, the rains diminished into infrequent sprinkles that came only during the winter months. In the summer, searing winds blew across the unprotected plain. Each year, the streams swelled up over their banks and washed away fields before receding back into their beds, leaving silt behind. The silt began to build up on the banks of the interweaving streams, pushing them apart. And the Gulf continued to creep northwards.

The people who lived on the southern plain, closest to the Gulf, scratched for survival in a shifting and unpredictable landscape. Once a year, far too much water covered their fields. As soon as the floods subsided, the ground dried hard. They had no stone, no forests to provide timber, no wide grass-

* There are other problems with the king list, including missing pieces where the tablets are broken, and the apparent elimination of rulers who are attested to by inscriptions and other independent evidence; still, the list is the best guide we have to the distant past of the Sumerians.

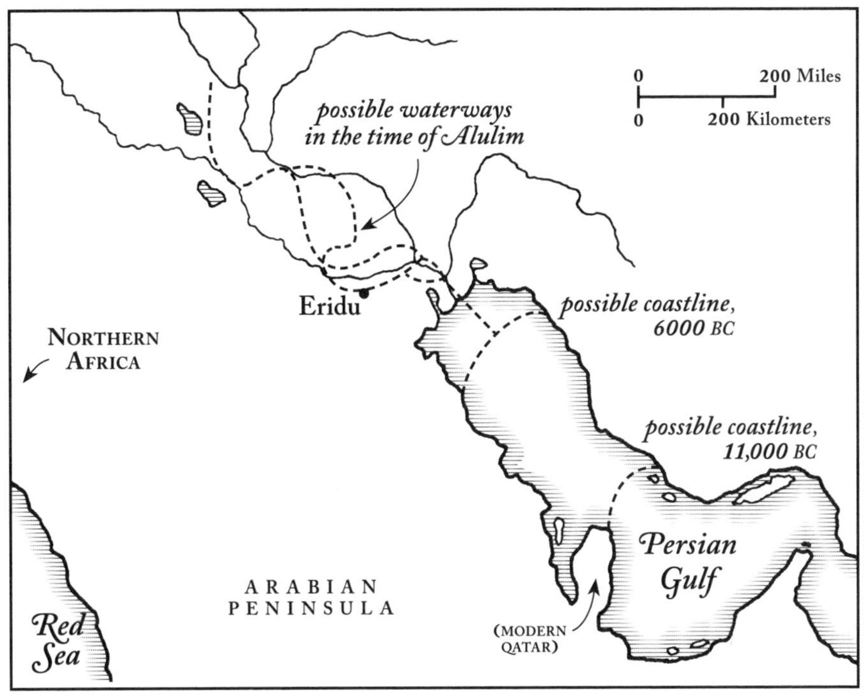

1.1 Very Ancient Mesopotamia

lands; just reeds, which grew along the streams, and plenty of mud. Mud, molded and dried, mixed with reeds and baked, became the foundations of their houses, the bricks that formed their city walls, their pots and dishes. They were people of the earth.*

* In many histories, these villagers are not called "Sumerians." Historians have reserved that name for the culture that occupied the Mesopotamian plain from about 3200 BC onwards, because for many years the evidence seemed to suggest that while early villages did exist from about 4500 BC on, the Sumerians themselves were a distinct group who invaded from the north and took over sometime after 3500 BC. However, more recent excavations and the use of technology to sound the land below the water table shows that Sumer was occupied long before 4500 BC. Closer examination of the remains that are accessible to archaeologists shows that a foreign invasion did *not* impose a new culture over the "native Mesopotamians"; early villages have the same patterns of house building, settlement, decoration, etc., as later "Sumerian" villages. It is much more likely that the earliest villagers were joined by peoples wandering down from the north, up from the south, and over from the east, not in one overwhelming invasion, but in a constant seepage of settlement. Despite this, the old names for the most ancient Sumerian settlements have stuck; the people in the lower Mesopotamian plain are called "Ubaid" for the period 5000–4000 BC, and "Uruk" for the period 4000–3200 BC. Another period, called "Jemdat Nasr," has been suggested for 3200–2900 BC, although these dates seem to be in flux. The settlements before 5000 are referenced, variously, as Samarra, Hassuna, and

The language that these settlers spoke—Sumerian—is apparently unrelated to any other language on earth. But by the time that the Sumerians began to write, their language was peppered with words from another tongue. Sumerian words are built on one-syllable roots, but dozens of words from the oldest inscriptions have unfamiliar two-syllable roots: the names of the two most powerful rivers that ran through the plain, the names for farmer, fisherman, carpenter, weaver, and a dozen other occupations, even the name of the city Eridu itself.

These words are Semitic, and they prove that the Sumerians were not alone on the southern plain. The Semitic words belonged to a people whose homeland was south and west of the Mesopotamian plain. Mountains to the north and east of Mesopotamia discouraged wanderers, but travelling up from the Arabian peninsula, or over from northern Africa, was a much simpler proposition. The Semites did just this, settling in with the Sumerians and lending them words. And more than just words: the Semitic loanwords are almost all names for farming techniques (plow, furrow) and for the peaceful occupations that go along with farming (basketmaker, leatherworker, carpenter). The Semites, not the Sumerians, brought these skills to Mesopotamia.

So how did the Semites learn how to farm?

Probably in gradual stages, like the peoples who lived in Europe and farther north. Perhaps, as the ice sheets retreated and the herds of meat-providing animals moved north and grew thinner, the hunters who followed these herds gave up the full-time pursuit of meat and instead harvested the wild grains that grew in the warmer plains, shifting residence only when the weather changed (as the native North Americans in modern Canada were still doing when Jacques Cartier showed up). Maybe these former nomads progressed from harvesting wild grain to planting and tending it, and finally gave up travelling altogether in favor of full-time village life. Well-fed men and women produced more babies. Sickles and grinding stones, discovered from modern Turkey down to the Nile valley, suggest that as those children grew to adulthood, they left their overpopulated villages and travelled elsewhere, taking their farming skills with them and teaching them to others.

Ancient stories add another wrinkle to the tale: as the Semite-influenced Sumerians planted crops around their villages, life became so complicated that they needed a king to help them sort out their difficulties.

Halaf. These eras, based partly on innovations in pottery styles, are named after archaeological sites where the most typical remains of the period were first identified. (Linguists use a different set of names, just to confuse the issue; the Ubaid people become "Proto-Euphrateans," for example.) I find it simpler—and more accurate—to use "Sumerian" throughout.

Enter Alulim, king of Eridu, and the beginning of civilization.

It's easy to wax lyrical over the "beginning of civilization." Civilization, after all, is what divides us from chaos. Civilized cities have walls that separate the orderly streets within from the wild waste outside. Civilization, as archaeologist Stuart Piggott explains in his introduction to Max Mallowan's classic study of ancient Sumer, is the result of a courageous discontent with the status quo: "Sporadically," Piggott writes, "there have appeared peoples to whom innovation and change, rather than adherence to tradition, gave satisfaction and release: these innovating societies are those which we can class as the founders of civilization."[3]

Actually, civilization appears to be the result of a more elemental urge: making sure that no one seizes too much food or water. Civilization began in the Fertile Crescent, not because it was an Edenic place overflowing with natural resources, but because it was so hostile to settlement that a village of any size needed careful management to survive. Farmers had to cooperate in order to construct the canals and reservoirs needed to capture floodwaters. Someone needed to enforce that cooperation, and oversee the fair division of the limited water. Someone had to make sure that farmers, who grew more grain than their families needed, would sell food to the nonfarmers (the basketmakers, leatherworkers, and carpenters) who grew no grain themselves. Only in an inhospitable and wild place is this sort of bureaucracy—the true earmark of civilization—needed. In genuinely fertile places, overflowing with water and food and game and minerals and timber, people generally don't bother.*

In the Fertile Crescent, as villages grew into cities, more people had to sustain themselves on the same amount of dry land. Strong leadership became more necessary than ever. Human nature being what it is, city leaders needed some means of coercion: armed men who policed their decrees.

The leaders had become kings.

For the Sumerians, who struggled to survive in a land where water either washed away their fields in floods, or retreated entirely, leaving the crops to bake in the sun, kingship was a gift from the gods. No primordial gardens for the Sumerians: cities, protected from invading waters and hungry raiders by thick mud-brick walls, were man's first and best home. The city of Eridu,

* This is not quite the same as explaining the rise of bureaucracy by the need to control large-scale irrigation systems; as Jared Diamond points out in *Guns, Germs, and Steel,* the centralized bureaucracies of cities were generally well in place before "complex irrigation systems" formed, and "in the Fertile Crescent food production and village life originated in hills and mountains, not in lowland river valleys" (p. 23). The formation of bureaucracies was necessary before those systems could be properly built and maintained; and the fact that "civilization" had its beginnings in the hills, which were far less hospitable than the river valleys, demonstrates my point.

where kingship first descended from heaven, reappears in the myths of the Babylonians as the Sumerian Eden, created by the king-god Marduk:

All the lands were sea. . . .
Then Eridu was made. . . .
Marduk constructed a reed frame on the face of the waters.
He created dirt and poured it out by the reed frame. . . .
He created mankind.[4]

Eridu never disappears, as the Eden of Genesis does. The sacred city stood as the division between the old world of the hunters and gatherers, and the new world of civilization.

But the hunters and gatherers were not entirely gone. From the earliest days of kingship and the first building of cities, settled farmers quarrelled with nomadic herdsmen and shepherds.

The fifth king in the Sumerian list is Dumuzi, who is (as the list tells us, with an air of faint surprise) a shepherd. That a shepherd who becomes king is a meeting of opposites becomes clear in "The Wooing of Inanna," a tale starring Dumuzi and the goddess Inanna.* In this story, Dumuzi is not only a shepherd and king, but also has the blood of gods in his veins; despite his divinity, Inanna finds Dumuzi unworthy. "The shepherd will go to bed with you!" exclaims the sun-god Utu, but Inanna (who generally bestows her favors without a whole lot of hesitation) objects:

The shepherd! I will not marry the shepherd!
His clothes are coarse; his wool is rough.
I will marry the farmer.
The farmer grows flax for my clothes.
The farmer grows barley for my table.[5]

Dumuzi persists with his suit. After a fair amount of arguing about whose family is better, he wins entrance to Inanna's bed by offering her fresh milk with cream; she promptly suggests that he "plow her damp field." (He accepts the invitation.)

Inanna's preference for the farmer echoes a real tension. As the southern plain grew drier, cities clustered along the riverbanks. But beyond the cities, the desert wastes still served as pasture for sheep and goats and as the home of

* Inanna is known as Ishtar, slightly later, by the Semitic peoples of Mesopotamia; she evolves into the goddess of both love and war, a combination fairly common in ancient times.

nomads who kept the ancient wandering ways alive. Herdsmen and farmers needed each other; herdsmen provided farmers with meat, fresh milk, and wool in exchange for life-sustaining grain. But mutual need didn't produce mutual respect. City dwellers scoffed at the rustic, unwashed herdsmen; herdsmen poked fun at the effete and decadent townspeople.

In this land of cities and kings, farmers and nomadic wanderers, the first eight kings of Sumer ruled until catastrophe struck.

Chapter Two

The Earliest Story

In Sumer, slightly later,
a very great flood occurs

NO RAIN HAS FALLEN for months. In a field near the salty head of the Gulf, a woman is harvesting the shrivelled heads of wheat. Behind her, the walls of her city rise up against a lead-colored sky. The ground is stone beneath her feet. The reservoirs, once filled with water from the yearly floods, hold only an inch of liquid mud. The irrigation channels are empty.

A drop of water dents the dust on her arm. She looks up to see clouds creeping from the horizon towards the peak of the sky. She shouts towards the walls of the city, but the streets are already filled with men and women, thrusting pots, basins, and hollowed shells into every open space. Far too often, the squalls blow across the plains in moments.

But not this time. The drops strengthen and stream down. Water collects, pools, and swells. In the distance, an unfamiliar roar strengthens and shakes the earth.

ANCIENT PEOPLES without deep wells, dams, or metropolitan water supplies spent a large part of their lives looking for water, finding water, hauling water, storing water, calculating how much longer they might be able to live if water were not found, and desperately praying for water to fall from the sky or well up from the earth beneath. But in Mesopotamia, an unexpected *fear* of water exists alongside this vital preoccupation. Evil and malice lurk in deep water; water may bring life, but catastrophe is not far behind.

The history of the earth (so geologists tell us) has been punctuated by great catastrophes which apparently wiped out entire categories of life forms. But only one echoes down in the words and stories of a dozen different races. We don't have a universal story that begins "And then the weather began to grow

VERY, VERY COLD." But at some point during the living, storytelling memory of the human race, water threatened man's fragile hold on the earth. The historian cannot ignore the Great Flood; it is the closest thing to a universal story that the human race possesses.

Apart from the brief mention of the flood in the king list, the Sumerian story of the flood comes to us only indirectly, translated thousands of years after the event into Akkadian (a Semitic language spoken later in Mesopotamia) and preserved in an Assyrian library. Enlil, king of the gods, grows exasperated because the roar of men on the earth keeps him from sleeping; he convinces the other gods to wipe out mankind, but the god Ea, who has sworn an oath to protect mankind, whispers news of the plot to the wise man Utnapishtim in a dream.* And then

> the gods of the abyss rose up
> the dams of the waters beneath were thrown down
> the seven judges of hell lit the land with their torches
> daylight became night,
> the land was smashed as a cup
> water poured over the people as the tides of battle.[1]

Utnapishtim, warned, escapes in a boat with his family, a few animals, and as many others as he can save.

The Babylonian version of this story is called the "Poem of Atrahasis" (Atrahasis, translated, means something like "Super Wiseman"). Atrahasis, the wisest king on earth, is warned of the coming disaster. He builds an ark and—knowing that he can spare only a few—invites the rest of his subjects to a great banquet, so that they may have one last day of joy before the end. They eat and drink, and thank him for his generosity; but Atrahasis himself, knowing that the feast is a death meal, paces back and forth, ill with grief and guilt.

> So they ate from his abundance
> and drank their fill,
> but he did nothing but come in, and go out,
> come in, and go out,
> never seated,
> so sickened and desperate was he.[2]

* In some versions, the Sumerian Noah-figure is named Ziusudra.

Even the wisest king on earth cannot always assure the survival of his people, in the face of overwhelming disaster.

But the most familiar flood story is undoubtedly the one told in Genesis. God determines to cleanse his creation of corruption, so he tells Noah, "blameless among his people," to build an ark which will save him and his family from destruction. Rain falls, and the "great springs of the deep burst, and the floodgates of the heavens were opened," and water swallows the earth.

Three cultures, three stories: too much coincidence of detail to be dismissed.*

Nineteenth-century geologists, with Genesis as their guide, searched for traces of the Great Flood and often found them: disordered geological layers, shells on tops of mountains. But the slow movement of ice sheets across land, a theory first suggested by Louis Agassiz in 1840, also explained many of those geological formations previously attributed to a universal flood. It was also more in tune with the growing scientific consensus that the development of the universe was uniform, gradual, always affected by the same logical processes, moving evenly forwards in a predictable pattern in which unique, unrepeatable events had no part.†

Yet the stories of a Great Flood remained. Students of Mesopotamia continued to champion the existence of a real flood—not a universal flood, since this was no longer philosophically respectable, but a Mesopotamian flood destructive enough to be remembered for thousands of years. Archaeologist Leonard Woolley, known for his excavations of Ur, wrote, "The total destruction of the human race is of course not involved, nor is even the total destruction of the inhabitants of the delta . . . but enough damage could be done to make a landmark in history and to define an epoch."[3] Looking for the footprints of a flood, Woolley (not surprisingly) found them: a ten-foot layer of silt, dividing early Mesopotamian settlements from later.

Seventy years or so later, the geologists William Ryan and Walter Pitman suggested that the flood stories represent, not a devastating Mesopotamian flood, but a permanent inundation, "a flood that never subsided . . . [that] expelled a people from their former homeland and forced them to find a new

* When the Sumerian flood story was first translated, most historians assumed that the Genesis account was derived from it; further study of the substantial differences between the two stories suggests that they are far more likely to have arisen separately from the same source event.

† This view of the universe has been somewhat dented by proof that unrepeatable catastrophes do in fact afflict the earth and, quite often, change the climate or bring an end to an entire species: for example, the asteroid thought to have ended the Cretaceous period. For a layman's overview of ancient global disasters, see Peter James and Nick Thorpe, *Ancient Mysteries*.

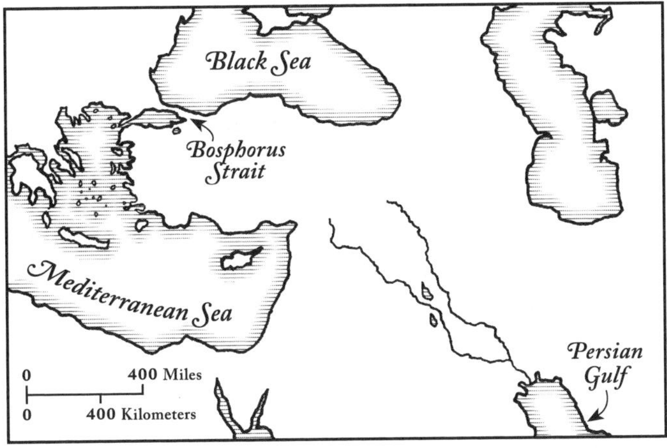

2.1 Before the Ryan-Pitman Flood

place to live."[4] As ice melted and the Mediterranean Sea rose, the Bosphorus Strait, at that point a solid land plug, burst open. The Black Sea overran its banks and settled into a new bed, forever drowning the villages on its edge; the people who escaped travelled south, and took with them the memory of the disaster.

Less spectacular answers have been suggested as well. Perhaps the flood story represents a sort of generalized anxiety about flooding, which undoubtedly was a regular occurrence near the braided stream that ran through Mesopotamia.[5] Or maybe the story of the earth-changing flood reflected the reshaping of the Sumerian homeland as the Gulf crept northwards, swallowing villages in its rising tide.

All of these explanations have their difficulties. Leonard Woolley's silt layer, as further excavation revealed, was far too localized to strike the Mesopotamian residents as civilization-ending. (It also dates to around 2800 BC, which puts it right in the middle of Sumerian civilization.) It is difficult to see how centuries of rising and falling floods, each of which receded and then came again, could be transformed into one single cataclysmic event which forever changed the face of the earth. And although the rising of the Gulf probably inundated villages, the waters crept up at a rate of one foot every ten years or so, which is unlikely to have produced a huge amount of angst.

Pitman and Ryan's theory—based on samples taken from the bottom of the Black Sea—is more engaging. But their flood dates to about 7000 BC, which leaves a question unanswered: How did stories of a universal flood make their way into the oral traditions of so many peoples who, by any reckoning, were far away from Mesopotamia by 7000 BC?

In China, where two independent farming cultures—the Yang-shao and the Longshan—grew up during the centuries that the Sumerians were building their cities, a treacherous warleader tears a rent in the sky's canopy and water rushes through, covering the whole earth and drowning everyone; the only survivor is a noble queen who takes refuge on a mountaintop along with a small band of warriors. In India, a fish warns the wise king Manu that an enormous flood is coming, and that he should build a ship and climb into it as soon as the waters begin to rise. "The waters swept away all the three heavens," the Rig Veda tells us, "and Manu alone was saved."[6]

More intriguing are the flood stories from the Americas, some of which bear an uncanny resemblance to the Mesopotamian stories (and seem to predate Christian missionaries who brought the book of Genesis with them, although this is not always certain). In the Mayan version, "four hundred sons" survive the flood by turning into fish; afterwards, they celebrate their deliverance by getting drunk, at which point they ascend into the heaven and become the Pleiades. (Alert readers will notice the odd parallels to the Noah story, in which signs also appear in the sky, and in which Noah gets insensibly drunk once he's on dry land.) In Peru, a llama refuses to eat; when its owner asks why, the llama warns him that in five days water will rise and overwhelm the earth. The man climbs the highest mountain, survives, and repopulates the earth. (No woman climbs up with him, which seems an unfortunate oversight.) If these American flood stories are related to the Mesopotamian tales, the flood could not have happened in 7000 BC; as the historian John Bright suggests, the shared disaster must have taken place before 10,000 BC, when hunters migrated across the Bering Strait.[7]

So what happened?

Water flooded man's world; and someone suspected, before the flood crashed down, that disaster was on its way.

AFTER THE WATER, the earth dries out. Man starts again, in a world redder in tooth and claw than it was. Something has been lost. In Genesis, Noah is told that it is now acceptable to kill an animal for its meat; in the Sumerian flood story, the gods lament the destruction of the world that was:

> Would that famine had wasted the world
> Rather than the flood.
> Would that pestilence had wasted mankind
> Rather than the flood.[8]

Surely it is not a coincidence that the creation stories of so many countries begin with chaotic waters which must recede so that man can begin his existence on dry land. In the Akkadian creation story, discovered on fragmented tablets along with the Epic of Gilgamesh, the first lines read:

When above were not raised the heavens:
And below on earth a plant had not grown up;
The abyss also had not broken open their boundaries:
The chaos Tiamat was the mother of the whole of them.[9]

In the creation of the world, the sea-being Tiamat is killed, and half of her body is tossed into the heavens, so that death-bringing salt water will not cover the newly dry land.

"In the year and the day of the clouds," the Mixtec creation legend begins, "the world lay in darkness. All things were orderless, and water covered the slime and ooze that then was the earth."[10] "Truly," the Indian Satapatha-Brahamana tells us, "in the beginning was water, nothing but a sea of water." "In the beginning, in the dark, there was nothing but water," the Bantu myth begins. And perhaps best known to those of us born into Christianity or Judaism, the words of Genesis: "In the beginning, the earth was without form and void, and darkness covered the waters; and the Spirit of God hovered over the deeps."

There is no way of knowing what was destroyed by the waters. But like many other peoples, the Sumerians had a tale of lost paradise. In the very ancient Sumerian poem "Enki and Ninhusag," this paradise is described as a place where

the lion does not kill,
the wolf does not seize the lamb,
the wild dog, devourer of kids, is unknown,
he whose eyes hurt does not say: "My eyes hurt."
He whose head aches does not say, "My head aches."[11]

But this dream city, filled with fruit trees and watered by fresh streams uncorrupted by salt, is lost to man.

We are still fascinated by water, and its inundation of the dry and orderly spaces where we live. Witness our ongoing obsession with the *Titanic;* the decks began to tilt, the water crept upwards, and the officers who had certain foreknowledge of the coming catastrophe could do nothing to avert it. Stories of deep water still frighten and attract us; as though, philosopher Richard

Mouw suggests, "images associated with 'the angry deep' have an enduring power in the human imagination that has little to do with our geography."[12]

But this is the territory of theologians and philosophers. The historian can only observe that the brewing of beer seems to have gone on as long as farming, and that the world's oldest wine (found at a village site in the present-day country of Iran) dates to the sixth millennium. For as long as man has grown grain, he has tried to recapture, if only temporarily, the rosier and kinder world that can no longer be found on a map.

Chapter Three

The Rise of Aristocracy

In Sumer, around 3600 BC,
kingship becomes hereditary

After the Great Flood, the Sumerian king list tells us that the city of Kish—to the north, surrounded by cornfields—became the new center of kingship. The list begins over again, with a series of kings generally known as "The First Dynasty of Kish." The first ruler of Kish was a man called Gaur; next came the magnificently named Gulla-Nidaba-annapad; after that, another nineteen kings led right down to Enmebaraggesi, the twenty-second king after the flood. Thanks to inscriptions, we know that Enmebaraggesi ruled around 2700, the first date that we can assign to a Sumerian king.

Which still leaves us with the problem of describing Sumer's history between the Sumerian flood (whenever it was) and 2700 BC. After the flood, kings no longer rule for neat multiples of thirty-six hundred years. Instead, the reigns trail raggedly off, growing shorter and shorter. Altogether, 22,985 years, 3 months, and 3 days elapse between the flood and before Enmebaraggesi comes to the throne—a figure which is not as helpful as its precision may imply. (Scholars of Sumerian literature tend to call the kings before the flood "mythical" and the kings afterwards "quasi-historical," a distinction which eludes me.)

Most of the twenty-one kings who rule before Enmebaraggesi are described with a single phrase: a name, a length of reign, no more. The one exception to this rule comes a little more than halfway through the list, when Etana, the thirteenth king after the deluge, is suddenly set apart from his colorless predecessors.

Etana, he who ascended into heaven,
He who made firm all the lands,
He reigned 1,560 years as king;

And Balih, the son of Etana,
He reigned 400 years.

There is more history here than might appear at first glance.

BY THE TIME the king list resumes, the valley has assumed something like its present shape. The head of the Gulf has advanced northwards. The braided steam that once watered the valley, its branches pushed apart by accumulating silt, has become two large rivers fed by meandering tributaries. Today we call these rivers the Euphrates and the Tigris, names given them by the Greeks; in more ancient times, the western river was called Uruttu, while the quicker and rougher east river was named after the swiftness of an arrow in flight: Idiglat.*

Between these two rivers, cities grew up. Archaeology tells us that by 3200, large groups of country-dwellers were shifting their whole way of life, moving into walled cities in a phenomenon called "streaming-in."

The transition was not always peaceful. The book of Genesis and its parallel flood story give us an intriguing glimpse of disruption: When Noah begins again, his descendants spread out across the land. In Shinar, the Semitic name for the southern Mesopotamian plain, city-building is taken to a particularly high level. Carried away by their own skill, the city-dwellers decide to make themselves a tower that reaches up to heaven, a tower that will give them place of pride not only over the earth, but over God himself. This act of arrogance brings confusion of language, estrangement, and eventually war.

The Tower of Babel, like the biblical flood, lies in the undatable past. But it gives us a window into a world where mud-brick cities, walled and towered, spread their reach across Mesopotamia.[1] A dozen walled cities, each circled by suburbs that stretched out for as much as six miles, jostled each other for power: Eridu, Ur, Uruk, Nippur, Adab, Lagash, Kish, and more. Perhaps as many as forty thousand souls lived in these ancient urban centers.

Each city was protected by a god whose temple drew pilgrims from the surrounding countryside. And each city sent tentacles of power out into the countryside, aspiring to rule more and more land. Shepherds and herdsmen came into the city to bring gifts to the gods, to sell and buy—and to pay the

* Of the four rivers named in Genesis 2—Pishon, Gihon, Hiddeqel, and Perat—it appears that Pishon and Gihon disappeared, while Hiddeqel became known as Idiglat, later the Tigris, and Perat ("Great River") as Uruttu, later the Euphrates. Modern English translations of Genesis 2 tend to cheat and translate Hiddeqel (חדקל) as "Tigris" and Perat (פרת) as "Euphrates."

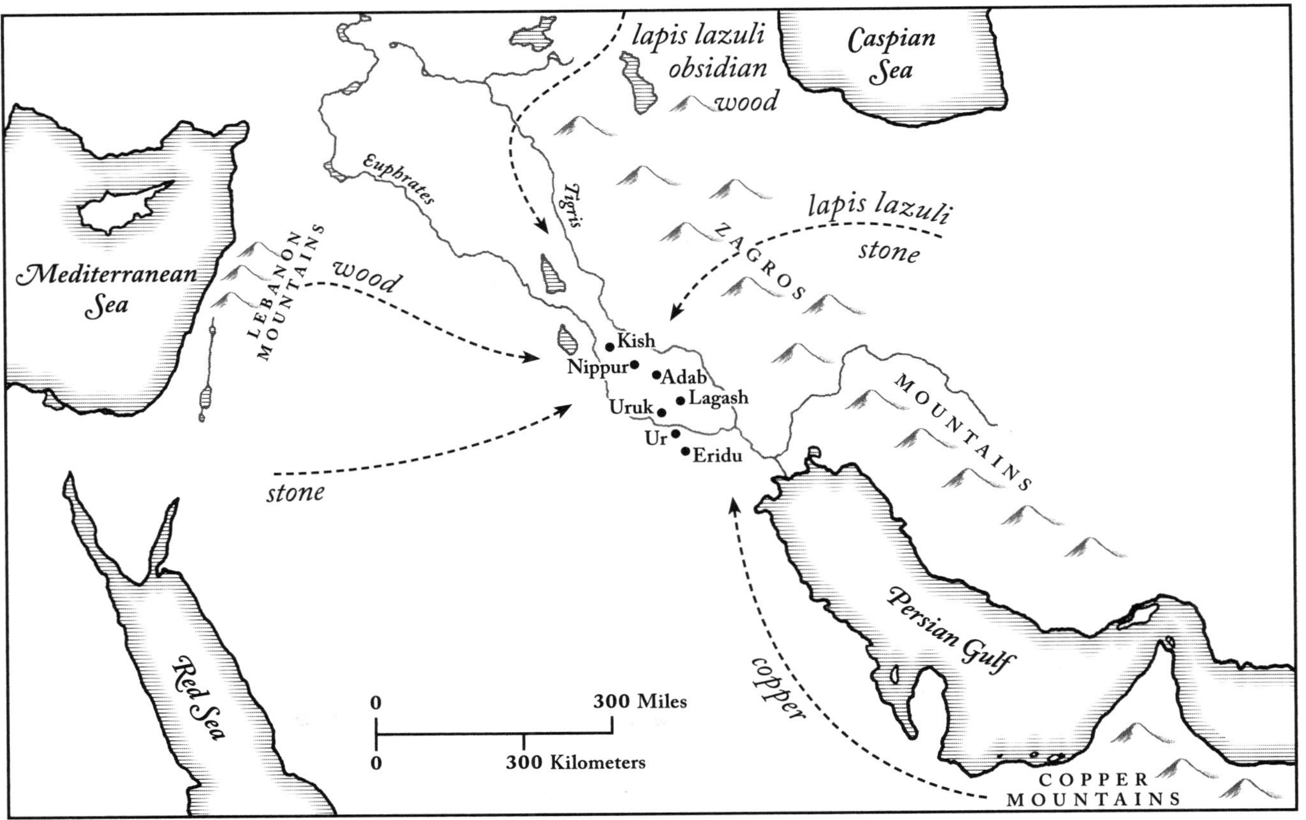

3.1 *Early Cities of Sumer*

taxes demanded by priests and kings. They relied on the city for trade and for worship, but the city demanded as much as it gave. The egalitarian structure of earlier hunter-gatherer groups had shattered. A hierarchy now existed: the city first, the countryside second.

Ten generations (or so) after the deluge, hierarchy took on a new form. Men claimed the right to rule, for the first time, not by virtue of strength or wisdom, but by right of blood.

The tenth king of Kish after the flood, Atab, is the first to be succeeded by his son and then by his grandson. This three-generation dynasty is the earliest blood succession in recorded history. But when the next king, Etana, takes the throne, he faces a brand new difficulty.

Of Etana, the king list tells us only that he "ascended into heaven"—a detail given without clarification. To discover more, we have to turn to a much later poem, which appears to preserve an older Sumerian story. In this poem, Etana is a pious king, faithful to the gods, but he has one great sorrow: he has no child. He laments, in his prayers,

> I have honoured the gods and respected the spirits of the dead,
> The dream-interpreters have made full use of my incense,
> The gods have made full use of my lambs at the slaughter . . .
> Remove my shame and provide me with a son![2]

In a frightening dream, Etana sees that his city will suffer if he can provide no heir to his throne:

> The city of Kish was sobbing
> Within it the people were in mourning . . .
> Etana cannot give you an heir![3]

Almost without remark, another huge change has come to man. Kingship has become hereditary. The leader who takes on the burden of his people's good is now born to that task, fitted for it by blood. For the first time, we see the rise of an aristocracy: a class born to rule.

The gods have pity on Etana and show him an answer. He must ride on an eagle's back up to heaven, where he will find the plant of birth, the secret to fathering a son. The tablet breaks off, and the rest of the story is lost. But the king list tells us that Balih, the son of Etana, reigned after Etana's death, so we can assume that the quest succeeded.

Inequality has been enshrined in blood. Like the idea of kingship itself, the idea of a born aristocracy never really goes away.

SINCE THOSE who are born to lead should clearly control as much territory as possible, Etana then "makes firm the land" for his son.

The cities of Mesopotamia were independent, each ruled by a local prince. But Kish lay between the two rivers, a position which simply cried out for some exercise of overlordship. Sumer, after all, had no native wood; only a few imported palm trees, which make for third-rate building material. There was no stone, no copper, no obsidian, nothing but mud and a few deposits of bitumen (asphalt, used as "pitch" in torches and as a mortar-binder). Wood had to be shipped down from the northeastern Zagros Mountains, or brought from the Lebanon Mountains to the northwest. Copper came from the southern Arabian mountains, lapis lazuli from the rocky lands north and east; stone from the desert to the west and obsidian from the far north. In exchange, the Sumerian cities traded the goods of an agricultural society: grain, cloth, leather, pottery. Sumerian pots and bowls show up in a wide swath of little settlements and towns all across eastern Europe and northern Asia.

Some of this trade took place across the deserts to the east and west, but a huge proportion went up and down the Tigris and Euphrates; the old name of the Euphrates, the Uruttu, means "copper river." The Mesopotamian valley, as archaeologist Charles Pellegrino points out, was a linear civilization: "an oasis thousands of miles long with a width of less than ten miles."[4] If a city downstream intended to send upriver to the mountains of Lebanon for cedar logs, the goods had to pass Kish. The king of Kish, collecting some percentage from the traffic passing by his city, could feather his own nest by plucking a few feathers from other princes.

By the time that Etana's son inherited, Kish had replaced the old southern city of Eridu as the most powerful city on the plain. By 2500, kings of other cities sometimes claim the title "king of Kish" as though it has become an honorary label, showing some sort of authority over other Sumerian cities.[5]

Collecting tribute is one thing, though, and actual conquest is another. Etana and his kin never extended imperial rule to the other cities of Sumer. The difficulty of moving armies up and down the length of the plain may have dissuaded the kings of Kish from actually conquering other cities; or perhaps they simply had, as yet, no thought of imperial leadership to complement the ideas of kingship and aristocracy. The first empire-builder would come from another nation entirely.

Chapter Four

The Creation of Empire

In the Nile river valley, around 3200 BC,
the Scorpion King unites northern and southern Egypt,
and Narmer of the First Dynasty makes the union permanent

SOUTHWEST OF SUMER, beneath the coast of the Mediterranean Sea, the first empire-builder stormed through the Nile river valley.

Like the first kings of Sumer, the Scorpion King hovers on the border between history and myth. He appears on no king list; he exists only as a carved image on the head of a ceremonial weapon. But unlike the first kings of Sumer, who occupy the vague distant past, the Scorpion King lives almost within the realm of written history. He made his effort to conquer his world around 3200 BC.

The Scorpion King was the descendant of an African people who had once lived on either side of the Nile valley. Centuries before his birth—in the days when the legendary Alulim ruled over a damper, cooler Sumer—the Nile valley was probably uninhabitable. Every year, when heavy rains poured down on the southern mountains, the gathered waters cascaded down the length of the Nile, northwards to the Mediterranean, and rushed far out over the surrounding land. The flooding was so violent that few groups of hunters and gatherers dared to linger. Instead, they lived in the more hospitable lands to the east and west: settling close to the shores of the Red Sea, and wandering through the Sahara. In those milder, wetter years, the Sahara was grassy and watered. Archaeologists have discovered leaves, trees, and the remains of game animals beneath the sands.

But the hotter, dryer weather patterns that changed the Mesopotamian plain also withered the Sahara. The people of the Sahara journeyed east, towards the well-watered Nile valley. Thanks to the decreasing rains, the Nile flood had become more moderate; the refugees found that they could manage the yearly inundation, digging reservoirs to hold the water at flood-time, and canals to irrigate their fields in the drier months. They built settlements on the banks, planted grain in the dark silt left by the floods, and hunted the wildlife of the marshes: wild cattle, ibex, crocodiles, hippopotami, fish, and birds. Other peoples travelled over from the western shores of the Red Sea to join them. They were the first full-time residents of the Nile valley: the first Egyptians.*

Unlike Sumer, the Nile valley had game and fish, stone, copper, gold, flax, papyrus—everything but wood. The Egyptians did trade west for ivory, east for shells, and north for semiprecious stones, but to survive they needed only the Nile.

The Nile, the bloodstream of Egypt, ran through a valley five hundred miles long, bordered by cliffs in some places and by flatlands in others. The yearly floodwaters began upstream, in what are now the Ethiopian highlands, ran down past the Second Cataract towards the First Cataract, careened around a bend where kings would one day be buried, and thundered towards a flat plain where the river finally fell away into a dozen streams: the Nile Delta.

Because the Nile flowed from south to north, it was clear to the Egyptians that every other river ran backwards. Judging from later hieroglyphs, they used one word for *north, downstream,* and *back of the head,* and another for *upstream, south,* and *face;*[1] an Egyptian always oriented himself by turning south, towards the oncoming Nile current. From the days of the earliest settlements, the Egyptians buried their dead at the edge of the desert, with their heads pointed south and their faces turned west towards the Saharan waste. Life came from the south, but the Land of the Dead was westward, towards the desert they had fled as grass and water disappeared.

The Egyptians gave their country two different names. The land where the yearly flood laid down its silt was Kemet, the Black Land; black was the color of life and resurrection. But beyond the Black Land lay Deshret, the deathly Red Land. The line between life and death was so distinct that a man could

* Like early Sumerian history, early Egyptian history before about 3000 BC ("predynastic Egypt") is divided into archaeological periods, each period defined partly by pottery styles, and named after towns where typical pottery was found. The earliest settlements, from about 5000 to 4000, are called Badarian. Between 4000 and 3000 BC is known as the Naqada Period, and was once divided into three phases: the Amratian, which runs from 4000 to 3500 BC; the Gerzean, from 3500 to 3200 BC; and the Final Predynastic, from 3200 to 3000 BC. Some Egyptologists divide Naqada into two periods, Naqada I (ends 3400) and II (3400–3200 or so). Yet others label 4000–3500 as Naqada I, 3500–3100 as Naqada II, avoid the labels Amratian and Gerzean altogether, and assign yet a third period, Naqada III, to 3100–3000—a century also sometimes called Dynasty 0. Since there is little reason to think that Egyptian culture is somehow unrelated to these earlier settlements of the Nile valley, I will use "Egyptian" throughout. (It was once traditional to suggest that Egyptian culture came from outside the Nile valley and was brought by invaders around 3400, but continued excavations have not supported this theory.)

bend over and place one hand in fertile black earth, the other on red, sun-baked desert.

This doubleness, an existence carried on between two extremes, was echoed in Egypt's growing civilization. Like the cities of Sumer, the Egyptian cities saw "streaming-in" by 3200 BC. Nubt (also called Nadaqa), on the east-west route that led to gold mines, became the strongest city of the south, with Hierakonpolis, home to at least ten thousand, not far behind. Very early, these southern cities identified themselves not as separate and sovereign, but as part of a kingdom: the White Kingdom (also called "Upper Egypt," since it lay upstream from the Mediterranean), ruled by a king who wore the cylindrical White Crown. In the north of Egypt ("Lower Egypt"), cities banded together in an alliance called the Red Kingdom; the cities of Heliopolis and Buto grew to prominence. The king of Lower Egypt wore the Red Crown, with a cobra shape curling from its front (the earliest portrayal of the crown dates to around 4000 BC),[2] and was protected by a cobra-goddess who spat venom at the king's enemies.[3] The two kingdoms, White and Red, like the Red and Black Lands, mirrored that basic Egyptian reality: the world is made up of balanced and opposing forces.

Unlike the Sumerian king list, which apparently intends to chronicle the beginning of time, the oldest Egyptian king lists do not go all the way back to the White and Red Kingdoms, so the names of their kings are lost. But for the existence of the Scorpion King, we have a different kind of testimony: a macehead, unearthed at the temple at Hierakonpolis. On it, a White King, wearing the distinctive White Crown, celebrates his victory over defeated soldiers of the Red Kingdom (and holds an irrigation tool, showing his power to sustain his people). To his right, a hieroglyph records his name: Scorpion.*

The Scorpion King himself may well have been a native of Hierakonpolis, which was itself a double city. Hierakonpolis was originally two cities divided by the Nile: Nehken, on the west bank, was dedicated to the falcon-god, and Nekheb on the east was guarded by the vulture-goddess. Over time, the two separate cities grew into one, watched over by the vulture. Perhaps the Scorpion King, seeing the two halves united, first conceived his plan of drawing White and Red Kingdoms together under one king.

His victory, which probably took place around 3200 BC, was temporary. Another carving records the reunion of the two kingdoms under another White King, perhaps a hundred years later. Like the Scorpion King macehead,

* Some studies of predynastic Egypt mention two Scorpion Kings; Scorpion II is the first empire-builder. An earlier king, Scorpion I, may have ruled in the south, but apparently made no effort to unite the country; he may be buried in the tomb at U-jat Abydos.

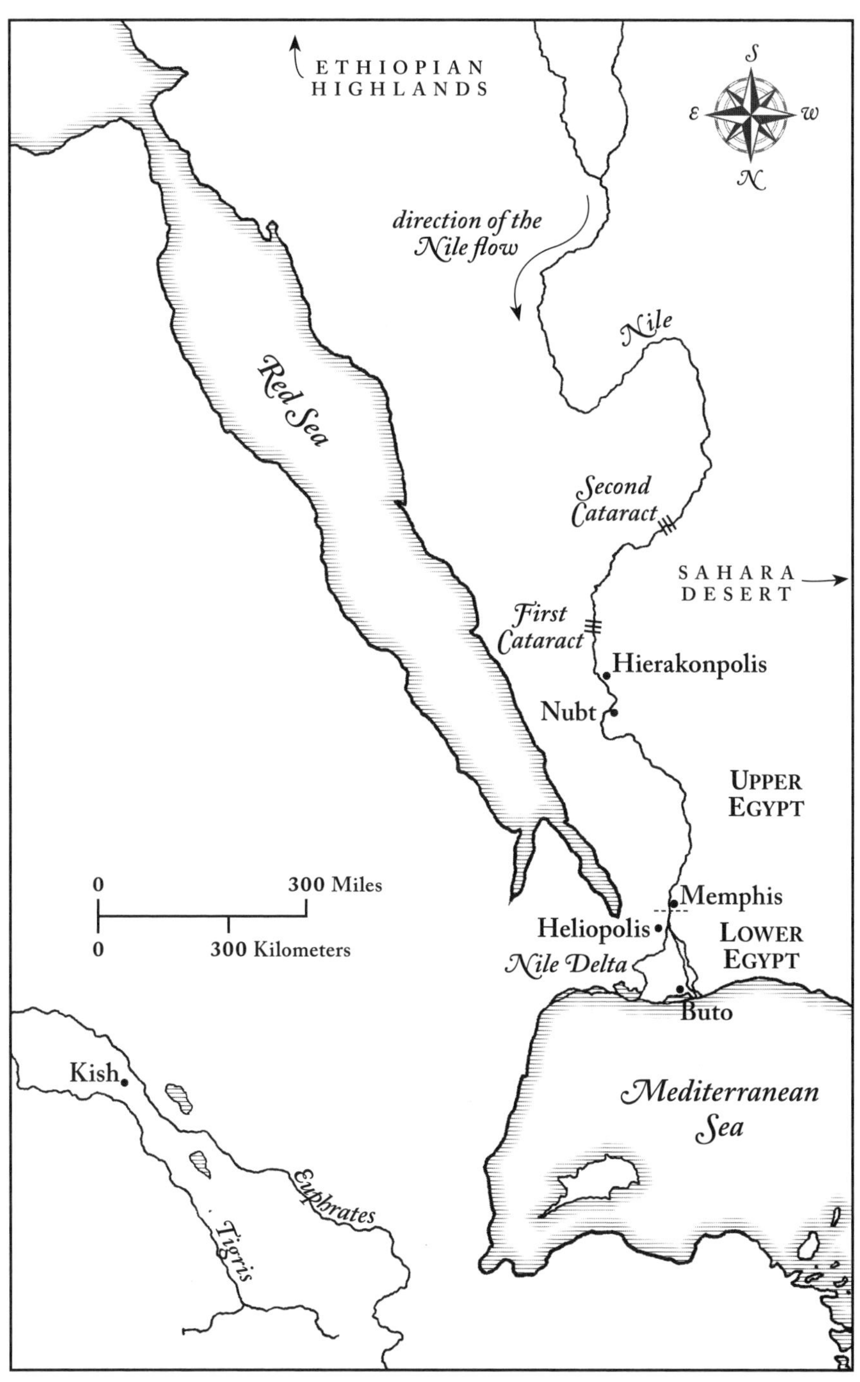

4.1 Upper and Lower Egypt

4.1. Scorpion King Macehead. On this ritual macehead, the "Scorpion King" is identified by the scorpion just to the left of his head. Ashmolean Museum, Oxford. Photo credit Werner Forman/Art Resource, NY

the carving was found at the temple at Hierakonpolis. Done on a palette (a flat piece of stone that served as a "canvas"), the carving shows a king who wears the Red Crown on the front of the palette, and the White Crown on the back. A hieroglyph names the king: Narmer.

The name Narmer means "Raging Catfish," or, more poetically, "Baleful Catfish." It is a compliment, as the catfish was the bravest and most aggressive of all fish. On the back of the Narmer Palette, Narmer, in his role as White King, holds a warrior of the Red Kingdom by the hair. On the front, Narmer—having doffed the White Crown and put on the Red Crown instead—parades in victory past the bodies of decapitated warriors. He has drawn the Red Kingdom under White Kingdom rule at last.

It seems likely that Narmer is another name for Menes, who appears in the

4.2. Narmer Palette. The unifier of Egypt strikes a conquered Egyptian enemy, while the Horus falcon delivers another captive to him. Egyptian Museum, Cairo. Photo credit Werner Forman/Art Resource, NY

Egyptian king lists as the first human king of Egypt.* Of him, the Egyptian priest Manetho writes:

> After the [gods] and the demigods,
> the First Dynasty comes, with eight kings.
> Menes was the first.
> He led the army across the frontier and won great glory.[4]

* There is, naturally, an ongoing debate about this. From 1500 BC on, inscriptions call the unifier of Egypt "Meni." This could be the "Menes" of Manetho, the "Narmer" of the palette, a later king named Aha, or—a suggestion which will probably gum up the identification of Egypt's unifier permanently—it could even be a grammatical form meaning "The one who came." Whoever he is, he seems to have spearheaded the unification of the two kingdoms.

The breach of the frontier—the border between the kingdoms—created the first empire, and one of the world's longest lived: great glory indeed.

Manetho's account comes long after the fact. Manetho served in the temple of the sun-god Ra at Heliopolis twenty-seven centuries later; around 300 BC, he took it upon himself to reconcile different versions of the Egyptian king lists into one document, using (among other records) a papyrus called the Turin Canon, which also identifies Menes ("Men") as the first king of Egypt.* When he compiled his list, Manetho organized the scores of Egyptian rulers since 3100 into groups, beginning a new group each time a new family rose to power, or the kingship changed locations. He called these groups *dynasteia,* a Greek term for "power of rule." Manetho's "dynasties" are not always accurate, but they have become traditional markers in Egyptian history.

The First Dynasty begins, for Manetho, when the two parts of Egypt were united under the first king of all Egypt. According to the Greek historian Herodotus, Menes/Narmer celebrated his victory by building a brand new capital at Memphis, the central point of his brand new kingdom. Memphis means "White Walls"; the walls were plastered so that they shone in the sun. From the white city, the ruler of united Egypt could control both the southern valley and the northern delta. Memphis was the fulcrum point on which the two kingdoms balanced.

Another scene, carved on a macehead, shows Narmer/Menes wearing the Red Crown and taking part in some ceremony that looks much like a wedding; possibly the victorious founder of the First Dynasty married the princess of the Red Kingdom in order to unite both kingdoms in the bodies of the Double Crown's heirs.

For the rest of Egypt's history, the doubleness of its origin was enshrined in its king. He was called the Lord of Two Lands, and his Double Crown was made up of the Red Crown of Lower Egypt set on top of the White Crown of Upper Egypt. The southern vulture and the northern cobra, one crawling on the earth and the other inhabiting the sky, guarded the united kingdom. Two contrary powers had been brought together into a mighty and balanced whole.

Narmer himself reigned for sixty-four years and then went out on a hippo hunt, a quest traditionally undertaken by the king as a display of his power over civilization-threatening enemies. According to Manetho, he was cornered by the hippopotamus, and killed on the spot.

* Many of the king lists, found on tomb or palace walls, are clearly written to boost the reputation of one pharaoh or another; the Turin Canon, written about 1250 BC, is a reasonably independent listing that seems to preserve a much older oral tradition.

TIMELINE 4	
MESOPOTAMIA	EGYPT
Warming begins (11,000 BC)	
Sumerian and Semitic peoples mingle	
Beginning of kingship	
The deluge	
	First Egyptians settle in the Nile valley
Ubaid period (5000–4000)	Badarian period (5000–4000)
Uruk period (4000–3200)	Naqada period (4000–3000)
Jemdat Nasr period (3200–2900)	
Atab	Archaic period (3100–2686)
Etanah	*Dynasty 1* (3100–2890)
Balih	**Menes (Narmer)**

Note: On all timelines, names of rulers are in bold type.

Chapter Five

The Age of Iron

In the Indus river valley, in 3102 BC, northern wanderers settle and build towns

IN THE YEARS when the king of Kish collected tribute from the ships sailing up and down the Euphrates, and when the white walls of Memphis rose at the balanced center of Egypt, the third great civilization of ancient times was still a string of tiny villages on a river plain. There would be no great cities and no empire-building in India for at least six hundred years.

The people who settled along the length of the Indus river were not city-dwellers. Nor were they list-keepers, as the Sumerians were. They did not carve the likeness of their leaders on stone, or set down their achievements on tablets. So we know very little about the first centuries of India.

We can try to mine the Indian epics for clues. Although they were written down very late (thousands, not hundreds, of years after the first settlements), they likely preserve a much older tradition. But even in this tradition, only one king, and one date, stand out with any clarity. In the year 3102, the wise king Manu presided over the beginning of the present age, and his age still has well over four hundred thousand years to go.

LONG BEFORE 3102, shepherds and nomads wandered into India. Some came down from central Asia, through the gap in the northern mountains now called the Khyber Pass. Others may have climbed straight over the Himalaya themselves (the occasional skeleton suggests that this route was as treacherous then as now).

They found both warmth and water on the other side of the mountains. The Himalaya acted as a barrier to frost, so that even in winter the temperature barely dropped below fifty degrees. In summer, the sun lit the Indian countryside into blazing heat. But two great rivers kept the subcontinent from

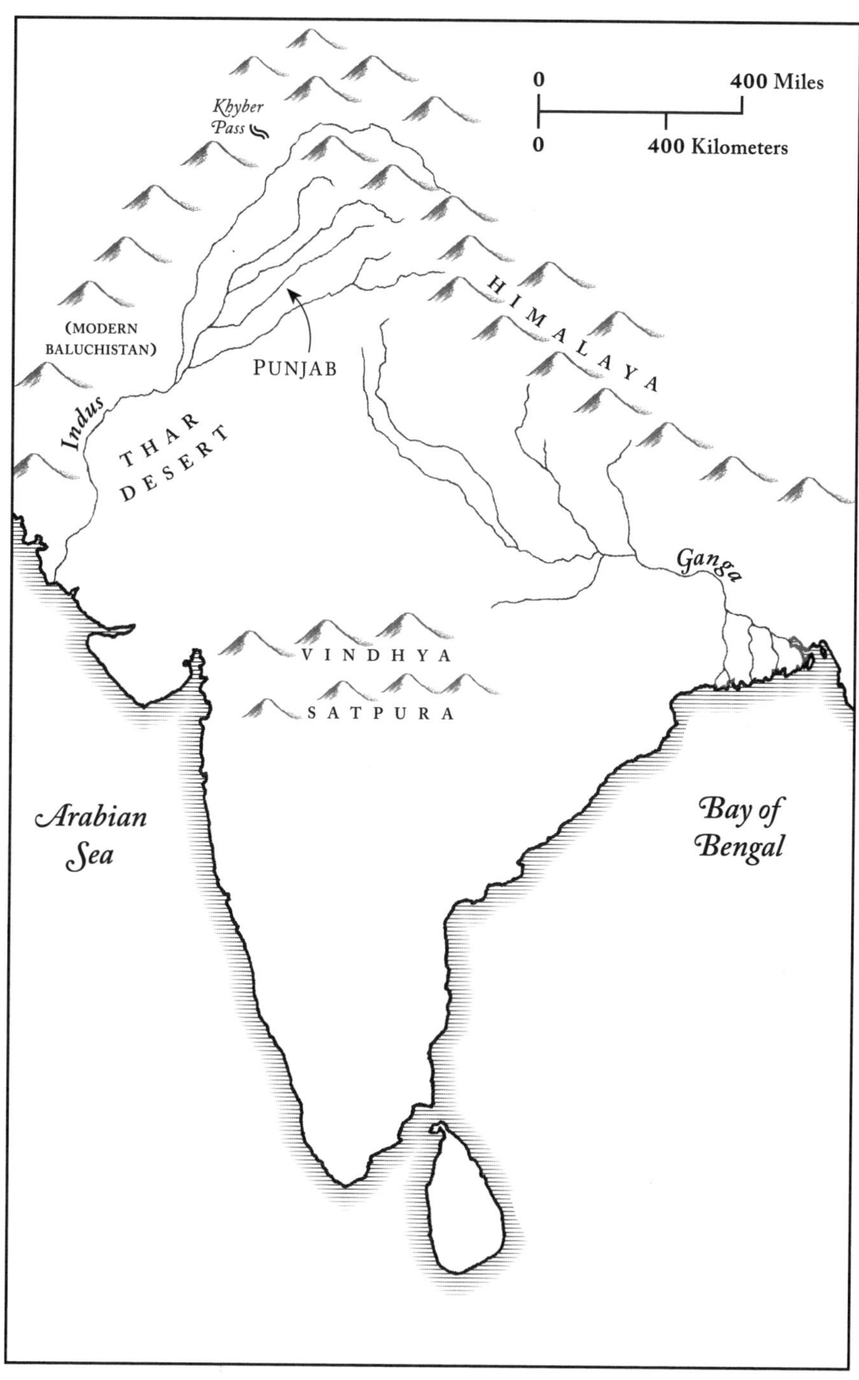
0
400 Miles
0
400 Kilometers
Khyber Pass
(MODERN BALUCHISTAN)
PUNJAB
HIMALAYA
Indus
THAR DESERT
Ganga
VINDHYA
SATPURA
Arabian Sea
Bay of Bengal

5.1 India

desert barrenness. Melted snow and ice streamed down from the mountains into the Indus, which flowed northwest through India into the Arabian Sea; the mountains also fed the Ganga, which poured down from the Himalayan slopes and into the Bay of Bengal, far on the eastern coast. In the days when the Sahara was green, the Thar desert east of the Indus river was also green, and yet another river, now long dry, ran through it into the Arabian Sea.[1]

Perhaps two thousand years after crops were first grown in Mesopotamia and Egypt, northern wanderers settled in the hilly land just west of the Indus, today called Baluchistan. Tiny villages spread along the lower Indus river, and along the five branches of its upper end: the Punjab (the *panj-ab,* the "Five Rivers"). Other villages grew up along the Ganga. Down in the south of India, tools much like those used in southern Africa suggest that a few intrepid souls may have shoved off from the coast of Africa, sailed to India's southwest shores, and settled there.

But these three areas—the south, the east, and the northwest—were divided from each other by enormous physical barriers. Hundreds of miles of plains and two mountain ranges, the Vindhya and Satpura, separated the north from the peoples of the south, whose known history comes much later. As the weather warmed, a desert three hundred miles wide spread its sands between the Ganga valley and the settlements in the northwest. From the very beginning of Indian history, the peoples of the south, the east, and the northwest lived independent of each other.

The villages near the Indus, in the northwest, grew into towns first.

The earliest houses in the Indus river valley were built on the river plain, perhaps a mile away from the river, well above the line of the flood. Mud bricks would dissolve in river water, and crops would wash away. The first reality of life in the Indus valley—as in Egypt and Sumer—was that water brought both life and death.

Which brings us to the first king of India, Manu Vaivaswata. Before Manu Vaivaswata, so the story goes, six semidivine kings had reigned in India. Each bore the name-title of Manu, and each ruled for a Manwantara, an age longer than four million years.

We are here clearly in the realm of mythology, but according to tradition, myth began to cross history during the reign of the seventh Manu. This Manu, sometimes simply called "Manu" and sometimes known by his full name of Manu Vaivaswata, was washing his hands one morning when a tiny fish came wriggling up to him, begging for protection from the stronger and larger fish who preyed on the weak, as was "the custom of the river." Manu had pity and saved the fish.

Past danger of being eaten, the fish repaid his kindness by warning him of

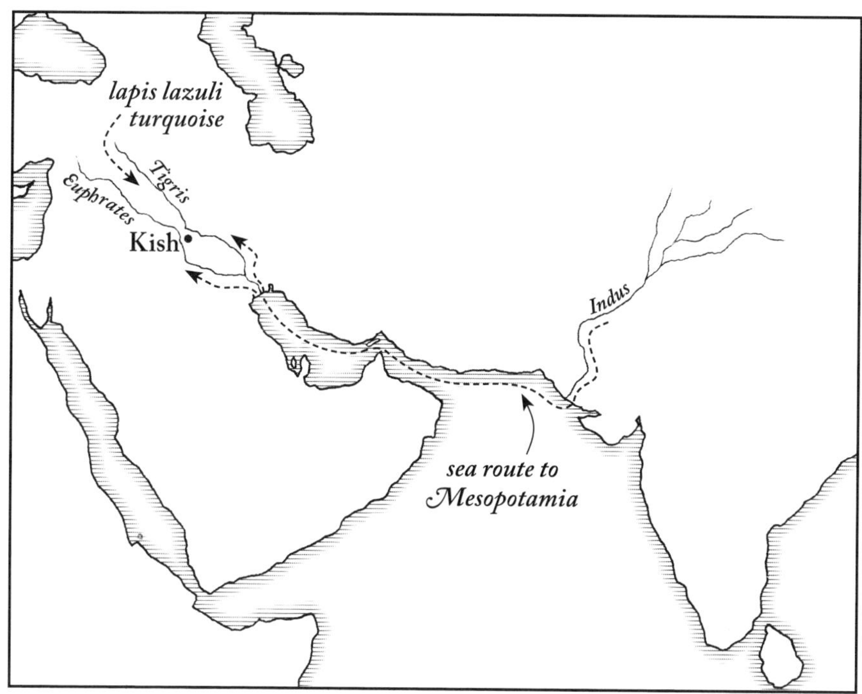

5.2 Indian Trade Routes

a coming flood that would sweep away the heavens and the earth. So Manu built a wooden ark and went on board with seven wise sages, known as the Rishis. When the flood subsided, Manu anchored his ship to a far northern mountain, disembarked, and became the first king of historical India; the seven Rishis, meanwhile, became the seven stars of the Big Dipper. The year was 3102.

For the purposes of reconstructing Indian history, this story is more smoke than fire. Manu Vaivaswata has less claim to actual existence than the Scorpion King of Egypt, even though they seem to occupy the same century, and the oddly precise date 3102 is a result of backfiguring done by literary scholars at least two thousand years later, when the oral traditions began to be set down in writing. But the date itself appears in many histories of India; firm dates in ancient Indian history are hard to come by, so historians who cling to this one do so more from relief than from certainty. ("It is the first credible date in India's history," John Keay writes, "and being one of such improbable exactitude, it deserves respect.")[2]

The only certainty about 3102 is that, around this date, villages in the Indus valley did indeed start to grow into towns. Two-story houses began to rise; the

Indus settlers began to throw pots on wheels and to make tools of copper. They began to cut the forests and bake their clay in kilns. Oven-burned brick, more durable than brick dried in the sun, was less vulnerable to the swirling waters of floods. After 3102, water no longer had quite so destructive a power.

Turquoise and lapis lazuli, brought from the plains north of Mesopotamia, lie in the ruins of the richest houses. The townspeople had left their valley to trade above the Tigris and the Euphrates, with those same merchants who supplied semiprecious stones to the kings of Kish and Nippur and Ur.

But despite the growing prosperity and reach of the Indus towns, the epics of India tell not of advance, but of decline. The flood had washed away the previous age and begun a new one; the age of towns was the Kali Yuga, the Age of Iron. It began when Manu descended from the mountain, and it was an age of wealth and industry. It was also an age in which truthfulness, compassion, charity, and devotion dwindled to a quarter of their previous strength.* In the Iron Age, the sacred writings warned, leaders would commandeer the goods that belonged to their people, pleading financial need. The strong would take property from the vulnerable, and seize hard-won wealth for themselves. Rich men would abandon their fields and herds and spend their days protecting their money, becoming slaves of their earthly possessions rather than free men who knew how to use the earth.

Given the relatively late date at which these dreadful warnings were put down, they probably reflect the worries of a more mature society—one which already had a large, unproductive bureaucracy draining the national coffers. But the storytellers themselves put the beginnings of this declension all the way back to 3102, the year when villages along the Indus began to grow into towns.

Manu himself, kneeling down by the water that will soon wash away the previous age and bring on the decline of the Kali Yuga, finds himself speaking to a little fish forced to beg for protection from the larger and stronger who prey upon the weak. In India, the journey towards civilization had just begun; but as in Sumer itself, it was a journey which took its people that much farther from paradise.

* In the Indian cosmology, the previous three ages of Gold, Silver, and Copper (Satya Yuga, Treta Yuga, and Duapara Yuga, respectively) had each seen spiritual awareness diminish by one quarter; the Iron Age, being the fourth, is the most wicked of all.

TIMELINE 5	
EGYPT	INDIA
First Egyptians settle in the Nile valley	
Badarian period (5000–4000)	
Naqada period (4000–3000)	Early settlements along the lower Indus and in the Punjab
Archaic period (3100–2686)	Kali Yuga, the Age of Iron (3102–present)
Dynasty 1 (3100–2890)	Villages begin to grow into towns
Menes (Narmer)	**Manu Vaivaswata**

Note on sources for Indian history: Historians of India work in a fraught political arena. The written sources which we have, including those which tell of the mythological Manu and the Ages of Gold, Copper, Silver, and Iron, are oral traditions which were set down, much later, in the language Sanskrit. The political movement in India known as "Hindu nationalism" or "Hindutva" claims that this later "Hindu" (or "Brahmanical") tradition is essentially native to India. Many academic historians, most notably Romila Thapar, argue instead that what we now call "Hinduism" arose as an interplay between native traditions and later immigrants from central Asia (the so-called "Aryan invaders"; see Chapters Twenty-Five and Thirty-Seven), and that the Sanskrit writings represent the thought of a small, elite group of Aryan immigrants. In terms of history, this would mean that the written accounts of Manu and the Age of Iron have practically no continuity with the earliest civilizations of India. However, the theory of Aryan invasion was distorted in the late nineteenth century by racist assumptions and political agendas, so that "Hindu nationalists" now see any version of the Aryan invasion theory as an offensive racist ploy. In reaction, scholars who believe that linguistic evidence supports some kind of invasion from the outside often paste the label "Hindutva fundamentalist" on anyone who uses later Sanskrit mythology to elucidate early Indian history. Manu is clearly mythological; his relationship to India in the fourth millennium remains extremely uncertain.

Chapter Six

The Philosopher King

In the Yellow river valley, between 2852 and 2205 BC, the early villages of China acquire kings but reject their heirs

FAR EAST OF MESOPOTAMIA AND INDIA, the familiar pattern repeated itself once more.

This time, settlement began around the Yellow river, which ran east from the high plateau now called Qing Zang Gaoyuan—the Plateau of Tibet—and ended in the Yellow Sea. Farther south, the Yangtze river also ran to the eastern coast.

In the days when the Sahara was green and the Thar desert watered by a river, the wide expanse of land between the two great rivers of China was probably an earth-and-water patchwork of swamps, lakes, and mud. The peninsula of Shandong, between the two rivers, was almost an island. Hunters and gatherers might wander through the marshes, but there was little reason to settle on the water-soaked land.

Then the Sahara warmed; the Nile floods lessened; the river that once watered the Thar Desert disappeared; the braided stream of Mesopotamia slowly became two separate rivers as soil built up between them. Between the two great rivers of China, the land dried.

By 5000 BC, the expanse between the rivers was a wide plain, with forests on its high places. The wanderers had begun to settle, planting rice in the wet ground around the rivers. Houses multiplied and villages grew up. Archaeology reveals the first significant clusters of houses near the Yellow river. Here, settlement slowly became something like a culture: people with the same customs, the same methods of building houses, the same style of pottery, and presumably the same language.

This Yellow river culture, which we now call the Yang-shao, was not the only cluster of settlements in China. On the southeast coast of China, facing the East China Sea, another culture called Dapenkeng appeared; in the Yangtze

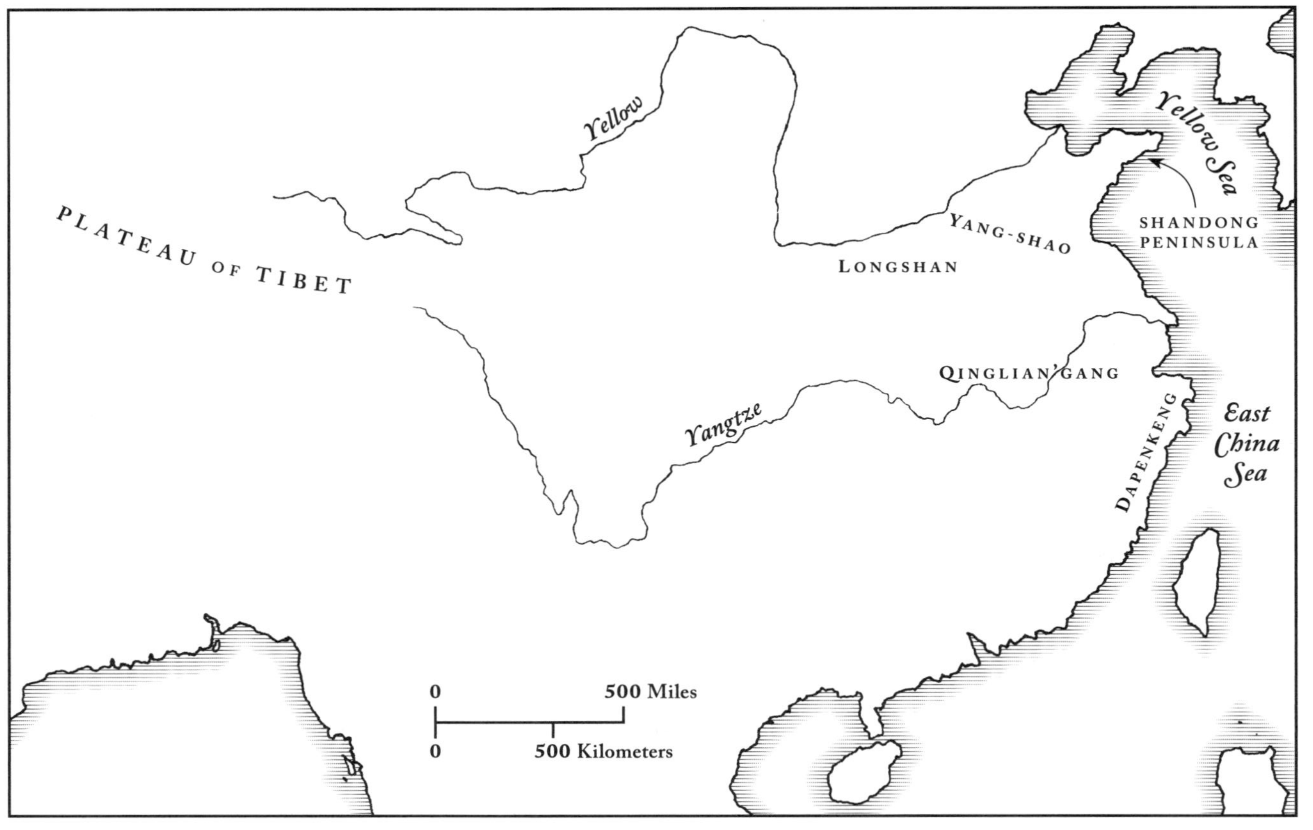

6.1 China's Early Settlements

river valley farther to the south, the Qinglian'gang grew up.[1] Beneath the great southern bend of the Yellow river, a fourth cluster of settlements, the Longshan, sprang up. Excavations show Longshan ruins overtop of Yang-shao remains, suggesting that the Longshan may have peacefully overwhelmed at least part of the Yellow river culture.

We know almost nothing about the lives and customs of any of these four groups of people. All we can do is label them with different names because they have different styles of pottery and different methods of farming and building; a Yang-shao settlement might be surrounded by a ditch, while a Longshan village might be set off from the surrounding waste by a wall of earth. But apart from very general speculations (perhaps the arrangement of a cemetery near a village on the south bank of the Yellow river hints at a very early form of ancestor worship; perhaps the burial of food along with the dead shows belief in a pleasant afterlife), we have no clues: only the stories which claim to tell of China's beginnings.

Like the stories of the Mahabharata, the stories of early China were set down several thousand years after the times they describe. But insofar as they keep older traditions alive, they tell of a first king who discovered the essential order of all things. His name was Fu Xi.

Sima Qian, the Grand Historian who collected the traditional tales of China into an epic history, tells us that Fu Xi began his rule in 2850. He invented the Eight Trigrams, a pattern of straight and broken lines used for record-keeping, divination, and interpretation of events. As he meditated on the appearance of birds and beasts, Fu Xi

> drew directly from his own person,
> and indirectly he drew upon external objects.
> And so it was that he created the Eight Trigrams
> in order to communicate the virtue of divine intelligence
> and to classify the phenomenon of all living things.[2]

The patterns of the Eight Trigrams are modelled after the markings on turtle shells. The first Chinese king didn't save his people from a flood, receive authority from heaven, or bring two countries into one. No; *his* great accomplishment was, for the Chinese, far more important. He found a connection between the world and the self, between the patterns of nature and the impulse of the human mind to order everything around it.

IN CHINESE LEGEND, Fu Xi is followed by the second great king, Shennong, who first made a plow from wood and dug in the earth. The *Huai-nan Tzu* says that he taught people to find the best soil, to sow and grow the five grains that sustain life, to thresh them, and to eat good herbs and avoid the poisonous. The Farmer King was followed by the third great king, perhaps the greatest of all: Huangdi, the Yellow Emperor.*

Huangdi is traditionally thought to have ruled from 2696 to 2598 BC. In his reign, he first conquered his brother, the Flame King, and spread his rule over his brother's land. Then the southern warleader Chi You, who had been faithful to the Flame King, launched a rebellion against the victorious Yellow Emperor. Chi You was an unpleasant character; he invented war, forged the first metal swords, ate pebbles and stones with his unbreakable teeth, and led an army of evildoers and giants. He charged against the army of Huangdi on a battlefield covered with fog; Huangdi had to use a magic chariot, equipped with a compass, to find his way to the center of the fight (which he won).

This is anachronistic. There were no compasses in China in 2696, magic or otherwise. Nor were there any cities. When Memphis and Kish were flourishing, the Yellow river settlements were still wood-posted, wattle-and-daub clusters surrounded by earthen ditches and walls. The people who lived in these settlements had learned to fish, to plant and harvest grain, and (we assume) to fight against invaders. Huangdi, if he fought for his empire against his brother and his brother's warleader, won not an empire of thriving cities and merchants, but rural clusters of huts surrounded by rice and millet fields.

But some kind of transition in the structure of Chinese government took place after Huangdi's conquests. Back in Sumer, the idea of hereditary power was well-established by this time. Apparently, the same issue reared its head in China almost at once. Huangdi, the last of the three great kings, was followed by a king called Yao. Yao, who was filled with wisdom (he is the first of the Three Sage Kings), apparently lived in a China where it was already customary for a king to pass his power to his son. Yao, though, realized that his own son was unworthy to inherit his throne. Instead, he chose as his successor a poor but wise peasant named Shun, who was famous not only for his virtue, but for his dedication to his father. Shun, who became a wise and just king (and the second of the Three Sage Kings), followed his own king's model; he passed over his son and chose another worthy man, Yü, as his heir. Yü, the third Sage King, is credited with establishing the first dynasty of China, the Xia.

In other words, in China the earliest tales of royal succession show, not a

* There is not total agreement among ancient Chinese accounts about this arrangement of Three God-Kings followed by Three Sage Kings. In some accounts, three Demigod Kings—Fu Hsi, Shennong, and Kan Pao, the thresher of grain—are followed by Five Emperors, who are Huangdi, Ti K'u (the maker of musical instruments), Yao, Shun, and Yü, who founds the semilegendary Xia Dynasty. The Xia Dynasty is followed by the Shang in 1776, the first dynasty for which significant historical records exist.

TIMELINE 6

INDIA	CHINA
Early settlements along the lower Indus and in the Punjab	Early cultures of China: Yang-shao, Dapenkeng, Qinglian'gang, and Longshan
Kali Yuga, the Age of Iron (3102-present)	
Villages begin to grow into towns	
Manu Vaivaswata	
	Fu Xi (2850)
	Shennong
	Huangdi (2696)
	Yao Shun (2598)
	Xia Dynasty (2205–1766)
	Yü

desperate quest for a blood heir, but sons disinherited in favor of virtue. They celebrate kingly power while rejecting too heavy an exercise of it. Authority is all very well, but no man should assume that he'll automatically be gifted with it because of his birth. Wisdom, not birth, qualifies a man to rule. The people of Kish may have mourned because their king Etana was childless. The towns of the Yellow river valley had no such longing.*

* Any Western account of Chinese history is complicated by the fact that no system of transcription of Chinese characters into the Roman alphabet is universally accepted. The Wade-Giles system, devised between 1859 and 1912 by two Cambridge men named (not surprisingly) Wade and Giles, was widely used until 1979, when the government of the People's Republic of China officially chose the Pinyin ("Chinese Phonetic Alphabet") system in order to try to standardize the spelling of Chinese names in other languages. Pinyin has not entirely caught on, however, in part because the Wade-Giles romanizations became so well known that many Westerners found the Pinyin versions of Chinese names disorienting (the *I ching* becomes *Yi jing;* the Yangtze river becomes the Chang Jiang) and in part because many Chinese terms have become familiar to non-Chinese readers in forms which are neither Wade-Giles *nor* Pinyin. For example, the northeastern region of China is properly called Tung-pei in Wade-Giles romanization and Dongbei in the Pinyin system, but most historians seem to have given up the battle and just call it by its sixteenth-century name, Manchuria.

Since Pinyin (so far as I can judge) seems the most accurate of the systems, I have tried to use Pinyin whenever possible. However, when another version of a name seems to be so much more familiar that the Pinyin version might cause confusion, I have defaulted to the better-known spelling (as with the Yangtze river).

Part Two

FIRSTS

Chapter Seven

The First Written Records

Between 3800 and 2400 BC
Sumerians and Egyptians begin to use seals and signs

WRITTEN HISTORY BEGAN sometime around 3000 BC. At the beginning of that millennium, there were only two things important enough to communicate across space and time: the deeds of great men, and the ownership of cows, grain, and sheep. In the cities of Sumer, a great epic literature started to form, and a bureaucracy coalesced to take care of the bean counting.

People being what they are, the bureaucracy came first. The genesis of writing lay, not in the celebration of the human spirit, but in the need to say with certainty: *This is mine, not yours.* But as they evolved their artificial code for keeping track of possessions, the accountants gave a gift to the storytellers: a way to make their heroes immortal. From its earliest days, literature was tied to commerce.

SINCE THE DAYS of cave paintings, people have made marks to keep count of objects. We can call these marks the seeds of writing, since a mark means not *Here is a mark,* but something else. But the marks do not reach beyond space and time. They are voiceless unless the maker of the marks is standing there, explaining: *This line is a cow; this one, an antelope; these are my children.*

In Sumer, the use of marks took a step forwards. Very early, a Sumerian who owned valuable resources (grain, or milk, or perhaps oil) would tie closed his bag of grain, smooth a ball of clay over the knot, and then press his seal on it. The seal, square or cylindrical, was carved with a particular design. When the ball of clay dried, the mark of the owner (*This is mine!*) was locked into the clay. The mark represented the owner's presence. It watched over the grain while he was absent.

These seals, like the marks made by the cave-painter, depended on shared knowledge. Everyone who saw the seal had to know whose presence the mark represented, before it could convey the message *This belongs to Ilshu.* But unlike the cave-painter's mark, a seal was distinctive. A mark could mean woman or sheep, man or cow. A seal—once you knew the meaning of it—could represent only one Sumerian: Ilshu. Ilshu no longer needed to be present to explain it.

A step had been made towards triumphing over space.

Perhaps simultaneously, another type of sign came into use. Like the cave-painters, the Sumerians used marks and tallies to keep track of the number of cows (or sacks of grain) that they owned. The tallies that counted their belongings were often stored on small clay circles ("counters"). These counters had been used for as long as farmers owned cows: perhaps for centuries. But sometime before 3000 BC, the richest Sumerians (those with many, many counters to keep track of) laid their counters out on a thin sheet of clay, folded the sheet up around them, and placed a seal on the seam. When the clay dried, it formed a kind of envelope.

Unfortunately, the only way to open the envelope was to break the clay, in which case (unlike a padded paper mailer) it was unusable. The more economical way to keep track of how many counters were inside the envelope was to keep a new tally on the outside, showing how many counters were inside.

Now the marks on the outside of the "envelope" represented counters inside, which had on them marks representing cows. In other words, the outside marks were *two* removes away from the objects represented. The relationship between *thing* and *mark* had begun to grow more abstract.[1]

The next advance was to move beyond the simple mark altogether. As the Sumerian cities grew, ownership became more complex. More *kinds* of things could be owned and transferred to others. Now, the accountants needed something more than marks. They needed pictograms—representations of the things counted—as well as tallies.

The pictograms used became increasingly simplified. For one thing, they were generally drawn on clay, which doesn't lend itself to careful detail. And it was time-consuming to draw a realistic cow, every time a cow was needed, when everyone looking at the tablet knew perfectly well that a square with a rudimentary head and tail meant *cow;* just as a child's stick figure is obviously Mommy, even though unrecognizable (and barely human), because Mommy is, after all, standing right there.

This was still a marking system. It doesn't quite deserve the name *writing* just yet. On the other hand, it was a marking system that had grown more and more complex.

Then the seal reappeared, this time conveying a whole new message. Ilshu, who once used his seal only to mark his grain and oil, could now set it at the bottom of a tablet which recorded, in pictographs, the sale of cows from the neighbor on the left to his neighbor on his right. Not trusting each other entirely, the two asked him to be present at the sale; he put his seal on the tablet as a witness to the transaction. At the bottom of the tablet, Ilshu's design no longer says *Ilshu was here,* or even *This is Ilshu's.* It says *Ilshu, who was here, watched this transaction and can explain it, if you have any questions.*

That is no longer simply a mark. It is a speech to the reader.

Until this point, Sumerian "writing" depended on the good memories of everyone involved; it was more like a string tied around the finger than a developed system of symbols. But cities traded, the economy grew, and now those clay tablets needed to bear more information than the number and kind of goods traded. Farmers and merchants needed to record when fields were planted, and with what kind of grain; which servants had been sent on what errands; how many cows had been sent to the Temple of Enlil, in exchange for divine favor, in case the priests miscounted; how much tribute had been sent to the king, in case he miscounted and demanded more. To convey this level of information, the Sumerians needed signs that would stand for *words,* not just for things. They needed a pictogram for *cow,* but also signs for *sent* or *bought;* a pictogram for *wheat,* but also signs for *planted* or *destroyed.*

As the need for signs multiplied, the written code could take one of two directions. Signs could multiply, each standing for yet another individual word. Or pictograms could evolve into a phonetic system, so that signs could represent *sounds,* parts of words rather than words themselves; in this way, any number of words could be built from a limited number of signs. After all, whenever a Sumerian saw the pictogram for *cow* and formed his lips into the Sumerian word for *cow,* sounds were involved. It was not such a stretch for the pictogram for *cow* to become, eventually, a sign representing the first sound in the word *cow.* It could then be used as the beginning sign in a whole series of words that all began with the *cow* sound.

Over the course of at least six hundred years, Sumerian pictograms took this second road and evolved into phonetic symbols.* These symbols, made in wet clay by a stylus with a wedge-shaped edge, had a distinctive shape, wider at the top than at the bottom of the incision. What the Sumerians called their

* The development of writing is a subject on which volumes have been written; this chapter is only an attempt to put it within its historical context. For a more detailed account written by an actual expert in linguistics, try Steven Roger Fischer's *A History of Writing*; for a readable account of the earliest systems of writing and their development, see C. B. F. Walker's *Cuneiform: Reading the Past,* as well as the second volume in the series, *Egyptian Hieroglyphs: Reading the Past* by W. V. Davies.

7.1. Cuneiform Tablet. This cuneiform tablet, from around 2600 BC, records the sale of a house and field. Louvre, Paris. Photo credit Erich Lessing/Art Resource, NY

writing, we will never know. It is almost impossible to recognize a world-changing technology in its very earliest stages, and the Sumerians did not remark on their own innovation. But in 1700 an Old Persian scholar named Thomas Hyde gave the writing the name *cuneiform,* which we still use. The name, derived from the Latin for "wedge-shaped," does nothing to recognize the importance of the script. Hyde thought that the pretty signs on clay were some sort of decorative border.

IN EGYPT, pictograms came into use slightly later than they did in Sumer. They were already common by the time Egypt became an empire. On the Narmer Palette, just to the right of King Narmer's head lies the pictogram for *catfish;* it is Narmer's name, written on his portrait.

Egyptian pictograms, which we now call hieroglyphs, don't seem to have evolved from a counting system. Most likely, the Egyptians learned the technique of pictograms from their neighbors to the northeast. But unlike Sumerian cuneiform signs, which lost their resemblance to the original pictograms, Egyptian hieroglyphs retained their recognizable form for a very long time. Even after the hieroglyphs became phonetic signs, standing for sounds and not objects, they were recognizable as *things*: a man with hands raised, a shepherd's crook, a crown, a hawk. Hieroglyphic script was a mixed bag. Some of the signs remained pictograms, while others were phonetic symbols; sometimes a hawk sign stood for a sound, but sometimes it was just a hawk. So the Egyptians evolved something called a *determinant,* a sign placed next to a hieroglyph to show whether it served as a phonetic symbol or as a pictogram.

But neither hieroglyphic script nor cuneiform evolved into a fully phonetic form: into an alphabet.

Sumerian never had the chance. It was replaced by Akkadian, the language of Sumer's conquerors, before its development was complete. Hieroglyphs, on the other hand, existed for thousands of years without losing their character as *pictures.* Probably this can be chalked up to the Egyptian attitude towards writing. For the Egyptians, writing brought immortality. It was a magic form in which the lines themselves carried life and power. Some hieroglyphs were too powerful to be carved in a magic place; they could only be written in a less powerful area, lest they bring unwanted forces into existence. The name of a king, carved in hieroglyph on a monument or statue, gave him a presence that went on past his death. To deface the carved name of a king was to kill him eternally.

The Sumerians, more practical, had no such purpose in their writing. Like the Egyptians, the Sumerians had a patron deity of scribes: the goddess Nisaba, who was also (so far as we can tell) the goddess of grain. But the Egyptians believed that writing had been invented by a god: by Thoth, the divine scribe, who created himself with the power of his own word. Thoth was the god of writing, but also the god of wisdom and magic. He measured the earth, counted the stars, and recorded the deeds of every man brought to the Hall of the Dead for judgment. He did not mess around counting bags of grain.

This attitude towards writing preserved the pictorial form of hieroglyphs, since the pictures themselves were thought to have such power. In fact, far from being phonetic, hieroglyphs were designed to be indecipherable unless you possessed the key to their meaning. The Egyptian priests, who were guardians of this information, patrolled the borders of their knowledge in order to keep this tool in their own hands. Ever since, the mastery of writing and reading has been an act of power.

As a matter of fact, hieroglyphs were so far from intuitive that the ability to read them began to fade even as Egypt still existed as a nation. We find Greek-speaking Egyptians, as late as AD 500, writing long explanations of the relationship between sign and meaning; Horapollo, for example, in his *Hieroglyphika,* explains the various meanings of the hieroglyph written as a vulture by desperately (and incorrectly) trying to figure out the relationship between sign and meaning. "When they mean a mother, a sight, or boundaries, or foreknowledge," Horapollo writes,

> they draw a vulture. A mother, since there is no male in this species of animal. . . . the vulture stands for sight since of all other animals the vulture has the keenest vision. . . . It means boundaries, because when a war is about to break out, it limits the place in which the battle will occur, hovering over it for seven days. [And] foreknowledge, because . . . it looks forward to the amount of corpses which the slaughter will provide it for food.[2]

Once the knowledge of hieroglyphs had disappeared entirely, the writing of the Egyptians remained obscure until a band of Napoleon's soldiers, digging out the foundations of a fort Napoleon hoped to build in the Nile Delta, uncovered a seven-hundred-pound slab of basalt with the same inscription written in hieroglyphs, in a later Egyptian script, and also in Greek; this rock, which became known as the Rosetta Stone, gave linguistics the key they needed to begin to break the code. Thus the military establishment, which had already provided material for centuries of literary endeavor, helped recover the means of reading the earliest poems and epics. (Great literature has never been independent of war, any more than it can shake itself free from commerce.)

HIEROGLYPHS could preserve their magical and mysterious nature only because the Egyptians invented a new and easier script for day-to-day use. *Hieratic* script was a simplified version of hieroglyphic writing, with the careful pictorial signs reduced to a few quickly dashed lines (in W. V. Davies's phrase, the "cursive version" of hieroglyphic script). Hieratic script became the preferred handwriting for business matters, bureaucrats, and administrators. Its existence depended on another Egyptian invention: paper. No matter how simple the lines were, they could not be written quickly on clay.

Clay had been the traditional writing material of both the Sumerians and the Egyptians for centuries. It was plentiful and reusable. The writing on a smooth-surfaced clay tablet that had been dried in the sun would last for years; but simply dampen the surface of the tablet, and the writing could be smoothed and altered, to correct or change a record. Records which had to be protected from tampering could be baked instead, fixing the marks into a permanent, unalterable archive.

But clay tablets were heavy, awkward to store, and difficult to carry from place to place, severely limiting the amount of writing in any message. (Think of it as the opposite phenomenon to the prolixity encouraged by word processors.) Sometime around 3000 BC, an Egyptian scribe realized that the papyrus used as a building material in Egyptian houses (reeds softened, laid out in a crossed pattern, mashed into pulp, and then laid out to dry in thin sheets) could also serve as a writing surface. With a brush and ink, hieratic script could be laid down very rapidly on papyrus.

Up in Sumer, where the raw material for such a substance didn't exist, clay tablets continued in use for centuries. Fifteen hundred years later, when Moses led the Semitic descendants of the wanderer Abraham up out of Egypt into the dry wastes of the Near East, God carved their instructions on tablets of stone, not on paper. The Israelites had to build a special box for the stone tablets, which were hard to transport.

Paper, on the other hand, was much simpler to carry. Messages could be rolled up, stuffed under one's coat or in one's pocket. The widely separated bureaucrats of the Nile River valley needed some such simple method of communication between north and south; a messenger travelling up the Nile with forty pounds of clay tablets was at an obvious disadvantage.

The Egyptians embraced the new, efficient technology. Hieroglyphs continued to be carved on the stone walls of tombs and on monuments and statues. But letters and petitions and instructions and threats were written on papyrus—which dissolved when it got wet, and cracked when it grew old, and disintegrated into heaps of dust not long after.

Although we can trace the family difficulties of the Sumerian king Zimri-Lim on the unwieldy clay tablets that travelled back and forth between the sunbaked cities of Mesopotamia, we know very little about the daily life of pharaohs and their officials after the invention of papyrus. Their sorrows and urgent messages are lost; the careful histories of their scribes have disappeared without a trace, like electronic messages wiped clean. Thus, five thousand years ago, we have not only the first writing, but also the first technological advance to come back and bite mankind.

SUMERIAN CUNEIFORM died and was buried. But the lines of hieroglyphs have survived until the present day. A later form of writing, which we call Protosinaitic because it shows up in various places around the Sinai peninsula, borrowed almost half of its signs from Egyptian hieroglyphs. Protosinaitic, in

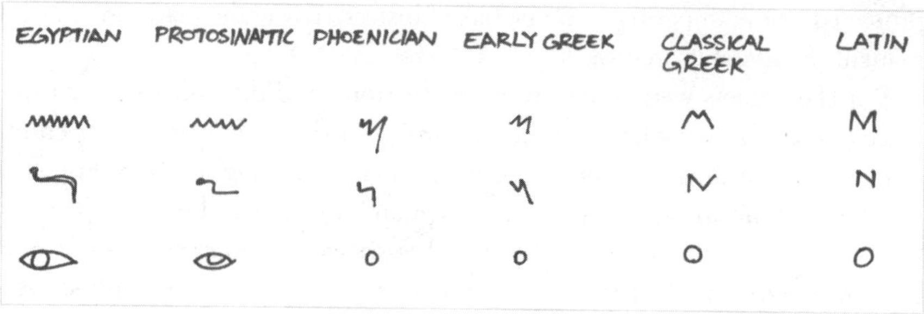

EGYPTIAN	PROTOSINAITIC	PHOENICIAN	EARLY GREEK	CLASSICAL GREEK	LATIN
				M	M
				N	N
		o	o	O	O

7.2. Alphabet Chart. The transformation of three letters from Egyptian to Latin. Credit Richie Gunn

turn, appears to have lent a few of its letters to the Phoenicians, who used it in their alphabet. The Greeks then borrowed the Phoenician alphabet, turned it sideways, and passed it on to the Romans, and thence to us; so that the magical signs of the Egyptians have, in fact, come as close to immortality as any mortal invention that we know.

Chapter Eight

The First War Chronicles

In Sumer, around 2700 BC*,*
Gilgamesh, king of Uruk, conquers his neighbors

WHEN THE SUMERIANS began to use cuneiform, they moved from *once upon a time* into the knowable past. They began to set down accounts of battles won, trades negotiated, and temples built. The king list can now be elaborated by official tablets and inscriptions.

Epic tales, which often preserve the body of earthly accomplishments beneath the fancy dress of demonic opponents and supernatural powers, remain useful. But now we can anchor them in accounts which are intended to be more or less factual. Which is not to say that inscriptions display a new and startling objectivity; they were written by scribes who were paid by the kings whose achievements they recorded, which naturally tends to tilt them in the king's favor. (According to Assyrian inscriptions, very few Assyrian kings ever lost a battle.) But by comparing the inscriptions made by two apparently victorious kings at war with each other, we can usually deduce which king actually won.

In Sumer, where civilization arose in order to keep the have-nots separate from the haves, battles between cities erupted sporadically from at least 4000 BC. From temple inscriptions, the king list, and a collection of tales, we can put together a story of one of the earliest series of battles: the first chronicles of a war.

In the year 2800 BC (more or less), the Sumerian king Meskiaggasher ruled in the city of Uruk. Uruk, known today as the southeastern Iraqi city Warka, was one of the oldest cities in Sumer, occupied since at least 3500 BC.* In

* Archaeologists refer to the period of Sumerian history which stretched from 4000 to about 3200 BC as the Uruk Period, a designation which refers to a certain type of pottery characteristic of these years rather than directly to the city of Uruk itself. The name Early Dynastic Period is generally assigned

Meskiaggasher's day, it was also (so far as we can tell) the largest. Its walls were six miles long; fifty thousand people lived in and around it. Two huge temple complexes lay within its gates. In the complex called Kullaba, the Sumerians gathered to worship the remote and reticent sky-god An; in the complex Eanna, they carried on a much more vigorous devotion to Inanna, the very accessible goddess of love and war.*

It must have galled Meskiaggasher that his great and historic city was not in fact the crown jewel of Sumer. That honor still belonged to Kish, the city whose king could claim the formal right of overlordship. By this point, Kish had extended its protection (and control) over the sacred city of Nippur, where the shrines of the chief god Enlil stood and where kings of every Sumerian city went to sacrifice and to seek recognition. Although not the strongest city in Sumer, Kish seems to have exerted a disproportionate influence over the area. Like New York City, it was neither a political nor military capital, but nevertheless stood for the heart of the civilization—particularly to those outside.

Meskiaggasher does not seem to have been a man who could happily stand second in line. He probably seized the throne of Uruk from its rightful holder; in the Sumerian king list, he is described as the son of the sun-god Utu, which is the sort of lineage a usurper often used to legitimize his claim. And, as the king list tells us, during his reign he "entered the seas and ascended the mountains." This seems more straightforward than Etana's ascension to the heavens. Once in control of Uruk, Meskiaggasher expanded its sway; not over other Sumerian cities (Uruk was not quite powerful enough to pitch into Lagash, or Kish, head-on), but over the trade routes that led through the seas and over the surrounding mountains.

The control of these trade routes had to come before war. Meskiaggasher needed swords, axes, helmets, and shields, but the plains between the rivers lacked metal. The swordsmiths of Kish could count on getting their raw materials from the north, down Kish's direct river route; Uruk needed to find a southern source for these raw materials that the plains between the rivers lacked.

---

to the years 2900–2350 in Sumerian history. The period is often subdivided into ED I (2900–2800), ED II (2800–2600), and ED III (2600–2350).

* During Meskiaggasher's reign, a tiny statue of Inanna stood in the Eanna complex, probably on an altar. The statue's face, known as the Mask of Warka, was dug up in 1938. It was stolen from the Iraqi National Museum in April of 2004, in the looting that took place during the U.S. invasion. The culprit, ratted out by a neighbor, admitted to Iraqi police that Inanna's head was buried in his backyard; in September of the same year, police dug it up with a shovel and returned it to the Ministry of Culture.

8.1 *Meskiaggasher's Trade*

A southern source lay at hand. The fabulous Copper Mountains stood in Magan—southeast Arabia, modern-day Oman. Mentioned in cuneiform tablets from Lagash and elsewhere, the Copper Mountains (the Al Hajar range) had mines sixty-five feet deep, and ovens for smelting ore, from very early times.

There was no easy path to Magan across the Arabian desert. At the ports of Magan, though, Sumerian reed boats—caulked with bitumen, capable of carrying twenty tons of metal—could trade grain, wool, and oil for copper. Meskiaggasher's first, logical preparation for war was to assure (either by negotiation, or by battle) that Uruk's merchants had a clear path down the Gulf of Oman to Magan.

But Sumerian smiths needed more than pure copper. Three hundred years or so before Meskiaggasher, they had begun to add ten percent of tin or arsenic to their copper, a combination which produced bronze: stronger than copper, easier to shape, taking a sharper edge when ground.*

To get the best bronze, Meskiaggasher needed tin. Bronze made with arsenic was a little weaker, a little harder to hone. It also tended to kill off your skilled craftsmen over time, which was no good way to build an arsenal. So Meskiaggasher's ascension of the mountains was likely carried out in search of this tin, which lay under the rocky slopes of the Zagros Mountains, or possibly even farther north, in the steep icy Elburz Mountains below the Caspian Sea. Meskiaggasher took his soldiers deep into the mountain passes and forced the mountain tribes to provide him with the metal he needed to turn copper to bronze.

Now Uruk was armed, but Meskiaggasher didn't live to see it victorious. After his death, his son Enmerkar inherited the throne.

Enmerkar had the unenviable job of living up to his father's reputation; it's difficult to go one better on a man who entered the seas and ascended the mountains. We're given a glimpse of his efforts to grasp fame in a long epic tale from somewhat later, called "Enmerkar and the Lord of Aratta."

Aratta was not a Sumerian city. It lay in the eastern mountains, somewhere south of the Caspian Sea. Its inhabitants were Elamites, a people who spoke a language entirely unrelated to Sumerian (and which, in fact, hasn't yet been

* In other words, Sumer had been in the Copper Age and out of the Stone Age for some time. These particular designations are like moveable feasts, changing from civilization to civilization. So the Copper Age of Sumer ran from around 5500 to 3000 or so, at which point smiths began to make bronze and Mesopotamia moved into the Bronze Age; for northern Europeans, who learned much later how to work soft copper into tools and weapons, the Stone Age lasted longer, and the Copper Age stretched until 2250 or so, so that the Bronze Age began seven hundred years later than in Sumer.

deciphered). The Elamite cities sat not on tin or copper, but on precious metals and stones—silver, gold, lapis lazuli—and for some years had been swapping semiprecious stone to the Sumerians in return for grain.

Enmerkar, standing in the shadow of the man who had entered the seas and ascended the mountains, decided to pick a quarrel with his trade partner. He had no compelling political reason to do this, but Aratta was a choice prize. If he could bring it under his sway, he would dominate a city that Uruk had long admired for its riches, its metalworkers, and its skilled stonecutters. His fame would be assured.

So he sent a message to the king of Aratta, announcing that Inanna—who also happened to be the chief deity of Aratta—preferred Uruk to Aratta, and that Aratta's people should acknowledge this by sending Enmerkar their gold, silver, and lapis lazuli at no charge.

This was a declaration of war, and it was met with defiance. Unfortunately, Enmerkar seems to have overestimated his strength. In the epic tale, after a series of testy exchanges between the two kings, the goddess Inanna settles the issue by assuring Enmerkar that while she most certainly loves Uruk best, she has an affection for Aratta as well and would prefer him not to flatten it. At the tale's end, the Elamites of Aratta are still free from Enmerkar's rule.[1]

Given that the story has come down to us from the Sumerians, not the Elamites, this ambiguous ending probably represents a shattering Sumerian defeat. Enmerkar died, childless, without expanding his father's empire, and brought Meskiaggasher's dynasty to an early end.

He was succeeded by one of his fellow warriors, a man named Lugulbanda, the star of several epic tales in his own right. After Lugulbanda, yet another unrelated warrior assumed control of the city. The succession of fathers and sons seems to have been broken, and Uruk made no more attempts to enclose other cities within its grasp.

Then, perhaps a hundred years later, Uruk again made a bid for the reins of Sumerian power. Uruk had a new king: yet another usurper, a young man named Gilgamesh.

According to the king list, Gilgamesh's father was not a king at all. He was most likely a high priest in the Kullaba temple complex, devoted to the worship of the god An, and the possessor of a certain reputation. The king list calls him a *lillu,* a word which implies demonic powers. Although the kings of Sumer had once been priests as well, this time had passed. For some years, the priestly and political administration of Sumerian cities had diverged; Gilgamesh may have inherited the priestly power, but he seized the kingly authority that he had no right to as well.

In an epic tale told not long after his reign, we find Gilgamesh claiming

Lugulbanda, the warrior-companion of Enmerkar, as his father. On the face of it, this is silly; Lugulbanda had occupied the throne decades (at least) before Gilgamesh's birth. But from the point of view of a man rewriting his personal history, Lugulbanda was a fine choice. He had been a brilliantly successful warrior-king, a man with a knack for surviving long brutal campaigns and emerging fresh and ready to fight at the far end. By Gilgamesh's day, Lugulbanda—perhaps thirty years dead, or even more—was well on his way to achieving the status of a Sumerian hero. A hundred years later, he would be considered a god. He lent Gilgamesh a sheen of secular power.

Once Gilgamesh's first venture—to seize the throne of Uruk—had succeeded, he was ready for a new task. And Kish still lay unconquered, its king protecting sacred Nippur, and claiming that vexing indefinable superiority of prestige.

When we detach this young king of Uruk, Gilgamesh, from the epic tales which predated him and later became attached to his person, we are still left with a vivid personality. Gilgamesh wanted it all: loyal companions, the throne, a royal title, the title "king of Kish," and eventually immortality.

Gilgamesh's first preparation, before declaring war on his neighbors, was to fortify his own walls. "In Uruk [Gilgamesh] built walls," the prologue to the Epic of Gilgamesh tells us, "a great rampart. . . . Look at it still today: the outer wall . . . it shines with the brilliance of copper; and the inner wall, it has no equal."[2]

The copper is a later exaggeration. Uruk's walls at this time weren't stone, let alone copper; they were made of wood, brought from the north. Gilgamesh's journey to get wood is reflected in the Epic. In it, he ventures to the cedar forests of the north in order to set up a monument to the gods, but before he can build it he has to fight the giant of the woods: "a great warrior, a battering-ram" known as "Hugeness"; or, in Sumerian, "Humbaba."[3] In fact, Gilgamesh would have faced, not a giant, but Elamite tribes who lived in the forest and were disinclined to hand over their most valuable resource peacefully.

With walls fortified, Gilgamesh was ready to pick his own quarrel with the king of Kish.

THE KING OF KISH was named Enmebaraggesi, and he had ruled in Kish for years before the upstart Gilgamesh came to power in Uruk.* He was not only the king of Kish, but also the protector of sacred Nippur. An inscription

* Enmebaraggesi is the first Sumerian king whose reign can be estimated; he was on the throne roughly around 2700, which allows us to date Gilgamesh's life as well. See chapter 3, p. 17.

found there tells us that Enmebaraggesi built in Nippur the "House of Enlil," a temple for the great Sumerian chief god of air, wind, and storms, who held the Tablets of Destiny and thus wielded power over the fates of all men. Enlil, who was credited with the sending of the flood in a grouchy moment, was not a god to be messed with. But since the temple built by Enmebaraggesi became known as Enlil's favorite, the king of Kish was confident in the god's favor. He was unlikely to have worried much about the juvenile challenger from the south.

Meanwhile, Gilgamesh was mobilizing Uruk's forces. All the machinery of war was put into motion: the foot soldiers with their leather shields, their spears and axes; the siege engines made of northern timber, hauled by oxen and sweating men; a huge cedar log, floated upstream on the Euphrates, to be used as a battering ram to bash down Kish's gates. War was the most highly developed skill in the ancient world. From as early as 4000 BC, carved scenes show us spearmen, prisoners both alive and executed, gates broken down and walls besieged.

So the attack began—and failed. We know this because the king lists record Enmebaraggesi's death from old age, and the peaceful succession of his son Agga to the throne of Kish.[4]

Why did Gilgamesh retreat?

In all the legends that accrue around Gilgamesh, the central figure remains vividly the same: a young, aggressive, impetuous man, of almost superhuman vitality, the kind of man who sleeps three hours a night and hurtles out of bed to get back to work, who starts an airline before the age of twenty-five, or founds and sells four companies by twenty-eight, or writes an autobiography before thirty. It is also a constant in the tales that this vitality wears Gilgamesh's people to a frazzle. In the epics, they are so exhausted by his constant bounding around that they call out to the gods for deliverance. In reality, they probably just balked; and without the support of his citizens, Gilgamesh was forced to retreat.

The king of a Sumerian city, after all, was not an absolute ruler. In the story of Gilgamesh's expedition to the north, he has to seek the approval of a council of elders before he sets off. Sumerians, formed by a country in which every man needed to keep his elbows out against his neighbor's trespasses in order to survive, seem to have had a keen sense of their own rights. They were the first people to write down their law codes, inscribing the limits of others' freedom, so that there could be no mistake. They were not likely to suffer a king's encroachments for long without objecting, and in this case, they declined to go to war any more.

Gilgamesh was still determined to conquer Kish. Agga of Kish, on the other hand, was inclined to make peace. A poem-story called "Gilgamesh and Agga of Kish" records that he sent envoys to Gilgamesh, apparently to establish friendly relations.

Gilgamesh seems to have taken this as a sign of weakness, rather than a sign of peace. According to the tale, he first brings together the elders of the city and tells them about Agga's message. Rather than recommending peace, though, he suggests another attack: "There are many wells of the land to be claimed. So should we submit to the house of Kish? Instead, we should smite it with weapons!"[5]

The assembly of elders declines to smite Kish, telling Gilgamesh to go finish his own wells rather than romping after the wells of others. But Gilgamesh instead turns to another assembly: the assembly of young ("able-bodied") men. "Never before have you submitted to Kish!" he tells them. After a little more rhetoric, they are ready to cheer him on. "Standing on duty, sitting attendance, escorting the son of the king [of Kish]—who has the energy?" they shout to him. "You are beloved of the gods, a man of exuberance!"

> "Do not submit to the house of Kish!
> Should we young men not smite it with weapons?
> The great gods created Uruk,
> and its great walls touch the clouds.
> The army of Kish is small,
> and its men cannot look us in the face."

So supported, Gilgamesh decides to attack Kish once more.

This double parliamentary assembly of elders (wise but past fighting) and younger men (able-bodied but hotheaded) was common in Sumerian city government. It endured for centuries in the ancient Near East; much later, the son of the great Hebrew king Solomon, on ascending the throne, would split his country in half by ignoring the peaceful counsel of the assembly of elders in favor of the rash actions suggested by the assembly of younger men.

Gilgamesh follows the same course, and comes to grief. Again, the attack on Kish drags on; again, the people of Uruk protest; and again, Gilgamesh withdraws. We know this because it is not Gilgamesh who finally defeats Kish and claims the titles of king of Kish and protector of Nippur, but another king entirely: the king of Ur.

Ur, farther south than Uruk and far away from Kish, had been quietly growing in strength and power for decades. Its king, Mesannepadda, seems to have been extraordinarily long-lived. By the time that Gilgamesh's second attack on Kish trailed off into retreat, Mesannepadda had been on his throne for decades. He was far older than Gilgamesh, perhaps even older than the now-dead Enmebaraggesi. He too wanted Kish; and he was no ally of Uruk.

But he had been willing to wait before launching his own assault. When Gilgamesh withdrew, leaving Kish weakened, Mesannepadda attacked Kish, and triumphed. Mesannepadda, not Gilgamesh, brought the First Dynasty of Kish to an end and took control of the sacred city of Nippur. Gilgamesh's superhuman energy was still locked behind walls, confined by his people's unwillingness to support another attack.

Once again, the dynamics of inheritance came into play. Kish had fallen when Enmebaraggesi died and left the defense to his son; now Gilgamesh waited until the old and powerful Mesannepadda died and left his own son, Meskiagunna, as ruler over the triple kingdom of Ur, Kish, and Nippur. (And, perhaps until the elders who had seen him twice defeated were dead as well.) Then, Gilgamesh attacked for a third time.*

This time he was triumphant. In a bitter struggle, he brought Meskiagunna down, claimed his city, and took over the other territories Meskiagunna had won through war. In one last push, Gilgamesh had finally become master of the four great cities of Sumer: Kish, Ur, Uruk, and the sacred Nippur.

After decades plotting Kish's conquest, Gilgamesh now ruled more of Sumer than any king before him. But only for a little while. Even Gilgamesh's superhuman energy could not ward off old age. When he died, very shortly after his victory, his four-cornered kingdom, the title of king of Kish, and all the stories surrounding his towering figure devolved on his son.

* The sequence of rulers seems to have run something like this:

	Uruk	Kish	Ur
2800	**Meskiaggasher**		
	Enmerkar		
	Lugulbanda		**Mesannepadda**
		Enmebaraggesi	
2700	**Gilgamesh**		
		Agga	
			Meskiagunna

TIMELINE 8

CHINA	MESOPOTAMIA
Early cultures of China: Yang-shao, Dapenkeng, Qinglian'gang, and Longshan	Uruk period (4000–3200)
	Jemdat Nasr period (3200–2900)
	Atab
	Etanah
	Balih
	Early Dynastic I (2900–2800)
Fu Xi (2850)	
Shennong	Early Dynastic II (2800–2600)
Huangdi (2696)	**Gilgamesh**
Yao Shun (2598)	Early Dynastic III (2600–2350)
Xia Dynasty (2205–1766)	
Yü	

Chapter Nine

The First Civil War

In Egypt, between 3100 and 2686 BC,
the First Dynasty pharaohs become gods,
the Second suffer civil war,
and the Third rule a reunited Egypt

THE BATTLING CITIES OF MESOPOTAMIA had no national identity; each was its own little kingdom. At the beginning of the third millennium, the only nation in the world stretched from the southern shores of the Mediterranean Sea at least as far upriver as the city of Hierakonpolis. Egypt was a kingdom like a knotted piece of string, over four hundred miles long, and so narrow in places that an Egyptian could stand on the desert that marked its eastern border and see right across the Nile to the wastes beyond the western frontier.

The nation's capital, the white city of Memphis, lay just south of the Delta, on the border between the ancient Lower and Upper Kingdoms. The site had little else to recommend it; the plain was so wet that, according to Herodotus, Narmer's first job was to build a dam to keep the water back. Even twenty-five hundred years later, Herodotus adds, "this bend in the Nile is closely watched . . . they strengthen the dam every year, because if the river decided to burst its banks and overflow at this point, Memphis would be in danger of being completely inundated."[1]

Narmer's unification, and his establishment of Memphis as a single Egyptian capital, brings an end to predynastic Egypt. His son followed him to the throne, and was in turn succeeded by six more kings assigned by Manetho to the so-called First Dynasty of Egypt; an actual, formalized, royal succession.*

* Traditionally, the eight kings of "Dynasty 1" are Narmer, Hor-Aha, Djer, Djet (sometimes called Wadj), Den, Adjib, Semerkhet, and Qaa. Hor-Aha is probably Narmer's son, the pharaoh known to Manetho as Athothis. Given the lack of certainty over Narmer's actual identity, it is possible that

What these eight kings were up to, in the six hundred years that they governed over unified Egypt, is more than a little obscure. But we can glimpse the growth of a centralized state: the establishment of a royal court, the collection of taxes, and an economy that allowed Egypt the luxury of supporting citizens who produced no food: full-time priests to sacrifice for the king, skilled metalworkers who provided jewelry for the court's noblemen and women, scribes who kept track of the growing bureaucracy.[2]

The third king of the dynasty, Djer, sent Egyptian soldiers out on the first official expeditions past the borders of Narmer's kingdom. On a rock 250 miles south of Hierakonpolis, near the Second Cataract, an engraved scene shows Djer and his army triumphant over captives; these were most likely the indigenous people of Lower Nubia, who before long would be entirely gone from the area, driven out by bad weather and Egyptian invasions. Egyptian troops also marched northeast, along the coast of the Mediterranean, towards the area which would later be called southern Palestine.

Den, two kings later, extended another cautious finger outside Egypt's borders. He led his men over into the Sinai peninsula, the triangle of land between the northern arms of the Red Sea. Here Den, according to a carved scene in his tomb, clubbed the local chieftains into submission, in a victory labelled, "The first time that the east was smitten."

These victories were theoretically won on behalf of all Egypt, both north and south. But in death, the First Dynasty rulers reverted to their Upper Egyptian identity. They were buried in their homeland: at Abydos, far, far south of Memphis.

This was no simple graveyard. Common Egyptians might still be laid at the desert's edge in the sand, faces turned west. But Egyptian noblemen, society's second rank, lay in a grand graveyard on the high desert plain of Saqqara, just west of Memphis.* And the kings buried at Abydos were entombed in brick or stone rooms sunk into the ground, surrounded by a positive embarrass-

---

Menes should be identified with Hor-Aha rather than with Narmer (in which case Manetho's Athothis would have to be Djer). As a way of dealing with this, some sources will list Narmer as belonging to a sui generis "dynasty" nicknamed "Dynasty 0" along with the Scorpion King. I have maintained the identification of Narmer/Menes, so I've eliminated any reference here to "Dynasty 0." The Scorpion King didn't begin a royal line, so he should remain in predynastic Egypt, where he belongs. (Dating the ancient dynasties of Egypt is an uncertain business. I have here generally followed the dating used by Peter Clayton in his *Chronicle of the Pharaohs,* although I've rejected his "Dynasty 0.")

* Some Egyptologists hold that the earliest pharaohs were buried at Saqqara and had honorary tombs also constructed at Abydos, so that they could rest in both north and south; opinion now seems to favor Abydos as the sole royal burying ground for the First Dynasty.

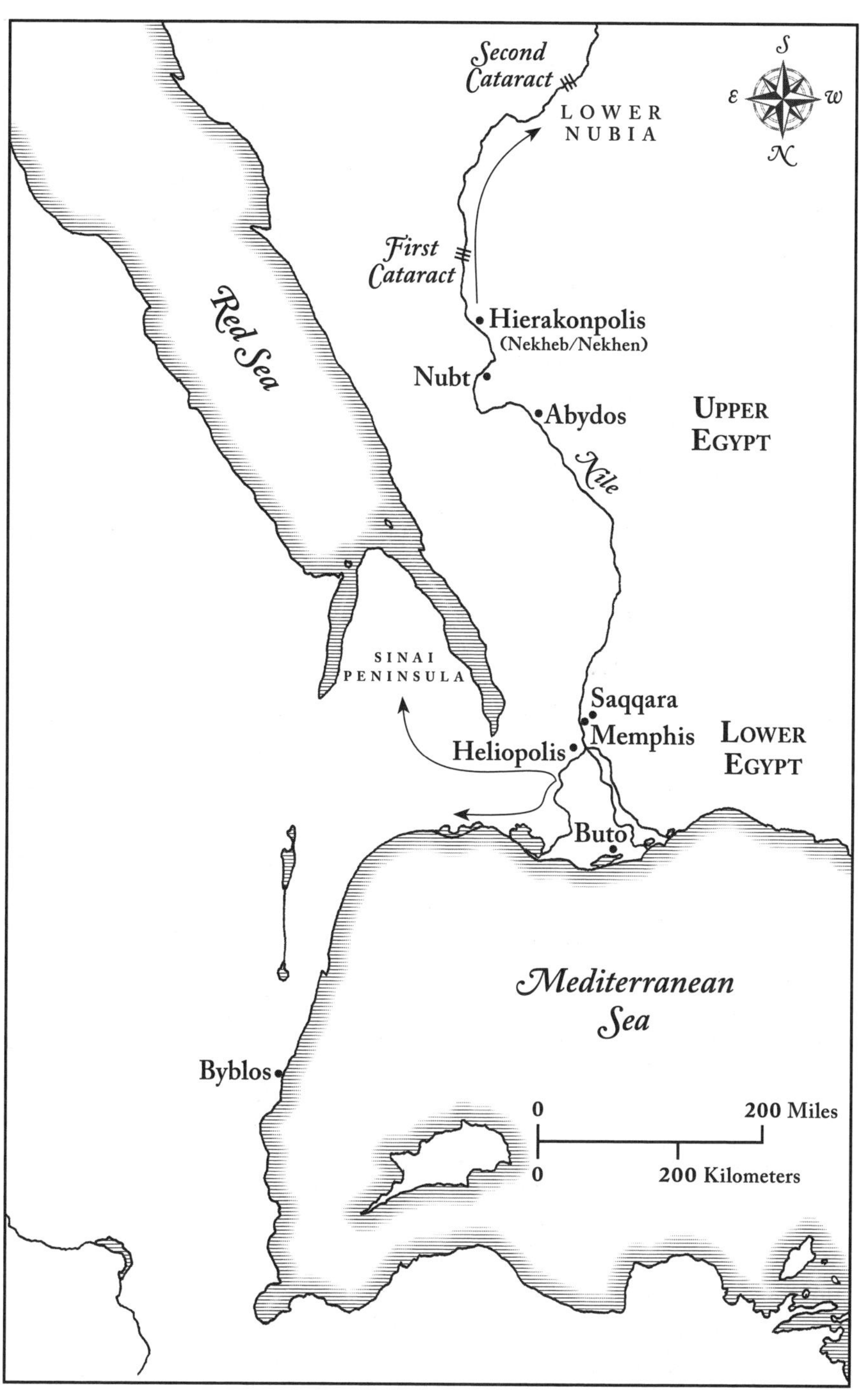

9.1 Egyptian Expansion

ment of human sacrifice. Almost two hundred dead attendants cluster around Den, while Djer was buried in the company of three hundred courtiers and servants.

These kings may have been uneasy about the loyalty of the north, but in their deaths they wielded a startling autocracy. Any man able to compel the deaths of others as part of his own funerary rites has advanced well beyond the tentative force employed by the earliest Sumerian rulers.

It isn't easy to tease out exactly why this power was expressed by way of human sacrifice. By the time that the pharaohs of the Fifth and Sixth Dynasty were laid to rest, the Egyptians were carving along the walls of their tombs an entire postburial agenda for the dead: the ascent from the pitch-black chambers of the pyramids to the sky, the crossing of the waters that divide life from afterlife, a warm welcome from the waiting gods. But these "Pyramid Texts" date, at the earliest, from half a millennium after the sacrificial burials at Abydos. When the First Dynasty kings were interred, the Egyptians had not even begun to embalm their dead. The royal bodies were wrapped in rags, sometimes soaked in resin, but this did nothing to preserve them.

We can deduce, though, that the kings were going to join the sun in his passage across the sky. Buried beside the kings at Abydos lie fleets of wooden boats, some a hundred feet in length, in long pits roofed over with mud brick. On First Dynasty engravings, the sun-god is shown travelling across the sky in a boat.[3] Presumably the pharaoh and the souls buried with him would use their boats to accompany him (although one of the grave complexes at Abydos has, not boats, but a herd of sacrificial donkeys for the king's use, suggesting that he at least might have been heading somewhere else).

Assuming that the kings reached the next life on the other side of the horizon, what were they going to do there?

Possibly, the pharaoh would continue his royal role; we have no Egyptian proof for this, but Gilgamesh, once dead, joined the gods of the underworld to help run the place. If the early pharaohs were believed to continue their kingly functions in the afterworld, the sacrificial burials make a kind of sense. After all, if a king's power only lasts until his death, he must be obeyed during his life, but there is no good reason to follow him into death. If, on the other hand, he's still going to be waiting for you on the other side, his power becomes all-encompassing. The passage to the undiscovered country is simply a journey from one stage of loyalty to the next.

Given the tensions between north and south, the First Dynasty kings needed this kind of authority to hold the country together. The theological underpinnings for the king's power are laid out by the "Memphite Theology," written on a monument called the Shabaka Stone (now in the British

Museum). The stone itself dates from much later in Egypt's history, but the story it bears is thought by many Egyptologists to go all the way back to the earliest Egyptian dynasties.

There are many later elaborations of the tale, but its center is simple. The god Osiris is given the rule of the entire earth, but his brother Set, jealous of his power, plots his death. He drowns Osiris in the Nile. The wife (and sister) of Osiris, the goddess Isis, hunts for her missing husband-brother. When she finds his drowned body, she bends over him and half-resurrects him. Osiris is alive enough to impregnate her, but not quite alive enough to stay on earth. Instead he becomes king of the underworld. The son born to Isis after Osiris descends to his new realm, Horus, becomes king of the living realm.

As king of the living, the god Horus was associated with the sun, the stars, and the moon: in other words, he was (as Egyptologist Rudolf Anthes suggests) "that celestial body which appeared conspicuous either at day or night . . . the permanent ruler of the sky, who unlike the sun did not vanish at night time."[4] The power of Horus did not wax and wane.

The early pharaohs of Egypt claimed to be the earthly embodiment of Horus, carrying with them that power which does not "vanish at night time," or with death. Nevertheless, all kings die. So Egyptian theology adapted to the inevitable. When the pharaoh died, he was no longer considered to be the incarnation of Horus. He became instead the embodiment of Osiris, who was both king of the underworld and the father of Horus, king of the living realm.* The earthly son of the dead pharaoh now took on the role of the incarnate Horus, which demonstrates the practical uses of such a system; it provides a neat way to legitimize succeeding rulers. The new king wasn't just the son of the old king. He was, in a sense, his father's reincarnation. Pharaohs might die, but the real power of kingship never bit the dust. The king of Egypt was not, first and foremost, an individual: not Narmer, or Den, or Djer. He was the bearer of a Power.

Sociologists call this arrangement "positional succession." It explains the growing tendency of Egyptian kings to claim the names of their predecessors; these names aren't just names, but descriptions of particular aspects of the undying kingship.[5] It also makes a little more sense out of the tendency to marry sisters (and sometimes daughters). When a pharaoh succeeds his father, his mother (the previous pharaoh's wife) is, in a sense, his wife as well; he has, after all, become (in some sense) his father.[6] It is still a number of centuries

* When considering Egyptian theology, it is useful to keep in mind Rudolf Anthes's observation that "Egyptian religion is . . . completely free of those logics which eliminate one of two contradictory concepts" ("Egyptian Theology in the Third Millennium B.C.").

before Oedipus runs into difficulties over this. For the Egyptians, family was the obvious place to find a wife.

Adjib, the fourth king of the First Dynasty, added a new descriptive title to his royal appellations: the *nesu-bit* name. Although these two Egyptian words have the sense of "above" and "below," *nesu-bit* doesn't express the pharaoh's rule over Upper and Lower Egypt. Rather, the *nesu-bit* seems to refer to the realms above and below. The *nesu* is the divine power of government, the *above kingship* that passes from king to king; the *bit* is the mortal holder of this power, the *king below.*[7]

Adjib, the first king to claim this title, had trouble hanging onto the *bit;* perhaps the first historical example of protesting too much. His grave is surrounded by sixty-four sacrificed Egyptians, tribute to his position as holder of the kingship above. On the other hand, his tomb, the earthly monument to the king below, is the shabbiest at Abydos. Worse, his name has been chipped away from various monuments where it was originally carved.

The man who did the chipping was Semerkhet, the next pharaoh. His removal of his predecessor's name was his attempt to rewrite the past. If the names that the pharaohs gave themselves expressed their eternal hold on the kingship above, writing them down, in the magically powerful signs of the hieroglyphs, carved them into the fabric of the world below. To deface the written name of a pharaoh was to remove him from earthly memory.

The attempt to erase Adjib suggests that Semerkhet was a usurper at best, and an assassin at worst. His seizure of the kingship below seems to have succeeded; he built himself a lovely tomb, much bigger than Adjib's, and poured so much sacred incense into it that the oil soaked three feet down into the ground and could still be smelled when the tomb was excavated in the early 1900s.[8] But his efforts to claim the *nesu,* the kingship above, were less triumphant. "In his reign," Manetho records, "there were many extraordinary events, and there was an immense disaster."

This cryptic remark isn't glossed by any later commentator. But the land around the Nile reveals that towards the end of the First Dynasty, the Nile floods lessened dramatically. By the Second Dynasty, the flooding was, on average, three feet lower than it had been a hundred years before.[9] If lessening floods had slowly pinched Egypt's farmers in a vise of lessening harvests, a tipping point of discontent might have arrived just as the usurping Semerkhet was busy defacing Adjib's monuments all over Egypt.

Egypt relied for its very life on the regular return of the Nile flood, an event which varied from year to year in its details, but remained essentially the same. In his role as sun-god, Horus carried with him the same combination of change and stability: each sunrise and sunset is different, but each morning the sun reappears on the eastern horizon. The title of nesu-bit suggests that the king himself had begun to represent this doubleness of unchanging eternal power and its mutating, earthly manifestation. The king, buried, came back again as his own son, like but different. He was like a perennial plant that returns with a different color of flower but the same root.

For Semerkhet to be erasing a pharaoh's name—the first time, so far as we know, that this happens—must have been a shocking insult to this budding conception of kingship, a little like the sudden discovery that a pope who has been issuing ex cathedra declarations for years was elected by a miscount of the College of Cardinals.* If the Nile flood then began to drop, with no apparent end to the receding waters in sight, one of those unchanging verities which the king was supposed to embody was also suddenly in flux. What would happen next; would the sun fail to come up?

Semerkhet's reign ended with an upheaval in the royal house extreme enough to cause Manetho to start a "Second Dynasty." Most ominous of all—for the pharaohs, if not for the courtiers—the sacrificial burials stop.

It's unlikely that the Egyptian kings suddenly developed a new respect for human life, as some historians tend to imply ("The wasteful practice of human sacrifice ended with the First Dynasty"). More likely, the believability of the claim to the unquestioned power of Horus took a nosedive. The Second Dynasty king could no longer compel human sacrifice, perhaps because he could no longer guarantee that he and he alone held the position of nesu-bit. He could no longer promise that he had the undoubted right to escort those souls past the horizon in royal procession.

In this Second Dynasty, which is generally considered to have begun around 2890, an indeterminate number of kings reigned. Following on the drought (proof of the king's uncertain control over life and death), civil war broke out and raged for years. The war reached its height during the reign of the next-to-last king, Sekemib, when an inscription notes that the southern army fought "the northern enemy within the city of Nekheb."[10] Nekheb, the ancient city of the vulture-goddess, was the eastern half of Hierakonpolis. It lay over a hundred miles south of Abydos, far into Upper Egypt. For a northern, Lower Egyptian rebellion to get this far suggests that during the Second Dynasty, the southern, Upper Egyptian hold on the empire was almost broken.

Although Sekemib himself was a southerner, the inscriptions that bear his name suggest that he may have been a ringer: a northern sympathizer, perhaps even of northern blood. Instead of writing his titles with the sign of the god Horus beside them, he wrote them next to the sign of the god Set.

* Yes, I am aware that this is not actually possible. But it would be shocking.

Set, the brother and murderer of Osiris (and the enemy of Osiris's son Horus), had always been more popular in the north. In later years he was pictured with red hair and a red cloak, reflecting the color of the Red Kingdom, Lower Egypt. He was the god of wind and storm; the bringer of clouds and sandstorms, the only powers strong enough to blot out the sun and bring it to the horizon before its time.

Set's hatred for his brother Osiris and for his brother's son Horus was more than simple jealousy. After all, Set was a blood relation of the king of the gods. He too felt that he had a claim to rule over Egypt. Old tales assured the Egyptians that, even after the murder, Set and Horus quarrelled over their competing claims to be the strongest, the most virile, the most deserving of rule over the earth. At one point, their arguments degenerate into a wrestling match. Set manages to tear out Horus's left eye, but Horus gets the better of his uncle; he rips off Set's testicles.

It's hard to imagine a less ambiguous resolution. The two, both kin and enemy, are struggling over the right to pass along the succession. Horus removes his uncle's ability to do so, and eventually inherits the throne. But Set's jealousy has already led him to commit the world's most ancient crime, the murder of a brother.

The hatred between Set and Horus is a reflection of the hostility between north and south, between two peoples with the same blood. Sekemib's allegiance to Set rather than Horus shows that the quarrel over who should control Egypt was alive and well. And when he died, a Horus-worshipper named Khasekhem came to the throne and took up the sword. He rallied the southern army and, after vicious fighting, overcame the northern enemy. Two seated statues of this triumphant king, both found at Nekhen (the western half of Hierakonpolis), show him wearing only the White Crown of Upper Egypt; around the base of his throne, the broken bodies of northerners lie in defeated heaps.

Egypt had survived its first civil war. Under Khasekhem, a king who deserves to be better known, it entered into the Third Dynasty, a time of peace and prosperity during which Egypt's pyramid-builders were able to develop their art.

The Third Dynasty owed its wealth to Khasekhem's efforts to rebuild Egypt's trade routes. Armed excursions out of the Delta had been abandoned, but during Khasekhem's reign inscriptions at the coastal city of Byblos, which did a huge trade in cedar logs cut from the mountain slopes nearby, began to record the arrival of Egyptian merchant ships. It owed its existence to Khasekhem's political marriage; he took as wife a princess from Lower Egypt, Nemathap, whose name and identity have survived because she was later given divine honor as the Third Dynasty's great founding matriarch. And it owed its peace not only to Khasekhem's generalship, but to his shrewdness in dealing with the Set problem.

After the war's end, Khasekhem changed his name. But rather than adopting a northern name that would honor Set, or claiming another title that would glorify the southern Horus, he chose a middle course. He became known as Khasekhemwy, "The Two Powerful Ones Appear"—a name which was written with both the Horus falcon and the Set animal above it. Temporarily, the two powers had been reconciled.

The reconciliation is reflected in the ancient myths as well. After the battle between Horus and Set, Horus recovers his missing eye from Set and gives it to his father, now ensconced as Lord of the Dead, as tribute. But Set also gets his own back; he rescues his testicles.

The conflict between the two powers, while balanced, has not gone away. Horus manages to keep hold of his power over Egypt, but Set, whose ability to father heirs is (theoretically, anyway) restored, continues to plot a hostile takeover. In a whole series of stories from a few centuries later, Horus and Set carry on an ongoing battle of wits that involves, among other things, Horus's sperm and a piece of lettuce. The jokes, which almost always involve someone's genitals, cover a real and present threat. Set's power doesn't diminish. He

TIMELINE 9

MESOPOTAMIA	EGYPT
Uruk period (4000–3200)	Naqada period (4000–3200)
Jemdat Nasr period (3200–2900)	
Atab	Archaic period (3100–2686)
Etanah	*Dynasty 1* (3100–2890)
Balih	**Menes (Narmer)**
Early Dynastic I (2900–2800)	
	Dynasty 2 (2890–2696)
Early Dynastic II (2800–2600)	
	Old Kingdom (2696–2181)
Gilgamesh	*Dynasty 3* (2686–2613)
Early Dynastic III (2600–2350)	

never leaves. He's always there, hovering, threatening to upset the orderly passing down of the nesu-bit name by pressing his own claims.

In later versions of the Osiris story, Set doesn't simply drown his brother; he dismembers him and scatters the pieces across Egypt in an attempt to obliterate his name. A thousand years later, Set has become the Egyptian Lucifer, a red-eyed prince of darkness, the Loki who threatens to bring the whole pantheon down in flames.

Khasekhemwy, the king who reunited north and south, has a huge tomb at Abydos, rich with gold, copper, and marble. But no human sacrifices. No courtiers followed him into death. The struggle over the throne had shown that the pharaoh was not a god; others could mount a claim to his power.

Chapter Ten

The First Epic Hero

In Sumer, by 2600 BC,
Gilgamesh has become a legend

BARELY A HUNDRED YEARS after his death—at the same time that the kings of Egypt were struggling to establish their own divine authority—the Sumerian king Gilgamesh had become a legendary hero. He had killed the Giant Hugeness, done away with the Bull of Heaven, turned down the romantic advances of the goddess Inanna, and made his way into the garden of the gods, where the smell of his mortality startled the sun-god himself. Because of the Epic of Gilgamesh (the oldest epic tale we know of), the personality of the historical Gilgamesh still echoes down to us, five thousand years after his death.

The relationship between the literary and the historical Gilgamesh is not unlike that between Shakespeare's Macbeth and the Maormor Macbeda who paid with his life in 1056 for murdering his king and kinsman. The real life provides a kind of springboard for an enormous, larger-than-life tale; the core of the man himself survives, magnified, distorted, but essentially true.

It's considerably simpler to isolate the historical echoes in *Macbeth.* For one thing, the details of Maormor Macbeda's actual life are described by other sources. Outside of the Epic, though, Gilgamesh's life is chronicled only by a couple of inscriptions, the Sumerian king list, and a poem or two. The story of Agga's fruitless peace-mission to Gilgamesh, quoted in the last chapter, is one such poem; it is written in Sumerian, and was likely told orally for some decades (or centuries) before being written down on clay tablets. The copies we have come from sometime around 2100 BC, when the king of Ur assigned a scribe to write out the tales of Gilgamesh. This king, a gentleman named Shulgi, wanted to keep a record of the great king's life because he claimed Gilgamesh as his ancestor (which, in all likelihood, means that Shulgi was a usurper with no relationship to Gilgamesh at all).[1] These poems date to within striking distance of Gilgamesh's lifetime, so we can (carefully) theorize that they do indeed convey some of the facts about the historical king's actions.

The Epic does as well, but sorting them out is a much more complicated matter.

Glance through a copy of the Epic of Gilgamesh in your local bookstore, and you'll see that the Epic is made up of six linked tales, like related short stories that together make up a novel. First comes "The Tale of Enkidu," in which Gilgamesh makes a friend of the monster sent by the gods to tame him; second, "The Journey to the Cedar Forest," in which he defeats Humbaba; third, "The Bull of Heaven," in which Gilgamesh irritates the goddess Inanna and Enkidu suffers for it; fourth, "Gilgamesh's Journey," where he reaches the land of the immortal Utnapishtim, the Sumerian Noah-figure, who has lived here ever since surviving the Great Deluge; fifth, "The Story of the Flood," told to Gilgamesh by Utnapishtim; and sixth, "Gilgamesh's Quest," in which Gilgamesh tries, fruitlessly, to find eternal life—or at least restored youth—and fails. A brief postscript then laments Gilgamesh's death.

This neat, six-chapter version of Gilgamesh's adventures is more than a little deceptive. The Epic was copied numerous times onto clay tablets, which, as clay tablets do, broke into bits. The bits, scattered across the ancient Near East, are written in an array of languages, from Sumerian to Assyrian, and were made anytime between 2100 and 612 BC. The oldest Sumerian copies, dating from the time of Shulgi's scribe, contain only the first two tales and the ending lament. It is impossible to know whether the other four stories were part of the cycle early on and were then lost, or whether they were added later. Parts of the third and fourth tales, "The Bull of Heaven" and "Gilgamesh's Journey," begin to appear on clay tablets, along with the first two, sometime between 1800 and 1500 BC, translated into Akkadian (the language which followed Sumerian, spoken by the people who occupied the river plain as the Sumerian cities declined). By 1000 BC or so, pieces of all four tales appear along the Mediterranean coast and scattered through Asia Minor. The story of the flood, which existed in a number of different versions well before 2000 BC, was likely shoehorned into Gilgamesh's story, as the fifth tale, at least a thousand years after Gilgamesh's death; it is clearly independent from the rest of the epic. ("Sit down and let me tell you a story," Utnapishtim orders Gilgamesh, and launches into the tale as though he's had little opportunity to tell it since getting off the boat.) And all we can say about the story of "Gilgamesh's Quest," in which he finds and loses the Plant of Youth, is that it had become attached to the rest of the Epic by 626 BC.

This is the date of the oldest surviving copy of the entire six-story Epic. It comes from the library of Ashurbanipal, the Assyrian king with the soul of a librarian. Ashurbanipal became king in 668. During the thirty-odd years of his reign, he destroyed Babylon, killed his own brother (who had become Babylon's king), and was annoyed by a Hebrew prophet named Jonah who insisted on bellowing that Nineveh, Ashurbanipal's capital, was doomed. By the time he died in 626, Ashurbanipal had also collected twenty-two thousand clay tablets into the world's first real library. Twelve of these tablets hold the Epic of Gilgamesh in more or less its current form.

Only the first two tales, then, can be placed, with any confidence, within striking distance of Gilgamesh's life. The trouble that Gilgamesh's tremendous energy brings on his subjects, and his journey north to the cedar forest, and his funeral lament: these can be treated as reflecting, however distorted, some historical truth.

More than that, they serve as the undoubted center of the world's first epic, in which death comes both as devastation and as deliverance.

IN THE FIRST STORY, "The Tale of Enkidu," the king of Uruk runs roughshod over his people, until they begin to mutter:

> Gilgamesh sounds the war-call for his own amusement,
> There are no limits to his arrogance,
> neither by day nor by night:
> He takes the sons from the father,
> although a king should be his people's shepherd.[2]

The kingship given to Sumer by the gods, the strong authority which helped the cities survive, has tipped over into tyranny. Uruk's citizens appeal to the gods for deliverance. In response, the gods make a creature named Enkidu from clay and set him down in the wastelands of Sumer. Enkidu

> knows nothing of cultivated land,
> nothing of civilized men, their ways of living,

nothing of the walled cities that have become the center of Sumer's culture. He looks like a strong and godlike man, but acts like a beast, roaming through the plains eating grass and living with the animals; he is, in fact, a caricature of the nomads who have always been at odds with the city-dwellers.

When Gilgamesh gets word of this newcomer, he sends a harlot out into the wilds to seduce and thus tame him. ("She made herself naked," the poem tells us.) Conquered by this fairly straightforward strategy, Enkidu spends six days and seven nights in carnal satisfaction. When he finally rises and tries to return to his life with the animals, they flee from him; he has become human.

Enkidu was lessened,
grown weak, and the wild creatures fled from him;
but also he was broadened,
for now wisdom had come to him,
now he had the mind of a man.

Now that he has the mind of a man, Enkidu must go to the city, the proper place for him to live. The harlot offers to take him to "strong walled Uruk, where Gilgamesh lords it over his people like a wild bull."

When they arrive in Uruk, Gilgamesh is in the middle of disrupting a wedding with his claims of droit du seigneur, which he has been exercising on a lavish scale for years: "The king of Uruk demanded to be first with the bride," remarks the Epic, "as his birthright." Enkidu, indignant over this abuse of power, blocks his way to the bride's bedchamber. The two wrestle; it is a close contest, closer than Gilgamesh has ever known. And although the king wins, he is so impressed by Enkidu's strength that the two swear a bond of friendship. This tames Gilgamesh's tyrannical impulse. The people of Uruk take a deep breath, as peace descends on their streets.

The wrestling match, of course, is more than just a wrestling match. Threaded through this whole story is a Sumerian ambiguity about kingship. Kingship was a gift of the gods for man's survival; kings were supposed to bring justice, keep the strong from driving the weak into poverty and starvation. Clearly, a king who had to enforce justice had to be strong enough to carry out his will.

Yet this strength was also dangerous, giving rise to oppression. And when that happened, the fabric of the Sumerian city began to twist and fray. In Uruk, the king was the law, and if the king himself became corrupt, the nature of law itself had been distorted.

This was frightening enough to be approached only obliquely. Gilgamesh fights, not with himself, but with a creature from outside the walls. The wrestling match at the bride's door is carried out against his uncivilized mirror image; Enkidu, after all, has been created

as like him as his own reflection,
second self, equal to his stormy heart:

let them fight each other,
and leave the city in peace.

The tale of Gilgamesh's journey to the cedar forest is not so very different. Again Gilgamesh shows a tendency to go bullheaded after his own desires.

I will conquer the Giant Hugeness,
I will establish my fame forever

he tells Uruk's council of elders. They try to restrain his ambitions:

You are young, Gilgamesh.
Your heart carries you away.
The Giant is not like men, who die.

In the face of his insistence, though, the elders yield. Gilgamesh and Enkidu head out to fight the giant, with Enkidu charged by the elders with the job of keeping the king safe.

Gilgamesh's journey north is driven by his desire for fame, the same longing that impels him to drive his people forward into war. But once again, the danger to Uruk's peace is cast as an outside force. Evil lurks, not in the soul of the king, but in the forests to the north.

Another danger lurks there too. In this earliest tale, Gilgamesh is already troubled by death. Even before setting out, he muses on his own mortality. He sounds resigned to the inevitable:

Who can go up to heaven?
Only the gods dwell forever.
Men number their days.
But even if I fall I will win fame,
Fame will last forever.

But the possibility that he will fall in the battle grows in his mind. On his way to fight Humbaba, the Giant Hugeness, he dreams three times, each time waking to cry out, "A god has passed; my flesh shivers!" The third dream is the most alarming:

Daylight was silenced, darkness swelled up,
Lightning struck, fire broke out,
Death rained down.

He is frightened enough to turn back, but Enkidu convinces him to keep on. Then, on the eve of the battle with Humbaba, Gilgamesh falls into a sleep so deep that Enkidu barely rouses him in time to fight.

Despite the omens, death is averted. By the end of the tale, Uruk is safe, and the Giant Hugeness lies dead. But Gilgamesh's admission that his days are numbered, and the fears that grow out of his mortality, become the core around which the rest of the Epic shapes itself. Whenever the rest of the tales were folded into the story, each shows a growing preoccupation with the descent into death, a growing determination to avoid it. Gilgamesh sets off to the garden of the gods in hopes that he will be able to somehow bring the fallen Enkidu back from the dead; he hears the story of the flood while searching for the causes of immortality; he manages to find the Plant of Youth, which will delay if not destroy death, but then allows it to be stolen by a water snake. In his fight to avoid death he schemes, he travels, he begs, he searches; but he never succeeds.*

This turns out to be a very good thing, as far as the Sumerians are concerned. The funeral lament that closes the Epic is part of the story from its earliest days. It isn't included in Ashurbanipal's copy; apparently the Assyrians found its finality too jarring, too unlike the quests for immortality that have come before. But the lament wraps the Sumerian worries about kingship into a single set of lines, approaching it more directly than anywhere else.

> You were given the kingship,
> everlasting life was not your destiny.
> You had power to bind and loose,
> supremacy over the people,
> victory in battle.
> But do not abuse this power.
> Deal justly with your servants in the palace.

* The world of the Sumerian dead was a particularly unpleasant place. So far as we can tell, the Sumerian afterlife was carried on in a kind of underground realm neither truly light nor completely dark, neither warm nor cold, where food was tasteless and drink thin, a place where (according to one Sumerian poem) all of the residents wandered around totally naked. It was a place reached across a river that devoured flesh, a world so distant and unpleasant that Gilgamesh refused to allow Enkidu to enter it for an entire week after his death, until the need for burial became imperative.

> Enkidu, my friend . . .
> For six days and seven nights I wept over him,
> I did not allow him to be buried
> Until a worm fell out of his nose.
> (Tablet X of Epic of Gilgamesh, translated by Stephanie Dalley, *Myths from Mesopotamia,* p. 106)

An eternal existence in this gray and unattractive place was a horrific prospect for any Sumerian.

The king has laid himself down,
He has gone into the mountain;
he will not come again.
The enemy that has neither hand nor foot,
that drinks no water and eats no meat,
the enemy lies heavy on him.[3]

In Sumer, Gilgamesh was held to be a god startlingly close to his actual lifetime. But his godship, apparently earned by his enormous efforts on behalf of his city (after all, it was the function of both king and god to protect cities, to make them great) is still limited by death. Like Baldar in much later Norse mythology, Gilgamesh is divine, but this is not somehow coterminous with immortality.

As a matter of fact, Gilgamesh's tremendous energies make death even more vital. Even had he remained evil, his power would have, eventually, come to an end. Even the strongest king of Sumer dies. The enemy without hand or foot limits that frightening power that could work either for or against his people. In the world's first epic tale, as in Sumer itself, the king Gilgamesh defeated, or outwaited, or persuaded with rhetoric, every opponent except for the last.

Chapter Eleven

The First Victory over Death

In Egypt, from 2686 to 2566 BC,
Third and Fourth Dynasty pharaohs build houses for the dead

BACK DOWN IN EGYPT, the pharaohs of the Third Dynasty began their own version of the epic quest to conquer death.

In relative peace, the early Third Dynasty pharaoh Djoser made his own expeditions to the copper and turquoise mines of the Sinai.* The Egyptian bureaucracy began to settle into shape; Egypt was divided into provinces, each watched over by a governor who reported to the royal family. Djoser did his own bit of empire-building, pushing Egypt's southern border as far as to the First Cataract. According to a later tradition, recorded in an inscription at Aswan, he dedicated some of this newly conquered land to the local deity Khnum, in gratitude for the ending of a seven-year famine.[1] "Seven" may simply be a traditional expression of "too long"; either way, this goes a long way to support the theory that diminished Nile floods had been causing difficulties for the pharaoh's claim to divine power.

By Djoser's day, the pharaoh's role as a buffer against change had solidified into ritual. A relief shows Djoser taking part in a jubilee festival, the *heb-sed* festival, in which the king took a ceremonial run around a race course. He was expected to win this physical contest, suggesting that in some way his strength was linked to the good of his country. Winning the heb-sed race reaffirmed the pharaoh's power to protect Egypt and to assure the continuing, regular rise and fall of the waters.

The fact that the Egyptians felt the need for a renewal festival at all suggests a certain fear that the pharaoh's power might fade if not ritually reinforced. The pharaoh was undoubtedly still credited with a kind of divinity, but the struggles of the first two dynasties had made his human side very obvious.

* Except for Djoser, the Third Dynasty kings are just as obscure as those of the Second Dynasty.

When an idea begins to lose some of its original heart-stopping force, it becomes surrounded with ritual and structure, a supporting affirmation that wasn't necessary before. In this case, charismatic leadership gave way to a machinery of rule and succession. Natural displays of power became enshrined in festivals; the mortal side of the pharaoh was blotted from view by an exercise of the national will.

When Djoser did finally die, he wasn't buried in the traditional graveyard at Abydos. He had already built his own tomb all the way back north, at Saqqara. He also abandoned the traditional mud brick of the Second Dynasty tombs. His tomb would be stone, and it would last forever because it was not a departure place for his spirit's journey to the next world. It was a place where the pharaoh *still lived.*

Laid out around Djoser's tomb was an entire city for his spirit. A heb-sed course was built to the south, so that the king could continue to run his rejuvenating race. Around the tomb complex, buildings recreated in stone the materials of traditional Egyptian houses: walls of stone, carved to look like reed matting; stone columns shaped into bundles of reeds; even a wooden fence with a part-open gate, chiselled from stone. The reeds and wood would not disintegrate; they would remain on earth forever. So would the pharaoh's spirit. In a small chamber called the *serdab,* a life-sized statue of Djoser sat, facing east, wrapped in a white limestone cloak. The wall of the serdab had two drilled eye-holes, so that the statue could look out at the rising sun. Below the eye-holes was an altar where priests offered food; Djoser could feast spiritually on the aromas.

Far from travelling to the realm of Osiris (with or without sacrificed courtiers), the pharaoh was still very much present: using the buildings, eating the sacrifices, rejuvenating himself, and Egypt, on the heb-sed course. There was no more need to sacrifice attendants for his comfort. The living could tend him, in his city of the dead.

At the center of the city of the dead, built overtop of the tomb itself, stood the first Egyptian pyramid: the Step Pyramid. Six levels of stone blocks rose up stepwise to a height of around two hundred feet. Beneath it, shafts reached down into the tombs of the royal family, dug beneath the lowest layer.

Apparently Djoser's vizier, Imhotep, thought up, designed, and directed the building of this odd structure. Manetho tells us that Imhotep was the first man in history to design a building of hewn stone. We don't know exactly what inspired Imhotep to come up with this novel sort of tomb, although archaeologists have suggested that the Step Pyramid's shape is simply an extension of an early Egyptian form. The graves at Abydos were roofed over by stone-walled and square-topped covers, or buildings, called *mastabas.* The Step Pyramid is, in essence, a huge mastaba with five smaller mastabas stacked on top of it. Perhaps Imhotep designed a huge mastaba tomb for the center of Djoser's complex, and then started stacking other mastabas on top of it.

But there's no compelling reason to stack mastabas. More likely, Imhotep borrowed the shape for the Step Pyramid from the Sumerians, who used stair-step temples called *ziggurats* for their worship. Given the extent of trade routes in the ancient world, Egyptians undoubtedly saw these temples rising against the Sumerian sky.

The function of the Sumerian ziggurats themselves is not entirely clear. They may have been designed by default. At the holiest places in Sumer, like the ancient city of Eridu, the temples that grew shabby were knocked down and ceremonially sealed within a layer of hard-packed earth and clay. A new temple was then built on top. Done enough times, this produced a steplike series of platforms, each layer surrounded by a retaining wall to keep the earth in place. It is possible that, over the course of a few centuries, the stepwise construction became an accepted form in its own right: hallowed by age, and useful because the top of the ziggurat, where Sumerian priests carried out rituals that remain unclear, was close to the sky.* The tops of the ziggurats may have been pedestals for the gods, places on earth where they could set their feet.†

We're not exactly sure what Djoser's spirit was intended to do with the Step Pyramid, but Imhotep's innovation earned him a whole array of honors. A statue of Imhotep dating from Djoser's reign lists his titles on its base; he is the Treasurer of the King of Lower Egypt, First after the King of Upper Egypt, the Palace Administrator and High Priest of Heliopolis, servant of the sun-god.[2] After his death, he was also honored as the greatest priest and wise man of Egypt. Not too long afterwards, he was deified as the god of medicine, another field of endeavor created by men to ward off death.[3]

The Step Pyramid, the first of the great Egyptian pyramids, shows more

* During the 1980–1988 war between Iran and Iraq, Saddam Hussein used the greatest ziggurat at Ur—the ziggurat of Ur-Nammu—as a base for a battery of antiaircraft guns; it was higher to the heavens than any surrounding spot.

† Building a place for the god to set his feet remains a constant in ancient Near Eastern forms of worship, right up to the building of Solomon's Temple, which featured two bronze pillars, each twenty-seven feet high, at its portico. The south pillar was called, in Hebrew, *he establishes* and *in him is strength;* in all likelihood they were meant to serve as symbolic pedestals for the God of Abraham. (Their presence in 1 Kings may suggest that Solomon's attempt to build the temple was less than theologically pure; see chapter 45.)

than an effort to redefine death as the absence of the body and the presence of the spirit. It shows the beginning of a new kingdom of Egypt, a peaceful and united one with an orderly bureaucracy. Djoser reigned only nineteen years, which was a relatively brief time span for such a huge building project in stone. In those nineteen years, stone had to be quarried with copper tools and brought from a fair distance; according to Herodotus, the stone for the pyramids was quarried from the mountain range east of Egypt and west of the Red Sea.[4] The pyramid itself needed to be constructed by an organized work-force of strong men who could be spared from farming and fighting. Pyramid-building required prosperity, peace, and tax money; Imhotep's title of "vizier" or "chancellor" suggests that the overseeing of tax collection was part of his job. For the first time, Egypt had a formal Internal Revenue.

Only a strong and well-to-do state could order workers to the quarries and afford to feed and clothe them. Egypt had reached a new level of prosperity and organization. For this reason, the beginning of the pyramid age also marks the beginning of a new era in Egyptian history: the "Old Kingdom of Egypt."

There are nine surviving efforts at pyramid-building in the first two Old Kingdom dynasties, some more successful than others, but all displaying the same mastery of men and resources. After Djoser, the next pharaoh, Sekhemkhet, attempted the same feat. We don't know much about Sekhemkhet except that he apparently suffered from insecurities; in a classic display of mine-is-bigger, Sekhemkhet's pyramid was planned to rise seven steps, not six as Djoser's had. But Sekhemkhet's pyramid was never completed. He died six years into his reign, and the construction on the Unfinished Pyramid halted at the first layer.

The fourth king of the Third Dynasty, Khaba, also built a pyramid. Khaba's Layer Pyramid was constructed not at Saqqara, but a few miles farther north, presumably over into the Lower Kingdom, although tensions at this point between the north and south seem to have ebbed. It too was (in all likelihood) to have seven steps, bringing it to a higher place than Djoser's. Khaba's reach exceeded his grasp; this pyramid too remained unfinished. The final pyramid of the Third Dynasty, the Meydum Pyramid, was also unfinished; it was built by the Third Dynasty's last king, Huni, and it would have had *eight* steps.

Unlike the two that came before, this pyramid was finished off by the first king of the next dynasty. From our perspective, the Fourth Dynasty is distinguishable from the Third mostly because the Fourth Dynasty kings finally got the pyramid thing right.

Snefru started off with a bang. First, he finished off the Meydum Pyramid and put a few innovations into place. For one thing, the Meydum Pyramid's burial chamber was in the pyramid itself, rather than in the ground below or nearby, as had been the case for the Step, Layer, and Unfinished Pyramids that preceded it. He also gave the Meydum Pyramid a causeway—a broad path leading down from the pyramid to a "mortuary temple," a sacred building to the east, facing the rising sun, where offerings could be made. Both of these innovations became standard a little later on.

Most interesting of all is the attempt Snefru apparently made to coat the Meydum Pyramid with a casing of some kind. The first four pyramids had all been step pyramids, with the stairlike sides of ziggurats. But the heaps of rubble around the Meydum Pyramid show that workmen tried to cover the steps with a smooth layer of facing stones.[5]

Had this worked, the Meydum Pyramid would have been the first of the familiar smooth-sided pyramids that we know. However, Snefru's architect (who was not deified later on) did not have the skills of Imhotep. The pyramid collapsed. The remaining core of the Meydum Pyramid still juts up like a half-eaten wedding cake, surrounded by heaps of collapsed stone.

No one was ever buried in the failed pyramid. Nor did the tiny, windowless temple at the end of the causeway really strike anyone as a spectacular achievement. A few centuries later, some Egyptian wandering past the drab little box scribbled on it "The Beautiful Temple of King Snefru," the first example of sarcastic graffiti in history.

Snefru didn't give up. We know little about this first pharaoh of the Fourth Dynasty, apart from records of now-standard expeditions to the mines of the Sinai and to the trading ports of Lebanon. (There is also a random story in the Westcar Papyrus of a day when Snefru, bored, ordered the twenty most beautiful girls from his harem to row him around on the palace lake, dressed in nothing but fishnets.) But he was, if nothing else, tenacious. He turned from the failed Meydum experiment and began a new pyramid, this one in a new location: Dahshur, a little bit south of Saqqara.

From the beginning, this pyramid was different. It was designed from the start to be slope-sided, with a smooth facing of limestone which made it glitter in the sun.

Much speculation has been centered around the pyramids, but one of the more fascinating unsolved mysteries is why Snefru, who has not been given enough credit for inventing a new architectural form, thought up the innovation of making the pyramids smooth-sided rather than stepped. Did this have some religious significance? Did it symbolize a new way of thinking about the pyramids—as markers on the landscape, rather than centers of a complex for the spirit?

We have no idea. But Snefru's new smooth-sided pyramid became known as the Bent Pyramid for the unfortunate reason that Snefru still hadn't quite

11.1. Bent Pyramid. The sides of the Bent Pyramid change angle sharply.
Photo credit Richard Seaman

managed to figure out the angles. The pyramid was to have smooth and very steep sides—but partway through the construction, Snefru and his chief of works seemed to realize that their measurements were off. If the pyramid continued up at its current steep angle, the weight of the stones over the relatively narrow base would likely collapse it. So they made a quick alteration in the angle, with the result that the pyramid turned out hunch-shouldered; one of its sides makes a right-hand turn.

This pyramid was completed, but never used. Snefru hadn't yet managed to build an eternal resting place to his satisfaction. Near the end of his reign, he began work on his third pyramid.

The Northern Pyramid, which stands a little more than a mile north of the Bent Pyramid, was wider, broader, and shorter than the pyramids which came before. The Bent Pyramid had shifted its steep angle from 52 degrees to a more gradual 43 degrees; the Northern Pyramid was designed from its conception with sides that sloped at a 43-degree angle. In this last attempt, Snefru's design was so well planned that even now, over four thousand years later, no cracks have appeared in the walls or ceilings of the chambers that lie beneath two million tons of stone weight.

The Northern Pyramid (also nicknamed "the Red Pyramid," since the limestone facing began to flake off and left the red sandstone beneath to glow in the sun) was probably Snefru's final burial place. Archaeologists found a body in it and shipped it off to the British Museum for identification; it was lost on the way and never found again.

Wherever Snefru's body ended up, the implication of his triple-building project suggests that Egyptian beliefs about the still-present nature of the dead pharaoh had solidified into ritual. Snefru was determined to make a final resting place for himself that was not only a good place for his spirit to walk after death, but also would stand apart from the walking-places of the pharaohs who had come before him. In some sense, death had now been tamed. The pharaohs had settled into the fairly comforting belief that they would still live among their people. Now, they could give attention to outdoing the pharaoh that had come before.

The fact that Snefru was able to complete one pyramid and build two more suggests that Egypt was now even richer, and more peaceful, and more subject to the authority of the pharaoh, than ever before. Snefru's son Khufu inherited his power and exercised it to its fullest.* He continued on in the military expeditions that had become, more or less, usual for an Egyptian king; he sent expeditions to the Sinai; he traded for turquoise; and he planned his own pyramid.

According to Herodotus, Khufu reigned for fifty years. Egyptologists reckon on a reign about half this long, but twenty-five years was long enough for him to begin the biggest building project in history. His pyramid, the Great Pyramid, was laid out with a full complex, based on Snefru's perfected designs: the pyramid itself, a causeway leading down to a valley temple, a temple for offerings to the east, and three smaller pyramids, probably for Khufu's queens.

The pyramid, built in a new location, on the Giza plain, peaked at 481 feet. Its slope is 51°52′, sharper than Snefru's successful Northern Pyramid but not quite as steep as the failed Bent Pyramid; Khufu's chief of works had benefited from the example of his predecessors. The sides of the Great Pyramid are remarkably even; each is right around 755 feet long, and even with the others to within 8 inches. The northern shaft that gives onto the King's Chamber was designed to point to the Pole Star.

Although we know very little for certain about Khufu's life, various stories about his reign have trickled their way down to us. One tells us that in order to provide water for the hundreds of thousands of workers who labored on the Great Pyramid, Khufu built the world's first dam: the Sadd al-Kafara, twenty

* Herodotus refers to Khufu by the Greek name Cheops.

miles south of Cairo. The lake created by the dam, which was almost eighty feet thick at the bottom, was thus the world's first public reservoir. Another records that the builder of the Great Pyramid was scornful of the gods and spent years in sneering until he repented and composed a set of Sacred Books.[6] And Herodotus writes that, in order to build the Great Pyramid, Khufu "reduced Egypt to a completely awful condition . . . and also commanded all the Egyptians to work for him."[7] He adds, primly, "He was a very bad man."

11.1 Pyramids of the Old Kingdom

Herodotus, who has all of the pharaohs in the wrong order, is far from reliable on this subject, and the Sacred Books have never been found; probably they never existed. But the tradition of Khufu's evil, which echoes down from more than one source, is an interesting one. To build his monument—a stone structure with something like two and a half million blocks of stone in it, each block an average weight of two and a half tons—Khufu mobilized one of the largest work forces in the world. Even if the laborers were not reduced to abject slavery, the king's ability to recruit such an enormous number of workers keenly illustrated his ability to oppress his people. The pyramids themselves stand as signposts to that power.

The stories of Khufu's cruelty suggest that his willingness to exercise power, for his own gain, at the expense of his people, did not go over particularly well. His ambition also led to impiety; he was so busy building that he closed down the temples and told the people to stop offering sacrifices. One particularly acid story related by Herodotus tells us that Khufu, running low on funds and needing to raise a little more money, installed his daughter in a room with orders to entertain any men who might want to visit her and pass the cash along to him; she did so, but told every man, as he left her, to pile a stone at the worksite for her. The result was the middle Queen's Pyramid, which stands near the Great Pyramid and which would have represented some kind of world record of courtesanship.[8]

By Khufu's day, the original purpose of that first necropolis built by

Imhotep had been well obscured. The Great Pyramid and the monuments that came after are the oldest surviving example of what we call "monumental architecture"—buildings which are much more elaborate in size or design than practicality requires. In the words of archaeologist Bruce Trigger, "The ability to expend energy, especially in the form of other people's labour, in non-utilitarian ways, is the most basic and universally understood symbol of power."[9] The less necessary and useful the pyramids were, the more they testified to the power of their builders. The house of the spirit had become the glittering testament to power.

Almost all that we know of Khufu is centered around his pyramid. His other accomplishments, whatever they were, are lost to history.

THE GREAT PYRAMID has been at the center of more theories than any other structure (possibly barring Stonehenge) in history. Pyramid theories range from the rational-but-difficult-to-prove to the out and out ridiculous. Among them: the layout of the Pyramids on the Giza plain reproduces on earth the constellation Orion (possibly, but too many stars are missing to make this compelling); the Great Pyramid is at the geographical center of the earth (this only works if you use a Mercator projection, which is unlikely to have been a common practice of the ancient Egyptians); the Egyptians used an energy coil called the "Caduceus Coil" which tapped into the "planetary energy grid" and allowed them to levitate the blocks into place. Charmingly, if anachronistically, "the main control panel for the grid is the Ark of the Covenant."[10] It has also been suggested that the Great Pyramid was built by the residents of Atlantis, who sailed from their mythical continent in mythical boats to build the pyramids, for no particular reason, and abandon them. Other theorists insist that mathematical calculations show that the Great Pyramid is a "scale model of the hemisphere," and that whoever built it "knew the precise circumference of the planet, and the length of the year to several decimals."[11]

The granddaddy of weird pyramid theories was Erich von Däniken, a Swiss hotelkeeper who turned writer in the early 1960s and published a book called *Chariots of the Gods.* Däniken insisted that the pyramids could not have been built by the Egyptians because they didn't possess the necessary technological ability; and, further, that the pyramids suddenly appeared without any precedent, which meant that they had most likely been built by aliens.

It is true that the Egyptians were not inclined to abstract mathematical thought. However, sighting the straight lines of a pyramid's base is not that complicated a task; it requires competent calculation, but not a grasp of higher mathematical concepts. The task of moving the huge blocks is an enormous one, but this, again, was a merely mechanical difficulty. Herodotus says that the blocks were hauled up earthen ramps, a task which is far from impossible; experiments have shown that a hundred men are capable of lifting a two-and-a-half-ton block of stone with a papyrus rope,[12] particularly if balls of the hard mineral dolomite are slid beneath the stone to act as rollers.

As for Atlanteans and aliens, the progression of failed pyramids before Khufu shows clearly enough that pyramid-building didn't spring full-blown from the head of some alien race. The pyramids travelled, in an easily traced line of development, right straight from Djoser's original city for the spirit to Khufu's gargantuan resting place. They stand as testaments, not to alien visits, but to the Egyptian reluctance to release power in the face of death. Gilgamesh had gone into the mountain and would not come again. But for the Egyptians, who could always see the house of the king's spirit looming in the distance, the might of the pharaoh was ever present.

TIMELINE II

MESOPOTAMIA	EGYPT
Jemdat Nasr period (3200–2900)	
Atab	Archaic period (3100–2686)
Etanah	*Dynasty 1* (3100–2890)
Balih	**Menes (Narmer)**
Early Dynastic I (2900–2800)	
	Dynasty 2 (2890–2696)
Early Dynastic II (2800–2600)	
	Old Kingdom (2696–2181)
Gilgamesh	*Dynasty 3* (2686–2613)
	Djoser
Early Dynastic III (2600–2350)	*Dynasty 4* (2613–2498)
	Snefru
	Khufu

Chapter Twelve

The First Reformer

Around 2350 BC, a Sumerian king makes war on corruption and poverty and loses his throne

IT IS DIFFICULT TO IMAGINE the Sumerians, with their spiky independence, ever granting a ruler as much power as the pharaohs of Egypt were given. Sumerian citizens would likely have rebelled if asked to sweat for twenty years over a monument to their ruler's magnificence. Nor were the kings of Sumer in any state to compel this kind of obedience. Gilgamesh's four-city coalition was the closest thing to a unified kingdom that Sumer had ever seen, and this coalition barely outlasted Gilgamesh's lifetime. His son Ur-Lugal inherited his kingdom and managed to keep it together, but the cities had all been weakened by the constant fighting. And while Egypt did not face any immediate threat from outside its borders, the same was not true of Sumer. To the east, the Elamites were waiting.

The Elamites had been living in their own small cities, over to the east of the Gulf, almost as long as Sumerians had occupied the Mesopotamian plain. Their ultimate origin, like that of most ancient people, is unknown, but their cities grew up not only just south of the Caspian Sea, but also along the southern border of the large salt desert plateau that lay east of the Zagros Mountains.

From about 2700, the Elamites too had kings. Twinned cities, Susa and Awan, served as the center of their civilization. Awan (whose exact location is unknown) was the more important of the two. Insofar as any king had jurisdiction over the whole Elamite collection, the king of Awan did, not unlike his Sumerian counterpart in Kish.

Inscriptions from the two centuries after Gilgamesh give us a glimpse of a churning mass of competition. The Elamites and the cities of the Sumerian plain—Uruk and Kish, but also the cities of Ur, Lagash, and Umma, now increasing in strength—fought an unending series of battles for primacy.

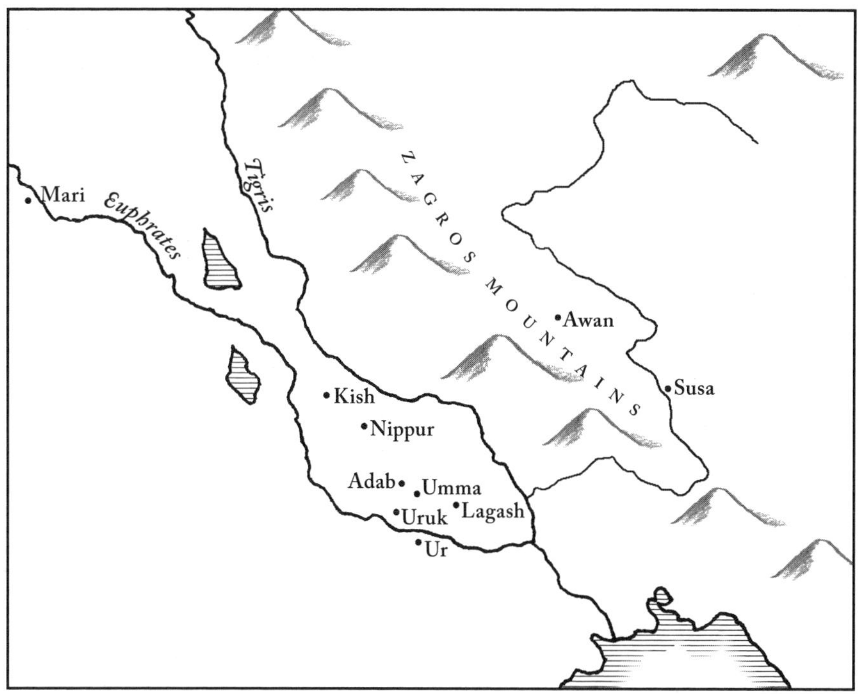

12.1 Battling Cities of Sumer and Elam

The Sumerian king list is missing quite a few names, and since it tends to list kings of different cities who reigned simultaneously as though they followed each other, it's not easy to construct an exact chronology. We do know that sometime after Gilgamesh's son inherited his father's kingdom, the city of Uruk was conquered by Ur, and that Ur was then "defeated in battle, and its kingship was carried off to Awan." This seems to indicate an Elamite invasion of great strength; and indeed the kings of Kish's next dynasty have Elamite names.

Not all of Sumer's cities fell under Elamite rule by any means. Sometime after the Elamite invasion, the Sumerian king of another city, Adab—almost in the exact center of the Mesopotamian plain—gathered his men around him and challenged their supremacy.

This king, Lugulannemundu, ruled sometime around 2500 BC. To drive out the Elamites, he fought an enormous coalition of thirteen Elamite-dominated cities. According to his own victory inscription, he triumphed; he calls himself the "king of the four quarters" (the whole world, in other words) and declares that he "made all the foreign lands pay steady tribute to him [and] brought peace to the peoples . . . [he] restored Sumer."[1]

If he did indeed carry out these conquests, he put together a temporary empire much larger than Gilgamesh's. But Lugulannemundu's exploits, which may have rescued Sumer from the Elamites and preserved its existence as an independent culture for a little while longer, didn't fire the imagination of his contemporaries. No epic poems elaborate on this conquest. Nor did his kingdom last any longer than Gilgamesh's. The next incident of note on the Sumerian plain is a border dispute between the cities of Lagash and Umma; a boring, run-of-the-mill quarrel over an undistinguished piece of land which would eventually bring the Sumerian culture to an end.

THE INSCRIPTIONS which record the start of the argument were written only two or three generations after Lugulannemundu's rule, but his kingdom had already disintegrated. Sumerian kings ruled by force of arms and charisma. Their kingdoms had no settled bureaucracy to sustain them. When the crown passed from the dynamic warrior to the less talented son, the kingdoms inevitably crumbled.

Lugulannemundu's kingdom had crumbled so quickly that his home city of Adab was no longer even a power on the Sumerian scene. When Lagash and Umma quarrelled, another king—the king of Kish, which had once again risen into prominence—stepped in. The two cities, which lay about fifty miles apart, had been trespassing on each other's land. Kish's king, Mesilim, intervened and announced that Sataran, the Sumerian judge-god, had shown him the proper border for both cities to observe. He put up a *stele* (inscribed stone) to mark the line: "Mesilim, the king of Kish," says an inscription commemorating the event, "measured it off in accordance with the word of Sataran."[2] Both cities apparently agreed to this judgment; the claim that a god had spoken directly to you was as hard to refute then as now.

However, the agreement didn't last long. After Mesilim's death, the new king of Umma knocked the stele down and annexed the disputed land (which suggests that fear of Mesilim, rather than respect for the god Sataran, had imposed the temporary peace). Umma held the land for two generations; then a military-minded king of Lagash named Eannatum took it back.

We know more about Eannatum than many other Sumerian kings because he was much inclined to inscriptions and monuments. He left behind him one of the most famous monuments of Sumer, the Stele of Vultures. On this stone slab, scenes carved comic-strip style show Eannatum's victory over Umma. Rank on rank of Eannatum's men march, helmeted and armed with shields and spears, over the bodies of the dead. Vultures pick at the strewn corpses and fly off with their heads. "He heaped up piles of their bodies in the plains," an inscription clarifies, "and they prostrated themselves, they wept for their lives."[3]

The Stele of Vultures shows an advanced state of warfare. Eannatum's men

12.1. Stele of Vultures. Vultures carry away heads of the conquered on the Stele of Vultures, carved to celebrate the triumphs of the king of Lagash.
Louvre, Paris. Photo credit Erich Lessing/Art Resource, NY

are armed not only with spears, but with battle-axes and sickle-swords; they are armed identically, showing that the concept of an organized army (as opposed to a band of independent warriors) had gained ground; they are marching in the tightly packed phalanx that would later prove so deadly to the countries that lay in the path of Alexander the Great; and Eannatum himself is shown riding in a war-chariot, pulled by what appears to be a mule.*

Eannatum of Lagash used this well-organized army to fight not only with Umma but with practically every other city on the Sumerian plain. He fought with Kish; he fought with the city of Mari; on the side, he fought with invading Elamites. After a lifetime of war he was apparently killed in battle. His brother took the throne in his place.

For the next three or four generations, Lagash and Umma fought over the

* Similar battle scenes are shown on the Standard of Ur, the other memorable war monument from Sumer in the years between 3000 and 2500 BC. Found in the Royal Graves of Ur, a set of graves that date from the Early Dynastic III Period (2600–2350), the Standard—still brightly colored after all these millennia—shows phalanxes of soldiers, war-chariots, and even forms of armor: cloaks that appear to be sewn over with metal circles. Lagash was not the only city to engage in highly organized and specialized warfare.

exact placement of their boundary line, a bitter and bloody domestic squabble occasionally interrupted by the odd band of trespassing Elamites. The next king of Umma burned the steles, both Mesilim's and the strutting Stele of Vultures; this was basically pointless, since both were stone, but may have relieved his feelings. Eannatum's brother passed the throne of Lagash on to his son, who was then overthrown by a usurper.[4]

A hundred years or so after the quarrel began, it was still going on. Lagash was now ruled by a king named Urukagina. Urukagina, the Jimmy Carter of the ancient Middle East, was the first Sumerian king with a social conscience. This great strength was also his weakness.

War with Umma was not the sole problem facing Lagash. A series of inscriptions from Urukagina's reign describes the state into which the city had fallen. It was entirely run by corrupt priests and the rich, and the weak and poor lived in hunger and in fear. Temple land, which was supposed to be used on behalf of Lagash's people, had been taken by unscrupulous temple personnel for their own use, like national parklands seized by greedy rangers. Workmen had to beg for bread, and apprentices went unpaid and scrabbled in the rubbish for scraps of food. Officials demanded fees for everything from the shearing of white sheep to the interment of dead bodies (if you wanted to bury your father, you needed seven pitchers of beer and 420 loaves of bread for the undertaker). The tax burden had become so unbearable that parents were forced to sell their children into slavery in order to pay their debts.[5] "From the borders to the sea, the tax collector was there," one inscription complains, an expression of frustration that has a rather contemporary ring.[6]

Urukagina got rid of most of the tax collectors and lowered the taxes. He cancelled fees for basic services. He forbade officials and priests to seize anyone's land or possessions in payment of debt, and offered amnesty to the debtors. He slashed Lagash's bureaucracy, which was bloated with pork-barrel positions (these included the head boatman, the inspector of fishing, and the "supervisor of the store of the cereals"). He also, apparently, took authority away from the priests by dividing religious and secular functions, thus preventing exactly the kind of authority that had allowed Mesilim to set up his stele by the authority of the god Sataran: "Everywhere from border to border," his chronicler tells us, "no one spoke further of priest-judges. . . . The priest no longer invaded the garden of the humble man."[7]

Urukagina's intent was to return Lagash to the state of justice intended by the gods. "He freed the inhabitants of Lagash from usury . . . hunger, theft, murder," the chronicler writes. "He established *amagi.* The widow and the orphan were no longer at the mercy of the powerful: it was for them that Urukagina made his covenant with Ningirsu."[8] *Amagi:* the cuneiform sign seems to stand for freedom from fear, the confidence that the life of Lagash's citizens can be governed by a certain and unchanging code and not by the whims of the powerful. This is, debatably, the first appearance of the idea of "freedom" in human written language; *amagi,* literally "return to the mother," describes Urukagina's desire to return the city of Lagash to an earlier, purer state. Urukagina's Lagash would be a city that honored the wishes of the gods, particularly the city-god Ningirsu. It would be Lagash the way it had once been, back in an idealized past. From the very earliest times, nostalgia for a shining and nonexistent past goes hand in hand with social reform.*

There wasn't much in this of benefit to Urukagina himself. It is impossible, at a distance of nearly five thousand years, to know what was in the man's mind, but his actions show a man possessed by a piety that overruled any thought of political gain. Urukagina's moral rectitude proved to be political suicide. His curtailment of priestly abuses made him unpopular with the religious establishment. More seriously, his actions on behalf of the poor made him unpopular with the rich men of his own city. Every Sumerian king ruled with the help of the double-barrelled assembly of elder and younger men, and the elder assembly was inevitably stuffed with the rich landed men of the city. These very men, the *lugals* ("great householders") of Lagash, had been severely criticized in Urukagina's inscriptions for abusing their poorer neighbors.[9] They were unlikely to have suffered this public chastisement without resentment.

Meanwhile, the throne of Lagash's old enemy Umma had been inherited by a greedy and ambitious man named Lugalzaggesi. He marched on Lagash, and attacked it, and Urukagina's city fell.

The conquest apparently went swimmingly, with very little resistance from the city. "When Enlil, king of all the lands, had given the kingship of the land to Lugalzaggesi," the victory inscription announces, "[and] had directed to him the eyes of the land from the rising of the sun to the setting of the sun, [and] had prostrated all the peoples for him . . . the Land rejoiced under his rule; all the chieftains of Sumer . . . bowed down before him."[10] The language of this inscription suggests that the priests not only of Lagash, but also of Nippur, the sacred city of Enlil, were cooperating with the conqueror.[11] The powerful priests of Nippur were not likely to have been thrilled by the curtailment of priestly power down to the south; it set a very bad precedent. And if the assembly of elders did not actually aid in Urukagina's overthrow, certainly they did not fight vigorously on his behalf. His reforms had brought his political career, and possibly his life, to a violent end.

An account written by a scribe convinced of Urukagina's righteousness,

* When Sumerian scholars proposed this interpretation of the cuneiform sign, the sign itself was immediately adopted as a logo by the Liberty Fund, simply proving that no good social reform goes unexploited.

promises that the good king will be avenged: "Because the Ummaite destroyed the bricks of Lagash," the scribe warns, "he committed a sin against Ningirsu; Ningirsu will cut off the hands lifted against him." The record ends with a plea to Lugalzaggesi's own personal deity, asking that even this goddess visit on Lugalzaggesi the consequence of his sin.[12]

Encouraged by his easy victory over Lagash, Lugalzaggesi cast his net wider. He spent twenty years fighting his way through Sumer. By his own account, his domain stretched "from the Lower Sea, along the Tigris and Euphrates to the Upper Sea."[13] To call this an empire is probably an exaggeration. Lugalzaggesi's boast to reign as far as the Upper Sea is probably a reference to the odd raiding party that made it all the way up to the Black Sea.[14] But there is no question that Lugalzaggesi made the most ambitious effort yet to bring the scattered cities of Sumer under his control.

While Lugalzaggesi was surveying his new empire, with his back turned to the north, retribution arrived.

TIMELINE 12

MESOPOTAMIA	EGYPT
Jemdat Nasr period (3200–2900)	
Atab	Archaic period (3100–2686)
Etanah	*Dynasty 1* (3100–2890)
Balih	**Menes (Narmer)**
Early Dynastic I (2900–2800)	
Early Dynastic II (2800–2600)	*Dynasty 2* (2890–2696)
	Old Kingdom (2696–2181)
Gilgamesh	*Dynasty 3* (2686–2613)
	Djoser
Early Dynastic III (2600–2350)	*Dynasty 4* (2613–2498)
	Snefru
Lugulannemundu (c. 2500)	**Khufu**
Mesilim	
Lugalzaggesi (Umma) **Urukagina** (Lagash)	

Chapter Thirteen

The First Military Dictator

In Sumer, between 2334 and 2279 BC, the cupbearer Sargon builds an empire

IN THE CITY OF KISH, a cupbearer named Sargon was laying his own plans to build an empire.

Sargon was a man of absences and disappearances. In the inscription that chronicles his birth, the voice of Sargon speaks:

My mother was a changeling, my father I knew not,
The brother of my father loved the hills,
My home was in the highlands, where the herbs grow,*
My mother conceived me in secret, she gave birth to me in concealment.
She set me in a basket of rushes,
she sealed the lid with tar.†
She cast me into the river, but it did not rise over me,
The water carried me to Akki, the drawer of water,
He lifted me out as he dipped his jar into the river,
He took me as his son, he raised me,
He made me his gardener.[1]

This birth story tells us nothing about Sargon's origins. We do not know his race or his childhood name. The name "Sargon" doesn't help us out, since he gave it to himself later on. In its original form, Sharrum-kin, the name

* The line here is literally "My city is Azupiranu," but Azupiranu is not a real city; as the Assyriologist Gwendolyn Leick points out, it refers to the mountainous area in the north where aromatic herbs (*azupiranu*) grow. See Leick's *Mesopotamia: The Invention of the City*, p. 94.

† As anyone who has ever been to Sunday School will immediately wonder what possible relationship this has to the story of Moses, I have speculated on this in chapter 32.

simply means "legitimate king" and (like most protestations of legitimacy) shows that he was born to no lawful claim whatsoever.*

If he came from the highlands, he may well have been a Semite rather than Sumerian. Semites from the west and south had mingled with Sumerians on the Mesopotamian plain since the beginning of settlement; as we noted earlier, dozens of Semitic loanwords appear in the very earliest Sumerian writing, and the earliest kings of Kish had Semitic names.

Nevertheless, there was a real division between the Sumerians of the south and the Semites, who lived mostly in the north. The two races traced their ancestry back to different tribes who had wandered into Mesopotamia, long before, from different parts of the globe. A Semitic language, related to the later tongues of Israel, Babylon, and Assyria, was spoken in the north; in the south, the Sumerian cities spoke and wrote Sumerian, a language unrelated to any other that we know. Even in the areas where Sumerians and Akkadians had mingled, a racial divide of some sort still existed. When, a century and a half earlier, Lugulannemundu of Adab drove out the Elamites and temporarily asserted himself over the "four quarters" of Sumer, the thirteen city chiefs who united against him all boasted Semitic names.[2]

But Sargon's story doesn't confirm his Semitic origins, because the man was careful to obscure the details of his parentage. He claims no knowledge of his father, which neatly removes the problem of a low or traitorous ancestry. The "changeling" mother is just as elusive. Presumably she had changed her own identity at some point. Maybe she rejected a secular life for a religious role (some translators choose to render the word "priestess"), or managed to rise from a low class to a higher one, or settled among people of another race.

Whatever her place in life, the changeling mother did not share it with her son. By abandoning him on the river, she left his own identity to chance. The very act of being pulled from the water carried then the same resonance that echoes later in the writings of both Hebrews and Christians; Sumerians thought that a river divided them from the afterlife, and that passing through the water brought an essential change of being. Drawn from the water, Sargon took on the persona of his adopted parent. The man who rescued him, Akki, bears a Semitic name; Sargon became a Semite. Akki was employed in the palace of the king of Kish; he raised his adopted son to be the king's gardener.

By the time Sargon was a grown man, he had risen much higher. Accord-

* Sharrum-kin, elided to Sharken, is spelled Sargon in Hebrew; it appears in Isa. 20:1 (in reference to Sargon II, who adopted his great predecessor's name fifteen hundred years later, around 700 BC), and the Hebrew rendering has become the best-known version of the name.

ing to the Sumerian king list, he had become "the cupbearer of Ur-Zababa," the Sumerian king of Kish.[3]

Ancient cupbearers were not merely butlers. The Sumerian inscriptions do not describe the cupbearer's duties, but in Assyria, not too long afterwards, the cupbearer was second only to the king. According to Xenophon, the cupbearer not only tasted the king's food but also carried the king's seal, which gave him the right to bestow the king's approval. He was the keeper of the king's audiences, which meant he controlled access to the king; the cupbearer of the Persian kings, writes Xenophon in *The Eduation of Cyrus,* "had the office of introducing . . . those who had business with [the king], and of keeping out those whom he thought it not expedient to admit."[4] The cupbearer had so much authority that he was required to taste the king's wine and food, not to protect the king from random poisoners (the cupbearer was too valuable an official to use as a human shield), but so that the cupbearer himself might not be tempted to increase his own power by poisoning his master.

While Sargon was serving Ur-Zababa in Kish, Lugalzaggesi was busy sending out raiding parties and adding bits of Sumerian territory to his kingdom. While Sargon carried the king's cup, Lugalzaggesi attacked Lagash and drove Urukagina out; he besieged Uruk, Gilgamesh's old home, and added it to his realm. Then, as every Sumerian conqueror did, Lugalzaggesi turned his eyes towards Kish, the jewel-city of the plain.

A fragment of an account tells us what happened then. "Enlil," the fragment announces, "decided to remove the prosperity of the palace." In other words, Lugalzaggesi was the aggressor; Enlil was his special deity. Ur-Zababa, learning that the army of the conqueror was approaching his city, grew so frightened that he "sprinkled his legs." In the face of the coming attack, he was "afraid like a fish floundering in brackish water."[5]

This aimlessness was aggravated by Ur-Zababa's growing suspicions of his cupbearer. Something in Sargon's bearing had made him wonder (with justification) whether his trusted second was in fact on his side. So he sent Sargon to Lugalzaggesi with a message on a clay tablet. The message, ostensibly an effort to come to terms, instead bore a request that his enemy might murder the bearer. Lugalzaggesi declined the assignment and kept on marching towards Kish.

This part of the story may be apocryphal. Stories of Sargon were much embroidered by later Assyrian kings, who claimed him as their great progenitor; certainly the next part of the tale, in which Lugalzaggesi's wife welcomes Sargon by offering "her femininity as a shelter," falls into a very long tradition of portraying great conquerors as sexually irresistible. However, the attack on Kish itself suggests that Sargon was not fully behind his king. Lugalzaggesi marches triumphantly into Kish while Ur-Zababa is forced to flee. Sargon, presumably Ur-Zababa's right-hand man, is nowhere in sight.

Apparently, while Lugalzaggesi was revelling in his victory, Sargon was collecting an army of his own (perhaps culled from Ur-Zababa's forces through careful recruiting, over the previous years) and marching towards Uruk; we can deduce this because accounts of the battle reveal that Lugalzaggesi was absent, when Sargon first hove into view on the horizon, and his city was taken by surprise. "He laid waste the city Uruk," Sargon's victory inscription tells us, "destroyed its wall and fought with the men of Uruk and conquered them."[6]

Lugalzaggesi, getting news of the attack, left Kish and headed home to destroy this threat to his power. But by now Sargon was unstoppable. He met Lugalzaggesi on the field, captured him, put a yoke around his neck, and marched him as a prisoner to the sacred city of Nippur. At Nippur, he forced the defeated king to go as a captive through the special gate dedicated to Enlil: the god Lugalzaggesi had thanked for his own victories, the god who had given Lugalzaggesi the right to "shepherd" the whole land. It was a bitter mockery. Two decades after the conquest of Lagash, Urukagina's curse had finally drifted home to roost.

Immediately Sargon took the title of king of Kish. In the same inscription that describes his conquest of Lugalzaggesi, he records that he travelled south, conquered the city of Ur, wiped out Umma, and blew through all remaining Sumerian resistance in an all-conquering march south to the head of the Persian Gulf. There he "washed his weapons in the sea" in a mysterious gesture of victory.

Sargon's relatively speedy conquest of the entire Mesopotamian plain is startling, given the inability of Sumerian kings to control any area much larger than two or three cities. A combination of his own strength and Sumerian weakness tipped the scale in his favor. His army was stronger than the Sumerian defenders, thanks to their heavy use of bows and arrows. Thanks to a lack of wood, bows were an uncommon weapon in Sumer; Sargon appears to have had a source for yew, suggesting that very early he extended his reach over to the Zagros Mountains, just east of the Gulf. His soldiers also seem to have shifted formation. Where the Stele of Vultures and the Standard of Ur show armed soldiers clustered together, moving in something like the later phalanx, Sargon's soldiers appear in engravings as lighter, less loaded down, and more mobile, moving freely through the battlefield to attack and re-form at will.[7]

In addition, the Sumerians were probably crippled by a rift in their cities. Sumerian cities just before the conquest were suffering from an increased gap between elite leadership and the poor laborers. The abuses that Urukagina swore to correct were symptomatic of a society in which aristocrats, allying themselves with the priesthood, used their combined religious and secular power to claim as much as three-quarters of the land in any given city for themselves. Sargon's relatively easy conquest of the area (not to mention his constant carping on his own non-aristocratic background) may reveal a successful appeal to the downtrodden members of Sumerian society to come over to his side.[8]

Whatever Sumerian weaknesses played into the conqueror's success, the outcome was a new thing. Sargon did what no Sumerian king had yet done successfully; he turned a loose coalition of cities into an empire.*

ONCE CONQUERED, the new territory needed to be controlled.

As part of his strategy for ruling far-flung cities, Sargon built a new capital, Agade; it is from the Hebrew spelling of this city's name, Akkad, that his empire drew its name.† The remains of Agade have never been found, but the city probably stood on the northern Sumerian plain, possibly near present-day Baghdad, in the bottleneck where Sippar lay. From this position, a little bit north of Kish, Sargon could control river traffic and keep an eye on both ends of his kingdom.

In this kingdom, the Sumerians rapidly found themselves living as foreigners in their own cities. Sargon's men were Semites from the northern plain. Their dialect, which became known as Akkadian, was Semitic. Their customs and their speech were unlike those of the southern Sumerians. When Sargon took over a city, it became an Akkadian stronghold, staffed with Akkadian officials and garrisoned with Akkadian troops.

Unlike his predecessors, Sargon was willing to run roughshod over the natives. When Lugalzaggesi conquered Kish, he claimed overlordship but didn't remove the Sumerian officials, the lugals, who ran Kish's bureaucracy. They were, after all, his countrymen, and he left them in place as long as they were willing to change allegiance. Sargon had no such mildness. When he conquered a city, he replaced its leadership with his own men. "From the sea above to the sea below," his inscription reads, "the sons of Akkad held the chiefdoms of his cities." The Semitic Akkadians, long mingling with the Sumerians, now triumphed over them. Agade alone had a standing garrison

* Sargon's accession is tentatively dated to 2334, a date which is reached by counting seven hundred years backwards from the reign of the Babylonian king Ammisaduga; the date 2334 may be off by as much as two hundred years. However, it has become the traditional dividing point in Mesopotamian history between the Early Dynastic Period (2900–2334) and the Akkadian Period (2334–2100).

† Gen. 10:10 makes specific reference to Babylon, Uruk, and "Akkad, in Shinar."

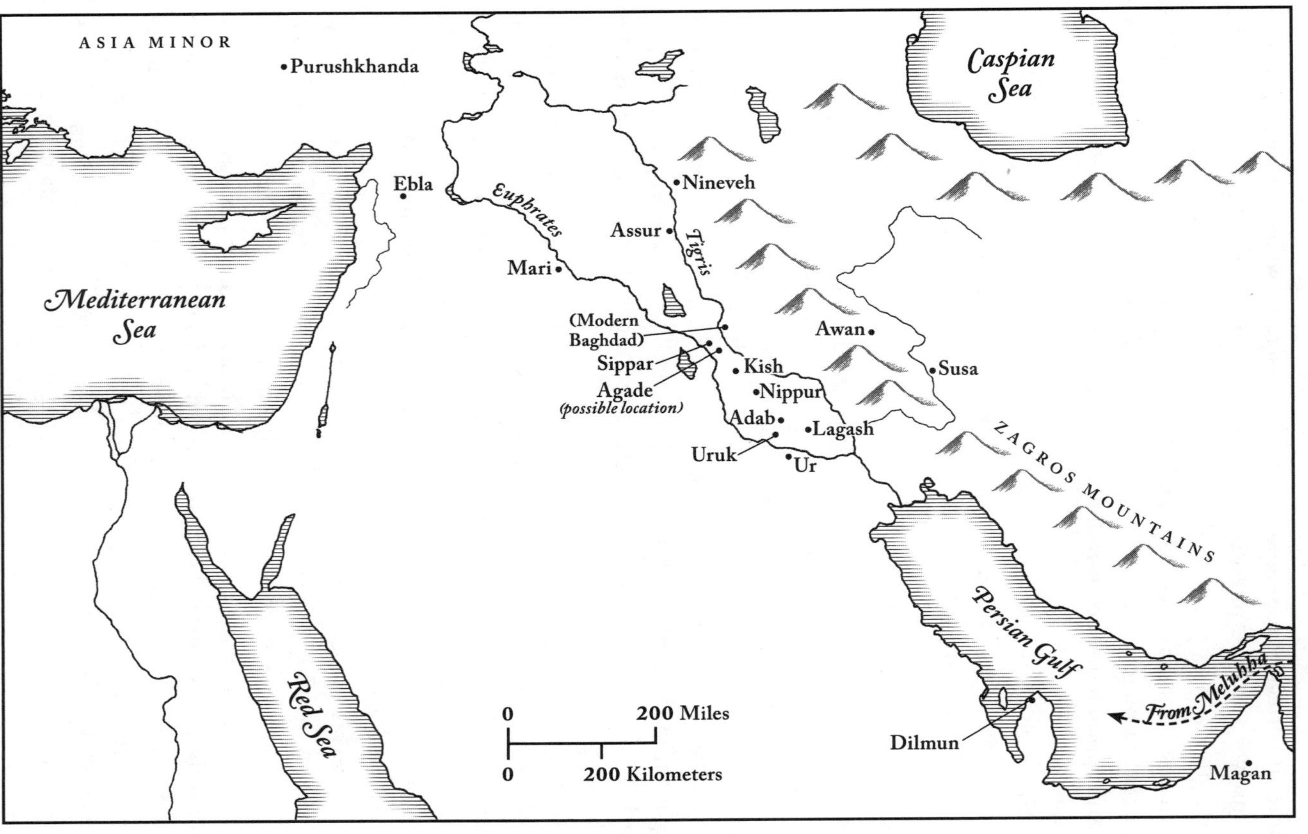

13.1 Sargon's Empire

of fifty-four hundred soldiers who "ate bread daily before" the king. Thousands more were spread throughout Mesopotamia.

With the Mesopotamian plain under his control, Sargon set out to build an empire that stretched beyond Mesopotamia. He led these soldiers in campaign after campaign; "Sargon, the king of Kish," reads one of his tablets, "triumphed in thirty-four battles."[9] He crossed the Tigris and seized land from the Elamites, who in response apparently shifted the center of their kingdom from Awan to the slightly more distant Susa, where the capital remained. He fought his way north to the city of Mari, which he captured, and then pushed even further into the land of another Semitic tribe, wilder and more nomadic than his own Akkadians: the Amorites, who ranged across the land west of the Caspian Sea. Campaigning up the Tigris, he reached and conquered the little northern city of Assur, which had been a center for Ishtar-worship for perhaps three hundred years before Sargon's birth. After this, he ranged even farther north and asserted his rule over the equally small city of Nineveh, a hundred miles on. Nineveh was a distant outpost; from this northern vantage point, his sons watched out over the wild northern conquests, while Agade remained his eye on the south.[10]

Sargon may even have invaded Asia Minor. A later story, "Sargon, King of Battle," describes his journey to the city of Purushkhanda, whose people had sent him a message asking for his help against Nur-daggal, the cruel local king. In the verses that survive, Nur-daggal scoffs at the possibility that Sargon will show up:

> He will not come this far.
> Riverbank and high water will prevent him,
> The massive mountain will make a thicket and tangle in his way.

No sooner had the words left his mouth, when Sargon crashed through his city gate:

> Nur-daggal had not spoken,
> when Sargon surrounded his city,
> and widened the gate by two acres![11]

Whether or not Sargon actually reached Purushkhanda, the story is revealing. He must have seemed as unstoppable as a juggernaut, almost magically ever-present all across the known world. He claimed himself to have marched all the way west to the Mediterranean,[12] and even boasted of controlling ships from Meluhha (the Indus), Magan (in southeast Arabia), and Dilmun (on the southern coast of the Gulf).

Keeping control of this vast expanse of land required a standing army; the men who "ate bread" in Sargon's presence daily may have been the first professional soldiers in history. Holding onto the varied peoples under his rule also required a certain amount of religious canniness, which Sargon had in spades. He paid tribute to pretty much every important local god he ran across, built temples at Nippur like a good Sumerian, and made his daughter the high priestess of the moon-god of Ur.

Records from Sargon's court show that this empire had a bureaucracy far beyond anything developed to this point in Sumer. Sargon tried to standardize weights and measures within his borders; he also put into place an Egyptian-style tax system, run by state officials who managed the empire's finances.[13] And his political strategy encompassed more than taxes and administration. He kept representatives of the old ruling families at his court, in a move which would become standard for much later empires; these representatives, ostensibly hosted by Sargon in honor for their exalted lineage, were hostages for the good behavior of their cities.[14]

This strategy reveals the continuing fault lines in his empire. This far-flung kingdom was continually on the edge of revolt.

The Sumerian king list credits Sargon with a reign of fifty-six years. Near its end, when he was most likely past seventy, a serious rebellion broke out. Old Babylonian inscriptions record that the "elders of the land," now deprived of their authority, gathered together and barricaded themselves into the Temple of Inanna, in Kish.

Sargon, naturally, claimed to have crushed the uprising at once. But according to the Old Babylonian records (which, granted, are late and generally anti-Sargon), at least one campaign against the revolutionaries went so poorly that the old man ended up hiding in a ditch while the rebels marched past.[15] It is beyond dispute that, almost as soon as Sargon died, his son Rimush had to mount an attack on a five-city coalition of rebels that included Ur, Lagash, and Umma.[16] Rimush reigned less than ten years and died suddenly. A later inscription says that his servants assassinated him.

Despite this scuffle after Sargon's death, his descendants kept the throne of Agade for over a hundred years—far longer than any Sumerian dynasty. The Akkadian empire was held together by more than charisma. Sargon's bureaucracy and administration, like those of Egypt, had finally provided Mesopotamia with a structure that could hold an empire together even when the throne passed from great father to struggling son.

TIMELINE 13

MESOPOTAMIA	EGYPT
Early Dynastic I (2900–2800)	
	Dynasty 2 (2890–2696)
Early Dynastic II (2800–2600)	
	Old Kingdom (2696–2181)
Gilgamesh	*Dynasty 3* (2686–2613)
	Djoser
Early Dynastic III (2600–2350)	*Dynasty 4* (2613–2498)
	Snefru
Lugulannemundu (c. 2500)	**Khufu**
Mesilim	
Lugalzaggesi (Umma) **Urukagina** (Lagash)	
Akkadian Period (2334–2100)	
Sargon	
Rimush	

Chapter Fourteen

The First Planned Cities

Sometime before 2300 BC,
the Indus villages have become Harappan cities

THE "MELUHHA" from which ships came to trade with Sargon the Great was India, where a great civilization had grown up. But from this great civilization, not a single personality has survived.

In the seven hundred years between Manu Vishnu and Sargon, the villages along the Indus had turned into a network of cities. The people who lived in these cities were related, not too distantly, to the Elamites. Just as the Amorites and Akkadians were offshoots of the same migrating group of people, so the original inhabitants of the Elamite plain north of the Arabian Sea and the people who built cities along the Indus seem to have come from the same original stock.

This is about all we know. What remains of the Indus city-civilization, generally called the "Harappan civilization" after the city of Harappa (one of its earliest-discovered sites), consists of city ruins, a whole assortment of seals used to identify goods for trading, and brief inscriptions that no one can read, since the script has never been deciphered. The two largest Harappan cities are Harappa itself on a northern branch of the Indus and Mohenjo-Daro, farther to the south.* With an effort of imagination we can people them with faceless artisans, merchants, and laborers, but the Harappan civilization has no recorded battles, sieges, power struggles, or tales of heroes.

This may not bother anthropologists and archaeologists particularly, but it annoys the historian no end. "[We have] history complete with approximate dates, cities, industries, and arts," John Keay complains, "but absolutely no

* Neither of these names originate with the Harappan civilization itself. "Hara" is a later name for Shiva, a divinity who may or may not have been worshipped this far back, and "Mohenjo-Daro" means "Mound of the Dead," a name given to the city's ruins by its excavators.

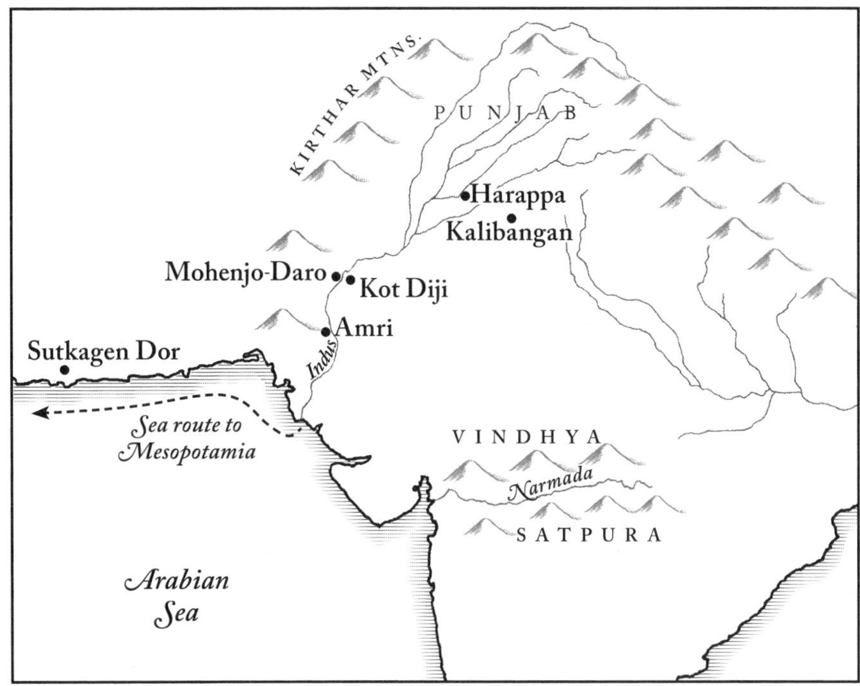

14.1 Harappan Cities

recorded events . . . [and] barring some not very helpful bones, no people."[1] We can speculate that the cities had kings; one of the only distinctive portraits found in the ruins is the statue of a bearded man, wearing an ornate robe and a headpiece, his eyes half closed and his face expressionless. Perhaps he is the king of Mohenjo-Daro, where his portrait was discovered. The city has a series of buildings that appear to be barracks, or servants' quarters, suggesting that a king or priest-king may have needed a staff to run his affairs.[2] But maybe there was no king at all. No clay tablets, texts written on papyrus, or any other examples of record-keeping exist in the Harappan ruins, even though the writing system (whatever it is) seems capable of producing them.[3] And it is difficult to see how priests, kings, and bureaucrats could carry on their business without feeling the need to keep track of their doings.

With or without a bureaucracy, the Harappan merchants traded their goods far afield. Harappan seals turn up in the ruins of Ur, dating from the time that Sargon controlled the city. Possibly the two civilizations first met in southeast Arabia, where both bought copper from the mines at Magan, and then began their own direct trade. Ur, close to the head of the Persian Gulf, is a reasonable center for the exchange of Indian and Akkadian goods. Indian

14.1. Mohenjo-Daro Man. Limestone figure of an Indus valley man, c. 2000 BC. National Museum of Pakistan, Karachi. Photo credit Scala/Art Resource, NY

merchants could avoid the Kirthar mountain range, which blocked the northern plain, by sailing out of the Indus into the Arabian Sea, up through the Gulf of Oman, north into the Persian Gulf, and from there into the Euphrates. A Harappan trading post has been discovered at Sutkagen Dor, which lies almost within Elamite territory. Presumably the two cultures had at least a working peace.

For some time, Harappa and Mohenjo-Daro were thought to be the only two Harappan cities. But now over seventy Harappan towns have been uncovered, stretching from the mouth of the Indus almost all the way to its northern streams, ranging from the western Sutkagen Dor over to the Narmada river on the east. The Harappan civilization covered perhaps half a million square miles.[4]

The cities are low and wide, made of mud brick baked hard in ovens. The houses, rarely more than two stories high, line well-planned streets, wide enough for two oxcarts to pass each other.[5] Storage buildings, probably granaries for feeding the populace, stand near the largest cities; Mohenjo-Daro and Harappa could have supported a population of somewhere around thirty thousand people each.

These people apparently put a high value on washing. The streets are equipped with elaborate gutter and drainage systems for waste water; the houses are generally supplied with bathrooms; and among the most distinctive features of the large cities are the enormous swimming-pool-sized baths surrounded by smaller chambers, perhaps for changing clothes. No one can say for certain whether the Harappan desire for cleanliness was religious or simply personal. The ruins of Harappan towns and cities have not provided archaeologists with a single building that they unanimously identify as a temple.

The most distinctive feature of the Harappan cities were the citadels, high sections of buildings surrounded by walls and watchtowers. Generally many more houses sprawled out away from the citadels, mostly to the east. Around the entire city stood another thick mud-brick wall. If this wall were breached, the population could still retreat into the citadel, their last resort of safety.

Which causes us to wonder: what were the Harappans so afraid of that they needed two sets of walls? Neither the Sumerians nor the Elamites ever sent an army quite so far to the east. Nor is there much evidence of savage nomadic tribes in the area. Yet the double walls are high and thick, with ramparts and watchtowers: built to keep out enemies.

Maybe these reinforcements give us a clue to the Harappan character.

It has long been thought that the citadel cities were a natural maturing of the villages that had rooted themselves in the valley nearly a thousand years before. Yet there is another possibility. Thirty miles from Mohenjo-Daro, on the opposite bank of the Indus, stands a town known as Kot Diji. Careful excavation of the layers of settlement show that, in the centuries before the Harappan cities grew to full size, Kot Diji's walls were reinforced against attack again and again. During the early years of Harappan dominance, they were rebuilt yet again. Then a great fire swept over the city, destroying not only the walls but the city itself. A new city was built overtop of old Kot Diji. This city had wide streets, brick gutters, houses with bathrooms. It was a Harappan city, its pattern unlike that of the town that had stood there before.[6]

Kot Diji is not the only site that seems to show a forcible takeover during the days of the Harappan cities. At Amri, on the same bank of the Indus as Mohenjo-Daro but a hundred miles south, a very ancient settlement was abruptly abandoned by half of its villagers. Over the old ruins, a Harappan city rose, with wide streets, brick gutters, and houses with bathrooms.

At Kalibangan, up in the north and not so far from Harappa, another old and durable city was deserted by its people. Overtop of the abandoned ruins, a Harappan city rose, with wide streets, brick gutters, and houses with bathrooms.[7]

Traces of actual warfare are hard to find. Yet the pattern is suggestive; the Harappan civilization, as it spread, was not always an organic development. For at least some cities, the spread was a takeover by a warlike segment of Indians. Judging others by themselves (or perhaps fearing retaliation), they built walls against attack and retribution.

Armed takeover is nothing unique, but the spread of Harappan architecture is very peculiar indeed. Even across half a million square miles of settlement, the Harappan cities are remarkably similar. The general plan of the cities was the same, with the citadel separate from the sprawl of houses and shops, and always to the west. The houses and shops, or "lower village," were organized around carefully planned streets. Depending on the level of traffic they were expected to bear, they were designed as main arteries (inevitably twenty-four feet wide), streets (eighteen feet wide, or three-quarters of the width of the arteries), or side lanes (twelve feet, or half the width of an artery). They ran, inevitably, directly north-south or east-west, in a planned grid pattern. The cities used standardized weights, which was not so unusual, as Sargon's Akkadian empire and the Egyptians had begun to move in the same direction; what is a little weirder is that the standardization also extended itself to the mud bricks used for building, which begin to conform to exactly the same dimension: in centimeters, 17.5 x 15 x 30.[8]

This was eminently practical, as anyone who has built with Legos will testify, but it also testifies to some oddly strong conformity, enforced in some unknown manner. John Keay calls this "obsessive uniformity," and notes that it even extends to the building tools and artisans' utensils, which were organized into a "standardised kit" which would have instantly been recognizable from the shore of the Arabian Sea all the way north into the far Punjab.

Most likely, the pattern of daily life still varied from city to city. The spread of Harappan civilization was not exactly the ancient equivalent of an invasion by the Borg.* But the similarity between such widely separated cities must have required close communication (not to mention enforcement), and even so no messages have survived for us. During this period the Harappan script (whatever it says) also became standardized in its form and, presumably, its use.

Yet it has no message for us. The cities of Harappa remain free of personality. If they are like the Borg, it is in the absence of any voice who emerges as an *I* from the collectiveness of the Harappan experience.

* For readers who may be too young, or too literate, to recognize the reference: the Borg, the scariest civilization ever invented, threatened the entire universe in various episodes of *Star Trek: The Next Generation.* The Borg were cyborg creatures linked together in a collective, with a mass identity so strong that they were unable to use the word "I." They rumbled through the universe sucking other cultures into the collective and making them Borg, while announcing, "We are Borg. Resistance is futile. You will be assimilated." They were entirely unstoppable until the scriptwriters of the eighth *Star Trek* movie apparently got drunk and gave the collective an individual identity, at which point the crew of the *Enterprise* mopped them up (*Star Trek: First Contact*). For an explanation of why this all has intellectual value, see *The Well-Educated Mind,* pp. 186–187.

TIMELINE 14	
MESOPOTAMIA	INDIA
Early Dynastic I (2900–2800)	
	Farming villages grow up along the Indus
Early Dynastic II (2800–2600)	
Gilgamesh	
	Harappan civilization spreads along the Indus and up into the Punjab
Early Dynastic III (2600–2350)	
Lugulannemundu (c. 2500)	
Mesilim	
Lugalzaggesi (Umma) **Urukagina** (Lagash)	
	Trade with Mesopotamia
Akkadian Period (2334–2100)	
Sargon	Maturity of Harappan civilization
Rimush	

Chapter Fifteen

The First Collapse of Empire

Between 2450 and 2184 BC*,*
the excesses of the pharaohs trouble the people of Egypt
and the Old Kingdom ends

MEANWHILE, EGYPT was suffering from the opposite problem: too many personalities, all of them wanting to be remembered forever.

Khufu, builder of the Great Pyramid, was succeeded first by his eldest son, who didn't reign long enough to build anything in particular, and then by his next son, Khafre. Khafre ruled for sixty-six years according to Manetho and fifty-six by Herodotus's count.* Either way, he kept the throne for a very long time.

Khafre, Herodotus tells us, "carried on in the same manner" as his father. Like Khufu, he spent so much energy in building that he neglected the gods and did not reopen the sanctuaries. "The Egyptians loathe Chephren [Khafre] and Cheops [Khufu] so much that they really do not like to mention their names," Herodotus adds.[1] Whatever severe measures Khufu had resorted to in the building of his pyramid were repeated in the reign of his son. Khafre's own pyramid, the so-called Second Pyramid, was only thirty-four feet shorter than the Great Pyramid. But Khafre built it, craftily, on higher ground, so the casual spectator is tricked into thinking that the Second Pyramid is taller.

He also left another spectacular monument: the Sphinx, a mysterious limestone sculpture, part lion and part falcon, with a man's face (probably a portrait of Khafre himself, although there is still plenty of argument over this point). The huge creature gazes to the east. It is usually referred to as a statue made from "living rock," which simply means that it was carved on a piece of

* Manetho gives Khafre the name Suphis II; Herodotus calls him Chephren.

15.1. Sphinx. The Sphinx at Giza, with the Great Pyramid behind it.
Photo credit Galen R. Frysinger

rock already sticking out of the ground, rather than constructed elsewhere and moved into place.

The origin of the sphinx-figure itself is totally unknown. Later, the Greeks tell marvelous stories about it which had no currency at all in the third millennium. Khafre may even have invented it, since the only sphinx which may be older* is a small female sphinx-figure which was discovered in the ruins of his oldest son Djedefre's unfinished tomb. There is no way to know whether it dates from Djedefre's day, or was tossed there later.[2]

Like the Great Pyramid, the Sphinx has attracted its share of nutty theories: it dates from 10,000 BC and was built by a disappeared advanced civilization; it was built by Atlanteans (or aliens); it represents a zodiacal sign, or a center of global energy.

The elaborate explanations are totally unnecessary. The falcon was identified with Horus, while the lion was identified with the sun and thus with the

* The lion and falcon appear combined into one creature in a predynastic carving, but the creature looks entirely different and has come to be known as a "griffin."

sun-god, Ra, and Ra's divine colleague Amun (this was a local god who came to be identified with Ra, sometimes as the composite god Amun-Ra). To have a statue half-lion, half-falcon, guarding the place where your soul would exist eternally, was to claim the protection of Egypt's most powerful gods. To put your own face on the statue was to claim their identity. The name "sphinx" is a Greek corruption; the original Egyptian name for the figure was probably "shesepankh," or "living image."[3]

Possibly Khafre needed to invent a new proof of his divinity because, as Herodotus hints, the Egyptians were getting fed up with the exacting demands of their ruler. In fact, Khafre was the last builder of a huge pyramid and the last big spender of his people's energy. His son Menkaure was forced to retrench and reform.

Herodotus tells us that, according to Egyptian tradition, Menkaure reopened Egypt's temples and sanctuaries, raised the people from the misery which his predecessors had inflicted on them, and ruled them kindly.* Menkaure's pyramid stands as additional proof of change: the Third Pyramid is only 228 feet tall, half the size of Khufu's. It still required vast use of resources, but nothing like the lifetime of man-hours demanded by the previous pyramids.

Menkaure's relative benevolence, Herodotus explains, came from conscience; he "disapproved of what his father had done."[4] Perhaps Menkaure did indeed object to the monumental architecture of his father and grandfather. However, it is just as possible that he was bowing to the inevitable: a slump in the ability of the Fourth Dynasty pharaohs to command the kind of obedience from the huge mass of Egyptian workers necessary to build a Great Pyramid. If he suspected that a revolt was on the way, a visible and public retrenching, leaning towards the merciful, was not only shrewd but unavoidable.

It was also lasting. The huge Fourth Dynasty pyramids, which have come to represent all of Egyptian history for so many students, stand as historical curiosities in the Egyptian landscape; no later pharaoh ever topped them. The pharaohs had tested the limits of their divine authority, and had come to the end of it. Menkaure could not compel the same unquestioning service as his father and grandfather.

The discovery of the limits of divine power seems to have led to an increasing decline in pharaonic fortunes, as if Menkaure's admission of his

* Herodotus calls Menkaure by the Greek name Mycerinus. He also tangles up the geneaology, making Khafre ("Chephren") the brother of Khufu ("Cheops"), and then identifying Menkaure as Khufu's son rather than his grandson.

own limitations had started Egypt down a slippery slope that ended in a swamp of anarchy.

The traditional account of Menkaure's reign, related to Herodotus by the priests at Memphis, suggests that Menkaure found himself in a bind. The gods were so displeased with Menkaure's rule that they sent him a message: Menkaure would die before the end of his seventh year of rule. At this, Menkaure was indignant. He found it horribly unfair that Khufu and Khafre, who had

> closed the sanctuaries, ignored the gods, and ruined men's lives, had lived a good many years, while a god-fearing man like himself was going to die so soon. A second message came from the oracle, explaining that it was precisely because he was a god-fearing man that his life was being cut short—that he had not behaved as he should. Egypt was supposed to suffer for a hundred and fifty years, and his two predecessors had understood that, while he had not.[5]

This extremely strange punishment tale suggests that there was an inherent tension between divine identity and merciful rule. The pharaoh's godlike status was related, in fact, to his willingness to exploit it. To show compassion was to show weakness. In that case, the unlimited power of a godlike ruler was inherently self-limiting; it would only run itself up to the point where the pharaoh either backed down or the people revolted.

And in fact this is exactly what happened to the Fourth Dynasty. Menkaure died abruptly and left the throne to his son Shepseskaf, who only managed to hold onto power for four years, and who didn't even rate a pyramid; he was buried in a mastaba tomb, an old-fashioned grave at the old graveyard at Saqqara, where his Third Dynasty predecessors lay. The Fourth Dynasty was ended.

TYRANNY MAY HAVE LED to the dynasty's end, but there is another possible factor.

Since the king was divine, he obviously needed to marry another divinity to maintain the divinity of his heirs. The royal family did not admit that any other mortal in Egypt shared in this quality. So the king's siblings were the only possible wives on offer.

Following the example of his predecessors, Khafre married his half-sister, Khamerernebty I; Khamerernebty I gave birth to a son and daughter, Menkaure and Khamerernebty II. Menkaure, on ascending the throne, then married his full sister, who was also his cousin, since Khamerernebty I, by marrying her half-brother, became her own daughter's half-aunt. (She also became both Menkaure's mother *and* his mother-in-law, a challenging role for any woman.) Shepseskaf was thus his father's son, his grandmother's great-nephew, and his mother's first cousin once removed.

The alert reader is probably wondering, at this point, why all these people didn't have three heads. Intermarriage of blood relations tends to reproduce a limited genetic pool, so damage in the genes is more likely to show up. In Europe, thousands of years later, decades of royal matches between blood relatives produced a slew of illnesses and imbecilities. Ferdinand I of Austria, whose mother was also his double first cousin once removed, liked to pack himself into a wastepaper basket and roll down the hall, and his most coherent utterance was reportedly, "I am the emperor! I want dumplings!"

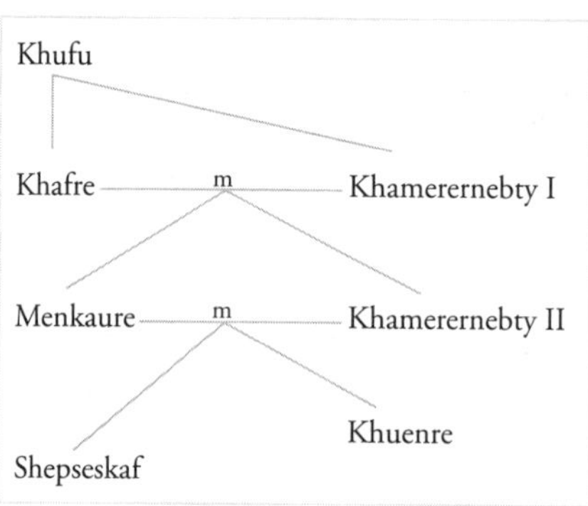

15.2. Khafre's Descendents.

It is possible that the genetic code was a little less fragile, so long ago. There also may have been a certain self-selection going on; if you had the choice of a handful of siblings for your spouse, you were likely to pick the most vigorous and healthy, thereby perhaps avoiding damaged genes. On the other hand, the rapid falloff of the pharaoh's power after Menkaure might hint at trouble in the royal bloodline. Statues of Menkaure himself show a slightly odd-shaped head with weirdly prominent eyes, although Menkaure himself seems to have been in full possession of his wits. However, his oldest son by his sister Khamerernebty II, Prince Khuenre, lived just long enough to be proclaimed heir, and then succumbed to some unknown illness before his father's death; Menkaure himself seems to have died very suddenly; and Menkaure's second son, Shepseskaf, had an entirely undistinguished and very brief reign.

There is also the peculiar survival of a story (again transmitted via Herodotus) that Menkaure fell in love with his own daughter and raped her, after which she hanged herself in grief. Herodotus himself remarks, "But this is all nonsense, in my opinion,"[6] and it probably is; given the usual cheerful incest in the Egyptian royal family, it is unlikely that an Egyptian princess would find this act as shocking as we do, and the story also says that the daughter was Menkaure's only child, which is demonstrably false. But this legend of inbreeding is the only one which survives as an explanation for the dynasty's end.

THE PHARAOHS of the Fifth Dynasty were not marked by a huge infusion of fresh blood. The first Fifth Dynasty pharaoh, Userkaf, was Menkaure's first cousin once removed; he also married his second cousin, Menkaure's daughter. Nevertheless, the breaking of the father-to-son succession also hinted at other changes.

A papyrus which is probably five hundred years later than Userkaf, but much much earlier than Manetho, chalks up the change in dynasty to a prophecy; Khufu was told that his son and grandson would rule, but that the throne would then go to three sons of the high priest of the sun-god Ra, the priest who served at the sun-god's chief temple in Heliopolis. These children, gold-skinned, would be attended at their births by the gods themselves.[7]

In other words, power was shifting from the palace towards the temples. The Fifth Dynasty pharaohs—there were probably nine, all of them more or less undistinguished—built very small pyramids, but during this century five new temples were built to the sun-god. The first was erected by Userkaf himself; a boat for Ra's use lies at its south edge, and it boasted in front of it an obelisk, a stone tower pointing upwards at the sky, the home of Ra. The top of the obelisk was a miniature pyramid covered in gold that glowed in the rays of the sun like a miniature sun itself.

During the Fifth Dynasty, the pharaoh also became more closely identified with the sun-god. He had been Horus and Osiris; now he was the son of Ra.[8] This likely brought him further under the control of the sun-god's high priests, who could convey to him his father's words.

Instead of the earthly incarnation of a god, the king was now the son of a god, a subtle but meaningful demotion. The rings of divine power had rippled outwards, and the pharaoh was no longer the central and unquestioned conduit of it. And the idea of the pharaoh's continuing presence on earth after death had also begun to fade. During the Fifth Dynasty, the entire progression of the spirit after death into another world was laid out in writing for the first time. The last pharaoh of the dynasty, Unas, was buried in a small pyramid with detailed incantations written along the walls, intended to make sure that he got where he was going. These Pyramid Texts, which became standard decoration for the burial chambers of the next dynasty of pharaohs, clearly indicate that Unas was leaving his people.* "Oh Ra," begins Spell 217, "This king Unas comes to you, your son comes to you." King Unas's identification with Horus and Osiris is mentioned in passing. But more attention is given

* The Pyramid Text inscriptions eventually migrate to the tops and sides of coffins and become the Coffin Texts; from the coffins, they travel to papyri and become the well-known Book of the Dead, which elaborates on the destiny of the soul after death. This, however, is not fully developed until the New Kingdom, nearly a thousand years later.

to the fact that he will now ascend with Ra, rise to the sky, and "go up on high," there to live "in the embrace of [his] father, the high and distant Ra."[9]

When Unas left his people, he apparently did so without issue, and a brief tussle over the throne ensued. The next dynasty that came to the throne, the Sixth Dynasty, had an even foggier vision of its own divinity; its pharaohs married commoners. This could have infused the royal family with new vigor and brought it back to power, but it was too late. Other blood successions had risen to challenge the power of the royal line. Over the course of a hundred years or so, the governors of various Egyptian provinces, bureaucrats who had always been appointed by the crown, had seized on periods of chaos at Memphis to pass their power to their sons.*

As a result, the first pharaoh of the Sixth Dynasty, Teti, now ruled an Egypt that contained, in essence, small hereditary states with their own "royal families." Teti himself took as his Horus-name the title Seheteptawy, which means "He who pacifies the Two Lands."[10] The startling return of the north-south hostility, something which had sunk from view beneath the surface of Egyptian unity, is only one hint of the currents now pulling at Egypt. Others are glimpsed in Manetho, who adds that Teti was assassinated by his own bodyguard; the divinity of the pharaoh had once made him untouchable, but this had now begun to fracture. Teti's successor, Pepi I, had to put down an assassination plot in his own harem.[11] His oldest son was dethroned and replaced by a six-year-old named Pepi II, clearly a figurehead for a powerful palace faction.

Pepi II is credited with a ninety-four-year rule, the longest in Egyptian history. But rather than representing a time of stability, this century stands as one when the pharaoh ruled in name only. Noblemen, priests, and palace officials increasingly broke the kingdom apart between them. Pepi II, the last king of the Old Kingdom of Egypt, stayed in power for so long because he had so little actual power.

Towards the second half of Pepi II's long reign, Egypt—already practically divided into smaller kingdoms, united only by the conventional agreement that the throne in Memphis in fact governed the whole country—began to unravel in earnest. It is difficult to point to one precipitating event, but it seems almost certain that the Nile floods dropped once again, as they had towards the end of the First Dynasty. The western desert seems to have been pushing at the edges of Egypt's cultivable land, an event which may have caused a certain level of panic.

Documented events related to the end of the Sixth Dynasty are scarce. Our

* The Greeks called these governors *nomarchs* and their provinces *nomes,* and the anachronistic names have become traditional.

TIMELINE 15	
INDIA	EGYPT
	Dynasty 2 (2890–2696)
Farming villages grow up along the Indus	
	Old Kingdom (2696–2181)
	Dynasty 3 (2686–2613)
	Djoser
Harappan civilization spreads along the Indus and up into the Punjab	*Dynasty 4* (2613–2498)
	Snefru
	Khufu
	Khafre
	Menkaure
	Dynasty 5 (2498–2345)
Trade with Mesopotamia	*Dynasty 6* (2345–2184)
Maturity of Harappan civilization	
	First Intermediate Period (2181–2040)

best source is the Egyptian king list, which, as Colin McEvedy remarks in his atlas of the ancient world, follows Pepi II with a "downright goofy dynasty": a Seventh Dynasty with seventy pharaohs in seventy days.[12] The numerical repetition must be symbolic. The number seven didn't yet have the significance of completion that it gained later on, in the sacred writings of the Israelites; more likely the scribes keeping the king list multiplied the number of the dynasty by ten to demonstrate total chaos.*

After the wasteful Fourth Dynasty squandering of Egyptian lives and money, the weakness of the royal family's genes, and the natural self-limiting nature of the pharaoh's divinity, drought provided the final push over the edge. For a little more than a hundred years, rival dynasties would rule in different cities and Egypt would be divided between battling kings. The Sixth Dynasty was the last of the Old Kingdom of Egypt; the next four dynasties would belong to the disorganized time known as the First Intermediate Period.

* The plagues visited on Egypt just before the Exodus numbered ten, with the tenth as the most devastating: this may also reflect an understanding of the number ten as an intensifier of sorts. (See the footnote on p. 262 for another example.)

Chapter Sixteen

The First Barbarian Invasions

Between 2278 and 2154 BC,
Gutian hordes invade the Akkadian lands and the Third Dynasty of Ur drives them out

THE AKKADIAN EMPIRE, now under Sargon's son Manishtushu, was looking to expand. Unlike Egypt, Agade found that its greatest enemies still lay outside its own borders.

Manishtushu's inscriptions boast that he was just as warlike as his father. He brags of conquering yet more territory for the empire, even travelling across the Persian Gulf by ship in order to fight against "thirty-two kings gathered against him," where "he defeated them and smote their cities."[1] There may be more smoke than fire in this. Although he brags of his conquests, the areas that appear to have paid tribute to him seem to be those which Rimush had already subdued. "These are no lies!" one victory inscription ends up. "It is absolutely true!"[2] (which tends to suggest the opposite, like the title "Legitimate King" in the mouth of a usurper).

Manishtushu's fourteen-year reign is mostly interesting because he fathered Naram-Sin the Great, the grandson of the great Sargon and the Akkadian king who would spread the empire to its greatest extent. Like his grandfather, Naram-Sin fought constantly. One of his steles announces nine victories in a single year; another, the unimaginatively titled Victory Stele, shows his victory over a tribe in the western Elamite territory. The Akkadian borders also crept over to swallow Susa, one of Elam's twinned capital cities. But Awan remained free, with Elamite resistance to the growing western threat centered there.

Ignoring the Elamite king's independence, Naram-Sin gave himself the titles "King of the Four Quarters of the World" and "King of the Universe," in self-puffery excessive even for ancient Mesopotamia. His name in cuneiform appears next to a sign that indicates godship,[3] and the Victory Stele shows his huge figure standing above his battling armies, in the position that the gods occupy in earlier engravings. Naram-Sin did not need any gods to bless his battles. He could do that all by himself. So far as we can tell, Naram-Sin was the first Mesopotamian king to lay hold of godlike status during his life; it is an action that shows a certain maturity in the power of the throne.

By Naram-Sin's day, the Akkadians themselves had reached a certain maturity as a people. Sargon had corralled the warring cities of Mesopotamia into a single empire, but the Akkadian culture itself was never exactly identical with the Akkadian political sphere. You could live in the Akkadian empire, obeying its Akkadian king, and still be a Sumerian. Sargon's sons and grandson described their victories in Sumerian cuneiform (for the sake of the conquered) and in Akkadian as well (for the sake of themselves). The officials and their garrisoned troops lived in the cities of Sumer, but also knew themselves to be part of a culture that was separate from them.

This growing sense of a *cultural* identity is most on display at the time of the empire's greatest peril. Down from the Zagros Mountains, the rocky rise east of the Tigris, swept the Gutian tribes, and hurled themselves against the edges of Naram-Sin's kingdom.

Chaos threatening the established order of a kingdom was nothing new. The Chinese tradition records the struggle of rulers against internal chaos: an impulse towards oppression and cruel exploitation. The Egyptians tell stories of the battles between brothers, as the kingdom along the Nile breaks apart into separate kingdoms. Gilgamesh fights a wild man, but this enemy proves also to be his shadow self.

But Naram-Sin faced something new: the invasion of *barbarians,* those from outside, the others who want to wreck and destroy. The Akkadian takeover of Sumer was violent and forceful, but Sargon's people had a language and a writing of their own. By the time of Naram-Sin's reign, the Akkadian empire had become more like a nation and less like a spreading army that occasionally stopped to eat. It had a history of its own; it had its own founding father. Only now was it even possible to speak of a contrasting kind of people: of "barbarians."

"No one calls himself a barbarian," historian David McCullough has remarked, "that's what your enemy calls you."[4] The culture of the Akkadians stood in opposition to the scattered piecemeal world of the Gutians, who—although they shared a spoken language—left no inscriptions, no traditions, and indeed no histories behind them. Certainly none of the Akkadian inscriptions ever use the word "barbarian," which comes from the Greeks much later on. But the Akkadians saw, in the Gutian hordes, an outside force that came simply to destroy—not to set up another culture in place of their own. The Assyriologist Leo Oppenheim has pointed out that the sheer hatred found in

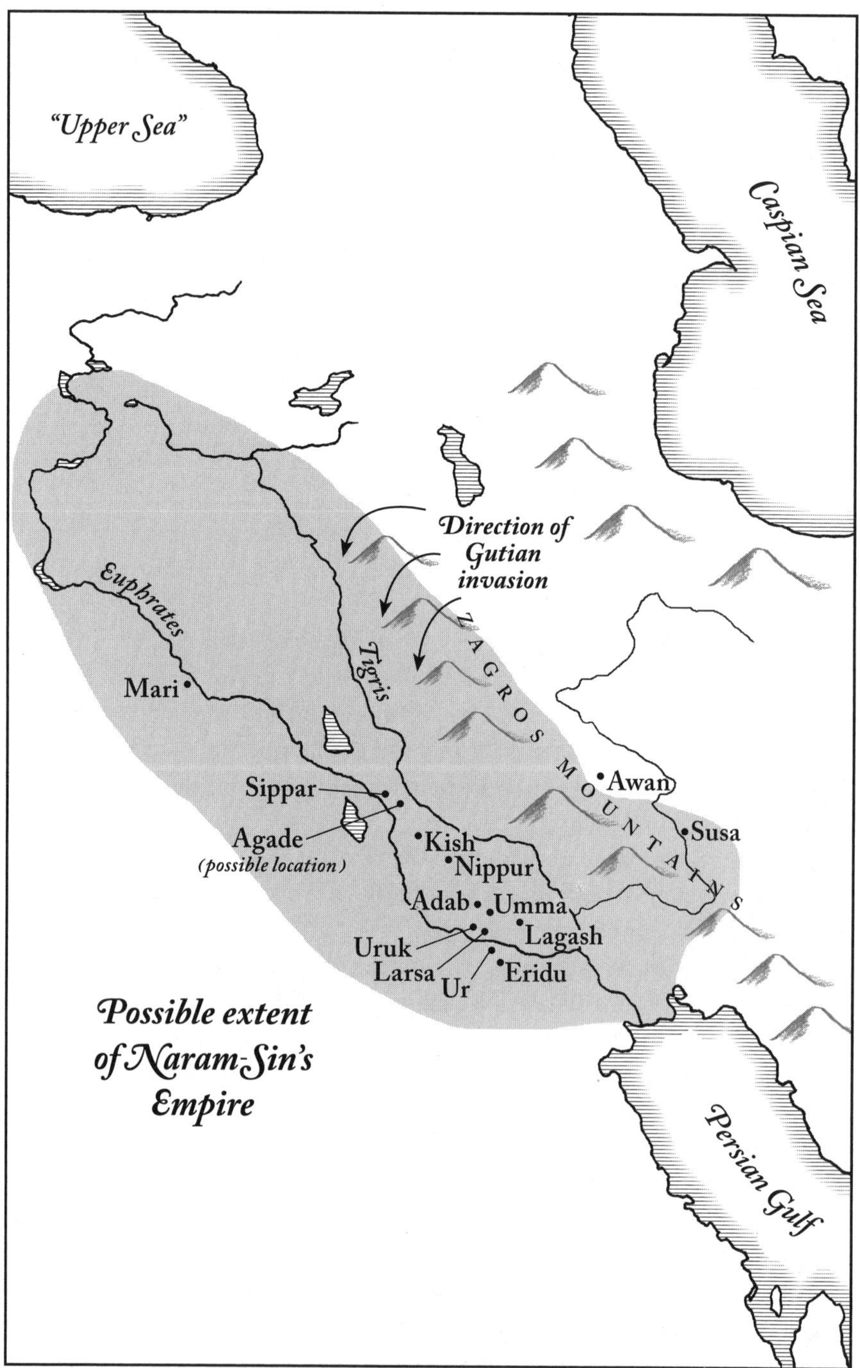

16.1 The Mesopotamia of Naram-Sin

the Akkadian chronicles of the Gutian invasion is new in the ancient world; it is, he remarks, "comparable only with the hatred of the Egyptians for the Hyksos,"[5] an event which came two hundred years later and represented the first time that Egypt was invaded by a destructive wandering people from outside. The Sumerians called the Gutians snakes and scorpions and parodies of men:

> those who are not part of the Land:
> the Gutians, a people with no bridle,
> with the minds of men, but the feelings of dogs,
> with the features of monkeys.
> Like small birds, they swooped over the ground in great flocks. . . .
> nothing escaped their clutches,
> no one escaped their grasp.[6]

Naram-Sin's armies were unable to keep the Gutian hordes away; they streamed in and took over city after city. The Gutian occupation of Akkadian cities turned the rightful order of things upside down.

> The messenger could no longer travel the highway,
> the boat of the courier could no longer travel the river. . . .
> Prisoners manned the watch,
> bandits occupied the roads. . . .
> They planted gardens for themselves inside the cities,
> not, as is usual, on the wide field outside.
> The fields gave no grain, the floods no fish,
> the orchards no syrup or wine,
> the clouds did not bring rain. . . .
> Honest men were confused with traitors,
> heroes lay dead in heaps on top of heroes,
> the blood of traitors streamed over the blood of honest men.[7]

The overthrow of order by the barbarians was so unsettling that a long story was written, only slightly later, to account for the devastation. The gods were angry: the first, but not the last time that barbarian invasions produced this explanation.

In "The Cursing of Agade," Naram-Sin destroys the great Temple of Enlil in his capital city and steals its gold, silver, and copper. It is an act of sacrilege that dooms his country; he loads the treasures into ships and sails them away, and "as the ships moved away from the docks, the city lost its intelligence."

Lost its wits: its distinctive, civilized, human character. Enlil, who then decides to unleash the Gutian hordes in revenge, comes against Agade like "the roaring storm that subjugates the entire land, the rising deluge that cannot be confronted." The barely human hordes are instruments of the god's anger. "And so it was," the story ends. "On the tow-paths of the canal banks, the grass grew long; on the highways, the grass of mourning grew." The cleared spaces of civilization had begun to disappear.

From the king list, we know that Gutian warriors seized control of Uruk, the ancestral home of Gilgamesh, early on. Since they worked their way so far to the west, they almost certainly broke the Akkadian hold on southern Sumer.

By Naram-Sin's death in 2218, the Gutian hordes had managed to shrink his kingdom to half of its former size. Naram-Sin left the whole mess to his son Shar-kali-sharri, who was faced with the task of attempting to drive the barbarians back out again. He didn't succeed; Lagash too fell to the Gutians, and by the end of Shar-kali-sharri's reign, the south of Sumer was irretrievably gone. Gutians moved into some of the southern cities, but other cities, including those in Elam, simply took advantage of Shar-kali-sharri's preoccupation with the Gutians to finally free themselves from an allegiance to the Akkadian king which had probably been nominal for some time.

What followed in the Akkadian lands was, apparently, anarchy. After Shar-kali-sharri's death sometime around 2190, the center of the kingdom still barely held together. But the Sumerian king list asks, "Who was king? Who was not king?" which implies that no one actually managed to hold on to power for any length of time.[8] Finally, a warrior unrelated to Sargon took the throne, managed to hold onto it for twenty-one years, and then pass it to his son.

But this non-Sargonic dynasty, of which we know absolutely nothing, was doomed. Inscriptions lament the fall of Agade itself, sometime around 2150 BC, as Gutian invaders broke through its walls. Since we haven't found the ruins, we don't know whether the city was sacked and burned. Perhaps the very absence of the site suggests a thorough destruction. And since the city left no mark on the landscape, it was probably not reoccupied afterwards. Most city sites in the ancient Near East show layer after layer of succeeding occupation, but a city considered to be under a curse sometimes lay deserted for centuries.*

* A Palestinian parallel may be the city of Jericho, which fell to Israelite attack and had a curse laid on it by Joshua, the Israelite leader (Josh. 6:26); likely because of its reputation as a cursed city, Jericho, one of the world's oldest cities, was deserted for several centuries before it was reoccupied. The biblical account treats the rebuilding of Jericho, which takes place under the rule of the wicked Ahab of Jericho, as a further sign of the corrupt times; apparently the builder used human sacrifice to guarantee that the walls built on evil-omened ground would remain standing (see 1 Kings 16:34).

For almost half a century, the Gutian "barbarians" ranged across the entire Mesopotamian plain. They left little behind them to suggest that they developed a culture of their own: no writing, no inscriptions or statues or cultic centers. The Gutian invasion brought an end to an existing civilization without building another in its place.

The king list draws a stark line between the reigns of the Akkadians and the Gutian "kings," who clearly have no idea of how to establish a succession. Manishtushu ruled fifteen years, Naram-Sin fifty-six; even Naram-Sin's son, who was faced with the difficulty of protecting the remnants of his father's kingdom against steadily encroaching hordes, is credited with a stable reign of twenty-five years. But the Gutians who seized Agade and the cities nearby were a shifting and unstable mass. An unnamed king is followed by twenty-one kings, only one of which manages to hang on to his power for more than seven years; most rule for only a year or two, and the last reigns for forty days.

The old and powerful Sumerian cities—now, presumably, occupied by a mix of Sumerians, Akkadians, and Gutians—did not long tolerate the rule of the barbarians.

The resurgence began in Lagash, the city closest to the Elamites. The warrior Gudea of Lagash rid his own city of Gutians, took Lagash's reins as king, and then began to purify and rebuild the temples of the Sumerians, which had apparently been wrecked either by the Akkadians or the Gutians.

Gudea doesn't appear in the Sumerian king list at all, which most likely means that his control never stretched beyond the borders of his own city. However, he is impressed enough with his own victories to call himself the "true shepherd" of his people. He also claims, in celebratory tablets, to have reestablished trade with the Elamites in the mountains, who sent copper; with India, from which "red stones" were procured; and even with the northern parts of Mesopotamia. He claims that he

> made a path into the cedar mountains . . . he cut its cedars with great axes . . . like great snakes, cedars were floating down the water from the cedar mountain, pine from the pine mountain.[9]

If this is true, the Gutians were not capable of guarding the river, which was still open for trade.

Gudea also brought stone from Magan (Oman, in Arabia) to build statues of himself. These statues show the king as a worshipper of the gods, unarmed and dressed in ceremonial clothes, his hands clasped in supplication. A greater contrast to Naram-Sin's arrogant striding divinity could hardly be found; Gudea was not going to risk the wrath of the gods by copying his predecessor's errors.

16.1. Gudea. Gudea, King of Lagash, depicted as humble worshipper of the gods. Louvre, Paris. Photo credit Scala/Art Resource, NY

Lagash's freedom was followed, very shortly, by the freedom of Gilgamesh's home city of Uruk, where the king Utuhegal had much bigger plans than simply freeing his own city. He drove the Gutians out of Uruk, and then his soldiers (fiercely loyal to him; in his own words, they followed him "like one man") marched in their wake out in a spreading ripple of circles: to Ur, to Eridu south of Ur, probably as far north as the ancient sacred city of Nippur.

Freeing Nippur from the Gutians symbolized the final freedom of the plain from the Gutian hordes. With his soldiers garrisoned in the cities which had once been under the chaos of Gutian rule, Utuhegal began to describe himself in inscriptions with a title no one had claimed for years, perhaps since Sargon's sons ruled his empire: King of the Four Quarters. He is, in his own victory accounts, "the king whose orders cannot be countermanded."[10] He captured the strongest Gutian leader, a man he describes as a "snake from the mountains," marched him into his court in handcuffs, and—in a posture which would become familiar in the reliefs of the next great empire to arise on the plain—"set his foot upon his neck."[11]

But although Utuhegal brought an end to the dominance of the invaders, he did not live long enough to enjoy his domain. The real snake in the grass appears to have been his right-hand man Ur-Nammu, who was also married to Utuhegal's daughter.

After driving the Gutians out of Ur, Utuhegal left Ur-Nammu in charge of the city, with troops on hand. Shortly afterwards, Ur-Nammu sent his soldiers against his own king. The king list records that Utuhegal's reign over his newly freed land had lasted seven years, six months, and fifteen days—the only time that a king's rule is specified in more detail than simply years. The precision argues for a sudden and shocking end to Utuhegal's reign: perhaps his death, in battle, at the hands of his own son-in-law.

Despite this bloody beginning, Ur-Nammu, once in control of both Ur and Uruk, behaved not primarily as a warleader but as a king. He mounted the occasional campaign against lingering Gutians, but records of treaties made, and alliances sworn out, suggest that Ur-Nammu's empire was spread largely through negotiation (although undoubtedly the soldiers standing behind the smiling diplomat had a great deal to do with Ur-Nammu's success). Where Ur-Nammu did not conquer, he befriended. He made a match with the daughter of the king of the city of Mari (we have no record of the reaction of his first wife, daughter of the slain Utuhegal, to this strategy). He built temples in cities all up and down the plain, including a new temple to the great god Enlil. Even Susa acknowledged his overlordship, although Awan remained aloof.

Under Ur-Nammu, the Sumerians enjoyed their last renaissance. His rule over this neo-Sumerian empire, and the reigns of the kings who followed him, is known as the Third Dynasty of Ur. Ur-Nammu was not only the conquerer of the plain, but the reestablisher of civilization. He rebuilt roads and walls; he dug canals to bring fresh water back into the cities where brackish water had stood. "My city is full of fish," he claimed, "the air above it is full of birds. In my city honey-plants are planted."[12]

Ur-Nammu's praise poems boast not only of his rebuilding projects, but of his reestablishment of order and law:

I am Ur-Nammu,
I protect my city.
I strike those guilty of capital offenses, and make them tremble. . . .
My judgments set Sumer and Akkad on a single path.
I place my foot on the necks of thieves and criminals,
I clamp down on evildoers. . . .
I make justice apparent, I defeat wickedness. . . .
In the desert, the roads are made up as for a festival,
and are passable because of me. . . .
I am the good shepherd whose sheep multiply greatly.[13]

Chaos had been temporarily beaten back, the rule of law and order asserted. For a little while longer, the cities on the Sumerian plain were safe.

TIMELINE 16

EGYPT	MESOPOTAMIA
	Early Dynastic II (2800–2600)
Old Kingdom (2696–2181)	
Dynasty 3 (2686–2613)	**Gilgamesh**
Djoser	
Dynasty 4 (2613–2498)	Early Dynastic III (2600–2350)
Snefru	
Khufu	**Lugulannemundu** (c. 2500)
Khafre	**Mesilim**
Menkaure	
Dynasty 5 (2498–2345)	**Lugalzaggesi** (Umma) **Urukagina** (Lagash)
Dynasty 6 (2345–2184)	Akkadian Period (2334–2100)
	Sargon
	Rimush
	Gutian invasion
First Intermediate Period (2181–2040)	
	Fall of Agade (c. 2150)
	Third Dynasty of Ur (2112–2004)
	Ur-Nammu

Chapter Seventeen

The First Monotheist

Abram leaves Ur sometime after 2166 BC and travels to the Western Semitic lands, while the neo-Sumerian empire grows stronger

SOMETIME DURING THE SUMERIAN STRUGGLE with the Gutians, a citizen of Ur named Terah collected his servants, his livestock, his wives, his sons and their families, and set off westwards. Among the household was Abram, Terah's son, and Abram's wife Sarai, who had the misfortune to be still childless.*

Terah was not a Sumerian, but perhaps an Akkadian or a member of a related tribe; he traced his ancestry back to Shem, the biblical progenitor of the Semites.[1] Born sometime during the rule of Naram-Sin, Terah had probably never lived in an Ur that was free of the Gutian threat. During his childhood, Ur had taken advantage of the weakening power of the Akkadian kings to free itself from Akkadian domination. By the time he became the father of three sons, the last Akkadian king was making a final stand for the throne; as his young family grew, the Gutians wrecked Agade and ranged freely across the northern plains.

Sometime around the time that Utuhegal was marching towards Ur, to take it over and then lose it again to his son-in-law, Terah and his family decided (understandably) that they would be better off out of the city. They set off,

* The traditional dating of Abraham's lifetime is 2166–1991 BC, based on a straightforward reading of the Masoretic text. There is, naturally, no agreement whatsoever on this. The text itself makes other readings possible; Genesis is a theological history, not a political chronicle, and does not provide an exact chronology. No archaeological evidence points irrevocably to Abraham; scholars comparing the world of Genesis 14 to ancient Mesopotamian conditions have come up with birth dates ranging from 2166 to 1500 BC, or have argued that he never existed at all. In keeping with my general practice up to this point, I have retained the traditional dating, but it ought to be held very loosely. However, Abraham's adventures fit well into the world of 2100 BC, as the rest of this chapter should make clear.

according to the book of Genesis, towards "Canaan"—to the west, towards the Mediterranean shore and away from barbarian Gutians, vengeful Elamites, and ambitious Sumerians.

The theological explanation for the journey, in Genesis 12, is that Abram had heard the voice of God. This was not a Sumerian god, or an Akkadian god, but *the* God: a God who gave himself the puzzling name יהוה, YHWH, possibly a form of the verb "to be."*

This seems to have been a new idea for Abram. Terah and his sons were likely to have been worshippers of the moon-god Sin and his daughter Inanna, the patron deities of the city of Ur, simply because all Ur natives paid at least lip service to the moon cult. Also, the family names show a fairly standard homage to the Akkadian/Sumerian pantheon. Terah's own name expresses kinship with the moon-god Sin. Sarai, Abram's wife, was also his half-sister, Terah's daughter by another wife; her name is the Akkadian version of Sin's wife, the goddess Ningal. Terah's granddaughter Milcah was apparently named after Sin's daughter Malkatu.[2] Abram's own name, which means "exalted father," is ambiguous. Nevertheless, we can assume that both Abram and Sarai's names were connected with moon worship, in part because later in the story, YHWH renames both of them as part of the making of a covenant. The new names, Abraham and Sarah, both contain the new syllable *ah,* the first syllable of the covenant name YHWH, a name which reclaims them from the possession of Ur and transfers ownership to the God of Genesis.

From this God, Abram gets both a promise and a command. The promise is that Abram will be made into a great nation and will be blessed; the command is that he leave his country and his people (the city of Ur and its mixed blend of Akkadians, Sumerians, and other Semites) and go "to the land I will show you": to the land of Canaan, almost due west.†

* The familiar "Jehovah" is a non-name. The name God gives to himself when speaking to Abraham is YHWH (see, for example, Gen. 15:7); this name, later known as the "Tetragrammaton" in Greek, is thought by some linguists to be related to the Hebrew verb that expresses existence (see, for example, Jack M. Sasson, *Hebrew Origins: Historiography, History, Faith of Ancient Israel,* p. 81). The name simply consists of the four consonants; the Masoretic text of Genesis has no vowels anywhere, since the reader was meant to insert these as he went. Vowels were added to the Hebrew text much later to help fix its meaning; at this time, the name was rendered YAHWEH. However, to avoid impious use of the name, many readers subsituted the name ELOHIM (the generic "my lord") when they reached YAHWEH. From about 1100 on, scribes unfamiliar with Hebrew began with increasing frequency to insert the ELOHIM vowels into the YHWH consonants, yielding the nonsensical YEHOWIH, which eventually travels into English (by way of Latin) as JEHOVAH.

† The chronology in the Genesis account is ambiguous. Either Abram heard the call of God in Ur, convinced his father to head for Canaan, and then got sidetracked to Haran; or else Terah headed towards Canaan for other reasons and then got sidetracked to Haran, where Abram then received the

Plenty of races have claimed to trace their ancestry back to one particular god-favored individual, but this is the first time it happens within recorded history. By blood Abram was no different from the Semites around him, and not so different from the people who inhabited the land he was headed towards. But by divine fiat, he was separated from the rest and began something new: one Semite out of the rest, one God rising above the chaos of polytheism. He was the first monotheist.

RATHER THAN HEADING DIRECTLY WEST, a route which would have taken them across desert, the clan travelled northwest along the easier route of the Euphrates. Eventually this would have brought them out on the northern corner of the Mediterranean coast. But they got as far north as the Bilikh river, which runs into the Euphrates at the point where they should have made a left-hand turn. Instead, they turned eastwards, followed the little river over to the small city of Haran, and settled there. Haran lay on a well-travelled trade route; it was, like Ur, a center of moon worship, and perhaps it felt familiar. Terah was growing old, and Haran was relatively peaceful.

Back down south, Ur-Nammu had taken his father-in-law's throne and extended his rule into a neo-Sumerian empire, but his reach never came as far north as Haran. Around 2094 he died, after an eighteen-year reign; his funeral poem praises him as a wise and trustworthy shepherd of his people, a king who had restored Sumer to itself, a man worthy of sharing a throne in the afterlife with Gilgamesh himself.[3]

Ur-Nammu's son Shulgi took his place. Not long afterwards—perhaps within four or five years—Abram left Haran and resumed his journey towards the land God had promised him. He travelled southwest and arrived, eventually, at Shechem, west of the Jordan river and halfway between the two bodies of water later known as the Sea of Galilee and the Dead Sea.

There, he required reassurance from God that the land would be his, because as far as he could see, it was full of Canaanites.

"CANAAN" is an anachronistic name for the land which would be known in the first millennium BC as Israel, to the Romans as Palestine, and to the Crusaders as "the Levant." The earliest occurrence of the word "Canaanite" comes

divine command to strike back out in the original direction. Both readings of the text itself are possible. I merely note this so that I won't get (any more) letters accusing me of not having read my Bible.

from a tablet found at Mari, Zimri-Lim's walled city, and dates from around 1775; it appears to be an uncomplimentary reference to roving bandits from somewhere around the Jordan river.[4] In 2090 BC there was no name for the land God promised to Abram, because it had neither a racial nor a political identity.

The people who lived along the expanse of the eastern Mediterranean shore were "Western Semites."* We met their close relations all the way back in chapter 1, when Semites mingled with the Sumerians in the earliest days of the Sumerian cities. Instead of settling down on the Mesopotamian plain, the Western Semites kept on going. While their relations taught the Sumerians to farm, the Western Semites spread up and down the coast and built their own cities.

Abram is the first personality to bob up from the surface of the history of this particular area. Without any unified culture, the Western Semites produced no chronicles, and what we know of them comes only from the ruins of their cities. By 7000 BC, farmers with domesticated goats and sheep occupied towns all through the area. Sites such as Catal Huyuk in the far north and Jericho, farther south and close to the Dead Sea, claim the honor of being among the oldest cities in the world. Jericho, down in the land that Abram's descendants would eventually claim, stands out; most of the Western Semitic sites are villages with no particular defenses, this far back, but by 6800 BC, the people of Jericho had built themselves a startlingly huge stone wall. At the corner of the wall, a circular tower rose thirty-five feet high so that watchmen could keep a constant eye on the surrounding land.

What the people of Jericho were expecting to come at them is not entirely clear. It is true that Jericho is located at the site of a steady and constant stream of fresh water,[5] but after all, the Jordan river was not so very far away. Nevertheless, the people of Jericho, alone among the Western Semites, built huge defenses against some frightening threat from the outside, and watched constantly lest it arrive unannounced.

By the time Abram arrived,† the Western Semitic cities had built up their own trade routes, particularly with Egypt. Byblos, halfway down the coast (and known as Gubla to the Akkadians, Gebal to the Semites), had built its entire economy on shipping cedars down to Egypt in exchange for Egyptian linen and precious metals. The northern city of Ebla was collecting taxes from cities that sent caravans its way.[6] The city of Megiddo, built on the pass between the Jordan valley and the plain of Sharon, had been growing in size

* This name originates with religion scholar Mark Smith, who suggests using it because it is not as horribly anachronistic as every other name used for the early inhabitants of the area. (See *The Early History of God: Yahweh and the Other Deities in Ancient Israel*, p. 19.)

† In "Canaan," the eras after prehistoric times are divided (based on pottery styles) into Early Bronze I, 3300–2850; Early Bronze II/III, 2850–2400; and Early Bronze IV, 2400–2000.

since at least 3500 BC. Shechem, where Abram first asked God to confirm his promise, was at least as old, and was perhaps settled because of an ancient well that rarely ran dry. The original Western Semitic settlers had been joined by various immigrants who filtered in from the north and south; most notably the Amorites, nomadic peoples speaking a Semitic language of their own, who may have come from the Arabian peninsula.

Abram can't be blamed for wondering how this patchwork country was ever going to be his. Nevertheless, he did not get the opportunity to wonder for long, because not five years after arriving in his promised land, he left again.

He wasn't alone. The archaeological record shows that, sometime between 2400 and 2000, the culture of the Western Semites—which had been moving increasingly towards urbanization—took a turn back towards a less organized, more nomadic lifestyle, with many cities temporarily abandoned.* A combination of overplanting and drought had shrunk streams and croplands; large settlements that consumed a lot of water had to disperse to survive.[7] Add to this the collapse of the Old Kingdom to the south, and the Western Semites had lost not only cropland, but also their wealthiest and most consistent trading partner, the country which had once lavished riches on Byblos and a dozen other cities in exchange for goods. The Old Kingdom chaos had radiated north. In response, Abram went south.

"There was a famine in the land," reads Gen. 12:10, "and Abram went south into Egypt for a while, because the famine was severe." There was more water in Egypt; and, temporarily, a little more order. The "goofy" Seventh Dynasty had been followed by an Eighth Dynasty, slightly more stable but entirely unremarkable; it had 27 kings spanning 146 years, and not a single pharaoh's name has survived.

Around 2160, though, a powerful nobleman from Herakleopolis named Akhtoy had managed through force of personality, canny alliances, and sheer force to pull all of Egypt together under his reign. Manetho calls Akhtoy "more terrible than his predecessors," probably a comment reflecting the amount of bloodshed that the temporary reunification demanded.[8] For the next hundred years, the descendants of Akhtoy—seventeen successive kings, comprising Manetho's Ninth and Tenth Dynasty—ruled over an Egypt that had lost almost all of its former greatness. It suffered not only from internal troubles, but from the inability to defend its edges from Western Semitic invaders, who constantly raided the Nile Delta in small nomadic bands.

* The theory was once that Amorites had mounted an armed invasion, which would account for such a drastic change in lifestyle; but since there does not seem to be any change in the culture of the area, this is unlikely.

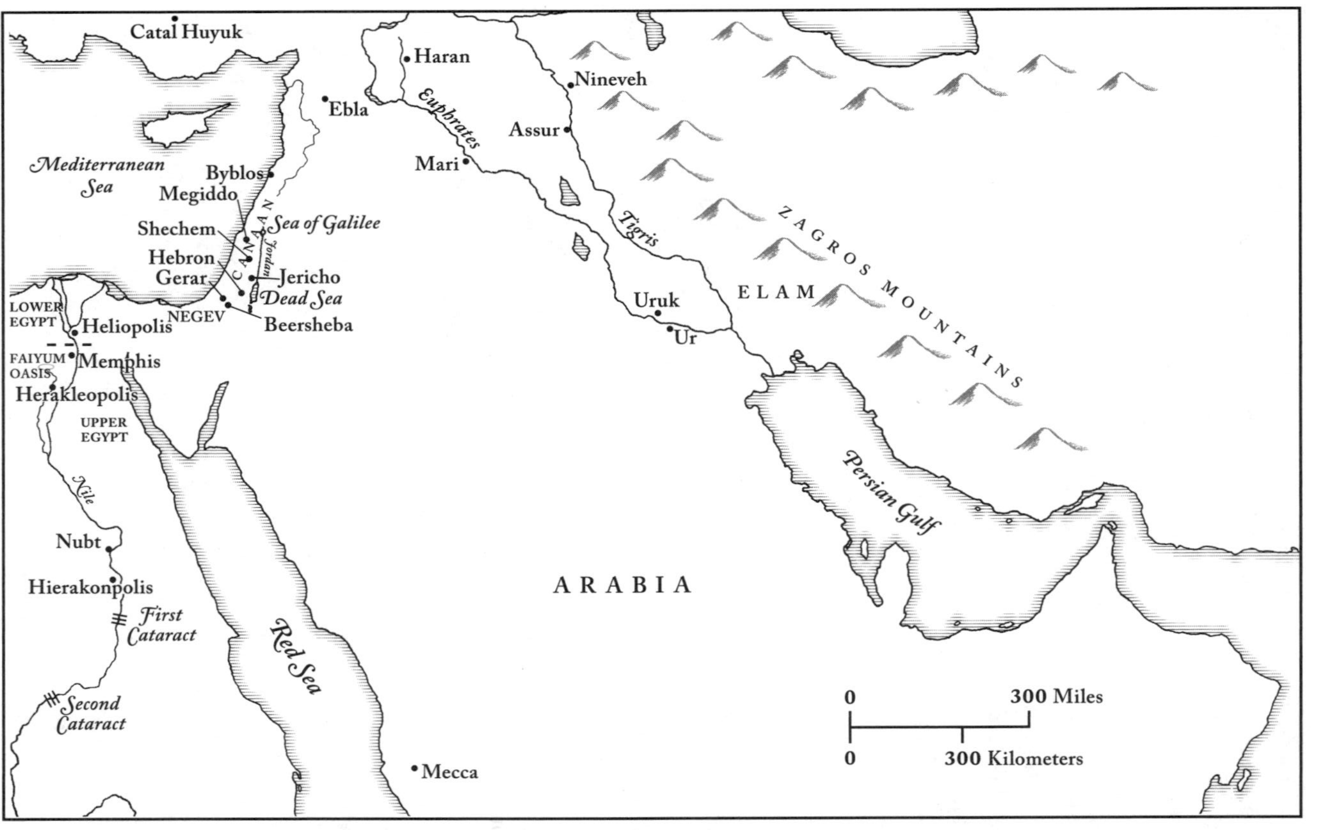

17.1 *Abram's World*

According to the traditional dating, Abram arrived down in Egypt with his wife, his servants, and his livestock sometime around 2085. This was not very distant from the time of Akhtoy III of the Tenth Dynasty, a pharaoh who wrote of the Western Semitic invaders:

> The vile Asiatic! It goes ill with the place where he is, lacking in water and covered in brushwood. . . . He never dwells in one place but has been forced to stray through want, traversing the lands on foot. . . . The Asiatic is a crocodile on the riverbank: he snatches on the lonely road.[9]

Perhaps this hostility explains why Abram, once down in Egypt, announced that Sarai was his sister rather than his wife. According to Genesis, Abram looked at Sarai, somewhere on the trip down to Egypt, and thought to himself: She is beautiful, so the pharaoh of Egypt is likely to order me killed so that he can have her (which certainly suggests that Semites had an equally low opinion of Egyptians).

Abram's fears came true. The pharaoh (one of the nameless, faceless, unremarkable kings of the Tenth Dynasty) co-opted Sarai and gave Abram thank-you gifts for bringing his beautiful sister to Egypt. Abram ended up with Egyptian sheep, cows, donkeys, camels, and servants. Meanwhile, the pharaoh and his household fared less well. Gen. 12 informs us that Sarai's presence in the pharaoh's harem brought a divine curse on it; the pharaoh and all of his household were inflicted with something called *neh-ga.* English translations tend to render this, politely, as "plague," perhaps because it involved nasty running sores. It rendered the pharaoh totally uninterested in any visits from any women of his household, let alone Sarai.

This odd story makes more sense if set beside the rest of the Genesis epic. Escaping from Egypt (and the pharaoh, who declined to kill Abram, clearly fearing further divine retribution), Abram returned to Canaan and settled near Hebron, significantly south of Shechem. The promise that he would be the father of a whole new nation did not seem to be coming true. The couple continued childless until Sarai was far too old for any hope of conception.

Twenty years or so after the original message from God, Abram decided to give the promise a helping hand. He borrowed Sarai's servant Hagar as a second and unofficial wife, promising Sarai that any child of Hagar's would be officially considered as her offspring.

This was not a practice unknown in the Sumerian cities—it is regulated in a set of Sumerian codes called the Nuzi Tablets—but it didn't work for Abram. God's promise of a new nation had been specific not just to Abram, but to Abram and Sarai together. Abram was to be the father of a new nation, but

Sarai, not just any fertile and available woman, was to be its mother. Like the one God himself, the new nation was going to resemble what came before it, and yet be entirely different. The God of Genesis shared some of the qualities of the nature-bound pantheon, but was beyond nature and uncontrolled by it. The new nation would be different from the peoples around it because it was created by the promise of the one God. That promise had been given to Abram and Sarai, not Abram alone. Any contribution from a Tenth Dynasty pharaoh or an Egyptian maidservant ("Hagar" is an Egyptian name that means something like "immigrant"; this woman was one of the maidservants given to Abram by the afflicted pharaoh) was not welcome; any more than the one God would have welcomed Enlil or Ishtar dropping by to give him a hand. It is after the episode with Hagar that God repeats his promise to Abram and renames him Abraham, showing his divine ownership of this man and his descendants.

Not long afterwards, Abraham again met a king with a roving eye. This time the king ruled Gerar, a city south of Hebron, in the area between Canaan and Egypt called the Negev. Once again afraid of being casually removed, Abraham again insisted that Sarah was his sister, and again Sarah was taken to the royal harem.

As a result, every woman in the entire household was rendered barren until Sarah was returned (and the king, Abimelech, was "kept from touching her," which seems to suggest that the women weren't the only ones temporarily deprived of their natural functions). Once again the story is preoccupied with the racial identity of this people God had promised to create.

Genesis was written, by any reckoning, well after the events it describes, with a deliberately anachronistic style of telling. The biblical accounts typically use names which would be familiar to contemporary readers, rather than the names in use during the historical past: "Ur of the Chaldees" is one such reference, since the land at the head of the Persian Gulf was not known as the land of the "Chaldeans" until the reign of Ashurnasirpal II of Assyria (884/883–859 BC) at the earliest.* Abram has dealings with "Amorites"; Abimelech, king of Gerar, is called a Philistine. These names refer to later political identities that evolved as Western Semitic tribes staked out territory and began to battle for it.

Yet even if the names in the text are deliberately anachronistic, the events in the story itself show a clear understanding of the difference not only between Abraham's blood and Egyptian blood, but between Abraham's race

* See chapter 48 for the entry of the "Chaldeans" into Assyrian and Babylonian history.

and the race of Abimelech. For the first time, it was possible to speak of Western Semites as belonging to different races.

In Sumer, from the earliest times, the primary identity of its people had not been as "Sumerians." They had been citizens of Ur, citizens of Lagash, citizens of Uruk, each paying primary loyalty to a different deity while acknowledging the existence of the others. The rise of Sargon's Akkadian empire, with its clear differentiation between Sumerians and Akkadians, had brought about a change: two peoples within one set of political boundaries, with a common identity ("subjects of Sargon") that nevertheless had not removed their basic difference. The raiding Gutians had further clarified this: two different peoples could nevertheless share an identity as *civilized* that set them off, together, against the contrast of a third.

Now Abraham, wandering west, speaking a language so like that of the Western Semites that he was able to communicate without too much difficulty, is set apart in a more sophisticated way yet. He is unlike Abimelech, another Western Semite, because of *choice.*

When the promise of God is finally fulfilled and Isaac is born, a new race is created and given a physical mark; God orders Abraham to circumcise his sons, himself, and his family as a sign of their separateness. (Presumably the sign would remind them, at the crucial moment, that they were not to mingle their blood with other races.) Later, when Abraham wants to find a wife for his son, he refuses to allow Isaac to marry any of the Western Semites around him. Instead he sends his servant all the way back to northwest Mesopotamia to bring back a blood relative, his great-niece Rebekah, from those relations who had remained behind in Haran.

Out of the old, a new race had come.

HAGAR'S SON too was different.

Sarai, with Abram's permission, chased the pregnant Hagar away. Hagar set out on the road that went from Hebron, past Beersheba, south towards Egypt. She was going home.

But Abram's son was not to be reabsorbed back into the chaos of Egypt during the First Intermediate Period. Hagar, according to Gen. 16, encountered a messenger of God on the road, and she too was given a promise. In a mirror image of the promise given to Sarai, Hagar's children would also become a nation too numerous to count.

So Hagar returned to Abram's household; and the baby, when born, was named Ishmael and grew up in his father's household. To him, the Arab peoples have traditionally chalked up their heritage. According to the Qur'an (written at an even greater distance than Genesis from the events described), Abram—Ibrahim, in the Arabic spelling—was the first to worship Allah, the one God, rather than the stars, the moon, or the sun. When grown, Ishmael went with Ibrahim down into Arabia, to the city of Mecca on the southwestern corner of the peninsula, and together they built the Ka'ba, the first house for the worship of Allah. To this house, the Qur'an orders all of Allah's followers—the "People of the Book"—to turn: "Wherever you are," the Qur'an says, "turn your faces in that direction. . . . From wherever you start forth, turn your face in the direction of the Sacred Mosque; wherever you are, turn your face there."[10]

BACK IN the neo-Sumerian empire that Terah's family had fled, the unrest of earlier days had settled into an empire.

Shulgi, who had succeeded his father, the ambitious Ur-Nammu, on the throne of Ur, had spent the first part of his reign taking stock of his situation. After twenty years on the throne—less than halfway through his reign, as it turned out—Shulgi began to reorganize his domain.[11] This organization involved a certain amount of conquest; Shulgi campaigned his way up north as far as the little cities of Assur and Nineveh and then back over across the boundary of the Tigris, into the land of the Elamites, taking back Susa. He never pushed his way up north into the Elamite highlands, where Elamite kings from a long-lasting Elamite dynasty called the Simash kept their claim on sovereignty. But where his fighting ended, his negotiation began. Shulgi made treaties and covenants with a score of small princes and warleaders, marrying three of his daughters to the rulers of territories that lay over in the Elamite lands. He divided his growing territory into a series of provinces, with governors who reported back to him. This was an empire under the rule of law and treaty, bound by regulations that his people were to obey. They were to be obedient not simply because Shulgi had soldiers who could enforce his demands, but because he was the chosen one of the gods, selected by the divine for special favor:

> Mother Nintu nurtured you,
> Enlil raised your head,
> Ninlil loved you . . .
> Shulgi, king of Ur.

He is, in particular, beloved of the goddess Inanna, who has set her love on him thanks in part to his sexual prowess:

Since he ruffled the hair of my lap. . . .
Since on the bed he spoke pleasant words. . . .
A good fate I will decree for him.[12]

He is also beloved of the moon-god Nanna. In gratitude to his divine protectors, Shulgi built the largest ziggurat of Ur, the neo-Sumerian equivalent of the Great Pyramid; an enormous structure for worship, named in Sumerian "The House Whose Foundation Is Clothed in Terror."[13] And in his attempt to rule righteously, as the gods required, Shulgi established a new set of laws. They are fragmentary, but these laws bear the distinction of being the first written code in history to prescribe set penalties for set offenses.[14]

WHILE SHULGI REIGNED IN UR, Abraham fought constantly to keep his family safe. It was a rough time to be in Canaan. During this time, the walls of Jericho alone were damaged and repaired seventeen different times.[15]

Abraham had fathered not one but two nations; both of his sons were marked with the sign of the covenant, the ceremonial removal of the foreskin that created a physical difference between them and the other Semites who were battling over the rough land between the Mediterranean coast and the Jordan river.* But this difference gave them no edge in the struggle for territory. When Sarah died, almost thirty years after giving birth to Isaac, the clan still had so little land that Abraham had to buy a cave from a nearby Western Semitic landlord in order to bury his wife.

* Muslims still practice male circumcision, or *khitan,* which tradition traces back to Abraham. Tradition says that the Prophet was born circumcised, but Muslim scholars disagree about the meaning of this miracle. Since the Qur'an does not specifically command circumcision, the practice is less strongly mandated in Islam than in Judaism; scholars disagree over whether circumcision is *wajib,* an obligation, or *sunna,* a custom. See M. J. Kister, " '. . . and He Was Born Circumcised . . .': Some Notes on Circumcision in Hadith," in *Oriens* 34 (1994), pp. 10–30.

TIMELINE 17

EGYPT	MESOPOTAMIA
Dynasty 4 (2613–2498)	Early Dynastic III (2600–2350)
Snefru	
Khufu	**Lugulannemundu** (c. 2500)
Khafre	**Mesilim**
Menkaure	
Dynasty 5 (2498–2345)	**Lugalzaggesi** (Umma) **Urukagina** (Lagash)
Dynasty 6 (2345–2184)	Akkadian Period (2334–2100)
	Sargon
	Rimush
	Gutian invasion
First Intermediate Period (2181–2040)	
Dynasties 7 & 8 (2181–2160)	
Dynasties 9 & 10 (2160–2040)	Fall of Agade (c. 2150)
	Third Dynasty of Ur (2112–2004)
	Ur-Nammu
	Shulgi Abram travels to Canaan

Chapter Eighteen

The First Environmental Disaster

In Sumer, between 2037 and 2004 BC, the Third Dynasty of Ur is conquered by invasion, rebellion, and famine

IN THE NEO-SUMERIAN EMPIRE ruled by the Third Dynasty of Ur, the reign of law and order was impressive but short-lived.

After his enormously long and prosperous forty-seven-year reign, Shulgi passed the throne to his son, who by then was well along in years himself; after his brief eight-year rule, Shulgi's grandson Shu-Sin inherited in turn. Under this fourth generation of the Ur III Dynasty, the empire began to fall apart.

Shu-Sin's reign faced a threat which had been steadily growing: Amorites, the Western Semitic nomads who were now roving along the western border, between Canaan and the borders of the neo-Sumerian realm. The Sumerians called them "the Martu" (or "Amurru") and were doomed to meet them in head-to-head rivalry for something that was in increasingly short supply: fertile land.

FOR CENTURIES NOW—perhaps for millennia—the cities on the plain had grown enough wheat to support their burgeoning populations through irrigation: digging channels from the riverbanks into reservoirs, so that rising waters would flow into storage tanks, from where they could be channelled in dryer months over the fields.

But the waters of the Tigris and the Euphrates, although fresh enough to support life, were very slightly salty. When this faintly brackish water sat in reservoirs, it collected more salt from the mineral-rich land. It then ran out over the fields and stood in the sun. Most of the water soaked into the earth, but some evaporated, leaving slightly more salt on the ground than had been there before.

This process, called *salinization,* eventually led to such a concentration of salt in the ground that crops began to fail.* Wheat is particularly sensitive to salt in the earth. Accounts from the Sumerian cities show, in the years before 2000 BC, a progressive switchover from wheat to barley, which can tolerate more salt. But in time even barley refused to grow in the salty soil. Grain grew scarce. So did meat, since there was not only less grain for humans, but less for animals, who had to be taken farther and farther afield to find grass.

Right around the reign of Shu-Sin, a Sumerian scribe notes that the earth in certain fields has "turned white."[1] An occasional proverb shows that the problem of rising salt was on farmers' minds; in a collection from the same time, one proverb asks, "Since beggars don't even know enough to sow barley, how can they possibly sow wheat?" Another proverb remarks that only a "male" rising of the river—presumably, a particularly powerful one—will "consume the salt" in the soil.[2]

The farmers of Sumer were not so ignorant of basic agriculture that they did not understand the problem. But the only solution was to avoid planting every other year, in a practice called "weed fallowing"—allowing weeds with deep roots to grow, lowering the water table and allowing salt to wash back down beneath the topsoil.[3] In the meantime, what would the cities of Sumer eat? And how would the increasingly strict tax burden, made necessary by a large and highly structured bureaucracy organized by Shulgi and preserved by his heirs, be shouldered?

In the absence of weed fallowing, fields could grow so toxic that they would have to be abandoned entirely, perhaps for as long as fifty years, to allow the soil to recover. This made the Amorite trespass on Sumer's fertile fields not a matter of annoyance, but of life and death. The Mesopotamian plain did not have an unlimited expanse of fields; it is what anthropologists call "circumscribed agricultural land," sharply defined by surrounding mountains and deserts.†

The growing scarcity of grain made the Sumerian population generally hungrier, less healthy, more fractious, and less able to defend itself. Lacking the full measure of grain tax, the court of the Ur III Dynasty could not pay its soldiers. The trespassing Amorites could not easily be driven away.

* Technically, salinization involves not only the accumulation of salt, but an actual chemical reaction that changes the soil's mineral content; it is "the process by which soluble chemical salts accumulate in soils and change their chemical composition" (D. Bruce Dickson, "Circumscription by Anthropogenic Environmental Destruction," in *American Antiquity* 52:4 [1987], p. 711). Dickson points out that the waters of the Tigris and Euphrates are also high in calcium, magnesium, and sodium, which tend to precipitate soluble salts out of the soil.

† Compare this with the wandering populations that later occupied the North American continent, who could move across a practically unlimited expanse of fertile land (R. L. Carneiro, "A Theory of the Origin of the State," *Science* 169 [1970], pp. 734–735).

In the first three years of his reign, Shu-Sin lost progressively more of his frontier. By the fourth year, he was desperate enough to try a brand-new strategy, one unused before: he ordered a huge wall, 170 miles long, built across the plain between the Tigris and the Euphrates, in a frantic attempt to keep the Amorites away.

The wall was ultimately useless. Shu-Sin's son, Ibbi-Sin, soon gave up even the pretense of defending the fields behind it. Poverty, disorder, and invasion led to bits of his realm flaking off, falling not only to marauding Amorites but to his own hungry and discontent people. When Ibbi-Sin had been on the throne for two years, Eshnunna, in the far north of his remaining empire, rebelled and refused to pay tribute, and Ibbi-Sin did not have the soldiers to bring the city back into the fold. The year afterwards, the Elamite king of Anshan—a principality which had been technically free from Sumerian domination, but which had made an alliance with Shulgi by marriage, fifty years before—rejected the half-century-old treaty and drove the Sumerians back out of Susa. Two years later, Umma broke free; three years later, in the eighth year of Ibbi-Sin's reign, the prestigious city of Nippur refused to acknowledge his lordship any longer.

Worse was to come. As his power declined, Ibbi-Sin had taken to granting his military commanders more and more autonomy. In the tenth year of his reign, one of these commanders, a man of Semitic descent named Ishbi-Erra, made his own play for power.

Ur was suffering from famine, thanks to those salty fields and a lack of grain and meat; Ibbi-Sin sent Ishbi-Erra, his trusted commander, north to the cities of Isin and Kazallu to fetch supplies. A series of letters preserved on clay tablets reveal Ishbi-Erra's strategy. First, Ishbi-Erra wrote to his king, explaining that if Ibbi-Sin sent more boats up the river and gave Ishbi-Erra even more authority, he could bring the grain; otherwise, he simply was going to have to stay in Isin with it.

> I have spent twenty talents of silver on grain, and I am here in Isin with it. Now, though, I have heard reports that the Martu have invaded the center of the land between us. I can't get back down to you with this grain unless you send me six hundred boats and put me in charge of both Isin and Nippur. If you do this, I can bring you enough grain for fifteen years.[4]

This was bald-faced extortion, which became clear to Ibbi-Sin when the governor of Kazallu also wrote him, complaining that, under cover of collecting grain for his king, Ishbi-Erra had seized Nippur, plundered a couple of nearby cities, asserted his dominance over several more, and was now threatening to take over Kazallu as well. "Let my king know that I have no ally," the governor complained, pathetically, "no one to walk at my side."

18.1 The Disintegration of Sumer

Ibbi-Sin was helpless to do anything against Ishbi-Erra, who had many of his soldiers and most of the food. His return letter to the governor of Kazallu has the testiness of desperation:

> I gave you troops, and I put them at your disposal. You are the governor of Kazallu. So how is it that you did not know what Ishbi-Erra was up to? Why didn't you . . . march against him? Now Ishbi-Erra can claim to be king. And he isn't even Sumerian. Sumer has been prostrated and shamed in the assembly of the gods, and all the cities that were your responsibility have gone straight over to Ishbi-Erra's side. Our only hope is that the Martu will capture him.[5]

The Amorites didn't capture Ishbi-Erra, and—as Ibbi-Sin had feared—the straying commander announced himself the first king of "Isin Dynasty," with his capital city at Isin and his territory the northern lands that had once belonged to Ur. The Isin Dynasty would resist Amorite capture and rule over the northern part of the plain for two hundred years. Meanwhile, Ibbi-Sin was left with only the very heart of his disintegrating empire, Ur itself, under his control.

At this point, the vultures landed. In 2004, the Elamites—now reunited into one, Sumerian-free realm under the rule of a king named Kindattu—were ready to revenge themselves for decades of domination. They swept over the Tigris, broke down the walls of Ur, burned the palace, levelled the sacred places, and brought a final and shattering end to the Sumerian era. The fields that were not already barren from salt were burned, and Ibbi-Sin himself was dragged away as a captive to Anshan.

Later poems mourn the fall of Ur as the death not just of a city, but of an entire culture:

> Corpses were piled at the lofty city gates,
> on the streets where festivals had been held, heads lay scattered,
> where dances had been held, bodies were stacked in heaps. . . .
> In the river, dust has gathered,
> no flowing water is carried through the city,
> the plain that was covered in grass has become cracked like a kiln.[6]

Ur's collapse showed not just the weakness of Ibbi-Sin but, more ominously, the impotence of the moon god Nanna and the patron deities of the fallen cities, gods who could not protect their own.

> Father Nanna,
> your song has been turned into weeping,

TIMELINE 18

EGYPT	MESOPOTAMIA
Dynasty 5 (2498–2345)	**Lugalzaggesi** (Umma) **Urukagina** (Lagash)
Dynasty 6 (2345–2184)	Akkadian Period (2334–2100)
	Sargon
	Rimush
	Gutian invasion
First Intermediate Period (2181–2040)	
Dynasties 7 & 8 (2181–2160)	
Dynasties 9 & 10 (2160–2040)	Fall of Agade (c. 2150)
	Third Dynasty of Ur (2112–2004)
	Ur-Nammu
	Shulgi Abram travels to Canaan
	Fall of Ur (2004)

your city weeps before you, like a child lost in a street,
your house stretched out its hands to you,
it cries, "Where are you?"
How long will you stand aside from your city?[7]

Abram and Terah had fled from Ur and from the worship of the moon-god, afraid that he could not protect them. Ultimately he could not even protect his own temple. The old nature-god, like the fields of Ur themselves, had lost his potency.

The age of the Sumerians was finally over. Semites, both Akkadian and Amorite, and Elamites dominated the plain, which would never again be as fertile as it had been back in the days of the earliest kings, when fresh water ran through green fields.*

* Even today, something like 60 percent of the previously fertile land of Iraq (the country which now claims much of Mesopotamia) is uncultivable because of centuries of built-up salt and chemicals.

Part Three

STRUGGLE

Chapter Nineteen

The Battle for Reunification

Between 2181 and 1782 BC, Mentuhotep I reunites fractured Egypt, and the Middle Kingdom begins

FOR A CENTURY AND A HALF, Egypt had no pharaoh worthy of the name.

Abram had arrived in the country sometime during the rule of the Ninth or Tenth Dynasty, two families of kings who probably overlapped. According to Manetho, the Ninth Dynasty was founded by a king named Achthoes, who began a royal line and ruled all of Egypt from Herakleopolis, farther south. Achthoes, he tells us, was the most cruel ruler Egypt had ever seen; he "hurt people all over Egypt."[1]

This king, who appears in inscriptions as "Akhtoy I," was actually the governor of the province centered at Herakleopolis; the tradition of his cruelty most likely stems from his armed attempt to seize all of Egypt. Almost as soon as Akhtoy was dead (Manetho says that he went mad and was eaten by a crocodile, the instrument of divine vengeance), another "pharaoh" announced himself much farther to the south. His name was Intef, and he claimed to rule all of Egypt from Thebes.

Manetho says that Akhtoy's Ninth Dynasty was followed by a Tenth Dynasty, and then neatly by an Eleventh Dynasty. What actually happened was that the Ninth and Tenth Dynasties and the Eleventh Dynasty ruled simultaneously. "Rule" is a kind word; unruly sets of warlords were fighting each other for the right to claim nominal control of Egypt, while other provincial governors went on doing as they pleased. An inscription from one of these governors (or *nomarchs*; the territories ruled by the *nomarchs* were known as *nomes*) shows a complete disregard for the royal pretensions in Herakleopolis and Thebes. "[I am] overseer of priests, overseer of desert-countries, overseer of mercenaries, great overlord of the nomes," Ankhtifi boasts. "I am the beginning and the peak of mankind. . . . I surpassed the feats of my ancestors. . . . All of Upper Egypt was dying of hunger and people were eating their children, but I did not allow anybody to die of hunger in this nome. . . . Never did I allow anybody in need to go from this nome to another one. I am the hero without equal."[2] In his own eyes at least, Ankhtifi is the equal of any pharaoh.

Manetho's neat succession of dynasties is produced by his determination to stuff all of this chaos into the framework of the old dynastic successions. Even more than fifteen hundred years after the fact, Manetho cannot quite admit that the authority of Horus-on-earth has entirely disappeared. In this, he is far from alone. What inscriptions survive from the period show that Egyptian scribes either ignored the reality of their kingdom's breakdown (other ancient king lists pretend that the Ninth and Tenth dynasties never happened and pick up partway through the Eleventh),[3] or tried to put it in slightly less threatening terms. Egypt had not fallen into anarchy. No; the old north-south hostility had just made a temporary return. Clashes between the north and south were nothing new, and in the past a pharaoh had always risen to reunify the whole mess.

So we find Intef I, the Theban pretender, calling himself "King of Upper and Lower Egypt" in his own inscriptions.[4] This was more than a little grandiose, as he certainly was not king of Lower Egypt and probably didn't control all that much of Upper Egypt either. Nevertheless, it put him firmly into the tradition of Upper Egyptian pharaohs who had managed to bring the rebellious north back under control. Intef's soldiers fought, more than once, with troops from Herakleopolis, in a re-creation of those old battles between north and south. Meanwhile, rival nomarchs clashed, Western Semites wandered into the Delta, and Egypt's great past receded a little further. "Troops fight troops," an account from the period reads. "Egypt fights in the graveyard, destroying tombs in vengeful destruction."[5]

Then, halfway through the Eleventh Dynasty, Mentuhotep I came to the throne of Thebes.

Mentuhotep, who was named after the Theban god of war, spent the first twenty years of his reign fighting his way north into Lower Egypt. Unlike Narmer and Khasekhemwy before him, he had to campaign not only against the soldiers of the northern king, but also against the nomarchs in his way. One of his first great victories was against the governor of Abydos; the ferocity of the takeover is marked by at least one mass burial, a tomb containing sixty soldiers all killed in the same battle.[6]

As he fought his way north, the soldiers of the Tenth Dynasty ruler at Herakleopolis retreated in front of him. Just before Mentuhotep reached Herakleopolis, the Tenth Dynasty king who reigned there died. The scramble for succession threw the defense of the city into disorder, and Mentuhotep marched into it with ease.

Now he held both Thebes and Herakleopolis, but Egypt was far from united. The nomarchs were not keen to give up their long-held powers; battles with the provinces continued for years. Portraits of Egyptian royal officials during this time tend to show them carrying weapons, rather than papyri or other tools of office, suggesting that going to the office remained chancy for quite a long time.[7]

But by the thirty-ninth year of his reign, Mentuhotep was finally able to alter the writing of his name. His new Horus-name was, unsurprisingly, "Uniter of the Two Lands." In fact, his forty-year struggle for power had almost nothing to do with north-south hostility; but the old paradigm of civil war gave him a much better chance to cast himself as a great pharaoh who had rescued Egypt once again.

His spin was successful. Not long afterwards, his name begins to appear in inscriptions next to that of Narmer himself. He is praised as a second Narmer, equal to the legendary king who had first pulled Upper and Lower Egypt together into one.

MENTUHOTEP'S REIGN was the end of the First Intermediate Period and the beginning of Egypt's next period of strength, the Middle Kingdom. He ruled, according to Manetho, for fifty years.

Although tomb inscriptions identify at least five different women as his wives, no inscriptions that date from his reign mention a son.[8] The next two kings had no blood link to him or to each other, and the third was a commoner: Amenemhet I, who had served Mentuhotep III as vizier. It seems that the idea of a divine royal bloodline, if honored in theory, had passed away in practice.

Amenemhet I is the first king of Dynasty Twelve. A southerner by birth (according to inscriptions, his mother was from Elephantine, far into Upper Egypt), Amenemhet immediately put himself into the line of great unifiers by building himself a brand-new capital city, just as Narmer had, to celebrate his hold over the country. He called this new city, twenty miles south of Memphis, "Seizer of the Two Lands" ("Itj-taway").[9] It would serve him as his own balancing point between north and south; Memphis, still a center of worship of the Egyptian pantheon and home to Egypt's most sacred temples, was no longer the place where the pharaoh made his home.

Amenemhet also commissioned scribes to write a "prophecy" about him, a document which began to circulate through Egypt very near the beginning of his reign. This "Prophecy of Nerferti," supposedly from the reign of King Snefru five hundred years before, begins with King Snefru brooding over the possibility that Egypt will fall to Asiatic invaders from the east (a clear case of a later worry imposed on a much earlier time, since this possibility probably never occurred to Snefru). Fortunately, Snefru's sage has a happy prediction:

A king will come from the South. . . .
He will take the White Crown,
He will wear the Red Crown. . . .
Asiatics will fall to his sword,
Rebels to his wrath, traitors to his might. . . .
[He] will build the Walls-of-the-Ruler
To bar Asiatics from entering Egypt.[10]

Amenemhet then proceeded to carry out the prophecy. With the help of his son Senusret, he led an expedition against the "sand dwellers" who had infiltrated the Delta.[11] He also built a fortress east of the Delta to keep other invaders out and named it, not surprisingly, Walls-of-the-Ruler.

Near the end of his reign, Amenemhet was powerful enough to build himself a pyramid near his new city of Itj-taway. It was only a small pyramid, but it stood as a monument to the return of the old order. Amenemhet must have felt himself to be walking in the footsteps of his great predecessors Narmer and Khufu and Khafre. The pharaoh's might was on the upswing once more.

Then Amenemhet was murdered.

SENUSRET I WROTE the story of his father's assassination shortly afterwards, in his father's own voice. "I awoke to fighting," the dead Amenemhet says, "and I found that it was an attack of the bodyguard. If I had quickly taken weapons in my hand, I would have made the wretches retreat. . . . But there is none mighty in the night, none who can fight alone. . . . my injury happened while I was without you, my son."[12]

A few more details are contained in a story from slightly later, the "Tale of Sinuhe." According to this account, Senusret was campaigning down south in "the land of the Libyans," the desert west of the Nile, where desert-dwellers had long troubled the Egyptian border. Hearing the news of his father's murder, Senusret left his army behind and flew like a hawk back north to Itj-taway, a long and difficult journey. As the crown prince approached, the courtier Sinuhe fled from the palace up into the land of the Asiatics because he was certain that he would be suspected of involvement in the crime.

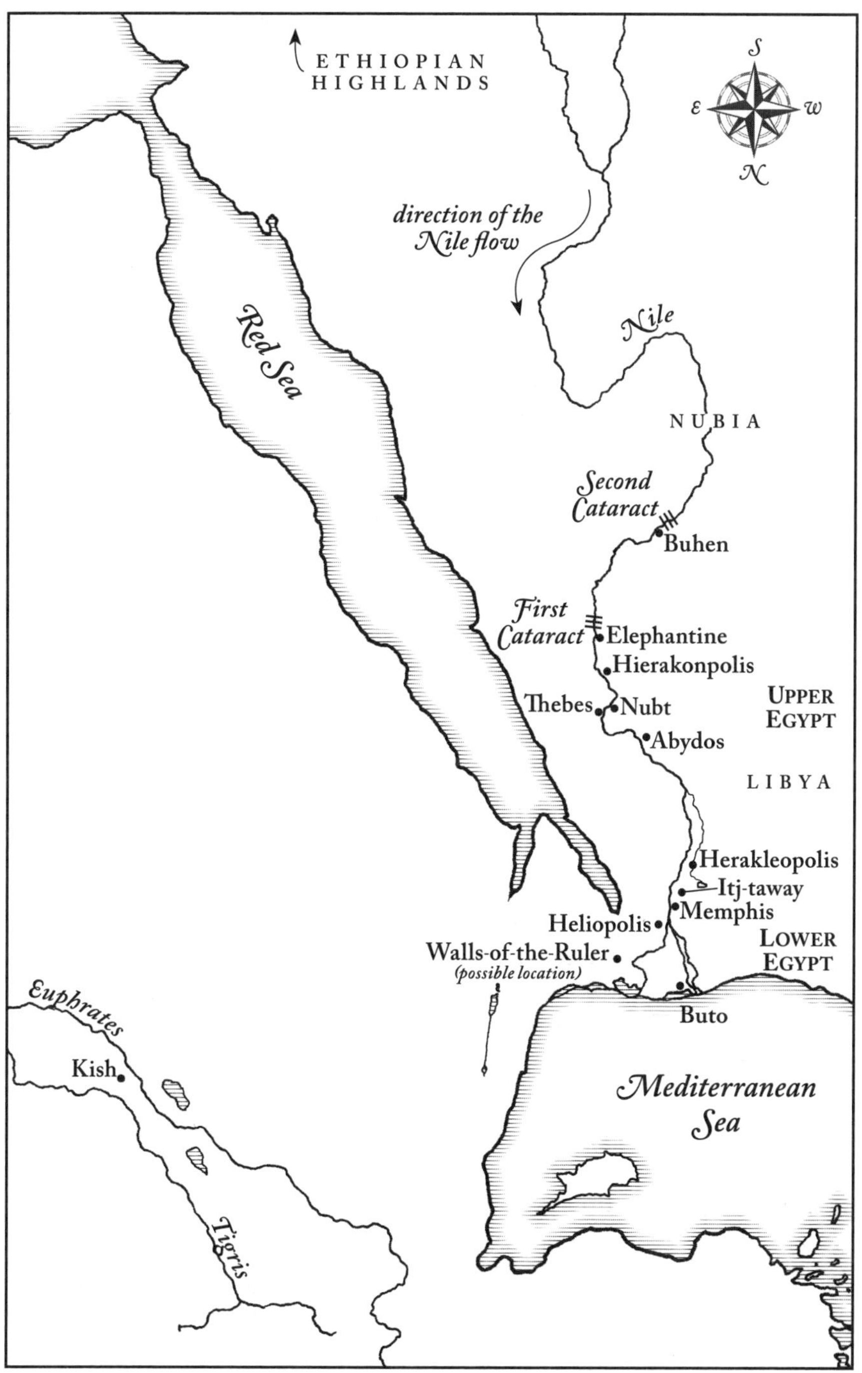

19.1 The Middle Kingdom

To flee into Canaan was a desperate act indeed for any Egyptian. Sinuhe had a difficult journey; he had to sneak past the Walls-of-the-Ruler fort ("I bowed down in the bushes, for fear the sentinels on the fort . . . should see me") and travel over desert sands for hot thirsty days. Finally, he reached Canaan, which he calls "Yaa," and found a land flowing with milk and honey. "There were figs," he exclaims, "and vines; more plentiful than water was its wine, copious was its honey, plenteous its oil."

Much later, Sinuhe would return to his native land to be pardoned by Senusret, who had taken his father's place and made Egypt both stronger and wealthier. Lest the listener get any idea that the land of the Canaanites was a good place to be, however, Sinuhe points out that before he rejoined polite Egyptian society, he had to be recivilized after his years among Asiatics; this was a lengthy process that apparently involved shaving him all over, since exile among the Western Semites had made him shaggy.

SENUSRET HIMSELF, having avenged his father's murder by executing the bodyguard, had a prosperous rule of his own. He made his son his co-regent a few years before his death, a practice which became standard for Twelfth Dynasty pharaohs. Co-regencies made the changeover from one pharaoh to the next both simpler and more peaceful. They were also a concession of sorts; the establishment of a co-regency must have flown in the face of the old tradition of the king's death and rebirth in his son. But by now, the pharaoh was clearly less god than man. His changing status is reflected in Twelfth Dynasty statues of the kings, which are portraits of real people very unlike the immobile god-faces of the Fourth Dynasty rulers.

The succession rolled on; Egypt, in relative peace, had regathered itself to something like its previous prosperity. Senusret's son was followed by his grandson and then his great-grandson, Senusret III, who is memorable for his enormous size (apparently he was over six and a half feet tall) and his instantly recognizable statues, which show him with a lined face, wide-set eyes with heavy eyelids, and ears that stick out far enough to hold his headdress back. He built more forts down in Nubia than any other pharaoh; according to his own records, at least thirteen of them. The fortresses are huge, like medieval castles with towers and ramparts and moats. One of the largest, the fortress at Buhen, near the Second Cataract, had mud-brick walls thirteen feet thick, five tall towers, and a massive central gate with double doors and a drawbridge across a protective ditch. Inside the fortress was enough space for a whole town, streets, and a temple.[13]

The Egyptians who lived at Buhen did not sleep outside these walls, where

19.1. Senusret III. Granite head of Senusret III, Pharaoh of Egypt, found near Karnak. Photo credit Bridgeman-Giraudon/Art Resource, NY

Nubians might find them. During Senusret's brutal campaigns, Egyptians had slaughtered Nubian men, brought women and children north as slaves, torched fields, and destroyed wells. The Nubians hated their overlords too much to live side by side with them.

But this savage treatment of Egypt's most troublesome province temporarily halted its resistance. By the time that Senusret III passed Egypt on to his own son, the Egyptian territories were peaceful. Egypt had again begun to trade with Byblos for cedar. The Sinai mines were worked to their full extent. And the Nile floods were at the highest point in years. The Middle Kingdom was at its height, even though a man rather than a god was on its throne.

TIMELINE 19

EGYPT	MESOPOTAMIA
First Intermediate Period (2181–2040)	
Dynasties 7 & 8 (2181–2160)	
Dynasties 9 & 10 (2160–2040)	Fall of Agade (c. 2150)
Middle Kingdom (2040–1782)	
Dynasty 11 (2134–1991)	Third Dynasty of Ur (2112–2004)
Intef I-III	**Ur-Nammu**
Mentuhotep I-III	**Shulgi** Abram travels to Canaan
	Fall of Ur (2004)
Dynasty 12 (1991–1782)	
Amenemhet I	

Chapter Twenty

The Mesopotamian Mixing Bowl

Between 2004 and 1750 BC,
the kings of Larsa and Assur build kingdoms in the south and north, while Hammurabi of Babylon waits for his chance

When Egypt began its journey back up to prosperity, the Mesopotamian plain was still a mess.* After sacking Ur and hauling off Ibbi-Sin in triumph to Susa, the Elamites had occupied the remains of the city and fortified the walls, ready to use it as a base to conquer more territory. But they had reckoned without the treacherous and canny commander Ishbi-Erra, still firmly in control of the city of Isin to the north. Ishbi-Erra needed Ur in order to carry out his charade of establishing a new Sumerian dynasty, as great as the Ur dynasty that had fallen.

He didn't have much competition. After the sack of Ur, most of the scattered cities which had once been under the protection of the Third Dynasty kings had not managed to reassert themselves as powers in their own right. There were only three possible challengers: two ancient Sumerian cities that had managed to retain some independent power after the Ur III collapse, and the Elamites themselves.

The first of these cities, the city of Eshnunna, was far to the north, along the right-hand bend of the Tigris river. Almost as soon as Ibbi-Sin began to run into difficulties, Eshnunna had taken advantage of its distance from the capital and rebelled. The city was certainly a threat to Ishbi-Erra's power, but

* The time from the fall of Ur through about 1600 BC is generally called the Old Babylonian Period, an incredibly inaccurate designation since Babylon doesn't become an important city until the reign of Hammurabi, beginning in 1792, and even after this doesn't dominate the whole Mesopotamian plain for another thirty years or so.

it was also a long way away from Isin (and there were Amorites in the path). On the other hand, the second independent city of old Sumer, Larsa, was right on the southern plain that Ishbi-Erra coveted. It too had rebelled against Ibbi-Sin's rule, but its kingship had been claimed by an Amorite.

Rather than weakening his forces by battling against Larsa, Ishbi-Erra fortified his own city of Isin, and built up his army in preparation for an attack on the crown jewel: Ur itself.

He took his time. It was near the end of his reign—perhaps ten years after the Elamite conquest of Ur—that he swept down from the north, went right past Larsa, and mounted an attack against the Elamite occupiers. An extremely fragmentary poem records his victory over the Elamites and his recapture of Ur from the enemy:

> Ishbi-Erra approached the enemy,
> and they did not escape his power, there on the plain of Urim.
> On a great chariot,
> he rode into the city in victory,
> he took its gold and jewels,
> and the news was brought to . . . [the] king of Elam.[1]

Ishbi-Erra had to be content with his crown jewel; he never did get to attack either Larsa or Eshnunna. He died shortly after and left his son in charge of his four-city kingdom of Isin, Nippur, Uruk, and Ur.

FOR THE NEXT FIFTY YEARS the Isin dynasty of Ishbi-Erra and the Amorite kings of Larsa fought it out against each other on the southern plain. Neither gained the upper hand.[2]

Up in the north, cities which had once been under the watchful eye of the Third Dynasty of Ur started to reassert their own independence. Assur, which had been added first to the Akkadian expanse by Sargon, and then to the Ur kingdom by Shulgi, rebuilt its walls and began trading with the Western Semites near the Mediterranean coast; merchants from Assur even built their own little trading colonies on the eastern edge of Asia Minor.[3] West of Assur, the northern city of Mari, on the banks of the Euphrates, was doing the same. Between Assur and Mari, and between the two rivers, lay a shifting patchwork of Amorite chieftains, mostly ruling over little patches of agriculture, who wandered and quarrelled and redrew each other's boundary lines.

Sometime around 1930 BC, the balance of power in the south began to shift.

The fifth king of Larsa, an Amorite named Gungunum, took the throne

20.1 Mesopotamian Mixing Bowl

after the death of his brother and made his own play to build an empire. He fought his way over to Susa and left an inscription with his name on it there; he fought his way up to Nippur and took it away from the control of Isin; and then he mounted a campaign against Ur, the pride of the Isin dynasty. We have from this campaign several frantic letters between the king of Isin, Lipit-Ishtar (Ishbi-Erra's great-great-grandson, so far as we can tell), and his general as they try to cope with the advancing troops. The general writes, "Six hundred troops of Gungunum have arrived; if my lord does not send reinforcements, they will soon build brick fortresses; do not delay, my lord!"

Lipit-Ishtar's response echoes the same desperation that Ibbi-Sin had felt at the advance of Ishbi-Erra, eighty years before: "My other generals are better servants to their king than you!" he writes. "Why haven't you kept me better informed? I have sent you in haste two thousand spearmen, two thousand archers, and a thousand axe-men. Chase the enemy away from their camp and guard the cities nearby. This is urgent!"[4]

The reinforcements arrived too late, or were too few; the enemy troops of Larsa overran Ur. Not long afterwards, Gungunum had declared himself the divine protector of the ancient city and was commissioning poems that—his Amorite ancestry notwithstanding—promise the moon-god that he longs to restore the ancient ways: "You, Nanna, are beloved of the king Gungunum," one reads. "He will restore your city for you; he will bring back for you the scattered peoples of Sumer and Akkad; in your Ur, the ancient city, the city of the great divine powers, the house which never diminishes, may Gungunum live for many days!"[5] Claiming the right to restore someone else's heritage: this would became the strategy of more than one later conqueror.

Gungunum's successor inherited Larsa and Ur, and decided to add the city of Nippur to his collection. When the king of Isin (a usurper; Ishbi-Erra's descendants had lost their throne in the wake of the Ur disaster) objected, the two cities revived their old rivalry. Once again Larsa and Isin waged a war that went on for years, this time over hapless Nippur, which changed hands at least eight different times in the course of the fighting. Meanwhile the other cities of the plain—Isin, Larsa, Uruk (now ruled by another Amorite chief), Eshnunna, Assur, Mari—existed alongside each other for some years in a state of high alert, but in heavily armed neutrality.

A new city rose to join them when yet another Amorite chief settled in the riverside village of Babylon and decided to make it into his headquarters. This chief, Sumu-abum, built walls around the settlement and made it into a city, with himself as king and his sons as heirs. The inscriptions he left behind him, commemorating his rule, name him (like Gilgamesh of old) as the great builder of his city: the second year of his reign is described as "The year in which the wall was built," and the fifth year as "The year in which the great temple of Nannar was built."[6]

Apart from Sumu-abum, none of the cities were blessed with distinguished leadership. Petty king succeeded petty king without leaving much in the way of tracks behind. Isin suffered from an embarrassing shift of power when its ninth king, Erra-imitti, was told by a local oracle that disaster was heading his way. Erra-imitti decided to avert the coming catastrophe by following a scapegoat ritual familiar from later Assyrian practice; he picked one of the palace workmen, a groundskeeper, to be king-for-a-day. At the end of a prescribed period, the faux king would be ceremonially executed. In this way, the omen would be fulfilled, since disaster had already come upon the king, and the real king would escape unscathed.

Unfortunately, as the chronicle that preserves the event tells us, once the groundskeeper was temporarily crowned, Erra-imitti went to eat a bowl of soup and died sipping from it.[7] Soup is hard to choke to death on; probably a palace poisoner was at work. With the king dead, the groundskeeper refused to give up the throne and reigned for twenty-four years.

The fight with Larsa had gone on all this time, and Larsa, weakened by constant battle, was an easy target when the Elamites staged a partial comeback. Sometime around 1834, a warrior-chief from northwest Elam rounded up an army and struck back across the Tigris. He took Larsa for his own and—not long afterwards—captured Ur and Nippur as well. He gave Larsa to his younger son, Rim-Sin, to rule on his behalf.

Rim-Sin's new domain was shabby and unhappy from years of war; Rim-Sin set out to bring Larsa back to its previous glories. We don't know exactly how he spent the first years of his reign, but we know that by 1804, eighteen years after he ascended Larsa's throne, three cities were worried enough about Larsa's growing might to put aside their historic differences and join together against the common threat. The king of Isin, the Amorite ruler of Uruk, and the Amorite chief of Babylon fielded a joint army against Rim-Sin.

Rim-Sin wiped it out and marched over to Uruk, which he occupied by way of reprisal. The kings of Babylon and Isin retreated to meditate on their next move.

At this point, the king of Eshnunna decided to take advantage of the southern chaos to extend his own territory northwards. He marched up the Tigris, knocked the Amorite king of Assur off his throne, and entrusted the city to his son to run for him. But before he could plan further campaigns, an invader appeared outside Assur's damaged walls.

This warrior, a man named Shamshi-Adad, was probably an Amorite, like many of the armed power-players of the day. The Assyrian king list (which records the succession of king after king to Assur's throne, in the same style as the Sumerian list) tells us that Shamshi-Adad had spent some years in Babylon, and then had moved up from Babylon and "seized the town Ekallatum," a military fortress that stood just north of Assur, on the opposite bank of the Tigris, and probably served Assur as an outpost.[8] Here he stayed for three years, apparently planning his takeover. Then he marched on Assur, deposed the Eshnunna deputy, and ascended the throne himself.*

Then he set out to build an empire that would be the northern reflection of the Larsan kingdom, now growing to the south under Rim-Sin. Shamshi-Adad put his older son Ishme-Dagan in charge of Ekallatum and Assur's northwest lands, and then seized control of the land between the Tigris and Euphrates. He marched west as far as Mari, defeated Mari's defensive line, and executed Mari's king; one of Shamshi-Adad's officials wrote to him, a little later, asking how much effort to put into the dead king's funeral.

The king's sons were put to death. Only one, the young prince Zimri-Lim, escaped. Zimri-Lim fled west to the Western Semitic city of Aleppo, north of Canaan; sometime earlier he had married the daughter of the king of Aleppo, and in the face of Shamshi-Adad's invasion, he took cover with his father-in-law. Shamshi-Adad put his younger son Yasmah-Adad on Mari's throne instead, to serve as its governor-king under his authority.

Shamshi-Adad not only commissioned the usual inscriptions, recording his victories, but also corresponded copiously with both of his sons. These letters, recovered from the ruins of Mari, tell us that Shamshi-Adad took control not only of the westward plain, but also some of the land east of the Tigris—in some places as far over as the Zagros Mountains, encroaching on Elamite holdings—and northwards conquered both Arbela and Nineveh. Under Shamshi-Adad, for the first time, the triangle of land between the upper Tigris and the Lower Zab river, cornered by the three cities of Assur and Arbela and Nineveh, became "Assyria": the center of an empire.

This was the largest extent, outside of Egypt, of any king's reign, and Shamshi-Adad was not slow to trumpet his own worth and the favor of the gods, which he courted by building elaborate temples. "I am Shamshi-Adad, king of the universe," one of his dedicatory inscriptions on a new temple read, "builder of the temple of Assur, who devotes his energies to the land between the Tigris and the Euphrates. . . . I have roofed the temple with cedars, and in the doors I placed door-leaves of cedar, covered with silver and gold. The walls

* The traditional start of Shamshi-Adad's reign is 1813; this may not be quite right, but it serves as one of the benchmarks of ancient history.

of that temple I have laid upon foundations of silver, gold, lapis lazuli, and stone; with cedar-oil, honey, and butter I have anointed its walls."[9]

Shamshi-Adad's empire was marked by his tight control, both of his bureaucratic servants and of the people he conquered. "I installed my governors everywhere," he records of his own kingdom, "and I established garrisons everywhere."[10] He had to worry about more than the revolt of his subjects; his empire was also threatened by the Elamites, who were massing troops to his east. The official who watched over the far eastern reach of Shamshi-Adad's territory wrote, more than once, warning him that the king of Elam had twelve thousand soldiers ready to march.[11] But Shamshi-Adad drafted enough of his subjects to man his garrisons and assemble an impressive defensive force, and the Elamite attack held off a little longer.

Back down south, Rim-Sin had finally managed to conquer Isin, which had been Larsa's rival in the south now for almost two hundred years. With the dynasty of Isin ended, he was unquestioned ruler of the south, as Shamshi-Adad was of the north. By 1794, the two men held almost all of the Mesopotamian plain between them.

IN 1792, the Amorite chief of Babylon died, and his son Hammurabi succeeded him.

Hammurabi, according to the Babylonian king list, was the great-great-great-grandson of Sumu-abum, that first Amorite to build walls around Babylon. He may even have been a very distant relation of Shamshi-Adad, since the Babylonian list has, as the earliest ancestors of the Babylonian rulers, twelve of the same names that show up as the "kings who live in tents" from Shamshi-Adad's own list; the two men shared a common descent from those Amorite nomads.[12]

The massive holdings of Rim-Sin and Shamshi-Adad sat on either side of Hammurabi's Babylon like two giants on either side of a man with a slingshot. But Babylon's central location was also an advantage. The city was a little too far south of Assur to worry Shamshi-Adad, too far north of Larsa to threaten Rim-Sin. Hammurabi began, cautiously, to claim control of the nearby cities in central Mesopotamia. Not long after his accession, we find him attaching his name to the old Sumerian city of Kish and to Borsippa, south on the Euphrates.[13]

If he wanted to expand his holdings any more, Hammurabi had to look either north or south. He turned south; Rim-Sin's conquest of Isin had left the city's defenses shattered. In 1787, five years after taking the throne of Babylon, Hammurabi attacked Isin and took control of it away from its Larsan garrison. He also campaigned across the Tigris and took the city of Malgium, which lay on the very western edge of Elamite territory.[14]

But he didn't yet try to take over the center of Rim-Sin's kingdom. Nor was he ready to challenge the north at all. Nine years into his reign, he made a formal alliance with Shamshi-Adad. A Babylonian tablet records the oath, which both men swore to; the language implies that although both were bound by it, Hammurabi acknowledged Shamshi-Adad as the superior. Certainly he knew himself not yet strong enough to take the king of Assur on, headfirst. Conceivably, he could see the future. Two years later, Shamshi-Adad was dead; probably of old age, although the date of his birth (like his parentage) remains a mystery.

Even then, Hammurabi did not immediately move north into Assyrian territory. He bided his time, building canals and temples, reinforcing cities, and strengthening his army. He even established more-or-less friendly relations with Shamshi-Adad's son Yasmah-Adad, still ruling as king at Mari, and also with the king of Eshnunna, north of Babylon. He was on good enough terms with both monarchs to send officials as ambassadors (and spies) to their courts; playing both sides of the card, he also made a gesture of friendship towards Aleppo, where the ousted rightful heir to Mari's throne was in exile, by receiving a delegation from Aleppo's king.[15]

To the south, Rim-Sin was in no doubt about the growing threat in the center of Mesopotamia. Hammurabi might be sitting relatively still, but he was dangerous. Rim-Sin was already building alliances. He was sending messages to the Elamites and the king of Malgium to the east of Babylon, to the king of Eshnunna north of Babylon, even to the Gutians who lived north of Elam: hoping to arrange a pincer move that would trap Hammurabi from both north and south.

Meanwhile Hammurabi waited, in relative peace, strengthening the center of his kingdom against the coming storm.

TIMELINE 20

EGYPT	MESOPOTAMIA
First Intermediate Period (2181–2040)	
Dynasties 7 & 8 (2181–2160)	
Dynasties 9 & 10 (2160–2040)	Fall of Agade (c. 2150)
Middle Kingdom (2040–1782)	
Dynasty 11 (2134–1991)	Third Dynasty of Ur (2112–2004)
Intef I-III	**Ur-Nammu**
Mentuhotep I-III	**Shulgi** Abram travels to Canaan
	Fall of Ur (2004)
Dynasty 12 (1991–1782)	
Amenhemhet I	Isin Dynasty Amorite kings of Larsa
	(Larsa) **Gungunum** (c. 1930)
	(Larsa) **Rim-Sin** (1822–1763)
	(Assur) **Shamshi-Adad** (1813–1781)
	(Babylon) **Hammurabi** (1792–1750)

Chapter Twenty-One

The Overthrow of the Xia

In the Yellow river valley,
the Xia Dynasty grows corrupt
and falls to the Shang in 1766 BC

MEANWHILE THE KINGS OF CHINA were still perched on the edge of myth.* According to Sima Qian, the Grand Historian, the Xia Dynasty founded by Yü kept the throne for four hundred years. Between 2205 and 1766, seventeen Xia monarchs ruled. But although archaeologists have discovered the remains of a Xia palace and capital city, we have no direct evidence from these centuries for the existence of any of the personalities that Sima Qian describes, more than fifteen hundred years after the fact.

Taken as oral tradition that reflects, however dimly, a real succession of rulers, the story of the Xia Dynasty and its fall shows that the struggle for rule in China was very different from the clashes on the Mesopotamian plain. In China, there were as yet no barbarians invading civilized people, no struggle between one nation and another. The greatest struggle was between a king's virtue and his wickedness. The threat to his throne came first from his own nature.

The Three Sage Kings who came just before the Xia Dynasty had chosen as their successors not their sons, but worthy and humble men. Yü, the third of these kings, gained his position by sheer ability. Sima Qian records that he was a vassal, recruited by the Sage King just before him to solve the problem

* Using the name "China" is an anachronism, like using "Iran" for the territory of Elam (which is something I've tried to avoid). During this millennium, the states that lay on the eastern part of the Asian continent were called by the names of their ruling families. However, it's marginally easier to justify the use of "China" for this area than the use of "Iran" for the Elamite lands, since the country of China has been coterminous with the land where the ancient Xia state lay for so very long (something certainly not true of modern Iran, which had its borders drawn in the twentieth century in places that do not match any of the ancient countries that occupied the same land).

of Yellow river floods so violent that they "surged towards the heavens, so vast that they embraced the mountains and covered the hills."[1] Yü worked for thirteen years, planning ditches and canals, building embankments and dikes, directing the Yellow river floods into irrigation and away from the settlements threatened by waters, and showing himself to be a man "both diligent and indefatigable."[2] At the end of his efforts, "the world was then greatly ordered."[3] Yü did not protect his people from outside forces, but from threats that lay within their own land.

The land that Yü ruled would have overlapped that occupied by the predynastic Chinese culture called the Longshan,* a people who built walled villages in the valley at the southern bend of the Yellow river. These villages were most likely governed by patriarchs, strong family heads who allied themselves with other village patriarchs through intermarriage and, occasionally, through conquest. The accounts of the early Xia Dynasty speak of the "feudal lords" or "dukes" who support or trouble the Xia kings; these are anachronistic titles for the Longshan patriarchs.[4]

We don't know where the capital city of Yü, the king who struggled with the river, might have lain. But at some point between 2200 and 1766, a Xia capital seems to have been built just below the southern bend of the Yellow river; excavations there have uncovered extensive buildings which appear to be royal palaces.†

Erlitou, just below the southern bend of the Yellow river, lies in a valley formed by the Lo river, which flows into the Yellow river from the south. The land around it is unusually good, since it is fertilized by silt deposits, and the ring of mountains surrounding the valley on three sides made Erlitou so easy to defend that the city had no walls.[5]

Despite the presence of a palace at Erlitou, the chiefs of the walled settlements (or *yi*) along the Yellow river seem to have kept plenty of independence of their own, directing their own trade with other villages and keeping their own small armies.[6] But tradition says that there was at least some sort of kingly power exercised along the valley. Possibly Yü's struggle with the devastating Yellow river floods preserves an ancient change in the rising of the

* Compared with the divisions of Mesopotamian history, the traditional archaeological divisions of Chinese history are pure simplicity: the Yang-shao culture (5000–3000) was followed by the Longshan culture (3000–2200), the Bronze Age (2200–500), and then the Iron Age.

† Until these excavations, carried out in the late 1950s, historians widely assumed that the Xia Dynasty was entirely legendary; archaeology has demonstrated that there was indeed a Yellow river kingdom during the traditional Xia dates. The relationship between the Erlitou site and the Xia dynasty is still a matter of debate, although the connection is primarily questioned by Western historians and archaeologists (see Li Liu and Xingcan Chen, *State Formation in Early China*, pp. 26–27).

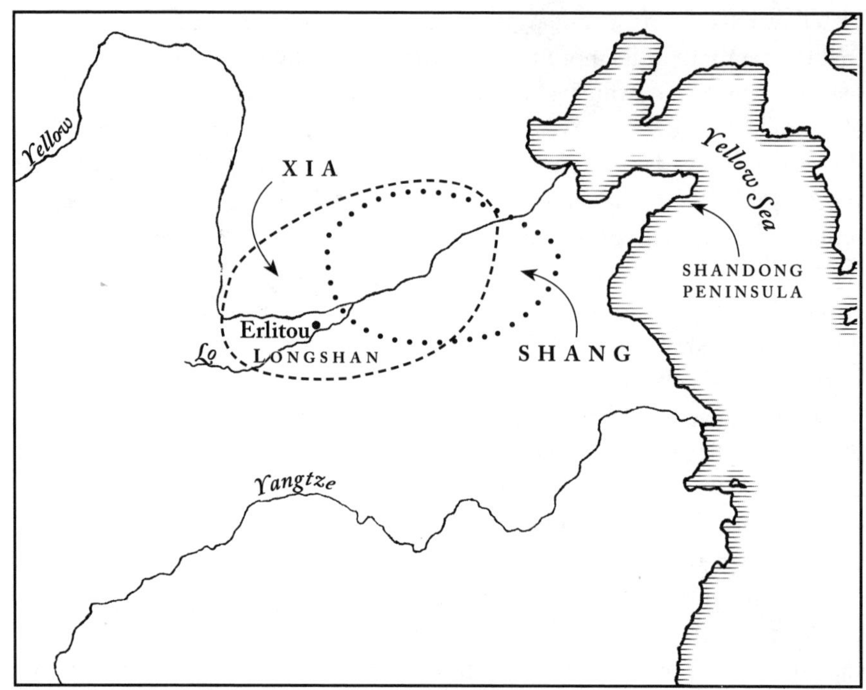

21.1 Xia and Shang

waters, a more severe flooding; if so, the increased difficulty of surviving in a more hostile environment might well have led the villages to accept the unifying and protecting power of a leader.

The hereditary assumption of this power began with Yü, who did his best to follow the example of the Sage Kings who preceded him. Like them, he rejected blood inheritance by choosing a worthy man as his successor and bypassing his son. Unfortunately the powerful patriarchs of the villages disagreed with his choice and instead supported Yü's son Qi; it was their will to have a hereditary dynasty. This rebellious action carried the Yellow river settlements from the days of the Sage Kings into an era of blood succession.

This innovation did not go unchallenged. One village, the village of the Youhu, so objected to this refusal to pass the crown from one family to another that all of the Youhu boycotted Qi's accession feast. Qi was having no such principled refusals. He sent his army to round up the rebels, defeated what resistance the Youhu could muster, and destroyed the village, claiming to be "carrying out Heaven's punishment" for their rebellion.[7] Force had trumped sagacity.

The first years of the blood succession did not go smoothly. After Qi's death, his five sons fought over the kingship; there were no conventions to guide the Xia state in the peaceful transfer of the crown from one generation to the next. The son who managed to triumph justified every Youhu fear about the dangers of a hereditary monarch. He immediately applied himself to carousing and womanizing, rather than ruling. At this, a powerful village patriarch mounted an attack on the palace and took the throne away. In turn, he was murdered by a court official, who seized the throne for himself.

In the absence of the sage choice of one king by his predecessor, chaos was reigning. Even a blood succession was better than this; and the blood relative who eventually rounded up enough support to challenge the usurper was Shao Kang, the great-great-nephew of Qi.

Shao Kang had fled the bloodshed in the capital city to hide in another village. Now with his followers behind him, he marched back to Erlitou, defeated the official who sat on the throne, and claimed the right to rule. The Xia Dynasty, barely begun, had already required rescuing.

AFTER THIS ROUGH START, the Xia succession bumped along for centuries. But Chinese historians tell us that the right to rule, based on no quality but that of accidental birth, slowly corrupted those who held it. The Xia kings entered into a cycle which would repeat again and again throughout Chinese history: The first kings of a dynasty earn their right to rule by their wisdom and virtue. They pass their rule to their sons, and as time goes on those sons become lazy. Laziness becomes decadence, decadence becomes dissolution, and dissolution leads to a dynasty's fall. A new man, wise and powerful, takes the throne, a new dynasty rises, and the pattern repeats. At the end of each cycle, tyrants fall and virtuous men return to the foundational principles; but they cannot hold those principles for long. Good faith deteriorates into mistrust, piety into superstition, refinement into pride and hollow exhibition. "For the way," Sima Qian writes, "is a cycle; when it ends, it must begin over again."

Sima Qian, who inherited his father's position as Prefect of the Grand Scribes in the second century BC, may have had a slightly jaundiced view of the world; after offending his own emperor with an unflattering remark or two about the emperor's father, he was given the choice between execution and castration. (He chose the latter, so that he could finish his history; a dedication to his work possibly unmatched in historiography.) But his description of the cycle of history was based on long tradition, and on long observation. The ideal of Chinese kingship was rule by wisdom, but as soon as a king could claim power over those villages along the Yellow river, corruption, oppression, and armed conflict inevitably followed.

In the Xia Dynasty, conflict reached a head during the reign of the Xia king Jie, who slowly alienated his courtiers by emptying the palace treasury in order to build palaces for himself. He alienated his people by taking as his mistress a beautiful but unpopular woman, both cruel and evil, and spending his days cavorting and drinking with her rather than ruling. And he alienated the lords of the villages by arresting anyone who might pose a challenge to his rule and either imprisoning or killing them. Jie, Sima Qian sums up, "did not engage in virtuous government but in military power."[8]

One of the village patriarchs arbitrarily jailed was a man named Tang, a member of the Shang clan, who held enough power over the lands east of Erlitou to appear threatening. After a little while, though, Jie (perhaps addled by wine and late nights) seems to have forgotten his original objections. He set Tang free. Immediately Tang set about strengthening his position among the leaders of the other cities that were nominally under the Xia rule. As Jie's unpopularity grew, Tang lived a conspicuously righteous life in contrast; Sima Qian says that he "cultivated his virtue" (and presumably exercised plenty of diplomacy). He even used his own men to march against one of the other feudal lords who was himself tyrannizing the people nearby.

Eventually Tang claimed the divine right to take vengeance against evil, and led his followers against the emperor.[9] Jie fled from the capital city, and in 1766 (the traditional date of his accession) Tang became the first Shang emperor.

Jie died in exile. His last words, apparently, were, "I should have killed Tang when I had the chance."[10]

The Shang conquest was not the establishment of a brand-new rule, but the extension of an existing power over a weakening palace at Erlitou. For decades, the Shang family had been growing in power to the east of the Xia capital. Just as the prehistoric Longshan culture itself extended overtop of the Yang-shao and the Xia grew up overtop of the Longshan, so the Shang state lay overlapping the Xia land. The takeover of Tang, who was given the title Tang the Completer, was an internal affair. The Xia kingdom struggled with itself; when it fell, it fell to its own people.

The cycle had begun again. Tang's rule was a model of justice, in which he threatened the feudal lords with punishment if they did not "do good deeds for the people." Like his great predecessor Yü, he also tackled the flooding problem; Sima Qian says that he "regulated" four troublesome streams, producing new fields and new village sites. The Shang Dynasty began in hard work and in virtue: for the way is a cycle, and it must begin again.

TIMELINE 21

MESOPOTAMIA	CHINA
	Xia Dynasty (2205–1766)
	Yü
Fall of Agade (c. 2150)	**Qi**
Third Dynasty of Ur (2112–2004)	
Ur-Nammu	**Shao Kang**
Abram travels to Canaan **Shulgi**	
Fall of Ur (2004)	
Isin Dynasty Amorite kings of Larsa	
(Larsa) **Gungunum** (c. 1930)	
(Larsa) **Rim-Sin** (1822–1763)	
(Assur) **Shamshi-Adad** (1813–1781)	
(Babylon) **Hammurabi** (1792–1750)	
	Jie
	Shang Dynasty (1766–1122)
	Tang

Chapter Twenty-Two

Hammurabi's Empire

Between 1781 and 1712 BC,
the king of Assur and his allies fall to Hammurabi of Babylon,
who then makes laws to control his empire

AFTER YEARS OF BIDING HIS TIME, Hammurabi had begun to see fractures in the empire to his north.

When Shamshi-Adad died of old age in 1781, the crown of Assur had gone to Ishme-Dagan, who had been ruling as his father's co-regent over a territory consisting of Ekallatum and the northward expanses. Ishme-Dagan now controlled the entire empire, including the city of Mari, where his younger brother Yasmah-Adad was reigning as his deputy.

Ishme-Dagan and Yasmah-Adad had never been good friends. The older son had been Shamshi-Adad's pride; the younger had suffered from his father's disdain since the very beginning of his term as governor-king of Mari. In letter after letter, Shamshi-Adad had compared the brothers, always to Yasmah-Adad's disadvantage. "Your brother has won a great victory in the east," Shamshi-Adad writes to the younger son:

> [But] you remain there, reclining amongst the women. Can't you behave like a man? Your brother has made a great name for himself; you should do the same in your own land.[1]

Rarely did Yasmah-Adad manage to please his father; Shamshi-Adad's letters criticize him for everything from not choosing a steward to manage his household affairs ("Why haven't you appointed a man to the post yet?") to not sending a requested official quickly enough. The constant criticism drained away whatever assertiveness Yasmah-Adad had. We find him writing back to his father in an agony of uncertainty over the reassignment of another minor official: "You have asked me to send Sin-iddinam to help you, and I will do as you say," he begins. "But if I do, who will stay here and govern? I honor my father, and I will be glad to send him to you. But then, what if you come here and say, 'Why didn't you tell me that you would have to leave his post empty? Why didn't you keep me informed?' So I am informing you, so that you can decide what you want me to do."[2]

Meanwhile, Ishme-Dagan peppered his younger brother with reports of his victories.

> *In eight days I became master of the city of Qirhadat and took all the surrounding towns. Rejoice!*
>
> *I marched against Hatka, and in one day, I flattened the town and made myself master of it. Rejoice!*
>
> *I raised siege-towers and battering rams against the town of Hurara, and took it in seven days. Rejoice!*[3]

No wonder Yasmah-Adad hated him.

After Shamshi-Adad's death, Ishme-Dagan wrote to his brother, apparently in an effort to improve their relationship. Unfortunately he had inherited his father's hectoring tone:

> I have ascended the throne in my father's house, and I've been extremely busy, or I would have sent you news before. Now I will say—I have no other brother than you. . . . You must not be anxious. As long as I am alive, you shall sit on your throne. Let's swear brotherly loyalty to each. Oh, and be sure to send me your complete report right away.[4]

It is hard to know how sincere this gesture of friendship was. The indecisive Yasmah-Adad was soon facing a siege; Zimri-Lim, the prince of Mari, who had been forced to run west by Shamshi-Adad's attack, was planning a return. He was reinforced by soldiers given to him by his father-in-law, the king of Aleppo. Six years after Shamshi-Adad's death, Zimri-Lim was ready to move against Yasmah-Adad.

No reinforcements arrived from Assur. Alone, Yasmah-Adad faced the besiegers, and died in the waves of the attack.

Now, Zimri-Lim was king of Mari once more. Given that three large and greedy kingdoms now lay to his east (Ishme-Dagan's centered at Assur, Hammurabi's at Babylon, and Rim-Sin's to the south), Zimri-Lim knew that Mari needed to make an alliance with the strongest in order to survive the other two.

But it was far from clear who the strongest might be. One of Zimri-Lim's own letters from this point in his reign reads:

> There is no king who, by himself is strongest. Ten or fifteen kings follow Hammurabi of Babylon, the same number follow Rim-Sin of Larsa, the same number follow the king of Eshnunna. . . .[5]

After surveying the territory, he finally settled on Hammurabi as his best bet.

Hammurabi accepted the alliance. Undoubtedly he had his eye on the forces gathering against him. Ishme-Dagan had negotiated a two-way treaty with the king of Eshnunna, that independent city east of the Tigris, and the country of Elam. This created a force to be reckoned with. Since the fall of Ur, Elam had been more or less a unified country; the southern realms had, at various times, fallen under the rule of various Mesopotamian kings, but the northern lands had always remained an Elamite stronghold. Now a new dynasty, the Eparti line, had taken control of the entire region and was ready to join in the fight against Babylon.*

Down in the south, Rim-Sin appears to have thought better of joining the anti-Hammurabi coalition of Assur, Eshnunna, and Elam. Possibly he now believed that Hammurabi could not be defeated. Just as possibly, he was too tired and too old to join a fight so far to his north. He had now been on the throne for nearly sixty years, longer than any other known Mesopotamian king.

Ishme-Dagan and the kings of Eshnunna and Elam moved without him. In 1764, nine years after Zimri-Lim returned to the throne of Mari, the joint army began its march against Hammurabi.

Hammurabi, his own Babylonian army reinforced with Zimri-Lim's soldiers, wiped the floor with them. He seized Assur and made it part of Babylon; he took Eshnunna as his own; and although he did not drive eastwards all the way into the Elamite highlands, he captured Susa and sacked it. He also carried off various statues of Elamite goddesses and had them taken, ceremonially, to Babylon, accompanied by their priestesses. This was a polite and sacred version of carrying off your enemy's wives and ravishing them.

The year after, he turned against Rim-Sin, whose neutrality had done him no good. Hammurabi used this very neutrality as a reason to attack the southern king. Why had Rim-Sin not joined him against the northern aggressors? When Rim-Sin could not answer the question satisfactorily, Hammurabi diverted the flow of a river across a heavily populated section of Rim-Sin's

* The previous dynasty had bee the Simash. This dynasty was named after its first king, Eparti; it is also referred to as the Sukkalmah, or "grand regent," Dynasty, possibly so named because the Elamite king ruled with the help of a viceroy (the "grand regent") whose succession was governed by unbelievably complicated rules.

kingdom. Apparently Rim-Sin buckled without too much of a fight, agreeing to do homage (and, according to his own records, draining land elsewhere so that he could hastily resettle the men and women who had been flooded out).

Hammurabi then turned against his own ally.

Apparently Zimri-Lim was too powerful a warrior, and too strong a personality to make Hammurabi feel entirely comfortable. He didn't attack his former partner; instead, he demanded the right to examine (and control) all of Zimri-Lim's correspondence with other powers. This particular sort of domination—the right to manage another country's foreign relations—would be much exercised in later centuries, when it generally spelled the end of actual independence. Zimri-Lim knew this. Indignant, he refused. Hammurabi threatened reprisal. Zimri-Lim defied him. Hammurabi marched to Mari and began executing prisoners outside its walls. When the gates stayed closed, Hammurabi besieged the city, broke down its walls, hauled its people off into slavery, and set it on fire.[6]

Zimri-Lim's fate is not recorded; nor that of Shiptu, his queen, nor that of his daughters. He had two young sons, but neither appears again in the annals either of Mari or of Babylon.

THE YEAR AFTER THIS ATTACK, Hammurabi turned again towards Larsa. We can assume that Rim-Sin had thought better of his homage and mounted a resistance. After a six-month siege, Larsa fell.

This time, Hammurabi took Rim-Sin prisoner, removing him from his throne. His sixty-year rule was over. Now all of the old Sumerian cities—not to mention a good many west and north of old Sumer—were part of the empire centered at Babylon. "May all men bow down in reverence to you," Hammurabi's scribes wrote. "May they celebrate your great glory; may they give their obedience to your supreme authority."[7]

This was no unruly empire; it was ruled by law. Hammurabi managed his growing conquests, in part, by enforcing the same code over the entire extent of it. The only surviving copy of this code was discovered centuries later in Susa, carved onto a black stone stele. Clearly the laws were intended to embody a divine code of justice (the top of the stele shows the god of justice, bestowing his authority on Hammurabi), but their showy presence in conquered cities also kept control over the conquered people. According to the stele itself, the laws were observed faithfully in Nippur, Eridu, Ur, Larsa, Isin, Kish, Mari, and other cities.

Hammurabi was not the first lawgiver—Ur-Nammu had scooped him in this regard—but his laws are certainly the most complete to survive from

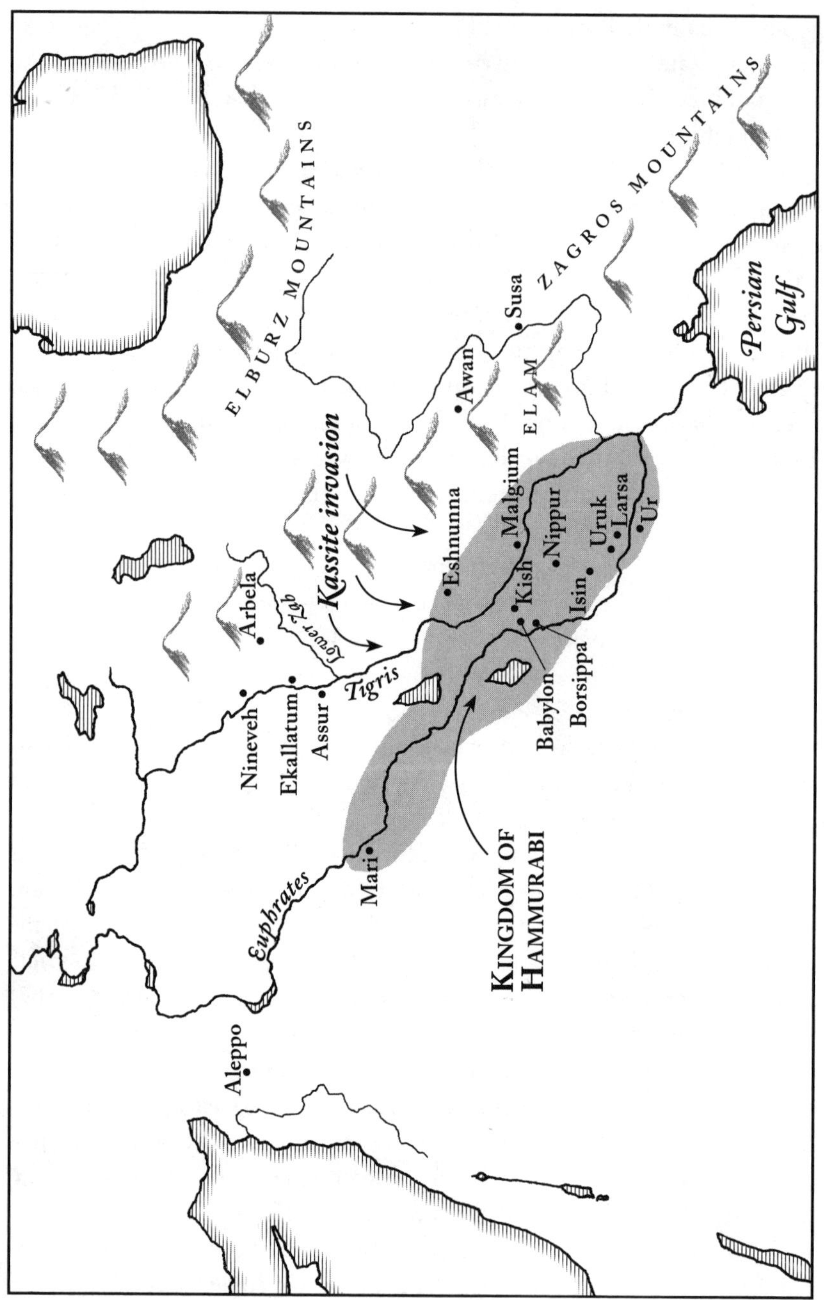

22.1 Hammurabi's Empire

ancient times, and they show an amazingly wide range of concerns. Penalties for robbery (death), aiding in the escape of a slave (death), kidnapping (death), designing a house that collapses on someone else's head (death), and the poor performance of an obligation to the king (death) are accompanied by regulations on marriage (a contract was required; husbands could obtain divorce from a judge, but so could a wife whose husband had disgraced her), injury (any man who puts out the eye of another free man will lose his own, but putting out a slave's eye only costs a fine of silver), inheritance (widows can inherit land but can't sell it; they must keep it for their sons), and firefighting (if a man goes to fight a fire at his neighbor's house and pinches any of his neighbor's goods under cover of smoke, he "shall be thrown into the fire").[8] All of these laws and codes of Hammurabi, handed down and reinforced from the center of the empire, were meant to convince conquered peoples of the justice and rightness of Babylonian rule. But they also served to keep a very tight rein on Hammurabi's subjects.[9]

A tight rein characterized almost all of Hammurabi's relations with his realm. Thanks to his wide conquests, he controlled all of the shipping routes from upstream downwards to the south; cedar and lapis lazuli, stone and silver, metal and bronze, all had to pass by his checkpoints, where only ships given a royal passport were allowed to continue on.[10] Not only did this guarantee the full payment of taxes, but it allowed the king to keep a very close eye on the goods going down into the troublesome south. No city in Hammurabi's empire would be able to arm itself in secret. Hammurabi liked to call himself the shepherd of his people; nevertheless, he seems to have been more worried that the sheep would grow wolf's teeth and break out of the fold, than that wolves would approach from the outside.

He knew perfectly well that his empire would only hang together as long as he appeared in complete control. In a letter written to one of his generals, we find him, after a run of bad luck in battle, trying to figure out a way to get the statues of those Elamite goddesses back to their homeland, so that they will bless his campaigns. He can't quite see how this will be accomplished, though. He doesn't want to fight his way in, and if he were to just hand them over, the Elamites might see the act as one of weakness.[11]

Particularly in the north and east, Hammurabi's rule was almost entirely one of subjection and coercion. Not ten years after claiming Eshnunna, he was again campaigning against the city, in a siege that lasted two full years and ended with Babylonian soldiers sacking, burning, and levelling it. He fought at the eastern border; he fought up near Nineveh, where more rebels were attempting to break away; he fought for almost the entire time that he ruled over his hard-won empire. By the end of the 1740s, he was an old man, ill from years of rough travel and in constant pain from partly healed battle wounds. He died only five years after the destruction of Eshnunna, and left his son Samsuiluna with a very big mess.

For some years, small bands of nomads—the Kassites—had been wandering over the Zagros Mountains, across the Tigris, and into the center of Mesopotamia. Babylonian accounts occasionally mention them as wandering workers, cheap immigrant laborers hiring themselves out.

The ninth year of Samsuiluna's reign was known as the year "in which the army of the Kassites came"; the laborers had armed themselves and were raiding the northeastern borders. Eshnunna had served as a barrier against the invaders. With the city gone, they streamed over the edge of the empire in larger and larger numbers.

At the same time, Samsuiluna was facing the rebellions that his father had spent his life putting down; Uruk, Isin, Larsa, and Ur all revolted in turn, requiring soldiers to go down and herd them back into the Babylonian fold. In the process, Ur was destroyed so thoroughly that it lay unoccupied for centuries afterwards; a little later, Nippur suffered the same fate.[12]

Already fighting on multiple fronts, Samsuiluna then discovered a new threat on his east. The Elamites had a new king, the warlike Kutir-Nahhunte I; ten years after the Kassite attacks began, Kutir-Nahhunte came across the Tigris with an army. The thin Babylonian ranks retreated out of Elamite territory, well back into their own, and then finally back to Babylon itself. This defeat of the Babylonian soldiers was so resounding that a thousand years later, Babylon's enemy Assyria was still taunting the Babylonians with it.

Samsuiluna couldn't keep his father's tight hand on his empire while fighting off these threats. By 1712, the end of his reign, he had lost all of the south. Without a ceaselessly campaigning warrior behind it, Hammurabi's code was helpless to hold the far reaches of the empire together.

TIMELINE 22

MESOPOTAMIA	CHINA
Third Dynasty of Ur (2112–2004)	
Ur-Nammu	**Shao Kang**
Abram travels to Canaan **Shulgi**	
Fall of Ur (2004)	
Isin Dynasty Amorite kings of Larsa	
(Larsa) **Gungunum** (c. 1930)	
(Larsa) **Rim-Sin** (1822–1763)	
(Assur) **Shamshi-Adad** (1813–1781)	
(Babylon) **Hammurabi** (1792–1750)	
	Jie
Hammurabi seizes Ashur and Eshnunna (1764)	Shang Dynasty (1766–1122)
	Tang
Samsuiluna (1749–1712)	

Chapter Twenty-Three

The Hyksos Seize Egypt

Between 1782 and 1630 BC,
Western Semites capture the throne of Egypt,
and the Middle Kingdom ends

THE PROSPERITY of the Middle Kingdom lasted for a relatively short time. The rule of Senusret III's son, Amenemhet III, was its high point. When he died, the power of the pharaoh to hold the country safe against invaders, and united with itself, began to fade.

Once again the Nile was lapping at the feet of the pharaoh. After reaching its highest point during the high noon of Amenemhet III's reign, the flood began to decrease year by year.[1] As always in Egypt, the dropping of the Nile and a diminishing of royal power went hand in hand.

Troubles with the succession probably had something to do with the slump as well. Amenemhet III ruled for forty-five years; by the time he died, his heir apparent was not only quite old, but also childless. Amenemhet IV, who had waited his whole life to ascend the throne, died almost as soon as he was crowned, and his wife, Queen Sobeknefru, took his place. Few details from the queen's reign have survived; but in ancient Egypt, a woman on the throne was a sign of serious palace trouble.

Manetho begins a new dynasty after Queen Sobeknefru, since there was no male heir waiting in the wings. The king who does eventually ascend the throne to begin the Thirteenth Dynasty is a nonentity, a shadowy figure followed by a handful of even more obscure personalities.

Down in Nubia, the governors who watched over the southern lands for the crown began to act with more and more independence; the Nubian lands that Senusret III had trampled on with such ferocity during the Twelfth Dynasty were easing out of the crown's grip. There was trouble in the north as well. Ruins show that the border fortresses on the eastern border between the Delta and the "land of the Asiatics" were crumbling. The border had once been so well protected that the courtier Sinuhe had trouble getting *out* of Egypt. Now the "Asiatics," those wandering Western Semitic nomads, came into the Delta in increasing numbers. Some of them settled down to live side by side with the Egyptians. Others were less domesticated; around 1720, sixty years or so after the Thirteenth Dynasty began its ineffectual rule, a particularly aggressive band of nomads invaded and burned parts of Memphis, the old Egyptian capital. Unlike the Egyptians, they fought with horse and chariot, an advantage that offset their relatively small numbers.

Despite this humiliation, the Thirteenth Dynasty managed to keep temporary control of the country. But their hold on Egypt was so shaky that historians have traditionally considered the Thirteenth Dynasty the end of the Middle Kingdom and the beginning of the Second Intermediate Period. Near the end of the Thirteenth Dynasty, the pharaoh's power had wilted so drastically that a second royal family appeared. We know almost nothing of this "Fourteenth Dynasty" except that it existed alongside the Thirteenth for some years. While the Thirteenth Dynasty pottered around in the Middle Kingdom capital Itj-taway, doing nothing useful, the so-called Fourteenth Dynasty claimed the right to rule the eastern reaches of the Nile Delta.

Some thirty or forty years later, yet another dynasty appeared alongside the waning Thirteenth and Fourteenth Dynasties. This Fifteenth Dynasty had its headquarters at the city of Avaris, which lay in the desert just east of the Delta. The first Fifteenth Dynasty king, a man named Sheshi, organized his followers into an army and began to spread his rule to the west and the south by force. Some twenty years later, around 1663, the Fifteenth Dynasty had managed to destroy both the Thirteenth and Fourteenth, and ruled supreme.

According to Manetho, Sheshi was a foreigner; he and his followers belonged to a race called the "Desert Princes," or *Hikau-khoswet*: the "Hyksos."[2] Manetho describes the Hyksos takeover as a violent and sudden overwhelming of Egyptians by savage invasion:*

> For what cause I know not, a blast of the gods smote us; and unexpectedly, from the regions of the East, invaders of obscure race marched in confidence of victory against our land. By main force, they easily overpowered the rulers of the land; they then burned our cities ruthlessly, razed to the ground the temples of gods, and treated all the natives with a cruel hostility, massacring some and leading into slavery the wives and children of others, and appointing as king one of their number.[3]

* The original account by Manetho is lost, but the Jewish historian Josephus preserved it by copying parts of it, word for word, into the work *Against Apion*.

Manetho, an Egyptian, can perhaps be excused for believing that his great ancestors could only have been overcome by a sudden and vigorous attack. But the traces left behind by these Fifteenth Dynasty rulers suggest that most of the Hyksos had actually been in Egypt for quite a while. Semitic names begin to appear in Middle Kingdom inscriptions and lists well before the 1663 takeover. So many Western Semites settled at the town of Avaris (the name means something like "Desert Mansion") that, over time, it became almost entirely Semitic. When the Thirteenth and Fourteenth Dynasties divided the already weakened leadership of Egypt between them, the inhabitants of Avaris took the opportunity to claim their own piece of the pie. The invasion of Egypt by foreigners was real, but it was primarily an invasion from within.

Manetho's hyperbole aside, the Hyksos—who, after all, had more likely been in Egypt for at least a generation or two—didn't raze too many cities. Although their names are Semitic, they had already adopted Egyptian dress and Egyptian customs. Egyptian continued to be the official language of inscriptions and records; Egyptians served the Hyksos as administrators and priests.

Despite the destruction of the Thirteenth and Fourteenth Dynasties, the Hyksos were never in sole possession of the country. A vassal line of kings ruled, probably with Hyksos permission, in the northwest; few names survive, but Manetho calls them the Sixteenth Dynasty. More serious was the announcement of the Egyptian governors of Thebes, to the south, that they would not submit to Hyksos rule and that true Egyptian authority was now centered in Thebes. This is the "Seventeenth Dynasty" of Manetho: the Fifteenth, Sixteenth, and Seventeenth Dynasties all existed side by side.

The Hyksos kings, aware of their own limitations, do not appear to have made a serious push to the south. The Egyptian rulers of Thebes controlled Egypt as far as Abydos; in this southern kingdom, the Middle Kingdom traditions carried on, free of foreign influence. But there was no peace between the two. Manetho writes, "The kings of Thebes and the other parts of Egypt made an insurrection against the foreign princes,* and a terrible and long war was made between them."[4]

The long-distance hostility between the two dynasties is revealed by the determined attempt of the fifth Hyksos king, Apepi I, who probably ruled around 1630, to pick a fight with the king of Thebes. A papyrus in the British

* Josephus actually translates the word used by Manetho as "shepherds." He deduces, incorrectly, that the term "Hyksos" comes from the Egyptian *hyk*, or "captive," and that the Hyksos were thus connected to the Israelite captivity in Egypt; in fact, it refers not to an invading race, but narrowly to the warrior-chiefs who rose up to claim rulership over Egypt; "chieftain" or "prince of the hill country" is closer to the sense of the word.

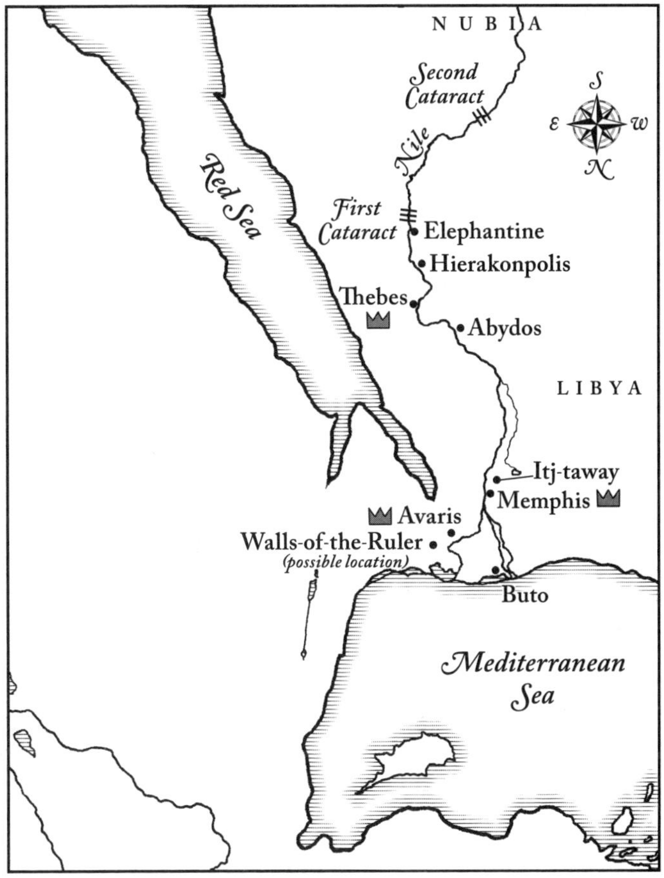

23.1 Three Simultaneous Dynasties

Museum preserves part of a letter sent by Apepi I all the way down to Thebes and addressed to Sequenere, the Seventeenth Dynasty king currently occupying the Theban palace. "Get rid of the hippopotami at Thebes," the letter demands, imperiously. "They roar all night, I can hear them all the way up here at Avaris, and their noise is ruining my sleep."[5]

Sequenere, five hundred miles away, took these as fighting words. His body, now in the Cairo Museum, suggests that he went and rounded up an army and started to march north. When he encountered the Hyksos border guard, he led his soldiers into battle. During the fight, Sequenere fell, his skull crushed by a mace. While he lay on the ground, he was stabbed and hacked with dagger, spear, and axe. His body was embalmed in a hurry, after a fair amount of decomposition had already set in; apparently the Theban pharaoh lay on the battlefield for several days before the Hyksos backed off enough for the southern soldiers to gather it up.[6]

The skirmish did not, quite, turn into a war. The Hyksos and Theban armies apparently retreated back to their home ground. Sequenere's older son Kahmose took the throne in Thebes, and began to lay plans to avenge his father's death.

TIMELINE 23

MESOPOTAMIA	EGYPT
	Middle Kingdom (2040–1782)
Third Dynasty of Ur (2112–2004)	*Dynasty 11* (2134–1991)
Ur-Nammu	**Intef I-III**
Abram travels to Canaan **Shulgi**	**Mentuhotep I-III**
Fall of Ur (2004)	
	Dynasty 12 (1991–1782)
Isin Dynasty Amorite kings of Larsa	**Amenhemhet I**
(Larsa) **Gungunum** (c. 1930)	
	Amenemhet III
(Larsa) **Rim-Sin** (1822–1763)	**Amenemhet IV**
(Assur) **Shamshi-Adad** (1813–1781)	**Queen Sobeknefru**
(Babylon) **Hammurabi** (1792–1750)	
	Second Intermediate Period (1782–1570)
Hammurabi seizes Ashur and Eshnunna (1764)	*Dynasty 13* (1782–1640)
Samsuiluna (1749–1712)	
	Dynasty 14 (1700–1640)
	Hyksos takeover (1663)
	Dynasties 15, 16, & 17

Chapter Twenty-Four

King Minos of Crete

On Crete, between 1720 and 1628 BC, the Minoans sacrifice to the god of the sea

NORTH OF THE NILE DELTA, far up in the Mediterranean Sea, a long mountainous island lay southeast of the unnamed messy peninsula that jutted down from the European mainland. The inhabitants may have come over from Asia Minor long before; by the time of the Hyksos, they too had joined the ranks of countries with kings, and had built a palace for their unknown monarch.

The palace stood at the center of Knossos, a settlement just inland from the very center of the northern coastline, and a strategic place from which to keep tabs on the east and west ends of the island. Not long after it was built, other, slightly smaller palaces went up at other key locations: at Mallia, east of Knossos on the northern coast itself, and Phaistos, just in from the southern coast.[1]

Since these early people left no writing behind them, we don't know exactly who lived in these palaces. But they stood at the centers of sprawling towns, networks of roads and houses. The people of these towns traded with the civilizations across the water. Their brightly painted pottery jars (possibly once holding wine or oil for trade) have been uncovered not only on the surrounding islands, but also along the Nile river and on the Mediterranean coast where the Western Semites lived.

They also practiced human sacrifice. Earthquakes shook the mountainous island with regularity; one of them collapsed a temple, situated on the mountain now called Mount Juktas and facing the northern sea, onto the inhabitants inside. Their skeletons lay undisturbed for almost three thousand years, until archaeologists uncovered the scene: a young man bound and lying on his side on a stone-and-clay altar, a bronze blade dropped on top of his body, and in front of the altar, a man in his forties, wearing a ceremonial ring and seal. A woman lay on her face in the southwest corner.[2]

Human sacrifice wasn't carried out very often. Traces of sacrifice have been uncovered in only one other location: a house in the western part of the town of Knossos, where two children had apparently been not only sacrificed, but carved up and cooked along with snails in some sort of ritual feast.[3] The ruins don't tell us what the sacrifice meant, or what horrible dilemma drove the priests and priestesses of Knossos to such an extreme act of worship.

But we can make a good guess.

SOMETIME AROUND 1720, an earthquake knocked down the early palace at Knossos. A new palace was built overtop of it and partially incorporating its ruins. This second palace was much more elaborate. The people of Knossos had progressed to the point where they needed a more royal king.

The Greeks, who called the island Crete, believed that a powerful king named Minos lived in Knossos in the days of this "Second Palace."* According to Greek myth, Minos was the stepson of a Cretan nobleman. Wishing to rule over the country, he told the people of Crete that he could prove he was divinely chosen for the kingship; whatever he prayed for would be given to him by the gods. The people challenged him to prove his boast, so Minos asked Poseidon to send him a bull for sacrifice. Immediately a magnificent bull walked up out of the sea onto the Cretan shore. It was so magnificent, in fact, that Minos couldn't bring himself to sacrifice it. He herded it into his own flock and sacrificed a lesser bull instead.

The Cretans acclaimed Minos as king. But Poseidon was displeased by Minos's greed, and cursed his wife Pasiphae with a lust for the bull. With the help of the legendary architect Daedalus, Pasiphae and the bull managed a rather odd coupling in which a wooden cow on wheels figured prominently; Pasiphae then gave birth to a horribly deformed child, a human figure with the face of a bull. Minos, seeing the baby, shut it up in a prison beneath the Knossos palace. The prison, which was designed by Daedalus as punishment for helping out Pasiphae, was made up of so many winding passages that the child—named Asterius by his mother, but known as the Minotaur—could never escape. In this prison, the Labyrinth, the Minotaur grew to adulthood. Minos fed it on human flesh; after a battle with the inhabitants of the Greek mainland, he ordered them to send seven young men and seven young women each year to be eaten by the Minotaur.[4]

* The early history of Crete is conventionally divided into the Prepalatial Period (3200–2000), before the building of palaces began; the Protopalatial, or First Palace, Period (2000–1720); the Neopalatial, or Second Palace, Period (1720–1550; it runs to 1450 if the eruption of Thera is placed in 1520 rather than 1628 [see the footnote on p. 188]; and the Final Palatial Period (1550 [1450]–1350).

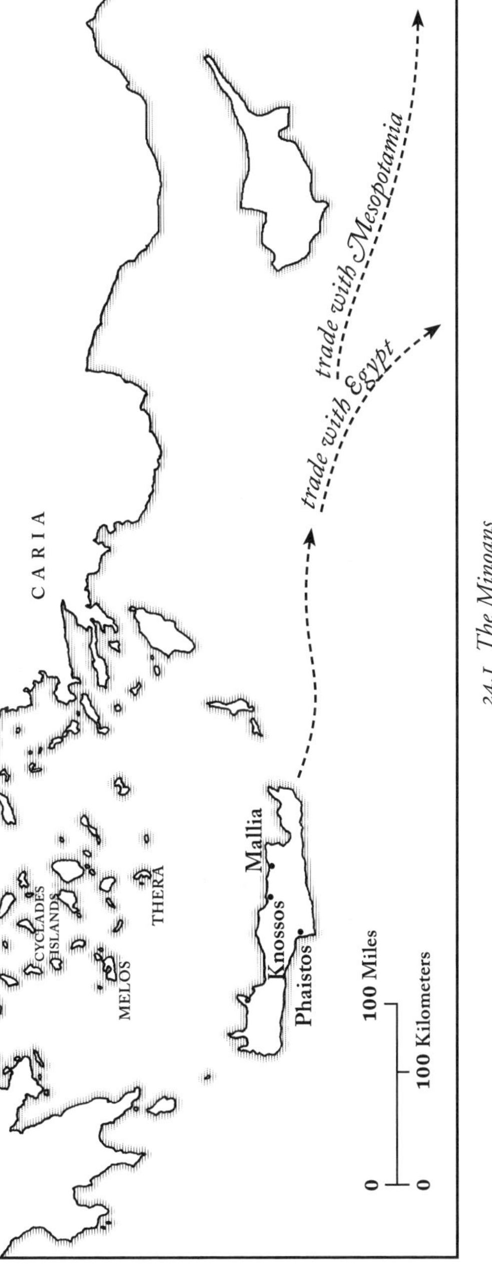

24.1 The Minoans

This story appears in the *Library*, a Greek collection of stories from the second century BC.* Behind the fog of this myth, we may be able to achieve a glimpse of a civilization which has left no other stories behind it.

Minos may well have been the name not just of one legendary ruler, but a line of kings who governed in Knossos and lent their name to Crete's earliest civilization. The story of the Minotaur, with its exchange of cargo between cities, reflects the ongoing international sea trade carried on by the Minoan people. So do the remains of Second Palace goods found around the ancient world. An alabaster jar lid uncovered at Knossos is marked with the name of the third Hyksos king, and the Hyksos palace at Avaris has on its walls the remains of a fresco painted in the Minoan style. Contact with the eastern coast of the Mediterranean was regular; possibly the Minoans even traded as far over as Mesopotamia. Some of the pictorial representations (most notably on seals) of Gilgamesh and his fight with the Bull of Heaven—a story which begins to appear on clay tablets between 1800 and 1500 BC, right at the height of Minoan civilization—show Gilgamesh grappling with a partly human bull who wears a kind of wrestling belt. The monster has a bull's body and man's head, which is a reversal of the Minotaur's deformity, but the resemblance between the two monsters suggests that Minoan and Mesopotamian sailors swapped stories in port.[5]

Although the organized Greek civilization from which Minos was theoretically compelling this yearly tribute is an anachronism (there were only scattered settlements on the peninsula this early), Minos's ability to demand payment from abroad reflects the military power of Crete during the Second Palace Period. The *Library* says that Minos was "the first to obtain the dominion of the sea; he extended his rule over almost all the islands." Minoan towns have been uncovered on a number of the nearby islands, including Melos, Kea, and the small unstable Thera. The towns served not only as trading stops, but as naval bases. The Greek historian Thucydides writes that Minos was the first ancient king to have a navy. "He made himself master of what is now called the Hellenic Sea," Thucydides says, "and ruled over the Cyclades [the Aegean islands to the north], into most of which he sent the first colonies, expelling the Carians [settlers from southwest Asia Minor] and appointing his own sons governors; and thus did his best to put down piracy in those waters, a necessary step to secure revenues for his own use."[6] According to Herodotus, the Carians remained on the islands but became Minos's subjects, a pool of

* The *Library* was generally attributed to Apollodorus, a Greek historian who lived in Athens around 140 BC; it is probably not by him.

experienced sea-hands who would "man ships for him on demand."[7] The Minoan empire was built on water.

Around 1680 or so it reached the full extent of its power. Pirates had always been a problem in the Mediterranean—Thucydides explains that Knossos was originally built inland, away from the sea, "on account of the great prevalence of piracy"—but Minos's navy put an end to piracy, at least in the sea around Crete. This new peace meant that the peoples on the islands and coast were able to "apply themselves more closely to the acquisition of wealth, and their life became more settled."[8] Trade flourished, new buildings went up, painting and sculpture reached a new level of sophistication.

But there is a lingering threat in the story of King Minos: the bull-monster beneath the palace. That malicious presence, just out of sight, is the visible sign of Poseidon's ill will. It threatens not just the peoples who pay tribute to Minos, but Minos himself. It is an untamed and hungry power that literally undermines the foundation of his palace and demands constant sacrifice.

The palace at Knossos was ornamented with frescoes: wall paintings created by laying bright colors made from carbon, yellow ochre, iron ore, and other minerals directly onto a damp layer of lime plaster. In these frescoes, sacred bulls lower their horns in threat while worshippers vault over the horns onto

24.1. Bull-dancer. A Minoan bronze of an acrobat, leaping over the back of a bull. British Museum, London. Photo credit HIP/Art Resource, NY

the bull's back, and from there spring to the ground. The most famous bronze sculpture from the Knossos ruins preserves the same bull-dance, frozen at its most dangerous moment.

Presumably the worshippers who took part in this ritual were young, athletic, and ready to die. The story of the Minotaur may well preserve a very old form of human sacrifice in which the dedicated victims were not laid on an altar, but set loose in front of the bull. Excavation of the so-called Bull Courts, the central courts at Knossos where the bull-dancing apparently took place, show an entire network of doors, stairs, and corridors opening onto the courts from the surrounding buildings: a veritable labyrinth.[9] There is another connection between the Minotaur story and the religious practices of Crete. The fourteen victims are eaten by the Minotaur; the sacrificial site uncovered at Knossos indicates some sort of ritual feasting on the dead.

What sort of divine anger required this kind of sacrifice?

In the later Greek version of the Minotaur story, Poseidon, the god of the sea, is also called Earthshaker, and the bull is his sacred animal. The island of Crete and the sea around it were constantly shaken by earthquakes and the destructive waves that followed. Only constant pleading to Earthshaker could stave off the threat that came from the sea.

SOMETIME AROUND 1628, the earthquakes around nearby Thera grew more frequent.* The island was an active volcano, and more than one eruption had already taken place. But for some years, the island had been quiet enough for Thera's only large town, Akrotiri, to grow large and prosperous.[10]

When the earthquakes first intensified, the inhabitants of Akrotiri rebuilt the walls that the earthquakes knocked down. As the tremors grew more

* The date of the eruption of Thera continues to be a topic for much argument. Radiocarbon dating of volcanic ash suggests a date around 1628. There is also evidence from tree rings in various places around the Northern Hemisphere suggesting that their growth was interrupted around 1628, which is certainly a possible result of a massive eruption such as may have taken place at Thera. However, there is no definitive way to link this for certain with the Thera eruption. Archaeologists argue that the eruption can't have happened in 1628 because the archaeological period (based on pottery styles) during which the eruption occurred ended about thirty years after the eruption; if Thera erupted in 1628, this period (called LM IA) must have ended around 1600; but the similarities between LM IA pottery and those of other cultures which traded with Crete suggest that LM IA went on until around 1500. This is a simplification of J. Lesley Fitton's condensed overview of the debate between 1628ers and 1530ers; for the overview itself, see Fitton's *Minoans*, pp. 25–36; for a recent survey of all the various theories, in way more detail than most of us need, see Paul Rehak and John G. Younger, "Review of Aegean Prehistory VII: Neopalatial, Final Palatial, and Postpalatial Crete," in *American Journal of Archaeology* 102:1 (1998), pp. 91–173.

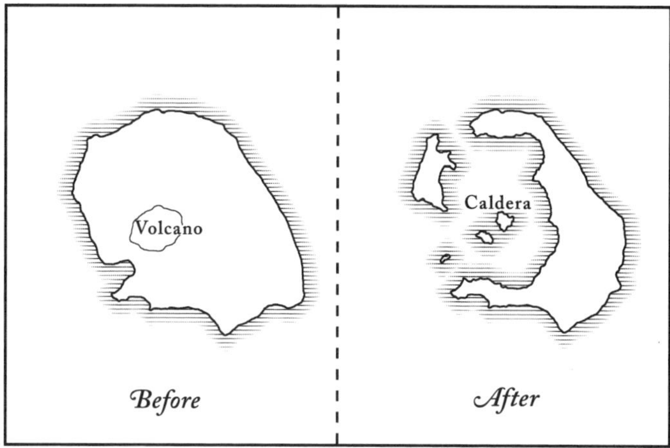

24.2 *Thera Before and After*

severe, they began to flee. Excavations of the ruins have revealed no skeletons, and the city seems to have been emptied of precious items such as jewelry and silver.[11]

Shortly afterwards, the volcano at the center of the island began to spew out pumice. The pumice that coats the ruins appears to have crusted over, meaning that it was exposed to the air (before being coated by the ash of the final eruption) for some time—any amount of time from two months to as much as two years. The rumblings at Thera went on a long time while the nearby islands listened in trepidation. Two years is a long time to wait for a looming catastrophe; long enough to sacrifice in hopes that the disaster will go away.

And then the volcano literally turned the island inside out, hurling fifteen feet of ash over the city. Enormous boulders flew from the depths of the volcano and rained down with the ash like gargantuan hail.[12] A gash opened in the side of the island, allowing the sea to pour into the crater left by the volcano. When the eruption finally succeeded, Thera was no longer a round island with a volcano at its center; it was a ring of land around a central inland sea, an enormous caldera.

This was the end of the Minoan town of Akrotiri, which would remain preserved under ash until it was excavated, beginning in the 1960s. It's less clear how much damage this gigantic eruption had on the Minoans of Crete. For a little while after Thera's explosion, the Minoan civilization continued as usual. Eventually, though, the population began to shrink; the houses grew shabby; trade trickled to a halt.

The decline may well have been related to the volcanic eruption.* Indications on Thera itself suggest that the volcano erupted in late June or early July, just before the harvest.[13] Ash fall, blown by the wind, missed the western end of Crete, but certainly reached the eastern half of the island, perhaps destroying a season's worth of food. Traces of ash on the shores around Thera suggest that the eruption caused a tsunami that submerged nearby islands, and that may still have been over thirty feet high when it crashed against the shores of Crete, twenty-five minutes after the eruption.[14] The huge cloud probably blocked the sun for some time. Electrical storms, heavy and violent thunderstorms, and sinking temperatures followed. For months, the sunsets would have been a deep blood red.

Even if the volcano were not directly responsible for the Minoan decline, all of these weird manifestations were likely to have had much the same effect as the dropping of the Nile down in Egypt. Such portents showed that Poseidon was angry. The royal house was no longer pleasing the gods. Very likely the catastrophe had been merely the forerunner of more extreme divine displeasure, looming on the horizon. The Earthshaker was not to be trifled with; and he always lurked in the depths, ready to bring an end to fragile prosperity. It was best to get away from such fury as quickly as possible.†

* It is impossible to make a more positive assertion, thanks to the fact that at least four different dates have been suggested for the eruption of Thera, and that archaeologists also disagree on the dates of the Minoan decline. (The landscape is further confused by the sheer number of different specialists who have gotten in on the act: historians, archaeologists, vulcanologists, and oceanographers, all using different methods and quarrelling over the results.)

† Much has been written, some serious and some not so serious, about the possibility that the eruption of Thera and the sinking of the island's center is the source of Plato's description of the lost island of Atlantis, which sank into the sea after violent earthquakes and floods; Plato calls Atlantis the strongest sea power in the region, which is a possible connection to the Minoan civilization. While this sort of speculation is fascinating, unfortunately I don't have room in this history to treat even *real* civilizations in detail, let alone investigate imaginary ones.

TIMELINE 24

EGYPT	CRETE
Middle Kingdom (2040–1782)	
Dynasty 11 (2134–1991)	
Intef I-III	
Mentuhotep I-III	
	Protopalatial Period (2000–1720)
Dynasty 12 (1991–1782)	
Amenhemhet I	
Amenemhet III	
Amenemhet IV	
Queen Sobeknefru	
Second Intermediate Period (1782–1570)	
Dynasty 13 (1782–1640)	
	Neopalatial Period (1720–1550)
Dynasty 14 (1700–1640)	**Minos**
Hyksos takeover (1663)	
Dynasties 15, 16, & 17	
	Eruption of Thera (c. 1628)
	Final Palatial Period (1550–1350)

Chapter Twenty-Five

The Harappan Disintegration

In India, from 1750 to 1575 BC,
the Harappan cities crumble
and northern nomads settle in the ruins

FAR EAST OF THE MEDITERRANEAN, the obsessively uniform Harappan cities faced a calamity of their own.

Sometime between 1750 and 1700, the people of Mohenjo-Daro began to flee their homes. Not all of them escaped. Excavation has revealed skeletons lying unburied in streets, an entire family trapped and killed in their home, their bodies left uninterred. Here and there, a house caught on fire and collapsed. Escaping inhabitants dropped their treasured items (tools for carrying on a livelihood, jewelry and silver) so that they could flee faster.[1] North at Harappa, much the same scene unfolded. The evidence from the smaller Harappan sites is not clear, but without a doubt the Harappan civilization ceased to exist.

The Harappans were not brought down by hostile invasion. The ruins show no dropped weapons, no bodies wearing armor, no systematic destruction of buildings, and no signs of struggle around the citadel (which, after all, had been built for just such an occasion).[2]

The collapse of various buildings, along with the fires (which may have started when kitchen-fires were overturned), could have been caused by earthquake or flood. If by flood, the waters must have been sudden and unusually violent. Silt layers show that the Indus, like other rivers that ran through major ancient civilizations, flooded regularly and left fertile soil behind in a predictable pattern.[3] The baked bricks of the citadels probably served as protection against unusually high waters. Only a wall-high wave could have caused the destruction found at the Harappan cities.

Hydrologist R. L. Raikes has suggested that a silt dam formed upstream from Harappa, stopped the flooding altogether for some time (thus reducing the fertility of the fields and possibly throwing the city into a minor famine), and then broke under the accumulated weight of water, sending enormous floods rushing down into the city. In fact, something like this happened in 1818, when a silt dam stopped up the Indus for almost two years, forming a block fifty miles long and fifty feet high.[4] But silt traces at the two largest Harappan cities don't prove a flood, one way or the other. In any case, even if a flood destroyed buildings throughout the cities, why weren't they rebuilt?

We have to assume that some kind of natural disaster descended on a civilization that was already suffering from internal rot. Many of the skeletons show evidence of illness, the most common being severe anemia, probably caused by malnutrition.[5] The banks of the Indus were not prone to salinization, but no field is immune to exhaustion; the growing populations undoubtedly required a greater and greater yield of grain. Those mud-brick buildings required plenty of small wood to use as fuel in the baking ovens. As the cities grew, the builders must have deforested larger and larger areas. Possibly the floods were simply a coup de grace given to an urban civilization already overextended. And once the cities had begun to disintegrate, the Harappan system was unable to turn the decay around. Perhaps that obsessive uniformity had so removed flexibility that, once driven out of their neat cities with the uniform bricks and familiar tools, they simply could not reorganize themselves from the ground up.

The cities were not entirely deserted. Some people remained, or returned, or wandered in from the countryside. The sketchy occupation above the Harappan layers shows crude pottery, little organization, and no attempt to rebuild or use the complicated drainage and sewer systems of the cities; far less sophistication than the Harappan. Archaeologists call this the post-Harappan, or Jhukar, culture,[6] after a village where the crude pottery was first made. But there is no organized culture about it. The "Jhukar culture" is, more accurately, the people who lived in the Harappan remains once the Harappan civilization had ended.

INVADERS DID COME down into India from the north, but they did not arrive until sometime between 1575 and 1500. They were nomads who had been wandering east of Elam and north of the mountains on India's western corner (now called the Hindu Kush Mountains). Eventually they made their way through the passes, down into the valleys formed by the upper branches of the Indus. Their own literature—not written down until a thousand years later—calls their earliest home in India the "Land of the Seven Rivers," which probably means that they first lived in the Punjab: the upper branches of the Indus, where it divided into six branches flowing into the one main river (in the millennia since, one of these branches, the Sarasvati, has dried up).[7]

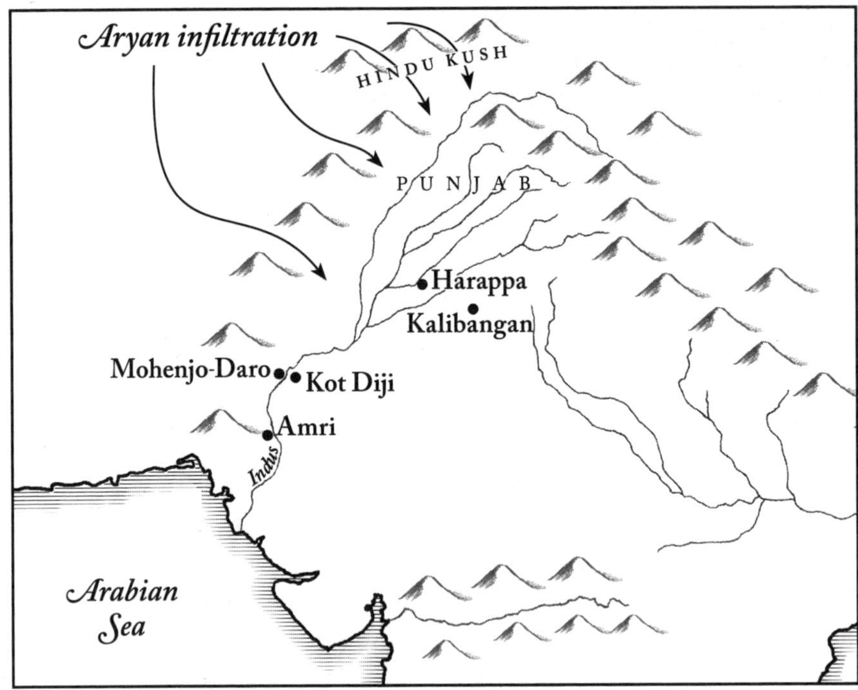

25.1 Newcomers to India

Their civilization was, at first, barely a civilization at all. They were accustomed to living in roving bands headed up by warleaders. So they did not build; they did not write; they had, so far as we know, no art; their language had no agricultural words such as "plough" or "threshing floor."

What they could do was fight. They are most distinguished by their weapons: not only horses, but also chariots with spoked wheels, bronze axes, and longbows with range unlike anything the Harappan people had used.[8] As with the Hyksos of Egypt, who also came from desert plains, these battle innovations had helped them plow a path through enemies before them.

However, they did not immediately set out to conquer the Indus valley. They lived among the Seven Rivers for at least a century before moving farther south and east. By the time they made their way down to the Harappan cities, the Harappan civilization had already tottered and fallen. Although they probably drove out the occasional band of squatters, this was the extent of their conquest. They took advantage of deserted buildings that they found, since they had none of their own (their language also lacked any word for "mortar"), and settled in. The sophisticated and highly organized Harappan civilization had been replaced by roving tribes with less culture, less technol-

TIMELINE 25

CRETE	INDIA
Protopalatial Period (2000–1720)	
	Desertion of Harappan cities begins (1750)
Neopalatial Period (1720–1550)	
Minos	
Eruption of Thera (c. 1628)	
Final Palatial Period (1550–1350)	Beginning of Aryan settlement

ogy, and no experience in running a city—but infinitely more experience in adapting to strange surroundings.

Later, the descendants of these invaders referred to themselves as *arya,* an adjective which has been given at least seven different English translations, ranging from "respectable" to the more ominous "pure."*[9] At its beginning, the Aryan civilization was anything but pure. Even though the citizens of Harappa and Mohenjo-Daro had lost the bureaucratic structure that held the Harappan *state* together, they were hardly removed en masse from northern India, like a massive alien abduction. They were scattered, but they survived. They mingled with the arriving Aryans, lent them the words for "plough" and "threshing floor" and "mortar," and presumably taught the ex-nomads how to use these civilized tools. The Aryan culture that spread across the north was woven through with threads from the world of the disappeared Harappans.

* The early twentieth-century theory that the Aryans swept in and conquered the Harappan cities through sheer might had more to do with politics than evidence; European scholars were anxious to find that the Aryans, with their European roots, were superior in every way to the natives of the Indian subcontinent. This motivation has also colored English understanding of the word *arya,* which (although it refers to a particular people group) probably did *not* originally bear the implication of "pure." As historian Stuart Piggott points out, it very likely bears the connotation "noble" (as opposed to "servant-class"); the invading Aryans, setting themselves up as conquerors, became the ruling class in the lands where they settled.

Chapter Twenty-Six

The Rise of the Hittites

Between 1790 and 1560 BC, the Hittites build an empire in Asia Minor, while Kassites take over in Babylon

By the time Samsuiluna died, around 1712, the Babylonian empire of his father Hammurabi ("Old Babylonia") had lost most of its holdings to the south and east. Elam had revolted. The ancient power centers of Sumer had mostly been destroyed and lay almost deserted. The land was desolate and infertile; an upstart line of kings about which absolutely nothing is known, the so-called Sealand Dynasty, claimed to rule the wasteland. The king seated at Babylon could still wield his power over land to the north and to the west, but only as far over as Mari. Past Mari, the king of Aleppo kept his independence.

After Samsuiluna, a succession of unremarkable kings claimed the throne of Babylon. Very little is known of them. The most detailed document to survive from the Babylonian court, in the hundred years after Samsuiluna, is an account of the exact behavior of the planet Venus as it rose and set.

The decline of one power coincided with the strengthening of another. Back in the days when Semites were wandering down into Mesopotamia and over into Canaan, another people with a different kind of language lived farther north, between the Caspian and Black Seas. Some of these northern peoples made their way east and became the ancestors of those Aryans who eventually travelled down into India. But others had gone west, into Asia Minor, and settled in a series of villages along the coast.

By around 2300, this particular Indo-European tribe had spread up through the entire western side of the peninsula and along the Halys river.* They

* This people group is often called "Indo-European," a not terribly helpful designation that means they weren't Semitic, Elamite, or Egyptian. "Indo-European" is primarily a linguistic term, referring to commonalities between the languages spoken across Europe and down into India which are not

carried on a healthy trade with islands to the west and also with the peoples to the east, especially with the city of Assur; for this reason the merchants of Assur built their trading posts here.

While Hammurabi was storming through Mesopotamia, uniting it by force, the villages of the Indo-Europeans in Asia Minor were coalescing into small kingdoms under various warleaders. We don't know who any of them were, so it's impossible to be any more vivid about this process. All we know is that the Egyptians had heard of these kingdoms, and knew them to be a single people. The Egyptians called them *Ht,* a designation taken from the peoples' own name for their homeland: *Hatti,* the territory of the Hittites.

The Hittites learned to write from the merchants of Assur who lived nearby; their early inscriptions and accounts are all in the cuneiform script used by the ancient Assyrians. By 1790, the chief of the Hittite city of Kussara was keeping his own records. The Hittites had entered history.[1]

This chief, Anittas, had inherited a very small two-city kingdom from his father, who had managed to conquer the nearby (and unsuspecting) city of Nesa by mounting a nighttime raid on it and kidnapping its king. In his father's day, Anittas had served as official Lord of the Watchtower, a job which required him to keep track of the reports from all the lookouts, who were spaced around the border of the tiny kingdom in watchtowers.[2] When his father died, Anittas—who at that time called himself merely the "prince of Kussara"—began his own wars of conquest. He campaigned against the nearby strong city of Hattusas, which he finally sacked when it continued to resist him.[3] He also cursed it, the same fate which may have overtaken Agade: "On its site I sowed weeds," he announced. "May the Storm God strike down anyone who becomes king after me and resettles Hattusa!"[4] Then he turned towards the city of Purushkhanda, which occupied, among the Hittite peoples, much the same place as Nippur occupied in the land of Sumer: it was a capital of the mind, a city whose ruler could claim a sort of moral authority over the cities of others. The king of Purushkhanda, perhaps with one eye on the distant column of smoke rising from Hattusas, surrendered without a fight.

Like his contemporary Hammurabi, who was at that moment fighting his way across the land between the Tigris and Euphrates, Anittas had created a nation. "I have conquered every land where the sun rises," Anittas announced, somewhat grandly, and began to refer to himself not as "prince" but as "great

---

shared by the Semitic languages, by Egyptian, or by Elamite. (Incidentally the Minoans are still a wild card in this four-way division; they are probably Indo-Europeans who migrated from Asia Minor over to Crete, but it's possible that they represent a fifth, totally different people group. The languages of the Far East fall into an entirely separate category.)

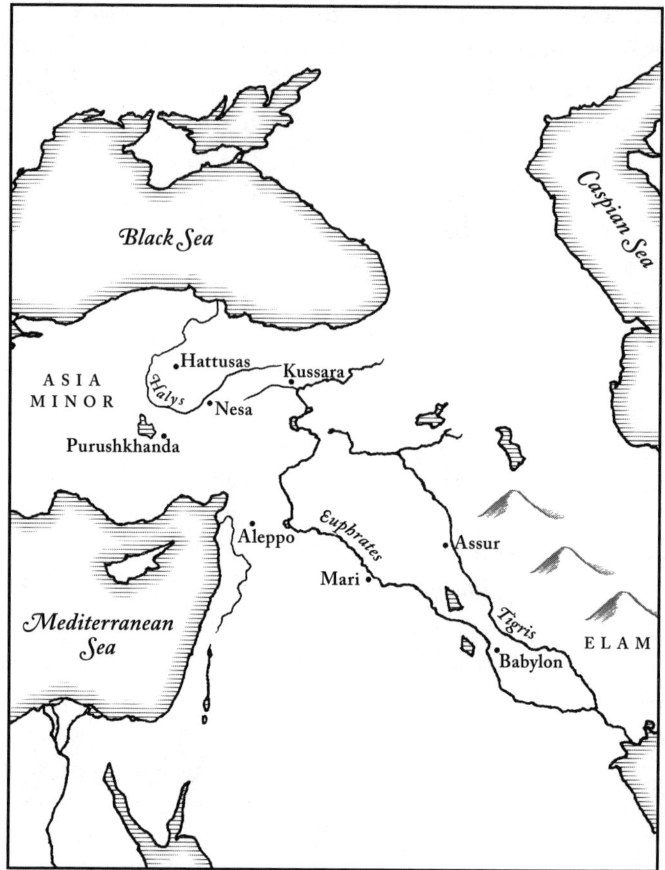

26.1 The Hittite Homeland

king."[5] He ruled his kingdom for a full forty years, a more than respectable period for any ancient king; he died within a year of Hammurabi, although there is no indication that the two ever exchanged messages.

The kingdom built by Anittas remained centered at his home city of Kussara until a couple of generations later, when a later king decided to ignore the curse and rebuild Hattusas. There were seven springs nearby, fertile land around it, and a cliff where a palace could be built and easily defended. The site was too good to leave deserted.

As soon as he had transferred his capital from Kussara to Hattusas, this king became known as Hattusilis I: "the one from Hattuses."[6] He began to make armed expeditions out of Asia Minor, down into the Western Semite kingdoms on the northeastern Mediterranean coast, and captured some of the smaller cities for himself. Anittas had created the Hittite nation, but Hattusilis

I made it into an empire that ruled over more than one people. He was a great warrior, possibly the greatest in the world at his time: the Harappan cities were sinking, Hammurabi was dead, in Egypt the kings of Thebes and Avaris were at war, and the reign of Minos was long past.

Despite his successes, Hattusilis died wretchedly unhappy, not in Hattusas but back in his old home of Kussara, where he had asked to be carried on his deathbed. A Hittite document called the *Testament* records his deathbed speech to his grandson Mursilis. Hattusilis breaks out in savage condemnation of his son and daughter, who had listened to discontented Hittite nobleman and allowed their minds to be poisoned against him. "They said to you: Revolt against your father," Hattusilis complains, "and they became rebellious, and they began to conspire."[7]

He has already disinherited the two grown children, and appointed his nephew heir instead. But in his last hours, Hattusilis rejects his nephew as well. He is, according to the *Testament*, "without compassion . . . cold and pitiless . . . heedless of the word of the king." His character, apparently, is partly his mother's fault; Hattusilis next turns on this woman, his own sister, and in furiously mixed metaphors calls her a snake in the grass who bellows like a cow.[8] The old king chooses another nephew named Mursilis as his heir instead and then dies, after a lifetime of military victories and family disappointments.

Mursilis, only thirteen or fourteen, was surrounded not only by the regents who were supposed to watch over him, but also by his seething disinherited cousins, uncles, and aunts. Despite this sticky beginning, the young Mursilis managed to survive to the age of accession (no mean feat in those days). He seems to have been lucky in his guardians; one of his regents, the Hittite prince Pimpira, was particularly concerned that he be not just a king, but a just and compassionate king. "Give bread to the one who is hungry," a Hittite chronicle records Pimpira as ordering, "clothing to the one who is naked; bring those distressed by cold into the heat."[9]

Once on the throne, though, Mursilis was more concerned with the conquest of new land than with the compassionate administration of the empire he already owned. A later Hittite treaty with Aleppo, by way of reviewing the previous relations between the two treatying parties, spells out his next move: "After Hattusilis, Mursilis the great king, the grandson of Hattusilis the great king, destroyed the kingship of Aleppo and Aleppo itself."[10]

Spurred on by his success at Aleppo, Mursilis began to march towards Babylon. He found various Kassite warleaders in his path, but he either conquered or made alliance with them. By 1595, he had arrived at Babylon's walls. The explosion that followed was more like a damp splutter. Babylon, under the rule of Hammurabi's great-great-grandson, put up little resistance. According to Mursilis's own accounts, he overran the city, took its people prisoner, and put the king in chains.[11] The final fate of this last descendant of Hammurabi is unknown.

Mursilis decided not to add Babylon to his empire. He had made his point: he was, like his grandfather, the most powerful conqueror in the world. Babylon was too far away from Hattusas to be governed with any security. Instead, Mursilis left the city desolate and marched back to his capital in victory. When he was well away, Kassite chiefs from nearby moved in to take over the ruins. The Amorite domination of Babylon had ended.*

Mursilis paraded into Hattusas hauling both captives and treasure with him. Behind the cheers, though, an assassination plot was slowly taking shape.

The culprit was his cupbearer, Hantili, a trusted official who also happened to be his brother-in-law. In Mursilis's absence, Hantili had grown accustomed to ruling on behalf of the throne; he was not likely to have welcomed the sudden curtailment to his authority. Not long after Mursilis returned from Babylon, Hantili and another palace official murdered the king, and Hantili took the throne. "They did an evil thing," the Hittite chronicles tell us. "They killed Mursilis; they shed blood."[12]

Hantili managed to keep the throne for almost three decades, during which the Hittites settled into their role as major players on the world scene. But he had set an unfortunate precedent. As soon as Hantili was dead, a court official killed Hantili's son and all of his grandsons and seized the throne. He, in turn, was killed by his own son, who was later murdered and replaced by a usurper, who then fell victim himself to assassination.

The dynastic succession of the Hittites had settled into a game of hunt-the-king. During these years, the royal palace at Hattusas acquired a twenty-five-foot-thick wall around it.[13] For the Hittite rulers, life within the borders of the kingdom was more dangerous than any military campaign.

* The standard Mesopotamian chronology follows the Old Babylonian Period (the reign of Hammurabi's dynasty, 1800–1600) with the Kassite era (1600–1150 BC).

TIMELINE 26

INDIA	ASIA MINOR/MESOPOTAMIA
	Anittas (c. 1790)
Desertion of Harappan cities begins (1750)	
	Death of Samsuiluna (1712)
	Hattusilis I (1650–1620)
	Mursilis I (1620–1590)
	Hittite conquest of Babylon (1595)
	Hantili
Beginning of Aryan settlement	

Chapter Twenty-Seven

Ahmose Expels the Hyksos

In Egypt, the pharaoh at Thebes defeats the Hyksos between 1570 and 1546 BC

After Sequenere of Thebes fell in battle against the Hyksos, his older son Kahmose took the throne.* Apepi I, the longest lived of the Hyksos kings, was still on the throne, and Kahmose needed to avenge his father's death.

His plans had to take account of an unpleasant reality: his Theban kingdom was sandwiched between a hostile power to the north, and that power's ally in the south. During the chaos just before the Hyksos takeover, the Egyptian governors of Nubia had gone their own way. Native Nubians had risen to official positions, and for years Nubia had been behaving like an independent country. Rather than attempting to subdue them, the Hyksos kings of the Fifteenth Dynasty had made a treaty with them. The Nubians agreed to come to the aid of the north against Theban Egypt, which would then have to fight a two-front war.

Kahmose of Thebes knew this. When he began to move his soldiers north along the Nile, he also spread out spies all across the south, hoping to intercept any Hyksos attempt to call their Nubian allies to arms. According to Kahmose himself, this strategy was brilliantly successful. In an inscription dedicated to Amun the sun-god, a deity much favored by the Hyksos, Kahmose claims that he conquered his way all the way to Avaris, where the Hyksos, frightened of his approach, "peeped out of the loopholes on their walls, like baby lizards." Meanwhile, his men managed to intercept the Hyksos messenger on his way down to Nubia. The letter he carried is preserved in Kah-

* Kahmose's place in the family is not entirely clear; he may have been Sequenere's brother, since there appears to have been a substantial gap in age between Kahmose and Ahmose, who comes next (Aidan Dodson and Dyan Hilton, *The Complete Royal Families of Ancient Egypt*, p. 126).

mose's records: "Kahmose has chosen to ruin both our lands, yours and mine," the Hyksos king told his Nubian counterpart. "Come north, then, and don't be afraid. He is already right here in my own area. . . . I will harass him until you arrive, and then you and I will divide up the towns of Egypt."[1]

The capture of this letter was cause for much boasting on the Egyptian side: "I caused the letter to be taken back to Apepi," Kahmose bragged, "so that my victory should invade his heart and paralyze his limbs."[2] He then marched back to Thebes, claiming victory the entire way and timing his arrival to coincide with the flooding of the Nile.

This fairly transparent attempt to remind everyone that he was the rightful king of all Egypt, responsible for the rising of the waters, suggests that Kahmose's victory wasn't quite as shattering as he claims. If he did indeed terrify the Hyksos with his might, it is difficult to see why he didn't go on and reclaim the north. At the very least, he could have attempted to occupy Memphis, the secondary Hyksos power center, from which the Hyksos appear to have kept an eye on the southern part of their realm; Avaris was too far north to be an effective center for the administration of the whole country.

He did neither, which suggests that his attack on Avaris was nothing more than a successful raid. Kahmose had little time to follow up on it. He died in that same year, after a reign of only three years; possibly he was wounded during the campaign, and lingered for a while before succumbing to his injuries. Since he died without sons, his brother Ahmose took the throne. He was still very young, and his mother Ahhotep ruled as his regent.

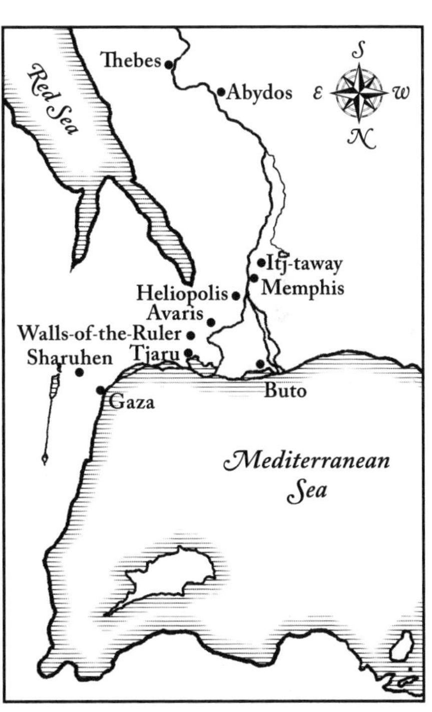

27.1 Ahmose Against the Hyksos

Around the same time, the long-lived Apepi I finally died in Avaris. The Hyksos throne was inherited by another king of much less personality; no contemporary records say much about him, and the scribes even disagree on his name. Apparently Queen Ahhotep took advantage of this northern weakness to follow up on her son's raid with a campaign of her own. In inscriptions, she is called "the one who has looked after her soldiers . . . has pacified Upper Egypt, and expelled her rebels."[3] She was buried with a ceremonial axe in her coffin, along with three medals, the Egyptian equivalent of medals of valor.

With this head start, Ahmose, when he inherited the throne, managed to battle his way successfully all the way to Avaris. By the twentieth year of his reign, he had captured both Heliopolis (just south of Avaris) and the eastern border fortress Tjaru. With these southern and eastern strongholds under his control, he was ready to pinch Avaris between the two wings of his army.

Manetho, quoted in the pages of Josephus, describes the next phase of the war:

> [The Hyksos] built a wall round all [Avaris], which was a large and strong wall, in order to keep all their possessions and their prey within a place of strength. But [Ahmose] made an attempt to take them by force and by a siege, with four hundred and eighty thousand men to lie round about them. When he despaired of taking the place by that siege, they came to an agreement. They would leave Egypt, and go, without any harm done them, wherever they would. After this agreement, they went away with their whole families and effects, not fewer in number than two hundred and forty-thousand, and took their journey from Egypt, through the wilderness.[4]

We should take this account with a grain of salt, since Egyptian accounts describe much more bloodshed. The tomb inscriptions of Ahmose's general (who is, confusingly, also named Ahmose) describe at least three different savage battles at Avaris: "I fought there, and I brought away a hand," he says proudly. (Egyptian scribes used amputated hands to tot up enemy casualties.) "This was reported to the royal herald, and I was given a medal of valor."[5] Egyptian relief sculptures commemorating the event show warships, battles, and herds of Hyksos led captive. Ruins show that Avaris was sacked. The Hyksos palace was flattened, and a new building, commissioned by pharaoh Ahmose, was built overtop of it.[6] Other traces of Hyksos occupation were so thoroughly obliterated that it is exceedingly difficult to reconstruct the details of their reign over Lower Egypt at all.

Nevertheless, the city's ruins show no evidence that a general slaughter, often the final phase of a long siege, ever took place at Avaris. Nor are there very many Semitic names in servant lists for the next fifty years, so it is unlikely that many Hyksos were enslaved. So it is indeed possible that a mass exodus, particularly of noncombatants, marked the end of Hyksos domination in Egypt.

We do know that, after the surrender of Avaris, the pharaoh Ahmose kept on marching north into Canaan, finally halting at Sharuhen near Gaza. Here, General Ahmose helped lead another successful siege. This may well have been a follow-up to the expulsion of the Hyksos from Avaris; if they fled just far enough to hole themselves up in another fortress, Ahmose would not have wanted them to regather their strength anywhere near Egypt.[7] Sharuhen was a danger to Egypt in any case. Excavations on its site show that it had become the center of a Western Semitic kingdom, the strongest military headquarters in the south of Canaan.[8] Conquering Sharuhen did more than simply make Egypt a little safer from reinvasion; it turned the south of Canaan into an Egyptian province.

According to General Ahmose's tomb inscriptions, the siege of Sharuhen took six years.[9] If this is true, pharaoh Ahmose probably left his general in charge and headed back home to take care of matters in Memphis, because he died not too long after the capture of Avaris.

It had taken Ahmose twenty years to take back Lower Egypt, and both Manetho and Josephus give him a rule of twenty-five years. He did not enjoy his position as king of all Egypt for long. But for his reunification of Egypt, and his reassertion of native Egyptian rule over the kingdom, Manetho names him the first king of the Eighteenth Dynasty. With this reunification, Egypt enters into a new phase of building, of peace and prosperity, of art and literature: the New Kingdom.

TIMELINE 27

ASIA MINOR/MESOPOTAMIA	EGYPT
Anittas (c. 1790)	Second Intermediate Period (1782–1570)
	Dynasty 13 (1782–1640)
Death of Samsuiluna (1712)	
	Dynasty 14 (1700–1640)
	Hyksos takeover (1663)
Hattusilis I (1650–1620)	*Dynasties 15, 16, & 17*
Mursilis I (1620–1590)	
	Kahmose
Hittite conquest of Babylon (1595)	
Hantili (1590–1560)	
	New Kingdom (1570–1070)
	Dynasty 18 (1570–1293)
	Ahmose I (1570–1546)

Chapter Twenty-Eight

Usurpation and Revenge

In Egypt, between 1546 and 1446 BC,
Tuthmosis III loses the throne to his aunt Hatshepsut
but regains it and conquers the Western Semitic lands

AFTER AHMOSE'S DEATH, his son Amenhotep I took up the reins of power, trampled on the Nubians until they were firmly back within the Egyptian fold, and consolidated his father's victories. But the family line ended there. Amenhotep remained not only childless, but also unmarried for most of his life. His first wife (and full sister) died young, and Amenhotep did not take another.[1]

In an age where pharaohs boasted multiple wives and dozens of concubines, this suggests that Amenhotep's taste didn't run to women. Even so, it is unusual that he didn't marry again. Most ancient rulers who preferred the company of their own sex still managed to produce the heir required for dynastic stability; Amenhotep I remained alone, deeply solitary, and appointed his trusted general to be the next king.

This general, Tuthmosis, was also his brother-in-law. Technically, this made him a member of the royal family; still, his coronation was a major break in the normal father-to-son succession. The mummies of Ahmose, Tuthmosis I, and two of Tuthmosis I's descendants—his son Tuthmosis II and great-grandson Tuthmosis IV—have been so well preserved that their features can be clearly seen. The family resemblance in the Tuthmosis line is startling, and markedly different from the face of Ahmose I.*

Tuthmosis I, elderly when he became king, reigned for only six years. Very

* These four mummies, along with fifty-two more, survived in good shape because they were gathered up and hidden in two groups by Egyptian priests around 1000 BC; the priests hoped to protect them from the increasingly destructive threat of tomb robbers. The first group was discovered in 1881, the second in 1898.

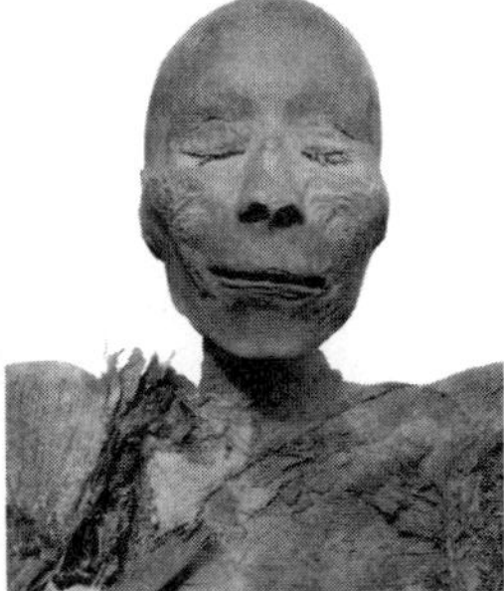
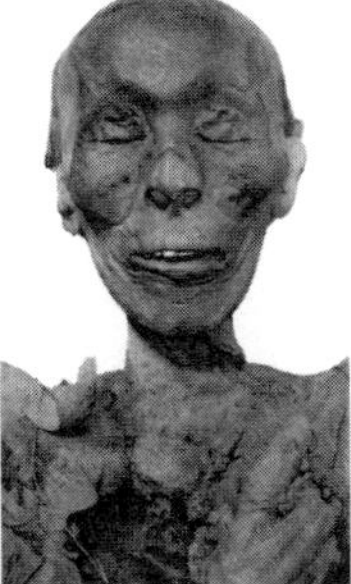
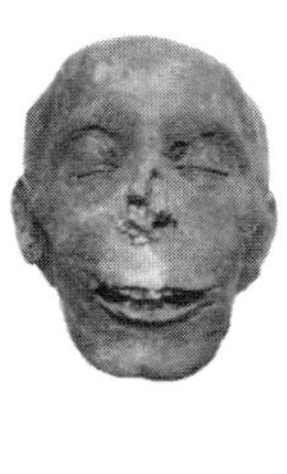

28.1. Kings of Egypt. Ahmose I (far left) does not share the family resemblance of Tuthmosis I, II, and III. Photo credit G. Elliot Smith, Catalogue Général des Antiquités Egyptiennes du Musée du Caire, Cairo

early in his rule, he began to plan his tomb. For some time, the pyramids, which were supposed to inspire awe, had been less than sacred to rank-and-file Egyptians. Tomb robbers had managed to break into almost every pyramid in Egypt; they were, after all, enormous treasure markers that pointed down to burial chambers stuffed with gold. To avoid losing his grave goods, Tuthmosis I planned a new, secret burial place: a cave with painted walls, just as ornate as the inside of any pyramid, but with a hidden entrance. The valley where his cave was located later became known as the Valley of the Kings.*

Unlike his predecessor, Tuthmosis I married at least twice. His most royal wife was Amenhotep's sister, the daughter of the great Ahmose, and mother of two sons and two daughters. But he had also married a lesser wife, who bore him a son.

When he became pharaoh, Tuthmosis appointed first his elder son, and then his second son, as heir. Both died before him. He had no intention of passing the crown to a trusted friend, and his only living male heir was his son by the lesser wife. So in order to strengthen this son's dynastic position, Tuthmosis not only appointed him heir, but married him to one of the daughters of his primary wife: the princess Hatshepsut. When Tuthmosis died, after a reign of only six years, his son became Tuthmosis II; Hatshepsut became queen.

Tuthmosis II had suffered from bad health all his life, and his physical weakness was complicated by his wife's readiness to take over any (or all) of his duties. Hatshepsut is mentioned alongside Tuthmosis II as co-ruler from

* Tuthmosis I was *likely* the first pharaoh to use the Valley of the Kings, but because his mummy itself hasn't been identified (and his name appears on two different Valley sarcophagi), some scholars believe he was buried elsewhere.

the very beginning of his reign. Apparently this did nothing for their marriage; Hatshepsut had only one child by her half-brother, a daughter. After this valiant gesture, during which he apparently closed his eyes and thought of Egypt, Tuthmosis II had no more children by Hatshepsut. He preferred the company of a woman named Iset, whom he never married. When Iset gave birth to a son, Tuthmosis II immediately named the illegitimate baby his heir, which was a slap in the face for his wife.

When Tuthmosis II died before the age of thirty-five, his only son—now Tuthmosis III—was still a child. At once Hatshepsut claimed her right, as the baby's aunt and stepmother, to rule as his regent.

For three or four years at the beginning of the regency, she appears in carvings standing behind the young Tuthmosis III in a properly supporting role. But sometime around 1500, Hatshepsut began to build a huge temple: a mortuary temple, a place of worship which had once stood at the foot of a walkway from a pyramid, and now often served as the primary burial monument itself. This temple was theoretically built in honor of the sun-god Amun. On the east, it faced directly across the Nile at Amun's other, larger temple, the temple at Karnak.[2] Across one wall, Hatshepsut ordered a relief carved: Amun, properly impressive, paying a visit to Hatshepsut's mother. The implication was that Hatshepsut had been conceived by the god himself.

Playing both sides of the paternity card, she also commissioned an engraving announcing that Tuthmosis I, her earthly father, had ordered her crowned true ruler of Egypt before his death. This coronation had taken place in front of the entire court on New Year's Day, and showed that Hatshepsut had the right to claim a Horus-name and rule as King of Upper and Lower Egypt.

Since this story was a complete fabrication, someone from the court might have been expected to protest. But no protest is recorded, which suggests that Hatshepsut had managed to convince powerful court officials that she would be a better ruler than Tuthmosis III, now rapidly approaching the age of accession. Certainly she had the strong support of one of the most powerful men in Egypt, the Chief Steward of Amun: Senenmut. She awarded him, over the course of several years, a dizzying array of titles. He became Chief Architect, Steward of the Royal Ship, Overseer of Amun's Graineries, Overseer of Amun's Fields, and also Overseer of Amun's Cows, Amun's Gardens, and Amun's Weavers.

This made him powerful, but not popular. Senenmut, it was whispered, was much more to Hatshepsut than an advisor. A scrawled graffiti found on the wall of a cave near Hatshepsut's mortuary temple shows a very small Senenmut with a very erect member sneaking cautiously up behind a very large and very masculine Hatshepsut: a rude commentary on the powerful female pharaoh and the ambitious steward.[3]

Hatshepsut never actually deposed the young Tuthmosis III. She simply portrayed herself as the senior of the two rulers. More than one of her statutes show her with the royal headdress and even the formal square beard of a crowned pharaoh. In the mortuary temple, she also had her figure carved celebrating a heb-sed festival, the ritual renewal of power. Tuthmosis III is in these reliefs as well, celebrating alongside the queen. But only Hatshepsut is pictured actually performing the running ritual central to the heb-sed renewal, the ritual that recognizes the pharaoh's ability to make the waters return.[4]

Tuthmosis III's own inscriptions tell us where he spent most of Hatshepsut's reign: well away from Memphis, sent by his aunt to fight in one campaign or another, mostly in the new northern province of Egypt, where the Western Semitic subjects were always threatening to revolt.

She probably hoped that he would fall in battle. That he didn't succumb either to injury or to assassination says much for his wariness, and also suggests that the army may have been less enthralled with Hatshepsut than Senenmut and the folks back at home. Certainly Hatshepsut put almost all of her energy into domestic projects, particularly buildings; in the ancient world, the number of buildings a king put up was considered a direct index of his success, and Hatshepsut wanted no question as to her greatness. The army, meanwhile, had no great triumphs—for almost twenty years.[5]

Twenty-one years after her husband's death, with her co-ruler and stepson now well into his twenties and hardened by years of fighting in exile, Hatshepsut died. Her steward and factotum Senenmut also died, just afterwards.

There is no direct evidence that Tuthmosis III was involved. But just after the deaths, Tuthmosis III returned from the front and began a savage wiping away of his stepmother's name. Her titles were scraped off every monument he could find. The reliefs showing her divine appointment were smashed. He had her statutes thrown into a nearby quarry. Hatshepsut had ordered sunward-pointing obelisks built, in honor of Amun; Tuthmosis III did not smash these, perhaps fearing the god's wrath, but he had walls built around them so that they could not be seen.[6] He also ordered Senenmut's tomb destroyed. He was thirty years old, and it was long past time for him to get to work.

Technically, Tuthmosis III had been king of Egypt for twenty-two years by the time he actually gained the throne. All of those years of impotence had stored up a great deal of ambition. His campaigns, over the next years, were Napoleonic in their intensity.* He became the anti-Hatshepsut, carrying out his greatest endeavors in the area that she had neglected.

* Historian James Henry Breasted was the first to call Tuthmosis "the Napoleon of Ancient Egypt," a title which has stuck.

Tuthmosis III appointed a scribe to travel with the army and record his campaigns. This account is long gone, but the parts of it that were copied into other documents show us the pharaoh's first moves. In the same year that Hatshepsut died, Tuthmosis III made a pass through Canaan. The king of Kadesh, more than halfway along the coast, organized a group of allies to march against the invader. Tuthmosis met them at the city of Megiddo, which stood at a pass through the mountains that ran crossways, cutting off Egypt from Mesopotamia.*

The battle was a rout. Before long, the allies led by the king of Kadesh were retreating back into the city so quickly that soldiers were hauling each other over the walls by their clothing. The Egyptians stopped to plunder the tents outside, which allowed the defenders to swing the gates of Megiddo closed.

Unlike the Assyrians, the Egyptians did not have much experience in attacking city walls; no siege towers or ladders.[7] They had to starve the enemy out. Seven miserable months later, the king of Kadesh surrendered, followed by his allies. The Egyptian army returned home in triumph with treasure, armor, chariots, livestock, prisoners, and grain: the first booty of the restored army, post-Hatshepsut. The men who had refused to assassinate Tuthmosis III were now rewarded for their pains.

This campaign appears to have frightened the countryside. Semitic warlords from nearby cities began sending gifts to Tuthmosis III, doing their best to make peace with the angry young man in the south. Those cities that resisted were attacked, and sacked, in Egyptian campaigns that stretched over the next few years. Joppa, on the coast, tried to make a deal instead of surrendering unconditionally; according to a later story, the king of Joppa agreed to visit the Egyptian commander in order to discuss peace terms, was served a banquet, and then was knocked unconscious and stuffed into a back room. The Egyptian commander went out and told the king's charioteer that the Egyptians had decided to surrender to Joppa, and that the charioteer should return quickly and tell Joppa's queen that her husband was on his way with prisoners. A procession of captive Egyptians soon appeared on the horizon, carrying baskets of plunder from the Egyptian camp. But each basket contained an armed warrior; when the queen of Joppa threw the gates open, the warriors burst out of their baskets and forced the city to surrender.[8]

The city of Ardata was conquered and plundered in a more traditional way.

* This is the first appearance of the city of Megiddo, which had been a crossroads since the days of Abram (see pp. 130–131), as a place of strategic importance. Thanks to its location, Megiddo would be the site of further crucial battles, the last fought in the twentieth century. In Rev. 16:16, armies gather at Megiddo, which the Greek text calls "Armageddon," just before the destruction of the world.

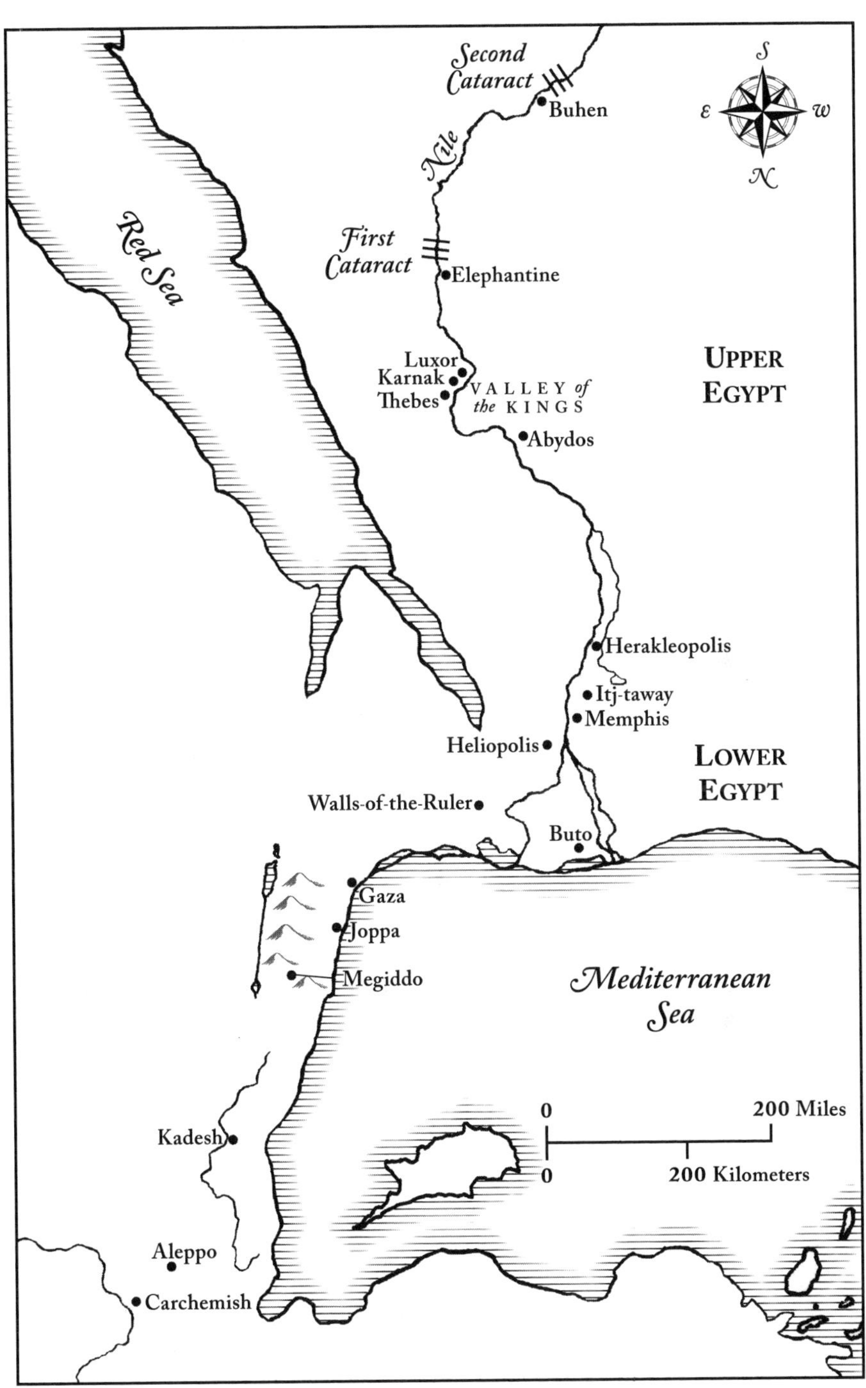

28.1 *Egypt's Greatest Northern Extent*

The walls were stormed and the gates broken down, upon which the Egyptian troops discovered to their great joy that the cellars were all full of wine. They got drunk every day, until Tuthmosis III had had enough of rejoicing. He ordered them to burn the fields and fruit trees, and dragged his soldiers off to the next target.[9]

Tuthmosis III spent almost two decades campaigning into the northern reaches. He worked his way to Kadesh itself and forced its surrender; he claimed Aleppo; he even seized Carchemish, which brought him to the edge of Asia Minor. By the last years of his reign, Tuthmosis III had succeeded in redeeming the years of his exile. His Egypt stretched almost to the Euphrates, a northern border never matched again.

TIMELINE 28

ASIA MINOR/MESOPOTAMIA	EGYPT
Anittas (c. 1790)	Second Intermediate Period (1782–1570)
	Dynasty 13 (1782–1640)
Death of Samsuiluna (1712)	
	Dynasty 14 (1700–1640)
	Hyksos takeover (1663)
Hattusilis I (1650–1620)	*Dynasties 15, 16, & 17*
Mursilis I (1620–1590)	
	Kahmose
Hittite conquest of Babylon (1595)	
Hantili (1590–1560)	
	New Kingdom (1570–1070)
	Dynasty 18 (1570–1293)
	Ahmose I (c. 1570–1546)
	Hatshepsut-Tuthmosis III (c. 1504–1483)
	Tuthmosis III (alone) (c. 1483–1450)

Chapter Twenty-Nine

The Three-Way Contest

Between 1525 and 1400 BC, the northern Mitanni take away Hittite land in the west and make a treaty with the Egyptians in the south

THE NORTHERN EDGE OF EGYPT, now up near the Euphrates, was never very secure. It was too far away from Memphis, and too close to the Hittites. It also brought the Egyptian border far too close to another enemy.

Centuries earlier—around 2000 BC—a mountain tribe from the slopes of the Zagros had started to wander west. These people, the Hurrians, crossed the Tigris into the center of Mesopotamia and settled in small groups on the edges of cities. By 1700, a few tiny independent Hurrian kingdoms lay in the northern reaches of Mesopotamia, above Assur and Nineveh, and a few Hurrians had wandered even farther west. Hurrian names show up in merchants' records from the Assyrian trading posts, all the way over in Hittite lands.[1]

These Hurrians were nothing like an organized nation, and probably would have remained in their separate scattered villages and walled cities, had a new batch of invaders not shown up to organize them. A splinter group of the Aryans who eventually made their way down into India broke off from their kin, sometime before the migration south, and travelled west into Mesopotamia. Welcomed by the Hurrians, they not only settled in and intermarried with them, but bullied their way into becoming the Hurrian ruling class: the *maryannu*. Maryannu and Hurrians together became the upper and lower strata of a kingdom called, by the surrounding rulers, "the Mitanni."

The Hurrians were not much for writing, so it is difficult to trace exactly what was going on in their lands between 1700 and 1500. But by the time Tuthmosis III began his northwards drive, the Mitanni kingdom had its own established capital at Washukkanni, a little east of the far northern reaches of the Euphrates. The first maryannu king whose name surfaces from the obscurity is Parattarna, who came to the throne during Hatshepsut's dominance,

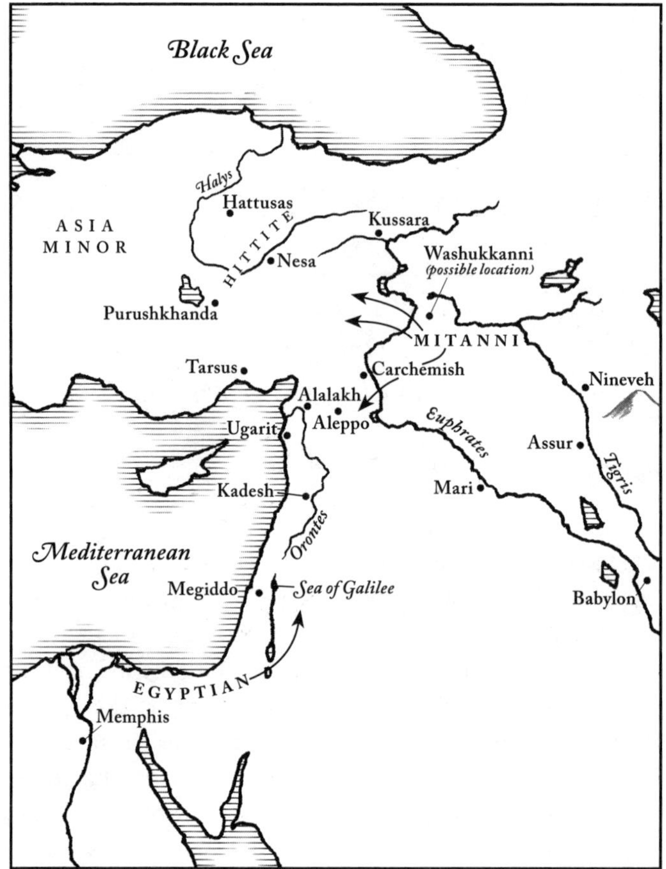

29.1 The Mitanni

probably sometime around 1500. Under his guidance, Hurrian troops marched as far down into Mesopotamia as Assur. This city, which had been swept into the Babylonian kingdom of Hammurabi, had been lost by Samsuiluna; since, it had been ruled by whatever warlord could hold onto it. Now it became a province of the Mitanni kingdom, with its king a vassal serving the Mitanni king.[2]

The Mitanni were not yet strong enough to resist Egypt. In the face of Tuthmosis III's vigorous forwards push, they backed up; one of Tuthmosis III's victory monuments stands on the east bank of the Euphrates, well within Mitanni territory. Egyptian excursions into this land yielded few prisoners, though. The Mitanni king and his forces retreated, strategically, away from possible harm.[3]

In the same year that Tuthmosis III returned to Egypt to die, a king named Saustatar came to the Mitanni throne at Washukkanni.* He began his own empire-building; his troops marched as far east as the distant bank of the Tigris, as far west as Tarsus on the Asia Minor peninsula, and as far south as Kadesh.

The eastern claim doesn't seem to have bothered anyone powerful enough to object. But the push west brought Saustatar into conflict with the Hittites; and his push south, through the Western Semitic lands, ran him head-on into Tuthmosis III's successors.

THE HITTITES, now faced with an aggressive Mitanni king in command of a well-organized army, were not having a good century.

Years of assassinations and constant changes at the palace meant that each new Hittite ruler who came to the throne had to begin from scratch, building support among his own officials and persuading the people of Hattusas that he had the right to rule. This was time-consuming, and left less time and energy for guarding the borders of the empire. Cities on the edge began to break away.[4]

Seventy-five years before Saustatar's push west against the Hittite border, a Hittite named Telepinus had tried to solve this problem. Telepinus was not exactly in the royal line. His brother-in-law, himself a man with no claim to the throne, had hired assassins to carry out an extensive clearing of the royal family. The slaughter wiped out not only all of the princes who currently stood in line to the throne, but also all the heirs of an entirely different family who might claim power once the current rulers were out of the way. Telepinus watched as his brother-in-law planned his coronation, but then got word that the king-to-be was also planning to remove Telepinus himself, as a possible threat. Proactively, Telepinus drove his brother-in-law out of town and proclaimed himself king.[5]

This probably places Telepinus in the best light possible, since this account comes from his own records. However, he was at least well-placed to understand why the Hittite empire was failing: internal struggles over the succession had distracted the rulers from the job of ruling. Early in his reign, he set out to fix this. In a document known as the Edict of Telepinus, he laid out long and detailed rules for the orderly conveying of the crown from one

* No Mitanni archives have been discovered, which means we have no king list, no correspondence to speak of, and no way to establish a definitive king list; all constructions of a Mitanni royal succession are open to question.

generation to the next. The Hittites, he explained in the preface, could only survive if the rules were properly followed. "A prince, the son of the first rank [that is, of the king's chief wife], should become king," he wrote. "If there is no prince of the first rank, a prince of the second rank [son of a lesser wife] can inherit. If there is no prince at all, the husband of a first-rank daughter of the king shall inherit."[6]

The Edict also prescribed penalties for various crimes from sorcery to murder, as Hammurabi had done over two hundred years before. Despite his irregular beginnings, Telepinus was trying to impose the rule of law on a kingdom which had operated almost entirely as a military state. For the first time, the Hittites were presented with the challenge of becoming something like a real kingdom.

By the time of Telepinus's death in 1500, just before Hatshepsut's seizing of the Egyptian throne, the empire had recovered somewhat from the shattering conflicts of the previous years. Unfortunately, Telepinus's Edict, like Hammurabi's Code, did not hold much power without the force of his personality and generalship behind it. His oldest son had died before him, so Telepinus (as prescribed) left the throne to his son-in-law, the husband of his oldest daughter. But this son-in-law soon lost the throne to an assassin, and for the next hundred years the Hittite empire went through another internal struggle during which almost no coherent records were kept. Six kings gained and lost the throne in obscurity, while the edges of the empire again began to flake away. The Hittite army, divided and disorganized, had no chance of resisting Tuthmosis III. When his armies stormed into Carchemish, the Hittites retreated and gave up their land.

Saustatar's invasion of Hittite territory began shortly afterwards. The Hittite army could not resist the Mitanni either; Saustatar pushed westwards to Tarsus with little difficulty. Aleppo paid tribute to him. So did the Hittite cities of Alalakh and Ugarit.

In the middle of all this, the people of Assur took the opportunity to revolt against their Mitanni overlord. Saustatar, without a lot of patience, sent troops down to remind the city who it belonged to; in a gesture both symbolic and practical, he hauled its gold-studded gate back to the capital city of Washukkanni.[7]

As soon as the news of Tuthmosis III's death spread up into the Egyptian-held lands of the north, the Western Semitic cities revolted. Saustatar did everything he could to encourage the revolt against Egypt, including sending his own army down to help out the rebels in Kadesh. Tuthmosis III's son

Amenhotep II, who had just been enthroned, immediately marched an army northwards. By the second year of his reign, he was all the way up near the Mitanni border.

But no major battle took place. The truth was that, under Saustatar, the Mitanni kingdom had grown strong enough to cause Amenhotep II serious trouble. He made a treaty, rather than risk open war.

He did his best in his own land to portray this as a victory: an inscription at Karnak claims that the Mitanni crept to him on hands and knees, asking for peace:

> The Chiefs of the Mitanni came to him, their tribute upon their backs, to seek the peace of His Majesty. . . . A notable event, one not heard of since ancient times. This land which knew not Egypt was asking for His Majesty's pardon![8]

But this was sheer face-saving; Amenhotep II didn't dare attack. No copy of the treaty has survived, but centuries later, a traditional boundary line between the two countries was still observed; it ran along the Orontes river.[9]

Within a twelve-year period, both Amenhotep II and Saustatar passed their thrones to their sons. In Egypt, Tuthmosis IV was enthroned; in the Mitanni capital of Washukkanni, Artadama took over. Sometime around 1425, the two kings reestablished the peace sworn out by their fathers. A formal treaty was put into place, and, even more important, Tuthmosis IV agreed to marry one of Artadama's daughters.

A letter written by Artadama's grandson, some decades later, explains that Tuthmosis IV wrote to Artadama "and requested for himself the daughter of my grandfather. . . . he wrote five and six times, but he did not give her; then he wrote to my grandfather for a seventh time, and then [my grandfather] agreed."[10] This is about as unlikely as Amenhotep's story about the Mitanni abasing themselves in hopes of a treaty. Egyptian pharaohs did not beg for foreign princesses. But the treaty with Egypt had given the Mitanni a whole new respect for their own greatness. Like the palace at Memphis, the Mitanni royal house saw itself as sovereign and mighty, granting its favors graciously to the pleading kings of other countries.

Even if Tuthmosis IV didn't beg for it, the alliance was very good for Egypt, which thereafter dominated its Canaanite holdings with the promised alliance of its good friends. No Western Semitic city, glancing at the huge empire to the south and the equally huge one to the north, dared to revolt, and a frightened peace followed.

TIMELINE 29	
ASIA MINOR/MESOPOTAMIA	EGYPT
Anittas (c. 1790)	Second Intermediate Period (1782–1570)
	Dynasty 13 (1782–1640)
Death of Samsuiluna (1712)	
	Dynasty 14 (1700–1640)
	Hyksos takeover (1663)
Hattusilis I (1650–1620)	*Dynasties 15, 16, & 17*
Mursilis I (1620–1590)	
	Kahmose
Hittite conquest of Babylon (1595)	
Hantili (1590–1560)	
	New Kingdom (1570–1070)
	Dynasty 18 (1570–1293)
	Ahmose I (c. 1570–1546)
Telepinus (1525–1500)	
	Hatshepsut-Tuthmosis III (c. 1504–1483)
Parattarna (Mitanni)	**Tuthmosis III** (alone) (c. 1483–1450)
Saustatar (Mitanni)	
Artadama (Mitanni)	**Tuthmosis IV** (1419–1386)

Chapter Thirty

The Shifting Capitals of the Shang

In China, between 1753 and 1400 BC, the Shang kings move their capital city five different times and finally settle at Yin

TO THE EAST, the Shang dynasty was ruling, in conspicuous virtue, over the territory once held by the Xia.

Little detail survives from these early years of the Shang Dynasty. But the ruins of Shang cities reveal that in the first half of the dynasty's rule—from its traditional beginnings in 1766 until around 1400—the Shang rulers had no single capital. Tradition tells us that the capital city moved five different times in these 350 years. The sites cannot be identified with complete certainty, but archaeologists believe that all of them fell within a circle drawn around the Yellow river, east of the Xia capital, in the land which was most likely Tang's ancestral home.

These shifts reveal a dynasty which, although it managed to keep the crown in the family, did not yet rule with complete authority. During the reign of Tang's heirs, the chaos that had marked the last years of the Xia Dynasty still rippled through the new regime.

TANG'S MOST POWERFUL OFFICIAL was Yi Yin, a man who rose to power either because he gained such a reputation for wisdom, while farming outside the capital Po, that Tang begged him to come and serve in the court; or because he served as Tang's cook and produced extraordinary meals (the Grand Historian Sima Qian records both stories).[1]

Whatever his origins, Yi Yin was a capable administrator but a wild card in the Tang court. A later story suggests that he temporarily defected at one point, going over to the Xia enemy for some time before returning to his previous loyalty.[2] More ominously, he was at the helm of the palace during a wholesale dying off of the Shang heirs.

When Tang died, after a respectably long rule of thirty years, Yi Yin was still serving as chief court official. Tang had appointed his oldest son to be his heir, but the young man "died before he was enthroned." The second son (presumably younger and more malleable) took the throne instead, but died after two years; then the third and final son was coronated and, after four years, died as well. Barring hemophilia or suicidal tendencies, this pattern of deaths is more than a little odd.

Sima Qian, who relates these details, attaches no suspicion to Yi Yin; and indeed, Yi Yin made no direct attempt to seize the throne after the death of the final son. Instead, he presided over the accession of Tang's grandson T'ai Jia, the child of the oldest son who had died six years before. But his actions suggest canniness, not loyalty. Yi Yin knew that the nobles of China would not accept the enthronement of an ex-cook (or ex-farmer); he was working his way towards a kingship in all but name. Thanks to the rapid decease of all of Tang's sons, the throne was now held by a child, and that child was under Yi Yin's guidance.

According to Sima Qian, Yi Yin spent the first year of T'ai Jia's rule writing out precepts for the young king to follow. These precepts were apparently not followed: three years after T'ai Jia's coronation, "he became dull and tyrannical; he did not follow Tang's precepts and discredited Tang's prestige."[3] As the boy was probably still very young, it's difficult to see how tyrannical he could have been. More likely, he had yanked with impatience at the puppet-

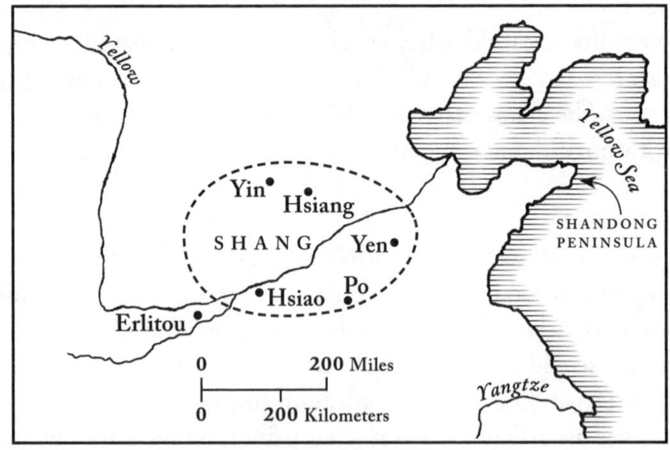

30.1 The Shang Capitals

master's strings. In response, Yi Yin promptly declared that the virtue of the throne was in danger, and sent the young king off into detention at a palace twenty-five miles out of town. For the next three years, "Yi Yin was in charge of the administration on the emperor's behalf, and in doing so received the feudal lords."

Sima Qian ends the story on a happy note. After three years in exile, the young emperor "repented his errors, accepted the blame himself, and returned to good behavior." Presumably this means he was now ready to be guided by Yi Yin, who welcomed him back and turned the kingdom over to him. "Yi Yin," Sima Qian concludes, "thought him to be excellent."

A variant on this story, told in other sources, may be closer to the truth; T'ai Jia escaped from the palace where he was guarded, returned to his capital city, and assassinated the kingmaker.

No detailed accounts of the reigns of the next fourteen Shang kings have survived, but we know that under the tenth Shang king, Chung Ting, a certain unrest seized the dynasty. Chung Ting moved his capital to Hsiao. Excavations at the site thought to be Hsiao have revealed a city surrounded by a stamped earth wall ninety feet thick in places, and nearly thirty feet high. The wall took, perhaps, eighteen years for ten thousand laborers to complete.[4] The Shang king may not have governed his realm with the authority of the Egyptian pharaoh, but he had enough power to compel labor from the multitudes.

Despite the immense Shang investment in this wall, less than two generations later, the twelfth Shang king moved the capital again, this time to Hsiang. His heir, the thirteenth Shang king Tsu Yi, packed up and went to a fourth capital, Keng. When Keng was destroyed by a flood, Tsu Yi transferred the Shang headquarters to the city of Yen, thus becoming the only Shang king to occupy three capital cities during his reign.

This constant migration of the Shang capital city is puzzling. Every other ancient kingdom (so far as we know) tried to maintain a particular city as a capital, only deserting it in the face of hostile invasion or natural disaster. Yellow river flooding may have had something to do with the wandering Shang capital. But Shang China was even more isolated than Egypt had been centuries before; it had no water trade with other nations, no land routes to the outside.

The hostility of nearby village patriarchs may have been the nearest equivalent to foreign invasion. Sima Qian says that these were years of rising and falling power. During the reigns of some Shang kings, the feudal lords "came to pay homage," but other monarchs found that the feudal lords stayed away and refused to visit the capital with tribute.[5] The power of the Shang king was anything but unquestioned. Possibly that huge stamped wall was built for protection against the Shang's own countrymen.

Sometime around 1400, the nineteenth Shang king, P'an Keng, decided to move the capital city to the other side of the Yellow river. The courtiers objected, resisting to the point of revolt. But P'an Keng was adamant.

A story surviving from P'an Keng's reign hints at the wily flexibility that preserved the Shang crown, even in the face of upheaval. Three different ancient texts record P'an Keng's response to his courtiers when they balked at his announcement that it was time to desert the old capital city:

> I have consulted the [oracle] and obtained the reply: "This is no place for us." When the former kings had any important business, they gave reverent heed to the commands of Heaven. In a case like this especially they did not indulge the wish for constant repose; they did not abide ever in the same city. Up to this time the capital has been in five regions. . . . [We must] follow the example of these old times . . . following the meritorious course of the former kings.[6]

In this tale, P'an Keng takes the constant shifting of the capital from city to city—a history which surely demonstrates weakness—and offers it as a tradition hallowed by age and stamped with divine approval. His ancestors did not move their seat of government because they could not control the turmoil around them. Instead, they moved because they refused to wallow in "constant repose." The difficulties of the past are recast as proof of strength.

The strategy worked, and Yin became the center of a newly strong court. "The Yin way of government again prospered," Sima Qian writes, "and all the feudal lords came to court to pay homage, for [P'an Keng] followed Tang's virtuous conduct."[7] P'an Keng himself, despite forcing his followers into an unwanted migration, became the object of his people's love. After his reign, his younger brother took his place, at which point those same noblemen of China who had "borne resentment, not wanting to move," instead "longed for P'an Keng."

The Hittite kings tore their kingdom apart fighting over the seat of power. Instead of resisting, the Shang bent. Instead of taking up arms against opposition, they shifted and changed their ground, and held China's throne for centuries.

TIMELINE 30

EGYPT	CHINA
	Shang Dynasty (1766–1122)
	Tang
Dynasty 14 (1700–1640)	**T'ai Jia**
Hyksos takeover (1663)	
Dynasties 15, 16, & 17	
	Chung Ting (Hsiao)
Kahmose	**Ho T'an Chia** (Hsiang)
New Kingdom (1570–1070)	
Dynasty 18 (1570–1293)	**Tsu Yi** (Keng, Yen)
Ahmose I (c. 1570–1546)	
Hatshepsut-Tuthmosis III (c. 1504–1483)	
Tuthmosis III (alone) (c. 1483–1450)	
Tuthmosis IV (1419–1386)	**P'an Keng** (Yin) (c. 1400)

Chapter Thirty-One

The Mycenaeans of Greece

On the Greek peninsula, between 1600 and 1400 BC,
Mycenaean cities fight with their neighbors
and carry on trade by sea

WHILE THE MINOANS of Crete were descending into increasing shabbiness and disorder, the cities on the peninsula north of the island were growing greater.

By 1600, the people of Mycenae had begun to bury their rulers in graves well stocked with treasure, high on a central hill. Whoever these kings were, they had gained enough power over their subjects to be treated with honor in death. But their authority didn't extend very far beyond Mycenae's walls. The royal palace at Mycenae was matched by another that dominated the city of Thebes, to the northeast; a third palace stood at Pylos, on the southwest coast, and a fourth was built at Athens, just across a short expanse of land.[1] The cities on the Greek peninsula, divided from each other by mountain ridges, ruled over themselves from their earliest days.*

Despite this independence, the cities shared trade, a language, and a culture. It is from the city of Mycenae, the largest on the peninsula, that the culture takes its name; as far as the historian is concerned, Thebes, Athens, and Pylos were all inhabited by Mycenaeans.

A tradition preserved by the Greek historian Plutarch (among others) tells us that the Minoans and the Mycenaeans fell out with each other very early.

* The term "Greek" is anachronistic. The classical civilization of "Greece" comes much later; but "Greece" is a convenient name for the peninsula, which, like China, is a fairly well defined geographical area. Also there is a connection, however weak and mythological, between the Mycenaean cities and the culture of classical Greece; the Mycenaeans are, most likely, the people Homer calls the Achaeans (or, elsewhere, Danaans or Argives: the earliest of the "Greek" heroes). For an extensive discussion of Greek origins and the timetable of Mycenaean culture, see William Taylour, *The Mycenaeans*.

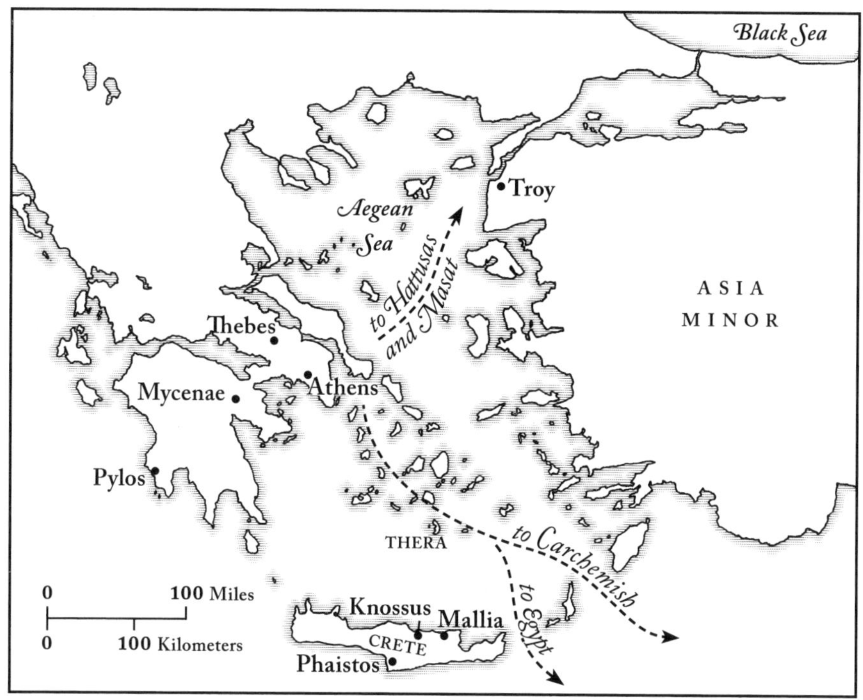

31.1 The Mycenaeans

One of Minos's sons, wandering around on the northern peninsula for some unknown reason, was killed by Mycenaeans; as blood-price for his son, Minos ordered the Mycenaean cities to take up the burden of supplying live boys and girls for the upkeep of the bull-man beneath the Knossos palace.

According to Plutarch, this burden was borne by the city of Athens, on the southeastern coast. For two years the people of Athens sent their sons and daughters to the Minotaur. By the third year, though, the Athenian parents were muttering with increasing bitterness against their king Aegeus, who seemed helpless against the Minoan tyrant. In the face of their swelling rage, the prince Theseus—eldest son of Aegeus—stepped forwards; he would join the third shipful of tribute, the seventh of the young men, and try to fight the Minotaur.

Aegeus, without a lot of hope that his son would return, nevertheless gave the black-sailed tribute ship an additional sail of white. Theseus promised to hoist the white sail if he overcame the Minotaur and came back unharmed. If he fell, like the others, to the Minotaur's appetite, the pilot would unfurl the black sail, so that the father would know the worst before the ship reached port.

Once in Crete, Theseus and the other victims were sent into the Labyrinth, to be hunted through the passages by the Minotaur until they were either eaten or died from exhaustion, unable to find their way out. But Theseus caught the eye of Minos's daughter, Ariadne. She gave him, in secret, a ball of string; when he was taken to the maze, he placed the ball on the ground at the Labyrinth's gate and followed it as it rolled slowly down towards the sunken center. He reached the monster's lair, killed the Minotaur, and then traced the string back out (having had the forethought to attach the end of it to the doorpost).

He then collected the other prisoners and fled back towards home, having first "bored holes in the bottom of the Cretan ships to hinder their pursuit."[2] But in the flush of triumph, Theseus forgot to change the ship's sail. Seeing the ominous black triangle on the horizon, Aegeus threw himself off the cliff near Athens into the sea. Theseus arrived, in victory, to a weeping city; the emerald sea just beyond it was known as the Aegean afterwards, in his father's memory.

BITS OF HISTORY glint from the facets of this myth. The Mycenaean skill at sea is on display in Theseus, staving in ship bottoms and piloting his ship home. In the Iliad, set down in writing some eight centuries later, the city of Mycenae is credited with sending a hundred ships to the combined Greek fleet: an enormous number of ships which makes Mycenae's king one of the most powerful leaders of the expedition against Troy. But in Homer's day, Mycenae was a shabby little town with no might.[3] The catalogue of ships in the Iliad preserves a much older tradition of Mycenaean naval might.*

The Mycenaean ships were more likely to be loaded with merchandise than with living tribute. Mycenaean pottery made it as far east as Carchemish, and up northeast as far as Masat, to the north of Hattusas; Mycenaean ships sailed south to Egypt, where a cup from Mycenae was buried in style with an official of Tuthmosis III.[4]

But the Mycenaean trade went on chiefly with Minoans of Crete. The kingly graves of Mycenae, the burial places of the so-called Royal Grave Circle, are filled with Minoan pottery, paintings done in Minoan style, and portraits of Mycenaeans in Minoan clothing. The oxhide shields of the soldiers of Knossos are painted with dapples that mimic animal hide; the shields of Mycenae bear the same pattern.[5] And it was from the Minoans that the Myce-

* The exact relationship between the Homeric epics (the Iliad and the Odyssey) and the early cultures on the Greek peninsula is not at all clear. And since archaeologists, historians, and literary scholars all have their own theories, all based on different materials, the relationship is not likely to grow much clearer. Nevertheless it seems safe to assert that the epics, like the Epic of Gilgamesh and the Chinese histories, were passed down orally for many generations and reflect, however weakly, a much earlier time.

naeans learned to write. The Minoans had evolved their own distinct script, following the old pattern that had developed thousands of years before: from seals on goods to pictograms, from pictograms to a streamlined pictographic script. The earliest form of this script survives on a scattering of tablets and stone engravings across Crete, and is generally called "Linear A" to distinguish it from its more sophisticated descendent: "Linear B," the version of Minoan script which spread north to the Mycenaeans.[6]

Despite some shared culture, there was war between the two peoples from the earliest times. The victory of Theseus—a victory of wits and civilization over a brutal and unsophisticated people—mirrors the later Greek disdain for other civilizations. Herodotus himself voices this scorn, explaining that the Greek ruler Polycrates was the first man to field a navy, and establish his rule over the sea: "I discount Minos of Knossos and anyone earlier than Minos who gained control of the sea," Herodotus remarks, in passing; "it remains the case that Polycrates was the first member of what we recognize as the *human* race to do so."[7]

This dislike was sharpened by the competition between the two peoples. The navies of both patrolled the Mediterranean, and it is unlikely that the two fleets existed in perfect peace. The trade with Egypt, which had gold and ivory, was too valuable; any king would have seen the advantage of a monopoly. And Crete boasted a strategic location, right on the trade route south into Egypt.

The Minoan goods found in Mycenaean graves reflect a temporary Cretan dominance. But after the eruption of Thera, the cultural influence between Crete and Greece began to run the other way. Distinctively Mycenaean pottery and cups appeared with greater frequency in Minoan houses, and by 1500 or so, Cretan tombs began to show a distinctively Mycenaean design that had not appeared on the island before.[8] The tribute of Athens to Knossos had reversed itself. Like the victorious Theseus, the Mycenaean cities had gained the upper hand over the island to the south.

Sometime around 1450, the city of Knossos was sacked, although its palace remained standing. The palaces of Mallia and Phaistos were flattened. Across Crete, some towns were abandoned; others shrank, abruptly, as if their young men had fought and fallen, or fled.

No traces of a new culture appear on the landscape. We can only assume that the Mycenaean-Minoan relationship had degenerated still further, from thorny jousting into out-and-out war. The survival of the Knossos palace implies that someone in the invading force needed the Minoan center of government for his own uses; whatever Mycenaean king led the invasion may have used Knossos as his own headquarters.[9]

But life in Crete after the invasion does not appear to have changed remarkably. The tombs remained more or less the same in design, Linear B continued in use, the pottery of the Minoans did not suddenly alter.[10] By the time of the takeover, the Mycenaean invaders were much like the Minoans. Their arrival was more like a sibling takeover, a formal change in leadership between two countries that had already been exchanging breath for centuries. The Minoans had been infiltrated, changed from within; the Labyrinth had been breached.

TIMELINE 31

CHINA	GREEK PENINSULA
Shang Dynasty (1766–1122)	
Tang	
T'ai Jia	
Chung Ting (Hsiao)	
Ho T'an Chia (Hsiang)	
	Mycenaean royal graves (c. 1600)
Tsu Yi (Keng, Yen)	
	Mycenaean invasion of Crete (c. 1450)
P'an Keng (Yin) (c. 1400)	

Chapter Thirty-Two

Struggle of the Gods

Between 1386 and 1340 BC, one pharaoh makes strategic alliances, the next changes the religion of Egypt, and the captive Hebrews disappear into the desert

THE ALLIANCE BETWEEN the Mitanni princess and the Egyptian pharaoh Tuthmosis IV, which sealed the treaty between the two countries, was apparently a success; their son Amenhotep became the next pharaoh.*

Judging from the length of his reign, Amenhotep III was still in his teens when he came to the throne around 1386. His reign was marked by the growing peace and wealth of Egypt's cities. Amenhotep III's inscriptions don't record battles; they describe the feats of a king with plenty of leisure time on his hands. According to one inscription, he killed 102 lions in the first ten years of his reign, a favorite sport of Egyptian kings.[1] Another credits him with killing fifty-six wild bulls in a single day on a wild-cattle hunt. (Apparently the bulls were penned into an enclosure before he started hunting, which made the task a little easier.)[2]

Egypt's trade flourished; among the objects found at Mycenae are several with Amenhotep III's name inscribed on them. And although the king made the obligatory trip down into Nubia to put down yet another revolt, the battle was small in scope. The palace account of the campaign tells us that Amenhotep,

> . . . heir of Ra, son of Ra, beloved of Ra. . . . His Majesty led on to victory; he completed it in his first campaign of victory.[3]

* There is an ongoing debate about this. Amenhotep III's mother, Mutemwai, cannot be absolutely identified with Artadama's daughter, but there are strong arguments in her favor (for one, she was not Tuthmosis IV's chief wife).

This single-campaign war is the only one of Amenhotep's whole reign. Although he gave himself the title "Smiter of the Asiatics," this was pure public relations; he never smote any Asiatics at all. He didn't actually need to, as his father and grandfather had established the kingdom for him.

Instead, he built. He dug a lake a mile long so that his chief wife could go boating in comfort, in a royal boat named *Aten Sparkles*, after the god of the sun-disk. He built a huge new palace for his own use; he added to the Temple of Amun, at Karnak, and built a virgin temple to the sun-god in the nearby city of Luxor; he constructed a huge mortuary temple for himself, with two enormous seated statues of himself, one on either side. The statue on the right, according to ancient witnesses, moaned loudly at dawn and dusk: "It gives out the sound of a voice, when the sun's rays strike it," the Roman historian Tacitus noted.[4] This was probably because the stone warmed and cooled quickly, but it gave the locals the shivers. He opened new quarries and mines, built a Memphis residence for himself, and erected shrines at various places farther south along the Nile.[5] And he married, promiscuously, as many princesses as he could find. At least seven daughters of minor kings from the Mesopotamian and Western Semitic lands came to Amenhotep III's palace as brides.

This was politically expedient, but apparently also to his tastes. A tablet sent to the governor of Gaza, who watched out over the southernmost Western Semitic lands for the pharaoh, remarks, "I have sent you this to inform you that I am sending you [a court official] . . . to fetch beautiful women. . . . Total women, forty, at forty pieces of silver each. Send very beautiful women, but make sure none of them have shrill voices. And then the king your lord will say to you, 'That is very good.' "[6]

Like his father, Amenhotep III made a gesture of peace towards the Mitanni kingdom, still strong and a looming threat in the north. The Mitanni king Artadama—his own maternal grandfather—had passed the throne on to his son Sudarna II. When Amenhotep III came to the throne, Sudarna had been ruling his own Mitanni empire for ten or twelve years.

Amenhotep III sent to his uncle for a bride and was given in return a royal princess (probably his own cousin). She arrived with 317 attendants,[7] reflecting her importance in her own kingdom if not in Amenhotep's; she became one of the pharaoh's minor wives. When Sudarna II was succeeded, not too much later, by his own son Tushratta (the brother of Amenhotep's princess), Amenhotep III sent north again with another offer of marriage. Tushratta agreed to the alliance, which bound the Mitanni and Egyptian royal houses together with a double knot, and sent his own daughter south. Now Tushratta's sister and daughter were both in the Egyptian harem,[8] and Tushratta himself had become simultaneously Amenhotep's father-in-law, brother-in-law, and cousin, thus continuing the Egyptian tradition of unsnarlable genealogical knots.

But it seems that Amenhotep III was not above playing a double game against his cousin/father-/brother-in-law and his cousin/father-/brother-in-law's empire. He was also receiving, quietly, envoys from the city of Assur, which lay under Mitanni overlordship; the vassal king of Assur, Assur-nadin-ahhe II, was surreptitiously strengthening his city's fortifications in preparation for revolt.[9]

Amenhotep III had no business welcoming Assur's diplomats at all. Mitanni vassals were not supposed to negotiate with foreign powers as though they were independent. However, the pharaoh not only welcomed the envoys, but sent them back home with money for the fortifications, earning Assur's gratitude and a possible ally against any aggression from the north.

Around the same time, he negotiated a secret treaty with the new king of the Hittites, sworn enemies of the Mitanni. This king, an energetic young man named Suppiluliuma, had inherited his position from a long line of entirely undistinguished predecessors; and he too was slightly worried about the looming Mitanni juggernaut. When Amenhotep III approached him for an alliance ("Let us establish only the most friendly relations between us," the pharaoh had proposed), the Hittite king agreed.[10]

Nor was that the end of Amenhotep's arrangements. He also married the daughter of the Kassite king of Babylon, a man much older than himself; when the king's son succeeded, he sent off with an offer for the son's daughter as well.

This was the same technique he had used with the Mitanni royal house. But the king of Babylon showed an unexpected willingness to cross the will of the pharaoh. In his letters, he objects that he hasn't heard anything from his sister in years:

> Here you are asking for my daughter in marriage. But my sister, whom my father gave you, is already there with you. And no one has seen her, to know whether she is alive or dead.[11]

Amenhotep III retorted,

> Did you ever send an ambassador here who knows her, who could speak with her and recognize her? You've only sent me nobodies instead—an assherder as a messenger![12]

He then pointed out, tartly, that the Babylonian king had a reputation for giving daughters happily away to anyone who offered gold in return.

The rude implication that Babylon's real concern was a better bride-price was ignored by the Babylonian king, who apparently didn't expect courtesy from Egypt anyway. By return message, he suggested that he take an Egyptian princess as *his* wife instead, but this met with no joy from Amenhotep: "From time immemorial," the pharaoh snapped, "no daughter of a king of Egypt is given to anyone."[13] Amenhotep would negotiate, scheme, and marry to create alliances, but he always had the inferiority of his allies firmly in mind.

As THE THIRTIETH YEAR of his reign approached, Amenhotep III planned his first jubilee festival, the heb-sed renewal of his power.

In this particular jubilee, the Nile and its waters were less in view than another divine entity: the sun. The sun-god Ra was one of Egypt's oldest, and since the beginning of his reign, Amenhotep III had proclaimed a special devotion to him. He had taken, as one of his royal names, the title "Ra is the lord of truth," and his inscriptions refer to him variously as "heir of Ra," "chosen one of Ra," and "image of Ra in the Two Lands."[14]

Like Amenhotep's marriages, this devotion was a convenient combination of personal tastes and political shrewdness. After a Fifth Dynasty surge in power,* the priests of Ra had given way somewhat to the priests of Amun, the ancient father-god, the First Cause in the Egyptian pantheon. Amun had always been a rather amorphous deity; in fact, one of his appearances was a non-appearance, as an invisible presence. He was nicknamed "The Hidden One," and was prone to borrow identities, temporarily claiming the powers of some other deity to mask his mysterious true nature.[15] This gave his priests plenty of flexibility. As the titles of Hatshepsut's vizier reveal, to be a priest of Amun was to claim ownership over practically any part of Egypt's wealth.†

By worshipping Ra as his personal deity, Amenhotep III freed himself from the authority of Amun's priests—and also avoided contributing any more land or wealth to Amun's temple. Apparently the sun-god Ra showed his gratitude by welcoming Amenhotep III into the pantheon; on a relief from around the time of the festival, Amenhotep's son bows down to worship his father, who stands high in the place of the sun.[16]

This is slightly unusual, since Amenhotep IV, the son of the king, rarely appeared on his father's monuments, almost as though Amenhotep III hoped to keep him out of the view of his future subjects. He had already assigned the young man a position as viceroy of the kingdom of Kush, the name for the far south of Nubia (or "Upper Nubia"; the Upper Nubian kingdom of Kush was centered around the Third Cataract, while the northern part of Nubia,

* See chapter 15, p. 115.
† See chapter 28, p. 208.

"Lower Nubia," was known as Wawa). Putting the heir to the throne so very far away suggests that Amenhotep III hoped to keep the next claimant as far from the throne as possible.

But he could not put off the inevitable forever. In the thirty-seventh year of his reign, Amenhotep III began to suffer from a sickness which drew itself out into an approach to death. His teeth, preserved in his mummy, were badly abscessed and must have pained him continually; perhaps this final sickness was a spreading infection.[17] His Mitanni cousin/father-/brother-in-law Tushratta sent help, in the form of a statue of the goddess Ishtar, taken from Assur decades before. We have Amenhotep's words of thanks, but the Mesopotamian goddess apparently had no power in Egypt; not long after Ishtar passed the Delta, Amenhotep III died.

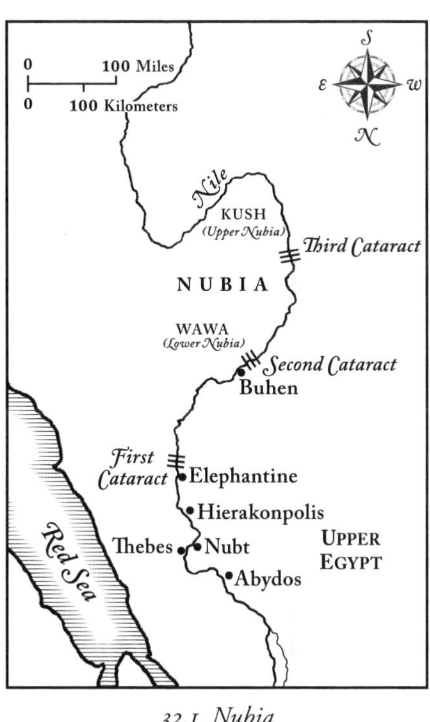

32.1 Nubia

During his extraordinarily long reign, Egypt had reached an unprecedented peace and prosperity. Amenhotep IV, returning from his Nubian exile to take his father's place, had a lot to live up to. He chose to outdo his father in devotion. Amenhotep III had worshipped the sun-god Ra; Amenhotep IV started an entire new religion, the worship of the sun itself.

The disk of the sun itself was called "the Aten," and had not gone unrecognized in the past; it was simply one aspect of the sun-god Ra. But in the hands of Amenhotep IV, the sun-disk became something new. Rather than a god shaped like a mortal being, as Osiris and Horus and Ra himself were, the sun-disk was an abstract representation of the divine itself: the manifestation of a single power. In its glare, the other gods of the pantheon vanished. The sun was not merely the chief power. It was the only power. The gods of the Egyptian pantheon had wives and consorts; Aten was alone and self-sufficient. The gods of the Egyptian pantheon appeared in the shapes of mortal beings; Aten had no form. The gods of the Egyptian pantheon had stories; Aten had no story at all.

Amenhotep IV was on his way to becoming a monotheist.

In the fifth year of his reign, Amenhotep IV announced to his priests and to his courtiers that he had received a divine word: Aten had pointed out to him a place, never before built on, where a new capital city would be erected in honor of the god.

The site was a dry, sandy, waste plain, east of the Nile, beneath a half-circle of cliffs, with hardly any fertile land nearby. It was a boiling hot hole where the stone walls collected the sun's heat while the cliffs blocked breezes. But here, Amenhotep IV intended to build the city of Akhet-Aten. As construction began, he also changed his own name. From the ninth year of his reign, he was almost universally inscribed as *Akhen-aten*: worshipper of the sun.[18]

Now the ruler of Egypt was no longer simply "beloved of Ra"; he was the child of Aten, son of the sun. Aten had no other god before it, but the pharaoh remained the sole earthly incarnation and representative of this deity. Akhen-aten's own power came directly from his knowledge of the One. He was at pains to explain this in a long creed, which he wrote himself:

> You arise on the horizon of Heaven, O Living Aten, Beginniner of Life. . . . When you set on the horizon, the earth is in darkness, as though it were in death. . . . The earth brightens when you arise on the horizon. . . . How many are your works! They are hidden from the sight of men, Only Divine, to whom there is no one who bears a likeness. . . . You are in my heart, but there is none other who knows you except for your son, Akhenaten. You have made him wise in your plans and in your power.[19]

Once he was settled in his new city, Akhenaten ordered the name of Amun wiped out of inscriptions. Workmen were to cover it with plaster and re-inscribe it with the name of Aten.[20] Amun was not a true god; he was a distorted, corrupted version of the true divine, and his powerful priests were now out of luck. The destruction was so complete that barely an instance of Amun's name survived.

The other gods fared no better. Akhenaten ordered new temples built to Aten, with open centers where the sun could fall; but other temples were closed, the priests turned out and forbidden to sacrifice. No other priests replaced them. Aten needed no priests, no religious bureaucracy that might thwart the pharaoh's aims. Neither the god nor the god's representative on earth would tolerate shared power.

Name-change notwithstanding, Akhenaten was a true son of his father.

Sometime within a hundred-year span of Akhenaten's reign, another religious and political upheaval took place, when the descendents of Abraham fled from Egypt.

According to the Pentateuch, Abraham's descendents had multiplied into a nation: the Hebrews, who had lived as shepherds and nomads in the Western Semitic lands until a famine threatened to wipe them out. They took themselves and their flocks down to well-watered Egypt, where they settled somewhere in the north and prospered.

The biblical story describes an Egyptian population uncomfortable with this energetic and—more to the point—fertile people, who showed signs of outgrowing the borders of their settlement and spilling over into the rest of the country. The Egyptians had always despised the "vile Asiatics" to the north, and invasions from the Western Semitic lands were a constant danger. Not only that, but Egypt had in recent memory been captured by Western Semites—the Hyksos, who (like the Hebrews) had lived in Egypt for decades before making their move. So it is hardly surprising that the presence of yet another prospering immigrant people might make them nervous.

The book of Exodus tells us that the pharaoh of Egypt rounded up the Hebrews as pressed labor for his building projects, and (when this did not decrease the surplus population) ordered all male Hebrew children thrown into the river. The mother of one of these children hid him for three months. When she realized that he had become too noisy to conceal any longer, she made a papyrus basket, sealed it with tar, put the baby in it, and set it in the reeds by the side of the Nile, right near the place where the Egyptian princesses came down to bathe. A princess arrived, with a flock of attendents behind her, and found the baby. She recognized him as one of the Hebrews, but decided to adopt him anyway. The baby grew up in the palace, under the name of Moses.

On the face of it, a princess's adoption of a Hebrew baby seems unlikely to exist alongside this hostility. But we know that the pharaohs from Tuthmosis IV on married the daughters of eastern royalty with regularity, meaning that this princess could easily have been of Western Semitic stock. She may well have known the story of Sargon, who floated as a baby down the Euphrates:

> My mother conceived me in secret, she gave birth to me in concealment.
> She set me in a basket of rushes,
> she sealed the lid with tar.
> She cast me into the river, but it did not rise over me.

Sargon's birth story served as a seal of chosenness, a proof of his divinity. Surely the mother of the Hebrew baby knew it, and made use of it in a desperate (and successful) attempt to place her own baby in the line of the divinely chosen.

The reality followed on her masquerade. Moses, grown, left Egypt and then heard the call of the God of Abraham: he was to return to Egypt and lead all the Hebrew people out of slavery, back up to the land God had promised to Abraham's descendents. When he arrived at court, the pharaoh (no doubt recognizing the Hebrew adoptee who had grown up in the palace; possibly the two men were much of an age) refused, indignantly. Each refusal was followed by divine reprisal: ten plagues, each worse than the one before, until the Egyptian resistance finally buckled and the pharaoh agreed to let the Hebrews go.

The Exodus became the central event in the history of the Hebrews, the defining moment around which the entire story of the Jewish nation was structured. But it shows up nowhere in Egyptian chronicles.

This is hardly surprising. The exodus of the Hebrews was a nose-thumbing directed not just at the power of the pharaoh and his court, but at the power of the Egyptian gods themselves. The plagues were designed to ram home the impotence of the Egyptian pantheon. The Nile, the bloodstream of Osiris and the lifeblood of Egypt, was turned to blood and became foul and poisonous; frogs, sacred to Osiris, appeared in numbers so great that they were transformed into a pestilence; the sun-disk was blotted out by darkness, Ra and Aten both made helpless. These are not the kinds of events that appear in the celebratory inscriptions of any pharaoh.

The most conservative dating of the Exodus puts it at 1446, which would have placed it near the end of the reign of Amenhotep II, Akhenaten's great-grandfather.* Other estimates put the Exodus a couple of hundred years later, in the mid–1200s and over a century from Akhenaten himself. A whole range of possibilities exists around this, with a subsection of historians suggesting that the Exodus was more of a gradual seeping out of Egypt back up into the land of the Western Semites, and a smaller subsection suggesting there was no Exodus at all.

For our purposes, it is enough to note that the Hebrews disappear into the

* The 1446 date is based on a straightforward reading of 1 Kings 6:1, which claims that 480 years passed between the Exodus and the building of Solomon's temple (c. 966). Other suggestions for the pharaoh of the Exodus are Rameses II (chapter 34), whose massive building programs provide a good match for the tasks given to the Israelites in slavery, and his successor Merneptah (chapter 38), who is the first pharaoh to make explicit reference to the Israelite nation as such; his victory stele from 1207 reads "Israel is devastated, her seed is no more, Palestine has become a widow for Egypt" (quoted in Peter Clayton, *Chronicle of the Pharaohs*, p. 157). It is actually difficult to see how this quote might line up with a massive departure of the Israelites from Egypt, even though it does testify to the early existence of the Israelites as a recognized people.

TIMELINE 32

MESOPOTAMIA AND ASIA MINOR			EGYPT
MITANNI	ASSYRIA	HITTITE	
			New Kingdom (1570–1070)
			Dynasty 18 (1570–1293)
			Ahmose I (c. 1570–1546)
Telepinus			**Hatshepsut-Tuthmosis III** (c. 1504–1483)
Parattarna			**Tuthmosis III** (alone) (c. 1483–1450)
Saustatar			
			Exodus (earliest date)
Artadama			**Tuthmosis IV** (1419–1386)
Sudarna II			
	Assur-nadin-ahhe II		**Amenhotep III** (c. 1386–1349)
Tushratta		**Suppiluliuma**	
			Akhenaten (c. 1349–1334)

desert, and off the international scene, for some centuries. These years are historically invisible, but theologically central. It is in the desert that their own sacred book is born; in this book, the Hebrew God appears as a single power with no consort, the divine First Cause, the one and only God, who brings life in his own name.

Despite this description, the Hebrew *I am* and the Aten of Egypt share almost no quality beside that of self-sufficiency. The Hebrew God, although not anthropomorphic, is most definitely a personality; Aten is a force. Aten *is* the sun, but the Hebrew God is in no way identified with the created world, and certainly *never* with either sun or moon. He is so far beyond the disk of the sun that it could not begin to represent him. The two monotheistic movements were close in time—but in no other way.*

* For at least a century, the theory that Akhenaten trained Moses in monotheism and then set him loose in the desert has floated around; it still pops up occasionally on History Channel specials and PBS fund-raisers. This has absolutely no historical basis, and in fact is incredibly difficult to square with any of the more respectable dates of the Exodus. It seems to have originated with Freud, who was certainly not an unbiased scholar in his desire to explain the origins of monotheism while denying Judaism as much uniqueness as possible.

Chapter Thirty-Three

Wars and Marriages

Between 1340 and 1321 BC, Assyrians and Hittites destroy the Mitanni, Tutankhamun undoes Egypt's religious reforms, and a Hittite prince almost becomes pharaoh

UP IN THE LAND OF THE MITANNI, the king Tushratta was growing increasingly worried about the Hittites. Their energetic new king Suppiluliuma was building up his army, over there on the other side of the Taurus Mountains, and Tushratta needed help to keep the Hittites away.

Egypt was the logical choice of ally. Akhenaten, for all his preoccupation with devotional matters, was still the king of the most powerful empire around. He also happened to be Tushratta's nephew (as well as something like a grandson-in-law, since two generations of Mitanni women had already married into the Egyptian royal family). Tushratta proposed one more match, between the pharaoh and his own daughter; Akhenaten agreed to the marriage, and Tushratta's daughter went south.

But the Mitanni king found himself increasingly annoyed by the offhand treatment he got from his nephew. In letters exchanged by the two kings, Tushratta complains that the gold sent north as a bride-price isn't up to snuff: "It doesn't look much like gold," one letter remarks. "My people say that gold in your country is more common than dirt, and perhaps, because you love me so much, you did not wish to send me something so common and so have sent dirt instead."[1]

After this tart comment, Tushratta's notes to his new son-in-law grow steadily more annoyed. He reminds Akhenaten that his father Amenhotep IV treasured Tushratta's friendship (which, given Akhenaten's attempts to outshine his father's shade, may not have been the wisest move); he complains that his envoys have been hanging around the Egyptian court for almost four years, waiting for the pharaoh to pay attention to them; soon after, he points out that he has been waiting six years for an answer to a query sent down to Egypt by messenger.[2]

Despite the ties of marriage, Akhenaten was backing away from the Mitanni alliance. He had a shrewd enough guess about which way the northern wind was blowing: the Hittites were arming, they were strong, and Suppiluliuma was a canny strategist. The Hittite king had already sent the new pharaoh presents as soon as Akhenaten took the throne, a two-edged gesture of kindness meant to remind the new king that the secret treaty between Egypt and Hattusas was still active. "Just as your father and I were desirous of peace between us," Suppiluliuma wrote, not long afterwards, "so now too should you and I be friendly with one another. . . . Let us be helpful to each other."[3] Faced with choosing between the two countries, Akhenaten chose the Hittites.

Tushratta likely knew nothing of the secret treaty, but he could soon see the results. Suppiluliuma, now certain that Egypt would not come to the defense of the Mitanni, began to march east towards the capital city: towards Washukkanni itself. If Tushratta looked south for help, he looked in vain. The court of Akhenaten preserved a dignified silence.

What did arrive was not alliance, but yet another enemy. Assur, which had been subject to the Mitanni for years, had been rearmed in secret by Egypt; now the aid bore fruit. The Assyrian king Assur-uballit (probably the grandson of the king who had first received aid from Amenhotep III) marched his own men up and joined the Hittites, attacking Washukkanni from the south.

Tushratta, assailed from both south and west, pulled his men back out of north Mesopotamia. Assur-uballit instantly claimed the territory for Assur. For the first time since the overthrow of Shamshi-Adad's dynasty, Assur was a kingdom.* Indeed, in his next letter to Egypt, Assur-uballit reclaims the title Great King (while simultaneously asking for further handouts):† "From Assur-uballit," the letter reads, "king of Assyria, Great King, your brother. Gold in your country is like dirt; one simply gathers it up. Why are you so sparing of it? I am building a new palace. Send me more gold for it. When Assur-nadin-ahhe my ancestor wrote to your father, he received twenty talents of gold. . . . If your purpose to me is friendship, send me as much."[4]

This letter, unlike similar messages from Tushratta, apparently gave no offense at all. Perhaps Akhenaten expected no more from Assyrians.

* It is from this point that historians date the Assyrian "Middle Kingdom."

† The salutations in the letters found at Akhenaten's city (the "Amarna letters") do not always make clear which king is writing to which king; in this case, Assur-uballit names himself, but simply calls the pharaoh Great King of Egypt. Because of this ambiguity, and because absolute dating of all of these ancient monarchs is impossible (we can only line them up against each other, and then only when they address each other by name), slightly different reconstructions of the relationship between the countries are possible.

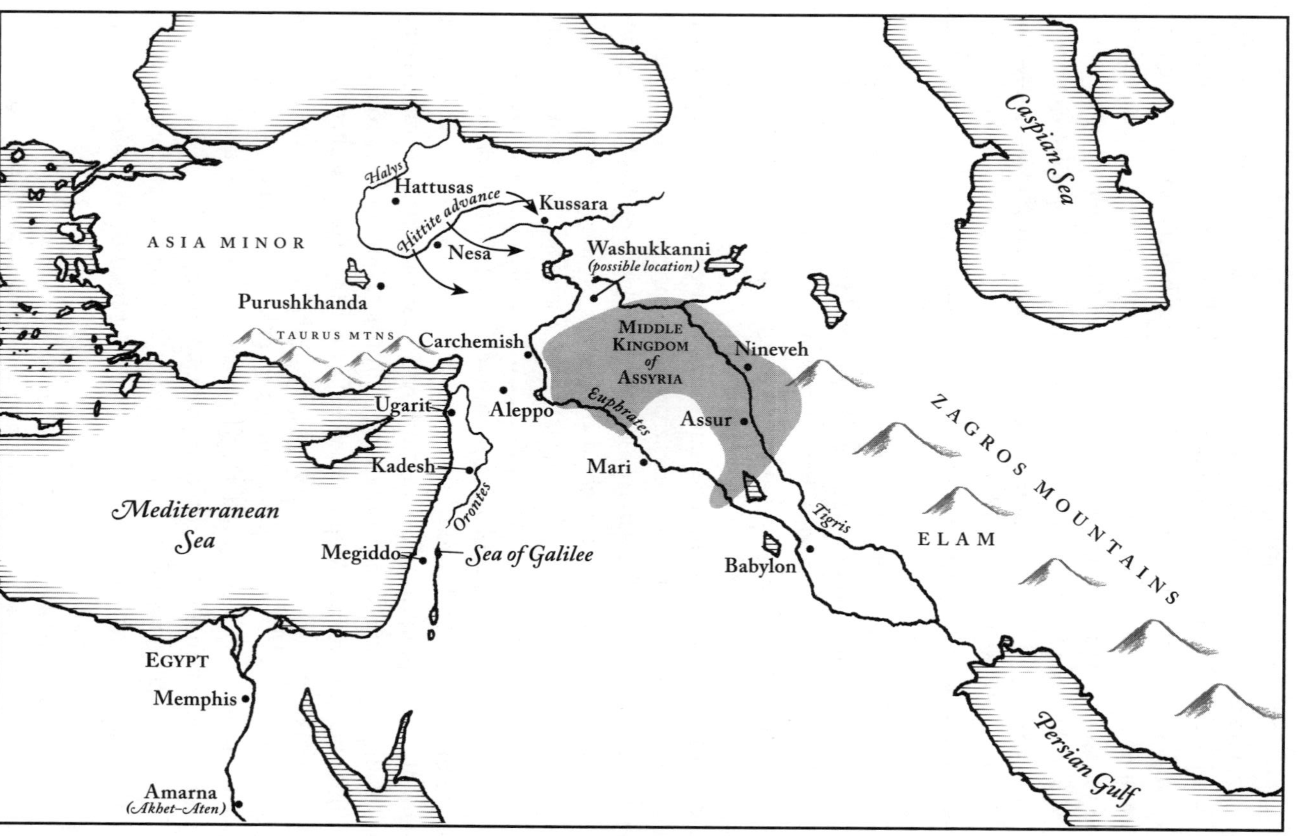

33.1 Assyria's Middle Kingdom

Meanwhile, Tushratta was faring badly on his western front. The Hittites got to the walls of Washukkanni much more quickly than he had expected. Unprepared for a siege, he fled from the city with a few courtiers. But he chose his companions poorly; he was assassinated by one of his own men as he ran.

His oldest son and heir, realizing that resistance was futile, turned back towards the enemy, surrendered, and was treated with honor. But he had no throne. In fact, after the fall of Washukkanni, there was no Mitanni kingdom at all. The Hurrians retreated, in the face of advancing Hittite troops, back across the Euphrates. Here, on the slopes of the Zagros Mountains from which they had come, they lingered: a weak tribal kingdom, ignored for a time by the great powers.

Meanwhile, Suppiluliuma marched down south along the Mediterranean as far as he could without actually starting a fight with the Egyptians. Every city he took had belonged to the Mitanni, not to Egypt (although he did march through Egyptian-held land on his way).[5]

Akhenaten made no objection to this empire-building. But by this point, his inaction was less from friendship than from necessity. The Egyptian army had fought little under Amenhotep IV and less under his son; the soldiers were now unused to war. Plague was spreading across Egypt and up the Mediterranean coast. With plague came poverty. A minor Western Semite king wrote, apologizing for the scarcity of the copper he was sending as tribute; plague had flattened his workforce.

And the royal family itself was suffering. Around the fourteenth year of Akhenaten's reign, his chief wife died, followed not long after by his second wife. Akhenaten, who had three daughters and no sons, decided that his best hope was to try for a male heir by impregnating all three royal princesses.

The strategy failed. All of the babies were girls, and the middle daughter died in childbirth.

Akhenaten married off his oldest girl to a vaguely royal cousin and named the young man his heir. Not long after, the crown princess died. The old pharaoh himself sickened and followed her. The heir was crowned, and sat on the throne for mere days before dying himself. Apparently the plague had reached the royal house.

The courtiers chose a nine-year-old boy named Tutankhaten as king. Whether he was of royal blood is very unclear; certainly he was no son of Akhenaten, although he seems to have grown up in the palace. At nine, he was brought from his schoolroom and made pharaoh, his claim to rule strengthened by a ceremonial marriage to Akhenaten's only surviving daughter: the youngest, who was older than he and already the mother of a princess (by her father).

Tutankhaten was surrounded by advisors and courtiers who had watched Egypt lose hold of the north and battle plague while Akhenaten built his temples to Aten. He had himself seen the royal family die off, one by one. The throne must have seemed like a death sentence: now he sat directly beneath the wrath of the old gods.

So he ignored Suppiluliuma's campaigns from the north and, directed by his regents, took care of more urgent matters. He rejected the name Tutankhaten and renamed himself Tutankh-Amun, to show his loyalty to the ancient First Cause. He followed his advisors' wishes and ordered Akhenaten's name excised from monuments, his inscriptions scraped off reliefs, his statues smashed.* The great city of Aten became known instead as Amarna.

With this done, Egypt had to turn again and face the rest of the world. The Mitanni were no longer a problem, but the Hittites were huge and threatening to the north; Assur-uballit was behaving like an emperor up in the city of Assur; and in the southern part of Mesopotamia, the Kassite warrior-chief ruling in Babylon, Burnaburiash I, had decided to register a protest. He wrote to the young Tutankhamun, suggesting that the new king quit treating Assur-uballit with respect. Now that the Mitanni had relinquished their hold on Assur, Burnaburiash said, the city should belong by right to Babylon. *He* should have control of it, not Assur-uballit, and it was entirely inappropriate for Assur-uballit to be calling himself "Great King."[6] Furthermore, Tutankhamun ought not to be receiving envoys from Assur as though it had the right to conduct its own foreign affairs. "I didn't send those Assyrian vassals to you," Burnaburiash wrote. "Why, on their own authority, have they come to your country? If you love me, they will conduct no business whatsoever. Send them off to me empty-handed."[7]

Tutankhamun appears to have ignored this, since Assyrian envoys continued to show up at the Egyptian court. Assur-uballit, treated as a king, retained his power and built his army; in fact, he kept his throne for almost thirty years.

Eventually Burnaburiash gave up any hope of getting Egypt on his side against Assyria, and took another tack. He suggested that Assur-uballit send his daughter down to marry the Babylonian crown prince, Karaindash. Assur-uballit agreed, likely seeing the marriage as a way to insulate his new empire from southern attacks. The wedding was duly celebrated. Karaindash soon

* The destruction was so complete that it is only with great difficulty (and uncertainty) that we can even reconstruct Akhenaten's reign, so details of his rule vary from historian to historian.

fathered an heir of his own, and the two states, Assyria and Babylon, existed in a delicate peace side by side.

The peace lasted only until Burnaburiash died. Just before his death, he decided to pass over his son in favor of his half-Assyrian, half-Babylonian grandson (leaving the unfortunate Karaindash in the position of royal stud). Perhaps he hoped that the boy would have a chance of claiming Assur's throne too, by right of his royal heritage; this would have brought Babylon and Assur under one crown.

Instead, he had sentenced his grandson to death. The Kassites of the army revolted. As far as they were concerned, the new king was a half-breed with no right to Babylon's throne. They mounted an attack on the palace, assassinated the half-Assyrian king, and put a military government into place.[8]

At this, Assur-uballit claimed the right to come in and straighten things out. The fragmentary letters and inscriptions that survive don't make his actions entirely clear; probably he killed his grandson's murderer. A new king was proclaimed, but it is impossible to say exactly who this new king was, or what part Assur-uballit played in his crowning. All we can say for certain is that Assyria did not take over Babylon's rule. A Kassite king, possibly a younger son of Burnaburiash, remained on the city's throne. At some point during the chaos, Karaindash had apparently been killed.

THE ASSYRIAN-BABYLONIAN MATCH was not the only odd marriage around.

After sitting on the throne for less then a decade, Tutankhamun died, unexpectedly; the circumstances of his death will never be known, but he may have been hit by an arrow. He was buried with great magnificence. Probably his tomb was no more ornate than the tombs of his predecessors, but (unlike the others) it remained unrobbed until November of 1922.

He left behind him no children. His wife Ankhesenamun (like her husband, she had changed her name to honor Amun) had become pregnant twice. Both times she gave birth prematurely and the babies were born dead. Their tiny bodies, embalmed with care, were buried with their father in the royal tomb.[9]

Now, her husband dead, no other male relatives in the royal line living, and with no child of Tutankhamun to look after, Ankhesenamun began to worry about her future. The Egyptian court, after all, was not short on ambitious men who would be glad to take over (perhaps after her unexpected death). Chief among them was her own maternal grandfather, Ay. Ay had served Akhenaten as chief minister, had remained as Tutankhamun's advisor, and was still in the palace: an old weary man who knew where all the bodies were buried. Just as powerful, if lacking the same venerability, was the army's chief general, Horemheb, whose military service had begun all the way back during the reign of Amenhotep III. Despite this long tour of duty, he was only in his forties; he had joined the army at thirteen.

Ankhesenamun, fearing both of these men, came up with an insane plan. She wrote to the Hittite king Suppiluliuma and asked him to send one of his sons down to Egypt. If he would do this for her, she promised, she would marry the son and make him pharaoh.

There is no copy of the letter in Egypt, which suggests that this was a secret arrangement. The letter survived only in the ruins of Hattusas, the Hittite capital:

> My husband died, and I have no son. But you have many. If you would give me one of your sons, I would make him my husband. I cannot pick out one of my servants and make him my husband. . . . and I am afraid.[10]

This was entirely unexpected, and Suppiluliuma was startled. He was on good terms with Egypt, but not *that* good. According to his own records, he sent several spies south to find out whether Ankhesenamun was serious.[11] When they reported back that yes, indeed, there was no heir on the horizon, Suppiluliuma agreed to the proposal and prepared one of his sons for the journey south.

The prince never got there. He was met at the border by a welcoming committee organized by Horemheb; apparently Ankhesenamun, with Suppiluliuma's consent in hand, had broken the news of her plan. Horemheb had not served in the army for decades without knowing that frontal assaults were always more risky than chance happenings. Travelling through the Delta towards his wedding, the Hittite prince accidentally died.

What negotiations then went on in Egypt are unknown. But immediately afterwards, Ay married his granddaughter Ankhesenamun and claimed the throne. His first act was to write Suppiluliuma denying any hand in the prince's death (and shifting the blame neatly over to Horemheb). Suppiluliuma may not have believed this, but he had no chance to avenge his son's death. Before he could get down south with his army, plague struck the Hittite camp, and the greatest Hittite king died.

Ay died soon after, of uncomplicated old age. He had ruled for less than four years. As soon as he was buried, Horemheb declared himself pharaoh. What happened to Ankhesenamun is a mystery. After her marriage to the old man, the Egyptian records never mention her again.

TIMELINE 33

MESOPOTAMIA AND ASIA MINOR			EGYPT
MITANNI	ASSYRIA	HITTITE	
			New Kingdom (1570–1070)
			Dynasty 18 (1570–1293)
			Ahmose I (c. 1570–1546)
Telepinus			**Hatshepsut-Tuthmosis III** (c. 1504–1483)
Parattarna			**Tuthmosis III** (alone) (c. 1483–1450)
Saustatar			
			Exodus (earliest date)
Artadama			**Tuthmosis IV** (1419–1386)
Sudarna II			
	Assur-nadin-ahhe II		**Amenhotep III** (c. 1386–1349)
Tushratta		**Suppiluliuma**	
	Assur-uballit Middle Kingdom of Assyria		**Akhenaten** (c. 1349–1334)
			Tutankhamun (c. 1333–1325)
			Ay (c. 1325–1321)
			Horemheb (c. 1321–1293)

Chapter Thirty-Four

The Greatest Battle in Very Ancient Times

Between 1321 and 1212 BC, the Nineteenth Dynasty of Egypt begins, Rameses II fights the Hittites to a draw at Kadesh, and the Assyrians begin a century of conquest

HOREMHEB MANAGED to hang onto Egypt's throne for twenty-eight years. He finished restoring the Temple of Amun, a job Tutankhamun had started; he ordered the rest of the temple to Aten levelled; and he restored the priesthood of Amun by simply choosing his old army comrades to be priests. Since he was the highest ranking Egyptian officer around, he could be fairly certain that army discipline would trump any tendency for the priest-officers to usurp power.[1] And then he died, well into his eighties, having outlived five sitting pharaohs.

He had no son, and so appointed another soldier to be his heir. This soldier, Rameses I, was the first pharaoh ever with absolutely no blood connection (real or imagined) to any previous royal line. He was not much younger than Horemheb and he died after a year on the throne, having done nothing of interest.

But from this undistinguished beginning, the great Nineteenth Dynasty of Egypt had its beginnings.* Rameses I passed the throne on to his son Seti

* You might wonder why, considering the double break in bloodline after Tutankhamun (and possibly before him, since his lineage is not at all clear), Manetho does not begin a new dynasty with either Ay or Horemheb. The short answer to this is that the general chaos at the end of the Eighteenth Dynasty wreaked havoc not only on the succession itself, but on its later records. Ay took over some of Tutankhamun's monuments as his own; Horemheb did the same to Ay; and the two best-known versions of the Egyptian king list skip straight over Tutankhamun and Ay and go straight to Horemheb. He appears as the last pharaoh of the Eighteenth Dynasty primarily because he claimed that his wife was a sister of Akhenaten's chief wife, which (barely) qualified him as an heir through

(remembered mostly for building temples in every available spot); Seti in turn left the crown to *his* son, Rameses II. Rameses II earned fame for the length of his reign, the number of his building projects, the legendary strength of his army, and for accidentally surviving the biggest battle in the world.

After the murder of Suppiluliuma's son and the great Hittite king's death from plague, the Hittite-Egyptian concord had pretty much shattered. Along the border between the two countries, armed clashes were common. By the time Rameses II came to the Egyptian throne, the Hittite crown had gone to Suppiluliuma's grandson Muwatalli, and Egypt had lost its northernmost holdings; the city of Kadesh, held by Egypt for over a century, had passed into Hittite hands.

At twenty-five, the new pharaoh had already been living an adult life for at least ten years. He had married for the first time at fifteen or so, and had already fathered at least seven children. He had already fought in at least two of his father's campaigns up into the Western Semitic lands.[2] He did not wait long before picking up the fight against the Hittite enemy. In 1275, only three years or so after taking the throne, he began to plan a campaign to get Kadesh back. The city had become more than a battle front; it was a symbolic football kicked back and forth between empires. Kadesh was too far north for easy control by the Egyptians, too far south for easy administration by the Hittites. Whichever empire claimed it could boast of superior strength.

Late in 1275, Rameses II heard from his spies that Muwatalli was nowhere near Kadesh. These were perfect conditions for an attack, and so Rameses II collected an unheard of number of soldiers (according to his own count, twenty thousand divided into four companies, named Amun, Ra, Ptah, and Set) and began his march north. It took at least two months to get anywhere near Kadesh, but Rameses II was reassured when guards at a Hittite outpost, captured and questioned, told him that the Hittite army was still far up in Hittite territory, unlikely to get near Kadesh any time soon. He drew his divisions into battle order, in order of importance of the gods (Amun first, Ra following, Ptah behind, and Set to the rear) and began his approach to the city.

But the outpost had been a plant. Muwatalli was actually just behind

---

the female line; and because he did his best to wipe out all traces of Akhenaten, Tut, and Ay, adding their years of reign to his own so that king lists engraved under his patronage go straight from Amenhotep III to Horemheb. Later, though, he is occasionally listed as the founding pharaoh of the Nineteenth instead of the last of the Eighteenth.

Or you may not have wondered this at all.

Kadesh with forty-eight thousand soldiers, both Hittites and hired mercenaries collected for the occasion. Almost three thousand were mounted in chariots, each containing a driver, an archer, and a shieldman to protect the archer as he shot.[3] While Rameses had his back turned, pitching camp just west of Kadesh with his first division of soldiers, Muwatalli's army poured out from behind Kadesh like a sweeping thunderstorm. The Hittite forces swung around behind Amun and flattened the second division, Ra, cutting off Rameses II and his five thousand men of Amun from the remaining two divisions behind.[4] Nearly seventy thousand men clashed outside the walls of Kadesh.

It should have been relatively easy to wipe out both Amun and the king, but the Hittites found themselves with a problem. The Amun division had camped in a fairly small plain, and when the chariots thundered into it, they scraped against each other and piled up in heaps.[5] The Hittite foot soldiers still outnumbered the Egyptians, but Rameses II had put a backup into place: he had sent reinforcements up the coast, probably by sea, in case the main body of the army ran into trouble on land.[6] The reinforcements reached the battlefield from the north just as Ptah arrived to attack from the south, and the two-front battle seems to have confused the Hittites; their army, swelled with mercenaries, was less disciplined than the smaller, tightly organized Egyptian force. Muwatalli did have men in reserve, but he held them back (possibly suspecting that even more Egyptian reinforcements were on the way). When dusk began to fall over the battlefield, the Hittites drew back to regather themselves.

At dawn, the battle began again. But the element of surprise was now missing, and the experience of the Egyptian soldiers paid off. The fight was a stalemate, and Muwatalli suggested a truce.

Rameses II declined to agree to an ongoing peace, but eventually he did agree to go home with his prisoners and booty, leaving Kadesh in Hittite hands. He then marched back to Egypt and proclaimed victory.

If this doesn't sound like an overwhelming triumph, it mutated into one later on, when Rameses II had flattering accounts of the battle carved at least nine times onto the walls of Egyptian temples, with plenty of graphic illustrations of Egyptians slaughtering Hittites. Accounts of the battle became school exercises for children to practice their penmanship on, like Caesar's victories in Gaul centuries later.[7] The Battle of Kadesh, even though it was more or less a draw, became an emblem of Egyptian superiority.

Which shows how far Egypt had come from its previous greatness. Egypt was still mighty, but it had become an empire that depended on reputation as much as actual strength to keep its position as a world leader. Had Egypt's army truly been as powerful as it appears in the reliefs of Rameses II, he would not have turned and marched home again, leaving Kadesh in the hands of the

34.1. Statue of Rameses II. Rameses II built colossal figures of himself at Abu Simbel. Photo credit Galen R. Frysinger

Hittites. Instead, Rameses devoted himself to the symbols of dominance; he built, within the safe territories of his own land, more temples, statues, and monuments than any pharaoh before him. So it happens that Rameses II gained a reputation as one of the greatest pharaohs in Egyptian history, when in fact he had lost part of the northern holdings gained by Tuthmosis III, two hundred years before.

THAT OTHER GREAT EMPIRE to the north had its own difficulties. By this point the Hittites seem to have made a treaty with the kings of Babylon, far to the south; at least we can assume so, since Muwatalli sent down to Babylon for a doctor to come and help him with some personal medical problem. A letter has survived, written by Muwatalli's brother after the king's death, answering a Babylonian inquiry after the doctor, who had been expected to return to the Babylonian court. ("He married a relative of mine and decided to settle here," the letter says, more or less, "so quit accusing me of keeping him in jail; what good would an imprisoned doctor do me?")[8]

Relations between the Hittites and the Assyrians were less friendly. The new king of Assur, Adad-nirari, was steadily fighting his way north through the territory fractured by the Mitanni flight, claiming it as his own. He also mounted at least one border war with Babylon, to the south, during which Assyria was able to claim a good bit of Babylon's northern territory. The conquests were impressive enough for Adad-nirari to call himself, in what was becoming a time-honored Assyrian tradition, the King of the World: "Adad-nirari, illustrious prince," one inscription begins, "honored of the gods, lord, viceroy of the land of the gods, city-founder, destroyer of the mighty hosts of Kassites . . . who destroys all foes north and south, who tramples down their lands . . . who captures all people, enlarges boundary and frontier; the king to whose feet Assur . . . has brought in submission all kings and princes."[9]

In the middle of planning a strategy against this growing Assyrian threat to his east, the Hittite king Muwatalli died after a long reign. He left his throne to his son, who promptly stripped the next most powerful man at court—Muwatalli's brother (and his own uncle)—of his court positions and attempted to exile him. The brother, Hattusilis, declined to be exiled. He rounded up his followers, put the king under guard, and pronounced himself King Hattusilis III.

The longest surviving document from Hattusilis III's time is a heartfelt argument known as "The Apology," in which he explains, with more or less circular logic, that (1) the gods had given him the right to rule, and (2) his successful seizing of the throne *proved* that the gods had given him the right to rule.[10] This was not entirely convincing to the Hittites; fragmentary records from Hattusas show that the king spent most of his reign struggling to win a civil war.

Fairly early on, Hattusilis III realized that he could not keep on fighting his own people, the Egyptians to the south, and the increasingly threatening Assyrians to the southeast. The Assyrian Adad-nirari had been succeeded by Shalmaneser I, who was even more aggressive than his predecessor, and who was in the process of taking over the rest of the previously Mitanni territory. Hittite soldiers had joined Aramaean forces in one battle against Shalmaneser I already, and had been pushed backwards: "I killed countless numbers of [the] defeated and widespreading hosts," Shalmaneser I boasted. "I cut down their hordes, 14,400 of them I overthrew and took as living captives"; this meant that he captured and blinded them, a gratuitous bit of cruelty which became standard practice in Assyrian warfare. Shalmaneser also claimed to have captured 180 cities, turning them into ruins: "The army of Hittites and Aramaeans, the allies, I slaughtered like sheep."[11]

Assyria on the east would make no peace, so Hattusilis turned to secure his southern border; he decided to negotiate a truce with Egypt.

This was slightly tricky for Egypt's Rameses II, since the rightful heir to the throne, Muwatalli's son, had escaped from his uncle's prison and shown up at the Egyptian court, asking for asylum.[12] (He had also written to the Assyrian king Shalmaneser on the same errand, but Shalmaneser was not in the business of providing refuge, and had refused.)

Faced with the perfect opportunity to take over the Hittite empire, Rameses II declined. He sent Muwatalli's son packing, agreed to a peace with the usurping uncle, and even sealed the terms by marrying two of Hattusilis III's daughters. The peace was inevitable; Rameses II was no longer in control of most of the Western Semitic territories that had once belonged to Egypt. The petty kings scattered along the Mediterranean coast had not been privileged to see Rameses's reliefs explaining that the Battle of Kadesh had been a great Egyptian victory. They had simply seen the Egyptians retreating, beaten, and since then had been in constant revolt. There was no way that the Egyptian army could get up to the Hittite land without fighting for every step of the way.

Egypt had been forced into alliance with its enemy. But Rameses II was still working on the spin. He had the treaty, which promised that Egypt would not attack the Hittites, carved into the temple walls at Karnak, with an introductory note explaining that the Hittites had come to him begging for peace. And he refused to send a daughter north to marry a Hittite prince, even though he had plenty to spare; by this time Rameses II, a man who liked women, had

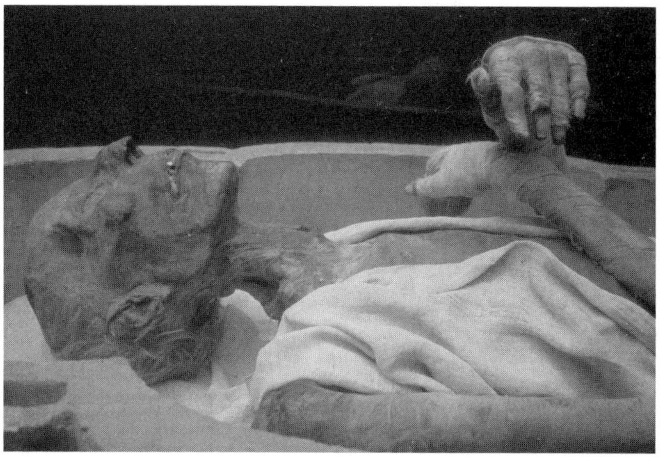

34.2. Mummy of Rameses II. The mummy of Rameses II retains his beaked nose, thanks to its peppercorn stuffing. Egyptian Museum, Cairo. Photo credit Scala/Art Resource, NY

well over a hundred children, who trail behind him in temple reliefs as though he were the Pied Piper. Egyptian princesses did not go to foreign lands.

The Hittite version of the treaty, uncovered at Hattusas, remarks that the Egyptians were the first to ask for peace.[13]

WHEN HE DIED, well into his nineties, Rameses II could claim the second longest reign in Egyptian history. He had left his tracks all across Egypt; his temples to Amun and the rest of the pantheon, his monuments and his statues, his cities and his inscriptions were everywhere. His embalmers had the forethought to stuff his distinctively large nose with peppercorns, so that the tight bandaging of his body didn't flatten it across his face. And so his personality stands out not only from the countryside of Egypt, but from his mummy as well.[14]

TIMELINE 34

MESOPOTAMIA AND ASIA MINOR			EGYPT
MITANNI	ASSYRIA	HITTITE	
			Tuthmosis III (alone) (c. 1483–1450)
Saustatar			
			Exodus (earliest date)
Artadama			**Tuthmosis IV** (1419–1386)
Sudarna II			
	Assur-nadin-ahhe II		**Amenhotep III** (c. 1386–1349)
Tushratta		**Suppiluliuma**	
	Assur-uballit Middle Kingdom of Assyria		**Akhenaten** (c. 1349–1334)
			Tutankhamun (c. 1333–1325)
			Ay (c. 1325–1321)
	Adad-nirari I		**Horemheb** (c. 1321–1293)
		Muwatalli	*Dynasty 19* (1293–1185)
	Shalmaneser I	**Hattusilis III**	**Rameses II** (c. 1278–1212)

Chapter Thirty-Five

The Battle for Troy

Mycenaeans attack the city of Troy between 1260 and 1230 BC and suffer greatly from their victory

All the way over on the northwest coast of Asia Minor, the city of Troy stood in a corner of the peninsula that had never been reached by the Hittite kingdom, not even at its greatest.

In the years that Babylon and Assyria, Washukkanni and Hattusas had battled over the right to control the land from the head of the Gulf over to the Mediterranean coast and up almost to the Black Sea, scores of mountain tribes, desert chieftains, and ancient cities had remained independent, outside the control of the grasping kingdoms. Troy was one of those cities. It had been settled almost two thousand years before, and its king had built walls around his tiny village to protect his people from the grasp of the greedy on the outside. Over centuries, the city burned and was rebuilt, grew shabby and was renovated, shrank and then grew again, over and over, producing layer on layer of occupation.

In the days that Rameses II and Hattusilis III negotiated their treaty, Troy—not so far to the west of the thriving Hittite kingdom—was on its seventh incarnation (called by archaeologists "Troy VIIa").* It was a wealthy city, without much need of imported food or goods; Troy stood on a plain with plenty of

* Most archaeologists assign the first five layers of occupation (Troy I–V) to the years between 3000 and 1900 BC. Troy VI stood on the site between 1900 and 1300 BC and was flattened by an earthquake; Troy VIIa was built on the ruins, but burned down (possibly as a result of siege) around 1240 BC. Troy VIIb was rebuilt over the ashes, but never achieved a very high standard of sophistication and wilted away. By 1100 BC or so the site was abandoned and left unsettled for four hundred years. The Greeks built a city on the site around 700 BC, well after the development of the Trojan War epic tales, and called it Ilion; archaeologists call Ilion Troy VIII. The Romans took the Greek city over in the first century BC (Troy IX, the city's last major occupation).

fertile farmland. There were fish in the nearby waters, and sheep in the meadows, and Troy was famous for the herds of horses which ate its surplus grain.[1]

Sometime between 1260 and 1230 BC, Troy was ravaged by fire and war. Its walls were broken down, and a slaughter took place; human bones lay unburied in the streets.

THE STORY OF the war's beginning was set down, five hundred years later, in the Iliad.

Peeled away from the skeleton of divine hostilities, the meat of the tale is straightforward enough. Menelaus, king of the Greek city of Sparta, married a princess from Argos, a city which lay north of his own. This princess, Helen, attracted the roving eye of Paris, son of the king of Troy, a brave enough warrior but a relentless womanizer. (This, incidentally, did not boost his reputation for masculinity among his own countrymen, one way in which the Trojans differed from our own time: "Paris, you pretty boy," his own brother shouts at him, "you woman-struck seducer!")[2] Paris seduced Helen and then carried her off to Troy. Helen's husband Menelaus, determined to have his revenge, recruited his brother Agamemnon to help him attack Troy.

Agamemnon was the high king of the Greeks (Homer's name for his own people is the Achaeans), and so called all of the Greek cities to join their forces together and sail in a united fleet towards Troy, to avenge the insult to his brother (the insult to Helen is not so much in view here). They arrived on the shores of Asia Minor but found themselves stymied by the valor of the Trojan soldiers and the height of Troy's walls. There they sat, besieging the city for ten long years.

The siege is the setting for the central drama of the Iliad, which is the behavior of the great warrior Achilles, who hailed from Thessaly (a mountainous region on the northern Greek peninsula). At the end of the Iliad, we have learned quite a lot about Achilles, but the Greek army is still sitting outside the walls of Troy, and the king of Troy, Priam, is still on his throne. The war itself takes place offstage. By the beginning of the companion epic, the Odyssey, the siege has ended, Troy has been sacked, and the Greeks are on their long way home.

The tale of Troy's actual fall to the besieging Greek forces is told in pieces by various Greek poets, but appears in its most complete form much later, in the second book of the Aeneid by the Roman poet Virgil:

> Broken in war and foiled by fate,
> With so many years already slipping away, the Greek staff

Constructed a horse. . . .
It was high as a hill, and its ribs were made from planks of pinewood. . . .
. . . Choosing warriors by lot they secretly
Put them in on the blind side of the horse, until its vast
And cavernous belly was crammed with a party of armed men.[3]

When the Greeks noisily and obviously depart, the Trojans—taking the horse as an offering to the Roman war-goddess Minerva—haul it into the city (while ignoring various evil omens). They feast in triumph, fall asleep dead drunk, and the Greek warriors climb out of the horse's belly.

They broke out over a city drowned in drunken sleep;
They killed the sentries and then threw open the gates, admitting
Their main body, and joined in the pre-arranged plan of attack. . . .
. . . The city's on fire; the Greeks are masters here.[4]

Both Virgil and Homer describe this thirteenth-century war using the language and convention, the armor and weapons, the political problems and heroes, of their own time. But once again a poem preserves the kernel of a historical event. Troy was burned, its people slaughtered or put to flight.

So who actually fought this war against Troy?

The city certainly did not fall during Homer's lifetime, whenever that was. General scholarly opinion has temporarily put him around 800 BC or so; he may have lived a little earlier, but there is no way that he was alive as far back as 1230 BC, which is the latest possible date that archaeology allows for the burning of Troy VIIa. Homer was telling the story of an older time. The details of the epics show us a writer creating historical fiction. The translator E. V. Rieu points out, for example, that Homer's Nestor (the king of Pylos, the Mycenaean city credited with sending sixty ships to the anti-Troy alliance) drinks from a cup topped with two doves; an identical cup was found in the ruins of Mycenae.[5]

By 1260 BC, when the dove-topped cup was in use, the Mycenaean kings of Mycenae, Thebes, Athens, and Pylos had built their cities into small kingdoms, surrounded by walls and connected by chariot-smooth roads. Knossos, down across the Sea of Crete, may have once been governed by a Mycenaean ruler, but by 1350 the city had been finally destroyed altogether.* The city of

* J. Lesley Fitton notes, "A complex literature covers the date of the final destruction at Knossos, and no consensus has yet been reached" (*Minoans,* p. 181). By any reckoning, though, Knossos had ceased to be a power center around 1450, and never regained its former importance.

Mycenae now claimed the largest territory, with Thebes, Pylos, and Athens not far behind. The king of Pylos ruled over so much land that he divided it into sixteen districts, each with a governor and deputy governor who sent the king a tax of bronze each year.[6] These great centers carried on an active trade with the Hittites and Egyptians, neither of which made any effort to conquer the cities on the Greek peninsula. The Hittites were not sailors at all, and although the Egyptians were used to boating on the Nile, they disliked the sea, which they called the "Great Green" and generally avoided.[7]

What sparked off a battle between the Mycenaean cities and the Trojans isn't known. The quarrel may indeed have involved a captive princess. The diplomatic marriages taking place all over the ancient world show that a great deal of pride was involved in the delicate negotiations; those who sent princesses were inferior, those who accepted them boasted the greater power.

Herodotus, writing later, also tells the story of Helen's abduction by the son of Priam. In his *Histories,* he claims to have heard the tale from an independent source: the Persians, who think that the Greeks overreacted.

> Although the Persians regard the abduction of women as a criminal act, they also claim that it is stupid to get worked up about it and to seek revenge for the women once they have been abducted; the sensible course, they say, is to pay no attention to it, because it is obvious that the women must have been willing participants in their own abduction, or else it could never have happened.[8]

This observation (which could demonstrate a rather charmingly high view of women's agency, but probably doesn't) leads Herodotus into an explanation of the ongoing hostility between Greeks and Persians:

> [T]he Greeks raised a mighty army because of a woman . . . and then invaded Asia and destroyed Priam and his forces. Ever since then, the Persians have regarded the Greeks as their enemies. . . . They date their hostility towards Greece from the fall of Ilium [the Greek name for Troy].[9]

This is another anachronism, as Persia didn't yet exist during the sacking of Troy VIIa. Still, it shows that the cities of the Greek peninsula and those in Asia Minor had hated each other for a long time. Robert Graves has suggested that the kidnapping, though real, was an act of revenge for a previous Mycenaean raid on Trojan land;[10] Helen's abduction fanned a hostility which had existed for years already.

However it began, the Mycenaeans won the struggle, and Troy fell. But not long afterwards, the Mycenaeans began on a long slide downwards from the height of their glory. The cities shrank; they grew shabbier; they grew less secure.

Possibly this had begun even before the siege. Thucydides tells us that the war lasted for so many years because the Mycenaean attackers didn't have enough money to supply themselves properly; since they ran out of food, they had to spend part of their time growing food and making piratical raids into the Aegean, rather than fighting nonstop.[11]

The war with Troy just accelerated the decline. In the Odyssey, we learn that the triumph over Troy was the sort of victory to which the later king Pyrrhus would lend his name: a victory which damaged the winner almost as much as the vanquished. The Odyssey has a mournful tone. In the words of Nestor, king of Pylos, even though the Mycenaeans won, their story is one of sorrow:

> This is the story of the woe we endured in that land,
> we sons of the Achaeans, unrestrained in fury,
> and of all that we bore. . . .
> There the best of us were slain . . . and many other ills
> we suffered beside these . . .
> After we had sacked the steep city of Priam,
> and had departed in our ships . . .
> even then, Zeus was fashioning for us a ruinous doom.[12]

The Mycenaean heroes limped home to unsettled households, murdered heirs, thieving nobles, sacked crops, and wives claimed by others. Their arrival brought even more unrest: the "late return" of the heroes home, Thucydides tells us, "caused many revolutions, and factions ensued almost everywhere."[13] The peak of Mycenaean glory had passed and would not come again.

TIMELINE 35

MESOPOTAMIA AND ASIA MINOR		EGYPT
ASSYRIA	HITTITE	**Amenhotep III** (c. 1386–1349)
Assur-uballit Middle Kingdom of Assyria		**Akhenaten** (c. 1349–1334) **Tutankhamun** (c. 1333–1325)
		Ay (c. 1325–1321)
Adad-nirari I		**Horemheb** (c. 1321–1293)
	Muwatalli	*Dynasty 19* (1293–1185)
Shalmaneser I	**Hattusilis III**	**Rameses II** (c. 1278–1212)
Mycenaean attack on Troy VIIA (c. 1260)		

Chapter Thirty-Six

The First Historical King of China

Around 1200 BC, in China,
Shang craftsmen cast bronzes,
Shang priests carve bones for divination,
and the Shang king rules from Yin

AFTER THE MOVE of the Shang capital to Yin under the wily and flexible P'an Keng, the Shang Dynasty bumped along in more or less silence for a century or so. The next ruler who emerges as a personality is the twenty-second Shang king, Wu Ting, who probably ruled sometime around 1200 BC.

Wu Ting, according to the ancient history *Shu ching* (written hundreds of years after the fact, but before the time of Sima Qian, who used it as one of his sources), spent his formative years among "lower people," the poor and the farmers. He then began his rule in complete silence: "He did not speak for three years," the history tells us. "Afterwards, he was still inclined not to speak, but when he did speak, his words were full of harmonious wisdom. He did not dare to indulge in useless ease, but admirably and tranquilly presided over the regions of Yin until throughout them all, small and great, there was not a single murmur."[1]

Silence, followed by taciturnity: this is an unexpected kingly virtue, not unlike P'an Keng's claim that a shifting capital showed strength rather than weakness. The power of the Shang king during this time clearly did not depend on the kind of might wielded by the Hittite, Babylonian, Assyrian, and Egyptian rulers, with their constant stream of threatening and cajoling letters, their self-puffery, their boasting, their envoys and messengers and diplomats. The Shang authority had some other source.

But like Wu Ting, history is almost silent about the years when the Shang ruled in Yin. Rather than letters and tablets, the Shang left bits and pieces of houses, bones, and bronzes. These tell us something about the Shang way of life. They do not, in the end, tell us a tremendous amount about who the Shang rulers *were*.

THE MOST FAMOUS Shang artifacts—vessels, weapons, beautifully turned farming tools, ornaments—are those made of cast bronze. They stand as a testament to the Shang ruler's authority. Like pyramid-building, the casting of bronze needed a king who could force multitudes of men to a nasty and labor-intensive job; in this case, digging ore out of the mines that lay in the hilly country north of the Yellow river.

The work of the miners and craftsmen produced, in the words of one scholar of ancient China, "one of humankind's great artistic achievements."[2] No other ancient nation was able to cast bronze into such sophisticated

36.1. Shang Bronze. A Shang cooking vessel, made of bronze from Ningxian, China. Photo credit Bridgeman-Giraudon/Art Resource, NY

forms.[3] Bronze-hafted spears were set with turquoise and topped with blades of white jade; ornate bronze buckles fastened the bridles of horses; bronze masks gave their wearers snarling or comic faces. Vessels for food and wine, the most elaborate of the bronze designs, were shaped like dragons or oxen or other creatures, finished with elaborate patternings and handles. Some are engraved with names, others with signs to show the vessel's use. Sometimes an inscription makes note of a year, or a festival.

This scattered information, brief though it is, testifies that the Shang people had progressed to using writing. In China, writing developed along the same pattern as in Mesopotamia and Crete: it began as marks of ownership as far back as 4000 BC and then became more complex. But Chinese script seems to have developed in complete independence from writing elsewhere in the ancient world. The earliest Yellow river signs were pictures, but the writing of China was the first to move beyond the pictorial by *combining* pictures: putting pictorial signs (called "ideograms") together into "composite ideograms" which represented abstractions and ideas.[4]

By the time of the Shang court's establishment at Yin, these "composite ideograms" were sophisticated enough to record divine answers to questions. In the ruins of the Shang capital, archaeologists have uncovered hundreds of signs engraved on bones; these served the Shang court much as entrails later served Greek priests and priestesses. A man or woman who sought guidance went to the Shang court to pose a question to the priests there. The priests brought out the cleaned and dried shoulder bones of cows or sheep (or, occasionally, a turtle shell), carved with patterns or marked with an inscription, and then touched the bone or shell with a heated metal point. When the bone cracked, the path of the crack through the pattern or inscription was "read" by the priests and interpreted as a message, sent by ancestors who now passed their wisdom back to the living. The priest carved the results of the inquiry into the bone or shell, in signs cut by a knife and filled with paint.[5]

The oracle bones show that the questions, no matter who asked them, were always posed in the name of the king.

THE KING WU TING is praised, by the ancient historian of the *Shu ching*, for his hard work, for his refusal to sink into luxury, and for the contentment he brought to his people: in all of his reign, "there was not a single murmur." At the same time, the ancient philosophical text *I ching* (Book of Changes) describes Wu Ting, approvingly, as going on a three-year campaign against rebellious tribes to the northwest; and seven hundred years later, the *Shih ching* (Book of Songs), credits him with rule over an improbably enormous land:

Even the inner domain was a thousand leagues. . . .
He opened up new lands as far as the four seas.
Men from the four seas came in homage,
Came in homage, crowd on crowd.[6]

These two portraits—the humble and hardworking man concerned for his people's contentment, and the conqueror demanding homage—are oddly in tension. The role of the king seems to be shifting, and the chroniclers are uncertain whether he is to be a spiritual leader, holding to the virtues of the past, or a general taking charge of the country's future.

We can say, without question, that the Shang king had gained considerably in his power since the move to Yin. In the royal cemetery, a little north of the capital city, the kings were buried in graves that were the reverse of Egypt's pyramids. Rather than rising into the sky, the graves are enormous pits, dug so deep into the ground that years must have gone into their construction. In these pits are human sacrifices; not the intact bodies of loyal subjects who have gone to their deaths in faith that their king would lead them across the horizon into another world, but decapitated bodies.* One grave has seventy-three skulls lined along the four ramps that sink down into it, with a cluster of fifty-nine skeletons (minus heads) on the southernmost ramp.[7] In Yin itself, archaeologists have uncovered the foundation of an altar where the sacrifices were most likely made.

This suggests a great deal of autocratic authority on the part of the king, particularly since he was able to compel death even after his own. Yet Sima Qian also makes constant mention of court officials and ruling noblemen with clout of their own. Probably the area over which the Shang king exercised his imperiousness was fairly small. On the edges of this, his nobles and officials governed in his name—but acted more or less as they pleased. Farther out lay plains and valleys of settlements where the people sent tribute to the king to avoid arousing his anger, or simply knew that he existed, or perhaps didn't know that he existed at all until armed men clattered through their village, seizing their goods in the king's name.

The two conflicting portraits of the king might boil down to a simple reality: the Shang king was the spiritual head of all his people, but his real and earthly power existed inside a much smaller domain. Wu Ting himself could not reign without help. According to Sima Qian, he spent his three-year silence searching for an official who could serve as his right hand. Finally he

* Scholar J. A. G. Roberts points out that the sacrifices were often multiples of ten, which perhaps goes to my theory in chapter 15 that the number ten could serve as an intensifier of sorts.

found the assistant he was looking for: a sage named Fu Yueh, who was working as a common laborer in a city to the east of Yin. Only then did Wu Ting break his silence and take up his role as ruler. The king, his spiritual virtues notwithstanding, had to rely on others to carry out the governing of his people: not just the sage assistant, but also the noblemen who were actually in control of those farther-flung provinces of the Shang kingdom.

But this is all speculation, since the story of Wu Ting is built around fragments of bone and bronze, and tales set down a thousand years after the fact.

TIMELINE 36		
MESOPOTAMIA AND ASIA MINOR		CHINA
ASSYRIA	HITTITE	
Assur-uballit Middle Kingdom of Assyria		Shang Dynasty, cont.
Adad-nirari I		
	Muwatalli	
Shalmaneser I	**Hattusilis III**	
Mycenaean attack on Troy VIIA (c. 1260)		
		Wu Ting (c. 1200)

Chapter Thirty-Seven

The Rig Veda

Around 1200 BC, the arya *of India spread into the river valleys and plains*

LIKE THE SHANG DYNASTY OF CHINA, the rulers of India remain just out of sight beneath the surface of history. Occasionally a face glimmers beneath the ripples, but its features remain indistinct.

Those tribes who referred to themselves as *arya* had settled along the Indus, south of the mountains, remaining almost entirely in the western part of the continent. They had intermarried, in all likelihood, with the people they found there. They were prospering much more vigorously than their relatives who had gone west to triumph so briefly as the Mitanni. In the three hundred years since their arrival, the infiltrators had adopted lives that were patterned much more after the vanished Harappan culture than after the nomadic, tribal rovings of their distant past. Their wandering ways had begun to fade from memory; the Sanskrit word *grama,* the name for a settled and walled village, originally meant a wandering wagon-centered clan.[1]

The arya have not left much trace of these lives behind them, but by 1200 or so they had begun to make sense of their new incarnation as a settled people with myths of their own. The earliest collections of Indian hymns, the poetic Rig Veda, were composed in their own tongue. Like most ancient poems, those in the Rig Veda were set down in writing long after they were first told around fires, but they can still give us a glimpse of the world that the arya were building for themselves.*

* Complicated linguistic calculations have led most scholars to agree that the hymns of the Rig Veda, first written down around 600 BC, entered the process of oral composition sometime between 1400 and 1100 BC (for a brief explanation, see Stanley Wolpert's chapter "The Aryan Age" in *A New History of India*). Given this date, it is notable that even the earliest of the stories in the Rig Veda say nothing about the existence that these tribes presumably led up in the deserts of central Asia, north

For one thing, the Rig Veda was devoted almost entirely to explaining the nature and requirements of the Indian gods. Any people with complicated gods who make complicated demands stand in need of priests as well as warlords; they are on the edge of becoming a more complicated society. By the time of the later verses in the Rig Veda, the priests of the arya had become not simply specialists in god-care, but a hereditary *class* of specialists. Priests fathered sons who were trained to become priests, and who married daughters of other priests. The hymns in the Rig Veda were the first writings of the arya, and the priests their first true aristocracy.

The people who were in the process of becoming Indians were held together by a common philosophy and a common religion, not by political organization or by military might.[2] So the Rig Veda tells us a great deal about the worship of the gods, but very little about the spread of the arya across the land that had become their home. The collection is divided into ten cycles, called *mandala*.[3] Each mandala contains hymns in praise of the gods, and chants to be said during sacrifices and other rituals. The Indian gods are nature-gods, as is common to peoples who live in harsh environments and along fierce rivers (the Yahweh of Abraham is a notable exception): Varuna, the sky-god; Ratri, the spirit of the night; Agni, the god of fire; Parjanya, the rain-god who "shatters the trees" and pours down water on cattle, horses, and men as well; Mitra, god of the sun; and Indra, the calmer of chaos and the ruler of the pantheon, he "who made firm the shaking earth, who brought to rest the mountains when they were disturbed . . . in whose control are horses, villages, and all chariots."[4] (Indra, Varuna, and Mitra, incidentally, appear as witnesses in a treaty between the Mitanni king and Suppiluliuma, the Hittite empire-builder; this shows not only that the Mitanni were arya, but that the arya were worshipping these gods long before they separated and went their different ways to the west and south.)

Books II to VII of the Rig Veda, the oldest of the hymns, give us glimpses of political and military structure through the dim glass of ritual. The fire-god Agni is credited with attacking "walls with his weapons," which suggests that as the arya flourished and spread, they made war on wooden-walled villages in their path by burning them.[5] One hymn mentions a battle between "dark-hued" peoples and the arya, a description which scholars seized on, a century ago, as proof that an inferior native people had been wiped out by light-skinned "Aryans." But the seventh mandala describes a battle among ten arya kings against each other. The arya seem to have fought each other quite as

of the mountains; this must signify a large gap of time between the settlement along the Indus and the first of the oral tales preserved for us in the Rig Veda.

much as they fought the other inhabitants of the river valleys and the plains beyond.

Apparently the years of the first hymns in the Rig Veda were a time in which not only a priest-clan, but also a clan of aristocratic warriors, had begun to form, a hereditary class of ruling chiefs who passed down power from father to son.[6] But we can go no further than this; and so far, none of these priests and warrior-chiefs have names.

TIMELINE 37

MESOPOTAMIA AND ASIA MINOR		INDIA AND CHINA
ASSYRIA	HITTITE	
Assur-uballit Middle Kingdom of Assyria		Oral composition of the Rig Veda begins (c. 1400)
Adad-nirari I		
	Muwatalli	
Shalmaneser I	**Hattusilis III**	
Mycenaean attack on Troy VIIA (c. 1260)		
		Wu Ting (c. 1200)

Chapter Thirty-Eight

The Wheel Turns Again

Between 1212 and 1190 BC, the Assyrians fight with Hittites, Babylonians, and Elamites, while the Nineteenth Dynasty of Egypt collapses

BACK OVER A LITTLE FARTHER to the west, the patchwork Hittite empire was beginning to gape at the seams.

The Egyptian-Hittite treaty was still holding; Egypt governed the Western Semitic lands as far as Kadesh, while the Hittites claimed the cities farther to the north. When Rameses II died, well into his nineties, his elderly son Merneptah succeeded to the throne (he was the thirteenth son of Rameses II, since the tough old man had already outlived his first twelve male offspring).[1] At the news of a new pharaoh on the throne, a few of the cities in the Egyptian provinces to the north tried their luck at a revolt, but Egyptian forces marched up and mashed them with little ceremony.[2]

The Hittites, meanwhile, had been struck by drought. Crops had been ruined, livestock were dying, villagers were tormented by hunger. One of the letters from the Hittite capital down to the Egyptian court suggests that, since the pharaoh has arranged to marry a Hittite princess, he had better come and get her; the Hittite stables had no more grain, and the herds of cattle set aside as her dowry would starve if not fetched right away.[3]

Hattusilis III had made his son Tudhaliya his Chief of Bodyguards, a position that proved his father's complete trust in him (not necessarily a given in Hittite royal families).[4] When Hattusilis III died, his son became King Tudhaliya IV. He inherited not just the throne, but a famine that was worsening by the year.

Tudhaliya IV sent down to Egypt for food, and Merneptah, now sitting on his father's throne, honored the alliance; his own inscriptions remark that he sent enough grain "to keep the land alive."[5] A letter from Tudhaliya himself to one of his subject cities, directing it to provide ships to help transport the grain, reveals that a single shipment was 450 tons.[6] The Hittite granaries were bare.

A king who has to beg foreign aid simply to keep his people alive is not in a good position, and the Hittites, precariously perched on top of the turning wheel of fortune, were on their way down. A country without grain is a country without money. A country without money inevitably delays paying its soldiers until the last possible moment. Underpaid soldiers are always less disciplined than well-fed and satisfied ones. The Hittite army was ripe for defeat.

Tudhaliya was a competent commander-in-chief and a seasoned warrior who had first gone out fighting in his father's army at the age of twelve.[7] But along with famine and poverty, he also had to worry about his throne. His father had usurped the crown, after all, and the kingdom was full of men with royal blood. "The descendants of Suppiluliuma, the descendants of Mursili, the descendants of Muwatalli, the descendants of Hattusili are numerous!" he complains in one letter.[8]

To prove his power as rightful king, Tudhaliya IV gave orders for the most massive building program of any Hittite king ever: new shrines; additions to the already-large palace complex; a new suburb of the capital city Hattusas that included twenty-six new temples and doubled the size of the old city.[9] This was the sort of project expected of a great king, and may have been in imitation of Rameses II, who had just died. But although the new buildings trumpeted Tudhaliya's royal authority, they also drained his treasury. In a kingdom already suffering from famine and poverty, Tudhaliya IV was pouring money into construction, and this left him even less royal silver with which to pay his soldiers.

The conquered peoples under Hittite rule clearly saw the army weakening year by year. Not long into his reign, Tudhaliya learned that twenty-two cities along the western edge of his empire had joined together in an alliance against him. He marched west and broke up the coalition, but the vultures were already circling.[10]

Down to the southeast, the new king of Assyria saw an opportunity to expand. Shalmaneser I had already swallowed the old Mitanni lands. Now his son, Tukulti-Ninurta, launched an attack against the Hittite borders to his west.*

* From the time of Tukulti-Ninurta's great-grandfather on, the Assyrian kings began to keep detailed accounts of all military campaigns fought during each year of their reign; these provide much of our information about Assyria's conquests at this time (the other details come from letters found at Nineveh, now in the British Museum; see Jorgen Laessoe, *People of Ancient Assyria*, pp. 94–96, for a fuller description of the nature of the source material).

Tudhaliya carried his defense into the enemy's land, and the two armies met on the plain of Erbila. If the Assyrian account of the battle is to be believed, Tudhaliya was not at all sure that he could win the fight. The Assyrian king wrote in a letter sent to an ally:

> Tudhaliya wrote to me, saying, "You have captured merchants who were loyal to me. Come on, let's fight; I have set out against you for battle."
>
> I prepared my army and my chariots. But before I could reach his city, Tudhaliya the king of the Hittites sent out a messenger who was holding two tablets with hostile words and one with friendly words. He showed me the two with a hostile challenge first. When my army heard about these words, they were anxious to fight, ready to set out at once. The messenger saw this. So then he gave me the third tablet, which said, "I am not hostile to the king of Assur, my brother. Why should we brothers be at war with each other?"
>
> But I brought my army on. He was stationed with his soldiers in the city Nihrija, so I sent him a message saying, "I'll besiege the city. If you are truly friendly to me, leave the city at once." But he did not reply to my message.
>
> So I withdrew my army a little ways back from the city. Then a Hittite deserter fled from Tudhaliya's army and reached me. He said, "The king may be writing to you evasively, in friendship, but his troops are in battle order; he is ready to march."
>
> So I called my troops out and marched against him; and I won a great victory.[11]

Tukulti-Ninurta boasted afterwards that he had taken 28,800 Hittites as prisoners of war, a hugely improbable figure. But he certainly carried off thousands of Hittites and brought them back to Assyria. Settling a conquered people in a foreign land weakened their sense of themselves as a nation; an exiled race was less likely to revolt.

The conquest made enough of a splash in the ancient Near East to figure in the oldest Greek chronicles, where Tukulti-Ninurta (under the Greek name Ninus) appears as the distant ancestor of the ruler of Sardis, all the way over in Asia Minor; this was a distant and distorted reflection of Tukulti-Ninurta's rampage through Hittite territory.*

* The chronology is difficult, but Tukulti-Ninurta is probably the king called Nimrod in Gen. 10:10: a mighty hunter and warrior whose kingdom included Babylon, Erech, Akkad, and Nineveh, the same expanse as that claimed by Tukulti-Ninurta for Assyria. Weirdly enough, this Hebrew version of the name of the Assyrian great king has become an English synonym for a foolish and ineffectual man ("What a nimrod!"). The only etymology I can find for this suggests that, thanks to some bib-

Tudhaliya himself retreated to his capital city, abandoning the outskirts of his empire. The Hittite military might was fading rapidly. In a letter sent to the vassal king of Ugarit, Tudhaliya complains that the city has not sent in its quota of soldiers for the Hittite army; is Ugarit arming itself for revolt? Another tablet lists all the ships from the city of Carchemish which are no longer in any shape to sail.[12] The edges of Tudhaliya's kingdom were cracking away.

TUKULTI-NINURTA, meanwhile, went back home to face a new problem to the south.

Babylon had had an ambiguous relationship with Assyria for years. Each city had, at various times, claimed the right to rule the other. Babylon and Assur were not only balanced in strength, but also twins in culture. They had once been part of the same empire, under Hammurabi, and the essentially Babylonian stamp on the whole area remained visible. Assyria and Babylon shared the same gods, albeit with occasionally different names; their gods had the same stories; and the Assyrians used Babylonian cuneiform in their inscriptions and annals.[13]

This likeness made Assyrian kings generally reluctant to sack and burn Babylon, even when they had the chance. But Tukulti-Ninurta was not much inclined to restraint. He boasted in his inscriptions of the fate of all those who defied him: "I filled the caves and ravines of the mountains with their corpses," he announces, "I made heaps of their corpses, like grain piled beside their gates; their cities I ravaged, I turned them into ruinous hills."[14]

Counting on Tukulti-Ninurta's preoccupation with the Hittites up north, the king of Babylon tried to seize some of the disputed land between the Assyrian and Babylonian borders. We know almost nothing about this king, Kashtiliash IV, except that he was a poor judge of men; Tukulti-Ninurta marched down and plundered Babylon's temples. In this he broke a long Assyrian tradition of respect for Babylon's sacred sites. He even took the images of the gods away, a particularly risky move since it was generally thought that sacrilege of this sort would peeve the Assyrian gods as well. "He removed the great lord Marduk from his dwelling-place," the Assyrian chronicle of the conquest tells us, "and set him on the road to Assur."[15] And he per-

---

lically literate scriptwriter, Bugs Bunny once called Elmer Fudd a "poor little Nimrod" in an ironic reference to the "mighty hunter." Apparently the entire Saturday-morning audience, having no memory of Genesis genealogies, heard the irony as a general insult and applied it to anyone bumbling and Fudd-like. Thus a distorted echo of Tukulti-Ninurta's might in arms bounced down, through the agency of a rabbit, into the vocabulary of the twentieth century.

sonally confronted the Babylonian king in battle: "In the midst of that battle," his inscriptions announce, "my hand captured Kashtiliash, I trod on his royal neck with my feet like a footstool. . . . Sumer and Akkad to its farthest border I brought under my sway. On the lower sea of the rising sun I established the frontier of my land."[16] He then proclaimed himself king of Babylon as well as Assyria. For the second time, the identity between the two kingdoms had been merged into one.

Tukulti-Ninurta marched Kashtiliash back to Assur, naked and in chains, and put Babylon itself under the authority of an Assyrian governor. This extended the border of the Assyrian empire from the northern part of the Western Semitic lands all the way down into the south of Mesopotamia. Tukulti-Ninurta, now the only great king in the entire region, embarked on the usual great king activities. He built new temples, fortified Assur's city walls, and constructed an entirely new royal mini-city for himself, a little north of the main sprawl of Assur; it had its own water supply and its own prison labor force, and could be run without any provision from the capital itself.

Tukulti-Ninurta claimed that the god Assur had desired him to build a new city "where neither house nor dwelling existed." But his haste to put himself behind walls and away from the people of Assur hints that all was not well. Babylon itself had been shocked by the plunder of the temples: "He put Babylonians to the sword," the Babylonian Chronicle says, "the treasure of Babylon he profanely brought out, and he took the great lord Marduk off to Assyria."[17] Nor had the destruction gone over well with the devout in his own land. The Assyrian epic that Tukulti-Ninurta commissioned to celebrate the victory over Babylon has an unmistakably defensive tone; it goes to great lengths to explain that Tukulti-Ninurta really wanted to have peace with Babylon and tried his best to be friends with Kashtiliash, only the Babylonian king insisted on coming into Assyrian territory to thieve and burn, which is why the gods of Babylon deserted the city and left it for punishment to the Assyrians.[18] Clearly the great king was under pressure to explain not only why he sacked Babylon, but why he took its sacred images back to his own capital.

The explanation didn't convince, and Tukulti-Ninurta's sacrilege brought about his end. The Babylonian Chronicle tells us, with subdued satisfaction, "As for Tukulti-Ninurta, who had brought evil upon Babylon . . . his son and the nobles of Assyria revolted, and they cast him from his throne [and imprisoned him in his own palace complex] . . . and then killed him with a sword."[19] He had reigned as great king for thirty-seven years.

After his death, his son took the throne. In an effort to reverse his father's misdeeds, he sent the statue of Marduk back down to Babylon,[20] but this did

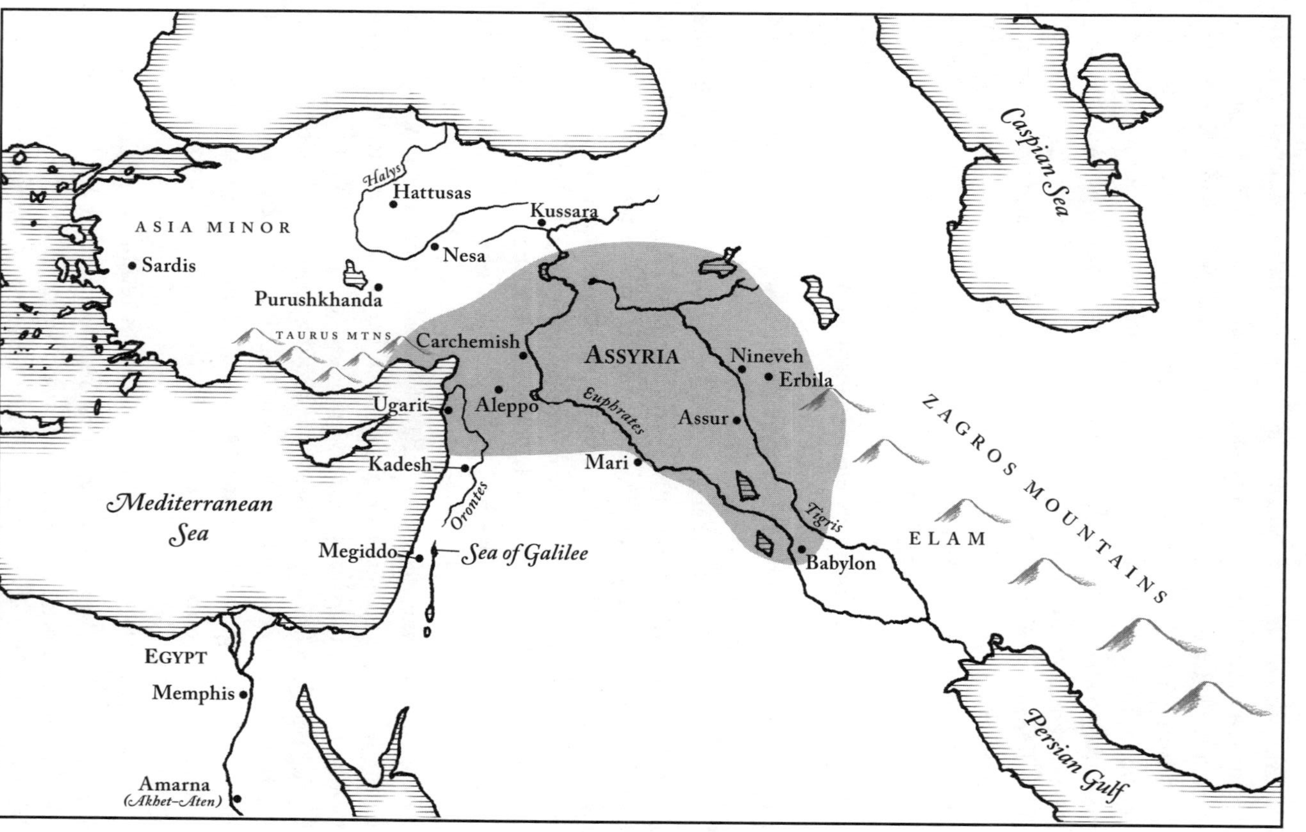

38.1 Tukulti-Ninurta's Assyria

not console the outraged Babylonians. Babylon rebelled almost at once, its Assyrian governor fled, and another Kassite nobleman seized the throne and declared the city's freedom from Assyrian domination.

At this display of Assyrian weakness, the Elamites (who had never really ceased to be a threat) began to prod at the eastern border of Assyrian land. They came as far in as Nippur, and knocked the Assyrian-appointed king of that city off his throne two separate times.[21] They also invaded Babylon with enough force to march through the streets, ascend the temple steps, and nab the statue of Marduk (again), which they took off to Susa in victory. (They also took Hammurabi's law stele, which remained at Susa until it was uncovered by archaeologists a couple of millennia later.) They kidnapped Babylon's king, as an afterthought, and took him as well. He was less important than either Marduk's statue or Hammurabi's laws, and disappears from the historical record at once.

Tukulti-Ninurta's son, an entirely unimportant Assyrian king named Assur-nadin-apli, was helpless in the face of all this tumult and managed to hold onto his throne for only three years. Although we know little about his death, it probably came before its natural time; he was succeeded not by his son, but by his nephew. This nephew held the throne for only six years before losing it to another uncle, who after five years was forcibly removed (and probably murdered) by a usurper whose only right to the throne was that he claimed a distant descent from the great-great-great-uncle of Tukulti-Ninurta.

Over in Babylon, things were not much better. Another family of uncertain descent, the so-called Second Dynasty of Isin, had taken possession of the throne after the Elamite removal of the reigning sovereign; the first four undistinguished kings rose and fell in the space of fifteen years. And up in Hittite territory, Tudhaliya IV died, probably of old age (a rarity at this point). His sons and cousins quarrelled over the Hittite throne and its tiny raggedy remnant of an empire.

Even down in Egypt, the throne was under attack. The elderly Merneptah's mummy was scarcely interred when the succession suddenly failed; Merneptah's son and co-regent, Seti II, was temporarily run off his throne by a half-brother and only got it back after a three-year hiatus. He died shortly afterwards and left the crown to his son, who (judging from his mummy) suffered from polio and died young. At this point, the dead young king's step-mother Twosret tried to seize power, and the king lists trail off into anarchy. The chaos was aggravated by wandering raiders who came down into the Delta, as they generally did when Egypt's defenses languished. "The land of Egypt was overthrown from without," a later papyrus reads, "and every man done out of his right. . . . the land of Egypt was in the hands of chiefs and rulers of towns; each slew his neighbor."[22] The Nineteenth Dynasty had come to an undistinguished end.

The wheel had gone sideways; no one sat on top. After decades of war making, the energy poured into conquest had drained the kingdoms dry.

TIMELINE 38

MESOPOTAMIA AND ASIA MINOR			EGYPT
BABYLON	ASSYRIA	HITTITE	
			Amenhotep III (c. 1386–1349)
	Assur-uballit		**Akhenaten** (c. 1349–1334)
Burnaburiash	Middle Kingdom of Assyria		**Tutankhamun** (c. 1333–1325)
			Ay (c. 1325–1321)
			Horemheb (c. 1321–1293)
	Adad-nirari I		
		Muwatalli	*Dynasty 19* (1293–1185)
	Shalmaneser I	**Hattusilis III**	**Rameses II** (c. 1278–1212)
	Tukulti-Ninurta	**Tudhaliya IV**	
Kashtiliash IV			**Merneptah** (1212–1202)
	Assur-nadin-apli		
Second Dynasty of Isin			

Chapter Thirty-Nine

The End of the New Kingdom

Between 1185 and 1070 BC, Rameses III defeats the Sea People, but Egypt declines

AT SOME POINT during the muddle at the end of the Nineteenth Dynasty, a completely unknown king named Setnakhte came to the throne of Egypt and restored order. He may have been a grandson of Rameses II; he may simply have been an army officer with troops under his command. Whoever he was, he led an attack on the Asiatic invaders who were pressing into the Delta, and was so successful that his next move was to claim the crown.

The same papyrus that tells of the unrest at the Nineteenth Dynasty's end (a papyrus that comes from the reign of Setnakhte's grandson) credits Setnakhte with temporarily righting the Egyptian mess: not only driving off the usual "vile Asiatics," but restoring law and order so that local noblemen were no longer fighting with each other over control of land, opening temples which had closed out of fear or poverty, and putting priests back on duty.[1] And he did all this, apparently, within the span of three years, at which point he died and left the throne to his son.

This son took the name Rameses III, in imitation of the great pharaoh who had lived a hundred years before. He built a mortuary temple patterned after Rameses II's; like Rameses II, he added to the various temples of Amun and gifted their priests with land, hoping to make a name for himself as god-chosen. "You, Amun, established me on the throne of my father, as you did for Horus on the throne of Osiris," reads a prayer composed by Rameses III and written down by his son. "So I made you a house with towers of stone, rising to heaven; I built a wall before it; I filled its treasury with gold and silver, barley and wheat; its lands and its herds were like the sand of the shore."[2]

The gifts to Amun didn't keep invaders away. Like Rameses II, Rameses III found himself fighting a great battle against invaders from the north. Unlike

Rameses II, he fought not in the northern provinces of the Western Semitic lands, but at the border of Egypt itself.

RAMESES III had an early hint of trouble coming in the fifth year of his reign, when a peaceful migration swelled suddenly into an attack. Libyan tribes, Africans from the western desert, had been wandering, a few at a time, into Egypt: moving from the dry red land into the black. Since the Hyksos disaster, no foreign people had been allowed to rule themselves within Egypt's borders. When the Libyans showed signs of gathering together and appointing a king of their own, Rameses III sent his soldiers in to inflict a general slaughter. Shattered, the Libyans fled back into the desert, or were taken into slavery.[3]

Scarcely had this western threat been dealt with than all hell broke loose to the northeast. Setnakhte's expulsion of the "Asiatics" had been temporary. The Western Semitic lands were a general seething mess from Troy all the way over to Assur and down to Babylon, with local chiefs asserting their independence, Hittite borders shrinking, Assur and Babylon at odds, the Elamites rampaging along the eastern borders, and—to make matters worse—a growing migration of tribal peoples who were coming in a steady stream into the area from past the Aegean and the Black Sea (from what we would now call the mainland of Eastern Europe). The wanderers of the ancient world were gaining the edge over the organized kingdoms: "The foreign lands burst forth and scattered in the strife," Rameses III wrote on his temple wall, "no land could stand before them. They laid their hands on countries as far as the circuit of the whole earth."[4]

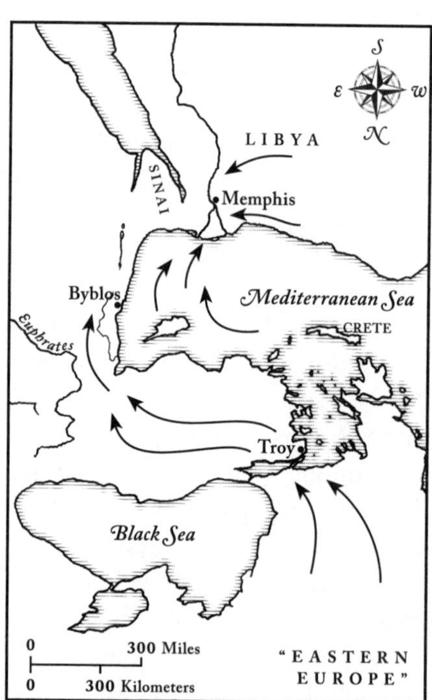

39.1 Sea Peoples Invade

Most of the "whole earth," as it happened, had been suffering through a decade of on-again, off-again drought, the same famine-producing dryness that probably sent the Libyans into the Delta. To thirsty wanderers, Egypt, with its always-watered lands, began to look like the world's prize jewel. Not long into Rameses III's reign, an organized alliance of invaders headed his way.

Invasions of the Delta were nothing new. But this particular invasion force was made up of a startling number of different tribes who swore allegiances with each other, with African tribes, and with Mycenaean seafarers (possibly mercenaries, leaving the Greek peninsula as the Mycenaean cities grew poorer). It is a little difficult to match the names Rameses III used for the invaders with our own names for the peoples in the area. Rameses's "Weshesh" were probably African tribes; the "Shekelesh" were most likely from the Aegean; the "Peleset" were a seafaring folk of vaguely Aegean origin, who probably came over by way of Crete in the wake of Mycenaean unrest. The Peleset seem to have been responsible for arming the force; Egyptian reliefs of the attackers show the whole force in crested helmets of Cretan style.[5]

Together, the invaders had a frightening strength. "Not one stood before their hands," Rameses III wrote, ". . . and they came with fire, prepared before them, forward to Egypt."[6] And perhaps the most alarming news came from the spies who told Rameses III that the armies, moving forwards towards Egypt, were trailed by oxcarts filled with women and children. These tribes didn't want to attack and raid Egypt. They wanted to move in and take over.[7]

The Egyptian soldiers marched up to meet the invasion at the border, and won the first clash. The reliefs carved onto the walls of Rameses III's mortuary temple gave the pharaoh credit for leading an enormous victory. In the carvings, the rejoicing Egyptian warriors are surrounded by piles of hands; it was customary for soldiers to sever the right hands of the dead and bring them back to the scribes, so that an accurate count of enemy casualties could be recorded.*

But the greater peril, given the Egyptian dislike for the Great Green, was yet to come: invasion by sea.

This second wave of the attack was directed by the experienced sailors in the alliance, probably those from the Aegean. Their skill on water was so great that the Egyptians, who had little sea experience and no fighting ships, knew the whole alliance by the name "Sea People."

Egyptian paintings of the battle show the Sea People on ships very different from the oar-driven Egyptian craft, which were designed for rivers. These were sailing ships, wind driven, with birds'-head prows.[8] Knowing that the Egyptians could never meet the expert sailors who manned them on equal terms, Rameses III filled his riverboats with soldiers until they were "manned completely from bow to stern with valiant warriors," and then clogged the harbor entrances in the Delta with them, "like a strong wall." He then lined his foot soldiers along

* The technique of "counting by hand" was varied, once or twice, in earlier battles, when the soldiers apparently decided to cut off penises and bring them for accounting instead (making for one particularly interesting relief, in which a scribe is comparing the hand-count with the penis-count to see if they agree).

39.1. Relief at Medinat Habu. An Egyptian scribe counts the severed hands of dead enemies; this scene is found on the victory relief of Rameses III at the temple of Medinet Habu. Photo credit Z. Radovan/www.BibleLandPictures.com

the banks with orders to pelt the incoming enemy ships with arrows and spears. "A wall of metal upon the shore surrounded them," he boasts.

The strategy worked. The sea warriors were overwhelmed by the sheer numbers that faced them. "They were dragged, overturned, and laid low upon the beach," the inscriptions conclude, "slain and made heaps from stern to bow of their galleys."[9] Temple paintings show lines of prisoners, manacled and on foot, paraded in front of the victorious Rameses III. The greatest threat since Kadesh had been beaten off.

THE FAULT LINE running through Egypt, temporarily plastered over by victory reliefs and building projects, was still liable to crack open at any point. Rameses III held the throne by right of his father's coup, and he was not immune to power plays.

Towards the end of his reign, one of his lesser wives hatched a plot to assassinate the king by mob violence. Scribes who recorded the affair during the reign of Rameses's successor say that she began a campaign to "stir up the people and incite enmity, in order to make rebellion against their lord."[10] Apparently she hoped that the mob would not only remove Rameses III, but also his appointed successor—his son by another wife—so that her own son would become king.

A harem plot to kill the pharaoh was hardly unknown, but this one was remarkable for the number of people involved. The court recorder lists, among others, the two royal standard-bearers, the butler, and the chief scribe. The overseer of the herds was accused of making wax figures of the king, apparently for use in an Egyptian form of voodoo;[11] the chief steward was convicted of spreading dissension. The conspiracy apparently stretched all the way down into Nubia: "Benemwese, formerly captain of archers in Nubia . . . was brought in because of the letter which his sister, who was in the harem, had written to him, saying, 'Incite the people to hostility!' "[12]

The records of the conspiratorial accusations end, in monotonous regularity, with either "He took his own life" or "The punishments of death were executed upon him." The exceptions were three conspirators who merely had their noses and ears cut off, and a single acquittal: a standard-bearer named Hori, who undoubtedly lived the rest of his years in disbelief that he alone had survived the purge.[13]

By the time the trials dragged to a close, the intended victim was offstage. Rameses III himself had died of old age.

Over the next eighty years, eight kings named Rameses ruled, most of them in such obscurity and chaos that only fragments of records and inscriptions survive. Egypt held onto its Nubian territories, but one by one its other holdings dropped away. The mines across the Sinai fell silent. Eventually the Nubian gold mines were abandoned by their workmen as well. By the 1140s, Egypt had stopped even trying to defend its Western Semitic holdings; the frontier forts lay just east of the Delta.[14] The tombs in the Valley of the Kings had not only been discovered, but plundered by thieves. Libyans near the Delta had taken to attacking Egyptians who strayed near the western border. A court official named Wenamun, attempting to travel up the coast in order to negotiate a good price for cedar logs from Byblos, was set upon and robbed of his money; the thieves had no fear of Egyptian reprisals. Wenamun finally did reach Byblos, but his mission failed. The king of Byblos was not inclined to accept Egyptian credit, which was no longer any good up north. "I am not your servant," he remarked to Wenamun, "nor am I the servant of the one who sent you. The logs stay here on the shore."[15]

Meanwhile, the priests of Amun were growing richer. Amun's reenthronement as chief god, under Tutankhamun, meant that pharaoh after pharaoh made rich offerings to the Temple of Amun. Rameses III gave Amun so much land that at the time of his death, the priests of Amun controlled almost a third of all the cropland in Egypt.

Horemheb's appointment of military officers to the priesthood—done to assure priestly loyalty to the throne—eventually backfired. Sometime around the twelfth year of Rameses XI, a general named Herihor managed to have himself appointed High Priest of Amun. He now controlled not only the army, but also the greatest treasure in Egypt. When he began to make demands, Rameses XI seems to have buckled without a fight. Less than five years later, Herihor became the Viceroy of Kush; not long after that, he began to style himself as Vizier of Egypt; and ten years later, his name began to appear as co-ruler of the entire country. His portrait was carved into the temple walls beside that of Rameses XI, the two men equal in size and power.[16]

When both men died within five years of each other, neither leaving a son and heir behind, their sons-in-law began a civil war. Rameses XI's son-in-law enthroned himself in the north, while Herihor's son-in-law claimed a divine right to rule the south from the city of Thebes.

This time, no great unifier appeared on the horizon. The New Kingdom had ended. Egypt remained divided, and soon sank into a confused and battling disaster: the Third Intermediate Period.

TIMELINE 39

MESOPOTAMIA AND ASIA MINOR			EGYPT
BABYLON	ASSYRIA	HITTITE	
		Muwatalli	*Dynasty 19* (1293–1185)
	Shalmaneser I	**Hattusilis III**	**Rameses II** (c. 1278–1212)
	Tukulti-Ninurta	**Tudhaliya IV**	
Kashtiliash IV			**Merneptah** (1212–1202)
	Assur-nadin-apli		*Dynasty 20* (1185–1070)
Second Dynasty of Isin			**Setnakhte** (c. 1185–1182)
			Rameses III (c. 1182–1151)
			Invasion of the Sea People
			Rameses IV-XI
			Herihor (c. 1080–1074)
			Third Intermediate Period (1070–664)

Chapter Forty

The Dark Age of Greece

In Greece, between 1200 and 1050 BC,
Dorian invaders bring a Dark Age

After the devastating victory at Troy, the Mycenaean ships had limped or blown back to the mainland of Greece, there to find that their homes had grown poor and troubled. Odysseus battled for ten years to get home and found his house overrun with enemies; Agamemnon returned to his wife and was murdered in his bath by her and her lover.

This was only a foretaste of disaster to come.

Around 1200 BC, a rash of fires spread across the peninsula. The Mycenaean city of Sparta burned to the ground. The city of Mycenae itself fought off an unknown enemy; the fortress survived, although damaged, but the houses outside the walls were left in ashes and never rebuilt.[1] The city of Pylos was swept by fire. A score of towns were shattered by some other disruption.

Archaeology suggests that the cities were resettled by a new people, who had no knowledge of writing (none appears in their remains), no skill in building with stone or brick, and no grasp of bronzeworking.[2] These new settlers came from the northern part of the peninsula, and were now moving south. Later historians called them the Dorians.

Both Thucydides and Herodotus credit the Dorians with a massive armed takeover of the Mycenaean cities. Herodotus tells of four Dorian invasions of Attica (the land around Athens), the first happening in the days when "Codrus was the king of Athens."[3] The later Greek writer Konon preserves the traditional story of the earliest attack: An oracle at the Dorian camp told the savage invaders that they would win the battle for Athens, as long as they didn't kill the Athenian king Codrus. When Codrus heard of this, he disguised himself as an ordinary Athenian, left his city, and went into the Dorian camp, where he picked a fight with armed Dorian warriors. In the brawl afterwards, he was killed, thus fulfilling the oracle and saving his city.[4]

40.1 Dorian Greece

The Dorians, amazed at such nobility, lifted the siege of Athens, but the retreat was only temporary. By the time the invasion was over, Thucydides tells us, the Dorians had become the "masters of the Peloponnese" (the southernmost part of the Greek peninsula).[5]

Thucydides and Herodotus both write of a violent irruption that spread across the land of the heroes and destroyed it. Like the Egyptian historians who recorded the invasion of the Hyksos, they could not conceive of any reason why their great ancestors should be defeated except for overwhelming military might. But the ruins of Mycenaean cities tell a slightly different story. Pylos and Mycenae burned as much as ninety years apart, which means that the Dorian influx itself spread slowly down over the peninsula over the course of a century. It was hardly a surprise attack; the Mycenaean Greeks had plenty of time to organize some sort of resistance.

But whatever defense these experienced soldiers mounted was too feeble to protect them—even against the Dorian newcomers, who were neither sophisticated nor battle hardened. And in some cities, there is no evidence of fighting at all. The tales of Athenian resistance (among the Mycenaean cities, only Athens boasted of repelling the invaders) may preserve a slightly different reality: no one ever attacked Athens. Excavations at Athens show no layer of destruction, no fire scars.[6]

But even so, the population of Athens shrank alarmingly. By 1100, a century and a half after the war with Troy, the northeast side of the Athenian acropolis (the high rock at the city's center, its most secure and defensible spot) had been peacefully abandoned. The Sparta that the Dorians burned down was already empty; its inhabitants had gone some years before.[7] The northerners poured down into a south already weakened and disorganized.

The war with Troy certainly had something to do with the slow decay of the Mycenaean cities, something which Thucydides himself makes note of: the "late return of the Hellenes from Troy," he remarks, provoked strife so severe that many Mycenaeans were driven from their own cities. But there must have been other factors at work. Two or three years of bad weather in a row, lessening crops just at a time when the old reliable sources of grain from Egypt and Asia Minor had also been disrupted by wars in both places, would have forced the Mycenaean cities to compete for food; hunger can kindle wars between cities and send city-dwellers into exile. And in fact the rings of Irish oaks and some trees from Asia Minor show signs of a drought that came sometime in the 1150s.[8]

Another, more fearful enemy may have stalked the Mycenaeans as well.

In the opening scenes of the Iliad, the Trojan priest Chryses begs the god Apollo to send illness on the attacking Greeks, in repayment for the kidnapping of Chryses's daughter by the Greek warrior Agamemnon. Apollo answers his prayer and fires down arrows of sickness on the enemy ships. The result is deadly:

> He made a burning wind
> of plague rise in the army: rank and file
> sickened and died for the ill their chief had done.[9]

Very likely the Mycenaeans encamped on the shore *were* struck by plague, and the sickness was probably bubonic.

The Trojans didn't know, any more than other ancient peoples, exactly how bubonic plague was spread. But they knew that the sickness had something to do with rodents. The Apollo who spreads sickness was honored, at Troy, with a name peculiar to Asia Minor: he was called Apollo Sminthian, "Lord of the Mice."[10] The Iliad also tells us that Apollo Sminthian's arrows carried off not just men, but horses and dogs; this spreading of sickness through the animal population is a constant in ancient accounts of bubonic plague. ("This pest raged not only among domestic animals, but even among wild beasts," wrote Gregory of Tours, fifteen hundred years later.)[11]

The Mycenaean heroes, returning, would have brought death back with them. A ship with no sick people on board, docking on an uninfected shore, might still have plague-carrying rats in its hold. In fact, plague tended to follow famine; grain shipments from one part of the world to another carried rats from one city to the next, spreading disease across an otherwise unlikely distance.

Plague, drought, and war: these were enough to upset the balance of a civilization that had been built in rocky dry places, close to the edge of survival. When existence became difficult, the able-bodied moved away. And so not only Mycenaeans, but Cretans and residents of the Aegean islands spread out

TIMELINE 40	
EGYPT	GREEK PENINSULA
Dynasty 19 (1293–1185)	
Rameses II (c. 1278–1212)	
	Mycenaean attack on Troy VIIA (c. 1260)
Merneptah (1212–1202)	
	Dorian influx from the north
Dynasty 20 (1185–1070)	
Setnakhte (c. 1185–1182)	Beginning of Greek Dark Age
Rameses III (c. 1182–1151)	
Invasion of the Sea People	
Rameses IV-XI	
Herihor (c. 1080–1074)	
Third Intermediate Period (1070–664)	

from their homeland in small bands, looking for new homes and hiring themselves out as mercenaries. It is impossible to tell how many of the Sea People fighting against Egypt were hired hands. But Egyptian accounts tell us that in the years before the Sea People invasion, the pharaoh had hired troops from the Aegean to fight *for* Egypt *against* the Libyans of the western desert. By the middle of the eleventh century, the Dorians, not the Mycenaeans, were masters of the south; and Mycenaean soldiers were available to the highest bidder.

The Dorian settlers had no king and court, no taxes and tributes, and no foreign sea trade. They farmed, they survived, and they had no particular need to write anything down. Their occupation plunged the peninsula into what we call a dark age: we cannot peer very far into it because there are no written records.*

* It seems that most of the Chinese and Indian history that we've covered to this point would also fall within a dark age, but the term tends to be used only when written records have been kept and then trail off, rather than for times before written accounts are widely used.

Chapter Forty-One

The Dark Age of Mesopotamia

Between 1119 and 1032 BC, the Hittites collapse, and the prosperity of Assyria and Babylon withers

WHILE THE MYCENAEANS deserted their cities and the Dorians trickled down into them, disruption was rippling eastwards, past Troy (now shabbily rebuilt, resettled, and a ghost of its former magnificent self) and farther east, into the lands still held by the Hittites.

By this time, the Hittite empire was not much more than a shadow state. The poverty, famine, and general unrest of Tudhaliya IV's reign had worn away its outer edges, and fighting over the throne continued. During the Mycenaean slide downwards, Tudhaliya IV's younger son took the crown away from his older brother and claimed the country for himself. He called himself Suppiluliuma II, in an effort to evoke the great Hittite empire-builder of a century and a half earlier.

Suppiluliuma II's inscriptions brag of his own victories against Sea Peoples. He fought several naval engagements off the coast of Asia Minor, beating off Mycenaean refugees and mercenaries, and managed for a time to keep his southern coast free of invasion. But he could not bring back the golden days of Hittite power, when his namesake had almost managed to put a son on the throne of Egypt itself.

The same wandering peoples who had pushed towards Egypt—peoples fleeing famine, or plague, or overpopulation, or war in their own lands—were pressing into Asia Minor. Some came from the direction of Troy, across the Aegean Sea and into Hittite land. Others came from the sea; Cyprus, the island south of the Hittite coast, apparently served them as a staging point. "Against me the ships from Cyprus drew up in line three times for battle in

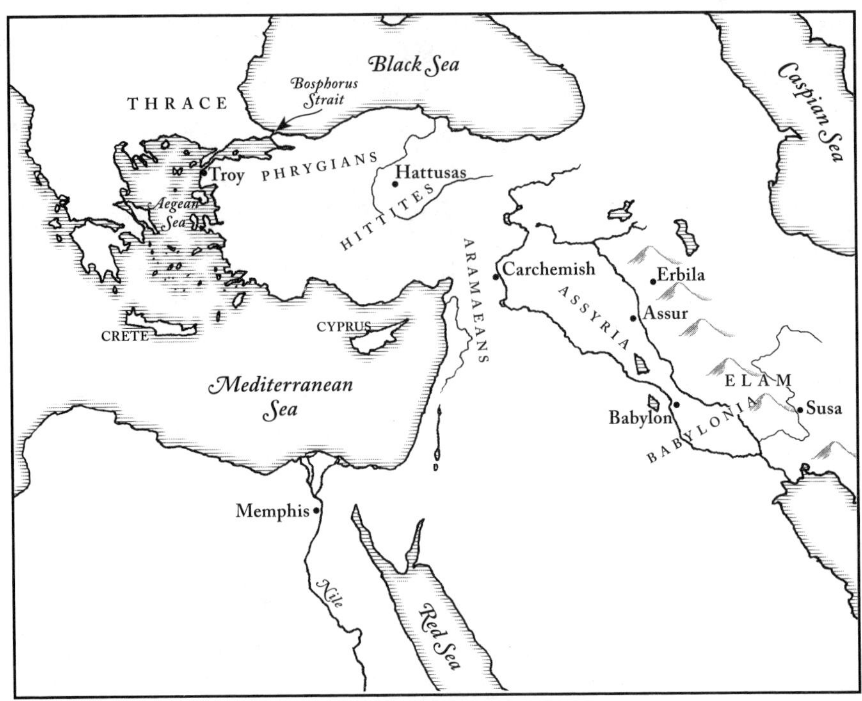

41.1 End of the Hittites

the midst of the sea," Suppiluliuma II writes. "I destroyed them, I seized the ships and in the midst of the sea I set them on fire. . . . [Yet] the enemy in multitudes came against me from Cyprus."[1] Still other enemies crossed over the narrow Bosphorus Strait, from the area north of the Greek peninsula called Thrace; these tribes were known as the Phrygians.

There were too many of them, and the Hittite army was too small. The newcomers moved right through Suppiluliuma's troops, scattered his defenses, and arrived in the heart of his kingdom. The capital city Hattusas burned to the ground; its people fled; the royal court dispersed like dust.

The Hittite language survived in a few separated cities around the southern edge of the old empire; Carchemish was the largest. In these last outposts of the Hittites, the Hittite gods hung onto life. But the kingdom that had worshipped them was gone.

THE EBB of three civilizations in a western crescent—the Hittites, the Mycenaeans, the Egyptians—coincided with a sudden burst of power to the east.

For a few brief years, while the wandering nomads and Sea Peoples were busy harassing the west, Assyria and Babylon brightened.

In Assyria, the king Tiglath-Pileser was crowned not long after the sack of Hattusas. His great-grandfather, grandfather, and father had each in turn ruled over the Assyrian heartland—an upside-down triangle with Assur at its bottom point, stretching up and over to Erbila on the west and Nineveh on the east. It was a nice little area, prosperous and easily defended, with the richest corn-growing land in all of Mesopotamia. All three kings had been content to hold it, defend it, and keep it safe.

Tiglath-Pileser wanted more. He was the first warlike king since Shalmaneser, eight generations and a hundred years earlier. He turned against the invaders and used their attacks to take more land for himself. And for a brief period—a little under forty years—Assyria regained something like its previous luminescence.

The Phrygians, having stormed through the Hittite territory, were approaching Assyria on the northwest. In one of his earliest victories, Tiglath-Pileser beat them off. His inscriptions boast that he defeated an army of twenty thousand Phrygians (he calls them "Mushki") in the valley of the northern Tigris: "I made their blood flow down the ravines and pour from the heights of the mountains," he explains. "I cut off their heads and piled them like grain heaps."[2]

And then he went on fighting his way northwest, heading right into the face of the approaching wave. "[I set out for] the lands of the distant kings who were on the shore of the Upper Sea, who had never known subjection," he wrote in his annals. "I took my chariots and my warriors and over the steep mountain and through their wearisome paths I hewed a way with pickaxes of bronze; I made passable a road for my chariot and my troops. I crossed the Tigris. . . . I scattered warriors . . . and made their blood to flow."[3]

For thirty-eight years, Tiglath-Pileser fought. An expanding list of cities, conquered by the king, sent taxes and laborers to the Assyrian palace and suffered under the rule of Assyrian governors.[4] Among them was Carchemish; Tiglath-Pileser had taken it (according to his own inscriptions, anyway) "in one day."[5] Other cities gave up without a fight, their kings greeting Tiglath-Pileser's approach by coming out and falling down to kiss his feet.[6] Tiglath-Pileser himself travelled all the way to the Mediterranean coast, where he went dolphin-hunting on a spear-boat rowed by his men.[7] The pharaoh of Egypt—one of the eight Rameses—sent him a crocodile for a present, which Tiglath-Pileser took back to add to his game preserve in Assur.[8] He built shrines and fortresses and temples, each proclaiming that at long last, Assyria had another great king.

Down to Assyria's south, Babylon also saw the rise of a great king.

Babylon and its surrounding lands had been ruled by nobodies ever since Burnaburiash, who had corresponded with Tutankhamun two hundred years earlier. Within three or four years of Tiglath-Pileser's accession up in Assur, the undistinguished line of the Second Dynasty of Isin spat out a genetic sport named Nebuchadnezzar.*

While Tiglath-Pileser fought his way west and north, Nebuchadnezzar turned east. The statue of Marduk, after all, was still in the hands of the Elamites of Susa; since its capture a hundred years before, no king of Babylon had proved himself mighty enough to get it back.†

Nebuchadnezzar's first invasion of Elam was met by a wall of Elamite soldiers. He ordered his troops to retreat, and made a cunning plan for a second attempt. He would march his men into Elam at the very height of summer, a time when no commander with any sense would force an army to march anywhere. The Babylonian soldiers, arriving at Elam's borders, caught the border patrols by surprise and made it to the city of Susa before anyone could raise the alarm. They raided the city, broke down the temple doors, kidnapped the statue, and departed to march in triumph back to Babylon.

Rather than waiting around for the priests of Marduk to acknowledge their debt to him, Nebuchadnezzar hired scribes to compose tales about the rescue, not to mention hymns in Marduk's honor. Stories and songs and offerings streamed from the royal palace to the Temple of Marduk until the god stood at the top of the Babylonian pantheon; it was in the reign of Nebuchadnezzar I that Marduk became the chief god of the Babylonians.[9] And in a classic circular argument, Nebuchadnezzar reasoned that, since he had rescued the chief god of Babylon, the chief god of Babylon had set divine favor on him. The undistinguished beginnings of the Second Dynasty were forgotten; Nebuchadnezzar had the god-given right to rule Babylon.

UNDER THESE TWO mighty kings, Babylon and Assyria were more or less balanced in power. Sharp border spats occasionally intensified into actual battles. A couple of Assyrian frontier towns were sacked by Babylonian soldiers, and Tiglath-Pileser retorted by marching all the way down to Babylon and burning the king's palace.[10] This sounds more serious than it was. Babylon lay so close

* This is Nebuchadnezzar I, who is less well known than his namesake Nebuchadnezzar II; it is the latter king (c. 605–561 BC) who captured Jerusalem, rebuilt Babylon, and (according to tradition) built the Hanging Gardens of Babylon for his homesick wife.

† See chapter 38, pp. 270–271.

to the Assyrian border that most of the Babylonian government offices had already been moved elsewhere. The city was a sacred site, but no longer a center of power. And Tiglath-Pileser, his point made, marched back home and left Babylon alone. He did not intend to provoke an all-out war. The two kingdoms were equally strong, and there were more serious threats to face.

The movement of peoples from the north and west had not stopped. Tiglath-Pileser was continually fighting border battles against roving wanderers who were rapidly becoming as pervasive as the Amorites had been, almost a thousand years before. These people were Western Semites who had lived in the northwest of the Western Semitic lands, until pushed onwards by the influx of people from farther west. The Assyrians called them Aramaeans, and by Tiglath-Pileser's own accounts, he made something like twenty-eight different campaigns to the west, each aimed at beating back Aramaean invasions.

Nor were Babylon and Assyria immune from the famine and drought, the crop failures and sickness plaguing the rest of the known world. Court records describe the last years of Tiglath-Pileser's reign as desperate and hungry, a time when the Assyrian people had to scatter into the surrounding mountains to find food.[11]

Babylon was in hardship too, and the city's suffering grew more intense as Nebuchadnezzar's twenty-year reign drew to an end. The city's troubles are described in the Erra Epic, a long poem in which the god Marduk complains that his statue is unpolished, his temple in disrepair, but he can't leave Babylon long enough to do anything about it, because every time he departs the city, something horrendous happens to it. The current horrendousness is the hovering mischief of another god, Erra, who because of his nature can't resist afflicting the city: "I shall finish off the land and count it as ruins," he says. "I shall fell the cattle, I shall fell the people." Babylon itself, shrivelled by the wind, had become like a "luxuriant orchard" whose fruit had withered before ripening. "Woe to Babylon," Marduk mourns, "I filled it with seeds like a pine cone, but its abundance did not come to harvest."[12]

The dryness and failed crops suggest famine; the falling of people and cattle, a repeat visitation of the arrows of Apollo Sminthian. Sickness and hunger did nothing to improve the defenses of either city. By the time that Tiglath-Pileser's son succeeded his father, the Aramaean problem had become so acute that he was forced to make a treaty with the new king of Babylon. Together, the two kingdoms hoped to beat off their common enemy.

The attempt failed. Not long after, Aramaeans rampaged across Assyria, seizing for themselves all but the very center of the empire. They invaded Babylon as well; the son of Nebuchadnezzar, the great king, lost his throne to an Aramaean usurper.

The Aramaeans, like the Dorians, did not write. And so as Egypt descended into fractured disorder and darkness spread across the Greek peninsula, a similar fog rolled from the old Hittite lands to cover Mesopotamia. The land between the two rivers entered its own dark age, and for a hundred years or so, no history emerges from the blackness.

TIMELINE 41

GREEK PENINSULA	MESOPOTAMIA AND ASIA MINOR		
	BABYLON	ASSYRIA	HITTITE
		Shalmaneser I	**Hattusilis III**
Mycenaean attack on Troy VIIA (c. 1260)		**Tukulti-Ninurta**	**Tudhaliya IV**
	Kastiliash V		
Dorian influx from the north		**Assur-nadin-apli**	
			Suppiluliuma II
Beginning of Greek Dark Age	Second Dynasty of Isin		Hattusus sacked (c. 1180)
	Nebuchadnezzar I (1125–1104)		
		Tiglath-Pileser (1115–1076)	
		Ashur-bel-kala (1074–1056)	
	Aramaean takeover		

Chapter Forty-Two

The Fall of the Shang

In China, between 1073 and 1040 BC, the Shang Dynasty falls to the virtue of the Zhou

FARTHER TO THE EAST, Wu Ting had passed his throne, after a sixty-year reign, to his son. The Shang kingship went on, for some years, from brother to brother or father to son, more or less in peace. The center of the Shang empire was the Yellow river, and the Shang capital remained at Yin.

By the time that the Mesopotamian kingdoms had begun to crumble, though, the kingship of China was also in crisis.

It was a very different crisis than any faced by Nebuchadnezzar I or Tiglath-Pileser. The Shang kings and their people were not dealing with the invasions of unknown foreign tribes; the Shang king's enemies were the cousins of his own people.

Just west of the Shang lands, the Zhou tribe lay across the Wei river valley. They were not exactly subjects of the Shang king, although their chief—the "Lord of the West"—paid lip service to the authority of the crown. Their land, after all, lay almost four hundred miles distant from the capital. Oracle bones travelled back and forth between the Lord of the West and the Shang palace, keeping a path of shared language and customs open.[1] But the Zhou noblemen were loyal first to their own lord, not to the distant Shang monarch. When rebellion broke out, they looked to the Lord of the West for their orders.

THE ANCIENT CHRONICLES make it very clear that the Shang kings brought this rebellion on themselves. They abandoned wisdom, and this wisdom (not military might, as in the west) was the foundation of their power.

The emperor Wu-yi, the fifth ruler to follow Wu Ting, showed the first signs of decay. His offenses, according to Sima Qian, were primarily against

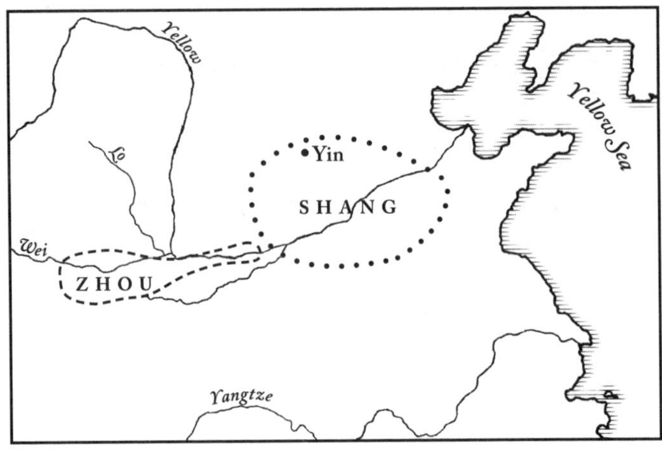

42.1 Shang and Zhou

the gods: he made idols, "called them heavenly gods," and played lots with them. When he won, he mocked the idols as lousy gamblers.

This was a serious breach of his royal responsibilities. With more and more weight being placed on the oracle-bone ritual, the royal court had become the center of divine revelations from the ancestors to the living. All queries to the ancestors were carried out in the name of the king; he was the conduit for the messages from the divine powers. For him to mock those powers was appalling.

The punishment fit the crime; Wu-yi was struck by lightning while out hunting. He was succeeded by his son and then his grandson, under whom (according to Sima Qian) the country declined still more. Then his great-grandson Chou inherited, and the Shang authority crashed.

Chou was gifted with natural graces—Sima Qian praises him for his strength, intelligence, articulateness, and perception—but he used them all for ill. "His knowledge was sufficient to resist remonstrance," Qian writes, "and his speech was adequate to cover up his wrongdoing. . . . He considered everyone beneath him. He was fond of wine, licentious in pleasure, and doted on women." Chou's love of wine and pleasure led him to raise taxes so that he could stock his hunting forests and pleasure parks with game; his love of women put him under the spell of a cruel and domineering courtesan named Ta Chi, whose words became the only ones he would hear. His love of spectacle grew so great that he built a pool and filled it with wine, hung meat like a forest around it, and "made naked men and women chase one another" around the pool and through the forest.[2]

Weird frivolity gave way to serious tyranny. Noblemen suspected of disloyalty were forced to lie on a red-hot rack. Chou had one court official flayed, and another carved up into meat strips and hung to dry. When his uncle remonstrated with him, he remarked that since the heart of a wise man had seven chambers, he would need to examine his uncle's heart with his own eyes before heeding his advice—and then carried out the threat. His cruelty worsened until "it knew no end." The noblemen—the "families of the hundred cognomens," those with honorable names—were "filled with resentment and hatred."

Finally he overstepped himself. The Zhou chief Wen, the Lord of the West, was in the capital on business, and Chou had set his spies to follow him. When the spies reported that the Lord of the West had "sighed in secret" over the behavior of the king, Chou had Wen arrested and thrown into jail.*

Hearing that their lord was in jail, the Zhou tribes brought Chou the kind of tribute likely to soften his heart: fine objects and beautiful women. Chou, properly touched, set Wen free. But the Lord of the West refused to return home without making some effort to shield Chou's oppressed subjects from the king's brutality. He told Chou that he had a proposition for him; if he would promise to stop using his red-hot rack, Wen would gift him with the fertile Zhou land around the Lo river, which flowed south to join the Wei. Chou, who had done very well out of Wen's imprisonment, agreed to the deal, took ownership of the land, and sent Wen home.

This turned out to be a mistake. Wen was much loved in his own lands as a warrior-king who was both good (as shown by his willingness to sacrifice his own lands for the people) and mighty (the later Chinese historian and philosopher Mengzi mentions, offhand, that he was ten feet tall).[3] Back in the west, he began quietly to round up opposition to the king. "Many of the feudal lords rebelled," Qian writes, "and turned to the Lord of the West." They were joined by the sages of the court who read the oracle bones and divine prophecies; they rose up en masse with all their instruments of ritual, left the court, and marched west.

Wen, by this time an elderly man (a hundred years old, according to Mengzi), died before he could lead his followers into the Shang capital.[4] But his son Wu took up his banner. Eight hundred of the feudal lords lined up behind him, each with their own soldiers. The Zhou army of fifty thousand marched towards the Shang palace at Yin. And Chou ordered his own troops out to meet the attack: seven hundred thousand strong.

* Wen and Wu appear as Wenwang and Wuwang in the Pinyin system; "Wang," or "king," becomes the suffix of all royal Zhou names. I have used "King Wen" and "King Wu" instead.

The two armies met about twenty miles outside Yin, at the Battle of Muye. By any measure, the imperial army should have crushed the tiny rebel force, but the Zhou had two advantages. The first was tactical: Zhou noblemen had provided three hundred war-chariots, while the royal army had none at all.[5] But it was the second advantage—the Zhou possession of the moral high ground—that turned the battle against the king. The king's men, disgusted with their leader's cruelty, were ripe for defection. As the Zhou line thundered towards them, the Shang soldiers in the front line reversed the direction of their attack and drove the men behind them back, turning the entire army around and throwing it into flight.[6]

Seeing the inevitable defeat looming, Chou retreated to his palace, where he donned jade armor in preparation for a last stand. But the invading Zhou forces burned the palace down around his ears. He died in flames, a poetic end for the man who had used fire to torture and kill.

There is in this story a strong whiff of discomfort with Wen's revolt. The ancient historians do not celebrate the overthrow of the tyrant, and Wu makes no boast of reigning from horizon to horizon, or of piling enemy heads by the gates. He is praised not for his skill at fighting, but for his restoration of proper order.

The rebellion of the Zhou is not exactly the disobedience of a governed people. Even before the revolt, the Shang king had an ambiguous power over the Zhou. Wen was a king in his own right, but the Shang king was able to throw him in jail and force a ransom. On the other hand, when Wen offered Chou a gift of land, the king recognized it happily as a present, rather than pointing out indignantly that he already ruled it.

But the ancient historians still find themselves forced to justify the Zhou defiance. The Zhou and Shang were sibling cultures, and battles between them were as disconcerting as the hostility between Set and Osiris in the early years of Egypt. It is positively necessary that the first Zhou king be, not a lawless subject, but rather a virtuous man who rises up to overthrow vice and begin the cycle again. For this reason, the Zhou rule is dated not from the victorious Wu, but from his father, who was unjustly imprisoned and who willingly sacrificed land for the good of his people. He, not his warlike son, is considered to be the first Zhou king. The Shang rule is said to have ended not at the gates of the burning palace, but back when the noblemen and the oracle-readers gathered under the leadership of the Lord of the West. And the Zhou takeover was not the invasion of an enemy people. Chou's own lawlessness was the cause of his death. For the Chinese chroniclers, rot always came from within.

Virtue notwithstanding, Wu of the Zhou claimed his new title by thrusting a pike into Chou's singed head and staking it out in front of Yin's gates for all to see. The old order had perished in fire; the new order had arrived.

TIMELINE 42

MESOPOTAMIA AND ASIA MINOR			CHINA
BABYLON	ASSYRIA	HITTITE	
	Shalmaneser I	**Hattusilis III**	
	Tukulti-Ninurta	**Tudhaliya IV**	
Kastiliash V			
	Assur-nadin-apli		
		Suppiluliuma II	**Wu-yi**
Second Dynasty of Isin		Hattusus sacked (c. 1180)	
Nebuchadnezzar I (1125–1104)			
	Tiglath-Pileser (1115–1076)		**Chou**
			Zhou Dynasty (1087–256)
	Ashur-bel-kala (1074–1056)		Western Zhou (1087–771)
Aramaean takeover			**Wen**
			Wu

Part Four

EMPIRES

Chapter Forty-Three

The Mandate of Heaven

Between 1040 and 918 BC, the Zhou kings of China come up with a justification for empire-building and discover its shortcomings

ALTHOUGH WU was the first Zhou king, Wen (who died before the final conquest of the Shang) very soon became the symbolic beginning of the new dynasty. Much later, Confucius would remark that although the music by which Emperor Wen celebrated his victories was perfectly beautiful and perfectly good, the victory music of the Emperor Wu "though perfectly beautiful, was not perfectly good."[1] Wu's violent scouring of the Shang capital was a dangerous violation of the emperor's divine authority.

No one wanted the Shang back, but Wu's new dynasty had to be justified with care. At the start of his reign, Sima Qian tells us, Wu sacrificed to the heavens to make up for the misdeeds of the last Shang ruler; he "put aside shields and pole-axes, stored his weapons, and discharged his soldiers, to show to the world that he would no longer use them."[2] The resulting peace was intended to make up for the frenzy of his accession.

This was all very ethical, but also a practical necessity. To keep his throne, Wu would have to rule by influence and tact, not sheer force. The Shang king had been unable to fight off the united force of the feudal lords, and Wu also had to face facts: he ruled over a kingdom filled with strong personalities who would resent too autocratic a rule. Sima Qian refers to the "Lords of the Nine Lands"—noblemen who governed their own territories, while still owing loyalty to the king. But there were many more than nine lands; the *Record of Rites*, written several hundred years later, counts up a total of 1,763 separately governed territories at the beginning of the Zhou Period.*[3]

* Ancient Chinese chronicles mingle history and philosophy to an extent that makes them difficult to use as sources for a traditional historical narrative. Perhaps the oldest Chinese text is the philo-

Inscriptions of gifts given and loyalties claimed seem to show a complicated pyramid-like structure with as many as five ranks of officials sloping down from the Zhou throne to a second rank of "enfeoffed" lords who had control of the states, through three more ranks of noblemen with decreasing territory and power.[4]

Many histories call these noblemen "feudal lords." The Zhou king did possess some sort of claim to the whole country; he did not "own" China's land, as a medieval feudal lord might, but he did claim the right to *run* it properly. This right of administration he granted to his noblemen, in exchange for their loyalty and (when necessary) military support. When a "lord" was "enfeoffed" by the king of the Zhou, he wasn't given a gift of his land; instead he was given gifts as a symbol that the Zhou king had awarded him a portion of sacred authority. Most often, these gifts were bronze vessels with inscriptions. A gift of bronze symbolized both wealth and power: enough power to control the miners who dug the metal out of the earth, the craftsmen who cast it into shape, and the priests who inscribed it.[5] The Zhou position at the top of the power ladder was represented by nine of these ceremonial vessels: the Nine Cauldrons, which resided in the Zhou capital city.

There's a big difference between this sort of "feudal" relationship and the

---

sophically oriented *I ching* (Pinyin *Yi jing*, Book of Changes). The bulk of it is traditionally ascribed to the founder of the Shang Dynasty; valuable commentaries were added to it during the Warring States Period (475–221 BC). The next continuous Chinese texts available to us come from the time of Confucius (551–479 BC). The *Shi jing* (Classic of Poetry) contains 305 poems collected (according to tradition) by Confucius, who is also credited with the first chronological Chinese history, the *Ch'un-ch'iu* (Pinyin *Chun qiu*, or Spring and Autumn Annals); this history covers events from 722 BC until just before the end of Confucius's lifetime. Sometime between 475 and 221 BC, an anonymous commentator added additional notes to the *Ch'un-ch'iu*; these are known as the *Tso chuan* (Pinyin *Zuo zhuan*). In the fourth century BC, the *Shu ching* (Pinyin *Shu jing*, also known as the *Shang shu* or Official History), came into circulation; it was a compilation covering history from the days of the Sage Kings down to the end of the Western Zhou Period. In 124 BC, these "Five Classics" (the *I ching*, *Shi jing*, *Shu ching*, and *Ch'un-ch'iu*, plus a text dealing with rites and rituals called the *Li ching*) were placed together as a central program for the training of Chinese scholars and became known collectively as the *Wu ching*. Sima Qian, writing between 145 and 85 BC, used all of these as sources.

Other useful sources for China's ancient history include the so-called Bamboo Annals (*Zu shu jinian*), copies of Eastern Zhou records from the years 770 to 256 BC; and the *Guanzi*, a collection of anonymous historical essays written (probably) between 450 and 100 BC and put together into one book by the scholar Liu Xiang in 26 BC.

Finally, historical information can be found in the "Four Books" (*Si shu*) published around AD 1190. The Four Books are a collection that includes two chapters from the *Li ching*, published separately and attributed directly to Confucius; the writings of Mengzi, the most famous disciple of Confucius; and a collection of Confucius's sayings called *Lun yu* and generally known in English as the Analects.

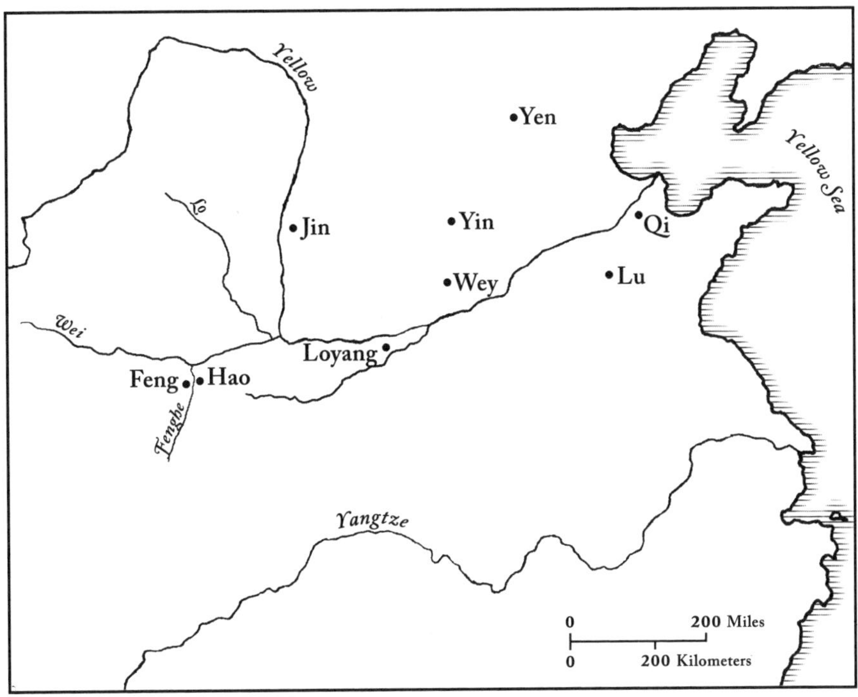

43.1 The Western Zhou

feudalism practiced in later times. For one thing, later feudal lords would claim actual possession of the land, not mere moral authority over it. Moral authority can disappear in an awful hurry. Wu himself leaned heavily on the justice of his court to prop up his power. "To secure Heaven's protection," he tells one of his younger brothers, not long after gaining the throne, ". . . we must single out the evil people and remove them. . . . Day and night we must reward and comfort the people to secure our western land."[6] He also did his best to pay homage to the divine authority which the Shang had held before him. He did move his capital city to the double city of Feng and Hao, separated by the Fenghe river;* but he appointed Chou's own son, the deposed heir to the throne, as one of his subject lords, with authority over a vassal center of the old Shang domain. According to Sima Qian, this son, Lu-fu, was given the old capital city of Yin as his base, and put in charge of the surrounding area, because "Yin had just been pacified, and [the situation] was not yet

* The Zhou Dynasty is generally divided into two. The first half, the period when the Zhou capital city was in the western part of the kingdom, is known as the Western Zhou and stretched from c. 1100 to 771 BC.

settled." Wu also detailed two of his younger brothers to "assist" the ex-prince; two watchdogs to make sure that Lu-fu behaved himself.[7]

As soon as Wu died, the shakiness of his authority became clear. His son was still young, and so his brother Tan took charge as regent. Almost at once, though, the two brothers who were supposed to be supervising Lu-fu organized an armed uprising in the middle of the old Shang territory. They intended to put Lu-fu back on the throne as their puppet-ruler.

Tan turned out the army in the name of the young king and overwhelmed the rebels with numbers. Lu-fu died in the fight, as did one of the brothers; and Tan then did his best to break up the remaining Shang resistance by deporting the obstinate Shang loyalists who lived around Yin to other parts of the empire.[8] Granting any recognition to the divine authority of the Shang was simply too dangerous.

Ancient accounts tell us that, after seven years of regency, Tan willingly stepped down as regent and turned the reins of power over to the now-grown Ch'eng. Perhaps he actually did. On the other hand, this relinquishment of power goes even further towards solving the knotty problem of the Zhou rise to power. The young king Ch'eng held his power only because his father was a regicide. When Tan, a man praised across his entire country for both wisdom and virtue, willingly handed authority over to him, his power was shifted onto a different foundation.[9] A virtuous man gives his power away only to a *more* virtuous man, and that man was Ch'eng.

Tan stayed on as one of the young king's ministers. As the "Duke of Zhou," he is credited with organizing the Chinese state into an efficient bureaucracy, perhaps for the first time. This organization involved the proper oversight of land, a tax system, appointments of officials, and other mundane details. But the Duke of Zhou's most important job was the gathering together of all the ceremonies surrounding the royal court into a book of ritual. If the Zhou king was to rule without constantly using his army to whip rebels into shape, his divine authority needed to be clearly on view. The rituals that surrounded him would be the outward show of his moral authority, the visible shadow cast by his invisible right to rule.

With his power at the center of the kingdom established, Ch'eng now had to worry about the edges of it. No book of ritual was going to convince peoples who lived a day's ride or more from the capital city that the Zhou king must be obeyed. That would have to be done by force.

The eastern side of his empire was, perhaps, the most worrying; the Shang remnant had been settled out there and needed to be watched. So the Duke of Zhou built a fortress to the east, in a strategic spot: it would dominate the Yellow river ford (which could be crossed by a hostile army) and protect the eastern approach to the Zhou capital.[10] This fortress became the center of a new city: Loyang.*

Ch'eng then sent his brothers out to build similar centers of Zhou watchfulness along the other edges of his domain. This had the additional advantage of getting them out of the capital and away from any temptation to steal his crown. As a result, the outer ring of the Zhou kingdom became a set of Zhou colonies, each ruled by a royal relative. The largest were at Jin, Wey, Lu, Qi, and Yen (the original city of the ancient Yen colony lay at the modern site of Peking).

Ch'eng fought a continual battle to keep the edges of his empire safe against the tribes who lived beyond his borders and did not recognize his authority. But he was careful to connect this use of force to his divine right to rule. "Heaven's mandate is not to be presumed upon," he tells his followers, as he prepares for another campaign of conquest against the east; he may have been granted the right to rule because of his virtue, but heaven did not expect him to relax and wait for *everyone* to recognize it. He is the first Chinese king, so far as we know, to use the phrase "Mandate of Heaven."[11] The Mandate of Heaven gave Ch'eng the right to take up arms; his success in battle demonstrated the reality of the Mandate of Heaven. It is a sort of circular reasoning that we have seen before.

CH'ENG DIED around 996 BC, after a thirty-year rule; his son K'ang took the throne.

Under King K'ang's chief general, the northern edge of the kingdom was pushed farther out. The Zhou army marched against a northern tribe known as the Guifang and subjugated them by force. "I captured 13,081 men," the general boasted, "along with horses, thirty chariots, 355 oxen and thirty-eight sheep."[12]

If this sounds more like an Assyrian boast than anything we have heard so far, it is; out on the edges of the empire, the Mandate of Heaven had to be backed up with armed troops. K'ang's son Zhao, who came to the throne around 977, followed his father's example and planned another campaign of expansion, this one to the south. Apparently he was encouraged in this by a comet, which seemed a fortunate portent.

But the comet was deceptive. "His six armies were lost," the Bamboo Annals tell us, "and the king died."[13] Sima Qian's account is a little more circumspect:

* The scholar Li Xueqin points out that Confucius calls the whole town Chengzhou, a name which other histories occasionally use. Chengzhou was technically the name of the entire city, which consisted of the twinned towns Loyang and Wangcheng; Wangcheng was the "king's town," the western area of the city where the later king P'ing and his successors resided. (See Li Xueqin, *Eastern Zhou and Qin Civilizations,* pp. 16–17.) For clarity's sake I have chosen to use Loyang throughout.

"In the time of King Zhao, the kingly way of government diminished," he writes. "King Zhao took an inspection tour to the south and did not return. . . . His death was not announced to the feudal lords; it was forbidden to speak of it. They enthroned King Zhao's son."[14] This is hardly surprising; Zhao's death suggested that he had not been protected by the Mandate of Heaven after all, and it was best to conceal this from his subject lords.

With the "six armies" (the primary royal army, stationed in the capital) wiped out, Zhao's son Mu soon discovered that he would have to redefine the Mandate in order to hold onto it at all. When he began to plan to use his remaining forces against another northern tribe, the Chuan-Jung, his noblemen remonstrated with him. The Mandate of Heaven did not stretch quite that far out, Mu was told. As a matter of fact, he should look at his empire as an onion with five rings: "Within the kingdom is the supply domain," the nobleman tells him; "just outside the supply domain is the warning domain; outside that is the subordinated domain; then the reinforcing domain; and then the wild domain."[15]

Each one of these domains had a decreasing responsibility to recognize the Mandate, a responsibility mirrored in the kinds of sacrifices sent to the capital city by the inhabitants of each. The central domain, the "supply domain," was expected to offer daily sacrifices, the warning domain monthly sacrifices, the subordinated domain seasonal sacrifices. The two outer rings of the kingdom had even less responsibility. Neither offered sacrifices. The reinforcing domain paid tribute once a year; the wild domain did homage only once for each king—at the king's funeral. The Chuan-Jung were out in the wild domain, and the Mandate did not dictate that they be treated in the same way as the peoples at the center of the kingdom. Attacking them was bound to be fruitless.

Mu took this to heart and "pacified" the Chuan-Jung; instead of campaigning against them, he made a royal journey north and brought back gifts: "four white wolves and four white deer." But there is a sting in the tail of this story: "From this time on," Sima Qian ends up, "those in the wild domain stopped coming to pay homage."[16]

The circular reasoning of the Mandate had come back and wound itself around Mu's feet. The Mandate justified war; the king had a sacred responsibility to protect his divinely granted powers. But defeat in battle cast doubt on the Mandate itself. In order to preserve it, the monarch could only go to war with the absolute certainty that he would win. He had strengthened his power at the center of his kingdom, where his court performed daily rituals that recognized his hallowed status; but only at the cost of perforating the edges of his empire until they tore away.

TIMELINE 43

MESOPOTAMIA AND ASIA MINOR			CHINA
BABYLON	ASSYRIA	HITTITE	
		Suppiluliuma II	**Wu-yi**
Second Dynasty of Isin		Hattusus sacked (c. 1180)	
Nebuchadnezzar I (1125–1104)			
	Tiglath-Pileser (1115–1076)		**Chou**
			Zhou Dynasty (1087–256)
	Ashur-bel-kala (1074–1056)		Western Zhou (1087–771)
Aramaean takeover			**Wen**
			Wu
			Tan (regent)
			Ch'eng
			K'ang (c. 996–977)
			Zhao
			Mu

Chapter Forty-Four

The Bharata War

In northern India, around 950 BC, the idea of kingship causes a great war between clans

WHILE THE ZHOU KINGS were negotiating with the outlying tribes, the people of India were spreading through the north of their adopted land. The Aryan-Harappan mixture had wandered farther and farther from the Indus, and now lived in the Doab, the land east of the modern city of Delhi, a curve lying between the northern flow of the Ganga and the branch known as the Jamuna. In the Mahabharata, a mythical later work which may preserve earlier tradition, the king Santunu falls in violent love with the goddess Ganga and marries her; this is very likely an echo of the Aryan journey into the river valley of the Ganga.

We do not know much about the peoples who lived here before the Aryan advance into their home. The Rig Veda makes reference to a people called *dasa* who lived in fortified cities which advancing Aryans broke down; a people who became servants of the conquerors. Dasa has sometimes been interpreted as a reference to the Harappans, but this is unlikely, since the Harappan cities had crumbled before the Aryan advance. And if the "Dasyu" refers to indigenous people of the Ganga valley, the fortified cities are an anachronism; they were village-dwellers.

Most likely, *dasa* is a general reference to other tribes encountered during the Aryan spread; some of the dasa may even have been Aryans who had migrated separately into other parts of India.[1] The Aryans fought the dasa as they fought each other. It seems likely that they also occasionally married them, since the related forms *dasa* and *daha* pop up in the names of legendary Aryan kings. There is no simple racial division here between Aryans and others; simply a shifting pattern of warrior clans moving east and claiming land for themselves, sometimes at the expense of other settlers.

Between 1000 and 600 BC, the fertile lands around the Ganga were tropi-

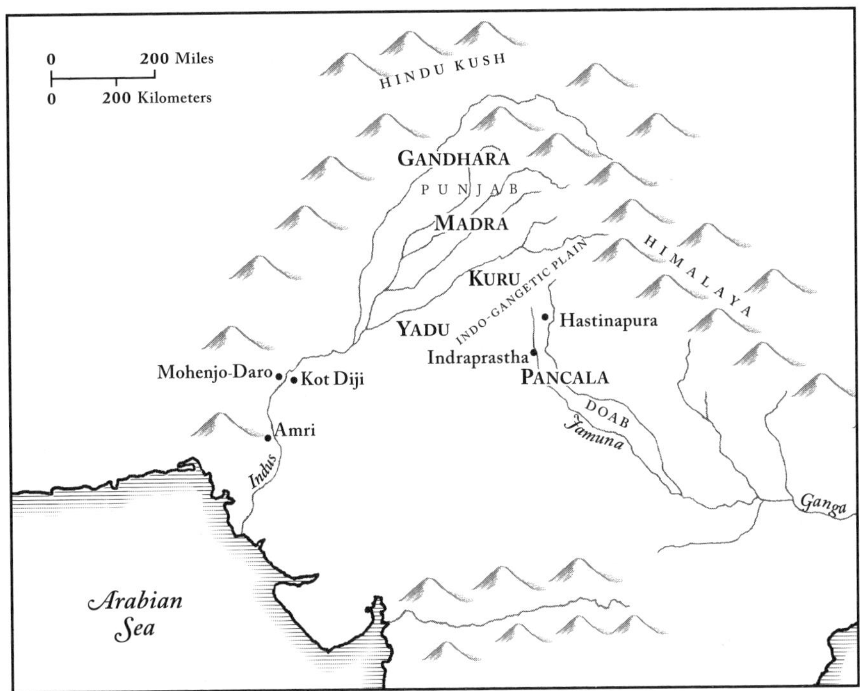

44.1 Aryan Clans of India

cal forest and swamp, covered over with a thick, mysterious, tangled green.[2] The earliest tales of these forests populate them with vicious demons, but this doesn't necessarily mean that the people who lived there put up violent resistance to the Aryan newcomers. The forest itself was an enemy. Trees had to be felled, by a people unaccustomed to such work. Roots, thicker and deeper than they had ever seen, had to be dug out of the ground. Poisonous snakes and unfamiliar animals lurked in the dark thickets.

But the warrior clans drove ahead. Iron—previously used mostly for weapons, blades, and arrowheads—now proved useful for axes and thick plows. In the Satapatha Brahamana (one of the prose commentaries attached to the poetic Rig Veda, sacred poems originating between 1000 and 700 BC), we find a vivid description of the fire-god Agni spreading his flame eastwards, eating forests; more than likely this describes the drastic clearing of the thick woods by fire.[3]

Over several centuries, the woods were cleared. The settled agricultural life that had been the norm in the Indus valley, centered around villages and small cities and their fields, was slowly established in the valley where unbroken forest had once lain.

And then a great war broke out. It took place between the northern reaches of the Ganga and the eastern reaches of the Indus, just south of the Himalaya mountain range, on a plain known to geographers as the Indo-Gangetic plain.

Although the historical details of this war are lost in time, later poets chronicled it as an epic struggle in the Mahabharata—just as the Trojan War would be immortalized by Homer, who overlaid a core of ancient truth with the customs and preoccupations of his own time.[4] According to the Mahabharata, the war grew out of a very complicated genealogical tangle.* The king of the Kuru clan has died without issue, which meant that the royal line of Kuru is almost extinct. The only remaining members of the royal family are the queen mother, the two surviving (and childless) wives of the dead king, and the dead king's older brother, Bhisma. Bhisma, however, is of no help, since some years earlier he had taken a solemn and dreadful vow to give up any claim to his brother's throne, and a second solemn and dreadful vow to remain celibate.

In such a fix, the queen mother decides on drastic measures to perpetuate the family line. She summons a great ascetic and sage named Vyasa—a mysterious wise man who is also known as Krishna, "on account of his dark complexion."[5] When Vyasa arrives, the queen mother asks him for a favor: she wants him to impregnate both of her daughters-in-law, so that they can give birth to royal heirs.†

Vyasa agrees to sleep with the senior of the two daughters-in-law. ("If she does not mind my body, my appearance, my garb, and my odour," he remarks, in passing.) The princess closes her eyes, submits, and "in due time" gives birth to a son and heir to the throne. But the baby, whom she names Dhritarashtra, is blind.

The queen mother, troubled by the prospect of a blind king, sends Vyasa

* The Mahabharata is a massive work, the longest known epic poem in any language; its shortest version has eighty-eight thousand verses. It developed over a long period of time and exists in several versions; plus it contains multiple myths, fables, and philosophical digressions which are unrelated to the main narrative. For the purposes of this history, I have used the free translation made by Chakravarthi V. Narasimhan as vol. 71 of the "Records of Civilization: Sources and Studies" project and published separately by Columbia University Press as *The Mahabharata: An English Version Based on Selected Verses.* Other translations may differ in their presentation of the story's details.

† As the tale is told in the Mahabharata, the queen mother has a little secret of her own: Vyasa is actually her son, born to her before her match with the king of Kuru, and then sent secretly away. As the story unwinds, she reveals the circumstances of his birth: when she was only a young girl, another wise man cornered her on a boat while she was crossing a river and "prevailed over" her, after promising her that she would still be a virgin afterwards, a useful pickup line unfortunately available only to magicians. (The queen mother also adds, apropos of nothing, "Till then my body had emitted a revolting odour of fish, but the sage dispelled it and endowed me with the fragrance that I now have"—a detail which we should perhaps leave unexplored.)

to the second daughter-in-law; in due time she too gives birth to a child, a son named Pandu. To provide backup, the queen mother then tells her oldest daughter-in-law to go back to Vyasa a second time, so that she might have one more son to stand in the royal line. But the princess, remembering Vyasa's "repellent odor," sends her maidservant instead. The girl becomes pregnant and gives birth to a third child of Vyasa, a boy named Vidura.

Now there are three half-brothers to stand in the royal line. All three are raised by their uncle, the celibate Bhisma, who trains them in the skills of kingship. Vidura grows to be one of the wisest and most devout of men; Pandu excels in archery; and Dhritarashtra, despite his blindness, becomes immensely strong and is appointed heir to the Kuru throne.

THIS MYTH catches the Indian clan of the Kuru at the point of a transition: from a nomadic life in which a network of warriors watched over the good of the clan, towards a more hierarchical idea of kingship, where one man in the clan can claim a hereditary right to rule over the rest. The knotted genealogy of the three brothers shows a culture in which the idea of direct royal succession is present, but disordered. The structures of kingship were just beginning to break apart the old blood relationships of the ex-nomadic clans, and the passing of power from father to son—as in the days of Etana—was still new enough to require supernatural intervention, as the next chapter of the story shows.

Dhritarashtra, the blind oldest son, marries a devout and beautiful woman named Gandhari, a princess from the clan of Gandhara to the north. She wants a hundred sons, so that her husband's royal line will be forever secure. So she appeals to her father-in-law Vyasa, who again appears and uses his powers to produce a supernatural pregnancy that lasts for two years. When Gandhari's child is finally born, it is not a baby but a lump; Vyasa cuts it into a hundred pieces, and they become children. Technically all of these sons are the same age, but the acknowledged "oldest son" and heir apparent is Duryodhana.

Meanwhile, the second brother, Pandu, has also married. Going one better on his older brother, he marries *two* princesses from *two* different neighboring clans, the Yadu and the Madra. His older wife gives birth to a son, Yudhishtra. Because of Gandhari's two-year pregnancy, this son is born *before* Gandhari's baby-lump; thus Yudhishtra can also claim to be the oldest royal heir in the family.

Unfortunately Pandu had been rendered impotent sometime before by the curse of a short-tempered sage. This suggests that someone else had been visiting his wife in secret—multiple times, since she then gives birth to two more sons, while Pandu's junior queen has twins.

In other words, there is not a single clear line of blood heritage in the entire Kuru clan. Clearly the whole idea of a hereditary kingship was fraught with all sorts of uncertainties.

With the uncertainties came conflict. Both Dhritarashtra and Pandu brought their families to live in the royal palace. Before long, a civil war broke out between the hundred sons of Dhritarashtra (the "Kauravas," led by the eldest prince, Duryodhana) and the five sons of Pandu (the "Pandavas," led by *their* oldest brother, Yudhishtra).

The territory over which they quarrelled was centered around Hastinapura, the Kuru capital which stood on the upper Ganga. The Kauravas first gained the upper hand, taking control of the city. Meanwhile, according to the Mahabharata, the five sons of Pandu all married the same woman (a rare case of polyandry)—the beautiful Draupadi, daughter of the king of Pancala, a clan which lay to the east.[6]

Draupadi is described as "dark in complexion, with eyes like lotus petals"[7]—physical details which, along with the eastern location of her homeland, suggest that she was the daughter of an indigenous king. As Vyasa is also described as dark complexioned, this does not mean that the "dark" Pancala clan was totally unrelated to the Aryans. Clearly the Aryans and the native clans had been intermarrying for decades.[8]

But the clans to the east likely had more indigenous and less Aryan blood. The Aryans had a name for the speech of the people who lived in the eastern Ganga valley: it was *mleccha*, language that had been changed and distorted.[9] The Pancala clan was one of these mostly indigenous clans. The Kaurava brothers had allied themselves with other arya clans, but the Pandava brothers were making strategic alliances with the native peoples.

Some years after completing the alliance with the Pancala, the Pandavas built a palace at Indraprastha, on the southeast edge of the land claimed by the Kauravas. They also coronated their oldest brother Yudhishtra as king, in an out-and-out challenge to the authority of the Kaurava king who ruled in Hastinapura.

This was obviously infuriating to the Kauravas, especially considering the magnificence of the palace (it was filled with golden pillars that glowed like the moon, and the assembly hall featured an enormous aquarium "embellished with lotuses . . . and stocked with different birds, as well as with tortoises and fish").[10] The Kaurava king Duryodhana visited his cousin's palace, by way of checking out the competition, and was embarrassed by its magnificence; when he reached a hall with a mirrorlike floor, he thought it was water, and drew his clothes up to his waist before realizing his error. Then, coming to a pond, he thought it was made of glass and fell in. "The servants laughed at this," the Mahabharata explains. So did all of the Pandava brothers, their great-uncle Bhima, and "everybody else. . . . And Duryodhana could not forgive their derision."[11]

But open war had not yet broken out between the cousins, and Duryodhana decided on a more subtle challenge: he invited the Pandavas to see his own palace, and then challenged them to a game of dice. Yudhishtra agreed to play on behalf of his brothers and lost first his jewels, then all his wealth, then his army, and then his queen Draupadi. Finally he waged his territory, agreeing that—should he finally lose—he and his brothers would leave Indraprastha and go into exile for twelve years.

Judging from a poem in the Rig Veda ("The abandoned wife of the gambler mourns! In debt, fear, and need of money, he wanders by night . . . !"), gambling fever was not unknown among the Indians of the first millennia.[12] This particular gambling fever proved fatal to Yudhishtra's crown. Unable to walk away when luck turned against him, Yudhishtra lost everything. His brothers followed him reluctantly into exile, while Duryodhana and the other Kauravas took over their palace and their land.

This exile was into the forest to the east, that mysterious and uncivilized place. But during their twelve-year exile, the Pandavas grew stronger at battle. Their new bows and arrows were, according to the stories, unbreakable because they were supernaturally blessed; more likely, they were made of new wood, green wood previously unfamiliar to the Indus-dwellers.[13]

In the thirteenth year, when the Pandavas returned, Duryodhana refused to give back the palace and their land. At this the hostility between the cousins broke out into open war: the Bharata War.

The Pandava cousins rallied behind them various relatives and native clans, including the Pancala clan; so did the Kauravas, who did a better job of claiming the loyalty of those wavering uncles and and generals who were equally related to both clans and torn between them. This made the Kaurava army slightly larger (eleven divisions to the Pandava seven). Judging from the traditional numbers assigned to a "division," the Kaurava forces had something like 240,000 chariots and an equal number of war-elephants, along with over 700,000 cavalry and over a million foot soldiers, with the Pandava army fielding three-quarters of a million infantry, 460,000 cavalry, 153,000 chariots, and the same number of war-elephants. These figures are unlikely, but certainly there was a massive clash when the two armies met.

The Mahabharata account, like the Homeric account of Troy, undoubtedly pastes the conventions of later, more stylized warfare over the primitive scramble for power that ensued. According to the epic, the fighting was governed by elaborate rules of fair play: a single soldier could not be set upon by a group, one-on-one combat could only take place between men with the same weapons; the slaughter of wounded or unconscious men was prohibited, as was any attack on a soldier from behind; and each weapon had its own elaborate rules for use which must be followed.

These sorts of courtly rules lend the war a very civilized air, but they spring from the preoccupations of men who lived centuries afterwards. Certainly the most famous section of the Mahabharata, the Bhagavad Gita or Song of the Lord, is centered around the sort of wartime dilemma which is unlikely to have worried the mythical combatants. In it, Krishna himself, disguised as the charioteer of the Pandava prince Arjuna (the middle brother, and the one most renowned for his might), helps Arjuna grapple with an ethical dilemma. Since so many of his own relatives are arrayed against him, in this civil war between cousins, should he attack—or would it be more righteous to allow himself to be killed?

But the ancient battle was fought between clans who were not so far away from their old days as nomadic warriors. Despite all the ethical concerns put into the mouths of the warriors, the Mahabharata gives us an occasional involuntary glimpse of the savagery. Bhisma, the great-uncle of both Pandavas and Kauravas, fights on the side of the Kauravas; when he slaughters the Pandava prince Dushasana, who is in fact his own cousin, he drinks the man's blood and dances a victory dance on the battlefield, howling like an animal.[14]

THE WINNERS of the great war were the Pandava brothers: those who had allied themselves with the indigenous people. But the victorious Pandavas won at enormous cost to themselves. Almost all of their soldiers were lost in a massacre just before the Kaurava surrender.

The Mahabharata itself laments this bloody resolution of the war. At the end of the tale, the Pandava prince Yudhishtra, ascending to the afterlife, plunges himself into the sacred and celestial Gangas and emerges, having washed away his human body. "Through that bath," the story tells us, "he became divested of all his enmities and his grief." He finds his brothers and cousins also in the celestial realm, also cleansed of their hatreds. And there they remain, the Pandavas and the Kauravas, "heroes freed from human wrath," enjoying each other's company without strife, in a world far removed from the ambitions of kings.*

* Although the details of the war may be mythical, there is archaeological proof for the spreading dominance of one particular clan or ruling group over the others. Right around 900 BC or so, the traditional date for the great war, the simple pottery which seems to have been native to Hastinapura

TIMELINE 44

CHINA	INDIA
Wu-yi	
	Aryan/Harappan people begin to wander east
Chou	
Zhou Dynasty (1087–256)	
Western Zhou (1087–771)	
Wen	
Wu	
Tan (regent)	
Ch'eng	
K'ang (c. 996–977)	
Zhao	
Mu	
	Bharata War

---

and the surrounding areas was replaced by a much more sophisticated kind of ware: PGW, or painted grey ware, thrown on a wheel and painted with patterns and flowers. Slightly later, a similar but distinctive pottery, called Northern Black Polished Ware, appeared: this NBPW overlapped the center of the PGW area, and extended a little farther to the south and much farther to the east. (See John Keay, *India: A History,* pp. 42–43, and Hermann Kulke and Dietmar Rothermund, *A History of India,* p. 363.) These pottery remains suggest that two related but different sets of settlers came in from the outside and settled in native territory, and that one of the settler groups then took over territory that belonged to the other. This is not so different from the tale told by the Mahabharata.

Chapter Forty-Five

The Son of David

Between 1050 and 931 BC, the Hebrews become a kingdom, and Egypt recovers its strength

On the coast of the Western Semitic lands, one of those wandering tribes that had taken part in the Sea People attack on Egypt had settled down near the Mediterranean. Their settlements grew into cities, the cities into a loosely organized alliance. The most powerful cities of the alliance were Gaza, Ashkelon, Ashdod, Gath, and Ekron, the "Pentapolis." The Egyptians had called them the Peleset; their neighbors called them Philistines.

The Philistines did not write, which means that their history is refracted to us through the chronicles of their enemies; this goes a long way to explain their reputation as ill-mannered, boorish, and generally uncivilized. But the remains they have left behind them suggest that their culture was, indeed, mostly borrowed. Philistine pottery was Mycenaean in style; their original language was soon eclipsed by a Canaanite dialect; and even the failed invasion of Egypt added its own flavor to the Philistine soup. They buried their dead in coffins carved to look like Egyptian sarcophagi, with clay lids surmounted by faces and out-of-proportion arms too short to fold. The faux Egyptian coffins were even decorated with hieroglyphs, painted by someone who had seen the signs often but had no idea what they meant; the hieroglyphs are meaningless.

Powerful as they were, the five cities of the Pentapolis did not have unquestioned domain over the southern Western Semitic territories. Almost from the moment of their settlement, they were challenged by competitors for the land: the descendants of Abraham.

After leaving Egypt, the Hebrews had disappeared from the international scene for decades. According to their own accounts, they had wandered in the desert for forty years, a span of time during which a whole new generation came of age. These years, which were historically invisible, were theologically crucial. The book of Exodus says that God gathered the Hebrews around Mount Sinai and gave them the Ten Commandments, carved on two tablets of stone—one copy for each of the covenanting parties, God as the greater party and the Hebrews as the lesser.

45.1. Philistine Coffin. An "Egyptian" style coffin from the Philistine cemetery of Deir el-Ballah. Israel Museum (IDAM), Jerusalem. Photo credit Erich Lessing/Art Resource, NY

This was the bedrock of Hebrew national identity, and led to a political reorganization. The Hebrew people had informally traced their ancestry back to Abraham and his twelve great-grandsons for centuries. Now, under divine direction, their leader Moses took a census and listed all the clans and families. They were divided into twelve tribes, each known by the name of the great-grandson who served as its ancestor. The tribe of Judah was by far the largest, turning out almost seventy-five thousand men of fighting age; the smallest tribe was that of Manasseh, with less than half as many.*

The formal recognition of the twelve tribes was preparation for the next move. The Hebrews had now wandered all the way to the southern border of the Western Semitic lands; Moses was dead; and Joshua, his aide and assistant,

* There were actually thirteen tribes of Israelites: Reuben, Simeon, Levi, Judah, Issachar, Zebulun, Ephraim, Manasseh, Benjamin, Dan, Asher, Gad, and Naphtali. Technically, the twelve sons of Jacob—Abraham's great-grandsons—were Reuben, Simeon, Levi, Judah, Issachar, Zebulun, Gad, Asher, Joseph, Benjamin, Dan, and Naphtali. However, Reuben lost his position as first-born by sleeping with his father's concubine Bilhah, the mother of his half-brothers Dan and Naphtali. Instead, his father Jacob decided to recognize Joseph's two sons, Ephraim and Manasseh, as clan leaders; in this way, his deathbed blessing still encompassed twelve "sons" and their families. Despite this, Reuben's clan retained its position as a Hebrew tribe. The number twelve is maintained by two different strategies: when the tribes are named for the purposes of recruiting soldiers or distributing land, the tribe of Levi is left out, since its men were all called to be priests and so neither fought nor owned land; and when all the tribes are reckoned up by ancestors, Levi is included but the tribes of Ephraim and Manasseh are counted as half-tribes, the "descendants of the sons of Joseph." (See Num. 1:20–53.)

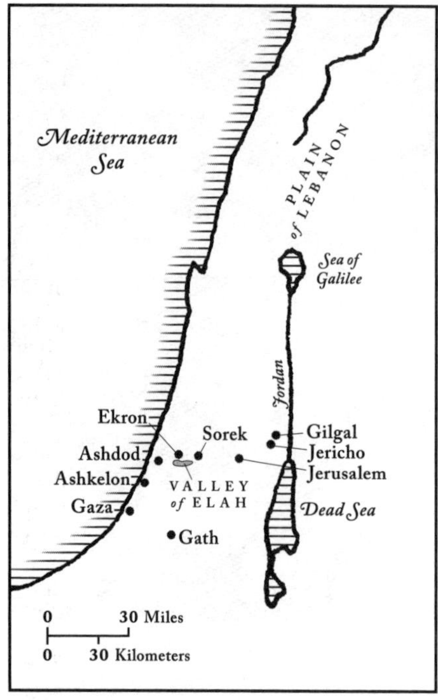

45.1 Israelites and Philistines

had become their commander. Under Joshua, the Hebrew tribes laid claim to the land along the coast, "from Lebanon to the Euphrates, all the Hittite country, all the way over to the Great Sea on the west."[1]

Joshua marched his followers to the east of the Dead Sea, up around to its northern tip, and across the Jordan river: the formal border of the Western Semitic kingdoms. Then he ordered all adult Hebrew men circumcised, since the circumcision ritual had been much neglected during the four decades in the desert. This might not seem the best beginning to a campaign that was going to involve a lot of walking, but Joshua needed his men to understand what they were about to do: the conquest of Canaan was the fulfillment of the promise made to Abraham, the first Jew and the first to circumcise his sons, six hundred years before.

Their chief military target was Jericho, the first stronghold west of the Jordan river, surrounded by its huge wall and its watchtowers. According to the biblical account in the book of Joshua, the battle ended after the Hebrews had marched around the walls of Jericho once per day for six days. On the seventh day, they marched around it seven times in a row and blew trumpets, and the walls fell down. The Hebrews poured over the ruined walls and destroyed every living thing: men and women and children, cows and sheep and donkeys.

When the city had been razed and sacked, Joshua cursed it. Two hundred years later, Jericho still lay uninhabited.[2] For six thousand years, the inhabitants of Jericho had been watching from the city's towers, waiting for the irresistible enemy to rise into sight on the horizon and break against Jericho's enormous walls.

The enemy had finally arrived, but the walls had broken instead.

JOSHUA DIED an old man, after a lifetime spent on the march. By the time of his death, Hebrews lived from Beersheba in the south all the way up to Kinnereth, on the northern shore of the little lake that would later be known as the Sea of Galilee, and as far west as Ramoth-Gilead. The conquered territory had been divided among the tribes. Joshua was succeeded not by a king, but by a series of chief judges, prophets who told the Hebrew tribes—now the nation of Israel—what God required.*

But large areas of Canaan remained unconquered. For one thing, the Philistines now governed the land from Ekron down along the Mediterranean coast, and they were unwilling to yield any space to the newcomers. During the years that Israel was ruled by judges, the Israelites fought battle after battle against the Philistines.[3]

It is impossible to date the "Conquest"—the Hebrew invasion of the Western Semitic lands under Joshua—with certainty. So it is also impossible to assign an absolute date to the years when the judges of the Hebrews led Israelite soldiers against the warlords of the Pentapolis.† But the most famous of the judges, the supernaturally strong Samson, probably exercised his guidance over this whole territory right around 1050: the time of the Third Intermediate Period in Egypt, the Aramaean dominance in Mesopotamia, and the Zhou rule farther east.

During the days of Samson, the Philistines were not only unconquered, but oozing over into Israelite territory. Down to the south, the two peoples had begun to mingle; Samson even married a Philistine woman, much to the despair of his devout parents. ("What? There's no suitable woman anywhere among our *own* people? Why do you have to go and get a wife from the uncircumcised?") The Philistine wife proved to be a mistake; after a falling-out with his father-in-law, Samson set fire to a vast swath of Philistine vineyards and grain fields, thus terrifying his countrymen at the thought of reprisals. "Don't you realize that the Philistines are rulers over us?" they demanded. "What do you think you're doing?"[4]

This seems to indicate that the Philistines, not the Israelites, had the upper hand in the very uneasy relationship between the two countries. But they did not actually *govern* Israelite land. Samson himself judged Israel for twenty years, during which he killed hundreds of Philistines in various fits of temper,

* "Israel," the name by which the Hebrew nation was known once it had settled into Canaan, was the new name given to Jacob by the angel of the Lord when they wrestled at the stream of Peniel; it meant *He struggles with God.*

† Like the Exodus, the Conquest has been assigned widely varying dates across a span of centuries. Like the Exodus, the Conquest has also been rejected entirely by some scholars, who prefer to interpret the archaeological evidence as indicating a gradual invasion carried out by various small groups of Hebrew invaders. Since the evidence is inconclusive, the debate will continue; the account in Joshua is the clearest guide we possess to the establishment of an Israelite kingdom in Canaan.

but the Philistines were never strong enough to launch an actual war against him. Instead, they commissioned a prostitute named Delilah—a woman who lived "in the valley of Sorek," or in other words, on the border right between Philistine territory and Israelite land—to betray him. Tricked and captured, Samson was blinded by his enemies and hauled off to Gaza, the strongest city of the Pentapolis; here, brought out and put on display by the Philistines during a festival to their chief god Dagon (a fish-god, reflecting their origin as an Aegean seafaring people), he used his tremendous strength to pull down the Temple of Dagon on top of himself and over three thousand of the enemy. "And so," the book of Judges tells us, "he killed many more when he died than when he lived."[5]

This sort of Pyrrhic victory over the Philistines reflects a stalemate. Philistines raided Israelite villages, Israelites burned Philistine fields, both sides knocked off the odd hunting party caught out of bounds, and neither kingdom triumphed. Politically, both nations suffered from the same indecisive leadership. No Philistine warlord could pull the armies of all five Pentapolis cities together behind him, and the judges of Israel, their theological authority notwithstanding, had even less power: "In those days, there was no king in Israel," is the repeated refrain of the book of Judges, "and everyone in Israel did what was right in his own eyes."

Finally, fed up, the Israelites demanded a king so that they could be like "other countries." Presumably they had Egypt in mind, the one country whose king had beaten the Philistines off. They wanted to make an impressively tall Benjamite named Saul their king and general, so that he could lead them to military victory.

He was properly anointed the first king of Israel by the last judge, an old and weary man named Samuel who believed kingship to be an enormous mistake. "He will draft your sons to be soldiers in his army," he warned the Israelites; "he will take them to plow his fields, to make weapons for his troops; he will take your daughters to work at his palace; he will take the best of your harvest, the best of your vines, a tenth of your grain, a tenth of your flock, the best of your servants and your cows; you will cry out for relief from the king you have chosen."[6]

Despite this warning, Saul was acclaimed king and commander. Immediately, he began to organize an attack against the Philistines.

Unfortunately, the Philistine hold over Israel had intensified to the point of an arms embargo: "There was no blacksmith anywhere in Israel," 1 Samuel tells us, "because the Philistines knew that otherwise the Israelites would make swords and spears."[7] Instead, the Philistines had arrogated to themselves the privilege of working with iron. Any Israelite who wanted a plow or axe sharpened had to go down into the Philistine land and pay a Philistine smith for the work.*

As a result, when Saul gathered the fighting men from the tribes beneath his new royal banner, he and his son the crown prince Jonathan were the only two men with swords. Everyone else had hoes and pitchforks. The Philistines, on the other hand, assembled three thousand chariots, six thousand charioteers (one to drive each chariot, and one to fight, hands free of the reins), and soldiers too great to count: "as numerous as the sand on the seashore." The Israelite forces, badly outnumbered and completely outarmed, scattered and hid. Saul holed up at Gilgal, north of Jericho, with only six hundred men left. For the remainder of his reign, the Israelite push against Philistine strength consisted of guerilla raids and inconclusive battles.

In one of those indecisive battles, this one dragging on in the Valley of Elah, on the western edge of Judah's territory, the fighting went on so long that the Philistines proposed a different kind of combat to settle the issue. Two champions would fight, one from each side, and the victor would take the loser's country.

The Philistines certainly expected the new Israelite leader, Saul, to answer the challenge. The Philistine champion was a giant: three meters tall, a height unusual but not entirely impossible (particularly since an occasional manuscript lists his height as seven, not nine, feet), and Saul himself was known for his height. The selection of Goliath, who was armed to the teeth and had been a fighting man since his youth, was an in-your-face gesture of superiority.†

Saul had no intention of facing down this giant, but another Israelite accepted the challenge: David, the younger brother of three siblings from Judah who had joined Saul's army. David, confident that God was with him, walked out with a slingshot, knocked Goliath out with a well-placed stone to the head, and cut off the giant's head with his own sword. "When the Philistines saw that their hero was dead," 1 Sam. says, "they turned and ran. Then the men of Israel and Judah surged forward with a shout and pursued the

* 1000 BC, around the time of David's rise, is the conventional beginning of the Iron Age in the ancient Near East. Anthropologists have suggested that knowledge of ironworking spread eastwards from Mycenae along the sea routes, during the days of the Dorian invasion. Colin McEvedy notes that this is "compatible with . . . the Bible's story of the Philistines' attempt to keep the Israelites in a position of military inferiority by forbidding them to manufacture any sort of iron tools" (*The New Penguin Atlas of Ancient History*, p. 48).

† The tallest man in history was Robert Wadlow, who topped out at eight feet, eleven inches. As of this writing, the tallest man living is Leonid Stadnik of Ukraine, who stands eight feet, four inches and is still growing (thanks to a pituitary disorder). Nine feet is an unlikely height, though, probably an approximation; in a day when the average Israelite man probably stood five and a half feet high, seven feet would have been staggeringly huge.

Philistines to the entrance of Gath and to the gates of Ekron. Their dead were strewn along the road to Gath and Ekron."[8] This victory made David so popular that Saul decided to get rid of him, as a possible competitor for the throne.

David, to preserve his own life, fled into Philistine territory. Here he acted as a double agent: sacking distant Philistine cities, and returning to his Philistine employers with the booty and a vivid description of the nonexistent Israelite settlements which had fallen to his might. When Saul was killed in a particularly violent clash with the Philistines, David returned and claimed the crown.

David was determined to weld the twelve tribes into not just a nation, but a *kingdom.* One of his first acts was to besiege the city of Jerusalem, which had remained unconquered and under the control of West Canaanites that the biblical account calls "Jebusites"—an uncertain mix of Western Semites and immigrants from the Arabian peninsula.* David conquered it by leading an invading force in through the water-shafts cut into the rock beneath the city's walls, and rebuilt it as his own.

With the twelve tribes under his authority, he extended his borders; he marched down to the southeast and defeated the Edomites, a people who had controlled the land as far as the Red Sea; he defeated the tribes of Moab, on the other side of the Dead Sea, and the tribes of Ammon to their north, just across the Jordan; and he decisively defeated the Philistines, who had marched on Israel as soon as they heard that David had assumed power. (They were, undoubtedly, more than peeved that their double agent had managed to deceive them for so long.) This was the end of Philistine dominance as a strong kingdom. Their summer of power had lasted barely more than a century.

David's kingdom was marked not only by extensive Israelite control over almost all of the Western Semitic lands, but also by something previous leaders had not managed to do: the establishment of friendly relations with the leaders of other countries.

His most productive alliance was with the king of Tyre, a gentleman known as Hiram. Tyre, on the northern Mediterranean coast (in the modern territory of Lebanon), had been built into strength by its inhabitants, a Western Semitic tribe who had fled their own home city of Sidon, farther up the coast, when the Sea People had sacked it on their way down to Egypt. These "Sido-

* In the rhetoric of Near Eastern politics, the identity of the Jebusites has become a charged issue: Yassir Arafat, chairman of the Palestinian Authority, claimed descent from the Jebusites (identified as a people originally from Arabia) and insisted that David, the first great Jewish king, took the city from his people, the rightful owners, by force. (Arafat's claim is documented by Eric Cline in *Jerusalem Besieged: From Ancient Canaan to Modern Israel,* among other places.) Israeli politicians responded by holding festivals celebrating the founding of Jerusalem by David (Cline, pp. 11–12).

nians" settled in Tyre, along with a few of the invading Sea People from the Aegean; the temples of Tyre, like those of the Philistines, honor the fish-god Dagon, betraying a common ancestry. By the time of David's reign, Sidon was resettled, and the same peoples occupied not only Tyre and Sidon but also the ancient trading city of Byblos. Their particular mix of Western Semitic and Aegean became known as Phoenician.[9]

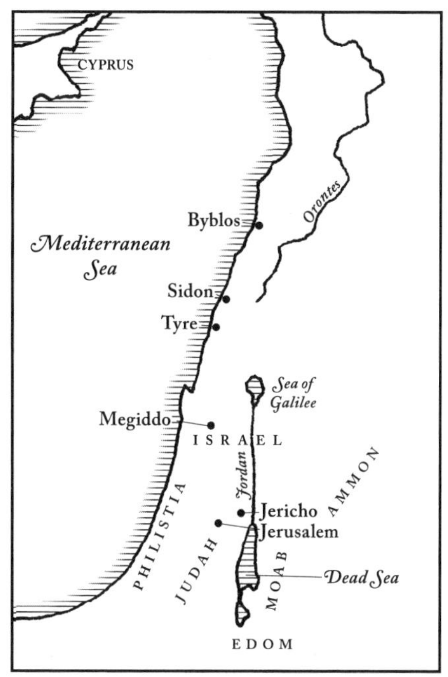

45.2 Israel and Surrounding Kingdoms

There was no country called Phoenicia, nor was there a Phoenician high king. The independent cities along the coast were united by a shared culture and language; their writing system was the first to incorporate an alphabet. And they had a virtual trading monopoly on one of the most valuable local resources: cedar logs which they cut from the nearby hills and sent abroad to Egypt, to Israel, and farther away. When David passed the kingdom on to his son Solomon (a transfer made with a bit of bloodshed before Solomon triumphed; Israel had as yet no tradition of hereditary monarchy), the trade with Tyre allowed Solomon to embark on the biggest building program ever seen in Western Semitic lands.

Solomon, honored in the biblical account as a man who longed after wisdom, reorganized David's kingdom into twelve administrative districts which did not always fall along the traditional tribal boundaries; he wanted to break up those old tribal divisions and any infighting that they might encourage. He revamped the tax system and pushed the borders of the kingdom out to their greatest extent. He also built an epically huge temple: forty-five feet high, constructed of quarried stone hauled from far away, lined with carved cedar, coated with gold in every possible place, filled with treasures. The God of Israel needed a temple, and Solomon was going to build him the best temple ever.

This was Solomon's usual mode of operation. In this he was very unlike his father. David had been a rough and scruffy fighter, a charismatic leader who killed hundreds of men with his own hands, refused to execute traitors until their treachery was too obvious to ignore, played the harp, and broke into fits of embarrassingly ecstatic dancing in public. His sheer force of personality inspired both insane hatred and cultish loyalty; three of his warriors once risked their lives and freedom by battling their way into Philistine-held territory to get David a drink from the well near the village where he had been born.

Solomon was a different man altogether. He was an executive with a fixation on size, a man determined to do everything bigger and better than his famous father and to turn a kingdom won by blood into a cushy and well-organized empire. In a more recent age, David would have been the American frontier evangelist who spoke in tongues and succumbed to visions and fainting fits; Solomon, the suburban megachurch pastor shepherding an increasingly huge congregation into his plush auditorium, convinced that the size and prosperity of his enterprise were proof of God's blessing. No king after Solomon ever wielded as much power over the Israelites, but no one ever risked his life out of love for Solomon.

Solomon's stables boasted twelve thousand horses, and his huge court ate 185 bushels of flour a day.[10] He was as powerful as any pharaoh. In fact, his kingdom now encompassed the Western Semitic province that had once belonged to Egypt, and Solomon even managed to marry an Egyptian princess; Egypt was long past the days when the pharaoh could sniff that daughters of the royal house did not travel out to other kingdoms.[11] And Solomon expanded David's connections with foreign countries. As well as dealing with Hiram of Tyre, he arranged to build his own ships at Byblos. He made marriage alliances with the far-flung Canaanite people that he could not conquer. He even received a delegation from Arabia: a delegation led by the most famous of ancient queens.

"When the queen of Sheba heard about Solomon's fame," 1 Kings tells us, "she came to test his wisdom; she arrived with a caravan of spices, gold, and precious gems."

The queen of Sheba is the first personality to struggle up out of the sandstorm covering the ancient history of the Arabian peninsula, and almost the only surviving face and name from the Arabia of very ancient times. Trade caravans were making their way to the Western Semitic kingdoms with greater frequency, and the queen of Sheba may have been leading such a caravan; she not only arrives with spices, gold, and gems, but leaves with "all she asked for, given to her out of the royal bounty."[12]

Clearly, trade and manufacture, metalwork and weaving, had been going on around the edges of the Arabian peninsula for a very long time. The Mesopotamian kings, after all, had been travelling down from the head of the Gulf to the Copper Mountains of Magan, in southeast Arabia, two thousand

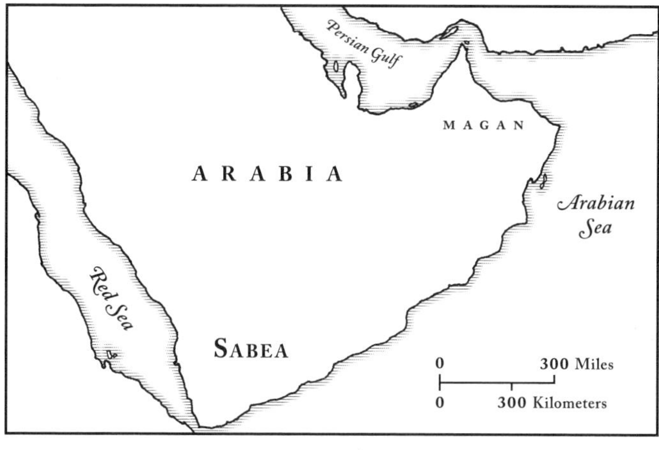

45.3 Arabia

years before. Farther north, the Arabian coast served as a staging post for ships making their way from Mesopotamia down to Indian ports; trading settlements here grew into cities.[13]

We know even less about the southern corner of Arabia, since the ancient inscriptions that exist there cannot be dated with certainty. But it was most likely the Sabean kingdom of southern Arabia that sent a royal representative up to see Solomon. Trade between Israel and Arabia probably continued after her visit; an ancient altar from the area just west of the Jordan river is inscribed with Arabic letters.[14] But all of the stories surrounding the enigmatic figure of the queen of Sheba, who may also be a queen of the Sabeans, are from much, much later; they tell us nothing at all about the Sabeans themselves.

Solomon's empire-building carved a rift through his kingdom that eventually split it apart.

In order to build his temple and palace, Solomon conscripted thirty thousand Israelite men as laborers. These conscripted laborers were paid for their services, but had no choice; they had to spend one out of every three months working for the king. Meanwhile they were supposed to keep up with their own fields and vines. Each district was required to feed the enormous court (along with thousands of royal horses, cows, sheep, goats, deer, gazelles, and chickens) for one month out of the year. As the court grew, it took the districts longer and longer to pay their debt to the court. In some areas, the people worked almost half the year to meet their obligations to the king, and the other half year to support themselves.

The huge court grew, in part, because of Solomon's tendency to make his political alliances by marriage; he had, according to his chronicler, seven hundred wives "of royal birth" who had been sent to him to seal alliances of various kinds. There is less excuse for the concubines, three hundred women with no political purpose whatsoever; the throng simply reflects Solomon's enormous appetite.

His appetite for size, which turned Israel into a kingdom important enough for other potentates to visit from afar, also destroyed it. Solomon's building programs ran him into tremendous debt, particularly to Hiram, the Phoenician king of Tyre. Lacking enough cash to pay off his shipments of cedar, pine, and gold, Solomon settled his account by giving Hiram "twenty towns in Galilee"[15]—a large section of the northern edge of his kingdom.

This was a no-win situation for everyone. Hiram, having gone to see the towns, nicknamed them "The Land of Good-for-Nothing." And the north of Israel was furious. Solomon was a southern king, from the large and powerful southern tribe of Judah; as far as the cluster of little northern tribes was concerned, he had overbuilt, overtaxed, and overworked his people, and then tried to fix his troubles by giving away twenty northern towns while refusing to touch his own native land.

Revolt began under one of Solomon's officials, a northern man named Jeroboam. When a prophet from Ephraim anointed Jeroboam king, Solomon got wind of the growing rebellion and sent out an assassination squad; Jeroboam fled down to Egypt and stayed there until old Solomon—who had now been on the throne forty years—died, leaving behind him a huge, rich, powerful, divided, and unhappy country.

Jeroboam returned, immediately, and organized a delegation to go to Solomon's heir Rehoboam and ask for changes: lower taxes, less conscripted labor. Rehoboam, in turn, asked for advice from the double assembly that helped him govern, as it had helped kings from Gilgamesh on. The assembly of elders, cautious and experienced, advised him to reverse Solomon's policies, to be less of a monarch and more of a shepherd; the assembly of young men told him to assert his power. "Tell them," the young men advised, "that your little finger is thicker than your father's penis."

Rehoboam liked this advice, which perhaps reveals certain unresolved issues. When the delegates returned, Rehoboam made what may have been the most tactless political speech in history: "My father put a heavy yoke on you," he told them, "but I will make it heavier." The political results were immediate: the northern tribes, already unhappy, seceded and proclaimed their northern leader Jeroboam as king.

Only the tribe of Judah, the ancestral home of David himself, and the tiny neighboring tribe of Benjamin remained loyal to David's grandson. The united kingdom of Israel had lasted barely two generations.

THE WEAKNESS of the kingdom did not go unnoticed by the Egyptians, who were experiencing a very brief renaissance.

Since the beginning of the Third Intermediate Period back around 1070, Egypt had been divided by civil war. The high priests of Amun, following the lead of Herihor, ruled from the southern city of Thebes, while the pharaohs of Dynasty 21 ruled the northern parts from the delta city of Tanis. The pharaohs at Tanis had the prestige of the royal bloodline, but the high priests had most of the money, thanks to the amount of land handed over to the Temple of Amun by previous pharaohs. Their wealth was so great that it echoed down into the Iliad: "The hell with him," Achilles announces of Agamemnon, when he refuses to join the attack against Troy. "I loathe his presents,"

> and for himself care not one straw.
> He may offer me ten or even twenty times what he has . . .
> he may promise me the wealth . . . of Egyptian Thebes,
> which is the richest city in the whole world,
> for it has a hundred gates through each of which two hundred men
> may drive at once with their chariots and horses.[16]

The priests used some of this wealth to keep control of the south; they hired mercenaries from Libya to back up their authority. This Libyan "police force" was known as the Meshwesh.[17] Around 950 or so, the "Great Chief of the Meshwesh" was a Libyan warrior named Sheshonq, with ambitions of his own. Although he headed up the armed forces of the north, he also managed to create an alliance with the south by marrying one of the daughters of the Tanis ruler Psusennes II, a pharaoh whose fourteen-year reign is almost completely obscure. When Psusennes II died, Sheshonq asserted his right, by marriage, to the throne of Egypt in Tanis. As Sheshonq had risen to prominence as the strong arm of the priests of Thebes, it did not take him long to assert his power over Egypt's other capital as well.

The relative stability of this temporarily reunited Egypt can be seen by Sheshonq's next action: he made a bid to recapture some of that land which had once belonged to Egypt, back in its glory days. And since Israel and Judah had now divided into weakened and quarrelling states, he set his eyes on the Western Semitic lands.

He marched up the coast, through the weakened Philistines, and laid siege to Jerusalem itself. "In the fifth year of King Rehoboam," 1 Kings says, "Sheshonq king of Egypt attacked Jerusalem. He carried off the treasures of the temple of the Lord and the treasures of the royal palace. He took everything, including all the gold shields Solomon had made. So King Rehoboam made bronze shields to replace them."[18]

Jerusalem's walls remained intact, though. In other words, Rehoboam bought off his attacker with the temple treasure. Everything valuable but the Ark of the Covenant itself went to Egypt. In all likelihood, he was also forced to swear a vassal oath, becoming formally subject to the king of Egypt.

Sheshonq's own reliefs tell us that he then marched farther north to subjugate the northern kingdom as well. Jeroboam, who had spent years hiding down in Egypt and waiting for Solomon's assassination order to expire, now found himself on the wrong side of the people who had once given him refuge. He was dreadfully outnumbered; Sheshonq had managed to assemble twelve hundred chariots and sixty thousand soldiers, largely drawn from Libya and from Kush to the south.

Jeroboam fled, thus living to fight another day. Sheshonq pushed through Israel as far as Megiddo, and then stopped. He had reached the city conquered by Tuthmosis III half a millennium before; he had made his point, that under him Egypt had been renewed; and so he went back home. When he died, his descendants held the north and south together for some years.

Sheshonq's invasion left a quivering and thoroughly demoralized divided kingdom behind him. For the next centuries, it would remain in two parts: the southern kingdom of Judah, under David's descendants; and the northern kingdom known collectively as Israel, under an unstable shifting line of kings which turned over every two or three generations as a new charismatic warrior seized control of the royal house.

TIMELINE 45

EGYPT	WESTERN SEMITIC LANDS
	Initial settlement of Philistine cities
Merneptah (1212–1202)	
	The Conquest (possible)
Dynasty 20 (1185–1070)	
Setnakhte (c. 1185–1182)	
Rameses III (c. 1182–1151)	
Invasion of the Sea People	
Rameses IV-XI	
Herihor (c. 1080–1074)	
Third Intermediate Period (1070–664)	**Samson**
Dynasty 21 (Thebes)	**Saul**
	David
Dynasty 22 (945–712)	**Solomon**
Sheshonq I (945–924)	
	Rehoboam (Judah) (931) **Jereboam** (Israel)

Chapter Forty-Six

From Western to Eastern Zhou

In China, between 918 and 771 BC, trouble both inside and out forces the Zhou king to move east

IN THE YEARS SINCE good King Wen's grandson had sent his brothers out to establish Zhou centers of power, the outposts had grown and spread into small kingdoms. The men who now ruled them, descendants of those original royal siblings, were the second and third and fourth cousins of the monarch; a blood tie so distant as to be merely formal.[1] The lands were now governed not by family relations, but by administrators (at best) and petty kings (at worst) who paid their dues of loyalty to the king not out of blood obligation, but out of duty.

Inevitably, the "Lords of the Nine Lands," centered around the old colonies, acted with more and more independence. In the remains of their capital cities, archaeologists have uncovered bronze vessels cast and inscribed by the lords of the lands themselves; the Zhou emperor had lost his control over the bronze casting which had once been a royal monopoly.[2] The inscriptions show that these same local governors were also beginning to celebrate their own feasts and rituals. They were not waiting for the king to act as the spokesman for heaven.

In response, the Zhou administration itself seems to have become slowly more and more structured, less dependent on personal loyalties, hedging its officials in with increasingly strict rules. Courtiers once simply called "lords," who had carried out the general function of enforcing the king's authority, now were awarded more specific titles: the Supervisor of the Land had one set of duties, the Supervisor of the Horse another set, the Supervisor of Works yet another. This growing bureaucracy, like the Mandate of Heaven itself, was intended to protect the king's power; yet it simultaneously reduced it, spelling out the truth that he could not compel all-encompassing, heartfelt obedience simply through the force of his character.[3]

Soon, trouble between king and "lords" (called "dukes" in many translations) began to rear its head. Mu's son Kung, according to Sima Qian, took a royal trip to visit the lord of a small state called Mi. The Duke of Mi had collected, for his harem, three beautiful girls from one family. Even his mother found this excessive: "A threesome of girls from one clan is too splendid a thing!" she scolded him. "Even a king does not consider himself deserving of this, much less should you, a petty lout!"

She suggested that he give the girls to the king instead. The duke refused, and King Kung apparently went home in peace. But a year later, he marched in and exterminated Mi.[4] He was not going to allow any of the lords of *his* lands the chance to wallow in greater luxury than that of the king.

During the reign of his successor, King Yih, the king's power was under threat from the outside as well. The Bamboo Annals tell us that barbarian tribes from outside the Zhou land mounted attacks on the capital itself. They had never accepted either Shang or Zhou rule, and did not intend to.[5]

The barbarians were beaten away, but the outside threat was compounded by treachery on the inside. Yih's brother, Hsiao, managed to seize his throne. The accounts of the overthrow are vague, but the Bamboo Annals say that King Yih departed from his capital abruptly, while his brother Hsiao succeeded him rather than his son and living heir, Yi.

Yih died in exile; eventually the usurper Hsiao died as well, and Yi managed to recapture his throne with the help of a coalition of lords who (in Sima Qian's words) "enthroned" him. But after this brief cooperation, he too had his difficulties with the lords of the lands. His particular bête noire turned out to be the Duke of Qi, up on the north Yellow river, which had grown into a stronger and stronger state in its own right. Bickering escalated to defiance; according to an inscription, Yi finally turned out the royal army and mounted a campaign against Qi. The Bamboo Annals add that he captured the Duke of Qi and boiled him in a bronze cauldron.[6]

Yi died the year after, and left the throne to his son Li. The quarrels between king and noblemen continued, and more than once erupted into actual fighting. Li, forced to battle constantly against challenges to his authority, grew more and more tyrannical. Sima Qian writes that his own people began to criticize him, and that in desperation the king ordered a Grand Inquisitor of sorts (a "shaman") to go out and listen for disloyal speech. Culprits were arrested and executed. "The criticism subsided," Sima Qian says, "but the feudal lords stopped coming to court. . . . The king became even more stern. No one in the capital dared to say a word, but only glanced at each other on the roads."[7]

Misfortune soon joined the king's repressive policies to make the people of China more miserable than ever: periods of famine and drought, punctuated by flooding rains, destroyed the harvests. An ode from Li's reign laments the state of the kingdom:

Death rains and chaos from heaven down
swamping the king and throne,
worms gnaw thru root and joint of the grain,
woe to the Middle Land, murrain and mould.[8]

Other songs passed down from these years talk of hunger, discontent, and rebellion.[9]

The lords who were still loyal to the king warned Li that an explosion was coming: "To block people's mouths is worse than blocking a river," the Duke of Shao told his king. "When an obstructed river bursts its banks, it will surely hurt a great number of people."[10]

Li, unconvinced, refused to recall his Grand Inquistor. Rebellion broke out; a mob gathered around the palace and shook the gates, but Li managed to get away, out of the capital and into the countryside. His young heir was less fortunate. Trapped in the city, the boy took refuge with his father's faithful advisor, the Duke of Shao. To save the life of the heir to the throne, the Duke of Shao "replaced the Heir . . . with his own son."[11]

Presumably the replacement "king" was killed; and the faithful advisor, who had sacrificed his own family for his king, raised the prince in his household. The rule of the Zhou kingdom passed into the hands of regents, until Li died in exile and the heir, King Hsuan, took the throne.

As far as Sima Qian is concerned, the cycle is progressing through its usual round. From Mu onwards, the Zhou rulers are becoming slowly more decadent. In all likelihood, drought, famine, and the constant encroachments of the lords on royal power were more than enough to make the capital city an unhappy place; but Sima Qian finds it absolutely essential that Li be self-indulgent and cruel, and his son and heir Hsuan be headstrong and blind to the wise advice of his counselors.

Headstrong or not, Hsuan also faced a massive invasion of barbarians.

These invasions had become a constant annoyance. Across the northern and western mountain ranges, tribes of nomads ranged. They were probably Indo-European, and so unlike the descendants of those first Yellow river settlers; they lived a horse-oriented nomadic life, travelling across the high steppes on horseback, hunting game with bows. When they grew hungry, they came down to raid the fields and granaries of the Zhou farmers.

During Hsuan's reign, the most threatening tribes were to the west.[12] The Zhou called them "Xianyun," which was probably not a tribal name; it was simply their designation for a coalition of different nomadic groups who had joined together to try to gain some of the Zhou prosperity for themselves.[13]

From the fifth to the twelfth year of his reign, the armies of King Hsuan marched out against the Xianyun, defending the center of his realm from those on the outside. They were a more troublesome tribe than the earlier invaders, in part because they used chariots in battle, and the wars against them dragged on and on. One of the poems from the Minor Odes ("Xianyun") section of the *Shi jing* laments the invasion; a soldier posted on the frontier complains,

> We have no house, no home
> Because of the Xianyun;
> We cannot rest or bide
> Because of the Xianyun . . .
> The year is running out.
> But the king's business never ends;
> We cannot rise or bide,
> Our hearts are very bitter.

Eventually the Xianyun dropped back, in the face of Zhou resistance, and for a time disappeared from the historical record. But Hsuan's victory over the barbarians did nothing to improve his authority with his own countrymen. Not long afterwards he was back to fighting his own feudal lords, and his fortunes grew bleaker and bleaker: "The many lords mostly rebelled against royal commands," remarks one chronicle.[14]

In the forty-sixth year of his reign, Hsuan died. His son Yu inherited, and the fall of the Zhou grew inexorably closer. An earthquake shook the capital almost as soon as Yu took power, and the resulting landslides apparently choked the river channels that supplied fresh water to the city: "When the source of the rivers is blocked," laments one of the court advisors, "the state will surely perish."

> If there is no way to imbue the soil and the people want for daily needs, then the state will perish all the sooner! . . . Now Zhou's deeds are like those of [the Xia and the Shang] in their final years, and the rivers and their

> sources are . . . blocked. . . . Landslides and dried up rivers are the signs a state will perish. And when the rivers dry up, landslides will surely follow.[15]

Sure enough, Sima Qian writes, "during that year, the three rivers dried up, and there were landslides."

The parallel between the action of Yu's grandfather Li, who had blocked the mouths of his people as a river is blocked, and the earth which slides down into the mouths of the rivers and cuts the capital city off from water, is unmistakable. The evils of the Zhou have overflowed into the earth itself; and in return Heaven will remove its Mandate from the Zhou, so that they no longer give life to their people.

Yu himself turned out to be a licentious, pleasure-seeking ruler. Having sired a son and heir on his senior wife, Yu then became infatuated with a harem woman and tried to depose the queen and crown prince on behalf of the concubine and her bastard son. His advisors resisted the suggestion, but Yu insisted; and finally the advisors stood aside. "The calamity has taken form," the Grand Historian observed, in despair, "and there is nothing we can do about it."[16]

This concubine, now queen, had ripped apart the royal family; not surprisingly, her chief pleasures were destructive. She liked best to hear silk tearing, and so she ordered enormous pieces of the expensive fabric brought to the palace to be torn up in order to amuse her.[17] Despite the wasteful occupation, she seldom smiled and never laughed.

Yu cast around in his mind for some way to amuse her, and decided that he would light all the beacon fires, and beat the alarm drums. This was a signal reserved to warn of barbarian invasion; at the uproar, the nearby lords turned out their armies and charged to the walls of the city. On their arrival, they found no barbarians. Their startled faces were so comical that the concubine laughed out loud (perhaps for the first time).[18]

But barbarian invaders did arrive, not too long later. They were known as the Quan Rong; their homeland was north and west of the Zhou lands. They poured over the borders and laid siege to the city. And they were joined in this by non-barbarians: relatives of King Yu's first wife, angry that she had been set aside. The outside and inside threats had coalesced into one dynasty-shaking attack.

King Yu ordered the beacon fires lit, but the feudal lords simply shrugged and went back to their own duties. They had no intention of being made fools of twice in order to entertain the emperor's fancy piece. Yu himself, fighting against the invaders, was killed in battle. The barbarians looted the palace, kidnapped the concubine, and returned home.

THE FALL OF the Zhou house, which took place in 771, was the end of the Western Zhou dominance. It was not, however, the end of the Zhou Dynasty. A few of the lords were still loyal to Yu's oldest son P'ing, the heir who had been disinherited in favor of the concubine's bastard son. Together, they declared him to be king.

But the capital city of Hao was clearly no place for P'ing. The barbarians may have gone home, but the western border was insecure, and Hao was too close to it. King P'ing decided to withdraw to the east, to a safer location: to

TIMELINE 46

WESTERN SEMITIC LANDS	CHINA
	Zhou Dynasty (1087–256)
Samson	Western Zhou (1087–771)
	Wen
	Wu
Saul	**Tan** (regent)
	Ch'eng
David	
Solomon	**K'ang** (c. 996–977)
	Zhao
Rehoboam (Judah) (931) **Jereboam** (Israel)	
	Mu
	Kung
	Yih (Hsiao)
	Yi
	Li
	Hsuan
	Xianyun invasion
	Yu
	Eastern Zhou (771–221)
	P'ing

the city of Loyang, which had been established centuries before by the Duke of Zhou.

So that he could march safely towards his new capital, the chief of the Ch'in—a minor state whose lord had not been officially recognized by the throne—sent soldiers to escort P'ing. In gratitude, according to the *Shu ching*, P'ing made the chief a lord, the Duke of Ch'in, and "also gave him sufficient land to sustain his new position, the chief city of which was the old capital which had just been abandoned."[19] The Zhou homeland was now in the hands of lesser lords; from his new eastern capital, leaning on the support of the dukes who would be loyal as long as it was in their best interest, King P'ing ruled over a newly shrunken kingdom.[20] The era of the Western Zhou had ended; the time of the Eastern Zhou had begun.

Chapter Forty-Seven

The Assyrian Renaissance

Between 934 and 841 BC,
Assyria makes itself a new empire,
and the Western Semites begin to lose their independence

THE ARAMAEANS, the tribes whose wandering invasion of Mesopotamia had disrupted business-as-usual in Assyria and Babylonia, had now settled down in a patchwork of tiny independent states. The strongest of these was centered at the city of Damascus, in the middle of the plain that lay across the Euphrates from Assyria. King David had managed to bring the Aramaeans of Damascus at least partly under his control: his chronicler boasts that the Israelite army under David "struck down twenty-two thousand of them," and afterwards received regular tribute from them.[1]

During the same years, the Assyrians called the entire area west of the Euphrates "Aram," a blanket term for the cities governed by Aramaean chiefs, and were almost helpless against them. Not until the reign of David's grandson Rehoboam and the fracture of Israel into two states did an Assyrian ruler manage to rally his troops and push back against Aramaean encroachment. His name was Ashur-dan II, and he was the first of the great Assyrian kings who would bring Assyria back out of its dark age, into its new and final renaissance.

Ashur-dan's inscriptions boast that he took vengeance on the wandering peoples who "committed destruction and murder" by burning the Aramaean cities which had been built on land that had once been Assyrian. In fact he came nowhere near re-establishing the boundaries of the old Assyrian empire. He did manage to ring the Assyrian heartland around with his troops, and make it secure; he brought back from the mountains the Assyrian villagers who had been driven from their towns by "want, hunger and famine," resettling them in their own land.[2] But he did not push any farther to the north or the east, where the Aramaeans still held the most power.

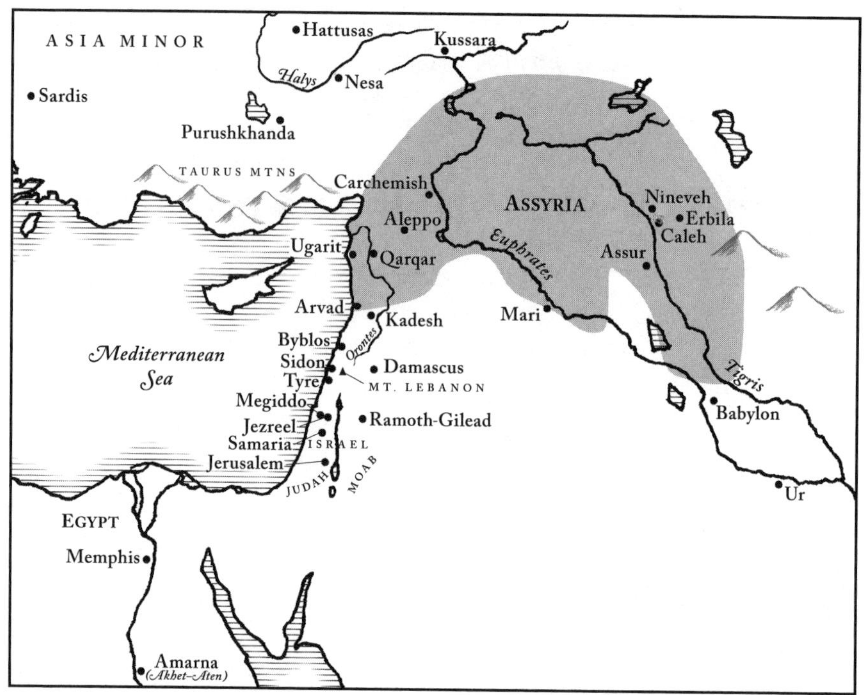

47.1 The New Assyrian Empire

And to the south, the ragged remnant of the Babylonian empire kept its independence, such as it was. The Babylonian throne had been claimed by family after family, its royal capital shifting from city to city, and Aramaeans had infiltrated the old Babylonian territory to such an extent that their language, a Western Semitic dialect known as Aramaic, was beginning to replace the ancient Akkadian which had once served Babylonians as a common tongue.[3]

Not until three generations later did the next great king of Assyria stake his claim to the title. Ashur-dan's great-grandson Ashurnasirpal II finally made Assyria into an empire again.* He fought up to the northwest of Nineveh, and made the city his northern base.[4] He crossed to the eastern bank of the Tigris and built himself a new capital city on the site of the old village of Caleh: "I have taken it anew as a dwelling," he announced. "The former city of Caleh, which Shalmaneser, king of Assyria, a prince who preceded me, had built, that city had fallen into decay and lay in ruins, it was turned into

* Historians date the "New Assyrian Empire," Assyria's last and most powerful incarnation, to the reign of Ashurnasirpal II.

a mound and ruin heap. That city I built anew. . . . I laid out orchards round about it, fruit and wine I offered unto Assur, my lord. . . . I dug down to the water level. . . . I built the wall thereof; from its foundation unto its top I built and completed it."[5]

Caleh, from now on, would be the center of his government; Assur itself became a purely ceremonial city. In Caleh he built not only office buildings, but a palace decorated with reliefs of the warriors and kings who had surrendered to him; at the doorways to the hall where he received tribute, he set up guardian statues, enormous winged bulls with human heads, their faces an idealized portrait of Ashurnasirpal himself.[6] When the palace was finished, Ashurnasirpal threw a huge banquet to celebrate it: his celebratory inscription explains that his guests were fed a thousand oxen, a thousand domestic cattle and sheep, fourteen thousand imported and fattened sheep, a thousand lambs, five hundred game birds, five hundred gazelles, ten thousand fish, ten thousand eggs, ten thousand loaves of bread, ten thousand measures of beer, ten thousand containers of wine, and more. By Ashurnasirpal's count, there were 69,574 guests at the tables, all celebrating his greatness. At the feast, he publicly claimed the titles "great king, king of the world, the valiant hero who goes forth with the help of Assur; he who has no rival in all four quarters of the world, the exalted shepherd, the powerful torrent that none can withstand . . . he who has overcome all of mankind . . . whose hand has conquered all lands and taken all mountain ranges."[7]

Grandiloquent rhetoric aside, Ashurnasirpal did do one thing his ancestors had not accomplished. He fought his way to the Euphrates and then crossed it. "I crossed the Euphrates at its flood in ships made of skins," he records. "I marched along the side of Mount Lebanon, and . . . in the Great Sea I washed my weapons."[8] It was exactly the same gesture of victory that Sargon had made, in the Persian Gulf, so many years before.

This brought him right across the top of the northern border of Israel, which was under the rule of a king named Omri. Omri doesn't get much play in the biblical account, which is more concerned about his disregard for the laws of God: all we learn from the book of 1 Kings is that Omri seized the throne of the north from another claimant and that he was more evil than any king who came before him.[9] But in political terms, Omri was a great warrior and builder (he built Samaria to be the new capital of the north), and the first Israelite king to be mentioned with awe in the inscriptions of another country; the Mesha Inscription, a stone found across the Jordan river in the territory of the tribe known as the Moabites, mourns that Omri "humbled Moab for many years."[10] He was a ruler of enough strength that Ashurnasirpal, who subdued pretty much all of the little states all the way to the coast and even demanded tribute from the Phoenician kings of Tyre and of Sidon, did not venture to attack him.

By now Ashurnasirpal's territory stretched across to the Euphrates, from there in a narrow band to the Mediterranean coast and down it as far as the port city of Arvad. He never actually claimed rule over either Tyre or Sidon, whose kings were friendly to Israel; nor did he attack Babylonia itself. He did march south down the Euphrates as far as the then-accepted borderline between Assyria and Babylonia, and there he sacked a town on the line in order to terrify the Babylonians (although he did not push farther).

His reputation undoubtedly preceded him. In Ashurnasirpal there appeared, full-blown, the delight in cruelty which tagged at the heels of almost every Assyrian king who followed. "I put up a pillar at the city gate," Ashurnasirpal explains, recording his dealings with a city which had revolted and killed its Assyrian-appointed governor, "and I skinned the chiefs who revolted against me, and covered the pillar with their skins. I walled up others in the middle of the pillar itself, and some of them I impaled on stakes and arranged them around the pillar. Inside the city, I skinned many more and covered the walls with their skins. As for the royal officials, I cut off their members."[11] He varied this, at other times, by making heaps of cut-off noses and ears, gouging out eyes, and tying heads to vines throughout the gardens of conquered cities like obscene and decaying fruit. "I made one pillar of the living," he remarks, a particularly nasty Assyrian invention where living prisoners were laid one on top of another and covered with plaster to make a column. "I cut off their ears and their fingers, of many I put out the eyes. . . . their young men and maidens I burned in the fire."[12]

AFTER A TWENTY-FIVE-YEAR REIGN of terror, Ashurnasirpal II died and left the throne to his son Shalmaneser, the third of this name. Shalmaneser III continued the campaign against the Western Semitic lands west of the Euphrates. Like his father, Shalmaneser crossed the Euphrates "at flood" (this seems to have become a point of pride), and advanced "to the shore of the sea of the setting sun," where "I washed my weapons in the sea."[13] Unlike his father, however, he did not shy away from the northern kingdom of Israel.

Israel, paradoxically, seemed stronger than ever. Omri's son Ahab had inherited his father's throne, and—watching the spreading Assyrian threat to his east and north—had negotiated a strategic marriage with the daughter of the Phoenician king of Sidon. This princess, Jezebel, became not just a wife, but his principal queen, which greatly strengthened the Phoenician-Israelite alliance against the Assyrian army.

For all this political savvy, Ahab made several very stupid moves. He showed a shrewd willingness to worship gods other than the God of Israel, including Baal, the chief god of the Phoenicians, and a number of other Western Semitic tribes and cities; this should have won him the friendship not only of Tyre and Byblos, but also the cities that lay between Israel and the advancing Assyrian front. But rather than pacifying his own people by keeping the worship of Yahweh alive as well, he allowed his Phoenician wife to round up and slaughter all the prophets of the God of Abraham. At least a hundred escaped and hid in the mountainous land to the east; from this refuge they became a voice calling the Israelites to rebel against their evil king.

Chief among the prophetic opponents of Ahab was the prophet Elijah, a wild man in animal skins who escaped Jezebel's attempts to assassinate him and did his best to upset the wicked monarch. In fact he anointed a young Israelite officer named Jehu to be God's choice as the next king and gave him divine permission to assassinate Ahab, Jezebel, and the entire royal house.

Given this level of hatred among Israelites themselves for their own king (and, even more virulently, for his foreign wife), it isn't surprising that the Aramaean king of Damascus chose to use this internal unrest as an opportunity to launch his own attack against Israel. He rounded up thirty-two Aramaean warlords, and with this enormous combined force set out to meet the relatively tiny Israelite force: "The Israelites camped opposite them," the writer of 1 Kings tells us, "like two little flocks of goats, while the Aramaeans covered the countryside."

Despite the overwhelming odds, the Israelite army, led by Ahab—who, despite his failings in devotion, appears to have been a perfectly competent commander—managed to fight the Aramaeans to a draw. The king of Damascus made a treaty with Ahab, a treaty which kept peace between Aramaeans and Israelites for two kings for three years.

In the third year, Shalmaneser marched against the Israelite border.

Israel was prepared. Ahab led into battle his own Israelite soldiers (including significant cavalry), Phoenician troops from his allies on the coast, and men sent by the king of Damascus, who did not wish to be the next victim of Assyrian expansion. They were joined by Egypt; the fifth pharaoh of the Twenty-Second Dynasty, Osorkon II, apparently feared that Assyria, once it plowed its way through the Western Semitic lands, might march down the Mediterranean into Egypt.

The troops broke against each other at the city of Qarqar in the year 853.

It is difficult to know exactly what happened next. Shalmaneser III claimed to be victorious: "I made the blood of my enemies flow down into the valley and scattered their corpses," he boasted, on an inscription known as the Monolith Inscription.[14] But the Assyrian reliefs depicting the battle show a highly uncommon sight: enemy soldiers charging forwards over the bodies of

Assyrian dead.[15] Given the usual Assyrian depictions of dead enemies and live warriors, this hints at a much different outcome.

And despite Shalmaneser's claim, he advanced no farther into the Western Semitic lands during the remaining thirty years of his rule. The Phoenician cities, the Israelite lands, and Damascus all remained free of Assyria's grasp.

Most likely the battle was a draw, but devastating enough to Assyria that Shalmaneser decided to withdraw. The Western Semitic kings returned to their cities, and the Egyptian soldiers marched back down to their homeland, which promptly fell apart again into civil war; Egypt, preoccupied with internal troubles, disappeared for a few years from the international stage.

Ahab did not stay put, though. Perhaps exalted beyond reason by his successful defense of his country, Ahab decided, just after the battle of Qarqar, that this was an opportune moment to turn against his ally, the king of Damascus. He sent south to Jehoshaphat, the king of Judah, and asked him to travel north and join with him in an attack against the border city of Ramoth-Gilead, which lay just over the Israelite border, in Aramaean land protected by the treaty.

Jehoshaphat, the great-great-grandson of Solomon, ruled a territory which consisted of the large tribe of Judah along with the minute tribe of Benjamin, a land known collectively as "Judah." He had no enormous military might, but since Ramoth-Gilead lay almost exactly on the north-south border, Jehoshaphat's alliance would have allowed Ahab to perform a pincer move on the city.

Jehoshaphat agreed to visit Ahab to discuss the matter, but once in Ahab's court—which, thanks to Jezebel's imported prophets and court attendants from Tyre, seemed more like a Phoenician than an Israelite court—he grew nervous. The Phoenician advisors, who were also soothsayers and omen-readers, were predicting certain victory against the Aramaeans, but Jehoshaphat asked whether Ahab had considered asking a Hebrew prophet what Yahweh thought about this plan.

"Yes," Ahab said, "there is one prophet I could call, but I don't like him; he never says anything good about me."

Jehoshaphat insisted, and the prophet, Micaiah, was summoned. Asked what he thought, he said, "Attack the Aramaeans and God will give you victory."

This was a prudent but untruthful answer, and Ahab knew it. He said, "How many times do I need to order you to tell me the truth?" upon which Micaiah remarked that not only would the attack fail, but Ahab himself would be killed.

"See?" Ahab said to Jehoshaphat. "I told you that he never says anything good about me."

Despite the prophecy, Jehoshaphat agreed to join in the attack. The events that followed suggest that he may have had his own arrangements with the Aramaean government. When the battle commenced, the Aramaean chariot commanders spotted Jehoshaphat's royal robes and headed directly for him, but when he called out, "I am the king of Judah, not the king of Israel!" they reversed direction and left him alone.[16]

Ahab, fighting in disguise, was not so lucky. An arrow shot at random from some enemy bow hit him between the joints of his armor, and he died.

Twelve years later, his son Joram tried again to conquer Ramoth-Gilead. Again the Aramaean forces proved too strong for him. Wounded in the unsuccessful battle, he retreated back across the Jordan river to the Israelite city of Jezreel to recover from his wounds. Immediately an Israelite prophet went to find Jehu—the young officer anointed by Elijah to kill off Ahab's family, almost fifteen years before—to tell him that his time had finally come.

Jehu had been lying low; the prophet finally ran him to earth in, of all places, Ramoth-Gilead itself, which suggests that he had taken refuge with Israel's enemy. As soon as he heard the news of Joram's weakness, he hitched up his chariot, slung his bow over his shoulder, and set off hell-bent for Jezreel.

Instead of hiding, as Ahab himself had done during the battle of Ramoth-Gilead, Joram put on his robes, harnessed up his own chariot, and rode out to meet the arriving soldier. Jehu put an arrow through him and continued on to Jezreel.

By the time he reached Jezreel, Jezebel the queen mother—who had apparently travelled to be with her wounded son—had heard of Joram's death and the approach of his assassin. She put on her own royal robes and waited at a window for his approach. Whether she was preparing to rally the court behind her, or whether she saw her death approaching, is unclear; but as Jehu drew to a halt in front of the royal residence, she leaned out of the window and called, "Are you coming in peace, you murderer of your master?"

Jehu, building on the anti-monarchical sentiment that had arrayed Joram's own officials behind him, called out for help; and three eunuchs from the queen mother's own household came up behind the old woman and threw her from the window. She fell to the pavement, and Jehu rode over her body. The half-wild dogs that skulked around every ancient city ate her, all but her hands and feet and her skull.

According to the book of 2 Kings, Jehu wiped out the rest of Ahab's family and killed Jezebel's Phoenician prophets.* These are the only two actions

* Right around the time of Jezebel's murder, the king of Tyre, Jezebel's grandnephew, had to fight off various challenges to this throne. He ended up by purging the royal family of all possible competitors. According to the tradition set down well after the fact by the Greek historian Timaeus (c. 270

47.1. Black Obelisk. This panel on the basalt victory stele of Shalmaneser III shows Jehu of Israel prostrating himself before the Assyrian king. British Museum, London. Photo credit Erich Lessing/Art Resource, NY

that characterize his reign: but in his days, "the Lord began to reduce the size of Israel."[17] The only defeat recorded is that at the hands of the Aramaean king of Damascus, who abandoned whatever support he had offered Jehu once the man was on Israel's throne, and took away everything east of the Jordan river.

The more serious defeat is not mentioned in the biblical account at all. It is, however, carved into Shalmaneser III's victory monument, the Black

---

BC), one victim of the purge was his brother-in-law; his sister, Jezebel's grandniece Elissa, managed to escape her brother's assassins and fled across the Mediterranean, along with a loyal band of followers. They landed on the coast of North Africa in 814 and founded a Phoenician colony there, the city of Carthage. Elissa, under the Greek version of her name—Dido—later became a central character in Virgil's epic tale, the Aeneid. Although most of this story is probably myth, it does reflect some very contemporary realities: unrest in the royal family of Tyre may have been related to Jezebel's death; the unrest may have also had something to do with the looming threat of Shalmaneser III's successor on the eastern horizon; and the story of Jehu shows that the purging of a royal family was a common occurence in ancient Near Eastern palaces.

Obelisk. On it, dozens of conquered kings come with tribute for Shalmaneser; on the second panel of one side, Jehu of Israel touches his forehead to the ground before the Assyrian king. Shalmaneser stands looking down at him, his head shielded from the sun by a parasol held over him by an obsequious attendant. Shalmaneser III had marched his army into Israel and had set up an image of himself in Israelite territory; the first Assyrian king to enter Israel, but by no means the last.[18]

Jehu had lost Ahab's old allies. The Aramaeans were against him, and the Phoenicians—infuriated by the slaughter of their royal princess Jezebel, her court, the priests who served her gods, and her descendants—were no longer willing to fight on his side.[19] Jehu, chosen to purify the house of Israel, had purified it of his allies. He had no choice left but to submit.

TIMELINE 47

WESTERN SEMITIC LANDS		ASSYRIA	EGYPT
		Ashur-bel-kala (1074–1056)	
		Aramaean takeover	
	Samson		Third Intermediate Period
			Dynasty 21 (Tanis)
	Saul		
	David		
			Dynasty 22 (945–712)
	Solomon		**Sheshonq I**
		Ashur-dan II (934–912) (945–924)	
Rehoboam (931)	**Jereboam**		
(Judah)	(Israel)	**Ashurnasirpal II** (911–859)	
	Omri		
Jehoshaphat	**Ahab**		
			Osorkon II (870–850)
	Ahaziah	**Shalmaneser III** (858–824)	
	Joram		
	Jehu		

Chapter Forty-Eight

New Peoples

In the fifty years after 850 BC,
Assyria attacks its neighbors,
while three kinds of Greeks invent a shared past

Not long after Jehu's submission, the old king of Babylon died. His two sons quarrelled over the throne, which gave Shalmaneser of Assyria the perfect chance to attack his southern neighbor.

He declined. In fact, Assyrian soldiers marched down to help the older prince get his throne back. "In my eighth year of reign," Shalmaneser III's inscription reads, "there revolted against Marduk-zakir-shumi his younger brother. . . . To avenge Marduk-zakir-shumi, I marched forth." At the approach of the Assyrians, the rebellious younger prince escaped, "like a fox, through a hole in the wall" and took off. The Assyrians followed and caught him: "The rebel officers who were with him, I cut down with the sword." Shalmaneser concludes.[1]

With the rebellion put down, Shalmaneser visited Babylon with gifts and arranged a match between one of Marduk-zakir-shumi's daughters and his own second-eldest son. In his own palace, he carved a relief that shows him clasping the hand of Marduk-zakir-shumi, the two kings standing side by side as equal rulers.[2]

The unwillingness to attack Babylon had nothing to do with weakness; Shalmaneser spent most of his reign in ceaseless campaigning. The kings of the Assyrian renaissance were particularly reluctant to attack the famous old city, and particularly worried about offending Marduk, Babylon's chief god. Instead, Shalmaneser III bypassed Babylon and sent troops east, northwest, and farther south, where three new peoples would soon be forced to pay tribute to Assyria.

At the head of the Persian Gulf, five Semitic tribes had claimed the land which once had formed the far southern edge of Sumer. The tribe of Bit-

Amukanni dominated the land near the old Sumerian city of Uruk; Bit-Dakkuri lay a little to the north, closest to Babylon; and the tribe of Bit-Yakin dominated Ur and the marshy land bordering the Gulf itself.[3] Two smaller tribes lay under the protection of these three.* Collectively, the Assyrians knew these tribes as the Chaldeans. They paid nominal allegiance to the king of Babylon, but they were only sketchily under any Babylonian control.

After helping Marduk-zakir-shumi get his throne back, Shalmaneser III marched down beneath Babylon's southern border and compelled tribute from the Chaldean tribes. The tribute was not minor; the Chaldeans sent gold, silver, ivory, and elephant hides, which suggests that they were trading down the Gulf with merchants as far east as India.[4] Shalmaneser's invasion was, theoretically, to help Babylon out, since the Chaldeans had happily joined in the younger brother's rebellion; but it didn't do Shalmaneser III any harm either. Respect Babylon he might, but now he controlled its northern and southern borders, which meant that the kingdom's growth was severely limited.

Then, around 840, Shalmaneser marched north up the Euphrates and turned west to cross over the top of the Aramaean-dominated lands. Here, on the northeast corner of the Mediterranean Sea, lay a little kingdom called Que.

Que was a new country, but it was populated by an old race. Three hundred years earlier, the Hittite capital Hattusas had burned, and the Hittite people had scattered. The center of their old kingdom was occupied by invaders from southern Europe who had crossed over the Bosphorus Strait; settling in Asia Minor, they built themselves a capital city at Gordium and became known as the Phrygians. The Hittites had lost most of their coastline as well. Mycenaeans, driven from their own homes by the Dorian influx, had settled along the western edge of Asia Minor and down along the southern coast as well.

The scattered Hittites regathered themselves on the only land they could still call their own, southeast of their old homeland. Here they worshipped the Hittite gods and lived in tiny independent neo-Hittite kingdoms, centered around walled cities. Carchemish, on the northern Euphrates, was the strongest of these.

Que, another neo-Hittite kingdom, had less military might but lay in a strategic position on the path through the Taurus Mountains, the best gateway into Asia Minor and also the road to the silver mines north of the moun-

* The smaller tribes were Bit-Sha'alli and Bit-Shilani. In the Chaldean language, which is not documented from this period, *bit* apparently meant "household of"; the rest of each tribal name referred to an ancestor from which the tribe was descended (see H. W. F. Saggs, *Babylonians,* p. 134). This shows a common heritage with the Western Semitic Israelites, both in tribal organization and in language; the Hebrew word for "household" was *bet.*

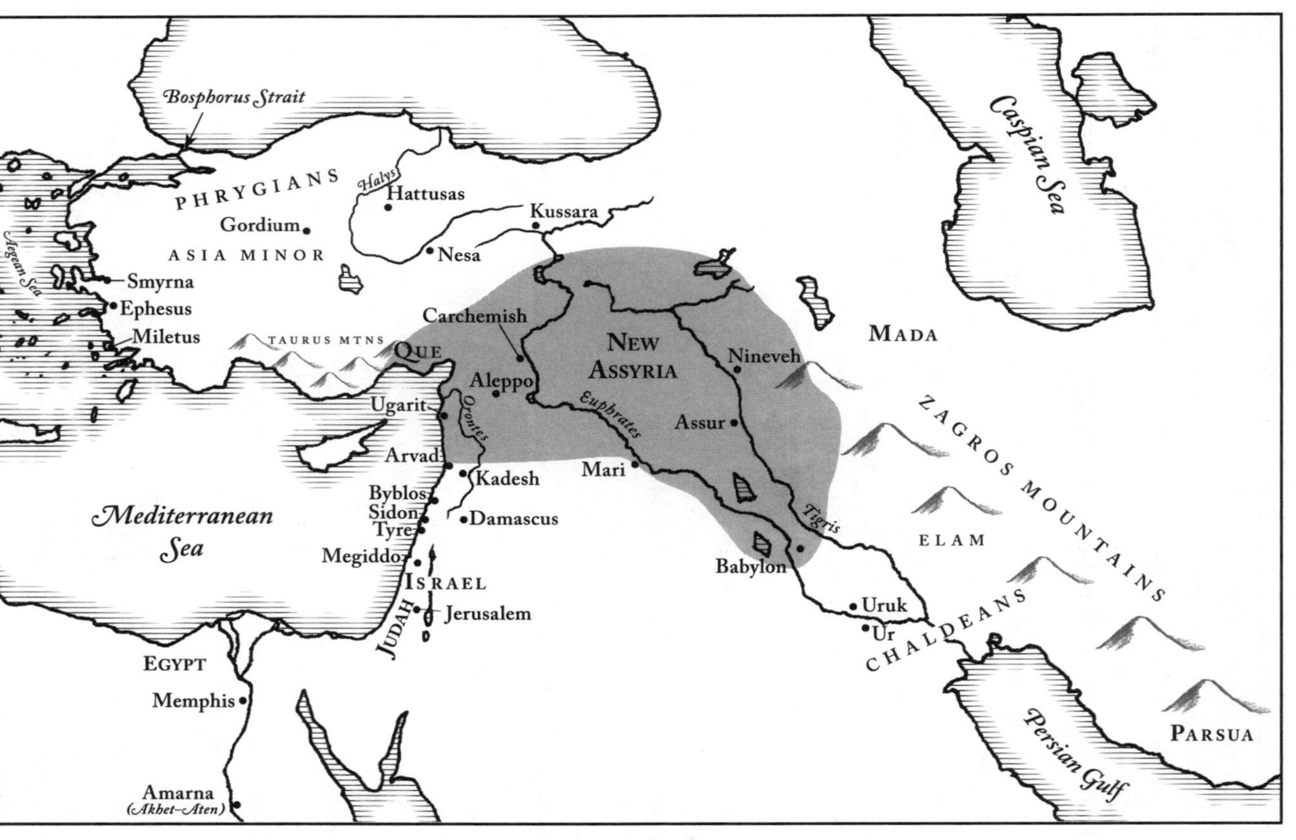

48.1 *Shalmaneser's Enemies*

tains. Shalmaneser attacked Que, marched into its capital, and claimed the silver mines for himself.[5]

Then he turned east. As always, the Elamites on the other side of the Tigris were a continual threat. The kings of the Elamite cities could see that Assyria was a much greater threat than the relatively small Babylon, and so they tended to ally themselves with the Babylonian kings when there was fighting to be done. Shalmaneser was a friend of Babylon too, but in the ancient Near East, the friend of your friend was more likely to be your enemy than otherwise. An alliance between Babylon and Elam might well threaten Assyrian power.

Shalmaneser did not attempt to add Elam formally to his empire, but he demanded tribute from its cities. A couple of Assyrian raids into Elamite land convinced the cities to pay up. Shalmaneser also strengthened his own position by making a quick journey across the Zagros Mountains in order to subdue the peoples who lived across the northern edge of Elam. As with Babylon, he could now claim to control two of Elam's borders.

These northern mountain-dwellers had probably divided off, perhaps a thousand years before, from those same wandering peoples who had then gone southeast into India. Shalmaneser's own annals name two tribes: the Parsua, who were settled just across the Zagros on the western side of Elam, and the Mada, who were still wandering nomadically all along the north.[6]

Neither the Parsua nor the Mada put up much of a fight against Shalmaneser, and he returned home boasting the allegiance of twenty-seven different mountain chiefs. He put no particular value on this conquest; the Parsua and the Mada were simply buffers against Elamite power. It would be a century or so before their names were given, by the Greeks, their more familiar form: the Persians and the Medes.

SHALMANESER III died in 824, in the middle of a rebellion launched by his own son. On his deathbed, Shalmaneser disinherited his heir and appointed his second son, Shamshi-Adad (husband of the Babylonian princess), in his place. He died before he could finish quelling the revolt; Shamshi-Adad, the fifth of that name, was now officially king of Babylon, but he was outnumbered by his brother's supporters and had to flee his own country.

It was a huge rebellion, as Shamshi-Adad V's own accounts reveal:

> Where [my brother] Assur-danin-apli, in the time of Shalmaneser, his father, acted wickedly, bringing about sedition, rebellion, and wicked plotting, caused the land to rise in revolt, prepared for war, brought the people of Assyria, north and south, to his side, and made bold speeches, brought

> the cities into the rebellion and set his face to begin strife and battle . . . 27 cities, along with their fortifications . . . revolted against Shalmaneser, king of the four regions of the world, my father, and . . . had gone to the side of Assur-danin-apli.[7]

The only king who could lend him enough soldiers to meet a challenge of this size was his father-in-law, the king of Babylon. So Shamshi-Adad fled to Babylon and asked Marduk-zakir-shumi for help. The Babylonian king agreed, and supplied troops to help the Assyrian heir retake his own capital city.

But Marduk-zakir-shumi made a ruinous error in judgment. He did not entirely trust his son-in-law, and forced Shamshi-Adad to sign a treaty as a condition of getting those Babylonian troops. The treaty is fragmentary, but it apparently required Shamshi-Adad to acknowledge Babylon's superiority. The wording did not give Shamshi-Adad the title *king*, which is granted to Marduk-zakir-shumi alone, and the accompanying oaths were sworn to in front of the Babylonian gods only, with the Assyrian pantheon dismissed.[8]

Shamshi-Adad signed the treaty, biting back his resentment for the sake of regaining his throne. He took the offered soldiers and mounted an attack against his own cities, winning Assur back by breaking through the walls.

Once Shamshi-Adad V had his throne back, he honored the treaty with Marduk-zakir-shumi. Either he was a man of his word, or he stood in fear of the deities overlooking the agreement. But when Marduk-zakir-shumi died and his son Marduk-balassu-iqbi took the throne in his place, Shamshi-Adad began to plan a campaign that no Assyrian king had undertaken for generations: the invasion of Babylon.

Not too many years after Marduk-balassu-iqbi's accession, the plans reached fruition. Shamshi-Adad organized his army for a march and headed south—not directly, but rather along the Tigris, in a rather leisurely manner that suggested he wasn't particularly worried about his brother-in-law managing to prepare much in the way of a fight; he records that he not only sacked a few villages along the way, but also stopped long enough for a lion hunt during which he killed three lions.[9]

Marduk-balassu-iqbi came up to meet him, fortified with a few Chaldean and Elamite allies. The alliance was shortly trounced, according to Shamshi-Adad's annals:

> He advanced against me offering battle and combat. . . . With him I fought. His defeat I accomplished. Five thousand of his hordes I cut down, two thousand I captured alive, 100 of his chariots, 200 of his cavalry. His royal tent, his camp bed, I took from him . . .[10]

which is to say that the Assyrian soldiers broke all the way through into the center of the Babylonian line. Among the captives marched off to Babylon was the king himself. We have no record of what the queen of Assyria, his sister, said to him when he arrived.

In his place, Shamshi-Adad V installed a puppet-king, a former Babylonian court official who was intended to act as vassal, not king. He was an unprofitable servant who immediately started to plan revolt. Shamshi-Adad V was forced to return after less than a year and take him too as a prisoner to Assyria.[11]

At this point, Shamshi-Adad V declared himself, in ancient and anachronistic terms, "King of Sumer and Akkad."[12] This was not at all the same thing as calling himself "King of Babylon." Rather, he was denying that any such entity as Babylon existed; there was only Assyria, the proper guardian of Babylonian culture and the Babylonian gods. His father-in-law's insult was revenged.

Not long afterwards, Shamshi-Adad, now king of Babylon and Assyria, died young. The year was 811; he had spent just over ten years on his throne, and his son, Adad-nirari III, was still a child. So Shamshi-Adad's queen, the Babylonian princess Sammu-amat, stepped into the place of power. A woman on the Assyrian throne: it had never been done before, and Sammu-amat knew it. The stele she built for herself is at some pains to link her to every available Assyrian king. She is called not only queen of Shamshi-Adad and mother of Adad-nirari, but also "daughter-in-law of Shalmaneser, king of the four regions."[13]

Sammu-amat's hold on power was so striking that it echoed into the distant historical memory of a people just arriving on the scene. The Greeks remember her, giving her the Greek version of her name, Semiramis. The Greek historian Ctesias says that she was the daughter of a fish-goddess, raised by doves, who married the king of Assyria and gave birth to a son called Ninyas. When her husband died, Semiramis treacherously claimed his throne.*

The ancient story preserves an echo of Adad-nirari's name in Ninyas, the son of the legendary queen; and it is not the only story to hint that Sammu-amat seized power in a manner not exactly aboveboard. Another Greek historian, Diodorus, tells us Semiramis convinced her husband to give her power just for five days, to see how well she could manage it. When he agreed, she had him executed and seized the crown for good.

* The works of Ctesias, who was a physician and a learned man, come to us only secondhand; the manuscripts have disappeared into dust, but a later Greek historian, Diodorus, borrowed large chunks of Ctesias's accounts and credits him with them. Diodorus is much given to fantastical tales, and it is difficult to know exactly how much of "Ctesias's accounts" should actually be credited (or debited) to the earlier writer.

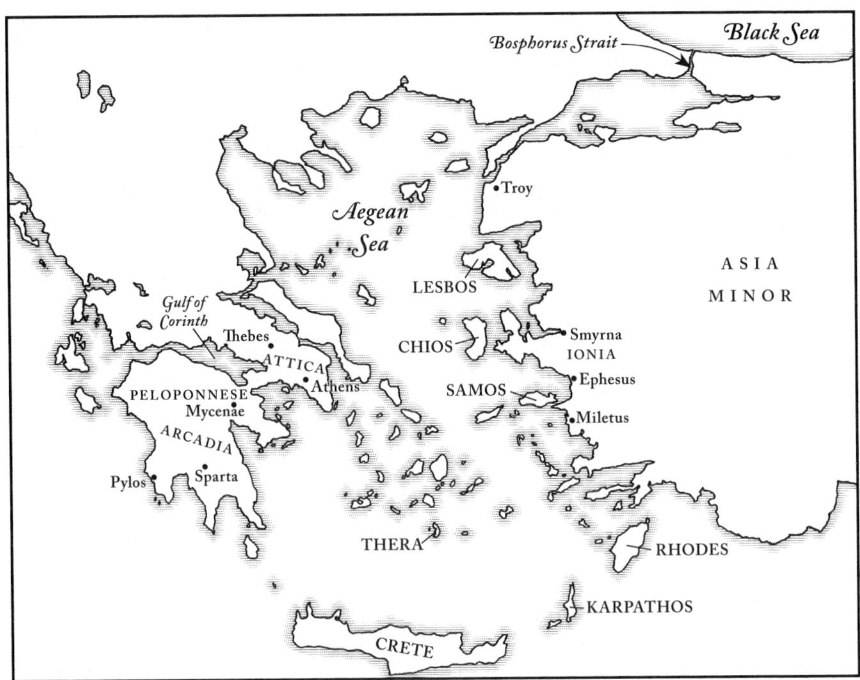

48.2 Mycenaeans, Dorians, and Ionians

By this time, the Greek cities had coalesced into three distinct clusters. The Mycenaean cities of the mainland had buckled, three hundred years earlier, in the face of overrunning Dorians. But they had not entirely disappeared. What remnants of Mycenaean civilization survived lay in the area known as Arcadia, in the center of the southern Greek peninsula, the "Peloponnese," below the arm of water that cut in from the eastern side, nearly dividing it into two (a body of water later known as the Korinthiakos Kolpos, the Gulf of Corinth).

Migrating Mycenaean Greeks, as well as wandering down and bothering Egypt, had also sailed across the Aegean Sea over to the coast of Asia Minor. Here they settled along the shore, in villages that grew into cities: Smyrna, Miletus, Ephesus, and others. The mixture of Mycenaean and Asian language and ways resulted in a distinctive culture which we now call Ionian; the Ionian Greeks then spread back across the nearby islands during the Dorian occupation, occupying the islands of Lesbos, Chios, and Samos, among others, and finally returning to the eastern coast of Greece itself.

Meanwhile the Dorians established their own stronghold on the south and the east of the Peloponnesian peninsula; they also spread down into Crete and as far east as the islands of Rhodes and Karpathos. The Doric dialect was distinct from the mainland Mycenaean version, and both were different from the Ionian dialect.

All three groups were, more or less, of the same race. The Ionians were Mycenaean at the root, and the Mycenaeans and Dorians came from the same Indo-European stock, both of them descended from wanderers who had come south into the Greek peninsula centuries before. Later, the Greeks would account for the similarities by claiming that the Dorians were descended from the sons of Heracles, who had been driven from their homeland in Mycenae by force and then had returned to reclaim their territory.[14]

But there was still no "Greece" here, only Mycenaeans ("Arcadians," to distinguish them from their ancestors), Ionians, and Dorians. The Greek peninsula, like the "Western Semitic" lands before the rise of Israelite and Aramaean kingdoms, was a land of independent kings and chiefs.

As the Dorian disruption receded into the distant past, the cities of the Greek peninsula entered into a period of relative peace. During this time, they were more likely to act as allies than as enemies, and to exchange even more of their customs and language.* Sometime around 800 BC—a very vague and general estimate—this growing sense of a single cultural identity led to the weaving together of a number of different historical traditions (many of them Mycenaean) into two related epic poems which would soon be claimed by the entire peninsula as the heritage of every city on it: the Iliad and the Odyssey.

According to later Greek tradition, the composer of these poems was an Ionian named Homer, who came either from the Asia Minor city of Smyrna, in the heart of the Ionian settlements, or from the island of Chios just off the Ionian coast. There is ongoing debate about who Homer was (or wasn't); theories encompass everything from a single genius to a whole school of poets writing under a single name. The poems themselves bear the stamp of the oral storyteller: two-word descriptions that occur again and again (wine-dark, swift-footed, fair-cheeked, lovely-haired) and give the poet an immediate way to fill out the rhythm of a spoken line; formal phrases that close off a scene ("so she said in winged words," "they sat still for a long time and in silence");[15]

* Historians generally divide Greek history into the Dark Age (1150–750 BC), the Archaic Period (750–490), the Classical Period (490–323), and the Hellenistic Period (323–30). Archaeologists, who base their very ancient chronology on shifts in styles of art and pottery rather than on recorded events, use a slightly different division; the early years of the Dark Age are known as the Submycenaean Period (1125–1050) and the later years as the Protogeometric Period (1050–900), while the emergence from the Dark Age is called the Geometric Period (after a pottery style) and is divided into the Early (900–850), Middle (850–750), and Late Geometric (750–700). These chronologies can be found in a number of standard reference works, including *Ancient Greece: A Political, Social, and Cultural History* by Sarah B. Pomeroy et al.

and the so-called ring compositions, in which the poet gives himself a convenient mental anchor for an episode by beginning in the middle of it, going back to the beginning, and then forwards to the end.*

No one is sure when these chanted or sung tales were set down in writing. During the Greek Dark Age, only the Mycenaeans had preserved any kind of writing at all, and they did very little of it. But no matter when the stories were reduced to writing, they clearly reflect a pre–800 BC world. Not just the Iliad and the Odyssey, but most of Greek mythology is (as classicist Ken Dowden puts it) "written on a Mycenaean geographical map";[16] details of armor (a boar's tusk helmet) and treasure reflect a world before the coming of the Dorians.[17] On the other hand, the epics also show a knowledge of overseas settlements unlikely to have been current in the Mycenaean era.[18] The language of the epic is itself that of the eighth century. And the name of Priam, king of Troy, belongs to the neo-Hittite language spoken by the inhabitants of Que and other scattered descendants of the Hittite empire.[19]

The stories of Troy and the heroes who fought against it offered the Dorians and Arcadians and Ionians a mythical shared past. In the Iliad, each city sends its ships instantly in response to Agamemnon's call, a unity of action that the Greeks never actually managed to achieve. But the story expresses the beginnings of a growing identification between Greek cities that separated them from other peoples.

In the Iliad, for the first time, we come across a word for those who live outside the triple circle of Greeks: Homer calls them *barbaro-phonoi,* "strange speakers."[20] It was a simple division of all peoples into two, those who spoke a dialect of Greek and those who didn't.

It was also the seed of an idea which would continue to twine itself, more and more tightly, around the minds of the Greeks. Human nature was binary; it was either Greek or non-Greek, and a man's identity as *Greek* was the core of his character.

The strength of this identification had its roots, paradoxically, in the separateness of the Greek cities, back in 800 BC. They had no political unity, no common aim, and not much in the way of shared life. They had different cities, different kings, different landscapes, but they all spoke some variation of Greek. The resemblance of their speech and their imaginary shared past were the threads that held them together.

* As this is a history rather than a literature survey, I am here resisting the urge to go deeper into the question of Homeric authorship, the structure of the epics, their language, their take on heroism, what they reveal about early Greek worship of the gods, and so on. These are subjects which could fill not one book, but many. Since they already have, I will refrain.

TIMELINE 48

ASSYRIA	EGYPT	GREEK PENINSULA/ASIA MINOR
		Neo-Hittite kingdoms form
Ashur-bel-kala (1074–1056)		
Aramaean takeover		
	Third Intermediate Period	
	Dynasty 21 (Tanis)	
	Dynasty 22 (945–712)	
	Sheshonq I (945–924)	
Ashur-dan II (934–912)		
Ashurnasirpal II (911–859)		
		Arcadian, Dorian, Ionian cultures (c. 900)
	Osorkon II (870–850)	
Shalmaneser III (858–824)		
Shamshi-Adad V (823–812)		
Sammu-amat		
		Homer (c. 800)

Chapter Forty-Nine

Trading Posts and Colonies

Between 800 and 720 BC,
the Olympic Games begin in Greece,
while Greek cities and the city of Rome are built in Italy

HOMER'S FLEETS OF SHIPS would have been a familiar sight to any Greek who lived near the water:

> Thus o'er the field the moving host appears. . . .
> The gathering murmur spreads, their trampling feet
> Beat the loose sands, and thicken to the fleet;
> With long-resounding cries they urge the train
> To fit the ships, and launch into the main.[1]

Greek merchants sailed across the Aegean Sea from island to island, to the Asia Minor coast, down to Crete, and back up to the mainland. By the time of Homer, ships from Greek cities were also making regular calls at the southern shores of the peninsula to the west, to trade with the peoples there.

Before 1200 BC, when the Mycenaeans were still at the height of their power over to the east, the Italian peninsula* was populated by widely scattered little settlements that ranged all along the peninsula, from boot-heel to boot-top. Despite the distance between them, they made the same kinds of pots, which suggests that they were all of the same descent. Because so many of the

* Italy was not a country until 1861, so to call the peninsula "Italian" at this point in history is more than stretching a point. However, like China, the Italian peninsula has been identified with the same culture and its descendents since very ancient times, so I will use "Italian" for convenience. (In the nineteenth century, when the Italian states were governed by Austria, the Austrian statesman Clemens von Metternich remarked that "Italy is merely a geographic expression"; he was immediately proved wrong, since Italian agitation for national identity erupted almost directly afterwards, but the comment applies much more accurately to the eighth century BC.)

settlements lay along the ridge of the Apennines, archaeologists assign these people to the "Apennine culture."[2]

During the Greek Dark Age, the Apennine culture put out branches. Differences began to appear not only in pottery, but in weapons and armor. Iron tools and weapons spread slowly through the peninsula. Population increased; the people of a single settlement now might number in the thousands.[3] Before 1200, all of the "Italians" had buried their dead. Now a good number of villages in the north began to burn the bodies instead.*

By the time the Greek ships arrived to trade, the peninsula was home to various customs which archaeologists use to distinguish the early Italians from each other. The villages that still buried their dead fell into three groups: the Fossa, which lay along the lower west coast and down into the toe of the Italian boot; the Apulian, just above the heel; and the Middle Adriatic, along the ridge of the Apennines.[4] The northern villagers who now cremated their dead divided into four groups: the Golasecca to the west, who buried chariots and armor with their warriors; the Este to the east, who did beautiful work in bronze; the Villanovan to the south, who not only burned the dead but then buried the ashes in urns; and the Latial, just below the Villanovans, and separated from them by the river Tiber.

The Latial peoples put *their* ashes not just in urns, but in tiny huts that were replicas of homes for the living, made as dwellings for the dead. Their own huts were simple, their settlements unprotected; the Roman historian Varro tells us that they "knew not the meaning of a wall or gate." The tiny villages, perched for safety on the tops of hills, were united by their common speech. They spoke an obscure tongue called Latin, one of at least forty different languages and dialects used throughout the peninsula.†[5]

The Greek ships landed on the southern Italian shores and traded for metal and grain; they also docked at the large southern island later known as Sicily. This successful trade led to the establishment of trading posts where Greek merchants not only docked but also lived, for at least part of the year.[6]

Around 775, the northwestern Greek city of Chalcis and the eastern city of Eretria sent a joint force of merchants to build a trading post a little farther to

* The archaeological division of the peninsula's history labels 2000–900 BC as the Bronze Age, with the period of the Greek Dark Age (1200–900 BC) assigned to the Late Bronze Age. The Iron Age begins around 900 BC.

† The identification of these languages, many of which are known only from a fragment or two of an inscription, and their relationship to each other is one of the elements which has gone into identifying the differences between the Iron Age Italian cultures. But it is a highly specialized field with its own lingo, so beyond the scope of this particular book. T. J. Cornell has a very compressed but helpful introduction to the whole subject in *The Beginnings of Rome*, pp. 41–44.

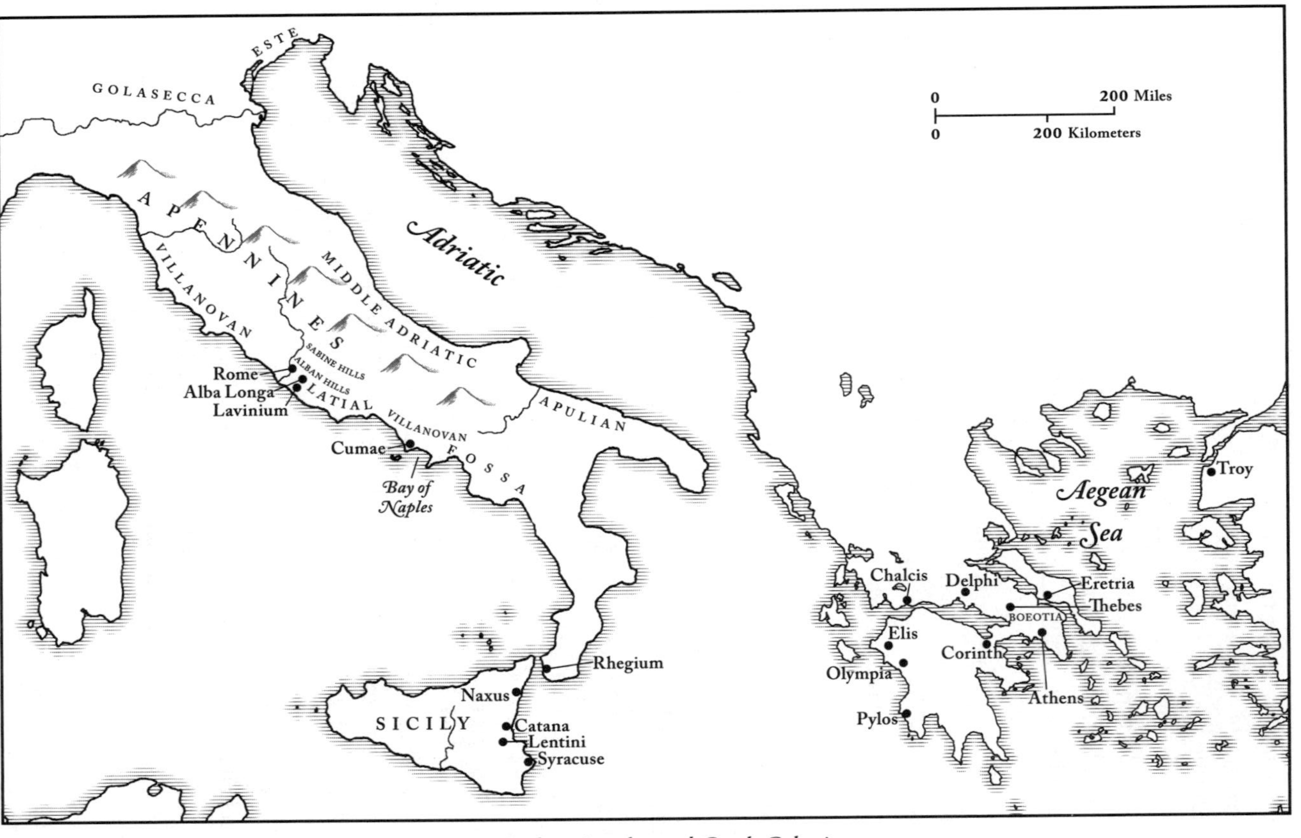

49.1 Italian Peoples and Greek Colonies

the north, on the upper shoreline of the little body of water today known as the Bay of Naples. This trading post was near the Villanovans, whom the Greeks called Tyrrhenians. Soon Greek vases began to appear among the grave goods in Villanovan graves; Greek lines began to appear in the carved reliefs of the Villanovans.

Chalcis and Eretria, cooperating for their mutual good, had forged a relationship that went beyond a shared dialect. Right around the same time, the temple of Zeus and Hera* at the Greek city of Olympia began to grow in size, thanks to pilgrimages made to it by Greeks from much farther away. Farther north, at Delphi, a slightly different kind of shrine—an oracle, where a priest or priestess consulted the gods on behalf of Greeks seeking guidance—also attracted distant visitors. On the island of Delos, the temple of Apollo and the martial goddess Artemis expanded. These sacred sites were rapidly becoming "pan-Hellenic," belonging not just to the nearest city, but to all speakers of Greek. They gave birth to the first Greek alliances as well. Cities joined together into *amphictyonys*, associations which shared responsibility for the upkeep of a temple or shrine; the ancient version of a building co-op.

Most remarkably, the Greek cities joined together in a single festival to honor the god Zeus. The first of these festivals was held (traditionally) in 776, not more than a year distant from the joint expedition of Chalcis and Eretria, and the worshippers met at Olympia.

Olympia had been a religious center for centuries, and races of various kinds had long been part of the sacrifices and rituals held there.† In 776, the king of Elis, a small city just northwest of Olympia, was said to have journeyed to the oracle at Delphi to ask how battles between Greek cities might be brought to an end. The oracle told him to make the games at Olympia into an official festival, during which a truce must be declared. From then on, according to the oldest sources, official games were held at Olympia once every four years. During the games, an Olympic truce was declared throughout the Greek world; it lasted at first for a month, and later was extended to three months so that Greeks from farther away could travel to Olympia and back safely.[7]

* A study of the Greek pantheon is beyond the scope of this book; I will just note that although cultic activity in honor of the gods had been going on for centuries, the Iliad and Odyssey are the earliest Greek works which show us anything about the personality and motives of Zeus and company, demonstrating that by 800 BC or so the pantheon had undergone quite a bit of development, elaboration, and ritualization.

† Judith Swaddling, curator of Greek and Roman antiquities at the British Museum, laments that there is no contemporary parallel to Olympia. Americans are better off; simply imagine a pro football game opened with prayer and played for the glory of God, with an altar call at halftime. Add in a presidential candidate flipping the initial coin, and you've got all three elements of the ancient games: religion, sport, and politics.

The games themselves never actually brought peace, as Elis's king had hoped. But they did remind the Greek cities that they were united not only by the same language, but by the worship of the same gods, and that war was not the only possible relation between them.

According to Roman legend, in 776 a king named Numitor was ruling over two Latin towns on the Italian peninsula, both of them just south of the Tiber. The first and older town was called Lavinium; the second, planted as a colony when Lavinium became crowded, was called Alba Longa and was built along the ridge of the Alban hills.

Numitor's wicked younger brother Amulius mounted an attack that forced the king to flee alone into exile, unable to return to his country to protect his family. Amulius then seized the throne, murdered his brother's sons, and decreed that his brother's daughter, the princess Rhea Silvia, should be a perpetual virgin, by way of preventing further claims to the throne by Numitor's grandchildren.

Despite this, she became pregnant; the Roman historian Livy remarks that she claimed to have been raped by the god Mars, and that while "perhaps she believed it, perhaps she was merely hoping by the pretense to palliate her guilt."[8] In any case, her twin boys, once born, were clearly a threat to the usurper's power, as they were in direct line of inheritance from the murdered king. (They were, the Greek biographer Plutarch adds, "of more than human size and beauty," which further alarmed Amulius.)[9]

Amulius ordered his baby grandnephews drowned in the river. As the Tiber was at flood, the servant sent to drop the children into the water dropped them near the bank instead, and went away. Here, according to legend, a she-wolf found them and nursed them, and not long after the king's herdsman found them and carried them off to his wife to raise.

The herdsman named them Romulus and Remus and raised them to manhood; Plutarch says that Numitor, in exile, sent money for their education. When they had grown, they got rid of their wicked great-uncle, and Numitor reclaimed his kingdom.

With their grandfather back on the throne, the twins—now recognized as the royal heirs—were, as Livy puts it, "suddenly seized by an urge to found a new settlement on the spot where they had been left to drown as infants."[10] The king approved; Alba had grown as large as Lavinium, and a third town was needed. But the sibling rivalry that had erupted between Numitor and Amulius was reborn in Numitor's grandsons; they could not decide who should be the ultimate ruler in their new settlement, and asked the gods to send them a sign. Things went downhill from there:

> For this purpose Romulus took the Palatine hill and Remus the Aventine as their respective stations from which to observe the auspices. Remus, the story goes, was the first to receive a sign—six vultures; and no sooner was this made known to the people than double the number appeared to Romulus. The followers of each promptly saluted their master as king, one side basing its claim upon priority, the other upon number. Angry words ensued, followed all too soon by blows, and in the course of the affray Remus was killed.[11]

Livy remarks that another, "commoner" tradition holds that Remus mocked his brother's attempt to build a wall around his new settlement by vaulting over it, and that Romulus killed him in a murderous rage. Either way, the newly built city was named after Romulus, who fortified the Palatine hill and made it the center of his new city of Rome. The year, according to tradition, was 753 BC.

This particular tale is almost entirely smoke and barely even a smoldering of actual fire. Archaeology suggests that settlers did indeed build houses on the site of Rome sometime between 1000 and 800 BC, but Roman writers were magpies, collecting bits of other peoples' stories for themselves; the story of Romulus and Remus contains a patchwork of parts from older Greek legends, not to mention hints of Sargon and Moses.* Livy himself, writing around 30 BC, begins his history by remarking, "Events before Rome was born, or thought of, have come to us in old tales with more of the charm of poetry than of a sound historical record."[12]

Perhaps the one historical echo we can dimly hear in this story comes through in the repeated struggle of brothers. A thousand years earlier, the struggle of Osiris and Set over Egypt reflected actual battles of succession between blood relatives. In the story of Romulus, we may also see a war between two related peoples. Ancient remains tell us that Rome began as two settlements, one on the Palatine hill, the other on the Esquiline, each hill held by a different Latial tribe.[13] Possibly one tribe did come down, like Romulus, from the Alban ridge, perhaps to feed a growing population with grain from the fertile Tiberian plain.

Very likely the other group came from the Sabine hills. According to Livy, once in control of the Palatine hill, Romulus built a big town ("the rapid expansion of the enclosed area was out of proportion to the actual population," Livy remarks) and was then faced with the problem of filling it with

* Classicist R. M. Ogilvie points out that the two sons of the Greek god Poseidon were put out onto the river Enipeus, and then were found and raised by animals; Remus's vault over the walls of Rome resembles the legends of Oeneus and Toxeus or Poimander and Leucippus.

people. He opened the gates to all fugitives and wanderers (Livy, a good republican, has some vested interest in proving that Rome's founding citizens were a "mob," as he puts it, who gave the city "the first real addition to the City's strength, the first step to her future greatness").[14] This filled the walls, but he had a problem: Rome's greatness "seemed likely to last only for a single generation," as there were almost no women.

This was aggravated by the tribal equivalent of sibling hatred: the neighboring villages, of the same racial makeup as the settlers at Rome, refused to send wives, since they "despised the new community, and at the same time feared . . . the growth of this new power in their midst.' "[15] So Romulus threw a huge festival for Neptune and invited the neighbors (the Sabines, from the largest nearby town). At the height of the festivities, when the Sabine men were distracted, the Roman men kidnapped all of the young women and carried them off.

The women, according to Livy, "in course of time lost their resentment," since their new husbands "spoke honeyed words" (one wonders what a female Roman historian might have made of the event), but the Sabine army marched on Rome in revenge and broke into the citadel, driving out the defenders. The Romans, now forced to attack their own city, advanced on the walls; as the two armies clashed, the Sabine champion, a great warrior named Mettius Curtius, gave out a war cry to his own men. "Show them that catching girls is a different matter from fighting against men!" he bellowed, at which point Romulus made straight for him with a band of the strongest Romans behind him, and Mettius Curtius went galloping off in a panic.

A massacre seemed likely to ensue, but the Sabine women now flooded out into the battlefield and put themselves between the warring tribes, begging the armies to cease, as either their husbands or their fathers would die if the battle continued. "The effect of the appeal was immediate and profound," Livy writes. "Silence fell and not a man moved. A moment later the rival captains stepped forward to conclude a peace. Indeed, they went further: the two states were united under a single government, with Rome as the seat of power." Romulus, descendent of the kings of Alba Longa and Titus Tatius, king of the Sabines, ruled jointly. (Although not for very long; Tatius was murdered in a riot a few years later, and Romulus "is said to have felt less distress at his death than was strictly proper.")[16]

These legends, however Greek-influenced, may well point to a real ancient Rome made up of two hills, one populated by Latins from the Sabine hills and the other by Latins from the Alban hills. More than that, it points to a basic hostility at the very center of Rome's origins. Like the Upper and Lower Egyptians, these people—of the same basic stock, with similar customs and language and gods—were nevertheless enemies at the core. The Greeks were trying to find common ground; the Latins were refusing to recognize others of their own race. In its most ancient incarnation, the city of Rome had two poles, and its people lived with their backs turned to each other.

ROME WAS not the only city growing on the fertile plains of the peninsula. Greek merchants, firmly rooted into their trading colonies, had proved to the folks back at home that the Italian coast was a good place for Greek colonies. And the Greek cities were under pressure from within. The population was growing (perhaps as much as sixfold, between 800 and 700 BC), and these people needed more: more metal, more stone, more grain, and more pastureland.[17]

Especially more land. The Greek cities were bounded by natural barriers: mountain ridges, clefts in the rocky land, or ocean. Like the Mesopotamian plain, the Greek peninsula was "circumscribed agricultural land."* Land was traditionally divided between the sons of a family equally, meaning that any family's land shrank inexorably, and faster if more sons were born. There was simply no more land for all of the sons born to each Greek family.

The Greek poet Hesiod, from the region of Boeotia, was born sometime around the mid-eighth century. In his poem *Works and Days*, he describes his plight: when his father died, the farm should have been divided between himself and his older brother Perses, but apparently Perses thought that this would give him too little land to support himself and his family, and so bribed the judges who were appointed to settle disputes of this kind in order to get the whole thing.

> Our inheritance was divided; but there is so much
> you grabbed and carried away as a fat bribe
> for gift-devouring kings, fools who want to be judges
> in this trial.[18]

This was the secondary, but equally fraught, difficulty faced by the Greek cities; limited resources led to desperate acts, and corruption among the landholders and officials was at plague-level.[19]

Hesiod longs for a day when men will benefit from their own labor rather than seeing it stolen by the more powerful, when they will

> know neither hunger or ruin,
> but amid feasts enjoy the yield of their labors.

* See chapter 18, p. 140.

For them the earth brings forth a rich harvest; and for them
the top of an oak teems with acorns and the middle with bees.
Fleecy sheep are weighed down with wool,
and women bear children who resemble their fathers[20]

which suggests that the rich were appropriating more than just land.

Hesiod spends dozens of lines explaining that hard workers should get what they deserve, that farmers who plan their crops carefully should reap their own grain, that wages should be paid promptly, and that crooked judges should expect a visitation of divine justice. None of this happened. Nor was it likely to, given the inability of the cities to expand.

Colonization, not reform, was the only solution. Around 740 or so, the leaders of Greek cities began to send out all of those younger brothers to farm new land. The earliest colonists came from the same two cities which had built those initial trading posts in Italy; Chalcis and Eretria sent colonists to the Bay of Naples, where they began to build the new Greek city of Cumae. Around 733, the city of Corinth put its aristocrat Archias at the head of an expedition to Sicily, where he founded a colony called Syracuse; not to be outdone, Chalcis and Eretria built no fewer than four colonies (Naxus, Lentini, Catana, and Rhegium) over the next twenty years. By 700 BC, cities on the southern Italian coast were almost as likely to be Greek as native.

TIMELINE 49

GREEK PENINSULA/ASIA MINOR	ITALIAN PENINSULA
Arcadian, Dorian, Ionian cultures (c. 900)	Fossa, Apulian, Middle Adriatic, Golasecca, Este, Villanovan, Latial cultures
Homer (c. 800)	
Greek trading posts established in Italy	
First Olympic games (776)	
	Founding of Rome (753)
	Romulus
	Greek colonies established in Italy

Chapter Fifty

Old Enemies

Between 783 and 727 BC,
the Assyrian empire declines,
until Tiglath-Pileser III restores it

IN 783, SHALMANESER IV came to the throne of Assyria and ruled for nine years. In a very un-Assyrian manner, he made few boasts of glory. The handful of subdued victory inscriptions that remain suggest that he spent most of his time trying to keep invaders out of Assyria. Damascus had grown to be the capital city of an Aramaean kingdom, called "Syria" in most ancient accounts, and the Syrians were strong enough to attack Assyria's border, rather than the other way around.[1] In one of his final battles against the Syrians, Shalmaneser IV was even forced to make an alliance with the king of Israel, Jeroboam II, in order to beat them off.[2]

He also faced a newly troublesome enemy to the north. In the mountains above Assyria, the Hurrians who had once belonged to the old Mitanni empire had built little tribal kingdoms. Since the fall of the Mitanni, Assyrian raiding parties had treated these backwoods Hurrians as a convenient source for metal, wood, and slaves. Shalmaneser I had boasted several centuries earlier of sacking fifty-one of their settlements, stealing their goods, and kidnapping their young men: "Their young men I selected and took for service," he wrote, "heavy tribute for all time I imposed on them."[3]

In the face of this constant invasion from beneath, the mountain peoples were forced to organize themselves into a coalition. They borrowed the Assyrian script for their inscriptions, and the Assyrian royal customs for their kings; the enemy's empire gave them the model for their own.[4] The Assyrians called them the Urartu, a name which is still preserved in the name of the high mountain in its ancient territory: Mount Ararat. Compared with Assyrian troops, the soldiers of Urartu were gnats swarming an elephant. But Assyrian attacks against the massive fortresses that guarded the Urartu mountain passes did not manage to breach their frontier.

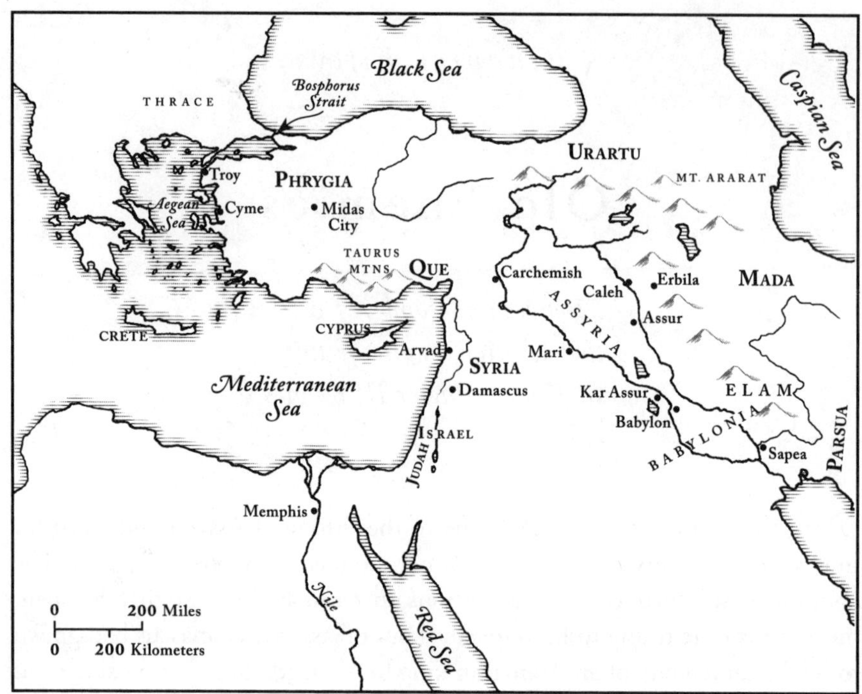

50.1 Assyria and Its Challengers

Stalled on both his western and northern fronts, Shalmaneser IV suffered his terminal embarrassment when he lost hold of Babylon. The city had been increasingly fractious, under its Assyrian governor. A jostling crowd of Chaldean warlords now fought over its throne, and the Assyrian governor seems to have fled.

In other far-flung provinces of the Assyrian empire, the governors had begun to act as petty kings without consulting Caleh; the governor of Mari, in his own annals, even dates the events of his tenure by the years of his own rule, with no mention of the king at all.[5] Under the reign of Shalmaneser IV's son, more than one governor made an armed attempt at freedom, forcing Assyrian troops to march on their cities. And by the time of his grandson, the king of Urartu was boasting in inscriptions that he had "conquered the land . . . of Assyria."[6]

Urartu had in fact managed to extend its rule not only south, into land once held by Assyria, but far to the west. In these new lands, they had built fortresses on the highest peaks they could find; they were mountain people, not happy unless they could stand on high ground and see around them. The

Urartu borders now encompassed much of the ancient Hittite territory,* and Sarduri I of Urartu sent east to make an alliance with the Mada and Parsua tribes against Assyria.

With these forces arrayed against him, it was all that Shalmaneser IV's grandson, Ashur-nirari V, could do to keep the heartland secure. Even in this he failed. The inner walls of Assur, the city's last line against invasion, had begun to disintegrate and collapse from neglect. No official or governor, nor the king, sent any order for their rebuilding; the people of Assur were gathering the fallen stones and building their own houses from them.[7]

Things must have been little better in Caleh, where the empire's headquarters were located. Seven years into his reign, the governor of Caleh, a man named Pul, led an insurrection against the king.

Pul was probably a royal cousin of some kind, given that he had been awarded the responsibility of governing the royal city itself, but if Ashur-nirari V had hoped for blood loyalty, he had miscalculated. Pul took advantage of his relative's weakness to round up his own supporters and murder not only Ashur-nirari V but also his family. He claimed the throne himself early in the month of May, 746. On his accession, he took a new name, one that recalled past Assyrian glories: Tiglath-Pileser, the third of that name.†

Almost simultaneously, a new and strong king had also taken the throne of Babylon.

Nabonassar was a Chaldean. However he managed to get control of Babylon, he then quelled the revolts and soothed the discontented. A historical tradition preserved by the Greeks insists that the strength of Babylon during his reign allowed the science of astronomy to flourish. (The Greeks, in fact, were so convinced of the Chaldean foundations of their own astronomical knowledge that they tended to use the words "Chaldean" and "astronomer" interchangeably, a usage which spread throughout the ancient world; it is for this reason that the book of Daniel explains that Nebuchadnezzar II, the king of Babylon two hundred years later, summoned his "Chaldeans" along with the other wise men of his kingdom when he needed advice.) During his years on the throne, Babylonian scribes first began to keep tables that correlate astronomical observations to daily records of the weather, the levels of the Tigris and Euphrates, and the price of grain and other important supplies: the sign

* See chapter 41, pp. 285–286.

† Tiglath-Pileser I reigned c. 1115–1077. Tiglath-Pileser II probably reigned 966–935, during a time of chaos in Assyria's records and just before Ashur-dan II began to push the Aramaeans back out of the country. See chapter 47, p. 335.

not only of a city at peace, but a city with leisure to search for ways to make itself more prosperous.[8]

As soon as he had control of Assyria, Tiglath-Pileser III headed south towards Babylon and offered himself as Nabonassar's ally. He had troubles on the north, east, and west; he didn't need an enemy to the south as well. Nabonassar accepted the alliance, and Tiglath-Pileser III sent Assyrian soldiers to help the new king of Babylon wipe out Chaldean and Aramaean resistance to his reign.

But the Chaldean and Aramaean chiefs ended up paying tribute to Tiglath-Pileser, not to Nabonassar. "The cities of Babylonia by the shore of the Lower Sea, I annexed," Tiglath-Pileser boasted in his own annals, "I annexed them to Assyria, I placed my eunuch over them as governor."[9] To the north of Babylon, where Aramaeans had been squelched, Tiglath-Pileser built a new city called Kar Assur, or "Wall of Assur." Ostensibly this city was to help protect Babylon against nomads trying to infiltrate Nabonassar's land. In reality, it became an Assyrian outpost in Babylonia, staffed with Assyrian officials, guarded by Assyrian soldiers, and populated by Assyrian conquests: "I named it Kar Assur," Tiglath-Pileser's annals explain. "I settled therein people of foreign lands, conquered by me, I imposed upon them tribute, and I considered them as inhabitants of Assyria."[10] When Tiglath-Pileser went home he announced himself (as Shamshi-Adad V had done before him) to be "King of Sumer and Akkad."

Nabonassar, down to the south, held his tongue. As long as the Assyrian king left him alone to rule his own country, he doesn't seem to have worried overmuch about what titles the other man boasted.[11] Tiglath-Pileser, in his turn, was content to leave the day-to-day running of Babylon to Nabonassar. He had business elsewhere.* He intended to replace the rebellious governors of the distant provinces with newly appointed officials, who were required to send him regular reports; he set up for this purpose an ancient sort of Pony Express so that relay riders could get reports to the palace in decent time.

Then, with his own house in order, he turned his attention to the north, where the Urartu were strutting across the provinces which had once belonged to Assyria. They had conquered their way as far down to the southwest as Carchemish. Even the city of Arvad farther south, technically bound to Assyria by treaty, had now joined the Urartu as an ally.[12]

* The exact retelling of Tiglath-Pileser III's conquests is complicated by the very poor state of his records, many of which were in the form of reliefs destroyed by later kings who used the stone slabs as building materials. "Extant records," to quote H. W. F. Saggs, "are so fragmentary that different reconstructions are possible, and academic throat-cutting still continues . . ." (*The Might That Was Assyria*, p. 88). This is one possible reconstruction.

Tiglath-Pileser besieged the city. It was a drawn-out attack, bloody on both sides. Two years later, Arvad finally fell.

Tiglath-Pileser's records say that he spent the year 740 "in Arvad"; the king had taken up residence temporarily in the conquered city, using it as a military headquarters to continue his battles into Urartu. He took both Que and Carchemish away from Urartian control. By 735, the Assyrians had marched into the center of Urartu, and the Urartian king Sarduri I and his soldiers had been forced northwards towards their own capital city. "The gorges and precipices of the mountains I filled with [their bodies]," Tiglath-Pileser III boasted, in the language which had now become as familiar as any governmental jargon. He adds, though, a distinct note: Sarduri "to save his life, escaped at night and was seen no more . . . up to the bridge across the Euphrates, the boundary of his land, I pursued him."[13]

There he stopped. Sarduri regathered and ruled over a smaller, although independent Urartu, in the area which had once been the northern part of his kingdom. The south remained in Assyrian hands.

Tiglath-Pileser III's redrawing of the map had the effect of creating a new country. His new province had swallowed the eastern tribes of the Phrygians, in central Asia Minor. Now the western tribes regathered themselves into a coalition, drawing together, in the face of the eastern enemy, into a Phrygian kingdom. Tiglath-Pileser III had accidentally created a new nation whose first real king exists in legend: King Midas.

Whoever Midas was, the story of his accession had entered into myth by the time of Alexander the Great, four hundred years later. Arriving in Phrygia, Alexander found himself faced with an ancient wagon, with the yoke attached to the wagon's pole by a huge knot. This, he was told, was the wagon of the first king of Phrygia. The Phrygian people, leaderless, had asked an oracle who should become their king; the oracle had answered that the first man who drove up in a wagon was the divine choice, whereupon a farmer named Midas came into sight, riding this very wagon.* He was at once crowned king, and in gratitude dedicated the wagon to Zeus.[14]

Midas, according to Herodotus, sent an offering to the oracle of Delphi, of his own throne, one of the few non-Greeks to do so.[15] According to other leg-

* The knot, as many readers will already know, was called the Gordian Knot; it seems to have received this name thanks to another tradition which held that Midas's father Gordius, not Midas himself, was the wagon-rider. However, as Ernest Fredericksmeyer points out, the historian Arrian puts Midas in the wagon; in this he was followed by Plutarch and others, and Alexander himself believed this version of events ("Alexander, Midas, and the Oracle at Gordium," *Classical Philology* 56:3 [1961], 160–168).

ends, Midas also married a Greek woman from Cyme. Both of these stories reveal that the Phrygians, now organized under a king and with a capital city named after him (Midas City; "Midas" became a traditional royal name), did a great deal of trade with the Ionian cities on the Asia Minor coast.

This trade made Phrygia immensely rich. The old Greek tale of Midas, in which he is given the magical ability to turn whatever he touches to gold, preserves the awe of Ionian merchants over the wealth of Phrygia's kings; the dreadful outcome, in which Midas's golden touch turns out to be curse as much as blessing, reflects their jealousy over all this prosperity.

WHILE PHRYGIA GREW, Tiglath-Pileser campaigned against all the usual enemies. He marched east and reconquered the rebellious Parsua and Mada. Once victorious he took up the cause against the troublesome west. When the king of Israel, a nobody named Menahem, saw the Assyrian forces on the horizon, he sent forty tons of silver to buy the enemy off.[16] Judah was even more cooperative; the current Davidic king, Ahaz, first raided Solomon's temple and sent all the sacred items to Tiglath-Pileser as a gesture of submission, and then offered to become Assyria's ally against Israel.

In the battle that followed, Israel lost most of its northern parts to Assyria. Now Tiglath-Pileser ruled Syria and controlled both Israel and Judah; the west was troublesome no more.

So far, Tiglath-Pileser had paid little attention to Babylon, but now Nabonassar died and the city fell into a frenzy of civil war. Tiglath-Pileser, who had just finished the conquest of Damascus, took notice of the mess and decided that it was now time to make Babylon part of his kingdom in fact as well as in name.

As Tiglath-Pileser crossed Babylon's northern border and marched towards the capital along the Tigris river, the country divided into two. Babylonian cities argued among themselves, as he approached, as to whether they should throw their lot in with the Assyrian monarch, or mount a (probably pointless) fight for independence. The Babylonian cities in the north tended to be pro-Assyrian; it was prudent to be pro-Assyrian if you lived just south of the Assyrian border, but their willingness to throw their lot in with Tiglath-Pileser suggests that they had more sympathy with Assyrian customs and gods than with the ways of the Semitic Chaldeans who were fighting over the throne.

Knowing this, Tiglath-Pileser sent officials down to Babylon ahead of him, with instructions to ask the citizens of Babylon for loyalty. They sent their report back to Tiglath-Pileser, behind them on the campaign trail, in a letter discovered at Caleh in 1952:

> To the king my lord, from his servants Samas-bunaia and Nabuieter. We came to Babylon on the twenty-eighth and took our stand before the Marduk Gate. We spoke to the Babylonians and said, "Why are you acting against us, for the sake of Chaldeans? Their place is down with their own Chaldean tribesmen. Babylon, showing favor to Chaldeans! Our king recognizes your rights as citizens of Babylon." To us, the citizens said, "We do not believe the king will come," but that they would submit, should the king arrive.[17]

Samas-bunaia and Nabuieter had played the race card, and Babylon preferred Assyria to the Chaldeans.

The Chaldean chief who currently occupied Babylon's throne fled, and Tiglath-Pileser swept past the city and down to the south, to the city where he had holed up: Sapea, a city with three walls, the shortest a good fifteen feet high and the other two ascending progressively higher. An Assyrian relief records the siege and the spoil of the city. Archers, shooting down from the walls, fall before the Assyrian assault and their bodies are piled in the stream that circles the city. Weeping women and children are carried off into exile.[18]

Tiglath-Pileser then marched to Babylon and entered the city in triumph. He declared himself king and swore allegiance to the great Babylonian god Marduk during the New Year's festival of 728. The Chaldeans, having been thoroughly terrified by the fall of Sapea, hurried to Babylon to honor their new king.

Among them was a local warlord named Merodach-baladan. He was, Tiglath-Pileser makes special note, a "king of the sealand who had not submitted to any of the kings, my fathers, and had not kissed their feet." But now he swore allegiance, and brought lovely presents as tribute: gold necklaces, precious stones, logs of valuable wood, dyed garments, and livestock.[19]

Merodach-baladan swore loyalty to Assyria with his fingers crossed behind his back, but Tiglath-Pileser III did not yet know this.[20] He was filled with exaltation, king of Babylon and Assyria together, and to demonstrate his power he sacrificed to the gods of Babylon in every major city: "In Sippar, Nippur, Babylon, Borsippa, Kutha, Kish, Dilbat, and Erech," he writes, "I offered pure sacrifices to . . . the great gods . . . and they accepted my priesthood. The wide land of [Babylonia] I brought under my sway, and exercised sovereignty over it."[21] He was the first Assyrian monarch to appear in Babylon's own king lists, the first to be recognized by the people of Babylon as their own king. All of the acclaim managed to paper neatly over the fact that he had no right to either throne.

TIMELINE 50

ITALIAN PENINSULA	ASSYRIA AND SURROUNDING LANDS	
Fossa, Apulian, Middle Adriatic, Golasecca, Este, Villanovan, Latial cultures		
	Ashurnasirpal II (911–859)	
Greek trading posts established in Italy		
	Shalmaneser III (858–824)	
	Shamshi-Adad V (823–812)	
	Sammu-amat	
	Adad-nirari III	**Argishti** (Urartu)
	Shalmaneser IV (782–770)	
	Ashur-Dan III (771–754)	
Founding of Rome (753)	**Ashur-nirari V** (753–746)	**Nabonassar** (Babylon)
Romulus		
Greek colonies established in Italy	**Tiglath-Pileser III**	**Sarduri I** (Urartu)
		Midas (Phrygia)

Chapter Fifty-One

Kings of Assyria and Babylon

Between 726 and 705 BC,
Egypt is reunited and Israel scattered,
as Sargon II conquers nearly the whole world

IN 726, TWO YEARS AFTER "taking the hand of Marduk," Tiglath-Pileser III died after almost twenty years on the Assyrian throne.

He left his son, Shalmaneser V, with a well-protected border and the joint rule of Assyria and Babylon. But down at the head of the Gulf, the reluctant Chaldean vassal Merodach-baladan was quietly gathering followers around him.

Shalmaneser V's reign suffers from an almost total lack of inscriptions, but he doesn't seem to have noticed this rising Chaldean threat. He was concentrating on his western front. His campaigns show an obsessive desire to bring it under total control; certainly this would have been one up on his great father, who received tribute from the Phoenicians and Israelites, but treated them as vassal states rather than Assyrian provinces. According to Josephus, Shalmaneser V spent almost five years besieging the Phoenician city of Tyre, which had sent tribute to Tiglath-Pileser.[1] Nor was this his only one-up on his father. Tiglath-Pileser had reduced Israel to a vassal state; Shalmaneser V wiped it out.

For this, he had some excuse. The current king of Israel, an ex-army officer named Hoshea, "no longer paid tribute to the king of Assyria, as he had done year by year."[2] Shalmaneser V's spies also reported to him that Hoshea had sent envoys down "to So, king of Egypt." Israel was planning a war against Assyria, and was searching for allies.

THE REENTRY OF EGYPT into the Western Semitic fray was only possible because the country had been temporarily reunified. In the century since the battle of Qarqar, Egypt had split again not only into north and south, but

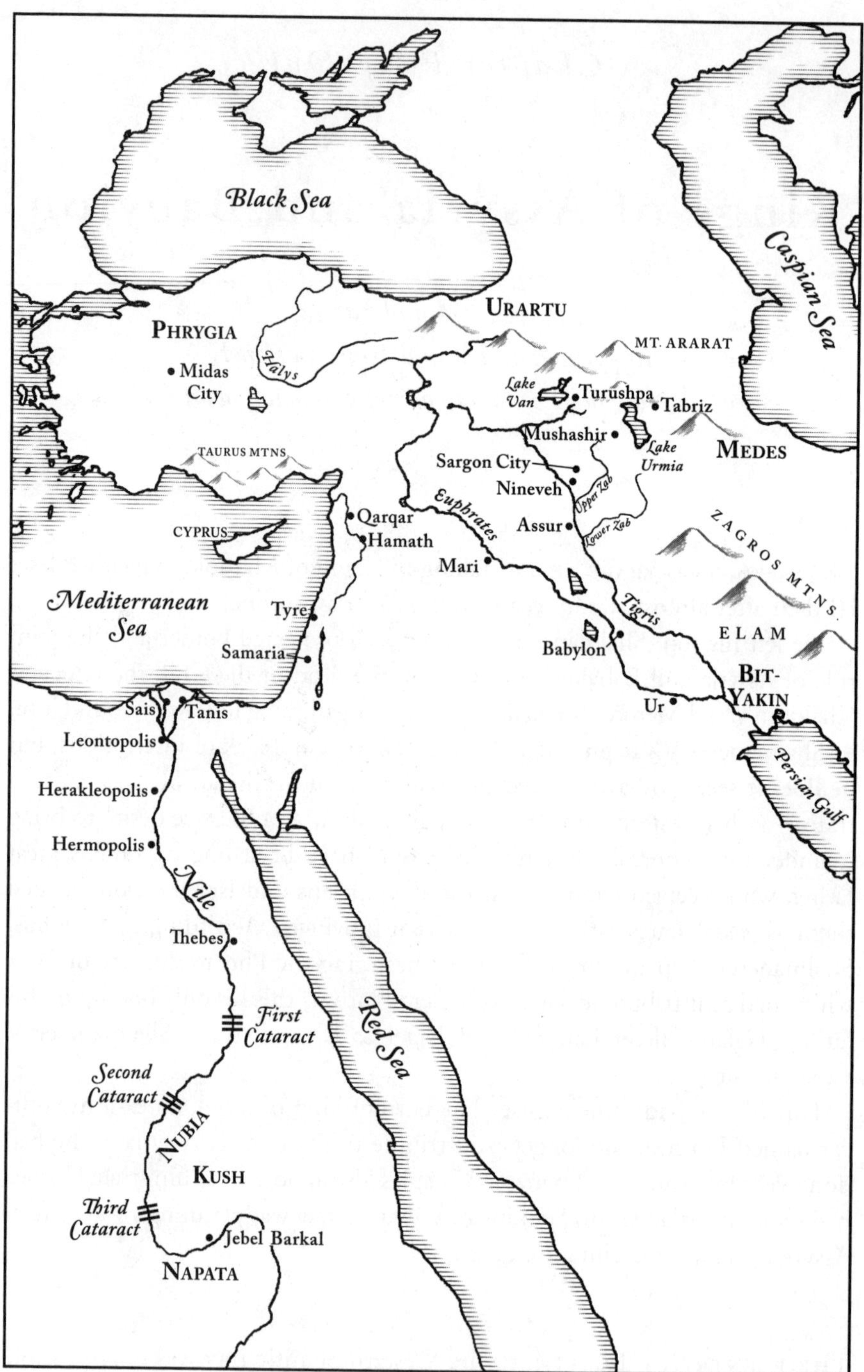

51.1 Egypt and Assyria

also into east and west kingdoms, yielding a dizzying array of pharaohs and three separate capitals: Thebes, Tanis, and the central Delta city of Leontopolis. For a brief time, there were also kings at Herakleopolis and Hermopolis, and at least fifteen other families claiming some sort of ruling title, from "king" and "lord" right down to the clan title of "chief."[3] Manetho attempts to reduce this mess into some sort of order by organizing the kings into the Twenty-Second, Twenty-Third, and Twenty-Fourth Dynasties, but all three "dynasties" were actually ruling simultaneously from different cities, and the local power of the Twenty-Second Dynasty lingered on into the dominance of the Twenty-Fifth.

During all of this messiness at the top, the southern lands on either side of the Nile—the African country of Nubia, its Egypt-governed section generally called "Kush" by the Egyptian overlords—had benefited from Egypt's preoccupation with its own troubles. Technically, various Egyptian viceroys were supposed to be governing the area, but in fact no one was really paying attention. By the time of Egypt's multiple dynasties, the Nubians, who were now a mixture of native African tribes and the Egyptians who had settled among them, were not actually governed by a viceroy, but rather by their own king. This kingdom, which its own people called Napata, was ruled from a Nubian palace at Jebel Barkal. It bore unmistakable traces of Egyptian occupation: its people worshipped the god Amun, and its Nubian rulers followed the ancient tradition of brother-sister marriages.[4]

In 727, the year just before Shalmaneser V inherited his father's throne, the king of Napata was a Nubian native named Piankhe. He had already been on the throne twenty years when he learned that the kings of Sais, Tanis, Herakleopolis, Hermopolis, and Leontopolis, nervous about the growing size of Napata, had formed an alliance to push Egypt's border back down into Nubian territory.

He fought back against the coalition, triumphed, and carved the details of his campaign into an elaborate relief: the god Amun bestows his blessing on Piankhe, true king of Egypt, while the warleader/kings approach him in humility.

Piankhe did not try to wipe out his enemies. Instead, he chose to see Egypt as a set of kingdoms, with himself as High King over them:

> Amun of Napata has appointed me governor of this land

he wrote in another inscription,

> as I might say to someone: "Be king," and he is it,
> or: "You will not be king," and he is not.

Amun of Thebes has appointed me governor of Egypt. . . .
Whoever is protected by me runs no risk of seeing his town conquered,
at least not if I can help it.[5]

This was the Egypt that Israel asked for alliance against the vast Assyrian threat.

The "So of Egypt" to whom the Israelite envoys appealed may not have been Piankhe himself; Egypt was now peppered with local "kings" serving as Piankhe's viceroys. In all likelihood, the Israelites ended up in the court of a Delta king named Osorkon IV. Hoshea may not have known exactly who was in charge down in Egypt, which had a political scene so complicated that even the Egyptians were confused. And possibly Piankhe did not even know that Israelite ambassadors had arrived in his country.

Whoever heard the appeal didn't respond, though; Hoshea was turned down. The trip down to Egypt turned out to be a major blunder. Shalmaneser V, already annoyed by the long siege of recalcitrant Tyre, was in no mood to put up with any resistance from the cities his father had reduced to obedience. "The king of Assyria invaded the entire land," reads II Kings 17:5, "marched against [Israel's capital] Samaria and laid siege to it for three years."

At this point the Assyrian accounts blink. When they reopen, Shalmaneser V—only five years on the throne and carrying on two sieges simultaneously—is dead. A new king has taken the throne under the royal name Sargon II.

If Shalmaneser V had died in battle, the writer of Kings would likely have said so. Most likely his successor Sargon II was a younger son of Tiglath-Pileser, taking advantage of his brother's weakness to seize power; those long and apparently fruitless sieges cannot have been popular with the army, and Shalmaneser V had also made himself unpopular back home by trying to introduce an obligation of forced labor to the people of Assur. This had not gone over well.[6]

Sargon II promised the citizens of Assur tax exemptions, by way of convincing them to forget about his brother's sudden death: "Shalmaneser did not fear the king of the universe," he told them, in his official annals. "He raised his hand to do evil against that city; he imposed on its people feudal dues and services, harshly, and counted them as his camp followers, whereupon the lord of the gods, in the anger of his heart, overthrew his rule. Me, Sargon, my head he raised on high. . . . Assur's freedom from dues I restored. . . . from the 'call to arms' of the land, the summons of the taskmaster, from tax, toll, and dues to all the temples of Assyria, I freed them."[7]

He also broke the stalemated sieges. In the first year of his annals, 721, he conquered Samaria, bringing to an end in short order an assault which had dragged on far too long. And then, with a ruthlessness that none of his predecessors had shown, Sargon II wiped the political state of Israel from the map. He took Hoshea captive, put him in jail, and then set to work deporting the Israelites, which was the typical Assyrian response to a vassal state that clung stubbornly to independence. Deportation was a kind of genocide, murder not of persons, but of a nation's sense of itself. Sargon's own inscriptions note that he removed 27,290 Israelites from their homeland, and settled them from Asia Minor all the way over to the territory of the Medes.[8] These Israelites became known as the "lost ten tribes," not because the people themselves were lost, but because their identity as descendants of Abraham and worshippers of Yahweh was dissipated into the new wild areas where they were now forced to make their homes.*

The scattered Israelites who still lived in the northern kingdom now found themselves invaded by exiles from elsewhere. "People of the lands my hand had conquered, I settled within," Sargon II notes.[9] This mishmash of Israelites and others eventually developed their own culture; it was a mix of different religions and bloodlines that the Jews of the first century BC called "Samaritans," and despised as half-breeds.

THIS WAS NOT the end of it. When the Aramaeans of Syria and Hamath joined to defy the Assyrian king, Sargon II met them at the city of Qarqar. This time, a hundred years after the first great clash of powers at Qarqar, there

* Students of modern history will recollect that a not-so-charming and peculiarly British movement whose adherents called themselves "British Israelites" grew up during the nineteenth-century renewal of interest in national identity. With practically no historical or geographical support, British Israelites proposed that the ten tribes had travelled across the Caucasus Mountains and ended up in Britain, which made white Western Christians of British descent the "true Israel." This served to act as a justification for anti-Semitism, weirdly enough, since the Jews of the present-day were labelled as pretenders. This is completely ridiculous simply from a political standpoint, given that Sargon II would never have allowed any sort of mass exodus of the Israelites; his whole goal was to destroy their identity as a nation. The ten tribes of Israel were not "lost," as though they had been misplaced in toto and could be rediscovered. They were very efficiently destroyed.

British Israelitism faded in the twentieth century, but has made a very ugly comeback in the so-called Christian Identity movement of the United States. I was startled to receive, only a few years ago, from a then-neighbor out in rural Virginia, a set of "teaching videos" from a Christian Identity "church" in the Midwest laying out, in great detail, how the Jews are actually "Edomites" cursed by God, and Caucasians are the true Jews, the chosen people of God. My attempt to explain that the supposed difference between cursed and non-cursed humans rested on a mistranslation of the Hebrew words for "man" was totally fruitless; it must have sounded like sophistry. This idiotic theology is alive and well.

was no ambiguity over the outcome. The king of Hamath was dragged off in chains to Assur, the Syrian leader "ran off alone like a shepherd whose sheep have been carried off," and Sargon sacked and burned Qarqar.[10]

Fully in control of the west, he crossed the Mediterranean as far as the island of Cyprus—occupied by a mix of Ionian Greeks and Phoenician settlers from the coast—and forced it to pay tribute to him. He also built himself a new capital, Dur-Sharrukin ("Sargon City"), northeast of Nineveh, just beyond the foothills of the Taurus Mountains where the Urartu still hovered as a threat.

Urartian soldiers could easily come down from their high places, attack, and then retreat back into the passes over which their fortresses loomed; marching into the mountains after them was a much more difficult proposition. And the Urartu had developed into a sophisticated and well-guarded kingdom. Sargon's own accounts speak, admiringly, of the Urartian king Rusas and the network of canals and wells which he built; of the herds of well-bred and guarded horses, raised in protected valleys until they were needed for war; of the splendid efficiency of Urartian communication, with watchtowers built high on mountain peaks, guarding heaps of fuel that could be lit at a moment's notice. One beacon, lit, flared up on its mountaintop into an enormous bonfire that appeared as a spark to the next distant post, where the next bonfire could then be lit. They shone like "stars on mountaintops," in Sargon's own words, and spread news of invasion faster than a messenger could ride.[11]

By 714, Sargon was ready to invade the mountains, in a dangerous and risky campaign which he chose to lead himself. Rather than marching straight north up into Urartian territory, which would have brought his army against the strongest of the Urartian fortresses, he led the army east towards the Zagros, intending to reach the relatively flat land on the other side and march up towards the weaker eastern border of the Urartu.

Sargon himself wrote an account of this campaign, in the form of an official royal letter to the god Assur and his divine companions, informing them all of the battles fought on their behalf (undoubtedly a letter to be read out loud to the gods in hearing of most of Assur's citizens). The army set off in early summer, forded the Upper and Lower Zab, and came soon to the Zagros Mountains.[12] Here the lowlanders came to looming and unfamiliar slopes, covered with thick forests where unknown enemies waited:

> [We came then to] high mountains, where trees of all kinds grew entwined; the midst of the mountains chaos, their passes stirring fear; over all stretched shade, like a forest of cedars; where he who treads their paths sees no rays of the sun.[13]

The cedar forests on the mountain slopes, like those into which Gilgamesh had ventured so many years ago, sheltered an enemy which was more terrifying because it was unseen.

Sargon set his men to chopping their way through the forest with copper tools, until the army had reached the flatlands on the east. Here the Medes, bound by treaty (and fear) to feed the Assyrian horde, offered water and grain.

With the army resupplied, Sargon led them up north to meet the Urartian army on the mountain slopes just south of the modern city of Tabriz.* He had chosen the battlefield well; it was far away from the imposing line of fortresses that guarded the southern frontier. But to reach it, the Assyrian army had marched over three hundred miles, in summer, through stifling woods and steep rock roads, low on water and lower on food. They were exhausted to the point of revolt:

> The harassed troops of Assur, who had come a long way, very weary and slow to respond, who had crossed and re-crossed sheer mountains innumerable, of great trouble for ascent and descent, their morale turned mutinous. I could give no ease to their weariness, no water to quench their thirst.[14]

Sargon was caught: he had reached his objective, and found himself powerless. Meanwhile the Urartian army, under the command of Rusas himself, had assembled to meet him.

His army refusing to follow, he gathered his own personal bodyguard around them and led them in a frantic and suicidal attack on the nearest wing of Rusas's force. The wing gave ground in the face of his desperate savagery; and according to his own account, Sargon's army, seeing him fling himself into the line, took courage and followed him in. The Urartian army wavered, broke, and began to retreat.

The retreat turned into a rout. The Assyrian army chased the disintegrating enemy westwards, past Lake Urmia and into their own territory. Rusas abandoned any attempt to hold his own capital city, Turushpa, and fled into the mountains.

At this point, Sargon's account announces, very abruptly, that the Assyrian army turned for home. He may have suspected that the Assyrian army would

* This is the most likely reconstruction, given Sargon's own accounts and inscriptions, but the exact actions of Assyrian armies at any given time are speculative: "The diversity of geographical reconstructions inspired by the account of [this campaign]," writes Assyriologist Paul Zimansky, "is a tribute to Assyriological ingenuity and Assyrian obscurity" ("Urartian Geography and Sargon's Eighth Campaign," in *Journal of Near Eastern Studies* 49:1 [1990], p. 1).

mutiny for good if he insisted on chasing the king farther into the unknown, tree-covered depths of the Urartu kingdom.

Instead, the army turned back south and, on its way, plundered and sacked the city of Mushashir, where the main temple of the Urartian chief god stood.[15] When this news reached Rusas in his distant retreat, he despaired. "The splendor of Assur overwhelmed him," Sargon's inscriptions read, "and with his own iron dagger he stabbed himself through the heart, like a pig, and ended his life."[16]

The troublesome kingdom to the north had been brought to heel, and Sargon marched home in victory. It was now November, and he could not have pursued the remnants of the Urartian forces any farther into the mountains without risking being trapped by winter weather, which might choke the mountain passes with ice and snow. The conquest of Urartu had taken place in less than six months.[17]

Now he was almost at the top of his world. He received ambassadors from Egypt and Ethiopia; gifts and envoys came even from the "king of Dilmun," who, according to Sargon's own inscriptions, "lives like a fish."[18] By this he probably meant the Sabean tribes of Arabia, whose queen had visited Solomon two centuries before. He was the admitted overlord of almost the entire world, except for the land directly to the south.

Down in Babylon, a drama had in the meantime been playing itself out. Merodach-baladan, the Chaldean chief of Bit-Yakin, had been collecting his own loyal following in the city of Ur. Almost directly after Shalmaneser V's death, Merodach-baladan uncrossed his fingers, marched on Babylon, drove off his rivals, and became king.* He had seen three changes in Assyrian kingship in less than a decade, and was sure that he could outlast Sargon II as well. To make this more likely, he sent envoys to the east, with a good chunk of his not inconsiderable personal wealth to buy Elamite support against Assyria.[19]

He needed an outside ally; Merodach-baladan's new country was not entirely behind him. Especially in the north, Babylonians tended towards pro-Assyrian feeling and disliked Chaldeans. Merodach-baladan attempted to get around this with a strategy that Napoleon would adopt a couple of millennia later; he announced that he was the country's liberator, the restorer of an ancient Babylonian tradition long trampled under the foot of northern invaders. If Assyrians had immediately arrived outside the city walls, this might not have worked. But Sargon was busy with the west, the Mediter-

* The Semitic name Merodach-baladan is used in the biblical accounts; as king of Babylon, Merodach-baladan took on the name Marduk-apla-iddina II. He sometimes appears in histories of Babylonia as Merodach-baladan II, a composite name.

ranean, his Egyptian and Arabian tributaries, and his Urartian enemies. He did not have much time for Merodach-baladan at first, and for almost a decade, the Chaldean king was able to work (and threaten) his way into total control of Babylon and much of the remaining land.

But by 710, Sargon found himself at leisure to turn south. And over in Elam, the experienced king-general who had agreed to be Merodach-baladan's ally had just died; his young and unseasoned nephew Shutruk-Nahhunte was now on the throne. So Sargon II attacked Babylon by first marching east into Elam.

Shutruk-Nahhunte fled almost at once into the sheltering mountains; Sargon, having cut off any possibility of Elamite aid coming to Merodach-baladan's rescue, then marched south and approached Babylon from the southeast. This canny strategy had the double effect of cutting Merodach-baladan off from his Elamite allies and also making it very dangerous for him to retreat to his homeland at the head of the Gulf, since Sargon's soldiers were actually nearer to the homeland of Bit-Yakin than they were to Babylon. Nor could he go north; the northern cities of Babylon welcomed Sargon with relief, opening their gates to him "with great rejoicing."[20]

Sargon's annals record that Merodach-baladan, clearly seeing that the battle was lost before it even began, considered fleeing into Elam with a small party, trusting to speed and the cover of darkness in order to get past the Assyrian camp:

> When Merodach-baladan . . . heard in Babylon of the victories of Assur . . . fear for his own safety befell him in the midst of his palace. He, with the warriors who supported him, left by night and headed for . . . Elam. To ask a favor from Shutruk-Nahhunte, the Elamite, he sent as presents his own royal furniture: a silver bed, throne, table, the royal ablution-pitcher, his own necklace. The Elamite scoundrel accepted his bribe but feared my military power; so he blocked Merodach-baladan's way and forbade him to go into Elam.[21]

Shutruk-Nahhunte may have been a scoundrel, but he made out well in this encounter, ending up with most of Merodach-baladan's treasure while still avoiding chastisement by the Assyrian king.

Deprived of refuge, Merodach-baladan had to turn around and make his dangerous way back down to Bit-Yakin. Here he suffered exactly the fate he had feared: he was besieged in his own native city. He did his best to resist; Sargon's account says that he "raised higher" the walls, fortifying them, and "cut a ditch . . . and flooded the city around with the mighty waves of the sea."[22]

But the jury-rigged moat did not protect the city for long. The Assyrian army splashed through it and broke through the defenses. "I burned it with fire," Sargon II boasts, "and even its foundations were torn up."[23]

Sargon II then played the Napoleon card himself, going through the festival in honor of Marduk and "taking the hand" of the god as true king of Babylon. He was restoring the city to its roots, so he claimed; he was their liberator, conqueror of the Chaldean invader who knew nothing of the shared heritage of the two cities. The Babylonians, who had probably lost sight of exactly who was actually restoring their heritage at this point, submitted.

At this point, Sargon's behavior towards the Chaldean warrior-chief stands in remarkable contrast to his attitude towards Israel. Rather than executing

TIMELINE 51

ASSYRIA AND SURROUNDING LANDS		EGYPT, ISRAEL, AND JUDAH	
	Ashurnasirpal II (911–859)		
		Osorkon II (870–850)	
	Shalmaneser III (858–824)		
	Shamshi-Adad V (823–812)		
	Sammu-amat		
	Adad-nirari III	*Dynasties 23 and 24*	
Argishti (Urartu)			
	Shalmaneser IV (782–770)		
	Ashur-Dan III (771–754)		
Nabonassar (Babylon)	**Ashur-nirari V** (753–746)	*Dynasty 25 (Nubian)*	
		Piankhi (747–716)	
Sarduri I (Urartu)	**Tiglath-Pileser III**		
Midas (Phrygia)			
		(Judah)	(Israel)
Merodach-baladan (Babylon)	**Shalmaneser V**	**Ahaz**	
	Sargon II (721–704)		**Hoshea**
		Hezekiah	
			Fall of Israel

Merodach-baladan, Sargon II accepted his surrender and (unwisely) allowed him to remain as vassal chief of Bit-Yakin. Apparently Sargon II was not entirely sure that the Chaldeans would be as easy to defeat as the Israelites had been, and preferred to leave his complete control of the far south untested.

Despite this hovering presence in the south, Sargon now celebrated complete victory over his enemies. The reliefs in his new palace at Sargon City show his greatness; his huge figure pushes even the forms of the gods into the background. He was the second Sargon, the second founder of the empire, the king of a second Assyria with new borders, a new capital city, and a newly fearsome power.

Chapter Fifty-Two

Spectacular Defeat

From 704 to 681 BC,
Sennacherib of Assyria defeats almost every enemy
but is remembered for one unsuccessful siege

FIVE YEARS AFTER HIS DEFEAT of Babylon, Sargon II died and left his throne to a son who hated him. In none of his inscriptions or annals does Sennacherib even acknowledge the existence of his father.

Sargon had, apparently, not been reticent in spreading his opinion of his son abroad. When Sennacherib came to the throne, the provinces—convinced that the crown prince was boneless and inadequate—celebrated their coming freedom from Assyrian rule. The old Philistine cities in the west began to plan revolt; and down at the head of the Gulf, Merodach-baladan started to make preparations for independence.

Not everyone agreed that Sennacherib was a weakling. A wise man in Jerusalem advised his king against joining the mutiny that was fomenting a little farther south. "The rod that struck them may be broken," the Hebrew prophet Isaiah warned, "but the Philistines should not rejoice; the snake has given birth to a dragon."[1]

The Babylonians were less circumspect. Sennacherib had not bothered to go through the ritual of "taking the hand of Marduk" in formal submission to the god; he had simply announced himself to be king of Babylon without ceremony, an insult to both Babylon and its chief deity.[2] Almost as soon as Sennacherib's coronation ceremonies had ended, the son of a Babylonian official declared himself king of Babylon.

He remained on the throne for one whole month. Old Merodach-baladan came hobbling up from his southern swamp, his kinsmen behind him, and removed the new king (with the help of eighty thousand archers and mounted soldiers, helpfully sent by the king of Elam, who was always ready to do Assyria a bad turn).[3]

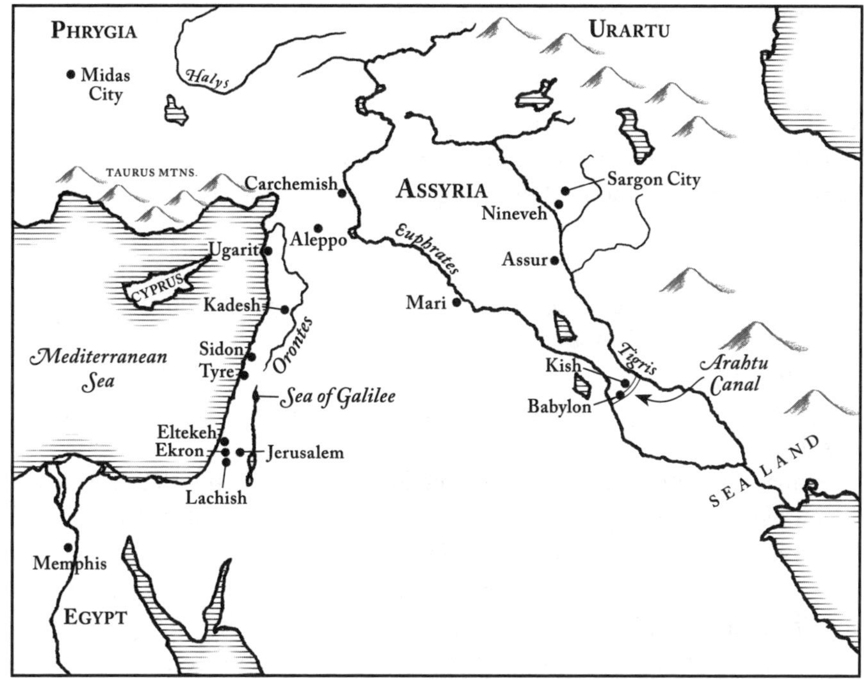

52.1 Sennacherib's Campaigns

Once again, Merodach-baladan announced that he was the true restorer of the ancient Babylonian traditions: "The great lord, the god Marduk," one of his inscriptions reads, ". . . looked with favour upon Marduk-apla-iddina II,* king of Babylon, prince who reveres him. . . . The king of the gods said, 'This is indeed the shepherd who will gather the scattered people.' "[4]

Sennacherib, irate, sent his chief general and a detachment of soldiers down to restore order in Babylon. Merodach-baladan made hasty arrangements with the other Chaldean tribes, the Aramaeans to his west, and the Elamites on the east. He marched out at the head of this combined force to meet the Assyrians at Kish, and drove them back.

That was the last straw. Sennacherib himself came sweeping down like the wrath of Assur and broke through the allied front line, barely pausing. Merodach-baladan ran from the battlefield and crept into the marshes of the Sealand, which he knew well, to hide himself; Sennacherib marched the rest of the way to Babylon, which prudently opened its gates as soon as it saw the

* This is Merodach-baladan's royal Babylonian name.

Assyrian king on the horizon. Sennacherib came through the open gate, but chose to send Babylon a message: he ransacked the city, took almost a quarter of a million captives, and destroyed the fields and groves of anyone who had joined the alliance against him.

He also spent almost a week hunting through the marshes for Merodach-baladan himself, but the aged fox had gone to ground and could not be found.

THE OLD PHILISTINE CITY of Ekron, taking no warning from Babylon's fate, now decided to mount a full rebellion, and put their Assyrian-loyal king in chains. The Phoenician cities of Tyre and Sidon had also revolted; King Hezekiah of Judah still sat undecided in the middle, considering Isaiah's warning.

Sennacherib prepared to leave Babylon and march on the rebels. He appointed a puppet-king to rule Babylon for him; this new ruler, Bel-ibni, had been raised in the Assyrian court. "He grew up like a puppy in my own house," Sennacherib observes in one of his letters, a simile which implies loyalty, if not fierce and competent government.[5]

The Assyrian army then moved towards the troublesome west. Sennacherib's annals report that he conquered and sacked his way through the Western Semitic lands until cities were rushing to submit to him. However, the time that it took him to work his way through the rebel lands suggests that he found the western frontier a more difficult challenge than expected.*

And then, suddenly, an unexpected threat appeared on the horizon. "Sennacherib received word," 2 Kings 19:9 reports, "that Tirhakah, the Kushite king of Egypt, was marching out to fight against him."

In fact, Tirhakah was not exactly the pharaoh yet. He was the younger son of the pharaoh Piankhe, who had died about fifteen years before. Piankhe's brother, Shabaka, had then succeeded to the throne, despite the fact that Piankhe had two living sons; it was a Nubian custom for brothers to trump sons in royal successions.[6] After Shabaka's death, Tirhakah's older brother inherited; Tirhakah served him as his general, and was also his appointed heir.

When Tirhakah and the Egyptian army appeared on the horizon, Hezekiah seems to have decided to throw in his lot with the anti-Assyrian forces.

* The campaign of 701 is recorded in Sennacherib's own annals, in 2 Kings, and in Isa. 36–37; it is also reported by Herodotus and Josephus. Some non-Assyrian chronicles also mention a second campaign against Jerusalem at the end of Sennacherib's reign (a campaign not recorded elsewhere). None of these sources gives a perfectly clear view of the order of events. What follows is a probable reconstruction of the sequence.

Merodach-baladan had been courting him with messages from hiding for some time. When Hezekiah fell sick with boils, Merodach-baladan even "sent Hezekiah letters and a gift, because he had heard of Hezekiah's illness."[7]

Hezekiah, who knew perfectly well what had really motivated this get-well gesture, accepted the presents and offered to show the Chaldean ambassadors around: "There was nothing in his palace," 2 Kings says, "that Hezekiah did not show them." This included the armory; Hezekiah was telling them just how much of a fight he could put up.

The court prophet Isaiah was horrified. "What did you show them?" he asked the king. When Hezekiah answered, "I showed them everything," Isaiah predicted doom: "Everything in your palace," he said, "and all that your fathers have stored up, and your own descendants, will be carried away."

Hezekiah was unworried. "This is good," he told Isaiah, and the writer of Kings adds, "He thought, 'There will at least be peace in my lifetime.' " Bolstered by this shortsighted hope, Hezekiah agreed, as his first anti-Assyrian gesture, to take charge of the imprisoned king of Ekron. The leaders of the Ekron rebellion were afraid that the king's continued presence in the Ekron dungeons might encourage other pro-Assyrian forces in the city to mount a countercoup; Assyria's fearsome reputation meant that there was always a strong countervoice in every plot, suggesting that it would really be better not to bring down destruction on their own heads.

The king of Ekron was escorted to Jerusalem and put under guard. When he heard of this act of defiance, Sennacherib—who was at the city of Lachish, directing a siege—sent messengers to Hezekiah. They were not just any envoys but Sennacherib's own general, chief officer, and field commander; and they arrived at the head of a large army. Three officials from Hezekiah's court came out to meet them.

Apparently Sennacherib had instructed them to try a bit of psychological warfare before launching an attack. The Assyrian officers stood on the grass in front of Jerusalem's walls, which had half the city's population hanging over it to hear what was going on, and announced (loudly, in Hebrew), "Tell Hezekiah that the king of Assyria has a message for him. You have no one to depend on; no strategy, no strength of your own. You may be depending on Egypt for chariots and horsemen, but Egypt is a splintered reed that you would try to use for a staff. It will pierce your hand if you lean on it."[8]

At this, Hezekiah's three representatives begged the commander to speak to them not in Hebrew, but in Aramaic, the language of the Aramaeans, which they understood (as did most Assyrians who had served in the outer parts of the empire). "Don't speak to us in the hearing of the people on the wall," they begged. But the Assyrian commander refused, in blunt and vulgar words:

"The message is for them too. Like you, they will have to eat their own dung and drink their own urine."

The people on the walls, forewarned by the king not to answer back to any threats, kept their silence. But the warnings, broadcast to the entire population of Jerusalem with a bristle of Assyrian spears standing stock still and threatening just beyond, shattered Hezekiah. He "rent his garments" and (less poetically) sent Sennacherib, at Lachish, eleven tons of silver and nearly a ton of gold as a bribe. He also unchained the king of Ekron and let him go; presumably the unfortunate man fled to the Assyrian camp and fielded a few hard questions about just how he had let the noblemen of Ekron overpower him.

For the moment, this lifted the crisis. Sennacherib had not forgiven Hezekiah, but he had to deal with the Egyptians. The two armies met at Eltekeh; details of the battle have not survived, but although the Egyptian army turned back home afterwards, Sennacherib did not follow them, which probably signals a very hard-won victory indeed.

However, now he could pay attention to the rebellious cities of the west without distraction. He besieged Ekron, which fell; and then he turned back to Jerusalem.

What followed was a siege that ended, abruptly, for some unknown reason, without Assyrian victory. Sennacherib does his best to claim triumph, with the sort of corroborative detail that Assyrian kings generally lavished only on less-than-successful campaigns.[9] "As for Hezekiah the Jew," the annals boast, "I levelled the cities around him with battering rams and siege engines, I gave them to the king of Ekron instead; I took off two hundred thousand of his people and animals without number. Himself, like a caged bird I shut up in Jerusalem, his royal city. I threw up earthworks against him and turned him back into his misery. And the terrifying splendor of my majesty overcame him."[10]

Well, not exactly. When Sennacherib marched back home to Assyria, the siege had lifted, Jerusalem's walls were still standing, and the city was still free.

According to 2 Kings, an angel of the Lord struck 185,000 of Sennacherib's men dead in the night: "When the people got up the next morning," the writer tells us, "there were all the dead bodies. So Sennacherib king of Assyria broke camp and withdrew. He returned to Nineveh and stayed there." Herodotus relays a slightly different version of events, which he says he heard from the priests of Egypt: Sennacherib decided to give up and go home because the Assyrian camp was overrun by mice, who "gnawed quivers and bows and the handles of shields."[11]

The host of Sennacherib was suffering from an invasion of rodents, and died in their tents. The combination suggests that the plague had arrived outside Jerusalem's walls, and that the king of Assyria retreated in the face of mounting deaths.

Back home, Sennacherib appointed the city of Nineveh to be his capital—a position which the city held for all the rest of Assyrian history—and built new palaces in it, decorating their walls with tremendous reliefs of battles won and cities besieged. The city of Jerusalem does not appear in the reliefs.

A year later, Babylon was back in his sights. The Chaldeans had soon realized that the puppy-ruler Bel-ibni was no Sennacherib, and were running the south as they pleased. After an Assyrian official or two went to check up on the situation, Sennacherib himself arrived to straighten things out.

He found, much to his frustration, that Merodach-baladan was once again busily attempting to put together an invasion force to take the throne back. At Sennacherib's approach, Merodach-baladan ran to the Sealand. But this time, Assyrian soldiers fanned out through the marsh, searching for the old man. With his hiding places in danger of discovery, Merodach-baladan collected his allies and made for the water, to sail for Elam. This did not give Sennacherib the satisfaction of striking Merodach-baladan's head off, but at least he had driven the man temporarily off the scene: "He fled alone to the Sealand," Sennacherib's account tells us, "with the bones of his fathers who lived before him, which he gathered from their coffins, and his people, he loaded on ships and crossed over to the other side of the Bitter-Sea [Persian Gulf]."[12]

Sennacherib ordered Bel-ibni back to Babylon and appointed his own oldest son Ashur-nadin-shumi, whom he loved, to rule Babylon instead. Then he started to make preparations to go across the water to Elam, after the thorn in his flesh. He hired Phoenician shipbuilders to make him a fleet of ships, and staffed them with mercenary sailors from Tyre and Sidon and from the island of Cyprus. Then he had to sail them down the Tigris river from Assur into the Gulf. But, wary of Elamite forces on the banks of the Tigris, he floated the ships down to the Tigris until they were level with the Arahtu canal, which ran into the Euphrates. He then ordered the ships hauled up onto the land and pulled over rollers to the canal, where they were relaunched and continued down to the head of the Persian Gulf by way of the Euphrates. (Sennacherib himself decided to stay on land the entire time).[13]

The journey across to Elam was successful. So were the campaigns; the Assyrian ships captured every city where they docked. But when Sennacherib arrived at Merodach-baladan's city of refuge, after this titanic expenditure of manpower and money, he learned that Merodach-baladan had died, of old age, just before his arrival.

SENNACHERIB went home to Nineveh in mixed victory and exasperation. But he had laid the foundation for disaster. The Elamites now knew where the Assyrian crown prince was stationed, and they were plotting revenge for the cities Sennacherib had sacked, and the unarmed families he had killed.

The plans took some time to lay; Elamite agents had to be installed in Babylon. But six years later, when Ashur-nadin-shumi was a little north of the city, an Elamite army under the energetic King Kahllushu charged across the border and captured him. They hauled him off to Elam and, before Sennacherib could arrive in fury, stormed into Babylon itself and threw their weight behind a Babylonian claimant to the throne.

It took Sennacherib almost three months to arrive at the scene. When he did, his army defeated the Babylonians outside the city, and took the pretender captive. But inside the city, a Chaldean named Musezib-Marduk seized the throne, stripped the temple of gold, and hired more Elamites.

This produced a full-blown war between Assyria, Babylon, and Elam. Fighting went on for four years. Sennacherib invaded Elam twice; the Elamite king himself came over to lead a retaliatory attack on the banks of the Tigris.

Sennacherib's account of the battle was the single most graphic description of Assyrian warfare ever made:

> With the dust of their feet covering the wide heavens like a mighty storm . . . they drew up in battle array before me . . . on the bank of the Tigris. They blocked my passage and offered battle. . . . I put on my coat of mail. My helmet, emblem of victory, I placed upon my head. My great battle chariot which brings low the foe, I hurriedly mounted in the anger of my heart. The mighty bow which Assur had given me I seized in my hands; the javelin, piercing to the life, I grasped. . . . I stopped their advance, succeeding in surrounding them. I decimated the enemy host with arrow and spear. All of their bodies I bored through. . . . I cut their throats, cut off their precious lives as one cuts a string. Like the many waters of a storm I made the contents of their gullets and entrails run down upon the wide earth. My prancing steeds, harnessed for my riding, plunged into the streams of their blood as into a river. The wheels of my war chariot, which brings low the wicked and the evil, were bespattered with filth and blood. With the bodies of their warriors I filled the plain, like grass. Their testicles I cut off, and tore out their privates like the seeds of cucumbers of June.[14]

The Babylonian Chronicle simple notes, laconically, that Assyria lost.

Sennacherib returned to Nineveh, leaving Babylon in the hands of the Chaldean king and his Elamite allies. Sennacherib's army had fought on every front of his empire, and there was simply a limit to how many men he could throw at the Babylonian problem, over and over again. Something needed to shift in the balance before Sennacherib could reclaim Babylon.

The shift came the next year. News began to filter out of Elam that the king who had led his forces into Babylonia had been struck down by illness; he could no longer speak or give commands. Probably he had had a stroke.

Sennacherib took the opportunity of Elamite absence to try once again. This time he succeeded, and Babylon's gates were broken down. Sennacherib captured the Chaldean pretender and sent him in chains back to Nineveh. And then he ordered the troublesome city razed:

> I destroyed, I devastated, I burned with fire. The wall and the outer-wall, temples and gods, temple-towers of brick and earth, as many as there were, I razed and dumped them into the Arahtu canal. Through the midst of the city I dug canals, I flooded its site with water. . . . That in days to come, the site of that city, and its temples and gods, might not be remembered, I completely blotted it out with floods of water and made it like a meadow. . . . I removed the dust of Babylon for presents to be sent to the most distant peoples and in that Temple of the New Year's Feast, I stored (some) of it in a covered bin.[15]

Turning Babylon into a lake—covering the civilized land with water, returning the city of Marduk to the primordial chaos—was an insult to the god. Sennacherib compounded this by ordering the state of Marduk hauled back to Assyria. The dust was by way of dreadful warning to the gods of other peoples.

The Babylon problem was finally solved. But nothing more was heard of the crown prince Ashur-nadin-shumi. The Elamites made no demands for ransom; in all likelihood they preferred to torture him to death out of sheer hatred for Assyria. The furious hunt for the Chaldean who had dared defy the king had doomed his oldest son to death.

Sennacherib was unlucky in his remaining children. Seven years later, in 681 BC, he was killed by two of his younger sons while sacrificing to the god Nabu, divine lord of the written word, in the god's temple at Nineveh.[16]

He died king of Assyria and Babylon, ruler over an Assyrian empire at the height of its glory. But despite all his victories, the empire he strengthened, the cities he devastated, the captives he took, and the treasure he claimed, Sennacherib was known for much of antiquity for his failure to take Jerusalem. Thanks to Lord Byron, it is also this single defeat—not the overwhelming success of his military career—that most English-speaking students remember.

The Assyrian came down like the wolf on the fold,
And his cohorts were gleaming in purple and gold;
And the sheen of their spears was like stars on the sea,
When the blue wave rolls nightly on deep Galilee. . . .

For the Angel of Death spread his wings on the blast,
And breathed in the face of the foe as he passed;
And the eyes of the sleepers waxed deadly and chill,
And their hearts but once heaved, and for ever grew still! . . .

And the widows of Ashur are loud in their wail,
And the idols are broke in the temple of Baal;
And the might of the Gentile, unsmote by the sword,
Hath melted like snow in the glance of the Lord!

TIMELINE 52

ASSYRIA AND SURROUNDING LANDS		EGYPT, ISRAEL, AND JUDAH	
	Shamshi-Adad V (823–812)		
	Sammu-amat		
	Adad-nirari III	*Dynasties 23 and 24*	
Argishti (Urartu)			
	Shalmaneser IV (782–770)		
	Ashur-Dan III (771–754)		
Nabonassar (Babylon)	**Ashur-nirari V** (753–746)	*Dynasty 25 (Nubian)*	
		Piankhi (747–716)	
Sarduri I (Urartu)	**Tiglath-Pileser III**		
Midas (Phrygia)			
		(Judah)	(Israel)
Merodach-baladan (Babylon)	**Shalmaneser V**	**Ahaz**	
	Sargon II (721–704)		**Hoshea**
		Hezekiah	
	Sennacherib	**Shabaka**	Fall of Israel
		Tirhakah (690–664)	

Chapter Fifty-Three

The Decline of the King

In China, from 771 to 628 BC,
the Hegemon gains kingly power
by driving barbarians away

P'ING, THE SURVIVING ZHOU HEIR, had fled east and settled into Loyang. Here he found himself in a city which was actually twinned towns. The Duke of Zhou, who had established the city three hundred years earlier, had built Loyang's palaces and temples on the western side; the Shang exiles who had been moved there to get them out of the center of the Zhou kingdom had settled mostly in the city's eastern suburb.[1]

Inside the royal complex on the west, P'ing considered the problems he now faced. His western frontier had crumbled, and was continually breached by invaders. Inside, noblemen with ambitions were ready to rule some—or all—of his kingdom for him.

He had coped with the western threat by handing his old royal territory over to the Ch'in; while this may have seemed like a defeat, it shifted the responsibility of dealing with the barbarians neatly over onto the shoulders of the Duke of Ch'in and his army. Now he coped with the internal troubles by ignoring them. Records are sketchy from the first century or so after this shift from Western Zhou to Eastern Zhou rule,* but in the traces that survive we see noblemen circling around each other, jockeying for position and keeping a cautious eye on the king. Meanwhile, in fifty years of reign, P'ing did almost

* The Eastern Zhou Period (771–221 BC) is further divided into two parts. The years 771–481 are known as the Spring and Autumn Period, after the account compiled by Confucius; it covered historical events from the beginning of the Eastern Zhou through Confucius's own lifetime, and was called Spring and Autumn Annals (*Ch'un-ch'iu,* or Pinyin *Chun qiu*). The second half of the Eastern Zhou, 403–221 BC, is known as the Warring States Period. The years 481–403 were occupied by complete chaos (see chapter 62, pp. 497–498). These divisions are widely but not universally used by historians.

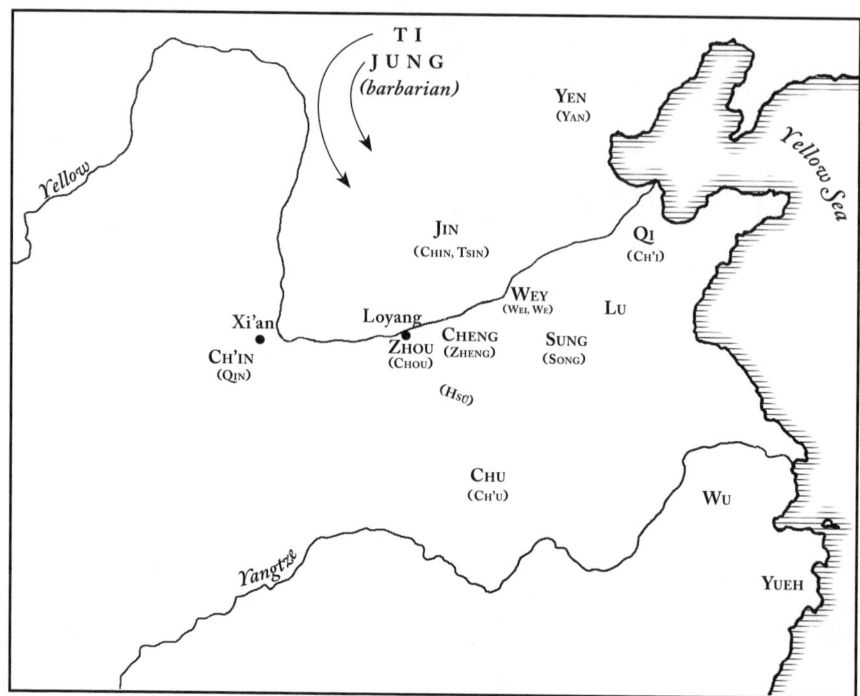

53.1 States of the Eastern Zhou (with Alternate Spellings)

nothing to interfere in spats between noblemen. This avoidance of war earned him the nickname "P'ing the Peaceful."

Almost immediately, powerful lords began to throw cautious nets over nearby, smaller kingdoms. "During the reign of King P'ing," Sima Qian writes, "among the feudal lords, the strong annexed the weak. Qi, Chu, Ch'in, and Jin emerged as major powers, and national policies were made by local lords."[2] Five hundred years earlier, China had been the home of 1,763 separate territories. Now states ran together like drops of water on a smooth surface, joining at last into at least twelve major centers of power: Qi, Chu, Ch'in, and Jin, as Sima Qian notes; along with these, the seven states Yen, Lu, Wey, Wu, Yueh, Sung, and Cheng; and finally the Zhou land centered around Loyang. Surrounding these were perhaps a hundred and sixty smaller chunks of land, each boasting its own walled city and warrior lord.*[3]

* There are multiple versions of the names of these states. In an attempt to reduce confusion, I have chosen to use distinct spellings for the major players rather than trying to hold to one system of transliteration. Other maps and histories most often use the following variants: Qi (Ch'i); Chu (Ch'u); Ch'in (Qin); Jin (Chin, Tsin); Yen (Yan); Lu (no variant); Wey (Wei, We); Cheng (Zheng); Sung (Song); Wu (no variant); Yueh (no variant); and Zhou (Chou).

The crown went from P'ing to his grandson (he had outlived his son during his long and peaceful reign). In P'ing's fifty-odd years on the throne, no one had challenged his assumption of rule; but now it began to be clear that the noblemen surrounding the Zhou land would not even bear ceremonial kingship for much longer.

The first burst of resentment came from the leader of the smallish Cheng state, on the Zhou's eastern side. "Duke Chuang of Cheng came to court," Sima Qian writes, "and King Huan did not treat him according to the norm."

Cheng should have been loyal to the Zhou; the Cheng and the Jin states, which now surrounded the Zhou land on three sides, had their roots in the same clan as the Zhou rulers.[4] But the Cheng state in particular was prickly. The "norm" apparently involved an acknowledgment of the duke's power in his own right, and King Huan had neglected to pay his distant relative the proper respect.

Duke Chuang responded by seizing one of the royal residences for his own use; it lay in the territory of Hsü, a small and unthreatening state south of both Cheng and the Zhou center of power. But it was the palace where the king worshipped, meaning that the duke of Cheng's seizure was a claim of authority both over Hsü, and over the king's religious observances: the ceremonial role which was one of the few powers left to him.

It took a full eight years for King Huan to screw himself up to a retaliation—or to get his soldiers into shape. "In the thirteenth year," Sima Qian goes on, "the king attacked Cheng."[5]

The attack was a disaster. King Huan himself was wounded by an arrow in the fighting and forced to retreat, leaving Cheng unpunished and Hsü still in the hands of his enemy. But although Cheng had defied the royal authority, the Duke of Cheng did not push his advantage further. The tenuous identity that linked the states of China together into a single people depended in large part on their willingness to accept the nominal lordship of the Son of Heaven. Without his unifying rule, cast like a net around the territories, they would break apart; and the northern and western barbarians would move in and destroy the separate states, one by one.

IN THE REIGN of King Huan's grandson, King Hsi, the threat of barbarians returned.

The attacking tribes were called the Yi and the Ti, more of those nomads who lived in the high grounds and had never accepted the authority of either lord or king. The Zhou army was in no shape to counter their attacks: "[The position of] the son of Heaven had become humble and weak," says the

Guanzi (a book of historical essays written at least two hundred years later and collected three hundred years after *that*). "The feudal lords used their energies in attacking [one another]. The Southern Yi and Northern Ti engaged the Central States in battle, and the continued existence of the Central States seemed [to hang by] a thin thread."[6]

The "Central States" were Cheng, Wey, Jin, and the Zhou land itself: the center of China. Seeing the threat of disorder swallowing his lands to the west, the new Duke of Qi was stirred into action. "He wished to keep alive what was dying," the *Guanzi* relates, "and to preserve what was ceasing to exist."[7]

The Duke of Qi, a young man who had just inherited his power, may have wished to preserve the existence of the Central States for the sake of their shared culture, but he was probably motivated by more practical concerns. Qi ran up the northeast edge of the plain, encompassed the mouth of the Yellow river, and stretched out to cover the Shantung peninsula. Disorder along Qi's long western border would have been disastrous for the duke.

But it seemed clear to the young duke that King Hsi was incapable of keeping the Central States safe. Three years after Hsi's enthronement, he announced himself as the new military leader of China: "In the third year of King Hsi," Sima Qian tells us, baldly, "Duke Huan of Qi* was first considered Hegemon."[8] The year was 679 BC.

The claim of the title *hegemon*, or "overlord," was a declaration of authority over the surrounding states. But the Duke of Qi intended to use this power to unite the bickering lands in defense against the invading Yi and Ti, not to mention the other nomadic peoples who roamed along the highlands and looked down with envy on the fertile Eastern Zhou lands. Led by the duke and his minister, Kuan Chung, the Qi army threatened the other states into submission for the common good. The bickering lords, faced with a bristling frontline of armed Qi, agreed to stop fighting among themselves long enough to donate soldiers to a coalition force which would march along the borders and beat back barbarian invasions.

The Duke of Qi never tried to claim the title of king; he was content to leave that in the hands of the Zhou representative. But "king" no longer meant "ruler," as it did in the west; the Duke of Qi could rule China without ever grasping for the word itself. And on the flip side, the king of China still held a kind of spiritual power which even a hegemon could not simply ignore. When Hsi died before his time, after a short five-year reign, his son took the

* The Duke of Qi, who was a contemporary of King Hsi, shares the same first name as Hsi's grandfather King Huan; I will simply call him the Duke of Qi to avoid confusion.

throne and then made official the power which the duke had taken for himself: "he conferred upon Duke Huan of Qi the status of Hegemon."[9]

Once again Duke Huan—who presumably had succeeded in pushing off the barbarian invaders with a coalition force—had been recognized as the chief general of the Chinese states. He had already been acting in this capacity for years. But now the role of Hegemon had been formalized, recognized by the king himself; and China had managed to turn itself into a two-headed country with both a military and a religious leader.

In the year that Hsi's grandson Hsiang was enthroned, the Hegemon—still Duke Huan of Qi, who had now spent decades fighting for China—found himself fighting off a different kind of barbarian invasion.

The invasion began as a contest between siblings. King Hsiang's half-brother Shu Tai wanted the throne for himself; to get soldiers for his coup, he sent to the barbarian tribes of the Ti and the Jung for alliance. His plan called for the Ti to descend down en masse on Jin, the state which lay between the barbarian north and the Zhou land itself. Meanwhile, the second tribe, the Jung, would march on down to the Zhou capital through Jin land, getting past the Jin soldiers while they were occupied fighting off the Ti invasion. They would invade the palace, kill Hsiang, and enthrone Shu Tai instead.

When King Hsiang found out about these secret negotiations, he ordered his brother arrested and killed. Shu Tai got wind of the arrest order and fled to the Hegemon, asking for sanctuary.

This was a tricky situation for the Hegemon. If he refused to protect Shu Tai, he would be admitting that he feared the king's power. If, on the other hand, he granted the asked-for protection, he would be proclaiming hostility for the king and might bring untold grief down on his own head.

He chose a middle path. Ignoring the whole issue of Shu Tai's treachery altogether, the Hegemon sent two of his own ministers to negotiate treaties between the Zhou and the Jung, and between the Jin and the invading Ti. The negotiations were apparently successful. The attacks were diverted; Shu Tai apparently did his best to pretend that he had never been involved; and disaster was averted.

This was a very different kind of power struggle than the clashes going on farther west. The kings of the ancient Near East were caught in a spiralling contest; any king who did not immediately set out to conquer territory risked losing some of his own to an opponent who was likely to speak a different language and worship a different god. The negotiations between the Chinese states were more like battles between cousins, all of whom were going to end up in the same vacation house during the summer months no matter how much they fought in between times. There was plenty of empire-building ambition in China, but it was considerably more subtle than the spear-clashing farther west. Empire-builders did best when they were able to portray themselves as guardians of China against the rest of the world, uniting the states together against the barbaric threat of the non-Chinese.

Six years after negotiating the safety of the Zhou and Jin lands against the barbarians, the Hegemon died without delegating his power to an heir. In the power vacuum left by the Hegemon's passing, King Hsiang made a tentative attempt to lasso the Hegemon's military authority and yank it back into the royal house.

He was given a marvellous excuse almost at once; the smallish state of Cheng showed the bad judgment to throw one of the king's ambassadors into jail. King Hsiang decided to punish, sharply, this insult to royal power.

Unfortunately, he chose exactly the wrong kind of strategy. He offered to marry the daughter of the Ti leader and make her a queen, if the Ti barbarians would help him invade and punish the Cheng.

The Spring and Autumn Annals, compiled at least three hundred years after the fact, put a dreadful caution into the mouth of one of King Hsiang's advisors. The Ti are not *like* the Zhou, the advisor warns; they are different in at least four ways. "Those whose ears cannot hear the harmony of the five sounds are deaf," he explains, "those whose eyes cannot distinguish among the five colors are blind; those whose minds do not conform to the standards of virtue and righteousness are perverse; those whose mouths do not speak words of loyalty and faith are foolish chatterers. The Ti conform to these four evils."[10]

King Hsiang paid no attention. "In the fifteenth year," according to Sima Qian, "the King sent down the Ti forces to attack Cheng," and prepared to make the barbarian Ti princess his queen.[11]

What exactly happened next is not recorded by Sima Qian, but apparently the invasion failed. The Cheng state remained standing, and the year after the invasion, King Hsiang decided to put his new wife away.

At this, the Ti turned and invaded the Zhou capital itself. Hsiang fled. Shu Tai, his half-brother, older but no wiser, then reappeared on the scene and offered himself for enthronement. The Ti, who (after all) had originally been summoned into the mix by Shu Tai himself, enthusiastically agreed; Shu Tai married his half-brother's discarded barbarian princess wife and made himself king. He also set up a new royal palace at Wen, thirty miles along the Yellow river from his brother's old royal residence.

However, Shu Tai's strategy for empire-building was no sounder than his brother's. King Hsiang travelled incognito to Jin and arrived at the court of the Jin leader, Duke Wen, asking for help against the barbarians. The Duke of Jin now had the opportunity to repeat the Duke of Qi's feat; he rounded up his own Jin soldiers, sent them down to drive the Ti out of the Zhou palace, and killed Shu Tai with his own hands. What happened to the Ti princess remains unknown.

He then used his own soldiers to reenthrone King Hsiang. And, not surprisingly, Hsiang then agreed to recognize Duke Wen of Jin as the Hegemon, heir to the power of the Overlordship. For good measure, Hsiang handed a good fertile chunk of land over to the Jin as well.

The new Hegemon exerted his power so lavishly that, unlike his predecessor, he almost made himself king. Three years after he was declared Hegemon, he was sending royal orders *to* King Hsiang: "In the twentieth year," Sima Qian writes, "Duke Wen of Jin summoned King Hsiang. And King Hsiang

TIMELINE 53

	ASSYRIA AND SURROUNDING LANDS	CHINA	
	Ashur-Dan III (771–754)	Eastern Zhou (771–221)	
		P'ing	
Nabonassar (Babylon)	**Ashur-nirari V** (753–746)		Duke Chuang of Cheng
Sarduri I (Urartu)	**Tiglath-Pileser III**		
Midas (Phrygia)			
Merodach-baladan (Babylon)	**Shalmaneser V** **Sargon II** (721–704)	**Huan**	
	Sennacherib		
		Chuang	
		Hsi	The Duke of Qi
		Hui	
		Hsiang	
			Duke Wen of Jin

went to meet him." In the annals of Hsiang's reign, this was recorded, euphemistically, as "The Heavenly King took an inspection tour.' "[12] He was inspecting the Hegemon's authority, and finding himself a nonentity.

DOWN TO THE SOUTH, the huge Chu state had made its own plans to deal with the barbarians storming back and forth through Jin and Cheng and in and out of the Zhou capital. The Duke of Chu had ordered a huge wall, the "Square Wall," erected along his northern border. It was a wall which served him not only against barbarians, but also against the ambitions of the new Hegemon. The Square Wall blocked the route that a Jin army might take, if it were to march straight down to the east of the Zhou land into Chu territory.

Now Chu and Jin faced each other from the north and south of the humbled Zhou king, staring each other down over his head. To the east and west, the Ch'in and the Qi faced each other as well; the Qi diminished from its previous prominence as the land of the Hegemon, but by no means out of the picture, and the Ch'in in possession of the old western Zhou lands. The Eastern Zhou rule had been transformed into this square of powerful states with the Zhou king cowering in the middle.

Chapter Fifty-Four

The Assyrians in Egypt

Between 681 and 653 BC,
Phrygia falls to barbarians,
while the Assyrians rebuild Babylon and lose Egypt

WITH SENNACHERIB DEAD in the temple of Nabu, all hell broke loose in Assyria.

The two assassins fled, according to the account preserved in the book of Isaiah, "to the land of Ararat."[1] This probably means that they ran up north, into the mountainous territory of the Urartu. The kingdom had gathered itself together again after the suicide of Rusas I; the new king, Rusas I's grandson Rusas II, was beginning to rebuild his army. He was happy to disaccommodate the Assyrians by offering hospitality to the king's killers.*

Meanwhile, competition between Sennacherib's remaining sons exploded into a full-blown war of succession. The eventual winner, the younger son Esarhaddon, wrote a victor's account on a prism (a stone pillar with six to ten sides) uncovered in the ruins of his palace:

> Of my older brothers, the younger brother was I,
> but by decree of Ashur and Shamash, Bel and Nabu,
> my father exalted me, amid a gathering of my brothers:
> he asked Shamash, "Is this my heir?"
> and the gods answered, "He is your second self" . . .
> And then my brothers went mad.

* The identity of the culprits remains a mystery. Isa. 37:38 reads, "One day, while he was worshiping in the temple of his god Nisroch, his sons Adrammelech and Sharezer cut him down with the sword." Adrammelech and Sharezer may possibly refer to Sennacherib's sons Ardi-Ninlil and Nabu-shar-usur, but there is no way to know for certain. The Babylonian Chronicle reads, simply, "His son killed Sennacherib, king of Assyria, in a rebellion." Esarhaddon never names the culprits who killed his father, and since Sennacherib's inscriptions certainly do not name all of his sons, we are ultimately left in the dark.

They drew their swords, godlessly, in the middle of Nineveh.
But Ashur, Shamash, Bel, Nabu, Ishtar,
all the gods looked with wrath on the deeds of these scoundrels,
brought their strength to weakness and humbled them beneath me.[2]

Obviously Esarhaddon won the contest for the crown, but the story of his recognition by his father before the old man's murder sounds very much like a tale invented for the sake of legitimacy. And it is peculiar, to say the least, that Esarhaddon does not refer directly to Sennacherib's murder. Perhaps he did not wish the act examined too closely.

Properly enthroned, Esarhaddon faced an empire whose edges had begun to fray. Official letters show that fifteen or sixteen major cities, centers of Assyrian provinces, had gotten well behind on their tribute, and Sennacherib had not bothered to follow up on the debts.[3] Worse, as soon as the news of Sennacherib's death spread down to the ruins of Babylon, a Chaldean rebellion began—led by none other than the son of old Merodach-baladan. His name was Nabu-zer-ketti-lisher, and he had been ruling over Bit-Yakin, down at the head of the Gulf, for some years. Now he collected his tribesmen and marched up to attack the city of Ur, the first stop on his way to claim the old Babylonian territory.[4]

Esarhaddon, who must have begun to feel that Merodach-baladan's ghost was always going to torment the kings of Assyria, sent soldiers to clean up the mess; Nabu-zer-ketti-lisher fled to Elam and discovered, to his great surprise, that the newly crowned king of Elam had no intention of provoking the new Assyrian ruler. He was arrested and, still startled, put to death.[5]

Esarhaddon himself began, almost at once, to pour money and men into Babylon.

Sennacherib's exasperated destruction of the city had not gone over well with much of the court, and many of his own people; Babylon's gods were far too close to their own, and the removal of Marduk's statue from Babylon struck many as an insult that simply begged for divine retaliation. Esarhaddon's own records announce that he desired to rebuild Babylon out of affection for Marduk. This left him with a bit of a problem, though; if he spent too much time promising to amend the insult to Marduk, he was condemning his own father for impiety (and potentially destroying his own claim to be part of a divinely appointed family of kings).

He got around this by managing to describe the destruction of Babylon without ever mentioning his father. His account of Babylon's flooding suggests that no human hand had any role in the devastation:

In the reign of an earlier king,
there were evil omens in Babylon.

There were crimes, injustices, lies,
The inhabitants mistreated the gods,
left off regular offerings and worship,
took the temple treasure to pay Elam,
took the treasure of Babylon for another.
Before my time, Marduk became angry with Babylon,
The Arahtu overflowed and turned the city into a ruin,
Babylon became a wasteland,
Reeds and poplars grew in the abandoned city,
its gods and goddesses left their shrines,
its inhabitants fled for refuge.[6]

This was dreadful history but brilliant propaganda: the repetition of "Before my time" which removed blame from Esarhaddon without pinning it on his father; the explanation that the gods deserted Babylon out of divine anger, as opposed to being hauled off in Assyrian wagons; the suggestion that the appeal to Elam had made Marduk particularly furious; the coy reference to "an earlier king"; and above all, the plaintive "The Arahtu overflowed" (as opposed to the more truthful, "Assyrian soldiers dammed it with broken bits of Babylon's own walls").[7]

The statue of Marduk remained in Assyria, as a reminder to the citizens of Babylon that their god had taken up residence with the *rightful* king of Babylonia. But Esarhaddon, acting as the god's agent, rebuilt temples and houses and relaid streets. He wrote his own praises into the very roads underfoot: scores of the bricks that paved the approach to the great temple complex of Esagila were stamped "For the god Marduk, Esarhaddon, king of the world, king of Assyria and king of Babylon, made the processional way of Esagila and Babylon shine with baked bricks from a ritually pure kiln."[8]

The Chaldean tribe Bit-Dakkuri, brother-tribe to the Bit-Yakin of Merodach-baladan, now decided to make friends. They sent a letter up to Babylon offering loyalty, but Esarhaddon, who was in no mood to trust Chaldeans, wrote back tartly. "The word of the king to the non-Babylonians," the letter begins, succinctly:

> . . . I am herewith sending back to you, with its seals intact, your completely pointless letter to me. Perhaps you will say, "Why did he return it to us?" When the citizens of Babylon, who are my servants and love me, wrote to me, I opened their letter and read it. But would it be good for me to accept and read a letter from the hand of criminals?[9]

The letter was followed by troops; Esarhaddon sent Assyrian soldiers to push the Chaldeans away from the southern lands of Babylonia, back into their marsh.

Meanwhile a new threat was coalescing to the northeast. Nomadic tribes who had long roamed around the shores of the Caspian Sea were gathering together above the tribes of the Medes and Persians. The Assyrians called the newcomers the Gimirrai; they were known to later historians as the Cimmerians.

The Cimmerians, like so many of the mountain nomads, were better at fighting than anything else.* Their excursions along the northern Assyrian border had reached all the way over into Cilicia, at the edge of Asia Minor, and they had also made friends with the Urartian king, Rusas II (still, apparently, harboring the patricidal princes somewhere up in his mountains).[10] This made Esarhaddon take notice: a Cimmerian/Urartian alliance could be dangerous.

In an attempt to strengthen his northern border, Esarhaddon made a tentative alliance with a second group of nomads who were filtering down from the Caucasus Mountains, north of the Black Sea. These Scythians would provide him with an extra arm to hold back the Cimmerians and Urartians, but he didn't entirely trust them. Divination tablets from Esarhaddon's rule, on which his formal inquiries to the sun-god Shamash were written so that they could be presented at the temple, record the king's difficulties:

> Shamash, great lord, will Rusas, king of the Urartu, come with his armies, and the Cimmerians (or any of his allies), and wage war, kill, plunder, and loot?
>
> Shamash, great lord, if I give one of my daughters in marriage to the king of the Scythians, will he speak words of good faith to me, true and honest words of peace? Will he keep my treaty and do whatever is pleasing to me?
>
> Shamash, great lord, will the troops of the Cimmerians, or of the Medes, or of any other enemy, attack? Will they try to capture cities by a tunnel, by scaling ladders, by ramps and battering rams, or by a treaty of peace—a ruse?[11]

There were no clear answers to any of these questions.

* This is probably why fantasy writer Robert E. Howard borrowed their name, in the 1930s, for the mythical warrior tribe that lived on a mythically distant past Earth, apparently, at some time between the drowning of Atlantis and the rise of the first pharaohs of Egypt. Their champion, Conan the Cimmerian, is better known as Conan the Barbarian, thanks to his movie incarnation. His most famous speech (in answer to the question "What is best in life?" he gets to intone, "To crush your enemies, to see them driven before you, and to hear the lamentations of the women") reveals a slightly more bloodthirsty point of view than that held by the average historical Cimmerian. On the other hand, the real Cimmerians did in fact make their way in the world by driving away enemies before them. Their exact origin is unknown, although they most likely did *not* come from north of the Black Sea as Herodotus claims (see Anne Katrine Gade Kristensen, *Who Were the Cimmerians, and Where Did They Come From?*, pp. 7–11).

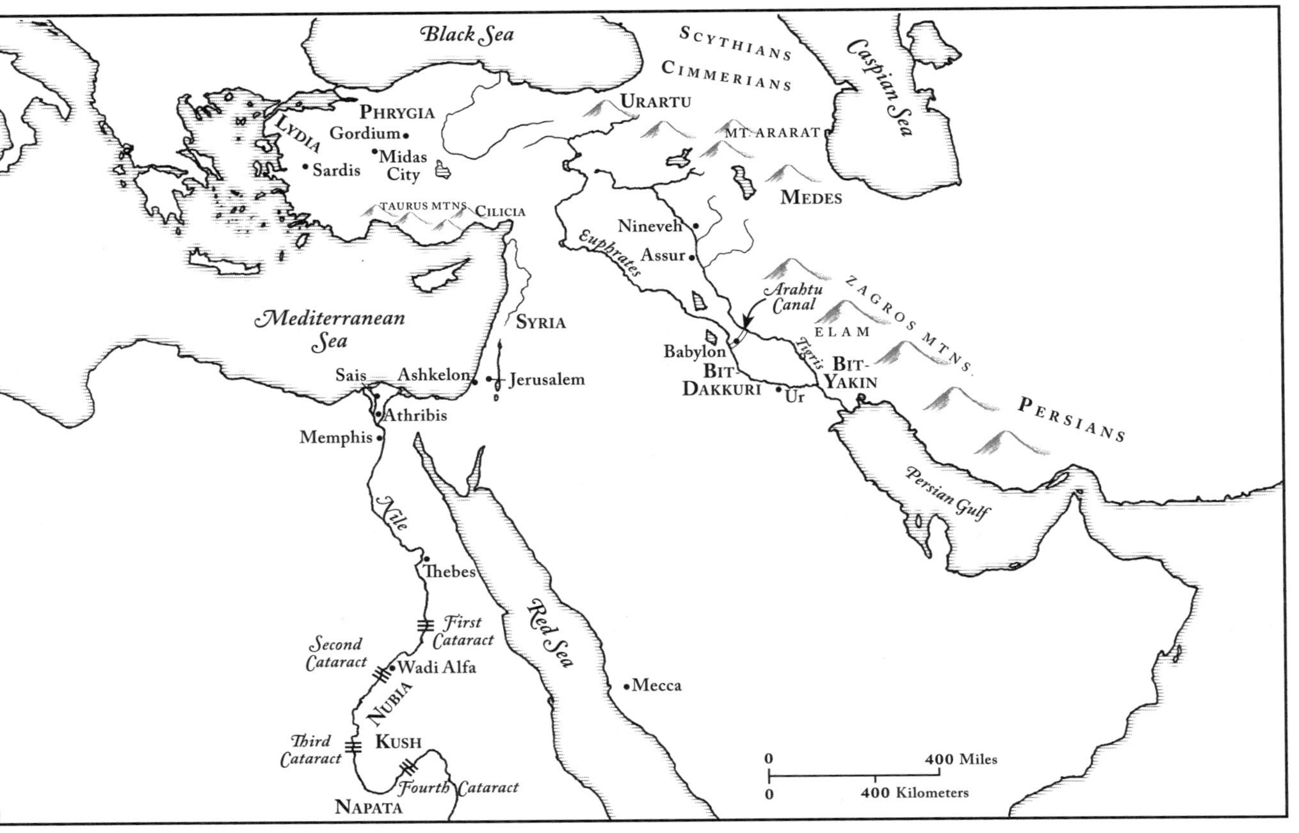

54.1 Esarhaddon's World

Esarhaddon was forced into war in 676, when the Cimmerian nomads pushed so far west that they arrived at the borders of Phrygia.

The prosperous Phrygians were not helpless. Their villages—stone buildings on hilltops, their foundations still visible thousands of years later—were built for defense. Their most characteristic monuments, the "facade monuments," still dot the landscape: slabs of stone jutting up into the air, one side carved into the likeness of a wall, with a sculpted door that can never be opened. The Midas Monument at Midas City faces the rising sun, as do almost all the other facade monuments. For a few moments at dawn, its gray surface turns bright and the false door glows.[12]

54.1. Midas Monument. The Midas Monument is carved to resemble the wall of a temple or tomb. Photo credit Chris Hellier/CORBIS

But the speed and savagery of the Cimmerian invasion took them by surprise. The Phrygian army was driven back towards the capital city of Gordium, as the people who lived in the countryside poured into the city, hoping to be protected by its walls. But the Cimmerians overran the walls and set the city on fire. Their king, Midas, grandson of the Midas who had ruled back in the years of Tiglath-Pileser, saw that defeat was inevitable. He killed himself in the citadel; the Roman geographer Strabo, writing six hundred years later, says that he committed suicide by drinking bull's blood.[13] It is an odd death, and a desperate one.

Esarhaddon marched his own army up to meet the threat. The two armies clashed in Cilicia, and Esharaddon claimed victory. He had killed the Cimmerian king Teushpa, he boasted in his inscriptions, with his own hands.[14]

Esarhaddon's attack halted the Cimmerian invasion, and saved the west of Asia Minor from destruction. But Phrygia had fallen. The shattered villages never did regather themselves, and the trade routes once dominated by Phrygian merchants now belonged to the villages farther west. These people were known as the Lydians, and with the plain to the east destroyed, their king Gyges became the strongest power in all of Asia Minor.

EGYPT HAD NOW been more or less united, under the Nubian pharaohs of the Twenty-Fifth Dynasty, for eighty years or so. Tirhakah, the prince who had fought Sennacherib to a draw years before, was now king. Esarhaddon was determined to finish the conquest that his father had begun: "Shamash, great lord," his next query begins, "should I go to Egypt, and wage war against Tirkhakah, king of Kush, and his troops; and in this war, will my weapons and army prevail?"[15] The answer must have been positive, because the Assyrian chronicles announce, "In the seventh year of Esarhaddon's reign, the Assyrian army marched on Egypt."[16]

Tirhakah had waited a long time for his throne, and he was not going to sit calmly in the Delta until Esarhaddon arrived. Egyptian forces marched up to meet the Assyrians at the Philistine town of Ashkelon, where the men of Ashkelon joined with them. Esarhaddon's men arrived at Ashkelon to face this joint enemy already tired and weakened. On the long march south, they had been forced to fight off nomadic Arabian tribes who saw the long Assyrian column as a good source of food and weapons.

The battle that followed was brief, and Tirhakah's army was victorious. Esarhaddon retreated from the Delta. Tirhakah went back to Egypt, where he splashed building projects (including an enormous sprawling Temple of Amun down in Nubia) all across the country, in the manner of a pharaoh secure in his own greatness.[17]

But Esarhaddon had not gone away. He had simply withdrawn to regather his forces. Two years later, in 671, he arrived with a rested army and drove through the outer defenses of Egypt, down through the Delta and all the way to Memphis, where Tirhakah and his army made a last stand. When it became clear that the Assyrian army would triumph, Tirhakah escaped the battlefield and fled down south towards his ancestral lands. Esarhaddon captured his son and wife, most of his family, and a slew of courtiers, and took the whole group back to Nineveh as captives. Along with Tirhakah's family, he had rounded up the sons of various noblemen—including the son of the king of Sais, a western Delta city—and hauled them back to Nineveh to educate them into Assyrians.

He left Egypt under the control of governors who had sworn allegiance to Assyria.[18] Their allegiance barely lasted until Esarhaddon was back in Nineveh. The governor of Sais, a man named Necho, remained loyal (his son, after all, was a hostage in Nineveh), but the vassals of other cities ceased following Assyrian orders almost as soon as the tail end of the procession was out of sight.

Esarhaddon reached Nineveh, turned around, and started back down to Egypt. He never reached it; he died on the march south.

Esarhaddon left his Assyrian throne to Ashurbanipal, his chosen and favorite son; but he appointed a younger prince, Shamash-shum-ukin, crown prince of Babylon, a sovereign ruler under his older brother's supervision. The year after Ashurbanipal's coronation, Shamash-shum-ukin was formally crowned in Babylon. His entrance into the city was accompanied by the image of the god Marduk, who was finally coming back home. "During my reign," Ashurbanipal announced in an inscription in Babylon,

> the great lord, the god Marduk
> entered Babylon amidst rejoicing and took up his residence
> and I re-established the privileged status of Babylon
> and I appointed Shamash-shum-ukin, my favorite brother,
> to the kingship of Babylon.[19]

Then he picked up his father's sword against Egypt. Tirhakah had crept back north and was trying to regain his throne; Ashurbanipal stormed through Egypt as far south as Thebes, killing every king who had forgotten his Assyrian allegiance, but sparing the pro-Assyrian Necho of Sais. In the place of the dead vassal kings, Ashurbanipal appointed those Assyrian-trained Egyptian sons that his father had taken to Nineveh. Necho's son, a young man named Psammetichus, was brought back from Assyria and installed in the eastern city of Athribis, across from his father's city. Together the father and son were given the joint overlordship of all the other cities.[20]

Tirhakah was still alive, though. This time he had been driven all the way south into Upper Nubia and was in Napata, almost at the Fourth Cataract. He had announced that his cousin would be his heir; apparently his own son had been executed, up in Nineveh. When he died, his cousin Tantamani inherited an empty title, the kingship of a land firmly under Assyrian control.

But then Tatanami had a dream:

> In Year 1 of his coronation as king . . . His Majesty saw a dream by night: two serpents, one upon his right, the other on his left. Then His Majesty awoke, and did not find them. His Majesty said, "Why have I seen this?" The answer came to him: "The Southland is yours; take the Northland also for yourself. The Two Goddesses shine upon your brow, the land is given to you in all of its length and breadth. No other divides it with you."[21]

He rose from his bed with the divine command echoing in his ears: take Egypt back from the Assyrians and their vassal kings.

His early victories were easy; the Assyrians had left, again, and the natives were not happy under their Assyrian governors. Tatanami progressed north along the Nile, welcomed by the towns he passed and collecting allies behind him. At Memphis, he came up against the first real obstacle: Necho of Sais, who had hurried south with an Assyrian-reinforced army to stop the Nubian conqueror.

In the battle that followed, Necho fell. His son Psammetichus took up his task, but found himself at once terribly unpopular with the other noblemen of the Delta, who preferred Nubian to Assyrian rule; Herodotus says that at one point Psammetichus was driven to hide in the marshes from eleven other Delta rulers, out for his blood. He was pushed steadily backwards into Sais, where he fenced himself in behind the Assyrian garrison stationed there.[22]

Meanwhile, the Delta was celebrating, and Tantamani was carving victory prayers to Amun ("He who is guided by Amun cannot go astray!") on memorial steles.[23]

But then Ashurbanipal returned, this time with more troops. In 663, he joined his forces with those of the struggling Psammetichus, and together, the two armies laid waste to the Delta. Tantamani ran down south for the second time; and Thebes was sacked and burned for the first time in its history. The Temple of Amun was crushed. Its treasure was stolen, its walls levelled, and the two silver obelisks that stood at its doors were hauled back up to Nineveh.[24] The destruction of Thebes was so shattering that it became a byword in the ancient Near East, proof of what could happen to those who defied Assyrian might. Decades later, the Jewish prophet Nahum could still describe it with violent detail:

> Thebes, on the river Nile, with water around her,
> defended by the river, the water her walls,
> Kush her strength, her ally—
> But she was taken captive, taken into exile,
> Her infants were dashed to pieces at the head of every street,
> Lots were cast for her noblemen,
> and all her great men were put into chains.[25]

Then Ashurbanipal got rid of every vassal king and appointed Psammetichus the sole pharaoh of Egypt. Egypt was just too far away for the Assyrians to keep a huge garrison there. If Ashurbanipal was to keep the country under his thumb, he needed an indestructibly loyal vassal king.

Despite his Assyrian indoctrination, Psammetichus was not that king. His willingness to fight on the side of Ashurbanipal's army had been craft, the strategy of a man who had spent his entire adolescence surrounded by enemies, powerless and homeless with his life hanging by a thread. As soon as he had the throne, he began to veer slowly away from the Assyrian straight and narrow. He began to negotiate with the various governors of Egypt, promising them power in a new regime. Not too long later, an Assyrian officer posted in Syria sent a message of complaint to Ashurbanipal, in Nineveh, about Psammetichus's increasingly independent behavior; the Assyrian viceroy was slowly but surely cleansing his cities of Assyrian soldiers stationed there. Ashurbanipal acknowledged the letter, but sent no cleanup crew. His men were busy elsewhere.[26]

By 658, Psammetichus was sending secret messengers to Gyges, king of Lydia, now the only powerful sovereign in Asia Minor. Sympathetic to the Egyptian cause (anything that reduced the looming power of Assyria made him happier), Gyges sent additional soldiers down to join Psammetichus in Egypt. They left their tracks; while waiting in boredom for the fighting to start, they scribbled graffiti which can still be read on the walls of the temple at Wadi Alfa.[27]

By 653, Psammetichus was ready to stake his future on the success of a rebellion. He turned on the Assyrian soldiers stationed in the Delta and drove them all the way out of his country, up into the Western Semitic territories. He then made Sais his royal capital; and by marrying his daughter to the most powerful nobleman at Thebes, he spread his authority down almost as far as the First Cataract.

Farther south, Nubia remained under a shifting patchwork of local rulers, progressively more independent of Egyptian influence. But north of the First Cataract, Egypt was once more under a real pharaoh (if an Assyrian-trained one), who claimed the ancient title Uniter of the Two Lands and the blessing of Egypt's chief god.[28] For the first time in many years, *maat*—divine order—had returned to Egypt. The Twenty-Sixth Dynasty, or Saite Dynasty, centered in Psammetichus's birth-city of Sais, had begun.

THE REVOLT IN EGYPT didn't work out nearly as well for Gyges. The Cimmerians, who had regathered themselves, were again on the march west. This time, the Assyrians refused to interfere; Ashurbanipal held a grudge against Gyges, thanks to those Lydian soldiers down in Egypt. The Cimmerians, under their king Dugdamme, attacked the Lydian army, drove it back, killed Gyges, and sacked Sardis. Dugdamme then moved southwards, which brought him a little too close to Assyrian territory; Ashurbanipal was willing to let the Cimmerians teach another nation a lesson, but he didn't want them on his own land.

He began to organize an expedition north, but was terrified by an eclipse which his court priests interpreted as a very bad omen indeed: "There will be an attack on your land," they told their king, "and the land will be destroyed."[29] Fortunately for Ashurbanipal, not long after the sack of Sardis, Dugdamme grew sick with a revolting disease that combined the vomiting of blood and gangrene of the testicles.[30] The illness carried him off, and a relieved Ashurbanipal was able to abandon the expedition north.

TIMELINE 54

ASSYRIA AND SURROUNDING LANDS		EGYPT, ISRAEL, AND JUDAH		
	Ashur-Dan III (771–754)			
Nabonassar (Babylon)	**Ashur-nirari V** (753–746)	*Dynasty 25 (Nubian)* **Piankhi** (747–716)		
Sarduri I (Urartu)	**Tiglath-Pileser III**			
Midas (Phrygia)			(Judah) **Ahaz**	(Israel)
Merodach-baladan (Babylon)	**Shalmaneser V**			**Hoshea**
	Sargon II (721–704)		**Hezekiah**	
		Shabaka		Fall of Israel
	Sennacherib (704–680)	**Tirhakah** (690–664)		
	Esarhaddon (680–668)	*Dynasty 26*		
Shamash-shum-ukin (Babylon)	**Ashurbanipal**	**Necho I**		
Phrygia falls to Cimmerians		**Psammetichus I**		
Gyges (Lydia)				

Chapter Fifty-Five

Medes and Persians

Between 653 and 625 BC,
Ashurbanipal makes a library and destroys Elam,
while the Medes and Persians become a nation

ASHURBANIPAL'S FAILURE TO STAMP ON Psammetichus was not his last loss of territory. During his rule, the borders of Assyria shifted, and caved slightly inwards. Ashurbanipal was a competent king, but no Sargon, to throw all of his energies into constant warfare so that his empire might be a little bit larger. He was preoccupied with a different sort of acquisition.

He was not the first Assyrian king to collect clay tablets, but he was the first to make their collection a priority all over his empire. He went about this in an organized fashion: he sent officers all over the kingdom to make an inventory of every library anywhere in the empire, and collected copies of every tablet he could find: spells, prophecies, medical remedies, astronomical observations, stories and tales (including a compilation of a thousand years' worth of stories about the ancient hero Gilgamesh), all put together.[1] Eventually the library at Nineveh had almost thirty thousand tablets in it

As far as Ashurbanipal was concerned, his library was the abiding accomplishment of his reign:

> I, Ashurbanipal, king of the universe,
> on whom the gods have bestowed vast intelligence,
> who has acquired penetrating acumen
> for the most recondite details of scholarly erudition
> (none of my predecessors having any comprehension of such matters),
> I have placed these tablets for the future in the library at Nineveh
> for my life and for the well-being of my soul,
> to sustain the foundations of my royal throne.[2]

Esarhaddon might have managed to keep Egypt, but Ashurbanipal's realm of the mind would last forever.

His earthly realm was more brittle. The Elamite king was preparing an invasion of Babylon, and to the north of Elam a new enemy was (again) coalescing into a threat.

In the same year as Psammetichus's rebellion, the Elamite king Teumann and his army began to march towards Babylon. Presumably Teumann had been promised a warm welcome. Hostility had been growing between Ashurbanipal and his younger brother Shamash-shum-ukin, viceroy of Babylon, for some time. Early inscriptions of Shamash-shum-ukin name Ashurbanipal, politely, as "my favorite brother" and "king of the four quarters of the earth," ask for blessings on Ashurbanipal's health, and threaten his enemies with disaster.[3]

But an equal number of inscriptions left in Babylon by Ashurbanipal himself suggest that he had micromanaged the city's affairs for years.[4] An Elamite army could help Shamash-shum-ukin shake free from Ashurbanipal's dominance.

When Ashurbanipal received news that the Elamites were on the march, he consulted his court prophets. They assured him that the omens were favorable, so he took the offensive: he crossed the Tigris and met the Elamites on their own land. His army drove them back to Susa, inflicting a great slaughter on them. "I dammed the river with the bodies of the people of Elam," Ashurbanipal boasts, in the epigraphs carved on his reliefs at Nineveh, "and when Teumann, king of Elam, saw the defeat of his troops, he fled to save his life."

> Teumann, king of Elam, was wounded; his oldest son took him by the hand, and they fled towards a forest. But the frame of his royal chariot broke and fell on top of him [and trapped him]. Teumann, in desperation, said to his son, "Take up the bow [and defend us]!" But the wagon pole that had pierced Teumann, king of Elam, had also pierced his son. With the encouragement of Assur, I killed them; I cut off their heads in front of each other.[5]

The reliefs themselves give one more detail; Ashurbanipal apparently brought the heads back with him and hung them in his garden, where he and his wife then dined beneath the decorated trees. Meanwhile Shamash-shum-ukin remained on the throne. There was, apparently, no proof that he had ever corresponded with the dead Teumann.

Almost immediately, another army marched on Nineveh itself.

The Madua tribes had managed to organize themselves into a Median kingdom a few years early. Sometime before Ashurbanipal's accession, a village

55.1 The Medes and the Persians

judge named Deioces had gained a reputation for fairness and integrity that spread throughout all the Median tribes until they proclaimed him leader of them all. "Once power was in his hands," Herodotus writes, "Deioces insisted that the Medes build a single city and maintain this one place."[6] The central city was Ecbatana, and when the tribes converged on it Ecbatana became the center of an emerging nation.

Ecbatana: one of the most startling cities of ancient times, built on the eastern slopes of Mount Orontes. Ecbatana was surrounded by seven circular walls, the outermost lying downhill from the next and so on, so that the top of each wall could be seen rising up beyond.[7] The city's bastions—the defensive positions on the walls, built out from the wall itself in a fortified wedge so that archers could stand on them—were painted with bright colors; the bastions of the outer wall white, the next black, then red, blue, and orange; the bastions of the penultimate circle were gilded with silver, and the final circle, within which lay the royal palace itself, gilded with gold. Ecbatana was one of the great sights of the ancient world: six thousand feet above sea level, shining on its hilltop like an enormous and threatening child's toy.

In 675, Deioces's son Phraortes had inherited his father's role as leader. From Ecbatana, Phraortes attacked the nearby Parsua: the Persians, who were a looser confederation led by their overlord Achamenes. They were conquered and made a subject state. And from there, Herodotus remarks, Phraortes, "with two strong countries under his command," set his eye on conquering Asia, "tribe by tribe." He had become a king.

By 653, Phraortes had also managed to make an alliance with the wild Cimmerians. Together, the Medes and Persians and Cimmerians decided to take advantage of Ashurbanipal's troubles in Assyria to march on the capital itself.

This was a miscalculation. The Scythians, allied to Assyria by marriage (Ashurbanipal's sister had married the Scythian king), came down and fought on the side of the Assyrian defenders. Not only were the forces of the Cimmerians, Medes, and Persians driven back from Nineveh's walls, but Phraortes was killed; and the Scythian warrior chief Madius claimed his place as Madius the Scythian, King of the Medes and the Persians.

THE YEAR AFTER, Shamash-shum-ukin's resentment of his brother burst into the open. He led Babylonian soldiers against Cuthah, an Assyrian outpost just north of Babylon, in an open attempt to drive his brother's forces out. Ashurbanipal rounded up his own armies for a return fight; his concerns are reflected in the queries to the sun-god Shamash that survive from this time. "Shamash, great lord," one of the earlier ones reads, "will the Elamites join the war?" (The answer was an affirmative, and indeed Elamite soldiers had soon arrived to reinforce Shamash-shum-ukin's rebellion. After Teumann's death, no one in particular had managed to claim the Elamite throne, and the army was apparently running itself.)

Shamash-shum-ukin dug himself in behind Babylon's walls to fight it out. "Will the army of Shamash-shum-ukin leave Babylon?" Ashurbanipal asks his god, not long after, and then, showing a certain lack of confidence, "Will the Assyrian army prevail over Shamash-shum-ukin?"[8]

The army did prevail, but not until after a three-year siege that ended in starvation and horror ("They ate the flesh of their sons and daughters because of starvation"). When the city finally fell, Ashurbanipal's soldiers showed no mercy on the rebels who had defended it. Ashurbanipal's own account justifies, obliquely, his grandfather Sennacherib's destruction of the city in the first place: Babylon was nothing but trouble. "The rest of those living, I destroyed in the place where my grandfather Sennacherib was killed," he wrote, "and their carved-up bodies I fed to dogs, to pigs, to wolves, to eagles, to birds of the heavens, to fishes of the deep."[9]

Shamash-shum-ukin himself died, not by any man's hand, but in a fire in his own palace. He had immolated himself to avoid his brother's vengeance.

Ashurbanipal ordered his body buried with proper ceremony, put his own agent, a man named Kandalu, on the throne, and ruled Babylon through this puppet. Kandalu served this role for more than twenty years, but his lack of authority is indicated by the absence of any royal inscriptions in Babylon that bear his name.[10]

And then Ashurbanipal fought the one war of his reign that would move Assyria's border outwards. To his east, civil war had broken out over the succession to the Elamite throne; Ashurbanipal went over the Tigris twice more with his army, each time acting with increasing ferocity as he brought the whole area directly under Assyrian rule. Elamite cities burned. The temples and palaces of Susa were robbed. For no better reason than vengeance, Ashurbanipal ordered the royal tombs opened and the bones of the kings bundled off into captivity:

> I took away their bones to Assyria,
> I made their ghosts restless,
> I deprived them of their food and drink offerings.[11]

He took anyone who could lay a future claim to the throne of Elam back to Nineveh in chains, and deported huge groups of Elamite citizens far away from their homeland; a slew of them were settled in the old territory of Israel, north of the small, resistant country of Judah.

This did not destroy their national identity quite as much as he could have hoped. Two hundred years later, the governor of the area wrote to his king naming the various groups under his supervision: among them, he mentions "the Elamites of Susa, and the other people whom the great and honorable Ashurbanipal deported and settled in the city of Samaria and elsewhere in Trans-Euphrates."[12] Even in exile, the descendants of Ashurbanipal's captives remembered both their names and their city of origin.

But after almost two thousand years of existence, the country of Elam had been obliterated. Ashurbanipal had two settings, in his dealings with trouble spots in his empire: full devastation or complete neglect. Egypt had been far enough away to benefit from the second setting; Elam, too close for neglect, received the first.

It was an unwise move. Ashurbanipal did not rebuild after the wrecking of the country. He installed no governors, he resettled none of the devastated cities, he made no attempt to make this new province of Assyria anything more than a wasteland; Elam lay open and undefended.

The first invasion was a cautious one: the Persian overlord Teispes moved gingerly into the old Elamite territory of Anshan and claimed it for his own. Ashurbanipal did nothing to stop him. Neither did Teispes's superior, Madius the Scythian, currently occupying the role of high king over both Medes and Persians. Even when Teispes began to style himself "King of Anshan," there was no retaliation. Presumably the title "king" was accompanied by a properly submissive attitude and the payment of tribute, even as Persian tribes began to spread across the land of the Elamites. It was this land, not the lands they had occupied in their earlier days, that became known by their name: Persia. It was here that they adopted the Elamite dress, the long ceremonial robes, that later on was identified as distinctively Persian.[13]

Just three or four years later, in 640, Teispes died and left the job of Persian overlord to his son Cyrus. Like his father, Cyrus exercised leadership of the Persian tribes under the umbrella of Madius the Scythian, and like his father, he called himself the King of Anshan. Madius the Scythian continued to exercise his own rule from Ecbatana, with Anshan as a subsidiary city.

THE LAST YEARS of Ashurbanipal's reign were marked by increasing chaos; the inscriptions are fragmentary, the chronicles incomplete. But if his behavior towards Elam is anything to judge by, the king had grown increasingly careless in the administration of his provinces. He may have been ill, or growing senile; from 630 until his death in 627, his son Ashur-etillu-ilani governed the empire in his name, and on his behalf.

Certainly the nearby states were doing what they pleased without fear of Assyrian interference. The Medes and Scythians had begun to make armed excursions into Urartu, closing down one pass after another, blocking one fortress and then the next; the walls of Urartian citadels, excavated two millennia later, had Scythian arrowheads dug into them like a spray of musket balls.[14] Up on the northern border of Urartu, the collapsed wooden roofs of the city of Teishabani (now Karmir Blur) were discovered, studded with charred Scythian arrowheads. Burning arrows, fired into the town, had set it ablaze.[15]

Over in the lands of the Western Semites, King Josiah of Jerusalem was making excursions up into the Assyrian province that had once been Israel, breaking down shrines and defiling the altars of the people settled there in Assyrian deportations by scattering human bones on them.[16] Meanwhile Scythian troops marched past Judah and down towards Egypt, threatening an invasion until Psammetichus came out and made a bargain with them: "With a combination of bribery and entreaty, he persuaded them to come no further," Herodotus writes.[17] And down at the head of the Persian Gulf, the curse of Merodach-baladan was still active; the Chaldean chief Nabopolassar, great-nephew of the old rebel, was inching his own men closer to the walls of Babylon.*

To all of this, Nineveh made no answer.

When Ashurbanipal finally died, in 627, disorder swallowed almost every part of the empire. Ashur-etillu-ilani became king of Assyria, but his brother immediately went down to Babylon and took it for himself. Meanwhile Nabopolassar was marching up from the south to make his own run at the Babylonian throne. For the next six years, three-way fighting went on between the Assyrians at Nineveh, the Assyrians in Babylon, and Nabopolassar, who was unable to take Babylon itself at first, but laid siege to the nearby cities one at a time.

In the middle of this mess, the Medians struck back against their Scythian overlords, who had now ruled over them for twenty-eight years. The Scythians, who were warriors and not administrators, had made themselves increasingly unpopular: "It was not just that they used to exact taxes from their subjects," Herodotus remarks, "but that, if the tax was not enough, they used to ride around and plunder people's belongings."[18]

The Medes, chafing under this treatment, used the Scythian greed to good account. The son of the dead Phraortes, Cyarxes, still lived on his father's estate (it had apparently not occurred to the Scythians that it might be a good plan to eliminate him). According to Herodotus, Cyarxes invited his Scythian ruler and his bodyguard to a banquet in their honor, got them thoroughly drunk, and killed them: "So the Medes regained their empire," Herodotus concludes, "and took control again of the same peoples as before." Cyarxes became high king over the Medes and Persians. At once he reorganized the army to make it stronger. He divided it into squads by specialty (foot soldiers with spears, cavalry, and archers) and began to drill them into perfection.

To the west lay nothing but chaos; to the north, disorganized and nomadic warrior tribes and a dying Urartian kingdom. The Medes and the Persians were poised to take it all over.

* The exact relationship between Nabopolassar and Merodach-baladan is unclear; great-nephew is the best possibility, but there is no direct proof.

TIMELINE 55

		ASSYRIA AND PERSIA	EGYPT AND JUDAH	
				Ahaz
		Shalmaneser V		
MEDIA **Deioces**	PERSIA	**Sargon II** (721–704)		**Hezekiah**
			Shabaka	
	Achamenes	**Sennacherib** (704–680)		
			Tirhakah (690–664)	
		Esarhaddon (680–668)		
Phraortes			*Dynasty 26*	
		Ashurbanipal (668–626)	**Necho I**	
Madius the Scythian	**Teispes** **Cyrus I**		**Psammetichus I**	
				Josiah
		Ashur-etillu-ilani		
	Cyarxes			

Chapter Fifty-Six

Conquest and Tyranny

In Greece, between 687 and 622 BC, Sparta and Athens try to eliminate sin

By the year of Ashurbanipal's death, Greek colonists had gone out to found scores of cities along a widely scattered southwest-to-northeast axis. Greek settlers rebuilt a new city on the Asian coast, on top of Troy's four-hundred-year-old ruins. The Greek cities of Chalcis and Eretria, which had already sent out colonists to found no fewer than nine cities on the Italian peninsula, dispatched more settlers up to the northern Aegean; Chalcis, in fact, sent so many that an entire area of the northern Aegean became known as Chalcidice.[1] The Aegean shore was ringed with Greek cities; the Greeks had become, in Plato's vivid simile, "like frogs around a marsh."[2]

The settlers who ventured out to these new Greek cities were forced to give up their citizenship in their home city, the *metropolis* or "mother city" from which they came.[3] Their entire identity as Greeks lay in their ability to establish a Greek enclosure in the new land. They took with them baskets of Greek grain to plant in foreign fields, and firepots with Greek brands to light the foreign hearthfires. Sustained by Greek food and warmed by Greek fire, they built Greek temples, told Greek tales, and sent their delegations to the Greek games, weaving a Greek net which stretched out from the peninsula itself to cover distant parts of the world.

The scarcity of land on the Greek peninsula had forced each metropolis to send out colonists well before the home city itself had reached maturity. Colonies, surrounded by other peoples, and mother cities grew together. From the very beginning, to be Greek was also to have elements of Asian, Italian, Phoenician, and African culture as well. Greek settlers populated Thrace, the land just north of the passage towards the Black Sea, where the Phrygians had long ago moved across the water into Asia Minor.* Greek adventurers moved through the Bosphorus Strait to the Black Sea itself, where men and women from Miletus—an Ionian city, which had itself been settled by Mycenaean colonists more than a century before—planted as many as seventy colonies around the Black Sea and even up to its north. Colonists sent out from the city of Megara (just west of Athens, on the bridge of land that connected the Peloponnese with the more northern parts of the Greek peninsula), seized two prime sites on either side of the Bosphorus Strait, and built twinned Megaran colonies on the shores: Byzantium on the western shore, Chalcedon on the east.

On the island of Thera, where hardy residents had returned to rebuild around the volcanic crater, the land shortage was particularly drastic. Towards the end of the colonization period, probably around 630 BC, the Therans chose one out of every two sons and sent them off to "Libya": the African coast to the south.

According to the Therans themselves, the expedition landed first on an island off the African coast, but then sent additional settlers ("one in two brothers . . . which one went was to be decided by lot") to extend the Theran colony over to the mainland. The Greek settlement on the North African coast became known as Cyrene.† But the Cyreneans themselves remembered an uglier history. They claimed that the original colonists had been so hungry and hard-pressed on their barren island that they tried to return to Thera. However,

> the Therans refused to let them land . . . they shot at them every time their boats got close to shore and told them to sail back to Libya. Since they had no choice in the matter, they returned.[4]

In the fifty-six years that the first two kings of Cyrene ruled, Herodotus says that "the Cyrenean population remained at pretty much the level it had been when they first set out to colonize Libya."[5] In other words, the conditions on the Libyan coast were so difficult that the colony barely survived. But despite the hardships, things were worse on Thera. The hostility of the Therans towards the returning colonists, who would again overcrowd the island, shows

* See chapter 41, p. 286.

† Cyrene was an unremarkable city until the fourth century BC, when it blossomed into a center of scholarship; it also became the home to many exiled Jews and gained fame for medieval hagiographers as the home city of Simon of Cyrene, the bystander who was pressed into carrying Jesus's cross and the father of Saint Rufus of Rome.

56.1 The Spreading Greek World

that the sending out of Greek families to colonies was literally a matter of life and death.

THE CITY OF SPARTA, in the center of the Peloponnese, took a different approach to the problem of growth.

The inhabitants of Sparta were Dorians who had settled on Mycenaean ruins and built a city of their own. Sparta lay in a river valley, on the eastern bank of the Eurotas, which flowed down from the mountains in the north. The river was useful as a water supply, but it was shallow, rocky, and unnavigable; so the Spartans had no ships. While the Greek cities on the coast were sending out boatloads of colonists to the east and to the west, the Spartans armed themselves, crossed over the Taygetus mountain range on their western border, and attacked the city of Messene, which lay on the other side. The motivation was mostly practical; seventy or so years later, the Spartan poet Tyrtaeus, writing of the war, calls the city "wide-spaced Messene . . . good for ploughing and good for planting."[6]

It was not an easy conquest; Tyrtaeus says that the Spartans and Messenians fought for twenty years. But by 630, Messene had become a subject city of Sparta. Sparta was no longer simply a Greek city: it was a little kingdom. In this Spartan kingdom, the conquered Messenians became a whole class of slaves, who grew food for their captors on terms as harsh as anything found in medieval feudalism: "Just like asses, worn out by their mighty burdens," Tyrtaeus says, "they bring to their masters through wretched necessity a half of all the fruit that the land brings forth."[7] The Spartans themselves became the aristocracy, a master race of warrior men and mothers of soldiers.

The Spartan state had a peculiarity not found anywhere else in the ancient world: it had two kings, descendants of legendary twin brothers who had ruled Sparta generations before, while spending "the whole of their adult lives quarrelling with each other."[8] The Spartan people preferred two kings at odds, rather than one directing affairs with unchallenged power.*

The two-king system, although it produced its own difficulties, did prevent the rise of a Mesopotamian-style monarchy. The Spartans did not, like the Assyrians, find it divinely ordained that the gods should select one man to rule over them. Ashurbanipal's claim to be king "by order of the great gods,"

* The oldest son of the senior twin, Eurysthenes, was named Agis; so the line of kings descended from Eurysthenes were called the Agiads. The junior twin, Procles, was succeeded by *his* eldest son, Euryphon, and so the junior line of kings became known as the Eurypontids. The Agiads and the Eurypontids ruled Sparta together until 192 BC.

appointed by them to "exercise sovereignty," was not only foreign but repulsive.[9] In Sparta, the Sumerian fear of inherited and limitless royal power, which had once found its expression in the ancient tales of that power ending by death, made a strong return.

Even with two kings playing tug-of-war with power, the Spartans kept on shoring themselves up against a concentration of power in the hands of the monarchy. Any ancient kingdom had three primary powers: the military power to declare war and lead the army; the judicial power to make laws and enforce them; and the priestly power to maintain good relationships with the gods. Israel was one of the earliest nations to fix this three-way power into law with any kind of formal division, with the official state roles of prophet, priest, and king. In Sparta, the kings held all three powers—but with significant limitations. They were priests of Zeus and received oracles from the gods, but four state officials also had the right to hear the prophecies; the kings could not ignore evil omens without the knowledge of the people. The kings had the unilateral right to declare war, but they were required to be first in the charge and last in the retreat, which undoubtedly kept them from sending the army out into needless battles. And by the time of Herodotus, the judicial power of the king had shrunk to two odd and particular roles. He was allowed to make the sole decision about "who should marry an heiress whose father has died without having betrothed her to anyone, and to adjudicate in cases concerning the public highways." The rest of the lawmaking fell on a council of twenty-eight elders.[10]

But the real power in Sparta was neither king, nor priest, nor even the Council of Twenty-Eight. The Spartan state was ruled by a strict and unwritten code of laws that governed every aspect of Spartan existence.

Our knowledge of most of these laws comes from Plutarch, who lived centuries later. But even allowing for distortion, the laws of Sparta seem to have governed every aspect of life from the greatest to the tiniest. Children did not belong to their families but to the city of Sparta; the council of elders had the right to inspect each baby and give it permission to live, or else order it laid out to die on the *Apothetai,* the "place of exposure," a wasteland in the Taygetus mountains. Boys were assigned at the age of seven to "boy herds" which ran in packs, learning to fight and forage for food. Any husband could choose to impregnate another woman, or to hand his wife over to another man, as long as the decision was made for the good of the master race: "Suppose an older man with a young wife liked and approved of a young man of nobility and virtue. . . . once the younger man had impregnated his wife with his noble seed, he could adopt the child as his own. Or . . . [if] a man of high principles admired a woman who was married to someone else for her modesty and fine children . . . he could prevail upon her husband to let him sleep with her, so that he could sow his seed in rich and fertile soil, so to speak."[11]

This minute regulation of public acts inevitably led to the legislation of private desires. The Spartans had most of their meals, by law, in common "messes," in order to prevent greed: "This stopped them spending time at home reclining at table on expensive couches," Plutarch explains, "fattening themselves up in the dark like insatiable animals . . . and ruining themselves morally as well as physically by indulging every whim and gorging themselves." Girls, who were the future mothers of Spartan warriors, were required to dance naked in front of crowds of young men; this gave them additional motivation to stay slim (Plutarch adds that the stakes were levelled somewhat by another law which gave the girls an opportunity to "taunt the young men one by one and helpfully criticize their errors.")[12] The doors and roofs of houses could be shaped only by axe and saw; to use more refined tools was illegal. This was meant to prevent a longing for fine furniture and fabrics, since these would look ridiculous next to rough-hewn wood.*

These laws were unwritten. Another oral law explained that it was against the law to write laws down. Legislation only works if it is written on the character and hearts of the citizens, a "steady inclination which recreates the intention of the legislator in each and every person." The Spartans themselves continually watched each other for violations of unwritten regulations: "It was not even possible for a rich man to eat at home first and then go to the common mess with a full stomach," Plutarch remarks, "because everyone else was alert to the possibility, and they used to watch out for people who would not drink or eat with them, and taunt them for their lack of self-control."[13]

Several generations later, the Spartan Demaratus tried to explain to Xerxes how this constant lawmaking had affected the Spartan character. "Although they're free, they're not entirely free," he told the Persian king. "Their master is the law, and they're far more afraid of this than your men are of you. . . . They do whatever the law commands, and its command never changes: it is

* Plutarch's description of Spartan life comes in his study of the life of Lycurgus, a legendary Spartan prince (brother to one king and uncle to the next) who single-handedly put Sparta's law code into place and then retired from public power and starved himself to death in order to show that he did not crave power. Plutarch himself says that there is absolutely no proof that Lycurgus ever existed, and he probably is entirely mythical; the scope of the laws he supposedly invented, the cultural institutions he was said to have put single-handedly into place, and his other accomplishments (he is credited with assembling the fragments of Homer's epics into a single tale, a most unlikely event) are none of them possible for a single man. But it is intriguing that Spartan tradition found it necessary to put a human face on the origins of the Spartan law system; it suggests a certain discomfort with the severity of the laws, even as those laws were followed.

that they should not turn tail in battle no matter how many men are ranged against them, but should maintain their positions and either win or die."[14]

They are far more afraid of the law, than your men are of you. The Spartan state, designed to escape the absolutism of an eastern monarchy, had exceeded it.

TO THE NORTH, across the land bridge that connected the Peloponnese to the rest of the peninsula, Athens had also grown to be something larger than a city, and had gone one further than Sparta by getting rid of its king altogether.

In very ancient times, the Mycenaean city of Athens had been ruled by the mythological Theseus, whose palace stood on the high rock—the Acropolis, "high point of the city"—at the center of Athens. During the fading days of Mycenaean domination, many of the people of Athens had either wandered away, or died of famine or plague. But some remained to keep the city alive.

Over two or three centuries, Athens slowly recovered from whatever catastrophes had drained its population away. When colonization began, Athens sent its own citizens east, to become part of the Ionian settlements along the Asia Minor coast.[15]

The happenings in these years before 650 or so are preserved only very sketchily, in accounts written long after the time. Around AD 310, Eusebius, the bishop of Caesarea in Palestine, put together a chronological table of ancient times which describes a seven-hundred-year succession of Athenian kings, beginning around 1500 BC:

> We will now list the kings of the Athenians, starting with Cecrops. . . . The total duration of the reigns of all [his descendants] . . . was 450 years.[16]

This list has about as much historical truth to it as the deeds of the Greek god Dionysius, who was supposedly born (out of Zeus's thigh) during the reign of the fifth Athenian king.* But it does tell us that Athens once had kings. Gradually, though, the power of the monarch was dispersed. After four and a half centuries, the role of king was renamed: the rule of Athens was still passed from father to son and lasted a lifetime, but the ruler was now called

* This is a roundabout source, to say the least; Eusebius is quoting the Greek grammarian Castor, whose original accounts (probably dating from around 200 BC) have been lost; and the original chronicle of Eusebius itself has been lost, surviving only in a Latin translation made by the Roman churchman St. Jerome around AD 365, and in an Armenian translation from the sixth century (both of which preserve overlapping but different parts of the text). It is still the most direct account we have of the earliest Athenians.

an *archon*: a chief justice. Another official, the *polemarch*, was given control of the military, while a third carried out priestly functions.

Thirteen archons later, the Athenians voted to give the *archons* ten-year terms; seventy years later, the office was transformed again, to become a one-year appointment. "The first annual *archon,*" Eusebius writes, "was Creon, in the year of the 24th Olympiad"—in other words, 684 BC.

This is all we get from Eusebius, who then wanders off into an interminable list of Olympic champions in various events over 249 consecutive Olympic Games. But other fragmentary accounts, pieced together, show a slow and crooked path away from monarchy towards an oligarchy: a sort of aristocratic democracy. By 683, a board of nine landowners carried out the job of archon. They were elected by other landowners, but an assembly of all Athenians—the *ekklesia*—had to confirm the elections. Ex-archons became members of the Council of Areiopagos, which met down below the western side of the Acropolis, on the top of a low rise called the "Hill of Ares."[17]

This was more complex and less efficient than the Spartan system. But then the Athenians were not continually repressing an unhappy subject population, and they did not need to fight to expand. By 640, Athens too had enfolded its neighbors within its borders, but the incorporation seems to have happened more or less peacefully, with the outlying villages seeing the advantage of falling beneath Athenian protection. The little jut of land south of the city, a district known as Attica, was almost entirely under Athenian control. Athens, ringed by low mountains on the east, west, and north, did not try to fling its control much farther away.

In 632, though, the seams of the semi-democratic practice gaped wide open. An Olympic champion named Cylon (he shows up in Eusebius's lists as the winner of the *diaulos*, or "double race," the 400-metre foot race, in the Olympic Games eight years previously)[18] made a bid to turn the archonship into something else.

"Cylon," Thucydides writes, "was inquiring at Delphi when he was told by the god to seize the Acropolis of Athens on the grand festival of Zeus." The Delphic oracle was a priestess who sat on a three-legged stool next to a sizable crack on top of the Sibylline Rock, a good-sized boulder on an outcropping of Mount Parnassas. Worshippers climbed to the rock and put a question to the priestess, who then asked the earth-goddess Gaia for an answer and received it by way of the crack. She then delivered the answer in a trance to a set of attendant priests, who cast it into hexameter verse and delivered it back to the questioner. The crack, the trance, and the hexameters combined to produce generally puzzling answers, open to interpretation (which also made it very difficult to prove the oracle wrong).

Cylon, mulling his answer over, decided that the "grand festival of Zeus" must refer to the upcoming Olympic Games. What more appropriate time for an Olympic victor to seize power? And so he borrowed a band of armed men from his father-in-law, rounded up his friends, and occupied the Acropolis, announcing "the intention of making himself tyrant."[19]

"Tyrant" was a technical term in Greek politics; it referred to a politician who leapfrogged the normal routes of power (election and then confirmation) and took control of a city's government by force. Tyrants were not necessarily cruel, although they tended to be autocratic in order to keep hold of their power; and various Greek cities scattered throughout the peninsula were governed by tyrants at different points (as a matter of fact, Cylon's father-in-law was the tyrant of the city of Megara, not far from Athens on the east, which explains why he had personal bands of armed soldiers to lend).

But Cylon had chosen the wrong "grand festival of Zeus." The oracle had apparently been talking about a later festival which took place well outside the city; Cylon had picked a bad time for his takeover.

This suggests that he was not an experienced conspirator; anyone who had been involved in political intrigue would have realized that a takeover would be most effective when all the men of the city had left it for a festival outside. Rather than rolling over, the Athenians grew indignant:

> As soon as the Athenians perceived [the takeover], they . . . sat down, and laid siege to the citadel. But as time went on . . . the responsibility of keeping guard [was] left to the nine archons, with plenary powers to arrange everything according to their good judgement. . . . Meanwhile Cylon and his besieged companions were distressed for want of food and water. Accordingly Cylon and his brother made their escape; but the rest being hard pressed, and some even dying of famine, seated themselves as suppliants at the altar in the Acropolis.[20]

The conspirators begged for mercy in the name of Athena, at whose altar they sat. The archons agreed to spare their lives, but when the men began to stagger out, the archons ordered them killed. Several flung themselves against the altars of the goddesses Demeter and Persephone, but were murdered anyway—a dreadful breach of protocol, since anyone who begged for the protection of a god at his altar was supposed to be spared.

For this crime, the other Athenians exiled the archons who had ordered the massacre. When they tried to return, they were driven away again, this time with more force; and the bodies of their colleagues were dug up and flung after them.[21] Cylon himself remained, prudently, vanished and did not reappear in Athenian history.

But the fighting and general unrest that followed showed that Athens was not at peace under its archons. Archons did, in most cases, as they pleased. In his history of the Athenian constitution, written several centuries later, Aristotle points out that Athenian "democracy" was in fact run by a few privileged and powerful men. Like the Spartans, who thought they were free but were enslaved by their law, the Athenians were free in name only: "In fact the poor themselves, and also their wives and children were actually in slavery to the rich," Aristotle writes. "[T]hey were called Sixth-Part-Tenants, for that was the rent they paid for the rich men's land which they farmed, and the whole of the country was in few hands. And if they ever failed to pay their rents, they themselves and their children were liable to arrest. . . . Thus the most grievous and bitter thing in the state of public affairs for the masses was their slavery; not but what they were discontent also about everything else, for they found themselves virtually without a share in anything."[22]

In response to the unrest, the Athenians did exactly what the Spartans had refused to do: they decided that it was time for the laws of Athens, which had always been oral, to be set down in writing. The good judgment of aristocrats was no longer sufficient to run the city; Athens needed a code.

The man who took on the job of taking down the most important of the massive oral traditions, systematizing them, and turning them into a written code was a councilor named Draco. Draco's version of the Athenian laws was remarkable not for what it outlawed (murder, theft, adultery) but for the penalty of death which was attached to so many crimes. Like the code of Hammurabi, the laws of Draco knew nothing of lesser and greater offenses: "The death penalty had been fixed for almost all crimes," Plutarch says, "which meant that even people convicted of not working were to be put to death, and the theft of vegetables or fruit carried the same penalty as temple-robbery and homicide."[23]

Draco himself, asked why so drastic a set of punishments, is reported to have said, "Even petty crimes deserve death, and I cannot find a more serious penalty for the greater crimes." It is a severity which gives us our English words *draconian* and *drastic*; and in its relentless expectation that men can be made perfect, it is oddly reminiscent of the Spartan view of crime.*

* Draco's law on homicide is the only one which directly survives, and even it is in fragments. However, the other laws in his code are mentioned frequently by Greek writers, and enough can be reconstructed from these references to give us a good idea of their content.

Plutarch writes that a Spartan, asked by another Greek how adultery was punished in Sparta, remarked, "He would have to pay a fine—a bull from his herd, large enough to reach over Mount Taygetus and drink from the Eurotas." "How could there be a bull that big?" the visitor protested, to which the Spartan replied, "How could there be an adulterer in Sparta?"[24] The laws were intended to eliminate all wrongdoing because they were engraved only on Spartan hearts. In Athens, that otherwise very different Greek city, the leaders also believed that in a just society, where the citizens are properly trained and warned, there will be no crime. Both cities had gotten rid of the power of their kings; both found the need for some other law-keeper to stand in the monarch's place.

And in both, the desire to give every citizen the ability to reach perfection led to a city in which citizens policed each other's lives. A stele uncovered in the ruins of Athens makes it clear that Draco's death penalty could be exercised by the Athenian citizens themselves: any man could kill a kidnapper, adulterer, or burglar caught in the act.[25] The laws which were intended to bring equality had made each citizen an enforcer.

Around 600 BC, an Athenian named Solon stepped forwards to make a second stab at establishing a fair law code. He was a young man from a good family, but his father had spent most of the family wealth in ill-judged generosity, forcing the son into the merchant trade. He was a lover of luxury, of good food and drink, and notorious for his love affairs: "Solon was not immune to good-looking young men," Plutarch remarks, primly.[26]

His business prospered, and like many later business luminaries, Solon got involved in local politics. Plutarch, from whom we have most of the details of Solon's life, writes that when it became clear that Athens was headed towards civil war, "the most sensible Athenians began to look to Solon" because he was respectably middle-class: "He had no part in the wrongdoing of the rich, and was not caught up in the afflictions of the poor either. . . . The rich found him acceptable because of his wealth, and the poor because of his integrity."[27]

Solon, elected archon, revoked the laws of Draco (except the penalty for homicide) and set about relegislating. He wrote new regulations that covered everything from the qualifications for holding public office to acceptable boundaries for mourning the dead (grief was fine, but sacrificing a cow, lacerating oneself, or visiting the tombs of people who weren't actually family members was over the top).

But the touchiest issues had to do with righting the inequalities of wealth in the city, which was a predictably thankless task. "Both sides had high hopes," Plutarch points out, which meant Solon was bound to disappoint someone. Which he did, almost at once, by cancelling the overwhelming debts of the poor, and by redistributing land so that the farmers who had cultivated it for generations now owned it.[28]

This didn't please the Athenian aristocracy. Nor did it please the debtors, who had hoped for a good deal more than debt cancellation; they had wanted land redistributed equally to all, but the poorest still had no holdings of their own. "We have his own words on the fact that he offended most of the people of Athens by failing to fulfill their expectations," Plutarch writes, and quotes a poem attributed to Solon: "Once their minds were filled with vain hopes, but now / In anger all look askance at me, as if I were their foe."

This state of affairs had actually been predicted by an acquaintance of Solon's, a stranger to Athens, who had visited the city earlier and found Solon busily writing out laws. The visitor laughed: "These decrees of yours are not different from spiders' webs," he said, according to Plutarch. "They'll restrain anyone weak and insignificant who gets caught in them, but they'll be torn to shreds by people of power and wealth."[29]

Solon disagreed. No one would break the laws, he insisted, if they were properly fitted to the needs of each citizen. It was an idealistic view of human nature, and Solon himself put it to the test by departing from Athens for ten years, as soon as the laws were enacted, in order to let them do their work free from any appeals to his person. "He claimed to be travelling to see the world,"

TIMELINE 56

ASSYRIA AND PERSIA			GREECE
		Shalmaneser V	Greek colonies spread through Asia Minor, the Aegean, Africa, and the land around the Black Sea
MEDIA	PERSIA	**Sargon II** (721–704)	
Deioces			
	Achamenes	**Sennacherib** (704–680)	**Creon of Athens**
			Sparta invades Messene
		Esarhaddon (680–668)	
Phraortes		**Ashurbanipal** (668–626)	Athens controls Attica
Madius the Scythian	**Teispes** **Cyrus I**		Cylon's revolt (632)
		Ashur-etillu-ilani	
	Cyarxes		Draco's laws
			Solon (600)

Herodotus writes, "but it was really to avoid the possibility of having to repeal any of the laws he had made."[30] (And also, possibly, from sheer annoyance: "Once his laws were in force," Plutarch writes, "not a day passed without several people coming up to him to express approval or disapproval, or to recommend the insertion of some point or other into the statutes, or the removal of something from them. . . . They would question him about it and ask him to explain in detail the meaning and purpose of every single point.")[31]

And how did this work?

With Solon gone, Athenian politics soon fell back into its old divisive squabbles. "The result of the laws," Plutarch says, regretfully, "justified the visitor's conjecture, rather than Solon's expectations." The Athenian experiment had again failed to bring justice, let alone peace; and a small group of Athenians began to plan for the inevitable tyranny.

Chapter Fifty-Seven

The Beginnings and End of Empire

Between 650 and 605 BC, Rome becomes Etruscan, and Babylon becomes queen of the world

On the Tiber river, the two-hill settlement of Rome had grown. The mythological Sabine co-ruler Titus Tatius, killed in a riot, had not been replaced; Romulus ruled alone. The dual population of Latial tribesmen and Sabine immigrants was now dominated by the Latials.

Rome's growth had not gone unnoticed by its neighbors. Not long after Titus Tatius's death, the men of Fidenae, just above Rome on the Tiber, sacked Roman farms along the river. Then the city of Veii, on the river's other side, started burning fields as well. Romulus fought off one threat and negotiated a peace with the other. But these attacks were signs of a bigger problem. "Veii," Livy observes, "like Fidenae, was an Etruscan town."[1]

The Etruscan towns stretched in a loose network of alliances up to the north. The Etruscans and Latials had once shared common customs, but the villagers north of the Tiber had been altered by newcomers. The Cimmerian sweep into Asia Minor had sent Phrygians and Lydians scrambling away into Thrace, across the narrow waters of the Bosphorus Strait and the Hellespont. This began a chain reaction of peoples shifting west; tribes driven into northern Italy filtered down into Villanovan land, where they mingled and traded and intermarried.[2] They were joined by refugees directly from Asia Minor, fleeing from cities that had fallen to fire, siege, and invasion. Roman legend told of the Trojan hero Aeneas carrying his father on his back away from the shattered city of Troy, making his way as an exile through Thrace, and then sailing to Sicily and from there to the Italian coast, where he settled and took a wife, sired sons, and became a king in his

57.1 Rome and Her Neighbors

own right: a mythical reflection of real immigration from the east.[3] This meld of Villanovans and newcomers was an alchemy of native tradition and eastern skills that produced a new people: the Etruscans, strong builders and wealthy merchants who did not intend to let the Latial upstarts to the south expand without challenge.

Etruscan hostility was not the only cloud on Romulus's horizon during his forty-year reign. "Great though Romulus was," Livy remarks, "he was better loved by the commons than by the senate, and best of all by the army."[4] The early kings of Rome were no more able to rule autocratically than the Greek monarchs were; Livy's use of the term "senate" is probably an anachronism, but some council of elders was keeping watch on the king's power. Even the semidivine Romulus had to reckon with them, as the circumstances of his death make clear: Livy writes that he was reviewing his troops one day when

> a storm burst, with violent thunder. A cloud enveloped him, so thick that it hid him from the eyes of everyone present; and from that moment he was never seen again upon earth. . . . The senators, who had been standing at the king's side . . . now declared that he had been carried up on high by a whirlwind. . . . Every man hailed him as a god and son of a god, and prayed to him. . . . However, even on this great occasion there were, I believe, a few dissenters who secretly maintained that the king had been torn to pieces by the senators.[5]

Whether or not Romulus had been assassinated by the senators, they were not long in asserting their power. They took control of the throne themselves, and declared a rule by committee. But the Sabine population of the city objected loudly. No Sabine had held power since the death of Romulus's co-regent, decades before, and they wanted a Sabine king.

The senators agreed to a Sabine king, as long as they could choose him. The Sabine they picked was Numa Pompilius. He was not a great general but a wise man, famous for his justice. "Rome had originally been founded by force of arms," Livy concludes; "the new king now prepared to give the community a second beginning, this time on the solid basis of law and religious observance."[6] Like Romulus, Numa Pompilius is probably legend, but his rule stands for a transition: Rome was moving from its roots as a colony established by war, towards a settled and mature existence as a city. Under Numa Pompilius, the gates to the Temple of Janus, god of war, were shut for the first time, symbolizing that Rome was at peace with the outside.

But the city continued at odds with itself. Dionysius of Halicarnassus (a Greek historian who went to Rome in the reign of Augustus Caesar and spent twenty-two years writing a history of the city) tells us that the "Alban element, who together with Romulus had planted the colony, claimed the right [of] . . . enjoying the greatest honours. . . . The new settlers thought that they ought not . . . to stand in an inferior position to the others. This was felt particularly by those who were of the Sabine race."[7]

None of the people who lived in Rome thought of themselves as *Romans*; they lived within the same walls, but that was their only point of agreement. This left "the affairs of State," in Dionysius's vivid phrase, "in a raging sea of confusion."

In addition, the peace with the outside was only temporary. The next two kings after Numa—the Latin Tullus Hostilius and the Sabine Ancus Marcius, both appointed by the Senate—led campaigns against the surrounding cities and tribes, doubling the size of Rome by force. If Rome ever did experience a time of tranquillity, it was brief; Rome had gone quickly back to its identity as an armed camp, threatening the peace of its neighbors.

The neighbors were not helpless, though. A native of the Etruscan city Tarquinii, on the northern coast above the Tiber, had set his sights on control of Rome.

This man, Lucumo, was mixed race by birth. His mother was Etruscan, but his father was a Greek from Corinth, a man named Demeter who had (according to Livy) been "forced by political troubles to leave his country."[8] Lucumo found himself facing the scorn of the "full-blooded" Etruscans around him, and with his wife decided to go to Rome, where race mattered less than opportunity: "There would be opportunities for an active and courageous man in a place where all advancement came swiftly and depended upon ability," Livy writes. After all, more than one Sabine had risen to be king over the Latins; foreign blood was no bar to ability.

Settled in Rome, the Etruscan Lucumo worked energetically (and scattered money around) until he became the right-hand man of the king himself. Ancus Marcius even appointed Lucumo guardian of the royal princes. When the king died, the two princes were still young: "one still a child in years," Dionysius records, "and the elder just growing a beard."[9] Lucumo sent the princes out of town ("on a hunting expedition," Livy remarks) and began at once to canvass for votes. He was proclaimed king by an overwhelming majority and, in 616, ascended the throne of Rome. Later historians knew him as Lucius Tarquinius Priscus, or Tarquin the Elder.

After nearly forty years of reign, he was succeeded by his son-in-law, Servius Tullius, whose destiny as king had been revealed to the Roman people when, as a child, his head burst into flame. (He was sleeping at the time; a servant offered to throw water on his head, but when he woke up of his own accord, the fire went out. "From that time," Livy explains, "the child was treated like a prince of the blood . . . he grew to be a man of truly royal nature," and Tarquin the Elder betrothed his own daughter to him and made him heir.)

Servius Tullius, like his father-in-law, was an Etruscan. These two kings stand for a historical truth: the city of Rome, quarrelsome and pious by turns, constantly at war with its neighbors, throwing its walls around the nearby hills one by one, was itself swallowed by the greater, stronger, and older culture to its north. Etruscan cities had already spread up all the way up to the Bottomless River: the old name for the Po, across the Apennines. To the northwest, Etruscan cities controlled the copper, iron, and silver mines in the so-called Metal-Bearing Hills.[10] This metal was traded to the Greek colonies along the

Italian coast, and contact with the Greek trading cities brought the Etruscans face-to-face with the Greek writing system. The Etruscans began to use the Greek alphabet to label their own goods, using their own language written in Greek characters.* Despite the recognizable letters, the language itself remains a puzzle: it appears almost entirely in brief inscriptions which have not been decoded.[11]

Rome did not become part of some entity called "Etruria." There was no "Etrurian empire," merely a set of Etruscan cities that shared a language and certain customs and were sometimes allies, sometimes enemies. The Etruscan move into Rome was the infiltration of a city already occupied by several different national groups by one more group—this one more influential than the rest.

Livy credits the Etruscan Tarquin the Elder with the planning of the Circus Maximus, the great Roman stadium that lay between the Palatine and Aventine hills, and the laying of the foundations for the Temple of Jupiter, on the Capitol; Dionysius adds that he squared off the walls and began the digging of sewers to drain the city's waste (a less dramatic but infinitely more useful accomplishment). The Etruscan Servius Tullius is praised for claiming the Quirinal and Viminal hills, and building trenches and earthworks to reinforce Rome's walls. These real structures were indeed built by Etruscans. Romans had little talent for building, but in Etruria, religious rituals governed the founding of towns, the laying out of walls, and the placement of gates.[12] Etruscan cities, excavated, show planned streets, laid out in a grid (something which the Romans had not yet considered). Like the long-ago cities of the Harappan Indians, Etruscan streets had standardized widths for main streets, the secondary roads that crossed them, and the minor roads that lay between. In Rome itself, excavation shows that sometime around 650, the huts in which most Romans lived (made of branches woven together, with walls of mud packed into the interstices) began to be knocked down in favor of stone houses. The huts on the western side of town were cleared away, and the open space was packed down hard, to serve as a city gathering place: later, this square became known as the Roman Forum.[13]

The very material of Rome was gaining an Etruscan stamp. So was its monarchy. Dionysius writes that Tarquin the Elder introduced to Rome the

* Etruscan history is generally divided into five periods: the Villanovan (900–700 BC); the Orientalizing (700–600), so named because Etruscan culture was borrowing heavily from the Greeks to the east; the Archaic (600–480), the height of Etruscan political power; the Classical (480–300), which saw the beginning of a decline in Etruscan might; and the Roman (300–100), during which the Romans became entirely dominant both politically and culturally.

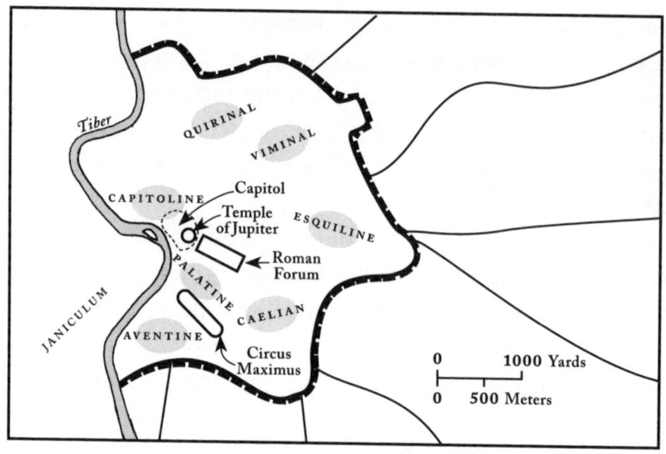

57.2 The City of Rome

Etruscan symbols of kingship: "a crown of gold and an embroidered purple robe . . . [he] sat on a throne of ivory holding an ivory sceptre in his hand." He was attended, when he went out, by twelve bodyguards (known as *lictors*), each of whom carried an axe bound into the middle of a bunch of rods: the *fasces*, which represented the power of the king both to discipline wrongdoers and execute serious criminals.[14]

Under Servius Tullius, "the size of the city was greatly increased," and he reigned forty-four years as king, Etruscan monarch over a mixed population of Etruscans, Latins, and Sabines. And Rome went on fighting: the city's soldiers fought with Sabine cities and Latin cities, and warded off assaults from other Etruscan kings who resented Roman control of the important ford at the Tiber river. Dionysius and Livy both tell the story of war after war, between Rome and Collatia, Rome and Fidenae, Rome and a five-city coalition of Etruscans, Rome and Eretum: unending war.

WHILE ROME struggled for its beginnings, an old empire was crashing to the ground to the east.

The three-way fighting in Assyria had continued. Ashurbanipal's heir at Nineveh, Ashur-etillu-ilani, had mobilized the Assyrian army against his brother Sin-shum-ishkun, now in command of a mixed Assyrian and Babylonian force headquartered at Babylon. The Chaldean king Nabopolassar, meanwhile, was driving his way up against the Babylonian forces from the south, taking away one ancient Sumerian city after another.

After years of fighting (how many is completely unclear, since the various

Babylonian king lists differ), Sin-shum-ishkun was forced to give up the defense of Babylon, and Nabopolassar marched into the city. But the confused accounts of the outcome suggest that Sin-shum-ishkun may have surrendered the south, only to go north and seize his brother's throne; Ashur-etillu-ilani disappears from the accounts from this point on. The heartland was in disarray, and now a Chaldean sat on the throne of Babylon.

Once established, Nabopolassar took up the fighting again—against the Assyrian empire itself. He had already planned his strategy: to fight his way first all the way up the Euphrates river, "liberating" one province after another, and then to turn and fight his way towards the Tigris to the east, towards Nineveh itself.

In this, he had help. Cyarxes, the Median king of the Medes and the Persians, knew an opportunity when he saw one. He offered his friendship to Nabopolassar, who accepted. They agreed to divide the Assyrian provinces, once Assyria had fallen; and Nabopolassar married off his son, the Babylonian crown prince (and his father's most trusted general) Nebuchadnezzar, to the Median princess Amytis, the daughter of Cyarxes.[15]

Together, the Medes and Persians fought with the Babylonians against the elderly empire that had dominated the world for so long. Babylonian chronicles record Assyria's slow fall: "In the tenth year," it begins, "Nabopolassar, in the month of Aiaru, mobilized the Babylonian army and marched up the bank of the Euphrates. The people . . . did not attack him, but laid their tribute before him."[16]

The tenth year—ten years after Nabopolassar had crowned himself king of the Chaldeans, in the wake of Esarhaddon's death—would have been 616/615 BC. The month of Aiaru was springtime, late April to early May; and the peoples along the Euphrates could see the writing on the wall.

After another year of fighting, Nabopolassar had reached Assur and laid siege to it. He had to retreat, after a mere month, and was forced to hole up in a nearby fortress for the summer. The Medes had apparently returned to their own land, but now they came back to aid their Babylonian ally. Rather than joining up with Nabopolassar, they made straight for the Assyrian heartland. Cyarxes crossed the Tigris and laid siege to Assur himself, and succeeded where Nabopolassar had failed. He captured the city and raided it for captives and goods; afterwards, he permitted the Median troops to massacre everyone left inside. Nabopolassar arrived, with his own army, after the city was thoroughly destroyed.[17]

The two kings planned, together, the final assault on Nineveh. Some months were spent in preparation; the Median army made a visit home to refurbish itself, and Nabopolassar took a few months to terrify various rebellious cities along the Euphrates into submission. But by 612, the assault troops were ready. "In the fourteenth year," the Babylonian Chronicle says, "the king of Babylon mobilized his army, and the king of the Medes came to where the Babylonians were encamped. They went along the banks of the Tigris to Nineveh. From the month of May to the month of July they made an assault on the city. And at the beginning of August, the city was taken."

Between May and August there was a bit of drama that the Babylonian Chronicle doesn't record, but which is preserved by Herodotus. Cyarxes, according to the *Histories,* was all set to destroy Nineveh, when his siege was disrupted by "a huge Scythian army, led by their king Madius."[18] (This was probably the grandson of the original Madius the Scythian, who had dominated the Medes fifty years or so earlier.) The Scythians chose the moment for attack well—but the Median and Persian troops, trained and organized by Cyarxes, turned from the siege and wiped them up.[19]

Then the soldiers turned back to Nineveh. A tributary of the Tigris ran through the city beneath the walls, providing it with water and making it difficult to besiege. But it seems likely that the attackers built a dam to divert more of the Tigris into the city, carrying away the foundations of the walls and breaking them away. Diodorus of Sicily, a Greek historian writing six hundred years later, says that the Ninevites put their confidence in a "divine oracle given to their fathers, that Nineveh the city would never be taken or surrender until the stream that ran through the city became its enemy; the king supposed that this would never come to pass." It is an after-the-fact prophecy that probably reflects an actual event.[20]

With the walls crumbling, the Babylonians stormed the city and sacked it. "A great slaughter was made of the people," the Chronicle tells us, "and the nobles, and Sin-shum-ishkun, king of Assyria, fled. . . . They turned the city into a mound and ruin heap."[21] The Jewish prophet Nahum, celebrating the destruction of the empire that had laid waste to the northern part of his country, offers a glimpse of the horror:

> The river gates are thrown open,
> the palace collapses.
> It is decreed: the city will be exiled, carried away. . . .
> Nineveh is like a pool,
> and its water is draining away. . . .
> She is pillaged, plundered, stripped,
> Hearts melt, knees give way,
> bodies tremble, every face grows pale. . . .
> Many casualties, piles of dead,

bodies without number,
people stumbling over the corpses. . . .
Nothing can heal your wound;
your injury is fatal.
Everyone who hears the news about you
claps his hands at your fall,
for who has not felt your endless cruelty?[22]

The Assyrians had flooded Babylon a hundred years earlier; now the Babylonians were returning the favor.

The Assyrian king fled towards the city of Haran.* The victorious Medes claimed the eastern territory, including the land which had once belonged to the Scythians; Babylon took over the old western provinces. And somewhere between Nineveh and Haran, Sin-shum-ishkun died or was killed. Assur-uballit, an army officer and royal cousin, took his title.

With a new king and a new capital, the depleted Assyrian army made one more attempt to gather itself. But Nabopolassar did not leave Haran long in peace. After putting down various Assyrian cities which had tried to take advantage of the chaos by declaring their independence from both Assyria and Babylon, Nabopolassar marched back towards Haran in 610, meeting up with Cyarxes and leading the joint force towards the city. When Assur-uballit got wind of this new front, he and his men deserted the city before the Median-Babylonian force had even shown up on the Orion. "Fear of the enemy fell upon them," the Babylonian Chronicle says, "and they forsook the city." Nabopolassar arrived at the defenseless city, looted it, and went back home.

But Assur-uballit was not quite done. He sent a message down south, to ask the pharaoh of Egypt for help.

The Assyrian-trained Psammetichus I of the Twenty-sixth Dynasty had died at a ripe old age, after a reign of more than fifty years. Now his son, Necho II, had assumed the throne.† Despite his father's fight against the Assyrians decades before, Necho II was not averse to helping out the Assyrians now. He had plans to make Egypt more important in world affairs (he was already hiring Greek mercenary sailors to strengthen his army, and one of his pet projects was the digging of a canal that would connect the Nile river to

* See map on p. 132.

† The pharaohs of the Twenty-Sixth Dynasty are known by both Greek and Egyptian names. I have used the Greek names since these are more familiar. The Egyptian names are Psamtik I (Psammetichus I), Nekau (Necho II), Psamtik II (Psammetichus II), Wahibre (Apries), Ahmose II (Amasis), and Psamtik III (Psammetichus III).

the Red Sea, improving Egyptian trade with the east by water),[23] and if Egypt was going to once again throw its net outside its own borders, the logical place for expansion was the Western Semitic lands along the Mediterranean. The rise of a strong Babylonian empire would not allow for Egyptian takeover of those Mediterranean territories. Anyway, if the Assyrians fell, one more barrier against the Scythians (who had already shown up at Egypt's borders once during Necho II's childhood) would be gone.

And so he agreed. Assur-uballit suggested that the city of Carchemish would be a good place to meet up and organize the joint force for an attack, and Necho II set out to march north.

He did not pass by Jerusalem unnoticed. "While Josiah was king," the writer of 2 Kings says, "Pharaoh Necho king of Egypt went up the Euphrates to help the king of Assyria."[24]

Josiah of Judah had taken advantage of the Assyrian disintegration to reassert his own independence; he had led a religious revival, getting rid of all traces of Assyrian shrines and cults; and he did not want to see Assyria resurrected. Nor did he want to find Necho II replacing Assyria as lord and master of Jerusalem. So instead of letting Necho go by, he marched out to attack the Egyptians when they drew close to Megiddo.

Necho, in a hurry, hadn't intended to take on the armies of Jerusalem quite so soon. He sent messengers to Josiah, offering a truce: "What quarrel is there between you and me? It is not you that I am attacking at this time, but the house with which I am at war."[25] Josiah ignored this. "King Josiah marched out to meet him in battle," says 2 Kings, "but Necho faced him and killed him at Megiddo." 2 Chron. 35 adds the detail that Josiah, in disguise, was struck by archers. His bodyguard took the wounded king away from the battlefield, but he died in his chariot on the way back to the capital city. He was thirty-nine years old.

Necho II did not pause to follow up on his victory. With the Judeans in retreat, he continued on up to meet the Assyrians under the command of Assur-uballit. Together, the joint armies tried to retake the Assyrian headquarters at Haran, which was now occupied by a Babylonian detachment. "They defeated the garrison which Nabopolassar had stationed there," the Babylonian Chronicle says, "but they were not able to take the city."[26]

Both armies retreated. Nabopolassar was not inclined to try again; his health was poor, he was no longer a young man, and Assur-uballit was not that much of a threat. Necho II decided to go down and finish his business at Jerusalem. He sent his soldiers again against Jerusalem, and took Josiah's son and heir Jehoahaz captive with ease. Necho II ordered Jehoahaz marched off to Egypt, where he died sometime later in exile. Then Necho picked one of

Josiah's younger sons, Eliakim, to be his puppet. He changed Eliakim's name to Jehoiakim—a traditional act of dominance and ownership—and demanded a heavy payment of gold and silver tribute (which Jehoiakim raised by collecting a new tax, by force, from the people).[27]

In 605, Nabopolassar turned his attention back to the resistance. The Egyptians and Assyrians had set up camp at Carchemish, but Nabopolassar was old and increasingly wretched with sickness. Instead he sent his son Nebuchadnezzar south to Carchemish at the head of his troops, to get rid of the Assyrian remnant.[28]

The two armies met outside the city. In heavy fighting, the Egyptian line broke. Necho II began the retreat back down towards the Delta, deserting the Western Semitic lands—a defeat celebrated by the Judean court prophet Jeremiah:

> This is the message against the army of Necho, king of Egypt
> defeated at Carchemish on the Euphrates by Nebuchadnezzar. . . .
> What do I see?
> They are terrified, they are retreating, their warriors are defeated.[29]

There is no mention of Assyrian fugitives in any ancient records of this battle; apparently the Assyrian forces were wiped out with no survivors. Assur-uballit fell, somewhere on the field, but must have been trampled into an unrecognizable corpse.

Nebuchadnezzar himself followed the trail of the retreating Necho II, apparently intending to catch and kill the pharaoh. But his pursuing army was caught by faster messengers who carried news: Nabopolassar had died while Nebuchadnezzar fought at Carchemish. At this, Nebuchadnezzar immediately gave up the chase and and turned back towards Babylon. The throne of Babylon was a ball that needed to be caught at once before someone else snatched it away.

Meanwhile, Necho II subsided back down south. He made no further attempt to assert Egyptian power over the Mediterranean coast. Instead, he concentrated his efforts on fortifying himself against further attacks from any claimants to the old Twenty-fifth Dynasty crown.[30]

And so two of the greatest ancient empires ceased to be world powers. Egypt was caged, and Assyria no longer existed. The Babylonian crown had become the most powerful in the world.

TIMELINE 57		
GREECE	ROME AND BABYLON	
Greek colonies spread through Asia Minor, the Aegean, Africa, and the land around the Black Sea	**Romulus**	
		Tiglath-Pileser III
		Shalmaneser V
		Merodach-baladan
	Numa Pompilius	
Creon of Athens		**Sargon II**
Sparta invades Messene		**Sennacherib**
	Tullus Hostilius	**Shamash-shum-ukin**
Athens controls Attica		
	Ancus Marcius	**Kandalu**
Cylon's revolt (632)		
		Sin-shum-ishkun
Draco's laws		
	Tarquin the Elder	**Nabopolassar**
	Fall of Nineveh (612)	
Solon (600)		**Nebuchadnezzar** (605)
	Servius Tullus (578)	

Chapter Fifty-Eight

A Brief Empire

Between 605 and 580 BC,
Egypt builds an army,
Babylon destroys Jerusalem,
and Nebuchadnezzar II goes mad

BACK IN BABYLON, the crown prince Nebuchadnezzar took the throne as Nebuchadnezzar II* and set out to take over the world which had once been Assyrian.

For several years, he had no serious opponents. Necho II, weakened by his defeat at Carchemish, had been driven back behind his own borders. The Lydians of Asia Minor were too small to be a threat; the wandering, belligerent Scythians were disorganized; the Greek cities were occupied with their own internal convulsions. The strongest possible challenger to Babylonian power was the Medes, who commanded the Persian army as well as their own. But Cyarxes, king of the Medes, was also Nebuchadnezzar's father-in-law; his daughter Amytis (whose husband had been on constant campaign since the match was made outside the walls of Nineveh) now lived in the palace at Babylon.

Nebuchadnezzar's conquests began in the Western Semitic lands. He posted a garrison outside the walls of Jerusalem, upon which Jehoiakim of Israel swapped alliances, away from Necho II (who had placed him on the throne), to Babylon. "For three years," says 2 Kings 24:1, "Jehoiakim became the vassal of Nebuchadnezzar, king of Babylon." And Josephus adds, "The king of Babylon passed over the Euphrates and took all of Syria, except for Judea . . . and Jehoiakim, affrighted at his threatening, bought his peace with money."[1]

Jehoiakim's payment was merely a stalling tactic until he could reestablish an alliance with some other king. Despite the conquest at Carchemish, Baby-

* See chapter 41, p. 288.

lon was still not regarded as a world power. But his court prophet Jeremiah warned him that Nebuchadnezzar's takeover was not only inevitable, but divinely ordained: "The king of Babylon will certainly come and destroy this land, and cut off both men and animals from it."

It was the same kind of warning that Isaiah had delivered about Sennacherib of Assyria, a hundred years earlier. Jehoiakim didn't want to hear it; when the scroll containing Jeremiah's warning was read to him, he chopped it up bit by bit with his knife and pitched it into the firepot that burned next to his throne.[2] He had begun to carry on plans for revolt with his old master, Necho II, behind Nebuchadnezzar's back. This didn't please Jeremiah either: "The pharaoh and his people will drink of the same cup of destruction," he promised, and added that Jehoiakim's body would be "thrown out and exposed to the heat by day and the frost by night."*

Unimpressed by this dire warning, Jehoiakim formally rebelled against Babylon as soon as Necho II was ready to attack. He stopped sending tribute to Babylon; Necho marched out of Egypt; and Nebuchadnezzar headed down to meet the threat.

In 602, Necho II and Nebuchadnezzar met in battle—and the two armies fought each other to a draw. The Babylonian Chronicle (which is in bits for this part of Nebuchadnezzar's reign) tells us that another battle was fought the following year, in 601: "They fought one another in the battlefield," reads the 601 entry, "and both sides suffered severe losses. . . . [Nebuchadnezzar] and his army turned and [went back] to Babylon."[3]

But Nebuchadnezzar was not the only loser. Necho II had spent too many men to keep hold of his Western Semitic lands. "The king of Egypt did not march out from his own country again," 2 Kings 24 says, "because the king of Babylon had taken all his territory, from the Wadi of Egypt to the Euphrates River."

Instead, Necho II turned back to his own country. He worked on his canal until it ran from the eastern Nile river through to the Red Sea. It was an enormous undertaking: "The length of the canal is such that it takes four days to sail it," Herodotus writes, "and it has been dug wide enough for two triremes to be rowed abreast."[4] A trireme was only fifteen feet wide, but a thirty-foot

* The book of Jeremiah, which is one of our main sources for the Egyptian-Judean-Babylonian confrontation, groups Jeremiah's predictions of doom thematically rather than chronologically; this prophecy comes after his account of Jehoiakim's death and Hezekiah's succession, but comparison with the events in 2 Kings and 2 Chronicles seems to place it before Hezekiah's accession. Cf. Jeremiah 37, 2 Kings 24:7 (which says that the king of Egypt did not come back out of Egypt again after Jehoiakim's reign), and 2 Chron. 36:5–7. (The relationship between the chronologies of Kings, Chronicles, and Jeremiah remains an unsolved problem.)

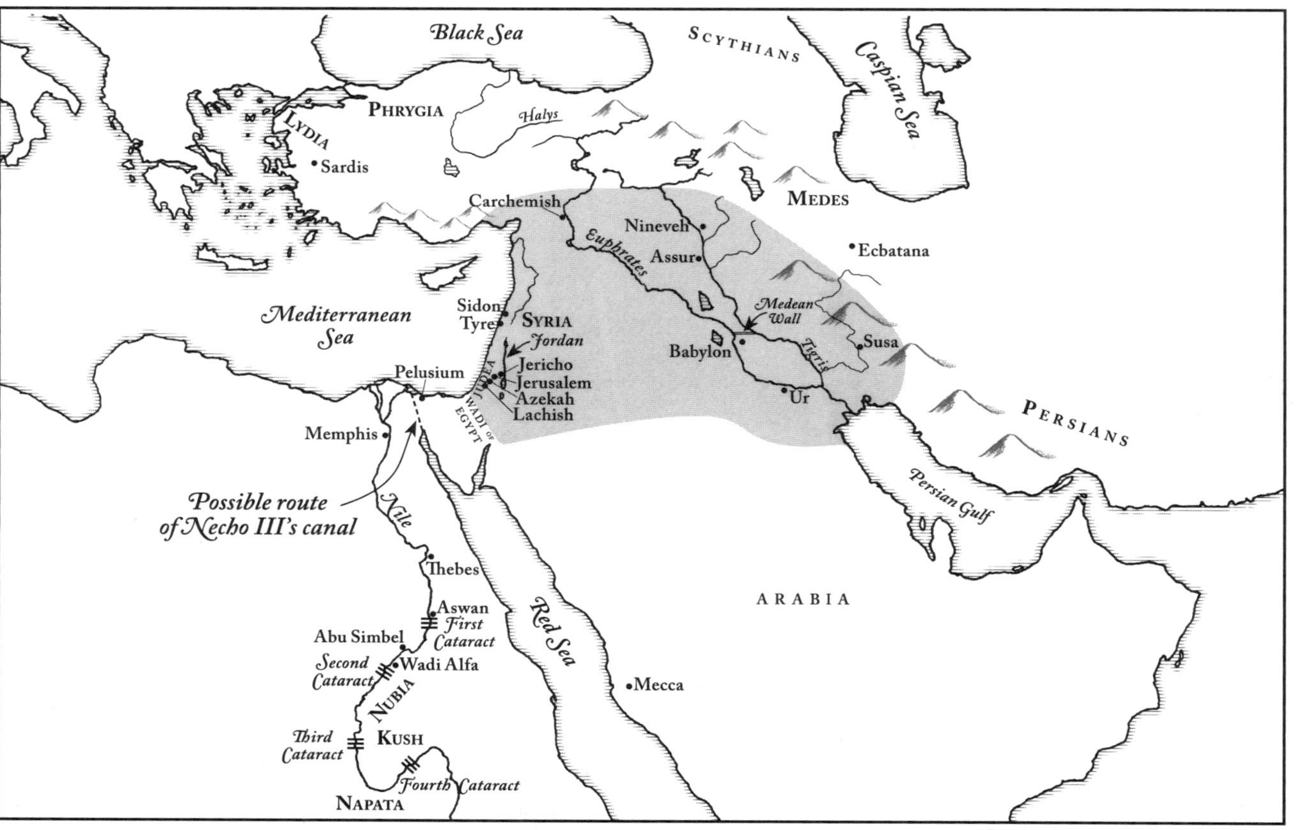

58.1 The Babylonian Empire

canal extending all the way to the Red Sea was nevertheless an enormous undertaking.* To guard its entrance to the Nile, he built a fortress: Pelusium.

He had hired two sets of mercenaries to come down and help him train a navy: Greek sailors from the Ionian cities around the Aegean Sea,[5] and also, according to Herodotus, Phoenician seamen, probably from one of the Phoenician cities (Tyre or Sidon, or perhaps the Phoenician-built city of Carthage on the North African coast, founded by Jezebel's great-niece Elissa, and rapidly growing). These helped him to build a fleet, which consisted largely of a primitive kind of trireme: a galley warship constructed so that it could ram other boats. These were anchored along the coast of the Red Sea.[6] Herodotus even insists that one crew of Phoenician sailors, told off to explore the Red Sea by Necho II, sailed down south and kept on sailing. Much to everyone's surprise, they showed up at the Pillars of Hercules—the mouth of the Mediterranean Sea—three years later, and sailed through the Mediterranean all the way back to the Nile Delta. They had, in fact, gone all the way around Africa.[7] All of this was an enormous break with tradition for the sea-hating Egyptians, but Necho II, forwards looking, could see that commerce was a better bet than warfare if he wanted to build an empire.

While all this exciting exploration was going on in Egypt, Judah was cut off. Jehoiakim had counted on Egyptian support; now he was alone. "He was disappointed of his hope," Josephus remarks, "for Egypt dared not fight at this time."[8]

But Jehoiakim, poised uneasily for Babylon's retaliation, had to wait four more years while Nebuchadnezzar rebuilt his army and then dealt with other business (fighting nomads in the northern deserts of Arabia, according to the Babylonian Chronicle).[9] What was going on in the city at this time, we do not know. But possibly some of Jerusalem's officials agreed with Jeremiah about the folly of opposing Babylon; Jehoiakim died in 597, at the relatively young age of thirty-six, and at once Nebuchadnezzar headed towards the city.

In Jerusalem, Jehoiakim's teenage son Jehoiachin was set on the throne. But as soon as Nebuchadnezzar reached Jerusalem's walls—mere weeks after

* Herodotus also says that Necho gave up digging the canal because of an evil oracle, and that it was completed by Darius; this is unlikely, as he also adds that Necho built a fleet of seagoing ships, which hardly seems to match up to his abandoning the canal. Darius probably repaired the canal and then took credit for it, which was one of the strategies which made him a Great King not only in deed but in reputation. Aristotle, Diodorus Siculus, Strabo, Pliny the Elder, Ptolemy, and other classical historians all mention the canal, although they differ on who dug it, who completed it, and where exactly it ran; apparently the canal was prone to silting (or sanding) up and required constant re-digging. A survey of the evidence for the canal is found in Carol A. Redmount's "The Wadi Tumulat and the 'Canal of the Pharaohs,' " in *Journal of Near Eastern Studies* 54:2 (1995), pp. 127–135.

Jehoiakim's death—the king, his mother, his court, the noblemen, and all the officials surrendered. Perhaps they had been offered some sort of immunity, in exchange for services rendered. Although they were taken into captivity, they were treated well; Babylonian records show that Jehoiachin spent the next forty years living in Babylon at the king's expense, provided for from the Babylonian treasury.[10]

The army was taken away into Babylon, but not scattered; the treasury and the Temple of Solomon were raided for gold, but the buildings were not razed or burned. Nebuchadnezzar didn't even take away all of the royal family. He assigned Jehoachin's uncle Mattaniah, brother of the dead king, the new, subject-name of Zedekiah, and put him on the throne; Josephus gives this arrangement the pleasant name "league of mutual assistance,"[11] but in fact Zedekiah was no more than a Babylonian governor. Nevertheless, Jerusalem had gotten off relatively easily.

Nebuchadnezzar did have concerns other than the control of a third-rate power to his west. He had his own position as great king to establish and maintain, and he set out to do this as Mesopotamian kings had done for two thousand years: he started to build. His own inscriptions record the restoration and addition of temple after temple in Babylon itself. Babylon was the home of the god Marduk, and Nebuchadnezzar's devotion to Marduk was also a celebration of Babylonian triumph. "O Marduk, my lord," reads one of Nebuchadnezzar's inscriptions, commemorating an effective campaign to put down rebellion to his west, "may I remain always your legitimate governor; may I pull your yoke until I am sated with progeny . . . may my offspring rule forever."[12]

His piety as a devotee of Marduk survives in almost every ancient account of his projects: "He most zealously decorated the temple of Bel and the rest of the holy places," writes Berossus.[13] He built a ceremonial road for the festival of Marduk, a seventy-foot-wide path from the central temple complex to the ceremonial Ishtar Gate, on the north side of the city, so that the god could progress along it in the New Year's festival. Walls on either side were glazed blue, decorated with carved lions.[14] Remnants of the Ishtar Gate and the path that led to it have become one of the most recognizable images of ancient Babylon, even though they come from the very end of Babylon's life.

Nebuchadnezzar also built himself at least three palaces, gilded with glazing, gold, and silver. And at one of these palaces, he built a garden.

The remains of this garden have not been identified with certainty (a huge arrangement of walls and chambers with vaulted ceilings, uncovered at the primary royal complex on the banks of the Euphrates, remains a possibility), but their fame lingers in the accounts of various writers from later times.

58.1. Ishtar Gate. A reconstruction of the Ishtar Gate, the main gate of Babylon during the reign of Nebuchadnezzar II. Vorderasiatisches Museum, Staatliche Museen zu Berlin. Photo credit Erich Lessing/Art Resource, NY

Diodorus of Siculus gives the best-known description of them in the third book of his *Bibliotheca Historica*:

> There was of old time a king who, for his lady's sake, prepared this garden, as you shall hear. This mistress, whom he so tenderly loved, was Persian-born, and as the nature of that country is, she had a great desire to stand upon high hills and see the country around her. So she entreated her sovereign lord to make her a ground, or an arbour of pleasure, artificially devised by curious workmanship.
>
> The entrance into it was in a hill, with building upon building made to a wondrous height, so that a man could see out of it far and wide. There were vaults made under the ground that bore up all the weight of this garden; one vault was set upon another, and the higher that the building proceeded, the bigger was the vault. On the uppermost vaults, the walls of this garden were founded and set, twenty-two feet thick. . . . There were cisterns of water in the pavement. And in this garden were all manner of trees,

> delectable to see, and fresh green meadows. Moreover, there was a conduit, that by craft conveyed water for the irrigation of the soil.[15]

The "Persian-born lady" is most likely not Persian at all, but Median: none other than Amytis, the daughter of Cyarxes, the Median high king.

These gardens—which acquired the name of the "Hanging Gardens" from this description of an upside-down ziggurat formation, each level overhanging the one below—became famous not only through time, but through space. Almost every ancient historian who describes Babylon mentions them, and from these snapshots we can build a picture of these most famous gardens of ancient times: the Eden of a warlord. "He had high stone terraces built that gave the appearance of being mountains planted with all kinds of trees," writes Berossus. "He had constructed and prepared what are called the Hanging Gardens for his wife, who had a love of the mountains since she had grown up in Media."*[16]

These were peaceful buildings. But Nebuchadnezzar had more serious issues in mind as well. He set his men to work on the double walls of Babylon, reinforcing them until the inner wall stood twenty-one feet thick and the outer wall was punctuated with watchtowers every sixty feet. A partly dug moat protected one side of the city already; Nebuchadnezzar had it dug the rest of the way around the city, until Babylon was surrounded by a forty-foot belt of water.[17] And then on the city's east side, he built yet another wall. This, later described by the Greek soldier Xenophon as the "Medean Wall," stretched from the Euphrates to the Tigris, reminiscent of the wall built long ago by the Sumerian king Shu-Sin to keep invading Amorites away.† But this wall had another purpose: "He fixed the walls," Berossus writes, "so that those who intended to besiege the city could no longer divert the river's course."[18] The recent destruction of Nineveh had left him wary of water.

Under Nebuchadnezzar, the city of Babylon had grown immense: Aristotle remarks, "It is said that when Babylon was captured, a considerable part of the city was not aware of it until three days later," thanks to the city's size.[19] But despite all of this building, it is possible that Nebuchadnezzar was not as

* The Great Pyramid of Giza (chapter 11) and the Hanging Gardens of Babylon are the first two of the Seven Wonders of the World, a list which was compiled by (among others) the architect Johann Bernhard Fischer von Erlach, in his 1721 work *Entwurf einer historischen Architektur*; in this, Fischer was following the lead of the North African librarian Callimachus, who sometime around 260 BC wrote out a list of great wonders round the world (we don't know what was on it, since the list was destroyed when the Library of Alexandria burned; see chapter 78, p. 693). As the gardens were long gone by von Erlach's day, he was clearly working from the descriptions in Berossus and Diodorus.

† See chapter 18, p. 141.

strong as he looked. In 595, he was forced to put down a rebellion in his own capital city; it took him two months to defeat the insurgents, which suggests that the army (perhaps tired of its endless fighting) was involved.[20]

And then there is the evidence from Egypt to consider.

Necho II, who had twice come up against Nebuchadnezzar without success, was now dead. He had died in 595, two years after the fight outside the Delta, and had been succeeded on the throne of Egypt by his son Psammetichus II.

Psammetichus II inherited an Egyptian military complex that now included a navy. He used it not for commerce, but for a return to an older style of Egyptian power. He made an expedition down into Nubia, long out of the grasp of the Egyptian pharaohs, bringing with him two divisions: an Egyptian division led by the Egyptian general Amasis, and a Greek division commanded by a separate officer. He stayed himself at Aswan, but his two divisions fought their way south.[21] This army is memorialized by graffiti which the Greeks, who had no particular awe of the Egyptian past, scribbled on the leg of the huge statue of Rameses II at Abu Simbel: "This was written by those who sailed with Psammeticus," it reads, ". . . [who] came beyond Kerkis as far as the river permits. Those who spoke foreign tongues were led by Potasimto, the Egyptians by Amasis."[22]

Napata was put to the torch, and 4,200 Nubians died or were taken captive.[23] Zedekiah, hearing of these conquests, sent word to Psammetichus II; if Egypt wanted to attack Nebuchadnezzar, Jerusalem would join him. He "revolted to the Egyptians," writes Josephus, "in hopes, by their assistance, of overcoming the Babylonians."[24]

Nebuchadnezzar must have looked vulnerable, because Psammetichus II agreed to come. He marched his army out of the Delta, a combined force of Egyptians and Greek mercenaries, travelling to battle over land in the traditional way. In response, the Babylonian army, which had already arrived at Jerusalem's walls to find out why Zedekiah's tribute was late, pulled away and headed down to meet the threat.

The prophet Jeremiah, still forecasting doom, warned Zedekiah that the worst was yet to come. "Pharaoh's army, which has marched out to support you, will go back to its own land," he announced. "Then the Babylonians will return. . . . Do not deceive yourselves, thinking, 'The Babylonians will surely leave us.' They will not! Even if you were to defeat the entire Babylonian army, and only wounded men were left in their tents, they would come out and burn the city down."[25]

This was a massive vote of no confidence, but Zedekiah didn't listen and Jeremiah ended up in a dungeon where no one else could hear him. ("He is discouraging the soldiers!" complained one of the officers, with some justification.) Meanwhile Nebuchadnezzar "met the Egyptians, and joined battle with them, and beat them; and when he had put them to flight, he pursued them, and drove them out of all Syria."[26] Psammetichus II went back home. Just weeks later, in February of 589, he died, and was succeeded by his son Apries. If Zedekiah sent south again for help from Egypt (as passages written later by the prophets Jeremiah and Ezekiel suggest), the messages were ignored. Apries had learned from his father's mistake and did not intend to defy the great king.*

Nebuchadnezzar then fought his way back towards the walls of Jerusalem. Zedekiah's army controlled the fortress cities of Azekah and Lachish, which were in the forefront of the defense against the Babylonian invasion; but these cities fell, one at a time. The agonizing and slow defeat is recorded on bits of pottery found at Lachish, sent there as messages by soldiers who were on the outer edges of the territory's defense, and who were bracing themselves for the onslaught. The attack would reach Azekah first.

"Let my lord know," one fragment reads, "that we can no longer see the signals of Azekah."[27] Azekah had fallen. Its lights had been quenched, and not long afterwards the dark Babylonian wave swallowed Lachish as well, and then washed up against the walls of Jerusalem.

The siege lasted two years. It was accompanied, according to Josephus, by "a famine and a pestilential distemper," and it was the famine that finally brought an end to the siege. In 587, Zedekiah had had enough. He tried to escape, apparently without thought for the rest of the people, left behind to face Babylonian wrath. "The famine had become so severe that there was no food for the people to eat," writes the historian of 2 Kings. "Then the city wall was broken through, and the whole army fled at night through the gate between the two walls near the king's garden, although the Babylonians were surrounding the city. They fled towards the Jordan Valley, but the Babylonian army pursued the king and overtook him in the plains of Jericho. All his soldiers were separated from him and scattered, and he was captured."[28]

Nebuchadnezzar, normally free from the gratuitous cruelty that had characterized the kings of Assyria, had been exasperated into vengeance. When Zedekiah was hauled in front of him in his army camp, he ordered the king's sons—still children—killed in front of his eyes, and then had Zedekiah's eyes put out, so that the last sight he ever witnessed was the execution of his family.

Zedekiah was taken back to Babylon in chains; all of his chief officials and

* The Hebrew accounts call Apries "Hophra"; the passages which may refer to him are found in Jer. 44:30, Jer. 46:25, Jer. 47:26, Ezekiel 29, and Ezek. 30:21–26.

the chief priests were executed just outside the army camp; and Nebuchadnezzar ordered his commander to set Jerusalem on fire. The walls were broken down; the city's people were marched off into exile; the palace of the king, the houses, the treasury, and the Temple of Solomon were all in flames. The Jews were resettled all over Babylon, and some fled down to Egypt as well. It was the beginning of a diaspora which lasted for two millennia. "And after this manner have the kings of David's race ended their lives," Josephus concludes.[29]

MEANWHILE, Nebuchadnezzar's allies the Medes, under his father-in-law Cyarxes, had been steadily fighting their way towards Asia Minor. By the time Jerusalem fell, the Medes had reached the Lydian border.

Lydia, which had been invaded by the Cimmerians a hundred years earlier, had been regathering its strength. Some Lydians had migrated across to Thrace, and perhaps from there farther west; but others had remained, and Gyges's great-grandson Alyattes was now their king. Under his leadership, the Lydian army came out to meet the Medes and fought them to a standstill.

From 590 to 585, the two armies faced each other across the Halys river, neither able to gain an advantage. Herodotus remarks that during this five years, "although plenty of battles went the Medes' way, just as many went the Lydians' way too."[30] So in 585, Nebuchadnezzar took a hand to resolve the stalemate. He sent up a Babylonian army officer named Nabonidus to help arrange a cease-fire between the two armies. Nabonidus seems to have done his job well; the two kings agreed to a peace, which was sealed by the marriage of Alyattes's daughter, Aryenis, to Cyarxes's son, the Median prince Astyages.[31]

It might have made more sense for Nebuchadnezzar to send an army to help the Medes conquer the Lydians, rather than messing about with a peace treaty. But Cyarxes had now been king of the Medes and Persians for forty years. He was an old man, and ill, and ready to stop fighting. Just after the swearing of the treaty and the royal marriage, he took to his bed, and died not long after. Astyages became king of the Medes and Persians in his place, but he did not pick the war back up; he took his wife and went back home.

Possibly Nebuchadnezzar did not send a Babylonian army because he too was suffering from illness.

Nebuchadnezzar's reign—particularly the end of it—is haunted by mysterious hints of something very wrong indeed. The most complete account of these difficult days is found in the book of Daniel, which describes the lives of four of the Jewish captives hauled off to Babylon and retrained, by Nebuchadnezzar's officials, to be Babylonians. One of these captives, Daniel himself, is called to interpret Nebuchadnezzar's troubling dream; the king has

TIMELINE 58

ROME AND BABYLON		PERSIA	
		PERSIA	MEDIA
	Sargon II		
	Sennacherib		
Tullus Hostilius	**Shamash-shum-ukin**		
		Cyrus I	
Ancus Marcius	**Kandalu**		
			Cyarxes
	Sin-shum-ishkun		
Tarquin the Elder	**Nabopolassar**		
Fall of Nineveh (612)			
	Nebuchadnezzar (605–562)		
Fall of Jerusalem (587)			**Astyages**
Servius Tullus (578)		**Cambyses I**	

seen, in the night, a huge tree with beautiful leaves, filled with fruit, giving shelter to animals beneath it and birds in its branches; and then he has seen the tree cut down, stripped and broken off, the stump bound with bronze.

Given that both Assyrian and Babylonian kings had shared a devotion to a sacred tree as the source of their power, this strikes Nebuchadnezzar as ominous. Daniel, asked to interpret, confirms the negative nature of the dream: he predicts that the king will be struck by madness and lose his power for a time. Sure enough, Nebuchadnezzar loses his wits: "He was driven away from people and ate grass like cattle. His body was drenched with the dew of heaven until his hair grew like the feathers of an eagle and his nails like the claws of a bird," a condition that lasts for seven years.[32]

This story, naturally, was much amplified by later Jewish commentary on the biblical books, attempting to make sense of this transformation; it is not common, in the biblical literature, to see men transformed into animals as punishment. A much later composition, the *Lives of the Prophets*—an anonymous account of the lives of various Jewish prophets, probably written around AD 100—sees the transformation as a symbol of Nebuchadnezzar's tyranny. The *Lives of the Prophets* describes Nebuchadnezzar as sane, but as part animal nonetheless:

> For his head and foreparts were those of an ox, his legs and hinder parts those of a lion. . . . It is in the manner of tyrants, that . . . in their latter years they become wild beasts.[33]

This is a reversal of the Gilgamesh epic, in which the wild man Enkidu looks human but roams through the fields, eating grass like an animal. In the Gilgamesh epic, Enkidu is the tyrannical, uncivilized, power-grasping, shadow side of the king, one who must be wrestled with and tamed before kingship can prosper. In the tale of Gilgamesh and Enkidu, a man becomes a good king (and his shadow side more human) when he resists the temptation to exercise his power without restraint. But Nebuchadnezzar goes the other way, increasingly autocratic and sinking from great king to animal existence.[34]

Despite the place it occupied in the imaginations of its neighbors, Babylon was the center of an empire for a very brief time. Hammurabi had been its first great king; the first Nebuchadnezzar its second; Nebuchadnezzar II was only its third great king, and its last. Babylon was not accustomed to emperors.

And so that ancient Sumerian unease with kingship is resurrected in the tale of Nebuchadnezzar's madness. Nebuchadnezzar too is conquered by the beast within him. Daniel, born into a nation which had chosen its kings against the will of its own God centuries before, provides a theological commentary to wrap the story up: men are frightened by kingship because every man desires power, and, desiring, is ruined by it.

Chapter Fifty-Nine

Cyrus the Great

Between 580 and 539 BC,
Cyrus takes over the Medes, the Persians,
and finally the Babylonians

To the east of Nebuchadnezzar, the Median king Astyages, high king of the Medes and the Persians, was having bad dreams of his own. His Lydian wife Aryenis had given birth to a daughter named Mandane some years before, and now Mandane was approaching the age of marriage. "He dreamt," Herodotus writes, "that she urinated so much that she not only filled his city, but even flooded the whole of Asia."[1] This was both disgusting and troubling; and his wise men, consulted, predicted that a child of Mandane would grow up to take the kingdom.

Astyages apparently had no son, and his grandson might well be his heir, so this interpretation was not necessarily bad news. However, he was very much aware that the *father* of Mandane's child might not be willing to watch the crown pass directly from grandfather to grandson.

So he chose his daughter's husband carefully: not any of the ambitious Median noblemen who surrounded him at Ecbatana, but a more subordinate (and more distant) man. He sent Mandane off to Anshan to marry his Persian vassal Cambyses, the son of Cyrus I, and the heir to the Persian leadership. Cambyses had sworn loyalty to his Median overlord, and Astyages apparently had no very high opinion of his ambitions.

Mandane became pregnant almost at once (Cambyses may not have been ambitious, but he was fertile). At this point Astyages had another dream, the reversal of Nebuchadnezzar's dream of a felled sacred tree; a vine grew out of his daughter and curled itself all around his territory. At this, his wise men told him that his daughter's son would not simply succeed him, but rule in his place.

So Astyages invited his daughter to Ecbatana for a visit, where she lived in

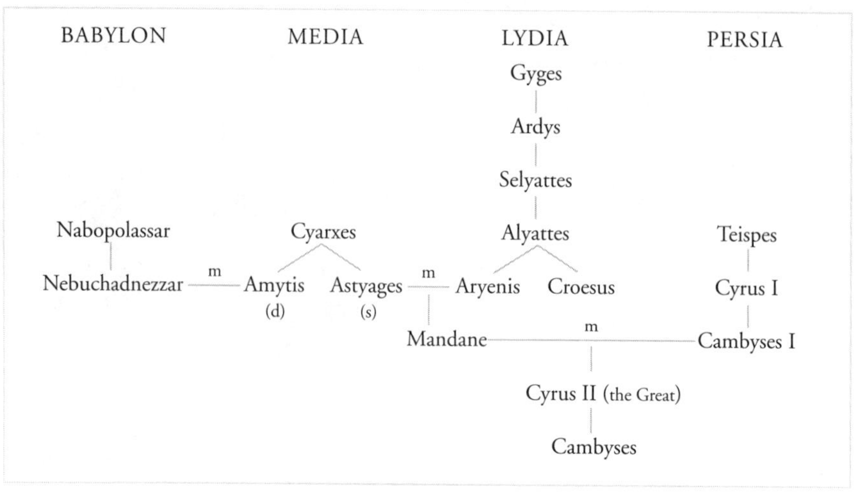

59.1. Cyrus's Family Tree. By marriage, Cyrus was related to the royal families of Babylon, Media, Lydia, and Persia. Credit Richie Gunn

luxury in the palace, waiting for her baby to be born. Meanwhile he planned to do away with the child. It seems that Cambyses had no choice but to relinquish his wife and unborn son; nor could Mandane refuse to come.

Mandane gave birth to a son, whom she named Cyrus after her husband's father. Astyages, who wished both to avoid the guilt of having killed a blood relative and to preserve his deniability, sent for his cousin and chief official, Harpagus, and told him to do away with the baby. Apparently Astyages hoped that they would all pretend that the baby had been stillborn, Mandane would go back home, and the threat to his throne would be gone.[2]

Harpagus also did not want to do something that would come back on his head later. His solution, not unlike Astyages's own, was to hand the job off: "The child has to die," he concluded, "but it must be one of Astyages's men who commits the murder, and not one of mine."

So he passed the baby on to one of Astyages's herdsmen, who promptly took it home and gave it to his wife, who had just been delivered of a stillborn baby. The herdsman laid the body of his own child out on the mountainside instead, and reported back to Harpagus that the deed was done. And Cyrus grew up in the herdsman's hut.

This story, related by Herodotus, is clearly a reprise of the standard peril that also shows a king's divine appointment: a baby, miraculously preserved, grows to be a great leader, thanks to the supernatural providence that so clearly lay upon his early life. But in the case of Cyrus, Herodotus's tale also demonstrates the uneasy political relationship between the Medes and the Persians. The Medes were the ruling race, but the child of the Persian vassal king could not simply be killed outright, even by his own high king.

The inevitable happened; Cyrus, grown to the age of ten, was discovered by his grandfather, who saw him playing a game in the public square in which he ruled over the other boys of the village. It was now too late to kill him, since no one could even pretend that it would be an accident. Making the best of the situation, Astyages acknowledged the boy's parentage. His wise men assured him that young Cyrus's playacting the role of king had fulfilled the omen of the vine, so Astyages sent Cyrus back to Anshan, to the house of the parents who had never seen him.

Then he sent for Harpagus. Caught, Harpagus admitted that he had dropped the duty into someone else's lap. Astyages behaved as though he planned to accept his cousin's apology: "Everything has turned out fine," he assured Harpagus. "I've been very upset by my daughter's hostility to me" (an understatement, we assume) "and I didn't feel at all good about what I'd done. Send your own son to the palace to meet his cousin, and we'll have a feast together."

Harpagus sent his own young son to the palace; Astyages had the boy murdered, baked, and set out as a main course at the feast that evening. "When he thought that Harpagus had eaten his fill," Herodotus writes, "Astyages asked him if he had enjoyed the meal. Harpagus said that he had, very much so. Then the servants brought in the boy's head, hands, and feet." Harpagus, seeing his son's remains, "retained his self-control." He told Astyages that "the king could do no wrong. Then he picked up what was left of his son's body and returned home."[3]

Should all of this be literally true, we could assume that the Medes went in for repressing emotion on a massive scale. Reading between the lines, we might see a more ominous and complicated picture: a Median king, sinking deeper and deeper into a nasty kind of paranoid psychosis, with enough despotic power to command his royal bodyguard to carry out awful acts against other Medians; a Median official, surrounded by his royal cousin's soldiers, watching his son marched off to a horrible death; a Persian royal family that had to obey the king's orders, yet could not be publicly humiliated; and a Persian underclass that had to be treated with some care, lest it rise up and protest.

Astyages was still the acknowledged overlord of the Medes and the Persians. He was still the brother-in-law of the king of Babylon, and he was still the second (or perhaps third) greatest ruler in the known world. But back in Anshan, Cyrus was growing up in the house of Cambyses, lord of Persia, mothered by a woman who hated her Median father. In the palace itself, Harpagus, still serving his cousin quietly, was planning long-term revenge: a dish served cold.

Astyages was not unaware of all of this resentment. He mounted a guard on every road leading from Anshan to Ecbatana, so that no one could march an army to his palace without his knowledge.

NEBUCHADNEZZAR died king of a vast territory, after forty-three years of rule. But we do not even know where his body was buried. What does emerge from the fragmentary records is a six-year period of chaos. His son Amel-Marduk* was the obvious heir; but it seems that all had not been well between father and son. A certain resentment comes to the surface in the biblical tale of Amel-Marduk's release of Jehoiachin, undoubtedly against Nebuchadnezzar's wishes, as soon as the old king died. "In the year Evil-Merodach became king of Babylon," 2 Kings tells us, "he released Jehoiachin from prison on the twenty-seventh day of the twelfth month. He spoke kindly to him and gave him a seat of honor. . . . So Jehoiachin put aside his prison clothes and for the rest of his life ate regularly at the king's table."[4] A much later tradition, relayed by the twelfth-century Jewish historian Jerachmeel, says that Nebuchadnezzar actually jailed Amel-Marduk for treachery, and that when Amel-Marduk was freed after Nebuchadnezzar's death, he took his father's body out of the grave and threw it out for vultures to eat.[5] If we are to gather anything from this, it is that Nebuchadnezzar and his son were on less than affectionate terms.

The Babylonian chronicles are fragmentary, but Berossus, chronicler of the pharaohs, preserves a dramatic tale: Amel-Marduk "ruled capriciously and had no regard for the law," so that his sister's husband planned his assassination and then took over after his death. He only ruled four years, however; and when he died, his son Labashi-Marduk, "still a child, succeeded to the throne and ruled for nine months. Because of his evil ways, his friends plotted against him and he was beaten to death."[6] Other writers from the same time tell the same tale: Amel-Marduk was "slain by his kinsman," according to the Greek historian Megasthenes, and Labashi-Marduk "also had suffered death by violence."[7]

The man who finally ended up with the crown of Babylon was Nabonidus, the army officer who had helped negotiate the treaty between the Medes and the Lydians thirty years before. He was now well into his sixties, with a son already in his forties, and had decades of experience as both a soldier and a courtier.[8] But he had no royal blood. Presumably he was from the city of Haran originally, since his long-lived mother, Adda-Guppi, had been a priestess of the moon-god Sin for many years there. An inscription at Haran iden-

* The Hebrew name Evil-Merodach is the same as the Babylonian Amel-Marduk (which reveals that old Merodach-baladan was a worshipper of Marduk of Babylon).

tifies her: "The king of Babylon, the son and offspring of my heart," the inscription reads, "one hundred and four propitious years in the presence of Sin, the king of the gods, to me he established and caused to live."[9]

This was an honorable, but not kingly, heritage, as Nabonidus himself admitted. In his own, most famous inscription, a cylinder describing his restoration of temples in the cities of Haran and Sippar, Nabonidus writes, "I am Nabonidus, who have not the honour of being a somebody; kingship is not within me."[10] Nevertheless, his accession seems to have been supported by both army officers and state officials. The Babylonian Chronicle is missing from the beginning of his reign, but his own inscriptions tell us, "To the midst of the palace they brought me, and cast themselves at my feet and kissed my feet and paid homage to my royalty. . . . As for Nebuchadnezzar who preceded me, I am [his] mighty delegate . . . troops have been entrusted into my hand."[11]

The Babylon over which Nabonidus came to power had been weakened by the six years of infighting, and Nabonidus no longer had the resources to push south against Egypt as his predecessors had. But he was still the king of a very great empire. And he had few enemies. To his east, Astyages was still king of the Medes and Persians, and still his loyal ally. Cambyses, king of Persia, had died in 559, three years before, and young Cyrus had become ruler of the Persians ("Cyrus became king of the Persians in the opening year of the Fifty-fifth Olympiad," the Greek historian Diodorus Siculus tells us, and adds that all historians agree on this date);[12] but so far he had not demonstrated any ill will over his grandfather's attempt to kill him in babyhood. He remained loyal to his Median high king, and so loyal to Babylon also.

To the northwest, the powerful Lydians of Asia Minor were now ruled by Croesus, son of Alyattes, who had extended his empire even further; the Phrygians were subject to Lydia, and the Lydians had alliances with the Greek Ionian cities along the coast. "Sardis was at the height of its prosperity," Herodotus remarks, "and was visited . . . by every learned Greek who was alive at the time, including Solon of Athens," who was on his ten-year exile from his city. The trade routes across Asia Minor had brought Croesus as much wealth as his predecessor Midas, two hundred years before; and like Midas, Croesus had gained the reputation of being one of the richest men in the world.

Nabonidus talked Croesus into making a formal alliance between Babylon and the Lydian throne. He was at peace with Egypt too. In fact, it must have seemed for a brief time as if he had no enemies at all.

But it was a very brief time indeed.

Cyrus had not forgotten his grandfather's offenses; his mother very likely helped him to remember them. He was "the bravest and best-liked of his generation," according to Herodotus. His own family, the Achaemenids, belonged to the Pasargadae tribe, which was the largest and most powerful of all the Persian clans. These men were already on his side, should he choose to rebel against Median dominance, and he set out to convince the other tribes, one by one, to join him. The Median rule had become increasingly burdensome to them, and Cyrus found willing ears to his message: "Free yourselves from slavery. . . . you are at least the equals of the Medes in everything, including warfare!"[13]

In addition, old Harpagus was on his side. "He had met with all of the most important Medes, one by one," Herodotus tells us, "and had tried to convince them of the necessity of setting up Cyrus as their leader and bringing Astyages' reign to an end." Presumably Astyages's behavior had grown more and more atrocious, because the Medes defected, one by one, to Harpagus's plan.

When all was in readiness, Cyrus and his Persians began to march towards Ecbatana. Astyages's watchmen raised the alert. The old king, still in enough command of his wits to remember the past, ordered the wise men who had interpreted his dream as already fulfilled to be impaled outside Ecbatana's walls. He then called up his own troops, and put Harpagus (who had been playing his part to perfection for many years now) at their head. Harpagus led all of the Medians out against the Persians, and promptly swapped sides, along with most of his commanding officers. It must have been a most satisfying moment for him.

Astyages's handful of loyal soldiers fled; Astyages was taken prisoner, and Cyrus took control of Ecbatana and pronounced himself king of the Medes and the Persians. "This is how Astyages' reign came to an end, after he had ruled for thirty-five years," Herodotus concludes. "Thanks to his cruel behaviour, the Medes became subject to the Persians after having dominated that part of Asia which lies beyond the River Halys for 128 years."[14] Cyrus, showing himself bound by the same reluctance to shed royal blood that had preserved his own life, did not kill his grandfather, but kept him in comfortable confinement until the old man died of natural causes.

Now the Achaemenid family of Persians ruled over the lands to the east. Cyrus did not intend to take on Babylon, his old ally, but he had ambitions to rule an empire. As soon as Astyages died, he considered the treaty between the Lydians and Medes dissolved and marched towards the domain of his great-uncle Croesus.

The two armies met at the Halys river and fought to a draw. Croesus drew back, intending to send to Babylon for aid, but Cyrus (knowing better than to allow time for this) pressed forwards into Lydia and finally cornered the Lydian army in front of Sardis itself. He scattered the Lydian cavalry by bringing in camels (which frightened the horses into bolting), laid siege to the city itself, and brought it down after only fourteen days.[15]

Cyrus thought that his men deserved a reward, so he let them pour into the city, plundering it of its fabled wealth. Meanwhile Croesus—taken prisoner and marched into Cyrus's presence—watched from the walls beside his captor. He said not a word, so Cyrus asked him why he wasn't distressed to see his wealth disappearing. "It isn't my wealth," Croesus remarked, "it's yours that they're stealing." Upon which Cyrus immediately ordered the plundering to stop.[16]

Cyrus, the ultimate pragmatist, rewarded others with great generosity as long as it would further his own advantage.* Even later writers who idealized him—such as the Greek general Xenophon, who fought on the side of the Persians for a time and who wrote *The Education of Cyrus* to explain exactly how the restraint, fairness, intelligence, and "benevolence of soul"[17] of Cyrus helped him to establish the greatest empire in the world—reveal inadvertently that the Great King's strategy was force, fear, and domination. "It is easier," Xenophon begins, "for a human being to rule all the other kinds of animals than to rule human beings." However,

> Cyrus, a Persian . . . acquired very many people, very many cities, and very many nations, all obedient to himself. . . . was willingly obeyed by some, even though they were distant from him by a journey of many days; by others, distant by a journey even of months; by others, who had never yet seen him; and by others, who knew quite well that they would never see him. Nevertheless, they were willing to submit to him, for so far did he excel other kings.[18]

For all Cyrus's justice and benevolence of soul, he excelled other kings primarily in creating terror. "He was able to extend fear of himself to so much of the world that he intimidated all," Xenophon remarks, before going off into

* The Greek historians, Herodotus most of all, are our most complete source of information for Persian and Median history. However, due to a long-running hostility between Greeks and Persians (which produced several wars and caused troubles for Alexander the Great), the Greeks almost universally portrayed Persians as lazy, pleasure seeking, and corrupt; anything good in Persian culture was attributed to Median influence. This allowed them to admire (for example) Cyrus the Great, even though he is Persian, because his education took place under the direction of his Median grandfather. This bias undoubtedly makes the Greek accounts much less reliable. More recent attempts to write Persian history have attempted to supplement the Greek accounts with careful studies of the structure of the Persian empire, based on the coins, inscriptions, and administrative documents left by the Persians themselves. Nevertheless, the Persians left no narrative history behind them, so the Greeks remain our only source for the actions taken by Persian *people*, as opposed to the shape of the empire in which they lived. (See Heleen Sancisi-Weerdenburg's preface to *Achaemenid History I*, pp. XII–XIII.)

paeans of praise over Cyrus's justice, "and no one attempted anything against him."[19] What he could not accomplish by fear, he bought; he was generous enough with his own wealth when the prospect of greater gain was in view. "He went far beyond everyone in courting with food," Xenophon says, much later, ". . . he surpassed human beings still much more in giving the most gifts . . . Who else, by the magnitude of his gifts, is said to make people prefer himself to their brothers, to their fathers, and to their children? Who else was able to take vengeance on enemies who were a journey of many months in distance as was the king of the Persians? Who else besides Cyrus, after overturning an empire, was called 'father' when he died?"[20]

This is a creepy use of the title "father," and becomes creepier when Xenophon goes on to point out that "Father Cyrus" used his gifts to convince people all over his empire to become "the so-called Eyes and Ears of the King," and to report to him anything "that would benefit the king. . . . There are many Ears of the king, and many Eyes; and people are everywhere afraid to say what is not advantageous to the king, just as if he were listening, and afraid to do what is not advantageous, just as if he were present."[21]

Nevertheless Xenophon insists on seeing, in Cyrus, something new: a new kind of emperor. He is wrong in thinking that this "newness" was the justice, benevolence, and fairness of the king. Cyrus, like every other great king before him, kept hold of his empire by force and by fear. But his empire was certainly "new" in the number of different peoples that it managed to unite together under one rule. Now the Medes, the Lydians (including Phrygia), and the northern provinces of Assyria (conquered by his grandfather) were all part of Persia. Cyrus gave to Harpagus the task of conquering the Ionian cities along the coast, and himself turned back to campaign to the east of the Median territory; inscriptions and mentions in ancient texts suggest that he fought his way almost all the way over to the Indus river, although he did not manage to enter the Indus valley.[22] Nor did he venture into the sea. The Persians were not yet a seafaring power.

Three kingdoms remained: the scattered dominion of the Scythians to the north, the Egyptians far to the south, and most powerful of all, the Babylonians to the west.

Nabonidus had not been paying much attention to his empire. In fact, he had made his son Belshazzar his co-regent, turned Babylon over to him, and trekked south into Arabia, where he had taken up residence far from the center of his own kingdom.

What exactly was Nabonidus doing down in Arabia?

The history of Babylon's fall composed right after his reign, the *Verse Account of Nabonidus,* was written by his enemies the Persians, who had a

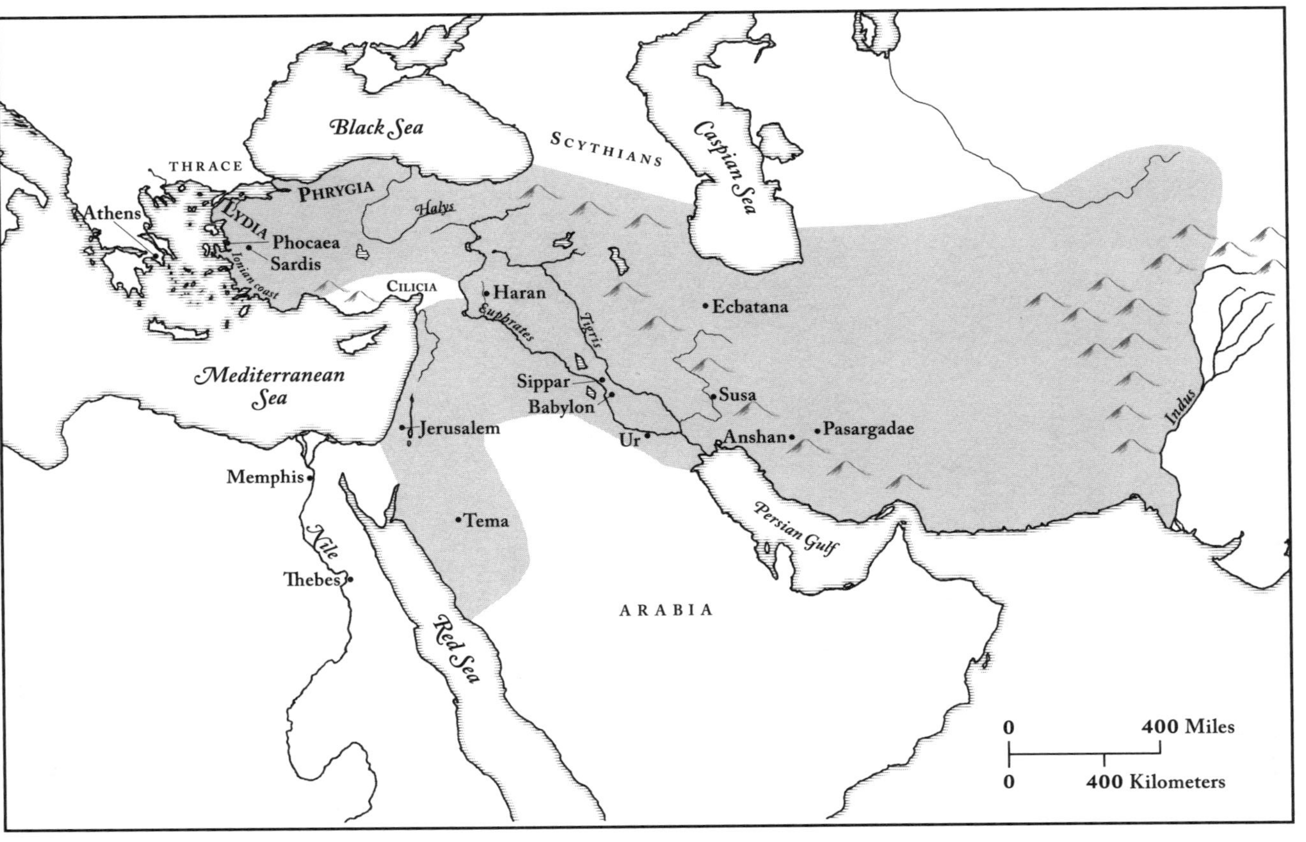

59.1 The Empire of Cyrus the Great

vested interest in demonstrating his unfitness to rule, and so should be taken with a spoonful of salt. But the *Account* inadvertently tells the truth, when it accuses Nabonidus of devotion to a god other than Marduk. The *Account* calls this god Nanna, and says that he was unfamiliar to the people of Babylon: a god

which nobody had ever seen in this country,
he placed it upon a pedestal,
he called it by the name of Nanna,
crowned with a tiara,
its appearance is like the eclipsed moon.[23]

This god may not have been familiar to the Persians, but he was certainly no stranger to the Babylonians. He was none other than the ancient moon-god Sin, of the old city of Ur.

Nabonidus certainly was devoted to Sin; his own mother, a priestess of the moon, mentions her son's piety. But Nabonidus's devotion brought him into difficulties. Although his own inscriptions attribute his rise to power (and the fall of Nebuchadnezzar's heirs) to the blessings of Sin, this very devotion led him away from the throne he had gained with such difficulty. He ran into difficulties almost at once with the priests of Marduk, who had gained enormous influence under the reign of Nebuchadnezzar, and found their hostility serious enough to make Babylon uninhabitable for him: "They disregarded [Sin's] rites," he complained in his own inscriptions, ". . . and [Sin] made me leave my city Babylon on the road to Tema. . . . For ten years I . . . did not enter my own city Babylon."[24]

His solution was simple: he turned the city of Babylon over to his son Belshazzar, whom he made co-regent, and left Marduk's chosen city. He travelled deep into Arabia and stopped at the desert city of Tema, as the *Account* points out:

He let everything go, entrusted kingship to his son,
And his army with him, he himself turned towards Tema, deep in the west,
when he arrived, he killed in battle the prince of Tema,
slaughtered the flocks of the city-dwellers and the country-dwellers,
and he himself took residence in Tema.[25]

This was not entirely a move of desperation. Tema was at the center of trade routes, a city through which valuable gold and salt passed continually. From the city, Nabonidus could keep his hand on Babylonian commerce, and his correspondence with Belshazzar makes clear that he did not in fact "let everything go." His son—who was on better terms with Marduk than the father—certainly ruled under his direction.

Nevertheless, he found himself in a dilemma arising from religious conviction. His sacred and secular duties clashed, and since he had to sacrifice one or the other, he sacrificed the secular. He did not even return to Babylon for the New Year's Festival, in which the king accompanied Marduk on his triumphal procession through the Ishtar Gate, in order to re-affirm his own right to the throne. Nabonidus, gripped by his love for his own deity, could not bring himself to do it.*

This ultimately weakened Babylon, and gave Cyrus his chance.

By 540, Cyrus had begun to send assault troops into skirmishes with the Babylonians along the eastern border. Their intrusions became serious enough that Nabonidus prepared himself to travel north, back up into the heart of his own country.[26]

By the time he arrived, Cyrus was planning an attack on Babylon itself. Nabonidus, now back in charge, ordered the Babylonian troops to march towards the enemy. They crossed the Tigris and met the Persian troops, under Cyrus, at Opis.

"The Babylonians engaged him," Herodotus remarks, baldly, "but they lost the battle and were driven back into the city."[27] Immediately the Babylonians barricaded themselves in under Nabonidus's direction. They were well supplied with food and water; according to Xenophon, enough to last twenty years.[28] Cyrus's rise to power had been gradual enough for the Babylonians to prepare themselves well for a siege (a prudent action, but one that suggests they did not have a great deal of faith in the army's ability to keep Cyrus off).

Cyrus, realizing that it would take months if not years to starve the defenders out of such a huge and well-supplied city, formed another plan. Xenophon explains it: The Tigris, which flowed right through the middle of Babylon, was deeper than two men's height. The city could not easily be flooded, thanks to Nebuchadnezzar's reinforcements, but Cyrus had another strategy in mind. He had trenches dug all along the Tigris, upstream from the city, and during one dark night he had his men open all the trenches simultaneously. Diverted away from its main stream in many directions, the level of the Tigris that ran through the city sank at once, enough that the Persian soldiers could march through the mud of the riverbed, under the walls of the city. The core assault

* Many scholars have argued that Nabonidus's absence from his palace is the source of the tale of Nebuchadnezzar's madness. The exile from Babylon is the primary similarity between the two events, but there are also significant differences.

unit climbed up out of the riverbed inside the city at night, covered with mud, and stumbled along through the streets, shouting as if they were drunken revellers, until they reached the palace and took it by storm. Xenophon points out that there was some sort of religious celebration going on which helped to mask the invasion; the book of Daniel agrees, saying that Belshazzar, the co-regent, was feasting in the palace with hundreds of his noblemen and had grown thoroughly drunk, when the Persians broke into the palace.

Nabonidus was apparently elsewhere in the city; he was captured and made prisoner without injury. But Belshazzar was killed in the fight that followed. The gates were opened from the inside. The rest of the Persians came in, and the city fell. The date was October 14, 539 BC.

Undoubtedly Cyrus had heard the grumblings that Nabonidus had slighted Marduk, and that Marduk was punishing the city for this insult. At once, Cyrus became the chosen of Marduk. He rode into the city to "take the hand of Marduk" in the traditional religious ceremony. He was, after all, Nebuchadnezzar's great-nephew by marriage, and thrones had been claimed on less of a blood relationship. And he had his scribes explain, in the Merodach-baladan/Napoleonic tradition, that he was in fact Babylon's liberator, the restorer of its ancient greatness.

He saved Babylon from need
Nabonidus, the king who did not venerate Marduk,
him Marduk delivered into the hands of Cyrus.
All the people prostrated themselves and kissed his feet,
They rejoiced in his sovereignty and their faces shone.
I, Cyrus, freed the inhabitants of Babylon from their yoke.
I repaired their dwellings, I removed the ruins,
Marduk the great lord rejoiced because of my deeds.
I returned the gods to their proper place
at the command of Marduk, the great lord.[29]

In exactly the same way, he announced to the Jews that he would restore the honor of their own God Yahweh. This made him very popular with the Jewish exiles. "In the first year of Cyrus king of Persia," begins the book of Ezra, meaning the first year of Cyrus's domination in Babylon, "the Lord moved the heart of Cyrus king of Persia to make a proclamation: 'The Lord, the God of Heaven, has given me all the kingdoms of the earth and he has appointed me to build a temple for him at Jerusalem in Judah. Anyone of his people among you, may his God be with him, and let him go up to Jerusalem in Judah and build the temple of the Lord, the God of Israel.' "[30] Cyrus also returned the valuables from the Temple of Solomon that he found in the treasury of Babylon, in another example of his using wealth (in this case, captured by others) to strengthen his own position. For this, he earned himself the title from the Jews "Anointed of the Lord."

A little more than a year after the return to Jerusalem began, the returned exiles laid the foundation of the Second Temple during a great festival of celebration. The priests were back in vestments that had not been used since Nebuchadnezzar's sack of the city; there were trumpets and cymbals and singing. But the new foundation, shabby and makeshift among the rubble, was so unlike the previous glories that the older onlookers could not bear the difference. While the younger exiles were shouting, "the older priests . . . and family heads, who had seen the former temple, wept aloud when they saw the foundation of *this* temple. . . . No one could distinguish the sound of the shouts of joy from the sound of weeping; and the sounds were heard from far away."[31]

TIMELINE 59

ROME AND BABYLON		PERSIA	
		PERSIA	MEDIA
	Sargon II		
	Sennacherib		
Tullus Hostilius	**Shamash-shum-ukin**		
		Cyrus I	
Ancus Marcius	**Kandalu**		
			Cyarxes
	Sin-shum-ishkun		
Tarquin the Elder	**Nabopolassar**		
Fall of Nineveh (612)			
	Nebuchadnezzar (605–562)		
Fall of Jerusalem (587)			
			Astyages
Servius Tullus (578)		**Cambyses I**	
	Amel-Marduk		
	Labashi-Marduk	**Cyrus II (the Great)** (559)	
	Nabonidus (556–539)		
Fall of Babylon (539)	**Cyrus II (the Great)**		

Cyrus's own victory was unmixed. He took over the great palace of Nebuchadnezzar as one of his royal houses, and kept Ecbatana as a summer residence; high in the mountains, it was snow-blocked for much of the winter, but much more pleasant than the hot Persian plain during the summer months. His palace in Anshan remained another of his homes. But for the administration of his new empire, Cyrus built himself a new capital city: Pasargadae.

In his Persian empire, the conquered peoples managed to carry on their daily lives without too much disruption. The newness of Cyrus's empire lay in his ability to think of it, not as a Persian nation in which the peoples must be made more Persian, but rather as a patchwork of nations under Persian rule. Unlike the Assyrians, he did not try to destroy national loyalties or identities. Instead he portrayed himself as the benevolent guardian of those very identities. And meanwhile, he continued to pay his Eyes and Ears to keep a watch out for trouble.

Chapter Sixty

The Republic of Rome

Between 550 and 501 BC,
Celts and Carthaginians enter the scene,
while Rome throws out its kings

THE NEWLY VICTORIOUS CYRUS had left Harpagus in Asia Minor to finish up the conquest of Lydia by capturing the Ionian cities, along the coast, that had been Lydian allies.

According to Herodotus, Harpagus's campaigning caused a domino effect. He began his operations with Phocaea, in the middle of the coast: a city whose people were "the earliest Greeks to make long voyages by sea." Besieged by Harpagus, who was busily building earthworks up against their stone walls, they told Harpagus that they might consider negotiations for surrender if he would pull back for a day and let them debate the matter in peace. He did so, and the Phocaeans "launched their penteconters" (ships with fifty oars and a square mainsail which were peculiarly theirs), "put their womenfolk, children, and all their personal effects on board . . . embarked themselves," and sailed away: "So the Persians gained control of a Phocaea which was emptied of men."

The Phocaeans had already built themselves a trading post called Alalia on the island of Cyrnus—the Greek name for Corsica. Half of the Phocaeans, overwhelmed by homesick longing, decided to go back to their deserted city and chance the Persian wrath. The other half set sail for Alalia.[1]

Once settled on Corsica, they set out to form a trading empire of their own. Penteconters were perfect for trade; they carried a large crew (fifty oarsmen plus the deck crew and captain, at a minimum), all of whom could fight, if necessary, which made the penteconter much more daunting to pirates than a merchant ship (which often had only five or six men aboard).[2] The Phocaeans planned to dominate the western Mediterranean trade routes, to which the other Greek cities had not yet paid much mind. To act as a trading post to the west, they built a colony on the coast of what is now southern France.

This new colony, Massalia, connected the Greek merchant net to a webwork of tribes that were, as yet, barely known. They were wild fighting barbarian tribes who came out of the depths of the rough lands farther away from the coast, bringing with them gold and salt, amber and fur, and (most valuable of all) tin.

The Phocaeans had come face-to-face with the Celts.

"CELT" IS AN ANACHRONISTIC NAME for the tribes who roamed around in western central Europe between 600 and 500 BC. Both the Greeks and the Romans referred to these peoples as "Gauls" or "Celts," a little later, but between 600 and 500 BC they had no kind of "ethnic identity."[3] They were merely a scattering of tribes with a common origin.

This origin was Indo-European, which meant that they had come, long ago, from that same homeland between the Caspian and the Black Seas once occupied by the peoples later known as Hittites, Mycenaeans, and Aryans.[4] Similarities between the languages of these four Indo-European peoples suggest that they wandered from a common point to settle in four different areas: the Hittites went west, into Asia Minor; the Mycenaeans west and then south into the northern Greek peninsula; the "Celts" to the north of the Alps; the Aryans first east and then south into India.

The particular Indo-Europeans later known as Celts did not write, so we can only try to read the graves and goods that they left behind. By the time that Massalia was built, around 630 BC, one particular style of burial had spread from modern Austria across to the southern Loire river. We call it the Hallstatt civilization, after its best-known site: a cemetery and salt mine south of the Danube.*

The Hallstatt tribes filled their graves with gold jewelry, swords and spears, food and drink and dishes for the use of the dead. Their dead chiefs were sur-

* The archaeological periods in central Europe are (naturally) different from those both to the east and west. They are, generally speaking, the Neolithic Age (before 2400 BC), the Copper Age (2300–1800), the Early Bronze Age (1800–1450), the Middle Bronze Age (1450–1250), the Late Bronze Age (1250–750), and the Iron Age (750–400). (See, for example, Marija Gimbutas, "European Prehistory: Neolithic to the Iron Age," in *Biennial Review of Anthropology* 3 [1963], pp. 79–92.) The Hallstatt culture was preceded by earlier Bronze Age settlements north of the Alps; archaeologists call these Bronze Age Indo-European cultures the Tumulus (characterized by the huge earthen mounds, or barrows, which they built over their dead), and the Urnfield (who cremated their dead and buried the bones in urns, not unlike the Villanovan and Latial tribes farther south; see chapter 49, pp. 354–355). The development of these cultures into iron-using tribes, which coincided with the Etruscan rise to power and the Greek colonization of Italy, produced the Hallstatt (See Daithi O'Hogain, *The Celts,* chapter 1, and Gimbutas, pp. 92–93.)

rounded by the graves of warriors who were interred with their long iron swords, their most precious possession.[5] Merchants from Hallstatt tribes drove their wagons to Massalia, loaded with amber, salt, and tin from as far away as the mines in modern Cornwall. These were all valuable and scarce items, and the trade made Massalia into a boom town.

The profitable Phocaean trade carried on from Massalia grew increasingly intolerable to the Etruscans. Cities from Etruria proper had been busy establishing cities farther and farther north. Now the aggressive Greeks were pushing into territory that the Etruscans considered their own to exploit. Greek colonies sprang up all along the southern coast of modern France; Monaco, Nice, and St. Tropez all had their origins as Greek trading posts.[6]

The pressure pushed the cities of Etruria—as spikily independent as those of Greece—into an association. Five Etruscan cities of Italy had joined together in an alliance against Rome a century before. Now, twelve Etruscan cities were ready to link their fates together into an association formed in imitation of the Greek amphictyonys, cities joined together for a common purpose while preserving their political independence. The Etruscan League, which formed around 550 BC, included Veii, Tarquinii, and Volsinii.[7]

Even united, though, the Etruscan League could not hope to fight successfully against the Phocaean invaders. The Phocaeans could call hundreds of allied Greek ships into any erupting war. And so, Herodotus continues, the Etruscans entered into league with the Carthaginians.

CARTHAGE, which lay on the northern coast of Africa at the bottom of the Mediterranean Sea, was already three hundred years old by 550. The two oldest cities of the loose Phoenician federation, Tyre and Sidon, now lay in Cyrus's dominion. But Carthage, farther away, was the center of its own little kingdom. In 550, its king was Mago, the first Carthaginian monarch of whom we have any historical record.[8]

By Mago's day, Carthage had planted trading colonies of its own in the Mediterranean. The Carthaginians were no happier than the Etruscans to see the Greeks busily colonizing around them, and they were very amenable to joining in an attack on the Phocaeans at Alalia.* A historical record of the alliance survives in Aristotle's *Politics,* which mentions that the "Etruscans and

* Possibly the Carthaginians had a bone of their own to pick with the Phocaeans; excavations at Marseilles have suggested that Phoenician settlers built a trading post of their own at Massalia before the Phocaean arrival, which may have driven the older merchant colony away.

60.1 Romans, Carthaginians, and Gauls

Carthaginians" once formed a community "for the sake of trade and of business relations."[9]

The Greeks on Alalia (or Corsica), getting wind of the plot, prepared for war: "The Phocaeans got sixty of their own ships ready," Herodotus writes, "and went out to meet the enemy in the Sardinian Sea." In the fighting that followed, forty Phocaean ships were destroyed, and the remaining twenty damaged so badly that they could no longer fight. But they could still float, so the Phocaeans sailed back to Corsica, loaded up their womenfolk and children once more, and retreated to Rhegium, a Greek city on the toe of the Italian boot.

The sea battle at Alalia was the second great naval battle ever fought (Rameses III against the Sea Peoples being the first). The immediate effect was that the Etruscans were temporarily top dog in the area. They took over Corsica and, untroubled by roving Phocaeans in penteconters, built trading colonies themselves, as far west as the coast of Spain (or so writes Stephanus of Byzantium.) They were at the height of their power, masters of the peninsula north of the Tiber.[10]

Massalia itself had its ties with Alalia cut, but the Etruscans did not destroy it. Having wiped out the mother city, they were not too worried about far-flung children. Massalia likely struggled for some time, but instead of collapsing, the city survived into the twenty-first century; it is now called Marseilles.

The battle had also given Carthage room to spread itself. By treaty with the Etruscans, they claimed rulership of Sardinia; and, untroubled by Greeks in the western Mediterranean, they too extended their reach to the Spanish coast.

WHILE THE GREEKS retreated and the Carthaginians and Etruscans sailed the Mediterranean, Rome was growing in both size and power. The more outlying areas that it claimed, the greater its internal troubles. How could a king of one race rule over a set of peoples so hostile to each other that they still refused even to intermarry? And how could that king deal with an aristocracy so opinionated and independent that it could be accused of assassinating its first, semidivine ruler?

In the days of Etruscan rule, Rome's king and Rome's people seem to have tried to work out some sort of compromise between monarchic absolutism, Cyrus style, and rule by the people, as in Athens. The history of the compromise is obscured by the early historians of Rome, who all seem to be reading later structures back into much earlier times. But it seems that, even in the days of the kings, Romans were already given a voice in the city's affairs.

The Roman historian Varro mentions an early division of Rome's people into three "tribes" of some kind, which may represent the three national groups of Sabines, Latials, and Etruscans (although the earliest accounts of Rome say nothing about this).[11] Livy, on the other hand, credits Servius Tullius with dividing the people of Rome into six "classes," based not on ancestry but on wealth; a useful way of starting from scratch, for a city in which the self-made man first made his appearance. The richest Romans were expected to defend the city with bronze helmet, shield, greaves, breastplate, sword, and spear; the poorest were required to bring only slings and stones.[12] Even under the kings of Rome, the citizens of Rome were expected to defend their own city—and, presumably, to decide when and where attack was needed. Given this much power over their city, the Roman citizens would not put up with the rule of a king for much longer.

At the end of Servius Tullius's forty-four-year rule, the monarchy imploded.

The culprit was Servius Tullius's nephew, Tarquin the Younger. He was not only ambitious but evil; his wickedness soon found an outlet when he started an affair with his younger brother's wife Tullia, who was also evil: "There is a magnetic power in evil," Livy observes, "like draws towards like." Tarquin the Younger was himself married, but rather than allowing this to get in their way, the lovers plotted the deaths of both of their spouses, and then married.

"From that day on," Livy writes, "Servius, now an old man, lived in ever increasing danger." Tullia, the prototype of Lady Macbeth, was filled with ambition that her new husband be king, and "soon found that one crime must lead to another. . . . she gave her husband no rest by day or night." "I didn't want a man who would be content just to be my husband," she lectured him, "I wanted a man who was worthy of a crown!"

Pricked into action, Tarquin the Younger broke into the throne room while Servius Tullius was out, seated himself on the throne, and declared himself king. Servius, hearing of the invasion, ran to the throne room to confront the usurper, but Tarquin, who had "gone too far to turn back," hurled the old king out into the street with his own hands, where his assassins finished the old man off. "With Servius," writes Livy, "true kingship came to an end; never again was a Roman king to rule in accordance with humanity and justice."[13]

Tarquin the Younger, now in control of the throne, quickly earned himself the nickname Tarquinius Superbus: "Tarquin the Proud." He formed a bodyguard to strong-arm the citizens of Rome into obedience; he executed Servius Tullius's loyal supporters; he accused innocent people of capital crimes so that he could confiscate their money. "He had usurped by force the throne to which he had no title whatever," Livy tells us.

> The people had not elected him, the Senate had not sanctioned his accession. Without hope of his subjects' affection, he could rule only by fear. . . . He punished by death, exile, or confiscation of property men whom he happened to suspect or dislike; he broke the established tradition of consulting the Senate on all matters of public business; he made and unmade treaties and alliances with whom he pleased without any reference whatever either to the commons or the Senate.

All of these were serious offenses. But the last straw came when his son, putative heir to the Roman throne, raped a Roman noblewoman named Lucretia, the wife of one of his own friends. Shamed, Lucretia killed herself. Her body lay in the public square while her husband shouted out to his countrymen to help him avenge his wife's death. It did not take long for indignation over the rape of Lucretia to morph into indignation over the tyrannical acts of the entire family.

Tarquin the Proud himself was outside Rome at the time, leading a campaign against the neighboring city of Ardea. When news of the uprising reached him, he started back to Rome; but by the time he arrived, the rebellion was in full swing, "Tarquin found the city gates shut against him," writes Livy, "and his exile decreed." The army joined "enthusiastically" into the insurrection, and Tarquin was forced to flee north into Etruria with his son.

Lucretia's bereaved husband and one of his trusted friends were elected leaders of the city, by the popular vote of the army: only members of the divisions which had been formed by Servius Tullius were allowed to vote. The two men were given kinglike powers to declare war and make decrees—but with a difference. Their power would last only for a single year, and each man could veto the other's decrees. They were now *consuls*: the highest office in Roman government. Rome had been liberated from its monarchy, and the Roman Republic had begun.*

Livy, our most thorough source for these years, gives this story a heavy pro-Republic gloss. As far as he is concerned, once Tarquin the Proud was thrown out of the city, the entire history of Rome makes a right-hand turn: "My task from now on will be to trace the history of a free nation," Livy declares, "gov-

* The traditional date for the expulsion of Tarquin the Proud, based on Livy's account, is 509 BC, although Rome's breaking away from Etruscan rule has been assigned dates as late as 445 BC. A detailed discussion of the evolution of Roman government after 509 BC is well beyond the scope of this work, but interested readers should consider consulting Gary Forsythe's *A Critical History of Early Rome* (chapter 6, "The Beginning of the Roman Republic") and H. H. Scullard's *A History of the Roman World, 753 to 146 bc* (chapter 3, "The New Republic and the Struggle of the Orders").

erned by annually elected officers of state and subject not to the caprice of individual men, but to the overriding authority of law."

The expulsion of Tarquin the Proud probably does have a historical base, but it is unlikely that the Romans suddenly realized the shortcomings of monarchy. Rather, the driving out of the Etruscan king represents the throwing off of Etruscan dominance.

Rome had been ruled by Etruscans since the accession of Tarquin the Elder a hundred years earlier. But since the sea victory at Alalia in 535, the Etruscans had been hard pressed to keep their power.

The events following Tarquin the Proud's expulsion show the slippage of Etruscan strength. In Etruria, he went from city to city, attempting to put together an anti-Roman coalition. "I am of the same blood as you," was his most potent argument. The men of Veii and Tarquinii responded. A double army marched behind Tarquin, back towards Rome, in an attempt to reassert Etruscan power over the most important city south of Etruria.

They were met by the Roman army and defeated in a fierce fight which was almost a draw; Livy remarks that the Romans won because they lost one fewer man than the Etruscans. The Etruscans then began to plan a second attack on Rome, this time under the leadership of Lars Porsena, the king of the Etruscan city of Clusium.

News of the coming attack was received in Rome with something close to panic. They had barely managed to fight off Veii and Tarquinii, and Lars Porsena had earned himself a reputation as a fierce fighter. In terror, the farmers on the city's outskirts abandoned their farms and fled inside the city's walls.

It was a peculiarity of the Roman defenses that the city was protected on three sides by walls, but on the fourth—the east side—only by the Tiber. The river was generally considered uncrossable, but there was one way that an army could get across the Tiber and directly into the city: a wooden bridge which stretched from the eastern lands outside the city, known as the Janiculum, across the river, right into the heart of Rome.

Lars Porsena made his first approach from this direction, eschewing the walls in favor of the Tiber. The Etruscan army swept in like a storm, and took the Janiculum without difficulty; the Roman soldiers posted there threw away their weapons and ran across the bridge to safety.

Except for one: the soldier Horatius, who took up his position at the western edge of the bridge, ready to hold it alone: "conspicuous amongst the rout of fugitives," writes Livy, "sword and shield ready for action."[14]

According to Roman legend, Horatius held off the Etruscans long enough for Roman demolition forces to arrive to destroy the bridge. Ignoring their shouts for him to retreat back across the bridge before it was taken down, he went on fighting until the supports were cut to pieces. "The Etruscan advance was suddenly checked by the crash of the falling bridge and the simultaneous shout of triumph from the Roman soldiers who had done their work in time," Livy writes. Horatius, now cut off from the city, plunged into the river in full armor and swam across. "It was a noble piece of work," Livy concludes, "legendary, maybe, but destined to be celebrated in story through the years to come."

Like Sennacherib's withdrawal from the walls of Jerusalem, Horatius's defense of the bridge was a minor military engagement that stands out in memory because of a poem; in this case, Thomas Babington Macaulay's *Lays of Ancient Rome*, in which Horatius becomes the model of patriotic British bravery:

Then out spake brave Horatius,
The captain of the gate:
"To every man upon this earth
Death cometh soon or late.
And how can man die better
Than facing fearful odds,
For the ashes of his fathers,
And the temples of his gods?"[15]

Gallant though it may have been, the defense of the bridge did not end the Etruscan attack. Porsena spread his forces across the Janiculum, barricaded the river so that Rome could not be supplied with food by ships, and besieged the walls. The siege, supplemented by various indecisive battles, dragged on until Porsena finally agreed to withdraw in return for Roman concessions. The two cities swore out a peace treaty that did little to change the relationship between the two cities, but at least halted hostilities.

The treaty revealed that the Etruscans and Romans were now balanced in power. Given that the Etruscans had been dominant for so many decades, this was a defeat for the cities of Etruria. And Rome made its own treaty with Carthage, sworn out in the same year, which recognized the coast south of the Tiber not as Etruscan, but as Roman territory.

Polybius records this treaty in his *Rise of the Roman Empire*. As he understands it, Rome and Carthage agreed to friendship on certain conditions, the most important being that Roman ships were not to sail farther west than "Fair Promontory," the modern Cape Bon.* A Roman captain who was blown off

* Two thousand years later, Fair Promontory was still a dividing line between armies. In 1943, the Axis forces in North Africa were forced into surrender when General von Arnim surrendered at Cape Bon—according to the *Guardian* (May 13, 1943), "on the extreme tip of the peninsula." Two days

course and landed in the forbidden territory was to repair his ship and leave within five days, without buying or carrying away "anything more than is required for the repair of his ship or for sacrifice."[16] Any trade that took place east of Fair Promontory had to be carried out in the presence of a town clerk (presumably to keep the Romans from trading arms close to Carthaginian land). In return, the Carthaginians agreed to leave the entire Latin population alone, to build no forts near them, and to refrain from entering Latin territory with weapons. Clearly the Romans were most concerned for their future political expansion, while the Carthaginians had their eye on a trading empire.

The Etruscans, on the other hand, were nowhere in sight. They were also just about to lose their grip on the land around the Po river; groups of Celtic warriors were on their way over the Alps, down into northern Italy.

According to Livy, they were driven by a population explosion; Gaul had become "so rich and populous that the effective control of such large numbers was a matter of serious difficulty." So the king of the Celts in Gaul sent his two nephews out, with two groups of followers, to find new lands. One nephew went north, into "southern Germany," while the other went south with a "vast host" towards the Alps. They crossed the mountains and "defeated the Etruscans near the river Ticinus, and . . . founded the town of Mediolanium"—that is, the city of Milan.

Nor was that the end of the invasion. Livy goes on to describe at least four successive waves of Gaulish invasion, each maurading tribe driving away the Etruscan inhabitants who lived in the cities south of the Alps, and building their own towns in the Po river valley. The fourth wave of arriving Celts found "all the country between the Alps and the Po already occupied" and so "crossed the river on rafts," expelled the Etruscans between the Po and the Apennine ridge, and settled there as well.[17]

The Celts must have been a fearsome sight, charging down the mountain slopes towards the walls of the Etruscan cities. The word "Celt," given to these tribes by the Greeks and Romans, comes from an Indo-European root meaning "to strike," and the weapons found in their graves—seven-foot spears, iron swords with thrusting tips and cutting edges, war chariots, helmets and shields—testify to their skill at war.[18] "They slept on straw and leaves," Polybius remarks, "ate meat, and practised no other pursuits but war and agriculture."[19]

---

earlier, the Allied forces had "cut off Cape Bon from the mainland and penned its enemy garrison in the mountainous roadless interior of the peninsula," while Allied naval and air forces blocked any attempts to evacuate Cape Bon by sea—a strategy which E. A. Montague, the *Guardian* war correspondent, referred to as Germany's "hope of a Dunkirk" (after the evacuation of Allied troops from occupied France in 1940, in the face of the German advance). (In "End of organised resistance in North Africa: Von Arnim captured at Cape Bon," *Guardian*, May 13, 1943.)

This particular invasion, which began around 505 BC, was part of a larger movement in the entire Celtic culture. Right around this time, new customs begin to overlay the old Hallstatt settlements; this was a culture that used knots, curves, and mazelike lines as decorations, and which buried leaders not with wagons, as in Hallstatt graves, but instead with two-wheeled war chariots. This was not a peaceful takeover. The Hallstatt burial ground at Heuneberg, in southern Germany, was thoroughly looted; the fortress on the Danube was burned.[20]

Archaeologists have given this next phase in Celtic culture the name "La Tène," after one of its most extensive sites, just west of the southern Rhine. In some places La Tène sites lie south of Hallstatt sites, or overwhelm them (as at Heuneburg and Dürrnberg), but generally they lie a little to the north.[21] It is the La Tène style of art which we now identify as "Celtic," and the characteristics of the La Tène culture which replaced those of the Hallstatt. This was not a foreign invasion, but a homegrown shift in power: one Celtic culture overwhelming another.

This internal struggle for dominance gave rise to the invasions southwards into Italy; its reality is preserved in the later account of the Roman historian Justin:

> The reason the Gauls came to Italy and sought new areas to settle in was internal unrest and ceaseless fratricidal strife. When they tired of this and made their way to Italy they drove the Etruscans from their homeland and founded Milan, Di Como, Brescia, Verona, Bergamo, Trento, and Vicenza.[22]

The unrest may have driven some of the Celts as far over as the western coast of Europe, and perhaps even across the water to the island of Britain. Britain had been inhabited for some centuries by a people we know almost nothing about, except that they dragged together huge rings of standing stones for a purpose which had something to do with the sky. Construction on Stonehenge, the most famous of these huge monuments, probably began around 3100 BC and continued over the next two thousand years.* But these people were soon infiltrated by the same warlike Celts who were pushing

* The general consensus seems to be that the earliest population of Britain entered the island all the way back before the change in climate that brought an end to the Ice Age, and was then isolated by the flooding of the land bridge between Britain and the mainland of Europe which occurred by 6000 BC (the same shift in water levels which pushed the head of the Persian Gulf northwards in the days of the early Sumerian cities). See chapter 1, pp. 3–4. What they did in their millennia of isolation, before the arrival of the Celts, is completely obscure to us.

south against the Etruscans. Right around 500 BC, graves in Britain begin to contain war chariots for the first time, just like the La Tène graves in southern Germany.

THE ROMAN REPUBLIC responded to the invasions in the north by altering its new government. "In these circumstances of mounting anxiety and tension," writes Livy, ". . . the proposal was made, for the first time, of appointing a dictator." The year was 501, only eight years after the Republic began.

Livy chalks up the willingness of the voting populace (which is to say, the army) to pass this proposal to a whole constellation of military emergencies: war with various nearby cities, hostility from the Sabines, looming attack from other Latin towns, unrest from "the commons." But certainly the ripples of displacement from the north, reverberating down south, put the entire peninsula on edge.

The office of dictator was not, as in modern times, license for unlimited power. The Roman dictators had power for only six months at a time, and had to be appointed by the ruling consuls. Often the dictator *was* one of the consuls. His role was to keep Rome secure in the face of extraordinary outside threats, but he also had unusual powers inside the city. Consuls were allowed to impose the death penalty on Romans outside the walls of Rome, in connection with military expeditions, but inside Rome they had to submit criminals to the will of the voting population for punishment. The dictator, though, was allowed to exercise that power of life and death inside Rome itself, with no obligation to consult the people.[23]

This first dictator may have been appointed to deal with marauding Gauls, Latins, and Etruscans, but getting Rome's unruly population back under control was also part of his job, as Livy makes clear. "The appointment of a dictator for the first time in Rome," he writes, "and the solemn sight of his progress through the streets preceded by the ceremonial axes, had the effect of scaring the commons into a more docile frame of mind. . . . From a dictator there was no appeal, and no help anywhere but in implicit obedience."[24]

Implicit obedience: Rome's first defense. It was the first time that the rights of the Republic were suspended for the sake of expediency, but not the last.

TIMELINE 60

PERSIA		ROME
PERSIA	MEDIA	
		Tarquin the Elder
	Astyages	
Cambyses I		**Servius Tullius** (578)
Cyrus II (the Great) (559)		
		Etruscan League
		Tarquin the Proud (535)
		Roman Republic begins (509)
		Celtic invasion
		First Roman dictator

Chapter Sixty-One

Kingdoms and Reformers

Between 560 and 500 BC,
India divides into kingdoms and alliances,
and the kingdom of Magadha begins its rise

BETWEEN THE MYTHICAL BATTLE of the Mahabharata and the middle of the sixth century BC, the warlike clans of India had battled, negotiated, and treatied their way into a semistable arrangement of kingdoms.

Sixteen of these kingdoms are mentioned in tales preserved by Buddhist oral tradition and later set down in writing.* Among them are the states of Kuru, Gandhara, and Pancala, kingdoms grown from the roots of the ancient clans that had fought in the Bharata War; the far southern state of Ashuaka, down below the Vindhya and Satpura mountain ranges, on the dry plateau now known as the Deccan; and the state of Magadha, below the curve of the Ganga.†

The sixteen kingdoms were called *mahajanapadas*, a word rooted in much

* Our best source for the very early history of the sixteen states is the Pali Canon (also called the *Tipitaka*), an enormous collection of Buddhist scriptures transmitted orally and set down in writing during the first century BC. The Pali Canon is divided into three sections: the *Vinaya Pitaka,* which prescribes the conduct of monks and nuns living in religious communities; the *Sutta Pitaka*, which consists of hundreds of teachings attributed to the Buddha (a "sutta" is a discourse or teaching) and is itself divided into five parts, called *nikayas*; and the *Abhidhamma Pitaka,* which is a systematic theology based on the teachings in the *Sutta Pitaka.* The Pali Canon is used by all four of the major schools of Buddhism (the Theravada, Mahasanghika, Sarvastivada, and Sammatiya) and is the *sole* sacred scripture for Theravada Buddhism. The texts in the Pali Canon are concerned with spiritual practice, not politics; the history we can gather from them has to be gleaned from passing remarks or from stories told to illustrate the source of a particular Buddhist practice.

† The most complete list is found in the sutta (teaching attributed to the Buddha) called the *Visakhuposatha Sutta.* The sixteen states and their alternate spellings are: Kamboja, Gandhar (Gandhara), Kuru (Kura, Kure), Pancala (Panchala), Malla (a kingdom that also included an alliance of eight clans called the Vajji or Vrijji Confederacy), Vatsa (Vatsya, Vansa), Kosal (Kosala), Matsya (Maccha), Surasena (Shurasena), Chedi (Ceti), Avanti, Ashuaka (Assaka), Kashi (Kasi), Magadha, Anga, Vanga.

older times. The early nomadic Aryan warrior clans had called themselves *jana* (Sanskrit for "tribe"); the warrior clans that had settled in the Ganga river valley and claimed land for themselves extended this word and called themselves *janapada*, tribes with land. The sixteen mahajanapada, or "great janapada," were tribes with land who had absorbed other tribes and become kingdoms. In these kingdoms, the king himself, his relatives, and his warriors remained the ruling clan. To be born into the ruling clan was to be *kshatriya* and to belong, by right, to the elite and powerful.

The kshatriya held political power, but the priests wielded a peculiar power of their own. Sacrifices and offerings had been part of the daily life of the Aryans since their journey south into India: "Indra helps, by his aid, the one occupied with sacrifice," reads one of the earliest hymns in the Rig Veda, "the one who chants hymns, who cooks the sacrificial food, who is strengthened by holy utterance . . . and by the gifts to the officiating priests. He, O people, is Indra."[1] Wound together with elements from the Harappan peoples and the other indigenous tribes, the old Aryan practices became the core of the most ancient form of practices later known as Hinduism. The priests who performed the sacrifices had been the first aristocracy of Indian society, and they continued to hold their influence in the sixteen mahajanapas. Like the ruling kshatriya, the priests had their own clans: to be born into a priestly family was to be *brahman* and to inherit the privilege of sacrifice.

This three-way division of society—priests, warrior-chiefs, and everyone else (the "everyone else" families were *vaishyas,* common people)—was far from unknown in ancient times. But in India, the priests dominated the rest. In most other ancient societies, the kings and warriors were at the top of the power heap; even those who paid lip service to the importance of the gods were likely to throw their prophets and priests in jail, or even execute them. And in almost every other ancient society, the king was able to carry out certain sacred functions, and sometimes held the highest religious office in the land.

But the brahman had an unshared power. During the days of the sixteen kingdoms, a man who had not been born kshatriya could still become king if the priests carried out a ritual to bestow sacred power upon him, but no one who was not born brahman could take up the job of a priest.[2] The brahman was, according to the later Hindu text *The Laws of Manu*, "the lord" of all other created orders, the most excellent of men: "born as the highest on earth, the lord of all created beings, for the protection of the treasury of the law;

(See *Anguttara Nikaya*, VIIII.43, in Bhikkhu Khantipalo, trans., *Lay Buddhist Practice*; Romila Thapar, *Early India: From the Origins to AD 1300*, p. 138; and John Keay, *India: A History*, p. 45.)

61.1 Indian Kingdoms

whatever exists in the world is the property of the brahman . . . the brahman is, indeed, entitled to all."[3]

By the time of the sixteen kingdoms, the animal sacrifices which had been so important to the wandering nomadic tribes had slowly fallen out of favor with the growing urban populations of India. But a power awarded by the universe itself to those "born as the highest on earth" could hardly be abridged. The importance of the priests was so built into the entire consciousness of the warrior clans that the brahmans—far from losing their job—kept their central role. Rather than sacrificing, they governed the proper performance of the bloodless rituals which now occupied the place of offerings: rituals carried out to honor the flame of the hearth, to acknowledge the coming of dusk, to honor deities by caring for their images, to mark marriages and funerals.[4]

Around the edges of the sixteen states lay a ring of tribes who still resisted being enfolded into any one of the sixteen mahajanapada. Instead of coalescing into kingdoms, these tribes formed independent alliances, called *gana-sanghas.*

It seems likely that the tribes of the gana-sanghas were not primarily of Aryan descent, but rather had their roots in the inhabitants of the Ganga valley who had been there before the warrior clans arrived. Intermarriage between the newcomers and the tribes (as illustrated by the alliance of the Pandava clan with the Pancala, back in the story of the Bharata War) had probably broken down any hard and fast racial divisions. But there is one strong proof that the gana-sanghas were, overwhelmingly, non-Aryan: they did not share the ritual practices so central to the lives of the Indians in the mahajanapada.

There were only two kinds of people in the gana-sanghas: the ruling families who claimed most of the land, and the hired servants and slaves who worked on it. The decisions (to go to war, to trade with another clan, to divert water from irrigation systems over particular fields) were made by the heads of the ruling families, and in these decisions, the laborers had no voice at all.[5]

The mahajanapada too had voiceless servants. They were a fourth kind of people: not ruling kshatriyas, or priestly brahmans, nor even common vaishyas who worked as farmers, potters, carpenters, and bricklayers. A late song of the Rig Veda, describing the mythical origin of each order, assigns pride of place to the brahman, who were born from the mouth of the huge, preexisting cosmic giant Purusha, whose death gave rise to the entire universe:

The brahman was his mouth,
his two arms became the kshatriya
his two thighs are the vaishya
and from his two feet the shudra was produced.[6]

The shudra were slaves and servants, the fourth and subordinate class of people. They were voiceless and powerless, unable to free themselves from servitude, allowed by law to be killed or exiled at any whim of their masters, barred from even hearing the sacred vedas read (the penalty was to have boiling lead poured into the offending ears).* They were not part of the society of

* By 600 BC, the Rig Veda—the oldest collection of hymns from ancient Aryan times—had been joined by three other collections of hymns: the Samaveda (a selection of Rig Veda hymns specially arranged for ceremonial use by singers), the Yajurveda (a combination of Rig Veda hymns plus newer texts, used by priestly specialists called *adhvaryu,* who carried out particular acts during religious

the mahajanapada; they were other, something else. Their origin is not clear, but perhaps the shudra were originally a conquered people.* [7]

In such highly stratified societies, someone was bound to be discontent.

The first objections to all of this hierarchy came from the gana-sanghas. Around 599 BC, the reformer Nataputta Vardhamana was born into a gana-sangha in the northeast of the Ganga valley: a confederacy of tribes known as the Vrijji.[8] His own particular tribe was the Jnatrika, and he was a prince and rich man, the son of a ruler.

According to his followers, his reforms began in 569, when he was thirty years old. At first he rejected the wealth and privilege of his birth, divested himself of all possessions except for a single garment, and spent twelve years in silence and meditation. At the end of this period, he had reached a vision of a life free from any priests: there were no brahmans in his universe. The goal of human existence was not to communicate with the gods through the agency of the priests. Nor was it to please gods by carrying out the duties to which one was born, as the Hindu scriptures taught.† Rather, man should free himself from the chains of the material universe by rejecting the passions (greed, lust, appetite) that chain him to the material world.

Around 567, he began to walk barefoot through India, teaching five principles: *ahisma,* nonviolence against all living things (the first systematic explanation of why animals have rights); *satya,* truthfulness; *asteya,* refraining from theft of any kind; *brahmacharya,* the rejection of sexual pleasure; and *aparigraha,* detachment from all material things (a commitment which the

---

rites), and the Atharveda (a collection not only of hymns, but of spells and rites for use in everyday life). (John Y. Fenton et al., *Religions of Asia,* pp. 27–28.)

* The word *caste* was a sixteenth-century invention of the Portuguese. Ancient Indians are more likely to have used the Sanskrit word *jati* ("birth") for the divisions.

† In the sixth century BC, Hinduism underwent massive new developments (not unrelated to the political shifts) and put out branches in three different directions. The Way of Action was a Hinduism particularly dominated by the priests, who emphasized that the role of every man and woman was to carry out the duties of the caste into which he or she was born. The Way of Knowledge focused, not on action, but on the achievement of high spiritual enlightenment through the study of *upanishads,* new teachings written down beginning around the time of the sixteen kingdoms. The Way of Devotion emphasized instead the worship of the highest deity in the Indian pantheon (either Shiva or Vishnu) as the center of the good life. All three traditions offer rebirth into a better human existence or (eventually) into a heavenly existence as a reward for those who excel in action, or in enlightenment, or in devotion.

This is a very simple summary of an immensely huge and complicated religious tradition. *Religions of Asia* by John Fenton et al. is a standard introduction that gives a slightly more detailed explanation of Hinduism's development. *Hinduism: A Very Short Introduction* by Kim Knott is another good overview. A more detailed (and academic, although still readable) resource is *Hinduism: Originis, Beliefs, Practices, Holy Texts, Sacred Places* by Vasudha Narayanan.

Mahavira illustrated by doing away with his single garment and going naked instead). Followers gathered behind him, and as a great teacher, Nataputta Vardhamana became known as the "Mahavira" (the Great Hero).[9]

None of these were brand new ideas. Mainstream Hinduism also taught the freeing of the self from the material world in various ways. The Mahavira was less an innovator than a reformer of already existing practices. But his explanations of the need for extreme self-denial, and the obligation to respect all life, were compelling enough to gather a following. His doctrines became known as Jainism, his followers as Jains.*

A few years later, another innovator appeared from outside the mahajanapadas, also born into a gana-sangha. Like Nataputta Vardhamana, he was born to power and money. He too rejected the privileges of his life around the age of thirty and walked away into a self-imposed exile. He too came to the conclusion that freedom could only be found by those who were able to reject their passions and desires.

This innovator was Siddhartha Gautama, a prince of the Shakya clan, which lay north of the Mahavira's native Vrijji alliance. According to the traditional tales of his enlightenment, he lived his earlier years surrounded by family and by comfort: he had a wife and a young daughter, and his father the king kept him in luxury within the walls of a huge palace, cut off from the lives of ordinary men.

But one day Siddhartha ordered his charioteer to take him for a drive in the park. There he saw an ancient man, "broken-toothed, gray-haired, crooked and bent of body, leaning on a staff, and trembling." Shocked by this extreme old age, he returned to his palace: "Shame on birth," he thought to himself, "since to everyone that is born, old age must come." He pushed the thought away, but on his next journey to the park, he saw a man riddled with disease, and after that a corpse. This cast him into even greater trouble of mind.

But the crowning revelation happened at a party some time later. He was entertained by the dancing and singing of beautiful women, but as the evening wore on, they grew weary, sat down, and fell asleep. The prince, looking around the room,

> perceived these women lying asleep, with their musical instruments scattered about them on the floor—some with their bodies wet with trickling

* Another simplified summary; for more, try the basic *An Introduction to Jainism* by Bharat S. Shah, or the more scholarly *The Jains* by Paul Dundas. The best-known modern follower of Jain principles is Gandhi, who made ahisma the center of his campaigns for nonviolent change. Gandhi was not himself a Jain, but grew up in a city where there was a large Jain population.

> phlegm and spittle; some grinding their teeth, and muttering and talking in their sleep; some with their mouths open; and some with their dress fallen apart so as plainly to disclose their loathsome nakedness. This great alteration in their appearance still further increased his aversion for sensual pleasures. To him that magnificent apartment . . . began to seem like a cemetery filled with dead bodies impaled and left to rot.[10]

It was in response to this that he set out on his own self-imposed exile. The year, according to tradition, was 534 BC.*

Siddhartha spent years wandering, trying to come to peace with the inevitability of decay and corruption. He tried meditation, but when his period of meditation was done, he was still faced with the reality of approaching suffering and death. He tried the Jain method of asceticism, starving himself to weaken his ties with the earth until, as a later text tells us, his "spine stood out like a corded rope," his ribs like "the jutting rafters of an old roofless cowshed," and his eyes were so sunken into their sockets that they seemed "like the gleam of water sunk in a deep well."[11] Yet this self-denial did not move him an inch beyond the common human condition.

Finally, he came to the answer that he had been searching for. It is not just desires that trap men and women, but existence itself, which is "bound up with impassioned appetite," and which always desires: "thirst for sensual pleasures, thirst for existence, thirst for non-existence."[12] The only freedom from desire was a freedom from existence itself.

The realization of this truth was Siddhartha's enlightenment, and from this point on he was known not as Siddhartha Gautama, but as a Buddha: an enlightened one who has achieved *nirvana,* the knowledge of a truth which is caused by nothing, dependent on nothing, and leads to nothing, a way of existence impossible to define in words.†

This was not merely a spiritual discovery, but (despite claims of detachment) a political position. It was both anti-brahman and anti-caste. The emphasis in brahmanical Hinduism on rebirth meant that most Indians faced a future of weary life after weary life after weary life, with no hope of leaving

* The traditional birth and death dates for both the Mahavira (599–527) and the Buddha (563–483) have been criticized in recent scholarship as about a hundred years too early, which would shift both men into the next century. Support for the later dates is widespread but not universal among scholars of India; as uncertainty remains, I have decided to use the traditional dates for the sake of consistency.

† For more, try the basic *Buddha* by Karen Armstrong, and Michael Carrithers's *Buddha: A Very Short Introduction.* A more comprehensive study of Buddhism is found in *An Introduction to Buddhism: Teachings, History, and Practices* by Peter Harvey.

their strictly circumscribed lives except through rebirth, which might face them with yet another long lifetime of similar or worse suffering. It was an existence which, in Karen Armstrong's phrase, did not so much promise the hope of rebirth as threaten with "the horror of redeath . . . [B]ad enough to have to endure the process of becoming senile or chronically sick and undergoing a frightening, painful death *once*, but to be forced to go through all this again and again seemed intolerable and utterly pointless."[13] In a world where death was no release, another kind of escape must be found.

Equally anti-brahman (and anti-kshatriya) was the Buddha's teaching that each man must rely on himself, not on the power of a single strong leader who will solve all of his problems. Much later, a ninth-century Buddhist master coined the command "If you meet the Buddha, kill the Buddha!" in order to emphasize to his students just how important it was not to submit to a single authority figure—even one who claims a divine mandate, whether king or priest.[14]

Soon the Buddha too had his followers, disciples drawn from all castes.

While Mahavira and the Buddha preached the relinquishment of material possessions, the kings of the mahajanapadas were fighting to gain as much territory as possible. Kashi and Kosal, just north of the Ganga, and Magadha to the south were prime enemies in the wars for land. They fought over the Ganga valley, and were joined in this competition by the gana-sangha Vrijji, home confederacy of the Mahavira.

Kashi and Kosal traded off power with each other, neither keeping dominance for long. But Magadha, below the Ganges, grew steadily stronger. The king Bimbisara came to the throne of Magadha in 544 BC, and became the first Indian empire-builder, albeit in a minor way. As the Buddha was reaching enlightenment, Bimbisara was rallying his armies against the delta kingdom of Anga, which controlled the river's access to the ocean (by way of the Bay of Bengal), and which contained the important city of Campa, the primary port from which ships sailed out for trade and down the coast to the south.[15] He marched against it, conquered it, and kept it.

This was not a huge conquest. But Anga was the first of the sixteen kingdoms to be permanently absorbed into another, which was a portent of things to come. And military campaigns were not Bimbisara's only victory. He treatied his way, by marriage, into control over part of Kosol, and by another marriage into friendship with the gana-sangha on his western border.[16] He built roads all across his kingdom, so that he could easily travel around it and call its village leaders together into conference. These roads also made it possible for him to collect (and police) the payment of taxes. He welcomed the Buddha, who had wandered down from the north; any doctrine which reduced the power of the brahmans was bound to increase the power of the king. He was well on his way to making Magadha not a set of warrior clans that held uncomfortably together, but a little empire. India, so long on an entirely different path of development than the empires to the west, was drawing closer to them.

TIMELINE 61

ROME	INDIA
	Sixteen kingdoms in the Ganga river valley
Tarquin the Elder	
	Birth of the Mahavira (trad. 599)
Servius Tullius (578)	
	Birth of the Buddha (trad. 563)
Etruscan League	**Bimbisara of Magadha**
Tarquin the Proud (535)	
	Death of the Mahavira (trad. 527)
Roman Republic begins (509)	
Celtic invasion	
First Roman dictator	
	Death of the Buddha (trad. 483)

Chapter Sixty-Two

The Power of Duty and the Art of War

In China, between 551 and 475 BC, *a philosopher and a general try to make sense of chaotic times*

As the Eastern Zhou rule began, a square of powerful states—Jin, Qi, Chu, Ch'in—surrounded the Zhou land. A fifth state was rising in power to join them: Yueh, on the southeast coast. Later histories call this the time of the Five Hegemonies, but in fact there were four more states that had swept enough smaller territories into their borders to tower as major powers: Lu and Wu, both with borders on the coast; Cheng, bordering the Zhou land; and the Sung on their eastern side.[1]

The Zhou sat in the middle, clinging onto a power which had become almost entirely ceremonial. The states were ruled by their own dukes, and *their* armies fought off the enemies at the borders. The Jin in particular were in a constant battle against the northern barbarian tribes known, collectively, as the Ti. The war went on for decades, and gradually extended the Jin border farther and farther to the north.

For some time, this patchwork country held an uneasy internal peace. King Hsiang died, after a long spell on the ceremonial throne, and was succeeded by his son (who ruled for six years) and then by his grandson (who ruled for seven). The grandson, too young for sons of his own, was succeeded by his younger brother, Ting, in 606 BC.

These clipped reigns seem to indicate some sort of trouble in the capital, and the lord to take advantage of it was the Duke of Chu.

The southern state of the Chu was not part of the original "central China," and it was still regarded as semibarbaric by the states of Jin and Cheng. Barbaric or not, Chu was strong. In the two and half centuries since the Zhou

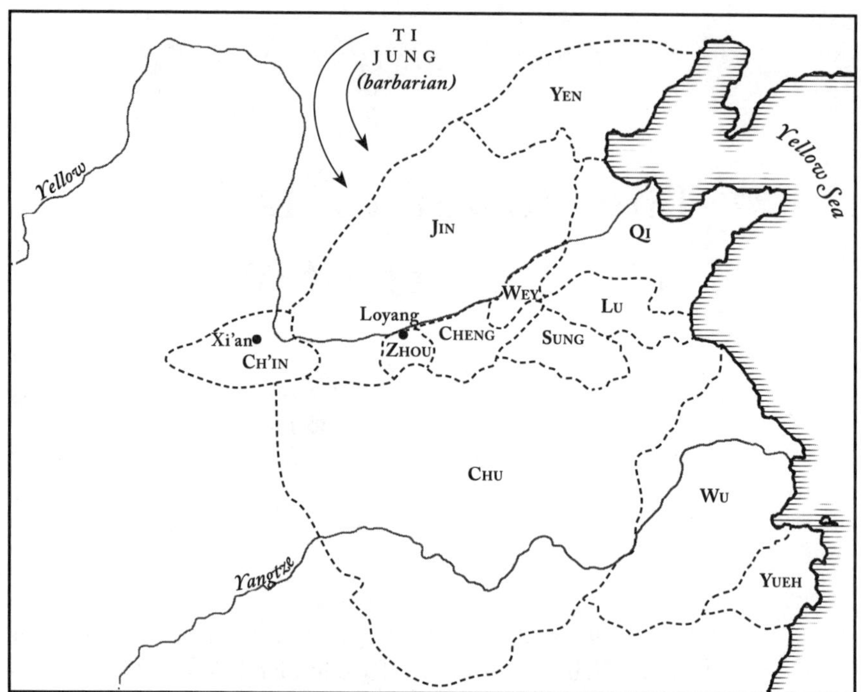

62.1 The Five Hegemonies

move, Chu soldiers had marched steadily to the north and east, invading and enfolding state after state. "In the ancient generations," wrote the eighteenth-century historian Gai Shiqi, "there were many enfeoffed states, which were densely distributed like chess pieces or stars." He lists a few of these, now disappeared forever from the map, which had once lain between the Chu and the Zhou border. "After the fall of Deng," he explains, "Chu troops made their presence felt by Shen and Xi, and after the fall of Shen and Xi the Chu troops made their presence felt by Jiang and Huang, and after the fall of Jiang and Huang, Chu soldiers made their presence felt by Chen and Cai. When Chen and Cai could no longer hold out, Chu soldiers reached the court directly."[2]

This Chu invasion of the Zhou land took place as soon as King Ting took the Zhou throne. It was not a direct attack on the palace; Chu's putative target was a band of the Jung, the northern barbarians who had allied themselves with King Hsiang's half-brother against the throne, eighty years earlier. They had been ricocheting around in China ever since. The Jin armies had shoved them over into the land of the Ch'in, the Ch'in army had shortly driven them farther south, and now they were on the western border of the Zhou.

The Chu did not attack these barbarians for the sake of protecting the sovereign; when the Duke of Chu marched against them, the Jung were not threatening the Zhou. And there is a hint in Sima Qian's records that the Duke of Chu did not have the good of the monarch in mind: "In the first year of King Ting," he writes, "the King of Chu attacked the Jung."[3] Never before had a duke been given the royal title. In fact, it was probably illegal for the Chu lord to call himself "king," but the Zhou ruler seems to have been in no position to object.

The King of Chu's campaign against the barbarians was halfhearted at best. As soon as he reached the north, he sent a messenger, not to the Jung with a demand for surrender, but rather to the Zhou palace with a somewhat ominous request: "He sent someone to inquire of Zhou about the Nine Tripods," writes Sima Qian—the Nine Cauldrons of the Zhou, which had served for half a millennium as the symbol of kingly power.*

We don't know why the King of Chu was inquiring after the Nine Tripods, but he probably wasn't motivated by idle curiosity. According to Sima Qian, King Ting sent a court official to talk his way out of actually answering the question; and the King of Chu, after a brief time, moved back to the south. What staved off the growing crisis is unclear. Perhaps the Zhou king agreed not to object to the Duke's use of "king," as the King of Chu went right on styling himself by the royal title.

Chu itself continued to grow. The *Tso chuan* (the additional notes to the Spring and Autumn Annals of Confucius) remarks that when the Chu overran the little state of Ts'ai, the King of Chu had the crown prince burned alive. Ten years after the attack on the Zhou, the King of Chu also invaded Cheng. Probably anxious to avoid being burned as well, the Duke of Cheng offered to become a faithful vassal: "Do not extinguish our altars," he begs, in the *Tso chuan*, "but let me change my course so that I may serve your lordship."[4]

The King of Chu agreed. Now his domain surrounded the Zhou by a large and threatening presence on two sides.

MEANWHILE, KING TING was succeeded by his son, grandson, and great-grandson. The great-grandson, King Ching, took the throne in 544 and had a more or less uneventful twenty-year reign. But although he intended to appoint his favorite son (a younger prince) as his successor, he died before he made the appointment formal. The year was 521.

Immediately Ching's oldest son seized the throne. The younger prince,

* See chapter 43, p. 300.

incensed, attacked and killed his older brother and took the throne himself, becoming King Tao. The other brothers fled the capital.

One of them, Prince Kai, made his way up into the Jin state of the north and appealed for help. The Duke of Jin agreed to throw the weight of the large and experienced Jin army behind Kai. He put together a coronation ceremony and proclaimed Kai to be the rightful king in exile; Kai took the name Ching II (as if to insist on his rightful claim to the throne, which seems to have been very shaky indeed). And then, with a Jin army behind him, Ching II marched back towards the walled Zhou city.

King Tao barricaded himself in. For three years, the brothers fought a civil war; in the fourth year, Ching II broke into the capital and reduced King Tao to a vassal, forced to swear allegiance to him.

By the time all this was over, the Eastern Zhou authority had almost completely broken down into anarchy and bloodshed. The Mandate of Heaven had splintered, and an even greater war between the surrounding states seemed likely to follow, as they jostled to take up the dropped Zhou authority.

In answer to the disorderly times, a reformer appeared in the state of Lu. His name was Kong Fuzi, and as a teacher he gained a following that lasted for millennia. Jesuit missionaries, arriving in China two thousand years later, spelled Kong Fuzi as *Confucius*, a Latinized version of his name by which he became known all over the world.

Like the Indian philosophers who were his contemporaries, Confucius was from a vaguely aristocratic family; he was the indirect descendent of an older half-brother of the last Shang king. Unlike those philosophers, he was raised in respectable poverty.

By the time he was twenty-one, he had married, fathered a son, and landed a job keeping track of state-owned grain shipments.[5] It was a job which required precision, attention to detail, and perfect record-keeping, all of which the young Confucius found himself naturally suited for. From his childhood, he had been a precise and orderly boy; as he grew, he was increasingly fascinated by the rituals performed to honor ancestors and divine beings, the rites that surrounded births and deaths and marriages, the ceremonies carried out in the courts of the state rulers and the court of the Zhou king himself.

These rituals were accompanied by poems and songs that described their proper performance; poems which, handed down orally from times before writing, acted as a living handbook of proper ceremony. Confucius, born with a naturally rententive memory, knew hundreds of them by heart.

For ten years or so, Confucius remained a government record-keeper. But he also gained a greater and greater reputation as a sort of walking repository of ritual performance. The Lu court called on him, when necessary, to make sure that visitors to the court were received with the proper rites. And he had begun to acquire pupils who were anxious to learn from the library inside his head.

By the time he was in his early thirties, the Duke of Lu consulted him on a regular basis. He was also hired away from his record-keeping to act as a tutor to the sons of at least one high Lu official.[6] Just as he entered into this new phase of his professional life—in which his knowledge of ceremony, ritual, and the proper performance of duties would be central to his entire working life—the civil war flared up in the Zhou lands.

The Zhou lack of clout had been partly masked by the general agreement among the lords of the surrounding states that the king still had some sort of ritual importance; that even if he did not actually *rule,* he stood at the center of some sort of cosmic order that they would prefer not to disrupt. The Chu demand for the Nine Tripods had, perhaps, been the first visible crack in that agreement. The bloody battles between two crowned kings, each boasting the authority conferred by ritual and ceremony, showed that the crack now reached all the way across the surface of Zhou power.

Confucius was a man who treasured order; and he began to teach his pupils how to find both order and stability in a world where neither was on conspicuous display.

His teachings tried to preserve the best aspects of the past—or at least a past that he believed had once existed. He collected the oldest poems and songs of China into the *Shi jing,* the Classic of Poetry, an anthology for future use. ("From them," Confucius remarked, "you learn the more immediate duty of serving one's father, and the remoter one of serving one's prince.")[7] He is also credited with collecting together a shoal of rituals and ceremonies into a text originally called the *Li ching,* which regulates everything from the proper attitude of mourners ("When one has paid a visit of condolence, he should not on the same day show manifestations of joy")[8] to the orderly succession of monthly tasks ("In the second month of autumn . . . it is allowable to rear city and suburban walls, to establish cities and towns, to dig underground passages and grain-pits, and to repair granaries.")[9] His sayings were gathered together by his followers into a third collection called *Lun yu,* or the Analects.

Confucius was not the inventor of the philosophy laid out in the Analects, any more than the Mahavira was the originator of Jainism. His innovation was in turning back to the past in order to find a way forwards. "I am not one who was born in the possession of knowledge," he told his followers, "I am one who is fond of antiquity and earnest in seeing it there."[10] His study of the past told him that, in a fractious China, both tranquillity and virtue lay in the orderly performance of duties. "It is by the rules of propriety that the character is established," he is reported to have said. "Without the rules of propriety, respectfulness becomes laborious bustle; carefulness, timidity; boldness, insubordination; and straightforwardness, rudeness."[11]

In a world where force of arms seemed to be the only glue holding a state together, Confucius offered another way for men to control the society that surrounded them. The man who understood his duties towards others and lived them out became the anchor of a country—in place of the king, or the general, or the aristocrat. "He who exercises government by means of his virtue," the Analects say, "may be compared to the north polar star, which keeps its place, and all the stars turn towards it. . . . If the people be led by virtue . . . they will become good."*[12]

BEFORE CONFUCIUS WAS FORTY, he was forced to flee from Lu when its duke was driven out by a rival aristocratic family. Confucius followed the exiled ruler of Lu up into the neighboring state of Qi, where both had to throw themselves on the mercy of the lord of Qi, who had not always been particularly friendly to his southern colleague.

However, it suited the Duke of Qi, for the moment, to play host; he offered his hospitality to the exiled ruler of Lu. Confucius, on the other hand, found his own welcome to the court ruined by jealous Qi courtiers, who banded together to block his access to the Duke of Qi.[13] Finding himself with no job, Confucius left Qi and went back to Lu, where he made it quite clear that he intended to stay uninvolved with politics. This was wise, as Lu was divided between three quarrelling families, none of whom had a clear upper hand. (Eventually, Confucius would return to civil service for a time, but he devoted most of his later years to writing out the history of Lu, an account now known as the Spring and Autumn Annals.)

A little farther to the west, Ching II, now nominally in control of the Zhou palace, was about to have troubles of his own. His vassal-brother, the onetime King Tao, remained in simmering submission for twelve years; and then rose up with his followers (who perhaps resented the Jin tampering in their affairs), reattacked the capital, and drove his brother back. Ching II returned to Jin and asked the duke for help. The following year, the Jin army once again "successfully escorted King Ching [II] back to Zhou."[14]

* Jonathan Clements's *Confucius: A Biography* is a good beginner's guide to the life and times of the philosopher; the Analects are readable by non-specialists in either the 1938 translation of Arthur Waley (Vintage, 1989) or the more recent Simon Leys translation (W. W. Norton, 1997); *An Introduction to Confucianism* by Xinzhong Yao (Cambridge University Press, 2000) is a more detailed and academic guide.

It was the last great Jin victory. Before long, the Duke of Jin began to find himself in difficulties. In the constant campaigning against the barbarians, several large families of Jin had grown steadily richer: one family claimed by birth the hereditary right to command the army; another had not only claimed huge amounts of barbarian land, but had also made alliances and treaties with the barbarian tribe. Men from these families and several others began to push against each other for more control of the Jin court. By 505, the divisions were serious enough to hamper the ongoing Jin fight against barbarians; according to the Spring and Autumn Annals, the Jin army, apparently divided by internal bickering, had to retreat from a siege laid against a barbarian town without success.[15]

In 493, Cheng and Jin waged a brief vicious war with each other; in 492, Qi, Lu, and Wey agreed to join with one of the Jin aristocrats and marched into Jin itself to push another Jin family off the map, in a combination civil war/invasion.

Now Lu was divided, Jin was fractious, and the Zhou were weak. Chu, which had been dominant in the south for a century, was fighting against the invasions of Wu and Yueh on its southeastern flank; Wu, temporarily gaining the upper hand, announced itself the ruling state of the entire south, at which the Yueh turned against its ally and attacked it.[16] The Zhou monarch had ceased to be even a blip on the political screen. The years between 481 and 403 were so confused that many historians, who divide the period when the Zhou occupied their eastern capital (the Eastern Zhou Period, 771–221) into two halves (the Spring and Autumn Period, 771–481, and the Warring States Period, 403–221), do not even try to give a name to the roil of years between the halves. It is a kind of interregnum.

During these years, another philosopher (of a sort) made another attempt to lay out principles by which China might find unity (of a kind). Sun-Tzu, the general who fought for the Duke of Wu,* had no illusions over what constant warfare was doing to his country: "There is no instance of a country having benefitted from prolonged warfare," he warned.[17] The *Art of War* is about conquering your enemies while avoiding as much actual fighting as possible. "Supreme excellence consists in breaking the enemy's resistance without fighting," Sun-Tzu wrote,[18] and "When you engage in actual fighting, if victory is long in coming, then men's weapons will grow dull, and their ardor will be

* Sun-Tzu's dates are debated. His treatise the *Art of War* directly mentions the Yueh at the southeast, which tends to place it in the period after the Wu declaration of primacy and the Yueh objection: "Though according to my estimate the soldiers of Yueh exceed our own in number," he writes, "that shall advantage them nothing in the matter of victory" (VI.21).

damped. . . . Cleverness has never been seen associated with long delays." Sieges, that staple of Middle Eastern warfare, were not recommended: "Do not besiege a town," Sun-Tzu ordered. "If you lay siege to a town, you will exhaust your strength. . . . Other chieftains will spring up to take advantage of your extremity. Then no man, however wise, will be able to avert the consequences."[19]

These are the words of a man who knew that enemies from your own state were just as dangerous as enemies in the next state over. In a country where your friends were as likely to be plotting against you as your enemies, deceit became a way of life: "All warfare is based on deception," wrote Sun-Tzu. "When able to attack, we must seem unable; when using our forces we must seem inactive; when we are near, we must make the enemy believe we are far away; when far away, we must make him believe we are near."[20] The good general not only deceives the enemy himself, but assumes that his enemy is always deceiving him: "Humble words and increased preparations are signs that the enemy is about to advance," Sun-Tzu explains. "Violent language and driving forward as if to the attack are signs that he will retreat . . . Peace proposals accompanied by a sworn covenant indicate a plot."[21]

Both Confucius and Sun-Tzu, roughly contemporary as they are, offer a philosophy of order, a way of dealing with a disunified country; stability through the proper performance of social duties, or stability through intimidation. Sun-Tzu's method is no less systematic and all encompassing than that of Confucius. And, for a time, it gained the upper hand. The states of the Eastern Zhou were, as the first-century Chinese historian Liu Xiang wrote, "greedy and shameless. They competed without satiety. . . . There was no Son of Heaven above and there were no local lords down below. Everything was achieved through physical force and the victorious was the noble. Military activities were incessant and deceit and falsehoods came hand in hand."[22]

China's government had become a constellation of military rulers, each holding onto his power by constant warfare. Without war, which acted to push the borders of the states outwards against the borders of the next state, the states would collapse inwards like pricked balloons; they had to stay inflated with the hot air of battle.

TIMELINE 62

INDIA	CHINA
	Ting
Sixteen kingdoms in the Ganga river valley	Duke ("King") of Chu
Birth of the Mahavira (trad. 599)	
Birth of the Buddha (trad. 563)	
	Birth of Confucius
Bimbisara of Magadha	**Ching**
Death of the Mahavira (trad. 527)	**Tao**
	Ching (II)
	Sun-Tzu, *The Art of War*
Death of the Buddha (trad. 483)	"Spring and Autumn" period ends (481)
	Death of Confucius

Chapter Sixty-Three

The Spreading Persian Empire

Between 539 and 514 BC,
Cyrus the Great falls in battle,
Cambyses conquers Egypt,
and the Indian kingdom of Magadha grows strong

AFTER THE CONQUEST OF BABYLON, Cyrus the Great ruled over his empire for a little less than nine years, and then fell in a skirmish with an unknown queen.

He was fighting his way up north into brand new territory, across the Oxus river and up into the wilds of central Asia, east of the Aral Sea. The mountain tribes up in this area were an offshoot of the Scythians: Herodotus calls them the Massagetae, fierce fighters who used bronze-tipped bows and spears, worshipped the sun, and "do not cultivate the land, but live off cattle and fish."[1]

Cyrus first tried to conquer the Massagetae by treaty. He sent a message to their queen Tomyris, offering to marry her. She not only declined, but sent her son to lead an attack against the rear wing of the Persian army. The attack failed and Tomyris's son was taken captive.

Unable to bear his shame, he killed himself. At this, Tomyris sent Cyrus a message, vowing, "I swear by the sun that I will quench your thirst for blood." Then she led the rest of her people against the advancing Persians. The two armies met in 530 BC, a minor clash with epic proportions: "I consider this to be the fiercest battle between non-Greeks there has ever been," Herodotus says, which (given his attitude towards non-Greeks) may mean that it was the most savage fighting ever seen. They fought with bows and arrows, and then with spears, and then with daggers.

The Massagetae did what the Assyrians could not: they wiped out most of the Persian troops. Cyrus himself, fighting on the ground among his men, fell. When the Massagetae had gained dominance over the field, Tomyris searched through the Persian bodies lying in their blood until she found the king's

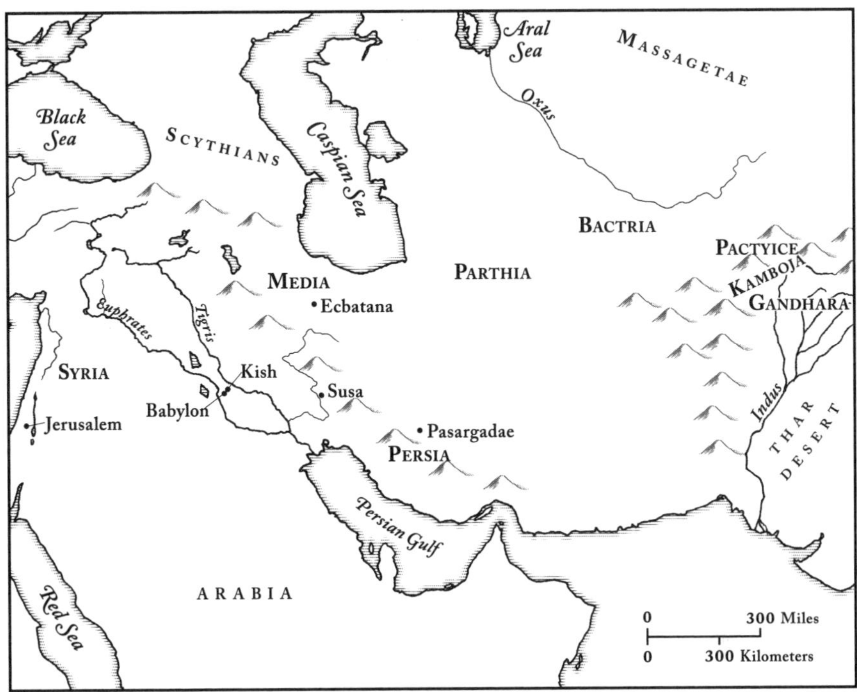

63.1 Persia and Central Asia

corpse. She lifted his head and shoved it into a wineskin filled with blood: "I warned you that I would quench your thirst for blood," she told the body.[2]

With her son avenged, Tomyris allowed the Persian survivors to take the body of the Great King from the battlefield. They washed the blood from his face and took the corpse in a defeated funeral procession back to Pasargadae.

Cyrus had already built himself a tomb: a gabled stone house, carved to look like timber, that stood on the top level of a seven-level ziggurat of steps. His body was dressed in royal robes and ornaments, provided with weapons, and placed on a gold couch. The tomb was sealed, and a cadre of Persian priests was given the task of living in a small house nearby as guardians of Cyrus's final resting place.

Cambyses II, the oldest son of the king, was crowned as his successor. He had acted as his father's commander for some years; in fact, he had been with Cyrus just before the crossing of the Oxus, but the king had sent his son back to Pasargadae to take care of matters there while he fought what must have seemed like a very minor engagement.

Surveying his father's empire, Cambyses seems to have suffered from the exact same impulse as so many other sons of great men: he wanted to outdo his father. This was not a matter of vengeance, since he left the northeastern frontier where Cyrus had died untouched. Instead, he first moved his palace and the center of the administration of the empire from his father's capital, Pasargadae, to a new city: the old Elamite capital of Susa, closer to the middle of the empire. And then he set his eye on Egypt.

DOWN IN EGYPT, the pharaoh Apries had led his armies straight into a huge disaster.

West of the Delta, the Greek settlement of Cyrene—the colony planted on the North African coast by the people of Thera—had finally begun to grow, after almost sixty years of bare survival. Its third king, Battus the Prosperous, had issued an all-points bulletin to every Greek city, begging for additional settlers and promising everyone who came a plot of land. Soon a "considerable mass" of people had gathered in Cyrene, mostly coming from the Greek mainland, and were claiming land all around the city.

This did not go over well with the native North Africans, whom Herodotus knows as "Libyans." They sent a message to Egypt asking for help, and "put themselves under the protection of the Egyptian king Apries." So Apries sent out an Egyptian army to help his fellow North Africans against the Greek invaders. Unfortunately the Egyptian army was decimated by the Greeks: they were, in Herodotus's words, "so thoroughly annihilated that hardly any of them found their way back to Egypt."[3]

This disaster turned the Egyptians against Apries, who was apparently already suffering from huge unpopularity: "They believed that Apries had deliberately sent them to certain death," Herodotus writes, so that after their destruction, with fewer subjects left to rule over, his reign would be more secure. The survivors who returned home from Cyrene took this hard: they "combined with the friends of those who had met their deaths and rose up in open rebellion."[4]

Apries sent out his chief Egyptian general, Amasis, to put down the rebellion.

This proved to be a mistake. The pharaoh had inherited Amasis from his father, Psammetichus II, which meant that Amasis had been around, and in power, longer than Apries had been king. Face-to-face with an armed Egyptian uprising that wanted to get rid of Apries, Amasis yielded to temptation and allowed it to be made known that, if the rebels pleased, they could make him king instead.[5]

Someone carried news of this treachery to Apries, who sent an official from his court demanding that Amasis return at once to the palace at Sais and give an account of his actions. "Amasis," Herodotus remarks, "happened to be on

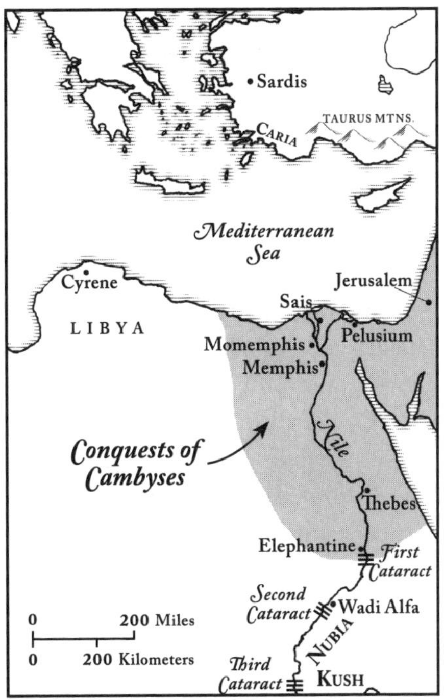

63.2 *Egypt and Cyrene*

horseback at the time; he lifted himself up in the saddle, farted, and told him to take that back to Apries."[6]

Apries, receiving the message, cut off the nose and ears of the messenger, which had the effect of turning even more Egyptians against him. It was clear that he would have to fight for his throne, but pretty much all he had left were his mercenary forces, of which he had about thirty thousand, both Ionian Greeks and Carians (mercenaries of Greek descent, from the southwest coast of Asia Minor).

The two armies met halfway between Memphis and Sais, at a battlefield called Momemphis. The Egyptian forces outnumbered the mercenaries, and Amasis was a shrewd general; the Egyptians won the day, and Apries was captured. He was taken off to the palace at Sais as a prisoner, but not killed.

Apparently Apries then escaped, because three years later, a fragmentary inscription from Elephantine relates that Amasis was in his palace at Sais when he received news that Apries was sailing down on him from the north with "Greeks without number," who were "wasting all Egypt" while the army of Amasis fled in front of them.[7] Apries had gone north to hire reinforcements.

The inscription is too damaged to know exactly how the battle progressed, but it concludes, "His majesty [Amasis] fought like a lion, he made a slaughter among them. . . . numerous ships took them, falling into the water, whom they saw sink as do the fish."[8] Among those caught on the sinking Greek ships was Apries, who died in the slaughter.

So Amasis was on the throne in Sais when word came down to Egypt that Cambyses, new king of the Persians, was preparing for an attack.

Cambyses had to begin by making himself a navy. The Persians had no seafaring tradition of their own; but Cyrus had provided his son with an empire that stretched all along the Mediterranean coast, and Cambyses considered the Ionian sailors of the Asia Minor coasts to be his subjects. He required them to build ships and staff them; and he made the same demand from the Phoenician cities under his control. The fledgling Persian navy combined the skills of Greeks and Phoenicians, two cultures who had been on the water since the beginning of their civilization.

Four years after his coronation, Cambyses began the attack on Egypt. His navy began its journey down the coast, while the Persian army marched across the desert. Cambyses, accompanied by his spear-bearer Darius, was in the lead; Darius, part of his personal bodyguard, was the son of a Persian nobleman who was in command of the conquered area called Parthia, in the northeastern part of the empire.[9]

Amasis readied his own forces to meet the Persians. But he was over seventy and had already led a long and very busy life. Before Cambyses could arrive, Amasis died of old age.

This was a bit of very good luck for Cambyses, since the job of defending Egypt now fell on Amasis's son, Psammetichus III, who was not a gifted general. Psammetichus III lined up his forces at the northeastern border of Egypt, centering his defense at the border fortress Pelusium, which had been built by Necho II to guard his canal. There was nothing wrong with this; but when the battle began to turn against the Egyptian forces, he pulled them back all the way to Memphis.

This gave the Persians almost free access to the waterways of the Delta and allowed them to besiege Memphis both by land and by sea. We have no details of the war that followed, but Psammetichus III was soon forced to surrender. He had been pharaoh of Egypt for less than a year.

Cambyses now styled himself pharaoh of Egypt, "King of Upper and Lower Egypt, Cambyses, beloved of the goddess Wajet"—this was the cobra-goddess of Lower Egypt whose likeness had appeared on the Red Crown, all the way back in the days of the unification.[10] He also apparently ordered Amasis's body exhumed and dismembered, but mummification had made it so tough that he had to resort to burning it instead.

Herodotus (who dislikes Cambyses) says that this was an act of gratuitous sacrilege. More likely, Cambyses was attempting to identify himself as the successor of the deposed Apries, and his desecration of Amasis's corpse was his attempt to portray the old general as a usurper whose rule had been fortunately ended. He told the people of Egypt that he was the "beloved of Wajet," and that he had come to liberate them: a now familiar strategy.

The "beloved of Wajet" didn't spend long in his new country; Cambyses put a governor in charge of Egypt and headed back into his empire to take care of other business. But his tenure as Great King was a short one. Three years after the conquest of Egypt, eight years after the death of Cyrus, Cambyses's reign ended suddenly and mysteriously.

Herodotus, who gives the most detailed account of Cambyses's reign, seems to have gathered and repeated every single anti-Cambyses story ever told: if he is to be believed, Cambyses was a madman who randomly executed his officials when they crossed him, killed his brother, married two of his sisters and murdered one of them, and set off to conquer Ethiopia in a temper without bothering to pack any food for his men. Given that Cambyses had managed to march an entire army across the Arabian desert and safely into Egypt, this seems unlikely. Herodotus's offhand remark that his sources for these stories are mostly Egyptian probably explains the hostility. Apparently Cambyses's attempt to portray himself as liberator was less than successful; he was not a popular pharaoh.

But Cambyses did indeed die suddenly, oddly, and without heirs.

The oldest sources say that Cambyses, when he began the Egyptian campaign, left his household under the management of a man Herodotus calls Patizeithes. Cambyses took his younger brother Bardiya on campaign with him, but after the conquest sent him back to Persia to check on how things were going back in the capital.

Somewhere between Egypt and Persia, Bardiya disappeared.

It so happened that the steward, Patizeithes, had a younger brother named Smerdis who looked so much like Bardiya that the two could be mistaken for each other.* This steward, receiving news by fast courier of Bardiya's disappearance, realized that he could keep the news under wraps. He convinced his younger brother to pose as the missing prince, set him on the throne, and then sent out messengers proclaiming Bardiya, full royal son of Cyrus, king in place of Cambyses.

Cambyses was over in Syria, checking on the western reaches of his empire. According to Herodotus, when Cambyses heard that his throne had been stolen, he ran for his horse, vaulted on to it, and in the process knocked the scabbard off his sword and sliced himself in the thigh. The wound turned; three weeks later, the Great King was dead from gangrene.[11]

With Cambyses dead, the imposter managed to hold onto the Persian throne for seven months; long enough for Babylonian documents to date themselves by his accession year.[12] During all this time, he escaped detection by never leaving the palace compound in Susa, or calling any of the Persian noblemen who had known the family well into his presence.

The charade could not go on forever, though, and soon more than one Persian aristocrat was asking why he was never called into the throne room.

* The accounts refer to this man as Smerdis or as Gaumata; it is also not always clear who is the moving force behind the usurpation, Smerdis/Gaumata (the false Bardiya) or his older brother, who is also referred to as the Magus, as he had a priestly function at the court.

Among them was Othanes, an experienced soldier and the father of one of Cambyses's wives; and also Darius, Cambyses's spear-bearer during the conquest of Egypt, who had returned to Persia after the campaign to Egypt and was now in Susa (for some reason unknown).

All together, seven Persian lords agreed to mount an assassination attempt against the pretender and his older brother. Othanes seems to have been the leader of the conspiracy, but Darius offered to get the group of men, their weapons hidden beneath their robes, past the palace guards; he could, he pointed out, claim that he had just come from his father, governor of Parthia, with a message for the king.[13]

The plan worked until the seven were almost at the doors of the royal chambers, when the king's eunuchs refused to let them in. Then they drew their weapons, killed the eunuchs, cut off the heads of both the imposter and his brother, and displayed them to the rest of the Persian aristocrats to prove that the man who had claimed to be Bardiya was, in fact, no son of Cyrus at all.

Now the Persian empire was balanced on a knife edge. It had no king, and both sons of Cyrus were off the scene. Each of the seven conspirators might have had his own ambitions (Herodotus writes that the seven had a reasonable, Greek-sounding, and very unlikely debate about the fair way to pick one of the seven, or whether Persia should perhaps become a democracy), but Darius was the natural choice. He was young and energetic, probably around thirty at the time of the conspiracy; he had been Cambyses's trusted aide, he was of the Achaemenid tribe by birth, and his father already held power over the soldiers in a large portion of the empire. In 521, he was acclaimed king of Persia by his six fellow conspirators, and started to smooth out the ripples caused by the death of Cyrus's heirs.

There are a lot of question marks in this story.

Cambyses's convenient death is probably the first. What actually happened to the Great King? Herodotus's story is not impossible, but shows uncharacteristic carelessness on the part of a man who had spent most of his life around sharp objects; the Greek historian Ctesias, who is rarely reliable, says that he was whittling out of boredom and cut himself on the thigh.[14] An Egyptian papyrus simply notes that Cambyses died "on a mat" (an odd phrase, which suggests that he was on a sickbed for some time) before reaching his own country, and that Darius then became king.[15] Darius's own accession inscription, the Bisitun Inscription, says without elaboration, "Cambyses died his own death," a phrase which usually implies natural causes of some kind.

Of course, it is possible that the death from gangrene was natural but the original wound was not; Darius's reticence on the subject is not necessarily in his favor. It was to his benefit that Cambyses die a natural death, just as it was to his benefit to discover that the man on the throne of Susa was an imposter.

Which brings us to the second mystery: what was the real identity of the "Bardiya" who died at the hands of the Persian seven? And is it really likely that an imposter could manage to hold power for almost a year, in a city where everyone knew the face of the king? Perhaps the real Bardiya didn't disappear in the desert; maybe he arrived safely at Susa, and then mounted a coup against his brother, which would make Cambyses's fury at the news even more understandable.

In this case, Darius is the villain. The man he killed at Susa was no imposter at all, but rather the last legitimate son of Cyrus the Great. A decapitated head is not easy to identify with certainty, particularly if it's been hacked up while being removed.

Darius's character is the big question mark in this scenario. It doesn't help his cause that we know the story of Bardiya the imposter mostly from Darius's own Bisitun Inscription, which puts Darius in the best possible light: "The people feared [the imposter] greatly," he insists, "since he used to slay in great number the people who previously had known Bardiya. . . . No one dared say anything . . . until I came. . . . Then I with a few men slew [him] . . . I restored Persia, Media, and the other lands."[16]

On the other hand, Darius's tale of a false Bardiya might actually be true. It is not at all unlikely that a young man who grew up in the court of Cyrus might bear a startling resemblance to one of Cyrus's legitimate sons, and if the Bardiya at Susa was indeed an imposter as Darius claims, the real Bardiya *did* disappear.

This brings us to the third mystery: what happened to Cambyses's younger brother?

Darius himself chalks up Bardiya's death to Cambyses: "Cambyses killed Bardiya," he writes, "and it did not become known to the people that Bardiya had been killed." But it is in Darius's best interest to make Cambyses the villain, since that gives Cyrus's dynasty a nice neat implosion and ends the line so that he can begin a new dynasty. If the story of the resemblance is true, and the Bardiya in Susa *was* an imposter, the villain in the story is probably neither Cambyses nor Darius. Cui bono: the steward Patizeithes did best out of Bardiya's disappearance. The accident of his brother's resemblance to Bardiya may have been the genesis of a plot to get rid of Cyrus's younger son.

But now Patizeithes was dead. And so were his followers (Darius had them executed), and so was Cambyses, and so was Bardiya. Darius himself married Cambyses's widow, and nothing more was heard from her about her first husband's death. The suspects were mostly dead, the rest were silent, and the mystery would remain unsolved.

In the meantime, more than one outlying territory of the empire had begun to plan revolt.

Darius went immediately to war to keep his new empire secure. Judging from the Bisitun Inscription, rebellions broke out among the Babylonians, the Scythians to the north, the Medians to his east, and even Parthia, where Darius's own father had lost control of the army. A scattering of smaller rebellions blazed up between them, all across the empire.

But in an amazingly brief time, Darius had corralled them back into the empire. However he had gotten into the position of power, Darius proved extremely capable of holding onto it: not through sympathetic tyranny, as Cyrus had before him, but by crushing his enemies.

Cambyses's army had been made up of a large number of draftees, soldiers sent to him as tribute. In an army made up mostly of draftees, the majority of the soldiers were disposable, numbers to throw in front of an opposing battle line in hopes of bearing down the opposition by sheer size. This was a strategy that had worked for Cambyses because of the inexperience of his opponent, and had not aided Cyrus, in his battle against the Scythian tribes, at all.

Darius had a different vision for his army. Instead of padding his ranks with mercenaries and tribute fighters, Darius planned for a professional army, one that would be smaller, but better fed, better trained, and more loyal. It would have a professional standing core of ten thousand foot soldiers and ten thousand cavalry, all of them Persians or Medes, and would move far faster than the huge and unwieldy armies of his predecessors.[17] "The Persian and Median army which was under my control was a small force," Darius writes, in his own inscription.[18] The troops were bound together by national feeling, with loyalty so strong that the ten thousand infantry soldiers called themselves the Companions and jealously guarded entrance into their own ranks.

One division of this new army put down the eastern rebellion of Media, while Darius in command of another small force tackled the Babylonian uprising, and yet another squad travelled to Asia Minor. The core troops—small, fast, flexible, well trained—were successful. In hardly more than a year, the revolts were over. Darius's huge celebratory relief, carved onto a cliff overlooking the road into Susa (where no one could miss it), shows him with his foot on the chest of the prostrate imposter to the throne, the false Bardiya, with the kings of Babylon, Scythia, Media, and six other lands roped and chained in front of him.

Darius was as brilliant an administrator as a general (a rare combination).

He organized the reconquered empire into a more orderly set of provinces, or *satrapies*, each governed by a trustworthy *satrap*, and assigned each satrap a tribute which had to be sent to Susa each year. Satraps who did not send the proper amount, or who did not manage to keep their satrapies in order, were liable to be executed. This seems to have worked quite well for Darius; it transferred the job of intimidating conquered peoples from the king to the governors, who were forced to be far more diligent in keeping an eye on their territories than any Eye or Ear of Cyrus could ever have been.

We get a glimpse of this in the biblical book of Ezra. The satrap who had the watch over Jerusalem noticed that the construction of the temple (and its defensive walls) had progressed to a worrying degree. The rising building must have looked suspiciously like the center of a fortress, because the satrap, a man named Tattenai, made a special journey down to ask the builders what they thought they were doing.

The Jews protested that Cyrus had given them permission to build, but Tattenai was not willing to take their word for it. He ordered them to stop building until he could report the activity to Darius. "The king should know," the report reads, "that the people are building it with large stones and placing the timbers in the walls; the work is making rapid progress."[19] Darius ordered the royal archives searched. Eventually a copy of Cyrus's decree was located, in (of all places) an old library at Ecbatana, and Darius gave the satrap permission to let the building go ahead. The biblical account is not sympathetic to Tattenai, but the man was undoubtedly worried lest he miss the seeds of rebellion and lose his head.

With the existing empire stable, Darius could turn his eyes to new frontiers. He hoped to march his army towards India.

INDIA WAS NOT, for the Persians, a strange and unfamiliar land, as Alexander of Macedonia would find it to be a century and a half later. The Indians of the north were, after all, descendants of the same Aryans who also stood in the Persian family tree. In the language of the Persians, the names of Darius's noblemen are recognizably kin to the names of the Indian princes who ruled the mahajanapadas: Utana, son of Thukra; Vidafarnah, son of Vayaspara; Bagabuxsa, son of Datuvahya.

While the Persians were expanding their grasp to the east and west, the Indian kingdom of Magadha was trying to swallow its own neighbors. The ambitious Bimbisara, who had conquered Anga and claimed part of Kosal as his wife's dowry, had sired an equally ambitious son. Unwilling to wait for his own chance at rule, this son, Ajatashatru, mounted a revolt against his father,

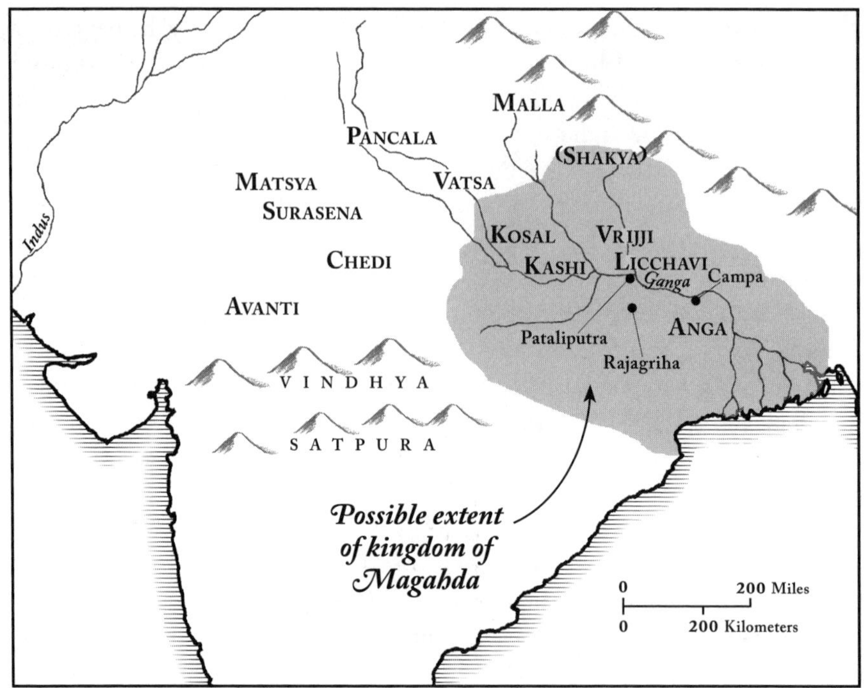

63.3 The Expansion of Magadha

imprisoned him, and allowed him to starve to death: "Bimbisara was imprisoned by his son in a tower," says the tale "The Jealousy of Devadatta."*

His mother grieved so harshly over her husband's loss that she died. At that point her brother, now king of Kosal, reclaimed the land that had been in her dowry, and Ajatashatru went to war to get it back.

At first, his soldiers were driven back by the Kosal defense forces, but Kosal had its own internal troubles. The crown prince, as ambitious as Ajatashatru himself, took advantage of the conflict to mount his own bid for the throne, and drove his father out of Kosal. Then he began a war of his own against the gana-sangha of Shakya, the tribal alliance that had produced the Buddha. He wiped them out; from this point, they disappear from the historical record.[20]

Meanwhile, his dethroned father had fled towards Ajatashatru's capital city of Rajagriha (a particularly well-fortified city, thanks to the natural walls

* According to other accounts, Bimbisara retreated from the kingship (which he handed over to his son) and ceased to eat. However, the amount of trouble that accompanied Ajatashatru's accession suggests that the more brutal account is accurate.

formed by five hills that ringed it).[21] When he reached the city, he begged for sanctuary. This may seem like an unwise decision, but he was Ajatashatru's uncle, and could claim some privilege of kinship. He was also an elderly man, and by the time he got to the wall, he was so worn out by his journey that he died before the gates could actually be opened.[22]

At this, Ajatashatru had yet another excuse to make war on Kosal. He regathered his forces, vowing loudly (and publicly) to avenge his uncle's death (never mind that his own attack on his uncle's land had brought about the original situation). But before he could get to Kosal, he had to turn and deal with his own family. His brother, who was serving him as vice-regent over the conquered kingdom of Anga, made a bid to become a king in his own right. He was preparing an alliance with the gana-sangha just to his north, Licchavi, against Ajatashatru. Ajatashatru built a fort on the frontier between the two territories, the fort Pataliputra on the shores of the Ganga, and went to war.

It was a war that lasted twelve years. At least Ajatashatru was spared from having to fight off his cousin in Kosol at the same time. A flash flood wiped out most of the army of Kosol, which had unwisely camped in a riverbed (later, a similar catastrophe drowned a number of Alexander's camp followers on one of his campaigns to the east). With the army gone, Ajatashatru simply marched in and took Kosol over.[23]

The twelve-year war with his brother, a few details of which survive in the Buddhist tales, forced Ajatashatru to make innovations. For one thing, he is credited with inventing a couple of new offensive weapons, including a huge rock-throwing catapult and a new kind of war chariot. Twelve years of war also required a professional army, one paid to do nothing but fight: India's first standing military force.[24]

His army was not Ajatashatru's only weapon. When the Buddha died, on a journey north into the kingdom of Malla, Ajatashatru at once claimed that Magadha had the right to guard the Buddha's sacred legacy. He ordered a council held in his capital, Rajagriha, in order to collect and set down into writing the Buddha's sayings, the suttas. This first Buddhist council presided over the first composition of those collected sayings which would become the Pali Canon, and it was held under Ajatashatru's watchful eye.

Empire-building, co-opting a religious tradition for political gain, family hostilities in the royal line, a professional army: northern India had joined the world to the west.

THE INDUS RIVER had probably been reached once by Persian soldiers, under Cyrus's command, although this is about all that we can surmise. Cyrus certainly didn't encounter any of the Indian tribes or fight his way into the Indus river valley. But Darius knew that the Indus was there. He just had no idea where it went.

So he hired a Carian sailor named Skylax, a Greek from southwest Asia Minor, to accompany an expedition down the river and make a map of what he saw. According to Herodotus, the starting point for the journey was the land he calls Pactyice, which is on the northern Indus: presumably both Cyrus and Darius reached the Indus by going through the Khyber Pass. Once through the pass, Darius's expedition must have built boats on the shore of the Indus river and then sailed down it, through the territory of the mahajanapada called Gandhara. They passed the Thar desert, before coming to the sea. Then they sailed west, around the entire southern coast of the Arabian peninsula, and came back up the Red Sea. Darius had ordered the canal from the Nile to the Red Sea dug out after it had begun to silt up, so the ships could then go through the Delta into the Mediterranean.

63.1. First World Map. The first known map of the world shows Babylon at its center, surrounded by a circular "Salt Sea." British Museum, London. Photo credit HIP/Art Resource, NY

"After this successful circumnavigation," Herodotus says, after describing a three-year journey, "Darius conquered the Indians."[25] The conquest was certainly not "all of the Indians," but Darius got some ways into the Punjab, perhaps dominating the Gandhara and Kamboja kingdoms: in an inscription at Susa, he lists goldwork from Egypt, Lydian stone, and timbers from Gandhara as the materials brought from the far places of his empire to build a new palace. Another inscription calls his far eastern conquest the "Hindush satrapy." It became the twentieth satrapy in his kingdom, with the duty of sending a yearly tribute of gold dust to Susa.[26]

During these years, some scribe in Babylon drew the earliest surviving map of the world. The clay tablet shows Babylon on the

Euphrates, Assyria to the east, and other cities, all of it ringed with "bitter water"—the Persian Gulf. Eight lands lie beyond, impossibly distant but nevertheless close enough to put on a map for the first time.

It is also in these years that a Babylonian inscription mentions a woman from India, Busasa, who kept an inn in the city of Kish. Presumably she had travelled down the Indus and up the Persian Gulf by sea: not moving from India to Babylon, but rather moving from one part of Darius's empire to another.[27] Persia had become a bridge between India and the peoples farther west.

TIMELINE 63

INDIA	PERSIA AND EGYPT		
	PERSIA	MEDIA	
Sixteen kingdoms in the Ganga river valley			
			Psammetichus II
Birth of the Mahavira (trad. 599)		**Astyages**	**Apries**
	Cambyses I		
Birth of the Buddha (trad. 563)			**Amasis**
	Cyrus II (the Great) (559)		
Bimbisara of Magadha			
Death of the Mahavira (trad. 527)	**Cambyses II** (530)		
			Psammetichus III
	Darius I		
Ajatashatru of Magadha			
Death of the Buddha (trad. 483)			

Chapter Sixty-Four

The Persian Wars

Between 527 and 479 BC,
Darius fails to defeat Athens,
and the cities of Greece unite against his son Xerxes

THE PERSIAN EMPIRE, bulging out in almost all directions, made little progress to the northwest, where the Scythians lived.

"Scythia," which Herodotus and other ancient historians refer to as though it were as easily located on a map as New Jersey, was no such thing. The Scythians had a score of tribes and a handful of kings, and they had been on the move for over two hundred years. In 516 BC, the center of their homeland lay between the two great rivers that ran into the Black Sea: the Danube to the west, and the Don river to the east.

These Scythians had been nomads when they first appeared in the records of the Assyrians, back before 700 BC, and they were still nomads in 516. "If we had towns, we might worry that they would be captured," one of the Scythian kings told Darius, when he first threatened Persian invasion, "and if we had farmland we might worry about it being laid waste. . . . but we don't have either."[1] Their customs were fierce. They made cups from the skulls of fallen enemies, and skinned their right arms ("fingernails and all," Herodotus remarks) to use as covers for arrow quivers; they hauled the dead bodies of their kinsmen to feasts for forty days after death, offering food and drink to the corpses; they threw cannabis seeds onto glowing stones and inhaled the smoke, "shrieking with delight at the fumes" (an exception to the common wisdom that a marijuana habit inevitably makes one dreamy and nonaggressive).[2]

By 516, Darius had begun to plan his campaign against the Scythians. He had already paid a good deal of attention to the northwest frontier. Sardis, in Asia Minor, had become his secondary center of administration. To give himself easy access to Sardis, Darius built a new road from Susa all the way into Asia Minor. This Royal Road was dotted with post stations for the change of

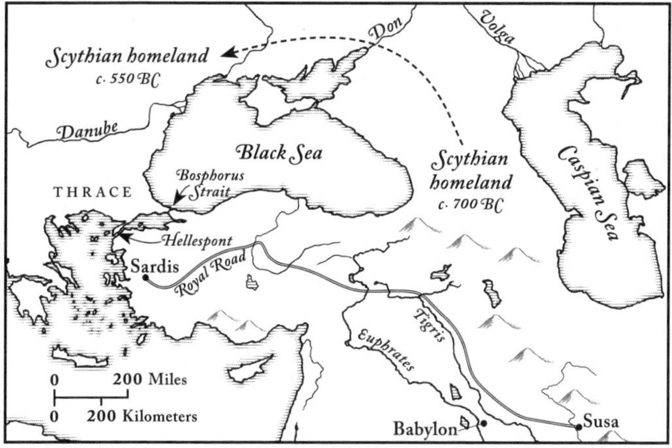

64.1 Homeland of the Scythians

horses, so that a messenger could get rapidly from the west to the capital and back again.

Now Darius himself rode along the Royal Road to Sardis, and then from Sardis to the edge of his territory. To attack the Scythians, he would bring his navy up the coast of Asia Minor, through the pass known as the Hellespont and into the Bosphorus Strait. From there, they would sail into the Black Sea and then up the Danube river (which Herodotus knew as the Ister), along the southern edge of Scythian territory.[3]

Meanwhile, his land forces would have to cross over the strait that separated Asia Minor from the land we now call Europe. It was not a particularly impressive expanse of water, but no eastern empire had yet crossed it. Darius assigned the job of building a bridge across the Bosphorus Strait to one of his Greek engineers, an Ionian named Mandrocles. Then he sent for his men.

The Persian army began the long march along the Royal Road towards Sardis, a force so concentrated that they shook the earth as they passed subjugated city after subjugated city. Meanwhile, the engineer Mandrocles had taken the measure of the strait. At its narrowest, it is around 650 meters, or 720 yards, wide (the length of seven American football fields), far too wide for a traditional bridge. Instead, Mandrocles designed a bridge built across galleys: low, flat-decked ships, roped together to form a floating foundation for a plank road covered with dirt and stones. This was the first pontoon bridge in history: "A bolted roadway, sewn with flax," in the words of the Greek poet Aeschylus.[4] It would still serve as a pattern for army bridge-builders centuries later.

Thousands of Persian foot soldiers and cavalry marched across the bridge, headed for a narrow place in the Danube. There they would meet the naval

64.1. Pontoon Bridge. Pontoon bridges remained a staple of military strategy for centuries; this pontoon bridge was constructed across the James River in Virginia during the American Civil War. Photo credit Medford Historical Society Collection/CORBIS

detachment and build another pontoon bridge into Scythian territory. The cities of Thrace on the other side did not attempt to block the advance. Most Thracians were afraid of the Scythians, and the Persian army might serve as protection against them.

The Scythians did not line up in opposition. Instead, the tribes retreated constantly in front of the Persians, filling in wells and springs and torching trees and grasslands as they went. The Persians, following on, found themselves marching through rough wastes, foraging constantly for food and water, horses and men growing ever hungrier. They were never able to set up and fight a pitched battle, so they were never able to use the skills in which they were trained. "The whole business dragged on endlessly," writes Herodotus, ". . . and things began to go badly for Darius."[5]

Badly enough that, finally, the Great King turned back. The entire Persian force marched *back* to the south, back over the pontoon bridge across the Danube, leaving the unconquered Scythians behind. Persian court historians, and later Persian kings, dealt with this problem by only writing the history of the lands south of the Danube. For all practical purposes, the land on the other side of the river simply ceased to exist. If the Persians couldn't take it, it clearly wasn't important.[6]

But Darius did not leave without spoils. He headed back to Sardis and left the army behind him under his most trusted general, the Persian Megabazus, with orders to conquer Thrace.

The Thracian cities which had hoped for deliverance from the Scythian threat now found themselves falling, one by one, under Persian dominance. Megabazus was a competent general, and the Persian soldiers skilled fighters, but their task was made easier by the fractured nature of Thrace: each city had its own warrior-chief and its own army. "If the Thracians were ruled by a single person or had a common purpose," Herodotus remarks, "they would be invincible and would be by far the most powerful nation in the world. . . . There is no way that it will ever happen, and that is why they are weak."[7]

Megabazus turned Thrace into a new Persian satrapy, Skudra.[8] Then he turned south and set his eyes on the next kingdom: Macedonia.

MACEDONIA, which stood between Thrace and the city-states of the Greek mainland, differed both from the Thracians above and the Greeks below. The cities of Macedonia belonged to a single kingdom, ruled by a single king.

The first Macedonian kings came from a warrior-chief clan called the Argead. The Argead hailed, originally, from the south, and were probably mostly Greek; the poet Hesiod provides the Macedonians with a mythological ancestry that makes them cousins of the Greek heroes and descendants of Zeus, probably reflecting a real ancient relationship of some kind.*

* The brothers Macedon and Magnes were (according to the geneaologies found in Hesiod's fragmentary *Catalogue of Women*) sons of Zeus; they "rejoiced in horses" and "dwelt near Olympus," both characteristic of the Macedonians. They were cousins of the Greeks because their mother, Thyria, was the sister of Hellen, father of the three legendary Greek heros Dorus (ancestor of the Dorians), Xuthus (Ionians), and Aeolus (Aeolians).

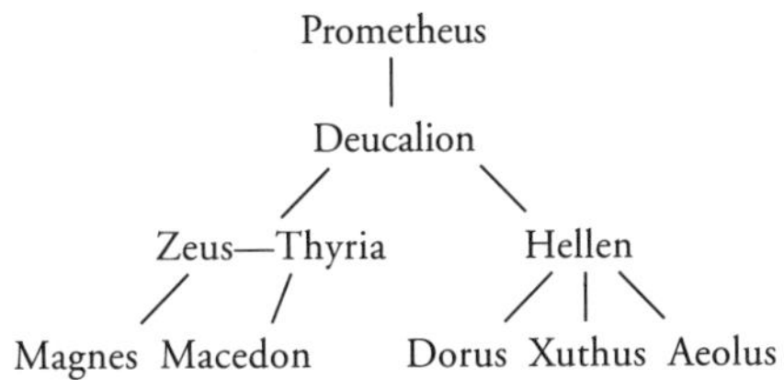

The relationship was not accepted, by Greeks, with a great deal of joy. They considered Macedonians uncouth and semibarbarian. Even the royal family, which was likely more Greek than any other

Moving north, the Argead conquered the land around the Thermaic Gulf and a little farther north, built a capital city (Aegae, near the ancient fortress of Edessa), organized an army, and collected taxes. Macedonia was the first state in Europe to achieve this level of organization.[9]

But it was a pretty rough and tumble kingdom. The kings of Macedonia did not come from the eastern tradition of divinely ordained kingship. They were warriors who held their thrones by force. And although the center of Macedonia was firmly under their control, their hold over the northern parts of Macedonia was much shakier. To the west lay a loose alliance of tribes called Illyrians (probably migrants down from the northwest, since the archaeological traces they have left behind bear a strong resemblance to those of the Celtic West Hallstatt, ranging north of Italy); to the north, Thracian tribes known collectively as the Paeonians.

In the year that Megabazus and his Persians appeared on the horizon with a well-conquered Thrace behind them, the king of Macedonia was Amyntas I (according to tradition, the ninth Argead king). The Persians rolled towards the Macedonian heartland, burning the towns of the Paeonians. Amyntas, seeing the smoke on the horizon, decided at once that resistance was futile.

When seven Persian delegates, led by Megabazus's own son, crossed the Macedonian border with a message, Amyntas received them with honor at his palace at Aegea. "They demanded earth and water for King Darius," Herodotus tells us,[10] a Persian custom symbolizing dominance over the land and sea of a captured country. Amyntas agreed at once. He also offered his daughter in marriage to Megabazus's son, by way of making him particularly welcome. This alliance turned out to be very good indeed for Macedonia; neither the Illyrians nor the remaining Paeonians would trouble their northern border, since to do so might be to risk Persian wrath.

Meanwhile, the Greeks to the south were rapidly approaching a state of panic. With Megabazus storming around to the north, and Amyntas of Macedonia now a Persian ally, there was little barrier now between Persian ambitions and the Greek peninsula.

Unfortunately the Greek cities had long been as divided as the Thracian tribes, and the two most powerful, Athens and Sparta, were suffering from internal convulsions.

Macedonian clan, had to argue for its Greekness. When Alexander I, son of the Macedonian king who ruled during Darius's advance, went down to Olympia to compete in the sprint at the Olympic Games, his competitors complained that he shouldn't be allowed to take part, since the games were only for Greeks. Alexander trotted out his genealogy and was eventually declared, by the Olympic officials, to qualify as a Greek. He then won the race, which suggests that his rivals were motivated by something more than racial pride. (Herodotus V.22.)

SOLON'S REFORMS had not legislated Athens into peace.

The famous code had reorganized the city's government. The top officials in Athens were still the archons, but there were two other levels of government below. The Council of Four Hundred, drawn by lot from the middle- and upper-class citizens of Athens, debated laws and decided which ones should be presented for a vote. The voting population of Athens made up the last level of government, the Assembly.

Every citizen of Athens belonged to the Assembly, which was not as democratic as it sounds; in order to be an Athenian citizen, you had to own property.[11] But Solon had also legislated that the sons of citizens inherited citizenship, even if their fathers had grown poor and lost their land. This was supposed to keep voting power from becoming concentrated in the hands of a smaller and smaller group of wealthy monopolists.

Like the legal reforms themselves, this didn't please two-thirds of Athenian citizens. Wealthy men wanted more influence than the Assembly gave them; the poorest Athenians were limited to membership in the lowest branch of Athenian government.

The Athenians divided into three squabbling groups over Solon's reforms, each with its own nickname. The Men of the Coast wanted to keep Solon's reforms, the Men of the Plain (the oldest families, the Main Line of Athens) wanted to return all power to the hands of the richest Athenians, and the Men of the Hills wanted complete democracy, with the poor and landless granted exactly the same privileges as everyone else. They were the wildest of the three, and their leader, Peisistratus, was, in the words of Aristotle, "an extreme democrat."[12] For one thing, he had been wounded fighting against the enemies of Athens, which gave him a lot of popular appeal (military service was always an advantage for a man who wanted the commoners on his side), and for another he seems to have been a very magnetic personality: "There was something subtly charming about the way he spoke," Plutarch remarks. "He was so good at simulating faculties with which he was not naturally endowed, that he was credited with them, more than those who really *did* have them."[13] He also complained that he was in constant danger of being assassinated by his enemies, which was not paranoid, but rather exceedingly clever; it gave him a reason to collect an increasingly powerful bodyguard around him.

His increasing rabble of armed men worried the most conservative Athenians, and even Solon, returning from his travels in wild lands, was concerned. But Solon was by now very old, his voice shaky and his commanding presence reduced. He could not make much difference in the unfolding of events.

In 560, Peisistratus and his club-wielding bodyguards stormed into the Acropolis, and Peisistratus announced that he would take control of the city.

64.2 Greece at the Time of the Persian Wars

Black Sea
Bosphorus Strait
THRACE
Byzantium
Chalcedon
Hellespont
Sigeum
Troy
Royal Road
Phocaea
Smyrna
Sardis
IONIAN COAST
SAMOS
Ephesus
Mycale
Miletus
Halicarnassus
CARIA
RHODES
KARPATHOS
0
100 Miles
0
100 Kilometers

The revolt was just about as successful as Cylon's. He had overestimated the strength of his followers, and the Men of the Coast and the Men of the Plain forgot their differences, joined together, and drove the Men of the Hills out of Athens.

Peisistratus regathered himself in exile. He had tried sheer force; now he would try strategy. He made a secret alliance with the aristocratic Megacles, leader of the Men of the Coast, promising to marry his daughter in return for helping him get rid of the Men of the Plain (apparently the two parties had begun to bicker with each other, now that they were no longer united against the poor rabble), and came back.

This time Peisistratus, with the combined support of his own followers and Megacles's, managed to hold on to power for a little longer. But soon he was in trouble again. This time, he annoyed his wife by "not having sex with her in the usual way," as Herodotus puts it, and "later she told her mother, who may or may not have questioned her about it."[14] Megacles, informed of this development (and presumably already regretting his alliance with the rough and ready Men of the Hills), decided to switch sides again, and joined the Men of the Plain in driving Peisistratus back out.

Peisistratus had tried revolt; he had tried political alliance; his only path back into power was to buy it, and this path he took. He spent ten years or so working in silver mines, and then, in 546, hired an army of mercenaries and reentered Athens with armed men at his back. He ordered them to take away all weapons of Athenian citizens (the right to bear arms was not, apparently, one of the democratic privileges on his agenda), and from then on ruled as tyrant.[15]

In his own eyes, he was dominating the Athenians for their own good. And in fact he became quite popular; he reduced the taxes for the poor, "advanced money to the poorer people to help them in their labour,"[16] and generally behaved like a mild and humble benefactor, as long as no one crossed him.

When he died in 528, his oldest son Hippias (from a previous marriage, before the irregular cavorting with Megacles's daughter) inherited his job as tyrant, in quite kinglike fashion. This didn't cause any heartburning until a family crisis ensued. According to Aristotle, Hippias's younger brother, Hipparchus, fell madly in love with a handsome young man named Harmodius, who refused to have anything to do with him. Spurned, Hipparchus publicly remarked that Harmodius was a degenerate.

Harmodius was infuriated. He recruited a friend, and the two of them rushed Hipparchus at the height of a religious festival and murdered him. They had hoped that noise and celebration would mask their actions, but royal guards killed Harmodius and arrested his accomplice.

The murder of his brother put Hippias into a frenzy of rage. He ordered the young accomplice tortured for an unspeakably long time, until the young man, maddened by pain, accused all sorts of Athenian citizens of plotting against Hippias and his household, and then finally was released by death.

"In consequence of his vengeance for his brother," writes Aristotle, "and of the execution and banishment of a large number of persons, Hippias became a distrusted and an embittered man."[17] He began a purge of everyone named by the young accomplice, and anyone else who got in his way.

The Athenians were delivered from this mess by an unlikely savior: the elder king of Sparta. This king, Cleomenes, had been told repeatedly by the prophetess at Delphi that it was his divine duty to overthrow the tyranny of Athens. In 508, he roused himself and marched towards Athens at the head of a Spartan army.*

The Delphic oracle was hardly unbiased (Athenian aristocrats, fleeing Hippias's paranoia, had paid to build a gorgeous marble temple in place of the oracle's old plain stone dwelling), and Cleomenes was likely *not* overwhelmed by a desire to see equality in Athens. In fact, the Spartan expansion across the center of the Peloponnese had produced a hugely *unequal* society. Native Spartan citizens were at the top. Beneath them lay a huge underclass of the conquered who could not be trusted as citizens: the *helots*, slaves and laborers. The Spartans liked it this way. The only equality in Sparta lay among male citizens over thirty, who were allowed to vote in the citywide assembly. Even there, Spartans were not permitted to debate. The airing of ideas was not considered useful in government. Young men spent their boyhoods, Plutarch tells us, trained into silent and ready obedience.[18] Argument was no part of this training, which is why the old Greek name for the Spartans—the Lyconians—has given rise to our English word *laconic*.[19]

Cleomenes's march to Athens was impelled not by a love for equality, but by fear of the advancing Persian juggernaut. If Athens fell completely apart into squabbling factions, it would scarcely be able to resist the Persian march south, and Athens was the biggest barrier left between Sparta and Persia. Cleomenes hoped to drive Hippias out, stop the squabbling, and restore Athenian strength.

The Spartan army chased Hippias out, and helped the Athenians hold elections. However, they refused to keep their fingers out of Athenian internal matters, and threw their weight behind one of the candidates.† The Atheni-

* The exact dates for events in Persia and Greece between 520 and 500 are unclear; it may have been 510 or even a little earlier.

† Behind this sentence lies a whole complicated series of events. With Hippias gone, a leader with aristocratic backing (Isagorus) and a leader with democratic backing (Cleisthenes) maneuvered for

ans, who saw in this a Spartan bid to fold Athens into its own orbit as a subject city, cast around for a powerful ally to help them against the dominant city of the south.

Someone in the Assembly (Herodotus does not say who) suggested that Spartan arrogance could only be checked if the Athenians made an alliance with some overwhelmingly huge army . . . like that of the Persians. So off went a delegation to Sardis, to ask the governor there (Darius's half-brother Artaphranes, who had been left in charge when Darius headed back to Persepolis) for an alliance against the Spartans.

The Athenians seem to have overestimated their place in the international scene; this seemed like a perfectly reasonable proposal to them, but Herodotus writes that the delegation "was in the middle of delivering its message when Artaphrenes . . . asked the Athenians who they were and where they were from." He undoubtedly knew the answer to this already, but this was a beautifully deflating inquiry, followed by a curt ultimatum: the Persians would only come to the aid of the Athenians if they agreed to send earth and water to Darius as a symbol of complete submission.

The delegates, surrounded by Persians, agreed, which at least got them safely out of Sardis, although they had to face the music back in Athens: "This got them into a lot of trouble on their return home," Herodotus remarks.[20] The Athenians had no intention of giving up any of their liberties. Instead, they turned to tackle the Spartan problem on their own, and fought a damagingly fierce set of skirmishes to get the remaining armed Spartans out of their city.

With the Spartans finally out of the picture, it took some time for the Athenians to reorder their tyrant-dominated government. When the dust cleared, the population had been divided into ten "tribes," with tribal lines cutting across old family alliances in an attempt to destroy the ancient web of highborn power. The Council of Four Hundred became the Council of Five Hundred, with fifty representatives from each tribe. In a final effort to get rid of the dominance of aristocratic families, the city itself was then divided into

---

power. Isagorus appealed to Cleomenes, who returned to throw his support behind Isagorus and drove out seven hundred Athenian clans; then the Athenian masses rose up, threw out both the Spartans and Isagorus, and acclaimed Cleisthenes leader.

This sort of convoluted negotiation within and between Greek city-states has its place in studies of the evolution of Greek forms of government, but if I were to continue to recount all of these internal events, this history would become impossibly long. From this point on, Greek crises that do not affect the broader world scene will be briefly summarized rather than covered in detail. Readers looking for a more comprehensive account of Greece's political development would do well to consult Herodotus's *Histories*, Aristotle's *Athenian Politics*, or a standard history of Greece such as *Ancient Greece: A Political, Social, and Cultural History* by Sarah B. Pomeroy et al.

thirty geographical units called *demes*, and the Athenians within each deme were ordered to use the name of the deme rather than their family names.*[21] This was an interesting idea, but didn't work particularly well; most Athenians eventually reverted to their old cognomens.

A new custom was introduced as well. Any citizen of Athens could be exiled from the city, should six thousand of his compatriots write his name down on pieces of pottery which were used as ballots. The pottery shards were called *ostraka*, and from this the custom of ten-year exile became known as "ostracism." It was yet another safeguard against tyranny: "Whenever someone . . . becomes greater in power than is appropriate . . . ," writes Aristotle, "such excessive superiority usually leads to one-man rule. . . . On account of this, some states have ostracism."[22]

According to Aristotle, the first Athenians to suffer ostracism were the friends of Hippias, who were forced to follow the ex-tyrant into exile.

MEANWHILE another Greek city had also decided to ask the Persian armies for help.

This was the Ionian city of Miletus, over on the edge of the Persian-ruled Asia Minor. The leader of Miletus was an ambitious warrior named Aristagorus, who had dominated his city as tyrant for years. Now he planned to cast his net wider. He went to the governor of Sardis and offered to conquer his way through the Greek islands called the Cyclades, all on behalf of Persia, if the Persians would just give him ships and soldiers.

Artaphranes agreed to this plan, and Aristagorus, delighted with his chance to become the tyrant of a whole mini-empire of islands, put together an invading force and sailed to his first target, Naxos.

Unfortunately the Greek city on Naxos proved impossible to break into. The inhabitants, rather than fighting, simply hauled all of their provisions inside the city and prepared to wait it out. After a four-month siege, Aristagorus had run out of Persian money, and Artaphranes, unimpressed with the tyrant's skill in conquest, declined to throw any more at the project. Aristagorus was forced to sail back to Miletus with mud on his face, his ambitions thwarted.

He had learned, however, from watching Greek politics from across the water; and, like any good Athenian politician, he switched his ground. He

* The Athenian politician credited with these reforms was Cleisthenes; he was himself aristocratic by birth, having belonged to the group of Athenians who went to Delphi and got on the good side of the oracle by building a temple, but Aristotle says that he had the loyalty of the masses.

decided to switch his alliance from pro-Persian to anti-Persian, sheerly out of expedience. He would lead the Greek cities of Asia Minor in a rebellion against the Persian overlords; and perhaps, eventually, unite them behind his leadership.

A few delicate inquiries showed him that other Ionian tyrants would undoubtedly be willing to join in a rebellion. But he had learned from his Naxos disaster that wars were expensive. He needed even more support to start a war against the Persians.

The obvious first ally for such a project was the warlike Sparta. Sparta was the chief and most powerful city in a loose alliance of Greek city-states called the Peloponnesian League—an association formed for mutual defense against enemies. If Sparta joined the war against Persia, so would other cities in the League. So Aristagorus travelled to Sparta and called on Cleomenes. Cleomenes not only refused to prod the Persian beast with a pin; he first laughed at Aristagorus, and then had Aristagorus pitched out of his city by force.

"After he had been thrown out of Sparta," Herodotus writes, Aristagorus "chose to come to Athens, because after Sparta it was the most powerful Greek state."[23] Here, he found more receptive ears.

Hippias, the expelled Athenian tyrant, was threatening to come back. He had fled Greece, crossed the Hellespont, and gone to the Persians in hopes that Persian armies might help him reconquer Athens. Artaphranes, listening to the plan, could see that Hippias would be the ideal Persian wedge into Greece. He sent a message to Athens, telling them to take Hippias back or suffer invasion; this message had just arrived when Aristagorus showed up, proposing rebellion.[24]

Athens, indignant at this Persian ultimatum, agreed to send twenty ships to help with Aristagorus's rebellion; its ally Eretria, on the coast, sent five.[25] And so, in 500 BC, war began.

THE WAR BETWEEN the Persians and the Greeks, which trailed on for a little more than twenty years, receives barely a mention in Persian histories. But in Greece, it was at the center of every man's life, and at the edge of every woman's, for over two decades. Our accounts are all from Greeks: Herodotus, who was five years old when the war ended, but who interviewed eyewitnesses to reconstruct the events; Thucydides, born twenty or so years later, who made use of Herodotus's accounts but corrected some of his interpretations based on other sources; and the Greek playwright Aeschylus, who was older than both the historians, and fought in the war himself. His play *The Persians* is the work of an eyewitness, but its spotlight is on Greek courage, not campaigns.[26] In the eyes of these men, the battles of the Persian Wars are central to the development of humanity. From the Persian point of view, they were small engagements which, when they went badly, were best ignored.

The Ionian cities that joined the revolt began on a high note by commandeering three hundred ships from Darius's navy, and staffing them with Greeks.[27] Darius immediately sent his fast and well-trained army to put down the Ionian revolt. Before they could arrive, Aristagorus and his allies had managed to surprise Sardis and enter it. The royal governor Artaphranes shut himself safely into the citadel, but the Ionians spread all through Sardis, intending to loot it. Unfortunately, the city began to burn almost at once. A soldier had torched a single house, and since the buildings of Sardis were mostly made of reeds, the fire spread through the whole city.

The "conflagration of Sardis," as Herodotus calls it,[28] made the Persians unredeemably angry. When the Persian and Ionian armies met up in Ephesus, the Ionians were thrashed. They scattered, and the Athenians, seeing that no good was going to come of this particular engagement, decided to go home. But the Ionians had no choice now but to keep on fighting. Burning Sardis was a point of no return. They could not now simply retreat without the most horrific consequences.

They did take the fighting offshore, though. A joint Ionian navy went up through the Hellespont and drove the Persian garrison stationed at Byzantium out of the city. Then the ships sailed back down the coast, collecting allies as they went.[29] The rebellion had grown strong enough to stalemate the Persians for years of weary fighting.

The tide turned against the Ionian cities in 494, when a Persian fleet of six hundred ships came up against the Ionian ships in the open sea, just off the coast near Miletus. The Persians had been collecting themselves for a huge encounter, and they knew the Ionian fleet well; 300 of the 353 ships in the Greek fleet had been kidnapped from Darius's navy at the beginning of the war.[30]

Scores of Ionian-manned ships were sunk. As the battle turned against the Greeks, scores more simply deserted. The admiral of the Ionian fleet sailed off to Sicily and turned pirate (although he only raided Carthaginian and Etruscan ships, and "left Greek shipping alone").[31] Aristagorus himself fled Asia Minor entirely and went over to Thrace, where he was killed while trying to seize a Thracian city for his own.

The victorious Persians landed on the coast at Miletus, the city of Aristagorus the troublemaker. They cut the city off from all outside aid, dug under the walls, and brought it down. "Most of the male population was killed," Herodotus says, "their women and children . . . reduced to slavery. . . . Those who remained alive were taken to Susa." Darius resettled them in the marshes at the mouth of the Tigris, the one-time home of the Chaldeans.[32] The Athenians, watching from afar, were distraught, despite their position as noncombatants. Miletus had once been a daughter city of Athens, and its destruction was a wound to the Athenian body.

Worse was to come. Darius had not forgotten the original Athenian and Eretrian participation in the rebellion. In 492, he put his general and son-in-law Mardonius in charge of a two-pronged invasion force: a land force that would march through Asia Minor, across the Bosphorus on the pontoon bridge, and down through Thrace and Macedonia, and a naval force that would sail through the Aegean and meet the land force for an attack on the northern Greek cities.

This first Persian foray into Greece was cut short. The Persian navy had almost reached its goal when a storm blew up and wrecked almost every ship on the rocks near Mount Athos. Without its planned reinforcements, the land force retreated.

It took the Persian navy two years to rebuild. But by 490, the new fleet was ready to go, and Mardonius (who had been called back to Susa for reproof) was back on the job.

Herodotus says that this second invasion force had six hundred ships; even if this is an exaggeration, the sea invasion was so enormous that the Persians did not bother to march a land force down to reinforce it. On one of the ships was Hippias, who had been promised that he could become the tyrant of Athens once more when the Persians had wiped out the opposition.

The Persian soldiers began their sweep inland by destroying Naxos (Aristagorus had indeed been an incompetent general; the Persian forces overran Naxos in a matter of days) and then besieging Eretria. The next goal was Athens: the queen of Attica, the key to dominating the Greeks.

The Eretrian defenses were gone. The Athenians, braced to face the Persian cataclysm, sent a messenger south to Sparta to beg for assistance. This messenger was Pheidippides, a "trained runner" by profession who is said to have covered the 140 miles between Sparta and Athens in barely twenty-four hours, an amazing feat of strength. (Likely Herodotus telescopes the time that the journey took, but there is no reason to doubt the distance covered.)* But the Spar-

* This was the original long-distance run from Marathon. Plutarch, who lived centuries later, says that the victory of the Athenians over the Persians spawned another run: this one by Thersippus or Euclus (sources differ), who ran from the battlefield to Athens proper with news of the victory and died from his wounds as soon as he had delivered the message. This particular story may be true, although it may also be a myth based on the original run by Pheidippides (who is sometimes credited, probably erroneously, with the postvictory run). Whoever originally ran it (and at what dis-

tans refused to answer the call. They were celebrating a religious holiday, and could not begin a march until the full moon.

The Spartans were a religious people (not to say superstitious), but it is very possible that they were attempting to avoid outright war with Persia. The Persians were arriving to punish Athens; their wrath was directed at those Greek cities which had joined in the Ionian rebellion, and the Spartans had declined.

Meanwhile, the Athenians had no choice but to face the Persians without aid.

Herodotus tells us that their commander, Miltiades, arranged the foot soldiers—the Athenian *hoplites*—in a slightly unusual formation, with a thin center line and massed troops on both wings. The hoplites were named after their shields, the Athenian *hoplon*s, which had grips at the side rather than the center. The hoplon was designed to leave the right arm free for spear use, which meant that it exposed part of the user's right-hand side, but it jutted out to the left far enough to cover the right side of the next hoplite over. It was, in other words, a style of armor that forced its users to stay in a tightly packed formation: the phalanx. A hoplite alone was terribly vulnerable. Only hoplites who remained jammed into the phalanx had a chance of survival.

This coerced discipline, plus desperation, made up for the smaller Athenian numbers. "The Athenians," Herodotus tells us, "charged the invaders at a run," which made the Persians think that perhaps they had all gone mad.[33] And in fact the Athenian center broke almost at once. The massed wings, though, pushed the Persians between them, until the invaders began to retreat out from the deathly space between the phalanxes. As they went backwards towards their ships, they stumbled into marshy ground, many of them bogging down, trapped by the weight of their armor.

Many of the Persians made it back out to the ships and escaped. But the Athenians captured seven ships and killed a huge number of the invaders; Herodotus's number of 6,400 Persian dead, as opposed to 192 Athenian casualties, is (like Henry V's numbers at the Battle of Agincourt) a patriotic exaggeration. But the Battle of Marathon was a staggering victory for Athens. They had fought off the monster.

The Spartans arrived in time to help count the dead.

THE MEN who fought at Marathon were known later by the name *Marathonomachoi*, honored in Athens as World War II veterans have been in

---

tance), the feat of endurance is still remembered in the name of the longest modern Olympic footrace, the marathon.

the United States for their role in freedom. Their victorious general Miltiades came to a thankless end, though, deprived of his command for failing to capture the island of Paros (which was Persian-loyal). He was brought to his trial suffering from a gangrenous wound received during the failed campaign, and died of it very shortly afterwards.

Darius, meanwhile, was considering ways of renewing the war with Greece. In 486, four years after Marathon, he raised taxes, probably to rebuild the army. Egypt rebelled almost at once, probably in reaction, but Darius had no time to deal with it. He grew ill in the fall of 486 and died before winter came.[34]

His oldest son, Xerxes, took his place.

Xerxes had been taking notes on his father's career. Like Darius, he first sent his army to put down the opportunistic rebellions that always accompanied a change in the royal house. The inevitable revolt in Babylon he dealt with by dividing the city into two smaller satrapies, thus short-circuiting some of its factionalism. Egypt he reconquered by sheer force of arms, and then had his own title of "Lord of the Double Country" carved into inscriptions in both Egypt and Persia.[35]

Then he turned his eyes back to Greece. By 484, ports all over his empire were building ships. Three hundred and twenty were manned by Greek mercenaries; two hundred came from Egypt. Egyptians also helped Xerxes to build another pontoon bridge, this one a little farther south than Darius's; it stretched across the Hellespont and was held together by Egyptian flax ropes.[36]

Meanwhile, Athens was building a fleet of triremes, long thin ships (around 120 feet long and only 15 feet wide) with room for 170 rowers, which meant they could knife through the water and ram other ships at high speed. In 481, Athens and thirty other cities joined together in a new league, the Hellenic League, formed specifically for the defense of Greece against the Persians. The Spartans, who had rejoined the anti-Persian cause, were the most experienced of the combined anti-Persian army.

In the fall of that same year, Xerxes in person marched his troops to Sardis, where they wintered, building up their strength and recovering from the journey. Then, in the spring of 480, he led them across the Hellespont.

The Greeks had little faith that the north would stand for very long. They established their front line of battle just below the Malian Gulf, with the army massed at Thermopylae, where the mountains divided to allow for passage. This was the only decent way for Xerxes to reach the southern part of the peninsula (although there was a hidden mountain road, which he was unlikely to discover). The navy was drawn up at the north end of Euboea.

There they waited. Meanwhile, behind them, Greece was in full preparation for disaster. The Athenians decided to expect the worst; a copy of a decree passed by the Council of five hundred has survived:

> Resolved by the Council and the People. . . . To entrust the city to Athena the Mistress of Athens. . . . The Athenians themselves and the foreigners who live in Athens are to send their children and women to safety in Troezen. . . . They are to send the old men and their moveable possessions to safety on Salamis. The treasurers and priestesses are to remain on the Acropolis guarding the property of the gods. All the other Athenians and foreigners of military age are to embark on the 200 ships that are ready, and defend against the barbarian for the sake of their own freedom and that of the rest of the Greeks.[37]

And then Xerxes swept down. In front of the invaders, Thrace surrendered; and then the cities of Macedonia, one by one. Xerxes was marching down into the Greek mainland, and if he could get through the mountains, the cities to the south would be doomed. A troop from Attica had been given the job of keeping an eye on the hidden mountain road, just in case. But the all-important pass of Thermopylae was entrusted to the Spartan troops, seven thousand men under the Spartan king Leonidas (successor to Cleomenes).

This would have been sufficient for the narrow ground on which the Persians and Greeks would meet, had a Greek traitor not gone over to Xerxes and drawn him a map of the mountain road. Xerxes sent a commander to climb through it with the most highly trained of the Ten Thousand, the elite fighters that Herodotus calls "the Immortals." When they came down on the other side of the mountains, they began to circle around to the rear of the Spartans.

Leonidas, seeing that his force was about to be sandwiched, realized that the battle had already been lost. He ordered all of his men but three hundred to retreat back down to the south. With these last three hundred, along with a few troops from the Greek cities of Thebes and Thespia who refused to leave, he fought a delaying action against Xerxes. Attica was doomed, but if his retreating Spartans could reach the Gulf of Corinth, they might still be able to hold the Peloponnese, along with Troezen, where the women and children were, and Salamis: all that would remain of Greece.

The Spartans fought until they were wiped out. In the battle, Immortals fell as well; two of Xerxes's own brothers died.[38] Later, the heroism of the soldiers who fell at the Battle of Thermopylae would become one of the most famous acts of heroism in history. Xerxes was unimpressed. He ordered Leonidas's body to be beheaded and nailed up on a cross, like that of an executed criminal.

Plutarch tells us that the Greeks, harassed and desperate, had a brief and violent internal quarrel about what to do next. The Athenian troops in the combined Greek army begged the rest to make a stand in Attica, to protect Athens; but the others had no confidence that they could hold a wide northern front against the huge Persian army. They won the day. The entire force retreated back down into the Peloponnese, where they could mass their ships in the waters around the island of Salamis and also erect a defensive line across the narrow land bridge—the Isthmus of Corinth—that linked the Peloponnese to Attica. The Athenians did so under protest: "angry at this betrayal," Plutarch writes, "and also dismayed and distressed at being deserted by their allies."[39]

At the head of his soldiers, Xerxes marched in triumph to great Athens and overran it. The Persian soldiers burned the Acropolis; from the other side of the water, the Athenians were forced to sit and watch the smoke of their city rise up.

The next events are chronicled by the playwright Aeschylus, who was there. In his play *The Persians,* a Persian herald returns to the capital city of Susa to report to the queen mother that her son Xerxes has decided to attack the Greeks in the Peloponnese at once:

> A Greek appeared from the enemy camp,
> whispering to your son that under
> cover of night every Greek to a man
> would leap to his oar and row madly in every
> direction to save his skin.[40]

The messenger had been sent by the Greek leader Themistocles, who knew that time was on the Persian side. The Greeks, penned up in the Peloponnese without allies, could most easily have been defeated with a slow and damaging war of attrition. The best possible strategy for Xerxes was to sit tight, send his navy around to ring the Peloponnese so that none of the outlying islands could provide aid, and regather himself for an attack.

So Themistocles sent a message to the Great King offering to change sides, and telling him that if he attacked at once, the weary and dispirited Greeks would scatter. Xerxes, convinced, did not bother to ring the island. Instead, he sent ships directly into the narrows to attack the Athenian triremes massed there.

> Your son, at once,
> deceived by Greek treachery, and the gods'
> jealousy, let it be known to all his

captains that when the
sun descended below the horizon, and
darkness covered the dome of the sky,
they were to divide the fleet into three divisions
and block the Greeks' escape to the open sea,
while other ships surrounded and circled the island.[41]

This was exactly what Themistocles wanted. The triremes, fast and maneuverable, could fight effectively in the cramped narrows around Salamis, while the more powerful Persian ships were unable to get out of the way of the ramming fronts.

Ship struck ship,
ramming with bows of brass,
breaking away whole prows.
The Greeks began it.
Men on opposing decks let fly their
spears.
We resisted at first, holding our own;
but soon our ships, so massed together,
struck each other head-on in the narrow strait,
bronze beak ramming bronze beak,
destroying oars and benches.
The Greeks then circled round in perfect
order and struck, and hulls were tumbled
wrong-side up, and the sea was no longer
seen for all the wreckage and floating bodies.
And all the shores and reefs bobbing with corpses.[42]

Persians, raised inland, were not swimmers. Those who fell overboard drowned, almost to a man.

Xerxes, who had sat himself down on a golden stool on high ground to view the battle, grew increasingly furious. This defeat need not have been the end for Xerxes, but his rage ruined him. He ordered the captains of his navy—all Phoenician, from the Phoenician cities that now lay under Persian control—put to death for cowardice. This turned every single Phoenician sailor against him. The Phoenicians, who were experienced at sea, knew exactly why their attack had failed.

Meanwhile, Babylon was rebelling again, and Themistocles was up to his usual schemes. He set free a Persian prisoner of war, who returned to Xerxes primed with the information that the Greek fleet intended to sail up to the Hellespont and rip up the pontoon bridge before Xerxes and his army could get back to it.[43] At this news Xerxes decided to go home.

He announced that there would be a substantial reward for anyone who captured Themistocles (a useless gesture) and then marched back up through Macedonia and Thrace with the bulk of his army, leaving behind him a force of soldiers commanded by his son-in-law Mardonius. In effect, Xerxes was leaving Mardonius to die, to save himself from the embarrassment of out-and-out retreat. The Athenians marched across the Isthmus of Corinth, and met Mardonius and his reduced force at Plataea. Pausanias, the nephew of the heroic Leonidas, had inherited his post as general (and was also serving as regent for Leonidas's young son, now king of Sparta). He led the assault; the Greeks were victorious and Mardonius died on the battlefield. "His corpse disappeared the day after the battle," Herodotus writes, and no one knows where it was buried.[44]

This was a two-pronged attack. The navy had simultaneously been sent to confront the remains of the Persian fleet, which had retreated back across the Aegean all the way to the coast of Asia Minor. The Persians, seeing Greek ships behind them, decided not to risk another sea battle; they beached their ships on the shores of Asia Minor, just west of the mountain called Mycale, and lined up to fight on land.

Tradition held that both battles, Plataea and Mycale, took place on the same day in 479. At Mycale, Persians relied on the Ionian fighters in their ranks to back them up. But when the Greeks approached, the Ionians melted away, back towards their own cities, and left the Persians standing alone. The combined Athenian and Spartan forces drove the Persians back all the way to Sardis, killing them as they went. Only a few ever reached the safety of Sardis's walls.

The Greek victories at Plataea and Mycale ended the Persian Wars. The loss didn't make an enormous dent on the Persian psyche, although the Persians did allow their navy to shrink rather than rebuilding it.[45] But Greek cities, from Sparta all the way over to the Ionian coast, had joined together in voluntary alliance to defeat a common enemy. It was the first joint action taken by the entire Greek world, a world held together not by political boundaries but by shared customs and language.

TIMELINE 64

PERSIA	GREECE
Cyrus II (the Great) (559)	
	Peisistratus of Athens
	Amyntas I of Macedonia
Cambyses II (530)	
Darius I	**Cleomenes of Sparta**
	Damaratus of Sparta
	Battle of Marathon (490)
Xerxes I (486)	**Leonidas of Sparta**
	Battles of Thermopylae and Salamis (480)
	Battles of Plataea and Mycale (479)

Part Five

IDENTITY

Chapter Sixty-Five

The Peloponnesian Wars

Between 478 and 404 BC, Xerxes dies, and Athens and Sparta declare a Thirty Years' Peace which only lasts fourteen years

WITH THE PERSIANS DRIVEN BACK, the newly united Greeks had to decide what to do about the Ionian cities. By joining with the Greeks, the Ionians had publicly declared their defiance of the Persian empire. The poet Aeschylus celebrated their new freedom:

> And those who live on Asia's broad earth
> will not long be ruled
> by Persian law
> nor longer pay tribute
> under empire's commanding grip
> nor fling themselves earthward
> in awe of kingship
> whose strength now lies dead.[1]

But the Persian strength was far from dead, and Persian troops were still occupying Asia's "broad earth." The Aegean lay between the Persians and the Greek mainland, but for the Ionians, the battered bully was standing just on the other side of their city walls.

The Spartans suggested that they simply evacuate the Ionian cities and abandon the land itself to the Persians, since they could not "stand guard over Ionia forever."[2] The Athenian soldiers at once took exception. These were mostly Athenian colonies that the Spartans were blithely proposing to abandon (much as they had abandoned Athens itself during the invasion, content simply to save the Peloponnese). "They put their objections forcefully," Herodotus says. After a vicious intercity argument, the Athenians managed to convince most of the other Greek contingents to join them in pushing the Persians back from the Ionian coast.

The Spartans, outargued, agreed to stay on; they didn't want to fight the Persians, but nor did they want Athens gaining power as the leader of the Hellenic League. By staying, they guaranteed that their own commander—Pausanias, victor at the Battle of Plataea, and still serving as regent for the young son of the Leonidas who had died at Thermopylae—would remain the supreme commander of the Hellenic League forces.

And so Pausanias and his navy sailed off to besiege Byzantium, which had been re-occupied by Persian soldiers. The Athenians regrouped under the command of their own native general, Xanthippus, and headed up to the Bosphorus to help out. The siege was successful, and then Persian Byzantium changed hands again and became Greek Byzantium once more.

It was the last time that Athens and Sparta would act as allies.

FURTHER THAN THIS, Herodotus does not go; his history ends right after Mycale. For the next sequence of events we have to go to Thucydides, who wrote his history some seventy years later, and Plutarch, whose *Life of Themistocles* adds a few details.

According to Thucydides, while the Athenian and Spartan soldiers were besieging Byzantium, the Athenians and Spartans were arguing back at home. After the defeat of Mardonius at Plataea, the Athenian soldiers under command of Themistocles had returned to Athens. Their city had been laid waste; the walls were broken down, the temples on the Acropolis had been hacked and burned, and the sacred olive tree which grew at the Temple of Athena had been chopped down, its stump charred. But in a mere matter of days, a green shoot was seen coming from the stump.[3] Athens still lived, and the returning Athenians set about the long task of rebuilding the shattered walls.

News of the rebuilding flew to Sparta. In just a few more days, a Spartan delegation arrived at Athens and demanded not only that the building stop, but that the Athenians "join them in throwing down the remaining walls of the cities outside the Peloponnesus."[4]

This was a blatant Spartan attempt to claim the overall lordship of Greece. The Athenians, who had few armed men and no wall, were in no shape to resist the demand. But Themistocles, who never told the truth in a sticky situation, had a plan. He told the Spartans that he would, naturally, come to Sparta right away along with a band of Athenian officials to discuss the problem. He then set out himself for Sparta, travelling at snail pace, and told the other Athenian officials to linger in Athens until the walls were built up to at least a minimum height. Meanwhile, every Athenian who could walk was to drop everything else and work on the walls, ripping down houses if necessary to serve as building material. "To this day," Thucydides writes, "the [wall] shows signs of the haste of its execution; the foundations are laid of stones of all kinds, and in some places not wrought or fitted, but placed just in the order in which they were brought by the different hands; and many columns, too, from tombs, and sculptured stones were put in with the rest."[5] Excavation has revealed these mismatched stones and columns built into the wall of Athens.

Down in Sparta, Themistocles sat around wondering out loud why his colleagues had not yet arrived, and hoping piously that they hadn't run into misfortune. By the time they did get there, the wall was up, and Themistocles was able to tell the Spartans that Athens now had defenses and wasn't about to get Spartan permission to run its own affairs. The Spartans swallowed this defiance, not really being in any condition to fight a walled city, and Themistocles went home.

Over at Byzantium, the Ionians were starting to complain about being under Spartan command. They came to the Athenian commander, Xanthippus, and complained that the Spartan general Pausanias was acting like a tyrant—and, more seriously, was carrying on secret negotiations with Xerxes. This was an accusation that could hardly be ignored, and when the Spartan assembly got wind of it, they summoned Pausanias home to stand trial. Xanthippus took supreme command in his place, which was one up for the Athenians.

Back in Sparta, Pausanias was acquitted. But his career was in ruins; a breath of scandal had done it in. The Spartans sent a replacement commander to Byzantium, but Xanthippus refused to surrender his command. Now Athens, not Sparta, was at the head of the combined forces. The Spartans, piqued, packed themselves up and went home—and so did all of the other soldiers from the Peloponnesian cities.

This was the death knell for the old Hellenic League. But the Athenians simply declared the formation of a new alliance, the Delian League, with Athens at its head. Back at home, Sparta claimed leadership of a Peloponnesian League that included the Peloponnesian cities and no one else.

Pausanias himself, under increasing suspicion and the target of more unproven accusations of treachery (largely fueled by the fact that he had occasionally been seen, in Byzantium, in Persian clothing), eventually realized that he was inevitably going to be re-arrested and tried again. He took sanctuary in an inner chamber of one of Sparta's temples. At this, Spartan officials walled him in, took the roof of the chamber off, and allowed him to starve to death.[6] The man who had saved the Peloponnese died while his own countrymen watched.

65.1 Greece and the Peloponnesian Wars

Nor was this the end of the matter. Back in Athens, Themistocles had started to push his own plans for Athenian security (these involved burning the ships of other Greek cities, and sailing around to shake money out of the smaller Greek islands).[7] Themistocles was, above all, a pragmatist, always willing to sacrifice personal dignity for the sake of getting his way. When other soldiers criticized his suggestions, Themistocles started making public speeches about the great debt that Athens owed him, and how the Athenians ought to do whatever he asked. After a whole course of these, he had managed to annoy enough Athenian men (who, after all, had fought at Mycale too) to get himself ostracized. "This," Plutarch remarks, "was their usual practice. . . . Ostracism was not a means of punishing a crime, but a way of relieving and assuaging envy—an emotion which finds its pleasure in humbling outstanding men."[8]

This was the shadow side of Greek democracy. The Greeks were not kind to their great men, unless those men had been fortunate enough to remove themselves from the political scene by dying. Marathon had not saved Miltiades; Plataea had done nothing for Pausanias; and Salamis would not save Themistocles. After his ostracism, the Spartans sent messages to Athens telling them that the investigation of Pausanias had found, "in the course of the inquiry," unspecified proof that Themistocles also had pro-Persian sympathies. The Athenians sent an assassin after their exiled general, but Themistocles was not to be caught so easily. He went on a long journey, always avoiding Greek ships and Greek ports, and finally (pragmatic as always) arrived at the Persian court and offered himself as an advisor on Greek affairs, on condition that Xerxes would agree to pay over the reward for his own capture.

Fortunately, Xerxes seems to have been entertained by this level of cheek. He made Themistocles a present of the reward and told him to "speak his mind about the state of affairs in Greece." Themistocles did so, but his conversation seems to have been mostly art without matter. His revelations, Plutarch remarks, did not give the Persians any military advantage, but mostly had to do with Greek dress, literature, and food.[9] He died in exile at sixty-five, either from illness or from a dose of poison, taken when he could no longer bear his banishment.[10]

Meanwhile, the soldiers of the Delian League, led by Athenian commanders, set about recapturing various islands and cities from the Persians. The Persians fought back, but not with a whole lot of conviction. The Persian empire had begun to grow unwell from internal canker. Xerxes's imperious refusal to take responsibility for the defeat at Salamis was just a symptom of a personality that would not brook any restraint, and accounts from several different sources suggest a man sinking deeper and deeper into sybaritic corruption. The biblical book of Esther tells of a week-long orgy hosted by Xerxes at his palace in Susa, at the end of which Xerxes (who, like his guests, had been drunk out of his mind for days) ordered his favorite wife to come out and parade in front of the entire party of men, so that they could admire her beauty. She refused; Xerxes, furious, sent word to her that she would never again come into his presence, and decided to replace her. He sent out word to all of his satraps to send the most beautiful girls in their satrapies to the court. Once they were in court, he spent a few pleasurable months calling them into his bedchamber, one per night, so that he could sample them all before choosing his favorite.[11] Xerxes's appetite for women is also mentioned by Herodotus, who says that he developed a great passion first for his brother's wife, and then for his brother's daughter.[12]

These stories are not written by friends. However, Xerxes was clearly not popular with either his court or his family by the time he died. The Greek historian Ctesias, who spent time at the Persian court some fifty years later, says that Xerxes was sleeping when the head eunuch, a trusted man who guarded his bedchamber, allowed a Persian army commander named Artabanos (a *chiliarch,* which meant that he commanded a thousand of the elite Persian fighters) in to see the king. Minutes later, Xerxes was dead. The year was 465.

When the body was discovered, Artabanos accused the oldest son, Darius, of the deed, and turned to the youngest son, the eighteen-year-old hothead Artaxerxes, exhorting him to avenge his father's murder. "With much shouting," Ctesias says, "Darius protested that he did not kill his father, but he was put to death."[13]

This left Artaxerxes as heir apparent, since the middle brother, Hystaspes, had been sent off to be satrap of the northern province Bactria and was nowhere around. Didorus Siculus picks up the story: as soon as Artabanos found himself alone with the brand-new king, he dropped all pretense and attacked Artaxerxes. The young man fought back, though, and although wounded managed to kill the treacherous captain.[14] As soon as the news travelled to Bactria, Hystaspes came charging down to try to get the throne for himself, but Artaxerxes met him in battle and was fortunate. A sandstorm came down while the battle raged, and behind its screen Artaxerxes killed his other brother and emerged victorious.[15]

As usual, chaos in the royal house produced rebellion all over the empire. The most serious was in Egypt, where news of Xerxes's death convinced one of Psammetichus III's surviving sons, Inaros (now well past middle age and living at Heliopolis), to drag his royal heritage out of the closet. Inaros sent to the Athenians, who were very happy to sail down and give him a hand with a rebellion.[16]

This combined guerilla force took Artaxerxes eleven years to defeat. When Persian forces finally managed to capture Inaros, who had been behaving like an elderly Egyptian Zorro for over a decade, Artaxerxes ordered him crucified.

Back in Greece, more Athenian troops were carrying on battles of their own. The Delian League had not been easy to hold together, and Athens found itself, perhaps without realizing it, using more and more force against its own allies. In 460, the island of Naxos declared that it no longer wanted to take part in the League (which meant "follow Athenian orders"), and war followed: "She had to return [to the League] after a siege," Thucydides writes. "[T]his was the first instance of the confederation being forced to subjugate an allied city."[17] It was not, however, the last. Other Delian League cities protested against the Athenian demands for tribute and ships, and Athens responded with force. They marched into Thrace; the Athenian navy fought against the city of Aegina and captured seventy ships; when the city of Megara, a member of the Peloponnesian League, complained loudly about a border dispute with Corinth (another Peloponnesian city), the Athenians not only welcomed Megara into the Delian League but helped the Megarans build new defensive walls and (unasked) sent Athenian troops to occupy the city. "They made themselves offensive," Thucydides concludes. ". . . .The Athenians were not the old popular rulers they had been at first."[18]

Athens and Sparta seemed to have exchanged places; the Athenians had become the bullies of the Aegean. The Delian League was still called the Delian League, but it had become something closer to an Athenian empire.* The beautiful city was also looking more and more like a fortress. Xanthippus's son Pericles had been elected to military command, and proposed that the Athenians build walls out from Athens down to the port of Pireus, a distance of eight miles, so that goods and soldiers could get to the water without fear of attack.[19] In 457, the construction on these "Long Walls" began.

Just after the walls were finished, the Athenian and Spartan armies themselves clashed. In 457, a Spartan army marched into the area called Boeotia, northwest of Attica, on the pretext that they had been invited in by the people of Doris, even farther to the northwest. This was not their only motivation: "Secret encouragement had been given to them by a party in Athens," Thucydides says, "who hoped to put an end to the reign of democracy and the building of the long walls."[20]

The Athenians marched out into Boeotia too, with fourteen thousand troops. When the dust had cleared, the Spartans claimed victory. Certainly they did cut down all the fruit trees they could find, before marching home; but since the Athenians went back out into Boeotia and claimed the area for themselves only two months later, it could hardly have been a decisive victory. In fact, the two forces were more or less equal. Athens, which had begun with the upper hand, had lost enough men in the unsuccessful fight in Egypt to even the balance.

In 446, the Athenians proposed a peace. The treaty itself has not survived, but remarks of various Greek politicians suggest that the Athenians were willing to give up some of the land they had seized on the Isthmus of Corinth and along the shore of the Peloponnese for an end to fighting. Both cities agreed not to interfere with the other's allies. This arrangement was supposed to hold for thirty years; and so the treaty became known as the Thirty Years' Peace.

* There was never an "Athenian empire," but many historians refer to 454 as the year when, for all practical purposes, the Delian League ceased to function as a "league" (an association of member cities) and became something more like an empire policed by the Athenian army.

Shortly after this, Herodotus left Athens. He had found the constant frenzy of politics uncongenial, and preferred to go to Thurii, a new pan-Hellenic colony that was drawing citizens from all across Greece.

Despite the frenzy, Athens was blooming. The commander Pericles, who had gained more and more popularity as a public speaker, oversaw the building of a new temple to Athena on top of the Acropolis. This temple, the Parthenon, was decorated with sculpted stone friezes showing legendary Greek victories over semihuman centaurs: a celebration of Greek triumph over non-Greek enemies. A forty-foot seated statue of Zeus was carved from ivory and placed at the temple at Olympia, where it became so well known that later list-makers called it one of the seven wonders of the ancient world. The philosopher Socrates spent his days talking and teaching, attracting scores of followers; like the Buddha, evolving a coherent and influential philosophy without writing a word, since all of his teachings were set down by his students.

But this beauty was all rotten at the core. Hatred between Athens and Sparta had not gone away. The Thirty Years' Peace held for fourteen years; and then it splintered.

THE FIRST FIGHTING actually broke out between Athens and one of Sparta's allies, the city of Corinth. In 433, a Corinthian colony called Corcyra tried to break away from Corinthian rule, and asked Athens for help.

Corcyra itself technically didn't belong to either the Peloponnesian or Delian League, so the Athenians could answer the call without breaking the peace. On the other hand, since Corcyra was a colony of Corinth, and Corinth was an ally of Sparta, the Spartans would undoubtedly take offense if Athens joined in a battle *against* Corinth.

The Athenians were unable to resist this chance to weaken the power of Corinth. After two full days of public debate, the Assembly decided to send ten ships.[21] In an attempt to have their cake and eat it too, the Assembly also warned the captain who was given command of this little fleet not to attack unless the Corinthians actually landed *in* Corcyra, or threatened Corcyra's own ships.[22]

The Corinthian ships, arriving, sailed directly into the ships that Corcyra had massed to meet them. The Athenian captain, trying to follow his orders, held back until the Corinthian ships had driven the Corcyreans well back and were pressing forwards, inflicting casualties. In Thucydides's words, they "butchered" the men "as they sailed through, not caring so much to make prisoners."[23]

At this, the Athenian ships not only joined the battle, but summoned reinforcements. Now Athens was at war with Corinth, and Corinth was an ally of Sparta. The Thirty Years' Peace had ended.

This sea engagement, the Battle of Sybota, was the first in a string of minor battles over the next year and a half. In 431, the string ended when the city of Thebes (a Spartan ally) attacked Plataea, the city in Boeotia which had been the site of the famous battle with the Persians and which was now under Athenian protection. This was the first attack to threaten a city's actual walls, and Thucydides says that this "overt act" finally broke the treaty beyond repair. "Athens at once prepared for war," he writes, "as did Sparta and her allies."*[24]

The Spartans whipped themselves up into fighting frenzy ("The Athenians aspire to rule the rest of the world!") and established their front line on the isthmus, ready to march into Attica. Athens made a hasty alliance with the king of Macedonia, Amyntas's grandson Perdikkas II, and Pericles ordered the country folk of Attica to come inside the walls of Athens for protection. When the first Athenians died in battle, Pericles gave a funeral oration to honor them, a speech in which he listed the superiorities of Athenian civilization: Athenian freedom, Athenian education (which gives its men "knowledge without effeminacy"), the ongoing Athenian war against poverty, the ability of its citizens to understand public matters. He ended with a patriotic call unlike any in history so far: "You must yourselves realize the power of Athens," he told them. "Feed your eyes on her from day by day till love of her fills your hearts; and then, when all her greatness shall break upon you, you must reflect that it was by courage, sense of duty, and a keen feeling of honor in action that men were enabled to win all this."[25] It was a call for loyalty not to a king, but to a concept; to identify themselves as Athenians, based not on race, but on a willing and voluntary association with an *idea*.

It was a stirring call, but most Athenians who died in the first two years of the Peloponnesian War met a less glorious, less patriotic death. In 430, plague struck Athens.

Thucydides himself, living in the city, survived it and gives an account:

> . . . [P]eople in good health were all of a sudden attacked by violent heats in the head, and redness and inflammation in the eyes, the inward parts, such as the throat or tongue, becoming bloody and emitting an unnatural

* The Peloponnesian War ran from 431 to 405. Some historians call the hostility between Sparta and Athens before the Thirty Years' Peace the "First Peloponnesian War" and the fighting between 431 and 405 the "Second Peloponnesian War," but since most direct fighting between the two armies took place in the second phase, I've chosen to name only one of the phases as an actual war.

> and fetid breath. These symptoms were followed by sneezing and hoarseness, after which the pain soon reached the chest, and produced a hard cough. . . . Externally the body was . . . reddish, livid, and breaking out into small pustules and ulcers. . . . [T]hey succumbed, as in most cases, on the seventh or eighth day, to the internal inflammation. . . . But if they passed this stage, and the disease descended further into the bowels, inducing a violent ulceration there accompanied by severe diarrhea, this brought on a weakness which was generally fatal. . . . [T]he disorder . . . settled in the privy parts, the fingers and the toes, and many escaped with the loss of these, some too with that of their eyes.[26]

Quite apart from the loss of able-bodied fighting men ("They died like sheep"), this was an unbearable blow to a city already apprehensive about its future. "By far the most terrible feature in the malady was the dejection which ensued when anyone felt himself sickening," Thucydides says, "for the despair into which they instantly fell took away their power of resistance, and left them a much easier prey to the disorder."[27]

The despair was worsened by the grim condition of the city. The residents of the Attica countryside were still making for the shelter of Athens. But when they arrived, the makeshift shelters built for them along the inside of the walls proved to be death pits: "stifling cabins where the mortality raged without restraint. The bodies of dying men lay one upon another . . . the sacred places also in which they had quartered themselves were full of corpses of persons that had died there."[28] Bodies burned in huge heaps at all hours of the day and night; petty thieves had free range through deserted households; no one bothered to sacrifice or observe any rituals. The distance between sacred and profane had been reduced by the need of survival.* Among the victims was Pericles, the great Athenian general, on whom the city had been depending.

The war, begun badly, continued to go badly. Thucydides, once recovered, was put in command of an Athenian force charged with protecting Thrace,

* Argument still rages over what the plague of Athens actually was. Thucydides makes no mention of the buboes which are usually described in accounts of bubonic plague. Typhoid is a possibility, but Thucydides does say that animals as well as humans suffer, which means that the epidemic may have been an animal disease which leaped hosts in the hot conditions of the Athenian summer of 430. John Wylie and Hugh Stubbs make a convincing case for tularemia, a bacterial infection which normally doesn't spread from person to person, but which may well have mutated since its first appearance in 430 BC. The puzzle remains unsolved; see J. A. H. Wylie and H. W. Stubbs, "The Plague of Athens, 430–428 BC: Epidemic and Epizootic," in *The Classical Quarterly* 33:1 (1983), pp. 6–11, for a summary of the various candidates.

but his soldiers were driven into retreat, and Thucydides was sent into exile as punishment. Greek ships, preoccupied at home, were unable to come to the aid of the Greek cities on the Italian peninsula when tribes from the Apennines (pushed, perhaps, by the Celtic waves from the north) came down from the slopes and attacked them. The Greek settlers were driven out; the Greek presence in the Italian peninsula almost disappeared.

THE GREEKS, tearing each other to shreds, were mostly ignoring the imperial power to the east. In 424, Artaxerxes died an obscure death after a fairly uninteresting reign. His wife died on the same day (we have no details, but it's a suspicious coincidence), and their one son, Xerxes II, reigned for a total of forty-five days. According to Ctesias (who, granted, generally puts the most interesting spin possible on Persian royal affairs), Xerxes II drank himself insensible one night, and while snoring in his bed was murdered by an illegitimate half-brother who then proclaimed himself king. This half-brother was violent, short-tempered, and unpopular. Messages must have gone out frantically from the household to the only possible rival to the throne: another illegitimate half-brother, who was married to his own illegitimate half-sister but at least was an experienced administrator who had been running a satrapy for some time in a competent manner.

This half-brother, Ochus, was also was on friendly terms with the satrap of Egypt, who sent him troops. He marched into Susa, caught the usurper, and had him put to death. He himself took the throne, giving himself a proper royal name to replace his bastard's name: Darius II.[29] His reign began near the end of the year 424, in which both his father and his half-brother had died: a year in which the Persian empire had had three different Great Kings.

BY 421, the Athenians and the Spartans found themselves back in the same position that they had been in back when the Thirty Years' Peace was sworn: losing soldiers constantly, facing famine if regular planting and harvesting didn't resume soon, neither of them with any hope of decisive victory. They agreed once more to a peace, known as the Peace of Nicias, after the Athenian leader who helped negotiate it.

The peace lasted for six years. Nicias's colleague in Athenian government, Alcibiades, was not inclined to let a peace go on for long; he wanted fame.

Alcibiades was a hard-drinking, extravagant man whose reputation for beauty outlasted his youth, an affected libertine who carried on affairs with both sexes: "[He] minces along with his cloak trailing behind him, tilts his head to one side and speaks with a pronounced lisp," Plutarch observes.[30] He was also driven by an obsessive need for public acclaim, which made him a bad match for the times. Athens needed to rebuild its strength and ignore Sparta, but Alcibiades knew that there was no glory for him in that. In 415, he seized an opportunity to play hero.

A Greek settlement on Sicily, called Egesta, asked the Athenian navy for support against two other Greek cities in Sicily, the cities of Selinus and Syracuse. Syracuse, originally a Corinthian colony, was one of the wealthiest Greek cities west of the Adriatic, and had kept its ties with the mother city. If the Athenians sailed to the aid of Egesta, they could replay the fight with Corinth and, perhaps, triumph.

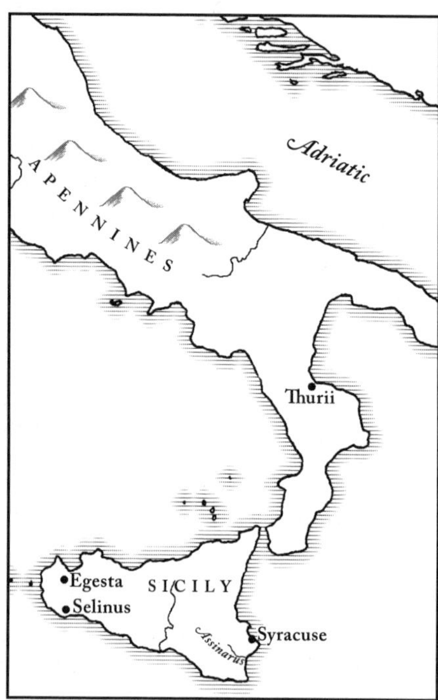

65.2 The War on Sicily

Alcibiades convinced the Athenians to throw a huge fleet at this distant and pointless target: 25,000 soldiers, over 130 triremes, and an equal number of boats carrying supplies.[31] A prank just before the fleet embarked (someone defaced a whole series of sacred images at the end of a long drunken evening) almost kept it on the shores, since many Athenians thought this to be a bad omen. But finally the ships were given their send-off and sailed towards Sicily, into total disaster.

Alcibiades and Nicias were in charge, along with a third experienced general. Almost at once, the three leaders quarrelled over when and how to attack. Then they received a message from Athens: Alcibiades was suspected of defacing those sacred images (he was probably guilty of this childish vandalism), and the Athenians had decided to haul him back to Athens to face trial.

No good ever came of such a summons, so Alcibiades took a ship and deserted the fleet. He sailed to Sparta, where he switched sides and offered to help the Spartans bring an end to their troubles with Athens once and for all. If he couldn't get fame in one way, he'd try another.

Back off the shores of Sicily, Nicias—who was not a decisive man, although a good peacemaker—delayed and deliberated until the Syracusans had collected a force of their own, including reinforcements from their allies in the Peloponnesian League. By then it was too late to win, even though the Athenians had managed to convince the Etruscans to join them.[32] Nicias wrote back to Athens, begging to be allowed to withdraw; given the size of the Syracusan opposition, he said, only a force twice as large as the one he currently commanded could win.

The Athenians had no idea of their precarious situation. They promptly raised, and sent, enough men to double Nicias's force.[33]

Nicias, aghast to see the reinforcements appear on the horizon, planned to take the whole army and retreat. But the Syracusans got wind of this scheme, and, in Thucydides's words, "became more eager than ever to press the Athenians, who had now themselves acknowledged that they were no longer their superiors either on sea or by land, as otherwise they would never have planned to sail away."[34] Syracusan ships blocked the Athenian retreat, whereupon forty thousand Athenian soldiers tried to escape across the island on foot to the other side. Their horrific march, in the summer sun with the enemy behind, ended in disaster: they hoped to reach the Assinarus river and launch a defense on the other side, but when they reached the shore,

> driven by their exhaustion and craving for water . . . they rushed in, and all order was at an end, each man wanting to cross first. . . . Meanwhile the opposite bank, which was steep, was lined by the Syracusans, who showered missiles down upon the Athenians, most of them drinking greedily and heaped together . . . in the hollow bed of the river. The Peloponnesians also came down and butchered them, especially those in the water, which was thus immediately spoiled, but which they went on drinking just the same, mud and all, bloody as it was, most even fighting to have it. At last, when many dead now lay piled one upon another in the stream, and part of the army had been destroyed at the river, and the few that escaped from there had been cut off by the cavalry, Nicias surrendered.[35]

Despite assurances from the Syracusan commander, Nicias was murdered as soon as he had laid down his arms. The captive Athenians were sent to the quarries, where they died in heat and filth, or lived among the piled bodies of those who had died before. The few survivors returned home to find that the Spartans, helped by Alcibiades, had already invaded Attica and were spreading across its edge.

But the Spartans still couldn't force an Athenian surrender, and after eight years the war was still dragging on. Most Greeks were, by now, very tired of fighting the Spartans. In these years, the playwright Aristophanes wrote the comedy *Lysistrata,* in which the women of Athens announce that they will all refrain from sex until their husbands bring the war to an end. "We need only sit indoors with painted cheeks," their leader Lysistrata exclaims, "and meet our mates lightly clad in transparent gowns . . . they will get their tools up and be wild to lie with us. That will be the time to refuse, and they will hasten to make peace, I am convinced of that!"[36]

No such solution presented itself. Instead, the Persians got reinvolved, and the troubles between the two cities became even more insoluble.

The Persians were brought into the picture by none other than Alcibiades, who had managed to get himself kicked out of Sparta. While Agis, the king of the junior line, was out of the city fighting, Alcibiades had carried on a raging affair with his wife so blatant that the whole city knew about it: "She got pregnant with his child," Plutarch observes, "and did not even deny it."[37] Agis himself, who could count, realized when he returned home that the baby wasn't his. Alcibiades, not wanting to meet with a fatal accident, fled to Sardis. There he introduced himself to the satrap now in charge of Asia Minor, one Tissaphernes, and offered to help the Persians work the ongoing war between Athens and Sparta in a way that might bring both cities down.

The scheme, as planned by Alcibiades and Tissaphernes (who didn't consult the king at Susa), was partially successful. Tissaphernes sent word to the Spartans, offering to fund their ongoing war on condition that, once Athens fell, the Spartans would abandon the Ionian cities to Persia. The Spartans agreed, which played directly into Tissaphernes's hands; he encouraged them to rely on the Persian bankroll and then did a lousy job of paying up. "Tissaphernes," says Thucydides, "was ruining their navy by payments made irregularly, and even then not made in full."[38]

Meanwhile Alcibiades wrote to Athens, offering to come and join *them* (again) with plenty of Persian gold in hand, as long as they would agree to reinstate him in his previous position. That the Athenians agreed was a measure of their desperation.

This was probably supposed to end in a huge sea battle in which the Athenians and Spartans would, theoretically, destroy each other's fleets. Alcibiades certainly did go back to Athens, in 407, with enough gold to help them refurbish the navy; and in the fall of that same year, he led a fleet of a hundred Athenian ships towards the Spartan navy.

Meanwhile, two changes of command had taken place. Darius II had gotten wind of the unauthorized negotiations, yanked Tissaphernes back to Susa, and sent his younger son Cyrus to Sardis with instructions to put Persian reinforcements firmly on the Spartan side. And the Spartan navy had been put under the command of a new admiral, a man named Lysander. Plutarch tells us that Lysander, bolstered by Persian reinforcements and Persian money, was paying his forces a third more than the Athenians got from Alcibiades, and that Alcibiades "was pinched to pay even the daily allowance."[39]

Outfunded and outmanned, the Athenian navy was doomed. In a series of battles between the fall of 407 and 405, Athenian ships were sunk and captured, sailors killed and drowned. In August, in a final devastating battle, the Athenian navy lost 171 ships in a single engagement.

Alcibiades himself disappeared, prudently; he turned up at the court of the satrap of Phrygia a little later and was treated "as an honoured member of the court."[40] His luck ran out shortly later, when Lysander (who remained on good terms with the Persians) asked the satrap to kill him off. The satrap agreed and sent men to burn down Alcibiades's house; Alcibiades woke up and crashed out through the flames, only to be spitted by a javelin.

Lysander followed up on his destruction of the Athenian fleet by burning every ship he could and then sailing for Athens. He reached the city in October and besieged it. The Athenians, seeing that resistance was only going to result in starvation, surrendered: "Besieged by land and sea," wrote the Greek soldier and historian Xenophon, "they had neither ships nor allies nor food."[41] The war was over.

Lysander ordered the Athenians to knock down the Long Walls, a condition which was carried out to the sound of celebratory flute music. Athens was also forced to give up all influence over the cities which had once belonged to the "Athenian empire."[42] This was not nearly as severe a punishment as it could have been; Athens still had its main city walls, it had not been sacked, and it had the freedom to reestablish its own government. Unfortunately the Athenians at once began a huge internal quarrel about how to do this. Eventually Lysander was forced to return and set up a junta of thirty aristocrats, known later simply as the Thirty.[43] They became infamous for the bloodbath which they instituted, putting to death on any pretext Athenians whom they suspected of wanting democracy restored. Lysander, whose initial reaction to Athens had been mild, turned a blind eye and even sent Spartan foot soldiers to help the new regime get rid of all opposition.

The executions soon moved beyond the political: "They aimed at removing all whom they had reason to fear," Aristotle later wrote, "and also those whose possessions they wished to lay hands on. And in a short time they put to death not less than fifteen hundred persons."[44]

In desperation, the remaining Athenians massed together, sent to nearby Thebes for help, and attacked the Thirty and the Spartan garrison that protected them. This could have started war with Sparta all over again, but the king of Sparta, seeing the mess, overruled Lysander and pulled the garrison out. Darius II had just died, and his son and heir, Artaxerxes II, was an unknown quantity; Sparta was not going to rely on Persian gold again.

The Thirty who had not died in the fighting fled. The following year, 403, was hailed by the Athenians as the start of a new era, in which democracy could finally make its return to Athens. But the Athens which welcomed it was broken and bankrupt.

TIMELINE 65

PERSIA	GREECE
Cambyses II (530)	
Darius I	**Cleomenes of Sparta**
	Damaratus of Sparta
	Battle of Marathon (490)
Xerxes I (486–465)	**Leonidas of Sparta**
	Battles of Thermopylae and Salamis (480)
	Battles of Plataea and Mycale (479)
Artaxerxes (465–424)	
	Perdikkas II of Macedonia
	Pericles of Athens
	Peloponnesian War (begins 431)
Darius II (424–404)	
Artaxerxes II (404)	

Chapter Sixty-Six

The First Sack of Rome

In Rome, between 495 and 390 BC, patricians and plebians quarrel, and Gauls burn the city

THE FIRST DICTATOR OF ROME, appointed to beat invaders away from the city walls, had succeeded in his task. His efforts had not brought a real peace, though. In the Roman countryside, Livy writes, there "was neither assured peace nor open war"; rather, an ongoing standoff between a rising and aggressive power, and the surrounding towns, not quite sure whether to challenge Rome or leave it alone.[1]

But while the Etruscans were no longer a serious worry—they had rallied their fading force behind the Athenians during the attack on Sicily, and had suffered for it—Rome had troubles of its own. "So deeply was the country divided by its political differences," says Livy, "that the people, unlike their oppressors in the governing class, hailed the prospect of invasion with delight."[2]

ROME HAD THROWN its net across peoples on the outside, and as it began to mutate towards an empire it faced the same difficulty as the Persians or Spartans: how to combine people with great power (the original conquerors) and those with no power (the conquered, now absorbed) into a harmonious whole.

In Sparta, the conquerors were called *citizens,* while the conquered were *helots.* In Rome, the two groups had slightly different origins. The *patricians* (from the Latin word *pater,* "father") were by tradition descendents of the Roman council of advisors that served the old kings. The *plebians* were everyone else: a term which is notoriously hard to define because it is a negation, the "not patricians." This included conquered peoples now living in Rome, but also men who traced their ancestry back to lowly inhabitants of the original city.

The plebians outnumbered the patricians, but the patricians held a disproportionate amount of land and wealth. Even in the early days of the Republic, the plebians managed to elect one of their own to be consul on a fairly regular basis, but Rome's magistrates and priests, landowners and generals, were all patricians.

As in Athens, the problem of debt had become acute. A plebian who had to borrow money in time of famine, or while away at war, to feed his family, had to pledge himself as security; if the money was not paid back, he and his dependents became slaves.[3] The patricians in this way were gaining not only land and money, but also ownership over the citizens of Rome themselves, in increasing numbers. The plebians found it particularly galling that they often fell into debt and slavery as a result of having gone off to fight for Rome.

In 495, their unhappiness was brought to public riot when an old soldier, once famous for his exploits, hobbled into the Forum. "With his soiled and threadbare clothes," Livy writes, "his dreadful pallor and emaciated body . . . his unkempt hair and beard . . . he was a pitiable sight." He was recognized, and a murmur went through the crowd; more and more people gathered to hear him. He ripped his shirt apart and showed his chest scarred with sword-cuts suffered during his service to Rome, his back marked with weals from beatings given him by his wealthy master. "While I was on service," the old man said, "during the Sabine war, my crops were ruined by enemy raids, and my cottage was burnt. Everything I had was taken, including my cattle. Then, when I was least able to do so, I was expected to pay taxes, and fell, consequently, into debt."[4]

At this, debt slaves (some still in chains) from all over the city thronged into the streets, shouting for the Senate to decide at once how to give them relief from their slavery. The senators were mostly missing, because they were hiding from the mobs. However, the consuls were determined to avoid unnecessary violence, so they went around and hauled senators out of hiding, into the Senate, so that they could begin deliberations on the problem of debt slavery. As the debates began between senators, angry debt slaves thronged around the Senate, pushing into doors and hanging through windows to hear just how the Senate would resolve the situation.

This was not the best setting for a reasonable debate over the problem of debt, and in fact the Senate was getting nowhere when help of a sort arrived on the horizon: news came that the nearby tribe of the Volscii, who lived south of Rome, were marching on the city. The Senate passed a hasty resolution that no man could in the future be reduced to debt slavery as long as he was on active military duty. At this, practically everyone in the streets joined the army and went out to fight the Volscians. The attackers were thoroughly thrashed, since the army of debtors that came charging out to meet them was, as Livy puts it, "spoiling for a fight."

But the larger problem of the imbalance of power hadn't yet been addressed. Rome, Livy writes, needed to find "a solution for the conflicting interests of the two classes in the state: by fair means or foul the country must recover its internal harmony."[5] The "or foul" is not particularly encouraging; it suggests that, even in Livy's day, a whiff of let's-just-get-rid-of-the-problem survived from those ancient senatorial deliberations. And in fact, with the Volscian threat beaten off, the plebian soldiers who had returned to the city (they couldn't stay on active military duty forever) soon saw that no permanent solution was on offer.

Their only strength in Rome was that of numbers, and they used it. In 494, they went on the world's first recorded strike: "They took themselves off in a body to the Sacred Mount, three miles from the city . . . ," Livy says, "and there . . . they made themselves a camp."[6] This became known as the Plebian Secession, and within Rome it threw both the patricians (who had lost their slaves and most of their army) and the remaining plebians (who had lost most of their strength) into a panic. The city froze up, vulnerable to attack, its daily work undone.

Finally the Senate and consuls proposed a solution. From now on, they would be joined in government by special magistrates called *tribunes*, who would always be appointed from the ranks of the plebians, and who would be "above the law" (which is to say, immune from pressures applied by Senate and consuls, since Rome had as yet no written law). Their job would be to protect the plebs from injustice. It was the first Roman office blocked off to patricians, as so many offices had been to the plebs.

The first two tribunes were appointed in 494, the same year as the Plebian Secession. The crisis had been, temporarily, averted.

Over the next half century, the jockeying for power between consuls, senators, priests, and tribunes threw into sharp relief Rome's need for a written law which would act as even further protection for the plebians. Roman ambassadors who had visited Athens came back talking of the laws of Solon, which had been written out in an attempt to reduce tensions between Athenian aristocrats and democrats. They even brought back a copy of the laws with them. Rome was now too big, and too diverse, to rely on unwritten tradition. The city needed laws "which every individual citizen could feel that he had . . . consented to accept."[7]

So in 451, a board of ten lawmakers—the *decemvirs*—was appointed in place of the regular Roman officers to serve during the year 450. Their task was not only to run the government but to draw up laws to govern Rome. Their appointment was not without controversy: "There was a certain amount of argument about whether men not of patrician birth should be allowed to serve," Livy says,[8] as some Romans were still unwilling to see plebians take any part in government. But with this issue resolved, the decemvirs spent their year working on the laws and then presented them to the people for public discussion. When the laws had been amended by the discussion, an assembly of all the people was held to approve them. There was a general feeling that a little more regulation was still in order, so decemvirs were appointed for the following year also to draw up two more tables.

The Twelve Tables that resulted were written out on wood and set in the Forum, where all could see them. Livy says that in his day they were still the foundation of Roman law. Unfortunately the Tables were lost; what we know of them is assembled from quotes in various Roman documents.

Reassembled, the incomplete Tables contain the expected provisions to keep peace between the two Roman classes. "*Eris confessi rebusque iure iudicatis XXX dies iusti sunto*," reads Table III: "You who admit to or have been judged to owe money have thirty days to pay it." After that, the debtor can be taken to court, and if he has no surety or income, he can be put in chains; but his accuser must pay for his food (which might end up being more costly than forgiving the debt). Anyone who makes a false claim, according to Table XII, can be brought in front of three judges; if they decide that he has lied, he has to pay a substantial penalty. And then there is Table IX, the bedrock of the whole arrangement: "*Privilegia ne irroganato*," "No private laws can be proposed." No longer could patricians simply impose their will on plebians without their agreement.

Along with these are regulations of injury and harm that recall the laws of Hammurabi: a man who breaks another's bone must pay a fine, but the fine is halved if the bone broken belongs to a slave; if roads are not kept up by those who own the property through which they pass, the users are permitted to trespass and drive their cattle alongside the road instead; a son who is sold into slavery three different times can declare himself emancipated from his father.

And along with these are hints that although the Laws of the Twelve Tables were a step in the right direction, there was still plenty of injustice in Rome. Some of the injustices are standard ancient practice: "A deformed child shall be killed," reads Table IV, baldly, and Table V explains, "Women, because of their light dispositions, shall always have guardians even when they are grown." And others are particular to Rome itself. "No one may hold meetings in the city during the night," reads Table VIII, a regulation meant to protect the patricians from another plebian plot; and, most infamously, Table XI decrees, "Marriage between a patrician and a plebian is forbidden." This particular law was finally repealed in 445 after savage debate in the Senate; not everyone was convinced that Rome would prosper if the blood of noble and common Romans mingled.[9]

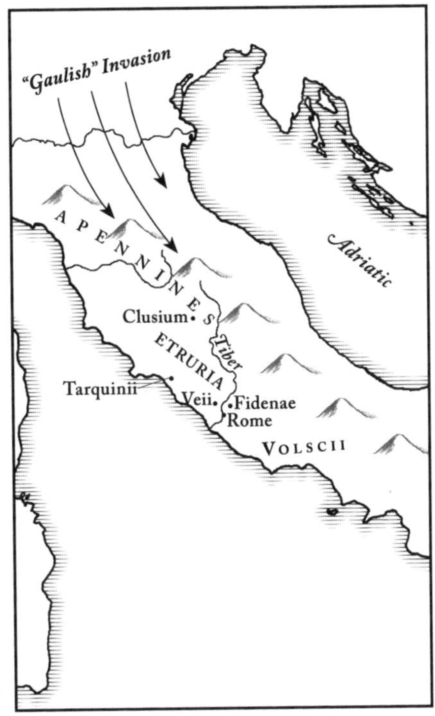

66.1 The Gaulish Invasion

The tribunes and Tables did not entirely soothe Rome's internal aches, but these reforms served to hold the population together long enough for the city to fix its gaze outwards. In 437, Rome began a long war with its old enemy Fidenae, upstream on the Tiber. Fidenae had first attacked the Latin upstart city back in the days of Romulus; Romulus had fought both Fidenae and Veii, the Etruscan cities, but had not destroyed either. Now the war with Fidenae began and dragged on until 426.

The next two decades were filled with minor battles, until the year 405, when Rome mounted a siege against Veii. This proved to be another drawn-out campaign; the Romans were still camped around the walls five years later, when news of another threat trickled down from the north. The Celts, whom the Romans knew as "Gauls," had been pushing south for a century now. They were drawing closer and closer to Rome.

But the Romans, busy claiming surrounding territory, do not appear to have paid much attention. Veii finally fell, in 396; it had been a bitter fight on both sides, as Veii was the richest and most resourceful of all the Etruscan cities.[10] The city of Veii, Livy writes, had "inflicted worse losses than she suffered," which means that the siege had significantly weakened the Roman army. And Veii had not been the only fish the army was frying; Roman soldiers had been all over the countryside, terrorizing farmers and seizing villages to add to the growing Roman territory.

The overstretched army was just taking a breath when a plebian named Caedicius came to the tribunes with an eerie warning. He had heard, "in the silence of the night," an inhuman voice saying, "Tell the magistrates that the Gauls are coming." The warning was "laughed off, partly because Caedicius was a person of no consequence";[11] Rome was still suffering from its patrician complex.

But hard on the heels of this vision came a message from the city Clusium to the north, the old home base of the fearsome Lars Porsena. Thousands of Celts had suddenly shown up at the city gates, waving weapons. "It was a terrible situation," says Livy, "and in spite of the fact that the people of Clusium had no official ties with Rome or reason to expect her friendship . . . they sent a mission to ask help from the Senate."[12]

The danger must have been extreme for Clusium to imagine that it would override the past hatred between the two cities. But the Gauls were an enemy that tended to unite the peninsula. If Rome had been able to send troops to fight them, it would have. But after the constant fighting of the last thirty years, the Senate had no real aid to give.

Instead, they sent ambassadors to convince the Gauls to settle peacefully in the area, rather than overthrowing Clusium by force. This might have been a fruitful discussion except that the Roman envoys lost their tempers when the Gauls defied them. The Romans drew their swords; the Gauls, who needed little encouragement, took this as a challenge. "They flamed into the uncontrollable anger which is characteristic of their race, and set forward, with terrible speed, on the path to Rome," Livy writes. ". . . And from all the immense host, covering miles of ground with its straggling masses of horse and foot, the cry went up 'To Rome!' "[13]

The Roman commanders hastily lined up their army at the Tiber, but the line was so thin that the Gauls at first held back, suspecting a trap since the Roman soldiers were so few. But when it became clear that these men were all that the overextended army could muster, the Gauls plunged into the front ranks of Romans. It was first a slaughter, and then a rout. Roman soldiers, fleeing, drowned in the Tiber, pulled down by the weight of their armor. Half of the survivors got to Veii and shut themselves in. The rest made it back to Rome, but their number was so obviously insufficient to defend the city that the whole population retreated into the Capitol, leaving the rest of the city unguarded.*

The Gauls flooded into it, killing anyone who had trailed behind in the flight to the Capitol and burning houses indiscriminately. The Romans, meanwhile, "could hardly believe their eyes or ears as they looked down on the barbaric foe roaming in hordes through the familiar streets. . . . now here, now

* There is some disagreement among scholars as to the exact dates of the Celtic attacks described in Livy.

there, the yells of triumph, women's screams or the crying of children, the roar of flames or the long rumbling crash of falling masonry. . . . not shut within their city but excluded from it, they saw all that they loved in the power of their enemies."[14]

Trapped in the Capitol, they could not fight back. On the other hand, the Celtic warriors down below could not get to them. Presumably a long enough siege could have starved them out, but the Gauls had no way of knowing how much food and water were inside the Capitol. And although conditions inside the Capitol were wretched, conditions down in the city soon grew just as bad. Food was limited, and the Gauls had camped on low ground, in a spot with little ventilation. Clouds of ash and dust from the fires of burning Rome blew over them and settled, in a lowland miasma that produced hacking coughs and lung infections. Eventually the crowded conditions led to epidemics. They started to die in tens and then in hundreds, until there were too many bodies to bury; the living burned them in huge heaps instead.[15]

So they were ready to listen when the Romans made a proposition: they would pay the Gauls off with gold, if the besiegers would back away from Rome's walls. In this, the Romans had been encouraged by an offer of help from an unexpected source. The Massalians, from the old Greek colony up on the southern coast of Europe, had had their own encounter with roving Celts, who had shown up and camped around Massalia's walls. The Massalians had bought them off, and the Celts had gone away. According to the Roman historian Pompeius Trogous, the Massalians then sent envoys to the shrine at Delphi to thank Apollo for their deliverance; Massalia had kept distant ties with the pan-Hellenic shrines of the homeland.

The envoys were on their way back when they heard news of the siege of the Capitol.[16] They took this news back to Massalia, where the city leadership decided that future good relations with Rome were worth cultivating. The Massalians raided their own treasury, convinced wealthy citizens to make private contributions, and added their gold to the ransom. The Gauls took the total and retreated back to the north, where the mountainous cool was a little more congenial than the hot south of the Italian peninsula.

The Romans emerged from the Capitol to rebuild, hastily, in case the enemy should return. "All work was hurried," Livy concludes, "and nobody bothered to see that streets were straight. . . . and buildings went up wherever there was room for them. This explains why . . . the general lay-out of Rome is more like a squatters' settlement than a properly planned city."[17] The first barbarian sack of Rome had not only smudged Rome's imperial ambitions, but left a permanent mark on the city itself.

TIMELINE 66

GREECE	ROME
Cleomenes of Sparta	
Damaratus of Sparta	Roman Republic begins (509)
	Celtic invasion
	First Roman dictator
	Plebian Secession (494)
Battle of Marathon (490)	
Leonidas of Sparta	
Battles of Thermopylae and Salamis (480)	
Battles of Plataea and Mycale (479)	
Perdikkas II of Macedonia	Laws of the Twelve Tables
Pericles of Athens	
Peloponnesian War (begins 431)	
	Rome burned by Gauls (390)

Chapter Sixty-Seven

The Rise of the Ch'in

In China, between 403 and 325 BC,
Jin divides and Ch'in dominates

AFTER DECADES OF UNENDING BATTLES against neighbors, barbarians, and its own noblemen, the northern state of Jin finally cracked apart. Its fall is recorded by Sima Qian in cryptic terms: "In the twenty-fourth year of King Wei-lieh," he writes, a year that works out to 403 BC, "the Nine Tripods shook. The king appointed Han, Wei, and Chao as feudal lords."[1]

Han, Wei, and Chao were three battling families of the Jin state who had each claimed part of the Jin territory for themselves. When they demanded that the Eastern Zhou monarch recognize them as lords over their three newly defined lands, he had no power to refuse. The Nine Tripods shaking is a very bad metaphor indeed; the Eastern Zhou king had now lost his authority even over his own sacred sanction.

The Jin state, as such, ceased to exist. A tentative reconstruction of the map of China at the onset of the fourth century shows that the thirteen states of the Spring and Autumn Period had now become nine, with the Zhou territory still perched uneasily at the center. Chu had claimed the two states to its east, nearly doubling its size. Sung and Qi had survived, as had the Lu state, although Lu had shrunk. The three new states of Chao, Wei, and Han overflowed the old Jin territory to swallow the old states of Hsü, Cheng, and the old Wey; Yen had lost some of its western territory, but had made up for it by spreading east along the coast.

But the state that emerged as the biggest winner was Ch'in, which at least quadrupled its original size. Evenutally, the eastern border of the Ch'in stretched from the Yellow river all the way down to the Yangtze.

THE WARRING STATES PERIOD, which began with these nine states, continued as one might expect from the name: with constant wars. It would be

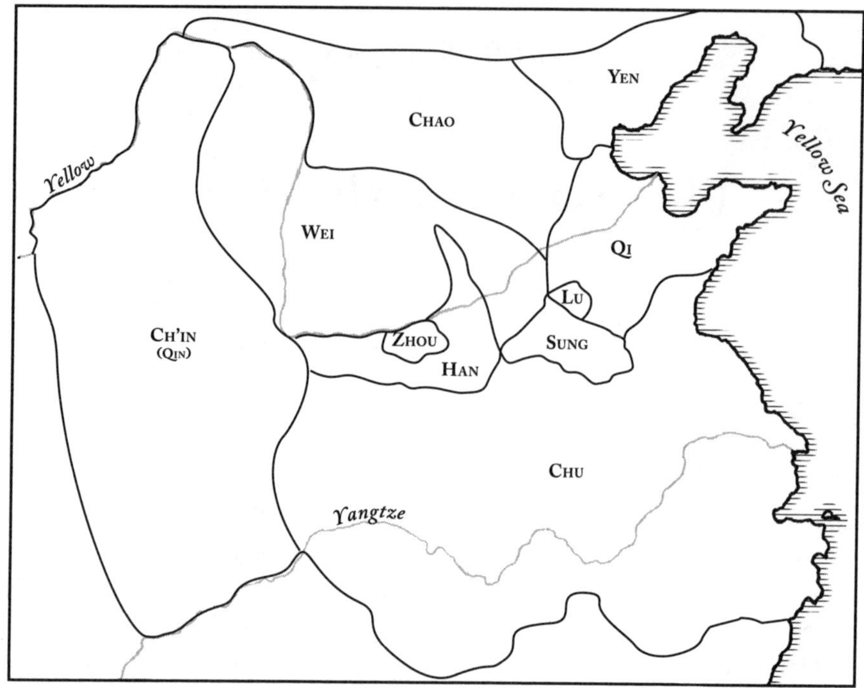

67.1 The Warring States

weary to recount all of them in detail, but between 403 and 361, the unending interstate squabbles slowly shook the nine states out into a pecking order. By 361, the most powerful states on the plain lay in a three-state line, from east to west: Qi, Wei, and Ch'in. The massive Chu, down to the south, was temporarily preoccupied by the two eastern states which it had swallowed, the Wu and Yueh; both were struggling to break away.

The Qi state was the most prosperous; it had an unusual run of competent dukes, who collected taxes in an orderly manner and also managed to corner a salt monopoly.[2] The Wei had the edge in military might. The Ch'in, all the way to the west, had a huge amount of territory, but it was a backwater state, far from the center of power, with a ridge of high lands separating it from the older Chinese states.[3] These still regarded the Ch'in as semibarbaric. "The feudal lords of the Central States . . . treated Ch'in as an uncivilized Yi or Ti people," Sima Qian comments.[4] Even a hundred years later, a Wei nobleman could sniff of Ch'in, "It is greedy, untrustworthy, and ignorant of polite manners, proper relationships, and upright behavior."[5]

This began to change in 361 BC, when a nobleman named Shang Yang arrived at the court of the lord of Ch'in, offering to help make Ch'in into a major power.

Shang Yang was born in the new state of Wei, the son of a royal concubine and so barred from rule. He felt himself deserving of more power than his birth allowed, so when the news worked its way east that the new lord of Ch'in, Duke Hsiao, had sent out an invitation to all capable men to join him in making Ch'in stronger, he left his native land and journeyed to the west.*

Duke Hsiao was so impressed by Shang Yang's ideas that he gave the man free rein to make whatever changes he thought necessary. At once, Shang Yang began a new regime by instituting strong penalties for treason and feuds; even private quarrels were punishable by law. To enforce this, he ordered Ch'in divided into a whole network of small squares, each containing not more than ten households, with each household given the responsibility of informing on any wrongdoing committed by the others. The people of Ch'in were, in the words of Shang Yang's biographer, "mutually to control one another and to share one another's punishments. Whoever did not denounce a culprit would be cut in half."[6] Nor was anyone allowed to escape the watchful eye of officials and neighbors by disappearing into the distance; innkeepers were forbidden to offer rooms to travellers unless those travellers carried official permits.

With this control mechanism in place, Shang Yang set about making Ch'in into a meritocracy. Rather than aping the ranks and privileges of the noble-dominated states to its east, Ch'in would turn its weakness—its lack of aristocracy, its blended heritage of Chinese and non-Chinese—into a strength. Titles would from now on be awarded by the duke solely on the basis of "military merit," and aristocrats who couldn't fight would be aristocrats no longer: "Those of the princely family, who had no military merit, could not be regarded as belonging to the princely clan."[7] Anxious to show that noble birth gave no privileges, Shang Yang even insisted that the duke's own son Huiwen be punished when he commited a minor infraction of the new laws. This seems to have created a bit of trouble in the palace; Shang Yang finally admitted that it wouldn't be a good idea to inflict capital punishment on the duke's heir, and instead consented to executing one of Huiwen's tutors and branding the other (or, according to some accounts, cutting off his nose).[8]

Furthermore, from now on no Ch'in citizen would be allowed to duck the task of performing useful labor for the good of the state. As far as Shang Yang was concerned, merchants were parasites who sold goods made by other men and took a cut of the proceeds. "Everyone had to assist in the fundamental

* We know the details of Shang Yang's life from the brief biography set down by Sima Qian as chapter 68 of the *Shih chi*.

occupations of tilling and weaving," writes Sima Qian, of Shang Yang's reforms, "and only those who produced a large quantity of grain or silk were exempted from labour on public works. Those who occupied themselves with trade were enslaved, along with the destitute and lazy."[9]

On the other hand, those who worked hard could look forwards to being rewarded with tracts of land. This was a new idea, and probably the first officially sanctioned private ownership of land in all of China.[10] This new private ownership was backed up with its own set of regulations: no one could now move to a new home without official permission, meaning that farmers could not exhaust their land and then shift to new farms. They had to manage their lands properly or else starve.[11]

Not everyone was pleased with the reforms. Shang Yang's biographer remarks that the protestors who "came to the capital and at first said that the laws were not appropriate could be counted by the thousands."[12] But the new importance given to farming meant that much of the Ch'in land now lying waste could be put into crops. And despite the severity of Shang Yang's penalties, his policies (which also allowed convicted criminals to earn their freedom by farming previously untilled land) attracted more and more poor peasants from other Chinese states. In Ch'in, they at least had the opportunity to rise in the hierarchy through military service. A hundred years later, the philosopher Xun Zi visited Ch'in and remarked on this: "The man who returns from battle with five enemy heads," he writes, "is made the master of five families in his neighborhood."[13]

Most ancient historians disliked Shang Yang intensely, but even Sima Qian had to admit that all this legislation established a kind of stability in a previously lawless state. He writes that, ten years into the new regime, "there were no robbers in the mountains; families were self-supporting and people had plenty. . . . great order prevailed throughout the countryside and in the towns."[14]

Despite this, Sima Qian thought the despotic Ch'in state a wretched place to live. The people were enslaved, if prosperous. Other worries had replaced the fear of thieves and riots: "None of the people dared to discuss the mandates," he notes, since Shang Yang had ordered malcontents to be banished.[15] Music and poetry were dismissed as unproductive; philosophy was scorned. As part of his campaign to make Ch'in strong, Shang Yang burned all of the teachings of Confucius that he could find.

By 344 Ch'in had grown strong enough for Duke Hsiao to exercise one of the privileges of the Hegemon and summon the other feudal lords into his presence. Sima Qian, who records this request, does not tell us how they reacted. He does add that, in 343, the Eastern Zhou king formally recognized Duke Hsiao of Ch'in as the Hegemon. It was the first time in a century that a duke could lay claim to the title, and the first time in history that a Ch'in lord had won it.[16]

Now the ultimate goal of all Shang Yang's reforms became clear. The new laws had produced a well-fed and growing population, and had made military service one of the most attractive careers for the new crop of young Ch'in men. In 340, Ch'in began to fight its way towards conquest of its neighbors.

Shang Yang's first target was Wei, and the new state fell to the Ch'in armies without too much of a struggle. But this victory was Shang Yang's last triumph. Duke Hsiao died and was succeeded by his son Huiwen—the Huiwen who had watched his tutors executed and disfigured, some twenty years ago, for his own trespassess. He had hated Shang Yang ever since. As soon as power was in his hands, he ordered Shang Yang arrested.

The minister disguised himself and fled from the Ch'in court, but when he sought shelter at an inn, the innkeeper refused to admit him. Neither would anyone else. He had no permit, as the law required.

Deprived of any hiding place, Shang Yang was soon overtaken by Huiwen's men and taken back to the Ch'in capital. There, he was sentenced to be tied to four chariots which were driven off in different directions, tearing him apart.

With Shang Yang's irritating presence gone, Huiwen decided not to revoke any of the minister's reforms. They had, after all, made Ch'in more powerful than it had ever been; so powerful, in fact, that in 325 he proclaimed himself king.

The other feudal lords reacted as you might expect: "Thereafter," Sima Qian writes, "all the feudal lords became kings." The wars of the Warring States continued as before, except that now they were conducted by kings rather than dukes.

In this continually disrupted world, teachers of philosophy continued to try to understand their lives and to ask the central question of their times: how can men be whole, in a world constantly torn apart?

The teachings of Confucius, which Shang Yang found so damaging to his own purpose, were carried on by his most famous pupil, Mencius (a Latinized form, like Confucius, of the name Meng-tzu). Mencius's writings paid particular attention (as is hardly surprising) to the relationship between a ruler and his people. The ruler governs by the will of Heaven, Mencius wrote, but since Heaven "did not speak," the ruler had to measure whether or not he was in fact carrying *out* the will of Heaven by listening to the opinions of the people.[17] If he listened closely enough, he would learn that warfare was never

Heaven's will. "One can guess what your supreme ambition is," he writes, addressing an imaginary king. "To extend your territory, to enjoy the homage of Ch'in and Chu, to rule over the Central Kingdoms. . . . Seeking the fulfillment of such an ambition [by force of arms] is like looking for fish by climbing a tree."[18] This was not a philosophy welcomed by kings, who preferred tree-climbing; Mencius, who offered to become an advisor to the dukes of several different states, was turned down by all of them.

Mencius was not the only voice offering solutions, though. His writings reveal a very Confucian emphasis on the basic perfectability of man, man's essential goodness, and the proper observation of forms as a way of finding peace in troubled times. And many in the Warring States found this totally insufficient. They had daily proof of man's essential self-centeredness and lust for power; they lived in such daily chaos that the observation of forms seemed pointless.

During these years, a new philosophy, quite different from that of Mencius, was drawing together mystical threads from more ancient times. This philosophy was finally set down in writing as the *Tao-Teh-Ching*. Tao: the Way. The Taoist believed that the way to peace lay in a passive acceptance of the way things are, which must have seemed eminently doable.

The Taoist makes no laws. All pronouncements on ethical behavior are inevitably flawed, reflections of man's own innate depravity.[19] All positive pronouncements must be avoided, in fact, along with all aggression and ambition. As the *Tao-Teh-Ching* explains,

> Tao inevitably does nothing,
> and yet there is nothing that is not done.
> If kings and dukes can preserve it,
> all things will go through their own transformation. . . .
> Absence of desires will lead to quietude;
> The world will, of itself, find its equilibrium.[20]

To withdraw from chaos, to wait in the faith that what will be, will be: this is a practical philosophy for evil times. Perhaps the most famous of Taoists was Chuang Tzu, who was born in the same year that Duke Hsiao inherited the rule of Ch'in and welcomed Shang Yang into his country. "The accomplishments of emperors and kings are superfluous affairs as far as the sage is concerned," he wrote, "not the means by which to keep the body whole and to care for life. Yet how many gentlemen of the vulgar world today endanger themselves and throw away their lives in the pursuit of mere things! How can you help pitying them?"[21]

Chuang Tzu himself put it into metaphor this way:

Once Chuang Tzu dreamt he was a butterfly, a butterfly flitting and fluttering around, happy with himself and doing as he pleased. He didn't know he was Chuang Tzu. Suddenly he woke up and there he was, solid and unmistakable Chuang Tzu. But he didn't know if he was Chuang Tzu who had dreamt he was a butterfly, or a butterfly dreaming he was Chuang Tzu.[22]

In such days, the Taoist found it most satisfying to let go of the material world. The next campaign that thundered by his door, the next law passed by his duke to restrict him: these were only incidental annoyances, not the true nature of things. No matter how many bars were placed around him, he remained as unconcerned as the butterfly.

TIMELINE 67

ROME	CHINA
Plebian Secession (494)	
	"Spring and Autumn" period ends (481)
	Death of Confucius
Laws of the Twelve Tables	
	Warring States period begins (403)
Rome burned by Gauls (390)	
	Duke Hsiao of Ch'in
	Shang Yang
	Huiwen of Ch'in (325)

Chapter Sixty-Eight

The Macedonian Conquerors

Between 404 and 336 BC,
ten thousand Greeks escape from Persia,
and a Macedonian takes on the task of creating Greek unity

THE WAR BETWEEN Athens and Sparta was over. Athens was desolate: broke, angry, the Long Walls ripped down, and as many as seventy thousand Athenians dead through plague, war, or political purge.[1] No one had a plan for the future, and the city was filled with widows and women who would never marry because so many men had died. Aristophanes gives bitter voice to the times in his play *The Assemblywomen:* "The situation can yet be saved," a woman of Athens proclaims. "I propose that we hand over the running of Athens to the women!"[2] Among their solutions for the city's troubles is a law proclaiming that any man who wants to sleep with a young woman has to "pleasure an older one first."[3]

Sparta, the nominal victor, was little better off. Planting and harvesting had been thrown entirely off schedule. The armies storming through the Peloponnese had crushed vines, flattened olive trees, and killed flocks. More and more Spartans despaired of feeding themselves at home, and became mercenaries instead.

Thousands of these Spartans went to work for the Persian royal family. In 404, Artaxerxes II had inherited the throne from his father, Darius II. But a big fight over the succession was de rigueur in Persia, and Darius's younger son Cyrus—now serving as satrap in Sardis—was planning to take the crown for himself. He was an ambitious and dashing young man, and Artaxerxes II was not a very imposing figure; he wasn't much of a horseman,[4] and Plutarch, who wrote a life of him, says that he had a "yielding and soft" nature.[5]

To bolster his support, Cyrus "sent orders to the commanders of his garrisons in the various cities to enroll troops from the Peloponnese, as many as possible and the best available" (this from the account written by Xenophon, a young mercenary who answered the call).[6] Ostensibly, Cyrus was hiring these soldiers for the defense of the Persian holdings in Asia Minor. But by 401, his force of over ten thousand Greek mercenaries had telegraphed an alarm. The Persian satrap of Lydia, the same Tissaphernes who had negotiated with Alcibiades, rode east in haste to warn the king.

With his cover blown, Cyrus headed towards the Euphrates with his army, crossed over it, and then turned south, marching towards Babylon with the river on his right; presumably he planned to use Babylon as a base for attacking the heart of the Persian empire. Most of the Persian army seems to have been at Ecbatana.[7] Artaxerxes II had to get his vast force assembled, provisioned, and on the march, which took him an unexpectedly long time (Plutarch says that he was afflicted with a "natural dilatoriness").[8] So Cyrus got almost all the way to Babylon before the king's army reached him; the long journey forced him to shell out extra pay for the Greek mercenaries, since they complained loudly about the distance.[9]

The Persian front line finally came into view as the rebel army approached Cunaxa, a battlefield about forty miles north of Babylon.* Xenophon, who was marching in full armor in the middle of the Greek ranks, describes their approach:

> In the early afternoon dust appeared, like a white cloud, and after some time a sort of blackness extending a long way over the plain. When they got nearer, then suddenly there were flashes of bronze, and the spear points and the enemy formations became visible . . . cavalry with white armour . . . soldiers with wicker shields . . . hoplites with wooden shields reaching to the feet (these were said to be Egyptians) . . . more cavalry and archers. . . . In front of them . . . were what they called the scythed chariots. These had thin scythes extending at an angle from the axles and also under the driver's seat, turned toward the ground, so as to cut through everything in their way. The idea was to drive them into the Greek ranks and cut through them.[10]

It was a huge defense force; Cyrus's army was outnumbered and outarmed.

Despite this, Cyrus was able to plunge forwards through the Persian lines until he met his brother face-to-face and struck him in the chest with a javelin, knocking him off his horse. The king's bodyguard dragged him away from the front to a little hill, where Ctesias dressed the wound; the javelin had gone through his armor, but had not pierced through to his heart. Cyrus, pushed

* The exact location of Cunaxa is unknown. Plutarch says that it was "five hundred furlongs" from Babylon, and descriptions of the battle suggest that it lay on the banks of the Euphrates.

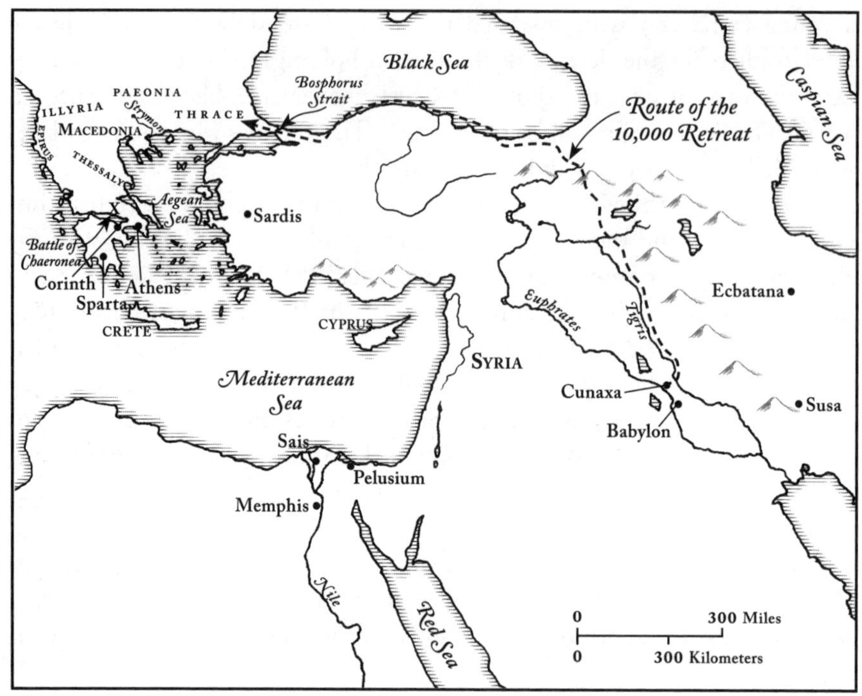

68.1 The March of the Ten Thousand

backwards by the fray, thought he had won; he spurred his horse forwards, shouting victory, when a stray arrow went through his temple.*

The Persian army had managed to keep back the attack, and the would-be usurper was dead. Many of the Greek officers had been captured. Artaxerxes II sent a message to the remaining Greek mercenaries offering to accept their surrender, but they refused. Instead, ten thousand Greeks regrouped and began to retreat from Cunaxa, back in the direction from which they had come. Young Xenophon was elected to be one of their leaders.

The journey, which began sometime in September of 401, dragged on for months. The Greeks plodded along the Tigris, short of food and water, constantly attacked from behind by a Persian detachment which had been assigned to harass them and from the sides and front by hostile residents of the lands through which they passed. They trudged through desert; they climbed through mountains; they marched through winter storms and six-foot snow drifts. They died from hunger and thirst, from cold, and from

* Xenophon, Ctesias, and Plutarch offer different versions of this encounter, which nevertheless all end up with Cyrus dead and Artaxerxes II alive but wounded.

battle wounds. Their shoes froze onto their feet; men who lost their toes were left behind to die.[11] They despaired of ever reaching the coast, from which they could return to Greece.

Almost a year after their journey began, they were struggling up yet another mountain when Xenophon, bringing up the rear, heard the men at the front shouting. He thought that the yells heralded yet another attack. But "the shouting got louder and drew nearer," he writes, "and those who were going forward started running towards the men in front, who kept on shouting, and the more there were of them, the more shouting there was."[12] At last the words became clear. They were shouting "The sea! The sea!"

The March of the Ten Thousand was an impressive feat of endurance, but not necessarily an extraordinary one. What was extraordinary was that the Persian army, under Artaxerxes, could apparently do little more than pester the retreating Greeks, who managed to escape from the very center of Persian power. "All [Artaxerxes II's] attempts to capture the Greeks that had come up with Cyrus," Plutarch concludes, ". . . proved unsuccessful, and they, though they had lost both Cyrus and their own generals, nevertheless escaped, as it were, out of his very palace."[13]

Artaxerxes II's Persian empire was weak enough to lose its grip on Egypt as well. An Egyptian nobleman from Sais named Amyrtaeus declared himself pharaoh, and the Persian satrap was unable to get enough support from the preoccupied Artaxerxes II to quell the revolt. Amyrtaeus was not the first Egyptian "freedom fighter" to organize a resistance, but he was the first in a long time to gain enough power to title himself as the first pharaoh of a new dynasty: the Twenty-Eighth. (Psammetichus III had been the last ruler of the Twenty-Sixth Dynasty, and Manetho lists the Persians as the Twenty-Seventh.) Amyrtaeus, who lasted four years, turned out to be the only Twenty-Eighth Dynasty pharaoh. We know very little about Egypt under his rule, although Aramaic documents from the time suggest that at least part of the country still considered itself to be under Persian rule. Inscriptions show that after Amyrtaeus died, another rebel took power as Nepherites I and announced himself as the founder of yet another dynasty, the Twenty-Ninth; after six years he was succeeded by a usurper named Achoris.[14]

Three years after he announced himself to be pharaoh of Egypt, Achoris sent up to Greece and asked Athens for help against Persian attempts to retake his country.

MEANWHILE, the Greeks had gone back to quarrelling with each other. Athens had not managed to get far in the rebuilding of its shattered peace; the city was still suffering from the political divisions caused by the purges of the Thirty. In 399, a year after the successful return of the Ten Thousand, the Athenians had convicted the philosopher Socrates of vague anti-Athenian wrongdoings. Socrates had been friendly both with Alcibiades and with the most ruthless of the Thirty, an aristocrat named Kritias who had died in the fighting that wrapped up the Thirty's horrendous rule. Sentenced to death, Socrates scorned flight and instead drank down hemlock; his death was recorded by one of his students, a young man named Plato.

Meanwhile Sparta had rethought its deal with Persia. At the end of the Peloponnesian War, the Spartans had promised to give up the Ionian cities to the Persians, in exchange for Persian gold. Now they reneged on the promise, and sent Spartan officials to run the cities instead. This was blatant empire-building, and the other Greek cities were not in the mood to tolerate it. The thirty years of fighting had barely ended when Athens, Thebes, Corinth, and Argos banded together with what was left of their armies to force Sparta to give up its claims.

Fighting in this so-called Corinthian War began in 395. After three years of pointless battling, Sparta backpedaled—not to the Greeks, but to the Persians, offering to give up those Ionian cities after all, if the Persians would come back in on the Spartan side.

Artaxerxes II agreed and sent Persian ships to help out. This made Athens quite willing to help Achoris of Egypt fight off the Persians; an Egyptian-Athenian alliance was a possible counter to a Persian-Spartan alliance.

Unfortunately, Athenian soldiers were too thin on the ground to keep it up, and the Spartans soon found that their soldiers were exhausted too. In 387, Artaxerxes II (happy to see that his potential enemies had once again worn themselves out against each other) decreed that unless the two cities agreed to a peace, the Persians would step in: "Should any of the parties concerned not accept this peace," he announced (according to Xenophon, who preserved the actual treaty in his *Hellenica*), "I, Artaxerxes, will war against him . . . by land and by sea, with ships and with money."[15]

Athens backed, regretfully, out of its Egyptian alliance, leaving Achoris to fight his anti-Persian war alone; Sparta disarmed; and for a little while everyone went back to rebuilding their cities. The so-called King's Peace was in full effect. "So it was," Xenophon writes, "that the Spartans and Athenians, with their allies, found themselves in the enjoyment of peace for the first time since . . . the demolition of the walls of Athens."[16]

The reclaiming of Asia Minor was the high point of Artaxerxes II's otherwise undistinguished reign. Egyptian inscriptions show that he did eventually sent a halfhearted party of soldiers down to brace Achoris in his den, but when

Achoris (who had managed to talk a few Greek mercenaries into becoming a part of the regular Egyptian navy) fought back, the Persians retreated.

When Achoris died and a new Egyptian seized command—an unknown soldier named Nectanebo I, founder of the Thirtieth Dynasty—Artaxerxes II made one more stab at getting Egypt back. This time he tried to turn the tables on Egypt by hiring Athenian mercenaries of his own and sailing down to the attack, entering the Delta on its western side rather than by the fortress of Pelusium on the east, in the usual way.[17] Nectanebo fought off this combined force, which was stronger than his own, with a brilliant bit of strategy. He made a stand at each stream in the Delta, fighting for a while before retreating a little bit farther south, pulling the invaders in further and further. He knew—as the Athenians and Persians did not—exactly when the flooding of the Nile was about to occur, and he managed to hold the combined invasion force off until the waters began to rise rapidly around him. At that he beat a quick retreat south; startled and overwhelmed by the flooding, the Persians and Athenians retreated back out of the Delta.[18] Nectanebo held onto his throne for eighteen prosperous years, and Artaxerxes II did not try again.*

THE RUIN OF GREECE had convinced at least one Athenian that the cities of Greece would only survive if they could manage to pull themselves together under one banner of Greek identity. Pan-Hellenism, not empire-building by force, was the only hope for the Greek world.

This Athenian was Isocrates, an orator and teacher of rhetoric who had been born before the Peloponnesian War began and had watched his city fall into tatters. In 380, seven years after the King's Peace, he published *Panegyricus,* a written speech begging for all Greek cities to recognize their common heritage.† Athens must be the leader in such an attempt, Isocrates writes, because "the city has made the name 'Greek' seem to be not that of a people but of a way of thinking; and people are called Greeks because they share in our education rather than in our birth."[19]

This was a resurrection of that call for willing identification with an idea that Pericles had first made in the throes of war, reshaped to bind Athens and Sparta together as Greeks against a non-Greek world. The *Panegyricus* is first

* This was not the end of fighting (naturally); in 366 the satraps in Asia Minor joined with Athens, Sparta, and Egypt to defy Artaxerxes II, but since the allies couldn't agree on a strategy the revolt fell apart before Artaxerxes II had to do much about it. The Greek historian Diodorus Siculus calls this the "Great Revolt of the Satraps," and although it was indeed extensive, the end result was more or less as though it had never happened (Diodorus Siculus XV.90).

† "Panegyric festival" (a "gathering together") was another name for "pan-Hellenic festival."

a summons to pan-Hellenic unity, but it is also a call for the Hellenes to join willingly against those who have not been educated as Greeks: against the Persians and their king Artaxerxes II, who rules "not by consent" of the parts of his empire, but rather "by having a greater army."[20]

This call for pan-Hellenism was answered from a slightly unexpected source.

In the year 359, two thrones were passed along at the same time. Artaxerxes II's oldest son, Darius, planned to kill his father, suspecting that Artaxerxes might be leaning towards declaring his younger son Ochus the heir. Artaxerxes got wind of the plot and sat up in bed on the night of the planned assassination, waiting. When Darius arrived, he called for his bodyguard. Darius was arrested, convicted, and put to death by having his throat cut.

Artaxerxes died of old age not long after; Ochus poisoned his other brothers and, his throne secure, became Artaxerxes III.

Over in Macedonia another king came to the throne in the same year. His name was Philip II; and he was the thirteenth king since Amyntas I had surrendered to Darius the Great, a hundred years before. Thirteen kings in a century works out to an average of less than eight years apiece; to be king of Macedonia was not a safe job.

Philip's elderly father, Amyntas IV, had married a much younger wife late in life, in order to get himself a legitimate heir for the throne (he had already fathered at least three illegitimate children who had their eye on it).[21] This woman, Eurydice, gave birth to the required heirs: three sons, Alexander II, Perdikkas, and Philip. She then started carrying on a blatant affair with a Macedonian courtier named Ptolemy; according to Macedonian accounts, the old king actually caught the two of them in bed at one point, but at nearly eighty decided not to make a fuss about it.

When ancient Amyntas died, Alexander II became king. He had troubles to his northwest, where the Illyrian tribes were threatening to invade. The Macedonian alliance with Persia had given Macedonia some protection from its enemies to the north and south, but by Alexander II's reign, the Persians were no longer casting such a long shadow. The third-century historian Justin tells us that Alexander II had to avoid conquest by paying the Illyrians off and sending his younger brother Philip (only ten years old) to live in Illyria as a hostage.

Eventually Philip was allowed to return home, but his older brother was doomed. Eurydice, Alexander's own mother, had arranged to have him murdered so that her lover Ptolemy could seize power. As soon as Alexander II was dead, Ptolemy announced himself to be regent on behalf of the legitimate heir, the second son Perdikkas. Philip, now fifteen, was sent off again as a hostage; this time he ended up in the southern Greek city of Thebes, which had been threatening to invade Macedonia.

Perdikkas, who was no fool, waited until he had reached the age of accession and then, with the support of the Macedonian noblemen who disliked Ptolemy, had his mother's lover dragged off and executed. (What happened to Eurydice is not recorded.) He then took the throne himself and did what he could to restore the royal family: he negotiated Philip's release from Thebes, married, and fathered a baby son. He then turned to face the Illyrians, who were once more threatening invasion.

In the sixth year of his reign, he made his younger brother Philip regent for his son and led the Macedonian army into war against the Illyrians. The battle was a disaster. Perdikkas was killed, along with four thousand Macedonian soldiers.[22] Philip, at twenty-four, was left to defend the kingdom against this northwestern threat.

He took command of the army as regent for the baby, but (Justin says) "dangerous wars threatened, and it was too long to wait for the cooperation of a prince who was yet so young, [so] he was forced by the people to take the government himself."[23] This may be accurate, or it may shield a more ominous appropriation of power. In any case, Philip's leadership was much needed. The Illyrians were not the only threat on the horizon; the Athenians were now making an attempt to put a candidate of their own on the Macedonian throne so that they could add Macedonia to the territory ruled by Athens.

Philip, unable to take on both Illyria and Athens, put off the Athenian threat by surrendering a border city to Athenian control. He then reorganized the Macedonian army by teaching the wild semi-savage Macedonian soldiers how to fight in a Greek phalanx, something he had learned during his years in Thebes.[24] The following year, the Macedonian army triumphed against the Illyrians.

By this point, the Macedonians were clearly too strong for Athenian invasion. Rather than fighting defensive wars, Philip was able to begin empire-building on his own account. He fought, and married (five different times), his way into alliance or dominance with the territories along the Thermaic Gulf, the border between Macedonia and Thrace, and the north and northwest borders of Macedonia. His third wife, the seventeen-year-old Olympias, was the daughter of the king of Epirus. Olympias, according to ancient accounts, was startlingly beautiful, but prone to frightening storms of temper and eccentric in her habits; she kept large snakes as pets and allowed them to crawl all over her bedchamber. Her father thought that he was protecting Epirus with the match; when he died, Philip simply annexed it.

In 356, Olympias gave birth to Philip's first son and heir. The baby was named Alexander, after Philip's dead brother.

Now Philip began to look south. When the ruler of the Greek city of Pherae

68.1. Philip of Macedonia. This marble head of Philip II shows his drooping eye, the result of an arrow wound. Photo credit Gianni Dagli Orti/CORBIS

was assassinated, Philip went down, restored order, and then kept control of the city. He campaigned into Thrace and seized the gold and silver mines around Mount Pangaeus, which would allow him to finance more campaigns. He took back the city he had yielded to Athens at his accession, and fought his way still farther south and east. During one of these campaigns an arrow went through his right eye; the missing eye can be seen in his statues.

There was, to all this, no organized Greek response. Sparta was too far south to be troubled, and Athens, which protested, was suffering from severe famine and could not mount another war. Philip went right on swallowing bits of Greece. His push southwards was not so much against a Greece that he wanted to conquer, as a Greece that he wanted to absorb. His infantry, his cavalry, his very court were salted with Greeks.

It was a Greek horse—a stallion from Thessaly named Bucephalas—that brought his son Alexander's precocious intelligence into public view. Plutarch says that Philip had paid a tremendous amount of money for this horse but found it to be completely unmanageable. He ordered it sent back, but Alexander protested; Philip told him to back up the protest by showing that he could ride the horse himself: "Alexander ran over to the horse," Plutarch writes, "took hold of the reins and turned him to face the sun—apparently because he had noticed that the horse was made jittery by the sight of his shadow stretching out and jerking about in front of him."[25] This allowed him to mount the horse, an incident which became famous throughout Macedonia (and, later, Greece). Even so early, Alexander was a strategist.

He continued to be Philip's only legitimate son. One of Philip's mistresses had given birth to a son a little younger than Alexander, also named Philip; but the unfortunate child was feebleminded. (Plutarch says that Olympias was responsible for this, having given the child a drug to damage his mind; but there is no other proof to support this.)

The Macedonian court was hazardous enough to suggest that Philip would have done well to produce a backup heir, but apparently he had started to avoid Olympias at all costs (local rumor said that the snakes in her bed had something to do with this: "A snake was once seen stretched out alongside Olympias's body while she was asleep," Plutarch writes, "and they say that it was this incident more than anything that cooled Philip's passion and affection").[26] He was pinning his hopes for an heir on Alexander. In 343, he invited the Greek philosopher Aristotle to come north into Macedonia to act as Alexander's tutor, a well-paid post which Aristotle accepted.

By 340, Philip was strong enough to declare war on Athens.

His invasion of Greece was made easier by the fact that more than one Greek city felt ambivalent about fighting back. The Greek philosopher Isocrates, now ninety, had given up on his hopes for willing Greek cooperation; he had followed up his *Panegyricus* with a speech called *To Philip*, asking the Macedonian king to take the lead. "You have obtained wealth and power such as no other Greek has," he announced, "and these alone are naturally suited both for persuading and for compelling. What I am about to suggest will require, I believe, both of these, for I am about to advise you to stand at the head of a Greek alliance and lead a Greek campaign against the barbarians."[27]

The association of Greek cities that looked after the shrine of Delphi followed Isocrates's advice, and invited Philip into Greece. Athens asked Sparta for help against the invasion, but Sparta declined to have anything to do with its old enemy. So when Philip's army finally marched down from the north, Athens had managed to round up only a few allied troops, mainly from Thebes and from the cities in Boeotia.

The armies met, in the hot summer of 338, on the plain of Chaeronea. The most complete account of the battle that remains is preserved in Diodorus Siculus's history:

> Both armies were now ready to engage; they were equal indeed in courage and personal valor, but in numbers and military experience a great advantage lay with [Philip]. For he had fought many battles, gained most of them, and so learned much about war, but the best Athenian generals were now dead. . . . About sunrise the two armies arrayed themselves for battle. The king ordered his son Alexander, who had just become of age . . . to lead one wing, though joined to him were some of the best of his generals. Philip himself, with a picked corps, led the other wing, and arranged the various brigades at such posts as the occasion demanded. The Athenians drew up their army. . . . At length the hosts engaged, and the battle was fierce and bloody. It continued long with fearful slaughter, but victory was

> uncertain, until Alexander, anxious to give his father proof of his valor—and followed by a courageous band—was the first to break through the main body of the enemy, directly opposing him, slaying many; and bore down all before him. His men, pressing on closely, cut to pieces the lines of the enemy; and after the ground had been piled with the dead, put the wing resisting him in flight.[28]

The Battle of Chaeronea, with relatively few casualties (a thousand Athenians dead, a large number for a single battle but minor compared to the toll of the war years), was remarkable for two things: this was Alexander's first try at major military command, and it marked the end of an era. The Greek city-states would never again be free from the bonds of empire.

Philip, who undoubtedly realized that he could not fight his way into the allegiance of the rest of the Greek cities, now switched ground. He treated Athens with great respect, releasing his prisoners and even putting together an honor guard to accompany the Athenian dead back to the city.[29] The Athenians, making the best of a bad situation, chose to pretend that Philip was now the friend of Athens.

The following year, Philip made a speech at Corinth, suggesting that Greek submission to his kingship would be good for Greece.[30] Sparta still refused to have anything to do with Philip's plans. But the rest of the Greek cities agreed (with Philip's army standing nearby, naturally) to join together in yet another Greek league. This was called the Corinthian League, and like the old Delian League of Athens, it was formed with the intent of attacking the Persians. Unlike the Delian League, it had the king of Macedonia as its supreme commander.

Persia was vulnerable, right in the middle of yet another chaotic change of command. Artaxerxes III had been on the throne for nineteen years; the greatest achievement of his reign was the retaking of Egypt, which he had done in 343 (six years earlier) by defeating the last native pharaoh of Egypt, Nectanebo II. Now Egypt was again under the control of a Persian satrap, and was ruled by the Persian king (Manetho calls this Dynasty Thirty-One).

And then, in the same year as the Battle of Chaeronea, Artaxerxes died. Details were sketchy, but although the king had been sick for a little while before his death, it seems almost certain that he did not die from illness but from poison, given to him under the pretext of medication by a eunuch named Bagoas. Bagoas had been one of Artaxerxes III's commanders in the victory over Egypt, and had grown pleased with his power.

With Artaxerxes III dead, Bagoas began running the kingdom himself as vizier. Two of the young princes also died, unexpectedly, from stomach troubles (Bagoas had been busy with his cups). Only one prince survived, a young man named Arses. Likely Bagoas planned to make him the puppet-king; when Arses showed signs of independence, Bagoas poisoned him too.

PHILIP was plotting his attack on the eunuch-led empire when catastrophe overtook him.

The catastrophe was mostly of his own making. Right after the Corinthian League meeting of 337, Philip decided to get married again. This had absolutely no political advantage for him, and was apparently impelled by lust; the girl was a native Macedonian, the beautiful niece of a courtier named Attalus. At the wedding feast, all of the Macedonians got staggering drunk (a tradition at Macedonian festivities) and Attalus proposed a toast: he waved his cup in the air and announced that the gods could now send Macedonia a legitimate heir to the throne.

Alexander was, of course, technically legitimate, but since his mother Olympias was Greek, he was only half Macedonian. Attalus's toast was a direct challenge to his position as crown prince, a suggestion that Macedonia's throne should only belong to full-blooded Macedonians (and a clear indication that Philip's love for all things Greek was not shared by all Macedonians).

Alexander, who was also drunk, threw a cup at Attalus and called him scum. Philip, probably the drunkest of all, drew his sword to attack Alexander and then fell flat on his face. "Gentlemen," Alexander said, standing over his father in scorn, "there lies the man who was getting ready to cross over from Europe to Asia, but who trips up on his way over to one couch from another!"[31]

Worse was about to come, and Attalus too was in this up to his neck. According to Diodorus, Philip had picked as his lover, some time before, a beautiful young man who was also a friend of Attalus. (Macedonians, like Greeks, tended to pay more attention to the mechanics of the sex act than to the gender of the partner involved; whether you were the penetrated or the penetrator was important, but who was on the other end was less relevant.) This beautiful young man unfortunately displaced Philip's previous lover, a member of his bodyguard named Pausanias. Pausanias, lovesick, insulted his replacement in public by calling him a "hermaphrodite," no true man. Shamed, the young man threw himself in front of Philip during a battle, intending to be killed, and died on an enemy sword.

Attalus, in revenge for his friend's suicide, invited Pausanias to dinner, got him thoroughly drunk, and then handed him over to be gang-raped by a group of cooperative friends, a punishment which fit the crime; to be penetrated was submissive, femalelike, the very qualities that Pausanias had used to slander his rival. Pausanias, when he sobered up, went to Philip in furious humiliation and complained, but Philip declined to punish Attalus, who was a trusted and valuable general. Instead he tried to pacify Pausanias by promoting him and giving him presents.

But he refused to love him again, and Pausanias nursed his rejection and humiliation until 336. Philip had organized a huge festival to celebrate the beginning of his attack on Persia; it was to begin with an opening parade, led by Philip, into a theater filled with cheering Macedonians. As Philip stepped over the threshold of the theater, Pausanias came up from behind him and put a knife into his ribs.

Pausanias ran for his horse. He tripped and fell, and was immediately stabbed multiple times by the rest of the bodyguard.[32] But Philip was already dead.

There were plenty of people who suspected that Alexander, who despised his father, had somehow been involved: "Alexander did not come out of the affair spotless," Plutarch says, although he gives no damning details.[33] But with Pausanias murdered and no proof of any treason, no one dared make any accusation. In any case Alexander was popular with the army, which acclaimed him as king the very next day.

He inherited, Plutarch says, a kingdom "surrounded on all sides by bitter resentment, deep hatred, and danger." The conquered territories to the north were unhappy under Macedonian rule; the Greeks, to the south, were not so fully resigned to their Corinthian League membership that Alexander could afford to rely on them; and the Persians were waiting for the Macedonians to attack.

But Alexander had one piece of business to take care of. Attalus had been sent on ahead into Asia Minor, to prepare the route that the Macedonian invasion force would follow into Persia. Alexander never forgot an insult; he sent an assassin after Attalus, and had him murdered.

TIMELINE 68

CHINA	GREECE
	Battle of Marathon (490)
	Leonidas of Sparta
"Spring and Autumn" period ends (481)	Battles of Thermopylae and Salamis (480)
Death of Confucius	Battles of Plataea and Mycale (479)
	Perdikkas II of Macedonia
	Pericles of Athens
	Peloponnesian War (begins 431)
Warring States period begins (403)	March of the Ten Thousand (401)
	Corinthian War (395)
Duke Hsiao of Ch'in	**Philip II of Macedonia** (359–336)
Shang Yang	
	Battle of Chaeronea (338)
	Alexander III of Macedonia (336)
Huiwen of Ch'in (325)	

Chapter Sixty-Nine

Rome Tightens Its Grasp

Between 367 and 290 BC,
Carthage fights Syracuse,
and Rome fights everyone within marching distance

WHILE THE GREEKS had been making useless stabs at unity—the Peloponnesian League, the Hellenic League, the Delian League, and the travesty of the Corinthian League—the cities in the old territory of Latium were also coalescing into an alliance: the "Latin League." The Romans called this league the *Nomen Latium*, and while they had been reasonably friendly with the Latin League cities for over a century (the first peace treaty between Rome and the League was probably signed around 490 BC), Rome never joined. The city was not inclined to become one among equals.

In the thirty-odd years since the Gauls had burned Rome, the Romans had rebuilt their walls, fought off various attacks from their neighbors, sent troops east to the Anio river to battle with more Gauls (the Roman soldiers approached the campaign in "great terror," Livy says, but "many thousands of barbarians were killed in battle,")[1] and suffered through yet another patrician-plebian standoff. This one ended in 367 with a patrician concession: the consulship would be formally opened to plebians, and the first plebian consul was installed that same year.

The Senate announced that this compromise needed to be celebrated with an extra festival day, and Livy himself calls it a "noteworthy" year, in which, "after their long dispute, the two orders were reconciled and in agreement at last."[2] "In agreement" is a bit strong, since patricians and plebians continued to aggravate each other, but the new arrangement does seem to have acted as grease in the squeaky relationship between the two classes. In the next decades there was enough peace within Rome's walls for the city to turn renewed attention to empire-building.

In 358, Rome convinced the Latin League to renew the old peace treaty.* As before, the two sides were obliged to defend each other in attack. But from now on, all booty from joint campaigns would be divided equally between the two sides; Rome would get as much out of any victory as all the cities of the League combined.[3] Rome was no longer simply another city on the peninsula; it was a power as great as the League itself.

In 348, the Romans updated another treaty, this one with Carthage. Roman ships still weren't supposed to sail farther west than Fair Promontory, and the Carthaginians still promised not to build any forts in the territory of the Latins. But a new condition turned the peace treaty into something slightly different: "If the Carthaginians capture any city in Latium which is not subject to Rome," the treaty specified, "they shall keep the goods and the men, but deliver up the city."[4] The Carthaginians were now partners in conquest; Rome was laying plans to control the countryside, even as its leaders swore friendship with the Latin League.

In the next fifty years, Rome's aggression would lead it into four wars and a revolt, and a fifth war would swirl just off its shores.

JUST ACROSS the Liri river lay an alliance of tribes known, collectively, as the Samnites. They came from the southern Apennines, and lived in a mesh of farms and villages below Rome and east of the coastal area of Campania.[5] Farms aside, they were known as an alarming set of fighters, "strong both in resources and in arms," as Livy puts it.[6]

Despite an earlier agreement that the Liri would serve as a boundary between them, Rome went to war against the Samnites in 343. Roman accounts put the best possible light on this; the Romans, Livy says, were simply responding to a desperate appeal for help, because the Samnites had "unjustly attacked" the people who lived in the region of Campania, on the southwestern coast. But the city's ambitions come out in Livy's version of events: " 'We have reached the point . . . when Campania will have to be absorbed by her friends or by her enemies," his Campanian ambassadors plead. "You, Romans, must occupy it yourselves rather than let [the Samnites] take it, a good deed on your part, an evil one of theirs. . . . Romans, the shadow of your help is enough to protect us, and whatever we have . . . we shall consider all yours."[7]

No matter how pressed the Campanians were, it is unlikely that any of Rome's neighbors were begging for absorption; this "First Samnite War" was

* This treaty was known as the *foedus Cassianum*, or "Cassius treaty."

69.1 Roman Enemies and Allies

the next move in Rome's imperial game. The gambit was not particularly successful. By 341, the First Samnite War was stalemated, and the two sides agreed to a treaty.

The second war, the Latin War, broke out right on the heels of the first. The cities of the Latin League, watching Rome's activities in the south, had finally decided that no treaty was going to halt Roman expansionism. Complicated political maneuverings resulted in the Latin cities attacking Rome, with the Samnites joining in the *Roman* side in order to keep *Latin* power from spreading farther to the south.

This war, Livy writes, was particularly difficult for the Roman army because the Latins marching towards them "were the same as themselves in language, customs, type of arms, and above all in military institutions." This concerned the consuls who were in command of the Roman army. In fear that the Roman soldiers would lose track of who were the allies and who the enemy, they "issued the order that no one was to leave his position to fight the enemy."[8]

The Latin soldiers and the Roman-Samnite troops met near Capua, in a savage battle. The Romans "broke up their enemy's formation with such slaughter that they left scarcely a quarter of their opponents alive," while the "entire army" of the Romans had been "cut to pieces. . . . before the standards and behind them was equally a bloodbath."[9] Even after so much bloodshed, the two armies regrouped and clashed again. This time the Romans were victorious.

After the Latin surrender, the Romans claimed an empire's worth of Italian land: not only Latium, but the north of Campania and southern Etruria as well.[10] The various peoples pulled within the Roman sphere were treated according to their loyalties. The Latins, Livy says, "were deprived of their rights to intermarry and trade with each other and to hold councils amongst themselves," which cut the ties between the League cities. The people of Campania who had fought on Rome's side "were granted citizenship without the vote," as were the residents of several other allied cities.[11] This was an odd category of privilege, the *civitas sine suffragio*; the new semicitizens were protected by the Laws of the Twelve Tables, but given no voice in Rome's decisions.

Rome also began to plant new colonies with increasing speed, spreading its boundaries by building as well as conquest.[12] The fledgling empire, however, was anything but stable; Livy uses the phrase "bad peace" to describe its relations with its newly conquered members and as-yet-unconquered neighbors.

In 326, even the bad peace ended, and the Samnites once again rose up in arms. Once again the aggression was on the Roman side; the Romans had crossed over that old boundary, the Liri river, to build a colony in Samnite land.[13] The "Second Samnite War" dragged on for over twenty years, in a series of dreary repetitive clashes between the two armies.

As Romans and Samnites battled, another fight was brewing offshore. With the Romans busy in Samnite territory, an ambitious Sicilian named Agathocles had seized the chance to do a bit of empire-building of his own. Agathocles was a Syracusan ex-potter who had married well and hired himself an army. In 317, he took Syracuse by force and made himself its tyrant, using the good old Merodach-baladan/Napoleon/Sargon II/Cyrus justification: "He declared that he was restoring to the people their full autonomy," writes Diodorus Siculus,[14] a claim which rang a little hollow when he then went on to conquer most of the rest of Sicily.

This involved shoving Carthaginians off the island, and Carthage did not ignore the challenge to its power in the Mediterranean. By 310, the Carthaginian navy had blockaded Syracuse. In response, Agathocles sent a Syracusan force to attack Carthage itself.[15]

The Carthaginians were so alarmed by this unexpected assault that the city fell into a panic. The priests of Carthage, who still followed a version of the old Canaanite religion brought over from Tyre centuries earlier, sacrificed as many as five hundred children to the Carthaginian deities in order to assure victory.[16] "They believed they had neglected the honors of the gods that had been established by their fathers," Diodorus tells us, and were anxious to make amends for the shortcomings that had brought Agathocles's invasion on them: "There was in their city a bronze image of Cronus [the Greek name for Baal, a Phoenician male god], extending its hands, palms up and sloping toward the ground, so that each of the children when placed thereon rolled down and fell into a sort of gaping pit filled with fire."*[17]

This horrific ritual didn't bring victory. Although Carthage did not fall, neither did Syracuse, and by 306 the two sides had to sign a treaty. Agathocles stayed on the throne of Syracuse, but Carthage kept control of the west part of the island.[18]

Just afterwards, in 304, the Romans finally made peace with the Samnites (again). Meanwhile, they had embarked on yet another empire-building proj-

* The Carthaginian habit of sacrificing children up to the age of ten is attested to in a number of classical authors, including Plutarch, Quintus Curtius Rufus (a first-century historian who used earlier, now-lost sources), and Cicero. The Canaanite (Phoenician) roots of this practice are mentioned in the biblical accounts, such as Deut. 12:31, which tells the Israelites not to sacrifice their sons and daughters in fire as the "nations around" do because this is detestable to the God of Abraham. Excavation near the ancient ports of Carthage has revealed the remains of the victims, although the statue Diodorus mentions has never been found. See David Soren et al., *Carthage*, for a review of the archaeological and literary evidence.

ect. Cyrus had laid out his Royal Road to link his original heartland with conquered territory, and the Romans, following suit, had begun to construct an official road to link the city with their own outlying lands. The consul Appius Claudius Caecus began the project in 312, and the road, which eventually ran along the coast all the way down to Capua in Campania, took his name: the Appian Way.

The peace with the Samnites lasted all of six years. In 298, just after the consular elections, Livy writes that a rumor began to spread through Rome: "the Etruscans and Samnites were enlisting huge armies. . . . The enemies of Rome were preparing for war with all their own might and that of their allies."[19] The anti-Roman coalition assembling across the Liri included not only Samnites and the remaning Etruscans, but also a contingent of Gauls down from the north and Umbrians, a federation of tribes from the Apennines northeast of Etruria. These disparate peoples were willing to band together to fight against Rome: a clear reflection of the growing sense of crisis over Rome's ongoing expansion.

The Roman campaign against this federation, the "Third Samnite War," began with three years of hard fighting that finally culminated at a huge battle in Sentinum, just across the Apennines in Umbria itself; the farthest away, in all likelihood, that the Roman army had ever campaigned, and the first time that many had ever crossed the mountains. "Great is the fame of that day on which the battle was fought in Sentinum," Livy says.

> A day was fixed for the battle, the Samnites and Gauls were chosen to engage in it, and during the actual fighting the Etruscans and Umbrians were to attack the Roman camp. These plans were upset by three deserters . . . who came over secretly by night to [the commanding consul] Fabius and told him of the enemy's intentions.[20]

The Romans, who had been seriously outnumbered by the four-way alliance, sent a detachment to go raid Etruscan and Umbrian land, at which point the Etruscan and Umbrian contingents went home to defend their families and farms. So when the battle began, the Romans were lined up against the Gauls and Samnites. They were "equally matched," Livy says; the Roman cavalry scattered in terror when the Gauls charged down in chariots, which many Romans had never seen before, and one of the consuls was killed; the Gauls, in turn, fell in such numbers that the heaps of bodies took days to remove. At last, with thousands dead on both sides, the Gaulish and Samnite line was breached, their camp invaded, and their retreat blocked.

Now the Romans had control of the countryside, but "there was still no peace" in the countryside, as Livy concludes. The worst of the fighting ended in 295, at Sentinum, but raids, battles, revolts, and rebellions continued for another five years. Another treaty in 290 brought an end to the Third Samnite War. But even afterwards, Roman soldiers marched out every year to fight in the north and center of the Italian peninsula; the Roman fist, closing over the countryside, was armored.

TIMELINE 69

GREECE	ROME
Battle of Marathon (490)	Plebian Secession (494)
Leonidas of Sparta	
Battles of Thermopylae and Salamis (480)	
Battles of Plataea and Mycale (479)	
Perdikkas II of Macedonia	Laws of the Twelve Tables
Pericles of Athens	
Peloponnesian War (begins 431)	
March of the Ten Thousand (401)	
Corinthian War (395)	Rome burned by Gauls (390)
Philip II of Macedonia (359–336)	
	First Samnite War (343)
Battle of Chaeronea (338)	Latin War (340)
Alexander III of Macedonia (336)	
	Second Samnite War (326)
	Third Samnite War (298)

Chapter Seventy

Alexander and the Wars of the Successors

Between 336 and 272 BC,
Alexander the Great makes most of the world part of one empire,
which his generals then divide

AFTER THE DEATH of Philip of Macedonia, his son Alexander had taken his place as king of Macedonia and head of the Corinthian League. But with Philip gone, various Greek cities declared their secession from the League, Thebes and Athens among them; Athens even had an ill-judged festival day and bestowed a posthumous gold crown on Pausanias.[1]

Alexander marched straight for the rebels with his Macedonian troops, reconquering Greeks as he went. When he arrived at the gates of Thebes, he offered to reinstate the city in his favor if the Thebans would just hand over the two noblemen responsible for leading the secession. Thebes refused, and Alexander ordered his men to break down the gates. "The city itself, being taken by storm," writes Plutarch, "was sacked and razed, Alexander's hope being that so severe an example might terrify the rest of Greece into obedience. . . . Thirty thousand were publicly sold as slaves. . . . upwards of six thousand were put to the sword."[2]

He then made the same offer to Athens, which agreed as quickly as possible. "Whether it were, like the lion, that his passion was now satisfied," Plutarch adds, "or that, after an example of extreme cruelty, he had a mind to appear merciful, it happened well for the Athenians; for he . . . forgave them all past offences."[3] The Athenians did their best to keep his good opinion by sending off into exile all the men who had opposed joining the Corinthian League.

After this, the rest of the Corinthian League fell into line within two months. Alexander marched down to the Isthmus of Corinth and there held a gathering of the League in which (as his soldiers stood by) the League's delegates hastily elected him to the position of leader in his father's place.

This show of democracy, backed up by force, would be characteristic of Alexander's dealings. Almost everything he did, he did by force of arms; yet somewhere in him there was a longing to be acclaimed by the free will of the conquered. The old idea of conquest by force, and the new idea that men could be bound together without coercion, by a shared loyalty or a joint identity, sat uneasily together in him.

ALEXANDER WAS NOW KING of the Greeks, which was something that no Spartan or Athenian hero had ever managed to pull off. He had behind him his elite Macedonian fighters, plus around forty thousand Greek troops; he was ready to brave the Persian lions.

70.1. Alexander the Great. Greek marble bust of Alexander the Great, King of Macedonia 336–323 BC. Museo Barracco, Rome. Photo credit Alinari/Art Resource, NY

Over in Persia, the eunuch Bagoas had come to a bad end. After the death of the prince Arses, Bagoas had chosen as his next puppet an impressive-looking (six and a half feet tall) but reputedly mild-mannered distant relative of Artaxerxes III, a man named Kodomannos.

Bagoas had not thought to get much resistance from Kodomannos, who had no experience of courts. He had underestimated his man, though. Once Kodomannos had been crowned under the royal name Darius III, he invited Bagoas into his throne room for a cup of wine. Bagoas, who knew what was coming, tried to beg off by pleading that he was getting sick, but the king suggested that, in that case, he'd better drink his medicine. An hour later Bagoas was dead, and Darius III was in control of Persia.[4]

In 334, Alexander marched over into Darius's realm with thirty-two thousand men; Diodorus says that almost fourteen thousand of these were Macedonian, the rest drawn from subject cities.[5] He had moved faster than the Persians expected, and the Persian army could not reach him in time to prevent this army from crossing the Hellespont.

Having lost their first advantage, the Persian commanders put their heads together for a new strategy (Darius III was not with them; he had just gotten rid of Bagoas and likely wanted to keep his royal eye on Susa a little longer). The Persian general Memnon suggested avoiding a land battle altogether. Instead, he said, the Persians should retreat while burning all of the supplies, luring Alexander's army across land bare of food and water, and meanwhile send ships around to attack the Macedonian homeland.[6]

This was a good plan, a combination of the Roman strategy against the four-way alliance in Italy and the Scythian strategy which had defeated the first Darius. But he was shouted down. Instead, the Persian army moved to the banks of the Granicus river, near the old site of Troy, and made its stand.

Against the advice of his own commander, Parmenio, Alexander drew up his forces and charged across the river at the Persian line. The first Macedonians who came up out of the water were slaughtered, but the weight of Alexander's attack soon pushed the Persians back. The Greek military historian Arrian chalks this up to the experience of Alexander's men and "the advantage of the long cornel-wood spear over the light lances of the Persians,"*[7] but Alexander's presence undoubtedly had something to do with the Macedonian ferocity as well. Unlike Darius, he was right in the middle of the first charge and fought on the front line until the end. In fact, he survived having a spear driven into his breastplate, and lost his helmet to an axe-blow from behind. He was saved from losing his head by one of his commanders, Cleitus the Black, who managed to cut off the attacker's arm at the shoulder before he could get his weapon up for a second blow.[8]

Ancient accounts record a Macedonian loss of around two hundred men, while the Persians lost something like four thousand; Darius's son, son-in-law, and brother-in-law were among the dead. The surviving Persians fled, and Alexander declared the Ionian cities liberated (which mean that they were now under his rule). He marched on towards Sardis, but Arrian says that he was still "eight or nine miles away" when the city's governor came out to surrender.[9] Asia Minor was his.

On his triumphant march through it, he stopped at the city of Gordium, Midas's old capital. There he saw, in the Temple of Jupiter, the cart that

* Cornel-wood comes from *Cornus sanguinea*, the "European dogwood," and is still used for making bows because it will flex without breaking.

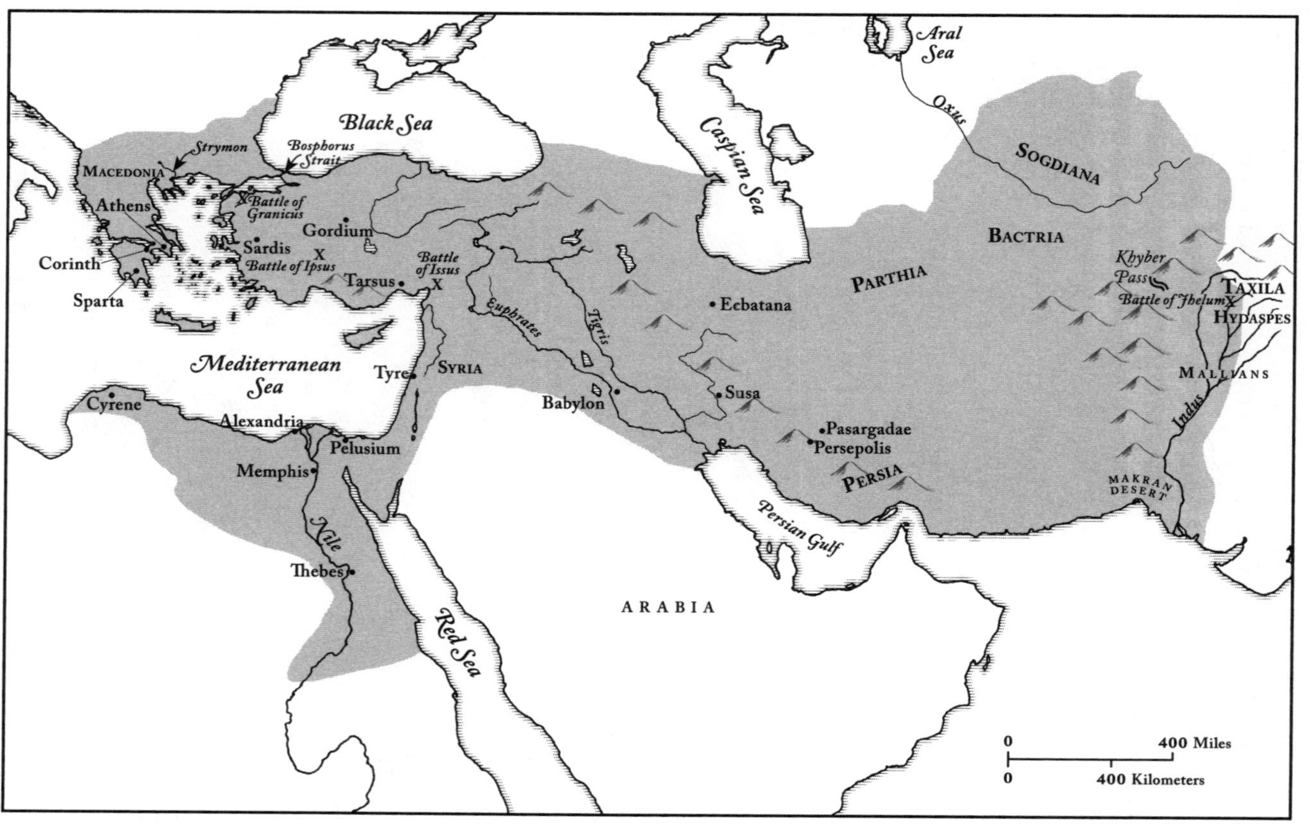

70.1 *Alexander's Empire*

Midas's father Gordius was said to have used when he first entered the country: "its remarkable feature being the yoke," according to the Roman historian Quintus Curtius Rufus, "which was strapped down with several knots all so tightly entangled that it was impossible to see how they were fastened." The locals said that the man who untied it would be king of all Asia, an irresistable challenge to Alexander. "For some time Alexander wrestled unsuccessfully with the knots," Rufus says. "Then he said: 'It makes no difference how they're untied,' and cut through all the thongs with his sword, thus evading the oracle's prophecy—or, indeed, fulfilling it."[10]

Darius, meanwhile, had grown worried enough to travel (with his wives, children, and most of his court) to Babylon, which would serve as his center of operations against the invader. Here he collected an absolutely mammoth army: over a quarter of a million Persians, Medes, and tribute fighters from various parts of his empire, according to Rufus. With this earth-shaking army, he then marched up from Babylon to open country in the old Assyrian heartland, where the Persian forces could spread out and crush the Macedonians.

But Alexander had grown ill with a high fever, and was delaying in Tarsus until it passed. Darius, impatient at his enemy's constant non-appearance, decided (against the advice of a Macedonian deserter who had shown up at the Persian camp) to make straight towards Asia Minor. As a result, the armies met at the Issus river, in Syria, where the huge Persian numbers gave no advantage; the troops couldn't all fit onto the smaller battlefield.[11]

Once again the Macedonian forces pushed through the Persian lines.* Darius, seeing that the battle was going against him, took to his heels: "He even stooped to throwing off his royal insignia so that they could not betray his flight," Rufus says.[12] Bagoas had not been entirely mistaken in Darius's mildness; he was frightened enough to leave his wife, his aged mother, and all his children behind. When Alexander arrived at the center of the Persian camp in victory, he found them all there, kept prisoner by the Macedonians in the royal tent to await his arrival. "They kept asking on which wing Darius had stood," Rufus says; they were convinced that Darius must be dead, if he had given up defending them. The news of his flight was a shock.

Alexander, who was generally kind to captives as long as they hadn't been part of a siege (which always put him in a bad mood), spared them. Darius got far enough away to make camp safely, and then sent a letter to Alexander

* Each stage of the battle is recorded in detail by Arrian (*The Campaigns of Alexander*, Book II) and Quintus Curtius Rufus (*The History of Alexander*, Book III), among others. I will not give a blow-by-blow description of Alexander's battles here, but interested readers might see the readable Penguin translations of both books, done by Aubrey de Selincourt and John Yardley, respectively, for a more complete account.

offering to become Alexander's ally, and also asking to ransom his wife and children.

By return letter, Alexander refused to make any treaties unless Darius came in person and addressed him as "Lord of the Continent of Asia." "In the future," his own letter ended, "let any communication you wish to make with me be addressed to the King of All Asia. Do not write to me as an equal."[13]

This pretty much guaranteed that talk of a treaty was at an end. Darius remained east of the Euphrates; Alexander provided for Darius's relatives to live in well-guarded comfort, and then began to campaign through Syria. In 332, he reached the city of Tyre, which refused to surrender and held out for seven months. When the siege finally ended, Alexander was so enraged by the delay that he allowed his men to massacre a good many of the thirty thousand people inside.

After this he marched down to Egypt and was proclaimed pharaoh in the place of Darius III, who had claimed the title as a matter of course when he reached the Persian throne. And then, in 331, he came back up to deal with Darius. Darius made another attempt to avoid war; he offered again to buy back his family, and also promised Alexander that he could have all the land west of the Euphrates without opposition, not to mention a Persian princess as wife, if Alexander would only agree to make a treaty of friendship. Alexander's general Parmenio thought this was a perfectly good idea which would allow everyone to go back home. "I would accept, if I were you," he told Alexander, to which Alexander retorted, "And if I were you, so would I."[14]

The two armies met yet again in battle, this time at Gaugemela, all the way up on the north Tigris. Again the Persians were defeated; again Darius fled. Alexander's men marched in triumph first to Susa, and then to Persepolis. Here, Alexander discovered a whole contingent of Greek prisoners of war, some of whom had been taken captive decades before in older wars, but all of whom had been made slaves. To keep them from escaping, their Persian masters had amputated whatever arms or legs they didn't need to fulfill their tasks. Alexander, once again moved to fury, told his men to sack the city; they were allowed to burn, kill, and enslave, but he forbade them to rape any of the women.[15] We have no way of knowing how far this order was followed, but the city was laid waste, and the palaces of Darius burned.

Darius himself ran towards Ecbatana. Alexander went after him with a small fast force, but before he could overtake the escaping Persian king, Darius's own men turned against him. His cavalry commander and one of his satraps stabbed him, and left him in a wagon to die in the hot July sun.[16]

Alexander was now Great King, and his men hoped that their tour of duty was over.[17] But Alexander was incapable of leaving land unconquered, and the northeastern satrapies, Bactria and Sogdiana among them, were not yet in his hands. He began campaigning farther and higher, above the high range that separated the Indian subcontinent from the central Asian lands. It was rough terrain, and over the next three years of fighting, his hold over his men's loyalties began to slip. First Parmenio's son was convicted of plotting against Alexander's life; Alexander had him tortured to death, and then ordered his father put to death as well (a brutal but not uncommon practice in Macedonia).

Then he arranged to marry a princess of Sogdiana, the beautiful Roxane. This was an unusually late first marriage, for a man of his age; like his father, he had carried on affairs with both sexes, but he spent most of his energy in battle, with sex a secondary pleasure. Now his queen would be a girl from a tribe that the Macedonians thought of as slaves and barbarians. And combined with this was a growing resentment over Alexander's increasing tendency to put on Persian dress and follow Persian customs. As far as they were concerned, he was becoming less and less Macedonian as he took more and more territory.

This resentment boiled out at a drunken dinner late in 328, when the very same Cleitus who had saved Alexander's life at Granicus accused him of taking credit for victories won by the blood of loyal Macedonians. Alexander leaped up, searching for a weapon; Cleitus's friends, who were slightly less drunk than he was, dragged Cleitus out of the room, but he insisted on returning by another door to taunt the king. Alexander grabbed a spear from his bodyguard and spitted his countryman.[18]

When he sobered up, he was horrified. But he did not give up his plans of campaigning farther east, even though his men were now following him with none of the joyful adoration that they had once shown. Whether or not they were fully with him, he intended to conquer India.

On the other side of the Indus river, the direct descendents of King Ajatashatru of Magadha (who had, so many years ago, conquered the surrounding kingdoms to make Magadha great) had lost their throne. In 424 BC, an illegitimate son of the royal line named Mahapadma Nanda had taken the crown of Magadha himself, and had gone on campaign.

He lived to be the greatest Indian conqueror yet. He was still fighting at the age of eighty-eight; and when he finally died, after decades of kingdom-building, he had pushed the territory of Magadha all the way down to the Deccan (the northern edge of the dry southern desert). He left the kingdom to his sons and grandsons. When Alexander came through the Khyber Pass into India, one of Mahapadma Nanda's descendents, Dhana Nanda, was on the throne of Magadha.

Before he had any chance of reaching this richest and most powerful Indian kingdom, Alexander had to pass through the lands that lay between them. But he never got quite far enough to face Dhana Nanda in battle.

The first Indian kingdom that lay between him and the northern kingdoms of India was Taxila, whose king took its name when he acceded. The current King Taxiles met Alexander with gifts and tribute soldiers as soon as he had crossed the Indus (perhaps using a pontoon bridge, although details of the crossing are unknown).[19] Taxiles hoped to make an alliance with Alexander against the next kingdom over: Hydaspes, which lay on the Jhelum river and was ruled by the seven-foot-tall King Porus.

Alexander took the gifts and soldiers, and agreed to help Taxiles against his enemy. The joint force of Indians and Macedonians marched to the Jhelum river, where they could see Porus and his army (which included "squadrons of elephants," Arrian says)[20] on the other side. With four of his hand-picked personal guard, men named Ptolemy, Perdiccas, Lysimachus, and Seleucus, he led his army across the river (some swimming, some wading, some on hastily built boats) and attacked both the elephants and the seven-foot Porus.

Both the Macedonians and the horses were a little alarmed by these monstrous beasts, but fought forwards and drove Porus's forces closer and closer together, until his elephants were trampling his own foot soldiers. Finally Porus was forced to surrender; Alexander, impressed by his courage, spared his life.

But Alexander's victorious army had suffered heavy losses; and when they found out that Alexander now intended to lead them across the Ganges river, which was even wider than the Indus and had more hostile Indian troops and elephants on the other side, they refused to go on.

This time, neither Alexander's fury nor his charm could persuade them. Finally, Plutarch says, he "shut himself up in his tent and lay there in sullen anger, refusing to feel any gratitude for what he had already achieved unless he could cross the Ganges as well."[21] He remained in his tent sulking for two days. And then, realizing that he had lost this particular battle, he emerged on the third day and agreed to turn back.[22]

But rather than marching back through the Khyber Pass, he led his soldiers along the Indus, south to the sea, and then to the west. This turned into a wretched, soul- and body-killing, seven-month voyage. The men had to fight their way through hostile riverside towns on their march down to the coast; in one of these attacks, on the town of the Mallians, Alexander was struck in the chest by an arrow and for some hours seemed to be dead. When they resumed the march he could barely sit on a horse, and the wound never completely healed. And once they were at the coast, the march west took them through salt desert: "through an uncultivated country," Plutarch says, "whose inhabitants fared hardly, possessing only a few sheep, and those of a wretched kind, whose flesh was rank and unsavoury, by their continual feeding upon sea-fish."[23] The heat was unbearable. All the water was salty. His men began to died fom starvation, thirst, and disease. Out of an army of 120,000 infantry and 15,000 cavalry, barely 30,000 reached home. It was a dreadful end to a brilliant campaign.

Back in Susa, Alexander put the Indian campaign out of his mind, insofar as he could, and instead concentrated on his duties as king rather than conquerer. He married again, this time one of Darius III's daughters, the princess Stateira (at least half a foot taller than he was). He also hosted a bizarre mass wedding between his Macedonian noblemen and hundreds of Persian noblewomen. To Hephaestion, his closest friend, his trusted general, and probably his boyhood lover, he awarded the privilege of marrying another one of Darius's daughters: Stateira's younger sister Drypetis.

The wedding festival was Alexander's attempt to deal with the ongoing hostility between the Persians, who found Macedonians uncouth, and the Macedonians, who found Persians effeminate. He also rounded up thousands of Persian boys and put them under the command of Macedonian officers, to be trained in Macedonian fighting. Both experiments backfired. Most of the mass marriages fell apart with speed, and the Macedonian foot soldiers hated the Persian youths with such vehemence that they threatened to go back to Macedonia. "They desired him to dismiss them one and all," Plutarch writes, "now he was so well furnished with a set of dancing boys, with whom, if he pleased, he might go on and conquer the world."[24]

Meanwhile, the idea that a joint Greek identity might somehow pull all of Alexander's subjects together had almost disappeared from view. But not completely. Alexander made an emotional appeal to the Persians ("Foreign newcomers though you are, I have made you established members of my force: you are both my fellow-citizens and my soldiers") and another to his old Macedonian comrades ("Everything is taking on the same hue: it is no disgrace for the Persians to copy Macedonian customs nor for the Macedonians to imitate the Persians. Those who are to live under the same king should enjoy the same rights").[25]

When he had managed to convince both Macedonians and Persians to coexist a little longer, he travelled from Susa to Ecbatana, where he intended to host a great festival in Greek style. He hoped that this might smooth out the very visible joints in his kingdom. But at Ecbatana, in mid-festival,

Hephaestion grew ill. He probably had typhoid; he was beginning to recover when, against the advice of his physicians, he had a huge meal of chicken and wine which perforated his stomach. He died just hours later.

Alexander never completely recovered from Hephaestion's death. He left Ecbatana and went to Babylon in deep mourning. Here, he too grew ill. Plutarch says he had a fever, which began on the eighteenth day of the month and grew continually worse. Ten days later, he was dead. The year was 323; he was thirty-three.

His body lay in his bedchamber unburied for several days, while his commanders argued over who would take control of the empire; he had never named a successor, and as he had learned not long before that Roxane was pregnant with an heir, had dismissed any need to do so. "During the dissensions among the commanders," Plutarch writes, "which lasted several days, the body continued clear and fresh, without any sign of such taint or corruption, though it lay neglected in a close sultry place."[26] Some took this as a miraculous sign; in all likelihood, Alexander was in deep coma for two or three days before finally dying. The delay saved him from being still alive when the embalming process finally began.

ALEXANDER'S CONQUESTS, made in a white heat of energy, had produced an empire with no administration to speak of, no bureaucracy, no organized tax system, no common system of communication, no national identity, and no capital city; Alexander himself, peripatetic, died in camp. It had been created at hyperspeed, and it did in hyperspeed what other ancient empires held together by dynamic personalities had done: it fell apart.

The disintegration began with Roxane. Five months pregnant, in a strange country, and familiar enough with Persian customs to feel entirely unsafe, she had just heard that Alexander's Persian wife Stateira, still in Susa, was also pregnant. She had probably also heard Ptolemy's remark that her own child, even if male, would be half-slave, and that no Macedonian would want to submit to him.[27] Stateira, on the other hand, was the daughter of a Great King.

Roxane wrote her a letter in Alexander's hand, under Alexander's seal, inviting her to Babylon. When Stateira arrived with her sister, Hephaestion's widow Drypetis, Roxane offered them both a cup of poisoned wine. Both were dead before night.[28]

Alexander's only heir was now Roxane's unborn child. But an unborn child could not rule, even through a regent. The empire needed a king before the news of Alexander's death spread through all those hard-conquered lands. The Macedonian army, which had gathered outside Alexander's bedchamber waiting for him to die, did not want to see anyone but a blood relative claim Alexander's title. They began to shout for Alexander's half-brother: the feebleminded child Philip, son of old Philip's mistress, known as Philip Arrhidaeus. This boy, now in his early thirties, was easily deceived, easily persuaded, and easily guided. He was also in Babylon, where Alexander, who was fond of him, had brought him in order to keep him safe.

When the army began to shout for him, one of Alexander's generals ran and got Philip, brought him out with a crown on his head, and managed to keep him quiet long enough for the army to acclaim him king. "But destiny was already bringing civil war," writes Quintus Curtius Rufus, "for a throne is not to be shared and several men were aspiring to it."[29] The men who wanted a piece of Alexander's conquests were the men who had spent the last decade fighting at his side: Ptolemy, a Macedonian who was rumored to be a bastard son of old Philip himself; Antigonus, one of Alexander's trusted generals; Lysimachus, one of his companions on the Indian campaign; and Perdiccas, who had served as commander of cavalry and then, after Hephaestion's death, as second-in-command.

Realizing that the mood of the army was against any one of them becoming supreme head of Alexander's empire, these men accepted a compromise. Feebleminded Philip would continue as nominal king, and if Roxane's baby was male, Philip and the infant would be co-rulers. Both would need a regent, and the man who took the job was Perdiccas.

He would stay in Babylon, which would serve as the center of the empire. The other men agreed to take positions as satraps, in imitation of the Persian system. Ptolemy would govern Egypt; Antigonus, most of Asia Minor ("Lycia, Pamphylia, and greater Phrygia," Rufus says); Lysimachus got Thrace; Antipater, a trusted officer who had served Alexander as regent of Macedonia during the king's absence, would continue in Macedonia and also keep tabs on Greece; Cassender, who was Antipater's son, got Caria (the southern Asia Minor coast). Five other officers were granted control of other parts of the empire.

This division of Alexander's domain into satrapies (the "Partition of Babylon") was a direct path to war. "Men who had recently been subjects of the king had individually seized control of huge kingdoms," writes Rufus, "ostensibly as administrators of an empire belonging to another, and any pretext for conflict was removed since they all belonged to the same race. . . . But it was difficult to remain satisfied with what the opportunity of the moment had brought them."[30] Neither their shared race nor their shared loyalty to Alexander could stave off the inevitable drama. The "Wars of the Diadochi," or "Wars of the Successors," broke out almost at once.

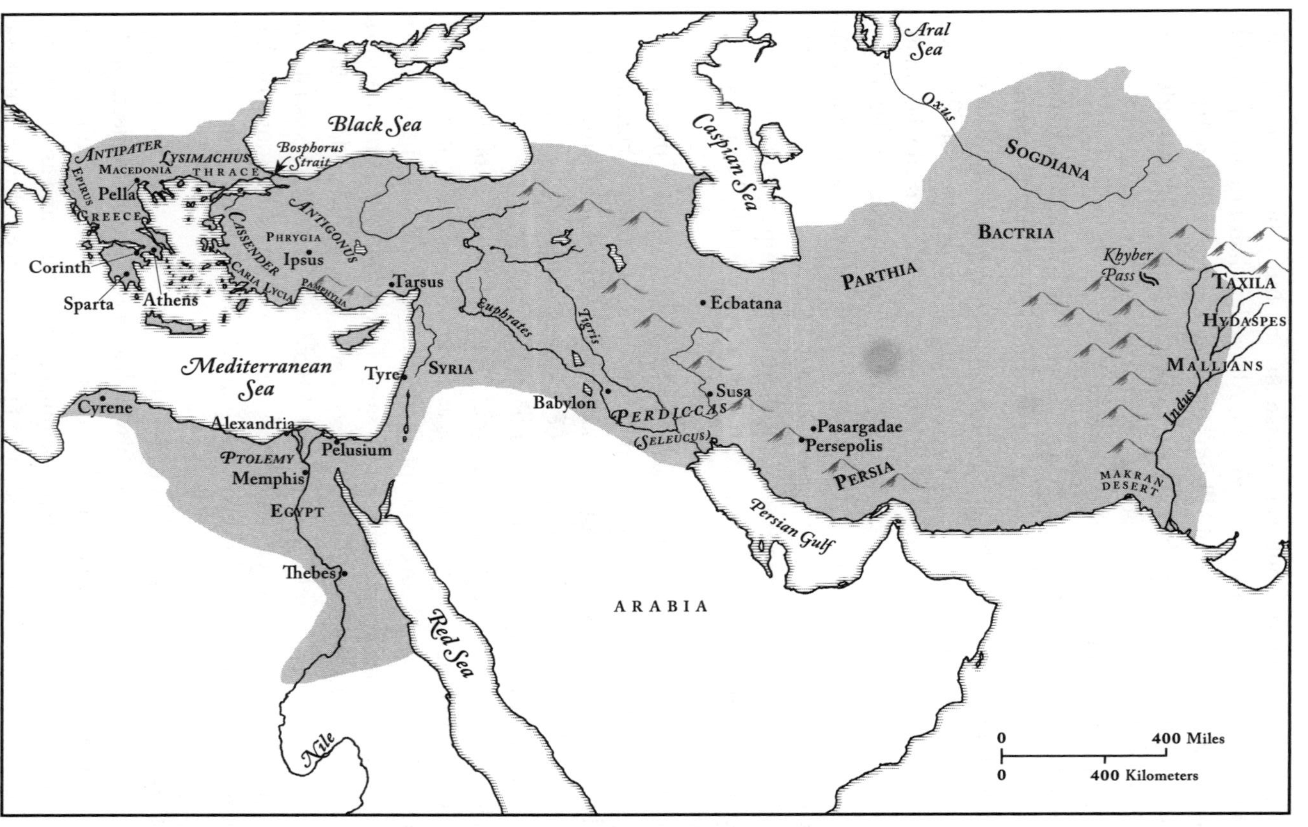

70.2 The Partition of Babylon

Scene One

Perdiccas's power as regent was increased when Roxane's baby, safely born, proved to be a boy: the infant Alexander IV of Macedonia. But Egypt had the potential to be the greatest military power of all the "satrapies"; Ptolemy had marched down to take charge with only two thousand men, but when word spread that he was offering generous pay, Greek mercenaries flocked to him. When his strength was great enough, Ptolemy made his intentions clear by kidnapping Alexander's body, which had been bound for Macedonia, and burying it in Egypt as though Alexander had been his ancestor.

Perdiccas knew that this was a move for control of the empire. He assembled his army and marched down to fight against Ptolemy. The attack was a disaster; Perdiccas's forces were embarassed. After the retreat, Perdiccas's officers banded together—led by the young officer Seleucus, who had also been with Alexander in Egypt—and assassinated him.

One general was now off the scene. Ptolemy ordered both Philip and the baby Alexander IV removed from Babylon and taken back to Macedonia, where they would be under the protection of Antipater. He rewarded Seleucus, who had gotten rid of Perdiccas, by giving him Babylon to rule—but as satrap, not as regent.

Scene Two

In 319, not long after, Antipater of Macedonia died. He left Macedonia not to his son Cassender (who already had Caria), but to another Macedonian. So both Ptolemy and Antigonus agreed to ally themselves with Cassander to help him capture his father's territory.

But fierce old Olympias, Alexander's mother, was still very much alive. She had her grandson Alexander IV brought to her own house at Pella, the royal capital of Macedonia, along with his mother Roxane. Then she rounded up supporters of her own to fight for control of Macedonia. Cassander's victory would have meant the establishment of a new royal house, and Olympias was too accustomed to being the mother of the king to watch that happen.

Olympias didn't manage to keep off the three powerful satraps for very long, but before they overran Macedonia, she did manage to get her hands on the feebleminded Philip. She had always hated him, and she loathed the idea that he would be co-king with her grandson. She had Philip stabbed to death before Cassander and his allies could arrive to rescue him. When Cassender did make it into Pella in 316, he arrested Olympias and ordered her stoned to death for murder. He put Roxane and young Alexander (now nine) under house arrest, theoretically for their own safety, in a castle called Amphipolis, overlooking the Strymon river.

Now the map had shaken itself out into five kingdoms: Cassender in Macedonia, Lysimachus in Thrace, Antigonus (nicknamed the One-Eyed, since he'd lost the other in battle) in Asia Minor, Seleucus controlling Babylon and the Persian heartland, and Ptolemy in Egypt.*

Scene Three

Up in Macedonia, in the castle of Amphipolis, the fate Roxane had feared ever since her husband's death came on her. Sometime around 310, the cup of wine at dinner had poison in it; and both Roxane and Alexander IV died. Alexander's only son was twelve years old, around the same age that his father had been at the taming of Bucephalus.

Cassander, who was acting as king of Macedonia, was undoubtedly the culprit. The other four generals knew exactly what had happened. But for the next half-decade, no one spoke of it. No one named himself king; no one abandoned the title of satrap. They all supported what they knew to be a lie: that young Alexander was still alive, in the fortress on the Macedonian river, and that they were all serving in his name. None of the five was willing to be the first to claim the title of king. Whoever first took it would find the other four allied against him.

Scene Four

Antigonus broke the balance, but only after two victories—both captained by his son Demetrius—had clearly demonstrated that he was the most powerful of the five. The first of these was the invasion of Athens in 307. Cassender, like Antipater before him, had been not only king of Macedonia but also the overlord of Greece. Demetrius marched into Athens and drove Cassender's men out of the city; and then he directed a naval battle against Ptolemy's ships which took place at Salamis. The Ptolemaic fleet was defeated.

After this, Antigonus—having triumphed over both Cassender and Ptolemy—took the title of king. Lysimachus (still in Thrace) and Seleucus (in Babylon) decided not to anger the one-eyed monster. Rather than allying against him, they began to call themselves kings as well. So did Ptolemy and

* I am, believe it or not, simplifying. There were other minor players on the scene: Laomedon in Syria, Philotas in Cilicia, Peithon in Media, Menander in Lydia, Eumenes in Cappadocia, Polyperchon in southern Greece, and a handful of others. Even the simplified version is enough to make one's head spin, and the full story of the Wars of the Diadochi requires a flow chart to follow. I am here trying to chart a middle course between giving every detail of the war (incomprehensible except to the specialist, and pointless for this sort of narrative since the end result was that the minor players all disappeared from the scene) and the usual textbook practice of saying that Alexander's empire was split into three parts, which is true but leaves a little too much unsaid.

Cassender. The death of Alexander IV, still unspoken, was now taken for granted.

Scene Five

All five kings then began to jostle at each other's borders, a process that reached its climax at the Battle of Ipsus in 301 BC. Ptolemy, whose power was concentrated in the south, sat this one out. But Cassander, Lysimachus, and Antigonus fought a three-way engagement which remained undecided until Seleucus arrived from Babylon with an overwhelming force and threw his weight onto Lysimachus and Cassander's side.

Antigonus, now eighty years old, fought until he died. His troops were scattered; his son Demetrius fled to Greece and set himself up as king there, abandoning the Asia Minor lands that had been the center of his father's empire. Lysimachus took the western part of Asia Minor for his own, adding it to Thrace; Seleucus took most of the rest. Cassander, who had done the dirty work of getting rid of Alexander IV, made very little out of the engagement; he added almost no land to Macedonia. Five kings remained (Ptolemy, Lysimachus, Cassander, Seleucus, and Demetrius), but the borders had shifted.

Scene Six

While fighting with the other successors, Seleucus had also been carrying on negotiations, with an Indian king named Chandragupta.

This king had come to power, sometime between 325 and 321, in his own small kingdom of Maurya. Not long after his accession, he had turned to make war on the last Nanda king of Magadha. The brutality of the Nanda Dynasty had long made these kings unpopular; Chandragupta found plenty of support. His capture of Magadha turned his little Mauryan kingdom into an empire.

His rise to power was partly due to the savvy of his closest advisor, Kautilya. Kautilya is traditionally given credit for writing the ancient political handbook *Arthashastra*; much of this text was probably set down somewhat later, but Kautilya's principles survive in it. The ruler, Kautilya taught, had two tasks. He was to enforce internal order, by making sure that his subjects properly observed the caste system:

> The observance of one's own duty leads one to *svarga* [Heaven] and infinite bliss. When it is violated, the world will come to an end owing to confusion of castes and duties. Hence the king shall never allow people to swerve from their duties; for whoever upholds his own duty, ever adhering

> to the customs of the Aryas, and follow the rules of caste and divisions of religious life, will surely be happy both here and hereafter.[31]

And he was to preserve outside order, by suspecting every neighbor of planning conquest, and taking the proper precautions.[32]

Whether or not Chandragupta's neighbors were planning on conquest, Chandragupta himself certainly was. He wanted to extend his own reach beyond the Ganges—but this brought him into the sphere of Seleucus, who had claimed Alexander's Indian territories along with his other gains.

Chandragupta proposed a bargain: he would give Seleucus war elephants, if Seleucus would yield the Indian territories to him. Seleucus, powerful though he was, realized that he would not be able to defend both the far eastern and far western borders of his kingdom. He agreed, and in 299 the two swore out a peace.

Scene Seven

In that same year, Demetrius took Macedonia. Cassander of Macedonia had died the year before, and his sons fought over the succession until one of them appealed to Demetrius, down in Greece, for help. This was a mistake; Demetrius campaigned northwards, drove out both of Cassender's heirs, and added Macedonia to Greece. The five kings had become four: Ptolemy, Lysimachus, Seleucus, and Demetrius in his father's place.

This was a temporary victory for Demetrius. A face from the past appeared: Pyrrhus, grandson of the king of Epirus, whose kingdom Philip had absorbed decades before. Pyrrhus was the son of Olympias's brother, and so the first cousin of Alexander the Great himself. As royalty in exile, he had had an unfortunate childhood (handed from relative to relative in an attempt to keep him out of harm's way), and he had an unfortunate face: Plutarch says that it had "more of the terrors than of the augustness of kingly power," since "he had not a regular set of upper teeth, but in the place of them one continued bone, with small lines marked on it, resembling the divisions of a row of teeth."[33] He was also rumored to have magical powers and could cure spleens by touching his right foot to the stomach of the afflicted person (his right big toe contained the magic).

Despite his personal disadvantages, Pyrrhus had made a smart marriage, to the stepdaughter of Ptolemy himself. He asked his father-in-law for help in getting his old kingdom of Epirus back again; Ptolemy was more than happy to attack Demetrius, who now had hold both of Greece and Macedonia. With Egyptian forces behind him, Pyrrhus took back Epirus. By 286, he had overrun the rest of Macedonia as well and driven Demetrius out.

Demetrius fled into Asia Minor and then, in an excess of hubris, decided to attack Seleucus in the east. He was likely an alcoholic and either suicidal or delusional by this time; Seleucus swatted him like a fly and put him under house arrest, where he drank himself to death.[34]

Pyrrhus's rule of Macedonia lasted for all of two years before Lysimachus came down from Thrace and drove him out. (Lysimachus, Plutarch says, "had nothing else to do.") Pyrrhus withdrew to Epirus, which Lysimachus—perhaps out of respect for Alexander's cousin—allowed him to keep.

The four kings had now become three: Ptolemy, Seleucus, Lysimachus. The satrapies had become three kingdoms: the Ptolemaic, the Seleucid, and the much smaller combined Thracian-Macedonian domain.

THE FOOTNOTE to the Wars of the Successors took place over in Italy. Rome, carrying on its dreary annual campaigns against its neighbors, was attacking the city of Tarentum, a Greek colony in the south. Tarentum sent messengers to Greece, asking for help; the call was answered by Pyrrhus, who was penned up in Epirus with no other chance of extending his power or winning any glory.

Pyrrhus left Epirus and sailed for Tarentum. Once there, he bought and borrowed war elephants (probably from Carthage) and mercenaries (largely Samnite) for the defense of the city. When the Romans attacked, Pyrrhus inflicted heavy losses on them; they had never seen elephants before. Then he drove them back to within forty miles of the city of Rome itself.

In the following year, 279, he tried to follow up on this with another pitched battle, this one fought at Asculum. He won this encounter too, but in such hard fighting that he lost as many men as the Romans. When another soldier congratulated him on the victory, he answered, "Another such victory will utterly undo me." "He had lost a great part of the forces he brought with him," Plutarch says, "and almost all his particular friends and principal commanders; there were no others there to make recruits. . . . On the other hand, as from a fountain continually flowing out of the city, the Roman camp was quickly and plentifully filled up with fresh men."[35] By 275, Pyrrhus had had enough campaigning against Rome. He left Tarentum to its own problems and went back to Greece.

Three years later, the Romans finally managed to conquer and sack Tarentum. In that same year, Pyrrhus—still looking for glory—was fighting in a nasty little Spartan civil war when an old woman threw a tile at him from a rooftop and knocked him unconscious. He was at once killed by his opponent, and his corpse was burned. Only the magical big toe survived.

TIMELINE 70

INDIA	GREECE	ROME
	Perdikkas II of Macedonia	Laws of the Twelve Tables
	Pericles of Athens	
	Peloponnesian War (begins 431)	
Mahapadma Nanda of Magadha		
	March of the Ten Thousand (401)	
	Corinthian War (395)	Rome burned by Gauls (390)
	Philip II of Macedonia (359–336)	
Dhana Nanda of Magadha		First Samnite War (343)
	Battle of Chaeronea (338)	Latin War (340)
	Alexander III of Macedonia (336)	
Chandragupta of Maurya		Second Samnite War (326)
	Philip Arrhidaeus/Alexander IV	
	Wars of the Successors	
	Battle of Ipsus (301)	Third Samnite War (298)
Ptolemy EGYPT	Seleucus SELEUCID EMPIRE Lysimachus THRACE-MACEDONIA	Battle of Asculum (279)

Chapter Seventy-One

The Mauryan Epiphany

In India, between 297 and 231 BC, the king pays more attention to dhamma *than to conquest, and his kingdom falls apart*

IN 297, CHANDRAGUPTA MAURYA abdicated his throne in favor of his son, the Mauryan prince Bindusara. Chandragupta had become a follower of Jainism; according to tradition, he then joined a group of monks and starved himself to death in an extreme demonstration of *aparigraha,* detachment from all material things.

Bindusara seems to have spent his own reign empire-building. The only records we have of his conquests come from Buddhist texts written several hundred years later. But one of them says that Bindusara conquered "the land between the two seas," which suggests that the Mauryan empire may have spread down south into the Deccan, as far as Karnataka.* Apart from this, little is known about Bindusara's twenty-five year rule except that the Greeks called him *Amitrochates,* "slayer of enemies," a name for a conqueror.[1]

The Mauryan empire was centered in the north. In the south lay different kingdoms: Kalinga in the southeast, Andhra in the center of the southern peninsula, Chera to the west and a little to the south; and at the very tip of the subcontinent, the land of the Pandyas.[2]

We know nothing of their history before about 500 BC. But we do know that while the language of Kalinga links its people to the more northern kingdoms (a Kalinga king, Srutaya, is credited in the Mahabharata with fighting on the side of the Kauravas), the more southern kingdoms speak a language that appears to have different roots.† No one knows where these southern peo-

* This would be the case if, as the scholar Romila Thapar suggests, the "two seas" are the Arabian Sea and the Bay of Bengal (*Asoka and the Decline of the Mauriyas*).

† The question of the relationship between the languages of the south, which were labelled "Dravid-

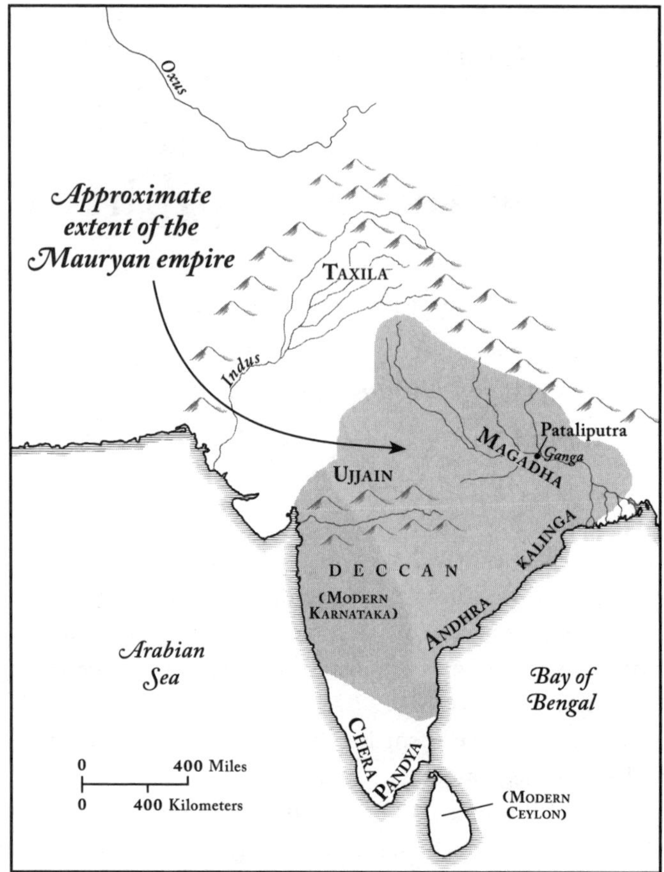

71.1 Mauryan India

ples originated, although their ancestry probably differs from that of the northern Indian rulers; possibly they were descended from intrepid sailors who made it across the Arabian Sea from Africa millennia earlier.

Kalinga resisted the spread of the Mauryan rule to the south. When Bindusara died, around 272 BC, Kalinga still remained unconquered. Bindusara's son Asoka was left the task of subduing it.

King Asoka is known to us mostly through the inscriptions which he ordered carved all around his empire, first on rocks (the Rock Edicts) and later on sandstone pillars (the Pillar Edicts). These Edicts give glimpses of Asoka's early life. His father sent him to Taxila, now part of the Mauryan empire, to

---

ian" by nineteenth-century linguists, and those of the north (the so-called Indo-Aryan languages), has been much muddied by politics, since later struggles for power in India were portrayed as a conflict between "natives" and "invaders." The relationship remains totally unclear.

put down a rebellion when he was a very young man. After this, he was sent to another part of the empire, called Ujjain, to govern one of the five *janapada,* or districts, into which the Mauryan empire had been divided.[3]

There he fell in love with a beautiful woman named Devi, the daughter of a merchant. He did not marry her, although he fathered two children by her; later, her son became a Buddhist missonary, which suggests that Devi also was a Buddhist.[4] But if she told Asoka about the principles of Buddhism, they made no dent in his consciousness. The early years of his reign showed no impulse towards peace.

When Bindusara died, Asoka had to fight his brothers for the throne, and after a four-year struggle he had done away with his competitors. We have no proof that he had them executed, but only one of the brothers is ever mentioned again.[5]

Asoka reigned alone for eight more years, carrying on his father's tradition of conquest. Then, in 260, he took an army down south to campaign against the resistant Kalinga.[6] The Edict which memorializes the battle gives a bleak picture of his cruelty to the people of Kalinga: "A hundred and fifty thousand people were deported," it reads, "a hundred thousand were killed, and many times that number perished."[7]

This horrific violence seems to have preyed on Asoka's mind until it brought about a conversion. "Afterwards," the Edict continues, "I felt remorse. The slaughter, death and deportation of the people is extremely grievous . . . and weighs heavy on the mind."[8]

From this point on, his reign shifts and grows oddly unpolitical. He seems to have spent his time, not in administration, but in the pursuit of *dhamma*: the Way, the Rightness, the Duty, the Virtue (it is a concept notoriously difficult to define). "I very earnestly practiced *dhamma,* desired *dhamma,* and taught *dhamma,*" the Kalinga Inscription says, and a little later in the same Edict, "Any sons or great-grandsons that I may have should not think of gaining new conquests . . . delight in *dhamma* should be their whole delight, for this is of value in both this world and the next."[9]

This was a bequest to a royal line like none ever seen in the west. The princes were not to follow on their father's conquests and do their best to outdo him in war; instead they were to refrain from war and choose heavenly delights instead. "As long as the sun and moon shall endure," Asoka's final Edict says, "[so] men may follow *dhamma.*"[10]

Asoka's greatest achievements after the conquest of Kalinga were religious, not political. Most lasting was his calling together of a Buddhist council to reassert the principles of *dhamma*; this Third Buddhist Council, held around 245 in the city of Pataliputra, gave birth to one of the books of the Pali Canon. At the council's end, Asoka's son Mahinda was sent to the large island off

India's southeast coast (modern Ceylon) as a missionary.[11] Other missionaries were sent out to Greece, under Asoka's sponsorship.

But Asoka's preoccupation with *dhamma* was not a total abandonment of his empire-building ambitions. He was making a genuine attempt to find a new unifying principle, other than force, that would hold the kingdom together.[12] It was the same problem Alexander had faced, in a slightly different setting. The clan system that had survived for so long in India, as a holdover from those very ancient nomadic days, was not one that lent itself easily to the establishment of empire; clan loyalties tended to pull the country apart into smaller political units, each negotiating friendship or hostility with those around it. The Mauryan conquest had temporarily united it by bloodshed, but Asoka had now turned away from that particular strategy. In place of the old clan loyalties, or loyalties enforced by conquest, Asoka tried for a third kind of loyalty: a common belief system that would make all Indians "my children" (as the Kalinga inscription puts it).[13]

And yet this too failed. After Asoka's death in 231, the Mauryan empire fell apart almost as quickly as Alexander's. The Edicts cease, no written records replace them, and a shadow falls over the next decades. Under cover of dark, Asoka's sons and grandsons lost hold of their kingdom and it separated again into smaller battling territories.

TIMELINE 71

GREECE			INDIA
			Dhana Nanda of Magadha
		Battle of Chaeronea (338)	
Alexander III of Macedonia (336)			
Philip Arrhidaeus/Alexander IV			**Chandragupta of Maurya**
		Wars of the Successors	
		Battle of Ipsus (301)	
			Bindusara of Maurya (297)
Ptolemy EGYPT	Seleucus SELEUCID EMPIRE	Lysimachus THRACE-MACEDONIA	
			Asoka of Maurya (272)
			Third Buddhist Council (245)

Chapter Seventy-Two

First Emperor, Second Dynasty

Between 286 and 202 BC,
the Ch'in extinguish the Zhou,
become the first rulers of unified China,
and are extinguished in turn

Back in China, where all the dukes had become kings by fiat (not unlike the satraps of Alexander's old empire), the time of the Warring States dragged on. After the rapid rise of the Ch'in state and Shang Yang's dismemberment at the hands of the new Ch'in king, the Ch'in army went on fighting. So did everyone else. Qi defeated Wei soundly, after which Wei diminished in power; Chu, which had finally absorbed Wu and Yueh for good, took Wei's place as one of the Big Three.[1] Now Ch'in, Qi, and Chu seemed certain to divide the rest of China among themselves.

For some years, none of them had a clear road to the very top. But the Ch'in army, conditioned by Shang Yang, was the most ruthless of the three. In 260, the Ch'in overran the new kingdom of Chao (one of the three states formed by the Jin breakup), which had shown unwelcome signs of ambition. On the wide plains of China, numbers could clash that would not fit into the mountainous passes of Greece or the Italian peninsula. Tens of thousands died in the battle between the two states. When the Chao army surrendered, the captives were massacred in huge numbers.[2]

Four years later, the Ch'in invaded the Zhou territory and put an end to centuries of sacred Zhou rule. "Ch'in exterminated Zhou," Sima Qian says, baldly, "and Zhou's sacrifices ceased."[3] It is a measure of the total lapse into irrelevance by the Zhou that no one really noticed. Like Alexander IV, the Zhou king had been merely a name for years.

In the invasion, a catastrophe took place. The Nine Tripods, removed by the Ch'in from their sacred site, were paraded in triumph along the river, but one of the tripods fell into the water and all attempts to get it back out again failed. Only eight tripods remained. The sign of the king's divinely bestowed power was marred, forever incomplete.[4]

IN 247, A NEW KING came to the Ch'in throne: the young Cheng. His father Chuang-hsiang had died before his time, after a two-year reign, and Cheng was only thirteen years old. His country was run for him by commanders, a chancellor, a magistrate, and various generals.

He was more fortunate in his guardians than other young kings had been. These officials took their task seriously; on Cheng's behalf, they beat off attacks from Ch'in's neighbors, including an attempt by a five-state coalition to wipe out Ch'in before Cheng could reach his majority.

At twenty-two, Cheng took full control of Ch'in.[5] He was planning the conquest not just of his neighbors, but of all China. By 232 he was raising an army larger than ever seen before; by 231, he was, as Sima Qian says, ordering "the ages of boys recorded" for the first time, which more than likely indicates a draft. And in 230, the other states of China began to fall, one by one. Han surrendered in 230; Chao, two years later. The crown prince of Yen, worried about the swelling size of Ch'in, sent an assassin, disguised as an ambassador, to Cheng's court, hoping to get rid of the western menace before it reached his borders. Cheng discovered the false ambassador's real purpose and had the man dismembered. The following year he marched into Yen, captured the crown prince, and beheaded him.

This ruthlessness would characterize the rest of Cheng's reign. It also led him to a peak of power which no other king of China had ever climbed. The states continued to fall to him: Wei in 225, Chu in 223, Qi, reluctantly, in 221. By the end of 221, a quarter-century after his father's death, Cheng was lord of the entire country. "Twenty-six years after Cheng, the King of Ch'in, was enthroned," writes Sima Qian, "he unified the world for the first time."[6]

Cheng was now more than a king; he was an emperor. He changed his name to Shi Huang-ti, "First Emperor." From this date we can actually speak of *China*, a country which draws its name from this first unification by the Ch'in.

This new country had never before been a single state, which mean that Shi Huang-ti had to create a single government, not from scratch (which would have been relatively easy), but instead from an unwieldy mass of existing customs and bureaucracies, laid at cross-purposes against each other.

Remodelling an old and crumbling house is a nightmare compared with the ease of laying out new foundations on a virgin site. It is a task that requires

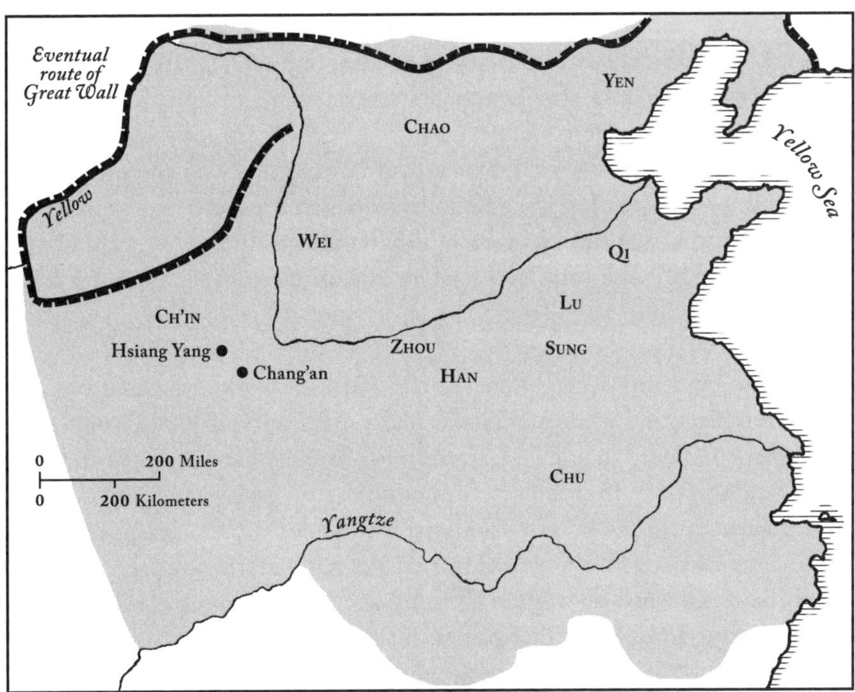

72.1 Ch'in China

relentless efficiency, which is exactly what Shi Huang-ti displayed. He broke down old lines of family influence, inherited wealth, and clan loyalties by dividing his empire into easily run sections: thirty-six *jun* (areas of command), with each jun divided into *xian* (roughly equivalent to the American system of states, divided into counties). A paired military commander and civilian administrator governed each jun, and a government inspector (which is to say, a spy) kept tabs on each pair.[7] No relatives of officials were handed plum positions; the First Emperor did not even give state jobs to his sons, in a return to the very old idea that hereditary kingship was bad for a country's health. In addition, he ordered the former noblemen of every state brought to the capital city and settled in new homes. Here they lived very comfortably—and very close to his watchful eye.[8]

Other reforms followed. He built roads out to every edge of China; he built canals for transportation and for irrigation; he restarted the calendar, so that everyone in his domain would follow the same system. "Exalting agriculture and suppressing the non-essential," reads a celebratory inscription, made two years into his emperorship, "he enriches the [people]. . . . With regard to implements, measurements have been unified, in writings, characters have been standardized. Wherever the sun and moon shine, wherever boat and cart can reach, people all live out their allotted span, and each is satisfied."[9] These reforms were more than efficient. They were messianic, the path to a newly happy life for Shi Huang-ti's subjects.

Like Shang Yang, the First Emperor had no patience with the precepts of Confucius, or with any kind of ambiguity. Efficient top-down rule, not metaphysical musing, was the key to a healthy country. And so he took Shang Yang's burning of books one step further. His prime minister announced his new regulations:

> Now the Emperor, having united and grasped the world, has discriminated between black and white and established a single authority. But [some subjects] are partial to their own learning and join together to criticize the laws and teachings. . . . In the court, they criticize it in their hearts, and outside, they debate it in the streets. To discredit the ruler is . . . a means of showing superiority. . . . If things like this are not banned, then the ruler's power will be diminished above and factions will form below. To ban them is appropriate. I would ask that you burn all the records in the Scribes' offices which are not Ch'in's. . . . Anyone who ventures to discuss songs and documents will be executed in the marketplace.[10]

The only books exempted from this sweeping decree were books of medicine, books of divination, and gardening handbooks.

This was a decision which didn't go over well with later generations ("The First Emperor got rid of the documents in order to make the people stupid," Sima Qian remarks tartly),[11] but made perfect sense for a man creating a new country out of a whole cluster of old ones. The states were filled with old records of how things had once been done; Shi Huang-ti intended to make a new China in which "there [could] be no rejection of the present by using the past." Alexander had fought, the Greeks had held festivals, Asoka had tried for a shared religious vision; Shi Huang-ti was doing his best to pull his own empire together into one by erasing the proofs that it had once been fatally divided. "In his twenty-eighth year," reads one of his own inscriptions, "the August Emperor makes a beginning."[12]

Perhaps this insistence on new beginnings gave birth to the tradition that Shi Huang-ti built the Great Wall of China. In fact, the Great Wall was not a brand-new barrier; the states of China had been building walls against the barbarians (and each other) for generations. Shi Huang-ti's innovation was in deciding that they should all be linked together, a project which he turned over to one of his officials, the general Meng T'ien.

Various western kings had built walls, at various times, against approaching invasions. But no one had ever tried to wall in an entire empire.[13] Shi Huang-ti's Great Wall was an earth-and-stone embodiment of his vision of China, a shared civilization held together by bonds stronger than mortar, all those within the Wall belonging to China, and those on the outside simply wandering and rootless barbarians.

But the embodiment cost scores of thousands of Chinese lives. The connecting walls were built with whatever materials lay at hand (stone in the mountains, packed earth in the plains, sand and pebbles in the desert); the builders were peasants, prisoners of war, soldiers, and farmers, all conscripted and sent to labor for the good of the state.[14]

Shi Huang-ti had left his mark on China's land itself during his life; he planned to make a similar mark in death. He built himself a final home, the likes of which had never been seen outside Egypt. Sima Qian gives a description of the tomb, which—according to his account—Shi Huang-ti, with an eye to his lasting fame, began to prepare just as soon as he took imperial power:

> After he had united the world, more than seven hundred convict laborers . . . were sent there. They dug through three springs, poured in liquid bronze, and secured the sarcophagus. . . . He ordered artisans to make crossbows triggered by mechanisms. Anyone passing before them would be shot immediately. They used mercury to create rivers . . . and the great seas, wherein the mercury was circulated mechanically. On the ceiling were celestial bodies and on the ground geographical features. The candles were made of oil of dugong, which was not supposed to burn out for a long time.[15]

Most startling of all, he filled his grave with life-size pottery soldiers and horses, almost seven thousand of them. They were armed with real bronze weapons, and sculpted from life; in the massive clay army, not a single face is alike.[16]

Like the first pharaohs of Egypt, the First Emperor was forced to pull together a scattered and separate country into one; like them, he had to impel obedience from a contentious kingdom. But the third millennium was long past. He could no longer express his power by compelling hundreds of courtiers to follow him to his grave. The pottery soldiers fill in instead: a perplexing substitution.

Shi Huang-ti went to this tomb in 210, after thirty-seven years as king of Ch'in and eleven as emperor of China. He was interred with care in his lavish grave; the tomb was covered over with earth, trees were planted above it so

72.1. First Emperor's Army. Life-size pottery soldiers, uncovered in the tomb of the First Emperor in 1974, in Xian, China. Photo credit Erich Lessing/Art Resource, NY

that its location would be obscured forever, and the architects who designed it were put to death so that its place would never be found.

His dynasty barely lasted past his death. The First Emperor's heir was his twenty-one-year-old son Hu-hai, the Second Emperor. The Second Emperor's crown sat uneasily on him; his father's empire had too recently been separate states to be fully subordinate yet to this central authority. "The great vassals have not submitted," he complained to his chancellor, "the officials are still mighty, and all the nobles will certainly contend with me."[17]

The chancellor suggested that the Second Emperor demonstrate his authority by force, eliminating all jun commanders and ex-nobles who seemed, in any way, to be reluctant to accept his authority. The Second Emperor took this advice with gusto, embarking on the slaughter of all he suspected of disloyalty. The purge, which ended with scores of deaths (and even included women, ten of whom were drawn and quartered in public), shocked the country. The Second Emperor, feeling more insecure than ever, drew up an army of fifty thousand crack soldiers and stationed them around the capital.

Only seven months later, the army stationed down in the former territory of Chu mutinied. The revolt spread from jun to jun, taken up by all those who had "suffered under Ch'in's officials," a number "too many to count." The Second Emperor's army could not hold off the rising rebellion. One by one, noble families reemerged from the anonymity of the Ch'in administration to reclaim rule: first a nobleman announcing himself to be king of Chao, then another of Wei, and then a third making himself king of Qi. The old states had begun to re-emerge from the smooth surface of China.

Civil war began, and raged on for the next three years. The Second Emperor grew more and more wild in his fury, until even the chancellor made excuses not to go to court out of fear that the emperor would kill him in a fit of temper. Instead, the chancellor pled sickness and retreated to his private home, from where he planned a palace coup that would be led by his own son-in-law; this coup would remove the Second Emperor and replace him with another royal prince, the Second Emperor's nephew.

The scene that followed suggests that the chancellor had in fact been counting on the unrest to help him with a takeover. In order to get his son-in-law, Yen Lo, to lead the invasion of the throne room, he had to kidnap Yen Lo's mother and hold her hostage. Meanwhile, he would stay carefully away, preserving his appearance of loyalty.

Yen Lo, caught in a bind, stormed the palace at the head of a shock troop and broke into the throne room, where he got the Second Emperor's attention by shooting an arrow into the draperies directly above his head. The Second Emperor, deserted by his palace bodyguard, demanded to see the chancellor; Yen Lo, properly instructed by his puppetmaster, refused. The Second Emperor then began to bargain. He offered to abdicate if he could be the commander of a jun; then he suggested a simple military command; then he offered to become a commoner in exchange for his life. Yen Lo refused and then, breaking his silence, told the Emperor that the chancellor had already decreed his death. His soldiers approached to carry out the sentence, but the Second Emperor killed himself before they could reach him.[18]

The chancellor then reappeared on the scene and carried out the enthroning of the Second Emperor's nephew, Tzu Ying; but the new emperor did not trust his kingmaker. Once crowned, he summoned the chancellor to his throne room and killed him with his own hands.*

Tzu Ying, the Third Emperor, held on to power for all of forty-six days before a Chu general, Hsiang Yu, arrived at the palace, at the head of a coalition force formed to wipe out the pretensions of the Ch'in. The troops overran the palace; Hsiang Yu killed Tzu Ying and massacred the court, burned the palace, and handed the royal treasures out to his allies. Three army officers claimed the Ch'in territory, dividing it up into three new kingdoms and declaring themselves king. "Ch'in," says Sima Qian, "was completely exterminated."

* The "Third Emperor" is not recognized as a genuine Chinese emperor by many ancient sources.

For five years, China returned to its old divided, battling, multi-kingdom ways. Then a new leader appeared, and fought his way to the head of the pack. His name was Liu Pang, and he had benefited from the Ch'in reforms in his own way: he was from a peasant family, and had become a minor official (a military policeman, in charge of a convict force), the sort of position which would not have been available to him in the old order.[19]

He had joined Hsiang Yu's army at the beginning of the rebellion. After the wholesale slaughter of the Ch'in court, Hsiang Yu himself claimed a territory in the old Chu and settled down to rule it. He awarded another, more distant territory in Han to Liu Pang, as a reward for his service. And as part of his strategy to assure his own power, Hsiang Yu had the man with the best claim to be the real Duke of Chu murdered.

This provided Liu Pang with his chance. He marched towards Hsiang Yu with an army of his own, announcing his righteous duty to punish the murderer of a king.[20] His initial attack on Hsiang Yu was unsuccessful, but he did manage to capture and claim rulership of a city called Hsiang Yang, on the Yellow river. From here, he fought an ongoing battle against other kingly claimants, rewarding his officers with captured land.

By 202 he had managed to fight his way into control of almost every one of the old kingdoms of China; and Hsiang Yu, who had remained his greatest (and now only) enemy, realized that his fight was in vain. He had grown increasingly unpopular thanks to his savagery; his butchery of the entire Ch'in court had not been forgotten, and he had won a reputation for leaving destruction and death behind him wherever he went. Cornered in a final battle, his supporters dwindling, he avoided capture and defeat by killing himself.

Liu Pang claimed the title of emperor, and gave himself the royal name Gao Zu. His dynasty, he decreed, would be named the Han, after that original territory given him by Hsiang Yu, and his capital would be at Chang'an.*[21] The Han Dynasty would be the first lasting dynasty of unified China; it would stand for four hundred years, built on the foundation that the Ch'in had laid during its brief and spectacular domination.

* This brings an end to the Ch'in Dynasty period (221–202) and begins the Han Dynasty period (202 BC–AD 220). Sources which do not recognize the legitimacy of the Third Emperor date these periods 221–206 and 206 BC–AD 220.

TIMELINE 72

INDIA	CHINA
Dhana Nanda of Magadha	**Huiwen of Ch'in**
Chandragupta of Maurya	
Bindusara of Maurya (297)	
Asoka of Maurya (272)	
	Fall of the Zhou (256)
Third Buddhist Council (245)	**Chuang-hsiang of Ch'in**
	Cheng of Ch'in
	Ch'in Dynasty (221)
	Cheng becomes *Shi Huang-ti*
	Second Emperor (209)
	Han Dynasty (202)
	Gao Zu

Chapter Seventy-Three

The Wars of the Sons

Between 285 and 202 BC,
Alexander's successors pass their kingdoms on,
and Hannibal takes his elephants across the Alps

OLD PTOLEMY, ALEXANDER'S ONE-TIME GENERAL and now king of Egypt, finally decided to retire at the age of eighty-two. In 285, he abdicated and handed his throne over to his younger son, Ptolemy II.* He spent his last years peacefully writing a history of Alexander's campaigns which put Ptolemy himself in the best possible light.†

The aftershocks were considerable. His older son, Ptolemy Ceraunus, promptly left the Egyptian court in a fit of pique. Later in that same year, he showed up in Thrace to visit his sister Arsinoe, who had been married off to Lysimachus.[1]

This particular match had been Lysimachus's insurance. He wanted to hang onto Thrace and Macedonia and his Asia Minor territories, despite Seleucus's increasingly huge presence over to his east, and making a marriage alliance with Ptolemy down south was a good way to assure that Seleucus would think twice about attacking him. The marriage was his second (Arsinoe was at least thirty years younger than her father's old army buddy), and his oldest son from his previous marriage, Agathocles, was his heir.

Ptolemy Ceraunus's troublemaking presence inspired Arsinoe, who wanted her own sons to inherit the kingdom instead. Together, the two of them

* The Ptolemies are distinguished both by surnames and by numbers; for the sake of simplicity I have used only the numbers. The surnames of the Ptolemies in this chapter are: Ptolemy I Soter; Ptolemy II Philadelphus; Ptolemy III Euergetes; Ptolemy IV Philopator; Ptolemy V Epiphanes. Ptolemy I's older son, Ptolemy Ceraunus, never got a number since he never ruled in Egypt, so I have retained his surname.

† This history was later lost, but one of my own sources, Arrian's *The Campaigns of Alexander*, is based on it; so Ptolemy's voice is still audible even in this book.

accused Agathocles of plotting with Seleucus to assassinate Lysimachus and take the Thracian-Macedonian throne away from him.

Lysimachus, elderly and paranoid, was an easy target. The year after Ptolemy Ceraunus arrived, he succumbed to his suspicions and tried to poison his son. When the poisoning failed, Lysimachus threw Agathocles into prison, where—in the dark, out of sight—he died.

Later historians believed that Ptolemy Ceraunus murdered him. Certainly the troublemaker was still active; he showed up not much later in Seleucus's court, asking Seleucus to join with him against the evil son-poisoning Lysimachus.[2] Seleucus, who by this time was turning eighty to Lysimachus's seventy-one, rounded up his forces and marched towards Lysimachus's domains.

Lysimachus came out to meet him and crossed the Hellespont to fight on Asia Minor's ground. In the battle, the two old men—who had known each other for forty years, ever since their days together in Alexander's officer corps—met hand-to-hand. Seleucus struck the final blow; Lysimachus died on the battlefield, and his body lay there for some days before his younger son arrived to take the battered corpse back home.

Seleucus got ready to march across the Hellespont and claim Macedonia. But before he could get very far, Ptolemy Ceraunus, still in his camp, still pretending alliance, turned on him and assassinated him. He had personally wiped out two-thirds of the remaining successors of Alexander.

Ptolemy Ceraunus promptly claimed the Macedonian-Thracian throne for himself and married his sister Arsinoe. This was an Egyptian custom, not a Greek one, and did not make him terribly popular in his new country. Neither did his next action, which was to kill two of Arsinoe's sons as threats to his rule. She left him and went down to Egypt to her *other* brother, Ptolemy II—and married him too. This earned him the Greek nickname "Ptolemy Philadelphus," or "Brotherly Love," which was not a compliment.

Meanwhile, old Ptolemy had died peacefully in his bed, almost the only successor of Alexander to do so.

Ptolemy Ceraunus kept his bloody throne for two years. In 279, the Celtic movement that had troubled the Italian peninsula reached Asia Minor. Gauls flooded down into Macedonia; Ptolmey Ceraunus went out to fight them and died in battle, ending his career as the most underappreciated villain of ancient times.* His throne ended up in the hands of Antigonus the One-Eyed's grandson, Antigonus II.[3]

Seleucus's son Antiochus I took control of his father's kingdom. Antiochus

* The exact date of Ptolemy Ceraunus's death is unknown.

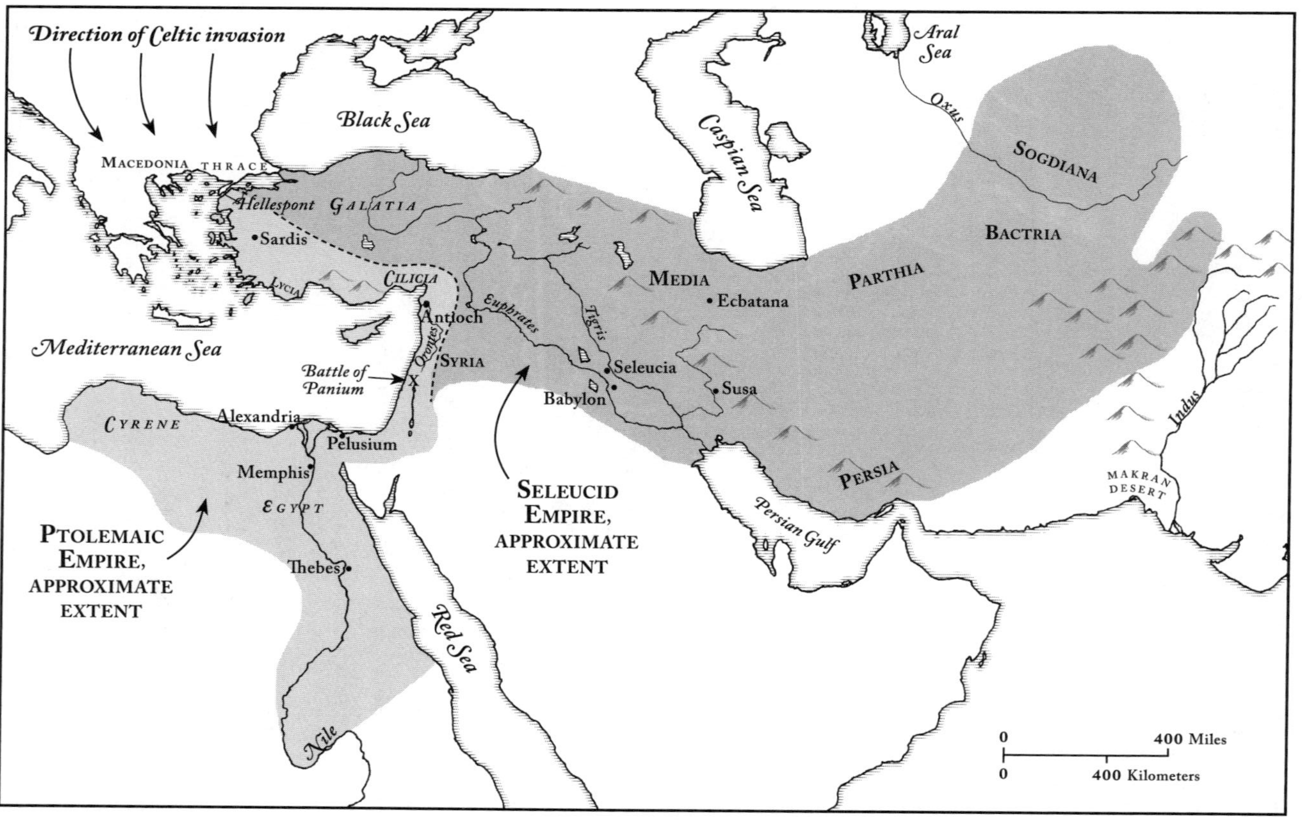

73.1 The World of the Seleucids

was half Persian (as a young man in Alexander's camp, Seleucus had been married to a Persian noblewoman in that mass wedding ceremony), and the empire he now headed had borrowed its basic structures from the Persians. Provinces were governed by satraps, and the empire was run from several royal capitals, each positioned to overlook a different part of the empire. The Persians had used Susa, Ecbatana, Sardis, and Babylon; Seleucus had kept the use of Sardis and Babylon, but had built himself two new cities to serve as adjunct headquarters. The city of Antioch lay on the Orontes river, in land which the Ptolemaic kings had once claimed. His largest and most favored city, though, was Seleucia, which he built on the western bank of the Tigris and linked with the Euphrates by a canal.

The year after Ptolemy Ceraunus's death, the Gauls crossed the Hellespont and threatened to breach the border of the Seleucid empire. Antiochus I fought them off, earning himself the nickname "Antiochus the Savior." The Gauls, retreating, settled in Asia Minor, where they eventually became known as "Galatians."

A DECADE LATER, Roman soldiers pushed off from the shores of the Italian peninsula, headed for Sicily. This was a historical moment, Polybius tells us. It was "the first occasion on which the Romans crossed the sea from Italy," and Sicily was "the first country beyond the shores of Italy on which they set foot."[4] Rome had entered into the next phase of its history; the Romans were getting ready to embark on their first overseas conquest.*

Like most fledgling empire-builders, the Romans had an excuse for this invasion. Sicily was still divided between the control of Syracuse and Carthage, and the Sicilian harbor city of Messina, originally a Greek colony, had fallen under Syracuse's power. But a band of renegade Italian mercenaries from Campania had sailed to Sicily and taken control of the city. The Messinians sent to both Carthage and Rome, asking for help in driving out the invaders.

Since Rome and Carthage were technically at peace, this was not all that unreasonable. But it lit the match under a long-building bonfire. The Carthaginians got there first and discovered that the tyrant of Syracuse, Hiero II (Agathocles had died some twenty years earlier), was already on the job; he had not appreciated Messina's turning to other powers for help, when the city

* Roman history is generally divided into the Kingdom (753–509), the Republic (509–31), and the Empire (31 BC–AD 476). The Republic is often subdivided into Early Republic (509–264), Middle Republic (264–133), and Late Republic (133–31). There is a fair amount of variation between scholars as to the exact years that these periods begin and end.

was supposed to be his. Rather than start a three-way war, the Carthaginians joined with Hiero II and occupied Messina, driving out the previous invaders.

The Romans, arriving second, refused to give up the project of besieging Messina and simply attacked the Carthaginian occupying forces instead. Afterwards, the Roman invaders spread out across the island, claiming Carthaginian-controlled land and laying siege to Syracuse as well.[5]

The Carthaginians reacted by crucifying (literally) the commander who had been in charge of the Messina garrison and settling in for a fight. They could see quite clearly that this overseas venture was Rome's first tentative prod at the land outside Italy's borders. For the next twenty-three years, the two powers would slog on through the First Punic War (264–241).

"Because they saw that the war was dragging on," Polybius writes, "[the Romans] first applied themselves to building ships. . . . They faced great difficulties because their shipwrights were completely inexperienced."[6] This was the second *first* of the First Punic War. To get over to Sicily, the Roman consuls had borrowed ships from Rome's allies and subject cities (a force called the *socii navales*).[7] But it soon became clear that Rome could not simply rely on the navies of other cities. When a Carthaginian warship ran aground on Roman shores, the shipbuilders took it apart and modelled their own ships on it; meanwhile, crews were practicing rowing on dry land. And with the ships finished, the new Roman fleet put to sea and was promptly captured by a Carthaginian commander.[8]

The Romans rebuilt and refitted and set to sea again. Two years later, Polybius says, the two navies were "equally matched." The Romans gleaned the best part of their strategy, their law, their government, and even their mythology from other cultures, but they were fast learners.

By 247, after seventeen years of almost constant fighting, the Romans had gained a little bit of advantage. Roman troops had landed in North Africa and established camps, although to attack Carthage itself was far beyond their capabilities; and Sicily was almost entirely in Roman hands. The leaders of Carthage removed their commanding general for incompetence and gave control of the army to a new officer, a man in his mid-twenties named Hamilcar Barca.

Hamilcar had under his command a mixed force of Carthaginians and mercenaries, about ten thousand in all, as well as seventy elephants. He captured himself a base in Sicily from which he harassed the Italian coast, and won himself several hard-fought victories; enough so that he was able to rescue the Carthaginians "from the state of absolute despair into which they had fallen."[9]

But by 242, the war—by now in its twenty-second year—had driven both nations to a state of exasperation. "They were worn out with the strain of an unbroken succession of hard-fought campaigns," Polybius says, "their resources . . . drained by taxes and military expenses which continued year after year."[10] Hamilcar's band of mercenaries and Carthaginians on Sicily had been fighting for over three years without losing—but without taking the island either. The Romans were unable to make any headway against the Carthaginian land forces, but the Roman navy made it harder and harder for Carthaginian supply ships to reach Hamilcar's soldiers on Sicily.

The Carthaginians were the first to call a halt. In 241, the home city sent Hamilcar a message: they did not want to abandon him, but it was now impossible to continue sending food and weapons. He had the power to handle the situation however he pleased. This powerless authority left Hamilcar with no option but surrender. He came down with his troops from their base, halfway up Mount Eryx, in "grief and rage,"[11] and under protest submitted to a treaty which required Carthage to give up all of Sicily, to release all prisoners, and to pay a sizable fine over the next ten years.[12]

The war was over. The Senate ordered the doors to the Temple of Janus shut, to symbolize peace everywhere in the lands that belonged to Rome. Sicily was now one of those lands; it had become Rome's first foreign province.

This peace had in it the seeds of a more terrible conflict.

BACK TO THE EAST, other battles dragged on. Ptolemy II of Egypt (now married to his sister) and Antiochus I (son of Seleucus) bickered about the Syrian border between their territories, and handed their quarrels on to their sons, but apart from this, the succession passed to the next generation without much change. Ptolemy II died in 246 and was succeeded by his son Ptolemy III; Antiochus I (following old Persian tradition) put his oldest son to death for treachery and left his throne to his second son, Antiochus II, instead.* Over in Macedonia, Antigonus II, grandson of the One-Eyed, died in his eighties after almost fifty years as king and was followed by his own son as well.

Down in Egypt, Ptolemy III had a prosperous twenty-two-year rule. Antiochus II did not fare nearly as well. Six years after he took over the Seleucid empire, he lost the satrapy of Bactria; it rebelled, under its Greek governor Diodotus, and declared itself to be an independent kingdom with Diodotus as king. Bactria was distant from any of Antiochus II's capital cities, over rough country, and the king was unable to reconquer it. Not long afterwards, a native Parthian nobleman named Arsaces declared his own homeland of

* There were thirteen Seleucid kings named Antiochus. The surnames of the first five were Antiochus I Soter ("Savior," possibly because he drove off the Gauls), Antiochus II Theos, Antiochus III the Great, Antiochus IV Epiphanes, and Antiochus V Eupater.

Parthia free as well. Antiochus II was preoccupied with his western border; he was fighting a war with Egypt over control of those old Western Semitic lands, including the old Phoenician, Israelite, and Judean territories, and he could not hold onto two borders of his huge empire at the same time.*

He finally managed to make a temporary peace with Ptolemy III, and the two kings sealed the bargain with a royal marriage; Ptolemy III's daughter went north and married Antiochus II as his second wife. The bargain didn't get Parthia and Bactria back, though, and Antiochus II's indignant first wife poisoned him, so the peace was a failure all around.

He was succeeded by his son (by his first wife) Seleucus II, who failed to retake the two rebellious satrapies and then died from falling off his horse. Seleucus II's oldest son only managed to rule for three years before his own commanders assassinated him; the throne then went to the younger son, Antiochus III.

He was only fifteen when he became king of the Seleucids in 223. With a boy on the throne, both Media and the old Persian heartland joined Bactria and Parthia in rebellion. But Antiochus III was made of stronger stuff than the three kings before him. He went on campaign and ticked off conquests one by one: the edges of his domain in Asia Minor which had started to flake away; Media and Persia, both forced to surrender to Antiochus when he personally led his army against them at the age of eighteen; eventually, Bactria and Parthia as well. These last two territories he did not try to reabsorb. He made a peace with both the Bactrian and the Parthian kings, which secured his eastern border and allowed him to pay a little more attention to the west.†

This was a good plan, as Egypt's hold on its own border was loosening. In 222, Ptolemy III had been succeeded by his son Ptolemy IV, who was universally disliked by all of his biographers. "He was a loose, voluptuous, and effeminate prince," Plutarch remarks, ". . . besotted with his women and his wine."[13] "He conducted his reign as if it were a perpetual festival," Polybius says with disapproval, "neglected the business of state, made himself difficult to approach, and treated with contempt or indifference those who handled his country's interests abroad."[14] As soon as his father died, he poisoned his mother so that she wouldn't plot against him, and followed this up by having his younger brother Magus scalded to death, since Magus was alarmingly popular with the army.[15]

* The ongoing trouble over the border is mentioned repeatedly in the biblical book of Daniel, which says that the "King of the North" and the "King of the South" will march against each other again and again with larger and larger armies (Dan. 11.2–29).

† At the time of Antiochus III's invasion, Parthia was ruled by Arsaces II, son of the original Parthian rebel king; Bactria had been taken away from Diodotus's heirs by a usurper named Euthydemus.

Ptolemy IV's affairs were mostly run by his mistress, her brother Agathocles ("that pimp," Plutarch calls him), and one of his advisors, a Greek named Sosibius who seems to have made the decisions for him while he gave his attention to "senseless and continuous drinking."[16] Ptolemy IV died in 204 (probably of liver failure), leaving his throne to his five-year-old son Ptolemy V. Sosibius and "that pimp" apparently then forged documents making them regents for the child.

Sosibius died months later, leaving Agathocles, his sister, and their mother at the top of the Egyptian power heap. Not for long; the trio had made themselves so unpopular that a mob, led by the army, stormed the palace, dragged them out into the street, stripped them naked, and tore them to pieces in a frenzy: "Some [of the mob] began to tear them with their teeth," Polybius says, "others to stab them, others to gouge out their eyes. As soon as any of them fell, the body was torn limb from limb until they had dismembered them all, for the savagery of the Egyptians is truly appalling when their passions have been roused."[17]

Young Ptolemy V was enthroned in Memphis with a proper Egyptian council of advisors, but when he was twelve, Antiochus III marched against the northern Egyptian border. Josephus records that Antiochus, whom he calls king "of all Asia," "seized on Judea."[18] The invasion ended in 198 at the Battle of Panium, when the Seleucid and Egyptian armies clashed near the head of the Jordan river. When the fighting was over, Egypt had lost hold of its Western Semitic territories for the last time. It would never again reach into those northern lands. Ptolemy IV's reign is described by almost every ancient historian as the end of Egypt's greatness. The ancient country's renaissance under its Greek rulers was over.

FARTHER WEST, Hamilcar Barca was still smarting under the Roman-imposed terms of peace. Carthage's greatness had been blocked; the Carthaginians had lost the Mediterranean islands which had formed their empire, and the Romans were planted firmly on them instead.

Hamilcar decided to make up for the loss by moving the Carthaginian empire a little farther west. He would take a force of soldiers and settlers to Iberia—modern Spain—and plant another Carthaginian colony to replace the losses at Sicily. This Iberian colony would be a new center of Carthaginian might—and it would also serve as an excellent base from which to launch retaliatory strikes against Rome. His humiliation at Sicily had turned into a loathing which he did his best to pass on to his young son Hannibal, as Polybius records:

> At the time when his father was about to set off with his army on his expedition to Spain, Hannibal, who was then about nine years old, was standing by the altar where his father was sacrificing. . . . Then [Hamilcar] called Hannibal to him and asked him affectionately whether he wished to accompany the expedition. Hannibal was overjoyed to accept and, like a boy, begged to be allowed to go. His father then took him by the hand, led him up to the altar and commanded him to lay his hand upon the [animal] victim and swear that he would never become a friend to the Romans.[19]

The oath of eternal hatred sworn, Hamilcar, with son and settlers, set sail.

The Carthaginian expedition reached the Iberian peninsula in 236 and set about conquering itself a new little kingdom. From his center of operations, Gadir (modern Cadiz), Hamilcar succeeded in setting up his new colony. It was here that Hannibal grew up, watching his father wheedle and browbeat the surrounding peoples into submission: "[Hamilcar] spent nearly nine years in the country," Polybius tells us, "during which time he brought many tribes under Carthaginian sway, some by force of arms and some by diplomacy."[20] He also sent spies across the Alps into the north of the Italian peninsula, to scout out a possible invasion route.[21] Hannibal grew to adulthood without ever setting foot in his home city of Carthage.

Meanwhile, the Romans sailed for the first time to Greece, where they had been invited to protect the island of Corcyra from the double threat of invasion by other hostile Greeks and the ongoing attacks of the northern Gauls. When the intervention was over, a Roman garrison remained, theoretically as a peacekeeping force; Rome was not yet ready to attack its Greek neighbors.

In that same year, 229, Hamilcar Barca died in battle while besieging a Celtic stronghold. Hannibal, now eighteen, was not considered quite old enough to take command. The governance of the Iberian colony went instead to his older brother-in-law, who does not seem to have shared the family loathing for Rome; he spent the next eight years governing the Iberian colony (and founding a city called, grandly, New Carthage) and ignoring the Romans to his east. Perhaps he might have built a new and lasting kingdom in the Iberian peninsula, but one of his slaves killed him in 221, and leadership of the Spanish forces fell to the twenty-six-year-old Hannibal.

Hannibal turned his back on New Carthage and immediately began to prepare for an overland invasion of Roman territory. He started to fight his way along the coast in order to clear a safe passage towards the Alps. When he drew near to Massalia, the city (which had been on good terms with Rome ever since helping the Romans buy off those invading Gauls) appealed to Rome for help.

The Romans sent a message to Carthage, warning that if Hannibal pro-

73.2 The World of the Punic Wars

gressed past the town of Saguntum, they would consider this an act of war. Hannibal promptly besieged and sacked the town, upon which Roman ambassadors travelled to Carthage itself to present the final ultimatum to the Carthaginian senate: Surrender Hannibal, or face a second Punic War.[22] The Carthaginians objected that Saguntum, which was a Celtic settlement, wasn't an ally of Rome; the ambassadors countered that Saguntum had once appealed to Rome for help, many years before, so Rome could now claim that the town was under Roman protection.

The bottom line was that both cities were determined to go to war. "On the Roman side there was rage at the unprovoked attack by a previously beaten enemy," Livy says, "[and] on the Carthaginian, bitter resentment at what was felt to be the grasping and tyrannical attitude of their conquerors."[23] When the senior Roman ambassador shouted that he carried both peace and war in the folds of his garment, and would let war fall from it if they weren't careful, the Carthaginian senators shouted back, "We accept it!"[24]

And so Hannibal headed for the Alps in 218. He left his brother Hanno in charge of the Iberian colony, and took with him an army that ultimately numbered over a hundred thousand foot soldiers, perhaps twenty thousand cavalry, and thirty-seven elephants.*

In response the Romans dispatched two fleets, one heading for the North African coast and the other, under the command of the consul Publius Cornelius Scipio, bound for the Iberian peninsula. Cornelius Scipio anchored at the mouth of the Rhône, intending to intercept Hannibal and his army before they could cross it, but Hannibal's army had moved so much faster than expected that Cornelius Scipio arrived at their crossing place three days too late. Hannibal was on his way towards the mountains.[25]

His men were a bigger problem than the Roman pursuit. They were mostly African-raised, and the Spanish coast was the coldest land they had known; they were terrified by the thought of ascending the steep unknown slopes, and their first sight of the Alps was no help. "The towering peaks," Livy says, "the snow-clad pinnacles soaring to the sky, the rude huts clinging to the rocks, beasts and cattle shrivelled and parched with cold, the people with their wild and ragged hair, all nature, animate and inanimate, stiff with frost: all this, and other sights the horror of which words cannot express, gave a fresh edge to their apprehension."[26] And they were constantly threatened by wild local tribes; in the first such attack, the Carthaginian horses panicked on a narrow mountain trail, and both soldiers and horses slipped and were thrown over the trail's edge, to break on the rocks thousands of feet below. As they marched

* This is an estimate; sources differ widely on the size of Hannibal's army when he arrived in Italy.

higher, glassy ice beneath a layer of snow sent more men and animals sliding to their death.

The crossing, Livy tells us, took fifteen days, and Hannibal himself reckoned that he lost a staggering thirty-six thousand men, as well as thirty-four of the elephants. He came down on the plain near the Po river with a demoralized and shrunken army, to face Cornelius Scipio, who had sailed as quickly as possible back to Italy with part of his own force in order to face him. News of the successful crossing soon reached Rome as well, and the Senate immediately recalled the invasion force in North Africa in order to strengthen the defense of the homeland.

Cornelius Scipio and Hannibal met at the Ticinus river in November of 218. Weary as they were, the Carthaginian cavalry broke through the Roman line almost at once. The Romans scattered; Scipio himself was badly wounded. "This showed," Livy says, "that . . . the Carthaginians had the advantage."[27]

Cornelius Scipio's forces retreated in order to meet up with the troops from North Africa, which had arrived back in Rome to great and dangerous acclaim; Rome was suffering from a perilous disconnect between public perception and reality. "The people's confidence in the ultimate success of Roman arms remained unaffected," Polybius writes. "Thus, when Longus [the commander of the North African contingent] and his legions reached Rome and marched through the city, the people still believed that these troops had only to appear on the field to decide the battle."[28] This was far from the truth. When the armies met again, a month later, at the Trebbia river, a full third of the Roman troops fell.

The news that the combined forces of two consuls had been defeated made its way back to Rome and caused a panic: "People fancied that at any moment Hannibal would be at the city gates," Livy writes.[29] Rome went on full alert, staffing the islands with garrisons, calling on the allies for reinforcements, outfitting a new fleet of ships. By 217, Hannibal was moving steadily south, devastating the countryside, marching through Etruria towards Rome itself. The consul Gaius Flaminus and a reinforced Roman army met the Carthaginians at Lake Trasimene, in an absolutely catastrophic engagement fought in thick fog. Fifteen thousand Romans died, and Flaminus himself was crushed in the press; his body was never found. Once again, news of the disaster swept down to Rome. "People thronged into the forum," Livy says, "women roamed the streets asking whom they met the meaning of the dreadful tidings which had so suddenly come. . . . No one knew what to hope for or what to dread. During the next few days the crowd at the city gates was composed of more women than men, waiting and hoping for the sight of some loved face, or at least for news."[30]

There was no good news. Hannibal's army seemed unstoppable. He continued to push south, temporarily bypassing Rome itself only in order to bring the lands below the city onto his side. "All the while the Romans followed the Carthaginian rearguard," Polybius writes, "keeping one or two days' march behind them but taking care never to approach any closer and engage the enemy."[31]

The following year, the two newly elected consuls Paullus and Varro joined together in an attempt to face Hannibal down. The Romans managed to field an army of over a hundred thousand, to meet a Carthaginian force of less than fifty thousand. On August 2, 216, the armies met at Cannae, on the southeastern coast.

Thanks to their huge numbers, the Romans seem to have counted on sheer weight to crush the invaders, arranging themselves in a solid mass of men that would storm forwards with unstoppable force. In response to this, Hannibal arranged a thin front line to meet the Roman attack, one that seemed entirely unequal to the task of holding them back. But on his far left and right, back behind him, he placed his strongest and fiercest men, hired mercenaries from Africa, in two groups. He himself took his place in the front line. Unless he put himself in the same danger as those troops, he could not expect them to carry out the difficult task he had in mind.

When the Romans advanced, the thin front line fought ferociously but retreated, slowly, as the Romans stormed forwards, drawing the Roman troops with them into a V. And then the mercenary troops on either side charged up either side of the V and attacked. The Roman force was neither prepared nor disciplined to fight on three sides at once. In the chaos that followed, fifty thousand Romans fell. Out of six thousand cavalry, seventy escaped and fled to the city of Venusia, led by Varro, who was disgraced both by the defeat and the flight.

When reports of the Battle of Cannae came back to Rome, almost every family in Rome found that they had lost a brother, or father, or son. "After this defeat," says Polybius, "the Romans gave up all hope of maintaining their supremacy over the Italians, and began to fear for their native soil, and indeed for their very existence."[32]

The situation only got worse when Carthaginian ships sailed for Greece and offered the king of Macedonia, now Philip V (great-great-grandson of Antigonus the One-Eyed), support to drive out the Roman "peacekeepers" on the Greek peninsula. Philip V accepted, and the Macedonians and Carthaginians together fought against the Roman occupiers and their Greek allies, which included both Sparta and the cities of the "Aetolian League" (an alliance of cities in the center of the peninsula, south of Macedonia and north of the Gulf of Corinth). Now this First Macedonian War overlapped with the Second Punic War, and the Romans were dealing with a two-front disaster.

As in the First Punic War, fighting in the Second dragged on and on.* In 211, the Romans managed to recapture part of Sicily by triumphing over Syracuse after a two-year siege; the Greek mathematician Archimedes, who was inside, died in the sack of the city. They were less successful in the Iberian peninsula. Roman forces led by two members of the Scipio family, the brothers Publius and Gnaeus, invaded and met Hannibal's brother Hasdrubal, who was still holding the fort for Hannibal back at home. Both Scipios died in the fighting that followed, although Hasdrubal was unable to push the Roman invaders entirely off his land.

This gave one Roman officer—Publius's son, known to later generations simply as Scipio—the personal hatred for Carthage which Hannibal had long felt for Rome. In 209, Scipio marched to New Carthage to avenge his father. His siege of the city was successful; Hasdrubal fled and followed his brother's route over to the Alps and across them.

This was not entirely a bad thing for the Carthaginians, since Hasdrubal brought with him not only his own forces, but eight thousand conscripted Celts, and had picked up yet more men on his journey from New Carthage to the Alps. He sent a letter to Hannibal, arranging to meet him and combine forces in Umbria.

The letter was intercepted by Roman officers, and was read. At once the nearest Roman forces turned to mount a surprise attack on Hasdrubal before he could get down to Umbria. Hasdrubal's allies did not acquit themselves well ("Gauls always lack stamina," Livy remarks).[33] Over fifty thousand of Hasdrubal's men fell, and Hasdrubal himself, seeing that he was doomed, galloped straight into the Romans massed ahead of him and died fighting. The Romans cut off his head, carefully preserved it, and took it with them; when they reached Hannibal's own outposts, they threw the head over into Hannibal's camp.[34]

Hannibal had lost both his brother and the Iberian colony, which had become a Roman province. The balance had begun, slowly, to tip towards Rome; and the Romans put a thumb on the scale by closing their second front in Macedonia in order to concentrate on Carthage. In 207, the same year of Hasdrubal's death, Roman soldiers began to withdraw from the fruitless fighting on the Greek peninsula. Both the Greek cities and Philip V himself were,

* Books XXI–XXX of Livy's *The History of Rome from Its Foundation* (the Aubrey de Selincourt translation is published separately by Penguin Books as *The War with Hannibal*) provides a detailed, year-by-year account of all major battles in the Second Punic War.

in Livy's phrase, "sick of the long and tedious war," and the Romans themselves could see that their troops were needed closer to home. Scipio had suggested that the new battleground should be North Africa; the Romans should go on the offensive and sail directly for Carthage, a strategy which might well pull Hannibal away from the Italian countryside.

In 205, Philip V signed an agreement with the Greek cities to his south, the Peace of Phoenice. It gave the Romans control of a few smaller cities, turned over other territories to Macedonia, and halted all hostilities between Macedonia and the Aetolian League. With all soldiers now free for a North African attack, Scipio put together an invasion force. In 204, he landed on the North African coast with a combined army of Romans and North African mercenaries.

His invasion had exactly the hoped-for effect: the Carthaginians sent a frantic message for help to Hannibal. And Hannibal came home. He was acting from patriotism, but it was a vague and reluctant patriotism; he had not been in the country of his birth since the age of nine, and he left most of his men in Italy, perhaps hoping to return soon. He had not yet fully carried out his father's wishes; Rome still stood. "Seldom has any exile left his native land with so heavy a heart as Hannibal's when he left the country of his enemies," Livy says. "Again and again he looked back at the shores of Italy . . . calling down curses on his own head for not having led his armies straight to Rome."[35]

Once at Carthage, he recruited himself an army of reluctant Carthaginians and African mercenaries to join the few veterans he had brought back with him. Then, in 202, Hannibal and Scipio met for peace talks at Zama, just south of Fair Promontory. Perhaps the peace talks were genuine, but Scipio had sent for reinforcements, and was waiting for them to arrive. The defeat of Cannae, fourteen years ago, was still fresh in Roman memory; the young sons of the dead were now in their twenties, battle ready and furious.

The Roman reinforcements arrived; the peace talks, inevitably, failed; and the Romans and Carthaginians joined in battle for the final time. Scipio had planned well. On the open country of Italy, always playing the aggressor, Hannibal had been unbeatable. But now the conditions under which he fought best had been reversed. He was fighting a defensive war in unfamiliar rocky land, with an army "composed of men who shared neither language, customs, laws, weapons, dress, appearance, nor even a common reason for serving."[36] They fought mostly for cash, and for a share of the plunder; and when Scipio's army thundered down on them, far too many of them broke line and retreated out of fear.

The Battle of Zama ended with Scipio in total control of the field; Hannibal had been forced, finally, to seek refuge in Carthage. Here he told the senate that he could not lead them to victory. Peace with Rome was the only option. The Carthaginian senate agreed, and Carthage surrendered itself to Scipio. For his triumph, Scipio earned himself the title Scipio Africanus from his countrymen. Carthage was forced to give up its fleet, bringing an end to its ambitions to spread across the west; five hundred of the ships were towed away from the shore, under Roman orders, and set ablaze, where they all burned to the waterline and then sank.[37] The Second Punic War had ended.

Hannibal, who had given up his Roman ambitions to defend a city he barely remembered, remained in Carthage, joining the senate in an attempt to help the Carthaginians rebuild their savaged world. For this, he got very little gratitude. Six years or so after the Battle of Zama, Hannibal got wind of a plot. His own countrymen were planning to turn him over to the Romans as a gesture of goodwill.

At once he took a ship and fled from Carthage. He had been back in his homeland for barely seven years. He would never return to it again.

TIMELINE 73

ROME	CHINA	SUCCESSORS OF ALEXANDER		
		Ptolemy EGYPT	Seleucus SELEUCID EMPIRE	Lysimachus THRACE-MACEDONIA
Battle of Asculum (279)		**Ptolemy II** (287)		
First Punic War (264)			**Antiochus I**	**Ptolemy Ceranaus**
	Fall of the Zhou (256)		**Antiochus II**	**Antigonus II**
	Chuang-hsiang of Ch'in	**Ptolemy III** (246)		
	Cheng of Ch'in		**Seleucus II**	**Demetrius II**
			Antiochus the Great	
	Ch'in Dynasty (221)	**Ptolemy IV** (222)		**Philip V**
Second Punic War (218) Battle of Cannae	**Shi Huang-ti** (formerly Cheng)			
	Second Emperor (209)			
Battle of Zama (202)	Han Dynasty (202)	**Ptolemy V** (204)		Peace of Phoenice
	Gao Zu		Battle of Panium (198)	

Chapter Seventy-Four

Roman Liberators and Seleucid Conquerors

Between 200 and 168 BC,
the Romans and Seleucids clash,
Greek Bactria stretches down into India,
and Latin becomes an official language

AT THE AGE OF FIFTY, Antiochus III was now in his thirty-second year of rule over the Seleucid empire. He had pushed the Seleucid border down through the old Egyptian holdings, and had forced both Parthia and Bactria to a peace, accomplishments that later earned him the title Antiochus the Great. Now he decided to embark on a new campaign: to go west and capture some more of Asia Minor, perhaps even crossing the Hellespont and taking Thrace as well.

He knew that if he didn't make some move to the west, he was likely to find Romans breathing down his neck. Buoyed by their victory over the Carthaginians, Roman troops were now looking back to the east. The largest power left in the world was the Seleucid empire, and with Hannibal conquered, Antiochus III was Rome's new enemy.

The king who was about to get pinched between these two powers was Philip V of Macedonia, who had managed to emerge from the First Macedonian War in pretty good shape. There were still Roman peacekeepers down in Greece, but Macedonia had increased its holdings in the Peace of Phoenice. And while the Romans were preoccupied with Carthage, Philip V had made a secret treaty with Antiochus III to divide up Egyptian territories which had once belonged to the Ptolemies.

The Romans were quite sure that Philip V was still planning to invade Greece, and they did not want the peninsula under the control of a pro-Seleucid king; Greece needed to remain a buffer between Rome and the power of Antiochus III. In 200, almost before peace with Carthage had been concluded, Roman troops marched on Philip V.

The Aetolian League once again jumped onto Rome's side, as did Athens, and this Second Macedonian War was brought to a speedy close by 197. In the final battle, fought at Cynoscephalae, Philip's soldiers were so thoroughly beaten that the king of Macedonia was afraid he might lose his throne itself.[1] But the Romans, who did not want to spend the next decades fighting to hang on to the Greek cities, proposed a peace that would allow Philip V to stay in Macedonia. Philip was to give up all thought of conquering Greek cities, surrender all of his warships, pay a fine, and withdraw all of his soldiers from Greek territory. The Roman consul Flaminus, who was in charge of the Roman forces in Macedonia, was given permission to play the Merodach-baladan/Napoleon/Sargon II/Cyrus card: he announced that the Romans had now liberated the Greeks from Macedonian oppression. "All the rest of the Greeks both in Asia and in Europe are to be free and to enjoy their own laws," the decree read.

Polybius notes that there were a few skeptical voices, at this; more than one Aetolian leader pointed out that "the Greeks were not being given their freedom, but merely a change of masters."[2] But the Romans insisted on their own disinterested benevolence ("It was a wholly admirable action . . . that the Roman people and their general should have made the choice to incur unlimited danger and expense to ensure the freedom of Greece," Polybius gushes),[3] and the cities of the Achaean League, which included Corinth, were pleased to sign a pro-Roman treaty, as long as it was also anti-Macedonian.

No sooner had the treaties all been signed than Antiochus III appeared in the north. By 196, he had blown through the disorganized resistance that met him in Asia, crossed over the Hellespont to claim Thrace, and was looking down on the new Roman allies. He was rather more inclined to start a war with Rome than not, partly because he now had a new military advisor: Hannibal, who had shown up at the Seleucid court after fleeing from Carthage. Hannibal had left his native city in bitterness and fury; his love for Carthage had faded, but his loathing for Rome remained. His arrival at the court of Antiochus III, the only power great enough to challenge the Romans, was a continuation of his lifelong obsession: "He impressed upon Antiochus," Polybius tells us, "that so long as the king's policy was hostile to Rome he could rely upon Hannibal implicitly and regard him as his most whole-hearted supporter . . . for there was nothing that lay in his power that he would not do to harm the Romans."* [4]

* This was a loathing of Rome as an entity, not necessarily a hatred for particular Romans. In the years after his exile from Carthage, Hannibal found himself in the same city as Scipio Africanus, who

Taking away Greece would undoubtedly harm the Romans. The Greek cities, caught between an old and frightening power to their northeast and a new and frightening power to their west, divided in their allegiances. The cities of the Aegean League kept their treaty with Rome, but the Aetolian League agreed to make an alliance with Antiochus III instead. More Roman troops arrived in the south of Greece while Antiochus's Seleucid troops (accompanied by Macedonian allies and elephants) came down from the north.

The two armies met in 191 at the Pass of Thermopylae. The Roman legions were exhorted by their consul in terms that tended to confirm the worst suspicions of the Aetolian leaders: "You are fighting for the independence of Greece," the consul bellowed, "to free now from the Aetolians and Antiochus a country which you earlier freed from Philip. And after that you will open up to Roman domination Asia, Syria, and all the wealthy kingdoms stretching as far as the rising sun. The entire human race will revere the Roman name only after the gods!"[5] It was not a particularly convincing speech of liberation, but it did the trick. The Romans drove Antiochus's army back, killing thousands, and he was forced to withdraw entirely from the peninsula.

The defeat was the beginning of the end for Antiochus the Great. As he backed up, he lost part of his Asia Minor conquests as well; the satrap of the Asia Minor province called Armenia, Artaxias I, set himself up as a king around 190. The Romans then carried the fight over into Seleucid land, under another member of the Scipio family. Antiochus gave Hannibal command of a naval force, and himself commanded a land defense, but both failed. Hannibal's fleet surrendered off the south coast of Asia Minor; Antiochus's army was defeated again, this time at Magnesia. Scipio earned himself the title Asiaticus for his victory, while Antiochus was forced to sign the Treaty of Apamea, which deprived him of most of his navy as well as his territory north of the Taurus Mountains.

Nor did Philip V escape. He was punished for his friendship with Antiochus by losing *his* navy, his border cities, and his son Demetrius, who was hauled off to Rome as a hostage for his father's good behavior.

Antiochus's defeat encouraged other satrapies to revolt. The following year, in 187, Antiochus the Great was killed in a minor battle against a rebellious satrap to the east. His son Seleucus IV inherited the Seleucid throne, but was forced, like Philip V, to send his oldest son and heir to Rome, also as a hostage.

Hannibal, deprived of his protector, fled. Plutarch says that he eventually

---

asked to meet him; the two spent some time amicably discussing military strategy, and Hannibal complimented Scipio on his ability as a commander (although he did remark that he himself was an even better general).

settled in an obscure little town on the coast of the Black Sea, where he had seven underground tunnels dug from his house that emerged a "considerable distance" away in all directions, so that he could not be cornered by Roman hit men.

But in 182, at the age of sixty-five, he was recognized by a Roman senator who happened to be visiting the local king. The senator threatened the king with the wrath of Rome should Hannibal be allowed to escape. So with reluctance, the king sent out his own local guard to block the seven passages and kill the old general. Rather than allowing himself to be taken alive, Hannibal drank poison. His last words, according to Plutarch, were "Let us ease the Romans of their continual dread and care."[6]

THE DIMINISHING THREAT of Seleucid invasion gave the Bactrians, to the east, a chance to expand their own territory. Their current king, a Greek Bactrian named Demetrius I, had his eye on the southeast: on India, which since the days of Alexander the Great had been a mirage of wealth, just waiting to be conquered.

There was no single strong king in India to resist invasion. After Asoka's death, his sons—inheriting their father's legacy of philosophical preoccupation—lost their grip on his land. In the fifty or so years between Asoka's death in 240 and Demetrius I's invasion, seven kings of Mauryan descent ruled over a diminishing territory.

The last of these Mauryan kings was Brhadratha, whose reputation as a devout Buddhist survives in sacred texts which describe his thousand-day penance in search of truth. During these thousand days, he is said to have left his oldest son in charge of the throne.[7] This suggests a king with a loose hold on power; and in fact Brhadratha lost his kingdom, sometime around 185, to the commander of his army, who assassinated him. The commander, a devout Hindu named Pusyamitra Sunga, took control of what was left of the empire. His reputation too survives in Buddhist texts; he is said to have led a persecution against Buddhists in an attempt to reestablish Hindu orthodoxy. Since several *stupas* (Buddhist sacred monuments) have been dated to his reign, this may not be entirely true. All we can say for sure is that Pusyamitra founded a dynasty, and began to expand the old kingdom of the Magadha. Unlike his predecessors, he was willing to fight for his power.

Right about this time, Demetrius I came down through the Khyber Pass, towards the Punjab. There is no written account of his invasion that followed; to reconstruct the conquests of the Greek Bactrian kings, we have to follow the trail of coins they left behind them (each king struck his own coins with

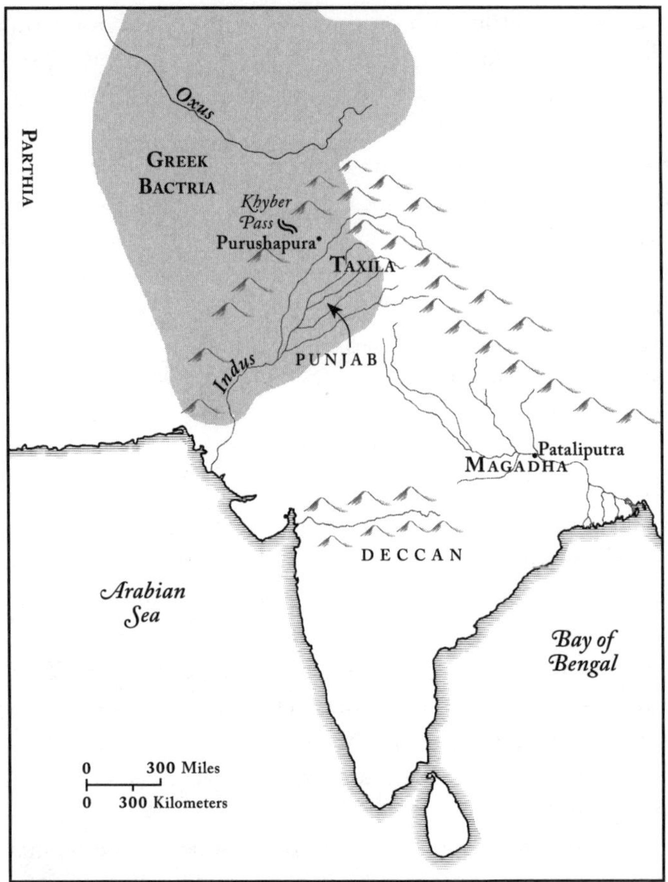

74.1 Bactria and India

his own portrait, with the result that although we know practically nothing about these kings, we have some idea of what they looked like). As far as we can guess, the first cities Demetrius I encountered were Purushapura and Taxila, which had been independent from the Mauryans for some time and had not yet been reconquered by Pusyamitra. He took both, and by 175 seems to have fought through the Punjab.

Meanwhile the Sunga king Pusyamitra spread his own grasp along the east and southwest. The two Indian kingdoms bordered each other, Greek and native side by side.

Back in Macedonia, Philip V's hostage son (also called Demetrius) had been returned from Rome, and had been welcomed by the Macedonians with enough joy to put his younger brother's nose out of joint. This young man, Perseus, had been heir apparent as long as Demetrius was a prisoner; now his chance of a throne was threatened.[8] He began to drop hints to Philip V that the newly freed Demetrius had been brainwashed by the Romans, who intended to put him on the throne of Macedonia as a Roman puppet. "We have in our bosom," he remarked, with apparent reluctance, "I don't want to say a traitor, but at least a spy. The Romans gave his body back to us, but they have retained his heart."[9] In 181, Philip gave in to his suspicions. Livy says that he ordered poison put into Demetrius's cup; the young man, feeling the first pains, realized what had happened and died screaming out against his father's cruelty.

Philip himself died two years later, and Perseus became king of Macedonia. He sent messages of friendship to Rome, but they were deceptive; he was gathering Macedonia to invade Greece once more.

His intentions were made clearer when he married one of the daughters of Seleucus IV. But he couldn't count on Seleucid help against Rome; Seleucus IV was murdered by his prime minister right after the wedding, and a big Persian succession-fight broke out. Seleucus IV's younger brother, Antiochus IV (later known as Antiochus Epiphanes), won the right to act as regent for Seleucus's baby son, whom he then murdered.

Perseus, meanwhile, set out to conquer Greece without raising Roman suspicions. Polybius says that he marched through central and northern Greece and called on various cities to "gain their confidence" while being very careful not to "inflict any damage" on the territory through which he passed.[10] This went on for three years or so before one of the Greek kings—Eumenes, ruler of the city of Pergamum, in Asia Minor—went to Rome in person to complain about Perseus's behavior. Perseus sent an assassin after Eumenes to silence him; this was a mistake, as the assassination failed and made the accusations that much more believable.

In 171, seventeen thousand Roman soldiers headed for Macedonia, inaugurating the Third Macedonian War. Perseus sent ambassadors to Rome to ask, in injured tones, why the Romans were harassing him. "Go back and tell your king that, if he really wants an answer, he should talk to the consul who will soon be in Macedonia with his army," the ambassadors were told.[11]

The Third Macedonian War lasted about three years, like the Second; as in the Second, the Romans finally crushed the Macedonians in one big disastrous battle, this one at Pydna. Unlike the Second Macedonian War, the Third brought an end to Macedonia. The Romans were fed up with fighting unpleasant little wars in the north of Greece. In 168, Perseus was hauled back to Rome as a captive, and the Roman consul oversaw the division of Macedonia into four separate subject countries. The Macedonian monarchy which had produced Alexander had ended.

ROMAN ENVOYS had come to the court of Antiochus Epiphanes to ask him whether he intended to support Perseus's war with Rome; Antiochus Epiphanes was able to assure them, with perfect truth, that he had no intention of joining with Perseus against Rome.[12]

He was planning on invading Egypt instead. The young Egyptian king Ptolemy VI, under the direction of his regents, had demanded that the Seleucid empire return its Western Semitic lands: the old kingdoms of Israel, Judah, Syria, and some of the surrounding land, which Antiochus the Great had taken away from the Ptolemaic dynasty. They had all been folded into a satrapy known as "Coele Syria," and Egypt wanted it back.

Instead, Antiochus Epiphanes marched his army down and laid siege to Alexandria while Rome was busy fighting in Macedonia. But he had overestimated the Roman preoccupation with Perseus. The Senate was not blind to this blatant bid for more territory; a Roman ambassador showed up at

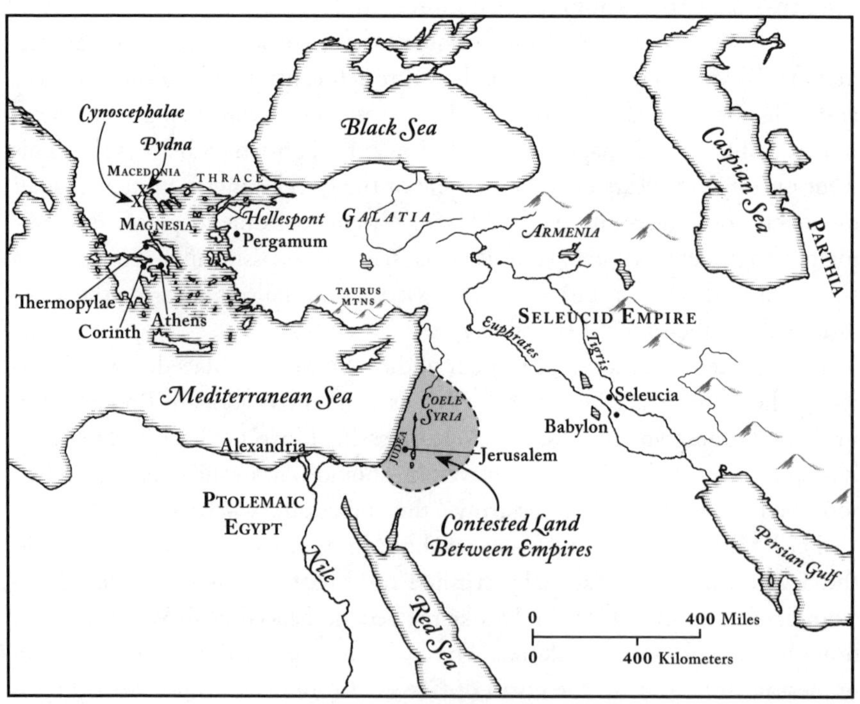

74.2 Contested Satrapies

Antiochus's camp with a letter demanding that Antiochus retreat and leave Egypt to the Ptolemys. Antiochus offered to talk the matter over with his advisors, but the ambassador (according to Livy) "drew a circle round the king with the stick he was carrying and said, 'Before you step out of that circle, give me a reply to lay before the Senate.' For a few minutes he hesitated, astounded at such a peremptory order, and at last replied, 'I will do what the Senate thinks right.' "[13] He was not prepared to take on the entire weight of Rome's anger.

Instead, he marched back up the coast and took his frustrations out on the satrapy of Coele Syria, beginning a purge among anyone who had shown sympathy for the Egyptians' request. This included a good many residents of Jerusalem: "At the same time that Antiochus, who was called Epiphanes, had a quarrel with the sixth Ptolemy about his right to the whole country of Syria," Josephus says, in his *Wars of the Jews*, ". . . [he] came upon the Jews with a great army, and took their city by force, and slew a great multitude of those that favored Ptolemy, and . . . spoiled the temple."[14]

The spoiling of the temple was pure opportunism; Antiochus was broke and needed the sacred treasures. On his pass through Judea, he not only plundered the temple treasury and butchered a great many citizens of Jerusalem, but also installed a garrison in Jerusalem to keep the Jews loyal.[15]

The garrison was standard procedure for a conqueror, but Antiochus Epiphanes's plan for keeping the Jews loyal was horrifically misguided. He knew nothing about the Jewish religion; his plan for folding the Jews more tightly into the Seleucid fold (and keeping them out of the Ptolemaic fence) was to change the temple cult so that their Yahweh became identified with Zeus. This chief god would then be worshipped as manifest in his own person: Antiochus Epiphanes, the "epiphany" or revelation of Zeus-Yahweh on earth.[16]

This was a fairly standard mixture of the Greek pantheon with Persian ideas about the king's divinity, as might be expected from a Greek ruler of the old Persian realm. For the Jews, who (unlike most ancient people) believed not only in a single God, but in that God's essential difference from man, it was hideous blasphemy. Antiochus wanted them to sacrifice to Zeus in the temple, and to celebrate his own birthday as a religious festival.

The Jews of Jerusalem went into hiding at this, or had to be flogged into obedience. Antiochus, infuriated by their stubbornness, declared Judaism an illegal religion. Anyone who refused to eat pork when required (this was against the Jewish regulations) or was found with a copy of the Jewish scriptures was put to death. "Two women were brought in for having circumcised their children," the book of 2 Maccabees records. "These women they publicly paraded about the city, with their babies hung at their breasts, then hurled them down headlong from the wall."*[17]

This level of savagery lasted for less than a year before revolt rose up among the Jews. It was led by a family of five brothers who were descended from the old tribe of priests. The oldest brother Judas was the general of the resistance; he went through the countryside, enlisting indignant Jews, until he had six thousand men who joined him in an ongoing guerilla war against the Seleucid occupiers. "Coming without warning," 2 Maccabees says, "he would set fire to towns and villages. He captured strategic positions and put to flight not a few of the enemy. He found the nights most advantageous for such attacks, and talk of his valor spread everywhere."[18] He earned himself a freedom-fighter's nickname, "Judas Maccabeus," or "Judas the Hammer," and the rebellion became known as the Maccabean War.

The fury of the Jews and Antiochus's own difficulties elsewhere (he had to send troops up north to fend off invading Parthians) prolonged the rebellion. So did another factor: Judas made "a league of friendship with the Romans," as Josephus puts it; Rome was anxious to go on checking Seleucid power.[19] The Jewish-Roman alliance did not last long, but it helped keep Jerusalem out of the hands of Antiochus for a full four years.†

At the end of that time, Antiochus Epiphanes died, and the usual internal fight over the succession commenced. No one had energy to send more soldiers down to Jerusalem, and Judas declared himself king of the city: the first king of the Hasmonean Dynasty of Jerusalem. Eventually Antiochus's nephew, Demetrius I (not to be confused with the Greek Bactrian Demetrius or the Macedonian Demetrius), managed to declare himself king of the Seleucid empire. When his crown was firmly on his head, he sent an army down to reconquer Jerusalem. Judas was killed in the fighting, and Jerusalem became once again part of Coele Syria under the Seleucid crown. But Demetrius I, taking his lesson from his dead uncle's catastrophic decisions, granted Judas's

* The books of 1 and 2 Maccabees are historical accounts in the Apocrypha proper, a set of biblical books which falls between the Old and New Testaments in the Christian Bible. These books were not universally accepted by the early church fathers as divinely inspired, and debate about their place in the canon continued until the sixteenth century. In 1546, the Catholic Council of Trent declared the Apocrypha proper "sacred and canonical," but Protestants generally rejected these books.

† In 165, Judas managed to bring the temple back under Jewish control, and set about ritually purifying it (the altar had been defiled, in the worship of Zeus, by having a pig sacrificed on it). According to 1 Macc. 4, the purification was finished and the temple rededicated in December 164, an event celebrated by the later Jewish festival of Hanukkah. According to the Talmud (a collection of written elaborations on the central texts of Judaism), the Maccabees did not have enough pure olive oil to use in the purification rituals, but the single flask that they used burned miraculously for eight days.

brother Jonathan a fair amount of freedom to govern the Jews as he saw fit, as long as he remained a faithful subject governor of the empire. Jonathan, Josephus says, "behaved himself with great circumspection," meaning that he was not a freedom-fighting hothead like his older brother.[20] He paid polite deference to the Seleucid authorities, and managed to stay in power in Jerusalem for almost twenty years.

MEANWHILE, Rome was doing splendidly.

Something extraordinary had happened a few years before. In 180, the city of Cumae, in Campania, had asked for permission to change its official language from its old dialect of Oscan to Latin.

The people of Cumae already had the privilege of *civitas sine suffragio*, citizenship without the vote; the *civitas sine suffragio* was more like an alliance than anything else, a right which did nothing to destroy the original identity of the cities which held it.[21] Now the people of Cumae were asking for a new level of identification with Rome. They did not become full Romans; nor did they entirely give up speaking Oscan. Without abandoning their identity as Cumaeans, they were making a willing identification not just with Roman politics, but with Roman culture.

The Greeks had never had to make such a formal outwards pledge of unity, as they all spoke Greek already. Perhaps their very shared language kept them from ever allowing that pan-Hellenic identity to trump their identity as Spartans, Athenians, Corinthians, Thebans. But the official status of Latin allowed Cumae to *remain* Cumaean. Latin would not be their only language, but it would be used for commerce and administration, binding Cumae together with other cities and peoples who retained their own identities, but glossed another above it.

Rome granted the request. Cumae could use Latin as its official language and be, in that sense, Roman. The Romans did not yet feel any need to further erase the old identities of their subject cities, to replace old customs with Roman customs, old allegiances with Roman allegiances, old gods with Roman gods.

But this bestowal of Roman identity only went so far. Conquests were flooding into Rome, with the result that free foreigners were in danger of outnumbering free men of Roman birth. In 168, the censor Sempronius Gracchus began to register all foreign-born free men as a single tribe. They could become Roman, like the Cumaeans. They could even have the vote. But no matter how many came to Rome, they would never be able to outvote the native Romans.

TIMELINE 74

ROME	SUCCESSORS OF ALEXANDER: EGYPT	SELEUCID EMPIRE	THRACE-MACEDONIA
	Ptolemy III (246)		
		Seleucus II	**Demetrius II**
		Antiochus the Great	
	Ptolemy IV (222)		**Philip V**
Second Punic War (218)			
Battle of Cannae			
Battle of Zama (202)	**Ptolemy V** (204)		Peace of Phoenice
Second Macedonian War		Battle of Panium (198)	
		Seleucus IV (187)	
Cumae changes its language to Latin	**Ptolemy VI** (180)		**Perseus**
		Antiochus Ephiphanes	
Third Macedonian War			Battle of Pydna (168)
		Antiochus V	
		Demetrius I	

Chapter Seventy-Five

Between East and West

Between 200 and 110 BC,
the Han Dynasty opens the Silk Road

GAO ZU, THE FIRST HAN EMPEROR,* had been born a peasant; now he ruled over a China in which the old noble families of the states had begun to re-emerge in answer to the Ch'in harshness. The old problem of unity had not gone away.

On the other hand, the Chinese states were weary of war, and Gao Zu managed to hold the empire together with a quick-witted combination of heavy-handed authority and the promise of independence. He marched with his army against any dukes who showed signs of revolt, but he also proclaimed a general amnesty throughout the empire, meaning that all noble families who were not currently planning rebellion could live free from the fear of random arrest and execution. To those who had helped him establish his power, he granted freedom from taxes and service. In one rebellious city, which he was forced to besiege for over a month, he granted complete pardon to every man who fought against him, as long as they had not cursed him; only those who cursed him were put to death.[1] The Ch'in emperors had clenched the imperial fist tighter and tighter; the Han king opened his fingers and gave freedom from oversight as a reward.

His greatest battles were fought against outsiders. China, unlike the civilizations to the west, did not face the constant encroachments of other organized armies. But nomads had roamed along the northern borders for centuries. The walls built along the northern edges of the old Chinese states, now being linked together into a Great Wall, had first been erected as a

* The years 206 BC–AD 9 are assigned by historians to the "Western Han," or "Earlier Han," Dynasty; a brief interruption between AD 9 and 25 separates this from the "Eastern Han," or "Later Han," Dynasty (AD 25–220).

defense against raiding nomads that the Chinese states considered to be barbarian, non-Chinese, outside the borders of real Chinese society.

These nomads were not quite so barbarian as the Chinese liked to think. In fact the nearest nomadic tribes had begun to organize themselves into a loose association, a nation of sorts: the Xiongnu.*[2] The association of tribes, each with its own leader, fell under the authority of a man appointed to be their king, or *chanyu.* In fact, the Xiongnu confederation was modelled after the Chinese government to the south.

The people themselves were probably descended from the Ti, the Jung, and the other "barbarians" who appear in earlier accounts.[3] They were not so very different from the "Chinese proper," as Sima Qian himself inadvertently reveals when he remarks that the Xiongnu were descended from a member of the Hsia Dynasty.[4] But this was a likeness that most Chinese ignored, as Qian also reveals when he adds, quickly, that they are, of course, something a little less than human.

During the earliest years of the Han, the Xiongnu chanyu was a general named Mao-tun; he is one of the few nomadic leaders whose name survives, and he had organized his confederation to the point where they had a regular annual gathering place (somewhere in Outer Mongolia) and something like a voting system.[5] Gao Zu collected a huge force of three hundred thousand men and marched up north to meet him. The nomads, like the Scythians a century before, used their mobility to their advantage; they retreated until the emperor and his personal force had ridden out ahead of the bulk of his army, and then turned—four hundred thousand horsemen strong—and attacked. It took seven days for Gao Zu to fight his way free.[6]

Afterwards, Gao Zu decided that it would be best to make peace. His empire was still filled with other generals who had fought in the war against the Ch'in, and who had not ended up with a throne; he did not want to start another war, against an outside power, with them at his back. He sent the Xiongnu gifts of money to pacify them, and—in a startling admission of Mao-tun's power—he also sent one of his daughters up to be the warrior-king's bride.

THE EARLY YEARS of the Han succession were less than smooth. Gao Zu died in 195 after a rule of only seven years, and was succeeded by his young son Hui-ti. But the real power in the Han court was held by Gao Zu's widow, Kao-hou, who ruled as empress dowager and regent for her son.

Kao-hou was not the emperor's only wife (he also had a whole constellation

* "Xiongnu" is the Pinyin spelling; many histories still use the Wade-Giles "Hsiung-nu" instead.

of sons born to noblewomen who became his wives and concubines after he took the title of emperor), but she had been his wife back in the days "when he was still a commoner." She was a "woman of very strong will," and her son Hui-ti was, "by nature, weak and soft-hearted."[7] She poisoned and put to death an array of royal sons and wives, in an excess of cruelty that sickened her son: "Emperor Hui gave himself up each day to drink," Sima Qian says, "and no longer took part in affairs of state."[8] At twenty-three, he died. His mother was less than heartbroken: "Mourning was announced and the Empress Dowager lamented," Qian writes, "but no tears fell from her eyes."[9]

In fact her son's death allowed her to install various brothers, sisters, and cousins from her own family as generals, ministers, secretaries, and dukes, which cemented her own power. With the cooperation of Hui-ti's widow, she produced a baby which she claimed to be Hui-ti's heir apparent; palace rumor said that the child was actually the son of a lady-in-waiting (Hui-ti had, apparently, been too consistently soused to father a son of his own). The new emperor was installed, but as he grew older he began to ask awkward questions about his parentage. The empress dowager then had him murdered and appointed another putative son of Hui-ti emperor in his place.[10]

This heir-juggling kept her in power for nine more years, but by the time she died in 179, she had grown so unpopular that the court rose up and slaughtered every relative of Kao-hou that they could get their hands on. The removal of her family left the throne and a good many government jobs open, but the Han Dynasty—unlike the Ch'in—survived this particular crisis. Despite the chaos in the court, the throne had not indulged in the harsh micromanagement of the people that had made the First Emperor's family so unpopular: "The common people succeeded in putting behind them the sufferings of the age of the Warring States," the Grand Historian sums up, "and ruler and subject alike sought rest in surcease of action. . . . Punishments were seldom meted out . . . while the people applied themselves to the tasks of farming, and food and clothing became abundant."[11] The throne had managed to keep the barbarians out and to leave the people alone to conduct their own lives, and as a result of this laissez-faire policy, China was prospering. Prosperous people are disinclined to revolt; once the unpopular family of Kao-hou had been cleared out, another son of the dead Gao Zu by a concubine was proclaimed emperor.

This young man, Wendi,* inherited an empire which still had no imperial

* "Wendi" is "King Wen" in Pinyin; the last syllable is the royalty marker. I have kept Pinyin spelling for most Han Dynasty monarchs, since it is easy to confuse their names with the names of the Chinese states.

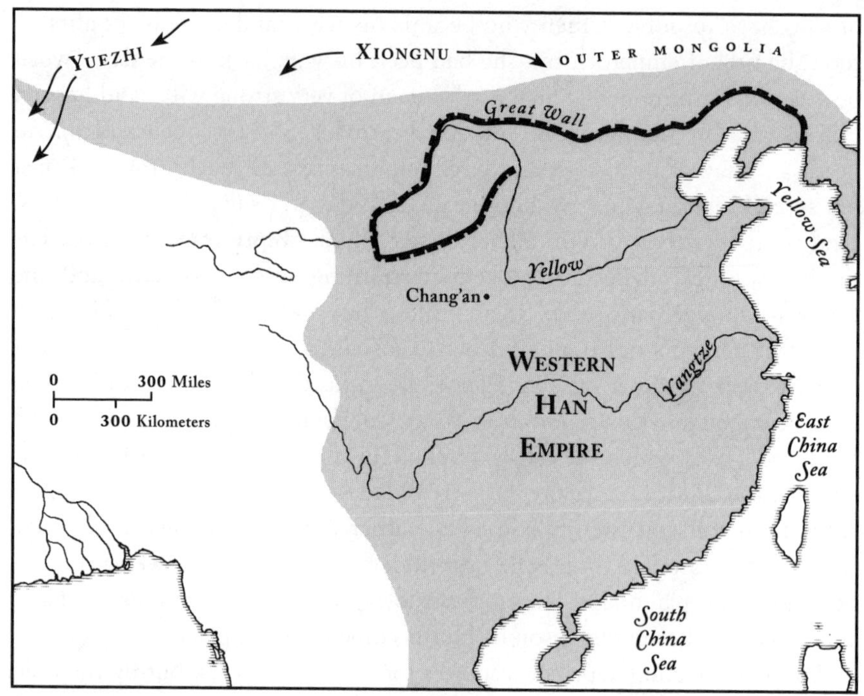

75.1 Han China

trappings: nothing to hold it together apart from the memory of previous unpopular and repressive rules which inclined the people to be on his side, as the anti-Ch'in king. Wendi's hold on power for over twenty years, until his natural death (he reigned from 179 to 156), displayed a great deal of tact; like his father, he capitalized on this negative bond and kept his hands out of local business as much as possible.

Like his father, he also faced the possibility of invasion. Nomads from even farther to the north—not part of the Xiongnu confederation, and called by the Chinese the Yuezhi—had begun to move down towards the Xiongnu territory. They were driven, like the Celtic tribes, by a complex intersection of hunger, overpopulation, and ambition, and their goal was to come south into China itself.

But the Xiongnu drove them away, deflecting them off to the west: "The Xiongnu had defeated the king of the Yuezhi," Sima Qian relates, "and had made his skull into a drinking vessel."[12] (Which suggests, if not identity, certainly a cultural relationship with the nomadic Scythians a little farther to the west, who had the same charming custom.) This move west had a domino-like effect: around 160 BC, they ran head-on into Bactria, overran it, and settled along its north, all the way to the Oxus river. It was one of the first lasting contacts between peoples from the far east and those closer to the Mediterranean. For the Han Dynasty, it was also a danger avoided. The Xiongnu had mustered itself against the barbarians, and Wendi was prevented from the necessity of recruiting a large army to fight back.

When he died around 157, he managed to pass his crown, without incident, on to his son, who in turn passed it along to *his* son: the emperor Wudi, who began his rule around 140. Wudi, who counts as either the sixth or seventh emperor of the Han Dynasty (depending on how many of the infants you include), began his fifty-three-year reign by campaigning up to push the encroaching Xiongnu back a little bit. This was the end of the tradition of pacification that Gao Zu had begun. The Han throne was now strong enough to survive a war.

Pushing back the Xiongnu was the least of Wudi's accomplishments. He had decades of relatively peaceful Han authority behind him, and the Ch'in oppression was far enough into the past so that, finally, the emperor could put his hands down into the dirt of his country long enough to shape it into something more like an empire. He reintroduced taxes; he took control of the trade of iron, salt, and alcohol as government monopolies; he cut back down to size local officials who had taken advantage of the Han hands-off policies to enrich themselves.[13] He began to rebuild a bureaucracy, introducing for the first time the requirement that officials take, and pass, a qualifying examination.[14]

Not long after taking the throne—probably right around 139 BC—he also sent an ambassador named Zhang Qian to find out what lay beyond his western border. We do not know exactly what impelled him to do this, but some trickle of commerce and exploration from the west must have made it all the way past the Han border. Sima Qian records the curiosity that this produced on both sides: "All the barbarians of the distant west craned their necks to the east and longed to catch a glimpse of China," he writes.[15]

Zhang Qian's trip did not go particularly well at first; he was captured by the Xiongnu and taken to the chanyu. Rather than killing him, though, they kept him a captive and even gave him a wife: and after he had lived there ten years, he "was less closely watched than at first" and managed to escape. After that he travelled through the west, visiting Bactria and Parthia, and seeing firsthand the movement of the Yuezhi nomads along the northern parts of the world. When he returned in 126, to great acclaim, he was able to report on both kingdoms.

Bactria, he told the emperor, was a land of settled farmers, but had no king: "only a number of petty chiefs ruling the various cities."[16] In fact, surviving coins suggest that the last Bactrian king of Greek descent was a man named

Heliocles, whose reign must have been brought to an end, around 130 BC, by the invading Yuezhi. Zhang Qian was arriving in Bactria just as the invading nomads were overrunning the country.

Most likely the ruling class had gone south into India, at the arrival of the nomads: Zhang Qian also reports that the Bactrians told him about a land they called Shen-tu, which lay "several thousand li southeast," where the people "cultivate the land." "The region is said to be hot and damp," he says, winding up the identification with "the inhabitants ride elephants when they go into battle, and the kingdom is situated on a great river." The flight of Bactrian Greeks across the mountains into India had broken the Bactrian kingdom into two: the original Greek Bactrians, now overrun by Yuezhi, and an "Indo-Greek" kingdom farther south.

In a matter of decades, these "Indo-Greeks" became much more Indian than Greek. Their most famous king was Menander I, who came to power around 150 BC. His coins show him in Greek armor and are inscribed in Greek, but he is remembered in a Buddhist sacred text called the *Milinda Panha* for his conversion to Buddhism. "None was equal to Milinda in all India," the text begins, "mighty in wealth and prosperity, and the number of his armed hosts knew no end." Despite this, he had unending questions about the nature of his own authority and the world in which he fought for dominance. One day, after reviewing his "innumerable host" of "elephants, cavalry, bowmen, and soldiers on foot," he asked to speak with a scholar who might help him resolve his difficulties, and in the conversation that followed was introduced to the principles of Buddhism.[17]

According to the *Milinda Panha*, this ultimately led to the king's abdication, after which he became a pilgrim: "Afterwards, taking delight in the wisdom of the Elder," it concludes, "he handed over his kingdom to his son, and, abandoning the household life for the houseless state, grew great in insight."[18] This is possible, but unlikely; Menander is remembered not only for his conversion but for the extension of the Indo-Greek border almost all the way to Pataliputra, a campaign which must have involved years and years of fighting. A later Buddhist scripture, the *Gargi-Samhita*, confirms this: it says that the "Yavanas," the Greeks, reached the "thick mud-fortifications at Pataliputra, all the provinces . . . in disorder."

Whether or not Menander then retired from warfare, his conquests pushed back a Hindu kingdom and extended a Buddhist one, which preserved his greatness in the Buddhist texts. When he died, in 130, his remains were enclosed into the sacred monuments known as stupas: "Sacred heaps," as the *Milinda Panha* calls them, "beneath whose solid dome the bones of the great dead lie."

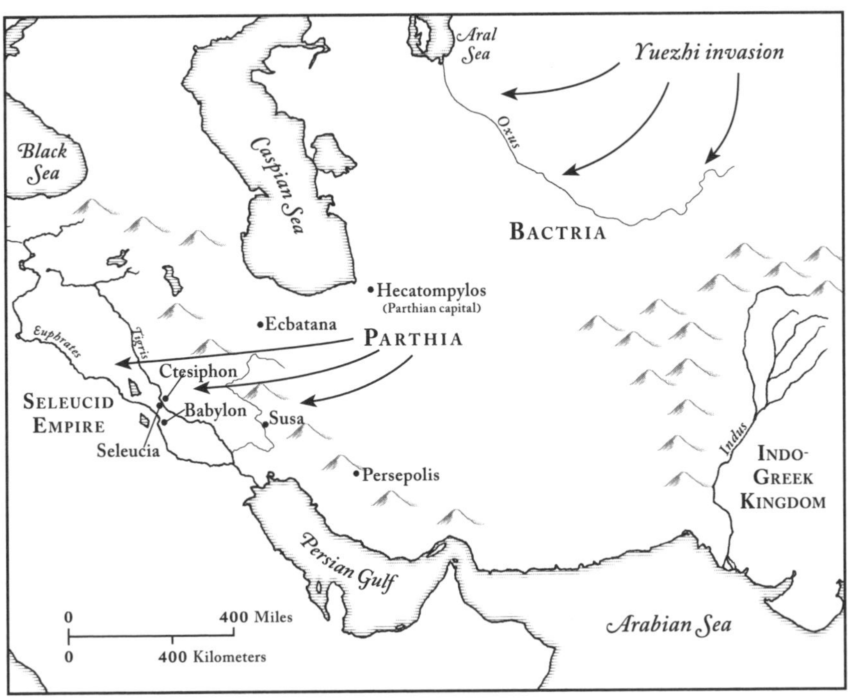

75.2 The Parthians

Zhang Qian's report also extended farther west, into Parthia, where a king was still very much on the throne. Antiochus Epiphanes had been forced to fight off Parthian attacks, and the three Seleucid kings who came after him had been faced with the same hostile invasions. The Parthians were, essentially, not very different in their origins than the Xiongnu; they were nomadic horsemen, hardy and good in battle, and they had begun to encroach further and further on the Seleucid border, pushing it closer to Syria. By the rule of the third king after Antiochus Epiphanes—Demetrius II, also called Nicator—they had run across the middle of the old Assyrian heartland between the Tigris and Euphrates. This land was firmly enough under Parthian control for the Parthians to build themselves defensive walls. These Parthian Walls were constructed from the large pieces of stone they found lying around, and used; the monuments of Ashurnasirpal were broken up and pressed into duty to guard his old domain from recapture by the Seleucids.

In 139, the Parthian king Mithridates I actually captured Demetrius Nicator in battle, and hauled him back to Parthia. Demetrius Nicator was treated well, held in comfortable confinement, but he spent ten years as a Parthian prisoner, which was horrendously embarrassing for the king of the once-great

Seleucids. Josephus claims that he died, still in captivity: "Demetrius was sent to Mithridates," he writes, "and the king of Parthia had Demetrius in great honor, till Demetrius ended his life by sickness."[19] Other accounts say that he escaped and died later, to be succeeded first by one son (who was murdered after less than a year) and then another.

Meanwhile the Parthians campaigned closer and closer to Babylon, and built themselves a camp at Ctesiphon, which they could use to penetrate even deeper into Seleucid land. This growing Parthian power was reflected in Zhang Qian's report to his king. The Parthians, he said, were an impressive and, to his eye, highly organized civilization: "They have walled cities," he related, "several hundred cities of various sizes." Parthian farmers grew rice, wheat, and grapes for wine; their merchants travelled far to trade with distant countries. And by this point, their empire stretched all the way out to a land which Zhang Qian called T'iao-chih, where it was "hot and damp," where there were "great birds which lay eggs as large as pots," where "the people are very numerous and are ruled by many petty chiefs," but where all the chiefs pay attention to the king of Parthia, who gives them orders "and regards them as his vassals."[20] The description is of the Mesopotamian valley. The Seleucids had been pushed all the way out of the land between the rivers; they were no longer an empire to concern the Romans.

That place had been taken by the Parthians themselves. Wudi's long and distinguished reign overlapped with that of the greatest Parthian king of all: Mithridates II, the Great. He came to the throne of Parthia in 123, and before long was alarming the Roman authorities in Asia Minor; one Lucius Cornelius Sulla, whose biography Plutarch records, was sent to keep an eye on "the restless movements of Mithridates, who was gradually procuring himself [a] vast new acquired power and dominion."[21] Sulla travelled as far as the Euphrates and there met an ambassador that Mithridates had sent to meet him: "As yet," Plutarch says, "there had been no correspondence between the two nations"; Sulla was "the first Roman to whom the Parthians made address for alliance and friendship."

Mithridates also sent merchants and envoys east. "When the Han envoys first visited the kingdom of An-hsi [Parthia]," says Sima Qian, ". . . the king of An-hsi dispatched envoys of his own to accompany them, and after the latter had visited China and reported on its great breadth and might, the king sent some of the eggs of the great birds which live in the region . . . to the Han court as gifts."

Envoys from the east were travelling west at the same time. After Zhang Qian's explorations, more men were dispatched from the Han court along his path: "After Zhang Qian achieved honor and position by opening up communications with the lands of the west," says Sima Qian, "all the officials and soldiers who had accompanied him vied with one another in submitting reports to the emperor . . . requesting to become envoys."[22]

These journeys west involved some fighting, as Han armies put down resistance from various local tribes in the lands through which the new trade route ran. But by 110, the trade route from west to east was thoroughly established. Outposts along the road, staffed by Chinese garrisons, protected traders from bandits. The Parthians bought Chinese goods, particularly silks and lacquer, which they did not make themselves. The Chinese emperor

TIMELINE 75

SUCCESSORS OF ALEXANDER			CHINA	
EGYPT	SELEUCID EMPIRE	THRACE-MACEDONIA		
			Fall of the Zhou (256)	
Ptolemy III (246)			**Chuang-hsiang of Ch'in**	
	Seleucus II	**Demetrius II**	**Cheng of Ch'in**	
	Antiochus the Great			
Ptolemy IV (222)		**Philip V**	Ch'in Dynasty (221)	
			Shi Huang-ti (formerly Cheng)	
			Second Emperor (209)	
Ptolemy V (204)		Peace of Phoenice	Han Dynasty (202)	
	Battle of Panium (198)		**Gao Zu**	**Mao-tun of the Xiongnu**
	Seleucus IV (187)		**Hui-ti** (195)	
Ptolemy VI (180)		**Perseus**	**Kao-hou** (188)	
	Antiochus Ephiphanes		**Wendi** (179)	
		Battle of Pydna (168)		
	Antiochus V			
	Demetrius I			
	Demetrius II		**Wudi** (140)	
			Zhang Qian's journey west	
	Mithridates II of Parthia (123)			

bought Parthian horses, which he admired for their speed and beauty. More and more foreign visitors came to the Han court, where the emperor would parade them along the coast to show them the size and wealth of the Han kingdom. And in Parthia itself, Mithridates II, who appears both in Plutarch and in Sima Qian, stood as a bridge between the two great and growing empires of the west and east.

Chapter Seventy-Six

Breaking the System

Between 157 and 121 BC,
Romans destroy Carthage,
put down a slave revolt,
and deal a death blow to the Republic

BACK IN ROME, trade had resumed with Carthage. The North African city was a good source for gold and silver, wine and figs; and so the two cities kept an uneasy but useful peace.[1]

But Carthage was in peril. The treaty that closed the Second Punic War had deprived Carthage of most of its army and navy, which made the city vulnerable to other attackers. The most feared of these were the Africans of Numidia, a kingdom which lay on the North African coast below Carthage. The king of Numidia, Masinissa, was a Roman ally; he had sent soldiers to fight with Scipio Africanus against Carthage, and Rome had helped him enlarge his own North African kingdom. (He had also tattled on the Carthaginians when they entertained messengers from Perseus of Macedonia, back when Perseus was trying to whip up support to drive the Romans out.) Since the end of the Second Punic War, Masinissa had been carrying on armed attacks against bits of Carthaginian territory and claiming them for himself: "An easy matter for a man who had no scruples," Livy remarks, since the Carthaginians were forbidden by Roman treaty to use weapons against any ally of Rome.[2]

In 157, a Roman delegation, led by the elderly statesman Marcus Cato, travelled down to North Africa in order to tell the Numidians to leave Carthage alone. But Cato, who had always been one of the most vehement anti-Carthaginians in the Senate, was horrified at what he found at Carthage. It was not "low and in an ill condition," as the Romans had assumed, but (in Plutarch's words) "well manned, full of riches and all sorts of arms and ammunition." He returned to Rome posthaste and warned the Senate that "they themselves would fall into danger, unless they should find means to check this rapid new growth of Rome's ancient irreconcilable enemy."[3]

Not all the Senators were convinced that Roman troops needed to march on Carthage at once; Cato, nearly eighty, sounded as though he were simply rehearsing past fears. When he was opposed, he resorted to annoying the senators by ending every single speech he made, no matter what the topic, with, "And to conclude, I think that Carthage ought to be utterly destroyed."[4]

So exhorted, the Senate made continual demands on Carthage to prove its loyalty. Finally, Rome demanded that the Carthaginians desert their city and rebuild it at least ten miles away from the coast. The Carthaginians refused, indignantly. In 149, Roman ships sailed for the North African coast under the command of Scipio Aemilius, grandson of the great Scipio Africanus, and a three-year siege began. It was purely a punitive measure, sometimes labelled the "Third Punic War."[5] As soon as the siege began, Cato died of old age; his epitaph, in the mouth of many Romans was that "Cato stirred up the third and last war against the Carthaginians."[6]

Carthage was not the only problem on the senatorial agenda. Over in Greece, Sparta was causing trouble.

Sparta was no longer the dominant city in the Achaean League, its old association, and the other cities of the League had been running roughshod over it. Unhappy with a League decision, Sparta announced its intention to appeal directly to Rome (now tacitly recognized as the real power on the Greek peninsula). The other League cities immediately passed a regulation saying that only the League as a whole could appeal to Rome.

The Spartans reacted to this as Spartans had reacted for centuries: they armed themselves and threatened to fight. Indignant letters went off to Rome from both sides of the debate. A Roman ambassador who was up in Macedonia settling another problem sent a message down, ordering them to knock it off until Roman officials could arrive and help them sort the matter out. But it was too late. By 148, swords had already been drawn.

The following year, Roman diplomats showed up to mediate the dispute. They held their deliberations in the city of Corinth, and came to a decision favoring the Spartans, which was not the cleverest of arrangements; the Corinthians, moved to fury, stormed out and mauled anyone who looked like a Spartan. The Roman officials, caught in the riot, got beaten up themselves.

The indignant Romans returned to Rome and put the worst possible spin on the incident: "They declared," Polybius says, "that they had a narrow escape of actually losing their lives. . . . they represented the violence which had been offered them as not the result of a sudden outbreak, but of a deliberate intention on the part of the Achaeans to inflict a signal insult upon them."[7]

In response, a Roman fleet sailed for Greece, where a force of twenty-six thousand men and thirty-five hundred cavalry, under the command of the consul Mummius, pitched camp at the Isthmus of Corinth. Some of the Achaean League cities tried to fight back, under the command of a Corinthian general, but the Greek army soon broke; the Corinthian commander fled, and then poisoned himself; the defeated Achaean League soldiers ran to Corinth and hid in the city. Mummius set the city on fire, and Romans overran it.

Rome had finally swallowed Greece.

As far as Polybius is concerned, the Greek cities brought this disaster on themselves: "The Carthaginians at any rate left something for posterity to say on their behalf," he writes, "but the mistakes of the Greeks were so glaring that they made it impossible for those who wished to support them to do so." He might have said the same about Macedonia, which continued to play host to men who claimed to belong to the Macedonian royal line until the Romans annexed it and turned it into a province, taking away even the small freedoms that the republics had been permitted.

Meanwhile Carthage, which had "left something for posterity to say on its behalf," was in flames. In that same year, Scipio Aemilius and his men finally brought the city down. Roman soldiers ran through the streets, setting buildings on fire. It took two weeks for Carthage to burn to the ground. Polybius himself was there, standing beside Scipio Aemilius as Carthage collapsed: "At the sight of the city utterly perishing amidst the flames," he writes, "Scipio burst into tears. . . . And on my asking him boldly (for I had been his tutor) what he meant . . . he immediately turned around and grasped me by the hand and said, 'O Polybius, it is a grand thing, but I know not how, I feel a terror and dread, lest someone should one day give the same order about my own native city.' "[8]

THE LAND where Carthage had once stood now became the Roman province of North Africa. Rome had conquered all of the ancient powers that lay within easy reach; Parthia, Egypt, and what was left of the Seleucids still lay beyond.

Before further campaigns, Rome had domestic troubles to settle. The success of the Roman wars to this point had brought thousands and thousands of foreign-born captives into the Roman provinces as slaves. Roman slaves were the property of their masters and could be beaten, raped, or starved at will, but as soon as a Roman master set his slave free, that slave became a Roman citizen, with all the rights of citizenship. This, as the historian M. I. Finley has pointed out, made Roman slavery a very odd institution indeed. In a single act, a piece of property became a human being, and since Roman slaves came in all shades (unlike slaves of the American South, who, even freed, carried in their skin color the reminder that they had once belonged to a slave class), freedmen then "melted into the total population within one or at the most two generations."*[9]

Practically speaking, badly treated slaves knew perfectly well how close they were, in essence, to their masters. By 136, there were thousands of these slaves in Sicily, which had prospered after its release from Carthaginian mastery. The Sicilians, writes Diodorus Siculus, "treated them with a heavy hand in their service, and granted them the most meagre care, the bare minimum for food and clothing. . . . The slaves, distressed by their hardships, and frequently outraged and beaten beyond all reason, could not endure their treatment. Getting together as opportunity offered, they discussed the possibility of revolt, until at last they put their plans into action."[10]

The rebellion broke out first in the city of Enna, where four hundred slaves banded together to murder a slaveowner notorious for his cruelty. They killed everyone in the slaveowner's house, even the babies, with the sole exception of one daughter who had shown kindness to her father's slaves. Then they appointed as their king and leader a charismatic slave named Eunus, who was rumored to have magical powers. Certainly he was a smooth and convincing talker, and proved himself to be no mean strategist either: "In three days," Diodorus writes, "Eunus had armed, as best he could, more than six thousand men. . . . Then, since he kept recruiting untold numbers of slaves, he ventured even to do battle with Roman generals, and on joining combat repeatedly overcame them with his superior numbers, for he now had more than ten thousand soldiers."[11]

His particular rebellion was soon joined by other slave leaders who acted as generals under his command. Somewhere between seventy thousand and two hundred thousand slaves eventually joined in this revolt, which became known as the First Servile War. Other sympathetic slave rebellions flared up in Rome, and then in several Greek cities. These were put down, but the Sicilian fighting continued.

The First Servile War dragged on for three years, in part because the plight of the Sicilian slaveholders did not rouse much pity in the breasts of Sicilian laborers: "When these many great troubles fell upon the Sicilians," Diodorus Siculus writes, "the common people were not only unsympathetic, but actually gloated over their plight, being envious because of the inequality in their

* Finley points out that this was markedly different from the Greek system, in which freed slaves became "free inhabitants who remained aliens in the political sphere" (*Ancient Slavery and Modern Ideology*, p. 97).

respective lots." Many peasants took the opportunity to set fire to the estates of the rich and blame the devastation on the rebellious slaves.[12] They did nothing to restore the old order, because they had suffered under it themselves.

In this, Sicily was not alone. Not only Rome's provinces but Rome itself was suffering from an increasing gap between rich and poor. Rome's constant warfare meant that hundreds of thousands of Roman foot soldiers had marched off to fight, and had returned, poorly paid and sometimes disabled, to badly kept farms, crumbling houses, and unsettled debts.[13] Meanwhile merchants were taking advantage of the newly opened trade routes to do a booming business, and public officials were earning higher and higher salaries from newly taxed lands.

Rome's management of its conquered lands had also been less than stellar. The Roman historian Appian, who wrote his *Civil Wars* some two hundred years later, describes the general procedure for territory seized on the Italian peninsula:

> As the Romans conquered the Italian tribes, one after another, in war, they seized part of the lands. . . . Since they had not time to [sell or rent] the part which lay waste by the war, and this was usually the greater portion, they issued a proclamation that for the time being any who cared to work it could do so for a share of the annual produce. . . . The wealthy, getting hold of most of the unassigned lands . . . and adding, part by purchase and part by violence, the little farms of their poor neighbors to their possessions, came to work great districts instead of one estate.[14]

To work these large tracts, landowners needed plenty of labor, but Roman law said that hired men, if free, could be drafted into military service. So the wealthy bought more and more slaves, who were exempt from the draft. "Thus," Appian says, "the powerful citizens became immensely wealthy and the slave class all over the country multiplied," while common laborers were held down "by poverty, taxes, and military service."

The most vocal opposition to this badly planned system was a tribune by the name of Tiberius Sempronius Gracchus, son of a consul. He had served under Scipio Aemilius in the campaign against Carthage, where he gained fame as the first man to mount the enemy wall.[15] In his other foreign service, he had seen the countryside of the Roman provinces dominated by the rich, with shepherds and farmers thrown off their land, and he returned to Rome and embarked on political office determined to bring reform. It was ridiculous, he argued in his public speeches, for Roman generals to order their soldiers to fight for home and hearth, when those very soldiers were on the edge of losing their homes: "He told them," Plutarch relates, "that they fought indeed and were slain, but it was to maintain the luxury and the wealth of other men. They were styled the masters of the world, but in the meantime had not one foot of ground which they could call their own."[16]

The reforms Tiberius Gracchus suggested, which would have crimped the estate-building of the rich, were naturally unpopular with wealthy Romans. They convinced his fellow tribunes to veto Tiberius's bill. This was perfectly legal; any tribune had the right to veto a law proposed by another. Tiberius suspected that bribes had been offered, though, and acted on his suspicions by breaching Rome's constitution. With the help of his supporters, he blocked a whole range of public services and announced that they would not start again until his bill was brought up for the popular vote.

This was breaking the law in order to do good, and it was this action which began to turn more and more Roman lawmakers against Tiberius Gracchus. No matter what his intentions were, he was introducing a dangerous precedent: he was using his personal popularity with the masses to get his own way.

Their fears were not calmed when the bill passed and Tiberius put himself, his father-in-law, and his younger brother Gaius in charge of seeing that it was enforced. More people began to mutter—not just lawmakers, but the commoners who had always been on Tiberius's side. He had bypassed the authority of his fellow tribunes, and the office of tribune was supposed to serve as a protection for the common people. They wanted his reforms passed, but many of them were worried about his methods.

The suspicions surrounding Tiberius Gracchus blazed up into a riot in 132, when he stood for reelection to the office of tribune. On the day of the elections, he was in the Capitol when rumors began to pass through the crowd: the wealthy would not allow a vote for him to be cast; assassins were coming to find him. The men around him began to grow more agitated. In the middle of all this, Tiberius put his hand to his head. Appian says that this was a sign to his followers that it was time to resort to violence to get him into office; Plutarch says that those around him thought he was asking to be crowned (a highly unlikely request). Clubs and sticks appeared. Whoever struck the first blow, the whole crowd erupted. Senators themselves were seen wrenching apart benches and using the legs as weapons. According to Plutarch, the first man to strike Tiberius himself was another one of the tribunes, who was armed with the leg of a stool. Tiberius fell and was beaten to death, along with three hundred other victims of the riot. He was barely thirty-one.

All of the bodies, including that of Tiberius Gracchus, were thrown without ceremony into the Tiber. "This," Plutarch says, "was the first sedition amongst the Romans, since the abrogation of kingly government, that ended

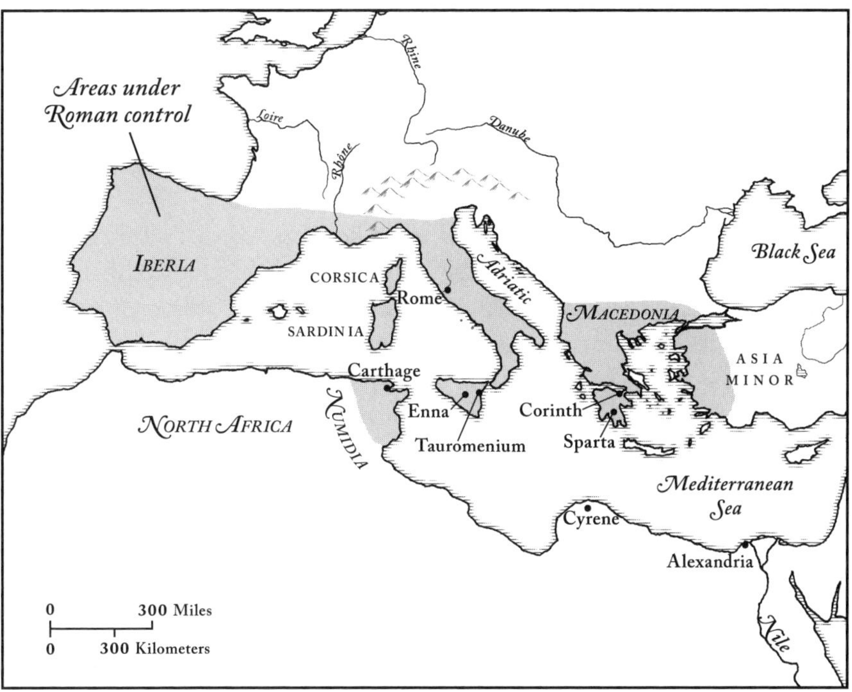

76.1 Slave Revolts

in blood."[17] Before, Senate and commons had managed to resolve their differences within the boundaries set by the Roman constitution; the murder of Tiberius Gracchus ripped those boundaries apart, and they were never fully stitched together again. Later, Romans themselves would look back to the blow that felled him as the fatal wounding of the Republic. But in fact Tiberius Gracchus had begun to insert the knife himself, when he had decided to bypass his fellow tribunes for the sake of the poor. "He lost his life," Appian concluded, "because he followed up an excellent plan in too lawless a way."[18]

In that same year, the First Servile War in Sicily finally came to an end when the consul Publius Rupilius crushed the rebellion with startling severity. He besieged the leadership of the revolt in the city of Tauromenium, and refused to lift the siege even when conditions inside became unspeakable: "Beginning by eating the children," Diodorus says, "they progressed to the women, and did not altogether abstain even from eating one another."[19] When the city surrendered, Rupilius tortured the slaves inside and then threw them, still living, over a cliff. He then pursued the slave-king Eunus across Sicily, captured him, and threw him into prison, where "his flesh disintegrated into a mass of lice."[20]

Eight years after Tiberius Gracchus's death, his brother Gaius Gracchus—nine years younger—stood for election to the tribunate as well. He was, Plutarch says, earnest and vehement where Tiberius had been calm and composed; passionate and zealous where his brother had been careful and precise in speech. He won enough votes to become a junior tribune, and soon showed that he intended to make good his brother's death. His reforms were even more radical than Tiberius's had been; he proposed that all public lands be divided between the poor, that foot soldiers should be clothed by the state, that all Italians should be given the vote as part of their citizenship, and half a dozen other enormous shifts in Roman practice. The consuls did their best to block his changes. In frustration, Gaius rounded up his own supporters to "oppose the consuls by force," and when the two parties came face-to-face another riot broke into bloodshed.[21]

Gaius Gracchus was murdered in the fighting. His killers hacked off his

TIMELINE 76

CHINA	ROME
Ch'in Dynasty (221)	
Shi Huang-ti (formerly Cheng)	Second Punic War (218)
	Battle of Cannae
Second Emperor (209)	
Han Dynasty (202)	Battle of Zama (202)
Gao Zu	Second Macedonian War
Hui-ti (195)	
Kao-hou (188)	Cumae changes its language to Latin
Wendi (179)	
	Third Macedonian War (171)
	Third Punic War (149)
Wudi (140)	Destruction of Carthage (146)
Zhang Qian's journey west	First Servile War (135)
	Death of Tiberius Gracchus
	Death of Gaius Gracchus

head and brought it to one of the consuls as a trophy. Three thousand other Romans fell in the riots as well. Once again the bodies were thrown into the Tiber, which this time came close to choking with the corpses. Tiberius Gracchus had died in a battle fought by clubs and wooden planks, but the riot that killed Gaius Gracchus was carried on with swords. The two sides had armed for war ahead of time.

Chapter Seventy-Seven

The Problems of Prosperity

Between 118 and 73 BC,
the allies of Rome demand citizenship,
the Han Dynasty spends too much money on conquest,
and Sulla and Marius fight for power inside Rome itself

AFTER THE DISASTER OF THE GRACCHI, it was clear that new laws were not going to bring any solution to the growing problems of poverty and landlessness. The Roman constitution, the elaborate system of tribunes and consuls, senators and judges, checks and balances, would neither bring nor prevent justice; the will of the rich or the charisma of the popular could always subvert it. New laws were not going to bring any solution to the growing problem of poverty and landlessness. Almost every Roman orator looked back wistfully to a golden age "before the destruction of Carthage," when the Republic was healthy: "Down to the destruction of Carthage," the Roman historian Sallust wrote a few years later, echoing the lament of the times, "the people and Senate shared the government peaceably and with due restraint, and the enemies did not compete for glory or power; fear of its enemies preserved the good morals of the state."[1]

That there had never been such a time was beside the point. Romans needed to look back with longing to an imaginary golden age, in order to cope with the present. Rome had once been pure, but now was filled with greed, corruption, pride, general decadence, and other fruits of prosperity, an evaluation which was only confirmed by a disaster called the Jugurthine War.

Down in North Africa, King Masinissa of Numidia had passed his throne on to his son Micipsa. This son, now getting on in years, had two sons of his own, plus a nephew named Jugurtha. The nephew was not in the line of succession, so Micipsa planned a military career for him and sent him off, in command of Numidian troops, to fight with Scipio Aemilius. Here Jugurtha was befriended by Roman officers, who assured him (so Sallust writes) that he

77.1 Numidia

could bribe the Roman government to put him onto his uncle's throne: "At Rome money could buy anything."[2]

When Micipsa died in 118, Jugurtha took the throne by force; his henchmen murdered one of his cousins, and the other, Adherbal, fled the country. To make sure that the Romans would not take the part of the rightful heir, Jugurtha "sent ambassadors to Rome with a quantity of gold and silver" to bribe senators with. This worked: "Their bitter resentment against Jugurtha was converted into favour and good will," Sallust remarks.[3]

Adherbal showed up in Rome, asking for help on his own account, to find that Jugurtha's money had already assured him a throne. The Senate decreed that the kingdom should be divided between the two of them; once they were both back down in Numidia, Jugurtha mounted a war against Adherbal, trapped him in his own capital city, captured him, and tortured him to death.

Public indignation meant that the Senate could not overlook this. In 111, a consul was sent down to Numidia with an army to punish Jugurtha. But like so many Roman officials, the consul was open to corruption: "Jugurtha sent agents who tempted him by offers of money," Sallust says, and he "quickly succumbed," subjecting Jugurtha to a token fine and then returning home.[4] Another official was then sent to drag Jugurtha to Rome, to stand trial, but once in Rome, Jugurtha paid off a tribune to halt the trial. The Senate sent him home. As he passed through the city gates, he is said to have looked back and said, "There is a city put up for sale, and if it finds a buyer, its days are numbered."[5]

This parade of bribes infuriated the Roman public, who saw in it everything they hated about their own corrupt government. Not until 109 did a

Roman officer gain a reputation for dealing honestly with Jugurtha. His name was Gaius Marius, and he was a "new man," meaning that he came from a family with no political power and no money. Given the mood of the Roman people, this worked in his favor. He spent two years fighting honorably in North Africa; in 107, he was elected consul.*

After the election he spent three more years campaigning against Jugurtha. Finally, with the help of his senior officer Lucius Cornelius Sulla (the same Sulla who had met with Mithridates II, inaugurating contact between Romans and Parthians, some fifteen years before), Marius managed to lure Jugurtha into a trap and capture him.

Jugurtha was paraded back into Rome in chains, a symbol not just of Roman victory, but of the triumph of common honesty over aristocratic corruption. Marius himself was hailed as Rome's champion. He was then elected consul five more times in succession.

This was actually against the Roman constitution, which was supposed to prevent consuls from serving year after year (and gaining more and more power). But Marius had become the people's darling, and the constitution hadn't prevented the wealthy and powerful from doing away with those earlier champions of the common man, the Gracchi brothers; so why should it stand in the way now?

Marius himself, awarding citizenship to a thousand Italian allies as a reward for their help in battle, was reproved for breaking the constitution: "I'm sorry," he replied, "but the noise of fighting prevented me from hearing the law."[6]

AFTER HIS SIXTH CONSULSHIP, Marius—realizing that he was unlikely to win a seventh—took himself off into self-imposed retirement. Rome had not fought a real war since Jugurtha's conquest, and Marius (so Plutarch says) "had no aptitude for peace or life as a private citizen."[7]

Real war was not long in coming, though. The Italian cities on the peninsula, Roman subjects all, had been asking for years to become full Roman citizens with voting rights, a privilege which the Senate had been stingy in granting. The general feeling that the common people of Rome were being trampled underfoot had spread outwards to encompass the Italian peoples as well, and little attention had been paid to their constant requests: "Tiberius Gracchus was persistent in support of the citizens," Cicero would remark later,

* Marius's original service in North Africa was as aide to the consul Metellus; Marius thought that Metellus was not bringing the war to a speedy enough end, and spent a year campaigning to be appointed in his commanding officer's place.

"but neglected the rights and treaties of the allies and the Latins."[8] Now the allies and the Latins wanted a voice in Rome's own affairs. They wanted, in the words of the ancient historian Justin, not just to be citizens, but to be partners in Rome's power.*[9]

When the Senate resisted sharing its authority, a swell of anti-Rome sentiment began. At first this took the form of a rejection of Roman customs and the Latin language, in favor of the old tongues of Italy; the historian E. T. Salmon has pointed out that inscriptions from Italian cities during this time contain an unusual number of archaic words.[10] This was followed by the joining together of a number of Italian cities into a new association which they called Italia. In 91, indignant Italians killed a Roman officer at the city of Asculum, and fighting began in earnest.

The struggle—the "Social War"—was an odd cross between civil war and reconquest of a foreign people. Rome slowly bargained and beat the Italian cities back into its fold. The consul of 90 BC, a member of the aristocratic but poor Julii Caesares clan, adopted the strategy that Gao Zu had used with success a century earlier, and offered citizenship to any Italian allies who refused to join the rebellion. Roman armies marched against the cities that remained hostile. Old Marius, now nearly seventy, came charging back from retirement to lead the campaign against the northern cities, but his ambitions were stronger than his body; he moved slowly, his decisions were hesitant, and finally, Plutarch says, "he felt that he was too incapacitated by his ill health to continue" and retired for the second time.[11]

Marius's former aide, Lucius Cornelius Sulla, did better out of the Social War. He was in charge of the campaigns in the south; twenty years Marius's junior, able to stand the rigors of camp life, he won victory after victory. "Sulla gained such remarkable successes," Plutarch says, "that he came to be regarded by his fellow citizens as a great leader."[12]

By 88, the Social War was over. Rome was master of the peninsula again, and the Italian cities had won the right of full Roman citizenship. Sulla stood for consul and was handily elected, thanks to his reputation as a great general. He fully expected to be given the plum military job of the year, which was to lead Roman legions into Asia Minor against a troublesome king there: Eupator Dionysius† of Pontus, a northwestern kingdom which was threatening to swallow more Asia Minor territory.

* The "Tiberius Gracchus" on behalf of the allies was a tribune named Drusus, who proposed that Rome give citizenship to all Italians, and also suggested that land be distributed to the poor. His reforms were blocked by the consul Philippus, who then arranged to have Drusus assassinated.

† Eupator Dionysius of Pontus (132–63) is more commonly known as Mithridates VI, and Roman

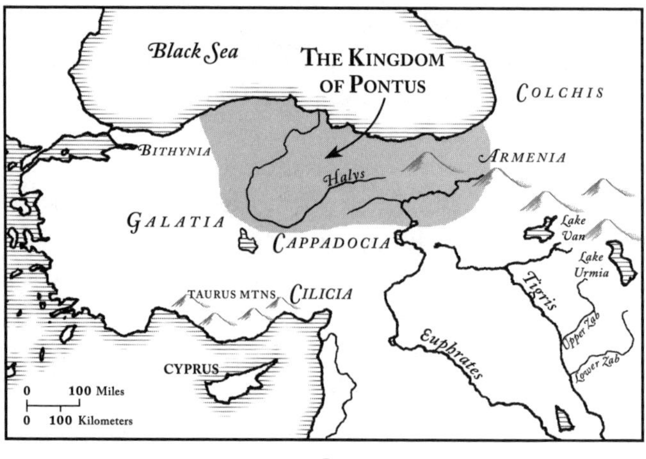

77.2 *Pontus*

Winning a war against Eupator Dionysius was a sure path to glory, and Sulla was the obvious choice for the job. As a matter of fact he was already out in the countryside with thirty-five thousand soldiers, preparing them for the upcoming campaign. But Marius had grown increasingly jealous of his old assistant. Even though he was now elderly, frequently ill, and overweight, he asked the Senate to award the campaign against Eupator Dionysius to him instead.

A good many Romans thought this was ridiculous. ("They suggested," Plutarch says, "that Marius should go to the warm springs and cosset himself instead, since he was worn out by old age and fluxes.")[13] Marius had not lived through decades of Roman politics to no avail, though. He bribed one of the tribunes to support his own claim to the generalship. The tribune, one Sulpicius, gathered himself a troop of armed men which he called the "Anti-Senate" and managed, more or less at swordpoint, to get the generalship awarded to Marius. He also sent two tribunes up to take command of Sulla's army and march it down to Marius.

When the tribunes arrived, the army stoned them to death.

"For many years there had been a festering sickness beneath the surface of Rome," Plutarch says, "and now the present situation caused it to erupt."[14] Full civil war broke out. Inside Rome, Marius, Sulpicius, and his armed ruffians "set about killing Sulla's friends." The senators, fearing for their lives,

sources often call him Mithridates the Great; I have decided to use his less common names to avoid confusion with the Parthian king Mithridates II (123–88), who was also known as "the Great" and whose reign overlapped that of Mithridates VI of Pontus.

sent another halfhearted message to Sulla asking him to surrender his army. Instead, Sulla called the legions together, and asked them to march on Rome.

This was a dreadful breach of the Roman constitution; no consul, awarded military powers, was supposed to exercise them within the pomerium, the domestic space set off from the outside world by Rome's walls. The inside of the city was solely the domain of the Senate. But as far as Sulla was concerned, Marius had already violated this restriction by employing those armed men of Sulpicius. He had to breach the constitution himself in order to fight back.

Some of Sulla's own officers refused to invade the *pomerium*. Sulla, knowing how serious an offense he was about to commit, did not even reprove them; he simply marched without them. When he got to the city, the Senate asked him to halt outside the walls, in order to give them time to sort the whole mess out. He refused, bursting through the gates with torch in hand and shouting to his men to set fire to the houses of his enemies. "In the heat of the moment, he let anger dictate events," says Plutarch. "All he could see were his enemies, and he . . . used fire as the agent of his return to Rome—fire, which made no distinction between the guilty and the innocent."[15]

Marius fled down to North Africa. Sulpicius was taken prisoner, and the Senate, convened by Sulla (and his armed men), dutifully sentenced Sulpicius to death (and also passed a death sentence on Marius in absentia). Sulla, walking a fine line between restoring order and acting like a military dictator, then pulled back a little and allowed a free election for consul held. The man who was elected, Lucius Cinna, was no friend of Sulla's. But he swore to be loyal to his fellow consul, and to obey the Senate.

Sulla, who had still not won his glory in Asia Minor, left the city in the hands of Cinna and the Senate and reassembled his army outside the walls. Then he marched on to the east, headed for Pontus and war.

THE OTHER GREAT EMPIRE, at the other end of the world, was also suffering growing pains. While Rome was struggling through the Social War, the Emperor Wudi—now close to the end of a fifty-year reign—was finishing up decades of campaigning against the nearby peoples: the Xiongnu, who were still trying to push down into the Han territory, and the lands to the west, along the new trade route, the Silk Road.

By 101 BC, the Han general Li Kuang had been put in charge of the most expensive campaign in Chinese history: the conquest of the northwestern land of Ferghana, or T'ai-yuan.[16] Li Kuang had been fighting for the Han emperors for over thirty years; his first military expedition had been against invading Xiongnu, back in the days of the Emperor Wendi. Sima Qian writes that,

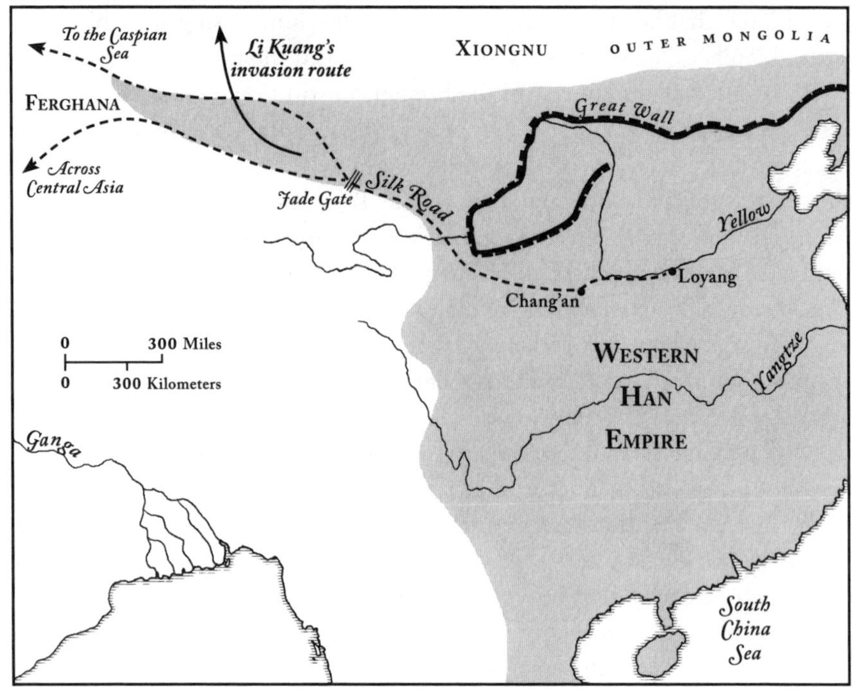

77.3 The Silk Road

on a later campaign, he demonstrated his intelligence by escaping from several thousand Xiongnu horsemen who had cut him off with only a hundred of his own men around him. He told his riders to get down from their horses and undo the saddles: "They expect us to run away," he said, "and if we show that we are not ready to flee, they'll suspect that something is up." His men obeyed him, and the Xiongnu, suspecting a trap, kept their distance. Dark was now creeping up on the trapped band, and Li Kuang told them to roll up in their blankets and lie down under their horses. The Xiongnu, seeing this, "concluded that the Han leaders must have concealed soldiers in the area and be planning to fall upon them in the dark." They all retreated, upon which Li Kuang and his men sprang up and rode back to the main body of the army.[17]

This sort of strategic thinking was still in short supply among the Roman commanders, who were far more likely to rely on sheer numbers to crush the enemy. It stood Li Kuang in good stead during his four-year campaign into Ferghana. He was now quite elderly, but unlike Marius he was still tough, active, and thoroughly capable of leading a difficult invasion into rough country.

The Xiongnu saw this as a direct challenge to their authority, and invaded

Ferghana from the other side to stop the Han armies. Li Kuang's first push into Ferghana was disastrous. He and his army marched up to the north through an area known as the Salt Swamp, which was about as hospitable as it sounds; their only source of food and water came from the walled cities along the way, and at the sight of the Han army on the horizon, most of these shut their gates tight and refused to come out. Li Kuang had the option of stopping to besiege them, and perhaps using up more supplies than the army would gain if the siege succeeded, and simply marching on. Sima Qian tells us that he took a middle way: if the town didn't surrender after a couple of days, the army abandoned it and continued the journey. By the time Li Kuang reached his original target, the major city of Yu-ch'eng, he had "no more than a few thousand soldiers left, and all of these were suffering from hunger and exhaustion."[18]

But he was unwilling to waste the journey, and set his men against Yu-ch'eng anyway. They were driven off in record time, and Li Kuang realized that he had no choice but to go back home. He turned and retraced his steps back to the edge of the Han land. The entire pointless journey had taken two years, and by the time it had ended, he had less than a fifth of his army left.

The Emperor Wudi, receiving word that the army was on its way home, flew into a fury and sent messengers to stand at the pass that led from Ferghana down into the Han territory: the Jade Gate. "Anyone who comes through the pass will be cut down on the spot," the messengers announced. Li Kuang came to a halt, unable to go home, unable to go back. For an entire summer he waited in limbo with the remnants of his army.

Wudi believed that the reputation of his empire was in jeopardy, and now that paths to the west had been opened, he could not afford to lose face. "Other lands would come to despise the Han," Sima Qian writes, "and China would become a laughingstock." So he emptied the royal treasury to hire soldiers and supply them, rounded up tribute fighters from his allies, and freed all the criminals in prison to go fight in Ferghana.

Li Kuang, receiving this new army of convicts and mercenaries, may not have felt particularly grateful. However, he had learned his lesson. He set off again for Yu-ch'eng. This time, the first walled city that refused to supply provisions for the passing soldiers was besieged, conquered, and sacked; all the inhabitants were massacred.[19] "After this," Sima Qian remarks, "his advance was unhindered."

Yu-ch'eng fell. Not long after, so did Erh-shih, the capital of Ferghana's ruling lord. The Xiongnu were unable to halt the Han advance. Four years after the campaign had first begun, the Han finally controlled all of Ferghana.

This was a major accomplishment; it demonstrated the Han superiority over the Xiongnu, and also put the states to the west, along the Silk Road, on notice that they had better yield to any Han parties passing through: "All of the states of the Western Region were shocked and frightened," one account reads.[20] The Han emperor had protected his empire's claim to greatness—its power to buy and sell with the west.

Pride came expensive, though. When Wudi died in 87, the same year that Sulla was marching towards Asia Minor at the head of his legions, the Silk Road remained open. But the Han treasury was drained, the army exhausted. The next two Han emperors, Zhaodi and Xuandi, would do little to advance the empire further.

Just as soon as Sulla was safely out of the Italian peninsula, Cinna's fellow consul threw him out of the city and locked the gates. Cinna, fuming outside the walls, began to collect himself an army, intending to fight his way back in. Marius, down in North Africa, heard the news and returned at once, meeting Cinna outside the city.

Marius indulged in a bit of theatrics, Plutarch says, dressing in rags and refusing to cut his hair during his entire exile from Rome, and limping slowly to meet Cinna like a persecuted elderly petitioner. News of this humility undoubtedly went to Rome, where the remaining consul was becoming increasingly unpopular (it was difficult to stay on anyone's good side for long in first-century Rome). Possibly bribes changed hands as well; in any case, the Senate sent messages inviting both Cinna and Marius to return to Rome.

Marius, rags notwithstanding, had used his considerable personal fortune to hire himself a large army of North African mercenaries. He and Cinna marched back to Rome at the head of this alarming force and passed through the gates.

Marius's behavior afterwards suggests that he was no longer thinking clearly. His personal bodyguard killed without question anyone at whom he pointed, and although this at first included anyone who might be a friend of Sulla's, the bloodbath soon expanded. "If anyone greeted Marius, but received no word or greeting in return," Plutarch says, "this in itself was the signal for him to be murdered right there in the street, until even his friends were riddled with anxiety and terror every time they came up to Marius to greet him."[21] Even Cinna began to look at him with alarm.

Meanwhile Sulla had been covering himself with glory (or shame, depending on whether you were a Greek or Roman historian) by taking back Asia Minor and then whipping various rebellious Greek cities back into shape.

When word of happenings in Rome flew eastwards to him, he turned back towards home with his army.

Sulla was coming! Plutarch writes. It sounded like deliverance for the people of Rome, and the news unhinged Marius even more. He began to drink uncontrollably, contracted pleurisy, and fell into delusions, imagining that he was in command of the legions that had gone to attack Pontus and shouting out battle orders at odd moments. On January 17, 86 BC, he died in his home.

77.1. Sulla. Roman bust of Sulla, consul of Rome in 88 BC. Museo Archeologico, Venice. Photo credit Scala/Art Resource, NY

Sulla was not, in fact, as near as Marius thought. He did not arrive in Italy until 83 BC; in the meantime, more and more prominent Romans fled from Cinna's "lawless thuggery" and travelled to meet Sulla, until he was "surrounded by what was to all intents and purposes a senate."[22] Cinna gathered together an army and set out to meet Sulla himself, but his men mutinied and killed him before he had gotten very far.

Clearly Roman opinion had turned more and more towards Sulla, as Cinna and Marius grew more savage; even so, Sulla had to fight his way into Rome when he finally arrived at the city. Marius's son, at the head of his father's old supporters, mounted fierce resistance. But Sulla was aided by two able younger officers named Pompey and Crassus, and under this three-way command, his army broke into the city.

Almost as soon as Sulla was inside Rome, he had six thousand prisoners (all men who had fought against him in his approach to Rome) herded into the Circus. He himself went to address the Senate. In the middle of his speech, screams began to rise up from the Circus. He had ordered the six thousand defenseless men butchered. "Sulla continued speaking with the same unmoved, calm expression on his face as before," Plutarch says, "and told them . . . not to pay any attention to what was going on outside, which was just some criminals being punished on his orders. As a result of this, even the densest person in Rome came to understand that they had merely exchanged one monstrous tyranny for another."[23]

It was true. The wound dealt to the Republic by Tiberius Gracchus's death had widened and festered. The only men ruthless enough to fight against tyranny were themselves inclined to it; and Sulla, once in charge of Rome (in 81 he was appointed dictator, despite the fact that there was no particular crisis on the horizon), began his own purge. "I am proscribing everyone I can think of," he said in one public speech, "but if I've forgotten anyone I'll get around to proscribing them later." Friends and relatives of Marius and Cinna died, or fled; Cinna's son-in-law, a young man named Julius Caesar, was one of the lucky escapees. The official murders soon progressed beyond the political and encompassed the personal as well: "More were killed for their property," Plutarch writes, "and even the executioners tended to say that this man was killed by his large house, this one by his garden, that one by his warm springs."[24] Sulla's two right-hand men were no more admirable than Sulla himself. Pompey was given the job of chasing those allies of Marius who had left the Italian peninsula; he tracked rebels down in Sicily and in North Africa, and was so successful in murdering them all that he demanded a victory parade when he returned to Rome.[25] Meanwhile, Crassus was helping out by setting fires to houses in Rome which he and Sulla wanted to claim. He also had a band of firemen and a real-estate agent on his payroll. As soon as the house began to burn, the agent would appear and offer to buy the property for a bargain price; the homeowner would agree, so that the house wouldn't be a dead loss; and then the firemen would appear from out of sight and douse the fire.[26]

Having gotten everything that he could out of Rome, Sulla then retired, in 80, and went to the country. Here he both married again *and* took a male lover, more or less simultaneously. All of this activity notwithstanding, he was in poor health, probably suffering from cirrhosis of the liver. "For a long time he failed to observe that his bowels were ulcerated, till at length the corrupted flesh broke out into lice," Plutarch writes. "Many were employed day and night in destroying them, but the work so multiplied under their hands, that not only his clothes, baths, basins, but his very meat was polluted with that flux and contagion, they came swarming out in such numbers." In this disgusting condition, he passed his last years; like the Republic, fatally ill, but lingering on and pretending to good health.

TIMELINE 77

CHINA	ROME
Han Dynasty (202)	Battle of Zama (202)
Gao Zu	Second Macedonian War
Hui-ti (195)	
Kao-hou (188)	Cumae changes its language to Latin
Wendi (179)	
	Third Macedonian War (171)
	Third Punic War (149)
Wudi (140)	Destruction of Carthage (146)
Zhang Qian's journey west	First Servile War (135)
	Death of Tiberius Gracchus
	Death of Gaius Gracchus
	Jugurthine War (112)
	Gaius Marius, consul
	Social War (91)
Zhaodi (87)	Lucius Sulla, consul
	Lucius Cinna, consul
Xuandi (73)	

Chapter Seventy-Eight

New Men

Between 78 and 44 BC, Spartacus leads a revolt, and Julius Caesar forms a partnership with Pompey and Crassus

IN 78, SULLA DIED at his country estate. He had married five times and sired twenty-three children; the last, Postumus Cornelius Sulla, was born after his death.

The aftershocks of the rivalry between Sulla and Marius rumbled on. Sulla's right-hand man Pompey led an army over to the Iberian peninsula to fight against one of Marius's allies. Another army went east in an attempt to wrap up the war against the king of Pontus, which Sulla himself had left unfinished when he returned to Rome. Between these two wars and an ongoing Roman battle against pirates in the Mediterranean, much of Rome's army was off the Italian peninsula.

This absence of armed men led another band of slaves to launch a revolt. But these slaves were skilled fighters, trained to take part in Rome's public games: gladiators.

Fights carried on by slaves for the entertainment of onlookers had been going on since the days of the Etruscans, and Roman public festivals had made increasing use of gladiatorial combats since the third century BC.* Rome's foreign wars had brought more and more slaves suitable for the games into Rome and the surrounding cities: captive soldiers from Gaul, the Iberian peninsula, Thrace, Syria, and Greece.[1] A successful gladiator could attract his share of hero worship ("Men give them their souls, women their bodies," the Roman theologian Tertullian wrote, a little later), but he remained a despised

* The first Roman gladiator fight is thought to have taken place in 264, when slaves were matched against each other as part of a private funeral festival.

member of Roman society. "[Romans] glorify and degrade and diminish them," Tertullian concluded, "indeed, they openly condemn them to ignominy and the loss of civil rights. . . . They belittle whom they esteem; the art they glorify, the artist they debase."[2]

One of the most notorious training schools for gladiators was in the city of Capua, south of Rome, where a gladiator master kept a whole assortment of slaves cooped up. "Most of them were Gauls and Thracians," Plutarch writes. "They had done nothing wrong, but, simply because of the cruelty of their owner, were kept in close confinement until the time came for them to engage in combat."[3] In 73, seventy-eight of these gladiators managed to break out of their quarters. They raided a nearby butcher's shop for knives and spits and headed out of the city. When troops came after them from Capua, the gladiators polished them off and took their weapons away.

This was the beginning of a fight that would go on for more than two years, and earned the title of the Gladiator War.* The gladiators elected as their leader a man named Spartacus; Plutarch says that he was a Thracian "from the nomadic tribes," but "most intelligent and cultured, being more like a Greek than a Thracian." (This was by way of a compliment.) He turned out to be a brilliant strategist. Three thousand Roman soldiers were sent out against the gladiators, and drove them up a mountain where there were only two routes of escape: through a pass guarded by the Romans, and down a steep cliff-face on the other side. But the ground was covered with wild vines. Under Spartacus's direction, the trapped gladiators cut them up and made them into ladders, which they dropped to the bottom of the cliff and scrambled down. Then they went around to where the Romans were camping, totally unprepared, and took the whole camp.[4]

After this, they routed several other Roman assault forces sent out against them, and began to gain a greater and greater opinion of their own strength. According to Appian, Spartacus's army grew to seventy thousand men, and the Romans had to entirely change their opinion about the contest: "Ridiculous and contemptible in the beginning," Appian says, the war had become "formidable to Rome."[5]

Spartacus, who apparently just wanted to go home, tried to convince them to turn their backs on Rome and march up through the Alps, where they could then scatter to their homelands of Thrace and Gaul. But they would not listen: "They were strong in numbers," Plutarch says, "and full of confidence, and they went about Italy ravaging everything in their way."[6]

* It was also known as the Third Servile War. The Second Servile War had been fought against a slave revolt in Sicily in 104; it was put down in less than a year.

This alarmed the Senate to such a degree that both consuls were sent out against the gladiator army. When both failed, the Senate appointed Sulla's junior lieutenant Crassus to the job of wiping out the revolt. His first foray against Spartacus ended with an ignoble Roman retreat; with the ruthlessness that characterized Sulla's associates, Crassus pulled out the five hundred foot soldiers who had been at the forefront of the flight and put fifty of them to death by lottery, while the rest of the army watched: a vicious punishment known as "decimation."

This had the intended effect of strengthening them for the next encounter. Spartacus was driven back towards the coast, where he made arrangements with a pirate fleet to ferry his army over to Sicily. However, the pirates took his money and then sailed away, leaving him standing on the shore at Rhegium, the very tip of the Italian boot.

This meant that his army was on a little peninsula, and Crassus ordered his men to build a wall across the neck of the peninsula, with a fifteen-foot ditch in front of it. Spartacus was trapped, but not for long; when a snowstorm descended on the two armies, he filled up part of the ditch with dirt, logs, and tree branches, and got a good part of his army out of it and away.

At this point the Romans back home decided that Crassus needed help: Appian says that the Senate "ordered up the army of Pompey, which had just arrived from Spain, as a reinforcement."[7] Crassus redoubled his efforts, desperately hoping to finish the war before his colleague (and competitor) Pompey should arrive to steal some of the glory. "A number of people were already loudly proclaiming that victory in this war belonged to Pompey," Plutarch writes; "it only remained for him to come and fight a battle, they said, and the war would be over."[8] Crassus was preparing for a last assault when Spartacus's men, who had been ruined by success (they were so overconfident that they no longer paid any attention to their general), made an ill-timed and badly judged attack on the Roman lines. The Roman troops were finally able to turn the attack back. Most of the gladiators fled; Spartacus himself, making straight for Crassus, was deserted by his fellows and killed.

Unfortunately for Crassus, Pompey had just arrived. He caught and killed many of the fleeing slaves as they ran past him. Six thousand of them, captured alive, were crucified along the road from Capua to Rome; the crosses stretched almost the entire length of the Appian Way.[9] Most people saw this as a monument to Pompey, not Crassus, which Pompey himself encouraged by sending a letter to the Senate saying that while Crassus had managed to win a battle, he himself had "dug the war up by the roots."[10]

The following year, 70 BC, both Crassus and Pompey were elected as consuls. Plutarch says that they quarrelled the whole time and got nothing done, but they made themselves popular with the people by giving out grain.[11] They were increasingly seen as champions of the common man; and for a little while, it must have seemed to the Roman voters as though the aristocratic control and corruption that had plagued Rome were finally on the wane. Crassus's shady moneymaking strategies were in abeyance; Pompey's biggest flaw was his propensity to claim credit for things that others had done. And another young politician, Cicero, was campaigning against senatorial corruption with zeal; in 70 BC, he prosecuted and convicted the aristocrat Verres of corruption, and the man was unable to escape.

78.1. Pompey. Pompey the Great, 106–48 BC. Carlsberg Glyptotek, Copenhagen. Photo credit Alinari/Art Resource, NY

So when piracy in the Mediterranean became a major problem, it seemed reasonable for the tribunes, representing the people, to suggest that Pompey be given the task of wiping it out. He would be given temporary command of a huge military force, which included not only all Roman ships in the Mediterranean but also over a hundred thousand Roman troops, in order to tackle the problem.[12] The Senate, disliking so much power concentrated in the hands of one man, objected; but the Assembly voted to approve Pompey's appointment.

His success was drastic and enormous and made him increasingly popular. His family was rapidly rising to become one of the most powerful in Rome; in fact, Julius Caesar (who had returned to Rome after Sulla's death) asked to marry his daughter Pompeia. Pompey agreed to the wedding, and immediately set off again on campaign. After his triumph against the pirates, he had been awarded command of the ongoing fight against Pontus in the east.

In 66, Pompey brought a quick end to this war and then swept down along the coast of the Mediterranean and conquered the Syrian holdings of the fading Seleucid empire. In Jerusalem, he went into the temple for a quick look, even sticking his head into the Holy of Holies. This shocked the priests, but they were reconciled to the heathen invasion when Pompey gave them control of the city. Under this new arrangement, Jerusalem would be

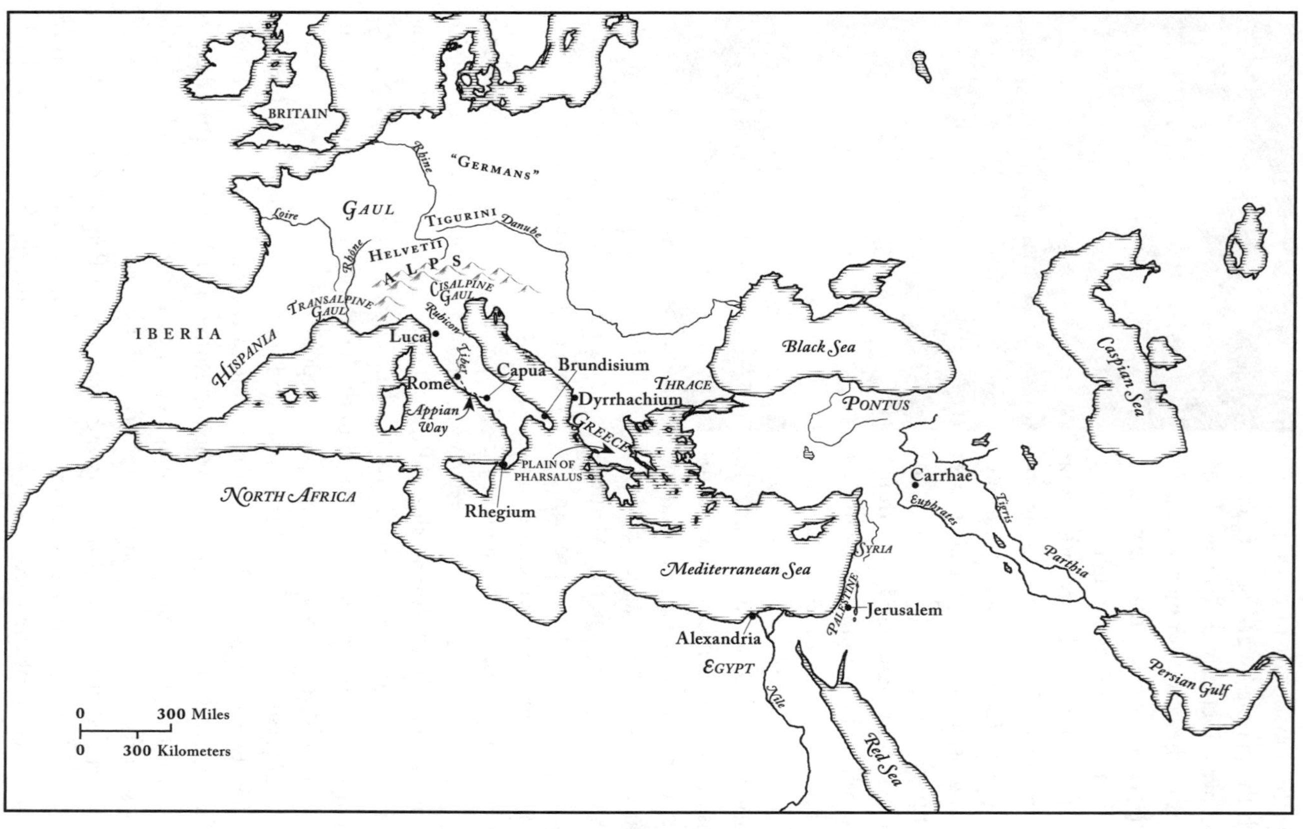

78.1 The Wars of Pompey and Caesar

part of the Roman province of Palestine, and would no longer have a Hasmonean king. Instead, Pompey appointed a priest named John Hyrcanus (known as Hyrcanus II) to be "High Priest and Ethnarch," a combined religious and secular office. The priests would run Palestine for Rome, and would report to a Roman governor who had charge over all of Syria, Rome's newest acquisition.

And then Pompey went home covered with glory.

BACK IN ROME, both Caesar and Cicero were rising in the political firmament. Cicero had been elected consul in 63, in a startling departure from tradition; it had been thirty years since a new man (a *novus homo*, from a family where no man had ever been consul before) had been appointed to the office. Julius Caesar too had been elected to two high-profile public offices: he became a financial official, an *aedile*, in 65, and Pontifex Maximus (high priest of the state religion) in 63.* Unfortunately, he ran so deeply into debt campaigning that by the end of his term as Pontifex Maximus, he was in danger of being arrested for unpaid bills. He needed to leave Rome, and he needed to make some money. He managed to get himself appointed to the governorship of Hispania, the Roman province on the Iberian peninsula, but his creditors caught him at the ports and tried to confiscate his luggage.

Crassus, who was a good businessman—he owned silver mines, huge tracts of farmland, and enough slaves to work it all—guaranteed Caesar's debts for him, and the creditors agreed to let him go.[13] Crassus was a good judge of men. In Hispania, Caesar made enough money to pay off the creditors and was able to return to Rome. Once there, he called together Pompey (the popular conqueror) and Crassus (the prosperous businessman) and suggested that the three of them have a private arrangement. If they would give him enough public support and money to make his run for the consulship of 59 a success, once he was in power he would push for whatever laws they wanted.

Pompey was willing; he wanted extra benefits for the veterans in his army. Crassus was harder to convince. He was still peeved by Pompey's self-glorification after the Gladiator War, and he did not trust Pompey now.

* The offices of consul and tribune had been joined by a whole array of positions. *Praetors* were assistants to the consuls and helped them carry out their duties; *quaestors* ran the state finances; *aediles* were responsible for keeping up with public buildings and organizing festivals; *governors* ran Rome's provinces; and *censors* supervised public behavior and punished the immoral (thus the English word "censorious"). Since Roman religion was state-run, religious officials also had secular duties; the Pontifex Maximus was a high priest who supervised the lesser religious officials (such as the *flamines*, who looked after the worship of specific deities, and the Vestal Virgins) and also kept Rome's state annals.

(When he first heard Pompey's nickname, "Pompey the Great," he snorted and asked, "As great as what?")[14] However, he could see the advantages of having Caesar press for new financial regulations that would benefit his business, rather than doing so himself, and eventually the triumvirate of politicians agreed on their three-way deal. Caesar also broke his daughter's engagement and offered her to Pompey, who was almost a quarter-century her senior and had already been married three times. Pompey agreed, and the wedding cemented the alliance.*

The campaign succeeded, and Caesar became consul. At once he introduced all sorts of measures to redistribute land to the poor. This made him extremely unpopular with his fellow consul Bibulus and with the Senate, which did not like to see a consul behaving like a tribune and championing the cause of the masses. ("This was a lowering of his great office," Plutarch sniffs.) The masses were pleased, though; the Assembly approved Caesar's measures, and Pompey sent armed men to the Forum to make sure that the Senators did not interfere. Bibulus himself got a bucket of manure dumped on his head when he came down to the Forum to object. After that, Plutarch says, he "shut himself up in his house and stayed there for the rest of his term of office."[15]

When his year as consul was over, Caesar (with the help of Pompey's armed men) got himself appointed as governor of "Transalpine Gaul," the western part of the province on the other side of the Alps (the eastern portion was known as "Cisalpine Gaul"). Here he set about building himself a reputation as a conqueror that would rival Pompey's own. First he pushed back the Celtic tribes of the Helvetii and the Tigurini, who were trying to invade Transalpine Gaul; then he took the war into the enemy territory, towards the Rhine river, against the tribes known collectively as "Germans." Taking a lesson from Pompey, he also made sure that the Romans back home knew about every single victory; he sent back constant reports on how well he was doing, always couched in terms of gains for the Republic. "On the receipt of the dispatches in Rome," he wrote, in his own history of his Gallic wars, "a public thanks-

* All of these people were related to each other anyway, in a big Faulknerian mess of marriages. Caesar's aunt was married to Marius. Caesar's first wife was Cinna's daughter, and his second wife was Sulla's granddaughter (Pompeia Sulla, whose mother was Sulla's daughter and whose father was a cousin of Pompey's). Pompey's second wife was Sulla's stepdaughter, and his fourth wife was Caesar's daughter, Julia. When Caesar broke Julia's engagement, Pompey offered the jilted fiancé *his* own daughter, even though she was already engaged to Sulla's son. Crassus married his own brother's widow and left it at that, although he was rumored to be carrying on an affair with one of the Vestal Virgins.

giving of fifteen days was decreed to celebrate [my] achievements—a greater honor than had previously been granted to anyone."*[16]

Meanwhile he was keeping a thumb in affairs at home. He came down into Italy as far as the Rubicon river, which was considered to be the northern border of Italy proper, and built himself a satellite camp at the city of Luca. From there, Plutarch says, he "employed his time in political intrigues," and handed out plenty of bribes: "Many people came to see him . . . everyone left him with something in hand for the present and with hopes for more in the future."[17]

In 56, two of those travellers were Crassus and Pompey, who came to work out the next stage of their three-way alliance. They decided that Crassus and Pompey would run for the consulship of 55; once they were in power, they would award Caesar another five years in Gaul, so that he could go on extending his power there. Then, after the consulships ended, Crassus would make himself general of an expedition to the east against the Parthians, now the strongest power on the other side of the Mediterranean, which would give him a chance for the military glory which had so far eluded him. Pompey, who was done with fighting, would give himself the governorship of Hispania and, like Caesar, make a profit from it.

With this agreement sealed, Pompey and Crassus went back to Rome. The Roman public was still suspicious of both of them, but neither one intended to leave the election to fair means. After an amount of vote-buying which exceeded any bribery ever seen before in Rome, they were both appointed to the consulship for the second time, fifteen years after their first term of service. The Senate duly voted to extend Caesar's command: "It was a question of compulsion," Plutarch notes, "and the senate groaned at the decrees for which it voted."[18]

But the people were still on Caesar's side: Caesar the compassionate, Caesar the all-conquering. The Triumvirate had succeeded again. They were poised, as far as all three were all concerned, on the very edge of glory and wealth beyond their wildest dreams.

As soon as the two consuls had taken office, Caesar launched a new offensive, against a brand-new frontier. In 55, he landed on the southeast coast of Britain for the first time for a reconnaissance.

* The opening words of *Bello Gallico*, the *Gallic War*, are *Omnis gallia est divisa in tres partes*, "All of Gaul is divided into three parts." This became one of the best-known Latin phrases in the English-speaking world, since generations of Latin students had to translate Caesar as their first "real" Latin assignment.

The inhabitants of this part of Britain were a mixture of the earliest residents of the island, perhaps living there since the days when Britain had been a peninsula instead of an island, and Celts who had moved west from the European mainland across the channel. In Britain, these tribes didn't have the space to be nomadic; they settled down into a network of little tribal kingdoms. What we know of them comes from Caesar's own account and, in distorted form, from a much later history: Geoffrey of Monmouth's *Historia Regum Britannia*, which combines Roman and medieval place names with Welsh legend, a thin thread of fact, and a strong patriotic bent ("Britain, the best island, is situated in the western sea between Gaul and Hibernia," he begins, showing his Roman orientation).[19]

78.2 Britain

The history starts out with the very unlikely story of a great-grandson of Aeneas, Brutus, setting out on an expedition and stumbling upon the island, which he named Britain after himself. This obligatory linking of British history with ancient myth is followed by Geoffrey's account of the earliest kings of Britain.* Prominent in this story is one Cassivelaunus, whom Geoffrey of Monmouth calls "king of the Britains," but who appears in Julius Caesar's account as a rogue warrior who usurped the throne of the Trinovantes tribe.

Pieced together, Monmouth and Caesar suggest that the king of the Trinovantes, King Lud, had managed to make the Trinovantes one of the most powerful tribal kingdoms of the south; he was best known for expanding and walling in the main settlement on the river Thames, which became known as Lundres in his honor. When Lud died, his brother Cassivelaunus claimed the

* Geoffrey of Monmouth says that one of the earliest kings of Britain was a man with the Welsh name Llur, who had three daughters named Koronilla, Rragaw, and Kordelia. To find out which of his daughters deserved the largest part of his kingdom, he asked which one loved him the most. Kordelia answered, "I will love you as a daughter should love her father," which angered Llur tremendously; this, of course, was Shakespeare's source for *King Lear*.

throne over the head of Lud's own son. The displaced prince, Mandubracius, fled across the water to Caesar's headquarters in Gaul and asked the Romans to help him get his kingdom back. Like most kings who asked for Roman intervention, he would regret it later.

On his first visit, Caesar evaluated the opposition. ("All the Britons dye their bodies with woad, which produces a blue color," he wrote on his return, "and shave the whole of their bodies except the head and the upper lip.")[20] The following year, 54, he returned with a fighting force to take over.

Cassivelaunus came out to meet him with a fleet of chariots, the first time Caesar and his men had encountered these in war. Fighting against charioteers demanded a swift change in tactics: "It was seen that our troops were too heavily weighted by their armour to deal with such an enemy," Caesar observes, especially since the British charioteers were able to leap down from the chariots, fight on foot, and then make a quick retreat: "They can run along the chariot pole, stand on the yoke, and get back into the chariot as quick as lightning."[21] Caesar sent his cavalry out front instead and managed to push Cassivelaunus back to the Thames, which was protected by sharp stakes driven into the riverbed beneath the surface of the water.

Here he halted, but the nearby tribes were already sending envoys to surrender to the Roman forces. Roman troops also managed to find and raid Cassivelaunus's headquarters, killing all of the cattle and making food very short indeed. Finally Cassivelaunus too sent a messenger offering terms of surrender. Caesar, who could see winter coming on, agreed to a peace as long as Mandubracius was put back in charge of the Trinovantes as a subject king of Rome; he extracted a promise from Cassivelaunus to leave the new king alone, and then went back to Gaul.

Caesar's fame was now unmatched, but dreadful news was waiting for him: his beloved daughter Julia, Pompey's wife, had died in childbirth.

Soon after, Crassus met with disaster in his war against Parthia. In 53, the year after Caesar's triumphs in Gaul, Crassus marched towards the Euphrates river (which was now the Parthian border) with about seventy thousand foot soldiers and four thousand cavalry. The Romans met the Parthian army at the town of Carrhae: old Haran, the city where Nabonidus was born and where Terah, father of Abraham, had died. Almost at once, they found themselves outarmed; the Parthian archers, shooting from a distance, could easily penetrate their armor. "They were thus hit and killed," Plutarch says,

> dying, not by a quick and easy death, but with miserable pains and convulsions; for writhing upon the darts in their bodies, they broke them in their wounds, and when they would by force pluck out the barbed points, they

> caught the veins, so that they tore and tortured themselves. Many of them died thus, and those that survived were disabled for any service . . . their hands nailed to their shields, and their feet stuck to the ground, so that they could neither fight nor fly.[22]

Crassus sent his son Publius, who had come with him as his second-in-command, to charge the line; the Parthians withdrew, pulling Publius and his men onwards, and then swung around and surrounded them. Almost all of Publius's troops fell fighting. Publius, seeing that defeat was inevitable, killed himself. The Parthians beheaded him and stuck his head on the end of a spear, waving it at his father as they harassed the remaining Romans.

Two days later Crassus was killed as well, with almost all of his men. The Parthian general, Surena, took Crassus's head back to Orodes, king of Parthia, who (according to the Roman historian Dio Cassius) used it as a prop in a victory play.

The eastern frontier of Rome's empire had been closed off. The Roman garrisons in Syria braced themselves under a Parthian attack which failed only because the Parthians were not yet experienced at sieges. King Orodes now ruled over a Parthia which stretched across much of the old Seleucid territory, from the Euphrates almost all the way to the border of China.

And the Triumvirate had been reduced to two. The year after the Parthian victory, Caesar—having put down a serious rebellion in Gaul—prepared to march back into Rome richer than Pompey and with more triumphs to his credit.

The Senate regarded this prospect with horror: Caesar's glorious reputation, his wealth, and his army together all spelled *dictator.* And they were no longer compelled by Pompey's armed men to grant Caesar's wishes. The deaths of Julia and Crassus had weakened the bond between the two men, and Pompey was increasingly jealous of Caesar's victories. "Pompey had come to fear Caesar," Plutarch says. "Up till this time, he had despised him."[23]

Together, Pompey and the Senate sent a message north: Caesar would not be allowed to enter Rome unless he surrendered his entire army.

Caesar suggested several compromises, including permission to enter with only a few legions, but Pompey convinced the Senate to refuse. Caesar knew that if he came to Rome unprotected, his career might end in hasty assassination. He decided that—like Sulla before him—he would enter with his army, as a conqueror; and so he set out, from Gaul, towards the north of Italy.

Plutarch says that Caesar knew perfectly well that this would start a bloody civil war, and that he halted, before he reached the Rubicon, and thought through the matter again. But finally, "in a sort of passion, as though casting calculation aside," he shouted out "*Alea iacta est!*" which was the gambler's traditional cry: "Let the die be cast!" He crossed the river, and "the broad gates of war were opened."[24]

Immediately Italy was struck with panic. Men and women fled from one coast to the other, trying to get out of the way of the inevitable clash. Reports constantly flew down to the city that Caesar was just over the horizon. Pompey, panicking himself, left Rome and told the Senate to come with him; clearly he was afraid that the people of Rome would throw the gates open to Caesar. He fled down south to Brundisium, on the eastern coast, set up a rump government there, and then sent his own army across the water to reassemble itself at the Greek city of Dyrrhachium.

Caesar thought that this showed tremendous weakness, and Cicero later thought it a bad decision as well. But the delay gave Pompey enough time to round up a huge army with a very strong fleet of ships, since Caesar (rather than chasing him on out of Italy) turned back towards Rome. And, like Sulla years before, Pompey soon found himself joined by hundreds of prominent Romans, including Cicero.

78.2. Julius Caesar. Roman marble bust of Julius Caesar, 100–44 BC. Uffizi, Florence, Italy. Photo credit Alinari/Art Resource, NY

Back in Italy, Caesar entered Rome and "found the city in a more settled state than he expected," with a good part of the Senate still in residence and inclined to pacify the great conqueror.[25] He did not, like Marius and Sulla, institute a purge; he simply took control of the city and scared the resistance out of everyone by sheer force of personality. When the remaining tribune objected to Caesar's raiding the treasury in order to prepare for war against Pompey, Caesar remarked, "Young man, if you don't stop interfering, I may just kill you. And I dislike *saying* this much more than I would dislike *doing* it." The tribune, Plutarch says, "went off in a fright," and for the rest of the war Caesar had all the money he needed.

It took him two years to defeat the expatriates over in Greece. Months of "desultory fighting," as Plutarch terms it, finally ended in 48, in a huge clash on the plain of Pharsalus. Caesar's infantry fought against Pompey's cavalry as they had learned to do against the Britons, by running up to the horses and aiming their javelins at the riders' faces. The cavalry was completely unaccustomed to this mode of fighting, and stampeded. The resistance collapsed. Pompey, watching his army fall apart, went back to his tent and sat down until he could hear Caesar's troops storming through the camp itself; then he changed into old clothes and slipped away unnoticed.

At news of the victory, the Senate proclaimed Caesar first dictator, and then, after eleven days, consul instead. Caesar's aide Mark Antony, who had led one of the wings of his army during the Battle of Pharsalus, ran the city as his deputy; Caesar had learned that Pompey had been sighted heading towards Egypt, and had decided to chase his enemy a little farther.[26]

Whatever personal reasons Caesar had for following Pompey to Egypt, his pursuit made good political sense as well. Egypt, much fallen from its old greatness, was still a rich and potentially troublesome kingdom, and it had a weak young king: Ptolemy XIII, distant descendent of the great Ptolemy himself.

The Ptolemys had followed each other in a bickering, contentious, but more or less unbroken line for the last century, since we saw Ptolemy VI quarrelling with the Seleucids over Coele Syria. However, Ptolemy XIII was in the middle of a quarrel with his sister, Cleopatra VII, over which one of them should have the throne. When Pompey sailed into view of Egypt's shores, Cleopatra was in Alexandria, while young Ptolemy was in Pelusium with an army, getting ready to attack his sister.[27]

Ptolemy, Plutarch says, was "a very young man," and his advisors made most of his decisions for him. They decided that since Caesar was already on the way down to Egypt to catch and punish Pompey, they would get on Caesar's good side by doing the job for him. So an official delegation of welcoming Egyptians sailed out to greet Pompey's approaching ship, saluted him as "Imperator," and invited him aboard so that they could ferry him ashore. Just as they were reaching the landing, as Pompey began to stand up to get off the boat, one of Ptolemy's men ran him through from behind; and then two more cut off his head and threw his body into the water. Pompey was sixty years old; he had just celebrated his birthday on September 28, the day before his murder.[28]

When Caesar arrived, the Egyptian officials brought him Pompey's head in a basket. He was, reportedly, furious: he had intended to humiliate his old ally, but not kill him. But this gave him a marvelous excuse for taking control of

Egypt, which he could now do by way of punishment. He ordered Cleopatra and Ptolemy XIII to both come to Alexandria, where he would choose one of them as rightful ruler of Egypt (under his supervision).*

His choice turned out to be less than objective. He was smitten with Cleopatra's beauty and ordered her brother deposed in her favor. Ptolemy XIII died fighting against the Roman troops who arrived to enforce Caesar's decision. Cleopatra was coronated and ceremonially married to her younger brother, an Egyptian custom that the Ptolemys had been following for some time.

Meanwhile Caesar carried on a furious affair with Cleopatra which kept him idle (politically, at least) in Alexandria for some months. When he was finally able to tear himself away, leaving her pregnant, he made a military tour around the edge of the Roman Republic: up the eastern border, where he destroyed the armies of Pontus; back down along the African border; up through the Iberian peninsula; and then back to Rome.

During his travels, he had been reelected consul four times, as a way of keeping up a legal pretense for his power. In 46, Caesar's supporters (and the Romans who were afraid of them) agreed to give him a victory parade into Rome that had in it uncomfortable echoes of the ancient Etruscan kingship. Statues of him were placed around the city, alongside those of the ancient kings. He was allowed to wear a purple robe, and was hailed with the ceremonial title Imperator; the parade was led by a placard that read *Veni, vidi, vici!* ("I came, I saw, I conquered!")[29]

After the parade, he took over the jobs of appointing magistrates, passing laws, and generally behaving as Senate, Tribune, Assembly, and Council all wrapped into one; all with the support of the army, which was loyal to him (he gave all the men who had fought in the Gallic Wars Roman citizenship), and the people, who still saw him as their benevolent guardian. He even changed the calendar: in order to institute the four-year system of leap years that we follow now, the year 46, that of his greatest public triumphs, was 445 days long.

Perhaps the Senate was afraid of the army's retaliation and of public resistance, should they cease to shower him with honors. In 44, the Senate agreed to name him dictator for life. But this was not the same as being king; and now it became clear that somewhere in his youth, Caesar had allowed the idea of becoming a king to take root in his imagination.

* During Caesar's invasion of Alexandria, his troops set fire to various parts of the city; several ancient authors say that the Great Library at Alexandria, the greatest collection of texts in the ancient world, burned down at this time.

On February 15 of 44, Mark Antony made a trial run at putting a crown on Caesar's head. Antony, as part of a religious festival, was carrying a diadem with a laurel wreath tied to it. He offered it to Caesar, but the crowd responded with only scattered applause. Caesar, reading their mood, pushed it away several times, which brought on a much bigger cheer. The people of Rome had made it quite clear that they would not like Caesar to become an actual king. Perhaps *king* had too many echoes of the Parthians to the east; perhaps the lingering idea that Rome should be a meritocracy made the hereditary nature of a kingship repugnant. Caesar had no legitimate sons (although Cleopatra had given birth to a son, Ptolemy XV Caesarion), but he had named his eighteen-year-old great-nephew Octavian, son of his sister's daughter, as his legal heir in his will.

Not long afterwards, the Senate agreed that Caesar *could* wear a crown, but only when he was out of Rome campaigning against Parthia—because myth said that only a king could conquer Parthia. Perhaps this was the last straw for those senators who were increasingly worried that the Republic would lose even its half-mythical reality. These hostile senators, which included Caesar's own cousin Marcus Brutus (one of the heirs named in his will), made plans to assassinate the Dictator for Life when he entered the Senate next, on March 15 of 44 BC: the Ides of March. Everyone knew that Caesar's right-hand man Mark Antony would not join in the plot, and so plans were made to stall him at the door while the act was done.

In his biography of Caesar's heir Octavian, the Greek writer Nicolaus of Damascus describes the assassination with clinical detail:

> When he came in and the Senate saw him, the members rose out of respect to him. Those who intended to lay hands on him were all about him. The first to come to him was Tullius Cimber, whose brother Caesar had exiled, and stepping forward as though to make an urgent appeal on behalf of his brother, he seized Caesar's toga, seeming to act rather boldly for a suppliant, and thus prevented him from standing up and using his hands if he so wished. Caesar was very angry, but the men held to their purpose and all suddenly bared their daggers and rushed upon him. First Servilius Casca stabbed him on the left shoulder a little above the collar bone, at which he had aimed but missed through nervousness. Caesar sprang up to defend himself against him, and Casca called to his brother, speaking in Greek in his excitement. The latter obeyed him and drove his sword into Caesar's side. A moment before Cassius [Longinus] had struck him obliquely across the face. Decimus Brutus struck him through the thigh. Cassius Longinus was eager to give another stroke, but he missed and struck Marcus Brutus

TIMELINE 78

PARTHIA	EGYPT	BRITAIN	ROME
			First Servile War (135)
			Death of Tiberius Gracchus
Mithridates II			Death of Gaius Gracchus
			Jugurthine War (112)
			Gaius Marius, consul
			Social War (91)
			Lucius Sulla, consul
			Lucius Cinna, consul
			Gladiator War (73)
			Crassus, consul
			Pompey, consul
		Cassivelaunus	Cicero, consul
Orodes II			Julius Caesar, consul
	Ptolemy XIII / Cleopatra XII		Battle of Pharsalus (48)
			Assassination of Caesar (44)

> on the hand. Minucius, too, made a lunge at Caesar but he struck Rubrius on the thigh. It looked as if they were fighting over Caesar. He fell, under many wounds, before the statue of Pompey, and there was not one of them but struck him as he lay lifeless, to show that each of them had had a share in the deed, until he had received thirty-five wounds, and breathed his last.[30]

Plutarch says that he died crying out for help; several Greek accounts, that he called out in Greek to Brutus, "Even you, my son?"* And Suetonius says that, as Caesar was first stabbed, he cried out in blank surprise: "But this is force!"[31]

Caesar's killers were simply at the logical end of a process that had begun with the Gracchi a hundred years before. No constitution or balance of pow-

* Either way, he did not utter the famous Latin phrase *Et tu, Brute?*, which was invented by Shakespeare, fifteen hundred years later.

ers had ever been able to restrain the ambitions of the powerful; Caesar himself had demonstrated this, and now he had fallen by the same methods he had used. But his shock reveals that the idea of the Republic still had a grasp on the Roman imagination. The official name of the Republic, engraved on the standards of the legions and on the buildings of Rome itself, was *SPQR: Senatus Populusque Romani,* The Senate and the People of Rome.

Rome is a place where the people have power: this had not been true for decades, but the Romans had no other way to think of themselves and no other name for their collective identity. It was a powerful lie, and even a dictator could still be aghast when its falsity was forced in front of his eyes.

Chapter Seventy-Nine

Empire

Between 44 BC *and* AD *14,*
Octavian becomes the First Citizen,
the Parthians reject Roman ways,
and the entire empire pretends that Rome is still a republic

WITH CAESAR'S BODY STILL LYING on the floor of the Senate, Mark Antony finally managed to shove his way into the Senate chamber. He was too late to help Caesar, but he did prevent the conspirators from throwing Caesar's body into the Tiber, as they had planned. Instead they deserted the Senate and marched in phalanx to the Capitol, swords still drawn, shouting to the people to come join them, and "resume their liberty." They were at a crucial juncture: the people in the street might spontaneously band together against them. A few of the better-known citizens of Rome fell into the march with them, and soon the city was past the immediate danger point. Meanwhile three of Caesar's household slaves came and got his body from the empty chamber and carried him home.[1]

Mark Antony, not sure how the public mood would break, fled to a friend's house, disguised himself as a slave, and got out of the city as quickly as possible. Brutus and Cassius, on the other hand, continued to make speeches about Caesar's death as a tragic necessity. The next day, they reassembled the Senate and suggested that Caesar be given a big honorable funeral and also be honored as divine, now that he was safely dead. The Senate agreed. This kept Rome calm, and also encouraged Mark Antony, who had not gone far, to come back; clearly no purges of Caesar's allies were about to begin.

But in the next days, the calm was wrecked when Caesar's will was made public, and it was found that he had divided his huge private fortune among the citizens of Rome. His body was then carried through the streets; Brutus and Cassius had agreed to this, as a necessary part of an honorable burial, but when the citizens to whom he had been generous saw the mutilated body, a riot began to form.

Mark Antony, who was in the Forum to give Caesar's funeral speech, encouraged the uprising. He had brought with him an armed guard, led by one of his allies: Marcus Aemilius Lepidus, who had been appointed by Caesar to be the governor of provinces in Gaul and Nearer Spain. Lepidus had not yet left for his new command, but he had been collecting troops in Rome to take with him. Now he surrounded Mark Antony with them. Safely guarded, Antony capped off his funeral speech with a show-and-tell: he took Caesar's ripped and bloodstained toga out from under his arm and shook it out so everyone could see how many times he had been stabbed.

The sight of Caesar's toga was the last push needed to send the people in the street over the edge. Citizens ran through the streets, waving torches and yelling for Brutus and Cassius to be found and torn to pieces.

No one could find them. They had managed to get out of the city in the early hours of the riot, and were now holed up in Antium. Mark Antony took control of the government and, by way of thanking Lepidus for his support, gave Lepidus the position of Pontifex Maximus, High Priest of Rome.

But Mark Antony's hold on power was very shaky. He was, as far as the Senate was concerned, Caesar Junior, as likely to become a tyrant as Caesar had been, and without Caesar's charisma to persuade any of them onto his side.

At the same time, Brutus was wooing the public from his exile at Antium, sending money back to Rome for public festivals, hoping to buy his way back into the good graces of the people. One of his allies in the Senate, the orator Cicero, helped him out by making continual speeches about his generosity and his willingness to fight tyranny. "By this time," says Plutarch, "the people had begun to be dissatisfied with Antony, who they perceived was setting up a kind of monarchy for himself; they longed for the return of Brutus."[2]

Brutus might have been able to return as a hero in a matter of weeks except for one factor: Caesar's adopted son Octavian, now eighteen, had been posted away from Italy on military duty, but as soon as he heard of his uncle's murder, he headed home.

When Octavian arrived, Cicero (who thought Mark Antony a fool and a tyrant in the making) saw the young man as his best possible ally against Antony's power. This naturally headed off any support for Brutus, the assassin. Plutarch writes that Brutus took this badly, and "treated with him very sharply in his letters."[3]

This did nothing to get Cicero back on his side, and Brutus gave up for the time being, left Italy altogether, and went to Athens to stay with a friend.

Antony, who had positioned himself as a friend of Caesar's, could not exactly oppose the man's nephew. But he quite rightly saw Octavian's arrival as a threat to his own power. He treated the young man with indulgence, asked him whether he really thought he was up to the task of dealing with Caesar's estate, laughed at his serious manner, and tried to block him from standing for tribune.

Opposed by Antony, Octavian began to make friends with all of Antony's detractors and opponents. Eventually a rumor got back to Antony that Octavian was planning to have him assassinated. The younger man denied the charge, but the suspicion was enough to transform the two men from political rivals into actual enemies. "Each of them hurried about all through Italy to engage, by great offers, the old soldiers that lay scattered in their settlements," says Plutarch, "and to be the first to secure the troops that still remained undischarged."[4] Cicero's silver tongue helped to tip the balance; he convinced the Senate to declare Antony a public enemy of the Roman people, which meant that Roman troops could drive him out of Italy.

Antony retreated to the north with the army he had managed to gather, and Octavian marched after him with another army and both consuls. The two met in battle at Modena, in 43 BC. But although Antony's men finally broke their line and fled, both consuls were killed along with many of Octavian's own men. It was not a joyful victory for the Romans.

Antony went through the Alps to the soldiers stationed in Gaul, and recruited them to his side. They had served with him before, they respected his abilities as a commander, and apparently the crisis was bringing out the best in him: "It was his character in calamities to be better than at any other time," Plutarch says. "Antony, in misfortune, was most nearly a virtuous man."[5]

Octavian at this point seems to have rethought his position. As long as Cicero and the Senate had hopes for the return of the Republic, they would never be fully behind him; their apparent support for him had merely been in order to get Antony out of Rome. But Octavian didn't want the return of the Republic. He wanted his great-uncle's power, and Cicero was not going to help him there: "Perceiving that Cicero's wishes were for liberty," Plutarch observes, "he had ceased to pay any further regard to him."[6]

So, following Caesar's example, he decided to make an alliance with his rival in order to strengthen his own position. Rather than attacking Antony, he dispatched friends to take a message: he had a proposal to make, if Antony would agree to meet with him.

In November, the two men met in a private location at Bologna, and for three days discussed a possible partnership. They decided to form a triumvirate, as their elders had done before them. As the third member of the triumvirate, they included Mark Antony's ally Lepidus; he was, after all, Pontifex

Maximus, and he commanded a good number of legions in his position as governor of provinces in Gaul and Nearer Spain.

This triumvirate was no informal arrangement, though: the pact of allegiance was written out. "The empire was soon determined of," Plutarch says, "it being divided amongst them as if it had been their paternal inheritance."

Each man then made up a list of the Romans he wanted to see killed in the takeover. This was far, far beyond even the pretense of legality. All together, there were three hundred persons on the death list, including Cicero (on Antony's list), Antony's own uncle (on Octavian's list), and Lepidus's brother (who had publicly opposed him) on Lepidus's own list.

The three returned to Rome at the head of an armed force and ruthlessly carried out the hits. After this, they divided the empire up. Octavian got the west, Antony the east. Lepidus, who was doomed to be the tail end of the triumvirate, lost his provinces in Gaul and Nearer Spain and instead was given Africa, which was hardly a plum job.

But he was pacified with temporary control of the city of Rome. While Lepidus looked out for the capital city, Antony and Octavian set out for Greece with part of the army to kill Cassius and Brutus.

Cassius and Brutus made a stand in Macedonia, dividing their army in two and stationing the troops in two different places. This forced Antony and Octavian to divided their forces as well. Octavian took the task of attacking Brutus; but on the day of the battle he was suffering from illness: "weak and unwell," Suetonius says, and soon driven back in a rout.[7] Antony, on the other hand, defeated Cassius, who killed himself without realizing that Brutus was still in good shape; he then turned and finished off Brutus for Octavian.

Octavian headed home, having grown sicker, and more than half-expecting to die before he could get back to Rome. Antony stayed east, to help protect the border. The Roman province of Syria was facing a possible invasion; the Parthians, by command of their king Orodes II, were massing on their western border, ready to invade the Roman-governed lands. And Antipater, the Roman governor of Syria, had just been poisoned; his son Herod was now governing in his place, but he was new to the job.

Antony arrived in Syria, but his attention was soon distracted from the coming attack. In 41, the year after the defeat of Brutus and Cassius, he met Cleopatra, who sailed up to Cilicia to see him and presented herself in a way bound to attract:

> in a barge with gilded stern and outspread sails of purple, while oars of silver beat time to the music of flutes and fifes and harps. She herself lay all alone, under a canopy of cloth of gold, dressed as Venus in a picture, and

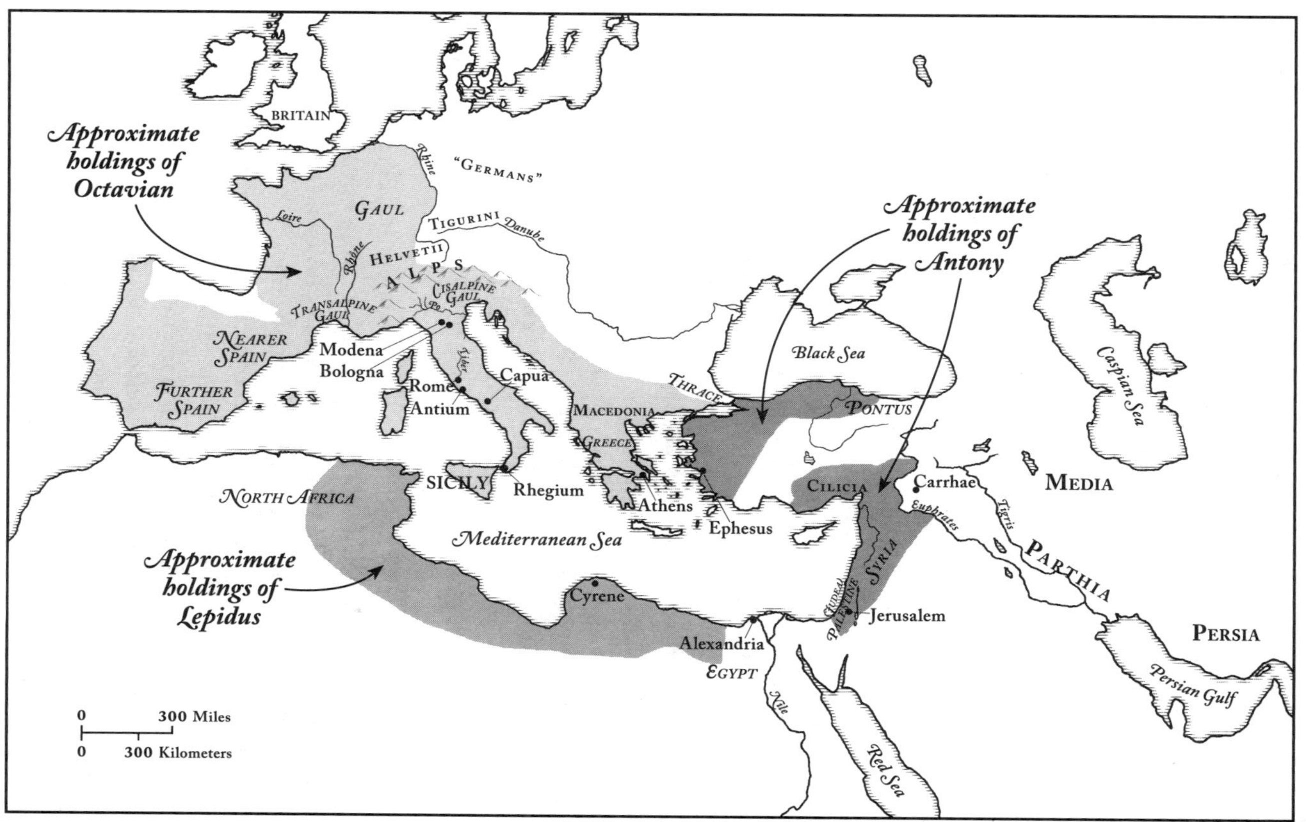

79.1 Rome Under the Triumvirate

> beautiful young boys, like painted Cupids, stood on each side to fan her. Her maids were dressed like Sea Nymphs and Graces, some steering at the rudder, some working at the ropes. The perfumes diffused themselves from the vessel to the shore, which was covered with multitudes, part following the galley up the river on either bank, part running out of the city to see the sight.[8]

Instead of remaining in Syria to protect the province, Antony, starstruck, followed Cleopatra back down to Alexandria.

The Parthian attack came in 40 BC, just months later. The Parthians swept down through Syria into Palestine, intending to kill the Roman governor Herod. He fled to Rome, so the Parthians instead dragged out Hyrcanus (who was the High Priest and Ethnarch of Judea, reporting to Herod) and cut both of his ears off. This kept him from serving as high priest any longer, as Jewish law dictated that the high priest be unmutilated.

Right after this success, Orodes was murdered by his son Phraates IV, who also killed off his brothers and his own oldest son, in an elimination of rivals that was excessive even by Parthian standards. Antony pulled himself away from Cleopatra and went back to Rome to consult with Octavian, who had, surprisingly, recovered from his illness. With a fresh army and the fugitive Herod in tow, Antony marched back east.

The Parthians, under Phraates IV, tried to defend the Syrian holdings, but Antony managed to drive them back out of Palestine. In 37 BC, he installed Herod as a vassal king of Rome: a secular King of the Jews, doing away with a combined priesthood and kingship.

Meanwhile, back a little farther to the west, Octavian had eliminated Lepidus. Lepidus had gotten terminally tired of being the weak sister in this setup. He sailed with troops to Sicily, which he claimed as his own. This was a clear message that he wanted more power in the triumvirate.

Octavian, however, landed on the shores of Sicily and begged Lepidus's soldiers not to resist him: they could save Rome from civil war, if they would simply desert Lepidus's cause. They did, legion after legion; Lepidus seems to have lacked the personal charisma to overcome Octavian's appeals. Finally Lepidus himself was forced to follow his troops to Octavian's camp, surrender, and beg for mercy. Octavian spared his life, but took his provinces, his soldiers, and his title of Triumvir away from him.[9] He also put him under house arrest, where Lepidus remained, for the rest of his life.

Octavian and Antony now shared the power between them, but Antony was in an increasingly weak position. After its initial success, his campaign against Parthia had turned inexorably towards disaster. He had tried to make a push into Media and was forced back on a retreat during which twenty thousand infantry and four thousand cavalry died.[10]

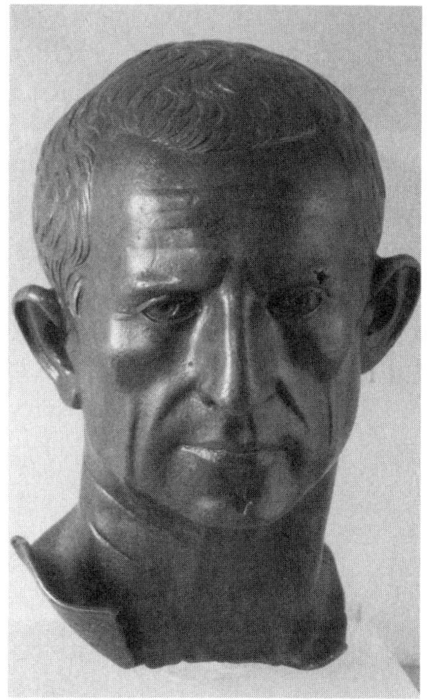

79.1. Octavian. Bronze head of Octavian, Caesar Augustus, 63 BC–AD 14. Museo Civico Archaeologico, Verona, Italy. Photo credit Cameraphoto Arte, Venice/Art Resource, NY

By 34 BC, Antony had given up. He went back to Egypt and to Cleopatra. The desertion gave Octavian the excuse he needed to declare war on Antony as an enemy of Rome, which would make him ruler of Antony's part of the empire as well as his own.

But he needed to convert any pro-Antony senators to his side. In 32 BC, Octavian had Antony's will read aloud to the Senate. This was illegal, but when the Senate heard that Antony had left most of his money to the half-Egyptian children that Cleopatra had borne him (these were twins, one boy and one girl) and also had asked to be buried in Egypt, they agreed to a formal pronouncement of war against Antony, as though he were a foreign enemy.[11] Octavian remarked that, given Antony's complete bewitchment by Cleopatra, he didn't expect any trouble removing him from the scene; he suspected that Antony's generals would be Cleopatra's beauty stylist and an Egyptian eunuch or two.

Antony, hearing news of this declaration, began to assemble himself an army and navy at Ephesus. His force was considerable: five hundred warships, Plutarch says, with a hundred thousand infantrymen and a handful of royal allies, one of whom was Herod, king of Judea.

Octavian journeyed towards him with a fleet and land forces of his own. After a series of pitched battles, the two navies met near the promontory of Actium, jutting from the northern coast of Greece. After Octavian's ships had destroyed three hundred of Antony's, Antony and Cleopatra left the scene of the fighting and sailed back towards Egypt. Most of his men deserted and joined Octavian, who was clearly on the winning side.

Octavian decided that it would be wiser not to leave Antony down in Egypt to plan more trouble for Rome. He waited through the winter, and then set out for Egypt.

When Antony heard of Octavian's approach, he stabbed himself in the stomach with a sword and bled to death slowly. Cleopatra managed to kill herself, although her body was unmarked and no dagger was found nearby; later, her servants suggested that perhaps she had allowed a poisonous snake to bite her, rather than remain a lifelong prisoner of Octavian's.

Octavian ordered Cleopatra's son by Caesar put to death as well. The year was 30 BC, and he alone was in control of the Roman territories.

IN 29, HE ARRIVED BACK in Rome, to a people sick of war.

Octavian threw himself a victory parade, and gave away money to the citizens. He also ordered the doors to the Temple of Janus closed to show that Rome had entered into a new time of peace. Octavian's victory at Actium was, in his own version of events, a new beginning. Not: *The Roman Republic has ended and the Roman Empire has begun* (as later historians would see it), but rather: *The Republic has been given a fresh new start.*

To keep this illusion alive, he could not dissolve the Senate: that would do away with half of Rome's official name. The Senate too was in a delicate position. Octavian had just finished fighting a war against a Roman citizen, and he had just put to death Caesar's only son. These were both autocratic actions, and if he acted too much like a king, protest was bound to swell up until it could no longer be ignored. If, on the other hand, the Senate compelled him to lay down all of his power, civil war might break out again. If one thing had become clear in the past years, it was that the original form of the Republic would not hold peace in the city for long.

The compromise between the Senate and Octavian was, like Octavian's own version of the victory at Actium, one of terminology. In 27 BC, Octavian walked into the January meeting of the Senate and formally announced the laying down of all the powers that had been granted to him in the years of crisis: this showed that they were extraordinary powers, not usual ones, and that the Republic was still in full force.

Octavian himself set down an account of this in his *Res Gestae*, a statement engraved on brass that later stood in front of his mausoleum: "After I had put an end to the civil wars," it said, "having attained supreme power by universal consent, I transferred the state from my own power to the control of the Roman Senate and people."[12]

In return, once Octavian had demonstrated that he respected the Republic, the Republic returned the favor. Octavian remained consul (a republican office), and the Senate gave him control over the outlying provinces—which, since most of the soldiers were stationed there and not in Rome, gave him control over the army. He was also allowed to establish something new, a large standing bodyguard in Italy itself: the "Praetorian Guard." This gave him, in effect, a private army, and broke the tradition that Rome did not keep an army close to home.[13]

He also retained the title Imperator, which he had held since 29; this title had always been a yearly honor, given to a successful general, but now it became part of his permanent name. So did another name, Augustus. Technically, the term meant consecrated, set apart and different; but it was a brand-new name, with no political baggage, so it could take on any shade of meaning that Octavian gave it.[14] Octavian himself saw the title Augustus (which became his primary name) as a reward for virtue, given to him by the Senate in recognition of his refusal to grasp power. He lays this out in the *Res Gestae*, where he lists all his conquests ("I extended the frontiers of all the provinces of the Roman people, which had as neighbours races not obedient to our empire. . . . I restored peace to all the provinces of Gaul and Spain and to Germany. . . . Egypt I added to the empire of the Roman people" and so on),[15] but these are not the basis for his authority. Rather, he deserves to be Augustus because "after I had extinguished the civil wars, having been put in supreme possession of the whole empire by the universal consent of all, I transferred the republic from my own power into the free control of the Senate and Roman people. For the which service I received the appellation of Augustus by decree of the Senate. . . . After that time I stood before all others in dignity, but of actual power I possessed no more than my colleagues."[16]

This was, of course, almost an exact reverse of the truth; Augustus had the actual power of an emperor, but not the title. Even to some of his contemporaries (such as the geographer Strabo), this so-called First Settlement seemed silly.

Over the next decades, Augustus combined acting like an emperor without a title and constant negotiations with the Senate over what formal privileges he should actually have. In the year 23, Augustus declined to be elected consul again, as he had successively for the past nine years. His exact motivation for doing this is not entirely clear. He may have realized that, if he were elected consul every year, a lot of senators were *not* getting the chance to run for an office which for many was the culmination of a lifelong dream. This was bound to produce discontented murmuring.[17] And he was also struck by a serious illness in 23; Suetonius remarks that he had ringworm, bladder stones, and spots all over him.[18] Possibly he did not like the idea of having to publicly display himself at an election while suffering from unsightly blemishes.

In any case, relinquishing the consulship was no sacrifice, because he still remained above the consuls in the power structure. The Senate had agreed to make him proconsul for life, which meant he could not only dabble legally in senatorial and consular affairs whenever he pleased, but could also exercise military power—the *imperium*—inside the city. This was an important privilege, particularly since he now had a standing army within march of Rome.

He had, in fact, every single power of royalty, including the legal means to strong-arm the city into doing what he wanted. But he still kept himself away from the word *emperor*. Augustus, Tacitus says, subjected the world to empire under the title of *princeps*: *fessa nomine principis sub imperium accepit.* Later translations would render this word "prince," but Augustus would have simply called himself the First Citizen.[19]

IN 20 BC, Augustus managed to work out a peace with the Parthian king Phraates IV. Antony's defeat had been a very good thing for Augustus, but it had been an embarrassment for Rome. The Parthians had taken Roman prisoners of war and had captured the Roman standards; Augustus needed to get them back.

Phraates IV agreed to return the prisoners of war and the standards. What he got from Rome is less clear. Augustus gave Phraates a slave girl, who soon became his lover, but there must have been some other inducement.

Phraates IV did send all four of his sons to Rome as hostages, an act which usually indicated weakness.[20] But given the state of intrigue in Parthian royal families, perhaps this was a Roman favor to Parthia; it gave Phraates IV a few more years in which he did not have to watch his back and sniff his cups. It also gave the Romans a chance to teach Roman ways to the Parthians (a technique that the Assyrians had used on Egyptian princes long before). Continued peace with the Parthians was important for Roman prosperity. It meant that the trade route to India and perhaps even farther to the east was now passable, rather than blocked by a solid wall of hostility.

Rome may have been prospering, but Augustus, who so needed the forms of the Republic to hold his empire together, was having trouble keeping up appearances. Senators had started trailing into the Senate later and later; this was understandable, since they were basically wasting their time passing any laws at all, but Augustus wanted Rome to see business-as-usual carried on. In 17 BC, he announced that senators who came in late would have to pay a fine.

Meanwhile he was accumulating even more powers. In 13, Lepidus died, still under guard. Octavian then "assumed the office of high priest," Suetonius writes, "which he had never presumed to do while Lepidus was alive."[21] This meant that the ruler of Rome's political affairs was now also the religious head

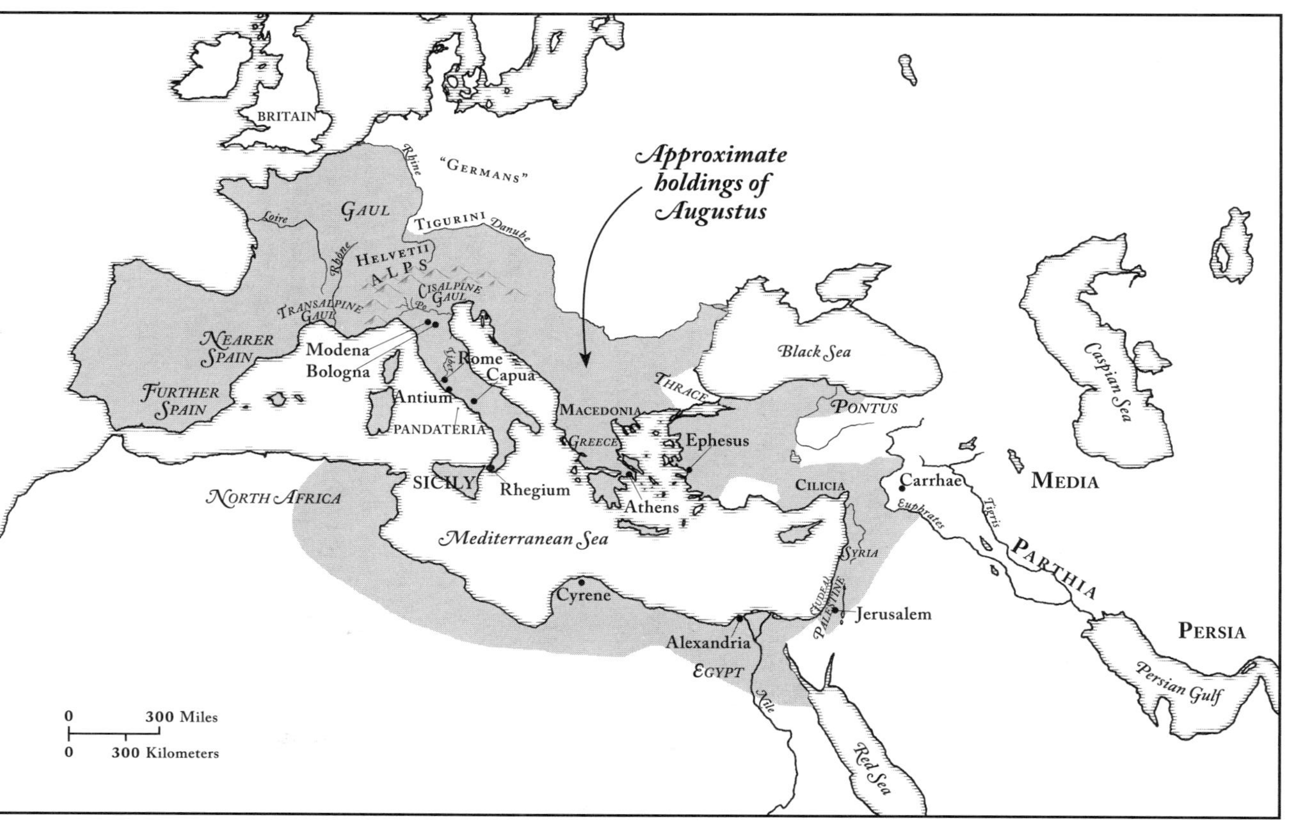

79.2 Rome Under Augustus

of state, a combination which considerably boosted his power and would remain the norm thereafter.

This made the Senate even more irrelevant. By 11 BC, Augustus had to change the regulations of the Senate so that business could be carried on even if the required minimum of four hundred senators (out of six hundred) didn't show up. He also announced that the members would no longer speak in order of seniority, since they had fallen into a habit of getting up one at a time and saying, "I agree with the last speaker." Instead, in an effort to keep everyone awake, he started calling on them to speak at random, like a college teacher with an inattentive freshman class.[22]

At the same time, Augustus was trying to find himself an heir and create a dynasty, a most unrepublican idea.

The Senate had some sympathy for the idea of an heir, since no one wanted a war to erupt as soon as Augustus died, but there was no legal way for him to appoint someone to be the next imperator of Rome. The more personal problem was that Augustus had no son of his own. He had considered making a son-in-law his successor, and so back in 24 BC he had married his fourteen-year-old daughter Julia off to her seventeen-year-old cousin Marcellus, his first choice for an heir. But Marcellus died just a year later. After that, Augustus married Julia to one of his officers, a man named Agrippa; but Agrippa too died, in 12 BC.

Instead of giving the poor woman some peace, Augustus then married her to his last candidate: his wife's son by a previous marriage, Tiberius. Tiberius was no one's first choice. He was cold and distant, generally silent, and he had odd tics: he walked stiffly, and made constant gestures with his fingers when he talked.[23] As Augustus's heir, Tiberius was a placeholder. The emperor hoped that one of Julia's sons would grow old enough to be appointed successor instead. But meanwhile he had created a wretched family life for his daughter. Julia hated Tiberius, and their life was so miserable that he went off to Rhodes, while she grew more promiscuous and drunken. Her behavior became so scandalous, in fact, that Augustus finally had her confined on Pandateria, a prison island.

His domestic troubles did not take him away from the business of running his empire for long. In 4 BC, Herod the Great—the vassal king put back on the throne by Mark Antony—died, leaving three sons and an enormously rebuilt temple. He had used his authority to turn the shabby, rebuilt Second Temple into a showpiece of his greatness as a king (albeit one under Roman supervision). The flat space on which it sat, the Temple Mount, was too small to allow for much expansion, so Herod dug all around it and built huge underground chambers to serve as foundations for more floor space.

Now Herod the Great was dead. But rather than choosing one of Herod's three sons to succeed him, Augustus divided Palestine into three parts; perhaps the size of the Temple had revealed family ambitions that needed to be squelched. In any case, Herod Antipas got Galilee, next to the Sea of Galilee; Archelaus got Samaria and Judea; and the third brother, Philip, got the north. Herod Antipas and Philip ruled without too much incident; but Archelaus turned out to be so cruel that in AD 6 Augustus yanked him from his throne and put a Roman official, a procurator, in his place to keep an eye on the area. This procurator had the final say over the whole area, particularly in serious legal matters such as executions, but as long as Herod Antipas and Philip behaved themselves, the Romans tended to leave them alone.

A little farther to the east, the Parthians were suffering from an anti-Roman reaction.

In 2 BC, Phraates IV's family life took a downturn again. His slave girl had borne him a son, and when this son reached his late teens, he turned and murdered his father. Coins from the reign of this boy, Phraates V, show his mother beside him; possibly she was a co-ruler, but she looks more like his consort, and it was not unheard of (although icky) to marry your mother in Parthia, particularly since she seems to have been barely fifteen years his senior.[24] Their joint reign made them terribly unpopular, and after barely four years, the Parthians drove them out into exile.

After this one of those Roman-educated sons of Phraates IV took the throne, under the royal name Vonones I. This was the sort of influence over Parthia that the Romans had hoped for, the next best thing to actual rule as they had in Palestine. Unfortunately, it didn't last. Vonones's portraits on his coins show him with western-style hair, undoubtedly learned in his days in Rome, and Vonones's Roman ways annoyed the Parthians in his court. Roman words in the mouths of Parthian men, Roman dress, Roman habits: these had become increasingly unpopular with the conservative part of Parthian society. During peace, it seemed even more important to stay vigilant about their native culture; a vigilance that wasn't necessary during wartime, when the hostilities acted as a natural check over cultural exchange.

Vonones I also lasted for only four years or so, before the Parthian patriot Artabanus drove him away (or killed him) and became king in his place. Parthia remained at peace with Rome, but it was a tentative peace, with Parthia consistently resisting all Roman influence and holding itself aloof on the other side of the Euphrates.*

* Internal Parthian politics are very obscure, and all reconstructions are uncertain; this is a probable course of events.

By AD 4, Augustus had given up on finding himself a blood heir. Two of Julia's grandsons had died young. The third, Agrippa Postumus, had grown to be so vicious that he was widely thought to be insane; Augustus had sent him to the prison island of Pandateria as well. He was stuck with Tiberius, so he formally adopted his son-in-law as his ward and part of his immediate family.

This did not make Tiberius his heir, since hereditary rule was still an unspoken possibility. But he did give Tiberius more and more control over the Roman army; and since the support of the Roman legions was the greatest prop of imperial power, this was almost as good as handing Tiberius a crown. In AD 13, the Senate confirmed Tiberius as proconsul and princeps alongside Augustus, which eliminated the immediate problem of a hereditary transfer of power.

TIMELINE 79

PARTHIA	ROME
	Social War (91)
	Lucius Sulla, consul
	Lucius Cinna, consul
	Gladiator War (73)
	Crassus, consul
	Pompey, consul
	Cicero, consul
Orodes II	Julius Caesar, consul
	Battle of Pharsalus (48)
Phraates IV	Assassination of Caesar (44)
	Octavian, consul
	Battle of Actium (31)
	First Settlement (27)
	Second Settlement (23)
	Octavian, pontifex maximus
Phraates V	
Vonones I	
Artabanus II	
	Death of Octavian (AD 14)

The action came just in time. In August of AD 14, the two men were travelling together when the seventy-five-year-old Augustus was struck with diarrhea. He grew progressively weaker, until he was unable to get out of his bed.

On his last day, he asked for a mirror so that he could arrange his hair, as though for an audience. "When the friends he had summoned were present," Suetonius writes, "he inquired of them whether they thought he had played his role well in the comedy of life." When they agreed, he quoted (almost as his last words) two lines from a popular drama:

> Since the play has been so good, clap your hands
> And all of you dismiss us with applause.[25]

In the last moments of his life, he could finally admit the truth that no one in Rome had dared to speak: his role as protector of the Republic had been playacting, and his refusal to accept the title of emperor had been nothing but pretense, all done for the sake of the audience.

Chapter Eighty

Eclipse and Restoration

In China, between 33 BC and AD 75, the Han Dynasty is temporarily replaced because of bad omens, and then is restored for the same reason

At the very end of the road east, China under the Han Dynasty was growing into an empire with its own surrounding provinces, not unlike the Roman empire at the very end of the road west. The chronicles of Sima Qian speak of tribe after tribe on its western border, conquered and folded into its borders. And just like the ruling family at the other end of the road, the Chinese royal clan suffered through its own personal dramas, which then weakened the borders of the empire itself.

In 33 BC, while Octavian was still building his powers, the Han emperor Yuandi died. He had inherited the throne from his father Xuandi, and now passed it to his son Chengdi.

Chengdi was eighteen, which in Chinese tradition was not quite old enough for full independent rule. His mother Cheng-chun became the empress dowager, with regentlike powers. When she suggested that Chengdi give her relatives from the Wang clan important government positions, Chengdi obediently complied. Her brothers became lords; her oldest brother, general-in-chief of the army. Other Wang family members were given other posts, until the highest posts in the Han government were overloaded with them.[1]

Chengdi died in 7, after a reign of over two decades—but with no son of his own. His nephew Aiti succeeded him. After this, the reigns of the Han rulers grow suspiciously short. Aiti died after only six years, also without children; and an eight-year-old cousin who next sat on the throne, Ping, died in AD 6 after a seven-year reign, also childless.

The empress dowager was still alive; she had now outlived four Han monarchs. Now she supervised the accession of yet another baby, a distant Han cousin named Ruzi who could claim to be the great-great-grandson of the earlier emperor Xuandi. As his regent, she appointed her own nephew Wang Mang, a well-respected and educated man who had been serving as a minister for years already. His biographer, the historian Ban Gu, remarked that he had managed to build himself up a loyal following by "distributing carriages, horses, gowns, and furs" to his "scholarly retainers," while keeping little for himself; in other words, he was proficient at bribery.[2]

Noblemen who resented the Wang power in government protested; one insisted that Wang Mang had poisoned at least one of the previous kings; another led a short-lived, armed uprising. But Wang Mang promised that he would hand the crown over to the baby king as soon as he was old enough. This gave him at least ten years of grace time.

It only took him three to convince the people of the capital city that the extraordinary bad luck of the Han succession showed that the Will of Heaven had turned against the Han, and that the absence of an adult emperor on the throne was encouraging banditry, murder, and all sorts of crimes. When omens began to favor Wang Mang (for one thing, a white stone discovered at the bottom of a well had written on it "Tell Wang Mang that he must become Emperor!"), he declared that the Han had ended, and that he was now emperor of China. "I am a descendant of the Yellow Emperor," he announced, "and have been given the Mandate for the continuation of the succession. The omens have indicated the clear commands of the Spirits, entrusting to me the people of the empire."[3]

The Han had already survived for 197 years, no mean feat. But for the next decade and a half after AD 9, Wang Mang's Xin Dynasty—the "New" Dynasty—would eclipse it.

The empress dowager, who finally died in 13 AD after having lived through the reigns of six emperors of China, did not live to see the end of the story. But the effects of the change in dynasty were obvious even before her death. Wang Mang was not a cruel man; he sent the baby prince away to be raised elsewhere, but spared his life (although rumor said that little Ruzi had been so carefully guarded that he did not know a chicken when he saw one). But his decisions were disastrous. He pronounced himself restorer of the old and honored ways, and tried to roll back all of the changes made during the Han to break the old ties of aristocratic privilege. He annoyed the peasants by giving the noble families some of their old feudal powers back; he annoyed the aristocrats by reviving the ancient idea that all of China belonged to the emperor (and even more by following through and claiming some of their territories for himself).[4] His policies were so sweeping, and so sudden, that his people were thrown into confusion and discontent. His biographer Ban Gu tells us:

> The people could not turn a hand without violating some prohibition. . . . The rich had no means to protect themselves and the poor no way to stay alive. They rose up and became thieves and bandits, infesting the hills and marshes.[5]

Wang Mang was also unlucky in the weather. Drought and famine over much of the capital region were joined, cruelly, by flooding; in AD 11, dikes on the Yellow river broke and thousands drowned. The omens that Wang Mang had depended on to sweep him into power turned against him. "Famine and pestilence raged," says Ban Gu, "and people ate each other, so that before Wang Mang was finally punished [by losing his throne] half the population of the empire had perished."

In response to this combination of political change and natural disaster, one of the first secret societies in Chinese history formed: the Red Eyebrows, who organized in a band to fight against the soldiers who came out into the countryside to enforce Wang Mang's decrees. In an age before uniforms, they painted their foreheads red so that, in battle, they could distinguish friend from foe.[6]

In AD 23, Wang Mang gave up his throne and fled. He left behind him a mess of Han relatives, none of whom had a clear right to the throne. Battles between them dragged on for two years before one of them, Liu Xiu, won enough support to claim the throne for himself.

Liu Xiu, better known by his imperial name Guang Wudi, set himself to reversing the damage Wang Mang had done. But he created some distance between himself and the earlier Han kingdom (which, after all, had disintegrated into disorder) by moving his capital city from Chang'an to Loyang, two hundred miles east; thus the second half of the Han empire is often called the Eastern Han to distinguish it from the earlier Han rule.

He also did not restore the Han custom of giving all important posts to royal family members, which was how Wang Mang had gotten into power to start with. Instead, he divided the old Han territory up into new counties, and gave more of the government posts to less important families. And as part of his struggle against the constant influence of the old noble families, he built over one hundred training schools for future bureaucrats, in which government-paid teachers taught the skills that government officials needed to run the empire properly. He also put into effect a system of examinations; candidates who passed the examinations could win government posts, regardless of family background. It was a meritocracy, based on Confucian ideas of order, and it became a system that would endure for centuries.[7]

But the counties which these new administrators would run were smaller, and fewer, than before; the famine, civil war, and flooding had killed many, many Chinese. Census figures suggest that as many as ten million people had died in the last years of the Western Han and the years of the New Dynasty, in one of the great hidden disasters of the past.[8]

GUANG WUDI REIGNED for a long and prosperous thirty-two years, and then passed the crown to his son Mingdi.

Mingdi was not the emperor's original heir. Guang Wudi had not entirely abandoned the old practice of building power through alliances with old families; his first marriage had been to a noblewoman of the north, and gave him a strategic link to the northern clans who might have given the emperor a run for the throne. Her son had been named crown prince. But almost twenty years into his reign, Guang Wudi felt in firm control of the north, and started to worry about the south instead. He put his first wife away and took a second, southern wife as official consort. When her son Mingdi was born, Guang Wudi pronounced this son, not his older child, to be his heir.

Mingdi was twenty-nine when he took the throne. He solved the problem of northern resentment by sending his general Pan Ch'ao north to campaign against the ongoing threat of the Xiongnu, above them. Gratitude assured him of the north's loyalty. And Pan Ch'ao's campaigns not only whipped the Xiongnu into submission, but also conquered the western area of the Tarim Basin: the so-called Oasis States, an act which reopened, from the eastern end, the road that had already been cleared from the west by the Parthian-Roman treaty.[9]

According to later biographers, Mingdi then had a dream: he saw a golden god in the sky, asking to be honored. His advisors assured him that this was the Buddha, a god of whom they had heard from India. This is a poetic expression of the reality of migration. Both merchants and missionaries from India had begun to travel regularly into China.

Mingdi sent men to India to learn more about the Buddha. According to Chinese tradition, they came back with the *Sutta in Forty-two Sections,* which were Buddhist sayings presented in much the same way as the Analects of Confucius.[10] Mingdi, pleased by the *Sutta*, began to adopt its teachings for himself and for his court.

This is probably a simplified presentation of a more gradual adoption of Buddhist principles by the court, but it does show that Buddhism was making its way into China—and that it was spreading in a way quite unlike Confucianism. Confucianism, now set into the structures of Han bureaucracy by Guang Wudi's schools, had begun among the people and had run along the grass roots of Chinese society, promising ordinary men and women principles that would get them through their day-to-day lives: a republican ethic. But Buddhism came into China at the top of the social tree; it was adopted first by the king, and spread from him downwards. In China, it was the religion of the educated, the powerful, and the well-to-do.

TIMELINE 80	
ROME	CHINA
Battle of Pharsalus (48)	**Yuandi**
Assassination of Caesar (44)	
Octavian, consul	
Battle of Actium (31)	**Chengdi**
First Settlement (27)	
Second Settlement (23)	
Octavian, pontifex maximus	
	Aiti
	Ping
	Ruzi
	Xin Dynasty (AD 9)
Death of Octavian (AD 14)	**Wang Mang**
	Eastern Han Dynasty (AD 25)
	Guang Wudi
	Mingdi

Chapter Eighty-One

The Problem of Succession

Between AD 14 and 69,
Roman emperors grow progressively madder,
the city burns, and
the persecution of Christians begins

With Augustus dead, Tiberius, at the age of fifty-four, now held the sole power of princeps.

Tiberius knew that the people of Rome were not automatically going to acclaim him as the next Augustus; most of them knew that Augustus had chosen him, as Suetonius puts it, "through necessity rather than preference."[1] The Senate might very easily turn against him altogether, particularly if he seemed too anxious. So when he went before the senators, a month after Augustus's death, to be formally recognized as head of state, he tried to follow Augustus's own strategy of laying powers down with apparent humility so that they could be willingly returned. He wasn't very good at apparent humility, though. When the Senate tried to return the powers, he kept on half-refusing them with ambiguous answers, until they were thoroughly frustrated and one of them shouted out, "Either do it, or have done with it!"[2] Finally, he did manage to get himself confirmed as Augustus's successor—but he never did end up with the title of Imperator, or with the new title of Augustus either.

He had appointed his own successor even before Augustus's death: his nephew Germanicus, who had been serving as general in command of the legions at the Rhine (the Romans knew this province as Germany, and the Celtic tribes who roved through it as Germans). Now he brought Germanicus back to Rome and had him elected consul, and then sent him to govern the province of Syria.

Not long after arriving in Syria, Germanicus died, leaving behind him his wife and young son Caligula. The people of Rome began to whisper that Tiberius had ordered his murder. Since Tiberius had been behind Germanicus's rise to power—preferring him over his own son Drusus, who was neither as handsome nor as popular—this was an unlikely accusation. But it took root. Tiberius was morose, unattractive, and heavy in speech; the man who kept power as emperor in all but name clearly needed to be personally magnetic, in order to paper over the crack between the appearance of republic and the reality of empire. Tiberius had none of the celebrated Caesarian charm.

Drusus, who lacked it as well, now became both consul and heir apparent. But in AD 23 he too died, apparently of stomach troubles. At this, Tiberius seemed to lose heart. He left Rome a little less than three years later and went first to Campania, and then to Capri. Here he remained, managing Roman affairs from a distance and never even visiting the city.

This kind of distant hand on affairs was not what the Senate had bargained for. The senators had given up their own authority so that a single authoritative presence could prevent civil war and revolt. But Tiberius was down in Capri, bathing in the surf with a gaggle of naked small boys whom he called his "minnows." He was inclined more and more to spend his days in pleasure, and since he was now emperor (in all but name) he had the wealth to make this pleasure quite extraordinary. He built little caves and grottoes all over his private island and hired boys and girls to dress up like nymphs and Pan; these he called his "haunts of Venus," and carried on in them exactly as the name suggests. He bought a famous work of pornography and kept it in his library "so that an illustration of the required position would always be available if anyone needed guidance in completing their performance."[3] The locals called him "that old goat." He was the third Roman princeps, and the first to indulge himself in the indiscriminate fulfillment of all his desires. It had not taken long for that particular power to corrupt its officeholders.

Meanwhile the Senate was doing the work of keeping the city running. And civil war seemed to be looming. Lucius Aelius Sejanus, the commander of the new Praetorian Guard (that standing "private army" of the princeps) was angling to seize power as soon as Tiberius died.

But in 31 Tiberius found out, in a way unrecorded by Tacitus, that Sejanus was not only the lover of his dead son Drusus's wife, but that the two of them had conspired to poison Drusus. He ordered Sejanus arrested and tried. Sejanus was convicted, and a purge ensued that swept up hundreds of citizens of Rome, including his own young children and even the son of the dead Germanicus, who starved to death in prison. From that time on, Tiberius's self-indulgence began to turn into cruelty: "He spared no one torture or execution," writes Suetonius.

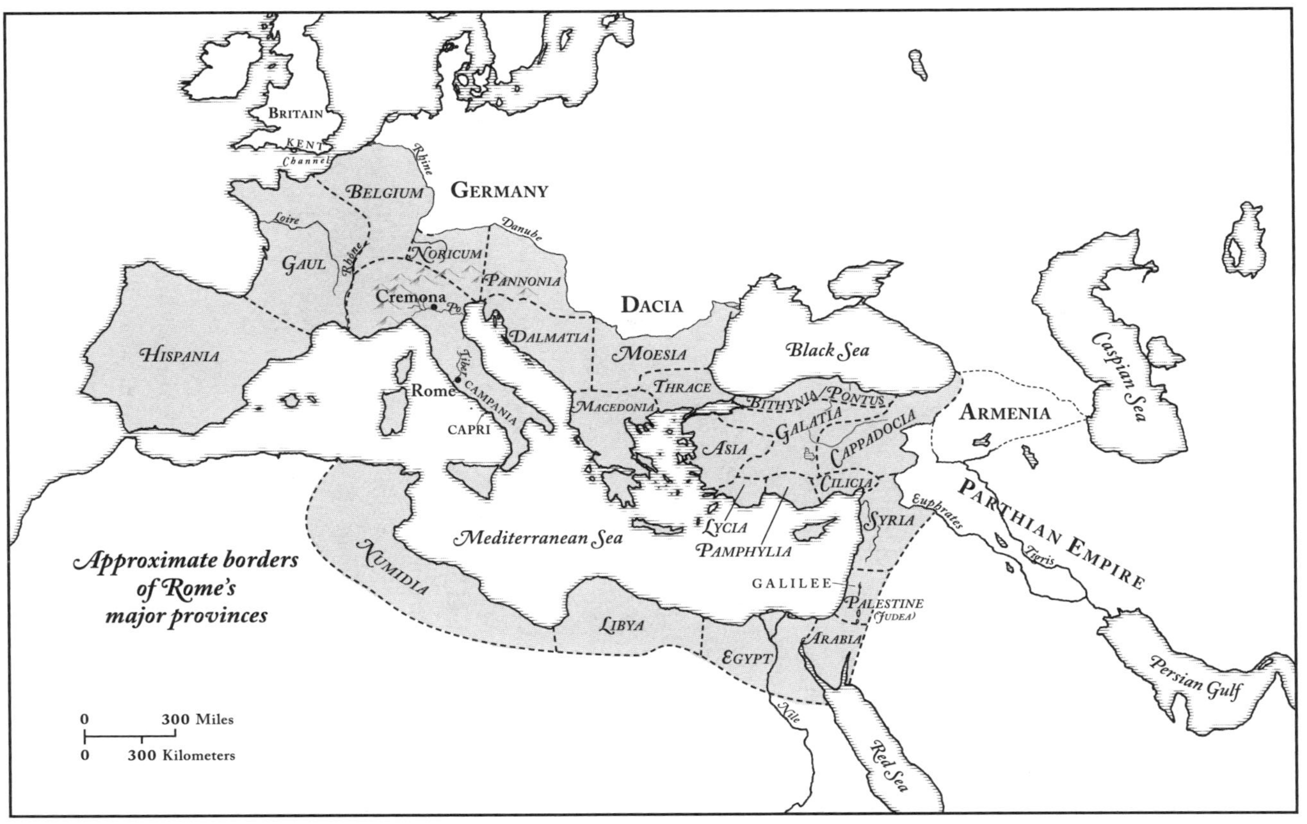

81.1 Rome Under Tiberius

While Tiberius was troubling the Romans at home, a wandering prophet named Jesus, down in Galilee, annoyed a large and powerful group of priests in Jerusalem by challenging their right to control the religious life of the Jews.* Since the abolishment of the office of High Priest and Ethnarch, the priests no longer had any political power, and they were particularly sensitive to guarding the religious power that remained to them.

But in order to silence Jesus, they needed help from the Romans. They had to maneuver him into looking guilty of some political offense in front of Herod Antipas, the vassal king who reported to Rome. The accusation they came up with was that Jesus had called himself "King of the Jews," something which was bound to irritate Herod.

But Herod, who had probably heard of the purges going on in Rome, was not about to do anything that smacked of independence; not when Tiberius was busy wiping out resistance. He sent Jesus directly to the Roman procurator who had replaced his brother Archelaus, with the message that the Romans, not he, had better do something about this problem.

This procurator, Pontius Pilate, was actually no surer of his own safety than Herod was. He too did not want to be suspected of doing anything that might undermine the power of that distant, angry, unpredictable princeps. A revolution in Palestine on his watch was not going to do him any good. So he agreed to execute Jesus, who had not contradicted him when Pilate had asked whether he was, in fact, claiming to be the king of the Jews. The method chosen, crucifixion, was the standard Roman punishment for revolutionaries; Spartacus's followers had also suffered it.

Pilate went on following a better-safe-than-sorry policy. Not too much later, in 36 AD, he reacted to a similar mild threat from a bunch of rebelling Samaritans by executing them all. This produced a backlash of anti-Roman sentiment in Palestine. The Roman governor of Syria, Pilate's superior, yanked him off the job and sent him back to Rome in disgrace.

In 37, Tiberius died of illness; it had taken him a long time to breathe his last, and someone finally smothered him. When Rome learned that he was safely dead, the people ran through the streets shouting, "Into the Tiber with Tiberius!"[4]

* The priests in Jerusalem had divided into two groups, the Pharisees and the Sadducees. The differences between them were mostly theological (chiefly, whether or not there would be a physical resurrection of the dead), but they formed distinct parties in the internal politics of Judea and Galilee. The Pharisees were the primary enemies of Jesus.

Neither Tiberius nor Augustus had ever claimed a royal title, but the transfer of powers was becoming a little more regal. Tiberius had chosen as his heir one of the dead Germanicus's sons, young Caligula.* But he had not bothered to go through the parade of making Caligula joint proconsul; Caligula had been given the job of quaestor (financial official) four years before, but never got any other title. The Senate awarded him the title of princeps, the authority of the Pontifex Maximus, and the military power of imperium without recognizing him first as the surviving member of a joint proconsulate, and without the formality of his surrendering his powers.

Caligula started off by relieving the grim suspicions that so many Romans were still living under, in the wake of Tiberius's purge. He pardoned all prisoners, invited exiles to return to the city, and made a few tax reforms that helped out poorer Romans.

But the good beginning was deceptive. Ancient accounts are divided about Caligula's behavior; some say that he was vicious from the beginning, but concealed it long enough to strengthen his power (Suetonius even says that his hand smothered Tiberius), while others claim that he suffered through a serious illness early in his reign and then emerged with a new personality. All of the accounts list shocking crimes: he murdered his cousin, his grandmother, and his father-in-law; he slept with all three of his sisters, as well as male and female prostitutes and other men's wives; he had a senator torn apart and his pieces dragged through the street; he forced his bodyguards to play war with him, and killed them when they hesitated to strike him; he raised taxes and then spent money wildly. Rumor said that he intended to make his horse a consul, and certainly he had no respect for the office. In 39, he fired both of the consuls and dissolved the Senate by force.

In less than a century, Rome had travelled a very long way from the city where the senators had killed a man because he might possibly want to be emperor. Now Rome was tolerating an unheard-of autocracy. The problem with Caligula's disintegration is that it didn't inconvenience everyone equally; he lavished money and privileges on those who managed to stay on his good side. So there were always tongues ready to carry reports of treason to the princeps, and Caligula's punishments were so inventively painful that few wanted to risk them.

This would not save him forever, although for a time he kept Rome's eyes fixed on him, waiting for the next outrage. But the business of empire had not stopped while the empire's central figure fell apart.

* In his will, Tiberius actually named Caligula joint heir along with Tiberius Gemellus, one of the sons of the dead Drusus, but Caligula first had the will declared void and then had Gemellus killed.

On Rome's eastern border, the Parthian king Artabanus III, son of the patriot who had taken the throne away from the Romanized Vonones I, ruled over Parthia with a restored nationalism. He appears on his coins (many of them found in Ecbatana) with the ancient square-cut Persian beard, and his traditionalism was matched by his attempts to reassert strong control over the Parthian cities; he put his kinsmen, now princes of a royal family, on minor thrones to rule over regions of his kingdom and report to him, in a system copied from the old Persian satrapies.

Pliny says that there were eighteen of these mini-kingdoms in Parthia, and Artabanus III had his eye on making Armenia the nineteenth. Armenia, which had once belonged to the Seleucid empire, lay as a buffer state between Parthia and Rome. It was not exactly a free country. Since the reign of Augustus, Armenia had been what was euphemistically called "Roman protected," meaning that Roman troops were propping up rule by a Roman-sympathizing king. Artabanaus planned to put his son Arsaces on the Armenian throne and make the state "Parthian protected" instead.

He attacked Armenia sometime in the thirties, with the help of hired Scythian troops from the north. Fighting in the capital city ended with Arsaces dead; Artabanus, unwilling to give up, seems to have made another assault with plans to crown another son.

The Roman commander, who did not necessarily want to carry on an out-and-out war so close to Rome's far eastern border, offered peace talks. In AD 37, Artabanus agreed to meet a Roman diplomat right on the Roman-Parthian border—the middle of the Euphrates. Both men, unwilling to set foot in the other's territory, walked forwards onto a bridge spanning the water, and carried on their negotiations right at the center. At the end, both Parthian and Roman troops had been committed to a partial withdrawal; Armenia would remain as a buffer state, with a certain shaky independence of its own.

Artabanus III wanted a pitched war with Rome as little as his Roman counterpart. Parthia was facing another enemy on its eastern border: the kingdom of Kushan.

The people of Kushan had originally been Yuezhi nomads. After the Yuezhi had invaded and broken down Greek Bactria, one Yuezhi tribe to the south had stretched its influence out over the clans around it, and had coalesced slowly into a country. The Kushan were an Asian people, but they used Greek script on their coins, learned on their journey south through Greek Bactria. The coins have Zeus on one side, and on the other a cross-legged seated figure who may be the Buddha; Kushan, which soon spread down as far as Gandhara, was woven through with influences from both west and south.

Around AD 30, the Kushan kingdom came under the rule of an ambitious

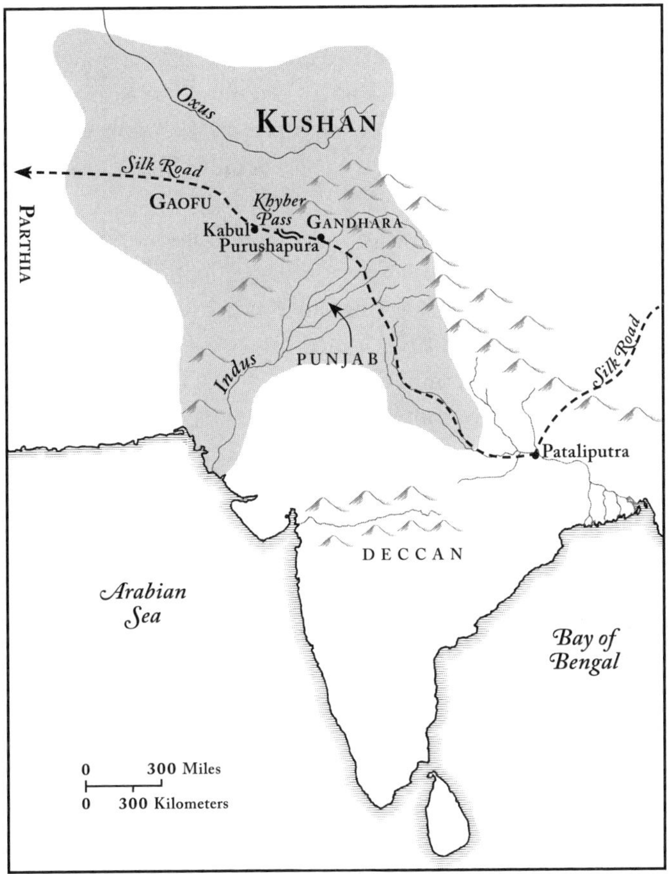

81.2 Kushan

man named Kujula Kadphises. Not a great deal is known about him, except that he held onto his throne for almost fifty years, and that during this time Kushan grew west far enough to start pushing on the eastern border of Artabanus III's Parthia. The ancient Chinese chronicle *Hou hanshi* says that he "invaded Anxi" (Parthia); the "invasion" seems to have been more of a taking away of territories on the east which had not been a full part of the Parthian system. "Gaofu," where Kabul now stands, is one of them. The Kushan, the *Hou hanshi* adds, became "very rich."

The growth of Kushan under Kujula Kadphises was abruptly checked when another warrior emerged from the shadows, conquered the area of the Punjab (which had been under Kushan's control), and spread his own new kingdom up as far as the modern valley of Kabul. His name was Gondophernes.

We know of him mostly through a story written a century or so later: the

Acts of Thomas, a text written by scholars who belonged to a theological offshoot of orthodox Christianity called Gnosticism. The story was first told in Syria, and relates the journeys of Thomas Didymus, the disciple of Jesus who is remembered in the New Testament gospels for refusing to believe in the Resurrection until he could see Jesus in the flesh. (This earned him the nickname Doubting Thomas.)

The story of Thomas's journey to meet Gondophernes begins, in the Acts of Thomas, at Jerusalem. Jesus, after being crucified, has risen from the dead and appeared to the disciples, giving them the task of spreading the news about him throughout the world. Thomas draws the job of going to India. He isn't enthusiastic about this, until he has a vision: "The Saviour appeared unto him by night and saith to him: Fear not, Thomas, go thou unto India and preach the word there, for my grace is with thee." Not long afterwards, Thomas encounters by chance a merchant "come from India whose name was Abbanes, sent from the King Gondophernes."[5]

The merchant agrees to be his guide into India. Eventually Gondophernes himself hears rumors of Thomas's arrival, since various miracles have surrounded him. He summons Thomas into his presence and asks him, as a holy man, to bless his daughter and her brand-new husband; the two have just celebrated their marriage. Thomas agrees to pray for the royal bride and groom, after which Jesus appears to the two in their bedchamber and tells them that if they abjure delights of the flesh ("abstain from this foul intercourse") and have no children, they will find enlightenment (a staple of gnostic theology). Both are convinced and become converts to Thomas's brand of gnostic Christianity. When Gondophernes learns, however, that the two have decided to live in chaste harmony (which meant "no heirs"),

> he rent his clothes and said unto them that stood by him: Go forth quickly and go about the whole city, and take and bring me that man that is a sorcerer who by ill fortune came unto this city; for with mine own hands I brought him into this house.[6]

Thomas manages to get away, and after various adventures makes his peace with the king, who is eventually converted and baptised himself.

For centuries, this story was dismissed as entirely mythical. But the discovery of Gondophernes's coins reveal that he did indeed exist, and that he ruled in the north of India. And the story suggests that his kingdom had a great deal of interaction with lands much farther to the west.

Whether Gondophernes actually became a Christian is unknown; but Christianity itself was beginning to take shape, in the first century, as a new means of identity. The Jewish theologian Paul, a Roman citizen, was writing about the death and resurrection of Jesus as a process that is repeated in the lives of Christian believers. Conversion, he says in a letter written to the Christians at Rome, brings death to an old corrupt self, and the power of Christ then raises it back up, restored and new. "Count yourselves dead to sin," Paul exhorts his readers, "but alive to God. Offer yourselves to God as those who have been brought from death to life."[7] The spreading cult of Christianity gave its adherents a brand-new identity in place of the old.

But the old identity, though it may be transformed, does not completely disappear. In another letter, to Christians in Galatia, Paul writes, "There is neither Jew nor Gentile, slave nor free, male nor female, for all are one in Jesus Christ." Yet elsewhere his letters make quite clear that Christians *remained* Jews and Gentiles, slave and free, not to mention male and female. A Christian had his (or her) core identity as a follower of Jesus Christ, but orthodox Christians did not relinquish their old nationalities, or their gender, or their place in the social hierarchy.

Christianity had, after all, originated in a conquered land—Judea—which had been allowed to keep its identity while donning another one at the same time. The Jews of Judea were Jews, not Romans; but they were also subjects of Rome, and some of them were even Roman citizens.

All Roman provincials faced this problem of balancing two different identities at the same time, but for Jews the problem was particularly acute. There was nothing inherently contradictory about being Roman and Christian, or Roman and Galatian, or even Roman and Egyptian. But Caligula was about to make it impossible to be both Roman and Jewish.

By AD 40, Caligula had decided that he was divine. He ordered statues of himself set up for worship: "He wished to be considered a god," writes the historian Josephus, "and to be hailed as such."[8] Caligula's decree stretched across the entire Roman domain. But in Jerusalem, the Jews, who were forbidden by their own laws to worship images, pled with the local Roman commander not to force them to do honor to Caligula's statue.

The commander, a reasonable man named Petronius, agreed to send a letter to Rome asking whether worship of the statues was really necessary. But the word that came back from the capital city was unexpected: Caligula was dead. The Praetorian Guard had finally murdered him. He had been princeps for three years and ten months.

Twenty-seven days after the news of Caligula's death arrived, another letter arrived: from the dead Caligula, threatening to put Petronius to death if the statues were not set up. The ship that carried the letter had been passed at sea by the faster ship bearing news of the madman's end.

The Senate now considered doing away with the office of princeps altogether, and dividing the powers which had been temporarily united in the person of the princeps back into their old republican offices. But two forces prevented them. Caligula's uncle Claudius, the brother of the dead Germanicus, had set his sights on the power of the *princeps.* The Praetorian Guard was willing to be bribed into supporting him; these elite soldiers had more say in Roman affairs now than soldiers had ever been granted before, and the restoration of the Republic would probably end in the guard's dissolution. Under a republic, they would lose their jobs, their livelihood, and (most seductive) their power.

Within a matter of days, Claudius had his power as princeps, Pontifex Maximus, and imperator firmly in his hands; he had paid off the guards, ordered the murderers of Caligula killed (everyone was grateful to them, but leaving them alive established a bad precedent), and planned out his next acts.

He had decided, apparently, on a combination of fear and mercy to establish his position; he gave back land Caligula had confiscated, and pardoned all those whom Caligula had suspected of treason. His mercy also extended a form of amnesty to those Caligula had convicted, by burning the records of their trials.

The mercy only extended to the point that he feared for his own life, however. Between 41 and 42, he executed senators and Roman aristocrats indiscriminately if he thought he might be in danger. In this he was encouraged by his wife Messalina, whose affairs were matched only by her willingness to denounce her enemies to her husband for execution.

Claudius's greatest achievement was in Britain, where a king named Caratacus had risen to challenge the power of the Romans. For some time, legions in Britain had been busy helping the little tribes in the southeast fight off takeover by Caratacus. This didn't commit Roman prestige to a full conquest of the island, but it did manage to keep Caratacus's kingdom from gaining so much power that it might be impossible, down the road, to begin such a conquest.

By 43, Caratacus had gained enough territory in the south to threaten Roman control of the Channel. So Claudius sent four legions, including many soldiers from Gaul itself, across to push the Britons back from the coast.

When they landed at Kent, Caratacus's men—who had never before seen such large Roman troops—were taken by surprise. The legions succeeded in fighting their way forwards and establishing a Roman frontier across the British southeast. When the Thames had been secured, Claudius himself arrived. For sixteen days, he took personal charge of the thrust forwards, an unusual act for a man who did very little personal fighting during his reign. Meanwhile the Second Legion advanced to the west under Claudius's trusted commander Vespasian. The establishment of Roman power in Britain* was the great political accomplishment of Claudius's reign.

But before long, Claudius's focus shifted to domestic troubles. His wife Messalina married her lover, a recklessly defiant act which may have been the first step in an attempt to overthrow Claudius himself. If so, it failed; Claudius had them both executed. After her death, Claudius married Caligula's younger sister, his own niece Agrippina (this required special permission from the Senate). She had a son by a previous marriage, a little boy named Lucius Domitius. Claudius adopted him, giving him the family name of Nero.

In 51, he declared Nero his heir. As soon as he did, Agrippina began to take steps to assure her own survival. She fully expected him to grow tired of her (Tacitus says she was "particularly frightened" when she heard Claudius, in a drunken stupor, remark that "it was his destiny first to endure his wives' misdeeds, and then to punish them"),[9] and she wanted to see him gone and her son on the throne before he turned against both of them.

Tacitus says that she chose her poison carefully: something that would appear to be a wasting disease rather than "a sudden, drastic effect" which might betray her crime. In AD 54, she put the poison on Claudius's dinner mushrooms. When Claudius was almost saved by an attack of diarrhea that emptied much of the poison out of his system, Agrippina ordered the doctor to make him vomit in order to save him. The doctor was in on the plot, and put more poison on the feather that he stuck down Claudius's throat.

AT SIXTEEN, NERO became princeps. He was by far the youngest man to ever assume it; he could not even claim to be qualified by previous government service. The position had begun to look more and more like a monarchy.

Nero began his reign, like Claudius, by paying off the Praetorian Guard to remain on their good side. He also promised the Senate, in a speech written by his tutor Seneca, that they would be given back some of their powers, as Augustus would have wanted. This was an extraordinary move which suggested that he (or Seneca) was fully aware of just how far away from the orig-

* Caratacus had been pushed back, but not defeated. Rome did not finally get rid of him until AD 49, when the queen of the Brigantes tribe, Cartimandua, agreed to trap and hand him over in return for Roman support.

inal Republic he had now strayed. It was a risky move, and Nero's decision to follow through on Seneca's guidance showed both courage and daring.

But he also resorted to Claudian tactics to protect himself. Claudius's natural son Britannicus (with the disgraced Messalina) died of an "epileptic fit" only four months later. Nero also ordered his mother's guards dismissed, and had her exiled from the royal residence; she had already removed one princeps to secure her own position, and he wanted to remain safe.

After this, the first five years of Nero's reign were markedly virtuous; later Romans gave them the name *Quinquennium Neronis*. Possibly his tutor Seneca was able to dominate him in his youth, or else he succumbed to the family curse of progressive dementia. In any case, from the age of twenty on his private behavior began to sink first towards overindulgence, and then towards insanity. In 58, he fell in love with Poppea, the wife of his friend Otho. Nero sent Otho off to a distant province and invited Poppea to stay in the palace; he was actually married already, but ignored his wife's protests.

In 59, he decided to get rid of his mother for good. He built a collapsible boat which was supposed to fold in upon her and drown her, and then sent her off on a river cruise; he was not yet mad enough to be unconcerned about appearances. But she swam to shore, much to his dismay; according to one account, he ordered a servant to stab her as soon as she got to land. He then divorced his wife and then had her murdered and her head brought back to Poppea as a trophy. He also declared a divorce between Poppea and her husband Otho, and married her himself.

Meanwhile, the Roman soldiers in Britain were taking their cue from their leader and behaving with complete lack of restraint. They had begun to build themselves a new city in Britain, over the ruins of Caratacus's old capital Camulodunum, a city which would be populated entirely by army veterans.[10] As free labor, they enslaved the nearby tribe of the Trinovantes, taking their land away and forcing the people to build for them.

In 60, the king of another smallish tribe, the Iceni, died; he left behind him a widow, Boudiccea, and two daughters. As he had no son, the Roman governor in Britain decided simply to absorb the Iceni territory into the Roman province. And then Roman soldiers stormed in, raped both girls, and beat up Boudiccea.

Boudiccea, insulted, dishonored, and seeing her country disappearing before her eyes, led a revolt. The oppressed Trinovantes joined her. They planned an assault on the partly built city at Camulodunum, an attack which the Romans later said had been presaged by omens: the statue of Victory fell down, unbodied yells and shrieks were heard in the unfinished buildings, the sea turned blood red, and "shapes like human corpses" were left by the ebbing tide.

It didn't take omens to see disaster coming, however. The new city had only a tiny garrison to guard it, and the swelling horde of Britons overran it without difficulty. The Ninth Division, which was headquartered there, was massacred, almost to a man; the governor fled to Gaul.

The Roman commander Paulinus saved the day by leading a violent retribution, and a properly organized wedge-force attack by armed soldiers soon broke the British resistance.[11] Boudiccea fled and then took poison.

The next governor walked more gingerly around the Britons, and shook the Roman troops in Britain into more temperate behavior. But there was no one to shake Nero into temperance. He had affairs, drank tremendously, raised taxes in the provinces to pay for his indulgences, and started once again to hold the infamous treason trials as Caligula had done.

81.1. Nero. Marble head of Nero, Emperor of Rome 54–68. Staatliche Antikensammlung, Munich. Photo credit Bildarchiv Preussischer Kulturbesitz/ Art Resource, NY

In AD 64, a fire began in Rome, and spread quickly through the poorer parts of the city. A wind picked it up and strengthened it. The city was crammed with dry wood houses, shoulder to shoulder, and the fire burned its way to a height never seen before. "The disaster which the city then underwent, had no parallel save in the Gallic invasion," wrote Dio Cassius. "The whole Palatine hill, the theater of Taurus, and nearly two thirds of the rest of the city were burned. Countless persons perished."[12]

Nero was out of the city at the time, but his cruelty had convinced Rome that he was capable of anything. At once, rumor flew: Nero had started the fire in order to clear land for his new palace . . . or, worse, for the sheer entertainment.

In fact, Nero's conscience was not yet entirely seared. He came back to the city and started relief operations, but he didn't help matters on the first night of his return, when he was so moved by the epic sight of flames sweeping across Rome that he climbed up onto a roof and sang his way through a whole lay of "The Taking of Troy." After that, his reputation was a lost cause. As Tacitus remarks, "All human efforts, all the lavish gifts of [Nero]. . . . did not banish the sinister belief that the conflagration was the result of an order."[13]

The fire, the insanity, and the treason trials together impelled a group of senators to plan an assassination in April of 65. The Senate had not been this desperate since Caesar's death, over a hundred years before. But the plan was discovered, the conspirators put to death, and Nero spiralled further into paranoia. His old tutor Seneca himself, learning that he was suspected of treason, killed himself with his wife, in their home, to avoid torture and execution.

Around this time the persecution of Christians began: Nero, while putting to death all suspected conspirators against him, needed to deflect attention from his own misdeeds. Christians provided him with a convenient scapegoat for the fire as well. But he also seems to have been motivated by genuine hatred. Sulpicius Severus's *Chronicle* says:

> Nero could not, by any means he tried, escape from the charge that the fire had been caused by his orders. He therefore turned the accusation against the Christians, and the most cruel tortures were accordingly inflicted upon the innocent. Nay, even new kinds of deaths were invented, so that, being covered in the skins of wild beasts, they perished by being devoured by dogs, while many were crucified or slain by fire, and not a few were set apart for this purpose, that when the day came to a close, they should be consumed to serve for light during the night. . . . At that time Paul and [the disciple] Peter were condemned to death, the former being beheaded with a sword, while Peter suffered crucifixion.[14]

Paul, the Roman Jew become Christian, who had put down in writing the clearest expression yet of the possibility that one identity could coexist in peoples of different nations and bind them together, was now seen as a potential danger to the empire.

In 66, Nero made a decision which put him on the path to disaster: he gave up Armenia. Parthia's current king, Vologases I, had refused to honor the agreement made in the middle of the Euphrates back in Caligula's day, and had sent Parthian troops into Armenia to capture it. Roman troops had begun to fight back in 53 BC, the year before Claudius's death, and the struggle had turned into an indecisive and draining war which had lasted nearly fourteen years. But there was trouble elsewhere in the Roman domains too; the provinces were restless and unhappy under too much tax, the army spread thin.

Nero decided that it would be best to make peace with Parthia. So he agreed to recognize Vologases's brother, Tiridates, as king of Armenia. Three thousand Parthians travelled with Tiridates to Rome, to watch the ceremony of Nero handing over the Armenian crown. Perhaps Nero meant this to be a brilliant spectacle of Roman greatness—he ordered the doors to the Temple of Janus closed, indicating that the entire empire was now at peace—but to the Romans looking on, the sight of thousands of Parthians thronging their streets in victory must have looked very like defeat.

In addition Nero's behavior had gotten, unbelievably, worse. He had kicked his pregnant wife to death in a rage, and then he had ordered a young boy named Sporus, who bore a resemblance to his dead wife, castrated so that he could marry Sporus in a public ceremony.

Two years after the capitulation in Armenia, the captain of the Praetorian Guard declared that the guard would support the governor of Hispania, an experienced soldier (and ex-consul) named Galba, if he wanted to claim the imperium: the supreme command of all Roman armed forces. Galba had the full support of his own troops in Hispania, plus the support of the governor of the neighboring province: this happened to be Otho, whose wife Nero had stolen and then murdered. He was glad to put his own army at Galba's disposal.

Nero, realizing that to lose the support of the Praetorian Guard was to lose his throne, ran to the port of Ostia and ordered a ship. The Guard was close behind him, and none of the captains at the port would allow him on board. He hurried out of the city, but the Guard cornered him in a house on the outskirts. The traditional gesture in such a situation was to kill oneself. Nero was helped; one of his aides held his hand and shoved the dagger in. "Such was the public rejoicing," Suetonius writes, "that the people put on liberty-caps and ran about all over the city."[15]

Galba was already past the age of seventy, hampered by arthritis, and had no connection whatsoever to any previous princeps of Rome. But it was becoming increasingly clear that the real power of the princeps lay not in his authority as proconsul, or Pontifex Maximus, or chief tribune, or in any of the civil offices which had been folded into the title of First Citizen. The real power of the princeps lay in the imperium, the supreme command of the army. And to keep the imperium, the ruler of Rome needed the support of the Praetorian Guard. The Republic had become an empire, and the empire was now run by something like a secret junta: a band of powerful soldiers who could put up or remove a figurehead ruler, but who held the real power themselves.

Galba turned out to be a bad figurehead. He marched to Rome at the head of his troops, with Otho at his side. But once there he declined to pay off the soldiers who had supported him, as the imperators before him had done.[16] Soon omens began to appear, suggesting that he would not reign long; the most serious was when the sacred chickens deserted him during a sacrifice.[17]

The omens were probably arranged by disgruntled members of the Praetorian Guard, who had decided to switch their allegiance from Galba to Otho. Seven months after claiming the power of imperator, Galba was sacrificing at the Temple of Apollo when the Praetorian Guard proclaimed Otho to be imperator in his place. Galba heard the news and charged into the Forum to confront the rebels. They killed him there, threw his body in the road, and stuck his head on a pole.

The Senate, unhappily, agreed to confirm Otho as imperator and princeps. Meanwhile, the army stationed at the Rhine river announced that they wanted Vitellius, the commander of the forces in Germany, to be imperator instead. Now there were two imperators in the Roman Empire, one confirmed by the Senate as princeps and supported by the Praetorian Guard, the other unconfirmed but with a vast army at his back.

Vitellius marched down towards Italy, where his men built a bridge across the Po and met Otho's smaller force at the Battle of Cremona. Otho's army was scattered; with rare resignation, Otho decided that it would do neither him nor Rome any good to embark on a full-scale civil war. He put his affairs in order, burned his papers, gave away his belongings, had a good night's sleep, and killed himself in the morning. It was the act of a man with a clear conscience and unusual courage, which was the kind of imperator Rome needed.

What Rome got instead was Vitellius, shrewd and unprincipled. He marched to Rome, where he showed his grasp of the power structure by dissolving the Praetorian Guard and recreating it from his own loyal troops.

The other Roman legions didn't like this preferential treatment of the soldiers from the German province. Before long the troops stationed in the eastern part of the empire declared that they would support yet another candidate: Vespasian, the Roman general who had already distinguished himself in the wars against Britain, and who had been rewarded with the governorship of Syria.

Vespasian was nowhere near Rome; he was in his own province, putting down trouble in Palestine. Ever since Caligula's threat to put his own statue in the temple, Jewish resistance to Roman rule had been growing; that demand had been avoided, but the Jews sensed that it would only be a matter of time before they were asked to do something truly appalling. In 66, a group of freedom fighters called Zealots had proclaimed war on the Roman soldiers stationed in Jerusalem. The local governor had marched troops in but had been defeated, and the situation had grown serious enough for Vespasian himself,

TIMELINE 81

ROME	CHINA	PARTHIA
Second Settlement (23)		
Octavian, pontifex maximus		
	Aiti	
	Ping	**Phraates V**
	Ruzi	**Vonones I**
	Xin Dynasty (AD 9)	
Death of Octavian (AD 14)	**Wang Mang**	**Artabanus III**
Tiberius, princeps		
	Eastern Han Dynasty (AD 25)	
Death of Jesus of Nazareth	**Guang Wudi**	
Caligula, princeps (41)		
		Vologases I
Nero, princeps (54)	**Mingdi**	
Galba, princeps (68)		
Vespasian, princeps (69)		

an experienced general, to intervene and wipe up the mess. With the help of his son and commander, Titus, Vespasian had managed to drive the rebels back inside Jerusalem, which was now under siege.*

Back in Rome, Vitellius was eating enormously, drinking, and indulging himself, while his soldiers prepared to defend his rule. Roman troops that supported Vespasian were marching towards them. The two armies met at Cremona, where the Vespasian-loyal soldiers eventually won a victory; but the victory began a four-day rampage of burning and destruction that stretched down to Rome itself. Vespasian's supporters in the city tried to seize the Capitol from Vitellius, and in the battle that followed both the Capitol and the great Temple of Jupiter Optimus Maximus burned to the ground. In Decem-

* The Roman army prepared for the siege of Jerusalem by gathering at the strategically located city of Megiddo (called "Armageddon" in the book of Revelation). The siege ended, eventually, with the destruction of Jerusalem, which lent Megiddo particular apocalyptic significance in the Jewish imagination.

ber of 69, soldiers broke into Vitellius's own quarters, killed him, and disposed of his body in the traditional way: by throwing it into the Tiber.

Vespasian was willing to take his place, but he did not want to come all the way west to Rome before the siege of Jerusalem was settled. So the Senate, which was desperate to satisfy his unruly supporters before they burned anything else down, declared Vespasian to be princeps, as Augustus, Tiberius, and Claudius had been before him. He was given the title without ever stepping foot in Rome.

The decree did not even list the names of Caligula, Nero, Galba, Otho, or Vitellius: they had been erased from the record, *damnatio memoria.* In the past year, four rulers had claimed the power of princeps, and it was clear that the fiction of power awarded by the Senate, on behalf of the people, was total fraud. The power in Rome was held by the strongest man with the most armed support. But by not listing the names of the men who had broken this illusion, the Senate denied their existence. The playacting that had characterized the rule of Augustus was still at the very center of Roman politics.

Chapter Eighty-Two

The Edges of the Roman World

Between AD 70 and 132, catastrophes trouble Rome, but a string of sane emperors occupies its throne

BY SEPTEMBER OF 70, the walls of Jerusalem had been broken down and the city burned, the Second Temple gone up in flames. The rebel Jewish army had not been entirely defeated, but Vespasian felt victory was sure enough for him to leave the area. He finally set out for Rome in September of 70 after nine months of princeps in absentia.

Vespasian was an experienced soldier; he understood the ways in which soldiers thought, and he did not underestimate the power of the army to make or break his power. His first action, once in Rome, was to reassign commanders and redivide troops so that old loyalties would be destroyed.

His ten-year rule was quiet, orderly, well administered: just as the Senate had hoped, a return to the days of Augustan procedure. There was some fighting on the outskirts of the empire: campaigns in Britain, Rome's least-conquered province, and a horrendous outcome to the war in Jerusalem. In 73, the remnants of the Jewish rebellion, trapped in their fortress of Masada, killed their children and then themselves, rather than finally surrender to the Romans. The last Jewish stronghold was gone, as was Judea and all remnants of the old nation of Israel; Palestine became part of the province of Syria.

But essentially Rome was at peace; Vespasian avoided treason trials and lowered taxes, both of which made him more popular and Rome more serene.

In AD 79, Vespasian died, probably of the flu, at the age of seventy.[1] The Senate confirmed his son Titus as his heir, a little apprehensively. During Vespasian's reign, Titus had gained a reputation as a ruthless and often cruel commander, and his conduct against Jerusalem had been particularly violent. But

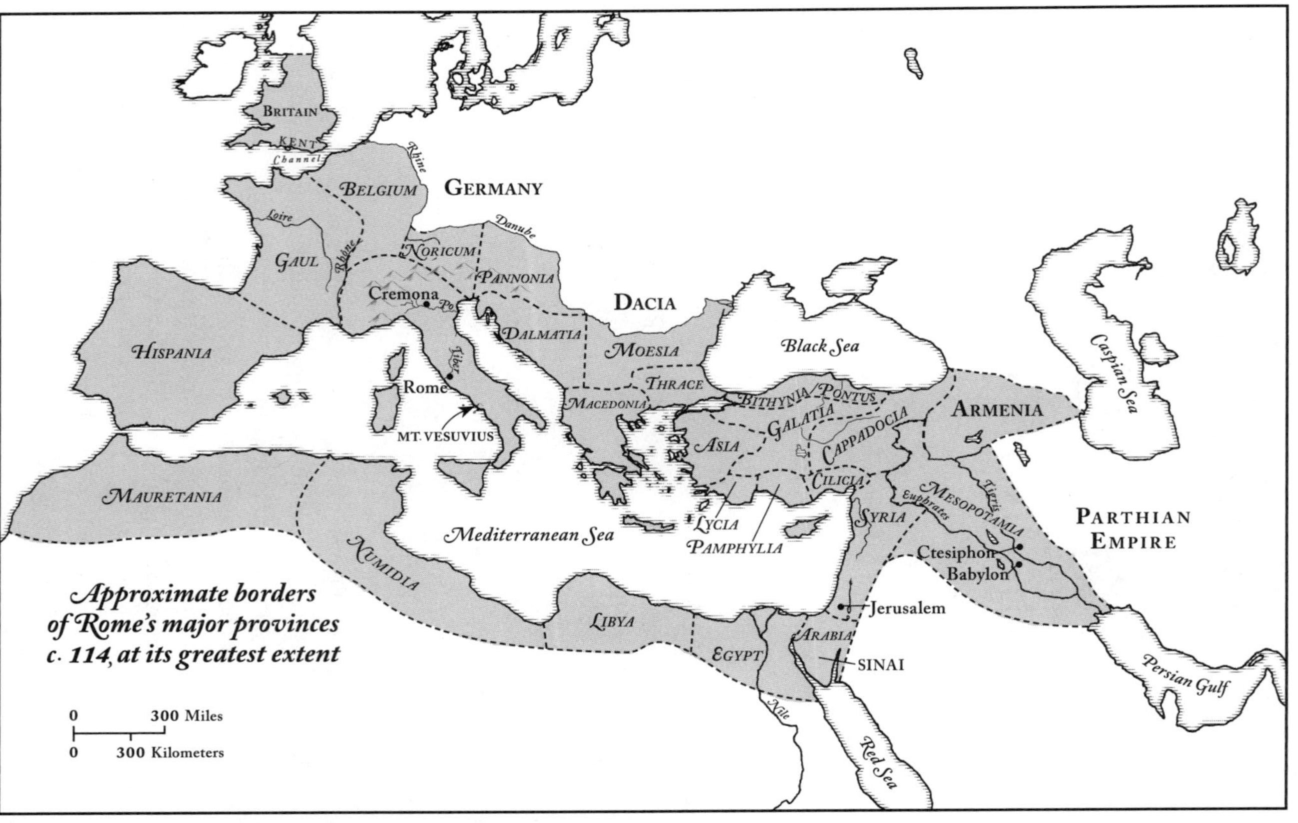

82.1 The Roman Empire

once given the title of princeps, he followed his father's orderly and decent example.

Rome had no chance to draw a deep breath, though. Three disasters hit Titus, one after the other.

The first was the eruption of Mount Vesuvius, only two months into his reign. The mountain Vesuvius lay near the southwest coast of Italy, not far from the Bay of Naples, and it had been rumbling in the background for as long as most Romans could remember. The people who lived in the city of Pompeii, near its foot, were accustomed to the earthquakes, and even though they had begun to grow stronger no one was alarmed; no one knew that quakes might be the first stages in an eruption.

The Roman writer Pliny the Younger was in Pompeii on August 23, 79, the day before the eruption. "There had been tremors for many days previously," he wrote, in a letter to a friend, "a common occurrence in Campania and no cause for panic."

> But that night the shaking grew much stronger; people thought it was an upheaval, not just a tremor. . . . Now the day begins, with a still hesitant and almost lazy dawn. All around us buildings are shaken. We are in the open, but it is only a small area and we are afraid, nay certain, that there will be a collapse. We decided to leave the town finally; a dazed crowd follows us, preferring our plan to their own (this is what passes for wisdom in a panic). Their numbers are so large that they slow our departure, and then sweep us along. We stopped once we had left the buildings behind us. Many strange things happened to us there, and we had much to fear. The carts that we had ordered brought were moving in opposite directions, though the ground was perfectly flat, and they wouldn't stay in place even with their wheels blocked by stones. In addition, it seemed as though the sea was being sucked backwards, as if it were being pushed back by the shaking of the land. Certainly the shoreline moved outwards, and many sea creatures were left on dry sand. Behind us were frightening dark clouds, rent by lightning twisted and hurled, opening to reveal huge figures of flame. These were like lightning, but bigger. . . . It wasn't long thereafter that the cloud stretched down to the ground and covered the sea. . . . Now came the dust, though still thinly. I look back: a dense cloud looms behind us, following us like a flood poured across the land. "Let us turn aside while we can still see, lest we be knocked over in the street and crushed by the crowd of our companions." We had scarcely sat down when a darkness came that was not like a moonless or cloudy night, but more like the black of closed and unlighted rooms. You could hear women lamenting, children

> crying, men shouting. Some were calling for parents, others for children or spouses; they could only recognize them by their voices. . . . It grew lighter, though that seemed not a return of day, but a sign that the fire was approaching. The fire itself actually stopped some distance away, but darkness and ashes came again, a great weight of them. We stood up and shook the ash off again and again. Otherwise we would have been covered with it and crushed by the weight. I might boast that no groan escaped me in such perils, no cowardly word, but that I believed that I was perishing with the world, and the world with me.[2]

Those who did not escape were buried in twenty-five feet of ash, or choked by the heat and gasses. Over two thousand people died in a single night.

Titus at once sent disaster relief from Rome, and visited the site himself as soon as it was safe. He was at Pompeii for the second time, checking to see what needs could still be relieved, when a small fire in Rome blazed up and burned an enormous area of the city. And on the heels of the fire came an epidemic, which swept through the overpacked refugees in the city, killing them in scores.

In 81, still struggling with the aftermath of the disasters, Titus came down with a fever and died at the age of forty-two. He had been princeps of Rome for less than three horrible years. Perhaps the fever was a relief.

On Titus's death, his brother Domitian was proclaimed imperator by the Praetorian Guard, and (inevitably) was confirmed as princeps by the Senate, twenty-four hours later. Domitian had never been his father's favorite; whatever self-doubts this had produced in him, he worked out in imperious behavior towards Rome and total disregard for the Senate.

This was not necessarily a bad thing. Suetonius says that his severity was generally exercised in the interests of law and order: "He administered justice scrupulously and conscientiously," he writes. "He degraded jurors who accepted bribes, together with all their associates. . . . He took such care to exercise restraint over the city officials and the governors of the provinces, that at no time were they more honest or just." He also kept a severe eye on public morals: "He expelled an ex-quaestor from the Senate because he was given to acting and dancing," Suetonius remarks. He made it illegal for prostitutes to receive inheritances, and when he found out that one of the Vestal Virgins had been having multiple flings, he decreed that the traditional punishment be meted out. She was buried alive, and her lovers were "beaten to death with rods" in public.[3]

This was all perfectly correct, although severe. Domitian was not inclined to show mercy; he took his power very seriously indeed. Not long after his accession, he adopted the title *dominus et deus*, which is to say "Lord and God," and ordered that all official letters be headed "Our Lord and our God commands that this be done." "And so the custom arose," Suetonius adds, "of henceforth addressing him in no other way even in writing or in conversation."[4]

Unlike Caligula, he was quite sane; and he did not use the claim of godhood to break the law. This scrupulous righteousness prevented the kind of popular outrage that had killed earlier abusers of the power of princeps. The Senate did not mount any sustained objection; the Praetorian Guard did not immediately assassinate him.

But we can look back at this title *dominus et deus* as the point at which the pleasant mask of republican government was finally put away for good. Even the worst princeps had been confirmed by the Senate, however unwillingly. But no one could claim that a ruler called "Lord and God" needed any kind of sanction from his people in order to rule. Domitian was not the first Roman ruler to wield kingly powers, but he was the first to *say* so. The First Citizen had finally become an emperor.*

Domitian's claim to ultimate power and his rigid law enforcement produced the same unhappiness that plagued China when rewards were given for reporting on the misdeeds of others, and vexed Sparta when each man was the enforcer of his brother's morals. The atmosphere in Rome grew so oppressive that Tacitus expressed gratitude that his much-loved and missed father Agricola had died before Domitian's reign:

> Domitian no longer left interval or breathing space. . . . Under Domitian more than half our wretchedness consisted in watching and being watched, while our very sighs were scored against us. . . . Happy you, Agricola, in your glorious life, but no less happy in your timely death.[5]

Relentless punishment of misdeeds led to discontent, discontent to muttering, mutterings to plot, plot to suspicion, suspicion to conviction, conviction to relentless punishment, in an unending circle of wretchedness.

* Latin had no word for "emperor" as such; the English word is derived from *imperator*. The histories of Tacitus and Suetonius use the word *princeps*, which is often translated "emperor" even when it refers to Augustus or another early ruler of the Empire. For example, in Tacitus's *Annals* I.7 he says that after Augustus's death, the people of Rome were careful *ne laeti excessu* ***principis*** *neu tristiores primordio, lacrimas gaudium, questus adulationem miscebant.* The relevant phrase is translated, in the classic English version done by Church and Brodribb, "neither to betray joy at the decease of one **emperor** nor sorrow at the rise of another." This tends to obscure the transition period in which republican ideals were slowly buried while the ruler of Rome mutated from First Citizen into Lord and God. I have chosen to use *princeps* before Domitian, and *emperor* afterwards, since it seems to me that his reign was the final transition point from one way of thinking to another.

Domitian, like Titus and Vespasian, knew the source of his power; he increased the pay for the army to assure himself of its loyalty. His household was less appreciative. In 96, his wife, his chamber attendant, his niece (whose husband he had put to death for atheism), and the leaders of the Praetorian Guard together stabbed Domitian to death in his bedchamber.[6] The Senate immediately declared as emperor one of their own number, the sixty-one-year-old consul Nerva.

This pleased the people of Rome, but not the army. In 97, the Praetorian Guard (which had not as a whole taken part in the conspiracy to kill Domitian and had shared the army's loyalty to him) shut Nerva up in his own palace, dragged out the chamberlain who had allowed the assassins into Domitian's rooms, hacked off his genitals, shoved them in his mouth, and then cut his throat.[7] Immediately afterwards, Nerva declared that his heir would be the general Trajan, a favorite of the army, currently stationed near the Rhine river. He had probably been told that this was the only way to avoid assassination, but none of the negotiations have survived. Just a few months later, Nerva died from fever. It was probably a welcome deliverance from a much nastier end.

Trajan, hearing the news that he was now emperor, took the time to make sure that his current command was properly wrapped up before heading for Rome. He journeyed along the frontier of the Rhine and Danube to see that it was safe, and only then turned back to the south. It was nearly eighteen months after Nerva's death that he arrived in Rome.

The city had remained calm during all this time, which is a measure of Trajan's perfect suitability for the job. The army respected his skill, and the people of Rome, relieved by Domitian's absence and the escape from civil war that could have followed Nerva's death, were ready to welcome him.

The Roman historians are almost unanimous in praising Trajan. He repaired roads and harbors, built libraries, dug canals, repaired sewers, and took "an oath that he would not shed blood," which pleased the people.[8] His campaigns pleased the army; by 106, he had added both the Sinai and the land north of the Danube to the Roman Empire. He led the attacks himself, and returned in triumph to a huge celebration. In honor of his victories, the story of his wars north of the Danube was carved, comic-book style, onto a column which still stands in Rome: Trajan's Column.

Trajan's reputation as a good emperor rested on his basic fairness, his lack of paranoia, his decent administration of the capital city, and his willingness to campaign for the greater glory of Rome. But it also had something to do with the punctilious manner in which he observed those empty forms of cooperation with the Senate. "He treated the Senators with dignity," says the fourth-century *Augustan History*,* and he was punctilious in carrying out senatorial regulations.

This was a relation between Senate and emperor that had not been seen for decades, or more; and in this atmosphere, thoughtful attempts were made to justify the domination of an emperor over a nation whose name itself denied any such possibility. The philosophy of stoicism had been taught in Rome for centuries; it had been foundational in the Roman idea of virtue. The stoic man was not dominated by his appetites. He was able to detach himself from both pleasure and pain, in order to decide with objectivity what course of action was good.

Now a philosopher named Epictetus turned to apply stoic principles to the problem of the emperor. The very word *Roman*, he wrote, now meant "a condition of submission to the emperor," but there was no reason for this to be incompatible with true freedom. Even men who are legally, constitutionally "free" struggle with compulsions that threaten to enslave them:

> Were you never commanded by her you loved to do anything you did not wish? Did you never flatter your precious slave-boy? Did you never kiss his feet? Yet if any one compel you to kiss Caesar's you count it an outrage, the very extravagance of tyranny. . . . Did you never go out at night where you did not wish, and spend more than you wished, and utter words of lamentation and groaning. . . . Why do you call yourself free then, any more?[9]

Epictetus was himself a slave from Asia Minor; he knew what it meant to live in submission. His Stoicism makes freedom a condition of the soul, not of the body. "That man is free," he wrote, "who lives as he wishes . . . who gets what he wills to get, and avoids what he wills to avoid." The emperors were there to stay; it was best, then, for Romans to simply redefine freedom.

IN THE LAST YEARS of Trajan's reign, the empire was troubled by a phenomenon it did not know what to do with: the presence of a growing number of Christians. The consul Pliny, who had gone on to serve as a provincial governor in Asia Minor, was so worried by these people that he wrote to Trajan, asking what he should do about them. They talked about belonging to a

* The *Augustan History* is a collection of biographies of the Roman emperors who ruled after 117. Although these biographies are attributed to six different authors, much of the collection was probably written by others, and there is no way of knowing what sources were used. It is not terribly reliable, but for some of the emperors, it is the only source that provides biographical detail.

kingdom with no earthly ruler; this was an attitude uncomfortably reminiscent of the Jews, who had first refused to worship the emperor and then had turned into a messy military problem.

In fact Christians, who did indeed look forward to a kingdom which would be ruled by God rather than Trajan, were quite different than Jews. Since Abraham, the Jewish worship of God had been tied to a particular piece of land; God had promised them the land of Israel which meant that their faith *had* to have a political dimension. The Jewish refusal to worship Roman emperors was based in theology (God had said: You will have no other gods but me), but it was also an assertion that the Romans had no right to rule over Israel, and particularly over Jerusalem. It belonged to God.

Christians, on the other hand, had never had a country of their own: the kingdom that they talked about was a spiritual one, existing in another dimension, side by side with the earthly nations where they lived. It was a city without foundations, whose builder was God, as the writer of the New Testament book of Hebrews put it. The name *Christian* itself implied that they found their identity as followers of the God-man who had been crucified in Palestine—not as residents of a particular place.

The emperors and governors of Rome never did figure this out. Pliny's letters were both cautious and puzzled: Should he hunt Christians down if they didn't come forwards? Should he allow them to carry on the strange rituals of their faith in public? How should he respond?

Trajan suggested a don't ask–don't tell policy; Pliny should discourage public professions of Christianity, but he was not to racket around finding Christians to kill. If they were behaving peacefully, they should be left in peace.

He was not overly concerned about the issue, in part because he was inclined to look outwards for his battles. Under Trajan, the Roman Empire reached its greatest extent. He had pushed the borders north and south; his final campaign was against Parthia, now ruled by the king Vologases III. In 113, he personally led Roman troops east through Armenia, which fell to Rome and became a Roman province, and directly into the Parthian land across the Euphrates river. The Parthians were forced to retreat; Trajan marched into Mesopotamia itself, occupied Babylon, and captured the Parthian capital Ctesiphon.

This was a great victory, but the Mesopotamian desert was notoriously difficult to hold onto; it was better suited to guerilla warfare than for occupation by a large army. Until 117, Trajan remained in Mesopotamia, fighting against the ongoing Parthian resistance, but was never able to entirely obliterate it. At the same time, another civil disturbance was troubling the Roman subjects. In 115, Jewish communities scattered across the empire, from Egypt northwards,

82.1. Hadrian's Wall. Photo credit Susan Wise Bauer

TIMELINE 82		
ROME	PARTHIA	JUDEA
Caligula, princeps (41)		
	Vologases I	
Nero, princeps (54)		
Galba, princeps (68)		
Vespasian, princeps (69)		
		Destruction of Second Temple
		Siege at Masada
Titus, princeps (79)		
Domitian, emperor (81)		
Nerva, emperor (96)		
Trajan, emperor (98)		
	Vologases III	
Hadrian, emperor (117)		

Chapter Eighty-Three

Children on the Throne

In China, from AD 88 to 182,
a succession of children inherit the Han title,
the palace eunuchs gain power,
and the Yellow Turbans rise

BY AD 88, THE LAST YEAR of Mingdi's son Zhangdi, the Han Dynasty had regained most of its former glory. The western states had been conquered almost as far as the Parthian border, and trade along the Silk Road had filled the empire with prosperity. Even the lack of a mature king to take Zhangdi's place—at his death, his successor Hedi was only nine years old—did not seem a catastrophe, as it had been for that earlier phase of Han rule. China was lucky to have a good regent: Pan Ch'ao, the old soldier, who had been around since the days of Zhangdi's father and knew as much about governing as any emperor.

In 91, at the age of twelve, Hedi ordered the palace eunuchs to kill off his mother's relatives, who were trying to take advantage of his youth to muscle in on government offices. We can probably chalk this ruthlessness up to old Pan Ch'ao, who was watching out for his young charge, and who remembered that the Han Dynasty had once been overthrown by relatives of a dowager empress.

In any case, this was the first appearance on the scene of a new group of power-players: the palace eunuchs. The use of palace eunuchs to serve the royal family had been part of a strategy to assure the loyalty of the king's servants; since they were castrated, they had no ambitions (theoretically) to seize land, wealth, or power on behalf of their children or clan. By some estimates, there were two thousand eunuchs at the Han court, and they had the emperor's trust.[1]

Hedi died in 105, still in his twenties, with no legitimate heir; neither of his wives had become pregnant. One of the palace concubines did have a three-month-old son of the emperor's; this baby, little Shangdi, died before he was a year old. The closest remaining relative was Hedi's nephew Andi, who was twelve when he took the throne in 106. But unlike his uncle, he did not have the benefit of a watchful guardian. Pan Ch'ao had died in 102, after a lifetime of constant warfare that had taken him as far west as the Caspian Sea.[2]

Once again, powerful relatives moved behind the scene. Andi was married, while still a child, to the daughter of an ambitious official. After this, he was encouraged to leave the political decisions to his wife's family.

Until 146, a whole succession of these too-young rulers were put on the throne by one ambitious noble family after another. Andi's son Shundi was crowned in 125, at the age of ten; his son Chongdi was crowned when barely a year old, and died before he was three; he was followed by his own third cousin, the seven-year-old Zhidi, who was poisoned when he was eight and replaced by another cousin, fourteen-year-old Huandi.

During all these years, Han China was run by uncles, cousins, aunts, and anyone else who could get a finger into the pie. Huandi's own policies were decided for him by his wife's older brother, the ambitious Liang Ji, who had already been running the capital city Loyang for some years. Deprived of his power, Huandi retreated totally into the palace, ignoring all political decisions, refusing to sleep with his wife, and—as it turned out—cultivating the friendship of the palace eunuchs.

These eunuchs had been gaining more and more power, thanks to gradual shifts in their legal status. Some decades before, a royal eunuch had adopted a son, which was not all that uncommon. But when the eunuch died, he left his land to the adopted son. For the first time, the son was allowed to keep it. Two decades later, another eunuch was permitted to pass down an honorary title to *his* adopted son.[3] These were not small changes. They allowed eunuchs to create a ruling clan of their own—one formed by adoptions rather than marriages, but a clan nonetheless. And like any clan, the palace eunuchs began to accumulate wealth, estates, and ambitions.

In 159, Huandi gave five eunuchs whose loyalty he had cultivated a job: they were to kill his brother-in-law, and he would reward them with both titles and land. His wife had just died, his blood ties to Liang Ji were broken, and he wanted his throne back.

The five eunuchs mobilized the palace guard and surrounded Liang Ji's house. He killed himself before they could break in and get their hands on him, but the rest of his family was slaughtered. The purge spread out to the entire clan.

But the return of Huandi to power came too late. In the decades when regents dominated China, no one had been paying much attention to the state of the country at large. Unwatched, the merit system instituted by Guang Wudi had started to backfire. It had put the government of China's provinces into the hands of trained and able men rather than aristocrats. But those able men were also ambitious. Many of them, over time, had seized the land of those who could not pay their taxes, and then had allowed the debtors to continue farming it.[4]

This was perfectly legal, and also more humane (and more productive) than throwing the debtors into prison. But as a result, government officials had accumulated wide tracts of land, worked by debtors who had become a new kind of feudal peasant. It was only human nature to pass that land on to sons and grandsons. Slowly, another network of powerful land-owning families had grown up. The names were different than those of the great families a century before, but the results were the same: wealthy landowners ran vast estates, and the poor farmers who worked the land had no power to protest their own low wages. The landowners had even begun to hire bands of security guards to keep their great estates safe—bands which grew to look more and more like private armies.[5]

At the same time, the opening of the road to the west brought in more and more trade. Merchants (who under the original Han system had been scorned as parasites and middlemen) were now able to make tremendous fortunes.[6] This was a phenomenon lamented by the scholar Wang Fu, who died sometime around 165: in *Qianfu lun,* "Criticisms of a Hidden Man" (he had never won much in the way of official favors), in the chapter "On excessive luxury," he complains that trade has replaced agriculture as the most profitable of occupations. And the trade was built partly on the backs of the poor laboring farmworkers, who had to pay higher and higher taxes so that the Silk Road could be kept up all the way west, and staffed with garrisons to keep merchant caravans safe from bandits.

Huandi did little to address any of these problems. He died in 168, leaving the throne and all of the Han Dynasty's problems to his twelve-year-old son Lingdi.

Lingdi's mother, the Empress Dowager Dou, was Huandi's third wife. She served as her son's regent, and since Lingdi was so young, she knew that she would be regent for some time. Her greatest worry was the power of the palace eunuchs, who had gained more and more wealth and power under Huandi's rule. In fact, a group of palace eunuchs had formed themselves into something like a voluntary clan, crossed with a secret society: it was called the Ten Regular Attendants, and its members were committed to getting as much as they could from the emperor for themselves.

One of her advisors, the Confucian scholar Chen Fan, suggested that it

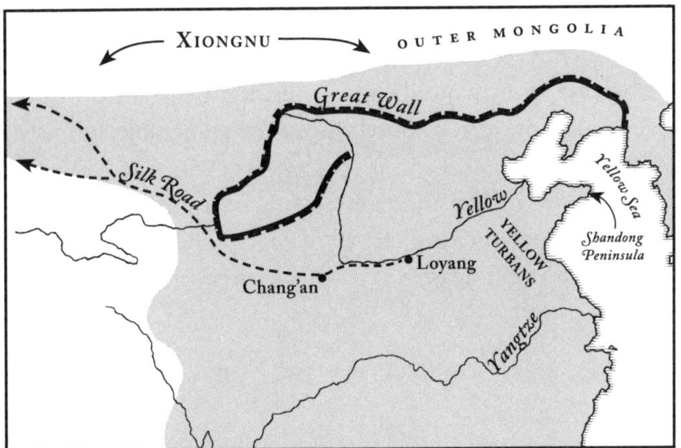

83.1 The Yellow Turbans

would be safest for the empire if all the eunuchs were simply wiped out. Word of this advice got back to the eunuchs themselves. The Ten Regular Attendants and their allies stormed the palace, put the empress dowager under guard, and told young Lingdi that they had come to free him from his mother's influence and keep him safe.

The empress dowager remained under guard for four years. When she died in 172, it was widely murmured that she had been murdered by Cao Jie, the leader of the Ten Regular Attendants. Meanwhile, Lingdi became so trusting of the Ten that he called another one of them, the much-hated Zhang Rang, by the honorary title "My Foster Father."

No one was at the helm of Han China, and its economic woes were soon joined by natural disasters. Widespread sickness in 172 was followed first by flooding, and then by an invasion of locusts. In 177, an army campaign against the barbarians ended in disaster. Two years later, in 179, another epidemic swept across the country.

These were the sorts of omens that had brought Wang Mang's new dynasty down. In his day, the Red Eyebrows had fought against the careless wealthy; now the cycle of violence began again. Now a new band of freedom fighters, the Yellow Turbans, took up the banner of the poor and downtrodden.

The Yellow Turbans were much more than a simple group of rebels: they were a millennial sect looking forward to the coming of a golden age. The millions of Chinese who lived unspeakably hard and grim lives were looking not just for political solutions, but for immediate hope. The Yellow Turbans offered exactly this. Their leader, a Daoist teacher named Chang Chueh, claimed that he had the power to do magic. He announced that he could heal sicknesses, a wonderful promise to a people who had just suffered through a horrendous epidemic. He promised that if they took his medicines, they would be immune from wounds and could fight in battle without fear, an equally marvelous notion for those who were vulnerable, underarmed, and weak with hunger.[7]

By 182, the Yellow Turbans had a following of over three hundred and fifty thousand poor, desperate, landless, and angry Chinese. By 184, they were ready to rise up and fight against their oppressors.

TIMELINE 83

ROME	CHINA
Nero, princeps (54)	
	Mingdi
Galba, princeps (68)	
Vespasian, princeps (69)	
Titus, princeps (79)	**Zhangdi**
Domitian, emperor (81)	
	Hedi
Nerva, emperor (96)	
Trajan, emperor (98)	
	Andi
Hadrian, emperor (117)	
	Shundi
	Chongdi
	Zhidi
	Huandi
	Lingdi (168)
	Rise of the Yellow Turbans

Chapter Eighty-Four

The Mistake of Inherited Power

Between AD *138 and 222, Marcus Aurelius breaks the tradition of imperial adoption, and the Han Dynasty finally collapses,*

HADRIAN'S UNAGGRESSIVE RULE was followed by more of the same. In 138, he adopted an heir: Antoninus Pius, a middle-aged politician who had served both as consul and as governor. Pius was fifty-two years old, and his new adoptive father was sixty-two.

In the same way, Augustus had adopted his son-in-law Tiberius, and Claudius had adopted Nero. This sort of adoption had nothing to do with nurturing. It created a "blood relationship" in law, the same sort of bond that the Han Dynasty eunuchs used to create their own clans. For the Roman emperors, it was a useful way to combine the great advantage of a father-to-son succession (it was always perfectly clear who the next emperor was supposed to be) with the great republican notion that only the deserving should have power. Adoption allowed each emperor to pass his throne not to the son he had, but to the son he had hoped for.

Like Hadrian, Antoninus Pius had a reasonably long and uneventful rule; the most exciting event during his twenty-three years was a big festival, in 148, celebrating Rome's 900th anniversary.[1] Pius himself formally adopted not one but two heirs: his nephew, Marcus Aurelius, and another boy nine years younger, Lucius Verus.*

* Roman emperors had two strings of names: birth names, and the names they chose when they were adopted as heirs. Other names were added when they acceeded to the imperial power. Antoninus Pius was originally named Titus Aurelius Fulvus Boionus Arrius Antoninus; when he was adopted he became Imperator Titus Aelius Caesar Antoninus; "Pius" was added to his name after his accession. Marcus Aurelius was Marcus Annius Verus at birth, became Marcus Aelius Aurelius Verus on adop-

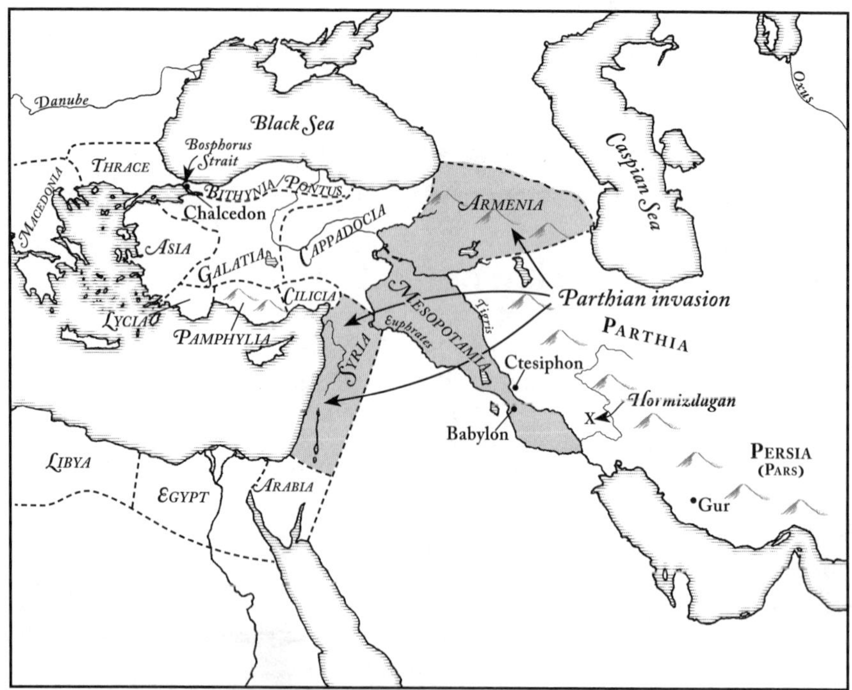

84.1 *The Parthian Invasion*

When Pius died in 161, his older heir Marcus Aurelius was forty. He had done his term of duty as a politican, including a year as consul, but he disliked politics. He was an intense introvert, a scholar by nature (the fourth-century *Augustan History* tells us that he "took a passionate interest in philosophy" before the age of twelve),[2] and he was not enthusiastic about becoming emperor of Rome. He was "compelled by the Senate" to take up his appointed task, and he retaliated by making his younger brother Lucius Verus, who was already serving as consul, his co-emperor.[3]

Immediately the two were forced to deal with a war. The Parthians were on the move again; King Vologases IV, perhaps encouraged by the placidity of the previous two emperors, was already marching through Armenia (which he had seized) and invading Syria.

tion, and then became Imperator Caesar Marcus Aurelius Antoninus Augustus on accession. Lucius Verus was born Lucius Ceionius Commodus, became Lucius Aelius Aurelius Commodus upon his adoption, and became Imperator Caesar Lucius Aurelius Verus Augustus as emperor. In an attempt to actually keep this readable, I have chosen to simply use the abbreviated popular designation of each emperor rather than striving for unintelligible accuracy.

The Parthians got a warm welcome in Syria, largely from the Jews who had fled the massacre that followed the Bar Kochba rebellion, and were able to defeat the Roman garrison stationed there. Lucius Verus took command of the Roman army and marched east, while Marcus Aurelius watched over the home front. By 162, Lucius was in Syria, and fighting a very effective war against the Parthian forces. He himself invaded Armenia and succeeded in taking it back; meanwhile one of his commanders marched southeast with another division, invaded Mesopotamia, and captured Ctesiphon. Vologases IV retreated, losing his palace, which the Romans destroyed.

The troops returned to Rome in triumph in 166, and brought plague with them. The disease was already sweeping through the city by the time the victory parades had ended.

The Greek physician Galen, who came to the city in 168 in answer to a desperate summons from the emperors, wrote down his own account of the plague in a treatise called *Methodus Medendi.* He describes his patients as suffering from fever, sore throat, and pustules: in all likelihood, this "Antontine Plague" was smallpox. The epidemic went on for three full years, with two thousand people a day dying at its height, and so many bodies to dispose of that Marcus Aurelius outlawed the building of new tombs in order to force Romans to haul their dead out of the city.[4] The sickness remained present in the city for years afterwards.

In the middle of this, with the army severely weakened by illness, the tribes along the Danube took the opportunity to attack the Roman frontier. Both emperors went up to deal with the threat, but it had been beaten back before they arrived. The catastrophe came on the way home, when Lucius Verus suddenly began to have seizures, and died before he could be brought back to Rome.

Marcus Aurelius came home to the city with the body of his adoptive brother and co-ruler, and saw him properly buried. Then he returned to the Danube. He spent almost the entire remainder of his reign—except for necessary journeys back to Rome to take care of imperial business, and one trip to the eastern frontier to deal with a rumored rebellion—in the German province, fighting against invasions which spread and intensified.

Absence from the capital often made an emperor unpopular, but Marcus Aurelius earned himself a reputation for keeping the empire safe, and for dealing gently with his people. When the treasury was drained by the constant wars in the north, he auctioned off the furniture, gold dishes, and jewels from the imperial palace, rather than raising taxes; this made him even more beloved. (The *Augustan History* says that he even sold "his wife's silk and gold-embroidered clothing," which may not have done much for him at home.)[5]

Life in an army tent, well away from a capital city filled with chattering senators and noisy Roman masses, was actually Aurelius's preferred place of residence. In his years on the German front, Marcus Aurelius was able to indulge some of his time in philosophy; his philosophical writings, the *Meditations of Marcus Aurelius*, became one of the classics of Stoicism. They are the musings of a man trapped by his own duty, carrying the weight of an empire that he was happiest when farthest from. "Let it make no difference to you whether you are cold or warm," he writes, "if you are doing your duty; or whether you are drowsy or satisfied with sleep, ill-spoken of or praised, dying or doing something else."[6] "Take care that you are not made into a Caesar," he adds, a little later, "that you are not stained with such a dye, for such things happen. Keep yourself simple, good, pure, serious, free from affectation, a friend of justice."[7]

He had never wanted to be Caesar himself, which probably accounts for his premature pushing of his son Commodus into leadership. Marcus Aurelius fathered fourteen children (rumor said that more than a few had been conceived by his wife in his absence; the *Augustan History* remarks that he once found his wife breakfasting with an overnight guest and pretended not to notice),[8] but Commodus was his only son to live past the age of four. He appointed Commodus to be his heir when the boy was only five, and in 176, when Commodus was fifteen, he declared Commodus co-emperor. Marcus Aurelius did not have much longer to live. He had been in pain for some time, possibly suffering from cancer; Dio Cassius says that he had become accustomed to take regularly a drug that made it possible for him to deal with his pain, which suggests that he may have been addicted to opium.[9] In 180, after a week of severe illness, he died at the front.

Commodus, emperor at nineteen, at once negotiated a peace with the Germans, halted the campaign on the frontier, and came back home. He was the first natural son to inherit the throne since Domitian, and Rome had been the better for it. The system of emperors adopting their heirs had avoided the worst pitfalls of hereditary kingship; once a wise and efficient ruler had the throne, he tended to appoint an heir of the same quality.

But Marcus Aurelius broke the system. Commodus's position as emperor was the biggest disaster to befall Rome during the century, and the mistake of a father who was too withdrawn to pay much attention to the personalities around him. Solitary by nature, finding close friendships exhausting, Marcus Aurelius did not find any man to replace him; he defaulted to his blood heir, a much simpler task.

Commodus's behavior was decadent almost from the moment of his accession. In his return procession to Rome, he brought his male lover into his chariot and kissed him during the parade. Homosexuality was certainly not uncommon in Rome, but it was considered Greek, and thus effeminate; if you were going to have a boy as your lover, it was tactful not to wave him in the face of the Roman public.

84.1. Commodus. Bust of Commodus, Emperor of Rome 180–192, as a child. Louvre, Paris. Photo credit SEF/Art Resource, NY

His misdeeds after that became the stuff of legend. He assembled an equal-opportunity harem of three hundred women and three hundred boys; he insisted on fighting in gladiatorial games, dressed as a gladiator himself; he murdered one of his sisters and forced another to sleep with him; he walked around Rome wearing "women's dress and a lionskin," striking down citizens with a club.[10] But if he had gone mad, he had not entirely lost touch with reality: "He used to singe his hair and beard from fear of the barber," the *Augustan History* tells us, which suggests that he knew how likely it was that someone might kill him for his behavior.[11]

Rome as a whole decided that he must be the product of one of his mother's affairs with a gladiator; he could not possibly be a blood relation of the saintly Marcus Aurelius. This did away with the problem of murdering a rightful emperor. In 192, a courtier and one of his concubines gave him poison. When he did not die fast enough, they went and fetched a wrestler to strangle him.

Civil war erupted at his death. Between 192 and 193, four different men tried for the support of the Praetorian Guard. The victor was a general in charge of an army near the troublesome Danube front: Septimus Severus, a small but energetic man who had been born in North Africa and had served in the Senate during Marcus Aurelius's rule.

He marched towards Rome with his army, but even before he arrived, the Senate made him emperor. He entered the gates on June 10, and immediately took steps to secure his position; he summoned the Praetorian Guard to a ceremonial parade (which meant that they came without their weapons) and then brought his own, German-tempered army out to surround them. Every guard suspected of preferring another candidate was warned to leave the city. When they fled, he at once appointed his loyal men to replace him.

After this, his reign was taken up with the usual campaigns against the Parthians, a standard journey into Britain to harass the Scots, and various other defenses of the border. But he had learned nothing from the drama played out in front of his eyes. In 198 he appointed his oldest son Caracalla as his heir.

In 209, two years before his death, he also appointed his younger son Geta to be co-emperor with his brother. Perhaps this was an attempt to make up for his first choice, which had begun to look like a mistake. Caracalla, a competent soldier, had already threatened to kill his wife, carried out the murder of his father-in-law, and had tried to kill his own father. Despite that, he remained his father's first choice as heir.

Marcus Aurelius had dealt the empire an almost-fatal wound. The Republic had died, but the empire had grown up to replace it, like an adopted cousin with a faint family likeness. The empire had sickened, under Caligula and the emperors who followed him, but it had made an unlikely recovery. The Romans had managed to figure out how to combine imperial rule with republican trappings, while avoiding the sort of dynastic declines which had been a problem ever since the Chinese had first cautioned about it back on the banks of the Yellow river valley three thousand years earlier. But now, the principle of hereditary succession was about to pull the power of the empire apart.

In 184, the brewing revolt of the Yellow Turbans finally boiled over.

The fighting was led by three brothers of the Zhang family: Jiao (or Jue), Bao, and Liang. In one of the classics of ancient Chinese literature, the *Romance of the Three Kingdoms*, they are portrayed as men who combined a millennial hope with a sort of proto-Marxism; their slogan was "The Han has perished, the rebellion will rise; let there be prosperity in the world!" and they hoped to take away the land of the wealthy and share it out evenly, among all Chinese.

But the most complete account of the Yellow Turban revolt and its aftermath is found in the history *Zizhi Tongjian,* written by the scholar and statesman Sima Guang in the middle of the eleventh century. This is long after the fact, but Sima Guang made heavy use of official records that stretched back for centuries.

Fighting began south of the Yellow river, near the Shandong peninsula. At first the Yellow Turban rebels were driven back by government soldiers, and Han officials—confident that the fighting would soon end—gave the celebratory name "Peace Achieved" to the year 184.[12] But the revolutionaries soon regathered themselves and pushed forwards again. By 189, fighting had reached the capital Loyang itself.

In May of that same year, the emperor Lingdi died. He had not named an heir at his death; instead he left the decision to his widow, the empress dowager, and the palace eunuch Jian Shi. Sometime before he had also given Jian Shi control of all the armed forces in Loyang, which made the eunuch one of the most powerful men in the country.

The two decided that the throne would go to Lingdi's fifteen-year-old son Shaodi. With the power of Loyang now firmly in his hands, the eunuch Jian Shi also made plans for a private purge; he intended to kill the Han chief general to increase his own power.

The chief general found out about this, and himself began to plan a wholesale extermination of all the palace eunuchs—a plot which in turn made its way to the ears of the eunuchs. The palace began to divide into suspicious factions, both armed. Finally the eunuchs made the first move; they seized and beheaded the chief general, upon which one of the other commanders ordered the gates of the palace locked and all of the eunuchs slaughtered. "Altogether some two thousand people died," says Sima Guang, "including several whole men, who had no beards and were killed by mistake."[13]

Another Han general who was outside the palace, Tung Cho, saw his opportunity to take over. He abandoned the fight against the Yellow Turbans and marched to the palace, taking control of the chaos. He ordered the empress dowager confined and began to appoint ministers of his own, using his army to back up his orders.

In fact, he was bluffing; he had fewer men than he needed for such a takeover. But every night he had a troop or so sneak out of Loyang in the dark, and then return loudly the next morning with flags flying and drums beating, so that it looked as though more and more soldiers were joining him at the palace.

The fifteen-year-old emperor and his younger brother fled from the palace, fearing for their lives. Out in the fields, they could find nowhere safe to go, nowhere to sleep, nothing to eat. Desperate, the two eventually came back to the palace and asked for sanctuary. Tung Cho granted it. He pronounced the younger brother, Xiandi, the new emperor, under his protection. But the fifteen-year-old Shaodi was old enough to be dangerous. Tung Cho broke his promise of sanctuary, and had the young man killed.

However, Tung Cho was not the only general with hopes of bettering himself. The Yellow Turbans had not yet been defeated—but now fighting broke out among the defenders themselves. Tung Cho was forced to retreat from Loyang, hauling the young Xiandi along with him. Another general, an able fighter named Ts'ao Ts'ao, who had inherited his own estate from the adopted son of a eunuch, cornered him in Chang'an and killed him.[14]

Ts'ao then offered *his* protection to Xiandi, who had little choice over accepting it; if he did not put himself under Ts'ao's control, he would die. He agreed, and Ts'ao promply married the young emperor to his own daughter and set about recapturing the north of China for his new son-in-law.

Fighting against the Yellow Turbans dragged on. Ts'ao finally managed to defeat the last Yellow Turban fighters in 205, but the years of war following on decades of mismanagement and corruption had already destroyed the country. Xiandi had returned to Loyang, and sat on the Han throne. But he was as powerless and unimportant as the Zhou emperor had been, back at the end of that dynasty's reign. Wars between would-be kings broke out all around the imperial territory. Ts'ao had been mostly successful in recapturing the north, but he had no allies in his quest to reunify the Han lands; too many rival generals did not want to see Loyang become powerful again.

In 208, Ts'ao's army met the troops of his two greatest rivals at the Yangtze river, at a place called the Red Cliffs. The two armies lingered on opposite banks of the river for days; both sides were exhausted by the unending fighting of the last years.[15] When Ts'ao finally launched an attack, he found that the wind had turned against him. The opposing commanders took the opportunity to launch a fearsome weapon towards the other bank. First they sent a letter of surrender to Ts'ao; and then they "took ten covered ships of war," in Sima Guang's words, "filled them with tinder grass and dried wood, poured oil inside, then covered them with tent curtains and set up flags." The dummy ships were sent across the water towards Ts'ao's own encampment and anchored ships; and when they were almost to the bank, soldiers in light boats behind them set them on fire. "The fire was fierce, and the wind was strong, and the ships went like arrows," says Sima Guang. "The whole of the northern fleet was burnt, and the fire reached the camps on the bank. In a very short time smoke and flame stretched across the sky and a multitude of men and horses were burned or drowned or died."[16] Ts'ao's men, fleeing, found themselves facing roads made impassable by mud. They tried to cover the road with enough grass to create a hard surface, but the grass sank beneath the horses' hooves, and more men and animals died in the muck.

The route ended Ts'ao's hopes of reuniting China. He retreated with only the north remaining to the Han king, and although battles continued he did not again challenge his competitors.

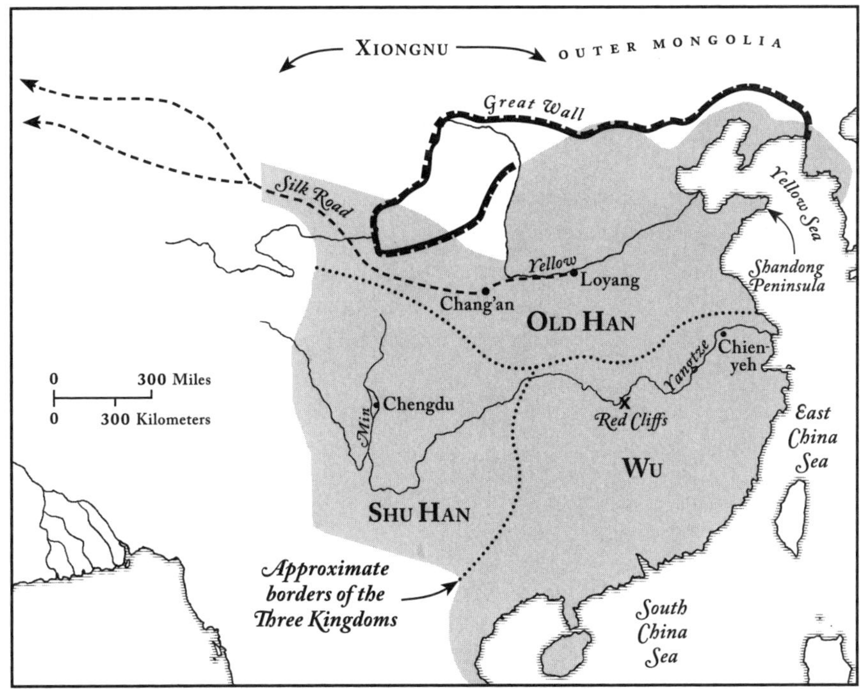

84.2 The Three Kingdoms

Xiandi himself must have known that his claim of emperorship was a fraud. When Ts'ao died in 220, Xiandi abdicated, handing power over to Ts'ao's son. After 426 years, the Han kingdom had ended.

China was now split into warring kingdoms. Ts'ao's son, Ts'ao P'ei, controlled the old Han land in the north. In the south, two rival dynasties were established by Ts'ao's two opponents at the Battle of Red Cliffs. Sun Ch'uan, in the Yangtze valley, boasted himself the founder of the Wu Dynasty and had a royal capital at Chien-yeh—modern Nanjing. Liu Pei ruled over the southwest from his own capital on the Min river, Chengdu, as first king of the Shu Han Dynasty.[17] The Three Kingdoms had replaced the Han Dynasty, and even the possibility of peace had passed. The next three centuries would see nothing but unending war.

To THE WEST, Septimus Severus had died, and the two brothers Caracalla and Geta were locked together in one imperial office. They had never been good friends, and Geta was the victim of their joint rule: Caracalla had him murdered in the imperial quarters and ordered his body burned.

The *Augustan History* suggests that Caracalla then had a tricky time of it, getting the Praetorian Guard on his side:

> After his father's death, he went to the camp of the [Praetorian] Guard and complained before the soldiers that. . . . his brother had prepared poison for him, and that he had been disrespectful to their mother, and he publicly rendered thanks to those who had killed [Geta]. Indeed, he gave them extra pay for being so loyal to him. Some of the soldiers took the killing of Geta very hard, and they all said that it was to two sons of Severus that they had promised allegiance, and that they ought to maintain it to both. The gates [of the camp] were shut, and for a long time the emperor was not admitted. The soldiers were only placated when their minds had been made easier, not only by the complaints and accusations that he uttered against Geta, but also by an enormous payment of money.[18]

He then began a purge of anyone who might resent Geta's murder. "During these days countless numbers were killed who had supported his brother," the *History* says, "slaughter everywhere. There was even murder done in the baths, and some were killed at dinner too."[19] Dio Cassius adds that Caracalla even abolished the observance of Geta's birthday.

Then he announced a new law: All free men in his empire were now Roman citizens.

Three hundred years earlier, Rome had gone indignantly to war at the suggestion that the Italian cities should be granted citizenship. Now the law passed without much debate or discussion, and with no public outcry.

From one point of view, the grant of Roman citizenship had grown more meaningless: Rome was no longer a republic, so being Roman was no longer a matter of getting the vote (which had been the biggest issue in the Social War). But from another direction, Roman citizenship looked far from meaningless. Hadrian's wall and the turning of client kingdoms (with a kind of independence and national pride of their own) into tightly controlled provinces both pointed to the same inevitable end, for those peoples enclosed within Rome's borders. They could not be allowed to remain a collection of countries "under Roman rule," like marbles in a jar; their first loyalty would always be to their first identity, and when crisis broke the jar, the marbles would escape. They had to be pulled away from the past, and pointed towards a new loyalty. They had to be made Roman.

But to be *Roman* no longer meant to have a vote in your nation's affairs. It no longer meant that Rome was your birthplace; the empire had spread across so many lands that hundreds of thousands of Roman citizens had never actually set foot in the city which now offered them its name. It did not mean that you knew the proper Roman way to eat a meal, or enjoyed the poetry of Seneca, or even spoke Latin.

In Caracalla's hands, Roman identity meant three things. It meant, as Epictetus had observed decades before, that you were obedient to the emperor. It meant that, like all Roman citizens, you had certain rights: if you were sentenced to death for a crime, you could appeal to Rome (unless you happened to get caught in a purge), your marriages and other contracts could be upheld as legal in Roman courts, your children were guaranteed to get their inheritance under your will. And it meant that you paid your taxes. Caracalla was broke. His bribes had drained the treasury, and he needed more citizens so that he could collect more money to refill them.

Roman citizenship, in short, had become a trade-off. In exchange for legal protections, the free men inside Rome's borders would pay out money. It was not a particularly bad bargain (or not yet; taxes had not yet begun to spike), but it certainly didn't have much in the way of bonding potential: nothing like Pericles's appeal to the Athenians to commit themselves to the idea of Athens, or like the Jewish conviction that God had promised the descendents of Abraham their own land. These were ideas that bound men together.

IN 212, THE SAME YEAR as Caracalla's announcement of citizenship, a Parthian vassal king named Ardashir was carefully waging small campaigns against the vassal kingdoms around him. Ardashir's own kingdom was in Pars, the Parthian province where Persians still lived; his capital was Gur, and his family was one of the last remnants of the old Persian empire. Later traditions say that he was a distant descendent of Darius himself, pushed into obscurity.[20] Quietly, without doing too much to alert the distant Parthian king, he was persuading or terrifying the nearby vassal kings into switching their allegiance over to him.

He probably wouldn't have gotten away with this for very long, except that the Parthian king Artabanus V was having troubles of his own. One of his own relatives had challenged his crown, and after a nasty bit of civil war had managed to occupy Ctesiphon and take control of the lower Mesopotamian valley. Artabanus had been driven out of his own capital and was uncomfortably camped to the west, in the northern plain between the Tigris and the Euphrates. He was not paying much attention to what was going on east of Ctesiphon.

Caracalla, seeing a chance to reduce the Parthians to vassals, sent a message to the displaced Artabanus V offering to help him, in exchange for a marriage alliance with Artabanus's daughter. Artabanus, seeing this not as a genuine alliance but a takeover attempt, refused; and so Caracalla journeyed to the east, with an army, and attacked the western Parthian border in the fall of 216. He campaigned until winter, and then set up a winter camp to wait and renew the attack in the spring.

In early April of 217, just before the renewed assault was planned, Caracalla was suffering from a badly upset stomach. He was riding with one of his bodyguard when he was seized with stomach cramps. He jumped off the horse and yanked down his breeches. The bodyguard took the opportunity to kill him while both his hands were occupied.

Mounted soldiers a little farther away rode up then and killed the assassin with javelins. Like Caligula's killers, he had done the empire a favor at the cost of his own life. Caracalla's body was cremated, the ashes sent to Rome; he had ruled for six years, and had died at the age of twenty-nine.

The eastern legions, left without an emperor, proclaimed their general Macrinus to be the new emperor. In late spring of 217, Macrinus led them again across the Parthian border. But Artabanus V had gathered himself, over the winter, and after hard fighting the Romans were forced to drop back without victory. Macrinus, unwilling to try another assault, offered to pay them off and handed over a staggeringly huge sum of money.

This infuriated many of his soldiers. An emperor who had gained his power solely because of his military abilities had nothing left, once he began to lose battles; and there was a rival candidate for emperor right at hand. He was Caracalla's first cousin once removed (the grandson of his mother's sister), a tall and handsome fourteen-year-old named Elagabalus, who looked something like Caracalla and was widely rumored to be his illegimate son.

On May 16, a few months after the defeat, a group of soldiers proclaimed Elagabalus emperor in Macrinus's place. Macrinus found more and more of his own followers abandoning him to follow the new emperor. Finally he fled, but pursuing soldiers found him, a month later, at Chalcedon, trying to cross the Bosphorus over into Thrace.[21] He was put under guard, and not long after was murdered in custody.

Elagabalus turned out to be weak minded and bizarrely self-indulgent; if even half of the stories related by the *Augustan History* are true, he went insane shortly after his accession. Most of the details are summed up in the *History*'s acid remark that the soldiers soon lost patience with "a princeps who was the recipient of lust in every orifice of his body."[22] He also indulged himself in strange religious rituals, one of which involved worshipping a stone which he had found and declared to be a god, and another of which led to him trying to circumcise himself (apparently he partly castrated himself instead).

By 222, the Praetorian Guard had lined up another candiadate for emperor, and a troop of guards went to find Elagabalus. He heard them coming and hid in a public latrine, but they dragged him out, killed him, and then dredged the body in a sewer, dragged it around a chariot-racing course, and finally pitched it into the Tiber with a stone tied to it. His blood relationship to a previous emperor had brought him to the throne; but it had not saved him.

TIMELINE 84

ROME	CHINA	PARTHIA
Trajan, emperor (98)		
	Andi	**Vologases III**
Hadrian, emperor (117)		
	Shundi	
Antoninus Pius, emperor (138)		
	Chongdi	**Vologases IV**
	Zhidi	
	Huandi	
Marcus Aurelius and **Lucius Verrus**		
Marcus Aurelius, sole emperor (169)	**Lingdi** (168)	
	Rise of the Yellow Turbans	
Commodus, emperor (180)		
	Yellow Turban Rebellion (184)	
Septimus Severus, emperor (193)	**Shaodi/Xiandi**	
Caracalla, emperor (211)	Battle of Red Cliffs (208)	
Macrinus, emperor (217)		**Artabanus V**
Elegabalus, emperor (218)	Three Kingdoms (220)	

Chapter Eighty-Five

Savior of the Empire

Between AD 222 and 312,
Parthia falls to Persia,
and Diocletian tries to save the Roman Empire,
leaving Constantine to finish the job

IN 222, THE SAME YEAR as Elagabalus's murder, the Parthian king Artabanus V managed to defeat his challenger and take back Ctesiphon.

He held his capital city for only two years. The young Persian Ardashir had managed to build a following from the old Median and Persian cities and their allies, and he had now fortified himself at his home city of Gur. In 224, he and his army advanced forwards to meet the Parthian hordes at the plain of Hormizdagan.

In the battle, Artabanus V was killed. The Parthian empire had ended; now Ardashir moved into the palace at Ctesiphon and declared himself, in the old Persian way, to be Ardashir I, King of Kings. His new dynasty took its name, the Sassanians, from his own native Persian clan.

The Parthian empire, which had evolved from a nomadic takeover, had operated as a set of vassal kingdoms that reported to an overall king. This, as Ardashir I knew from experience, gave rebel kings too much freedom to rebel. Instead, he organized his new empire into something more along old Persian lines. He divided it into provinces, or satrapies, under military governors; these were intentionally laid out across and through the old kingdom borders, to break up any alliances which might be tempted to form after the overthrow of Artabanus V. Governors who were members of his own royal Sassanian clan were known by the honorary Persian title of *shah.*

For the Romans, afflicted with one useless king after another, the resurrection of the Persians must have seemed like the return of a monster from an old dream. Ardashir I, the first Great King of the new and restored Persian dominance, ruled until 241 and then passed on to his son Shapur a well-organized empire, ready for expansion.

Coins from the end of his reign show Ardashir facing a younger prince; he seems to have crowned his own son co-ruler before his death. The ninth-century Arab historian Abu al-Mas'udi, who like Herodotus travelled through the known world and collected ancient traditions to weave into a history, says that Ardashir put his crown upon Shapur's head with his own hands, and then withdrew so that Shapur could rule alone.[1] This indicates a man with the future on his mind (something which had not been conspicuous in the Roman emperors of the last few decades).

Shapur I began his career as king by calling on the great god Ahuramazda to support his claim to the throne. Both Ardashir I and Shapur I were Zoroastrians, adherents of a mystical religion first preached by the prophet Zoroaster (or Zarathustra) back in the days of Darius I. Zoroastrianism had a complicated theology and even more complicated rituals, but by the time of Shapur I it taught that the universe was divided into two equally powerful opposing forces of good and evil. Good emanated from the being of the great god Ahuramazda; evil resided in the opposing deity Ahriman.*[2] This dualism meant that good and evil were in eternal conflict, and that the followers of Zoroaster were committed to an unending battle against the forces of wickedness, represented by demonic spirits called *daevas.* "I curse the Daevas," begins the ancient creed attributed to Zoroaster himself, "I declare myself a Mazda-worshipper, I ascribe all good to Ahuramazda. I want freedom of movement and freedom of dwelling for those with homesteads, to those who dwell upon the earth with cattle. . . . Of all religions that exist or shall be, [it] is the greatest, the best, and the most beautiful."[3]

Shapur had no hesitation in claiming Ahuramazda's sanction on his divine right to rule; there was no negotiating around the sensibilities of his people. As king of Persia, he was the champion of righteousness. Ardashir himself had proclaimed Zoroastrianism the state religion of his new empire, which drew every one of his subjects together into a holy community with a single purpose. Every subject of Shapur was a soldier against the daevas; the loyalty of every man and woman to Persia was also a commitment to the constant fight against evil. The official religion was also a tremendously powerful nation-maker.

Shapur's armed conquests began with the Roman giant. He managed to capture the Roman garrisons in Mesopotamia and then marched into Syria to

* This is a pocket definition only. A good historical survey of the development of Zoroastrianism is Mary Boyce's *Zoroastrians: Their Religious Beliefs and Practices,* revised ed. (Routledge, 2001). A less academic introduction to the influence of the religion on surrounding cultures is Paul Kriwaczek's *In Search of Zarathustra: Across Iran and Central Asia to Find the World's First Prophet* (Vintage, 2004). Zoroastrianism is generally considered to be the world's first creedal religion: one whose basic beliefs are defined in a set statement of faith.

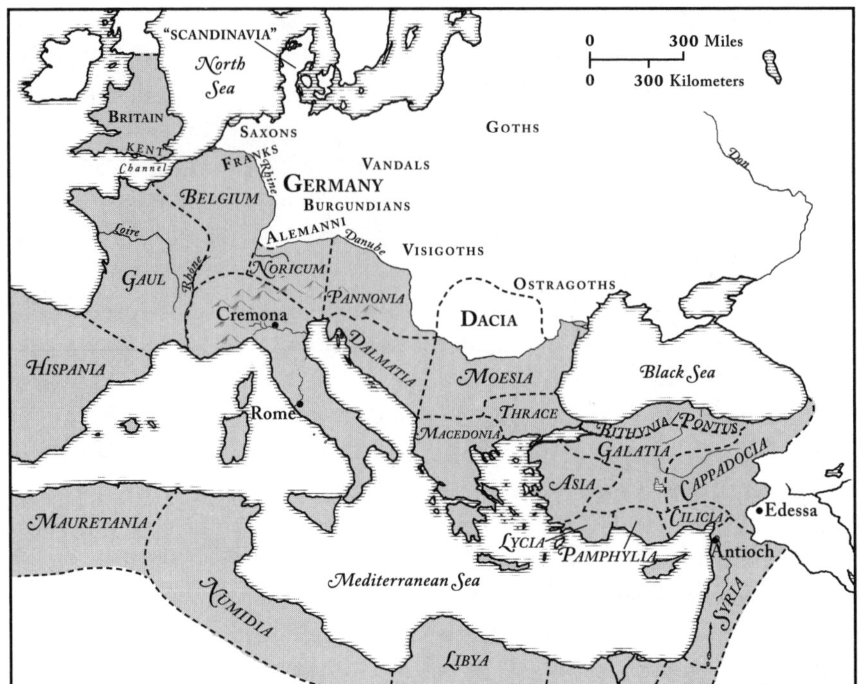

85.1 The Gothic Invasion

face the Roman forces in the Syrian province. This initial Persian thrust at Rome failed; Shapur's army was defeated by the Syrian legions, and the Persians were forced to retreat.* But despite this successful parry, Rome's ability to keep off Persian attacks was seriously strained. Rome was also facing a new enemy to the north.

Sometime in the second century, peoples who had long lived on the northern peninsulas which we now know as Scandinavia crossed the strait in boats and landed on coast of Europe. The sixth-century writer Jordanes, our best source for what happened next, begins their history here: In the "arctic region," he writes, there is "a great island named Scandza, from which my tale (by God's grace) shall take its beginning. For the race whose origin you ask to know burst forth like a swarm of bees from the midst of this island and came into the land of Europe."[4]

These newcomers were known to the Romans as the Goths. Jordanes calls them "many and diverse," and lists a whole array of tribes that fall under the

* The accounts left by Roman historians and by Shapur's own inscriptions are so contradictory that any reconstruction of the results is uncertain.

general name of *Goth:* Screrefennae and Finnaithae and Finns, Dani and Grannii and many more. They were a tough and resilient people, he adds, "like no other race in their sufferings and blessings, because during the longer days they see the sun returning to the east along the rim of the horizon, but on the shorter days it is not thus seen."[5] Accustomed to twenty-four-hour days and nights, the Goths were comfortable with extremes.

In Europe, they fought their way through the Germanic tribes down to the Danube, and some made their way over to the east, towards the old territory of the Scythians. Jordanes after this divides them into two groups: the Visigoths, or "Goths of the Western Country," and the Ostrogoths, the eastern half. The Visigoths were now threatening the Danube into Roman territory, while the Ostrogoths were overflowing into the old lands of Thrace and Macedonia.

By 249, the threat of invasion from the north had become acute enough for the army to take matters into its own hands. The current emperor, the forgettable Philip,* had tried to buy the Goths off with tribute payments, and had fallen behind on his installments, upon which the Visigoths crossed the Danube and ravaged the countryside. The troops near the Danube, disgusted, declared their general Decius emperor instead; some of them, Jordanes says, simply deserted and went over to join the Goths.

Decius lasted exactly two years. After he went down to Rome to accept his new power, he went back up again to fight the invaders. In 251 he was killed in battle, just below the Danube. He was the first Roman emperor to fall while fighting against an outside threat; all the others had been removed by their countrymen.

When Shapur I launched his next attack against the Syrian border in 252, the Roman legions were seriously put to it to defend both the eastern borders from Persian pressure and the northern border from Gothic attack. The east broke first. Shapur I pushed through the Syrian garrisons and took all of Syria for himself. In 253, he captured the great eastern city of Antioch and sacked it.

In that same year, Rome finally got an emperor who managed to hold onto the throne for more than a month or two. Valerian had served as consul and also as general; he was nearly sixty, but for a few years it looked as though he might be able to turn the Roman luck around. He gave his son Gallienus command of the legions in the west, and while Gallienus fought off invaders near the Rhine, Valerian began to win battles in the east.

* Rome had had eight emperors since Elagabalus's death in 222, four of whom ruled for mere months: Alexander Severus (222–235), Maximinus Thrax (235–238), Gordian I (238); Gordian II (238), Pupienus Maximus (238), Balbinus (238), Gordian III (238–244), and Philip (244–249).

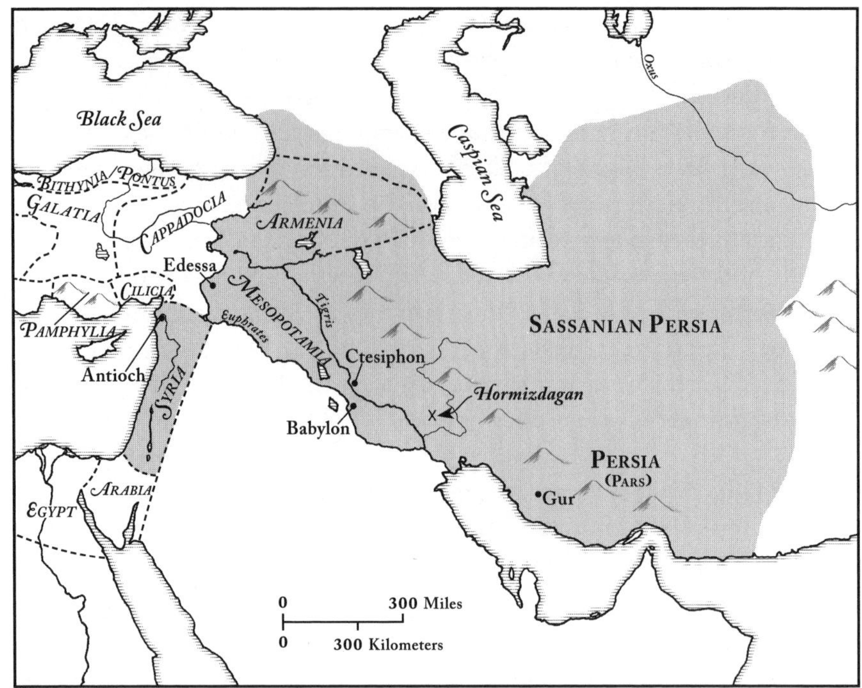

85.2 The New Persian Empire

Exactly how many is not known, but his coin of 257 calls him "Restorer of the World," which (given room for exaggeration) suggests significant success. But in 260, plague swept through his army and weakened it. When the Persians attacked him at Edessa, he was forced to retreat, and finally to ask for negotiations.

Shapur I agreed, as long as the emperor would meet him with only a small band of soldiers. Valerian arrived at the negotiation place with few guards; Shapur I killed his retinue and took him captive.

Later church historians, who were the most complete chroniclers of Valerian's life but who loathed him because he hated Christians, saw this as a judgment. "God punished him in a new and extraordinary manner," says Lactantius. "[Shapur], the king of the Persians, who had made him prisoner, whenever he chose to get into his carriage or to mount on horseback, commanded the Roman to stoop and present his back; then, setting his foot on the shoulders of Valerian, he said, with a smile of reproach, '*This* is true, and not what the Romans delineate on board or plaster.' Valerian lived for a considerable time under the well-merited insults of his conqueror; so that the Roman name remained long the scoff and derision of the barbarians."[6]

A Roman emperor, still crowned, in captivity to a Persian barbarian and acting as his footstool, was about as humiliating a turnaround as could be imagined. It was certainly a big deal to Shapur, who had carved on his tomb an enormous figure of himself, seated in triumph on horseback, dragging Valerian by the arm. The previous emperor Philip is kneeling humbly in front of the horse; another emperor sprawls under the horse's hooves.

Rome was suddenly less alarming, less all-overcoming. The provinces began to revolt. The Roman army was scraped thin dealing with rebellion and with more invasions from the north: the Germanic Alemanni tribe was making intrusions into Italy, the Franks (also Germanic in origin) were ravaging the Roman provinces on the Iberian peninsula, and the Gauls had broken away and announced themselves a kingdom in their own right.

Valerian was still captive, and still emperor; his son Gallienus was now acting emperor, more or less by default. He was a competent general, but this level of chaos was beyond fixing by any one man. He too would remain in power only as long as he proved his worth as a commander, and he could see that his days were limited. He made his enemies eat with him, in an effort to avoid poisoning; he kept around him at all times a small circle of soldiers he trusted; but in 268, one of those very soldiers killed him.

At some unknown point, his father Valerian had also died in captivity. Shapur treated his body like a trophy: "He was flayed," says Lactantius, "and his skin, stripped from the flesh, was dyed with vermilion, and placed in the temple of the gods of the barbarians, that the remembrance of a triumph so signal might be perpetuated, and that this spectacle might always be exhibited to our ambassadors, as an admonition to the Romans, that, beholding the spoils of their captived emperor in a Persian temple, they should not place too great confidence in their own strength."[7]

After Gallienus's murder in 268, the Roman Empire—just barely—held onto its existence. By 271, barbarian invaders had managed to make their way right into the middle of the peninsula. But the reigning emperor Aurelian, a soldier-turned-king whom the fourth-century historian Eutropius calls "a man of ability in war . . . much inclined to cruelty,"[8] directed the troops into a series of well-planned campaigns which almost restored the old borders. The disintegration had been temporarily reversed, and this made Aurelian respected if not popular. "He was indeed cruel and sanguinary," Eutropius concludes, "and rather an emperor necessary for the times, in some respects, than an amiable one. . . . He was, however, a reformer, in a great degree, of military discipline and dissoluteness of manners."[9]

But merely whipping the army back into shape was not going to solve Rome's difficulties. Aurelian himself acknowledged this when he ordered a wall built around the city itself. For three hundred years, Rome had had no wall; its citizens boasted that it was protected by the power of Rome's armies.[10] Now that protection could no longer be relied upon. The army's loyalties, on which the power of the emperor now rested, were too changeable. Aurelian himself would only last five years before the Praetorian Guard murdered him in the middle of a public road.[11]

The Senate had put power in the hands of the emperor, the emperor leaned on the strength of the army, and Rome had too many armies on too many frontiers for this to be anything like stability. In the nine years after Aurelian, six men were given the title of *emperor*, and each one was murdered.

The possible exception to this was the fourth: the emperor Carus. His men claimed that he had been struck by lightning while camping on the banks of the Tigris.[12] This was, just barely, plausible. On the other hand, when Carus was "struck by lightning," the commander of his bodyguard, Diocletian, was in the camp. Carus's son Numerian then became king, and died mysteriously while travelling with the army. He was riding in a litter because of some difficulty with his eyes that kept him out of the full sun, and when he died in the litter no one noticed. "His death . . . was made known by the odour of his dead body," Eutropius says, "for the soldiers, who attended him, being struck by the smell, and opening the curtains of his litter, discovered his death some days after it had taken place."[13]

This reeks of conspiracy (one wonders what "attending him" means, if the soldiers didn't notice that Numerian had been behind his curtains for days), and before long a culprit was fingered. The army gathered to appoint a new leader, and Diocletian cried indignantly that he knew who had killed Numerian: it was Numerian's own father-in-law, commander of the Praetorian Guard. Overcome with righteous indignation, he drew his sword and killed the man "in the sight of the army," which did away with the necessity of investigating the accusation.[14]

Then Carus's other son was acclaimed emperor by his father's friends. Diocletian's ambitions now came out into the open. He led his own supporters against the troops of the new emperor, and killed his opponent in the battle.

This left Diocletian at the head of the Roman empire: a man whom Lactantius called "that author of ill and deviser of misery."[15] Like his predecessors, Diocletian comes off badly in the church fathers because he too ordered edicts of persecution against Christians. Lactantius accuses him of corruption, cruelty, overtaxation, rape, and pretty much anything else he can throw into the pot, and winds up by announcing that he almost ruined Rome: "This man, by avarice partly, and partly by timid counsels, overturned the Roman empire," he complains. "For he made choice of three persons to share the government with him; and thus, the empire having been quartered, armies were multiplied, and each of the four princes strove to maintain a much more considerable military force than any sole emperor had done in times past."[16]

But in fact this division of the empire saved it. Diocletian was undoubtedly an ambitious man, but his ambition was more complex than Lactantius gives him credit for. He was not merely grasping for gain. He was looking for a solution to the problem of the empire, and he found it by giving most of his power away.

The year after he was acclaimed, Diocletian chose a right-hand man, another army officer named Maximian whom he knew well. He gave Maximian the imperial title Augustus, and offered him the job of co-emperor: the first time since the disastrous days of Caracalla and Geta that two emperors had shared the title.

He had come to the conclusion that the biggest problem of the empire was one of size. It was impossible for any one man to keep a hand on all the regions without autocratic tyranny, and autocratic tyranny led to death. Anyway, even the most autocratic emperor could not remain the favorite of troops spread from Gaul all the way over to the Euphrates. The legions were bound to favor the man who was closest to them; Diocletian gave both halves of the empire an emperor who could remain near.

The power of the army continued to worry Diocletian. In 293, Diocletian made a further arrangement to keep the army from getting involved in each change of power. He appointed two junior "emperors," two officials who were given the title of Caesar (the usual designation that an emperor gave to his successor). These two Caesars, Constantius and Galerius, were also tied to the emperors themselves in a more personal way: Galerius married Diocletian's daughter, while Constantius married Maximian's. ("Both being obliged to divorce the wives they had before" Eutropius remarks.[17] Stability came at a price.)

In 305, Diocletian did something no emperor yet had tried. He retired, abdicating in favor of his Caesar—and he insisted that Maximian do the same. He was growing older and wearier, but rather than clinging to power until his last breath, he preferred to supervise the transfer of power to the next generation. Maximian complied, with great reluctance, and the two men held abdication ceremonies on the same day, at opposite ends of the empire, both of them taking part in a victory parade and then, at its end, ceremonially doffing their imperial robes and putting on civilian clothes instead.[18]

Diocletian was making one more effort to refine that troublesome idea of

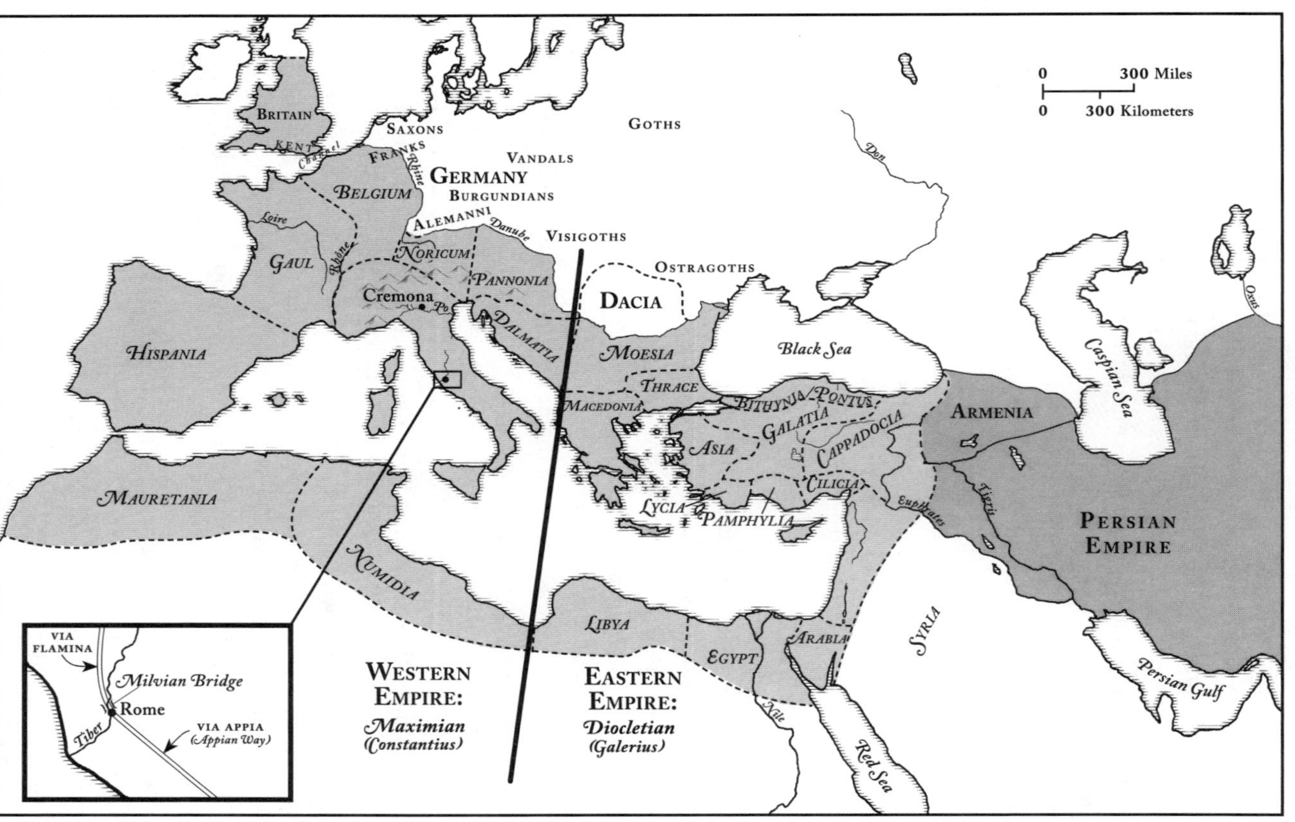

85.3 The Roman Empire, Divided

Roman. Instead of submission to an emperor, the citizens of Rome were now being asked to submit to the *idea* of imperial authority. The change of clothing was more than public theatrics. Diocletian was attempting to demonstrate that the emperor represented Rome, for a time, but that the task of representative was greater than the personality who undertook it.

Briefly, this worked. Constantius became emperor of Gaul, Italy, and Africa; Galerius became emperor of the east; and two more Caesars were chosen to become their junior colleagues. But when Constantius died in 306, only a year after his accession, the army pushed its way back into the succession. The troops had not grasped Diocletian's subtle redefinition of imperial power, and Constantius had been enormously popular with the army in the west. Now they demanded that young Constantine, his son from his previous marriage, inherit his power. The irrational desire for a king's son to inherit his power, no matter what his character, had existed in the human race ever since the days of Etana of Sumer. It was still strong three thousand years later.

This was exactly what Diocletian had hoped to avoid, but now the old habits clashed with his new institution. The eastern emperor, Galerius, insisted that Constantius's junior Severus become emperor of the west as planned. And then the lust for power (which had existed at least since Gilgamesh) reappeared as well. Maximian, who had never wanted to retire in the first place, threw his hat back in the ring. He marched on the unfortunate Severus—with the help of Constantine, who was Severus's rival for rule of the west—and defeated him.

Now the empire was in a more complicated mess than ever before. The only man with the legal right to rule was Galerius; Severus was dead and Maximian was supposed to be retired, Constantine was supporting Maximian's return to power and had also married Maximian's daughter, which meant that his step-grandfather was also his father-in-law. And Maximian's son, Maxentius, could now see that if his father became full emperor, he would be next in line—as long as Constantine, his brother-in-law, didn't interfere.

A whole welter of battles broke out, with power shifting from one man to another, and from east to west, while the inhabitants of the empire covered their heads and waited it out. By 312, the array of conflicts had funnelled down into one looming conflict: Constantine and his army, north of Rome, planning an attack on Maxentius. Maximian himself had committed suicide two years earlier, humiliated by his inability to reclaim his old throne; Maxentius was in control of Rome, with troops of his own.

Constantine began his march down towards Rome in October. According to the church historian Eusebius, whose source for his accounts seems to have been Constantine himself, he justified this attack in a very familiar way: "The

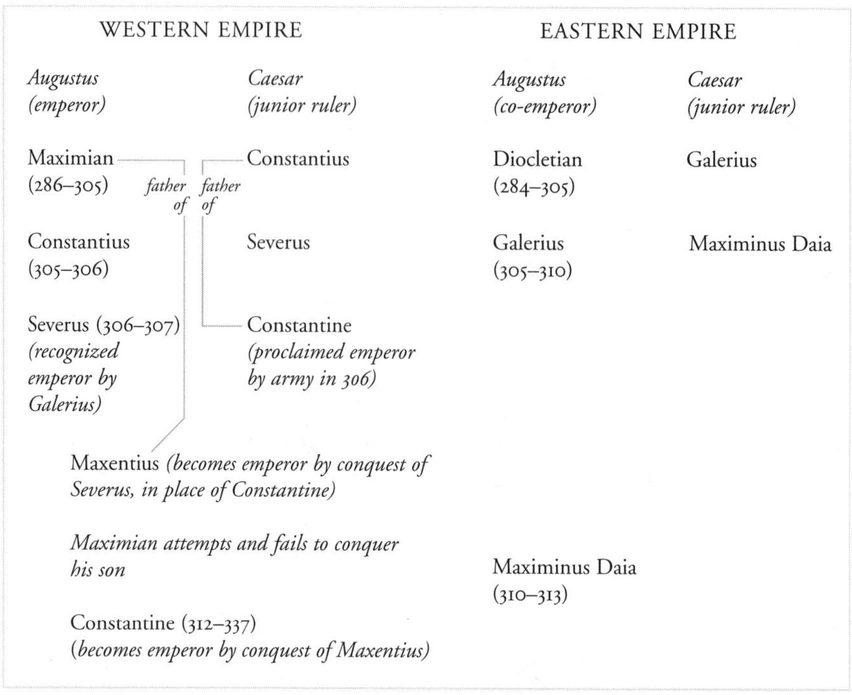

85.1 Shifts of Power in the Roman Empire.

royal city of the Roman empire, was bowed down by the weight of a tyrannous oppression," Eusebius writes, ". . . [and] he said that life was without enjoyment to him as long as he saw the imperial city thus afflicted, and prepared himself for the overthrowal of the tyranny."[19]

But the days were long past when the simple claim to be a liberator would serve to unite an empire behind a conqueror; the Romans in the capital city had seen too many liberators who offered a different version of enslavement. Constantine needed some more powerful flag under which to march.

Eusebius himself seems uncomfortable with what happened next. Constantine, considering whether he might claim some Roman god as the sponsor of his quest (something which had worked well for Shapur I over in Persia) had a vision.

> A most marvelous sign appeared to him from heaven, the account of which it might have been hard to believe had it been related by any other person. But since the victorious emperor himself long afterwards declared it to the writer of this history, when he was honored with his acquaintance and society, and confirmed his statement by an oath, who could hesitate to accredit

> the relation . . . ? He said that about noon, when the day was already beginning to decline, he saw with his own eyes the trophy of a cross of light in the heavens, above the sun, and bearing the inscription, *Conquer by this.* At this sight he himself was struck with amazement. . . . [W]hile he continued to ponder and reason on its meaning, night suddenly came on; then in his sleep the Christ of God appeared to him with the same sign which he had seen in the heavens, and commanded him to make a likeness of that sign which he had seen in the heavens, and to use it as a safeguard in all engagements with his enemies.[20]

Eusebius's gingerly account may reflect an orthodox Christian doubt about the latter part of this vision, since Christian theology generally discouraged this kind of magical thinking. But Constantine acted on it, engraving the first two Greek letters in the name of Christ, the *chi* and *rho*, onto his helmet and placing it on his standard.

At Constantine's approach, Maxentius and his army came out of the city and marched along the Via Flamina, across the Tiber river, to make their stand in front of the Milvian Bridge. Constantine would have to go through them to cross the bridge into the city.

Maxentius's army outnumbered Constantine's, but Eusebius mentions that there had been famine inside the city; possibly his soldiers were not at the strongest. Constantine's attack turned them back towards the Tiber. The Milvian Bridge was too narrow to hold their retreat, so the fleeing soldiers tried to build a makeshift pontoon bridge beside it. The overloaded boats sank, drowning hundreds of them. Among the retreating soldiers drowned was Maxentius, dragged down into the Tiber by his armor. Constantine was master of the city; before long, he would be master of the empire as well.

85.2. Constantine. Marble bust of Constantine the Great, Emperor of Rome 306–337. Palazzo dei Conservatori, Rome. Photo credit Archive Timothy McCarthy/Art Resource, NY

Eusebius, telling the story of Maxentius's end, cannot keep himself from quoting the words used by the victorious Israelites when they emerged from the Red Sea with the Egyptians drowning behind them: "So the victors might well say: Let us sing unto the Lord, for he has thrown the horse and chariot into the sea."[21] Those were words sung by a people whose faith was connected to their political existence as a nation; something Christians had never been. But Constantine saw in Christianity some hope for the future of his own nation. In three centuries of perseverance, that Christian identity—an identity that became absolutely central to those who held onto it, yet did not wipe out the other identities that had come before it—had proved itself stronger than any other.

The Roman Empire had drawn lines around itself, subjugated its allies, and demanded submission first to an emperor, and then to some ideal of the

TIMELINE 85

ROME	CHINA	PARTHIA
		Yellow Turban Rebellion (184)
Septimus Severus, emperor (193)	**Shaodi/Xiandi**	
Caracalla, emperor (211)		Battle of Red Cliffs (208)
Macrinus, emperor (217)		**Artabanus V**
Elegabalus, emperor (218)	Three Kingdoms (220)	
		PERSIA
		Ardashir I (226)
Decius, emperor (249)		**Shapur I** (241)
Valerius, emperor (253)		
Gallienus, emperor (260)		
Aurelian, emperor (270)		
Carus, emperor (284)		
Numerian, emperor (284)		
Diocletian, emperor (285)		
Diocletian/Maximian, co-emperors (286)		
Constantine/Galerius, co-emperors (305)		
Constantine, emperor (312)		

emperor's authority; and the empire had grown more and more ragged and contentious. Meanwhile, the Christians had survived bloody wars and had spread across a good part of the known world. Christianity had done what Rome had never managed: it had spread out from its land of origin, from its narrow beginnings as a Jewish cult, and had become an identity which had drawn Jews, Gentiles, Thracians, Greeks, Syrians, and Romans into a single fold.

In allying himself with the Christian God at the Milvian Bridge, Constantine had turned the empire into something new. He had abandoned that fruitless quest to find a Romanness that was rooted in the city of Rome, but could also transcend it. Instead, he had chosen something else to take its place. When he went forwards into the battle with the name of Christ on his standard, he was staking his future on the gamble that *this* would be the key to holding the whole thing together.

This was the end of the old Rome. But it would turn out to be the rise of something much more powerful, both for good and for evil.

Notes

Preface

1. From the collection published in *Archives royales de Mari*, vol. X, 123; translated and quoted by Bertrand Lafont in "The Women of the Palace at Mari," in *Everyday Life in Ancient Mesopotamia* by Jean Bottéro (2001), pp. 129–134. I am grateful to Mr. Lafont for summarizing the quarrel between Kirum and Shimatum.
2. Bottéro, p. 130.

Chapter One The Origin of Kingship

1. Translated by Samuel Kramer, as Appendix E of *The Sumerians: Their History, Culture, and Character* (1963), p. 328.
2. See, for example, Charles Pellegrino, *Return to Sodom and Gomorrah* (1994), p. 155 ff.
3. In M. E. L. Mallowan, *Early Mesopotamia and Iran* (1965), p. 7.
4. Translated by Gwendolyn Leick in *Mesopotamia: The Invention of the City* (2001), p. 1.
5. Translated by Diane Wolkstein and Samuel Noah Kramer in *Inanna, Queen of Heaven and Earth: Her Stories and Hymns from Sumer* (1983), p. 33.

Chapter Two The Earliest Story

1. My paraphrase, drawn from the prose translation by N. K. Sandars, *The Epic of Gilgamesh* (1972), p. 110.
2. My paraphrase, drawn from the translation offered by Bottéro, p. 69.
3. Quoted in William Ryan and Walter Pitman, *Noah's Flood: The New Scientific Discoveries about the Event that Changed History* (2000), p. 54. I am grateful to Mr. Ryan and Mr. Pitman for their cogent summary of scholarly research on the flood.
4. Ryan and Pitman, p. 57.
5. This is the position taken by Charles Pellegrino, for example, in *Return to Sodom and Gomorrah.*
6. Quoted in John Keay, *India: A History* (2000), pp. 1–2.
7. See Peter James and Nick Thorpe, *Ancient Mysteries* (1999), p. 13.
8. Sandars, p. 112.
9. Quoted in Ryan and Pitman, p. 50.
10. *Origin de los Indias,* quoted by Lewis Spence in *The Myths of Mexico and Peru* (1994), p. 108.
11. Translated by Samuel Kramer and quoted in Bottéro, p. 19.
12. Richard J. Mouw, " 'Some Poor Sailor, Tempest Tossed': Nautical Rescue Themes in Evangelical Hymnody," in *Wonderful Words of Life: Hymns in American Protestant History and Theology,* ed. Richard J. Mouw and Mark A. Noll (2004), p. 249.

Chapter Three The Rise of Aristocracy

1. Michael Rice, *Egypt's Making: The Origins of Ancient Egypt 5000–2000 BC* (2003), p. 73.
2. Stephanie Dalley, ed. and trans., *Myths from Mesopotamia* (2000), p. 196.
3. Ibid., pp. 198–199.
4. Pellegrino, p. 39.
5. Harriet Crawford, *Sumer and the Sumerians* (1991), p. 23.

Chapter Four The Creation of Empire

1. Rice, p. 11.
2. David P. Silverman, general ed., *Ancient Egypt* (2003), p. 107.
3. A. Rosalie David, *Religion and Magic in Ancient Egypt* (2002), p. 46.
4. Gerald P. Verbrugghe and John M. Wickersham, *Berossos and Manetho, Introduced and Translated: Native Traditions in Ancient Mesopotamia and Egypt* (1996), p. 131.

Chapter Five The Age of Iron

1. Stanley Wolpert, *A New History of India* (2004), p. 11.
2. Keay, p. 2.

Chapter Six The Philosopher King

1. J. A. G. Roberts, *The Complete History of China* (2003), p. 3.
2. Anne Birrell, *Chinese Mythology: An Introduction* (1993), p. 46.

Chapter Seven The First Written Records

1. Steven Roger Fischer, *A History of Writing* (2001), pp. 25–26. Fischer gives credit to Denise Schmandt-Besserat as the "leading proponent of this theory," and points out that this theory (like pretty much every other theory about the origin of writing) is still debatable.
2. Quoted in W. V. Davies, *Egyptian Hieroglyphs: Reading the Past* (1987), p. 47.

Chapter Eight The First War Chronicles

1. "Enmerkar and the Lord of Aratta," translated by J. A. Black, et al., in *The Electronic Text Corpus of Sumerian Literature* at http://www.etcsl.orient.ox.ac.uk/ (1998–); hereafter abbreviated as *ETC.*
2. Translated by Sandars, p. 61.
3. Sandars, p. 71. I am indebted to N. K. Sandars for highlighting, in the introductory essay to her translation, the various historical possibilities that might lie at the root of Gilgamesh's journey north.
4. The version of the Tummal Inscription I am working with is found in Kramer, *The Sumerians,* pp. 78–80. Dr. Kramer also matches the inscription to the king list to show the progress of the war between the three cities.
5. "Gilgamesh and Agga of Kish," in *ETC.*

Chapter Nine The First Civil War

1. Herodotus, *The Histories,* translated by Robin Waterfield (1998), 2.99.
2. Ian Shaw, ed., *The Oxford History of Ancient Egypt* (2002), pp. 68–69.

3. Rudolf Anthes, "Egyptian Theology in the Third Millennium B.C.," *Journal of Near Eastern Studies* 18:3 (1959), p. 171.
4. Ibid.
5. Ian Cunnison, *The Luapula Peoples of Northern Rhodesia* (1959), p. 98.
6. Edmund Leach, "The Mother's Brother in Ancient Egypt," *RAIN* [Royal Anthropological Institute of Great Britain and Ireland] 15 (1976), p. 20.
7. Shaw, p. 9.
8. William Flinders Petrie, *Researches in Sinai* (1906), p. 41.
9. Rice, p. 14.
10. Peter A. Clayton, *Chronicle of the Pharaohs: The Reign-by-Reign Record of the Rulers and Dynasties of Ancient Egypt* (1994), p. 28.

Chapter Ten The First Epic Hero

1. Dalley, p. 42 ff.
2. The quotes from the Epic of Gilgamesh are, more or less, mine. I have based them on the structure of the N. K. Sandars translation, but I have slightly condensed some of them, clarified the difficult words, and often modified them based on the translations supplied by Samuel Kramer, Maureen Gallery Kovacs, and Stephanie Dalley.
3. Drawn almost entirely from the Sandars translation, pp. 118–119.

Chapter Eleven The First Victory over Death

1. Clayton, p. 33.
2. Richard L. Zettler and Lee Horne, *Treasures from the Royal Tombs of Ur* (1998), p. 29.
3. This is J. M. Roberts's suggestion in *The Penguin History of the World* (1997), p. 71.
4. Herodotus, 2.12.
5. Paul Jordan, *Riddles of the Sphinx* (1998), p. 73.
6. Clayton, p. 45.
7. Herodotus, 2.124.
8. Herodotus 2.126.
9. Bruce G. Trigger, "Monumental Architecture: A Thermodynamic Explanation of Symbolic Behavior," *World Archaeology* 22:2 (1990), p. 119.
10. Dean Hardy and Marjorie Killick, *Pyramid Energy: The Philosophy of God, the Science of Man* (1994), p. 169.
11. Peter Tompkins, *Secrets of the Great Pyramid* (1971), p. xiv.
12. James and Thorpe, p. 208.

Chapter Twelve The First Reformer

1. Translated by Samuel Kramer, *The Sumerians,* p. 51.
2. Ibid., p. 313.
3. John Winthrop Hackett, ed., *Warfare in the Ancient World* (1989), p. 4.
4. Leick, *Mesopotamia*, p. 149.
5. I. M. Diakonoff, ed., *Early Antiquity* (1991), p. 82.
6. Translated by Samuel Kramer, *From the Tablets of Sumer* (1956), p. 48.
7. Diakonoff, p. 82.
8. J. S. Cooper, *Sumerian and Akkadian Royal Inscriptions*, vol. 1, *Presargonic Inscriptions* (1986), p. 78.

9. Nels Bailkey, "Early Mesopotamian Constitutional Development," *American Historical Review* 72:4 (1967), p. 1222.
10. Translated by Kramer, *The Sumerians,* pp. 323–324.
11. Leick, *Mesopotamia,* p. 150.
12. Translated by Kramer, *The Sumerians,* pp. 322–323.
13. Cooper, p. 95.
14. Crawford, p. 25.

Chapter Thirteen The First Military Dictator

1. Adapted from the translation provided by James B. Pritchard, ed., in *The Ancient Near East: An Anthology of Texts and Pictures* (1958), pp. 85–86, with clarification of certain terms from the explanation provided by Gwendolyn Leick in *Mesopotamia,* p. 94.
2. J. M. Roberts, p. 51.
3. Translated by Kramer, *The Sumerians,* p. 330.
4. Xenophon, *The Education of Cyrus,* translated by Wayne Ambler (2001), 1.3.8–9.
5. "The Sargon Legend, Segment B," in *ETC.*
6. Translated by Kramer, *The Sumerians,* p. 324.
7. Diakonoff, p. 85.
8. Ibid.
9. Translated by Kramer, *The Sumerians,* p. 324.
10. H. W. F. Saggs, *The Might That Was Assyria* (1984), p. 19.
11. Adapted from Benjamin R. Foster, *Before the Muses: An Anthology of Akkadian Literature,* vol. 1 (1996), p. 254.
12. Michael Roaf, *Cultural Atlas of Mesopotamia and the Ancient Near East* (1996), p. 97.
13. A. Leo Oppenheim, *Ancient Mesopotamia: Portrait of a Dead Civilization* (1977), p. 154.
14. Diakonoff, p. 86.
15. Bailkey, p. 1225. Bailkey's footnotes contain a full bibliography of the Old Babylonian inscriptions, the so-called Omen Texts, that record the revolt.
16. Leick, *Mesopotamia,* p. 99.

Chapter Fourteen The First Planned Cities

1. Keay, p. 6.
2. Wolpert, pp. 14–15.
3. Fischer, p. 61.
4. Wolpert, p. 18.
5. Keay, p. 13.
6. Hermann Kulke and Dietmar Rothermund, *A History of India* (1998), p. 23.
7. Ibid., pp. 22–23.
8. Terminology and measurements supplied by Kulke and Rothermund, p. 23, and Keay, pp. 8–9.

Chapter Fifteen The First Collapse of Empire

1. Herodotus, 2.127–128.
2. Jordan, p. 80.
3. Ibid., p. xvii.
4. Herodotus, 2.129.
5. Herodotus, 2.133.
6. Herodotus, 2.131.

7. Clayton, p. 60.
8. A. Rosalie David, *The Egyptian Kingdoms* (1988), p. 16.
9. Spell 217 translated by J. H. Breasted in *Development of Religion and Thought in Ancient Egypt* (University of Chicago Press, 1912); the following spell, 309, translated by R. O. Faulkner in *The Ancient Pyramid Texts* (Clarendon Press, 1969); both quoted by Jon E. Lewis, ed., *Ancient Egypt* (2003), pp. 27–29.
10. Clayton, p. 64.
11. Quoted in Clayton, p. 67.
12. Colin McEvedy, *The New Penguin Atlas of Ancient History* (2002), p. 36.

Chapter Sixteen The First Barbarian Invasions

1. Kramer, *The Sumerians*, p. 61.
2. Roaf, p. 98.
3. First noted by Hugo Radau, *Early Babylonian History Down to the End of the Fourth Dynasty of Ur* (1899), p. 307.
4. David Willis McCullough, ed., *Chronicles of the Barbarians* (1998), p. 8.
5. Oppenheim, *Ancient Mesopotamia*, p. 62.
6. "The Cursing of Agade," in *ETC.*
7. Ibid.
8. Kramer, *The Sumerians*, p. 330.
9. "A *tigi* to Bau for Gudea," in *ETC.*
10. "The Victory of Utu-hegal," in *ETC.*
11. Kramer, *The Sumerians*, p. 325.
12. "Ur-Namma the canal-digger," in *ETC.*
13. "A praise poem of Ur-Namma" in *ETC.*

Chapter Seventeen The First Monotheist

1. Gen. 10:11–24.
2. Victor P. Hamilton, *The Book of Genesis: Chapters 1–17* (1990), p. 363.
3. Adapted from "The death of Ur-Namma (Ur-Namma A)," in *ETC.*
4. Jonathan N. Tubb, *Canaanites: Peoples of the Past* (1998), p. 15.
5. J. M. Roberts, p. 41.
6. Tubb, p. 39.
7. Donald B. Redford *Egypt, Canaan, and Israel in Ancient Times* (1992), pp. 63–64.
8. Aidan Dodson and Dyan Hilton, *The Complete Royal Families of Ancient Egypt* (2004), p. 80.
9. Quoted in Redford, *Egypt*, pp. 67–68.
10. Qur'an 2.144–150.
11. Roaf, p. 101.
12. Quoted in Leick, *Mesopotamia*, pp. 132–133.
13. Leick, *Mesopotamia*, p. 126.
14. Roaf, p. 102.
15. Tubb, p. 38.

Chapter Eighteen The First Environmental Disaster

1. John Perlin, *Forest Journey: The Role of Wood in the Development of Civilization* (1991), p. 43.
2. Thorkild Jacobsen, *Salinity and Irrigation Agriculture in Antiquity* (1982), p. 468.

3. D. Bruce Dickson, "Circumscription by Anthropogenic Environmental Destruction: An Expansion of Carneiro's (1970) Theory of the Origin of the State," *American Antiquity* 52:4 (1987), p. 713.
4. Kramer, *The Sumerians,* pp. 333–334, adapted.
5. Ibid., pp. 334–335, adapted.
6. Slightly adapted from "The Lament for Urim," in *ETC.*
7. Ibid.

Chapter Nineteen The Battle for Reunification

1. Verbrugghe and Wickersham, p. 137.
2. Stephan Seidlmayer, "The First Intermediate Period," in *The Oxford History of Ancient Egypt,* ed. Ian Shaw (2002), pp. 128–129.
3. Verbrugghe and Wickersham, p. 194.
4. Clayton, p. 72.
5. "Instructions for Merikare," in Miriam Lichtheim, *Ancient Egyptian Literature,* vol. 1 (1975), p. 70.
6. Shaw, p. 161.
7. Ibid., p. 151.
8. Dodson and Hilton, p. 87.
9. Ibid., p. 90.
10. "The Prophecy of Nerferti," quoted in Shaw, p. 158.
11. Clayton, p. 79.
12. Shaw, p. 160.
13. Silverman, p. 79.

Chapter Twenty The Mesopotamian Mixing Bowl

1. Reconstruction of "Ishbi-Erra and Kindattu," segments A, B, D, and E in *ETC.*
2. Roaf, p. 110.
3. Saggs, *Assyria,* pp. 28–30.
4. Reconstructed from the somewhat fragmented "Letter from Nann-ki-ag to Lipit-Estar about Gungunum's troops" and "Letter from Lipit-Estar to Nann-ki-ag about driving away the enemy," both in *ETC.*
5. "An adab to Nanna for Gungunum (Gungunum A)," in *ETC.*
6. L. W. King, *The Letters and Inscriptions of Hammurabi,* vol. 3 (1976), p. 213, translation of "Reign of Sumu-abu."
7. Translated by A. K. Grayson, *Assyrian and Babylonian Chronicles* (1975), p. 155.
8. Assyrian king list quoted in Saggs, *Assyria,* p. 25.
9. Daniel David Luckenbill, *Ancient Records of Assyria and Babylon, Volume I: Historical Records of Assyria from the Earliest Times to Sargon* (1926), p. 16.
10. Saggs, *Assyria,* p. 37.
11. Roaf, p. 116.
12. Saggs, *Assyria,* p. 25.
13. Gwendolyn Leick, *The Babylonians: An Introduction* (2003), p. 33.
14. Oppenheim, *Ancient Mesopotamia,* p. 156.
15. H. W. F. Saggs, *Babylonians* (1995), p. 98.

Chapter Twenty-One The Overthrow of the Xia

1. Ssu-ma Ch'ien, *The Grand Scribe's Records,* vol. 1, ed. William H. Nienhauser, Jr., translated by Tsai-fa Cheng et al. (1994), p. 21.

2. Ibid., p. 22.
3. Ibid., p. 32.
4. John King Fairbank and Merle Goldman, *China: A New History* (2002), p. 37.
5. Li Liu and Xingcan Chen, *State Formation in Early China* (2003), p. 35.
6. Ibid., p. 35.
7. Ch'ien, p. 37.
8. Ibid., p. 38.
9. J. A. G. Roberts, p. 5.
10. Ch'ien, p. 38; the exact quote is "I regret failing to kill T'ang in Hsia-t'ai; that is what has brought me to this."

Chapter Twenty-Two Hammurabi's Empire

1. Jorgen Laessoe, *People of Ancient Assyria: Their Inscriptions and Correspondence* (1963), p. 47.
2. Slightly paraphrased for clarity, from Laessoe, p. 50.
3. Laessoe, pp. 68–69.
4. Ibid., p. 76.
5. Ibid., p. 78.
6. André Parrot's reconstruction, from the Mari letters, recapped in Jack M. Sasson, "The King and I: A Mari King in Changing Perceptions," *Journal of the American Oriental Society* 118:4 (1998), p. 454.
7. King, vol. 2, p. 176.
8. Pritchard, p. 142.
9. Norman Yoffee, "The Decline and Rise of Mesopotamian Civilization: An Ethnoarchaeological Perspective on the Evolution of Social Complexity," *American Antiquity* 44:1 (1979), p. 12.
10. Saggs, *Babylonians*, p. 101.
11. King, vol 1, p. xxxvii.
12. Roaf, p. 121.

Chapter Twenty-Three The Hyksos Seize Egypt

1. Shaw, p. 169.
2. Clayton, p. 93.
3. Josephus, *Against Apion*, 1.14.74–77, in *The Works of Josephus* (1987).
4. Ibid., 1.14.85.
5. Redford, *Egypt*, p. 126.
6. George Steindorff and Keith C. Steele, *When Egypt Ruled the East* (1957), p. 29.

Chapter Twenty-Four King Minos of Crete

1. J. Lesley Fitton, *Minoans* (2002), p. 67.
2. Ibid., pp. 104–105.
3. Ibid., p. 138.
4. Apollodorus, *The Library* (1921), 3.1.3–4 and 3.15.8.
5. Cyrus H. Gordon, *The Common Background of Greek and Hebrew Civilizations* (1965), pp. 51–52.
6. Thucydides, *The Landmark Thucydides: A Comprehensive Guide to the Peloponnesian War*, translated by Richard Crawley (1998), 1.4–5.
7. Herodotus, 1.171.
8. Thucydides, 1.8.
9. Rodney Castleden, *Minoans: Life in Bronze Age Crete* (1990), p. 148.

10. Fitton, p. 166.
11. Christos G. Doumas, *Thera, Pompeii of the Ancient Aegean* (1983), p. 134.
12. Ibid., pp. 134–135.
13. Ibid., p. 139.
14. Ibid., p. 147.

Chapter Twenty-Five The Harappan Disintegration

1. Wolpert, p. 21.
2. G. F. Dales, "The Mythical Massacre at Mohenjo Daro," in *Ancient Cities of the Indus*, ed. G. L. Possehl (1979), p. 291.
3. Gregory L. Possehl, "The Mohenjo-daro Floods: A Reply," *American Anthropologist* 69:1 (1967), p. 32.
4. Ibid., p. 35.
5. Romila Thapar, *Early India: From the Origins to AD 1300* (2002), p. 87.
6. Julian Reade, "Assyrian King-Lists, the Royal Tombs of Ur, and Indus Origins," *Journal of Near Eastern Studies* 60:1 (2001), p. 27.
7. Wolpert, p. 27.
8. Ibid., p. 24.
9. Keay, p. 20.

Chapter Twenty-Six The Rise of the Hittites

1. Robert S. Hardy, "The Old Hittite Kingdom: A Political History," *American Journal of Semitic Languages and Literatures* 58:2 (1941), p. 180.
2. Trevor Bryce, *Life and Society in the Hittite World* (2002), pp. 116–117.
3. G. G. Giorgadze, "The Hittite Kingdom," in *Early Antiquity*, ed. I. M. Diakanoff, trans. Alexander Kirjanov (1991), p. 271.
4. Bryce, p. 230.
5. Robert S. Hardy, p. 181.
6. Giorgadze, p. 272.
7. Robert S. Hardy, p. 194.
8. The Hittite *Testament,* quoted at length in Bryce, p. 11.
9. Bryce, p. 31.
10. Redford, *Egypt,* p. 134.
11. Leick, *The Babylonians,* p. 42.
12. Robert S. Hardy, p. 206.
13. Bryce, p. 107.

Chapter Twenty-Seven Ahmose Expels the Hyksos

1. Slightly paraphrased from Steindorff and Steele, p. 31.
2. Silverman, p. 30.
3. Clayton, p. 102.
4. Josephus, *Against Apion*, 1.14.
5. Lewis, p. 98.
6. Shaw, p. 216.
7. Redford, *Egypt,* p. 129.

8. Eliezer D. Oren, "The 'Kingdom of Sharuhen' and the Hyksos Kingdom," in *The Hyksos: New Historical and Archaeological Perspectives*, ed. Eliezer D. Oren (1997), p. 253.
9. Lewis, p. 98.

Chapter Twenty-Eight Usurpation and Revenge

1. Dodson and Hilton, p. 127.
2. Clayton, p. 105.
3. Edward F. Wente, "Some Graffiti from the Reign of Hatshepsut," *Journal of Near Eastern Studies* 43:1 (1984), pp. 52–53. Wente points out that the graffiti can be given alternate interpretations.
4. E. P. Uphill, "A Joint Sed-Festival of Thutmose III and Queen Hatshepsut," *Journal of Near Eastern Studies* 20:4 (1961), pp. 249–251.
5. I. V. Vinogradov, "The New Kingdom of Egypt," in *Early Antiquity*, ed. I. M. Diakonoff, trans. Alexander Kirjanov (1991), p. 178.
6. Ibid.
7. Ibid., p. 180.
8. Steindorff and Steele, p. 58.
9. Ibid., p. 57.

Chapter Twenty-Nine The Three-Way Contest

1. Laessoe, p. 83.
2. Ibid., p. 87.
3. Steindorff and Steele, p. 63.
4. Robert S. Hardy, p. 206.
5. Ibid., p. 208.
6. Bryce, pp. 28–29.
7. Laessoe, p. 89.
8. Redford, *Egypt*, p. 164.
9. Ibid., p. 167.
10. Alan R. Schulman, "Diplomatic Marriage in the Egyptian New Kingdom," *Journal of Near Eastern Studies* 38:3 (1979), p. 83.

Chapter Thirty The Shifting Capitals of the Shang

1. Ch'ien, p. 43.
2. Kwang-Chih Chang, *Shang Civilization* (1980), p. 11.
3. Ch'ien, p. 45.
4. Arthur Cotterell, *China: A Cultural History* (1988), p. 16.
5. Chang, p. 10.
6. Quoted in Chang, p. 11.
7. Ch'ien, p. 47.

Chapter Thirty-One The Mycenaeans of Greece

1. Lord William Taylour, *The Mycenaeans* (1983), p. 18.
2. Plutarch, *Plutarch's Lives*, vol. 1, The Dryden Translation (2001), p. 10.
3. Taylour, p. 41.
4. Ibid., p. 147; Robert Morkot, *The Penguin Historical Atlas of Ancient Greece* (1996), p. 29.

5. Taylour, p. 137.
6. John Chadwick, *Linear B and Related Scripts* (1987), pp. 44–49.
7. Herodotus, 3.122.
8. Taylour, p. 156.
9. Fitton, p. 179.
10. J. T. Hooker, "Homer and Late Minoan Crete," *Journal of Hellenic Studies* 89 (1969), p. 60.

Chapter Thirty-Two Struggle of the Gods

1. Clayton, p. 116.
2. David O'Connor and Eric H. Cline, *Amenhotep III: Perspectives on His Reign* (1998), p. 13.
3. Ibid., p. 11.
4. Tacitus, *The Annals of Imperial Rome* (1996), p. 111.
5. Details found in Ernest A. Wallis Budge, *Tutankhamen: Amenism, Atenism, and Egyptian Monotheism* (1923), p. 68, and also Clayton, p. 117.
6. Donald B. Redford, *Akhenaten: The Heretic King* (1984), pp. 36–37.
7. Clayton, p. 116.
8. O'Connor and Cline, p. 20.
9. Laessoe, p. 90.
10. O'Connor and Cline, p. 243.
11. William L. Moran, ed. and trans., *The Amarna Letters* (1992), p. 1.
12. Ibid., pp. 1–2.
13. Ibid., p. 8.
14. O'Connor and Cline, pp. 2–3.
15. Redford, *Akhenaten,* p. 162.
16. Dodson and Hilton, p. 142.
17. Redford, *Akhenaten,* p. 52.
18. Cyril Aldred, *Akhenaten, King of Egypt* (1988), p. 278.
19. Ibid., pp. 241–243.
20. Redford, *Akhenaten,* p. 141.

Chapter Thirty-Three Wars and Marriages

1. Slight paraphrase of the letter labelled El Amarna (hereafter EA) 20 by archaeologists, quoted in Moran, p. 48.
2. Redford, *Akhenaten,* p. 195.
3. EA 41, in Moran, p. 114.
4. EA 16, in Moran, p. 16.
5. Redford, *Akhenaten,* p. 197.
6. Laessoe, p. 90.
7. EA 9, in Moran, p. 18.
8. Saggs, *Babylonians,* pp. 118–119.
9. Clayton, p. 134.
10. Nicholas Reeves, *The Complete Tutankhamun: The King, The Tomb, The Royal Treasure* (1995), p. 23.
11. Clayton, p. 135.

Chapter Thirty-Four The Greatest Battle in Very Ancient Times

1. Clayton, p. 138.
2. Ibid., p. 146.

3. Bryce, p. 111.
4. Shaw, p. 298.
5. Diakonoff, p. 189.
6. Shaw, p. 298.
7. Clayton, p. 151.
8. Letter translated and quoted in Bryce, p. 172.
9. Luckenbill, *Ancient Records*, vol. 1, p. 27.
10. Bryce, p. 108.
11. Luckenbill, *Ancient Records*, vol. 1, p. 40.
12. Redford, *Egypt*, p. 188.
13. Clayton, p. 153.
14. Ibid., p. 155.

Chapter Thirty-Five The Battle for Troy

1. Taylour, p. 159.
2. Homer, *The Iliad*, Book 3; this translation is E. V. Rieu's (1950).
3. Virgil, *The Aeneid*, 2.13–20, translated by C. Day Lewis (1950).
4. Ibid., 2.265–267, 327.
5. E. V. Rieu, "Introduction," in Homer, *The Iliad* (1950), p. xiv.
6. Chadwick, p. 36.
7. Clayton, p. 162.
8. Herodotus, 1.4.
9. Herodotus, 1.5.
10. Barbara W. Tuchman, *The March of Folly: From Troy to Vietnam* (1984), p. 43.
11. Thucydides, 1.11.1.
12. Homer, *The Odyssey*, Book 3, Samuel Butler translation (1898).
13. Thucydides, 1.12.2.

Chapter Thirty-Six The First Historical King of China

1. J. Legge and C. Waltham translation, quoted by Chang, p. 12.
2. Fairbank and Goldman, p. 34.
3. J. A. G. Roberts, p. 67.
4. Ibid., p. 8.
5. Chang, pp. 32–35.
6. A. Waley translation, quoted in Chang, p. 13.
7. Cotterell, *China*, p. 24.

Chapter Thirty-Seven The Rig Veda

1. Keay, p. 26.
2. Ranbir Vohra, *The Making of India: A Historical Survey* (2001), pp. 3–4.
3. Keay, p. 29. A *mandala* can refer to anything with qualities of circularity.
4. The Rig Veda, translated by Franklin Edgerton in *The Beginnings of Indian Philosophy* (1965), pp. 52–56.
5. Kulke and Rothermand, p. 35.
6. Thapar, *Early India*, p. 114.

Chapter Thirty-Eight The Wheel Turns Again

1. Redford, *Egypt,* p. 247.
2. Clayton, p. 157.
3. Bryce, p. 94.
4. Ibid., p. 22.
5. K. A. Kitchen, trans., *Ramesside Inscriptions, Historical and Biographical,* vol. 4 (1969), 5.3.
6. Bryce, p. 95.
7. Ibid., p. 109.
8. Ibid., p. 26.
9. Ibid., p. 234.
10. Redford, *Egypt,* p. 245.
11. Adapted from the letter labelled RS 34, found in Sylvie Lackenbacher, *Le roi bâtisseur. Les récits de construction assyriens des origins à Teglatphalasar III* (1982).
12. Itamar Singer, "New Evidence on the End of the Hittite Empire," in *The Sea Peoples and Their World: A Reassessment,* ed. Eliezer D. Oren (2000), p. 22.
13. Laessoe, p. 98.
14. Leick, *Mesopotamia,* p. 209.
15. Chronicle P, quoted in Saggs, *Babylonians,* p. 119.
16. Quoted in Roaf, p. 148.
17. Luckenbill, *Ancient Records,* vol. 1, p. 49.
18. Saggs, *Assyria,* p. 52.
19. Luckenbill, *Ancient Records,* vol. 1, p. 49.
20. Leick, *Mesopotamia,* p. 251.
21. Saggs, *Babylonians,* p. 120.
22. The Great Harris Papyrus, quoted by A. Malamat in "Cushan Rishathaim and the Decline of the Near East around 1200 BC," *Journal of Near Eastern Studies* 13:4 (1954), p. 234.

Chapter Thirty-Nine The End of the New Kingdom

1. Clayton, p. 160.
2. Condensed slightly from the translation in Lewis, p. 219.
3. Jacobus van Dijk, "The Amarna Period and the Later New Kingdom," in *The Oxford History of Ancient Egypt,* ed. Ian Shaw (2000), pp. 304–305.
4. Condensed slightly from the translation in Redford, *Egypt,* p. 251.
5. Redford, *Egypt,* p. 252.
6. Lewis, p. 245.
7. David O'Connor, "The Sea Peoples and the Egyptian Sources," in *The Sea Peoples and Their World: A Reassessment,* ed. Eliezer D. Oren (2000), p. 95.
8. Ibid., p. 85.
9. Lewis, pp. 245–246.
10. van Dijk, p. 306.
11. Lewis, p. 247.
12. Ibid., p. 252.
13. Ibid., p. 254.
14. Clayton, p. 168.
15. See van Dijk, p. 308, and also Lewis, p. 265.
16. Clayton, p. 171.

Chapter Forty The Dark Age of Greece

1. Taylour, p. 159.
2. Morkot, p. 46.
3. Herodotus, 5.76.
4. Konon, *Narratives,* Sec. 26, in *The Narratives of Konon: Text Translation and Commentary of the Diegesis* by Malcolm Brown (2003).
5. Thucydides, 1.12.2–4.
6. Taylour, p. 161.
7. E. Watson Williams, "The End of an Epoch," *Greece & Rome,* 2d series, 9:2 (1962), pp. 119–120.
8. Philip P. Betancourt, "The Aegean and the Origin of the Sea Peoples," in *The Sea Peoples and Their World: A Reassessment,* ed. Eliezer D. Oren (2000), p. 300.
9. Homer, *The Iliad,* 1.12–14, translated by Robert Fitzgerald (1974).
10. Williams, p. 117.
11. Quoted in Williams, p. 112.

Chapter Forty-One The Dark Age of Mesopotamia

1. Translated by H. Otten in the journal *Mitteilungen des deutschen Orientgesellschaft* 94 (1963), p. 21, and quoted in Redford, *Egypt,* p. 254.
2. Roaf, p. 149.
3. A. T. Olmstead, "Tiglath-Pileser I and His Wars," *Journal of the American Oriental Society* 37 (1917), p. 170.
4. J. N. Postgate, "The Land of Assur and the Yoke of Assur," *World Archaeology* 23:3 (1992), p. 255.
5. Luckenbill, *Ancient Records,* vol. 1, p. 83.
6. Olmstead, "Tiglath-Pileser I and His Wars," p. 186.
7. Leick, *Mesopotamia,* p. 212.
8. Olmstead, "Tiglath-Pileser I and His Wars," p. 180.
9. W. G. Lambert, "Studies in Marduk," *Bulletin of the School of Oriental and African Studies,* University of London 47:1 (1984), p. 4.
10. Postgate, p. 249.
11. J. A. Brinkman, "Foreign Relations of Babylonia from 1600 to 625 BC: The Documentary Evidence," *American Journal of Archaeology* 76:3 (1972), p. 276.
12. Quoted in Leick, *Mesopotamia,* p. 254.

Chapter Forty-Two The Fall of the Shang

1. J. A. G. Roberts, p. 10.
2. Ch'ien, p. 51.
3. Mencius, *Mencius,* translated by D. C. Lau (1970), p. 172.
4. Ibid., p. 26.
5. J. A. G. Roberts, p. 13.
6. Cotterell, *China,* p. 28.

Chapter Forty-Three The Mandate of Heaven

1. Tsui Chi, *A Short History of Chinese Civilisation* (1942), p. 47.
2. Ch'ien, p. 64.
3. Cotterell, *China,* p. 42.

4. Claudio Cioffi-Revilla and David Lai, "War and Politics in Ancient China, 2700 BC to 722 BC: Measurement and Comparative Analysis." *Journal of Conflict Resolution* 39:3 (1995), p. 473.
5. Constance A. Cook, "Wealth and the Western Zhou," *Bulletin of the School of Oriental and African Studies,* University of London 60:2 (1997), pp. 254–275.
6. Ch'ien, p. 63.
7. Ibid,, p. 62.
8. Li Xueqin, *Eastern Zhou and Qin Civilizations* (1985), p. 16.
9. Sarah Allan, "Drought, Human Sacrifice and the Mandate of Heaven in a Lost Text from the 'Shang Shu,' " *Bulletin of the School of Oriental and African Studies,* University of London 47:3 (1984), p. 533.
10. Edward L. Shaughnessy, "Western Zhou History," in *The Cambridge History of Ancient China: From the Origins of Civilization to 221 BC,* ed. Michael Loewe and Edward L. Shaughnessy (1999), p. 311; also Xueqin, p. 16.
11. This is preserved in the *Shang shu*; see Shaughnessy, "Western Zhou History," p. 314.
12. Quoted in Shaughnessy, "Western Zhou History," p. 322.
13. Ibid.
14. Ch'ien, p. 66.
15. Paraphrased slightly from Ch'ien, p. 68.
16. Ibid.

Chapter Forty-Four The Bharata War

1. Kulke and Rothermund, p. 36.
2. Keay, p. 40.
3. Wolpert, p. 37.
4. Keay, pp. 3–4.
5. Chakravarthi V. Narasimhan, trans., *The Mahabharata: An English Version Based on Selected Verses* (1998), pp. 14–15.
6. Wolpert, p. 30.
7. Narasimhan, p. 34.
8. Kulke and Rothermund, p. 44.
9. Keay, p. 43.
10. Narasimhan, p. 44.
11. Ibid., p. 47.
12. Wolpert, p. 30.
13. Keay, p. 41.
14. Wolpert, p. 36.

Chapter Forty-Five The Son of David

1. Josh. 1:4, New International Version (hereafter NIV).
2. Pellegrino, p. 256.
3. Josh. 13:2–4, NIV.
4. Judg. 15:11, NIV.
5. Judg. 16:30, NIV.
6. 1 Sam. 8:11–18, NIV.
7. 1 Sam. 13:19–21, NIV.
8. 1 Sam. 17:51–52, NIV.
9. Dimitri Baramki, *Phoenicia and the Phoenicians* (1961), p. 25.

10. 1 Kings 4:22–26, NIV.
11. E. W. Heaton, *Solomon's New Men: The Emergence of Ancient Israel as a National State* (1974), p. 34.
12. 1 Kings 10:1–2, 13, NIV.
13. Robert G. Hoyland, *Arabia and the Arabs: From the Bronze Age to the Coming of Islam* (2001), p. 13.
14. Ibid., p. 38.
15. 1 Kings 9:11, NIV.
16. Homer, *The Iliad,* Book 9, 460–469, translated by Samuel Butler (1898).
17. Clayton, p. 184.
18. 1 Kings 14:25–27, NIV.

Chapter Forty-Six From Western to Eastern Zhou

1. Shaughnessy, "Western Zhou History," p. 324.
2. Constance A. Cook, "Wealth and the Western Zhou," p. 283.
3. Shaughnessy, "Western Zhou History," p. 326.
4. Ch'ien, p. 70.
5. Fairbank and Goldman, p. 18.
6. Shaugnessy, "Western Zhou History," p. 329.
7. Ch'ien, p. 71.
8. The Greater Odes 3.7, Ezra Pound, in trans., *The Confucian Odes: The Classic Anthology Defined by Confucius* (1954), p. 180
9. Constance A. Cook, "Wealth and the Western Zhou," p. 288.
10. Ch'ien, p. 71.
11. Ibid., p. 72.
12. Edward L. Shaughnessy, "Historical Perspectives on the Introduction of the Chariot into China," *Harvard Journal of Asiatic Studies* 48:1 (1988), p. 223.
13. Edward Kaplan, *An Introduction to East Asian Civilizations: The Political History of China, Japan, Korea and Mongolia from an Economic and Social History Perspective* (1997), sec. 12.3.
14. Shaughnessy, "Western Zhou History," p. 347.
15. Ch'ien, p. 73.
16. Ibid., p. 74.
17. Chi, p. 48.
18. Ibid., pp. 48–49.
19. Quoted in Cotterell, *China,* p. 39.
20. Chi, p. 49.

Chapter Forty-Seven The Assyrian Renaissance

1. 2 Sam. 8:5–6, NIV.
2. Saggs, *Assyria,* p. 70.
3. Joan Oates, *Babylon* (1979), p. 106.
4. Saggs, *Assyria,* p. 72.
5. Luckenbill, *Ancient Records,* vol. 1, pp. 158, 171.
6. Laessoe, p. 102.
7. Ibid., p. 104.
8. Luckenbill, *Ancient Records,* vol. 1, pp. 164–166.
9. 1 Kings 16:21–25, NIV.

10. John Rogerson, *Chronicle of the Old Testament Kings* (1999), p. 102.
11. A. T. Olmstead, *History of Assyria* (1923), p. 87–88.
12. Luckenbill, *Ancient Records*, vol. 1, p. 147.
13. Ibid., p. 201.
14. Charles F. Pfeiffer, *Old Testament History* (1973), p. 314.
15. Olmstead, *History of Assyria*, p. 136.
16. 1 Kings 22:7 ff., NIV.
17. 2 Kings 10:32, NIV.
18. Michael C. Astour, "841 B.C.: The First Assyrian Invasion of Israel," *Journal of the American Oriental Society* 91:3 (1971), p. 386.
19. Pfeiffer, p. 318.

Chapter Forty-Eight New Peoples

1. Luckenbill, *Ancient Records*, vol. 1, pp. 202–203, 264.
2. Oates, pp. 109–110.
3. Alan R. Millard, "Chaldeans," entry in *Dictionary of the Ancient Near East*, ed. Piotr Bienkowski and Alan Millard (2000), p. 70.
4. Brinkman, "Foreign Relations of Babylonia," p. 279.
5. Olmstead, *History of Assyria*, p. 144.
6. Saggs, *Assyria*, p. 77.
7. Luckenbill, *Ancient Records*, vol. 1, p. 254.
8. Olmstead, *History of Assyria*, p. 156.
9. R. W. Rogers, *A History of Babylonia and Assyria*, vol. 2 (1971), p. 95.
10. Luckenbill, *Ancient Records*, vol. 1, p. 259.
11. J. A. Brinkman, *A Political History of Post-Kassite Babylon, 1158–722 BC* (1968), pp. 169–170.
12. Brinkman, "Foreign Relations of Babylonia," p. 279.
13. Saggs, *Assyria*, p. 79.
14. Terry Buckley, *Aspects of Greek History, 750–323 BC: A Source-Based Approach* (1996), p. 35.
15. Donald Latimer, "The *Iliad:* An Unpredictable Classic," in Robert Fowler, ed., *The Cambridge Companion to Homer* (2004), p. 18.
16. Ken Dowden, "The Epic Tradition in Greece," in Fowler, p. 190.
17. Robin Osborne, "Homer's Society," in Fowler, p. 206.
18. Ibid., p. 218.
19. Robert Fowler, "Introduction," in Fowler, p. 5.
20. Sarah B. Pomeroy et al., *Ancient Greece: A Political, Social, and Cultural History* (1999), p. 79.

Chapter Forty-Nine Trading Posts and Colonies

1. Homer, *The Iliad*, Book 2, translated by Alexander Pope (1713).
2. T. J. Cornell, *The Beginnings of Rome: Italy and Rome from the Bronze Age to the Punic Wars (c. 1000–264 BC)* (1995), pp. 31–33.
3. David Ridgway, *Italy Before the Romans: The Iron Age* (1979), pp. 24–25.
4. Cornell, pp. 35–36.
5. H. H. Scullard, *A History of the Roman World, 753 to 146 BC* (2003), p. 39.
6. Buckley, p. 36.
7. Judith Swaddling, *The Ancient Olympic Games* (1999), pp. 10–11.
8. Livy, 1.4, from *The Early History of Rome, Books I–V of The History of Rome from Its Foundation*, translated by Aubrey de Selincourt (1971), pp. 37–38.
9. Plutarch, *Romulus*, in *Plutarch's Lives*, vol. 1: The Dryden Translation, p. 27.

10. Livy 1.6, *Early History of Rome*, p. 39.
11. Ibid., p. 40.
12. Livy, 1.1, *Early History of Rome*, p. 33.
13. R. M. Ogilvie, "Introduction: Livy," in Livy, *Early History of Rome*, p. 17.
14. Livy, 1.7–9, *Early History of Rome*, pp. 42–43.
15. Livy, 1.9, *Early History of Rome*, p. 43.
16. Livy, 1.13–14, *Early History of Rome*, pp. 48–49.
17. Buckley, p. 39.
18. Hesiod, *Works and Days*, ll. 37–40, in *Theogony, Works and Days, Shield* (2004), p. 66.
19. Ibid., ll. 220–221, p. 70.
20. Ibid., ll. 230–235, p. 71.

Chapter Fifty Old Enemies

1. Saggs, *Assyria*, p. 81.
2. 2 Kings 14:25–28.
3. Luckenbill, *Ancient Records*, vol. 1, p. 114.
4. Saggs, *Assyria*, p. 80.
5. Ibid., p. 83.
6. Ibid.
7. Olmstead, *History of Assyria*, p. 124.
8. Oates, p. 112.
9. Hayim Tadmor, *The Inscriptions of Tiglath-Pileser III, King of Assyria* (1994), p. 45.
10. Ibid.
11. Oates, p. 114.
12. Saggs, *Assyria*, p. 88.
13. Luckenbill, *Ancient Records*, vol. 1, p. 273.
14. Ernest A. Fredricksmeyer, "Alexander, Midas, and the Oracle at Gordium," *Classical Philology* 56:3 (1961), p. 160.
15. Herodotus, 1.14.
16. 2 Kings 15–16.
17. Reconstruction from fragmentary translations offered by Oates, p. 114, and Brevard S. Childs in *Isaiah and the Assyrian Crisis* (1967), p. 81.
18. Olmstead, *History of Assyria*, p. 179.
19. Luckenbill, *Ancient Records*, vol. 1, p. 285.
20. Daniel David Luckenbill, "The First Inscription of Shalmaneser V," *American Journal of Semitic Languages and Literatures* 41:3 (1925), p. 164.
21. Luckenbill, *Ancient Records*, vol. 1, p. 283.

Chapter Fifty-One Kings of Assyria and Babylon

1. Josephus, *Antiquities of the Jews*, 9.14, in *The Works of Josephus* (1987), pp. 264–265.
2. 2 Kings 17:4, NIV.
3. Clayton, p. 189; Jan Assmann, *The Mind of Egypt: History and Meaning in the Time of the Pharaohs* (2002), p. 312.
4. Assmann, pp. 317–319.
5. Quoted in Assmann, p. 320.
6. Saggs, *Assyria*, p. 92.
7. Daniel David Luckenbill, *Ancient Records of Assyria and Babylon*, Volume II: *Historical Records of Assyria from Sargon to the End* (1927), p. 71.

8. Ibid., p. 2; 2 Kings 17:6.
9. Luckenbill, *Ancient Records*, vol. 2, p. 2.
10. Ibid., p. 3.
11. A. Leo Oppenheim, "The City of Assur in 714 B.C.," *Journal of Near Eastern Studies* 19:2 (1960), pp. 142, 147.
12. Paul Zimansky, "Urartian Geography and Sargon's Eighth Campaign," *Journal of Near Eastern Studies* 49:1 (1990), p. 2.
13. Translated in Saggs, *Assyria,* p. 93.
14. Ibid., p. 94.
15. Oppenheim, "The City of Assur in 714 B.C.," p. 134.
16. Luckenbill, *Ancient Records*, vol. 2, p. 10.
17. Zimansky, p. 3.
18. Laessoe, p. 113; Hoyland, p. 19.
19. J. A. Brinkman, "Elamite Military Aid to Merodach-Baladan," *Journal of Near Eastern Studies* 24:3 (1965), pp. 161–162.
20. Oates, p. 116.
21. Slightly condensed from the annals of Sargon, as translated by Brinkman in "Elamite Military Aid," p. 163.
22. Luckenbill, *Ancient Records*, vol. 2, p. 15.
23. Oates, p. 116.

Chapter Fifty-Two Spectacular Defeat

1. Isa. 14:29, NIV.
2. Daniel David Luckenbill, *The Annals of Sennacherib* (1924), p. 9.
3. Ibid., p. 10.
4. Grant Frame, *Rulers of Babylonia from the Second Dynasty of Isin to the End of Assyrian Domination (1157–612 BC)* (1995), p. 137.
5. Luckenbill, *Annals,* pp. 10–11.
6. Assmann, p. 335.
7. This quote and following from 2 Kings 20:12 ff., NIV.
8. This quote and following from 2 Kings 18:1 ff., NIV.
9. Luckenbill, *Annals,* p. 10.
10. Condensed and language updated slightly, from Luckenbill, *Annals,* p. 10.
11. Herodotus, 2.14.
12. The Nebi Yunus Inscription (H4), translated in Luckenbill, *Annals,* p. 85.
13. Luckenbill, *Annals,* p. 15.
14. Ibid., p. 16.
15. Ibid., p. 17.
16. Emil G. Kraeling, "The Death of Sennacherib," *Journal of the American Oriental Society* 53:4 (1933), p. 338.

Chapter Fifty-Three The Decline of the King

1. Xueqin, p. 16.
2. Ch'ien, p. 74.
3. Fairbank and Goldman, p. 49.
4. Xueqin, p. 37.
5. Ch'ien, p. 75.

6. G. W. Ally Rickett, trans., *Guanzi*, vol. 1 (1985), p. 5.
7. Ibid., p. 6.
8. Ch'ien, p. 75.
9. Ibid.
10. *Tso chuan*, quoted by Nicola Di Cosmo in *Ancient China and Its Enemies: The Rise of Nomadic Power in East Asian History* (2002), pp. 98–99.
11. Ch'ien, p. 76.
12. Ibid., p. 77.

Chapter Fifty-Four The Assyrians in Egypt

1. Isa. 37:38, NIV.
2. Adapted from the translation by R. C. Thompson and quoted in Kraeling, pp. 338–340.
3. Olmstead, *History of Assyria*, p. 343.
4. Frame, p. 164.
5. Olmstead, *History of Assyria*, p. 351.
6. Adapted from J. A. Brinkman's compilation of the various versions of Esarhaddon's inscriptions, in "Through a Glass Darkly: Esarhaddon's Retrospects on the Downfall of Babylon," *Journal of the American Oriental Society* 103:1 (1983), p. 39.
7. Brinkman, "Through a Glass Darkly," p. 41.
8. Frame, 167.
9. Francis Reynolds, ed., *State Archives of Assyria*, vol. 18: *The Babylonian Correspondence of Esarhaddon and Letters to Assurbanipal and Sin-saru-iskun from Northern and Central Babylonia* (2003), p. 4.
10. E. D. Phillips, "The Scythian Domination in Western Asia: Its Record in History, Scripture, and Archaeology," *World Archaeology* 4:2 (1972), p. 131.
11. Slightly paraphrased for the sake of clarity from the translation by Ivan Starr in *State Archives of Assyria*, vol. 4, *Queries to the Sungod: Divination and Politics in Sargonid Assyria* (1990), Queries 18, 20, 24, and 43, pp. 22, 24–25, 30, 48.
12. C. H. Emilie Haspels, *The Highlands of Phrygia: Sites and Monuments*, vol. 1, *The Text* (1971), p. 73.
13. Strabo, *The Geography of Strabo in Eight Volumes* (1928), 1.3.21.
14. Luckenbill, *Ancient Records*, vol. 2, pp. 516, 530, 533, 546.
15. Starr, Query 84, p. 98.
16. Slightly condensed from Laessoe, p. 114.
17. Clayton, p. 193.
18. Shaw, p. 358.
19. Slightly condensed from Frame, p. 194.
20. Clayton, p. 195.
21. Gebel Barka Stele, translated by Assmann, pp. 336–337, language slightly modernized.
22. Herodotus, 2.151; also Redford, *Egypt*, p. 431.
23. Assmann, p. 337.
24. James Henry Breasted, *A History of Egypt* (1967), p. 468.
25. Nah. 3:8–10.
26. Olmstead, *History of Assyria*, p. 417.
27. Ibid., p. 422.
28. The Nitiqret Adoption Stele, paraphrased slightly from the translation in Shaw, p. 376.
29. Olmstead, *History of Assyria*, p. 423.
30. Phillips, "The Scythian Domination in Western Asia," p. 132.

Chapter Fifty-Five Medes and Persians

1. Konstantinos Staikos, *The Great Libraries: From Antiquity to the Renaissance (3000 BC to AD 1600)* (2000), p. 13.
2. Condensed slightly from Benjamin R. Foster, *Before the Muses: An Anthology of Akkadian Literature*, vol. 2 (1996), p. 714.
3. Frame, p. 255.
4. Ibid., p. 258.
5. Epigraphs arranged chronologically by John Malcom Russell, *The Writing on the Wall: Studies in the Architectural Context of Late Assyrian Palace Inscriptions* (1999), p. 159.
6. Herodotus, 1.98.
7. A. T. Olmstead, *History of the Persian Empire* (1959), p. 30.
8. Starr, pp. 267–270.
9. Saggs, *Babylonians,* p. 161.
10. Frame, p. 260.
11. Saggs, *Babylonians,* p. 114.
12. Ezra 4:9–10, NIV.
13. P. Calmeyer, "Greek Historiography and Acheamenid Reliefs," in *Achaemenid History II: The Greek Sources*, ed. Heleen Sancisi-Weerdenburg and Amelie Kuhrt (1987), p. 11.
14. David Frankel, *The Ancient Kingdom of Urartu* (1979), p. 19.
15. Phillips, p. 135.
16. 2 Kings 23.
17. Herodotus, 1.105.
18. Ibid., 1.106.

Chapter Fifty-Six Conquest and Tyranny

1. Buckley, p. 37.
2. *Phaedo* 109b, quoted in Robin Waterfield, *Athens* (2004), p. 41.
3. Pomeroy et al., p. 92.
4. Herodotus, 4.156–157.
5. Ibid., 4.159.
6. Fragment 5, quoted in Buckley, p. 66.
7. Fragment 6, quoted in Buckley, p. 67.
8. Herodotus 6.52.
9. Luckenbill, *Ancient Records,* vol. 2, pp. 291–292.
10. Herodotus, 6.57.
11. *Lycurgus* 15, in Plutarch, *Greek Lives*, translated by Robin Waterfield (1998), p. 24.
12. *Lycurgus* 12–14, in Plutarch, *Greek Lives*, pp. 18–22.
13. *Lycurgus* 10, in Plutarch, *Greek Lives,* p. 18.
14. Herodotus, 7.104.
15. Waterfield, p. 39.
16. Eusebius, *Chronicle,* in A. Schoene and H. Petermann, trans. *Armeniam versionem Latine factam ad libros manuscriptos recensuit H. Petermann* (1875), pp. 182–183.
17. Waterfield, p. 43.
18. Eusebius, *Chronicle*, p. 198.
19. Thucydides, 1.125.
20. Thucydides, 1.126.
21. *Solon* 12, in Plutarch, *Greek Lives,* p. 55.

22. *Athenian Constitution*, translated by H. Rackham, 2.1–3, in *Aristotle in 23 Volumes*, vol. 20 (1952).
23. *Solon* 17, in Plutarch, *Greek Lives*, p. 61.
24. *Lycurgus* 15, in Plutarch, *Greek Lives*, p. 25.
25. Michael Gagarin, *Drakon and Early Athenian Homicide Law* (1981), pp. 19–21.
26. *Solon* 1, in Plutarch, *Greek Lives*, p. 46.
27. *Solon* 14, in Plutarch, *Greek Lives*, p. 57.
28. Buckley, pp. 91–92.
29. *Solon* 6, in Plutarch, *Greek Lives*, p. 50.
30. Herodotus, 1.29.
31. *Solon* 25, in Plutarch, *Greek Lives*, pp. 69–70.

Chapter Fifty-Seven The Beginnings and End of Empire

1. Livy, 1.15, *Early History of Rome*, p. 50.
2. R. M. Ogilvie, "Introduction: Livy," in Livy, *Early History of Rome*, p. 18.
3. Livy, 1.1–1.2, *Early History of Rome*, pp. 34–36.
4. Livy, 1.15, *Early History of Rome*, p. 50.
5. Livy, 1.16, *Early History of Rome*, p. 51.
6. Livy, 1.19, *Early History of Rome*, p. 54.
7. Dionysius of Halicarnassus, *Roman Antiquities*, vol. 1, *Books I–II* (1937), 2.62.
8. Livy, 1.33, *Early History of Rome*, p. 72.
9. Dionysius of Halicarnassus, *Roman Antiquities*, vol. 2, *Books III–IV* (1939), 3.45.
10. Gary Forsythe, *A Critical History of Early Rome: From Prehistory to the First Punic War* (2005), pp. 39–40.
11. Salvatore Settis, ed., *The Land of the Etruscans: From Prehistory to the Middle Ages* (1985), p. 30.
12. Jacques Heurgon, *Daily Life of the Etruscans* (1964), p. 136.
13. Christopher S. Mackay, *Ancient Rome: A Military and Political History* (2004), p. 12.
14. Dionysius of Halicarnassus, *Roman Antiquities*, vol. 2, 3.61–62.
15. Ray Kamoo, *Ancient and Modern Chaldean History: A Comprehensive Bibliography of Sources* (1999), p. xxxi.
16. Luckenbill, *Ancient Records*, vol. 2, p. 417.
17. Kamoo, p. xxxiii; Luckenbill, *Ancient Records*, vol. 2, p. 419.
18. Herodotus, 1.103.
19. Christopher Johnston, "The Fall of Nineveh," *Journal of the American Oriental Society* 22 (1901), p. 21.
20. Diodorus Siculus, *Bibliotheca Historica*, vol. 1 (1956), p. 171; Paul Haupt, "Xenophon's Account of the Fall of Nineveh," in *Journal of the American Oriental Society* 28 (1907), p. 101.
21. Luckenbill, *Ancient Records*, vol. 2, p. 420.
22. Nah. 2:6–10, 3:3, 3:19, NIV.
23. Assmann, p. 338.
24. 2 Kings 23:29, NIV.
25. 2 Chron. 35:21, NIV.
26. Luckenbill, *Ancient Records*, vol. 2, p. 421.
27. 2 Kings 23:31–35.
28. Verbrugghe and Wickersham, p. 58.
29. Jer. 46:2–6, NIV.
30. Donald B. Redford, *From Slave to Pharaoh: The Black Experience of Ancient Egypt* (2004), p. 146.

Chapter Fifty-Eight A Brief Empire

1. Josephus, *The Antiquities of the Jews*, 10.6.1.
2. Jer. 36.
3. Quoted in Ronald H. Sack, *Images of Nebuchadnezzar: The Emergence of a Legend* (2004), p. 49. I am grateful to Mr. Sack for his thematic organization of the ancient and classical sources for the reigns of Nebuchadnezzar and Nabonidus.
4. Herodotus, 2.158.
5. Clayton, p. 196.
6. Herodotus, 4.42; Shaw, p. 381; Redford, *Egypt*, p. 452.
7. Herodotus, 4.42.
8. Josephus, *Antiquities of the Jews*, 10.6.2.
9. Sack, p. 49.
10. 2 Kings 24; Rogerson, p. 151.
11. Josephus, *Antiquities of the Jews*, 10.7.3.
12. The Wadi-Brisa Inscription, in Sack, p. 16.
13. Verbrugghe and Wickersham, p. 58.
14. Saggs, *Babylonians*, p. 167.
15. Paraphrased and slightly condensed from Diodorus Siculus, pp. 149–150.
16. Verbrugghe and Wickersham, p. 59.
17. Saggs, *Babylonians*, p. 166.
18. Verbrugghe and Wickersham, p. 58.
19. *Politics* 3.1276, in H. Rackham, trans., *Aristotle in 23 Volumes*, vol. 21 (1944).
20. Redford, *Egypt*, p. 461.
21. Redford, *From Slave to Pharaoh*, p. 146.
22. Clayton, p. 196.
23. Redford, *Egypt*, p. 463.
24. Josephus, *Antiquities of the Jews*, 10.7.3.
25. Jer. 37:7–10, NIV.
26. Jer. 38:4; also Josephus, *Antiquities of the Jews*, 10.7.3.
27. Letter 4, quoted in Rogerson, p. 153.
28. 2 Kings 25:4–6, NIV.
29. Josephus, *Antiquities of the Jews*, 10.8.4.
30. Raymond Philip Dougherty, *Nabonidus and Belshazzar: A Study of the Closing Events of the Neo-Babylonian Empire* (1929), p. 33; Herodotus, 1.74.
31. Herodotus 1.74.
32. Dan. 4:33, NIV.
33. Quoted in Sack, p. 44.
34. Matthias Henze, *The Madness of King Nebuchadnezzar: The Ancient Near Eastern Origins and Early History of Interpretation of Daniel 4* (1999), pp. 96–99.

Chapter Fifty-Nine Cyrus the Great

1. Herodotus, 1.107.
2. The following is all drawn from Herodotus, 1.108–119.
3. Herodotus, 1.119.
4. 2 Kings 25:27–29.
5. The *Chronicle* of Jerachmeel, quoted in Sack, pp. 58–59.
6. Verbrugghe and Wickersham, p. 60.

7. Quoted in Sack, p. 22. The work of Megasthenes is lost, but he is quoted in Eusebius.
8. Leick, *The Babylonians,* p. 64.
9. Dougherty, p. 24.
10. Quoted in Oates, p. 132.
11. Quoted in Dougherty, pp. 72–73.
12. Diodorus Siculus, 2.32.2–3.
13. Herodotus, 1.123–126.
14. Ibid., 1.129–130.
15. Ibid., 1.75–87.
16. Ibid., 1.88–90.
17. Xenophon, *The Education of Cyrus* (2001), 8.2.1.
18. Ibid., 1.1.2.
19. Ibid., 1.1.5.
20. Ibid., 8.2.8–9.
21. Ibid., 8.2.11–12.
22. Pierre Briant, *From Cyrus to Alexander: A History of the Persian Empire* (2002), pp. 38–40.
23. The *Verse Account of Nabonidus,* quoted in Sack, p. 17.
24. Harran Inscription of Nabonidus, translated by Oppenheim, quoted in Henze, pp. 59–60.
25. The *Verse Account of Nabonidus,* quoted in Sack, p. 18.
26. Gene R. Garthwaite, *The Persians* (2005), p. 29.
27. Herodotus, 1.189.
28. Xenophon, *Education of Cyrus,* 8.5.13.
29. The Cyrus Cylinder, slightly condensed from the translation in Dougherty, pp. 176–168.
30. Ezra 1:1–3, NIV.
31. Ezra 3:12–13, NIV.

Chapter Sixty The Republic of Rome

1. Herodotus 1.164–165.
2. A. Trevor Hodge, *Ancient Greek France* (1998), p. 19.
3. Barry Cunliffe, *The Extraordinary Voyage of Pytheas the Greek: The Man Who Discovered Britain* (2002), p. 16.
4. Daithi O'Hogain, *The Celts: A History* (2002), p. 1.
5. Ibid., p. 2.
6. Hodge, pp. 5, 190–193.
7. Heurgon, p. 13.
8. David Soren et. al., *Carthage: Uncovering the Mysteries and Splendors of Ancient Tunisia* (1990), p. 49.
9. *Politics,* 3.1280, Rackham, *Aristotle in 23 Volumes,* vol. 21.
10. Heurgon, p. 13.
11. Arnaldo Momigliano, "An Interim Report on the Origins of Rome," *Journal of Roman Studies* 53:1–2 (1960), pp. 108–109.
12. Livy, *Early History of Rome,* 1.41–43.
13. Ibid., 1.47.
14. This quote and the following from Livy, *Early History of Rome,* 2.10.
15. Thomas Babington Macaulay, "Horatius: A Lay Made About the Year of the City CCCLX," stanza 27.
16. Polybius, *The Rise of the Roman Empire* (1979), 3.22.

17. Livy, *Early History of Rome,* 5.34.
18. O'Hogain, p. 2; Bernhard Maier, *The Celts: A History from Earliest Times to the Present* (2003), pp. 44–45.
19. Polybius, *Rise of the Roman Empire,* 2.17.
20. Maier, p. 24; O'Hogain, p. 7.
21. Cunliffe, pp. 19–20.
22. *Epitome of the Philippic History,* quoted in Maier, p. 38.
23. Mackay, pp. 26–28.
24. Livy, *Early History of Rome,* 2.17–19.

Chapter Sixty-One Kingdoms and Reformers

1. Edgerton, p. 54.
2. Thapar, *Early India,* p. 152.
3. *The Laws of Manu,* translated by Georg Buhler (1970), 1.93–100.
4. Jan Y. Fenton et al., *Religions of Asia* (1993), pp. 46–48.
5. Thapar, *Early India,* pp. 146–148.
6. Rig Veda 10.90, in Edgerton, p. 68.
7. Wolpert, p. 39.
8. Thapar, *Early India,* p. 149.
9. Fenton et al., p. 90.
10. From the Introduction to the Jataka, 1.54, translated by Henry Clarke Warren in *Buddhism in Translation* (1896), pp. 56–61.
11. Quoted in Michael Carrithers, *Buddha: A Very Short Introduction* (2001), p. 46.
12. Ibid., p. 62.
13. Karen Armstrong, *Buddha* (2004), p. 9.
14. Ibid., p. xi.
15. A. L. Basham, *The Wonder That Was India* (1963), p. 47.
16. Thapar, *Early India,* p. 152.

Chapter Sixty-Two The Power of Duty and the Art of War

1. Xueqin, p. 5.
2. Gai Shiqi, *Zuozhuan Jishibenmuo,* vol. 45 (1979), quoted in Xueqin, p. 170.
3. Ch'ien, p. 77.
4. Cho-yun Hsu, *Ancient China in Transition: An Analysis of Social Mobility, 722–222 BC* (1965), pp. 59–60.
5. Jonathan Clements, *Confucius: A Biography* (2004), pp. 10–15. I am grateful to Mr. Clements for assembling the scattered details about the life of Confucius into a chronological record.
6. Clements, pp. 21–22.
7. James Legge, trans., *The Sacred Books of the East,* vol. 27: *The Texts of Confucianism, Li Ki, I–X* (1968), 17.9.6.
8. Ibid., 2.1.7.
9. Ibid., 3.2.1, 12.
10. James Legge, trans., *Confucian Analects, The Great Learning, and the Doctrine of the Mean* (1971), 7.19.
11. Ibid., 1.1.
12. Ibid., 3.1, 3.
13. Clements, p. 39.

14. Ch'ien, p. 787.
15. Jaroslav Prusek, *Chinese Statelets and the Northern Barbarians in the Period 1400–300 BC* (1971), p. 187.
16. Hsu, p. 69.
17. Sun-Tzu, *The Art of War,* translated by Lionel Giles (2002), 2.6.
18. Ibid., 3.2.
19. Ibid., 2.2–4.
20. Ibid., 1.18–19.
21. Ibid., 9.24, 26.
22. Quoted in Xueqin, p. 7.

Chapter Sixty-Three The Spreading Persian Empire

1. Herodotus, 1.216.
2. Ibid., 1.214.
3. Ibid., 4.159.
4. Ibid., 2.161.
5. James Henry Breasted, *Ancient Records of Egypt: Historical Documents from the Earliest Times to the Persian Conquest* (1906–1907), 4.1000, pp. 510–511.
6. Herodotus, 2.162.
7. Breasted, *Ancient Records,* 4.1003, p. 511.
8. Ibid., 4.1005, p. 512.
9. J. M. Cook, *The Persian Empire* (1983), p. 46.
10. Briant, p. 57.
11. Herodotus, 3.64–66.
12. J. M. Cook, *Persian Empire,* p. 50.
13. Herodotus, 3.72.
14. Maria Brosius, trans. and ed., *The Persian Empire from Cyrus II to Artaxerxes I* (2000), p. 21.
15. Ibid., p. 48.
16. Ibid., p. 23.
17. J. M. Cook, *Persian Empire,* p. 53.
18. Brosius, pp. 32–33.
19. Ezra 5:3–9, NIV.
20. Basham, p. 47.
21. Thapar, *Early India,* p. 154.
22. Keay, p. 67.
23. Ibid.
24. Thapar, *Early India,* p. 155.
25. Herodotus, 4.44.
26. Olmstead, *History of the Persian Empire,* p. 145; Herodotus, 3.94 and 4.44; Brosius, p. 40.
27. Olmstead, *History of the Persian Empire,* p. 145.

Chapter Sixty-Four The Persian Wars

1. Herodotus, 4.127.
2. Ibid., 4.64–65, 73–75.
3. Ibid., 4.89.
4. *The Persians,* in Aeschylus, *The Complete Plays,* vol. 2, translated by Carl R. Mueller (2002), p. 12
5. Herodotus, 4.126, 131.

6. Briant, p. 144.
7. Herodotus, 5.3.
8. Morkot, p. 65.
9. Peter Green, *Alexander of Macedon, 356–323 BC: A Historical Biography* (1991), pp. 1–2.
10. Herodotus, 5.18.
11. Waterfield, p. 51.
12. *Solon* 29, in Plutarch, *Greek Lives*, p. 73; *Athenian Constitution*, in Rackhain, *Aristotle in 23 Volumes*, vol. 20, secs. 13–14.
13. *Solon* 29, in Plutarch, *Greek Lives*, p. 74.
14. Herodotus, 1.61.
15. *Athenian Constitution*, in Rackham, *Aristotle in 23 Volumes*, vol. 20, sec. 15.
16. Ibid., sec. 16.
17. Ibid., sec. 19
18. *Lycurgus* 16, in Plutarch, *Greek Lives*, p. 26.
19. Pomeroy et al., p. 152.
20. Herodotus, 5.73.
21. *Athenian Constitution*, in Rackham, *Aristotle in 23 Volumes*, vol. 20, sec. 21.
22. *Politics*, in Rackham, *Aristotle in 23 Volumes*, vol. 21, 1302b; Buckley, p. 145.
23. Herodotus, 5.97.
24. Ibid., 5.96.
25. Ibid., 5.99.
26. Buckley, pp. 161–162.
27. H. T. Wallinga, "The Ancient Persian Navy and its Predecessors," in *Achaemenid History I: Sources, Structures, and Synthesis*, ed. Heleen Sancisi-Weerdenburg (1987), p. 69.
28. Herodotus, 5.102.
29. Herodotus, 5.103.
30. H. T. Wallinga, in Sancisi-Weerdenburg, p. 69.
31. Herodotus, 6.17.
32. Herodotus, 6.19.
33. Herodotus, 6.112.
34. John Curtis, *Ancient Persia* (1990), p. 41.
35. Garthwaite, p. 36; Briant, p. 547.
36. H. T. Wallinga, in *Sancisi-Weerdenburg*, p. 43; Shaw, p. 384.
37. M. Jameson, in Peter Green, *Xerxes of Salamis* (Praeger, 1970), p. 98, quoted in Pomeroy et al., p. 194.
38. Pomeroy et al., p. 195.
39. Plutarch, *Themistocles*, sec. 9, in *Plutarch's Lives*, vol. 1, The Dryden Translation.
40. Aeschylus, *The Complete Plays*, pp. 139–140.
41. Ibid., p. 140.
42. Ibid., p. 142.
43. Plutarch, *Themistocles*, sec. 16, in *Plutarch's Lives*, vol. 1, The Dryden Translation.
44. Herodotus, 9.84.
45. H. T. Wallinga, in *Sancisi-Weerdenburg*, p. 74.

Chapter Sixty-Five The Peloponnesian Wars

1. Aeschylus, *Persians* (1981), pp. 67–68.
2. Herodotus, 9.106.
3. Waterfield, p. 72.

4. Thucydides, 1.90.2.
5. Ibid., 1.93.2.
6. Ibid., 1.133–134.
7. Plutarch, *Themistocles*, secs. 19–21, in *Plutarch's Lives*, vol. 1, The Dryden Translation.
8. Plutarch, *Themistocles*, sec. 22, in *Plutarch's Lives*, vol. 1, The Dryden Translation.
9. Plutarch, *Themistocles*, sec. 29, in *Plutarch's Lives*, vol. 1, The Dryden Translation.
10. Thucydides, 1.138.4; Plutarch, *Themistocles*, sec. 31, in *Plutarch's Lives*, vol. 1, The Dryden Translation.
11. Esther 2:12–16.
12. Herodotus, 9.585.
13. Brosius, p. 54.
14. Diodorus Siculus, 11.69.2–6.
15. J. M. Cook, *Persian Empire*, p. 127.
16. Thucydides, 1.103.2.
17. Ibid., 1.99.4.
18. Ibid., 1.99.1–2.
19. *Pericles* 13, Plutarch, in *Greek Lives*, p. 156.
20. Thucydides, 1.108.4.
21. Pomeroy et al., p. 251.
22. Thucydides, 1.45.3.
23. Ibid., 1.50.2.
24. Ibid., 2.7.1.
25. Ibid., 2.43.1.
26. Ibid., 2.49.2–8.
27. Thucydides, 2.4.
28. Thucydides, 2.52.2–3.
29. J. M. Cook, *Persian Empire*, p. 129.
30. *Alcibiades* 1–3, in Plutarch, *Greek Lives*.
31. Pomeroy et al., p. 306.
32. Buckley, p. 388.
33. Pomeroy et al., p. 309.
34. Thucydides, 7.51.1.
35. Ibid., 7.84.2–5, 85.1.
36. Aristophanes, *Lysistrata* (1912), p. 1.
37. *Alcibiades* 24, in Plutarch, *Greek Lives*.
38. Thucydides, 8.78.
39. *Alcibiades* 35, in Plutarch, *Greek Lives*.
40. *Alcibiades* 37, in Plutarch, *Greek Lives*.
41. Xenophon, *Hellenica*, 2.2.10, translated by Peter Krentz.
42. Waterfield, p. 209; Xenophon, *Hellenica*, 2.2.23; Victor Davis Hanson, in Thucydides, p. 549.
43. Waterfield, p. 210.
44. *Athenian Constitution*, in Rackham, *Aristotle in 23 Volumes*, vol. 20, p. 35.

Chapter Sixty-Six The First Sack of Rome

1. Livy, *Early History of Rome*, 2.21.
2. Ibid., 2.24.
3. Mackay, p. 34.
4. Livy, *Early History of Rome*, 2.23.

5. Ibid., 2.32.
6. Ibid., 2.32.
7. Ibid., 3.35.
8. Ibid., 3.333.
9. Based partly on Oliver J. Thatcher, ed., *The Library of Original Sources*, vol. 3: *The Roman World* (1901), pp. 9–11.
10. Livy, *Early History of Rome*, 5.21.
11. Ibid., 5.32.
12. Ibid., 5.36.
13. Ibid., 5.38.
14. Ibid., 5.41.
15. Ibid., 5.47.
16. Cunliffe, pp. 21–22.
17. Livy, *Early History of Rome*, 5.55.

Chapter Sixty-Seven The Rise of the Ch'in

1. Ch'ien, p. 79.
2. Fairbank and Goldman, p. 54.
3. J. J. L. Duyvendak, trans., in his introduction to *The Book of Lord Shang: A Classic of the Chinese School of Law* (1928), p. 1.
4. Ch'ien, p. 108.
5. Cotterell, *China*, p. 53.
6. *Shih chi* 68, translated in Duyvendak, p. 14.
7. Ibid., p. 15.
8. Ibid., p. 16.
9. *Shih chi* 68, translated in Cotterell, *China*, p. 55.
10. Shu-Ching Lee, "Agrarianism and Social Upheaval in China," *American Journal of Sociology* 56:6 (1951), p. 513.
11. *The Book of Lord Shang*, translated by Duyvendak, p. 180.
12. *Shih chi* 68, in Duyvendak, p. 16.
13. *Shih chi* 68, in Cotterell, *China*, p. 57.
14. *Shih chi* 69, in Duyvendak, pp. 16–17.
15. Ibid., p. 17.
16. Ch'ien, p. 79.
17. Franz Michael, *China Through the Ages: History of a Civilization* (1986), p. 48.
18. Mencius, I.A.7.
19. Fairbank and Goldman, pp. 53–54.
20. Quoted in Michael, pp. 49–50.
21. "Giving Away a Throne," in *The Complete Works of Chuang Tzu*, translated by Burton Watson (1968), n.p.
22. "Discussion on Making All Things Equal," in Watson, *The Complete Works of Chuang Tzu.*

Chapter Sixty-Eight The Macedonian Conquerors

1. Pomeroy et al., pp. 327–328.
2. Scene 1, in Aristophanes, *The Birds and Other Plays*, translated by David Barrett and Alan H. Sommerstein (2003), p. 221.
3. Scene 3, Ibid., p. 257.

4. J. M. Cook, *Persian Empire,* p. 212.
5. Plutarch, *Artaxerxes,* in *Plutarch's Lives,* vol. 2, The Dryden Translation.
6. Xenophon, *The Persian Expedition* (also known as *Anabasis*) 1.1, translated by Rex Warner (1972), p. 56.
7. This detail from Ctesias comes to us via Diodorus Siculus; see George Cawkwell's "Introduction" to the Warner translation of Xenophon, *The Persian Expedition,* p. 40.
8. Plutarch, *Artaxerxes,* in *Plutarch's Lives,* vol. 2, The Dryden Translation, p. 646.
9. Xenophon, *The Persian Expedition,* 1.4.
10. Ibid., pp. 86–87.
11. Ibid., 4.5.
12. Ibid., 4.7.
13. Plutarch, *Artaxerxes,* in *Plutarch's Lives,* vol. 2, The Dryden Translation, p. 658.
14. Clayton, pp. 201–202.
15. *Hellenica,* 5.19, in *The Works of Xenophon,* vol. 2, translated by H. G. Dakyns (1892).
16. Ibid., 5.23.
17. Clayton, p. 203.
18. J. M. Cook, *Persian Empire,* p. 48.
19. *Panegyricus* 50, in Isocrates, *Isocrates II,* translated by Terry L. Papillon (2004), p. 40.
20. *Panegyricus* 166, in Isocrates, p. 68.
21. Green, p. 14.
22. Ibid., p. 22.
23. Justin, *The History,* 7.5, in William Stearns Davis, ed., *Readings in Ancient History,* vol. 1 (Allyn and Bacon, 1912).
24. Green, pp. 23–24.
25. *Alexander* 6, in Plutarch, *Greek Lives.*
26. *Alexander* 3, in Plutarch, *Greek Lives.*
27. *To Philip* 15–16, Isocrates, p. 78.
28. Diodorus Siculus, 16.14.
29. Pomeroy et al., p. 389.
30. Justin, *History,* 8.8.
31. *Alexander* 10, in Plutarch, *Greek Lives.*
32. Parts of the story are told by Diodorus Siculus, and by Aristotle in his *Politics* (translated by Rackham); see also Guy MacLean Rogers, *Alexander: The Ambiguity of Greatness* (2004), pp. 31–34.
33. *Alexander* 11, in Plutarch, *Greek Lives.*

Chapter Sixty-Nine Rome Tightens Its Grasp

1. Livy, *Rome and Italy: Books VI–X of The History of Rome from Its Foundation,* 6.42, translated by Betty Radice (1982), p. 95.
2. Ibid., 6.42.
3. Edward T. Salmon, *The Making of Roman Italy* (1982), p. 5.
4. Polybius, *Rise of the Roman Empire* 3.24.
5. Mary T. Boatwright et al,. *The Romans: From Village to Empire* (2004), p. 79.
6. Livy, *Rome and Italy,* 7.29, p. 135.
7. Ibid., 7.30, pp. 136–137.
8. Ibid., 8.6, pp. 164–165.
9. Ibid., 8.10–11, pp. 171–173.
10. Salmon, p. 40.
11. Livy, *Rome and Italy,* 8.14, p. 178.

12. Boatwright et al., p. 82.
13. Ibid., p. 84.
14. Diodorus Siculus, 9.9.
15. Soren et al., p. 91.
16. Ibid., pp. 90–91, 128–130.
17. Diodorus Siculus, 20.6–7.
18. Soren et al., p. 92.
19. Livy, *Rome and Italy*, 10.13, 304–305.
20. Ibid., 10.28, pp. 327–328.

Chapter Seventy Alexander and the Wars of the Successors

1. Green, p. 114.
2. Plutarch, *The Life of Alexander the Great*, translated by John Dryden (2004), p. 13
3. Green, p. 118; Plutarch, *Alexander the Great*, p. 13.
4. Diodorus, Siculus, 17.5–6.
5. Ibid., 17.17.
6. Quintus Curtius Rufus, *The History of Alexander* (lost, summarized by John Yardley), translated by John Yardley (2001), p. 23; also Arrian, *The Campaigns of Alexander*, 1.12, translated by Aubrey de Selincourt (1971).
7. Arrian, I.15, p. 73.
8. Didodorus Siculus, 17.20; Arrian, 1.16.
9. Arrian, 1.17.
10. Rufus, 3.15–18, p. 27.
11. Arrian, 2.8.
12. Rufus, 3.12, p. 42.
13. Arrian, 2.15, p. 128.
14. *Alexander* 29, in Plutarch, *Greek Lives*, p. 339.
15. G. M. Rogers, pp. 124–145.
16. Arrian, 3.23.
17. G. M. Rogers, p. 135.
18. Arrian, 4.9.
19. Ibid., 5.4, p. 259.
20. Ibid., 5.9, p. 267.
21. *Alexander* 63, in Plutarch, *Greek Lives*, p. 369.
22. Rufus, 9.19.
23. Plutarch, *Alexander the Great*, p. 64.
24. Ibid., p. 67.
25. Rufus, 10.3.14.
26. Plutarch, *Alexander the Great*, p. 71.
27. Rufus, 10.6.13.
28. Plutarch, *Alexander the Great*, p. 72; also Diodorus Siculus, 18 and 19.
29. Rufus, 10.9.1.
30. Ibid., 10.10.7–8.
31. Sarvepalli Radhakrishnan and Charles A. Moore, eds. *A Sourcebook in Indian Philosophy* (1957), p. 198.
32. Vohra, p. 25.
33. Plutarch, *Pyrrhus*, in *Plutarch's Lives*, vol. 1, The Dryden Translation, p. 520.
34. Plutarch, *Demetrius*, in *Plutarch's Lives*, vol. 2, The Dryden Translation, p. 480.
35. Plutarch, *Pyrrhus*, in *Plutarch's Lives*, vol. 1, The Dryden Translation, p. 537.

Chapter Seventy-One The Mauryan Epiphany

1. Keay, p. 88.
2. Thapar, *Early India,* p. 5.
3. Wolpert, p. 57.
4. Keay, p. 90.
5. Ibid., p. 91.
6. Thapar, *Early India,* p. 180.
7. Translated by Romila Thapar in *Asoka and the Decline of the Mauryas* (1998), p. 255.
8. Ibid., pp. 255–256.
9. Ibid., p. 256 and Keay, pp. 91–92.
10. Keay, p. 95.
11. Wolpert, p. 64. The story of Mahinda is found in the Dîpavamsa 7, 28–31; see Max Muller's introduction in *Sacred Books of the East,* vol. 10: *The Dhammapada* (1981).
12. Vohra, p. 25.
13. Ibid.

Chapter Seventy-Two First Emperor, Second Dynasty

1. Charles O. Hucker, *China's Imperial Past: An Introduction to Chinese History and Culture* (1975), p. 40.
2. Ibid., p. 41.
3. Ch'ien, p. 83.
4. Ibid., p. 123.
5. Ibid., p. 130.
6. Ibid., p. 123.
7. Fairbank and Goldman, p. 56.
8. Hucker, pp. 43–44.
9. Ch'ien, p. 140.
10. Ibid., p. 147.
11. Sima Qian, "The Biography of the Chief Minister of Qin," in *Historical Records,* translated by Raymond Dawson (1994), p. 31.
12. Sima Qian, "The Annals of Qin," in *Historical Records,* p. 69.
13. Jorge Luis Borges, "The Wall and the Books," in Daniel Schwartz, *The Great Wall of China* (2001), p. 10.
14. Ann Paludan, *Chronicle of the Chinese Emperors: The Reign-by-Reign Record of the Rulers of Imperial China* (1998), pp. 18–19.
15. Ch'ien, p. 155.
16. Arthur Cotterell, *The First Emperor of China* (1981), p. 28.
17. Ch'ien, p. 156.
18. Ibid., pp. 161–162.
19. Denis Twitchett and Michael Loewe, eds., *The Cambridge History of China,* Volume I: *The Ch'in and Han Empires, 221 BC–AD 220* (1986), p. 113.
20. Ibid., p. 117.
21. Sima Qian, *Records of the Grand Historian: Han Dynasty I,* translated by Burton Watson (1993), pp. 74–75.

Chapter Seventy-Three The Wars of the Sons

1. Plutarch, *Demetrius,* in *Plutarch's Lives,* vol. 2, The Dryden Translation, p. 465.
2. Diodorus Siculus, 21.12.

3. Plutarch, *Pyrrhus,* in *Plutarch's Lives*, vol. 1, The Dryden Translation, pp. 540–541, and Polybius, *Rise of the Roman Empire*, 2.43.
4. Polybius, *Rise of the Roman Empire*, 1.5, p. 45.
5. Ibid., 1.7–12.
6. Ibid., 1.20, p. 62.
7. J. H. Thiel, *A History of Roman Sea-power before the Second Punic War* (1954), p. 63.
8. Polybius, *Rise of the Roman Empire*, 1.21, p. 64.
9. Polybius, *The Histories*, 1.75, translated by Evelyn Shuckburgh (1889), pp. 83, 85.
10. Polybius, *Rise of the Roman Empire*, 1.58, p. 105.
11. Livy, *The War With Hannibal: Books XXI–XXX of The History of Rome from Its Foundation*, 21.41, translated by Aubrey de Selincourt (1965), p. 66.
12. Polybius, *Rise of the Roman Empire*, 1. 63, p. 109.
13. Plutarch, *Cleomenes*, in *Plutarch's Lives*, vol. 2, The Dryden Translation, p. 351.
14. Polybius, *Rise of the Roman Empire*, 5.34, p. 291.
15. Clayton, p. 211.
16. Polybius, *Rise of the Roman Empire*, 5.34, p. 292.
17. Ibid., 15.33, p. 491.
18. Josephus, *Antiquities of the Jews*, 12.3.3.
19. Polybius, *Rise of the Roman Empire*, 3.11, p. 189.
20. Polybius, *Rise of the Roman Empire*, 2.1, pp. 111–12.
21. Soren et al., p. 102.
22. Polybius, *Rise of the Roman Empire*, 3.20–21.
23. Livy, *The War with Hannibal*, 21.1, p. 23.
24. Polybius, *Rise of the Roman Empire*, 3.33, p. 209.
25. Ibid., 3.49.
26. Livy, *The War with Hannibal*, 21.32, p. 56.
27. Ibid., 21.47, p. 72.
28. Polybius, *Rise of the Roman Empire*, 3.68, p. 237.
29. Livy, *The War with Hannibal*, 11.57, p. 83.
30. Ibid., 22.7, p. 102.
31. Polybius, *Rise of the Roman Empire*, 3.90, p. 257.
32. Ibid., 3.118, p. 275.
33. Livy, *The War With Hannibal*, 27.48, p. 493.
34. Ibid., 27.51.
35. Ibid., 30.20, p. 644.
36. Ibid., 30.36, p. 664.
37. Leonard Cottrell, *Hannibal: Enemy of Rome* (1992), p. 242.

Chapter Seventy-Four **Roman Liberators and Seleucid Conquerors**

1. Livy, *The Dawn of the Roman Empire: Books 31–40* [of *The History of Rome from Its Foundation*], 33.19, translated by J. C. Yardley (2000), pp. 112–113.
2. Polybius, *Rise of the Roman Empire*, 18.45, p. 514.
3. Ibid., 18.46, p. 516.
4. Ibid., 3.11, p. 189.
5. Livy, *Dawn of the Roman Empire*, 36.17, p. 268.
6. Plutarch, *Flamininus*, in *Plutarch's Lives*, vol. 1, The Dryden Translation, p. 515.
7. The story is found, among other places, in the *Maitreyopanishad* of the *Sama-Veda*.
8. Polybius, *Histories*, 23.7.
9. Livy, *Dawn of the Roman Empire*, 40.5, p. 486.

10. Polybius, *Histories*, 27.1.
11. Livy, *The History of Rome*, vol. 6, translated by E. Roberts (1912), 42.36.
12. Ibid., 42.26.
13. Ibid., 45.12.
14. Josephus, *Wars of the Jews*, 1.1, in *The Works of Josephus*, p. 546.
15. John Bright, *A History of Israel* (1974), pp. 424–425.
16. Ibid., p. 424.
17. 2 Macc. 6:10, Revised Standard Version.
18. 2 Macc. 8:1, 7–9.
19. Josephus, *Wars of the Jews*, 1.4.
20. Ibid.
21. A. N. Sherwin-White, *The Roman Citizenship* (1973), p. 42.

Chapter Seventy-Five Between East and West

1. Sima Qian, *Records of the Grand Historian*, p. 77, 84.
2. Di Cosmo, *Ancient China and Its Enemies*, p. 157.
3. Ibid., p. 165.
4. Burton Watson, trans., *Records of the Grand Historian of China: Translated from the Shih chi of Ssu-ma Ch'ien*, vol. 2 (1968), p. 129.
5. Twitchett and Loewe, p. 384.
6. Ibid., p. 386.
7. Sima Qian, *Shih chi 9: The Basic Annals of the Empress Lu,* in *Records of the Grand Historian*, p. 267.
8. Sima Qian, *Records of the Grand Historian*, p. 269.
9. Ibid., p. 270.
10. Ibid., pp. 273–274.
11. Ibid., p. 284.
12. Sima Qian, *Shih chi 123*, in Watson, *Records*, vol. 2, p. 264.
13. Hucker, pp. 123–125.
14. Hucker, p. 128.
15. Sima Qian, *Shih chi* 123, in Watson, *Records*, vol. 2, p. 264.
16. Ibid., p. 269.
17. T. W. Rhys Davids, trans., *The Questions of King Milinda* (1963), Book 1, p. 7.
18. Ibid., Book 7, p. 374.
19. Josephus, *Antiquities of the Jews*, 13.14.
20. Sima Qian, *Shih chi* 123, Watson, *Records*, vol. 2, p. 268.
21. Plutarch, *Sylla*, in *Plutarch's Lives*, vol. 1, The Dryden Translation, p. 610.
22. *Shih chi* 123, in Watson, *Records*, vol. 2, p. 276.

Chapter Seventy-Six Breaking the System

1. Soren et al., p. 115.
2. Livy, *The History of Rome*, 6.42.23.
3. Plutarch, *Marcus Cato*, in *Plutarch's Lives*, vol. 1, The Dryden Translation, p. 478.
4. Ibid., p. 478.
5. Philip Matyszak, *Chronicle of the Roman Republic* (2003), p. 120.
6. Plutarch, *Marcus Cato*, in *Plutarch's Lives*, vol. 1, The Dryden Translation, p. 479.
7. Polybius, *Histories*, 38.3–11.
8. Ibid. 39, p. 530.
9. M. I. Finley, *Ancient Slavery and Modern Ideology* (1980), p. 97.

10. Diodorus Siculus, 34.1–4.
11. Ibid., 34.16.
12. Ibid., 34.48.
13. Finley Hooper, *Roman Realities* (1979), p. 155.
14. Appian, *The Civil Wars*, 1.1, translated by Oliver J. Thatcher in *The Library of Original Sources*, vol. 3: *The Roman World* (1901).
15. Plutarch, *Tiberius Gracchus*, in *Plutarch's Lives*, vol. 2, The Dryden Translation, pp. 357–358.
16. Ibid., p. 361.
17. Ibid., p. 369.
18. Appian, *Civil Wars*, 1.2.
19. Diodorus Siculus, 34.21.
20. Ibid., 34.23.
21. Plutarch, *Caius Gracchus*, in *Plutarch's Lives*, vol. 2, The Dryden Translation, pp. 381–383.

Chapter Seventy-Seven The Problems of Prosperity

1. *The Jugurthine War* 41, in Sallust, *The Jugurthine War/The Conspiracy of Cataline*, translated by S. A. Handford (1963), p. 77.
2. *The Jugurthine War* 8, in Sallust, p. 41.
3. *The Jugurthine War* 14, in Sallust, p. 47.
4. *The Jugurthine War* 28, in Sallust, p. 64.
5. *The Jugurthine War* 37, in Sallust, p. 73.
6. *Marius* 28, in Plutarch, *Greek Lives*, p. 148.
7. *Marius* 32 in Plutarch, *Greek Lives*, p. 152.
8. Cicero, *On the Commonwealth*, 3.41, in *On the Commonwealth and On the Laws*, translated and edited by James E. G. Zetzel (1999), p. 74.
9. Justin 38.4.13, quoted in Salmon, p. 128.
10. Salmon, p. 129.
11. *Marius* 33 in Plutarch, *Greek Lives*, p. 153.
12. *Sulla* 6 in Plutarch, *Greek Lives*, p. 179.
13. *Marius* 34 in Plutarch, *Greek Lives*, pp. 153–154.
14. *Marius* 35 in Plutarch, *Greek Lives*, p. 154.
15. *Sulla* 9, in Plutarch, *Greek Lives*, p. 185.
16. Twitchett and Loewe, p. 410.
17. *Shi chi 109*, in Watson, *Records*, vol. II, pp. 142–143.
18. *Shi chi* 123, in Watson, *Records*, vol. 2, p. 282.
19. Ibid., 123, p. 284.
20. *Han shu* 96, quoted in Twitchett and Loewe, p. 410.
21. *Marius* 43, in Plutarch, *Greek Lives*, p. 164.
22. *Sulla* 22 in Plutarch, *Greek Lives*, p. 199.
23. *Sulla* 30, in Plutarch, *Greek Lives*, p. 208.
24. *Sulla* 31, in Plutarch, *Greek Lives*, p. 210.
25. Hooper, p. 215.
26. Ibid., p. 223.

Chapter Seventy-Eight New Men

1. Carlin A. Barton, "The Scandal of the Arena," *Representations* 27 (1989), p. 2.
2. Tertullian, *De spectaculis* 22, in Barton, p. 1.
3. *Crassus* 8, in Plutarch, *Fall of the Roman Republic: Six Lives by Plutarch*, translated by Rex Warner (1972), p. 122.

4. *Crassus* 9, in Plutarch, *Fall of the Roman Republic*, p. 123.
5. Appian, *Civil Wars*, 1.118.
6. *Crassus* 9, in Plutarch, *Fall of the Roman Republic*, p. 124.
7. Appian, *Civil Wars*, 1.119.
8. *Crassus* 11, in Plutarch, *Fall of the Roman Republic*, p. 127.
9. Appian, *Civil Wars*, 1.121.
10. *Crassus* 11, in Plutarch, *Fall of the Roman Republic*, p. 127.
11. *Crassus* 12, in Plutarch, *Fall of the Roman Republic*, p. 128.
12. Hooper, p. 226.
13. Ibid., p. 121.
14. Ibid., p. 120.
15. *Pompey* 48 and *Caesar* 14, in Plutarch, *Fall of the Roman Republic*, pp. 207, 257.
16. Caesar, *The Conquest of Gaul*, 2.35, translated by S. A. Handford, revised by Jane F. Gardner (1982), p. 73.
17. *Caesar* 20, in Plutarch, *Fall of the Roman Republic*, p. 263.
18. *Caesar* 21, in Plutarch, *Fall of the Roman Republic*, p. 265.
19. Acton Griscom, *The Historia Regum Britannia of Geoffrey of Monmouth* (1929), p. 221.
20. Caesar, *Conquest of Gaul*, 5.14, p. 111.
21. Ibid., 4.36, p. 103.
22. Plutarch, quoted in Hooper, p. 273.
23. *Caesar* 28, in Plutarch, *Fall of the Roman Republic*, p. 271.
24. *Caesar* 32–33, in Plutarch, *Fall of the Roman Republic*, p. 276.
25. *Caesar* 35, in Plutarch, *Fall of the Roman Republic*, p. 279.
26. Plutarch, *Antony*, in *Plutarch's Lives*, vol. 2, The Dryden Translation, p. 487.
27. Clayton, p. 216.
28. *Pompey* 79–80, Plutarch, *Fall of the Roman Republic*, pp. 240–241.
29. Harriet I. Flower, ed., *The Cambridge Companion to the Roman Republic* (2004), p. 328.
30. Nicolaus of Damascus, *Life of Augustus*, translated by Clayton M. Hall (1923).
31. Suetonius, *The Deified Julius Caesar* 82, in *Lives of the Caesars*, translated by Catharine Edwards (2000), p. 39.

Chapter Seventy-Nine **Empire**

1. Suetonius, *The Deified Julius Caesar* 83, in *Lives of the Caesars*, p. 39.
2. Plutarch, *Marcus Brutus*, in *Plutarch's Lives*, vol. 2, The Dryden Translation, p. 586.
3. Ibid., p. 587.
4. Plutarch, *Antony*, in *Plutarch's Lives*, vol. 2, The Dryden Translation, pp. 490–491.
5. Ibid., p. 491.
6. Ibid., p. 492.
7. Suetonius, *The Deified Augustus* 16, in *Lives of the Caesars*, p. 49.
8. Plutarch, *Antony*, in *Plutarch's Lives*, vol. 2, The Dryden Translation, p. 496.
9. Suetonius, *The Deified Augustus* 16, in *Lives of the Caesars*, p. 50.
10. Hooper, p. 305.
11. Chris Scarre, *Chronicle of the Roman Emperors* (1995), p. 18.
12. Hooper, p. 331.
13. Mackay, p. 184.
14. Hooper, pp. 332–333; Mackay, p. 185.
15. *Res Gestae,* ll.38–41, 58, in *The Monumentum Ancyranum*, translated by E. G. Hardy (1923).
16. Ibid., ll.74–80, 85–87.
17. Mackay, p. 185.

18. Suetonius, *The Deified Augustus* 79, in *Lives of the Caesars*, p. 84.
19. Tacitus, *Annals of Imperial Rome*, 1.1.
20. Garthwaite, p. 80.
21. Suetonius, *Augustus* 31, in *The New Testament Background: Selected Documents*, edited by C. K. Barrett, p. 5.
22. Hooper, p. 334.
23. Suetonius, *Tiberius*, in *Lives of the Caesars,* p. 131.
24. Garthwaite, p. 80.
25. Suetonius, *The Deified Augustus* 98, in *Lives of the Caesars*, p. 95.

Chapter Eighty Eclipse and Restoration

1. Twitchett and Loewe, p. 225.
2. Clyde Bailey Sargent, trans. *Wang Mang: A Translation of the Official Account of His Rise to Power* (1977), p. 55.
3. Ibid., p. 178.
4. Hucker, p. 129.
5. Ban Gu, historian of the Former Han, quoted in J. A. G. Roberts, p. 57.
6. J. A. G. Roberts, p. 57.
7. Paludan, p. 45.
8. J. A. G. Roberts, p. 59.
9. Michael, p. 82.
10. Fenton, p. 141.

Chapter Eighty-One The Problem of Succession

1. Suetonius, *Tiberius* 25, in *Lives of the Caesars*, p. 111.
2. Ibid.
3. Suetonius, *Tiberius* 43, in *Lives of the Caesars*, p. 119.
4. Suetonius, *Tiberius* 75, in *Lives of the Caesars*, p. 134.
5. Acts of Thomas, 2.4.
6. Ibid., 1.16.
7. Rom. 6:8–14, NIV.
8. Josephus, *Wars of the Jews*, ii.184–203.
9. Tacitus, *Annals of Imperial Rome*, 12.62, 280.
10. I. A. Richmond, *Roman Britain* (1978), p. 30.
11. Ibid., p. 33.
12. Dio Cassius, *Roman History* (1916), 62.16–1.
13. Tacitus, *Annals of Imperial Rome*, 15.44.
14. Sulpicius Severus, "The Sacred History of Sulpicius Severus," in *Nicene and Post-Nicene Fathers, Second Series*, vol. 11, edited by Philip Schaff and Henry Wace (1974), book 2, chapter 29.
15. Suetonius, *Nero* 57, in *Lives of the Caesars*, p. 227.
16. Suetonius, *Galba*, in *Lives of the Caesars*, pp. 236–237.
17. Hooper, p. 393.

Chapter Eighty-Two The Edges of the Roman World

1. Hooper, p. 403.
2. Pliny, Letter 6.20 in *The Letters of the Younger Pliny* (1963).

3. *De Vita Caesarum: Domitianus*, in *Suetonius*, edited by J. C. Rolfe (1914), vol. 2, 339–385.
4. *Domitian* 13, in Suetonius, *Lives of the Caesars*, sec. 13, p. 289.
5. Tacitus, "Life of Cnaeus Julius Agricola," in *Complete Works of Tacitus*, translated by Alfred John Church and William Jackson Brodribb (1964), pp. 707–708.
6. Scarre, p. 83.
7. Scarre, p. 88.
8. *Trajan*, in Anthony Birley, *Lives of the Later Caesars* (1976), p. 44.
9. Epictetus, "Discourses 4," in *Discourses, Books 3 and 4*, translated by P. E. Matheson (2004), i. 128–131.
10. Dio Cassius, *Roman History*, p. lxix.
11. Eusebius, *Ecclesiastical History*, translated by A. C. McGiffert, 1890.
12. Ibid.

Chapter Eighty-Three Children on the Throne

1. J. A. G. Roberts, p. 60.
2. Hucker, p. 131.
3. J. A. G. Roberts, p. 60.
4. Fairbank and Goldman, p. 60.
5. Hucker, p. 131.
6. Michael, p. 84.
7. Ibid.

Chapter Eighty-Four The Mistake of Inherited Power

1. Scarre, p. 110.
2. *Marcus Antoninus* 2, in Birley, p. 110.
3. Birley, *Marcus Antoninus* 7, in Birley, p. 115.
4. Birley, *Marcus Antoninus* 12, in Birley, p. 122.
5. Birley, *Marcus Antoninus* 17, in Birley, p. 125.
6. Marcus Aurelius, *The Meditations of Marcus Aurelius*, translated by George Long (1909), 6.2.
7. Ibid., 30.
8. *Marcus Antoninus* 28, in Birley, p. 136.
9. Scarre, p. 122.
10. *Commodus* 9, in Birley, p. 170.
11. *Commodus* 16, in Birley, p. 175.
12. Rafe de Crespigny, trans., *To Establish Peace, vol. 1* (1996), p. xi.
13. Ibid., p. 17.
14. Michael, p. 133; Paludan, p. 55.
15. de Crespigny, vol. 1, p. xxxviii.
16. Ibid., vol. 2, p. 396.
17. Hucker, p. 133.
18. *Caracallus* 2, in Birley, p. 251.
19. *Caracallus* 4, in Birley, p. 253.
20. Darab Dastur Peshotan Sanjana. *The Kârnâmê î Artakhshîr î Pâpakân, Being the Oldest Surviving Records of the Zoroastrian Emperor Ardashîr Bâbakân, the Founder of the Sâsânian Dynasty in Irân* (1896), 1.6.
21. Scarre, p. 147.
22. Birley, *Heliogabalus* 5, in Birley, p. 293.

Chapter Eighty-Five Savior of the Empire

1. al-Mas'udi, *El Masudi's Historical Encyclopedia, Entitled "Meadows of Gold and Mines of Gems,"* Book 2 (1841).
2. Curtis, p. 61.
3. "Yasna 12: The Zoroastrian Creed," translated by Joseph H. Peterson (electronic text at www.avesta.org, 1997), sections 1, 3, 9.
4. Jordanes, *The Origin and Deeds of the Goths*, translated by Charles C. Mierow (1908), 1.9.
5. Jordanes, 2.20.
6. Lactantius, "Of the Manner in Which the Persecutors Died," in *The Anti-Nicene Fathers*, vol. 7: *Fathers of the Third and Fourth Centuries,* edited by Alexander Roberts and James Donaldson (1974).
7. Ibid.
8. Eutropius, *Abridgement of Roman History,* translated by John Selby Watson (Bohn, 1853), 9.13.
9. Ibid., 9.14.
10. Scarre, p. 193.
11. Eusebius, "The Oration of the Emperor Constantine," 24, in *Nicene and Post-Nicene Fathers,* Second Series, Vol. I, edited by Philip Schaff and Henry Wace (1974).
12. Eutropius, 9.18.
13. Ibid., 9.18.
14. Ibid., 9.20.
15. Lactantius, "On the Manner in Which the Persecutors Died."
16. Ibid.
17. Eutropius, 9.23.
18. Ibid., 9.27.
19. Eusebius, "Life of Constantine," in *Nicene and Post Nicene Fathers, Second Series,* vol. 1, edited by Philip Schaff and Henry Wace (1974), 26.
20. Ibid., 28, 29.
21. Ibid., 38.

Works Cited

Aeschylus. *Persians.* Trans. Janet Lembke and C. J. Herington. New York: Oxford University Press, 1981.

———. *The Complete Plays.* Vol. 2. Trans. Carl R. Mueller. Hanover, N.H.: Smith and Kraus, 2002.

Aldred, Cyril. *Akhenaten, King of Egypt.* London: Thames & Hudson, 1988.

Allan, Sarah. "Drought, Human Sacrifice and the Mandate of Heaven in a Lost Text from the 'Shang shu.' " *Bulletin of the School of Oriental and African Studies,* University of London, Vol. 47, no.3 (1984), pp. 523–539.

al-Mas'udi, Abu. *El Masudi's Historical Encyclopedia, Entitled "Meadows of Gold and Mines of Gems."* London: Oriental Translation Fund, 1841.

Anthes, Rudolf. "Egyptian Theology in the Third Millennium B.C." *Journal of Near Eastern Studies,* Vol. 18, no. 3 (Jul. 1959), pp. 169–212.

Apollodorus. *The Library.* Trans. Sir James George Frazer. Cambridge, Mass.: Harvard University Press, 1921.

Appian. *The Civil Wars.* Trans. Oliver J. Thatcher. In *The Library of Original Sources,* vol. 3: *The Roman World,* ed. Oliver J. Thatcher. New York: University Research Extension Co., 1901.

Aristophanes. *Lysistrata.* (Trans. anonymous.) London: Athenian Society, 1912.

———. *The Birds and Other Plays.* Trans. David Barrett and Alan H. Sommerstein. New York: Penguin Books, 2003.

Armstrong, Karen. *Buddha.* New York: Penguin Books, 2004.

Arrian. *The Campaigns of Alexander.* Trans. Aubrey de Selincourt. New York: Penguin Books, 1971.

Assmann, Jan. *The Mind of Egypt: History and Meaning in the Time of the Pharaohs.* Trans. Andrew Jenkins. New York: Henry Holt and Company, 2002.

Astour, Michael C. "841 B.C.: The First Assyrian Invasion of Israel." *Journal of the American Oriental Society,* Vol. 91, no. 3 (Jul.–Sep. 1971), pp. 383–389.

Bailkey, Nels. "Early Mesopotamian Constitutional Development." *American Historical Review,* Vol. 72, no. 4 (Jul. 1967), pp. 1211–1236.

Baramki, Dimitri. *Phoenicia and the Phoenicians.* Beirut: Khayats, 1961.

Barrett, C. K., ed. *The New Testament Background: Selected Documents.* Revised and expanded ed. San Francisco: HarperSanFrancisco, 1989.

Barton, Carlin A. "The Scandal of the Arena." *Representations* 27 (Summer 1989), pp. 1–36.

Basham, A. L. *The Wonder That Was India.* New York: Hawthorn Books, 1963.

Bauer, Susan Wise. *The Well-Educated Mind: A Guide to the Classical Education You Never Need.* New York: W. W. Norton, 2003.

Betancourt, Philip P. "The Aegean and the Origin of the Sea Peoples." Pp. 297–301 in *The Sea Peoples and Their World: A Reassessment,* ed. Eliezer D. Oren. Philadelphia: University of Pennsylvania Museum, 2000.

Biblia Hebraica Stuttgartensia. Stuttgart: Deutsche Bibelgesellschaft, 1984.

Bienkowski, Piotr, and Alan Millard, eds. *Dictionary of the Ancient Near East.* Philadelphia: University of Pennsylvania Press, 2000.

Birley, Anthony, trans. *Lives of the Later Caesars: The First Part of* the Augustan History, *with Newly Compiled Lives of Nerva and Trajan.* New York: Penguin Books, 1976.

Birrell, Anne. *Chinese Mythology: An Introduction.* Baltimore, Md.: Johns Hopkins University Press, 1993.

Black, J. A., G. Cunningham, J. Ebeling, E. Flückiger-Hawker, E. Robson, J. Taylor, and G. Zólyomi. *The Electronic Text Corpus of Sumerian Literature.* Oxford: Oriental Institute, University of Oxford, 1998–. http://www-etcsl.orient.ox.ac.uk/.

Boatwright, Mary T., Daniel J. Gargola, and Richard J. A. Talbert. *The Romans: From Village to Empire.* Oxford: Oxford University Press, 2004.

Bottéro, Jean. *Everyday Life in Ancient Mesopotamia.* Trans. Antonia Nevill. Baltimore, Md.: Johns Hopkins University Press, 2001.

Breasted, James Henry. *Ancient Records of Egypt: Historical Documents from the Earliest Times to the Persian Conquest.* Vols. 1–4. Chicago: University of Chicago Press, 1906–1907.

———. *A History of Egypt.* New York: Bantam Books, 1967.

Briant, Pierre. *From Cyrus to Alexander: A History of the Persian Empire.* Trans. Peter T. Daniels. Winona Lake, Ind.: Eisenbrauns, 2002.

Bright, John. *A History of Israel.* 2d ed. Philadelphia: Westminster Press, 1974.

Brinkman, J. A. "Elamite Military Aid to Merodach-Baladan." *Journal of Near Eastern Studies,* Vol. 24, no. 3, (Jul. 1965), pp. 161–166.

———. *A Political History of Post-Kassite Babylonia, 1158–722 BC.* Rome: Pontificium Institutum Biblicum, 1968.

———. "Foreign Relations of Babylonia from 1600 to 625 BC: The Documentary Evidence." *American Journal of Archaeology,* Vol. 76, no. 3 (Jul. 1972), pp. 271–281.

———. "Through a Glass Darkly: Esarhaddon's Retrospects on the Downfall of Babylon." *Journal of the American Oriental Society,* Vol. 103, no. 1 (Jan.–Mar. 1983), pp. 35–42.

Brosius, Maria, trans. and ed. *The Persian Empire from Cyrus II to Artaxerxes I* (LACTOR 16). Kingston upon Thames: London Association of Classical Teachers–Original Records, 2000.

Bryce, Trevor. *Life and Society in the Hittite World.* New York: Oxford University Press, 2002.

Buckley, Terry. *Aspects of Greek History, 750–323 BC: A Source-Based Approach.* New York: Routledge, 1996.

Budge, Ernest A. Wallis. *Tutankhamen: Amenism, Atenism, and Egyptian Monotheism.* London: Martin Hopkinson and Co., 1923.

Buhler, Georg, trans. *The Laws of Manu: Sacred Books of the East.* Vol. 25. Ed. F. Maxmuller. 1886. Reprint, Delhi: Banarsidass, 1970.

Caesar. *The Conquest of Gaul.* Trans. S. A Handford. Revised and updated by Jane Gardner. New York: Penguin Books, 1982.

Carneiro, R. L. "A Theory of the Origin of the State." In *Science,* Vol. 169 (1970), pp. 733–738.

Carrithers, Michael. *Buddha: A Very Short Introduction.* Oxford: Oxford University Press, 2001.

Castleden, Rodney. *Minoans: Life in Bronze Age Crete.* London: Routledge, 1990.

Chadwick, John. *Linear B and Related Scripts.* Berkeley: University of California Press, 1987.

Chang, Kwang-Chih. *Shang Civilization.* New Haven, Conn.: Yale University Press, 1980.

Chi, Tsui. *A Short History of Chinese Civilisation.* London: Victor Gollancz Ltd., 1942.

Ch'ien, Ssu-ma. *The Grand Scribe's Records,* Vol. 1: *The Basic Annals of Pre-Han China.* Ed. William H. Nienhauser, Jr. Trans. Tsai-fa Cheng, Zongli Lu, William H. Nienhauser, Jr., and Robert Reynolds. Bloomington: Indiana University Press, 1994.

Childs, Brevard S. *Isaiah and the Assyrian Crisis.* London: SCM Press, 1967.

Cicero. *On the Commonwealth and On the Laws.* Trans. and ed. James E. G. Zetzel. Cambridge: Cambridge University Press, 1999.

Cioffi-Revilla, Claudio, and David Lai. "War and Politics in Ancient China, 2700 BC to 722 BC: Measurement and Comparative Analysis." *Journal of Conflict Resolution,* Vol. 39, no.3 (Sep. 1995), pp. 467–494.

Clayton, Peter A. *Chronicle of the Pharaohs: The Reign-by-Reign Record of the Rulers and Dynasties of Ancient Egypt.* London: Thames & Hudson, 1994.

Clements, Jonathan. *Confucius: A Biography.* Phoenix Mill, U.K.: Sutton Publishing, 2004.

Cline, Eric. *Jerusalem Besieged: From Ancient Canaan to Modern Israel.* Ann Arbor: University of Michigan Press, 2004.

Cook, Constance A. "Wealth and the Western Zhou." *Bulletin of the School of Oriental and African Studies,* University of London, Vol. 60, no. 2 (1997), pp. 253–294.

Cook, J. M. *The Persian Empire.* New York: Schocken Books, 1983.

Cooper, J. S. *Sumerian and Akkadian Royal Inscriptions.* Vol. 1, *Presargonic Inscriptions.* New Haven, Conn.: American Oriental Society, 1986.

Cornell, T. J. *The Beginnings of Rome: Italy and Rome from the Bronze Age to the Punic Wars (c. 1000–264 BC).* New York: Routledge, 1995.

Cotterell, Arthur. *The First Emperor of China.* New York: Holt, Rinehart & Winston, 1981.

———. *China: A Cultural History.* New York: New American Library, 1988.

Cottrell, Leonard. *Hannibal: Enemy of Rome.* New York: Da Capo Press, 1992.

Crawford, Harriet. *Sumer and the Sumerians.* Cambridge: Cambridge University Press, 1991.

Cunliffe, Barry. *The Extraordinary Voyage of Pytheas the Greek: The Man Who Discovered Britain.* London: Penguin Books, 2002.

Cunnison, Ian. *The Luapula Peoples of Northern Rhodesia.* Manchester: Manchester University Press, 1959.

Curtis, John. *Ancient Persia.* Cambridge, Mass.: Harvard University Press, 1990.

Dales, G. F. "The Mythical Massacre at Mohenjo Daro." In *Ancient Cities of the Indus,* ed. G. L. Possehl. New Delhi: Vikas, 1979.

Dalley, Stephanie, ed. and trans. *Myths from Mesopotamia.* Rev. ed. New York: Oxford University Press, 2000.

David, A. Rosalie. *The Egyptian Kingdoms.* New York: Peter Bedrick Books, 1988.

———. *Religion and Magic in Ancient Egypt.* New York: Penguin Books, 2002.

Davies, W. V. *Egyptian Hieroglyphs: Reading the Past.* Berkeley: University of California Press, 1987.

De Crespigny, Rafe, trans. *To Establish Peace: Being the Chronicle of Later Han for the Years 189–220 AD as Recorded in Chapters 59 to 69 of the Zizhi Tongjian of Sima Guang.* Vol. 1: *Chapters 59–63, 189–200 AD.* Canberra: Australian National University, 1996.

———. *To Establish Peace: Being the Chronicle of Later Han for the Years 189–220 AD as Recorded in Chapters 59 to 69 of the Zizhi Tongjian of Sima Guang.* Vol. 2: *Chapters 64–69, 201–220 AD.* Canberra: Australian National University, 1996.

Diakonoff, I. M., ed. *Early Antiquity,* trans. Alexander Kirjanov. Chicago: University of Chicago Press, 1991.

Diamond, Jared. *Guns, Germs, and Steel: The Fates of Human Societies.* New York: W. W. Norton, 1997.

Dickson, D. Bruce. "Circumscription by Anthropogenic Environmental Destruction: An Expansion of Carneiro's (1970) Theory of the Origin of the State." *American Antiquity,* Vol. 52, no. 4 (Oct. 1987), pp. 709–716.

Di Cosmo, Nicola. *Ancient China and Its Enemies: The Rise of Nomadic Power in East Asian History.* Cambridge: Cambridge University Press, 2002.

Dio Cassius. *Roman History*. Loeb Classical Library. Trans. Earnest Cary. Cambridge, Mass.: Harvard University Press, 1916.

Diodorus Siculus. *Bibliotheca Historica*. Trans. John Skelton. Ed. F. M. Salter and H. L. R. Edwards. London: Early English Text Society, 1956.

Dionysius of Halicarnassus. *Roman Antiquities*. Vol. 1, *Books I–II*. Trans. Earnest Cary. Cambridge, Mass.: Harvard University Press, 1937.

———. *Roman Antiquities*. Vol. 2, *Books III–IV*. Trans. Earnest Cary. Cambridge, Mass.: Harvard University Press, 1939.

Dodson, Aidan and Dyan Hilton. *The Complete Royal Families of Ancient Egypt*. London: Thames & Hudson, 2004.

Dougherty, Raymond Philip. *Nabonidus and Belshazzar: A Study of the Closing Events of the Neo-Babylonian Empire*. New Haven, Conn.: Yale University Press, 1929.

Doumas, Christos G. *Thera, Pompeii of the Ancient Aegean: Excavations at Akrotiri 1967–79*. London: Thames & Hudson, 1983.

Dundas, Paul. *The Jains*. 2d ed. New York: Routledge, 2002.

Duyvendak, J. J. L., trans. *The Book of Lord Shang: A Classic of the Chinese School of Law*. London: Arthur Probsthain, 1928.

Edgerton, Franklin, ed. and trans. *The Beginnings of Indian Philosophy: Selections from the Rig Veda, Atharva Ved, Upanisads, and Mahabharata*. Cambridge, Mass.: Harvard University Press, 1965.

Epictetus. "Discourses 4." In *Discourses, Books 3 and 4*, trans. P. E. Matheson. New York: Dover, 2004.

Eusebius. *Ecclesiastical History*. Trans. A. C. McGiffert. New York: Select Library of Nicene and Post-Nicene Fathers, 1890.

———. "Life of Constantine." In *Nicene and Post Nicene Fathers, Second Series*, vol. 1, ed. Philip Schaff and Henry Wace. Reprint, Grand Rapids, Mich.: W. B. Eerdmans, 1974.

———. "The Oration of the Emperor Constantine." In *Nicene and Post-Nicene Fathers, Second Series*, vol. 1, ed. Philip Schaff and Henry Wace. Reprint, Grand Rapids, Mich.: W. B. Eerdmans, 1974.

Eutropius. *Abridgement of Roman History*. Trans. John Selby Watson. London: Henry G. Bohn, 1853.

Fairbank, John King, and Merle Goldman. *China: A New History*. Enlarged ed. Cambridge, Mass.: Harvard University Press, 2002.

Fenton, John Y, Norvin Hine, Frank E Reynolds, Alan L. Miller, Niels C. Nielson, Jr., Grace G. Burford, and Robert K. C. Forman, *Religions of Asia*, third edition. New York: St. Martin's Press, 1993.

Finley, M. I. *Ancient Slavery and Modern Ideology*. New York: Viking Press, 1980.

Fischer, Steven Roger. *A History of Writing*. London: Reaktion Books, 2001.

Fitton, J. Lesley. *Minoans*. London: British Museum Press, 2002.

Flower, Harriet I., ed. *The Cambridge Companion to the Roman Republic*. Cambridge: Cambridge University Press, 2004.

Forsythe, Gary. *A Critical History of Early Rome: From Prehistory to the First Punic War*. Berkeley: University of California Press, 2005.

Foster, Benjamin R. *Before the Muses: An Anthology of Akkadian Literature*. Vol. 1, *Archaic, Classical, Mature*. 2d edition. Bethesda, Md.: CDL Press, 1996.

———. *Before the Muses: An Anthology of Akkadian Literature*. Vol. 2m *Mature, Late*. 2d ed. Bethesda, Md.: CDL Press, 1996.

Fowler, Robert, ed. *The Cambridge Companion to Homer*. Cambridge: Cambridge University Press, 2004.

Frame, Grant. *Rulers of Babylonia from the Second Dynasty of Isin to the End of Assyrian Domination (1157–612 BC)*. Toronto: University of Toronto Press, 1995.

Frankel, David. *The Ancient Kingdom of Urartu.* London: British Museum Publications, 1979.

Fredricksmeyer, Ernest A. "Alexander, Midas, and the Oracle at Goridum." *Classical Philology,* Vol. 56, no. 3 (Jul. 1961), pp. 160–168.

Gagarin, Michael. *Drakon and Early Athenian Homicide Law.* New Haven, Conn.: Yale University Press, 1981.

Garthwaite, Gene R. *The Persians.* London: Blackwell Publishing, 2005.

Gimbutas, Marija. "European Prehistory: Neolithic to the Iron Age." *Biennial Review of Anthropology,* Vol. 3 (1963), pp. 69–106.

Giorgadze, G. G. "The Hittite Kingdom." Pp. 266–285 in *Early Antiquity,* ed. I. M. Diakonoff, trans. Alexander Kirjanov. Chicago: University of Chicago Press, 1991, pp. 266–285.

Gordon, Cyrus H. *The Common Background of Greek and Hebrew Civilizations.* New York: W. W. Norton, 1965.

Gosden, Chris. *Prehistory: A Very Short Introduction.* Oxford: Oxford University Press, 2003.

Grayson, A. K. *Assyrian and Babylonian Chronicles* (texts from Cuneiform Sources, vol. 5). Locust Valley, N.Y.: J. J. Augustin, 1975.

Green, Peter. *Alexander of Macedon, 356–323 BC: A Historical Biography.* Berkeley: University of California Press, 1991.

Griscom, Acton. *The Historia Regum Britannia of Geoffrey of Monmouth.* New York: Longmans, Green and Co., 1929.

Hackett, John Winthrop, ed. *Warfare in the Ancient World.* London: Sidgwick & Jackson, 1989.

Hamilton, Victor P. *The Book of Genesis: Chapters 1–17.* Grand Rapids, Mich.: W. B. Eerdmans, 1990.

Hardy, Dean, and Marjorie Killick. *Pyramid Energy: The Philosophy of God, the Science of Man.* Hagerstown, Md.: Tri-State Printing, 1994.

Hardy, E. G., ed. *The Monumentum Ancyranum.* Oxford: Clarendon Press, 1923.

Hardy, Robert S. "The Old Hittite Kingdom: A Political History." *American Journal of Semitic Languages and Literatures,* Vol. 58, no. 2 (Apr. 1941), pp. 177–216.

Harvey, Peter. *An Introduction to Buddhism: Teachings, History, and Practices.* Cambridge: Cambridge University Press, 1990.

Haspels, C. H. Emilie. *The Highlands of Phrygia: Sites and Monuments.* Vol. 1: *The Text.* Princeton, N.J.: Princeton University Press, 1971.

Haupt, Paul. "Xenophon's Account of the Fall of Nineveh." *Journal of the American Oriental Society,* Vol. 28 (1907), pp. 99–107.

Heaton, E. W. *Solomon's New Men: The Emergence of Ancient Israel as a National State.* New York: Pica Press, 1974.

Henze, Matthias. *The Madness of King Nebuchadnezzar: The Ancient Near Eastern Origins and Early History of Interpretation of Daniel 4.* Leiden: Koninklijke Brill, 1999.

Herodotus. *The Histories.* Trans. Robin Waterfield. New York: Oxford University Press, 1998.

Hesiod. *Theogony, Works and Days, Shield.* Trans. Apostolos N. Athanassakis. Baltimore, Md: Johns Hopkins University Press, 2004.

Heurgon, Jacques. *Daily Life of the Etruscans.* Trans. James Kirkup. New York: Macmillan Company, 1964.

Hodge, A. Trevor. *Ancient Greek France.* Philadelphia: University of Pennsylvania Press, 1998.

Homer. *The Iliad.* Trans. Alexander Pope. 1713. Online text available at Project Gutenberg, www.gutenberg.org/etext/6130.

———. *The Iliad.* Trans. Samuel Butler. 1898. Online text available at Project Gutenberg, www.gutenberg.org/etext/2199.

———. *The Odyssey.* Trans. Samuel Butler. 1898. Online text available at Project Gutenberg, www.gutenberg.org/etext/1727.

———. *The Iliad.* Trans. E. V. Rieu. New York: Penguin Books, 1950.

———. *The Iliad.* Trans. Robert Fitzgerald. New York: Doubleday, 1974.

Hooker, J. T. "Homer and Late Minoan Crete." *Journal of Hellenic Studies*, Vol. 89 (1969), pp. 60–71.

Hooper, Finley. *Roman Realities.* Detroit, Mich.: Wayne State University Press, 1979.

Hoyland, Robert G. *Arabia and the Arabs: From the Bronze Age to the Coming of Islam.* New York: Routledge, 2001.

Hsu, Cho-yun. *Ancient China in Transition: An Analysis of Social Mobility, 722–222 BC.* Stanford, Calif.: Stanford University Press, 1965.

Hucker, Charles O. *China's Imperial Past: An Introduction to Chinese History and Culture.* London: Duckworth & Co., 1975.

Isocrates. *Isocrates II*, trans. Terry L. Papillon. Austin: University of Texas Press, 2004.

Jacobsen, Thorkild. *Salinity and Irrigation Agriculture in Antiquity: Diayala Basin Archaeological Report on Essential Results, 1957–58* (Bibliotheca Mesopotamica, no. 14). Lancaster, Calif.: Undena Publications, 1982.

James, M. R. *The Apocryphal New Testament.* Oxford: Clarendon Press, 1924.

James, Peter, and Nick Thorpe. *Ancient Mysteries.* New York: Ballantine Books, 1999.

Johnston, Christopher. "The Fall of Nineveh." *Journal of the American Oriental Society*, Vol. 22 (1901), pp. 20–22.

Jordan, Paul. *Riddles of the Sphinx.* Photographs by John Ross. New York: New York University Press, 1998.

Jordanes. *The Origin and Deeds of the Goths.* Trans. Charles C. Mierow. Princeton, N.J.: Princeton University Press, 1908.

Josephus. *The Works of Josephus.* Trans. William Whiston. Peabody, Mass.: Hendrickson Publishers, 1987.

Justin. *The History.* In William Stearns Davis, ed., *Readings in Ancient History*, vol. 2, *Greece and the East.* Boston: Allyn and Bacon, 1912.

Kamoo, Ray. *Ancient and Modern Chaldean History: A Comprehensive Bibliography of Sources.* Lanham, Md.: Scarecrow Press, 1999.

Kaplan, Edward. *An Introduction to East Asian Civilizations: The Political History of China, Japan, Korea and Mongolia from an Economic and Social History Perspective.* Bellingham: Western Washington University, 1997.

Keay, John. *India: A History.* New York: Grove Press, 2000.

Khantipalo, Bhikkhu. *Lay Buddhist Practice: The Shrine Room, Uposatha Day, Rains Residence.* Kandy: Buddhist Publication Society, 1982.

King, L. W. *The Letters and Inscriptions of Hammurabi*, Vols. 1–3. 1900, Luzac & Co. Reprint, New York: AMS Press, 1976.

Kister, M. J. " ' . . . and He Was Born Circumcised . . . ': Some Notes on Circumcision in Hadith." *Oriens*, Vol. 34 (1994), pp. 10–30.

Kitchen, K. A., trans. *Ramesside Inscriptions, Historical and Biographical.* Vol. 4. Oxford: Oxford University Press, 1969.

Knott, Kim. *Hinduism: A Very Short Introduction.* Oxford: Oxford University Press, 2000.

Konon. *Narratives.* In Malcolm Brown, *The Narratives of Konon: Text, Translation and Commentary of the Diegesis.* Munich: K. G. Saur Verlag, 2003.

Kovacs, Maureen Gallery. *The Epic of Gilgamesh.* Stanford, Calif.: Stanford University Press, 1989.

Kraeling, Emil G. "The Death of Sennacherib." *Journal of the American Oriental Society*, Vol. 53, no. 4 (Dec. 1933), pp. 335–346.

Kramer, Samuel Noah. *From the Tablets of Sumer: Twenty-Five Firsts in Man's Recorded History.* Indian Hills, Colo.: Falcon's Wing Press, 1956.

———. *The Sumerians: Their History, Culture, and Character.* Chicago: University of Chicago Press, 1963.

———. *History Begins at Sumer: Thirty-Nine Firsts in Mom's Recorded History.* 3rd rev. ed. Philadelphia: University of Pennsylvania Press, 1981.

Kristensen, Anne Katrine Gade. *Who Were the Cimmerians, and Where Did They Come From?* Trans. Jorgen Laessoe. Copenhagen: Det kongelige Danske videnskabernes selskab, 1988.

Kulke, Hermann, and Dietmar Rothermund. *A History of India.* 3rd ed. New York: Routledge, 1998.

Lackenbacher, Silvie. *Le roi bâtisseur. Les récits de construction assyriens des origins à Teglatphalasar III.* Paris: Études assyriologiques, 1982.

Lactantius. "Of the Manner in Which the Persecutors Died." In *The Anti-Nicene Fathers,* vol. 7: *Fathers of the Third and Fourth Centuries,* ed. Alexander Roberts and James Donaldson. Reprint, Grand Rapids, Mich.: W. B. Eerdmans, 1974.

Laessoe, Jorgen. *People of Ancient Assyria: Their Inscriptions and Correspondence.* Trans. F. S. Leigh-Browne. London: Routledge & Kegan Paul, 1963.

Lambert, W. G. "Studies in Marduk." *Bulletin of the School of Oriental and African Studies,* University of London, Vol. 47, no. 1 (1984), pp. 1–9.

Leach, Edmund. "The Mother's Brother in Ancient Egypt." *RAIN* [Royal Anthropological Institute of Great Britain and Ireland], no. 15. (Aug. 1976), pp. 19–21.

Lee, Shu-Ching. "Agrarianism and Social Upheaval in China." *The American Journal of Sociology,* Vol. 56, no. 6 (May 1951), pp. 511–518.

Legge, James, trans. *The Sacred Books of the East.* Vol. 27, *The Texts of Confucianism, Li Ki, I–X.* Reprint of the original Oxford University Press ed. Delhi: Motilal Banarsidass, 1968.

———. *Confucian Analects, The Great Learning, and the Doctrine of the Mean.* Reprint of the original Clarendon Press 2d rev. ed. (vol. 1 in The Chinese Classics series). New York: Dover, 1971.

Leick, Gwendolyn. *Mesopotamia: The Invention of the City.* New York: Penguin Books, 2001.

———. *The Babylonians: An Introduction.* New York: Routledge, 2003.

Lewis, Jon E., ed. *Ancient Egypt.* New York: Carroll & Graf, 2003.

Lichtheim, Miriam. *Ancient Egyptian Literature.* Vol. 1. Berkeley: University of California Press, 1975.

Liu, Li, and Xingcan Chen. *State Formation in Early China.* London: Gerald Duckworth & Co., 2003.

Livy. *The History of Rome.* Vol. 6 (Books 40–45 of *The History of Rome from Its Foundation*). Trans. E. Roberts. New York: J. M. Dent and Sons, 1912.

———. *The War With Hannibal: Books XXI–XXX of The History of Rome from Its Foundation.* Trans. Aubrey de Selincourt. New York: Penguin Books, 1965.

———. *The Early History of Rome, Books I–V of The History of Rome from Its Foundation.* Trans. Aubrey de Selincourt. New York: Penguin Books, 1971.

———. *Rome and Italy, Books VI–X of The History of Rome from Its Foundation.* Trans. Betty Radice. New York: Penguin Books, 1982.

———. *Ancient Records of Assyria and Babylon, Volume II: Historical Records of Assyria from Sargon to the End.* Chicago: University of Chicago Press, 1927.

Luckenbill, Daniel David. *The Annals of Sennacherib.* Chicago: University of Chicago Press, 1924.

———. "The First Inscription of Shalmaneser V." *American Journal of Semitic Languages and Literatures,* Vol. 41, no. 3 (Apr. 1925), pp. 162–164.

———. *The Dawn of the Roman Empire, Books 31–40* [of *The History of Rome from Its Foundation*]. Trans. J. C. Yardley. Oxford: Oxford University Press, 2000.

———. *Ancient Records of Assyria and Babylon, Volume I: Historical Records of Assyria from the Earliest Times to Sargon.* Chicago: University of Chicago Press, 1926.

Macaulay, Thomas Babington. "Horatius: A Lay Made About the Year of the City CCCLX." In *Lays of Ancient Rome.* London: Longman, Brown, Green & Longmans, 1842.

Mackay, Christopher S. *Ancient Rome: A Military and Political History.* Cambridge: Cambridge University Press, 2004.

Maier, Bernhard. *The Celts: A History from Earliest Times to the Present.* Trans. Kevin Windle. Notre Dame, Ind.: University of Notre Dame Press, 2003.

Malamat, A. "Cushan Rishathaim and the Decline of the Near East around 1200 BC." *Journal of Near Eastern Studies,* Vol. 13, no. 4 (Oct. 1954), pp. 231–242.

Mallowan, M. E. L. *Early Mesopotamia and Iran.* New York: McGraw-Hill, 1965.

Macqueen, J. G. *The Hittites and their Contemporaries in Asia Minor.* London: Thames and Hudson, 1996.

Marcus Aurelius. *The Meditations of Marcus Aurelius.* Trans. George Long. Vol. 2 of *The Harvard Classics.* Ed. Charles W. Eliot. New York: P. F. Collier & Sons, 1909.

Matyszak, Philip. *Chronicle of the Roman Republic.* London: Thames & Hudson, 2003.

McCullough, David Willis, ed. *Chronicles of the Barbarians: Eyewitness Accounts of Pilage and Conquest from the Ancient World to the Fall of Constantinople.* New York: History Book Club, 1998.

McEvedy, Colin. *The New Penguin Atlas of Ancient History.* New York: Penguin Books, 2002.

Mencius. *Mencius.* Trans. D. C. Lau. New York: Penguin Books, 1970.

Michael, Franz. *China Through the Ages: History of a Civilization.* Boulder, Colo.: Westview Press, 1986.

Momigliano, Arnaldo. "An Interim Report on the Origins of Rome." *Journal of Roman Studies,* Vol. 53, Pts. 1–2 (1963), pp. 95–121.

Moran, William L., ed. and trans. *The Amarna Letters.* Baltimore, Md.: Johns Hopkins University Press, 1992.

Morkot, Robert. *The Penguin Historical Atlas of Ancient Greece.* London: Penguin Books, 1996.

Mouw, Richard J., and Mark A. Noll, eds. *Wonderful Words of Life: Hymns in American Protestant History and Theology.* Grand Rapids, Mich.: W. B. Eerdmans, 2004.

Muller, F. Max, trans. *The Sacred Books of the East.* Vol. 10, *The Dhammapada.* Oxford: Clarendon Press, 1991.

Narasimhan, Chakravarthi V., trans. *The Mahabharata: An English Version Based on Selected Verses.* New York: Columbia University Press, 1998.

Narayanan, Vasudha. *Hinduism: Origins, Beliefs, Practices, Holy Texts, Sacred Places.* Oxford: Oxford University Press, 2004.

Nicolaus of Damascus. *Life of Augustus.* Trans. Clayton M. Hall. Menasha, Wisc.: George Banta Pub. Co., 1923.

Oates, Joan. *Babylon.* London: Thames & Hudson, 1979.

O'Connor, David. "The Sea Peoples and the Egyptian Sources." Pp. 85–102 in *The Sea Peoples and Their World: A Reassessment,* ed. Eliezer D. Oren. Philadelphia: The University of Pennsylvania Museum, 2000.

O'Connor, David, and Eric H. Cline. *Amenhotep III: Perspectives on His Reign.* Ann Arbor: University of Michigan Press, 1998.

Ogilvie, R. M. "Introduction: Livy." In Livy, *The Early History of Rome, Books I–V of The History of Rome from Its Foundation,* trans. Aubrey de Selincourt. New York: Penguin Books, 1971.

O'Hogain, Daithi. *The Celts: A History.* Woodbridge, Suffolk: Boydell Press, 2002.

Olmstead, A. T. "Tiglath-Pileser I and His Wars." *Journal of the American Oriental Society,* Vol. 37 (1917), pp. 169–185.

———. *History of Assyria.* New York: Charles Scribner's Sons, 1923.

———. *History of the Persian Empire.* Chicago: University of Chicago Press, 1959.

Oppenheim, A. Leo. "The City of Assur in 714 B.C." *Journal of Near Eastern Studies,* Vol. 19, no. 2 (Apr. 1960), pp. 133–147.

———. *Ancient Mesopotamia: Portrait of a Dead Civilization.* Rev. ed. Chicago: University of Chicago Press, 1977.

Oren, Eliezer D., ed. *The Hyksos: New Historical and Archaeological Perspectives.* Philadelphia: University of Pennsylvania Museum, 1997.

Paludan, Ann. *Chronicle of the Chinese Emperors: The Reign-by-Reign Record of the Rulers of Imperial China.* London: Thames & Hudson, 1998.

Pellegrino, Charles. *Return to Sodom and Gomorrah.* New York: Avon Books, 1994.

Perlin, John. *Forest Journey: The Role of Wood in the Development of Civilization.* Cambridge, Mass.: Harvard University Press, 1991.

Peterson, Joseph H., trans. "Yasna 12: The Zoroastrian Creed." Electronic text at www.avesta.org, 1997.

Petrie, William Flinders. *Researches in Sinai.* New York: E. P. Dutton & Co., 1906.

Pfeiffer, Charles F. *Old Testament History.* Washington, D.C.: Canon Press, 1973.

Phillips, E. D. "The Scythian Domination in Western Asia: Its Record in History, Scripture, and Archaeology." *World Archaeology,* Vol. 4, no. 2 (Oct. 1972), pp. 129–138.

Pliny the Younger. *The Letters of the Younger Pliny.* Trans. Betty Radice. New York: Penguin Books, 1963.

Plutarch. *Fall of the Roman Republic: Six Lives by Plutarch.* Trans. Rex Warner. New York: Penguin Books, 1972.

———. *Greek Lives.* Trans. Robin Waterfield. Oxford: Oxford University Press, 1998.

———. *Plutarch's Lives.* Vols. 1 and 2: The Dryden Translation. Ed. Arthur Hugh Clough. New York: Modern Library, 2001.

———. *The Life of Alexander the Great.* Trans. John Dryden. New York: Modern Library, 2004.

Polybius. *The Histories.* Trans. Evelyn S. Shuckburgh. New York: Macmillan, 1889.

———. *The Rise of the Roman Empire.* Trans. Ian Scott-Kilvert. Ed. F. W. Walbank. New York: Penguin Books, 1979.

Pomeroy, Sarah B., Stanley M. Burstein, Walter Donlan, and Jennifer Tolbert Roberts. *Ancient Greece: A Political, Social, and Cultural History.* New York: Oxford University Press, 1999.

Possehl, Gregory L. "The Mohenjo-daro Floods: A Reply." *American Anthropologist,* New Series, Vol., 69, no. 1 (Feb. 1967), pp. 32–40.

Possehl, Gregory L., ed. *Ancient Cities of the Indus.* New Delhi: Vikas, 1979.

Postgate, J. N. "The Land of Assur and the Yoke of Assur." *World Archaeology,* Vol. 23, no. 3 (Feb. 1992), pp. 247–263.

Pound, Ezra, trans. *The Confucian Odes: The Classic Anthology Defined by Confucius.* New York: New Directions, 1954.

Pritchard, James B., ed. *The Ancient Near East: An Anthology of Texts and Pictures.* Princeton, N.J.: Princeton University Press, 1958.

Prusek, Jaroslav. *Chinese Statelets and the Northern Barbarians in the Period 1400–300 BC.* New York: Humanities Press, 1971.

Qian, Sima. *Records of the Grand Historian, Han Dynasty I.* Rev. ed. Trans. Burton Watson. New York: Columbia University Press, 1993.

———. *Historical Records.* Trans. Raymond Dawson. Oxford: Oxford University Press, 1994.

The Qur'an. Trans. Abdullah Yusuf Ali. Hertfordshire, England: Wordsworth Editions Ltd., 2000.

Rackham, H., trans. *Aristotle in 23 Volumes,* Vol. 21. Cambridge, Mass.: Harvard University Press, 1944.

———. *Aristotle in 23 Volumes,* Vol. 20. Cambridge, Mass.: Harvard University Press, 1952.
Radau, Hugo. *Early Babylonian History Down to the End of the Fourth Dynasty of Ur.* New York: Oxford University Press, 1899.
Radhakrishnan, Sarvepalli, and Charles A. Moore, eds. *A Sourcebook in Indian Philosophy.* Princeton, N.J.: Princeton University Press, 1957.
Reade, Julian. "Assyrian King-Lists, the Royal Tombs of Ur, and Indus Origins." *Journal of Near Eastern Studies,* Vol. 60, no. 1 (Jan. 2001), pp. 1–29.
Redford, Donald B. *Akhenaten: The Heretic King.* Princeton, N.J.: Princeton University Press, 1984.
———. *Egypt, Canaan, and Israel in Ancient Times.* Princeton, N.J.: Princeton University Press, 1992.
———. *From Slave to Pharaoh: The Black Experience of Ancient Egypt.* Baltimore, Md.: Johns Hopkins University Press, 2004.
Redmount, Carol A. "The Wadi Tumilat and the 'Canal of the Pharoahs.' " *Journal of Near Eastern Studies,* Vol. 54, no. 2 (Apr. 1995), pp. 127–135.
Reeves, Nicholas. *The Complete Tutankhamun: The King, The Tomb, The Royal Treasures.* London: Thames & Hudson, 1995.
Reynolds, Francis, ed. *State Archives of Assyria.* Vol. 18, *The Babylonian Correspondence of Esarhaddon and Letters to Assurbanipal and Sin-saru-iskun from Northern and Central Babylonia.* Helsinki: Helsinki University Press, 2003.
Rhys Davids, T. W., trans. *The Questions of King Milinda.* Originally printed in 1890 and 1894 as vols. 35 and 36 of the *Sacred Books of the East.* Reprint, New York: Dover, 1963.
Rice, Michael. *Egypt's Making: The Origins of Ancient Egypt 5000–2000 BC.* 2d ed. New York: Routledge, 2003.
Richmond, I. A. *Roman Britain.* 2d ed. New York: Viking Press, 1978.
Rickett, W. Allyn, trans. *Guanzi: Political Economic, and Philosophical Essays from Early China,* vol. 1. Princeton, N.J.: Princeton University Press, 1985.
Ridgway, David. *Italy Before the Romans: The Iron Age.* San Diego, Calif.: Academic Press, 1979.
Roaf, Michael. *Cultural Atlas of Mesopotamia and the Ancient Near East.* New York: Facts On File, 1996.
Roberts, J. A. G. *The Complete History of China.* Gloucestershire, U.K.: Sutton Publishing, 2003.
Roberts, J. M. *The Penguin History of the World.* New York: Penguin Books, 1997.
Rogers, Guy MacLean. *Alexander: The Ambiguity of Greatness.* New York: Random House, 2004.
Rogers, R. W. *A History of Babylonia and Assyria.* Vol. 2. Freeport, N.Y.: Books for Libraries Press, 1971.
Rogerson, John. *Chronicle of the Old Testament Kings.* London: Thames & Hudson, 1999.
Rolfe, J. C., ed. *Suetonius.* 2 vols. Loeb Classical Library. New York: Macmillan Co., 1914.
Rufus, Quintus Curtius. *The History of Alexander.* Trans. John Yardley. New York: Penguin Books, 2001.
Russell, John Malcolm. *The Writing on the Wall: Studies in the Architectural Context of Late Assyrian Palace Inscriptions.* Winona Lake, Ind.: Eisenbrauns, 1999.
Ryan, William, and Walter Pitman. *Noah's Flood: The New Scientific Discoveries about the Event That Changed History.* New York: Touchstone, 2000.

Sack, Ronald H. *Images of Nebuchadnezzar: The Emergence of a Legend.* 2d revised and expanded ed. Selinsgrove, Penn.: Susquehanna University Press, 2004.
Saggs, H. W. F. *The Might That Was Assyria.* London: Sidgwick & Jackson, 1984.
———. *Babylonians.* Norman: University of Oklahoma Press, 1995.
Sallust. *The Jugurthine War/The Conspiracy of Cataline.* Trans. S. A. Handford. New York: Penguin Books, 1963.
Salmon, Edward T. *The Making of Roman Italy.* Ithaca, N.Y.: Cornell University Press, 1982.

Sancisi-Weerdenburg, Heleen, ed. *Achaemenid History I: Sources, Structures and Synthesis.* Leiden: Nederlands Instituut Voor Het Nabije Oosten, 1987.

Sancisi-Weerdenburg, Heleen, and Amelie Kuhrt, eds. *Achaemenid History II: The Greek Sources.* Leiden: Nederlands Instituut Voor Het Nabije Oosten, 1987.

Sandars, N. K., trans. *The Epic of Gilgamesh.* New York: Penguin Books, 1972.

Sanjana, Darab Dastur Peshotan. *The Kârnâmê î Artakhshîr î Pâpakân, Being the Oldest Surviving Records of the Zoroastrian Emperor Ardashîr Bâbakân, the Founder of the Sâsânian Dynasty in Irân.* Bombay: Steam Press, 1896.

Sargent, Clyde Bailey, trans. *Wang Mang: A Translation of the Official Account of his Rise to Power.* Reprint, Westport, Conn.: Hyperion Press, 1977.

Sasson, Jack M. "The King and I: A Mari King in Changing Perceptions." *Journal of the American Oriental Society*, vol. 118, no. 4 (1998), pp. 453–470.

———. *Hebrew Origins: Historiography, History, Faith of Ancient Israel.* Hong Kong: Theology Division, Chung Chi College, 2002.

Scarre, Chris. *Chronicle of the Roman Emperors.* London: Thames & Hudson, 1995.

Schoene, A., and H. Petermann, trans. *Armeniam versionem Latine factam ad libros manuscriptos recensuit H. Petermann. Graeca fragmenta collegit et recognovit, appendices chronographicas sex adiecit A. Schoene* (vol. 1). Berlin [publisher unknown], 1875.

Schulman, Alan R. "Diplomatic Marriage in the Egyptian New Kingdom." *Journal of Near Eastern Studies,* Vol. 38, no. 3 (Jul. 1979), pp. 177–193.

Schwartz, Daniel. *The Great Wall of China.* London: Thames & Hudson, 2001.

Scullard, H. H. *A History of the Roman World, 753 to 146 BC.* 5th edition. New York: Routledge, 2003.

Seidlmayer, Stephan. "The First Intermediate Period." Pp. 118–147 in *The Oxford History of Ancient Egypt,* ed. Ian Shaw. New York: Oxford University Press, 2002.

Settis, Salvatore, ed. *The Land of the Etruscans: From Prehistory to the Middle Ages.* Florence, Italy: Scala Books, 1985.

Shah, Bharat S. *An Introduction to Jainism.* 2d U.S. ed. Great Neck, N.Y.: Setubandh Publications, 2002.

Shaughnessy, Edward L. "Historical Perspectives on the Introduction of the Chariot into China." *Harvard Journal of Asiatic Studies,* Vol. 48, no. 1 (Jun. 1988), pp. 189–237.

———. "Western Zhou History." Pp. 292–351 in *The Cambridge History of Ancient China: From the Origins of Civilization to 221 B.C.,* ed. Michael Loewe and Edward L. Shaughnessy. Cambridge: Cambridge University Press, 1999.

Shaw, Ian, ed. *The Oxford History of Ancient Egypt.* New York: Oxford University Press, 2002.

Sherwin-White, A. N. *The Roman Citizenship.* 2d ed. Oxford: Clarendon Press, 1973.

Silverman, David P., general ed. *Ancient Egypt.* New York: Oxford University Press, 2003.

Singer, Itamar. "New Evidence on the End of the Hittite Empire." In *The Sea Peoples and Their World: A Reassessment,* ed. Eliezer D. Oren. Philadelphia: University of Pennsylvania Museum, 2000.

Smith, Mark S. *The Early History of God: Yahweh and the Other Deities in Ancient Israel.* 2d edition. Grand Rapids, Mich.: W. B. Eerdmans, 2002.

Soren, David, Aicha Ben Abed Ben Khader, and Hedi Slim. *Carthage: Uncovering the Mysteries and Splendors of Ancient Tunisia.* New York: Simon and Schuster, 1990.

Spence, Lewis. *The Myths of Mexico and Peru.* London: George G. Harrop, 1913. Reprint, New York: Dover, 1994.

Staikos, Konstantinos. *The Great Libraries: From Antiquity to the Renaissance (3000 BC to AD 1600).* New Castle, Del.: Oak Knoll Press, 2000.

Starr, Ivan. *State Archives of Assyria*, Vol. 4, *Queries to the Sungod: Divination and Politics in Sargonid Assyria.* Helsinki: Helsinki University Press, 1990.

Steindorff, George, and Keith C. Steele. *When Egypt Ruled the East.* 2d ed. (revised by Keith C. Steele). Chicago: University of Chicago Press, 1957.

Strabo. *The Geography of Strabo in Eight Volumes.* Trans. Horace L. Jones. London: William Heinemann, 1928.

Suetonius. *Lives of the Caesars.* Trans. Catharine Edwards. Oxford: Oxford University Press, 2000.

Sulpicius Severus. "The Sacred History of Sulpicius Severus." In *Nicene and Post-Nicene Fathers, Second Series,* vol. 11, ed. Philip Schaff and Henry Wace. Reprint, Grand Rapids, Mich.: W. B. Eerdmans, 1974.

Sun-Tzu. *The Art of War.* Trans. Lionel Giles. Australia, Deodand Publishing, 2002.

Swaddling, Judith. *The Ancient Olympic Games.* 2d ed. Austin: University of Texas Press, 1999.

Tacitus. "Life of Cnaeus Julius Agricola." In *Complete Works of Tacitus.* Trans. Alfred Church and William Brodribb. New York: McGraw-Hill, 1964.

———. *The Annals of Tacitus.* Trans. Alfred Church and William Brodribb. Franklin Center, Penn.: Franklin Library, 1982.

———. *The Annals of Imperial Rome.* Trans. Michael Grant. Rev. ed. with new bibliography. New York: Penguin Books, 1996.

Tadmor, Hayim. *The Inscriptions of Tiglath-Pileser III, King of Assyria.* Jerusalem: Israel Academy of Sciences and Humanities, 1994.

Taylour, Lord William. *The Mycenaeans.* Rev. ed. London: Thames & Hudson, 1983.

Thapar, Romila. *Asoka and the Decline of the Mauryas.* 3d rev. ed. Oxford: Oxford University Press, 1998.

———. *Early India: From the Origins to AD 1300.* Berkeley: University of California Press, 2002.

Thatcher, Oliver J., ed. *The Library of Original Sources,* Vol. 3, *The Roman World.* New York: University Research Extension Co., 1901.

Thiel, J. H. *A History of Roman Sea-power before the Second Punic War.* Amsterdam: North Holland Publishing Co., 1954.

Thucydides. *The Landmark Thucydides: A Comprehensive Guide to the Peloponnesian War.* Trans. Richard Crawley. Ed. Robert B. Strassler. New York: Touchstone, 1998.

Tompkins, Peter. *Secrets of the Great Pyramids.* New York: Harper and Row, 1971.

Trigger, Bruce G. "Monumental Architecture: A Thermodynamic Explanation of Symbolic Behavior." *World Archaeology,* Vol. 22, No. 2 (Oct. 1990), 119–132.

Tubb, Jonathan N. *Canaanites: Peoples of the Past.* Norman: University of Oklahoma Press, 1998.

Tuchman, Barbara W. *The March of Folly: From Troy to Vietnam.* New York: Ballantine Books, 1984.

Twitchett, Denis, and Michael Loewe, eds. *The Cambridge History of China, Volume I: The Ch'in and Han Empires, 221 B.C.–A.D. 220.* Cambridge: Cambridge University Press, 1986.

Uphill, E. P. "A Joint Sed-Festival of Thutmose III and Queen Hatshepsut." *Journal of Near Eastern Studies,* Vol. 20, no. 4 (Oct. 1961), pp. 248–251.

van Dijk, Jacobus. "The Amarna Period and the Later New Kingdom." Pp. 272–313 in *The Oxford History of Ancient Egypt,* ed. Ian Shaw (New York: Oxford University Press, 2002).

Verbrugghe, Gerald P. and John M. Wickersham. *Berossos and Manetho, Introduced and Translated: Native Traditions in Ancient Mesopotamia and Egypt.* Ann Arbor: University of Michigan Press, 1996.

Vinogradov, I. V. "The New Kingdom of Egypt." Pp. 172–192 in *Early Antiquity,* ed. I. M. Diakonoff, trans. Alexander Kirjanov. Chicago: University of Chicago Press, 1991.

Virgil. *The Aeneid.* Trans. C. Day Lewis. New York: Doubleday, 1953.

Vohra, Ranbir. *The Making of India: A Historical Survey.* London: M. E. Sharpe, 2001.

Walker, C. B. F. *Cuneiform: Reading the Past.* London: British Museum Publications, 1987.
Warren, Henry Clarke. *Buddhism in Translation.* Vol. 3, Harvard Oriental Series. Cambridge, Mass.: Harvard University Press, 1896.
Waterfield, Robin. *Athens: A History, from Ancient Ideal to Modern City.* New York: Basic Books, 2004.
Watson, Burton, trans. *Records of the Grand Historian of China: Translated from the Shih chi of Ssu-ma Ch'ien. Vol. 2: The Age of Emperor Wu, 140 to Circa 100 BC.* New York: Columbia University Press, 1961.
———. *The Complete Works of Chuang Tzu.* New York: Columbia University Press, 1968.
Wente, Edward F. "Some Graffiti from the Reign of Hatshepsut." *Journal of Near Eastern Studies,* Vol. 43, no. 1 (Jan. 1984), pp. 47–54.
Werner, E. T. C. *Myths and Legends of China.* London: George G. Harrop, 1922. Reprint, New York: Dover, 1994.
Williams, E. Watson. "The End of an Epoch." In *Greece & Rome,* 2d series, Vol. 9, no. 2 (Oct. 1962), pp. 109–125.
Wolkstein, Diane, and Samuel Noah Kramer. *Inanna, Queen of Heaven and Earth: Her Stories and Hymns from Sumer.* New York: Harper and Row, 1983.
Woolley, C. L. *The Royal Cemetery, Ur Excavations.* Vol. 2. London: Trustees of the British Museum and Museum of the University of Pennsylvania, 1934.
Wolpert, Stanley. *A New History of India.* 7th ed. Oxford: Oxford University Press, 2004.
Wylie, J. A. H., and H. W. Stubbs. "The Plague of Athens, 430–428 BC: Epidemic and Epizootic." *Classical Quarterly,* New Series, Vol. 33, no. 1 (1983), pp. 6–11.

Xenophon. *The Persian Expedition.* Trans. Rex Warner. New York: Penguin Books, 1972.
———. *The Education of Cyrus.* Trans. and annotated by Wayne Ambler. Ithaca, N.Y.: Cornell University Press, 2001.
———. *Hellenika I–II.3.10.* Trans. and ed. Peter Krentz. Warminster, England: Aris & Phillips Ltd., 1989.
Xueqin, Li. *Eastern Zhou and Qin Civilizations.* Trans. K. C. Chang. New Haven, Conn.: Yale University Press, 1985.

Yoffee, Norman. "The Decline and Rise of Mesopotamian Civilization: An Ethnoarchaeological Perspective on the Evolution of Social Complexity." *American Antiquity,* Vol. 44, no. 1 (Jan. 1979), pp. 5–35.

Zettler, Richard L., and Lee Horne. *Treasures from the Royal Tombs of Ur.* Philadelphia: University of Pennsylvania Museum, 1998.
Zimansky, Paul. "Urartian Geography and Sargon's Eighth Campaign." *Journal of Near Eastern Studies,* Vol. 49, no. 1 (Jan. 1990), pp. 1–21.

Permissions

American Oriental Society: Thirteen lines from J. A. Brinkman's "Through a Glass Darkly: Esarhaddon's Retrospects on the Downfall of Babylon," *Journal of the American Oriental Society* 103, No. 1. Used by permission of American Oriental Society, University of Michigan.

American Oriental Society: Ten lines from "The Death of Sennacherib," translated by R. C. Thompson and quoted by Emil Kraeling in *Journal of the American Oriental Society*, University of Michigan.

Bar-Ilan University Press: Five lines from *Three Sulgi Hymns: Sumerian Royal Hymns Glorifying King Sulgi of Ur*, translated by Jacob Klein, Copyright © 1981, Bar-Ilan University Press. Used by permission of Bar-Ilan University Press, Ramat-Gan, Israel.

Cambridge University Press: Ten lines from "The Cyrus Cylinder" from *The Cultures Within Ancient Greek Culture: Contact, Conflict, Collaboration* by Carol Dougherty and Leslie Kurke, Copyright © 2003. Used by permission of Cambridge University Press.

CDL Press: Six lines from *Before the Muses: Anthology of Akkadian Literature, Vol. I,* and eight lines from *Before the Muses: Anthology of Akkadian Literature, Vol. II*, translated by Benjamin R. Foster. Used by permission of CDL Press.

Electronic Text Corpus of Sumerian Literature: Twelve lines from *Gilgameš and Aga*, nineteen lines from *The Cursing of Agade*, ten lines from *A Praise Poem of Ur-Namma* (Ur-Namma C), twelve lines from *The Lament for Urim*, and seven lines from *Išbi-Erra and Kindattu* (Išbi-Erra B) (segments A, B, D, and E), translated by J. A. Black, G. Cunningham, J. Ebeling, E. Fluckiger-Hawker, E. Robson, J. Taylor, and G. Zólyomi. Used by permission of the Electronic Text Corpus of Sumerian Literature, The Oriental Institute, University of Oxford.

George Allen and Unwin, Ltd: Four lines from "The Rigveda," translated in *The Beginnings of Indian Philosophy* by Franklin Edgerton, Copyright © 1965, Harvard University Press, reverted to the original publisher, George Allen and Unwin, Ltd. Used by permission of George Allen and Unwin, Ltd.

Indiana University Press: Excerpts from *The Grand Scribe's Records* by Ch'ien, Ssu-ma, edited by William H. Nienhauser, Jr., Copyright © 1994. Used by permission of Indiana University Press.

Johns Hopkins University Press: Ten lines from Hesiod's "Works and Days," *Theogony, Works and Days, Shield*, translated by Apostolos N. Athanassakis, Copyright © 2004, Johns Hopkins University Press. Used by permission of Johns Hopkins University Press.

Oxford University Press: Seven lines from "The Middle Kingdom Renaissance" by Gae Callender, from *Oxford History of Ancient Egypt*, Copyright © 2000, edited by I. Shaw. Used by permission of Oxford University Press.

Oxford University Press: Eleven lines from *Myths from Mesopotamia, Revised*, Copyright © 1989, edited by Stephanie Dalley. Used by permission of Oxford University Press.

Oxford University Press: Excerpts from *Greek Lives*, edited by Robin Waterfield, copyright © 1999, Oxford University Press, and excerpts from *Histories*, edited by Robin Waterfield, Copyright © 1998, Oxford University Press. Used by permission of Oxford University Press, UK.

Oxford University Press: Two lines from *New History of India* by Stanley Wolpert, Copyright © 2004, Oxford University Press. Used by permission of Oxford University Press, US.

Penguin Group: Twenty-five lines from *The Epic of Gilgamesh*, translated with an introduction by N. K. Sandars, Copyright © 1972, N. K. Sandars. Used by permission of Penguin Group, UK.

Penguin Group: Excerpts from *The Early History of Rome: Books I–V of the History of Rome from Its Foundation* by Livy and translated by Aubrey de Sèlincourt; Copyright © 1960, Estate of Aubrey de Sèlincourt. Used by permission of Penguin Group, UK.

Smith and Kraus Publishers: Thirty-eight lines from "The Persians," *Aeschylus: Complete Plays, Volume II*, translated by Carl Mueller, Copyright © 2002, Smith and Kraus Publishers. Used by permission of Smith and Kraus Publishers.

Sterling Lord Literistic Inc: Eighteen lines from Virgil's *The Aeneid*, translated by C. Day Lewis, Copyright © 1953 by C. Day Lewis. Used by permission of Sterling Lord Literistic, Inc.

University of California Press: Three lines from *Babylonians* by H. W. F. Saggs, Copyright © 2000, University of California Press. Used by permission of University of California Press.

University of Chicago Press: Excerpt from I. M. Diakonoff, *Early Antiquity*, translated by A. Kirjanov, Copyright © 1999. Used by permission of Chicago Distribution Services, a division of The University of Chicago Press.

University of Chicago Press: Excerpts from *Ancient Records of Assyria and Babylonia, Vol. I: Historical Records of Assyria from the Earliest Times to Sargon* by Daniel D. Luckenbill, Copyright © 1926, University of Chicago Press. Excerpts from *Ancient Records of Assyria and Babylonia, Vol. II: Historical Records of Assyria from Sargon to the End* by Daniel D. Luckenbill, Copyright © 1927, University of Chicago Press. Excerpts from *The Annals of Sennacherib* by Daniel D. Luckenbill, Copyright © 1924, University of Chicago Press. Used by permission of University of Chicago Press.

University of Chicago Press: Five lines from *A Babylonian Genesis*, translated by Alexander Heidel, Copyright © 1951, University of Chicago Press. Used by permission of University of Chicago Press.

University of Toronto Press: Seven lines from *Rulers of Babylonia from the Second Dynasty of Isin to the End of Assyrian Domination (1157–612 BC)* by Grant Frame, Copyright © 1995, University of Toronto Press. Used by permission of University of Toronto Press.

University of Toronto Press: Four lines from *Assyrian Royal Inscriptions* by Albert Kirk Grayson, Copyright © 1972, University of Toronto Press. Used by permission of University of Toronto Press.

Wolkstein, Diane: Four lines from "Wooing of Inanna," *Inanna, Queen of Heaven and Earth*, Copyright © 1983. Published by permission of Diane Wolkstein.

Index

Page numbers in *italics* refer to illustrations and maps.